DogFriendly.com's

United States and Canada Dog Travel Guide

2nd Edition

Tara Kain
DogFriendly.com, Inc.

DogFriendly.com's United States and Canada Dog Travel Guide, 2nd Edition
by Tara Kain, President of DogFriendly.com, Inc.

DogFriendly.com, Inc.
4570 Pleasant Valley Road #J55
Placerville, California 95667 USA
1-877-475-2275
email: email@dogfriendly.com
http://www.dogfriendly.com

PLEASE NOTE
Although the author and publisher have tried to make the information as accurate as possible, they do not assume, and hereby disclaim, any liability for any loss or damage caused by errors, omissions, misleading information or potential travel problems caused by this book, even if such errors or omissions result from negligence, accident or any other cause.

CHECK AHEAD
We remind you, as always, to call ahead and confirm that the applicable establishment is still "dog-friendly" and that it will accommodate your pet.

DOGS OF ALL SIZES
If your dog is over 75-80 pounds, then please call the individual establishment to make sure they allow your dog.

OTHER PARTIES DESCRIPTIONS
Some of the descriptions have been sent to us by our web site advertisers or other parties.

ISBN 0-9718742-3-9

Printed in the United States of America

Cover Photographs (top to bottom, left to right):
Vintage Inn, Yountville (Napa Valley), CA
FDR Memorial, Washington, DC
Park Bench Cafe, Huntington Beach, CA
Yosemite National Park, Yosemite, CA

Table of Contents

2. Accommodation Guides... 164

UNITED STATES – State Guides

3. Dog-Friendly Coastal Beach Guides... 413

4. Dog-Friendly Highway Accommodation Guides.. 441

5. Other Dog-Friendly Attractions **516**

Introduction by the Author and President of DogFriendly.com, Inc.

I grew up with dogs and have always loved dogs. When I moved away from home, I discovered a whole new world through traveling. But whenever I traveled, the last thing I wanted to do was leave my best friend behind. I practically spent the whole time worrying about my beloved pooch. So I began taking my dog with me. It was much tougher than I originally thought. I would often spend several days researching and planning where my dog and I would be accepted and what else I could do with my dog, aside from just staying in a hotel room. Unfortunately, many places did not allow dogs, especially a large dog like my standard poodle. Many times when I found a supposedly "dog-friendly" hotel or motel, they would allow pets only in smoking rooms. In my opinion, just because I have a dog should not limit me to a smoking room. So in June of 1998, I began to compile my list of dog-friendly places, notes and photos and began to post them on a web site called DogFriendly.com. This allowed me to easily keep track of my research and also help other dog lovers know about these dog-friendly places. I was devoted to finding the best pet-friendly places and then letting the rest of the world know about them.

In search of the best places, I have traveled over 100,000 miles across the United States and Canada with my dog. Today I continue to travel with my best friend. Together we scout out not just lodging but also great places to dine, sightsee, walk and shop. I believe it's important to make a complete travel guide which does not just list places to stay, but also fun and exciting places like dog-friendly attractions, parks, beaches, outdoor restaurants and retail stores. I still continue the tradition of focusing on establishments that allow all well-behaved dogs, regardless of size or breed as well as only listing places that allow dogs in your choice of smoking or non-smoking rooms. By using this guide, I hope you will spend less time researching and more time actually going places with your dog. We at DogFriendly.com believe that well-behaved dogs are an integral and wonderful part of people's lives and they should be as welcome as anyone, anywhere! And last, but not least, thank you! We know you have a choice when looking for dog-friendly resources. We want to thank you for choosing DogFriendly.com as your source for finding great dog-friendly vacation getaways.

Tara Kain, Author and President of DogFriendly.com, Inc.

Your Comments and Feedback

We value and appreciate your feedback and comments. If you want to recommend a dog-friendly place or establishment, let us know. If you find a place that is no longer dog-friendly, allows small dogs only or allows dogs in smoking rooms only, please let us know. You can contact us using the following information.

Mailing Address and Contact Information:
DogFriendly.com, Inc.
4570 Pleasant Valley Road #J55
Placerville, California 95667 USA
toll free phone: 1-877-475-2275
email: email@dogfriendly.com
website: http://www.dogfriendly.com

How To Use This Guide

General Guidelines

1. Please only travel with a well-behaved dog that is comfortable around other people and especially children. Dogs should also be potty trained and not bark excessively.

2. Always keep your dog leashed unless management specifically tells you otherwise.

3. Establishments listed in this book should allow well-behaved dogs of ALL sizes (at least up to 75 pounds) and in non-smoking rooms. If your dog is over 75-80 pounds, then please call the individual establishment to make sure they will allow your dog. We have listed some establishments which only allow dogs up to 50 pounds, but we try our best to make a note in the comments about the restrictions. All restaurants and attractions we list should allow dogs of all sizes.

4. Accommodations listed do not allow dogs to be left alone in the room unless specified by hotel management. If the establishment does not allow pets to be left alone, try hiring a local pet sitter to watch your dog in the room.

5. All restaurants listed as dog-friendly refer to outdoor seating only. While dogs are not permitted to sit in a chair at a restaurant's outdoor dining table, they should be allowed to sit or lay next to your table. We do not list outdoor restaurants that require your dog to be tied outside of a fenced area (with you at the dining table on one side and your dog on the other side of the fence). In our opinion, those are not truly dog-friendly restaurants. Restaurants listed may have seasonal outdoor seating.

6. Pet policies and management change often, especially within the lodging and restaurant industries. Please always call ahead to make sure an establishment still exists and is still dog-friendly.

7. After purchasing your book, please visit http://www.dogfriendly.com/updates for FREE book updates. We will do our best to let you know which places may no longer be dog-friendly.

Preparation for a Road Trip

A Month Before

If you don't already have one, get a pet identification tag for your dog. It should have your dog's name, your name and phone number. Consider using a cell phone number, a home number and, if possible, the number of where you will be staying.

Get a first aid kit for your dog. It comes in very handy if you need to remove any ticks. The kits are usually available at a pet store, a veterinary office or on the Internet.

If you do not already have a dog harness for riding the car, consider purchasing one for your dog's and your own safety. A loose dog in the car can fly into the windshield, out of the car, or into you and injure you or cause you to lose control of the car. Dog harnesses are usually sold at pet stores or on the Internet.

Make a trip to the vet if necessary for the following:

- A current rabies tag for your dog's collar. Also get paperwork with proof of the rabies vaccine.
- Dogs can possibly get heartworm from mosquitoes in the mountains, rural areas or on hikes. Research or talk to your vet and ask him or her if the area you are traveling to has a high risk of heartworm disease. The vet may suggest placing your dog on a monthly heartworm preventative medicine.
- Consider using some type of flea preventative for your dog, preferably a natural remedy. This is out of courtesy for the dog-friendly hotels plus for the comfort of your pooch.

- Make sure your dog is in good health.

Several Days Before

Make sure you have enough dog food for the duration of the trip.

If your dog is on any medication, remember to bring it along.

Some dog owners will also purchase bottled water for the trip, because some dogs can get sick from drinking water they are not used to. Talk to your vet for more information.

The Day Before

Do not forget to review DogFriendly.com's Etiquette for the Traveling Dog!

Road Trip Day

Remember to pack all of your dog's necessities: food, water, dog dishes, leash, snacks and goodies, several favorite toys, brush, towels for dirty paws, plastic bags for cleaning up after your dog, doggie first aid kit, possibly dog booties if you are venturing to an especially cold or hot region, and bring any medicine your dog might be taking.

Before you head out, put on that doggie seat belt harness.

On The Road

Keep it cool and well ventilated in the car for your dog.

Stop at least every 2-3 hours so your dog can relieve him or herself. Also offer him or her water during the stops.

Never leave your pet alone in a parked car - even in the shade with the window cracked open. According to the Los Angeles SPCA, on a hot day, a car can heat up to 160 degrees in minutes, potentially causing your pet (or child) heat stroke, brain damage, and even death.

If your dog needs medical attention during your trip, check the yellow pages phone book in the area and look under Veterinarians. If you do not see an emergency vet listed, call any local vet even during the evening hours and they can usually inform you of the closest emergency vet.

Etiquette for the Traveling Dog

So you have found the perfect getaway spot that allows dogs, but maybe you have never traveled with your dog. Or maybe you are a seasoned dog traveler. But do you know all of your doggie etiquette? Basic courtesy rules, like your dog should be leashed unless a place specifically allows your dog to be leash-free. And do you ask for a paper bowl or cup for your thirsty pooch at an outdoor restaurant instead of letting him or her drink from your water glass?

There are many do's and don'ts when traveling with your best friend. We encourage all dog owners to follow a basic code of doggie etiquette, so places will continue to allow and welcome our best friends. Unfortunately all it takes is one bad experience for an establishment to stop allowing dogs. Let's all try to be on our best behavior to keep and, heck, even encourage new places to allow our pooches.

Everywhere...

- Well-Behaved Dogs. Only travel or go around town with a well-behaved dog that is friendly to people and especially children. If your dog is not comfortable around other people, you might consider taking your dog to obedience classes or hiring a professional trainer. Your well-behaved dog should also be potty trained and not bark excessively in a hotel or other lodging room. We believe that dogs should be kept on leash. If a dog is on leash, he or she is easier to bring under control. Also, many establishments require that dogs be on leash and many people around you will feel more comfortable as well. And last, please never leave your dog alone in a hotel or other lodging room unless you have the approval from the establishment's management.

- Leashed Dogs. Please always keep your dog leashed, unless management specifically states otherwise. Most establishments (including lodging, outdoor restaurants, attractions, parks, beaches, stores and festivals) require that your dog be on leash. Plus most cities and counties have an official leash law that requires pets to be leashed at all times when not on your property. Keeping your dog on leash will also prevent any unwanted contact with other people that are afraid of dogs, people that do not appreciate strange dogs coming up to them, and even other dog owners who have a leashed dog. Even when on leash, do not let your pooch visit with other people or dogs unless welcomed. Keeping dogs on leash will also protect them from running into traffic, running away, or getting injured by wildlife or other dogs. Even the most well-behaved and trained dogs can be startled by something, especially in a new environment.

- Be Considerate. Always clean up after your dog. Pet stores sell pooper scooper bags. You can also buy sandwich bags from your local grocery store. They work quite well and are cheap!

At Hotels or Other Types of Lodging...

- Unless it is obvious, ask the hotel clerk if dogs are allowed in the hotel lobby. Also, because of health codes, dogs are usually not allowed into a lobby area while it is being used for serving food like continental breakfast. Dogs may be allowed into the area once there is no food being served, but check with management first.

- Never leave your dog alone in the hotel room. The number one reason hotel management does not allow dogs is because some people leave them in the room alone. Some dogs, no matter how well-trained, can cause damage, bark continuously or scare the housekeepers. Unless the hotel management allows it, please make sure your dog is never left alone in the room. If you need to leave your dog in the room, consider hiring a local pet sitter.

- While you are in the room with your dog, place the Do Not Disturb sign on the door or keep the deadbolt locked. Many housekeepers have been surprised or scared by dogs when entering a room.

- In general, do not let your pet on the bed or chairs, especially if your dog sheds easily and might leave pet hair on the furniture. Some very pet-friendly accommodations will actually give you a sheet to lay over the bed so your pet can join you. If your pet cannot resist coming hopping onto the furniture with you, bring your own sheet.

- When your dog needs to go to the bathroom, take him or her away from the hotel rooms and the bushes located right next to the rooms. Try to find some dirt or bushes near the parking lot. Some hotels have a designated pet walk area.

At Outdoor Restaurants...

- Tie your dog to your chair, not the table (unless the table is secured to the ground). If your dog decides to get up and move away from the table, he or she will not take the entire table.

- If you want to give your dog some water, please ask the waiter/waitress to bring a paper cup or bowl of water for your dog. Do not use your own water glass. Many restaurants and even other guests frown upon this.

- Your pooch should lay or sit next to your table. At restaurants, dogs are not allowed to sit on the chairs or tables, or eat off the tables. This type of activity could make a restaurant owner or manager ban dogs. And do not let your pooch beg from other customers. Unfortunately, not everyone loves dogs!

At Retail Stores...

- Keep a close eye on your dog and make sure he or she does not go to the bathroom in the store.

Store owners that allow dogs inside assume that responsible dog owners will be entering their store. Before entering a dog-friendly store, visit your local pet store first. They are by far the most forgiving. If your dog does not go to the bathroom there, then you are off to a great start! If your dog does make a mistake in any store, clean it up. Ask the store clerk for paper towels or something similar so you can clean up any mess.

At Festivals and Outdoor Events...

Make sure your dog has relieved himself or herself before entering a festival or event area. The number one reason that most festival coordinators do not allow dogs is because some dogs go to the bathroom on a vendor's booth or in areas where people might sit.

Customs Information for Traveling Between the United States and Canada

If you will be traveling between the United States and Canada, identification for Customs and Immigration is required. U.S. and Canadian citizens traveling across the border need the following:

People

- Proof of citizenship such as your passport or a certified copy of your birth certificate issued by the city, county or state/province where you were born.

- Photo identification such as a current valid driver's license.

- People with children need to bring their child's birth certificate. Single parents, grandparents or guardians traveling with children often need proof or notarized letters from the other parent authorizing travel.

Dogs

- Dogs must be free of evidence of diseases communicable to humans when possibly examined at the port of entry.

- Valid rabies vaccination certificate (including an expiration date usually up to 3 years from the actual vaccine date and a veterinarian's signature). If no expiration date is specified on the certificate, then the certificate is acceptable if the date of the vaccination is not more than 12 months before the date of arrival. The certificate must show that the dog had the rabies vaccine at least 30 days prior to entry.

- Young puppies must be confined at a place of the owner's choosing until they are three months old, then they must be vaccinated. They must remain in confinement for 30 days after the vaccination.

Quarantine Information for Hawaii

The State of Hawaii law states that pets are required to complete a 120-day confinement in the State Animal Quarantine Station. However, if specific pre-arrival and post-arrival requirements are met, animals may qualify for a 30-day quarantine or a new 5-day-or-less quarantine that became effective on June 30, 2003.

There is a three page checklist for the 5-day-or-less program on Hawaii's Agricultural web site at http://www.hawaiiag.org/AQS/aqs-checklist-5.pdf. In general, the program requires stringent rabies vaccine requirements, a rabies blood test (which states that the test was given *at least* 120 days before arrival into Hawaii), a readable microchip, complete documents filled out, payment of about $225 per pet, and a "direct release" from the airplane to the Airport Animal Quarantine Holding Facility located only at the Honolulu International Airport. All pets arriving into Hawaii must be in a sealed carrier or crate and the seal can only be removed by quarantine officials. If you remove the seal yourself, your dog may have to go into a 5 to 120 day quarantine. All requirements must be met exactly according to their documentation, otherwise dogs will go into the lengthy quarantine.

DogFriendly.com's Top 5 National Parks
(Ratings based on sights to see and places to walk or hike with dogs)

1. Grand Canyon National Park, Arizona, 928-638-7888

You and your dog can view the popular Grand Canyon along the South Rim where millions of visitors come every year. Dogs are allowed on the South Rim trails which includes a 2.7 mile scenic walk along the rim. And, well-behaved pooches are allowed on the Geology Walk, a one hour park ranger guided tour which consists of a leisurely walk along a 3/4 mile paved rim trail. The following is the remainder of the doggie regulations. Dogs are not allowed in park lodging, or on park buses. Pets are not permitted at all on North Rim trails with the exception of a bridle path which connects the lodge with the North Kaibab Trail.

2. Acadia National Park, Maine, 207-288-3338

Dogs are allowed on most of the trails and carriage roads. There is even an off-leash area within the park at Little Long Pond. Pets are not allowed on sand beaches or on the steeper hiking trails. Pets must be on a 6 foot or less leash at all times, except for the above mentioned off-leash area.

3. Shenandoah National Park, Virginia, 540-999-3500

This national park, located along a section of the Blue Ridge Parkway, offers miles and miles of dog-friendly hiking trails. There are some trails where dogs are not allowed, but your pooch is allowed on the majority of trails in this park. Pets must be on a 6 foot or less leash at all times, and are allowed in campgrounds, and picnic areas.

4.Yosemite National Park, California, 209-372-0200

Dogs are allowed on the paved trails throughout the Yosemite Valley. The valley is where the majority of tourists visit and you can see most of the popular landmarks and sights from the valley floor, with your pet. Dogs are not allowed on other trails, in wilderness areas, or on the shuttle buses. Owners must clean up after their pets.

5. North Cascades National Park, Washington, 360-856-5700

Dogs are allowed on one of the hiking trails, the Pacific Crest Trail. This scenic hiking trail runs through the park and is rated moderate to difficult. The trail is located off Highway 20, about one mile east of Rainy Pass. At the Bridge Creek Trailhead, park on the north side of the highway and then hike north (uphill) or south (downhill). A Northwest Forest Pass is required to park at the trailhead. The cost is about $5 and can be purchased at the Visitor's Center in Newhalem. For a larger variety of trails, including a less strenuous hike, dogs are also allowed on trails at the adjacent Ross Lake National Recreation Area and the Lake Chelan National Recreation Area. Both recreation areas are managed by the national park.

Top 10 National Parks

(Ratings based on number of visitors per year. Ratings are NOT based on dog-friendliness.)

1. Great Smoky Mountains National Park, Tennessee, 865-436-1200

Pets must be leashed or restrained at all times and are not allowed on hiking trails. They can accompany you in your car and at lookouts and stops near the road. However, there is one trail from the park headquarters to the city of Gatlinburg that allows leashed dogs. It is a nice 2 mile long dirt trail that follows a creek. There are spots along the way where your dog can take a dip in the water. If you want a longer hike, try the nearby dog-friendly Pisgah National Forest or the Nantahala National Forest. Both are in North Carolina, and they are located about a two hour drive from the national park.

2. Grand Canyon National Park, Arizona, 928-638-7888

This is one of the best national parks to exercise and sightsee with your pooch. Leashed pets are allowed on South Rim trails throughout the developed areas in the park. Dogs are not allowed on any trails below the rim. But do not feel too left out, as the majority of all visitors to the Grand Canyon never go on trails below the rim. One of the dog-friendly South Rim trails is about 2.7 miles long, follows the edge of the Grand Canyon, and offers excellent, awe-inspiring views of the Grand Canyon. Well-behaved dogs are even allowed on the Geology Walk, a one hour park ranger guided tour which consists of a leisurely walk along a 3/4 mile paved rim trail. The following is the rest of the park's doggie regulations. Dogs are not allowed in park lodging, or on park buses. Pets are not permitted at all on North Rim trails with the exception of a bridle path which connects the lodge with the North Kaibab Trail. If you are looking to stay near the canyon, pet-friendly lodging is available one hour away in Williams, Arizona.

3. Olympic National Park, Washington, 360-565-3130

Pets are not permitted on park trails, meadows, beaches or in any undeveloped area of the park. There is one exception. Dogs are allowed on leash, during daytime hours only, on Kalaloch Beach along the Pacific Ocean and from Rialto Beach north to Ellen Creek. For those folks and dogs who want to hike on a trail, try the adjacent dog-friendly Olympic National Forest. Leashed dogs are allowed on the national forest trails. Of particular interest is the Mt. Mueller Trail which offers great views of the Strait of Juan de Fuca and the mountains. Maps for this 13 mile loop trail and other trails can be picked up for free at a Forest Ranger Station including the one located at 551 Forks Avenue South, Forks, Washington.

4. Grand Teton National Park, Wyoming, 307-739-3300

Pets are only allowed in your car, on roads and road shoulders, campgrounds, picnic areas, parking lots, etc. Dogs must be leashed. Dogs are not allowed on any park trails or in the backcountry. With national parks like this, it is very nice to have an adjacent national forest that allows dogs on trails. The Bridger-Teton National Forest offers miles of trails for you and your pooch to enjoy.

5. Yellowstone National Park, Wyoming, 307-344-7381

While this national park is not dog-friendly, you will still be able to see, in a limited fashion, some of the major attractions. Dogs are allowed in parking areas, campgrounds and within 100 feet of roads. Pets must be on a 6 foot or less leash or crated or caged at all times. Pets are not allowed on the trails, boardwalks, or in thermal areas where the geysers, including Old Faithful, are located. While dogs are not allowed next to the Old Faithful Geyser, you and your pooch will be able to view its large eruptions from about 200 feet back. And if you drive the Grand Loop Road, you will be able to view some points of interest and perhaps see some wildlife including black bears, grizzly bears, bison and elk. If you are looking for some hiking trails, there are numerous dog-friendly trails in the nearby Shoshone National Forest, located between the town of Cody and Yellowstone National Park.

6. Yosemite National Park, California, 209-372-0200

This national park offers a fair amount of dog-friendly walking areas and sights to see with your dog. Leashed dogs are allowed on the approximately 2 miles of paved trails located on the floor of the Yosemite Valley. Dogs are not allowed on any other trails in Yosemite. However, there are many sights to see from the dog-friendly paved trails in the valley. Yosemite Valley is world famous for its impressive waterfalls, cliffs and unusual rock formations. From the paved trails, you can see El Capitan, Half Dome, Yosemite Falls and Bridal Veil Falls. You can pick up more trail information from the Visitors Center in the Yosemite Village area. The park's website also offers an online map which shows the paved trail path (green dots). Other pet rules are as follows: Pets are only allowed in developed areas, on roads and on paved trails (like the trails in Yosemite Valley). Dogs are not allowed on other trails, in wilderness areas, or on the shuttle buses. Owners must clean up after their pets.

7. Rocky Mountain National Park, Colorado, 970-586-1206

Dogs cannot really do much in this park, but as you drive through the park, you will find some spectacular scenery and possibly some sightings of wildlife. Pets are not allowed on trails, or in the backcountry. Pets are allowed in your car, along the road, in parking lots, at picnic areas and campgrounds. Dogs must be on a 6 foot or less leash. You can still take your dog for a hike, not in the national park, but in the adjacent Arapaho-Roosevelt National Forest. There are numerous trails in this national forest that allow dogs. Some of the trails are located off Highway 34 or Highway 36, near Estes Park. The trails, rated easy to difficult, are over 2.5 miles to 4.5 miles or more in length. Some of the dog-friendly trails include the North Fork Trail, the Lions Gulch Trail/Homestead Meadows Trail, and the Round Mountain Trail.

8. Acadia National Park, Maine, 207-288-3338

This national park ranks high on the tail wagging meter. In this park, dogs are allowed in the majority of the park. Dogs are allowed on most of the hiking trails and carriage roads. Pets are also allowed at the campgrounds, but must be attended at all times. They are not allowed on sand beaches or on the steeper hiking trails. Pets must be on a 6 foot or less leash at all times. There is one exception to the leash rule. There is an area in the park that is privately owned where dogs are allowed to run leash-free. It is called Little Long Pond and is located near Seal Harbor. Overall, this is a pretty popular national park for dogs and their dog-loving owners.

9. Zion National Park, Utah, 435-772-3256

Dogs are allowed on one walking trail at this national park. Dogs on a 6 foot or less leash are allowed on the Pa'rus Trail which is a 1.5 mile long trail that runs from the South Campground to Canyon Junction. You and your pooch can also enjoy a 10-12 mile scenic drive on the Zion-Mount Carmel Highway which goes through the park. If you are there from November through March, you can also take your car on the Zion Canyon Scenic Drive. If you arrive during the summer months, the Zion Canyon Scenic Drive is closed and only allows park shuttle buses. Other pet rules include no pets on shuttle buses, in the backcountry, or in public buildings. Pets are allowed in the campgrounds and along roadways.

10. Mammoth Cave National Park, Kentucky, 270-758-2251

At this national park, leashed dogs are allowed on hiking trails and in campgrounds. There are over 70 miles of hiking trails which go through valleys, up into hills, and next to rivers, lakes and waterfalls. However, dogs are not allowed in the cave, which is the main attraction at this park. The park does offer kennels that are located near the Mammoth Cave Hotel. The kennels are outdoor and not heated or air-conditioned. If you want to try the kennels at Mammoth Cave, be sure to check them out first. You will need to make a reservation for the kennels and there is a $5 key deposit fee for the cage lock and a $2.50 fee for half a day or a $5.00 fee for the entire day. To make kennel reservations, call the Mammoth Cave Hotel directly at 270-758-2225.

Chapter 1

Dog-Friendly City Guides

Bar Harbor - Acadia City Guide

Accommodations

Bar Harbor

Balance Rock Inn
21 Albert Meadow
Bar Harbor, ME 04609
207-288-2610
The oceanfront inn is within walking distance of many restaurants and shops in downtown Bar Harbor. Choose from fourteen individually decorated rooms at the inn, many of which offer an ocean view and private balcony. They also offer a heated outdoor pool and fitness room. Room rates for this inn average $200 to $300 per night but can start at $95 and go up to almost $600 per night. There is also a $30 per day pet fee.

Hanscom's Motel and Cottages
Route 3
Bar Harbor, ME
207-288-3744
This motel is located just 3 miles from downtown Bar Harbor. Rates for the motel range from $54 to $120 per night, with an extra $8 per pet.

Rose Eden Cottages
864 State Highway 3
Bar Harbor, ME 04609
207-288-3038
This small cottage complex offers ten non-smoking cottages and some of them have kitchenettes. They are located just 4 miles to the entrance of Acadia National Park and about 10 minutes from downtown Bar Harbor. Harbor Point Beach, which allows leashed dogs, is located within walking distance. Room rates range from about $40 to $80 per night depending on the season and size of the cottage. One dog is allowed per cottage and there is a $10 per

day pet charge.

Summertime Cottages
Call to arrange.
Bar Harbor, ME
207-288-2893
These vacation rental cottages border the Acadia National Park. They are located near downtown Bar Harbor. The rentals are available year-round. Children and family pets are welcome.

The Ledgelawn Inn
66 Mount Desert Street
Bar Harbor, ME 04609
207-288-4596
This bed and breakfast inn has a $15 one time pet charge. There are no designated smoking or non-smoking rooms.

Swans Island

Harbor Watch Motel

Swans Island, ME
207-526-4563
To get to this motel on Swans Island, take the ferry from Bass Harbor in Southwest Harbor to Swans Island. Leashed dogs and cars are allowed on the Maine State Ferries. Dogs are allowed for an additional $10 per day pet fee. Rooms rates range from about $60 to $80 per night.

Attractions

Bar Harbor

Acadia National Park
Eagle Lake Road
Bar Harbor, ME
207-288-3338
This national park ranks high on the tail wagging meter. Dogs are allowed on most of the hiking trails, which is unusual for a national park. There are miles and miles of both hiking trails and carriage roads. Pets are also allowed at the

campgrounds, but must be attended at all times. They are not allowed on sand beaches or on the steeper hiking trails. Pets must be on a 6 foot or less leash at all times. There is one exception to the leash rule. There is an area in the park that is privately owned where dogs are allowed to run leash-free. It is called Little Long Pond and is located near Seal Harbor. Overall, this is a pretty popular national park for dogs and their dog-loving owners. There is a $10 entrance fee into the park, which is good for 7 days. You can also purchase an audio tape tour of the Park Loop Road which is a self-guided auto tour. The driving tour is about 27 miles and takes 3 to 4 hours including stops. Audio tapes are available at the Hulls Cove Visitor Center.

Acadia Outfitters
106 Cottage Street
Bar Harbor, ME
207-288-8118
This boat rental company allows dogs on their lake canoes. Rent a tandem canoe for $35. Just make sure your pooch does not rock the canoe enough to tip it over and send everyone into the water!

Wildwood Stables Carriage Tours
Route 3
Bar Harbor, ME
207-276-3622
Take a horse and carriage ride with your pooch in Acadia National Park. The ride is along carriage roads which do not allow cars. Dogs are only allowed on the private tours which cost about $180 ($90 per hour, 2 hour minimum, holds up to 6 people including dogs).

Southwest Harbor

Maine State Ferry Service
Bass Harbor

2

Southwest Harbor, ME
207-596-2202
Dogs are allowed on the ferries if they are leashed, crated or caged. The ferries closest to Bar Harbor depart at the nearby Southwest Harbor and go to Swans Island. Cars can also be transported on the ferry.

Masako Queen Fishing Company
Beal's Wharf
Southwest Harbor, ME
207-244-5385
Take a water excursion on a fishing boat with your dog. This boating company offers five hour deep sea fishing trips. Prices are about $39 per person for a half day, and a little less for children and seniors. The boat goes out eight to twelve miles from the shore to fish for mackerel, codfish and more. You will even be able to bring back your own lobster.

Beaches

Bar Harbor

Hadley Point Beach
Highway 3
Bar Harbor, ME

Dogs are allowed on the beach, but must be leashed. The beach is located about 10 minutes northwest of downtown Bar Harbor, near Eden.

Restaurants

Bar Harbor

China Joy Restaurant
195 Main Street
Bar Harbor, ME
207-288-8666
Dogs are allowed at the outdoor tables.

Fishermen's Landing
35 West Street
Bar Harbor, ME

207-288-4632
Dogs are allowed at the outdoor tables.

George's Restaurant
7 Stephens Lane
Bar Harbor, ME
207-288-4505
Located in downtown Bar Harbor, this restaurant allows your dog to dine with you at the outside tables. This Mediterranean restaurant offers nice patio seating which overlooks a garden. Enjoy dinner entrees like the Lobster Strudel, Whole Maine Lobster, Filet of Beef and more.

Jack Russell's BrewPub
102 Eden St.
Bar Harbor, ME
207-288-5214
This restaurant serves a variety of beer as well as food. They allow dogs at the outdoor tables. And yes, they do have a Jack Russell Terrier as their mascot.

Jordon Pond House Restaurant
Route 3
Bar Harbor, ME
207-276-3316
Dine outdoors at the tables on the lawn with your leashed pooch. The outdoor seating area offers a beautiful view of the pond and mountains. They are open for lunch, afternoon tea and popovers, and dinner. Enjoy entrees like the Grilled Maine Salmon, Steamed Lobster, and Maine Crab Cakes. The restaurant also offers salads, beef, chicken, desserts and a children's menu.

Pier Restaurant
55 West Street
Bar Harbor, ME 04605
207-288-2110
Dogs are not allowed on the outdoor deck, but you can dine with your dog at the picnic tables on the pier.

Boston City Guide

Accommodations

Boston

Boston Harbor Hotel
70 Rowes Wharf
Boston, MA 02110
617-439-7000
There are no additional pet fees. Pet owners must sign a pet waiver.

Seaport Hotel
1 Seaport Lane
Boston, MA 02210
617-385-4000
Dogs up to 50 pounds allowed.

Sheraton Boston Hotel
39 Dalton Street
Boston, MA 02199
617-236-2000
Dogs up to 50 pounds are allowed. There are no additional pet fees. Pets may not be left alone in rooms.

Swissotel Boston
One Ave de Lafayette
Boston, MA 02111
617-451-2600
Pet owners must sign a pet waiver. You need to specifically request a non-smoking pet room if you want one. Dogs need to stay in the first through fourth floors only. Pets may not be left alone in the rooms. The hotel can recommend pet sitters if needed.

The Eliot Suite Hotel
370 Commonwealth Ave
Boston, MA 02215
617-267-1607
There are no additional pet fees. Pets may not be left alone in the rooms.

Braintree

Motel 6
125 Union Street
Braintree, MA 02184
781-848-7890

3

Well-behaved large dogs allowed. Dogs must be leashed on premises and may not be left alone in the room. There are no additional pet fees.

Burlington

Candlewood Suites
130 Middlesex Turnpike
Burlington, MA 01803
781-229-4300
There is a $150 one time pet fee.

Staybridge Suites
11 Old Concord Rd
Burlington, MA 01803
781-221-2233
There is a $150 one time pet fee.

Cambridge

Hotel Marlowe
25 Edwin H. Land Blvd.
Cambridge, MA 02141
617-868-8000
Dogs of all kinds and sizes are welcome at this pet-friendly and family-friendly hotel. The luxury boutique hotel offers both rooms and suites. Hotel amenities include a fitness room and 24 hour room service. There are no pet fees, just sign a pet waiver.

Sheraton Commander Hotel
16 Garden Street
Cambridge, MA 02138
617-547-4800
Dogs up to 80 pounds are allowed. There are no additional pet fees. The dog owner must fill out a pet agreement.

The Charles Hotel in Harvard Square
1 Bennett St
Cambridge, MA 02138
617-864-1200
There is a $50 one time pet fee. Pets may not be left alone in the rooms, and pet owners must sign a pet agreement.

Concord

Best Western at Historic Concord
740 Elm St
Concord, MA 01742
978-369-6100
There is a $10 per day charge for pets.

Danvers

Motel 6
65 Newbury St/US Rt. 1 N
Danvers, MA 01923
978-774-8045
Dogs are allowed up to around 75 pounds.

Residence Inn - North Shore
51 Newbury St, Rt.
Danvers, MA 01923
978-777-7171
There is a $100 one time pet fee and an additional $10 per day pet fee.

Dedham

Residence Inn - Dedham
259 Elm Street
Dedham, MA 02026
781-407-0999
There is a $100 one time pet fee and a $10 per day pet fee.

Foxborough

Residence Inn - Foxborough
250 Foxborough Blvd
Foxborough, MA 02035
508-698-2800
There is a $150 one time pet fee and a $10 per day pet fee.

Framingham

Motel 6
1668 Worcester Rd
Framingham, MA 01702
508-620-0500
There are no additional pet fees. A well-behaved dog is allowed and must be attended at all times.

Sheraton Framingham Hotel
1657 Worcester Road
Framingham, MA 01701
508-879-7200
Dogs up to 80 pounds are allowed. There are no additional pet fees.

Gloucester

Ocean View Inn
171 Atlantic Rd
Gloucester, MA
978-283-6200
Dogs are allowed, but not in the Main Building (restaurant building). There are no additional pet fees.

Lawrence

Hampton Inn Boston/North Andover
224 Winthrop Ave
Lawrence, MA 01843
978-683-7143
There are no additional pet fees.

Lexington

Holiday Inn Express
440 Bedford Street
Lexington, MA 02173
781-861-0850
There is a $75 one time pet fee per visit.

Sheraton Lexington Inn
727 Marrett Road
Lexington, MA 02421
781-862-8700
Dogs up to 80 pounds are allowed. There is a $15 one time pet fee. The only place dogs aren't allowed is in the food and beverage area.

Mansfield

Red Roof Inn
60 Forbes Blvd
Mansfield, MA 02048
508-339-2323
There are no additional pet fees.

Newton

Sheraton Newton Hotel
320 Washington Street
Newton, MA 02458
617-969-3010
Dogs of all sizes are allowed.
There are no additional pet fees.
Pets cannot be left unattended
in rooms.

Rockland

Holiday Inn Express
909 Hingham St
Rockland, MA 02370
781-871-5660
There is a $6 per day additional
pet fee.

Rockport

Sandy Bay Motor Inn
173 Main St
Rockport, MA 01966
978-546-7155
There is a $10 per day pet
charge. The hotel has two non-
smoking rooms in their pet
building.

Salem

Hawthorne Hotel
18 Washington Sq. W
Salem, MA 01970
978-744-4080
There is a $7.50 per night
charge for pets.

Tewksbury

Holiday Inn
4 Highwood Drive
Tewksbury, MA 01876
978-640-9000
Pet owners must sign a pet
waiver.

Motel 6
95 Main St
Tewksbury, MA 01876
978-851-8677
There are no additional pet fees.

Residence Inn by Marriott
1775 Andover St
Tewksbury, MA 01876
978-640-1003
There is a $100 pet charge per
stay and a $10 per day pet
charge.

Wakefield

**Sheraton Colonial Hotel and
Golf Club Boston North**
One Audubon Road
Wakefield, MA 01880
781-245-9300
Dogs up to 80 pounds are
allowed. There are no
additional pet fees.

Waltham

Homestead Village
52 Fourth Ave
Waltham, MA 02254
781-890-1333
$75 one time fee. This is a long
term stay hotel.

Winthrop

The Inn at Crystal Cove
600 Shirley Street
Winthrop, MA 02152
617-846-9217
Great view and wonderful dog-
friendly people. The inn is
located on Boston Harbor. The
inn is a comfortable, colonial-
style hotel located in a
residential neighborhood of
Winthrop, just minutes from
downtown Boston. Their
swimming pool and jacuzzi
make comfortable lodging at a
reasonable rate.

Woburn

Radisson Hotel
15 Middlesex Canal Park Rd
Woburn, MA 01801
781-935-8760
There is a $50 refundable pet
deposit.

Attractions

Boston

Boston T

Boston, MA
617-222-3200
The Boston T allows dogs of all
sizes to ride during non-rush
hour periods. Smaller dogs that
can be held can ride in rush hour
as well.

Bull and Finch Pub (Cheers)
84 Beacon St
Boston, MA 02108
Arlington and Charles Street
617-227-9605
We normally don't recommend
any places where a dog must
wait for "takeout" food to eat
elsewhere. However, since your
dog has probably had to put up
with you watching Cheers or
rerun after rerun of Cheers,
she's entitled. Just this once.

Faneuil Hall Marketplace
North St and Merchants Row
Boston, MA

A large and usually crowded
outdoor shopping and eating
area. If your dog isn't used to
crowds, this is not the place to
be. In the evenings, horse and
carriage rides leave from here.

Freedom Trail
Tremont and Temple
Boston, MA
Boston Common

This 2.5 mile tour marked by a
red line on the sidewalk takes
you by many famous sites. Your
dog may join you on the self-
guided tour.

**Horse and Carriage (Bridal
Carriage)**
Faneuil Hall Marketplace
Boston, MA
781-871-9224
Well behaved dogs are allowed
on the carriages that depart from

Faneuil Hall Marketplace in the evenings if the weather is appropriate.

Concord

Minute Man National Historical Park
Rt. 2A and I-95
Concord, MA

Dogs are allowed on all the paths and to all the markers here. The Battle Road path goes all the way through the park, with a few interruptions.

Salem

Salem Walking Tour

Salem, MA

A line on the sidewalk shows you the way for a two mile walking tour of Salem.

Beaches

Boston

Carson Beach
I-93 and William Day Blvd
Boston, MA
617-727-5114
Dogs are only allowed on the beach during the off-season. Pets are not allowed from Memorial Day weekend through Labor Day weekend. Dogs must be leashed and people are required to clean up after their pets.

Parks

Boston

Arnold Arboretum
125 Arborway
Boston, MA
near Centre St.
617-524-1718
Dogs must be on leash and must be cleaned up after at all

times. The arboretum has a collection of trees, shrubs, and vines on 265 acres.

Back Bay Fens
The Fenway and Park Drive
Boston, MA

Leashed dogs are allowed at this back bay park.

Boston Common
Tremont St and Park St
Boston, MA

Leashed dogs are allowed. This 50 acre park is one of the oldest parks in the United States and is the starting point of the Freedom Trail.

Charlesgate Dog Run
Massachusetts Ave and Beacon St
Boston, MA
Mass Ave Bridge (West Side)

This is a very small dog park but it is fenced in.

Fort Independence
William J. Day Blvd
Boston, MA
East end of the road

This park and a historical fort can be viewed by your dog.

Brookline

Larz Anderson Park
Goddard St and Newton St
Brookline, MA

Dogs are allowed on-leash only.

Cohasset

Whitney and Thayer Woods Park
Rte 3A
Cohasset, MA
opposite Sohier St
617-821-2977
Dogs on leash are allowed.

East Boston

Belle Isle Reservation
Bennington Street
East Boston, MA
617-727-5350
Dogs must be leashed in the park.

Framingham

Callahan State Park
Millwood Street
Framingham, MA
508-653-9641
Dogs are allowed on leash or in some areas, off-leash but under strict voice control. This 820 acre day use park offers 7 miles of hiking and walking trails, and a pond where dogs can swim. The park is located west of Boston. Take Route 9 to Edgell Road in Framingham, turn left on Belknap and then right onto Millwood St.

Hingham

Wompatuck State Park
Union St
Hingham, MA
781-749-7160

World's End Park
Martin's Lane
Hingham, MA
near route 3A
781-821-2977
Dogs are allowed on leash. There is a $4 fee per person to enter. This park offers over 240 acres and about 5 miles of shoreline.

Lexington

Lexington Battle Green
Massachusetts Ave and Bedford St
Lexington, MA

Minuteman Commuter

Bikeway
Massachusetts Ave and
Waltham
Lexington, MA

This 10 mile trail extends from
Arlington, thru Lexington, and to
Bedford. Dogs must be leashed
in this park.

Lynn

Lynn Woods Reservation
Great Woods Road
Lynn, MA
Rte 129
781-593-7773
Dogs must be leashed in this
park.

Milton

Blue Hills Reservation
1904 Canton Ave
Milton, MA 02186
617-698-1802
Leashed dogs are allowed in
this park which offers over 125
of trails.

Salem

Salem Common
Washington Square
Salem, MA

Leashed dogs are allowed. This
park is the second largest
municipal park in the United
States and offers over 30 miles
of trails.

Restaurants

Boston

Casa Romero
30 Gloucester Street
Boston, MA 02115
617-536-4341
This restaurant serves authentic
Mexican cuisine. Then are open
nightly for dinner. Well-behaved
leashed dogs are allowed at the
outdoor tables.

Kinsale Irish Pub
2 Center Plaza
Boston, MA 02108
617-742-5577
Dogs are allowed at the
outdoor tables.

Maison Robert
45 School Street
Boston, MA 02108
617-227-3370
This restaurant serves French
cuisine. Well-behaved leashed
dogs are allowed at the outdoor
tables.

Salty Dog Seafood Grille
206 Faneuil Hall Market Pl
Boston, MA 02109
617-742-2094
Dogs are allowed at the
outdoor tables.

Tremont 647
647 Tremont Street
Boston, MA 02118
617-266-4600
This restaurant offers
"adventurous" American
cuisine. Well-behaved leashed
dogs are allowed at the outdoor
tables.

Wisteria House Chinese
264 Newbury St
Boston, MA 02116
617-536-8866
Dogs are allowed at the
outdoor tables.

Brookline

Taberna de Haro
999 Beacon Street
Brookline, MA 02446
617-277-8272
This restaurant serves Spanish
cuisine. Well-behaved leashed
dogs are allowed at the outdoor
tables as long as they sit or lay
quietly under the table.

Cambridge

Au Bon Pain
1360 Massachusetts Avenue,

Harvard Square
Cambridge, MA 02138
617-497-9797
This chain restaurant offers both
baked goodies as well as a
variety of sandwiches. Well-
behaved leashed dogs are
allowed at the outdoor tables.

Cafe Paradiso
1 Harvard Square
Cambridge, MA 02139
617-868-3240
This restaurant serves Italian
cuisine. Well-behaved leashed
dogs are allowed at the outdoor
tables.

Cambridge Brewing Company
One Kendall Square
Cambridge, MA 02139
617-494-1994
In addition to the wide selection
of beer on tap, this brewery also
offers burgers, pizzas and fresh
seafood. They are open for
lunch and dinner. Well-behaved
leashed dogs are welcome at
the outdoor tables.

Henrietta's Table
1 Bennett Street
Cambridge, MA 02138
617-661-5005
This restaurant serves
homestyle American cuisine.
Well-behaved leashed dogs are
allowed at the outdoor tables.

Lexington

Dabin Restaurant
10 Muzzey St #1
Lexington, MA 02421
781-860-0171
This Japanese and Korean
restaurant is in historic
Lexington, near the Green.

Salem

Coffee Merchant
196 Essex St
Salem, MA 01970
978-744-1729
Dogs are allowed at the outdoor
tables.

Cape Cod City Guide

Accommodations

Brewster

Greylin House
2311 Main St
Brewster, MA 02631
508-896-0004
1 room, non-smoking for pets. Dog must be able to get along with the owners 2 dogs.

High Brewster Inn
964 Satucket Rd
Brewster, MA
508-898-3636
There are no additional pet fees.

Buzzards Bay

Bay Motor Inn
223 Main St
Buzzards Bay, MA 02532
508-759-3989
There is a $10 per day pet fee. The motel has no designated smoking or non-smoking rooms. Pets must be attended at all times.

Centerville

Centerville Corners Motor Lodge
369 S Main St
Centerville, MA 02632
508-775-7223
There is a $5 per day pet fee.

Hyannis

Sheraton Hyannis Resort
35 Scudder Avenue
Hyannis, MA 02601
508-775-7775
Dogs up to 80 pounds are allowed. There are no additional pet fees.

Hyannis Port

Simmons Homestead Inn

288 Scudder Ave.
Hyannis Port, MA 02647
800-637-1649
The B & B is at an 1800 Sea Captain's estate in Hyannis Port in the center of Cape Cod. 14 rooms in two buildings. Full breakfasts, wine hour(s), free bikes, beach stuff, billiards and a bunch more. A chance to see the collection of over 50 classic red sports cars behind the Inn at Toad Hall is probably worth the trip by itself.

Provincetown

BayShore on the Water
493 Commercial Street
Provincetown, MA 02657
508-487-9133
This five house complex has been converted to studios, one bedroom and two bedroom units. There are a few non-smoking units and the rest are not designated as smoking or non-smoking. There is a $15 per day pet fee for 1 dog, or a $20 per day pet fee for 2 dogs.

Keep Inn
698 Commercial St
Provincetown, MA 02657
508-487-1711
There are no additional pet fees. Pets must be attended at all times.

White Wind Inn
174 Commercial St
Provincetown, MA 02657
508-487-1526
There are no additional pet fees.

Sandwich

Sandwich Lodge and Resort
54 Route 6A
Sandwich, MA 02563
508-888-2275
There is a $15.00 one time pet fee.

The Earl of Sandwich Motor Manor

378 Rt. 6A
Sandwich, MA 02537
508-888-1415
There are no additional pet fees.

Yarmouth Port

Colonial House
Old Kings Hwy
Yarmouth Port, MA 02675
508-362-4348
There is a $5.00 per day pet charge.

Accommodations - RV Parks and Campgrounds

Brewster

Nickerson State Park Campgrounds
Route 6A
Brewster, MA
508-896-3491
This state park has 1900 acres of land and offers over 400 campsites. Your dog is welcome at the campgrounds, but they ask that your dog never be left unattended. Dogs are also allowed on the hiking trails, and paved trails. Dogs are not allowed in the pond or on public beaches. However, you can take your dog to an uncrowded beach, where there are not many other people. Dogs must be leashed and you must have proof of your dog's rabies vaccination.

Accommodations - Vacation Home Rentals

Provincetown

The Sandpiper Beach House
165 Commercial Street
Provincetown, MA 02657
508-487-1928
There is a $25 per visit pet fee.

Attractions

East Sandwich

8

Green Briar Nature Center
6 Discovery Hill
East Sandwich, MA
508-888-6870
The famous author Thorton Burgess grew up in Sandwich and wrote over 170 books and 15,000 stories about Peter Rabbit and his animal friends. As a child, he used to go for walks in what is now the conservation area next to the Nature Center. The Nature Center offers interpretive nature trails and a special wild flower garden. Leashed dogs are allowed on the nature trails and throughout the trails in the flower garden. Pets are not allowed inside the buildings. The adjacent 166 acre Briar Patch Conservation Area also allows dogs on their trails. Pets must be on leash, except during the months of September through March when dogs are allowed off-leash, but must be under voice control. The conservation area is the home of Peter Rabbit and other Burgess animal characters. The Nature Center offers trail guides for the conservation area. Green Briar is located off Route 6A.

Falmouth

Island Queen Ferry
Falmouth Heights Road
Falmouth, MA 02540
508-548-4800
This ferry carries passengers, bicycles and leashed dogs. It does not transport vehicles. The ferry runs between Falmouth in Cape Cod and Oak Bluffs in Martha's Vineyard (about 35 to 45 minutes).

Hyannis

Hy-Line Cruises Ferry Service
Ocean Street Dock
Hyannis, MA
508-778-2600
This ferry service runs from

Cape Cod to Nantucket Island (1 hour on the high speed ferry) or Martha's Vineyard (1.5 hours). They also offer the only Inter-Island Ferry between Nantucket and Martha's Vineyard (2.25 hours). Pets are allowed on the ferries, but not in the first class lounge. Pets need to be leashed. This ferry company provides year-round service to Nantucket and seasonal service to Martha's Vineyard. The Inter-Island Ferry is also seasonal. No vehicles are transported on these ferries. Call ahead to make reservations.

Hyannisport Harbor Cruises
Ocean Street Dock
Hyannis, MA
508-778-2600
Enjoy a one hour leisurely cruise on Lewis Bay and Hyannis Harbor. You will see vistas of historic interest, scenic islands and beaches, a few presidential summer homes, and more. Tours are held rain or shine. Dogs are allowed, but need to be leashed.

Nantucket Airlines
660 Barnstable Road/North Ramp
Hyannis, MA 02601
508-790-0300
This airline offers daily flights between Hyannis and Nantucket (20 minute flight). Dogs are allowed in the cabin with you on this airline! Dogs under 35 pounds can be carried on your lap and no kennel is required. For dogs over 35 pounds, there is a "shelf" which is just a few inches off the floor, in the back of the plane where your dog can sit or lay. While you cannot sit next to your dog, you can try to get the seat directly in front of him or her. There is no reserved seating, so you'll need to arrive early to try and make special arrangements to sit in front of your pooch. Large dogs must

be properly restrained with a leash, harness or similar device. No kennel is required. You will need to reserve a space for your pet in advance as the airline usually only allows one dog per flight. Their sister airline, Cape Air also allows dogs in the cabin, but most flights require your dog to be in a kennel, and they have a size limit for dogs.

Steamship Authority Ferry Service
South Street Dock
Hyannis, MA
508-477-8600
This ferry services runs from Cape Cod to Nantucket Island (2.25 hours) or Martha's Vineyard (1.5 hours). Pets are allowed on all ferries except for the M/V Flying Cloud fast ferry. Pets must be leashed or in a crate at all times. Pets are not allowed on the seats, tables, or in the concession areas. The ferries transport both passengers and cars. They provide year-round service to Nantucket and Martha's Vineyard. Call ahead to make reservations.

Onset

Cape Cod Canal Cruise
Town Pier
Onset, MA
508-295-3883
This 2 or 3 hour boat cruise starts at the pier in the Victorian village of Onset. The cruise will take you through the Cape Cod Canal to the Sandwich Yacht Basin. You will be able to enjoy live commentary about the history and sights. Some points of interest include Taylor Point, Massachusetts Maritime Academy Training Ship, Vertical Lift Railroad Bridge, Sagamore Bridge and more. Well-behaved, leashed dogs are allowed.

Provincetown

Dolphin Fleet of Provincetown Whale Watch

307 Commercial Street
Provincetown, MA 02657
508-349-1900

This whale watching tour company offers you and your well-behaved dog the opportunity to view a variety of whales including Baleen, Toothed, Humpback, Fin and Right Whales. Each tour is about 3 to 4 hours long. Small dogs are allowed on all of the boat tours. Large dogs are also allowed, but there are a few requirements. The smaller tour boats are recommended for large dogs, because these boats are less crowded and offer more space. They also recommend that you call first to make sure that there is space available. All dogs need to be leashed.

Beaches

Barnstable

Barnstable Town Beaches

off Route 6A
Barnstable, MA
508-790-6345

Dogs are allowed only during the off-season, from September 15 to May 15. Dogs must be on leash or under voice control. People need to clean up after their pets. The town of Barnstable oversees Hyannis beaches and the following beaches: Craigville, Kalmus, and Sandy Neck. Before you go, always verify the seasonal dates and times when dogs are allowed on the beach.

Chatham

Chatham Town Beaches

off Route 28
Chatham, MA
508-945-5100

Dogs are allowed only during the off-season, from mid September to end the end of May. Dogs

must be leashed and people need to clean up after their pets. The town of Chatham oversees the following beaches: Hardings, Light, and Ridgevale. Before you go, always verify the seasonal dates and times when dogs are allowed on the beach.

Dennis

Dennis Town Beaches

Route 6A
Dennis, MA
508-394-8300

Dogs are allowed only during the off-season, from after Labor Day up to Memorial Day. There is one exception. Dogs are allowed year-round on the four wheel drive area of Chapin Beach. Dogs must be leashed on all town beaches, and people need to clean up after their pets. The town of Dennis oversees the following beaches: Chapin, Mayflower, Howes Street and Sea Street. Before you go, always verify the seasonal dates and times when dogs are allowed on the beach.

Falmouth

Falmouth Town Beaches

off Route 28
Falmouth, MA
508-457-2567

Dogs are allowed during the summer, only before 9am and after 5pm. During the off-season, dogs are allowed all day. Dogs must be leashed and people need to clean up after their pets. The town of Falmouth oversees the following beaches: Menauhant, Surf Drive, and Old Silver. Before you go, always verify the seasonal dates and times when dogs are allowed on the beach.

Harwich

Harwich Town Beach

off Route 28
Harwich, MA
508-430-7514

Dogs are allowed only during the off-season, from October to mid-May. Dogs must be on leash or under voice control. People need to clean up after their pets. The town of Harwich oversees Red River Beach. Before you go, always verify the seasonal dates and times when dogs are allowed on the beach.

Orleans

Orleans Town Beaches

off Route 28
Orleans, MA
508-240-3775

Dogs are allowed only during the off-season, from after Labor Day to the Friday before Memorial Day. Dogs are allowed off leash, but must be under voice control. People need to clean up after their pets. The town of Orleans oversees Nauset and Skaket beaches. Before you go, always verify the seasonal dates and times when dogs are allowed on the beach.

Provincetown

Provincetown Town Beaches

off Route 6
Provincetown, MA
508-487-7000

Dogs on leash are allowed year-round. During the summer, from 6am to 9am, dogs are allowed off-leash. The town of Provincetown oversees the following beaches: Herring Cove and Race Point. Before you go, always verify the seasonal dates and times when dogs are allowed on the beach.

Sandwich

Sandwich Town Beaches

off Route 6A

Sandwich, MA
508-888-4361
Dogs are allowed only during the off-season, from October through March. Dogs must be leashed and people need to clean up after their pets. The town of Sandwich oversees the following beaches: East Sandwich and Town Neck. Before you go, always verify the seasonal dates and times when dogs are allowed on the beach.

Truro

Truro Town Beaches
off Route 6
Truro, MA
508-487-2702
Dogs are allowed during the summer, only before 9am and after 6pm. This policy is in effect from about the third weekend in June through Labor Day. During the off-season, dogs are allowed all day. Dogs must be leashed and people need to clean up after their pets. The town of Truro oversees the following beaches: Ballston, Corn Hill, Fisher, Great Hollow, Head of the Meadow, Longnook and Ryder. Before you go, always verify the seasonal dates and times when dogs are allowed on the beach.

Wellfleet

Cape Cod National Seashore
Route 6
Wellfleet, MA
508-349-3785
The park offers a 40 mile stretch of pristine sandy beaches. Dogs on leash are allowed year-round on all of the seashore beaches, except for seasonally posted nesting or lifeguard controlled beaches. Leashed pets are also allowed on fire roads, and the Head of the Meadow bicycle trail in Truro. Check with the visitor center or rangers for details about fire road locations. To get there from Boston, take Route 3

south to the Sagamore Bridge. Take Route 6 east towards Eastham.

Wellfleet Town Beaches
off Route 6
Wellfleet, MA
508-349-9818
Dogs are allowed during the summer, only before 9am and after 6pm. During the off-season, from after Labor Day to the end of June, dogs are allowed all day. Dogs must be leashed and people need to clean up after their pets. The town of Wellfleet oversees the following beaches: Marconi, Cahoon Hollow, and White Crest. Before you go, always verify the seasonal dates and times when dogs are allowed on the beach.

Parks

Brewster

Nickerson State Park
Route 6A
Brewster, MA
508-896-3491
This state park has 1900 acres of land and miles of trails. Dogs are allowed on the hiking trails, and paved trails. Dogs are not allowed in the pond or on public beaches. However, you can take your dog to an uncrowded beach, where there are not many other people. Dogs must be leashed and you must have proof of your dog's rabies vaccination. Your dog is also welcome at the campgrounds, but they ask that your dog never be left unattended.

Wellfleet

Cape Cod Rail Trail
off Route 6
Wellfleet, MA
508-896-3491
This paved trail extends 25 miles through the towns of

Dennis, Harwich, Brewster, Orleans, Eastham and Wellfleet. The paved trail is for bicycles, and there is a wide unpaved shoulder for walkers, runners, and horseback riders. Dogs on leash are allowed. There are multiple parking areas along the trail. One is located off Route 6 at LeCount Hollow Road in Wellfleet. Another is located in Nickerson State Park, off Route 6A.

Restaurants

Brewster

Cobie's outdoor restaurant
3260 Main St
Brewster, MA
508-896-7021
This clam shack offers fried clams, seafood rolls, burgers, smoothies and more. They are open from about the end of May to mid September. Well-behaved, leashed dogs are allowed at the outdoor tables.

Harwich Port

Schoolhouse Ice Cream and Yogurt
749 Route 28
Harwich Port, MA
508-432-7355
This popular ice cream shop offers over 30 flavors, including sherbet, low-fat yogurt and fruit ices. Well-behaved, leashed dogs are allowed at the outdoor tables. Outdoor seating is seasonal. They are located on Route 28, just past Saquatucket Harbor and Brax Landing Restaurant heading towards Chatham.

Hyannis

Bobby Byrnes Restaurant
Route 28 and Bearses Way
Hyannis, MA 02601
508-775-1425
Well-behaved, leashed dogs are

allowed at the outdoor tables. Outdoor seating is seasonal.

Mashpee

Starbuck's Coffee House
38 Nanthan Ellis Hwy
Mashpee, MA 02649
508-477-5806
Well-behaved, leashed dogs are allowed at the outdoor tables. Outdoor seating is seasonal.

The Tea Shoppe
13 Steeple Street
Mashpee, MA 02649
508-477-7261
Anyone who would like to eat outside at this restaurant, needs to get food in a to go container, because they cannot serve their porcelain outside. Well-behaved, leashed dogs are welcome to join you at the outdoor sidewalk tables. Outdoor seating is seasonal.

Zoe's Pizza
58 Falmouth Rd
Mashpee, MA
508-477-1711
This pizza place offers a variety of pizzas, hot and cold subs, and pasta. They have two small outdoor tables. Well-behaved, leashed dogs are allowed at the outdoor tables. Outdoor seating is seasonal.

Orleans

The Cheese Corner and Deli
56 Main Street
Orleans, MA 02653
508-255-1699
This deli offers homemade soups, and sandwiches on homemade bread. The variety of sandwiches include roast beef, meat loaf, turkey, pastrami, liverwurst, peanut butter and jelly, ham and cheese, veggie pocket, and more. They also offer espresso, and fresh baked goodies. The deli serves lunch daily, except for when they are closed on Sundays during the

winter months. Well-behaved, leashed dogs are allowed at the outdoor tables. Outdoor seating is seasonal.

Martha's Vineyard City Guide

Accommodations

Edgartown

Colonial Inn
38 North Water Street
Edgartown, MA 02539
508-627-4711
This family friendly inn offers two pet-friendly suites for travelers with dogs. You can enjoy the daily complimentary continental breakfast outside in the Garden Courtyard with your pooch. There is a $30 per day pet fee. The entire inn is non-smoking.

Shiverick Inn
5 Pease Point Way
Edgartown, MA
508-627-3797
Pets up to about 75 pounds are allowed in the three bedroom suite which is located just off the library. Dogs are not allowed in the indoor common areas, just inside your room and outside. There is a $50 pet deposit. Pets cannot be left alone in the room. The entire inn is non-smoking.

The Point Way Inn Bed and Breakfast
104 Main Street
Edgartown, MA 02539

All rooms are non-smoking, have private bathrooms and some have private entrances. This inn allows dogs and they have even had previous guests with large dogs like Newfoundlands and Mastiffs. Complimentary continental breakfast is included and you may dine with your pooch in your room, or in the garden.

Afternoon tea or espresso can also be enjoyed outside. There may be a 3 night minimum stay on weekends. There is a $50 per day pet fee during the summer, and a $25 per day pet fee in the off-season.

Accommodations - Vacation Home Rentals

Edgartown

Martha's Vineyard Vacation Homes
Call to Arrange.
Edgartown, MA
203-374-8624
Some of the vacation homes are pet-friendly. There is a $100 weekly pet fee, and a $150 security deposit for pet damage or additional cleaning.

Vineyard Haven

Martha's Vineyard Rental Houses
Call to Arrange.
Vineyard Haven, MA
508-693-6222
Select from a variety of pet-friendly rental homes. Pet fees may vary per property.

Attractions

Hyannis

Hy-Line Cruises Ferry Service
Ocean Street Dock
Hyannis, MA
508-778-2600
This ferry service runs from Cape Cod to Nantucket Island (1 hour on the high speed ferry) or Martha's Vineyard (1.5 hours). They also offer the only Inter-Island Ferry between Nantucket and Martha's Vineyard (2.25 hours). Pets are allowed on the ferries, but not in the first class lounge. Pets need to be leashed. This ferry company provides year-round service to Nantucket and seasonal service

to Martha's Vineyard. The Inter-Island Ferry is also seasonal. No vehicles are transported on these ferries. Call ahead to make reservations.

Steamship Authority Ferry Service
South Street Dock
Hyannis, MA
508-477-8600
This ferry services runs from Cape Cod to Nantucket Island (2.25 hours) or Martha's Vineyard (1.5 hours). Pets are allowed on all ferries except for the M/V Flying Cloud fast ferry. Pets must be leashed or in a crate at all times. Pets are not allowed on the seats, tables, or in the concession areas. The ferries transport both passengers and cars. They provide year-round service to Nantucket and Martha's Vineyard. Call ahead to make reservations.

West Tisbury

West Tisbury Farmer's Markets
State Road
West Tisbury, MA
508-693-0085
The farmer's market is a great place to buy local, fresh fruits and vegetables. The market is usually held from mid-June to mid-August on Saturdays, from 9am to 12pm. Well-behaved dogs are allowed, but they must be held on a tight leash and you will need to watch them closely and avoid letting them play with other dogs. You will also need to make sure that your pooch does not go the bathroom in the market area, or on a vendors booth or produce. Please let your dog relieve himself or herself before you get there. The farmer's market is located between the Grange Hall and the playground.

Beaches

Edgartown

Joseph Sylvia State Beach
Beach Road
Edgartown, MA
508-696-3840
Dogs are allowed during the summer, only before 9am and after 5pm. You will need to keep your dog away from any bird nesting areas, which should have signs posted. During the off-season, from mid-September to mid-April, dogs are allowed all day. This beach is about 2 miles long. Dogs must be leashed and people need to clean up after their pets. Before you go, always verify the seasonal dates and times when dogs are allowed on the beach.

Norton Point Beach
end of Katama Road
Edgartown, MA
508-696-3840
Dogs are allowed during the summer, only before 9am and after 5pm. You will need to keep your dog away from any bird nesting areas, which should have signs posted. During the off-season, from mid-September to mid-April, dogs are allowed all day. This beach is about 2.5 miles long. Dogs must be leashed and people need to clean up after their pets. Before you go, always verify the seasonal dates and times when dogs are allowed on the beach.

South Beach State Park
Katama Road
Edgartown, MA 02575
508-693-0085
Dogs are allowed during the summer, only after 5pm. During the off-season, from mid-September to mid-April, dogs are allowed all day. This 3 mile beach is located on the South Shore. Dogs must be leashed

and people need to clean up after their pets. Before you go, always verify the seasonal dates and times when dogs are allowed on the beach.

Oak Bluffs

Eastville Point Beach
At bridge near Vineyard Haven
Oak Bluffs, MA
508-696-3840
Dogs are allowed during the summer, only before 9am and after 5pm. You will need to keep your dog away from any bird nesting areas, which should have signs posted. During the off-season, from mid-September to mid-April, dogs are allowed all day. Dogs must be leashed and people need to clean up after their pets. Before you go, always verify the seasonal dates and times when dogs are allowed on the beach.

Restaurants

Oak Bluffs

Carousel Ice Cream Factory
15 Circuit Avenue
Oak Bluffs, MA 02557
508-693-7582
They do not have tables outside, but you and your pooch can enjoy the ice cream at the outdoor benches.

Coop de Ville Restaurant
Dockside Marketplace
Oak Bluffs, MA 02557
508-693-3420
This restaurant offers a variety of food including wings, soup, veggies, seafood, chicken, hamburgers and even veggie burgers. Well-behaved, leashed dogs are allowed at the outdoor tables.

Nancy's Snack Bar and Harborview Restaurant
29 Lake Avenue
Oak Bluffs, MA 508-693-0006

Well-behaved, leashed dogs are allowed at the downstairs tables only, not upstairs.

Vineyard Haven

John's Fish Market
State Road
Vineyard Haven, MA
508-693-1220
They are open for lunch and dinner. Well-behaved, leashed dogs are allowed at the outdoor picnic tables. Tables are seasonal.

Louis' Tisbury Cafe
350 State Road
Vineyard Haven, MA
508-693-3255
This cafe serves Italian favorites, pizza, ribs, chicken, lasagna, eggplant parmesan and more. Well-behaved, leashed dogs are allowed at the outdoor picnic tables.

Sodapops
79 Beach Road
Vineyard Haven, MA
508-693-5200
There is one outdoor table in the back, near the water. Well-behaved, leashed dogs are allowed at the outdoor table. The cafe is open for breakfast and lunch.

Nantucket City Guide
Accommodations

Nantucket

Brass Lantern Inn
11 North Water Street
Nantucket, MA 02554
508-228-4064
Dogs up to about 65 pounds are allowed. Call to inquire if you have a larger dog. There is a $30 per day pet fee. All rooms are non-smoking.

Safe Harbor Guest House
2 Harbor View Way
Nantucket, MA 02554
508-228-3222
Dogs are allowed at this guest house. All rooms have private bathrooms. If your dog will be on the bed, please bring a sheet with you to place over the bedspread. There is no pet fee, they just request that you give the housekeeper a tip for extra cleaning, if necessary.

The Cottages at the Boat Basin
P.O. Box 1139
Nantucket, MA 02554
866-838-9253
Dogs and cats are welcome in "The Woof Cottages." These cottages are one and two bedroom cottages which include special pet amenities like a welcome basket of pet treats and play toys, a pet bed, food and water bowls, and a Nantucket bandana. When you make a reservation, let them know what size your pet is, so they can have the appropriate size pet bed and bowls in the room. All cottages are non-smoking. There is a $25 one time per stay pet fee.

The Grey Lady
P.O. Box 1292
Nantucket, MA 02554
508-228-9552
Pets and children are welcome at this guest house. While there is no pet fee, they have certain pet rooms which cost more per night than a standard room. All rooms are non-smoking. There may be a two or three night minimum stay during the summer. They also offer weekly cottage rentals at the Boat House.

Accommodations - Vacation Home Rentals

Nantucket

Quidnuck Vacation Rental
Call to Arrange.
Nantucket, MA 02554
202-663-8439
One dog is allowed at this vacation rental home. They ask that you do not bring a puppy and to never leave your dog alone in the house. There is a $75 one time per stay pet fee which will be used towards spraying the house for fleas. Ask for Jack when calling.

Attractions

Hyannis

Hy-Line Cruises Ferry Service
Ocean Street Dock
Hyannis, MA
508-778-2600
This ferry service runs from Cape Cod to Nantucket Island (1 hour on the high speed ferry) or Martha's Vineyard (1.5 hours). They also offer the only Inter-Island Ferry between Nantucket and Martha's Vineyard (2.25 hours). Pets are allowed on the ferries, but not in the first class lounge. Pets need to be leashed. This ferry company provides year-round service to Nantucket and seasonal service to Martha's Vineyard. The Inter-Island Ferry is also seasonal. No vehicles are transported on these ferries. Call ahead to make reservations.

Nantucket Airlines
660 Barnstable Road/North Ramp
Hyannis, MA 02601
508-790-0300
This airline offers daily flights between Hyannis and Nantucket (20 minute flight). Dogs are allowed in the cabin with you on this airline! Dogs under 35 pounds can be carried on your lap and no kennel is required. For dogs over 35 pounds, there is a "shelf" which is just a few inches off the floor, in the back of the plane where your dog can

sit or lay. While you cannot sit next to your dog, you can try to get the seat directly in front of him or her. There is no reserved seating, so you'll need to arrive early to try and make special arrangements to sit in front of your pooch. Large dogs must be properly restrained with a leash, harness or similar device. No kennel is required. You will need to reserve a space for your pet in advance as the airline usually only allows one dog per flight. Their sister airline, Cape Air also allows dogs in the cabin, but most flights require your dog to be in a kennel, and they have a size limit for dogs.

Steamship Authority Ferry Service
South Street Dock
Hyannis, MA
508-477-8600
This ferry services runs from Cape Cod to Nantucket Island (2.25 hours) or Martha's Vineyard (1.5 hours). Pets are allowed on all ferries except for the M/V Flying Cloud fast ferry. Pets must be leashed or in a crate at all times. Pets are not allowed on the seats, tables, or in the concession areas. The ferries transport both passengers and cars. They provide year-round service to Nantucket and Martha's Vineyard. Call ahead to make reservations.

Nantucket

Nantucket Regional Transit Authority (NRTA)
22 Federal Street
Nantucket, MA 02554
508-228-7025
Well-behaved dogs of all sizes are allowed on Nantucket shuttle buses. Pets must be leashed or caged, well-behaved, clean and dry, and pets cannot sit on the seats. While you can still take a car onto Nantucket Island, the transit authority encourages

everyone to leave their cars on the mainland.

Beaches

Nantucket

Nantucket Island Beaches
various locations
Nantucket, MA
508-228-1700
Dogs are allowed during the summer on beaches with lifeguards only before 9am and after 5pm. On beaches that have no lifeguards, or during the winter months, dogs are allowed all day on the beach. Dogs must always be leashed. Before you go, always verify the seasonal dates and times when dogs are allowed on the beach.

Restaurants

Nantucket

Espresso To Go
1 Toombs Court
Nantucket, MA
508-228-6930
In addition to the variety of specialty coffees, this cafe also serves pizza, sandwiches, salads, pasta, muffins and baked goods. Leashed dogs are welcome to join you at the tables in the outside garden.

Henry's Sandwich Shop
2 Broad Street
Nantucket, MA
508-228-0123
They are open for breakfast, lunch and dinner. Well-behaved, leashed dogs are welcome at the outdoor tables.

The Chantieleer
9 New Street
Nantucket, MA
508-257-6231
This French restaurant is open for lunch and dinner. Well-behaved, leashed dogs are

allowed at the outdoor tables. Please call ahead to make sure they will have outdoor seating for any particular day.

The Farm Kitchen
33 Bartlett Farm Road
Nantucket, MA
508-228-9403
The Farm Kitchen, located on Bartlett's 100 acre Ocean View Farm, offers fresh vegetables and daily seasonal specialties for take-out to the beach, a picnic or to their outdoor tables. They have two outdoor picnic tables where you are welcome to sit with your leashed pooch.

Stores

Nantucket

Cold Noses
The Courtyard at Straight Wharf
Nantucket, MA 02554
508-228-5477
Dogs are welcome at this boutique store for dogs and cats. Find pet apparel and accessories, and even stuff for people. Open year-round.

Geronimo's of Nantucket
119 Pleasant Street
Nantucket, MA 02554
508-228-3731
Dogs can accompany you to this pet store which offers treats, unique pet accessories and gifts.

New York City Guide
Accommodations

East Rutherford

Sheraton Meadowlands Hotel and Conference Center
2 Meadowlands Plaza
East Rutherford, NJ 07073
201-896-0500
Dogs of all sizes are allowed.

There is a $75 one time per stay pet fee.

Edison

Red Roof Inn
860 New Durham Rd
Edison, NJ 08817
732-248-9300
There are no additional pet fees.

Sheraton Edison Hotel Raritan Center
125 Raritan Center Parkway
Edison, NJ 08837
732-225-8300
Dogs of all sizes are allowed. There are no additional pet fees.

Englewood

Radisson
401 S Van Brunt St
Englewood, NJ 07631
201-871-2020
There are no additional pet fees.

Hampton Bays

Bowen's by the Bays
117 West Montauk Highway
Hampton Bays, NY 11946
631-728-1158
Bowen's by the Bays offers a choice of one, two or three bedroom cottages. The resort is set on four lovely acres and amenities include lighted tennis, swimming pool, playground, shuffleboard courts and a putting green. Hampton Bays is located in the heart of the Hamptons - the ideal setting for a special vacation. Pets are welcome in the cottages and prior arrangements must be made. Pet owners are required to abide by the published pet rules,i.e. clean up after your pet, keep pets under their direct control, do not disturb other guests, etc. There is a $15.00 per day/per pet fee.

Kings Park

Villa Rosa B&B Inn
121 Highland Street
Kings Park, NY 11754
631-724-4872
Built in 1920, this bed and breakfast inn is surrounded by spacious landscaped grounds. Some of the inn's rooms have private baths. This dog-friendly inn offers a fenced dog park area. Guests are welcome to bring their well-behaved dog, but pets must be leashed when in shared areas. There is a $20 per day pet charge. Room rates start around $130 per night and up. Weekly and monthly rates are available. They also have parking for larger vehicles like motorhomes and trailers.

Lyndhurst

Quality Inn Meadowlands
10 Polito Ave.
Lyndhurst, NJ 07071
201-933-9800
There is no pet fee.

Mahwah

Sheraton Crossroads Hotel
1 International Boulevard
Mahwah, NJ 07495
201-529-1660
Dogs of all sizes are allowed. There are no additional pet fees.

Mt Kisco

Holiday Inn
1 Holiday Inn Dr
Mt Kisco, NY
914-241-2600
There is a $25 one time pet charge.

New York

Holiday Inn - Wall Street
15 Gold Street
New York, New York 10038
212-232-7700

There is a $25 one time pet fee.

Novotel Hotel
226 West 52nd Street
New York, NY 10019
at Broadway
212-315-0100
This hotel is located in Midtown Manhattan, in the Broadway theater district. Amenities include room service, an exercise room and gift shop. The hotel lobby is located on the 7th floor. The Novotel allows dogs up to 50 pounds. There are no pet fees, but owners must sign a pet waiver.

Regency Hotel
540 Park Avenue
New York, NY 10021
212-759-4100
All well-behaved dogs of any size are welcome. This upscale hotel offers their "Loews Loves Pets" program which includes special pet treats, local dog walking routes, and a list of nearby pet-friendly places to visit. There are no pet fees.

Renaissance New York Hotel
714 7th Avenue
New York, NY 10036
at W. 48th Street
212-765-7676
They allow dogs up to about 70 pounds. This hotel is located in Times Square. It is located at the intersection of Broadway and Seventh Avenue. Amenities include room service, an in-room refreshment center, and an exercise/weight room. The hotel lobby is located on the third floor. There is a $65 one time charge for pets.

Sheraton New York Hotel and Towers
811 7th Avenue on 53rd Street
New York, NY 10019
212-581-1000
Dogs up to 75 pounds are allowed. There are no additional pet fees.

Sofitel Hotel

45 West 44th Street
New York, NY 10036
212-354-8844
This French hotel overlooks 5th Ave. Amenities include a fitness room. There are no additional pet fees.

Soho Grand Hotel
310 West Broadway
New York, NY 10013
between Grand and Canal
212-965-3000
This hotel is VERY pet-friendly and there are no size restrictions at all for dogs. They are owned by the Hartz Mountain Company which manufactures the 2 in 1 pet products. The hotel is located in the artistic heart of New York's cultural capital SoHo (South of Houston Street), and within an easy walking distance to the surrounding neighborhoods of Tribeca, Greenwich Village, Little Italy and Chinatown. The hotel is also just steps from Wall Street, and only minutes from Midtown Manhattan. Amenities include 24 room service and a fitness center. One of our readers has this to say about the hotel: "This is the most incredibly dog friendly hotel. Bellboys carry dog treats, there is a dog room service menu, doggie day care is provided. It's also one of New York's super chic hotels." There are no pet fees.

Swissotel NY -The Drake
440 Park Avenue
New York, NY 10022
at 56th Street
212-421-0900
Located in Midtown Manhattan, The Drake is just a couple of blocks from several dog-friendly stores and only 5 blocks from Central Park. Amenities include 24 hour room service and a fitness center/spa. No extra pet charge, just sign a pet waiver. Dogs up to about eighty pounds are allowed.

The Muse

130 West 46th Street
New York, NY
212-485-2400
There are no additional pet fees. They offer a pampered pooch package for an additional fee.

Tribeca Grand Hotel
2 Avenue of the Americas
New York, NY 10013
212-519-6600
This dog-friendly hotel is located just 2 blocks from it's sister hotel, the dog-friendly Soho Grand Hotel. This hotel is located within walking distance of Little Italy, Chinatown, Greenwich Village, and many department stores. Room rates begin at $399 and up. There are no pet fees.

W New York
541 Lexington Avenue
New York, NY 10022
212-755-1200
Dogs up to 70 pounds are allowed. There is a $25 one time per stay pet fee.

W New York - The Court
130 East 39th Street
New York, NY 10016
212-685-1100
Dogs up to 80 pounds are allowed. There is a $100 one time pet fee and a $25 per day additional pet fee.

W New York - The Tuscany
120 East 39th Street
New York, NY 10016
212-686-1600
Dogs up to 80 pounds are allowed. There is a $25 per day additional pet fee.

W New York - Times Square
1567 Broadway at 47th Street
New York, NY 10036
212-930-7400
Dogs up to 80 pounds are allowed. There is a $100 per stay pet fee and a $25 per night additional pet fee.

W New York - Union Square

201 Park Avenue South
New York, NY 10003
212-253-9119
Dogs up to 80 pounds are allowed. There is a $100 one time per stay pet fee and a $25 per day additional pet fee. Dogs may not be left alone in the room.

Paramus

Radisson
601 From Rd
Paramus, NJ 07652
201-262-6900
Dogs up to 50 pounds are allowed. There is a $25 per week pet fee.

Peekskill

Peekskill Inn
634 Main St
Peekskill, NY 10566
914-739-1500
There are no additional pet fees.

Plainview

Residence Inn by Marriott
9 Gerhard Rd
Plainview, NY 11803
516-433-6200
There is a $150 one time pet charge and a $10.00 per day pet charge.

Rockville Center

Holiday Inn
173 Sunrise Hwy Rt. 27
Rockville Center, NY 11570
516-678-1300
There is a $15 per day pet fee.

Secaucus

Mainstay Suites Meadowlands
1 Plaza Drive
Secaucus, NJ 07097
201-553-9700
There is a pet fee of $10 per day.

Radisson Suite
350 NJ 3 W
Secaucus, NJ 07094
201-863-8700
There is a $25 one time pet fee.

Weehawken

Sheraton Suites on the Hudson
500 Harbor Boulevard
Weehawken, NJ 07087
201-617-5600
Dogs up to 70 pounds are allowed. There is a one time pet fee of $64.00 per stay.

Attractions

New York

Brooklyn Bridge Self-Guided Walk
Park Row
New York, NY
across from City Hall Park

Enjoy the sights and skyline of New York City from the Brooklyn Bridge! You and your pooch can stroll along the bridge on the wooden walkway which is elevated over the traffic. The Brooklyn Bridge, designed by architect John Roebling between 1867 and 1883, is the world's first steel suspension bridge. It was constructed to link Brooklyn and Manhattan. This popular walk takes about 20-40 minutes each way, depending on your pace, If you need a break along the way, benches located on the walkway. The footpath begins at a street called Park Row (across from the City Hall Park).

Horse & Carriage Rides
59th Street and Fifth Avenue
New York, NY
and up to 6th Avenue

You and your pooch are welcome to hop on the horse and carriage rides for a tour of Central Park and NYC. The carriage driver will also supply a blanket for humans (and possibly your pooch!) if it is a little chilly outside. Carriages are available seven days a week after 10am, weather permitting. Rates are $34 (for a half hour) and up. The carriages are located at the south end of Central Park, at 59th Street and Fifth Avenue (up to 6th Avenue).

NYC Dog Walking Tour
various (see below)
New York, NY
914-633-7397
Armascan and Zuckerman Family offer "dog-friendly" walking tours of New York City. The tours last from 3-5 hours. Each tour will include many historical facts about the most incredible city in the world. Some highlights of the tour are visits to the following neighborhoods : Greenwich Village, Soho, Lower East Side, Little Italy, Central Park and any other area in Manhattan that you wish to visit. A special highlight is a walk across the Brooklyn Bridge at dusk. Call for tour rates or to arrange a guided tour.

Pet Taxi
227 E 56th St
New York, NY 10022
212-755-1757
When want to get around town without driving, there are numerous taxi cabs. A typical New York yellow taxi cab is supposed to pick up people with pets, however, they don't always stop if you have a pooch. Don't feel too bad, many NY cabs don't stop even for people without pets! However, with a little advance planning, you can reserve the Pet Taxi. The Pet Taxi makes runs to the vet, groomer and other pet related stuff. But they are also rented to transport you and your pooch to a park, outdoor restaurant, across town, etc.

For example, if you are at a hotel near Central Park but would like to go to Little Italy and Chinatown for half a day, they will take you to your destination and then several hours later, they will pick you up and take you back to your hotel. Just be sure to reserve the Pet Taxi at least one day in advance during the weekdays. If you need the taxi on Saturday or Sunday, book your reservation by Thursday or Friday. They are open from 8am-7pm during the weekday and by reservation on the weekends. They can be reserved for $35 per hour or $25 each way for a pick up or drop off. Pet Taxi serves the Manhattan area.

Seastreak Ferry Rides
various (see below)
New York, NY
800-BOAT-RIDE
Want to enjoy the sights of New York City from the water, including the Manhattan Skyline and the Statue of Liberty? Or maybe you want to stay at a hotel in New Jersey and visit New York City during the day. Well, the nice folks at Seastreak allow dogs onboard their commuter ferries. Here are the rules: Dogs of all sizes must stay on the outside portion of the ferry and they need to be on a short leash. Dogs are not allowed on the inside area regardless of the weather unless you have a small dog and he or she is in a carrier. The ferries operate between Manhattan and New Jersey on a daily basis with up to 11 ferry rides during the weekday and about 4 ferry rides on the weekend. The ride lasts about 45 minutes each way and costs approximately $20 per round trip, half price for children and free for dogs! The ferries depart from Pier 11 (Wall Street) and East 34th Street in Manhattan and Atlantic Highlands and Highlands in New Jersey. Please visit their website

for current ferry schedules, times and fares.

TV Broadcasts
various (see below)
New York, NY

Ever watch the NBC or CBS morning shows and see people standing outside holding signs or just wanting to get captured on national TV? Well, the filming locations are right here in the Big Apple. Located just outside the NBC and CBS broadcast studio buildings are designated areas for the public to line up for a chance at 15 minutes of fame. The live cameras film the crowds between 8am and 9am every day. If you want to get in the front of the line, you must arrive around 6am during nice weather and around 7am during bad weather. There is usually a larger crowd on sunny days. Please note that your pooch may not like crowds, especially if you are in the front. People may be pushing to get to the front, so your pooch may prefer to watch from the back. While you are waiting, you can also watch the live morning broadcast and the well-known anchor people from the outside through the large windows at the studios. The NBC studio is located in Rockefeller Center near 49th Street and the CBS studio is located on Fifth Avenue between 58th and 59th Streets.

Times Square Walking Tour
1560 Broadway
New York, NY 10036
between 46th and 47th Streets
212-768-1560
The Times Square BID (Business Improvement District) holds free guided walking tours every Friday at Noon for a behind-the-scenes look at Times Square. Visit historic theatres and the best of the neighborhood during this walking tour. Your pooch is welcome on the outdoor part of

the tour. Sometimes the tour will enter a few Theatres and unless you can convince the Theatres to allow your pup, you will need to wait outside. However, the majority of the tour should be outside. The tour leaves, rain or shine, every Friday, from the new Times Square Visitors Center, 1560 Broadway between 46th and 47th Streets.

William Secord Gallery
52 East 76th Street
New York, NY 10021
between Madison and Park Avenues
212-249-0075
The William Secord Gallery, located in Manhattan's Upper East Side, specializes in nineteenth century dog paintings, bronzes and works on paper. The only gallery of its kind in North America, it was established by William Secord in 1990. Since then, it has become a popular destination for those interested in dog art and collectibles. In addition to creating the gallery, William Secord was the founding director of The Dog Museum of America and is the author of Dog Painting, 1840-1940, a Social history of the Dog in Art, as well as European Dog Painting, both books available at the gallery. And of course, your well-behaved dog is welcome inside! If you ask, they will serve your pooch cookies and water. If you want a portrait of your own pooch, this gallery can direct you to several painters like Christine Merrill and Barrie Barnett. Samples of their work are located at the gallery. Merrill has painted several pet portraits for celebrities like Oprah Winfrey and Bob Schieffer. Prices for consignment portraits start at $7,000 and up. The gallery is open Monday - Saturday 10a.m. to 5:00p.m. and by

appointment. It is located on the third floor, so when you enter from the street, press the "William Secord" button. One of the staff members will then buzz the door open. Once inside, you can either take the small elevator or use the stairs. The toll free number is 1-877-249-DOGS.

Beaches

Montauk

Camp Hero State Park
50 South Fairview Avenue
Montauk, NY 11954
631-668-3781
The park boasts some of the best surf fishing spots in the world. Dogs on a 6 foot or less leash are allowed on the beach year-round, but not in the picnic areas. To get to the park, take Route 27 (Sunrise Highway) east to the end. The park is about 130 miles from New York City.

Hither Hills State Park
50 South Fairview Avenue
Montauk, NY 11954
631-668-2554
This park offers visitors a sandy ocean beach. Dogs are allowed with certain restrictions. During the off-season, dogs are allowed on the beach. During the summer, dogs are not allowed on the beach, except for the undeveloped area on the other side of the freeway. Dogs must be on a 6 foot or less leash and people need to clean up after their pets. Dogs are not allowed in buildings or on walkways and they are not allowed in the camping, bathing and picnic areas.

Montauk Point State Park
50 South Fairview Avenue
Montauk, NY 11954
631-668-3781
This park is located on the eastern tip of Long Island. Dogs

are allowed on the beach, but not near the food area. Dogs must be on a 6 foot or less leash and people need to clean up after their pets. Dogs are not allowed in buildings or on walkways and they are not allowed in the camping, bathing and picnic areas. Please note that dogs are not allowed in the adjacent Montauk Downs State Park. The park is located 132 miles from Manhattan, off Sunrise Highway (Route 27).

Parks

New York

Battery Park
State Street
New York, NY
south of the Financial District

From this 23 acre city park, you can view the Statue of Liberty and Ellis Island in the distance. There are numerous picnic tables and several sidewalk vendors in the park. This park also contains several sculptures and the Clinton Castle Monument, a sandstone fort built in 1811. Your leashed dog is allowed in the park, but much of the grass area is fenced off.

Canine Court
Henry Hudson Parkway
New York, NY
in Van Cortlandt Park

In April of 1998, New York City's first public dog playground (agility course) opened in Van Cortlandt Park. Canine Court was also the first public dog agility course/playground in the country. Canines now have a fenced-in play area that totals 14,000 square feet - one half as a dog run and the other half as a dog agility course. The agility equipment consists of several chutes or tunnels for pooches to run through, a teeter-totter and a pair of hurdles. Canine Court

was made possible by $3,000 from the Friends of Van Cortlandt Park and $1,000 from the City Parks Foundation (CPF). The NYC event called PawsWalk, held every April/May helped to fund some of the equipment, fencing and benches. The doggie playground is located in Van Cortlandt Park in the Bronx. From the Henry Hudson Parkway, follow signs to Van Cortlandt Park. Canine Court is located across the Parkway from the horse barn/stable. It is located between a running track/soccer field area and the Parkway. You cannot really see it from the road, so you will need to park and then walk along the running path, towards the Parkway.

Central Park
Central Park W & Fifth Ave.
New York, NY
between 59th & 110th Streets

Central Park, located the heart of Manhattan, is the world's most famous park. This 843 acre park is so nice and refreshing that you'll find it hard to believe it is in the middle of the country's largest city. When we visited Central Park, it seemed very clean and safe, however there are two rules of thumb to follow. Only walk in the park during daylight hours and stay on the main paths. It is best to go on main paths where other people are walking. The park is 6 miles long and has an inner path which is a 4 mile loop. Also inside the park is a popular running track which is a 1.58 mile loop (between 86th and 96th Streets). When inside the park, be sure to stop by the Shakespeare Garden - leashed pooches are welcome on the paths. And don't miss Balto - a bronze sculpture of Balto, the sled dog. Balto is located between the Shakespeare

Garden and Fifth Street (around 67th Street). If 66th Street were to go through the Park, the statue of Balto would be on 66th Street. Another popular area for dog fanatics is "Dog Hill". On a nice day, you will find dogs of all shapes, sizes and breeds socializing here. It is located near Central Park West and 79th Street (north of 79th Street.) ***PLEASE NOTE: The official policy of the park is that dogs are not allowed off leash. However, the park rangers don't give out any tickets/fines between the hours of 9pm to 9am. But be aware that a police officer could still give out a ticket. ***

Riverside Park
Riverside Drive
New York, NY
between W 72nd and 158th

This waterfront park has a path which stretches for 4 miles alongside the Hudson River. Your leashed pooch is welcome.

Washington Sq. Park Dog Run
Washington Sq. South
New York, NY
near Thompson Street

This dog run is located in Washington Square Park in Greenwich Village. The run is located in the south side of the park near Thompson Street.

Restaurants

New York

Amaranth Restaurant
21 East 62nd St.
New York, NY
212-980-6700
This Italian restaurant welcomes dogs at their outdoor tables.

Cafe Nosidam
768 Madison Ave
New York, NY
212-717-5633

This Italian restaurant allows dogs at their outdoor perimeter tables.

Cascina
281 Bleecker St
New York, NY
212-633-2941
This Italian restaurant allows dogs at the outdoor tables.

Da Rosina Ristorante
342 W 46th St
New York, NY
212-977-7373
This Italian restaurant allows dogs at the outdoor tables.

Ferrier
29 E 65th St
New York, NY
212-772-9000
This French bistro allows dogs at the outdoor tables.

Fratelli Ristorante
115 Mulberry St
New York, NY
212-226-5555
Dogs are allowed at the outdoor tables at this Italian restaurant.

Gator's Southern Seafood
89 South St
New York, NY
212-571-4199
Dogs are allowed at this seafood restaurant, but need to be on a leash and tied to a chair or the table.

La Goulue
746 Madison Ave.
New York, NY
212-988-8169
This French restaurant allows pooches at their outdoor tables.

San Martin Restaurant
143 E 49th Street
New York, NY 10017
212-832-0888
This Italian restaurant has delicious food and allows dogs at the outdoor tables. There are only 3 tables and they are pretty close together, but even a large pooch can lay beside you

(assuming there is no one sitting at the table next to you).

Sorrento Restaurant
132 Mulberry St
New York, NY
212-219-8634
Dogs are allowed at the end outdoor tables at this Italian Restaurant. There is not much space in the outdoor seating area, so a large dog may need to lay under the table.

Stores

New York

Banana Republic
130 East 59th Street
New York, NY 10022
59th & Lexington Avenue
212-751-5570
Dogs are allowed in many of the Banana Republic stores in the area.

Bergdorf Goodman's
754 5th Ave (57th and 5th Avenue)
New York, NY 10019
212-753-7300

Bloomingdale's
59th Street and Lexington Avenue
New York, NY
212-705-2000
Thanks to one of our viewers who writes: "during one of our visits, Captain (my Dane) was invited to be apart of a photo shoot. He was then invited back for a fashion show."

Polo Ralph Lauren
72nd & Madison
New York, NY

Thanks to one of our viewers who writes: "they will bring your dog cookies and water on a silver tray. Very lovely."

Restoration Hardware
935 Broadway

New York, NY
212-260-9479
They love having dogs in the store!

The Gap
59th Street and Lexington Avenue
New York, NY 10022
212-751-1543
Dogs are allowed in many of the Gap stores in the area.

Tiffany's
Fifth Avenue at 57th Street
New York, NY 10022
212-755-8000

Tourneau
12 East 57th Street
New York, NY 10022
212-758-7300
Dogs are allowed in many of the Tourneau stores in the area.

Philadelphia City Guide

Accommodations

Berwyn

Residence Inn
600 W Swedesford Rd
Berwyn, PA 19312
610-640-9494
There is a $150.00 one time pet charge.

Essington

Red Roof Inn - Airport
49 Industrial Hwy
Essington, PA 19029
610-521-5090
There are no additional pet fees. Dogs up to 80 pounds are allowed.

Horsham

Residence Inn
3 Walnut Grove Rd
Horsham, PA 19044
215-443-7330

There is a $150.00 one time pet charge.

Kulpsville

Best Western
1750 Sumneytown Pike
Kulpsville, PA 19443
215-368-3800
This hotel was previously a Holiday Inn. There are no additional pet fees.

Langhorne

Sheraton Bucks County Hotel
400 Oxford Valley Road
Langhorne, PA 19047
215-547-4100
Dogs up to 80 pounds are allowed. There are no additional pet fees.

Lionville

Hampton Inn
4 N Pottstown Pike
Lionville, PA 19341
610-363-5555
There are no additional pet fees.

Malvern

Homewood Suites
12 E Swedesford Rd
Malvern, PA 19355
610-296-3500
There is a $150.00 one time pet charge.

Philadelphia

Crowne Plaza
1800 Market St
Philadelphia, PA 19103
215-561-7500
There is a $50 one time pet fee.

Loews Philadelphia Hotel
1200 Market Street
Philadelphia, PA 19107
215-627-1200
All well-behaved dogs of any size are welcome. This upscale hotel offers their "Loews Loves

Pets" program which includes special pet treats, local dog walking routes, and a list of nearby pet-friendly places to visit. There are no pet fees.

Philadelphia Marriott
1201 Market St
Philadelphia, PA 19107
215-625-2900
There is a $100 one time pet charge.

Residence Inn - Philadelphia Airport
4630 Island Ave
Philadelphia, PA 19153
215-492-1611
There is a $100 one time pet charge.

Sheraton Society Hill
One Dock Street
Philadelphia, PA 19106
215-238-6000
Dogs of all sizes are allowed. There are no additional pet fees.

The Rittenhouse
210 W Rittenhouse Square
Philadelphia, PA 19103
215-546-9000
There are no additional pet fees.

Pottstown

Comfort Inn
99 Robinson St
Pottstown, PA 19464
610-326-5000
There is a $25 refundable pet deposit.

Days Inn
29 High St
Pottstown, PA 19464
610-970-1101
There is a $10 per day pet charge.

Attractions

Philadelphia

Ben Franklin Bridge
5th St and Vine St
Philadelphia, PA

You can walk across the Ben Franklin bridge from 5th St and Vine St. The bridge connects Philadelphia with New Jersey.

Ben Franklin's Grave
5th St and Arch St
Philadelphia, PA

Dogs are not allowed in the burial grounds at the church. However, Ben Franklin's grave is accessible from the street sidewalk at 5th and Arch.

Horse and Carriage Rides
Independence Mall
Philadelphia, PA

The horse and carriage rides leave from next to Independence Hall on Independence Mall. Most drivers will allow well behaved dogs.

Independence Mall
Market St and 5th St
Philadelphia, PA

There is a lot to see while walking your dog here. However, if you want to go inside the Liberty Bell pavilion the dog needs to stay outside. He can see the bell through the glass, though.

South Street District
South St and 2nd Ave
Philadelphia, PA

There are a number of dog-friendly eateries and stores in this colorful district.

Valley Forge

Valley Forge National Historical Park
US 422 and PA 23
Valley Forge, PA

There is a self-guided tour and

lots of trails here.

Washington Crossing

Washington Crossing Historic Park
1112 River Rd
Washington Crossing, PA 18977
215-493-4076
Most of the park is visible from walking outside. You can even peek into some buildings. Dogs are allowed on leash in the park.

Parks

Evansburg

Evansburg State Park
US Route 422
Evansburg, PA

Pets must be leashed. This park is over 1000 acres.

Fort Washington

Fort Washington State Park
Bethlehem Pike
Fort Washington, PA
Between Ft Wash - Fourtown

Dogs must be leashed. This park offers over 3.5 miles of hiking trails.

New Hope

New Hope Towpath
3620 Windy Rd
New Hope, PA

This towpath dirt walking trail begins in the center of New Hope. There are a number of dog-friendly restaurants in New Hope.

Philadelphia

Ben Franklin Parkway
Ben Franklin Pkwy and 19th St.
Philadelphia, PA

Ben Franklin Parkway is a large

avenue surrounded by Grass and Trees. It is scenic and a good area to walk a dog in downtown Philadelphia.

Fairmount Park
4231 N. Concourse Dr
Philadelphia, PA 19131
215-685-0000
This address is the Park commission headquarters, in the park. The park is very big and stretches from the Center of Philadelphia to the northwest.

Manuyunk Towpath and Canal
Main Street
Philadelphia, PA

This is a two mile path in the Manayunk area of Philadelphia. There are a lot of dog-friendly eating places in the area, also.

Pennypack Park
Algon Ave and Bustleton Ave
Philadelphia, PA

Leashed dogs are allowed at this large 1600 acre city park.

Rittenhouse Square Park
Walnut St and 18th St
Philadelphia, PA

Located in downtown Philadelphia, this park is a gathering spot for people who wish to sit and rest on a bench or on the lawn. Leashed dogs are allowed.

Washington Square Park
Walnut St and 6th St
Philadelphia, PA

Leashed dogs are allowed at this city park.

Restaurants

Philadelphia

Brasserie Perrier
1619 Walnut St

Philadelphia, PA 19103
215-568-3000
Well-behaved dogs are welcome here.

Cafe Zesty
4382 Main St
Philadelphia, PA 19127
215-483-6226
Dogs are allowed at the outdoor tables.

Caribou Cafe
1126 Walnut St
Philadelphia, PA 19107
215-625-9535
Dogs are allowed at the outdoor tables.

Devon's Seafood
225 18th St F1 1
Philadelphia, PA 19103
215-546-5940
Dogs are allowed at the outdoor tables.

Garden Gate Cafe
8139 Germantown Ave
Philadelphia, PA 19118
215-247-8487
Dogs are allowed at the outdoor tables.

Le Bus
4266 Main St
Philadelphia, PA 19127
215-487-2663
Well-behaved dogs are welcome here at the outdoor tables.

Main-Ly Desserts
4247 Main Street
Philadelphia, PA 19127
215-487-1325
Dogs are allowed at the outdoor tables.

Pat's King of Steaks
1237 E Passyunk Ave
Philadelphia, PA 19147
215-468-1546
One of the original Philly steak places. You order food outside and eat outside here.

Philadelphia Java Company
518 4th St
Philadelphia, PA 19147

215-928-1811
Dogs are allowed at the outdoor tables.

Society Hill Hotel Rest.
301 Chestnut St
Philadelphia, PA 19106
215-925-1919
Dogs are allowed in the outdoor eating area. However, dogs are not allowed to stay at the hotel.

Sonoma
4411 Main Street
Philadelphia, PA 19127
215-483-9400
Dogs are allowed at the outdoor tables.

Baltimore City Guide
Accommodations

Baltimore

Brookshire Suites
120 E. Lombard Street
Baltimore, MD 21202
410-625-1300
All well-behaved dogs are welcome at this suites hotel. There are no pet fees.

Comfort Inn Airport
6921 Baltimore-Annap. Blvd
Baltimore, MD 21225
410-789-9100
There are no pet fees.

Pier 5 Hotel
711 Eastern Avenue
Baltimore, MD 21202
410-539-2000
The entire hotel offers a smoke free environment. All well-behaved dogs are welcome and there are no pet fees.

Sheraton Baltimore North Hotel
903 Dulaney Valley Road
Baltimore, MD 21204
410-321-7400
Dogs up to 100 pounds are allowed. There is a $100 one time pet fee.

Sheraton Inner Harbor Hotel
300 South Charles Street
Baltimore, MD 21201
410-962-8300
Dogs up to 80 pounds are allowed. There are no additional pet fees. The hotel has specific pet rooms.

Sheraton International Hotel on BWI Airport
7032 Elm Road
Baltimore, MD 21240
410-859-3300
Dogs of any size are allowed. There is a $25 one time additional pet fee.

Sleep Inn and Suites Airport
6055 Belle Grove Road
Baltimore, MD 21225
410-789-7223
There are no pet fees.

The Admiral Fell Inn
888 South Broadway
Baltimore, MD 21231
410-522-7377
All well-behaved dogs are welcome and there no pet fees.

Cockeysville

Chase Suite Hotel by Woodfin
1071 0 Beaver Dam Road
Cockeysville, MD 21030
All well-behaved dogs are welcome. All rooms are suites with a full kitchen. Hotel amenities include a complimentary breakfast buffet. There is a $5 per day pet fee. There are no additional pet fees.

Glen Burnie

Days Inn - Glen Burnie
6600 Richie Hwy
Glen Burnie, MD 21061
410-761-8300
There is a $10 per day additional pet fee per pet.

Timonium

Red Roof Inn - Timonium
111 W Timonium Rd
Timonium, MD 21093
410-666-0380
There are no additional pet fees.

Towson

Days Inn - Baltimore East
8801 Loch Raven Blvd
Towson, MD 21286
410-882-0900
There is a $15 per day pet charge.

Attractions

Baltimore

Fort McHenry
End of East Fort Avenue
Baltimore, MD 21230
410-962-4290
Dogs are allowed in the outdoor areas of the park. They must be well behaved and on leash.

Horse and Carriage Rides
Inner Harbor
Baltimore, MD

Well-behaved dogs are allowed on the carriage rides.

Parks

BWI Airport

BWI Bike Trail
Dorsey Road
BWI Airport, MD

This trail is a nice paved trail at the airport, near a number of the dog-friendly hotels.

Baltimore

Cromwell Valley Park
2175 Cromwell Bridge Rd
Baltimore, MD
410-887-2503
Dogs on leash are welcome.

Cylburn Arboretum
4915 Greenspring Ave
Baltimore, MD 21209
410-396-0180
Well behaved dogs on leash are welcome at this over 20 acre nature preserve and city park.

Druid Hill Park
Druid Park Lake Drive
Baltimore, MD

Druid Hill Park is a large city park in the center of Baltimore. Dogs on leash are allowed in the park.

Federal Hill
Key Hwy and Light St
Baltimore, MD

This small park is listed because its in easy walking distance from the Inner Harbor. Dogs on leash are welcome.

Gwynns Fall Trail and Park
Franklintown Rd and Holly Ave
Baltimore, MD

This is a city park with a paved bike trail. Dogs on leash are welcome.

Robert E Lee Park
Falls Road and Lake Ave
Baltimore, MD

Dogs must be on leash at all times in the park.

Cockeysville

Oregon Ridge Park
Beaver Dam Road
Cockeysville, MD
410-887-1818
Dogs on leash are allowed. This is a very large park with lots of trails.

Edgemere

Fort Howard Park
North Point Blvd
Edgemere, MD

410-887-7529
Dogs must be leashed in this park.

North Point State Park
Old North Point Rd
Edgemere, MD
410-592-2897
Dogs must be leashed in this park.

Glen Burnie

Baltimore & Annapolis Bike Trail

Glen Burnie, MD
From Glen Burnie to Annapolis

This is a 13 mile paved trail from Baltimore to Annapolis. Leashed dogs are allowed.

Hereford

Gunpowder Falls State Park

Hereford, MD
410-592-2897
This is a huge park with over 100 miles of trails. It follows the Gunpowder Falls River and extends as far as Pennsylvania. Dogs on leash are allowed.

Towson

Hampton Historical Site
535 Hampton Lane
Towson, MD 21286
410-823-1309
Dogs on leash are allowed in the outdoor areas. There is an admission fee to the park, which is an 1800's plantation.

Restaurants

Baltimore

Admiral's Cup Cafe
1647 Thames St
Baltimore, MD 21231
410-522-6731

Dogs are allowed at the outdoor tables.

Bonjour
6070 Falls Rd
Baltimore, MD 21209
410-372-0238
Dogs are allowed at the outdoor tables.

Caffe Brio
904 S Charles St
Baltimore, MD 21230
410-234-0235
Dogs are allowed at the outdoor tables.

Cannella's Italian Deli
9946 Harford Rd
Baltimore, MD 21234
410-661-3089
Dogs are allowed at the one outdoor table.

Ethel and Ramone's
1615 Sulgrave Ave
Baltimore, MD 21209
410-664-2971
This restaurant is in the Mt Washington district. Dogs are allowed at the outdoor tables.

Glas Z Cafe
6080 Falls Rd
Baltimore, MD 21209
410-377-9060
Dogs are allowed at the outdoor tables.

Greene Turtle
722 S Broadway
Baltimore, MD 21231
410-342-4222
Dogs are allowed at the outdoor tables.

J. Paul's Harbor Place
301 Light St
Baltimore, MD 21202
410-659-1889
Dogs are allowed at the perimeter tables.

Nile Cafe Egyptian Oven
811 S Broadway
Baltimore, MD 21231
410-327-0005
Dogs are allowed at the outdoor

tables.

Parkville

Checkers
1915 E Joppa Rd
Parkville, MD 21234
410-663-5798
Dogs are allowed at the outdoor tables.

Washington D.C. City Guide
Accommodations

Alexandria

Comfort Inn - Mount Vernon
7212 Richmond Highway
Alexandria, VA 22306
703-765-9000
There is a $20 per night pet fee (per pet per day). There is a $50 refundable pet deposit. There is a 2 pet limit per room. Please call for availability as there are a limited number of pet rooms.

Holiday Inn - Telegraph Rd
2460 Eisenhower Ave
Alexandria, VA 22314
703-960-3400
There are no additional pet fees.

Red Roof Inn
5975 Richmond Highway
Alexandria, VA 22303
703-960-5200
Dogs up to 80 pounds are allowed. There are no additional pet fees.

Arlington

Potomac Suites Rosslyn
1730 Arlington Blvd
Arlington, VA 22209
703-528-2900
Located just across the Potomac River from historic Washington, DC in a quiet neighborhood in Rosslyn, Virginia. Potomac Suites Rosslyn offers quick access to the shopping and

dining of Georgetown and the excitement of the museums and monuments on the National Mall. You and your pet will enjoy fully spacious suites with fully equipped kitchens, cable TV with HBO, high speed Internet access, and more.

Quality Inn - Iwo Jima
1501 Arlington Blvd
Arlington, VA 22209
703-524-5000
There is a $10 per day pet fee. Dogs are allowed in rooms with exterior entrances.

Bethesda

Residence Inn by Marriott
7335 Wisconsin Ave
Bethesda, MD 20814
301-718-0200
There is a $100 one time pet fee and an additional $5 per day pet charge.

Fairfax

Comfort Inn University Center
11180 Main St
Fairfax, VA 22030
703-591-5900
Pets are welcome and there are no pet fees.

Holiday Inn Fair Oaks - Fairfax
11787 Lee Jackson Memorial Hwy
Fairfax, VA 22033
703-352-2525
There is a $25 non-refundable pet fee per stay.

Gaithersburg

Comfort Inn at Shady Grove
16216 Frederick Rd
Gaithersburg, MD 20877
301-330-0023
There is no pet fee.

Holiday Inn - Gaithersburg
2 Montgomery Village Ave

Gaithersburg, MD 20879
301-948-8900
There are no additional pet fees.

Red Roof Inn - Gaithersburg
497 Quince Orchard Rd
Gaithersburg, MD 20878
301-977-3311
There are no additional pet fees.

Residence Inn by Marriott
9721 Washington Blvd
Gaithersburg, MD 20878
301-590-3003
There is a $100 one time pet charge and an additional $6 a day pet fee.

Herndon

Residence Inn by Marriott
315 Elden St
Herndon, VA 20170
703-435-0044
There is a $100 one time pet fee plus $6 per day.

Laurel

Comfort Suites Laurel Lakes
14402 Laurel Pl.
Laurel, MD 20707
301-206-2600
There is a $50 refundable pet deposit.

Red Roof Inn - Laurel
12525 Laurel Bowie Rd
Laurel, MD 20708
301-498-8811
One pet per room is permitted. Dogs up to 85 pounds are allowed. There are no additional pet fees.

Manassas

Red Roof Inn
10610 Automotive Dr
Manassas, VA 20109
703-335-9333
There are no additional pet fees.

Oxon Hill

Red Roof Inn - Oxon Hill
6170 Oxon Hill Rd
Oxon Hill, MD 20745
301-567-8030
There are no additional pet fees.

Rockville

Best Western Washington Gateway Hotel
1251 W Montgomery Ave
Rockville, MD 20850
301-424-4940
There is a $10 per day additional pet fee.

Quality Suites and Conference Center
3 Research Ct
Rockville, MD 20850
301-840-0200
There is a $25 pet fee.

Sleep Inn Shady Grove
2 Research Ct
Rockville, MD 20850
301-948-8000
There is a pet fee of $25.

Woodfin Suite Hotel
1380 Piccard Drive
Rockville, MD 20850
301-590-9880
All well-behaved dogs are welcome. Every room is a suite with either a wet bar or full kitchen. Hotel amenities includes a pool, free video movies and a complimentary hot breakfast buffet. There is a $5 per day pet fee per pet. If you are staying for one month, the pet fee is $50 for the month.

Springfield

Comfort Inn - Springfield
6560 Loisdale Ct
Springfield, VA 22150
703-922-9000
There are no additional pet fees.

Motel 6
6868 Springfield Blvd
Springfield, VA 22150
703-644-5311

There are no additional pet fees.

Vienna

Comfort Inn Tysons Corner
1587 Spring Hill Rd
Vienna, VA 22182
703-448-8020
There is a one time pet fee of $25. There is also a pet fee of $10 per day.

Residence Inn - Tysons Corner
8616 Westwood Center Dr
Vienna, VA 22182
703-893-0120
There is a $150 one time pet fee plus $5 per day.

Waldorf

Days Inn of Waldorf
11370 Days Court
Waldorf, MD 20603
301-932-9200
There is a $10 one time fee per pet.

Washington

Hotel Helix
1430 Rhode Island Ave
Washington, DC 20006
202-462-9001
Well-behaved dogs of all sizes are welcome at this hotel. The boutique hotel offers both rooms and suites. Amenities include room service, and a 24 hour on-site exercise room. There are no pet fees.

Hotel Madera
1310 New Hampshire Ave
Washington, DC
202-296-7600
Well-behaved dogs of all sizes are welcome at this boutique hotel. Amenities include an evening wine hour, and room service. There are no pet fees.

Hotel Rouge
1315 16th Street NW

Washington, DC
202-232-8000
Well-behaved dogs of all sizes are welcome at this luxury boutique hotel. Amenities include complimentary high speed Internet access in the rooms, 24 hour room service, and a 24 hour on-site fitness room. There are no pet fees.

Hotel Sofitel
1914 Connecticut Ave
Washington, DC 20009
202-737-8800
There are no additional pet fees.

Hotel Washington
515 15th St NW
Washington, DC 20004
202-638-5900
There are no additional pet fees.

Loews L'Enfant Plaza Hotel
480 L'Enfant Plaza
Washington, DC 20024
202-484-1000
All well-behaved dogs of any size are welcome. This upscale hotel offers their "Loews Loves Pets" program which includes special pet treats, local dog walking routes, and a list of nearby pet-friendly places to visit. There are no pet fees.

Park Hyatt Washington
1201 24th St NW
Washington, DC 20037
202-789-1234
There are no additional pet fees.

The Jefferson Hotel, a Loews Hotel
1200 16th St. NW
Washington, DC 20036
202-347-2200
All well-behaved dogs of any size are welcome. This upscale hotel offers their "Loews Loves Pets" program which includes special pet treats, local dog walking routes, and a list of nearby pet-friendly places to visit. There are no pet fees.

Willard Inter-Continental
1401 Pennsylvania Ave

Washington, DC 20004
202-628-9100
Pet owners must sign a pet waiver. There are no pet fees.

Attractions

Alexandria

Old Town Horse and Carriage
Duke St
Alexandria, VA
703-765-8976
Take a horse and carriage ride with your pup or just roam around the Old Town Alexandria area. Pick up the horse and carriage ride in Old Town.

Arlington

Arlington National Cemetery
Memorial Drive
Arlington, VA 22211
Memorial Bridge Circle

Well behaved, leashed dogs are allowed in Arlington Cemetery. Please respect the grounds here. Your well behaved dog can accompany you to the Kennedy grave and other outdoor sites at the cemetery.

Iwo Jima Memorial

Arlington, VA

Leashed dogs can accompany you to the Iwo Jima, or Marine Corp War Memorial as it is formally called.

Mt Vernon

Mount Vernon
George Washington Pkwy
Mt Vernon, VA
703-780-2000
Your leashed, well behaved dog can accompany you to all outdoor areas of Mount Vernon. If you would like to take the mansion tour then someone will need to watch the dog. Otherwise, most of the site is

outdoors.

Washington

Capitol River Cruises
31st and K St, NW
Washington, DC 20007
Washington Harbour
301-460-7447
Dogs are allowed on this water tour of Washington. The 1 hour tour passes most of the major attractions downtown.

FDR Memorial
National Mall
Washington, DC

Leashed dogs are allowed in the FDR memorial, which is entirely outdoors. There is a statue of FDR's dog for your dog to pose with. There are audio tours of the memorial available as well.

Fletcher's Boat House
4940 Canal Rd NW
Washington, DC 20007
202-244-0461
Rent a canoe or a boat on the C & O Canal or the Potomac River.

Jefferson Memorial
National Mall
Washington, DC

According to the National Park Service, well behaved dogs are allowed on leash except in the area underneath the dome.

Lincoln Memorial
National Mall
Washington, DC

According to the National Park Service, well behaved, leashed dogs are allowed at the memorial except underneath the dome. This allows a pretty close view of the statue for your pup.

National Mall
Independence Ave and 14th St.

Washington, DC

Dogs are permitted on the mall on leash. According to the National Park Service, they are permitted up to the monuments except in indoor or covered areas. The mall is two miles long and is an excellent place for dog walking downtown. Dogs are not permitted on the walkways at the Vietnam or Korean War Memorials or inside the Washington Monument.

Parks

Alexandria

Holmes Run Park
Holmes Run Pkwy and S Jordon St
Alexandria, VA 22304

This park has a bike trail, creek, and picnic areas. Dogs are allowed on leash. There is also an off leash dog park at the Duke St intersection with the park.

Huntley Meadows Park
3701 Lockheed Blvd
Alexandria, VA 22306
703-768-2525
Dogs on leash are allowed in most of the park. However, they are not allowed on the wooden boardwalk.

Mount Vernon Trail
George Washington Parkway
Alexandria, VA
703-285-2601
This bike trail is very scenic and connects Mt Vernon with Washington. Dogs on leash are allowed.

Arlington

Gravelly Point Park
George Washington Pkwy
Arlington, VA
Northbound only

You and your dog can watch the airline traffic at National Airport. It can get noisy. You need to access the park from the northbound direction on the George Washington Parkway. Dogs must be leashed in this park.

Theodore Roosevelt Island Park

George Washington Parkway
Arlington, VA
703-289-2500
Theodore Roosevelt Island park has nice dirt trails and a memorial to Theodore Roosevelt. Your dog will probably like this memorial the most in Washington as it has many acres of trails and nature. Dogs may accompany you on leash in the park.

Greenbelt

Greenbelt Park

6565 Greenbelt Rd
Greenbelt, MD 20770
301-344-3944
Dogs must be leashed in this park.

Washington

C & O Canal Towpath

M Street
Washington, DC
301-739-4200
The 184 mile towpath extends all the way from Georgetown, in Washington, DC to Cumberland, MD. It is a dirt trail and can be accessed at many points along the way. Dogs must be leashed on the towpath.

Capital Crescent Trail

Water Street, NW
Washington, DC
Between Georgetown and Bethesda

This paved bike trail starts in Georgetown and heads to the Maryland Suburbs. Dogs must be leashed on the trail.

National Arboretum

3501 New York Ave NE
Washington, DC
R Street
202-245-2726
The National Arboretum allows dogs on leash. There are miles of walking trails here.

Rock Creek Park

Washington, DC
202-426-6828
Rock Creek Park is a large city park run by the National Park Service. Dogs on leash are allowed in the park. There is a paved trail and lots of picnic areas, trails and activities. The park extends from near downtown Washington to Maryland.

Wheaton

Wheaton Regional Park

2000 Shorefield Rd
Wheaton, MD

An excellent park for kids and dogs. There are a number of annual dog events here and trails to jog or walk on. Dogs must be leashed in the park.

Restaurants

Bethesda

Wok Inn Restaurant

4924 Saint Elmo Ave
Bethesda, MD 20814
301-986-8590
Dogs are allowed at the outdoor tables.

Rockville

Chicken Out Rotisserie

1560 Rockville Pike
Rockville, MD 20852
301-230-2020
Dogs are allowed at the outdoor tables.

Takoma Park

Savory Cafe

7071 Carroll Avenue
Takoma Park, MD 20912
301-270-2233
Well-behaved leashed dogs are allowed at the outdoor tables. Thanks to one of our readers for recommending this dog-friendly cafe.

Washington

Alamo Grill of Georgetown

1063 31st St NW
Washington, DC 20007
202-342-2000
Dogs are allowed at the outdoor tables.

Ben and Jerry's Ice Cream

1333 19th St NW
Washington, DC 20036
202-667-6677
Dogs are allowed at the outdoor tables.

Furin's of Georgetown

2805 M St NW
Washington, DC 20007
202-965-1000
Dogs are allowed at the outdoor tables.

Paper Moon

1073 31st St NW
Washington, DC 20007
202-965-6666
Dogs are allowed at the outdoor tables.

Park Place Gourmet

1634 I St NW
Washington, DC 20006
202-783-4496
Dogs are allowed at the outdoor tables.

Riverside Grille

3000 K St NW
Washington, DC 20007
Georgetown Harbor
202-342-3535
This restaurant has a dog-friendly outdoor deck and is right next to the Capitol River Cruise,

which is also dog-friendly.

Wrap Works
1601 Connecticut Ave NW
Washington, DC 20009
202-265-4200
Dogs are allowed at the outdoor tables.

Wheaton

The Chicken Place
2418 University Blvd W
Wheaton, MD 20902
Georgia Avenue
301-946-1212
This restaurant serves Peruvian flavored food.

Williamsburg City Guide
Accommodations

Williamsburg

Best Western Colonial Capital Inn
111 Penniman Road
Williamsburg, VA 23187
757-253-1222
There is a $10 one time pet fee per visit.

Best Western Patrick Henry Inn
249 E. York Street NW
Williamsburg, VA 23187
757-229-9540
There is a $15 one time pet fee per visit. This hotel is within walking distance of Colonial Williamsburg.

Heritage Inn Motel
1324 Richmond Rd.
Williamsburg, VA 23185
757-229-6220
There are no additional pet fees.

Holiday Inn - Colonial District
725 Bypass Rd
Williamsburg, VA 23185
757-220-1776
Pets up to 50 pounds are

allowed. There is a $25 one time pet fee.

Motel 6
3030 Richmond Rd
Williamsburg, VA 23185
757-565-3433
There are no additional pet fees. One pet per room is okay. Pets must be attended at all times.

Ramada Inn 1776
725 Bypass Road
Williamsburg, VA 23185
757-220-1776
All well-behaved dogs are welcome at this pet-friendly inn. The inn is located about 1 mile from Colonial Williamsburg. Amenities include a guest laundry and a seasonal pool. There are no pet size restrictions and no pet fees.

Attractions

Williamsburg

Colonial Williamsburg

Williamsburg, VA

Colonial Williamsburg allows dogs in all outdoor areas. If you want to go inside the buildings, then someone will need to stay outside with the dog.

Mini-Golf America
1901 Richmond Rd
Williamsburg, VA 23185
757-229-7200
Play mini-golf while your leashed dog joins you.

Parks

Williamsburg

Quarterpath Park
Quarterpath Road and Rt 60 East
Williamsburg, VA
757-220-6170
This is a standard city park.

Waller Mill Park
Airport Road
Williamsburg, VA
Between I-64 and Rt 60 West
757-220-6178
This park has a number of trails and hiking areas. It is a little out of town.

Restaurants

Williamsburg

Aroma's
431 Prince George St
Williamsburg, VA
757-221-6676
Dogs are allowed at the outdoor tables.

Ben and Jerry's Ice Cream
7097 Pocahontas Trail
Williamsburg, VA 23185
757-253-0180
Dogs are allowed at the outdoor tables.

Lo-Dog
501 Prince George St
Williamsburg, VA
757-564-8036
Dogs are welcome at the outdoor tables.

Pierce's Bar-B-Que
447 Rochambeau Dr
Williamsburg, VA 23188
757-565-2955
Dogs are allowed at the outdoor tables.

Charlotte City Guide
Accommodations

Charlotte

Clarion Hotel
321 West Woodlawn Road
Charlotte, NC 28217
704-523-1400
Room amenities include a microwave, refrigerator,

hairdryers and more. Hotel amenities include a fitness center, onsite restaurant and more. There is a $25 one time per stay pet charge.

Drury Inn & Suites
415 West W.T. Harris Blvd.
Charlotte, NC 28262
704-593-0700
Dogs of all sizes are permitted. Pets are not allowed in the breakfast area of the hotel. Pets are not to be left unattended, and each guest must assume liability for damage of property or other guest complaints. There is a limit of one pet per room.

La Quinta Inn & Suites Charlotte Coliseum
4900 South Tryon Street
Charlotte, NC
704-523-5599
Dogs of all sizes are allowed at the hotel.

Residence Inn - South Park
6030 J.A. Jones Drive
Charlotte, NC 28287
704-554-7001
There is a $150 one time per stay pet fee. Every suite at this eight floor inn offers a separate living and sleeping area. Amenities include an indoor pool, complimentary buffet breakfast, free parking, dinner delivery from local restaurants and more.

Residence Inn - Uptown
404 South Mint Street
Charlotte, NC 28202
704-340-4000
There is a $100 one time per stay pet charge and an additional $5 per day pet fee. Every room in this eleven story inn is a suite with a living area, bedroom and kitchen. The inn is located within walking distance to downtown and Uptown. Amenities include a 24 hour exercise room, complimentary hot breakfast, complimentary evening happy hour and more. There is a fee for parking.

Residence Inn by Marriott
5816 Westpark Drive
Charlotte, NC 28217
704-527-8110
There is a $150 one time pet fee.

Sleep Inn
8525 N Tryon St.
Charlotte, NC 28262
704-549-4544
There is a $25 one time pet charge.

Staybridge Suites
7924 Forest Pine Drive
Charlotte, NC 28273
704-527-6767
There is a $75 one time pet fee.

Studio 6
3420 I-85 Service Rd South
Charlotte, NC 28208
704-394-4993
There is a $10 per day pet fee. Well-behaved dogs are allowed at the hotel.

Fort Mill

Motel 6
255 Carowinds Blvd
Fort Mill, NC 29708
803-548-9656
There are no additional pet fees.

Attractions

Fort Mill

Charlotte Knights-Dog Day Game
Gold Hill Road (Exit 88 off I-77)
Fort Mill, SC
704-357-8071
Once a year, the Charlotte Knights minor league baseball team invites four-legged fans to attend their Dog Day Game. This dog-friendly game is usually in August. Dogs are welcome to sit with their owners at any seat throughout the ballpark. If your pooch is

itching to walk around, dogs are also welcome on the concourse. Just remember to clean up after your pooch!

Westfield

Hanging Rock River Trips
3466 Moores Spring Road
Westfield, NC
336-593-8283
This company offers full and half day river adventures in canoes or kayaks. Your kids and dogs are welcome to join you. Be sure to bring a leash. They are open Wednesday through Sunday in early March to late November. It is about a one hour drive from Charlotte, NC.

Parks

Charlotte

Barkingham Park Dog Park - Reedy Creek
2900 Rocky River Rd.
Charlotte, NC
704-365-0750
Reedy Creek Dog Park opened in the Summer of 2003. It consists of 4 acres. Currently the park has an off-leash dog park. Expected to be added soon are a small dog area and an agility playground. Charlotte Dog Parks require a annual pooch pass which you can get by signing a liability form. Currently the fee is $35 per year for a pooch pass. More information is available from FidoCarolina at http: //www.fidocarolina.org.

Fetching Meadows Dog Park
McAlpine Park
Charlotte, NC
704-365-0750
Fetching Meadows Dog Park opened in late 2002. Charlotte Dog Parks require a annual pooch pass which you can get by signing a liability form. Currently the fee is $35 per year

for a pooch pass. More information is available from FidoCarolina at http://www.fidocarolina.org.

Freedom Park
1900 East Boulevard
Charlotte, NC
704-336-2884
This is a popular park complete with athletic fields, tennis and basketball courts, playgrounds, a 7 acre lake, picnic shelters, concessions, and paved trails. Pets must be leashed and under your control at all times. From this park, you can begin the Lower Little Sugar Creek Trail (1.3 mile trail).

Lower Little Sugar Creek Trail
1900 East Boulevard
Charlotte, NC
704-336-3854
Take your pooch out for some exercise on this 1.3 mile paved trail. Pets must be leashed and under your control at all times. Use the parking lot at Freedom Park and begin your walk.

Mallard and Clark's Creek Greenway
9801 Mallard Creek Road
Charlotte, NC
704-336-8866
Go for a walk or jog with your dog on this 3.6 mile paved trail. Pets must be leashed and under your control at all times. Parking is available at the Mallard Creek Elementary School, off Mallard Creek Road.

McAlpine Creek Greenway
8711 Monroe Road
Charlotte, NC
704-568-4044
You can go for a nice long walk with your dog at this trail system which offers over 8 miles of paved and gravel trails. Pets must be leashed and under your control at all times. There are many starting points, but you can park at either the McAlpine Creek Park (has a 5K championship cross country

course) located at 8711 Monroe Road or the James Boyce Park located at 300 Boyce Road.

Upper Little Sugar Creek Trail
2100 North Davidson Street
Charlotte, NC
704-336-3367
Go for a walk on this 1.1 mile trail which joins Cordelia Park and Alexander Park. Pets must be leashed and under your control at all times. You can begin your walk at the parking lot in Cordelia Park.

Pineville

McMullen Creek Greenway
Pineville-Matthews Road
Pineville, NC
704-643-3405
Enjoy a stroll with your pooch on this 1.5 mile paved and gravel trail. Pets must be leashed and under your control at all times. The parking lot as well as a picnic area is located off Pineville-Matthews Road (across from the McMullen Creek Marketplace.)

Restaurants

Charlotte

Brixx Wood Fired Pizza
225 East 6th Street
Charlotte, NC 28202
704-347-2749
Located in Uptown, well-behaved dogs are allowed at the outdoor tables. In addition to the wood-fired pizzas, this restaurant also serves a variety of salads, sandwiches, pastas and dessert.

Fat City Deli
3127 North Davidson Street
Charlotte, NC 28205
704-343-0240
Dogs are welcome to dine with you in the covered outdoor seating area. In addition to the meaty sandwiches, this deli

also serves up a large array of veggie sandwiches.

Fuel Pizza Cafe - Trade St.
319 West Trade Street
Charlotte, NC 28202
704-344-1767
Going with a gas station theme, drinks here are known as lubricants and appetizers are fuel starters. They also offer a large selection of pizzas, otherwise known as pizzas! Well-behaved dogs are allowed to accompany you to the outdoor tables.

Moe's Southwest Grill
1500 East Blvd.
Charlotte, NC
704-377-6344
Food here is fresh and made from scratch. Burritos, quesadillas, fajitas, margaritas and more are all on the menu. Well-behaved dogs are allowed at the outdoor tables.

Planet Grill
1531 East Blvd.
Charlotte, NC
704-372-1818
At this restaurant, you get to participate in preparing your own meal. Pile up ingredients from a buffet table and then at the end of the table, give it to a chef who will quickly cook everything for you. Dogs are allowed at the outdoor tables.

Providence Bistro and Bakery
8708 J.W. Clay Blvd.
Charlotte, NC
704-549-0050
Dogs are allowed to sit with you at the bar side of the patio.

Rock Bottom Brewery
401 North Tryon Street
Charlotte, NC
704-334-2739
This restaurant is part of a chain of nationwide restaurants. They offer handcrafted beers and a diverse menu with items such as Brown Ale Chicken, Texas Fire Steak, Garlic Tenderloin and of

course, handmade Beer Bread. Dogs are allowed at the outdoor tables.

Sir Edmond Halley's
4151-A Park Road
Charlotte, NC 28209
704-525-2555
A quiet, well-behaved dog is allowed to accompany you at the outdoor tables. They ask that you sit at a table next to the grass so your dog can sit or lay on the grass. Your dog will still be right next to you.

Thomas Street Tavern
1218 Thomas Ave.
Charlotte, NC
704-376-1622
Your dog is welcome to join you at the tables on the front patio.

Stores

Pineville

Barbara's Canine Cafe
315 Main Street
Pineville, NC 28134
704-588-3647
This dog bakery makes fresh cookies, treats and even cakes just for your pooch. The ingredients used to make these yummy treats are all natural with no preservatives, fillers, artificial colorings, or added fat. While your pooch chows down on the goodies, you can sit back and relax on a chair. There is even complimentary ice tea and coffee for people. And don't miss out on the special dog events held frequently at the cafe. Call or check out their website at http://www.k9treat.com for upcoming events.

The Smoky Mountains City Guide

Accommodations

Gatlinburg

Holiday Inn Sunspree Resort
520 Historic Nature Trail
Gatlinburg, TN 37738
865-436-9201
There are no additional pet fees.

Pigeon Forge

Heartlander Country Resort
2385 Parkway (US 441)
Pigeon Forge, TN 37863
865-453-4106
There is a $20 one time pet charge.

Holiday Inn
3230 Parkway
Pigeon Forge, TN 37868
865-428-2700
There are no additional pet fees.

Accommodations - Vacation Home Rentals

Franklin

Patterson Realty, Vacation Home Rentals
145 E. Palmer Street
Franklin, NC 28734
800-742-0719
Choose from several of their vacation rental homes that allow pets. The Armstrong's River House, located on the Cullasaja River, is a 2 bedroom, 2 bathroom home and accommodates up to 7 people. Courson's Cottages, located close to Franklin, are cute new 1 bedroom cottages which accommodate up to 4 people. They have porches with nice views of the mountains.

Gatlinburg

A & B Rentals
702 East Parkway Suite #2
Gatlinburg, TN 37738
865-430-9988

Stay in a beautiful private chalet or cabin in the Smoky Mountains. The busy season for Gatlinburg is April through October, but there is much to do year round. Dogs are allowed at some of the rentals. Mention that you will be bringing a dog when making reservations.

Riverside Rentals
P.O. Box 1296
Gatlinburg, TN 37738
865-436-9496
Riverside Rentals offers 1 - 12 Bedrooms fully furnished, some of which are pet friendly. In those units that allow pets, there is a $10 per night additional pet fee. Up to two dogs are allowed in a rental and a pet security deposit is required on your credit card. One night's deposit plus a $25.00 reservation fee is required to make a reservation.

Saluda

Spring Pond Cabin
640 E US Hwy 176
Saluda, NC 28773
828-749-9824
This cozy cabin in the woods is available for rent to you and your pets. There is a covered porch with fenced in area as well as a half mile hiking loop on the property which is wooded and has two spring fed ponds. The cabin is fully equipped and sleeps five. They ask that you bring your own linens if your dog sleeps on the bed.

Attractions

Gatlinburg

Great Smoky Mountains National Park
107 Park Headquarters Road
Gatlinburg, TN 37738
865-436-1200
Pets must be leashed or restrained at all times and are not allowed on hiking trails. They

can accompany you in your car and at lookouts and stops near the road. However, there is one trail from the park headquarters to the city of Gatlinburg that allows leashed dogs. It is a nice 2 mile long dirt trail that follows a creek. There are spots along the way where your dog can take a dip in the water. If you want a longer hike, try the nearby dog-friendly Pisgah National Forest or the Nantahala National Forest. Both are in North Caorlina, and they are located about a two hour drive from the national park.

Linville

Grandfather Mountain
near Blue Ridge Parkway
Linville, NC 28646
828-733-4337
Dogs are allowed on leash. It gets very windy near the top of the mountain and this can make for rugged hiking. There is calmer hiking lower on the mountain. The bridge is quite a spectacle.

Lookout Mountain

Rock City Gardens
I-24, Exit 174 or 178
Lookout Mountain, TN
Follow Signs
706-820-2531
This approximately 1 mile walk through rock formations, gardens, and views is great for people and dogs alike. Dogs must be on leash but are welcome everywhere.

Pigeon Forge

Alabama Touring Bus
2050 Parkway
Pigeon Forge, TN 37863
865-908-8777
A well behaved dog on leash can walk through the Country Music Band Alabama's touring bus with you.

Parks

Asheville

Nantahala National Forest
various
Asheville, NC 28802
828-257-4200
The forest offers miles of dog-friendly hiking trails. It is located about 2 hours from the Great Smoky Mountains National Park.

Pisgah National Forest
various
Asheville, NC
828-257-4200
The forest offers miles of dog-friendly hiking trails. It is located about 2 hours from the Great Smoky Mountains National Park.

Chattanooga

Chattanooga RiverWalk
Ross's Landing
Chattanooga, TN
Downtown

The Riverwalk is a two mile walking path along the Tennessee River in downtown Chattanooga. Dogs must be on leash.

Pigeon Forge

Patriot Park
Light #7, Parkway
Pigeon Forge, TN

This is a nice city park with a Jogging and Walking trail. Dogs on leash are welcome.

Restaurants

Blowing Rock

Tijuana Fats
1182 Main St
Blowing Rock, NC 28692
828-295-9683
Dogs are allowed at the

outdoor tables.

Gatlinburg

Heidelburg Restaurant
148 Parkway
Gatlinburg, TN
865-430-3094
Dogs are allowed at the outdoor tables.

Humdingers Frozen Yogurt
615 Parkway
Gatlinburg, TN 37738
865-436-5093
Dogs are allowed at the outdoor tables.

Subway
223 Airport Rd
Gatlinburg, TN 37738
865-436-6792
Dogs are allowed at the outdoor tables.

Pigeon Forge

Baskin Robbins Ice Cream
3668 Parkway
Pigeon Forge, TN 37863
865-453-3337
Dogs are allowed at the outdoor tables.

Townsend

Mountain Home BBQ
7305 E Lamar Alexander Hwy
Townsend, TN
865-448-9420
Dogs are allowed at the outdoor tables.

Subway
8213 State Highway 73
Townsend, TN 37882
865-448-6909
Dogs are allowed at the outdoor tables.

Nashville City Guide

Accommodations

Antioch

Holiday Inn
201 Crossing Place
Antioch, TN 37013
615-731-2361
There are no additional pet fees.

Goodlettsville

Motel 6
323 Cartwright St
Goodlettsville, TN 37072
615-859-9674
There are no additional pet fees. Pets must be well-behaved and leashed when outside the room.

Kingston Springs

Best Western Harpeth Inn
116 Luyben Hills Rd
Kingston Springs, TN 37082
615-952-3961
There is a $10 per day additional pet fee.

Nashville

Best Western Calumet Inn at the Airport
701 Stewarts Ferry Pike
Nashville, TN 37214
615-889-9199
There are no additional pet fees.

Drury Inn & Suites
555 Donelson Pike
Nashville, TN 37214
615-902-0400
Dogs of all sizes are permitted. Pets are not allowed in the breakfast area of the hotel. Pets are not to be left unattended, and each guest must assume liability for damage of property or other guest complaints. There is a limit of one pet per room.

Holiday Inn Select - Opryland
2200 Elm Hill Pike

Nashville, TN 37214
615-883-9770
There is a $125 refundable pet deposit and there is a $25 one time pet fee. They are located near Briley Parkway.

Loews Vanderbilt Hotel
2100 West End Ave
Nashville, TN 37203
615-320-1700
All well-behaved dogs of any size are welcome. This upscale hotel offers their "Loews Loves Pets" program which includes special pet treats, local dog walking routes, and a list of nearby pet-friendly places to visit. There are no pet fees.

Motel 6
420 Metroplex Dr
Nashville, TN 37211
615-833-8887
There are no additional pet fees.

Motel 6
311 W Trinity Lane
Nashville, TN 37207
615-227-9696
There are no additional pet fees.

Motel 6
95 Wallace Rd
Nashville, TN 37211
615-333-9933
There are no pet fees. Pets must be well-behaved and attended at all times.

Pear Tree Inn
343 Harding Place
Nashville, TN 37211
615-834-4242
Dogs of all sizes are permitted. Pets are not allowed in the breakfast area of the hotel. Pets are not to be left unattended, and each guest must assume liability for damage of property or other guest complaints. There is a limit of one pet per room.

Red Roof Inn-South
4271 Sidco Drive

Nashville, TN 37204
615-832-0093
Dogs under 75 pounds are allowed. There are no additional pet fees.

Residence Inn - Nashville Airport
2300 Elm Hill Pike
Nashville, TN 37214
615-889-8600
There is a $50 one time pet charge. They are located near Briley Parkway.

Sheraton Music City
777 McGavok Pike
Nashville, TN 37214
615-885-2200
Dogs up to 80 pounds are allowed. There are no additional pet fees. Pets are allowed on the first floor which has both smoking and non-smoking rooms.

South Drury Inn
341 Harding Place
Nashville, TN 37211
615-834-7170
Dogs of all sizes are permitted. Pets are not allowed in the breakfast area of the hotel. Pets are not to be left unattended, and each guest must assume liability for damage of property or other guest complaints. There is a limit of one pet per room.

Attractions

Nashville

BiCentennial Mall State Park
598 James Robertson Pkwy
Nashville, TN 37243
At Capitol
615-741-5800
This park has a large concrete map of Tennessee to explore. It has a history of mankind and Tennessee to read about. And it has green areas for your pup to play in. Dogs must be leashed in the park.

CityWalk

Nashville, TN
start at Fort Nashborough
615-862-7970
Follow the Green Line on the sidewalk for a 2 mile historic tour of downtown Nashville. The tour starts at Fort Nashborough but you can pick it up anywhere along its route. Dogs must be leashed.

Horse and Carriages
Broadway and 1st St
Nashville, TN
Downtown

Take a horse and carriage ride with your pup. Most drivers will accept dogs but you do need to ask.

Legends Corner
428 Broadway
Nashville, TN 37203
615-248-6334
This bar plays country music often. When they do, it is easy to hear from the sidewalk where you and your dog can listen. They don't have outdoor seats for eating or drinking, however. Next door you can get a map showing where the country stars live in the Nashville area.

Parks

Nashville

Bell Meade Plantation
5025 Harding Rd
Nashville, TN 37205
615-356-0501
Pets on leash are allowed on the grounds of the plantation, but not in the buildings.

Centennial Park
West End Ave and 25th Ave N.
Nashville, TN
615-862-8442
Leashed dogs are allowed at this urban park.

Grand Ole Opry Park
2804 Opryland Dr

Nashville, TN
Opryland Mall

This is a city park surrounding the world-famous concert hall. Leashed dogs are allowed.

J. Percy Priest Lake Park
I-40 and Stewards Ferry Pike
Nashville, TN

There are miles of trails next to this lake. The park is only 15-20 minutes from downtown. Leashed dogs are not allowed in the day use areas but are allowed on the trails.

Percy Warner Park
7311 Highway 100
Nashville, TN

Dogs are allowed on leash. There are many trails in this large park.

Riverfront Park
1st Ave and Broadway
Nashville, TN

Dogs on leash are allowed in this downtown park. There is also a fort, Fort Nashborough to view here. This is where the CityWalk walking tour of downtown starts.

Shelby Park
2021 Fatherland St
Nashville, TN 37206
615-862-8474
Dogs are allowed on leash in the park.

Restaurants

Nashville

Bruegger's Bagel Bakery
5305 Harding Rd
Nashville, TN 37205
615-352-1128
Dogs are allowed at the outdoor tables.

Jack's Barbecue
416 Broadway

Nashville, TN 37203
615-254-5715
This downtown restaurant has outdoor seating in the back of the building.

Schlotzsky's Deli
2117 Abbott Martin Rd
Nashville, TN
615-385-9550
Dogs are allowed at the outdoor tables.

Vets and Kennels

Nashville

Creature Comforts
536 Paragon Mills Rd
Nashville, TN 37211
615-833-4078
You can drop your dog off for a few hours or a day at this kennel. Its hours are 8 am - 5 pm (M-F) and 8 am - 1pm (Sat).

Atlanta City Guide
Accommodations

Atlanta

Airport Drury Inn & Suites
1270 Virginia Avenue
Atlanta, GA 30344
404-761-4900
Dogs of all sizes are permitted. Pets are not allowed in the breakfast area of the hotel. Pets are not to be left unattended, and each guest must assume liability for damage of property or other guest complaints. There is a limit of one pet per room.

AmeriSuites-Atlanta/Perimeter Center
1005 Crestline Parkway
Atlanta, GA 30328
770-730-9300
There are no additional pet fees.

Crowne Plaza - Airport
1325 Virginia Ave
Atlanta, GA 30344
404-768-6660

There is a $100 refundable pet deposit and a one-time $25 non-refundable pet fee.

Hawthorn Suites
1500 Parkwood Circle
Atlanta, GA 30339
770-952-9595
There is a $100 one time pet fee and there is a 2 dog limit per room. There is also a $50 refundable pet deposit.

Holiday Inn - Airport North
1380 Virginia Ave
Atlanta, GA 30344
404-762-8411
There is a $100 refundable pet deposit and a $25 one-time pet fee.

Holiday Inn Select-Atlanta Perimeter
4386 Chamblee-Dunwoody Rd.
Atlanta, GA 30341
770-457-6363
There is a $25 one time pet fee and a 2 dog per room limit.

Marriott Atlanta Airport
4711 Best Road
Atlanta, GA 30337
404-766-7900
There is a $50 refundable pet deposit, dogs allowed on first floor only, and limit 1 dog.

Motel 6 - Northeast (I-85)
2820 Chamblee - Tucker Rd
Atlanta, GA 30341
770-458-6626
There is a $50 refundable pet deposit.

Red Roof Inn
2471 Old National Pkwy
Atlanta, GA 30349
404-761-9701
There is no extra pet fee, limit 3-4 well-behaved dogs.

Red Roof Inn-Druid Hills
1960 N Druid Hills Rd.
Atlanta, GA 30329
404-321-1653
There is no extra pet charge, limit 2 dogs. There is an eighty pound weight limit.

Residence Inn by Marriott
134 Peachtree Street NW
Atlanta, GA 30303
404-522-0950
Located in downtown Atlanta.
There is a 2 dog limit and a $150 non-refundable pet fee.

Residence Inn by Marriott-Midtown
1041 W Peachtree Street
Atlanta, GA 30309
404-872-8885
There is a $100 one time pet charge, and a 2 dog per room limit.

Sheraton Midtown Atlanta at Colony Square
188 14th Street at Peachtree
Atlanta, GA 30361
404-892-6000
There is no size limit for dogs. There is a $25 one time additional pet fee. There is one floor for pets. It is a non-smoking floor.

Staybridge Suites - Perimeter
4601 Ridgeview Rd
Atlanta, GA 30346
678-320-0111
There is a $75 one time pet fee.

Summerfield Suites-Buckhead
505 Pharr Road
Atlanta, GA 30305
404-262-7880
There is a $150 one time pet charge. There is a 60 pound weight limit for dogs.

W Atlanta
111 Perimeter Center West
Atlanta, GA 30346
770-396-6800
Dogs up to 60 pounds are allowed. There is a $25 per day additional pet fee.

Austell

La Quinta Inn Atlanta West
7377 Six Flags Drive
Austell, GA

770-944-2110
Dogs of all sizes are allowed at the hotel.

College Park

Howard Johnson Express Inn
2480 Old National Pkwy.
College Park, GA 30349
404-766-0000
Dogs of all sizes are welcome. There is a $10 per day pet fee.

Duluth

Studio 6 - Gwinnett Place
3525 Breckinridge Blvd
Duluth, GA 30096
770-931-3113
There is a $10 per day pet fee.

Jonesboro

Holiday Inn - Atlanta South
6288 Old Dixie Hwy
Jonesboro, GA 30236
770-968-4300
There is a $15 one time pet fee.

Marietta

Comfort Inn
2100 Northwest Pkwy
Marietta, GA 30067
770-952-3000
There is a non-refundable pet charge of $75.

La Quinta Inn Atlanta Delk Road - Marietta
2170 Delk Road
Marietta, GA
770-951-0026
Dogs of all sizes are allowed at the hotel.

Motel 6 - Marietta
2360 Delk Rd
Marietta, GA 30067
770-952-8161
There are no additional pet fees.

Morrow

South Drury Inn & Suites

6520 S. Lee Street
Morrow, GA 30260
770-960-0500
Dogs of all sizes are permitted. Pets are not allowed in the breakfast area of the hotel. Pets are not to be left unattended, and each guest must assume liability for damage of property or other guest complaints. There is a limit of one pet per room.

Norcross

Northeast Drury Inn & Suites
5655 Jimmy Carter Blvd
Norcross, GA 30071
770-729-0060
Dogs of all sizes are permitted. Pets are not allowed in the breakfast area of the hotel. Pets are not to be left unattended, and each guest must assume liability for damage of property or other guest complaints. There is a limit of one pet per room.

Roswell

Studio 6 - Roswell
9955 Old Dogwood Rd
Roswell, GA 30076
770-992-9449
There is a $10 per day pet fee or a $50 per week pet fee.

Tucker

Studio 6 - Northlake
1795 Crescent Blvd
Tucker, GA 30084
770-934-4040
There is a $10 per day additional pet fee.

Attractions

Atlanta

Bark in the Park
Piedmont Park
Atlanta, GA
404-733-5000
Once a year, normally in August, the Atlanta Symphony Orchestra holds a Bark in the Park concert. It is usually located in Piedmont Park. So if you, or even your pooch loves the symphony, come for an evening of free music outdoors.

Centennial Olympic Park
Andrew Young International Blvd.
Atlanta, GA
404-223-4000
Come enjoy this 21 acre park which highlights and commemorates the 1996 Olympics that where held in Atlanta. Thousands of visitors come to this park every year. The park features both man-made and natural points of interest. During hot summer days and nights, the five-ring water fountain is a popular spot to cool off. Pets must be leashed and remember to clean up after your pet. Dogs are normally not allowed in concerts at this park. The park is bordered by Marietta Street, Baker Street, Centennial Olympic Park Drive and Andrew Young International Blvd.

Stone Mountain

Stone Mountain Park
Highway 78
Stone Mountain, GA
770-498-5600
Dogs are not allowed in most of this park which includes the attractions and many public areas. However, dogs are allowed on the Cherokee Trail which goes around the base of the mountain, and the Nature Trail and Gardens. You and your pooch will also be able to see the Memorial Carving on the mountain which depicts three Confederate heroes of the Civil War; President Jefferson Davis, General Robert E. Lee, and Lt. General Thomas "Stonewall" Jackson. Admission to the park is just under $20 per adult and less for children and seniors. The price includes the attractions, but unless you take turns watching the pooch, you will not be able to take advantage of the attractions. Dogs are also allowed at the campground and RV park. Pets must be leashed throughout the park. Dogs are not allowed at the Lasershow Lawn, the Walk Up Trail or Special Events Areas. The park is located 16 miles east of downtown Atlanta. To get there, take exit 39B off I-285 and go east on Highway 78 to exit 8, the Stone Mountain Park Main Entrance.

Parks

Atlanta

Chattahoochee River National Recreation Area
1978 Island Ford Parkway
Atlanta, GA
770-399-8070
Dogs are allowed, but must be kept on a leash and under control at all times. Please clean up after your pooch. There are many separate areas or units that make up this park. One of the more popular trails starts near the Park Headquarters at the Island Fort Unit. The Cochran Fitness Trail follows the Chattahoochee River and is a great place to walk or run. For a map and more details, call or visit the Park Headquarters at the Island Ford Unit at 1978 Island Ford Parkway. Take Highway 400/19 and exit Northridge Road. The park is located about 15 minutes north of downtown Atlanta.

Grant Park
840 Cherokee Ave., SE
Atlanta, GA 30315
404-875-7275
This park has over 125 acres and miles of scenic trails. While dogs are not allowed in the Zoo

or in the Atlanta Cyclorama, they can walk with you around this park. Dogs must be leashed and pet owners must clean up after their dogs.

Piedmont Park
400 Park Drive Northeast
Atlanta, GA
404-875-7275
Located in Midtown is the popular Piedmont Park, which consists of 185 acres. The park offers many paths for walking or running. Dogs must be leashed, except for the designated off-leash area located north of the Park Drive bridge. Dog owners are required to clean up after their dogs. Dogs are not allowed in the lake, in the botanical gardens, on the tennis courts, ball fields or playgrounds. Of special interest to dog lovers, is the Atlanta Symphony Orchestra's Annual Bark in the Park event. The event usually takes place in August and is held in Piedmont Park. To get to the park, take I-85/75 north and take exit 101 (10th Street). Go straight to the first light, then turn right on 10th Street. Turn left at Piedmont and the park entrance will be on the right.

Piedmont Park Off Leash Dog Park
Park Drive
Atlanta, GA
404-875-7275
Dogs can run leash-free only in this designated area of Piedmont Park. The dog park is just over 1.5 acres. To get there, take I-85/75 north and take exit 101 (10th Street). Go straight to the first light, then turn right on 10th Street. Go past Piedmont Park, then turn left onto Monroe Drive. At the first light, turn left onto Park Drive. The dog park is below the bridge on the north side.

Restaurants

Atlanta

Anis Cafe and Bistro
2974 Grandview Avenue
Atlanta, GA 30305
404-233-9889
This French bistro allows dogs at their outdoor tables. The cafe offers a variety of foods including soups, salads, lamb, chicken, raviolis and more.

Corner Bakery Cafe
3368 Peachtree Rd. NE
Atlanta, GA 30326
404-816-5100
This cafe is open for breakfast, lunch and afternoon dining. Dogs are allowed at the outdoor tables.

Corner Bakery Cafe
4400 Ashford Dunwoody Road
Atlanta, GA 30346
770-804-0233
Dogs are allowed at the outdoor tables. The cafe is open for breakfast, lunch and afternoon dining.

Mick's Restaurant
2110 Peachtree Rd
Atlanta, GA
404-351-6425
Dogs are allowed on the lower level patio.

Rocky's Brick Oven Pizza
1770 Peachtree Street
Atlanta, GA
404-870-7625
Dogs are allowed at the outdoor tables.

Zocalo
187 10th Street
Atlanta, GA
404-249-7576
This Mexican restaurant allows dogs at the outdoor tables.

Decatur

Margie's Pantry
653 East Lake Drive
Decatur, GA
404-377-3818

Dogs are allowed at the outdoor tables. This cafe is a European style bakery that serves brunch, lunch and dinner. They are not open for dinner on Sundays.

Mo Jo Pizza
659 East Lake Drive
Decatur, GA
404-373-1999
Dogs are allowed at the outdoor tables.

Stores

Atlanta

Junkman's Daughter Store
464 Moreland Avenue
Atlanta, GA 30307
404-577-3188
This novelty store allows well-behaved leashed dogs inside.

Orlando City Guide
Accommodations

Altamonte Springs

Embassy Suites Orlando North
225 East Altamonte Drive
Altamonte Springs, FL 32701
407-834-2400
There is a $15 per day pet charge.

Apopka

Howard Johnson Express Inn
1317 S. Orange Blossom Trail
Apopka, FL 32703
407-886-1010
Dogs of all sizes are welcome. There is a $10 per day pet fee. The hotel has two pet rooms, one smoking and one non-smoking.

Kissimmee

Holiday Inn
7601 Black Lake Rd

Kissimmee, FL 34747
407-396-1100
There is a $75 one time pet deposit of which $50 is refundable and $25 is not refundable.

Holiday Inn
7300 Irlo Bronson Memorial Hwy
Kissimmee, FL 34747
407-396-7300
There is a $125 refundable pet deposit.

Homewood Suites Orlando-Disney Resort
3100 Parkway Blvd.
Kissimmee, FL 34747
407-396-2229
There is a $250 pet deposit and $200 of the deposit is refundable. ($50 pet charge)

Howard Johnson Express Inn
4311 W. Vine Street/W Hwy 192
Kissimmee, FL 34746
407-396-7100
Dogs of all sizes are welcome. There is a $10 per day pet fee per pet and a $25 one time pet fee.

Howard Johnson Hotel
2323 Hwy 192 East
Kissimmee, FL 34744
407-846-4900
Dogs of all sizes are welcome. There is a $10 per day pet fee.

Howard Johnson Hotel
8660 W. Irlo Bronson Memorial Hwy
Kissimmee, FL 34747
407-396-4500
Dogs up to 50 pounds are allowed. There is a $25 per week pet fee.

Larson's Family Inn
6075 West U.S. Hwy. 192
Kissimmee, FL 34741
407-396-6100
There is a $150 refundable pet deposit and a $10 per day pet charge. Dogs up to 50 pounds are allowed.

Motel 6 - Main Gate East

5731 W Irlo Bronson Memorial Hwy
Kissimmee, FL 34746
407-396-6333
Pets must not be left unattended.

Red Roof Inn
4970 Kyng's Heath Rd
Kissimmee, FL 34746
407-396-0065
There are no additional pet fees.

Orlando

La Quinta Inn Orlando International Drive
8300 Jamaican Court
Orlando, FL
407-351-1660
Dogs of all sizes are allowed at the hotel.

Motel 6 - Winter Park
5300 Adanson Rd
Orlando, FL 32810
407-647-1444
There are no additional pet fees.

Quality Inn At International Drive
7600 International Drive
Orlando, FL 32819
407-996-1600
There is a pet fee of $6.66 per day.

Red Roof Inn
9922 Hawaiian Ct
Orlando, FL 32819
407-352-1507
Dogs up to 80 pounds are allowed. Only one pet per room is allowed. There are no additional pet fees.

Residence Inn SeaWorld
11000 Westwood Blvd.
Orlando, FL 32821
407-313-3600
There is a $150 one time pet fee.

Sheraton Suites Orlando Airport

7550 Augusta National Drive
Orlando, FL 32822
407-240-5555
Dogs of any weight are allowed. There is a $25 per day additional pet fee.

Travelodge Orlando Centroplex
409 N. Magnolia Ave.
Orlando, FL 32801
407-423-1671
There is a $10 per day pet charge. Dogs up to 50 pounds are allowed.

Sanford

Rose Cottage Inn & Tea Room
1301 S Park Ave
Sanford, FL 32771
407-323-9448
There is a $10 per day additional dog fee. Dogs are not allowed on the furniture.

Accommodations - Vacation Home Rentals

Kissimmee

Sun N Fun Vacation Homes
Bear Path
Kissimmee, FL 34746
407-932-4079
Vacation Homes are located just 5 minutes to Disney and very close to other area attractions. All homes have private screened pools and fenced yards. Most homes welcome well-behaved pets and their families. Their is a pet fee of $30 per pet, per week plus a $300 security deposit, which is refundable assuming no damage, etc.

Attractions

Celebration

Celebration
US 192 and I-4
Celebration, FL

Celebration is a town created by

Disney. It has dog-friendly walking trails, outdoor cafes, and stores. Also check for events at Celebration.

Kissimmee

Bonanza Golf
7761 W Irlo Bronson
Kissimmee, FL 34747
407-396-7536
Your dog is welcome to accompany players on the mini-golf course. However, please keep the dog outside of the building. You can walk him or her around the back.

Lake Buena Vista

Walt Disney's Animal Kingdom - Kennels
Walt Disney World Exit
Lake Buena Vista, FL
407-842-4321
Dogs aren't allowed inside the theme park, but Disney offers day kennels located at the main entrance. The kennels are air conditioned, attended, indoor pens. You are welcome to exit the park and walk your dog. Just be sure to get your hand stamped so you can re-enter the park. The kennels are open 1 hour before the park opens to 1 hour after the park closes. Proof of vaccinations is required. There is a $6 per day kennel charge.

Walt Disney's Epcot Center - Kennels
Walt Disney World Exit
Lake Buena Vista, FL
407-842-4321
Dogs aren't allowed inside the theme park, but Disney offers day kennels located at the main entrance. The kennels are air conditioned, attended, indoor pens. You are welcome to exit the park and walk your dog. Just be sure to get your hand stamped so you can re-enter the park. The kennels are open 1 hour before the park opens to 1

hour after the park closes. Proof of vaccinations is required. There is a $6 per day kennel charge.

Walt Disney's MGM Studios - Kennels
Walt Disney World Exit
Lake Buena Vista, FL
407-842-4321
Dogs aren't allowed inside the theme park, but Disney offers day kennels located at the main entrance. The kennels are unattended, locked, outdoor pens. You are welcome to exit the park and walk your dog. Just be sure to get your hand stamped so you can re-enter the park. The kennels are open 1 hour before the park opens to 1 hour after the park closes. Proof of vaccinations is required. There is a $6 per day kennel charge.

Walt Disney's Magic Kingdom - Kennels
Walt Disney World Exit
Lake Buena Vista, FL
407-842-4321
Dogs aren't allowed inside the theme park, but Disney offers day kennels located at the main entrance. The kennels are air conditioned, attended, indoor pens. You are welcome to exit the park and walk your dog. Just be sure to get your hand stamped so you can re-enter the park. The kennels are open 1 hour before the park opens to 1 hour after the park closes. Proof of vaccinations is required. There is a $6 per day kennel charge.

Sanford

St. Johns River Cruises
Celery Avenue
Sanford, FL
407-330-1612
Well behaved, leashed dogs are welcome aboard the narrated cruises. The cruise travels along the St. Johns

River and lasts about two hours. The boat tour is located about 30 minutes from Orlando. They are located in Blue Springs State Park.

Winter Park

Winter Park Shopping District
Park Avenue and Osceola Ave
Winter Park, FL

This is a dog friendly shopping district with outdoor cafes. Many of the stores will allow a well behaved, leashed dog inside.

Parks

Apopka

Wekiwa Springs State Park
Wekiwa Springs Road at
SR-434
Apopka, FL 32712
407-884-2008
Dogs are allowed in the park but are not allowed in the springs. Dogs must be leashed in the park.

Orlando

Cady Way Trail
Bennett Rd and Corrine Dr.
Orlando, FL
407-836-6200
There is a 3.5 mile paved bike and hiking trail which links Winter Park and Orlando. Dogs on leash are allowed.

Lake Eola Park
Rosalind and Washington St
Orlando, FL
407-246-2827
This is a downtown urban park with a 1 mile jogging trail, grassy areas and a lake. The park has outdoor entertainment periodically. Dogs are allowed on leash.

Sanford

Lake Jessup Park
South end of Sanford Ave
Sanford, FL

This is a small park for walking or picnicing. Dogs must be leashed in this park.

Lower Wekiva River State Preserve
S.R. 46
Sanford, FL
9 miles west of Sanford
407-884-2008
Dogs are allowed on the trails but are not allowed in the camping areas. Dogs must be leashed in this park.

Restaurants

Celebration

Columbia Restaurant
649 Front St
Celebration, FL 34747
407-566-1505
Dogs are allowed at the outdoor tables.

Max's Cafe
701 Front St
Celebration, FL 34747
407-566-1144
Dogs are allowed at the outdoor tables.

Orlando

Friday's American Bar
55 W Church St # 148
Orlando, FL 32801
407-649-7778
Dogs are allowed at the outdoor tables.

Sanford

Angelo's Pizzaria
107 W 1st St
Sanford, FL 32771
407-320-0799
Dogs are allowed at the outdoor tables.

Tin Lizzie Tavern

111 W 1st St
Sanford, FL 32771
407-321-1908
Dogs are allowed at the outdoor tables.

Winter Park

Three Ten Park South
310 S Park Ave
Winter Park, FL 32789
407-647-7277
Dogs are allowed at the outdoor tables.

Village Bistro
326 S Park Ave
Winter Park, FL 32789
407-740-7573
Dogs are allowed at the outdoor tables.

Tampa Bay City Guide

Accommodations

Bradenton

Howard Johnson Express Inn
6511 14th St. W (US 41)
Bradenton, FL 34207
941-756-8399
Dogs of all sizes are welcome. There is a $5 per day pet fee for pets under 20 pounds, $10 per day pet fee for pets over 20 pounds.

Motel 6
660 67 Street Cir E
Bradenton, FL 34208
941-747-6005
There are no additional pet fees.

Clearwater

Residence Inn by Marriott-St. Petersburg
5050 Ulmerton Road
Clearwater, FL 33760
727-573-4444
There is a $150 one time pet charge.

Clearwater Beach

Mar - Jac Apartment / Motel
144 Brightwater Drive
Clearwater Beach, FL 33767
727-442-6009
Located on Clearwater Bay, this pet-friendly motel is within walking distance to the Gulf of Mexico and its white sandy beaches. Also close by is big pier fishing, deep sea fishing boats, shopping and fine restaurants.

Sea Spray Inn
331 Coronado Drive
Clearwater Beach, FL 33767
727-442-0432
Sea Spray Inn is just a one minute walk to the Gulf of Mexico. There are 6 rooms, 4 with full kitchens, 2 rooms have refrigerators. Microwaves in rooms, phones, cable TV and a swimming pool. A quiet setting yet close to attractions, restaurants, marina and the pier.

Ellenton

Ramada Limited
5218 17th Street E
Ellenton, FL 34222
941-729-8505
There is a $10 one time pet fee.

Shoney's Inn-Bradenton
4915 17th Street East
Ellenton, FL 34222
941-729-0600
There is a $10 one time pet charge.

Madeira Beach

Snug Harbor Inn Waterfront Bed and Breakfast
13655 Gulf Blvd
Madeira Beach, FL 33708
727-395-9256
This bed and breakfast offers a location on the waterfront, continental breakfast, and a boat slip. Check for availability. Snug Harbor Inn is on the Suncoast Trolley line.

Palm Harbor

Red Roof Inn
32000 US 19 North
Palm Harbor, FL 34684
727-786-2529
There are no additional pet fees.

Sarasota

Calais Motel Apartments
1735 Stickney Point Road
Sarasota, FL 34231
941-921-5797
There is a $15 per day pet
charge and there are no
designated smoking or non-
smoking rooms.

Comfort Inn Airport
4800 N. Tamiami Trail
Sarasota, FL 34234
941-355-7091
There is a pet fee of $10 per
day.

Coquina On the Beach Resort
1008 Ben Franklin Drive
Sarasota, FL 34236
941-388-2141
There is a $30 one time pet
charge. There are no designated
smoking or non-smoking rooms.

Howard Johnson Express Inn
811 S Taimiami Trail
Sarasota, FL 34230
941-365-0350
Dogs of all sizes are welcome.
There is a $10 per day pet fee.

Siesta Key

Turtle Beach Resort
9049 Midnight Pass Road
Siesta Key, FL 34242
941-349-4554
This resort was featured in the
Florida Living Magazine as one
of the best romantic escapes in
Florida. There is a pet charge
added, which is about 10% of
the daily room rate.

St Petersburg

Valley Forge Motel
6825 Central Avenue
St Petersburg, FL 33710
727-345-0135
There is a $5 per day pet
charge or a fee of $25 per week
for a pet.

Tampa

Best Western All Suites Hotel
3001 University Center Dr
Tampa, FL 33612
813-971-8930
There is a $10 one time pet fee.

**Days Inn-Busch Gardens
North**
701 E. Fletcher Ave.
Tampa, FL 33612
813-977-1550
There is a $6 per day pet
charge.

**Holiday Inn Express Hotel &
Suites**
4732 N. Dale Mabry
Tampa, FL 33614
813-877-6061
There is a $25 one time pet fee.

Howard Johnson Express Inn
2520 N. 50th St.
Tampa, FL 33619
813-247-3300
Dogs of all sizes are welcome.
There is a $20 per day pet fee.

Howard Johnson Hotel
4139 E. Busch Blvd.
Tampa, FL 33617
813-988-9191
Dogs of all sizes are welcome.
There is a $25 one time pet fee.

**La Quinta Inn & Suites
Tampa Bay - Brandon**
310 Grand Regency Blvd.
Tampa, FL
813-643-0574
Dogs of all sizes are allowed at
the hotel.

**La Quinta Inn & Suites
Tampa Bay USF**
3701 East Fowler
Tampa, FL

813-910-7500
Dogs up to 50 pounds are
allowed at the hotel.

Quality Hotel Westshore
1200 N. Westshore Blvd
Tampa, FL 33607
813-282-3636
There is a non-refundable pet
charge of $25.

Red Roof Inn - Brandon
10121 Horace Ave
Tampa, FL 33619
813-681-8484
There are no additional pet fees.

Red Roof Inn - Fairgrounds
5001 North US301
Tampa, FL 33610
813-623-5245
There are no additional pet fees.

**Sheraton Suites Tampa
Airport**
4400 West Cypress Street
Tampa, FL 33607
813-873-8675
Dogs up to 80 pounds are
allowed. There are no additional
pet fees. There are certain
rooms designated as pet rooms.

Venice

Days Inn
1710 S. Tamiami Trail
Venice, FL 34293
941-493-4558
There is a $30 one time pet
charge.

Accommodations - Vacation Home Rentals

Indian Shores

Barrett Beach Bungalows
19646 Gulf Blvd
Indian Shores, FL 33785
727-455-2832
Beachfront bungalows plus a
cottage in the heart of
picturesque Indian Shores. One,
two and three bedroom
bungalows and a pool. Any

number and size of pets welcome. Private dog runs with each bungalow. Enjoy sunsets, volleyball and BBQs in your own backyard.

Pass-a-Grille

Pass-a-Grille Beach House
111 Eleventh Avenue
Pass-a-Grille, FL 33706
casita.111@prodigy.net
Enjoy Florida, the way it used to be, with no high rise condos blocking the beach views. This pet-friendly house has all the modern amenities, yet it is in the heart of the historic district at Pass-a-Grille Beach. Just a half block from the Gulf of Mexico in one direction, a half block from Boca Ciega Bay in the other direction, yet, you'll be staying three blocks from restaurants and shops, and minutes from downtown St. Petersburg. Pets are welcomed, no size limits. There is a $100 pet fee.

Attractions

Bradenton

De Soto National Memorial
P. O. Box 15390
Bradenton, FL 34280
941-792-0458
This memorial commemorates the Spanish explorer Hernando de Soto, who landed on the southwest Florida coast in 1539. He brought with him 600 soldiers and was under orders from the King of Spain to explore, colonize and pacify the Indians of the area known as "La Florida". The park depicts 16th century Spanish cultural values and the clash with the native cultures that the expedition encountered. From late December to early April, there is a reproduction of the 16th Century Indian village with park rangers dressed in period costume. They give

demonstrations of blacksmithing, cooking, armor repair and military weapons. Dogs are not allowed in the buildings, but they are allowed on the one half mile self-guiding interpretive trail which leads through mangrove and coastal environments. Dogs need to be on a 6 foot leash.

Hunsader U-Pick Farms
5500 C.R. 675
Bradenton, FL
941-322-2168
Bring your pup and pick your own strawberries, tomatoes, peppers, eggplant, beans and more at this farm. Produce seasons vary, but the the u-pick area is open from mid-September through mid-June. They also have a picnic area.

Beaches

Dunedin

Honeymoon Island State Park
1 Causeway Blvd.
Dunedin, FL 34698
727-469-5942
Dogs on a 6 foot or less leash are allowed on part of the beach. Please ask the rangers for details when you arrive at the park. The park is located at the extreme west end of SR 586, north of Dunedin.

St Petersburg

Gandy Bridge Causeway
Gandy Bridge east end
St Petersburg, FL

This stretch of beach allows dogs to run and go swimming. We even saw a horse here. Dogs should be leashed on the beach.

Pinellas Causeway Beach
Pinellas Bayway
St Petersburg, FL

This stretch of beach is open to humans and dogs. Dogs should be on leash on the beach.

Tampa

Davis Island Dog Park
Severn Ave and Martinique Ave
Tampa, FL

This dog beach is fenced and offers a large parking area and even a doggie shower. To get there go towards Davis Island and head for the Peter Knight Airport. Loop around until you reach the water (the airport should be on the left). Thanks to one of our readers for the updated information.

Parks

Hillsborough

Flatwoods Wilderness Park
Morris Bridge Road
Hillsborough, FL

There are a number of hiking trails here. Dogs are allowed on leash.

St Petersburg

North Shore Park
North Shore Dr and 13th Ave
St Petersburg, FL

Dogs must be leashed in the park.

Tampa

Lake Park
17302 N. Dale Mabry
Tampa, FL
Van Dyke Road
813-264-3806
Here your leashed dog will have to share the trails with horses and people. The park is 600 acres.

Upper Tampa Bay County

Park
8001 Double Branch Road
Tampa, FL 33635
813-855-1765
Dogs must be leashed in the park.

Ferg's Sports Bar and Grill
1320 Central Ave
St Petersburg, FL 33705
727-822-4562
Dogs can sit at the end with the picnic tables.

Foxy's Cafe
160 107th Ave
St Petersburg, FL 33706
727-363-3699
Dogs are allowed at the outdoor tables.

Bagels Plus
2706 E Fletcher Ave
Tampa, FL 33612
813-971-9335
This bagel shop closes at 5 pm each day. Dogs on leash may accompany you at outdoor tables.

Bernini Restaurant
1702 E 7th Ave
Tampa, FL 33605
813-248-0099
Dogs are allowed at the outdoor tables.

Mad Dogs and Englishmen
4115 S Macdill Ave
Tampa, FL 33611
813-832-3037
Dogs are allowed at the outdoor tables.

Rick's Italian Cafe
214 E Davis Blvd
Tampa, FL 33606
813-253-3310
Dogs are allowed at the outdoor tables.

Thai House
3200 W Bay To Bay Blvd
Tampa, FL 33629
813-839-4995
Dogs are allowed at the outdoor tables.

South Florida City Guide

Sheraton Bal Harbour Beach Resort
9701 Collins Avenue
Bal Harbour, FL 33154
305-865-7511
Dogs up to 80 pounds are allowed. There are no additional pet fees.

Radisson Suite
7920 Glades Road
Boca Raton, FL 33434
561-483-3600
There is a $100 one time pet charge.

Residence Inn by Marriott
525 NW 77th Street
Boca Raton, FL 33487
561-994-3222
The non-refundable pet charge is as follows; $75 for studios, $85 for 1-bedroom suites and $95 for penthouses.

Sheraton Fort Lauderdale Airport Hotel
1825 Griffin Road
Dania, FL 33004
954-920-3500
Dogs up to 80 pounds are allowed. There are no additional pet fees.

Hampton Inn-Miami
124 E. Palm Drive
Florida City, FL 33034
305-247-8833
There are no additional pet fees.

Birch Patio Motel
617 N Birch Rd
Fort Lauderdale, FL 33304
954-563-9540
There is a $10 per day pet charge.

Motel 6
1801 SR 84
Fort Lauderdale, FL 33315
954-760-7999
There are no additional pet fees.

Red Roof Inn
4800 Powerline Rd
Fort Lauderdale, FL 33309
954-776-6333
There are no additional pet fees. Pets under 85 pounds are allowed.

Sheraton Suites Cypress Creek Ft. Lauderdale
555 N.W. 62nd Street
Fort Lauderdale, FL 33309
954-772-5400
Dogs up to 80 pounds are allowed. There is a $100 one time per stay pet fee.

Days Inn
6651 Darter Court
Fort Pierce, FL 34945
561-466-4066
There is a $10 one time pet charge.

Holiday Inn Express
7151 Okeechobee Rd.
Fort Pierce, FL 34945
561-464-5000
There is a $25 one time pet charge.

Royal Inn
222 Hernando Street

Fort Pierce, FL 34949
561-464-0405
There is a $25 one time pet charge.

Hollywood

Days Inn
2601 N. 29th Avenue
Hollywood, FL 33020
954-923-7300
There is a $10 per day pet charge.

Juno Beach

Holiday Inn Express-North Palm Beach
13950 US Hwy 1
Juno Beach, FL 33408
561-622-4366
There is a $25 one time pet charge.

Miami

Amerisuites
3655 NW 82nd Ave.
Miami, FL 33166
305-718-8292
There is a $10 per day pet charge.

Hampton Inn-Downtown
2500 Brickell Ave.
Miami, FL 33129
305-854-2070
There are no additional pet fees.

Homestead Village-Miami Airport
8720 NW 33rd Street
Miami, FL 33172
305-436-1811
There is a $75 one time pet charge.

La Quinta Inn Miami Airport North
7401 NW 36th St
Miami, FL
305-599-9902
Dogs up to 70 pounds are allowed at the hotel.

Quality Inn South-Kendall

14501 S. Dixie Highway
Miami, FL 33176
305-251-2000
There is no pet fee.

Staybridge Suites
3265 NW 87th Avenue
Miami, FL 33172
305-500-9100
There is a $125 one time pet fee per visit.

Miami Beach

Brigham Gardens Guesthouse
1411 Collins Avenue
Miami Beach, FL 33139
305-531-1331
Hotel Rooms, Studios and one Bedroom Apartments - Each uniquely and comfort appointed in bright tropical linens and decor. Pets are welcome for a nightly fee of $6.00.

Hotel Leon
841 Collins Avenue
Miami Beach, FL 33139
305-673-3767
Stone's throw from the beach, in the heart of the Art Deco District of Miami Beach.

Hotel Ocean
1230 Ocean Drive
Miami Beach, FL 33139
800-783-1725
Hotel Ocean's accommodations, mostly suites, are appointed in a warm Mediterranean style, where decor varies from room to room in colors, shapes, and accents. Furnished with 1930's collectible pieces, original art-deco fireplaces and exquisite bathrooms all units feature sound proofed windows, central A/C, in room safes, complimentary breakfast and cable tv. Pets are welcome. They have created a special package that includes a bed, treats, and walking service for only $19.95 per pet per day. The regular pet fee is $15.00

per pet per day.

Loews Miami Beach Hotel
1601 Collins Avenue
Miami Beach, FL 33139
305-604-1601
All well-behaved dogs of any size are welcome. This upscale hotel offers their "Loews Loves Pets" program which includes special pet treats, local dog walking routes, and a list of nearby pet-friendly places to visit. While pets are not allowed in the pool, they are welcome to join you at the side of the pool or at the pool bar. There are no pet fees.

Miami Springs

Mainstay Suites
101 Fairway Dr
Miami Springs, FL 33166
305-870-0448
There is a non-refundable pet charge of $25.

Palm Beach

Heart of Palm Beach
160 Royal Palm Way
Palm Beach, FL
561-655-5600
There are no pet fees. Pet owners must sign a pet waiver.

Plaza Inn
215 Brazilian Avenue
Palm Beach, FL 33480
561-832-8666
This pet friendly hotel has accommodated dogs up to 100 pounds. This inn, located on the Island of Palm Beach, is a historic 50 room hotel which has been fully renovated with warm textures of lace, polished wood, antiques and quality reproductions. Take a look at their website for pictures of this elegant inn. There are no pet fees.

Plantation

Holiday Inn
1711 N. University Dr
Plantation, FL 33322
954-472-5600
There is a $10 per day additional
pet fee.

Residence Inn by Marriott-Ft. Lauderdale
130 N. University Drive
Plantation, FL 33324
954-723-0300
There is a $20 per day pet
charge.

Staybridge Suites
410 North Pine Island Rd
Plantation, FL 33324
954-577-9696
Dogs up to 70 pounds are
allowed and there is a $100 one
time per stay pet charge.

Pompano Beach

Motel 6
1201 NW 31st Ave
Pompano Beach, FL 33069
954-977-8011
One large dog is okay.

Singer Island

Days Inn-Oceanfront Resort, W. Palm Beach
2700 N. Ocean Drive
Singer Island, FL 33404
561-848-8661
There is a $10 per day pet
charge. This motel is located on
the beach.

Stuart

Pirates Cove Resort and Marina
4307 S.E. Bayview Street
Stuart, FL 34997
561-287-2500
There is a $20 per day pet fee.
The pet rooms are usually the
smoking rooms, but if you speak
with the hotel manager, they
should be able to give you a
non-smoking room.

West Palm Beach

Hibiscus House Bed & Breakfast
501 30th Street
West Palm Beach, FL 33407
561-863-5633
This bed and breakfast was
ranked by the Miami Herald as
one of the ten best in Florida.
The owner has a dog, and
there are no pet charges. Large
dogs usually stay in the
cottage.

Studio 6
1535 Centrepark Dr, North
West Palm Beach, FL 33401
561-640-3335
There is a $10 per day
additional pet fee. Large dogs
are allowed if well-behaved.

Attractions

Coopertown

Coopertown Airboat Tours
US-41
Coopertown, FL
11 miles west of Florida's
Turnpike
305-226-6048
Some of the boat drivers will
allow dogs, but not all will.
However, there are a number of
them here at any time. The
airboats are noisy. Only take a
dog that is experienced with
noisy boats and rides. A large
dog may go on the tour only if
the boat is not full with
passengers.

Coral Gables

Village of Merrick Park Shopping Plaza
358 Avenue San Lorenzo
Coral Gables, FL 33146
305-529-0200
Well-behaved leashed dogs are
allowed at this outdoor mall and
inside many of the stores
including Nordstrom,
Athropologie, Crabtree &

Evelyn, and Williams-Sonoma.
Several restaurants also allow
dogs at their outdoor tables,
including Cafe Ibiza, Java of
Merrick Park and Pescado.

Fort Lauderdale

Club Nautico
801 Seabreeze Blvd
Fort Lauderdale, FL 33316
954-467-6000
You can rent powerboats here
for use on the inland waterways.

Fort Lauderdale Riverwalk
2nd St and 4th Ave
Fort Lauderdale, FL
954-761-5784
Leashed dogs are allowed at the
Riverwalk which is a promenade
that follows the river for about
1.5 miles. The walk is located
along the New River's north
bank and links together many
historical landmarks. The walk
starts near the Stranahan House
and ends near the Broward
Center for the Performing Arts at
201 S.W. Fifth Ave. There is an
outdoor Jazz brunch on the first
Sunday of each month where
you can take you dog with you.
There are nearby outdoor
restaurants on Las Olas Blvd.

Las Olas District
Las Olas Blvd and Federal Hwy
Fort Lauderdale, FL

This shopping district has a
large number of outdoor
restaurants. It is near the
Riverwalk so you and your pup
can make a day of it here.

Key Biscayne

Club Nautica
4000 Crandon Blvd
Key Biscayne, FL 33149
At Crandon Park Marina
305-361-9217
You can charter any number of
fishing boats for a half day or
entire day or you can rent a
powerboat.

Lake Worth

Hoffman Chocolate Shop and Gardens
5190 Lake Worth Rd
Lake Worth, FL
561-433-GIFT
There is a nice garden to explore while you munch on chocolates and your dog sniffs the garden. You will have to go inside to order the chocolates without the pup, however.

Miami

Bal Harbour Shopping Center
9700 Collins Ave
Miami, FL 33154
95th Street
305-866-0311
An upscale outdoor shopping center where your dog is welcome in some of the stores and the outdoor restaurants.

Monty's Marina
2560 S Bayshore Dr
Miami, FL 33133
305-854-7997
You can rent a boat here at Club Nautica or charter a fishing boat as well. There is an outdoor restaurant, Cicero's, that you can take your pup to at the marina.

Miami Beach

Art Deco Self-Guided Walking Tour
1001 Ocean Drive
Miami Beach, FL
10th Street
305-672-2014
Audio tapes for a self-guided walking tour of Miami Beach's Art Deco District are available at the Welcome Center. The Welcome Center is located at 1001 Ocean Drive. The cost is $10 per person for the audio rental.

Lincoln Road Shops
Lincoln Road

Miami Beach, FL
305-531-3442
This pedestrian-only street mall in Miami beach has a number of dog-friendly establishments for eating and shopping.

Palm Beach

Worth Avenue Shopping District
Worth Avenue
Palm Beach, FL

This is a high-class outdoor shopping district on Palm Beach. Many of the stores will welcome your well behaved dog, but as always we suggest that you ask.

Beaches

Boynton Beach

Dog Beach
A1A
Boynton Beach, FL

Dogs can be leash-free at this beach. Please clean up after your dog. It is a county beach, located between the cities of Boynton Beach and Ocean Ridge. The dog beach is next to Nomad Surfshop which is at 4655 North Ocean Blvd. There is no parking lot for the beach.

Fort Pierce

Fort Pierce Inlet State Park
905 Shorewinds Drive
Fort Pierce, FL 34949
772-468-3985
Dogs are not allowed on the ocean beach, but they are allowed on the cove beach. Pets must be leashed and people need to clean up after their pets. The park is located four miles east of Ft. Pierce, via North Causeway.

Jupiter

Jupiter Beach
A1A at Xanadu Road
Jupiter, FL

The beach is about 2 miles long. Please follow the dog rules on the beach so that dogs will continue to be allowed here. Dogs must be leashed on the beach. Please clean up after your dog as well.

Jupiter Island

Hobe Sound National Wildlife Refuge
North Beach Road
Jupiter Island, FL
772-546-6141
This refuge has sea turtle nesting areas and endangered species like the scrub jay and gopher tortoise. Dogs on leash are allowed at the beach. The leash law is enforced and people need to clean up after their pets. The park headquarters is located 2 miles south of SR 708 (Bridge Road) on U.S. 1. The beach is located 1.5 miles north of Bridge Road on North Beach Road.

Miami

Rickenbacker Causeway Beach
Rickenbacker Causeway
Miami, FL
Key Biscayne

This beach extends the length of the Rickenbacker Causeway from Downtown Miami to Key Biscayne. Dogs are allowed on the entire stretch. There are two types of beach, a Tree lined Dirt beach and a standard type of sandy beach further towards Key Biscayne. Dogs should be leashed on the beach.

Parks

Boca Raton

South County Regional Park
11200 Park Access Rd
Boca Raton, FL 33498
561-966-6600
Dogs must be leashed in the park.

Coconut Grove

Barnacle State Historic Site
3485 Main Highway
Coconut Grove, FL 33133
McFarlane Road
305-448-9445
Dogs are allowed in the outdoor areas of the park. Dogs must be leashed in the park.

Davie

Tree Tops Park
3900 S.W. 100th Ave
Davie, FL 33328
Griffen Road
954-370-3750
Dogs must be leashed in the park.

Deerfield Beach

Quiet Waters Park
401 S. Powerline Rd
Deerfield Beach, FL 33442
Hillsboro Blvd
954-360-1315
Dogs must be leashed in the park.

Fort Lauderdale

Bike Trail - Fort Lauderdale
along A1A near the beach
Fort Lauderdale, FL
Las Olas Blvd

This trail follows A1A through the Fort Lauderdale beach area. Dogs must be leashed on the trail.

Canine Park
East End of Sunrise Blvd
Fort Lauderdale, FL
Ocean

There is a 100 yard stretch of beach which dogs can use. However, there are only certain hours and an annual permit is required. The current hours are 5 pm - 9 pm on Saturdays and Sundays. Permits can be purchased at Parks and Recreation Department, 1350 W. Broward Boulevard. Call (954) 761-5346 for permit information.

Hugh Taylor Birch State Park
3109 East Sunrise Boulevard
Fort Lauderdale, FL 33304
Ocean
954-564-4521

Fort Pierce

Heathcote Botanical Gardens
210 Savannah Rd
Fort Pierce, FL
561-464-4672
Well-behaved leashed dogs are welcome to walk with you on the self-guided tour of the botanical gardens. The 3.5 acre garden has orchid trees, over 40 species of palm trees, beds of ornamental annuals and an herb garden. Just remember to clean up after your pooch!

Key Biscayne

Bill Baggs State Park
1200 S. Crandon Blvd
Key Biscayne, FL 33149
At the south end of Crandon Blvd
305-361-5811
Dogs are allowed on leash. This park has trails and a lighthouse (to view from outside). Dogs are not allowed on the beach near the lighthouse.

Lake Worth

John Prince Park
2700 6th Ave. S

Lake Worth, FL

Dogs must be leashed in the park.

Miami Beach

Lummas Park
Ocean Drive
Miami Beach, FL
5th Street

This park borders the ocean in the Art Deco district of Miami Beach. Dogs must be leashed in the park.

North Miami

Oleta River State Park
3400 N.E. 163rd Street
North Miami, FL
Biscayne Blvd

This park has hiking, jogging, and waterfront on the Biscayne Bay. Dogs are allowed on leash.

Oakland Park

Easterlin Park
1000 N.W. 38th St
Oakland Park, FL 33309
Powerline
954-938-0610
Dogs must be leashed in the park.

Palm Beach

Lake Trail
Sunset Ave and Bradley
Palm Beach, FL

This is a 3 1/2 mile paved trail along the inter-coastal waterway. Dogs must be leashed on the trail.

Sunrise

Markham Park
16001 W. State 84
Sunrise, FL 33326
Weston Road

954-389-2000
This park is at the edge of the Everglades. Dogs must be leashed in the park.

Restaurants

Boca Raton

Bangkok in Boca
500 Via De Palmas
Boca Raton, FL 33432
561-394-6912
Dogs are allowed at the outdoor tables.

Downtown Deli
399 SE Mizner Blvd
Boca Raton, FL 33432
561-394-7827
Dogs are allowed at the outdoor tables.

Einstein Bros Bagels
9795 Glades Rd
Boca Raton, FL 33434
561-477-0667
Dogs are allowed at the outdoor tables.

Ichiban Japanese Restaurant
8841 Glades Rd
Boca Raton, FL 33434
Lyons
561-451-0420
Dogs are allowed at the outdoor tables.

Lion and Eagle English Pub
2401 N Federal Hwy
Boca Raton, FL 33431
561-447-7707
Dogs are allowed at the one outdoor table.

Coral Gables

Cafe Ibiza
370 San Lorenzo Ave
Coral Gables, FL
305-443-8888
This Mediterranean restaurant allows well-behaved leashed dogs at their outdoor tables. They are located in the dog-friendly Village of Merrick Park

shopping plaza.

Java of Merrick Park
380 San Lorenzo Ave
Coral Gables, FL
305-461-1113
This cafe offers freshly roasted coffee and pastries. Well-behaved leashed dogs are allowed at the outdoor tables. They are located in the dog-friendly Village of Merrick Park shopping plaza.

Pescado
320 San Lorenzo Ave
Coral Gables, FL
305-443-3474
This restaurant offers both local and international seafood plus sushi. Well-behaved leashed dogs are allowed at the outdoor tables. They are located in the dog-friendly Village of Merrick Park shopping plaza.

Delray Beach

City Oyster
213 E Atlantic Ave
Delray Beach, FL 33444
561-272-0220
Dogs are allowed at the outdoor tables.

Fort Lauderdale

China Yung Restaurant
720 E Las Olas Blvd
Fort Lauderdale, FL 33301
954-761-3388
Dogs are allowed at the outdoor tables.

Grill Room On Las Olas
620 E Las Olas Blvd
Fort Lauderdale, FL 33301
954-467-2555
Dogs are allowed at the outdoor tables.

Indigo Restaurant
620 E Las Olas Blvd
Fort Lauderdale, FL 33301
954-467-0045
Dogs are allowed at the outdoor tables.

Japanese Village
716 E Las Olas Blvd
Fort Lauderdale, FL 33301
954-763-8163
Dogs are allowed at the outdoor tables.

Samba Room
350 E Las Olas Blvd
Fort Lauderdale, FL 33301
954-468-2000
Dogs are allowed at the outdoor tables.

Stromboli Pizza
801 S University Dr
Fort Lauderdale, FL 33324
954-472-2167
Dogs are allowed at the outdoor tables.

Hollywood

Harrison Street Sushi Jazz
1902 Harrison St
Hollywood, FL 33020
954-927-8474
Dogs are allowed at the outdoor tables.

O'Hara's Jazz Cafe
1903 Hollywood Blvd
Hollywood, FL 33020
954-925-2555
Dogs are allowed at the outdoor tables.

Shuckums
1814 Harrison St
Hollywood, FL 33020
954-923-9394
Dogs are allowed at the outdoor tables.

Miami

Bal Harbour Bistro
9700 Collins Ave
Miami, FL 33154
305-861-4544
This restaurant is in the Bal Harbour shopping center.

Ciceros
2550 S Bayshore Dr

Miami, FL 33133
at Monty's Marina
305-854-0053
This restaurant is at Monty's
Marina, where you can rent a
power boat or charter boats as
well.

Groovy's Pizza
3030 Grand Ave
Miami, FL 33133
Main Hwy
305-476-6018
It's really an outside only
restaurant. You order and sit
down.

Johnny Rockets
3036 Grand Ave
Miami, FL 33133
305-444-1000
Dogs are allowed at the outdoor
tables.

Mambo Cafe
3105 Commodore Plaza
Miami, FL 33133
305-448-2768
Dogs are allowed at the outdoor
tables.

Senor Frog's
3008 Grand Ave
Miami, FL 33133
Main Hwy
305-448-0999
This patio restaurant is in the
Coconut Grove area of Miami.

Miami Beach

Sushi Rock Cafe
1351 Collins Ave
Miami Beach, FL 33139
305-532-4639
Dogs are allowed at the outdoor
tables.

Taste Bakery Cafe
900 Alton Road
Miami Beach, FL 33139
305-695-9930
The food served here is
hormone and pesticide free and
totally organic when possible.
The cafe is open for breakfast,
lunch and dinner. For breakfast,

try a smoothie, specialty coffee,
tea, a breakfast sandwich, or
bread with spread. For lunch or
dinner, they offer wraps, rolls,
sandwiches, salads, soups and
baked goodies. Well-behaved
leashed dogs are welcome to
join you at the outdoor tables.

Van Dyke Cafe
1641 Jefferson Ave
Miami Beach, FL 33139
305-534-3600
Dogs are allowed at the
outdoor tables.

World Resources Cafe
719 Lincoln Rd
Miami Beach, FL 33139
305-535-8987
Dogs are allowed at the
outdoor tables.

West Palm Beach

Buddy's Cafe and Deli
2431 Beach Ct
West Palm Beach, FL 33404
561-848-1506
Dogs are allowed at the
outdoor tables.

Dax Bar and Grill
300 Clematis St
West Palm Beach, FL 33401
561-833-0449
Dogs are allowed at the
outdoor tables.

Outback Steakhouse
871 Village Blvd
West Palm Beach, FL 33409
561-683-1011
Dogs are allowed at the
outdoor tables.

Pescatore Restaurant
200 Clematis St
West Palm Beach, FL 33401
561-837-6633
Dogs are allowed at the
outdoor tables.

Rooney's Public House
213 Clematis St
West Palm Beach, FL 33401
561-833-7802

Dogs are allowed at the outdoor
tables.

Stores

Coral Gables

Anthropologie
330 San Lorenzo Avenue
Coral Gables, FL
305-443-0021
This store offers women's
clothing and household items.
They are located in the dog-
friendly Village of Merrick Park
shopping plaza. Well-behaved
leashed dogs are allowed inside
the store.

Crabtree & Evelyn
320 San Lorenzo Avenue
Coral Gables, FL
305-448-4077
This bath and skincare store
allows well-behaved leashed
dogs inside. They are located in
the dog-friendly Village of
Merrick Park shopping plaza.

Nordstrom
4310 Ponce De Leon Blvd.
Coral Gables, FL
786-999-1313
This department allows well-
behaved leashed dogs inside
the store. They are located in
the dog-friendly Village of
Merrick Park shopping plaza.

Williams-Sonoma
350 San Lorenzo Avenue
Coral Gables, FL
305-446-9421
This store offers specialty
packaged foods, appliances,
cookbooks, tableware, and
kitchen products. They allow
well-behaved leashed dogs
inside and are located in the
dog-friendly Village of Merrick
Park shopping plaza.

Vets and Kennels

Miami-Homestead

KennelStation
23850 SW 129 Ave
Miami-Homestead, FL 33032
305-258-9030
Family owned kennel offering comprehensive K-9 Boarding and In-Home Pet Sitting services throughout South Florida since 1989.

Key West City Guide

Accommodations

Key West

Ambrosia House Tropical Lodging
622 Fleming Street
Key West, FL 33040
305-296-9838
This inn, located on almost two private acres, offers a variety of well-appointed rooms, suites, town houses and a cottage, all with private baths. The inn is located in the heart of historic Old Town. There is a one time non-refundable pet fee of $25. All pets are welcome. There is no weight limit or limit to the number of pets.

Center Court Historic Inn & Cottages
916 Center Street
Key West, FL 33040
305-296-9292
Dogs are allowed in the suites and cottages. There is a $10 per day pet charge.

Chelsea House
707 Truman Avenue
Key West, FL 33040
305-296-2211
There is a $15 per day pet charge.

Courtney's Place
720 Whitmarsh Lane
Key West, FL 33040
305-294-3480
This inn has historic guest cottages. There are no designated smoking or non-

smoking cottages.

Douglas House and Cuban Club Suites
419 Amelia St
Key West, FL 33040
305-294-5269
Small dogs are welcome at the Douglas House. Large dogs are welcome at the Cuban Club Suites. There is a $10 per day pet fee. There are no designated smoking or non-smoking rooms.

Francis Street Bottle Inn
535 Francis Street
Key West, FL 33040
305-294-8530
Dogs are allowed, including well-behaved large dogs. There is a $25 one time pet fee.

Key West's Center Court - Bed and Breakfast and Cottages
915 Center Street
Key West, FL 33040
800-797-8787
Special doggy treats upon check-in. Pets welcome in suites, cottages, condos and homes. Amenities include 4 pools and most suites offer private jacuzzis. Specializing in weddings, honeymoons, and romantic escapes. There is a $10 per pet per night charge. Dogs of all sizes and breeds are welcome.

Key West's Travelers Palm - Inn and Cottages
915 Center Street
Key West, FL 33040
800-294-9560
Special dog treats upon check-in. Dogs are welcome in the suites and cottages. Amenities include premier Old Town locations and 3 heated pools. Dogs of all sizes and breeds are welcome.

Seascape Tropical Inn
420 Olivia St
Key West, FL 33040
305-296-7776

Pets are allowed in all of the cottages and two rooms in the main guesthouse. There is a $25 one time pet fee. All rooms are non-smoking. Children are allowed in the cottages. The owner has two dogs on the premises.

Sheraton Suites Key West
2001 South Roosevelt Blvd
Key West, FL 33040
305-292-9800
Dogs up to 80 pounds are allowed. There are no additional pet fees. Pet treats are available as well.

Whispers
409 William St
Key West, FL 33040
305-294-5969
Dogs are allowed, but no puppies please. There is a $25 one time pet fee. Children over 10 years old are allowed.

Accommodations - Vacation Home Rentals

Key West

Key West Hideaways
915 Eisenhower Drive
Key West, FL 33040
305-296-9090
Cottages, condominiums, suites and rooms in Key West. Escape the real world while enjoying the perfect alternative to a luxury hotel with the added value of total privacy and many locations in Key West. Call to request pet policy and to inquire about which rentals allow pets.

Attractions

Key West

Duval Street Shopping District
Duval Street
Key West, FL

This street has a large number of dog-friendly specialty shops.

Guild Hall Gallery
614 Duval St
Key West, FL 33040
305-296-6076
Your well-behaved, leashed dog is allowed inside this co-op museum with art from 30 working artists.

Key West Aquarium
1 Whitehead St
Key West, FL 33040
305-296-2051
This aquarium is the only one we know of that allows you to take your pup along on leash. It has a large unfenced shark tank so please keep your pup under good control.

Lighthouse Museum
938 Whitehead Street
Key West, FL 33040
305-294-0012
Dogs must be leashed at all times on the premises.

Southernmost Point Monument
Whitehead St and South Street
Key West, FL
South Street

You and your pup can stand next to the monument at the southernmost point in the United States.

Stephen Huneck Art Gallery
218 Whitehead St
Key West, FL 33040
305-295-7616
This art gallery contains art about dogs and your well-behaved, leashed dog is very welcome to accompany you to the gallery.

Beaches

Key West

Dog Beach
Vernon Ave and Waddell Ave
Key West, FL
Waddell Ave

This tiny stretch of beach is the only beach we found in Key West that a dog can go to.

Restaurants

Key West

American Bar
526 Front Street
Key West, FL 33040
305-292-7551
Dogs are allowed at the outdoor tables.

Billie's Bar and Restaurant
407 Front Street
Key West, FL 33040
305-294-9292
Dogs are allowed at the outdoor tables.

Bo's Fish Wagon
801 Caroline St
Key West, FL 33040
305-294-9272
This is an outdoor restaurant that "appears" indoors and your dog is welcome where you order and where you sit.

Casablanca Cafe
904 Duval St
Key West, FL 33040
305-296-0815
Dogs are allowed at the outdoor tables.

Conch Republic Seafood Company
631 Greene St
Key West, FL 33040
305-294-4403
There is live entertainment here often.

Limbo At Mangoes
700 Duval St
Key West, FL 33040
305-292-4606
Dogs are allowed at the outdoor tables.

Old Town Mexican Cafe
609 Duval St
Key West, FL 33040

305-296-7500
Dogs are allowed at the outdoor tables.

Pepe's Cafe and Steakhouse
806 Caroline Street
Key West, FL
305-294-7192
Well-behaved leashed dogs are allowed at the outdoor tables. Thanks to one of our readers for recommending this dog-friendly restaurant.

Schooner Wharf Bar
202 William Street
Key West, FL 33040
305-292-9520
This open air waterfront bar and grill offers soups, salads, sandwiches, plates like chicken or mahi-mahi and more. This restaurant also regularly offers live musical entertainment. Well-behaved leashed dogs are allowed at the outdoor tables. Thanks to one of our readers for recommending this dog-friendly restaurant.

Willie T's
525 Duval St
Key West, FL 33040
305-294-7674
There is often live entertainment here.

Chicago City Guide
Accommodations

Arlington Heights

La Quinta Inn Chicago - Arlington Heights
1415 W Dundee Road
Arlington Heights, IL
847-253-8777
Dogs of all sizes are allowed at the hotel.

Motel 6 - North Central
441 W Algonquin Rd
Arlington Heights, IL 60005
847-806-1230

There are no additional pet fees.

Sheraton Chicago Northwest
3400 West Euclid Avenue
Arlington Heights, IL 60005
847-394-2000
Dogs up to 80 pounds are allowed. There is a $50 one time pet fee per stay. Pets may only be left alone in the room in a crate.

Chicago

Claridge Hotel
1244 North Dearborn Parkway
Chicago, IL 60610
312-787-4980
There is a $25 refundable pet deposit.

Holiday Inn - Mart Plaza
350 N. Orleans St
Chicago, IL 60654
312-836-5000
There are no additional pet fees.

Hotel Allegro
171 West Randolph Street
Chicago, IL 60601
312-236-0123
Well-behaved dogs of all sizes are welcome at this pet-friendly hotel. The luxury boutique hotel offers both rooms and suites. Hotel amenities include complimentary evening wine served in the living room, a gift shop, and an on-site fitness center. There are no pet fees.

Hotel Burnham
1 West Washington
Chicago, IL 60602
312-782-1111
Dogs of all kinds and sizes are welcome at this pet-friendly hotel. The luxury boutique hotel offers both rooms and suites. Hotel amenities include a fully equipped fitness room, and complimentary evening wine in the lobby. There are no pet fees, just sign a pet liability form.

Hotel Monaco Chicago
225 North Wabash

Chicago, IL 60601
312-960-8500
Well-behaved dogs of all sizes are welcome at this pet-friendly hotel. The luxury boutique hotel offers both rooms and suites. Hotel amenities include complimentary evening wine service, 24 hour room service, and an on-site fitness room. There are no pet fees, just sign a pet liability form.

Palmer House Hilton
17 East Monroe Street
Chicago, IL 60603
312-726-7500
No pet charge, just sign a pet waiver for any possible damages to the room.

Residence Inn by Marriott-Downtown
201 East Walton Place
Chicago, IL 60611
312-943-9800
There is a $15 per day pet charge.

W Chicago - Lakeshore
644 North Lake Shore Drive
Chicago, IL 60611
312-943-9200
Dogs up to 80 pounds are allowed. There is a $125 one time pet fee per stay and a $25 per day additional pet fee.

Downers Grove

Red Roof Inn
1113 Butterfield Road
Downers Grove, IL 60515
630-963-4205
There are no additional pet fees.

Glenview

Motel 6 - North
1535 Milwaukee Ave
Glenview, IL 60025
847-390-7200
Pets must be attended at all times.

Hammond

Holiday Inn - Southeast
3830 179th St
Hammond, IL 46323
219-844-2140
There is a $35 one time pet fee. Pets may not be left alone in rooms.

Joliet

Comfort Inn North
3235 Norman Ave
Joliet, IL 60435
815-436-5141
There is no pet fee. Pets are allowed on the first floor only.

Motel 6 - Joliet
3551 Mall Loop Drive
Joliet, IL 60431
815-439-1332
From I-80 take I-55 north to US 30 exit.

Palatine

Motel 6 - Northwest
1450 E Dundee Rd
Palatine, IL 60074
847-359-0046
There are no additional pet fees.

Rosemont

Holiday Inn Select
10233 West Higgins Rd
Rosemont, IL 60018
847-954-8600
There is a $25 one time pet fee.

Sheraton Gateway Suites Chicago O'Hare
6501 N. Mannheim Rd
Rosemont, IL 60018
847-699-6300
Dogs up to 75 pounds are allowed. There are no additional pet fees.

Schaumburg

Chicago - Schaumburg Drury Inn

600 N. Martingale
Schaumburg, IL 60173
847-517-7737
Dogs of all sizes are permitted. Pets are not allowed in the breakfast area of the hotel. Pets are not to be left unattended, and each guest must assume liability for damage of property or other guest complaints. There is a limit of one pet per room.

Skokie

Howard Johnson Hotel
9333 Skokie Blvd.
Skokie, IL 60077
847-679-4200
One large dog is permitted per room. There are no pet fees.

Attractions

Chicago

Antique Coach and Carriage Company
700 North Michigan
Chicago, IL
(at Huron)
773-735-9400
Your dog is welcome to join you on a scenic horse and carriage ride through downtown Chicago. Choose from a variety of carriage tours including the lakefront tour, Lincoln Park or Chicago's Magnificent Mile (a popular shopping district that attractions over 22 million visitors each year according to Chicago's Magnificent Mile(TM) Association.) Carriage rides depart at the corner of Michigan and Huron. During the Christmas season, you can also catch a carriage at 200 North State St (at Randolph) for a tour of the Chicago loop and the large Christmas tree on display. Reservations are recommended, usually one day in advance, for holidays including Valentine's Day.

Buckingham Fountain

In Grant Park
Chicago, IL
(Congress and Columbus)
312-742-7529
Dogs on leash are allowed at this popular Chicago landmark in Grant Park. The fountain, built in 1927, is noted for its artistic bronze sculpture, decorative details, and especially for its creative use of technology to present a brilliant music, light and water show. The shows take place every hour on the hour from dusk to 11pm, and last for twenty minutes. The show is seasonal and operates spring through early fall.

Chicago Horse and Carriage Rides
Michigan Avenue
Chicago, IL
(at Pearson Street)
312-944-9192
Dogs are allowed on the horse and carriage rides.

Chicago White Sox Dog Day
333 W. 35th Street
Chicago, IL
(Comiskey Park)
866-769-4263
Take your pooch to a Major League Baseball game once a year, usually in April, at the Dog Day game. On event day, come to Comiskey Park, take a seat in the left field bleachers, and enjoy the game. This event normally sells out, so be sure to purchase tickets early.

Dog Days of Summer Cruises
Michigan Ave. & Wacker Dr.
Chicago, IL
312-332-1353
Every Sunday during the summer months, bring your pooch and enjoy a Canine Cruise. Mercury Skyline Cruiseline offers a cruise just for dogs (and their people) every Sunday at 10am-11am from about June through September. The river and lakefront cruise highlights

downtown Chicago landmarks. Food and drinks are not sold on the boats, but you can bring your own in non-breakable containers. Tour prices are $15 per adult, $7.50 per child 11 and under, and $5.00 per dog. Prices are subject to change. Advance reservations are not required. Tickets go on sale at 9am on Sundays and cash only please (no credit cards). The boat departs at Michigan Avenue and Wacker Drive, on the Chicago River.

Navy Pier
600 East Grand Avenue
Chicago, IL
312-595-7437
Dogs are allowed at most of the outdoor areas of this Chicago landmark. The Navy Pier offers over 50 acres of parks, shops, and attractions. While dogs are not permitted in the attractions or shops, they are allowed to accompany you while you walk around outside. Dogs are also allowed at the outdoor seats at the Food Court. The Food Court offers a variety of foods including pizza, Chinese, Greek, sandwiches, pretzels, baked goods and more. In addition to the sights at this pier, your dog is allowed on the Architecture Boat Tours which depart from the Ogden Slip at the Navy Pier. See our listing for Shoreline Sightseeing Boat Tours for more information.

Retail Stores
See comments for details.
Chicago, IL

Well-behaved, leashed dogs are allowed in the following retail stores in Chicago: Neiman Marcus at 737 North Michigan Ave, 312-642-5900 and Billy Hork Galleries at 109 East Oak Street , 312-337-1199. As with all other establishments, please always call ahead to make sure a retail store is still dog-friendly.

Riverwalk Gateway/Riverwalk
Lake Shore Drive
Chicago, IL
(at the Chicago River)
312-744-6630
You and your pooch can walk through the Riverwalk Gateway, which to date, is the City of Chicago's largest work of public art. As you stroll through the lighted tunnel, you will learn about the history of Chicago and the Chicago river by viewing sixteen narrative panels and twelve decorative panels. This gateway connects the dog-friendly Chicago Riverwalk, a pedestrian path along the river and through downtown, with the Lakefront Trail. The Riverwalk parallels the Chicago River and Wacker Drive, between Michigan Avenue and Lake Shore Drive. Dogs are allowed on both the Riverwalk and Lakefront Trail (just not on any beaches). If you work up an appetite after walking, try dining at Cyrano's Bistro and Wine Bar. This French bistro allows dogs at the outdoor tables.

Shoreline Sightseeing Boat Tours
Illinois Street
Chicago, IL
(at Navy Pier)
312-222-9328
Dogs are allowed on the Architecture Cruises which highlight over 40 major buildings in downtown Chicago. Led by a knowledgeable guide, the cruises take about one hour. Board the boat tours at the Ogden Slip at the Navy Pier. Reservations are not required, but strongly recommended. Call or visit their website for days and hours of operation.

Parks

Chicago

Grant Park
Congress and Columbus

Chicago, IL
312-742-7529
Dogs on leash are allowed. The famous Buckingham Fountain is located in this park. The park offers some nice views of Lake Michigan. The Lakefront Trail is near this park.

Montrose Harbor Dog Beach
Lake Shore Drive
Chicago, IL
312-742-7529
Effective August 2003, dogs are allowed on part of the beach near Montrose. Dogs can run leash-free on the beach. Please note that people who violate the leash law by not having their dog on a leash between the parking lot and the beach are being fined with $75 tickets, so be sure to bring your dog's leash.

The Lakefront Trail
Lake Shore Drive
Chicago, IL
312-742-7529
This popular trail offers 18 miles of paved paths alongside Lake Michigan. Walkers, joggers, rollerbladers, bicyclists, and of course dogs, frequent this path. One of the starting points is at Lake Shore Drive and Wacker Drive, where the Riverwalk Gateway is located. Effective August 2003, dogs are allowed on part of beach near Montrose. Dogs can run leash-free on the beach but must be leashed from the parking lot to the beach.

Wiggly Field Dog Park
2645 North Sheffield Ave.
Chicago, IL 60614
(near Lincoln)

This dog park is located in Noethling Park which is north of downtown Chicago.

Restaurants

Chicago

A Taste of Heaven Bakery
1701 West Foster Avenue
Chicago, IL 60640
312-850-2663
This bakery offers fresh baked goodies, desserts and even sandwiches, salads, and hot entrees. Dogs are allowed at the outdoor tables.

Amarit
1 E Delaware Pl
Chicago, IL 60611
312-649-0500
This Thai restaurant allows dogs at some of their outdoor tables. If bringing your dog, you will need to sit at a perimeter table and your dog needs to be outside of the serving area, alongside your table.

Banana Leaf
3811 North Southport Avenue
Chicago, IL 60613
773-883-8683
Dogs can join you at the outdoor tables at this downtown Thai restaurant.

Ben Pao
52 W. Illinois
Chicago, IL
(corner of Illinois and Dearborn)
312-222-1888
Dogs are allowed to accompany you to the outdoor tables at this Chinese restaurant.

Bice
158 E. Ontario Street
Chicago, IL 60611
312-664-1474
This cafe allows dogs at the outdoor tables, most of which are covered with an awning or umbrellas. Bice is one of Chicago's top rated restaurants.

Bistrot Margot
1437 N Wells Street
Chicago, IL
312-587-3660
This French bistro is located in the heart of Chicago's Old Town. Well-behaved, leashed dogs are allowed at the outdoor tables.

Bordo's Eatery and Sauce
2476 N Lincoln Ave
Chicago, IL 60614
773-529-6900
Dogs are welcome to accompany you to the outdoor tables at this restaurant located in Lincoln Park. This downtown Chicago restaurant serves lunch and dinner including appetizers, salads, fresh pasta, sandwiches, burgers and pizza.

Brasserie Jo
59 West Hubbard St.
Chicago, IL 60610
312-595-0800
Your dog is welcome to join you at the outdoor tables at this French restaurant. This authentic brasserie is open for dinner only.

Brett's Cafe Americain
2011 West Roscoe
Chicago, IL
773-248-0999
This restaurant offers brunch on Saturday and Sunday, lunch Wednesday through Friday, and dinner on Wednesday through Sunday. Brett's was rated "One of The 10 Top Ten Brunches in Chicago" by the Chicago Tribune's P. Vettel. Dogs are allowed at the outdoor tables.

Cheesecake Factory
875 North Michigan Ave
Chicago, IL 60611
312-337-1101
In addition to cheesecake, this popular chain restaurant also serves an array of food like pizza, pasta, steak, sandwiches, salads, brunch with eggs and more. They are located on Michigan Avenue in the John Hancock Center. Dogs are allowed at the outdoor tables.

Chicago Flat Sammies
811 North Michigan Avenue
Chicago, IL
312-664-2733
Sandwiches are served at this restaurant and pooches are allowed at the outdoor tables.

Corner Bakery
1121 N. State Street
Chicago, IL 60610
(State/Cedar)
312-787-1969
Enjoy fresh baked breads, sandwiches, salads, soups and pastries for breakfast, lunch or early dinner. Dogs are allowed at the outdoor tables.

Corner Bakery
676 North St. Clair
Chicago, IL 60611
312-266-AJ70
Your pooch is allowed to join you for breakfast, lunch or early dinner at the outdoor tables. Try the bakeries fresh baked pastries, bread, sandwiches and more.

Corner Bakery
188 W. Washington Street
Chicago, IL 60602
(at Wells)
312-263-4258
Come for breakfast, lunch or early dinner and enjoy the fresh pastries, bread, sandwiches and more. Dogs are allowed at the outdoor tables.

Costello Sandwich and Sides
4647 North Lincoln
Chicago, IL
773-989-7788
Oven baked and deli sandwiches are the specialty here! Choose from a wide variety of sandwiches like The Mess or Italian Meatball. Or if you prefer a vegetarian fare, try the Cheesy Veggie Wrap or the Baked Caprese. Dogs are allowed at the outdoor tables.

Cucina Bella
543 W. Diversey
Chicago, IL 60614
773-868-1119
Open only for dinner, this Italian restaurant is very dog-friendly! They serve your pooch a complimentary bowl of pasta and a bowl of water.

Cucina Bella Osteria and Wine Bar
1612 N. Sedgwick
Chicago, IL 60614
312-274-1119
Dogs are allowed at this outdoor restaurant. Also, visit their other very dog-friendly restaurant on Diversey.

Cyrano's Bistro and Wine Bar
546 North Wells St.
Chicago, IL 60610
312-467-0546
Dine on Chicago's Riverwalk at this French restaurant. Dogs are welcome to join you at the outdoor tables.

Grecian Taverna
4535 North Lincoln Avenue
Chicago, IL 60625
773-728-1600
Located on Chicago's North Side, this restaurant serves authentic Greek food like shish kebobs, pasta and much more. Dogs are allowed at the outdoor tables.

Kitsch'n on Roscoe
2005 W. Roscoe Street
Chicago, IL 60618
773-248-SERA
According to Kitsch'n's, they offer a "funky and upbeat" atmosphere. Come here for breakfast, lunch or dinner and enjoy some comfort food. Dogs are allowed at the outdoor tables in the front.

MOD Restaurant
1520 North Damen
Chicago, IL
773-252-1500
Enjoy a wide variety of American food at this restaurant. Dogs are allowed at the outdoor restaurants.

Sauce
1750 North Clark St.
Chicago, IL 60614
312-932-1750
Dogs are allowed at the outdoor tables.

Wishbone
1001 W Washington Blvd
Chicago, IL 60607
312-850-2663
This restaurant specializes in "Southern Reconstruction Cooking." They offer omelettes, Jambalaya, Red Beans and Rice, Pan-Fried Chicken, Blackened Catfish, Grilled Salmon, Steaks and much, much more. Open for breakfast, lunch and dinner. Dogs are allowed at the outdoor tables.

Glencoe

Foodstuffs
338 Park Avenue
Glencoe, IL
847-835-5105
This gourmet food store also offers a deli where you can order sandwiches and baked goodies and then take them outside to the outdoor tables. Dogs are allowed at the outside tables.

Little Red Hen
653 Vernon Avenue
Glencoe, IL
847-835-4900
Their specialties are barbecue chicken and they also offer ribs and pizza. Dogs are allowed at the outdoor seats.

Highland Park

Las Palmas
474 Central Avenue
Highland Park, IL
847-432-7770
This Mexican restaurants offers a variety of fajitas, quesadillas, burritos and more. Dogs are allowed at the outdoor tables.

Little Szechwan
1900 First Street
Highland Park, IL
847-433-7007
Dogs are allowed at the outdoor tables at this Chinese restaurant.

Highwood

Hoagie Hut
17 Bank Lane
Highwood, IL
847-432-3262
As the name implies, they serve up a variety of hot and cold hoagies (sandwiches). They have a couple of outdoor tables. Dogs are allowed at the outdoor tables.

Vernon Hills

Cafe Pyrenees
701 North Milwaukee Avenue
Vernon Hills, IL
847-918-8850
This French Bistro allows dogs at the outdoor tables.

Wilmette

The Noodle Cafe
708 12th Street
Wilmette, IL 60091
847-251-2228
Open for lunch and dinner, this cafe serves a variety of fresh pasta, seafood, poultry and meat. Well-behaved dogs that don't bother other guests are allowed at the outdoor tables.

Vets and Kennels

Schaumburg

The 8Paws Petsitters
300 Islington Ln
Schaumburg, IL 60193
847-895-1358
Offer mid-day dog walking, pet-sitting for vacationers and local motels and hotels. Weekly packages. Serve Schaumburg, Streamwood and Western Elk Grove, IL.

Detroit City Guide
Accommodations

Auburn Hills

Staybridge Suites
2050 Featherstone Rd
Auburn Hills, MI 48326
248-322-4600
There is a $75 one time pet fee.

Belleville

Comfort Inn
45945 S. I-94 Service Drive
Belleville, MI 48111
734-697-8556
There is a pet fee of $10 per day.

Red Roof Inn - Detroit Airport-Belleville
45501 North Expressway Service Drive
Belleville, MI 48111
734-697-2244
Dogs up to 80 pounds are allowed and one dog is permitted per room. There are no pet fees.

Canton

Baymont Inn and Suites
41211 Ford Rd
Canton, MI 48187
734-981-1808
One large dog per room is permitted.

Dearborn

Red Roof Inn
24130 Michigan Ave
Dearborn, MI 48134
313-278-9732
There are no additional pet fees.

Residence Inn Detroit Dearborn
5777 Southfield Service Drive
Dearborn, MI 48228
313-441-1700
Amenities include a complimentary buffet breakfast,

guest laundry, outdoor pool and an exercise room. Room amenities include a full kitchen in each room. There is a $100 one time pet fee.

Ritz-Carlton
300 Town Center Drive
Dearborn, MI 48126
313-441-2000
There is a $150 one time pet fee.

TownePlace Suites
6141 Mercury Drive
Dearborn, MI 48126
313-271-0200
Amenities include full kitchens in each suite room. Hotel amenities include a guest laundry room, outdoor pool and an exercise room. There is a $100 one time per stay pet fee and a $5 per day pet fee.

Detroit

Hotel St. Regis
3071 West Grand Blvd
Detroit, MI 48202
313-873-3000
There are no pet fees. Amenities include room service.

Ramada Inn Downtown Detroit
400 Bagley Avenue
Detroit, MI 48226
313-962-2300
Dogs are welcome but must be on a leash. There are no pet fees.

Residence Inn by Marriott
5777 Southfield Service Dr
Detroit, MI 48228
313-441-1700
There is a $100 one time pet fee.

Farmington Hills

Motel 6
38300 Grand River Ave
Farmington Hills, MI 48335
248-471-0590
There are no additional pet fees. A large well-behaved dog is

allowed.

Red Roof Inn
24300 Sinacola Ct
Farmington Hills, MI 48335
248-478-8640
There are no additional pet fees.

Livonia

TownePlace Suites Detroit Livonia
17450 Fox Drive
Livonia, MI 48152
734-542-7400
Hotel amenities include an outdoor pool. There is a $125 one time pet fee.

Madison Heights

Motel 6
32700 Barrington Rd
Madison Heights, MI 48071
248-583-0500
There are no additional pet fees. One well-behaved dog is allowed per room.

Pontiac

Residence Inn Detroit Pontiac/Auburn Hills
333 Centerpoint Parkway
Pontiac, MI 48341
248-858-8664
Amenities include a complimentary buffet breakfast, guest laundry, indoor pool and an exercise room. Room amenities include a full kitchen in each room. There is a $100 one time per stay pet fee and a $5 per day pet charge.

Romulus

Romulus Marriott Detroit Airport
30559 Flynn Dr
Romulus, MI 48174
734-729-7555
There is a $75 one time pet fee.

Sterling Heights

TownePlace Suites
14800 Lakeside Circle
Sterling Heights, MI 48313
586-566-0900
Hotel amenities include an outdoor pool. There is a $125 one time per stay pet fee and a $5 per day pet charge.

Troy

Drury Inn
575 W. Big Beaver Road
Troy, MI 48084
248-528-3330
Dogs of all sizes are permitted. Pets are not allowed in the breakfast area of the hotel. Pets are not to be left unattended, and each guest must assume liability for damage of property or other guest complaints. There is a limit of one pet per room.

Holiday Inn
2537 Rochester Court
Troy, MI 48083
248-689-7500
At I-75 and Rochester Road. There is a $5 per day additional pet fee.

Warren

Residence Inn Detroit Warren
30120 Civic Center North
Warren, MI 48093
586-558-8050
Amenities include a complimentary buffet breakfast, guest laundry, outdoor pool and an exercise room. Room amenities include a full kitchen in each room. There is a $75 one time pet fee.

Attractions

Davison

Johnny Panther Quests
8065 E Coldwater Rd
Davison, MI 48423
N Irish Rd

810-653-3859
Your dog is welcome on these boat tours. The guided boat tours usually have 1-4 people and last at least 4 hours. You and your dog will be able to get off the boat and walk around at several different points along the river. You can customize your own tour by having a relaxing, laid back tour or a more adventurous tour which goes through a wooded wildlife refuge, stopping for walks along the river. They are open year-round, with springtime offering the best views of wildlife. Tours start at about $40. They also offer a cooler on the boat, so bring along your favorite beverage.

Waterford

Drayton Plains Nature Center
2125 Denby Drive
Waterford, MI
248-674-2119
Your leashed dog is allowed at this Nature Center and on the several miles of trails located along the Clinton River. The interpretive nature center allows leashed dogs inside the building. But there are many stuffed birds and other animals that might be tempt your pup, so make sure you keep him on a short leash! There is no park entrance fee.

Parks

Belleville

Lower Huron Metropark
Haggerty Rd and Huron River Dr.
Belleville, MI
800-477-3182
Dogs must be leashed in the park.

Dearborn

River Rouge Park
Lower Rouge Parkway

Dearborn, MI

Dogs must be leashed in the park.

Gibraltar

Lake Erie Metropark
Jefferson Ave and Lower Huron Dr.
Gibraltar, MI
734-379-5020
Leashed dogs are allowed at this Detroit area park. The park offers views of Lake Erie.

New Boston

Willow and Oakwoods Metropark

New Boston, MI
734-697-9181
Leashed dogs are allowed in the parks.

New Hudson

Kensington Metropark
I-96 and Kensington
New Hudson, MI
248-685-1561
Leashed dogs are allowed in the park.

Restaurants

Birmingham

Brooklyn Pizza
111 Henrietta
Birmingham, MI
248-258-6690
Enjoy a gourmet pizza with your pooch at the outdoor tables. Well-behaved, leashed dogs are allowed outside.

Dearborn

A & W Family Restaurant
210 Town Center Dr
Dearborn, MI 48126
313-271-1676
Dogs are allowed at the

outdoor tables.

Einstein Brothers Bagels
22171 Michigan Ave
Dearborn, MI 48124
313-792-9888
Dogs are allowed at the outdoor tables.

Spencer's Indoor Grill
1041 Howard St
Dearborn, MI 48124
313-359-2000
Well-behaved dogs are allowed at the outdoor tables.

Grosse Pointe Park

Tom's Oyster Bar
15402 Mack Avenue
Grosse Pointe Park, MI
313-884-6030
This restaurant offers fresh seafood as well as chicken, steak and pasta. Well-behaved, leashed dogs are allowed at the outdoor tables. The outdoor seating is seasonal.

Toronto City Guide

Accommodations

Brampton

Comfort Inn
5 Rutherford Rd S
Brampton, ON L6W3J3
905-452-0600
There is no pet fee.

Motel 6
160 Steelwell Road
Brampton, ON L6T 5L9
905-451-3313
A large well-behaved dog is okay if it is kept on a leash and is with you at all times.

Etobicoke

Quality Hotel & Suites Airport East
2180 Islington Ave
Etobicoke, ON M9P3P1

416-240-9090
There is a pet fee of $12 per day.

Ramada Hotel - Toronto Airport
2 Holiday Dr
Etobicoke, ON M9C 2Z7
416-621-2121
There is a $20 per day additional pet fee.

Mississauga

Motel 6
2935 Argentia Rd
Mississauga, ON L5N 8G6
905-814-1664
There are no additional pet fees.

Ramada Hotel Toronto Airport
5599 Ambler Dr
Mississauga, ON L4W 3Z1
905-624-9500
A large well-behaved dog is okay.

Studio 6
60 Britannia Rd East
Mississauga, ON L4Z 2T2
905-502-8897
There is a $25 one time pet fee.

Richmond Hill

Sheraton Parkway Toronto North Hotel & Suites
At Highway 404 and Highway 7
Richmond Hill, ON L4B 1B2
905-881 2121
Dogs of all sizes are allowed, but there is only one pet room. It is a non-smoking room. There are no additional pet fees.

Thornhill

Staybridge Suites
355 SOuth Park Rd
Thornhill, ON L3T 7W2
905-771-9333
There is a $75 one time pet fee. Dogs are welcome to stay in the hotel but are not allowed in the public areas such as the lobby and pool.

Toronto

Beaches Bed and Breakfast Inn
174 Waverley Road
Toronto, ON M4L 3T3
416-699-0818
This B&B, located in The Beaches neighborhood, is just 1.5 blocks from the beach. Pets and children are welcome at this bed and breakfast. Most of the rooms offer private bathrooms. The owner has cats on the premises.

Comfort Inn Downsview
66 Norfinch Dr
Toronto, ON M3N1X1
416-736-4700
There is no pet fee. Pets are allowed on the first floor only. Pets may not be left alone.

Crowne Plaza
1250 Eglinton Ave East
Toronto, ON M3C 1J3
416-449-4111
There is a $20 per day pet fee. Pets stay in first floor rooms.

Delta Toronto Airport Hotel
801 Dixon Rd West
Toronto, ON
416-675-6100
There are no additional pet fees.

Four Seasons Hotel
21 Avenue Road
Toronto, ON M5R 2G1
416-964-0411
There are no extra pet charges, just notify reservations that you will be bringing a pet. The hotel needs to know in advance because they have special pet rooms.

Holiday Inn on King
370 King Street West
Toronto, ON
416-599-4000
There are no additional pet fees.

Howard Johnson Hotel
89 Avenue Road
Toronto, ON
416-964-1220
Dogs of all sizes are welcome. There are no additional pet fees.

International Plaza Hotel and Conference Centre
655 Dixon Rd
Toronto, ON
416-244-1711
You must sign a pet waiver for your dog. There are no additional pet fees.

Novotel Toronto Centre
45 The Esplanade
Toronto, ON M5E 1W2
416-367-8900
There is a $20 per day pet charge.

Quality Hotel
280 Bloor Street West
Toronto, ON
416-968-0010
There are no additional pet fees.

Quality Hotel Downtown
111 Lombard St
Toronto, ON M5C2T9
416-367-5555
There is no pet fee. Pets may not be left alone.

Quality Suites Airport
262 Carlingview Drive
Toronto, ON M9W5G1
416-674-8442
There is no pet fee. Pets may not be left alone. A credit card will be required.

Sheraton Centre Toronto Hotel
123 Queen Street West
Toronto, ON M5H 2M9
416-361-1000
Dogs up to 80 pounds are allowed. There are no additional pet fees.

Travelodge Hotel
925 Dixon Road
Toronto, ON
416-674-2222
There are no additional pet fees.

Attractions

Toronto

Black Creek Pioneer Village
1000 Murray Ross Parkway
Toronto, ON M3J 2P3
416-736-1733
Leashed dogs are allowed in this 1860's village. The village shows how people lived in Upper Canada through the 1860's. Enjoy over 35 restored homes and shops, as well as costumed people who will demonstrate how the inhabitants lived during this time period.

Centreville Amusement Park
Centre Island
Toronto, ON
416-203-0405
Leashed dogs are allowed at this amusement park, but they are not allowed on any of the rides. The park offers over 30 rides and attractions and 14 food outlets. While there are no admission fees to enter the park, you will need to buy ride tickets if you plan on going on any rides. An average price for ride tickets for a family of four might cost about $72. The park is open daily from mid-May to the beginning of September and then open weekends only in May and September, weather permitting. The park is closed the rest of the year. To get there, you will have to take the ferry which departs from Queens Quay and Bay Street in downtown Toronto. Ferry prices are about $5 per person and less for children.

City Walks Guided Tours
Call to arrange.
Toronto, ON
416-966-1550
Take a guided walking tour of historic Toronto and bring your pooch along. Learn about Toronto's history and architecture plus hear stories and get tips about the culture.

There are many tours to choose from and they are normally held on the weekends. Tours are approximately 2 hours long. The cost is $12 Canadian per adult and free for children under 12 years old and pets. Reservations are required. Call 416-966-1550 between 8am and 10pm to reserve a space.

Great Lakes Schooner Company
Queen's Quay
Toronto, ON
416-203-2322
Take a Toronto boat tour onboard a large schooner (sailboat). Your well-behaved, leashed dog is allowed on the tours. Enjoy great views of Toronto's skyline from the water. Tours run from June to September and are about 1 to 2 hours long, depending on the tour. The cost is just under $20 per adult and less for children and seniors. Dogs ride for free. The tours depart off Queen's Quay, between Rees Street and Lower Simcoe Street.

Harbourfront Centre
York and John Quays
Toronto, ON
416-973-3000
Dogs are not allowed inside any buildings, but are allowed outside and at outdoor events. Dogs must be leashed. Located on Toronto's waterfront, this 10 acre centre provides entertaining and educational events and activities. Your pooch is welcome to join you at the summer outdoor concerts and festivals. Even if there are no outdoor events, you can enjoy a walk along the waterside. The centre is located on York Quay and John Quay, south of Queens Quay West (near University Avenue).

Toronto Islands Park
Toronto, ON

various islands
416-392-8186
These islands, located less than 10 minutes from downtown via ferries, have over 600 park acres with walking paths. Dogs on leash are allowed on the islands. Centre Island is home to the dog-friendly Centreville amusement park (no dogs on rides). The only way to the islands is via the ferries. Ferry prices for adults are about $5 per person, less for children and free for dogs.

Parks

Toronto

Bluffer's Park
Brimley Road South
Toronto, ON
416-397-8186
Leashed dogs are allowed in the park and on the beach. This 473 acre park is located east of the Toronto Harbour and The Beaches neighborhood. The park offers a beach and scenic overlooks from the bluffs. It is located at Brimley Road South and Kingston Road.

Dog Beach - Kew Gardens
2075 Queen Street
Toronto, ON

Located in The Beaches neighborhood, dogs are allowed to run leash-free on this section of the beach. Dogs can run leashless 24 hours a day. The dog beach area is located at the foot of Kew, on Beach, between snow fence and Lake.

Dog Park - High Park
1873 Bloor Street
Toronto, ON
416-397-8186
Dogs can run leash-free at the open area located west of the Dream Site and the allotment Gardens, and northeast of the Grenadier Restaurant. The dog park area is open 24 hours a

day, except for 6pm to 10pm during stage productions at the Dream Site. The park is located at Bloor Street and Parkside Drive.

High Park
1873 Bloor Street West
Toronto, ON
416-397-8186
Leashed dogs are allowed in this park. The park covers almost 400 acres and offers many nature hiking trails and a picnic area. High Park is located west of the Toronto Harbour.

Woodbridge

Kortright Centre
9550 Pine Valley Drive
Woodbridge, ON
416-661-6600
Dogs on leash are allowed, but must be cleaned up after and are not allowed in the Visitor's Center. This 800 acres of green space offers about 10 miles of nature trails, a river valley, marshes, meadows, forests, and more. The park also focuses on promoting green energy. It is located about 10 minutes north of Toronto. To get there, take Highway 200 north to Major Mackenzie Drive. Follow Major Mackenzie Drive about 2 km west to Pine Valley Drive. Follow Pine Valley Drive south 1 km to Kortright.

Restaurants

Markham

Carmelina
7501 Woodbine Avenue
Markham, ON L3R 2W1
905-477-7744
Dogs are allowed at the outdoor tables.

Toronto

Charlotte Room Restaurant
19 Charlotte Street

Toronto, ON
416-598-2882
Well-behaved, leashed dogs are allowed at the outdoor tables. Thanks to one of our readers for recommending this restaurant.

Erl's Bistro and Bar
700 University Avenue
Toronto, ON
416-595-0700
Dogs are allowed at the outdoor perimeter or corner tables.

Foster's on Elm
31 Elm Street
Toronto, ON M5G 1H1
416-581-1037
This British pub allows dogs at their outdoor tables.

Gabby's Grillhouse
2572 Yonge Street
Toronto, ON M4P 2J3
416-483-1020
Dogs are allowed at the outdoor tables.

Mitzi's Cafe and Gallery
100 Sorauren Avenue
Toronto, ON
416-588-1234
Dogs are allowed at the outdoor tables.

Reds Wine Country Bistro and Bar
77 Adelaide West
Toronto, ON
416-862-7337
Dogs are allowed at the outdoor tables.

Sassafraz Restaurant
100 Cumberland Street
Toronto, ON M5R 1A6
416-964-2222
Dogs are allowed at the outdoor tables. This restaurant, located in the posh Yorkville area, offers both French and California cuisine.

Whistler's Grille and Cafe Bar
995 Broadview Avenue
Toronto, ON

416-421-1344
Dogs are allowed, but need to be tied to the fence. They can sit right next to you on the same side of the fence.

Unionville

Jakes on Main
202 Main Street
Unionville, ON
905-470-6955
Dogs are allowed at the outdoor tables.

Vaughan

Windy O'Neill's Irish Pub
50 Interchange Way
Vaughan, ON
905-760-9366
Dogs are allowed at the outdoor tables. Choose from a variety of entrees as well as fine stouts.

Austin City Guide
Accommodations

Austin

Best Western Atrium North
7928 Gessner Drive
Austin, TX 78753
512-339-7311
There are no additional pet fees.

Comfort Suites
1701 E St. Elmo Rd
Austin, TX 78744
512-444-6630
There is no pet fee.

Hawthorn Suites-Austin South
4020 IH 35 South
Austin, TX 78704
512-440-7722
There is a $50 one time pet charge and a $5 per day additional pet fee.

Highland Mall Drury Inn
919 E. Koenig Lane
Austin, TX 78751
512-454-1144

Dogs of all sizes are permitted. Pets are not allowed in the breakfast area of the hotel. Pets are not to be left unattended, and each guest must assume liability for damage of property or other guest complaints. There is a limit of one pet per room.

Holiday Inn
8901 Business Park Drive
Austin, TX 78759
512-343-0888
There is a $25 one time pet fee.

Holiday Inn
3401 S. I-35
Austin, TX 78741
512-448-2444
There is a $35 one time pet fee. Well-behaved housebroken dogs are allowed.

Holiday Inn
20 N I-25
Austin, TX 78701
512-472-8211
There is a $100 refundable pet deposit and a $25 per day additional pet fee.

Holiday Inn
6911 N I-35
Austin, TX 78752
512-459-4251
There is a $15 one time pet fee.

Holiday Inn-Northwest Plaza
8901 Business Park Drive
Austin, TX 78759
512-343-0888
There is a $25 one time pet fee.

La Quinta Inn & Suites Southwest at Mopac
4424 S. Mopac Expressway
Austin, TX
512-899-3000
Dogs of all sizes are allowed at the hotel.

La Quinta Inn Austin Capitol
300 E. 11th St.
Austin, TX
512-476-1166
Dogs of all sizes are allowed at the hotel.

La Quinta Inn Austin North
7100 N IH 35
Austin, TX
512-452-9401
Dogs up to 50 pounds are allowed at the hotel.

La Quinta Inn Austin Oltorf
1603 E. Oltorf Blvd.
Austin, TX
512-447-6661
Dogs of all sizes are allowed at the hotel.

Motel 6
5330 N Interregional Hwy
Austin, TX 78751
512-467-9111
There are no additional pet fees.

Motel 6
2707 Interregional Hwy S
Austin, TX 78741
512-444-5882
There are no additional pet fees.

Red Lion Hotel
6121 I-35 North
Austin, TX 78752
512-323-5466
There are no additional pet fees.

Staybridge Suites - Northwest
10201 Stonelake Blvd
Austin, TX 78759
512-349-0888
There is a $12 per day pet fee. Up to two dogs are allowed and there is a weight limit of 50 pounds per pet.

Studio 6
937 Camino La Costa
Austin, TX 78752
512-458-5453
There are no additional pet fees.

Studio 6
11901 Pavilion Blvd
Austin, TX 78759
512-258-3556
There is a $50 one time pet fee.

Attractions

Austin

Austin Carriage Service
various downtown locations
Austin, TX
512-243-0044
You and your pooch can enjoy an elegant horse drawn carriage ride in downtown Austin. This carriage services offers one hour Historic Day Tours on Saturdays and Sundays from 10am to 4pm. You will view downtown Austin's Congress Avenue, the State Capitol and Grounds, the Bremond Area and much more. They also offer Downtown Evening Rides from 7pm to 11pm. There are two ways to take this carriage ride. You can either flag down one of the carriages located in downtown or call the dispatcher about 2 hours ahead of time and they will have a carriage pick you up from a downtown location like a hotel or restaurant (like the dog-friendly Carmelos at 504 E 5th). Rates are $45 for a half hour tour and $85 for one hour. There is a $5 discount if paying by cash.

Austin Guided Walking Tours
11th and Congress Avenue
Austin, TX
512-478-0098
From March through November, there are three guided walking tours which you and your pooch can choose from. They are all outdoor tours and your well-behaved leashed dog is welcome. The first tour is the Capitol Grounds. The tour highlights the lawns and gardens, and some interesting facts about the statehouse. This one hour tour is offered on Saturdays at 2pm and Sundays at 9am. The second tour is the Bremond Block. Walk through one of Austin's Victorian neighborhoods and view homes of the John Bremond Sr. family. These one and a half hour tours

are on Saturdays and Sundays at 2pm. The third tour is Congress Avenue and Sixth Street. This tour focuses on the history and architecture of downtown Austin. These one and a half hour tours are Thursdays through Saturdays at 9am and Sundays at 2pm. All tours start promptly at their designated times. They are all FREE and they all start at the south steps on the Capitol, near Congress Avenue and 11th Street. Be sure to meet at the Capitol's south steps and not on the street corner. Reservations are not required, but please call ahead to verify times and days.

Congress Avenue Bridge Bats
305 South Congress Avenue
Austin, TX
512-416-5700
Congress Avenue Bridge is the home to one of the most unusual tourist attractions, the largest urban bat colony in North America. Around sunset, from March to early November, you can watch 1.5 million Mexican free-tail bats fly out from under the bridge. They go out at around sunset in search of their food which are mosquitos and other small bugs. The best time for this bat viewing is late July through mid-August. If your pooch is a bird-watcher, he or she might just notice all the bats in the sky. To view the bats, some people stand on the bridge, some go to the shoreline of the Town Lake, while others watch from the Bat Observation area. There are even Bat Interpreters at the observation area Thursday through Sunday, from June through August. The observation site is located at the Austin American-Statesman (local newspaper) at 305 South Congress Avenue. Free but limited parking is available after 6pm. If this lot is full, extra parking is available at the Texas Department of Transportation office parking lot, off nearby Riverside Drive.

Zilker Botanical Gardens
2220 Barton Springs Drive
Austin, TX 78746
512-477-8672
Dogs on leash are allowed at this botanical garden. The 31 acre garden is on the south bank of the Colorado River, close to downtown Austin. Enjoy garden themes like the Fragrance Garden, Prehistoric Garden, Rose Garden, Oriental Garden and more. The grounds are usually open daily from 7am until dark. Food is not allowed in the gardens, except for certain special events. However, you can have a picnic in the adjacent dog-friendly Zilker Metropolitan Park. Admission to the garden is free. The garden is located in Zilker Park, south of Town Lake and east of MoPac (Loop 1). From MoPac (Loop 1), take the FM 2244/Rollingwood exit and follow the signs for Zilker Park. Watch for the Zilker Botanical Garden's dark green signs. The garden is located on the left at 2220 Barton Springs.

Parks

Austin

Barton Creek Greenbelt Preserve
3755 B Capital of Texas Hwy
Austin, TX
512-472-1267
This popular greenbelt follows a creek and offers about 7 miles of walking, hiking and mountain biking trails. There are also several popular swimming holes along the creek. Dogs are allowed, but must on a leash. Some of the more popular access points to the trails are Zilker Metropolitan Park, and Loop 360 (south of MoPac/Loop 1).

Bull Creek District Dog Park

6701 Lakewood Drive
Austin, TX
512-974-6700
This dog park is not fenced. It has access to the creek for water-loving pooches. Well-behaved dogs can roam and play off-leash, but must be under verbal control and within your sight. The off-leash area is located behind the restrooms.

Norwood Estate Dog Park
I-35 and Riverside Drive
Austin, TX
512-974-6700
This is a fully fenced dog park. Well-behaved dogs can roam and play off-leash, but must be under verbal control and within your sight. The dog park is located on the north end of Travis Heights at the northwest corner of Riverside Drive and I-35.

Town Lake
2100 Barton Springs Road
Austin, TX
512-974-6700
This is a popular walking and swimming spot for people and dogs. Dogs must be on a 6 foot or less leash. The park offers 10 miles of walking, hiking and bicycling trails. There are many beaches located along the lake. From March through early November at dusk, you can also watch the bats fly out from under the popular Congress Avenue Bridge at this park. Playgrounds, picnic tables, and restrooms are available at Town Lake. There are many access points to this park, including Zilker Metropolitan Park at 2100 Barton Springs Road. To get there from I-35, take the Riverside exit. Go west on Riverside towards downtown. After you pass Congress Avenue, turn left onto Barton Springs. Go about 2 miles to the park. The entrance will be on the left.

Zilker Dog Park

2100 Barton Springs Rd.
Austin, TX
512-974-6700
This dog park is not fenced. Well-behaved dogs can roam and play off-leash, but must be under verbal control and within your sight. The dog park is located in Zilker Metropolitan Park at 2100 Barton Springs Road. The leash free area is located near the soccer field area, between Great Northern Blvd. and Shoal Creek Blvd.

Zilker Metropolitan Park
2100 Barton Springs Road
Austin, TX
512-974-6700
This is one of Austin's most popular parks. There are about 350 acres and 1.5 miles of trails to enjoy. Leashed dogs are allowed, but not in buildings or areas like the theatre, nature center or the Umlauf sculpture garden. Dogs are welcome at the Zilker Botanical Gardens. A playground, picnic tables, and restrooms are also available at this park. To get there from I-35, take the Riverside exit. Go west on Riverside towards downtown. After you pass Congress Avenue, turn left onto Barton Springs. Go about 2 miles to the park. The entrance will be on the left.

Restaurants

Austin

Artz Rib House
2330 South Lamar Blvd.
Austin, TX
512-442-8283
Try some Texas barbecue, or choose some vegetarian items here. Well-behaved, leashed dogs are allowed at the outdoor tables.

Austin Java Company
1206 Parkway
Austin, TX 78703
512-476-1829

This restaurant offers a selection of beer and wine, coffees, and organic juices. For breakfast they have omelettes, pancakes and breakfast tacos. For lunch and dinner, choose from a variety of sandwiches and pastas. Well-behaved, leashed dogs are allowed at the outdoor tables.

BB Rover's Cafe and Pub
12636 Research Blvd.
Austin, TX
512-335-9504
Enjoy a variety of beer at this pub as well as salads, soups, pizzas, sandwiches, pasta, fajitas and more. Well-behaved, leashed dogs are allowed at the outdoor tables.

Bongo Barbecue
1004 West 24th St.
Austin, TX
512-478-7427
This restaurant has several picnic tables outside. Well-behaved, leashed dogs are allowed at the outdoor tables.

Carmelo's Italian Restaurant
504 East 5th St.
Austin, TX
512-477-7497
This Italian restaurant offers pastas, seafood, steak and chicken entrees. Well-behaved, leashed dogs are allowed at the outdoor tables.

Carrabba's Italian Grill
6406 North IH-35
Austin, TX
512-419-1220
Enjoy a variety of food from this Italian restaurant like antipasti, wood-fired pizza, pasta, Italian classics and more. Well-behaved, leashed dogs are allowed at the outdoor tables.

Carrabba's Italian Grill
11590 Research Blvd.
Austin, TX
512-345-8232
Try items like the shrimp scampi, Italian chicken pizza,

sirloin marsala, eggplant parmesan or lasagna at this Italian restaurant chain. Well-behaved, leashed dogs are allowed at the outdoor tables.

Central Market
4001 North Lamar Blvd.
Austin, TX
512-206-1000
Signature sandwiches, salads, pastas and entrees are on the menu at this cafe. Well-behaved, leashed dogs are allowed at the outdoor tables on the tree-shaded deck, but not at the tables on the roof covered deck.

Cipollina
1213 West Lynn St.
Austin, TX
512-477-5211
This Italian cafe serves wood-fired pizza, shrimp, pasta, chicken and more. Well-behaved, leashed dogs are allowed at the outdoor tables.

Dog & Duck Pub
406 West 17th Street
Austin, TX 78701
512-479-0598
This pub offers a large selection of both tap and bottled beers. Appetizers and sandwiches can also be ordered here. Well-behaved, leashed dogs are allowed at the outdoor tables on the front porch, not on the back patio.

Green Mesquite Barbeque & More
1400 Barton Springs Road
Austin, TX
512-479-0485
Enjoy smoked brisket, chicken, sandwiches, veggie items, fresh BBQ sauce and salsa, and more. Well-behaved, leashed dogs are allowed at the outdoor tables.

Mangia Chicago Stuffed Pizza
2401 Lake Austin Blvd.
Austin, TX
512-478-6600

Choose from a variety of thin or stuffed pizzas, pastas, burgers, salads and more. Well-behaved, leashed dogs are allowed at the outdoor tables. They are very dog-friendly.

Mangia Chicago Stuffed Pizza
3500 Guadalupe
Austin, TX
512-302-5200
There are two picnic tables outside. Well-behaved, leashed dogs are allowed at the outdoor tables.

Mozart's Coffee Roasters
3825 Lake Austin Blvd.
Austin, TX
512-477-2900
Enjoy variety of coffees and bakery items including cheesecake at this coffee shop. Well-behaved, leashed dogs are allowed at the lakeside outdoor tables.

Pizza Nizza
1608 Barton Springs Rd.
Austin, TX
512-474-7590
Choose from a variety of pizza toppings and pizza sauces. Well-behaved, leashed dogs are allowed at the outdoor tables.

Red River Cafe
2912 Medical Arts
Austin, TX
512-472-0385
This cafe serves breakfast, lunch and dinner. For breakfast, they offer pancakes, omelettes, and french toast. For lunch and dinner, burgers are the main fare. Well-behaved, leashed dogs are allowed at the outdoor tables.

Romeo's
1500 Barton Springs Rd.
Austin, TX
512-476-1090
This Italian restaurant offers a selection of salads, sandwiches, pizzas, pastas, specialties and desserts. Well-behaved, leashed dogs are allowed at the outdoor

tables.

Romeo's
5800 Burnet Rd
Austin, TX
512-419-7567
Well-behaved, leashed dogs are allowed at the outdoor tables at this Italian restaurant.

Scholz Beer Garden
1607 San Jacinto Blvd.
Austin, TX 78701
512-474-1958
Come to Texas' oldest German biergarten and the oldest restaurant in Austin. They serve up Texas BBQ, burgers (including a veggie burger), German food, and of course, a wide selection of bottled and draft beer. Well-behaved, leashed dogs are allowed at the outdoor tables.

Serranos Cafe and Cantina
1111 Red River Street
Austin, TX
512-322-9080
Items on the menu at this Tex-Mex restaurant include enchiladas, tacos, fajitas, and chicken, beef and vegetarian entrees. Well-behaved, leashed dogs are allowed at the outdoor tables.

Spider House
2908 Fruth St.
Austin, TX
512-480-9562
This coffee house serves up a variety of coffee as well as beer and wine. They also have food on the menu like chili, salads, and bakery goodies.

West Lynn Cafe
1110 West Lynn St.
Austin, TX 78703
512-482-0950
This vegetarian restaurant offers a wonderful selection of entrees for breakfast, lunch and dinner. They also serve smoothies such as the Pina Colada and Dreamsicle. Well-behaved, leashed dogs are

allowed at the outdoor tables.

Z Tejas Grill
1110 West 6th St
Austin, TX
512-478-5355
This Southwestern restaurant has appetizers, soups and salads, and entrees like salmon, chicken and stuffed shrimp. Well-behaved, leashed dogs are allowed at the outdoor tables.

Corpus Christi City Guide
Accommodations

Corpus Christi

Bayfront Inn
601 North Shoreline Blvd.
Corpus Christi, TX 78401
361-883-7271
There is a $20 pet fee for every 3 days of a stay.

Best Western Garden Inn
11217 IH-37
Corpus Christi, TX 78410
361-241-6675
There is a $5 per day additional pet fee.

Holiday Inn
5549 Leopard St
Corpus Christi, TX 78408
361-289-5100
There are no additional pet fees.

Holiday Inn
1102 S. Shoreline Blvd
Corpus Christi, TX 78401
361-883-5731
There are no additional pet fees.

La Quinta Inn Corpus Christi South
6225 South Padre Island Dr
Corpus Christi, TX
361-991-5730
Dogs of all sizes are allowed at the hotel.

Red Roof Inn - Airport
6301 Interstate 37
Corpus Christi, TX 78409

361-289-6925
There is a $10 per day pet fee.

Residence Inn by Marriott
5229 Blanche Moore Drive
Corpus Christi, TX 78411
361-985-1113
There is a $100 one time per stay pet charge and a $10 per day pet fee.

Surfside Condo Apartments
15005 Windward Drive
Corpus Christi, TX 78418
361-949-8128
Dogs up to 50 pounds are allowed. There is a $15 per day pet charge and a $200 refundable pet deposit.

Attractions

Corpus Christi

Corpus Christi Botanical Gardens
8545 South Staples Street
Corpus Christi, TX 78413

This 180 acre site offers more than 2500 orchids, 70 bright colored hibiscus, and about 300 roses all amongst natural wetlands, and a shady mesquite forest. Picnic tables and a playground are also available. Dogs on leash are allowed, but do not let your dog go to the bathroom on the flowers. The gardens offer free parking and parking space available for buses and RVs. They are located on Staples Street at Oso Creek. Upon entering Corpus Christi from the north areas (San Antonio, Houston, Austin), go north on Crosstown Expressway/Texas 286 North. Continue to follow Crosstown. Make a slight left onto Crosstown/David Street. Merge onto Texas 286 South via the ramp on the left. Take the Ayers Street exit towards Texas 286 South. Keep right at the fork in the ramp. Merge onto Ayers Street/Texas 286 BR South.

Turn left onto Texas 358 East. Turn right onto South Staples Street/FM 2444. Follow the green signs to 8545 South Staples Street.

Ingleside

Dolphin Connection
off 1069
Ingleside, TX
361-882-4126
Dogs are allowed on the boat tours, as long as other people on the boat do not mind. These trips focus on viewing and possibly touching dolphins in their own natural environment in Corpus Christi Bay. There are about one to three boat tours per day, year-round. The cost for an adult is $17, kids are $12, and children under 3 and dogs are free. Please call ahead as reservations are required. To get there from Corpus Christi, take Freeway 361 south to Portland/Ingleside via Port Aransas. In Ingleside, turn left onto 1069. Go about 3 1/4 miles and then turn right at the Public Boat Ramp. There is a pink dolphin at the entrance.

Beaches

Corpus Christi

Cole Park
Ocean Drive
Corpus Christi, TX
800-766-2322
Dogs on leash are allowed on the beach. People need to clean up after their pets.

Padre Island

Padre Island National Seashore
Highway 22
Padre Island, TX
361-949-8068
Visitors to this beach can swim, sunbathe, hunt for shells or just enjoy a walk. About 800,000

visitors per year come to this park. Dogs on leash are allowed on the beach. People need to clean up after their pets. There is a minimal day use fee. The park is located on Padre Island, southeast of Corpus Christi.

Parks

Rockport

Aransas National Wildlife Refuge
FM 2040
Rockport, TX
361-286-3559
This 70,000 plus acre refuge is home to cranes, alligators, deer and other wildlife. Dogs must be on leash and are only allowed on certain trails that do not have alligators. Check with park rangers upon arrival to get details about which trails allow pets. To get there from Rockport, take Highway 35 north about 20 miles. Turn right on FM 774 and go about 9 miles to FM 2040. Turn right and follow FM 2040 for 7 miles to the refuge entrance.

Restaurants

Corpus Christi

Les Succes Bakery
6537 Staples Street
Corpus Christi, TX
361-991-1003
This bakery offers a variety of sandwiches and a large selection of pastries. They are open for breakfast and lunch. Dogs are allowed at the outdoor tables.

Sonic Drive-In
14401 South Padre Island Drive
Corpus Christi, TX 78418
361-949-7886
Dogs are welcome at the outdoor tables. This Sonic even has doggie treats!

Dallas – Fort Worth City Guide

Accommodations

Dallas

Best Western Dallas North
13333 N Stemmons Fwy
Dallas, TX 75234
972-241-8521
There is a $20 one time pet fee
per visit.

Crowne Plaza Suites
7800 Alpha Rd
Dallas, TX 75240
972-233-7600
There is a $150 refundable pet
deposit and a $50 one time pet
fee.

**Dallas Marriott Suite Market
Center**
2493 North Stemmons Freeway
Dallas, TX 75207
214-905-0050
Amenities at this hotel includes
room service which might come
in handy if you want to dine in
with your pooch. There is a $50
one time per stay pet fee.

Harvey Hotel
7815 LBJ Freeway
Dallas, TX 75251
972-960-7000
There is a $125 deposit for pets
and $100 is refundable.

Hawthorn Suites
7900 Brookriver Dr
Dallas, TX 75247
214-688-1010
There is a $50 one time pet fee.
Dogs must be less than 75
pounds.

**La Quinta Inn & Suites Dallas
North Park**
10001 North Central
Expressway
Dallas, TX
214-361-8200
Dogs of all sizes are allowed at
the hotel.

**La Quinta Inn Dallas City
Place**
4440 N Central Expressway
Dallas, TX
214-821-4220
Dogs of all sizes are allowed at
the hotel.

**La Quinta Inn Dallas
Lovefield**
1625 Regal Row
Dallas, TX
214-630-5701
Dogs of all sizes are allowed at
the hotel.

**La Quinta Inn Farmers
Branch NW**
13235 Stemmons Freeway
North
Dallas, TX
972-620-7333
Dogs of all sizes are allowed at
the hotel.

Motel 6
2660 Forest Lane
Dallas, TX 75234
972-484-9111
Use 35E to 635 East. There are
no additional pet fees.

Motel 6
2753 Forest Lane
Dallas, TX 75234
972-620-2828
Use 35E to 635 E. There are no
additional pet fees.

Motel 6
4220 Independence Dr
Dallas, TX 75237
972-296-3331
There are no additional pet
fees.

Radisson - Mockingbird
1893 W Mockingbird Ln
Dallas, TX 75235
214-634-8850
There is a $50 pet deposit. Of
this, $25 is refundable.

**Residence Inn by Marriott -
Market Center**
6950 N Stemmons Frwy
Dallas, TX 75247

214-631-2472
There is a $50 one time pet fee.

Studio 6
2395 Stemmons Trail
Dallas, TX 75220
214-904-1400
Use I-35 E to the Northwest Hwy
exit. There is a $10 per day
additional pet fee.

The Mansion on Turtle Creek
2821 Turtle Creek Blvd
Dallas, TX 75219
214-559-2100
There is a $200 one time pet
fee.

Fort Worth

**Best Western Fort Worth Hotel
& Suites**
2000 Beach Street
Fort Worth, TX 76103
817-534-4801
There is a $25 one time pet fee.
Exit Beach Street from I-30.

Green Oaks Park Hotel
6901 W Frwy
Fort Worth, TX 76116
817-738-7311
There is a $50 refundable pet
deposit.

Motel 6
1236 Oakland Blvd
Fort Worth, TX 76103
817-834-7361
There are no additional pet fees.

Motel 6
3271 Interstate 35 W
Fort Worth, TX 76106
817-625-4359
There are no additional pet fees.

Motel 6
6600 S Frwy
Fort Worth, TX 76134
817-293-8595
There are no additional pet fees.
One pet per room is allowed.
Pets must be attended at all
times.

Motel 6

8701 Interstate 30 W
Fort Worth, TX 76116
817-244-9740
There are no additional pet fees.

Residence Inn by Marriott
1701 S University Dr
Fort Worth, TX 76107
817-870-1011
There is a $5 per day pet fee.

Attractions

Dallas

Dallas Foundation Self-Guided Walking Tours
900 Jackson St, Suite 150
Dallas, TX 75202
214-741-9898
The Dallas Foundation has put together many different suggested self-guided downtown sculpture walking tours which highlight over 30 public sculptures. The tour maps are available to order online at http://www.dallasfoundation.org. Take a tour of the Arts District, City Hall, Reunion Area or Downtown (North, Central or West). From the Downtown Central tour, check out the Pegasus Plaza. It is an urban park with carved stones and a fountain. Next to the Pegasus Plaza is the historic Magnolia Building, which in 1922 was the tallest building south of Washington, D.C. Check out these points of interest at Akard and Commerce Streets.

Old City Park
1717 Gano St.
Dallas, TX 75215
Gano and Harwood Streets
214-428-5448
Dogs on leash are allowed in this Historic Village of Dallas. Take a step back in time to the 1860's Living Farmstead. Farm life during the Civil War is displayed with buildings and people re-enacting scenes. The park is open every day from Tuesday through Saturday,

except on some major holidays. Tickets can be purchased at the ticket office.

Party Animals Carriage Rides
Market Street-West End Area
Dallas, TX
(at cross streets Corbin, Munger or Ross)
214-441-9996
Enjoy a historic and informative carriage ride with your pooch in downtown Dallas. One of the rides covers historical sites including the site where Lee Harvey Oswald shot and killed President Kennedy, and the JFK Memorial. Scenic tours cover the Uptown area of Dallas including Lincoln Plaza, Fountain Plaza, and Thanks-Giving Square. Rides start at $35 for a 15-20 minute ride and go up to $100 for a one hour ride. Prices are subject to change. Well-behaved, trained dogs are allowed in the carriages.

Pioneer Plaza
Young Street and Griffin Street
Dallas, TX
214-953-1184
This plaza is home to the world's largest bronze monument. The monument is on over 4 acres of land and consists of 40 longhorn steer sculptures and three cowboys on horseback sculptures. This monument represents settlers arriving in Dallas from about the 1840's until just after the Civil War. Pioneer Plaza is located next to the Dallas Convention Center, near Young and Griffin Streets.

Fort Worth

Stockyards Station

Fort Worth, TX
817-624-4741
The Stockyards National Historic District offers a variety of dog-friendly and people-

friendly activities. Start the day by observing the popular Fort Worth Herd Cattle Drive mosey on through the historic area. Cattle drives take place daily at 11:30am and 4pm, weather permitting. After the cattle drive, try a guided walking tour of the Stockyards which starts at the Visitor's Center. You and your pooch will tour the Livestock Exhange Building, Mule Alley, Cowtown Coliseum and more. Tours leave daily, Monday through Saturday, from 10am to 4pm and on Sunday from 12pm to 4pm. For details on the walking tour, call 817-625-9715.

Parks

Dallas

Bachman Lake Park
Bachman Drive
Dallas, TX
near W. Northwest Hwy & Webb Chapel
214-670-1923
This park offers a 3 mile path around a lake. The trail is popular with walkers and joggers. The park is located northwest of downtown Dallas, near the Dallas Love Field Airport. Dogs on leash are allowed and you must pick up after your pet. There are heavy fines for dogs off leash and for folks who do not clean up after their pets.

Dallas Nature Center
7171 Mountain Creek Parkway
Dallas, TX 75249
972-296-1955
Dogs are allowed on leash at this 600 acre park that offers 10 miles of hiking trails. The hikes are rated from very easy meadow trails to difficult steep hikes. The park is located on Mountain Creek Pkwy, about 2 1/2 miles south of Interstate 20.

White Rock Lake Dog Park
8000 Mockingbird Lane

Dallas, TX
214-670-8895
Dogs are welcome to run leash-free at this dog park. The fully enclosed park offers a separate section for large dogs and small dogs. The dog park is closed on Mondays for maintenance. To get there from Central Expressway (75), go East on Mockingbird Lane. After you pass the West Lawther exit, begin looking for the parking lot. If you go to Buckner Blvd., then you have passed the dog park. The dog park is located on Mockingbird Point.

White Rock Lake Park
8300 E. Lawther Drive
Dallas, TX
214-670-8895
Enjoy a 9 plus mile hiking and bicycling trail at this city lake park. Bring your lunch and enjoy it at one of the many scenic picnic areas. Dogs on leash are allowed and you must pick up after your pet. There are heavy fines for dogs off leash and for folks who do not clean up after their pets.

Restaurants

Dallas

Beau Nash at Hotel Crescent Court
400 Crescent Ct.
Dallas, TX 75201
214-871-3240
Located in the Hotel Crescent Court, this restaurant offers outdoor seating, weather permitting. There are a few table umbrellas that provide some shade. A well-behaved, leashed dog is allowed at the outdoor tables.

Cadillac Bar
1800 North Market St.
Dallas, TX 75202
214-999-0662
The Cadillac bars serves up authentic Mexican food including

homemade soup, quesadillas, tacos, fajitas and much more. Well-behaved dogs are allowed at the perimeter tables.

Cafe Italia
4615 West Lovers Lane
Dallas, TX 75209
214-357-4200
Dogs are welcome at the outdoor tables.

Corner Bakery Cafe
7615 Campbell Rd
Dallas, TX 75248
Coit and Campbell
972-407-9131
Dogs are allowed at the outdoor tables. Enjoy breakfast, lunch or an early dinner at this cafe which offers fresh baked breads, pastries, sandwiches, salads and more.

Dick's Last Resort
1701 North Market St.
Dallas, TX 75202
214-747-0001
Lunch and dinner are served at this restaurant. Menu items include sandwiches, salads, entrees with ribs or chicken and more.

Dubliner
2818 Greenville Avenue
Dallas, TX
214-818-0911
Dogs on leash are allowed at the outside tables.

La Calle Doce
1925 Skillman St.
Dallas, TX
214-824-9900
This Tex-Mex restaurant specializes in seafood. Well-behaved leashed dogs are welcome at the outdoor tables.

Metropolitan Restaurant
1525 Main Street
Dallas, TX 75201
214-977-9205
Dogs are welcome at the outdoor tables, but they need to be leashed.

Pappas Bar-B-Q
2231 West Northwest Hwy
Dallas, TX 75220
214-956-9038
Your pooch is allowed at the outdoor tables at this BBQ restaurant which serves slow smoked barbecued beef, pork, chicken and much more.

Pappasito's Cantina
10433 Lombardy Ln.
Dallas, TX 75220
214-350-1970
Enjoy fajitas, ribs, margaritas and more at this Tex Mex restaurant.

Paris Vendome
3699 McKinney Avenue
Dallas, TX
469-533-5663
Located in Uptown, this French restaurant welcomes dogs at their outdoor tables.

Ristorante Bugatti
3802 West Northwest Hwy
Dallas, TX 75220
214-350-2470
This Italian restaurant serves both lunch and dinner. Enjoy Italian dishes like lasagna, pasta, Gnocchi, antipasta or entrees like chicken or fresh salmon. Dogs are allowed at the outdoor tables.

Samba Room
4514 Travis St.
Dallas, TX 75205
214-522-4137
Dogs are not allowed in the patio, but are allowed at the tables located outside the fenced area. This restaurant serves Latin and Cuban food.

San Francisco Rose
3024 Greenville Ave
Dallas, TX
214-826-2020
Dogs are allowed at the outdoor tables. Thanks to one of our readers for recommending this place.

Sol's

6434 E. Mockingbird Lane
Dallas, TX
214-821-7911
Thanks to one of our readers for recommending this restaurant. Leashed dogs are allowed at the outdoor tables.

TCBY Frozen Yogurt
6402 E. Mockingbird Lane
Dallas, TX
214-821-5757
Dogs are welcome at the outdoor tables. One of our readers writes: "TCBY even puts a dog biscuit on top of (my dog's) yogurt."

Texas Land and Cattle Steakhouse
3130 Lemmon Avenue
Dallas, TX 75204
214-526-4664
Try the smoked sirloin and other choice steaks. Or try the mesquite grilled ribs, chicken or seafood. Dogs on leash are allowed to dine with you at the outdoor tables.

The Bronx
3835 Cedar Springs Rd
Dallas, TX
214-521-5821
Dogs are welcome at the outdoor tables.

The Old Monk
2847 North Henderson
Dallas, TX
214-821-1880
This brew pub offers a wide selection of beer. They also have some appetizers to enjoy with the drinks. Dogs are allowed at the outdoor tables.

Two Rows Brewery and Grill
5500 Greenville Avenue
Dallas, TX 75206
214-696-2739
In addition to the wide selection of beer, this restaurant also serves up wood-fired pizza, ribs, pasta, chicken, salads and more. Dogs on leash are allowed at the outdoor tables.

Fort Worth

Buckaroo's Soda Shoppe
140 E Exchange
Fort Worth, TX 76106
817-624-6631
This soda shop offers more than just soda. Enjoy hamburgers, hot dogs, salads, pizzas, ice cream or sodas. A well-behaved dog is allowed to accompany you on the patio. If you are dining around 11:30am or 4pm, you will be able to watch the Fort Worth Herd Cattle Drive meander through town.

Stores

Dallas

Big Bark Bakery
2538 Elm Street
Dallas, TX 75226
214-741-6173
Dogs are welcome at this bakery just for dogs. They use all natural ingredients to create treats, cakes and gift baskets for pooches.

Neiman Marcus
One Marcus Square
Dallas, TX 75201
214-741-6911
Your well-behaved dogs is allowed inside the very first Neiman Marcus store. It is located in downtown Dallas.

Pottery Barn
3220 Knox Street
Dallas, TX 75205
214-528-2302
A well-behaved dog is allowed inside this popular home furnishings store.

REI
4515 LBJ Freeway
Dallas, TX
(Farmers Branch)
972-490-5989
Dogs on leash are allowed in this outdoor gear retail store.

Galveston City Guide
Accommodations

Galveston

Motel 6
7404 Ave J Broadway
Galveston, TX 77554
409-740-3794
There are no additional pet fees. Well-behaved pets are allowed.

The Reef Resort
8502 Seawall Blvd.
Galveston, TX 77554
409-740-0492
The weight limit for dogs is usually 25 pounds, but they can allow a larger dog if he or she is well-behaved. There is a $20 per day pet fee and a $150 refundable pet deposit. There are no designated smoking or non-smoking rooms.

Accommodation - Vacation Home Rentals

Galveston

Sand 'N Sea Pirates Beach Vacation Rentals
13706 FM 3005
Galveston, TX 77554
800-880-2554
They offer several pet-friendly vacation home rentals.

Attractions

Galveston

Caribbean Breeze Boat Rental
1723 61st Street
Galveston, TX
409-740-0400
Enjoy the waters of Galveston Bay with your pooch. Dogs are allowed on the boat rentals, but you are responsible for any damage done by your dog. The rental company offers pontoon

boats for about $75 per hour with a 2 hour minimum, and fishing skiff boats with motors for about $25 per hour. You can also rent a pontoon boat with a captain. Receive a discount on the regular daily rental rates if you rent frequently.

Galveston Ferry
Ferry Road at Highway 87
Galveston, TX
409-763-2386
You can take a ride on the ferry between Bolivar and Galveston with your dog, but only if your dog stays in your car. Pets are not allowed on the ferry deck, unless you can carry and hold them. Ferries run about every 15 to 20 minutes during the day. There is no charge.

Island Carriages
Pier 21 or 22
Galveston, TX
409-765-6951
Enjoy a scenic horse and carriage ride with your well-behaved pooch. Tour Galveston's East End Historical District, or the Strand, Galveston's Historic Landmark District. Narrated tours are available upon request. The driver can point out historical points of interest and architectural details. The cost is $25 for a half hour tour or $50 for a one hour tour. You can find their carriages at the waterfront near Pier 21 or 22. But the best bet is to call for reservations and they will pick you up at your hotel or at a restaurant.

Beaches

Galveston

Big Reef Nature Park
Boddeker Drive
Galveston, TX
409-765-5023
Take a walkway to the beach which runs parallel to Bolivar Rd. Dogs on leash are allowed

on the beach. People need to clean up after their pets. There are no day use fees. This park is part of East Beach which does not allow dogs on the pavilion. The beach is located on the east end of Galveston Isle, off Boddeker Drive.

Dellanera RV Park
FM 3005 at 7 Mile Rd.
Galveston, TX
409-740-0390
This RV park offers 1,000 feet of sandy beach. Dogs on leash are allowed on the beach and at the RV spaces. People need to clean up after their pets. There are over 60 full RV hookups, over 20 partial hookups and day parking. Picnic tables and restrooms are available at this park. There is a $5 day parking fee. RV spaces are about $25 and up.

Galveston Island State Park
14901 FM 3005
Galveston, TX 77554
409-737-1222
Leashed dogs are allowed on the beach and at the campsites. There is a $3 per person (over 13 years old) day use fee. There is no charge for children 12 and under. The park can be reached from Interstate 45 by exiting right onto 61st Street and traveling south on 61st Street to its intersection with Seawall Boulevard and then right (west) on Seawall (FM 3005) 10 miles to the park entrance.

Stewart Beach
6th and Seawall Boulevard
Galveston, TX
409-765-5023
This is one of the best family beaches in Galveston. Many family-oriented events including a sandcastle competition are held at this beach. Restrooms, umbrella and chair rentals, and volleyball courts are available. There is a $7 per car admission fee. Dogs on leash are allowed

on the beach. People need to clean up after their pets. The beach is located at 6th Street and Seawall Blvd.

Restaurants

Galveston

Charlie's Burgers and Mexican Food
1110 Tremont (23rd St.)
Galveston, TX
409-765-7065
This restaurant has a few outdoor tables. Well-behaved, leashed dogs are allowed at the outdoor tables.

Fullen's Waterwall Restaurant
2110 Strand
Galveston, TX
409-765-6787
Come here for steak, hamburgers, chicken, and more. Well-behaved, leashed dogs are allowed at the outdoor tables.

Java's 213 Coffee Shop
213 Tremont (23rd St.)
Galveston, TX
409-762-5282
Leashed dogs are allowed at the outdoor tables at this pet-friendly coffee shop. This is the oldest coffee shop on the Strand. They serve fresh coffee, cappuccinos, expressos, lattes and hot chocolate.

Mosquito Cafe
623 14th Street
Galveston, TX
409-763-1010
This bistro was selected by the Zagat Survey as one of the Top 15 Restaurants in the Houston Metro Area. They are open for breakfast and lunch daily, and for dinner Thursdays through Saturdays. For breakfast, they offer a selection of items like pancakes, omelettes, bagels. For lunch there is a nice variety of salads and sandwiches, and for dinner there are beef, fish and vegetarian entrees. Well-

behaved, leashed dogs are allowed at the outdoor tables. The restaurant is located in Galveston's Historic East End District.

Phoenix Bakery and Coffee House
2228 Ship Mechanics Row
Galveston, TX
409-763-4611
This cafe is open for breakfast and lunch. They offer pastries and a selection of sandwiches. Well-behaved, leashed dogs are allowed at the outdoor tables.

Sonic Drive-In
6502 Seawall Boulevard
Galveston, TX 77551
409-740-9009
Well-behaved, leashed dogs are allowed at the outdoor tables at this fast food restaurant.

Houston City Guide
Accommodations

Channelview

Best Western Houston East
15919 I-10 East
Channelview, TX 77530
281-452-1000
There is a $15 one time pet fee.

Houston

Comfort Inn
9041 Westheimer Rd
Houston, TX 77063
713-783-1400
There is a pet fee of $25 per day.

Comfort Suites - Near the Galleria
6221 Richmond Ave
Houston, TX 77057
713-787-0004
There is a one time pet fee of $25.

Doubletree Guest Suites
5353 Westheimer Rd
Houston, TX 77056

713-961-9000
There is a $10 per day pet fee.

Holiday Inn - Airport
15222 John F. Kennedy Blvd
Houston, TX 77032
281-449-2311
There is a $25 one time pet fee.

Holiday Inn Hotel & Suites
7787 Katy Fwy
Houston, TX 77024
713-681-5000
There is a $25 one time pet fee.

Holiday Inn Select
14703 Park Row
Houston, TX 77079
281-558-5580
There is a $150 one time pet fee and a $100 one time pet fee.

Houston - Near the Galleria Drury Inn & Suites
1615 West Loop South
Houston, TX 77027
713-963-0700
Dogs of all sizes are permitted. Pets are not allowed in the breakfast area of the hotel. Pets are not to be left unattended, and each guest must assume liability for damage of property or other guest complaints. There is a limit of one pet per room.

Houston - West Drury Inn & Suites
1000 North Highway 6
Houston, TX 77079
281-558-7007
Dogs of all sizes are permitted. Pets are not allowed in the breakfast area of the hotel. Pets are not to be left unattended, and each guest must assume liability for damage of property or other guest complaints. There is a limit of one pet per room.

Howard Johnson Express Inn
9604 S Main St.
Houston, TX 77025
713-666-1411
Dogs of all sizes are welcome.

There is a $35 one time pet fee.

La Quinta Inn & Suites Houston - Bush Intercontinental
15510 John F Kennedy Blvd.
Houston, TX
281-219-2000
Dogs of all sizes are allowed at the hotel.

La Quinta Inn & Suites Houston Park 10
15225 Katy Freeway
Houston, TX
281-646-9200
Dogs of all sizes are allowed at the hotel.

La Quinta Inn Greenspoint
6 North Belt East
Houston, TX
866-725-1661
Dogs of all sizes are allowed at the hotel.

La Quinta Inn Houston Astrodome
9911 Buffalo Speedway
Houston, TX
713-668-8082
Dogs up to 50 pounds are allowed at the hotel.

La Quinta Inn Houston Brookhollow
11002 Northwest Freeway
Houston, TX
713-688-2581
Dogs of all sizes are allowed at the hotel.

La Quinta Inn Houston Cyfair
13290 Fm 1960 Road West
Houston, TX
281-469-4018
Dogs up to 50 pounds are allowed at the hotel.

La Quinta Inn Houston East
11999 East Freeway
Houston, TX
713-453-5425
Dogs of all sizes are allowed at the hotel.

La Quinta Inn Houston Hobby

Airport
9902 Gulf Freeway
Houston, TX
713-941-0900
Dogs of all sizes are allowed at the hotel.

La Quinta Inn Houston I-45 North
17111 North Freeway
Houston, TX
281-444-7500
Dogs of all sizes are allowed at the hotel.

La Quinta Inn Houston Wilcrest
11113 Katy Freeway
Houston, TX
713-932-0808
Dogs up to 50 pounds are allowed at the hotel.

La Quinta Inn Houston-Greenway Plaza
4015 Southwest Freeway
Houston, TX
713-623-4750
Dogs of all sizes are allowed at the hotel.

Mainstay Suites
12820 NW Freeway
Houston, TX 77040
713-690-4035
There is a non-refundable pet fee of $75.

Motel 6
3223 S Loop W
Houston, TX 77025
713-664-6425
There are no additional pet fees.

Motel 6
14833 Katy Frwy
Houston, TX 77094
281-497-5000
One well-behaved pet per room is allowed.

Staybridge Suites
5190 Hidalgo
Houston, TX 77056
713-355-8888
There is a $75 one time pet fee.

Studio 6
220 Bammel-Westfield Rd
Houston, TX 77090
281-580-2221
There is a $50 one time pet fee.

Studio 6
12700 Featherwood
Houston, TX 77034
281-929-5400
There is a $50 per week additional pet fee.

Studio 6
12827 Southwest Freeway
Houston, TX 77477
281-240-6900
There is a $10 per day or $50 per week additional pet fee.

Studio 6
1255 North Highway 6
Houston, TX 77084
281-579-6959
There is a $10 per day pet fee up to a maximum of $50.

Studio 6
3030 West Sam Houston Pkwy South
Houston, TX 77042
713-785-8550
There is a $50 one time pet fee.

The Lovett Inn
501 Lovett Blvd
Houston, TX 77006
713-522-5224
There is one pet room in this bed and breakfast.

Katy

Best Western Houston West
22455 I-10 West
Katy, TX 77450
281-392-9800
There is a $10 per day additional pet fee.

The Woodlands

Houston - The Woodlands Drury Inn & Suites
28099 I-45 North
The Woodlands, TX 77380

281-362-7222
Dogs of all sizes are permitted. Pets are not allowed in the breakfast area of the hotel. Pets are not to be left unattended, and each guest must assume liability for damage of property or other guest complaints. There is a limit of one pet per room.

Attractions

Houston

Houston Arboretum and Nature Center
4501 Woodway Drive
Houston, TX
713-681-8433
Pets are allowed on the trails only, but must be on leash. Trails are designed for hiking only, no biking or jogging. Enjoy over 5 miles of nature trails, including forests, pond and prairie habitats. This 155 acre nature sanctuary is located on the western edge of Memorial Park. It is open from 8:30am to 6pm daily.

La Porte

San Jacinto Battleground
3523 Highway 134
La Porte, TX
281-479-2431
While dogs are not permitted inside the museum or on the battleship, they are allowed to walk around on the battleground. You will find historical markers and monuments throughout the battleground. Dogs must be on leash. There is no fee to enter the battleground. This historic site is located 20 miles east of downtown Houston.

Parks

Houston

Hermann Park
Fannin
Houston, TX

713-845-1000
Features at this park include a reflecting pool and a 2 mile jogging trail. Picnic tables and restrooms are available. The park is located south of downtown Houston, bordered by South Main, Hermann Drive, Almeda, Brays Bayou and the Texas Medical Center. Dogs on leash are allowed.

Memorial Park
Memorial Drive
Houston, TX
713-845-1000
Leashed dogs are allowed at this park. At over 1,400 acres, this is the largest urban park in Texas. There is a 3 mile popular jogging course. The park is located on Memorial Drive, near the I-610 Loop.

Sam Houston Park
1000 Bagby
Houston, TX
713-845-1000
This 19 acre park is located in downtown Houston. Leashed dogs are allowed outside, but not in the historic houses. The park is located off I-45 and Allen Parkway.

Restaurants

Houston

Annabelle's Diner
705 Taft
Houston, TX
713-523-9959
Leashed dogs are very welcome on the outdoor patio and are treated to a bone and water. Items on the human's menu include pasta, fish and burgers.

Arcodoro
5000 Westheimer
Houston, TX
at Post Oak
713-621-6888
This Italian restaurant allows well-behaved, leashed dogs at their outdoor tables. They offer homemade pasta, pizza, baked fish, steaks and more.

Barnaby's Cafe
1701 S. Shepherd
Houston, TX
713-520-5131
This restaurant offers a variety of food like salads, meat loaf, hamburgers, sandwiches and more. Well-behaved, leashed dogs are allowed at the outdoor tables.

Becks Prime
2615 Augusta Drive
Houston, TX
713-266-9901
Order mesquite grilled burgers, chicken, fish, or steak from this fast food chain. Or try the chocolate or fresh strawberry shake. This particular location boasts the largest tree in Houston which covers their outdoor deck. Well-behaved, leashed dogs are allowed at the outdoor tables.

Bistro Provence
13616 Memorial
Houston, TX
713-827-8008
This French restaurant allows well-behaved, leashed dogs at their outdoor tables.

Cafe Toulouse
5750 Woodway
Houston, TX
713-977-6900
The menu at this restaurant includes soup, salad, pasta, fresh salmon, filet mignon and more. Well-behaved, leashed dogs are allowed at the outdoor tables.

Flemings Prime Steakhouse
2405 W. Alabama
Houston, TX
713-520-5959
The menu at Flemings includes prime beef, a variety of chops, fish, chicken, salads, side orders and desserts. They also offer a wide selection of wines. Well-behaved, leashed dogs are allowed at the outdoor tables.

Guerin's Bistro
11920 Westheimer
Houston, TX
281-497-1122
Pastas, pizzas, steak and vegetarian dishes are available at this restaurant. Well-behaved, leashed dogs are allowed at the outdoor tables.

McCormick and Schmick's Seafood Restaurant
1151 Uptown Park Blvd.
Houston, TX
713-840-7900
Enjoy fresh seafood with a Pacific Northwestern flavor. Well-behaved, leashed dogs are allowed at the outdoor tables.

Mission Burritos
2245 West Alabama St.
Houston, TX
713-529-0535
Well-behaved leashed dogs are welcome at the outdoor tables. Thanks to one of our readers for recommending this restaurant.

Shanghai River
2407 Westheimer Rd.
Houston, TX
713-528-5528
This award winning Chinese restaurants offers a wide variety of dishes, prepared without MSG. Well-behaved, leashed dogs are allowed at the outdoor tables.

Taco Milagro
2555 Kirby Drive
Houston, TX
713-522-1999
This restaurant offers fresh handmade food in a self-serve setting. The menu includes tamales, fajitas, enchiladas, and more. Well-behaved, leashed dogs are allowed at the outdoor tables.

West Alabama Icehouse
1919 West Alamaba
Houston, TX 77006

713-528-6874
Dogs are allowed at the outdoor tables.

San Antonio City Guide

Accommodations

San Antonio

Best Western Ingram Park Inn
6855 Northwest Loop 410
San Antonio, TX 78238
210-520-8080
There is a refundable pet deposit.

Clarion Suites Hotel
13101 E Loop 1604 N
San Antonio, TX 78233
210-655-9491
There is a pet deposit of $25 for a stay of 30 days or less. For a stay of 30 days or more there is a pet deposit of $100.

Comfort Inn
4403 I-10 e
San Antonio, TX 78219
210-333-9430
There is a one time pet fee of $10.

Comfort Inn Airport
2635 N. E. Loop 410
San Antonio, TX 78217
210-653-9110
There is a refundable pet deposit of $25.

Days Inn
1500 S. Laredo St.
San Antonio, TX 78204
210-271-3334
There is a $10 one time per stay pet fee.

Holiday Inn
318 W. Durango Blvd
San Antonio, TX 78204
210-225-3211
There is a $125 refundable pet deposit and a $25 one time pet fee.

Holiday Inn - Riverwalk

217 North St. Mary's St.
San Antonio, TX 78205
210-224-2500
There is a $100 refundable pet deposit and a $25 one time pet fee.

Holiday Inn Express
9411 Wurzbach Rd
San Antonio, TX 78240
210-561-9300
There are no additional pet fees.

Holiday Inn Riverwalk
217 St. Mary's St.
San Antonio, TX 78205
210-224-2500
There is a $25 one time pet fee.

Holiday Inn Select
77 NE Loop 410
San Antonio, TX 78216
210-349-9900
There is a $125 refundable pet deposit and a $25 one time pet fee.

Howard Johnson Express Inn
2755 IH-35N
San Antonio, TX 78208
210-229-9220
Dogs of all sizes are welcome. There is a $20 one time pet fee.

La Quinta Inn & Suites San Antonio Airport
850 Halm Blvd.
San Antonio, TX
210-342-3738
Dogs of all sizes are allowed at the hotel.

La Quinta Inn I-35 North at Windsor Park
6410 N IH 35
San Antonio, TX
210-653-6619
Dogs of all sizes are allowed at the hotel.

La Quinta Inn San Antonio Lackland
6511 Military Drive West
San Antonio, TX
210-674-3200
Dogs up to 50 pounds are allowed at the hotel.

La Quinta Inn San Antonio Wurzbach
9542 I-10 West
San Antonio, TX
210-593-0338
Dogs of all sizes are allowed at the hotel.

La Quinta Inn San Antonio-Convention Center
1001 East Commerce Street
San Antonio, TX
210-222-9181
Dogs of all sizes are allowed at the hotel.

La Quinta Inn Seaworld/Ingram Park
7134 NW Loop 410
San Antonio, TX
210-680-8883
Dogs of all sizes are allowed at the hotel.

Motel 6
138 N WW White Rd
San Antonio, TX 78219
210-333-1850
There are no additional pet fees. One well-behaved pet per room is allowed. Pets must be attended at all times.

Motel 6
16500 IH-10 W
San Antonio, TX 78257
210-697-0731
There are no additional pet fees.

Motel 6
7719 Louis Pasteur Court
San Antonio, TX 78229
210-349-3100
There is a $10 per day pet fee up to a maximum of $50 per visit.

Motel 6
2185 SW Loop 410
San Antonio, TX 78227
210-673-9020
There are no additional pet fees. One well-behaved pet of any size is allowed per room. Pets must be attended at all times.

Motel 6 - Ft Sam Houston

5522 N Pan Am Expwy
San Antonio, TX 78218
210-661-8791
There are no additional pet fees.
Pets must be attended at all
times.

Motel 6 - Med Center
9400 Wurzbach Rd
San Antonio, TX 78240
210-593-0013
There are no additional pet fees.

Motel 6 - North
9503 Interstate Hwy 35 N
San Antonio, TX 78233
210-650-4419
There are no additional pet fees.
Pets must be attended at all
times.

Motel 6 - Northeast
4621 E Rittiman Rd
San Antonio, TX 78218
210-653-8088
There are no additional pet fees.
One pet per room is allowed.
Pets must be attended at all
times.

Motel 6 - Riverwalk
211 N Pecos St
San Antonio, TX 78207
210-225-1111
There are no additional pet fees.

Quality Inn & Suites
222 South WW White Rd
San Antonio, TX 78219
210-359-7200
There is a one time pet fee of
$20.

Quality Inn NW Medical Center
6023 IH 10 west
San Antonio, TX 78201
210-736-1900
There is a one time pet fee of
$25.

**Residence Inn by Marriott-
Downtown**
628 S Santa Rosa
San Antonio, TX 78204
210-231-6000
This inn is 1.2 miles from the
Alamo and .5 miles from the
Riverwalk. There is a $5 per day

pet charge and a $50 one time
pet charge.

Staybridge Suites
4320 Spectrum One Rd
San Antonio, TX 78230
210-558-9009
There is a $75 one time pet fee.

Staybridge Suites - Airport
66 NE Loop 410
San Antonio, TX 78216
210-341-3220
There is a $75 one time pet fee.

Studio 6
11802 IH 10 West
San Antonio, TX 78230
210-691-0121
There is a $10 per day pet fee
not to exceed a maximum of
$50. One pet per room is
permitted.

Attractions

San Antonio

La Villita
King Phillip Walk
San Antonio, TX

La Villita was the original
settlement of Old San Antonio.
It is one square block in the
heart of downtown, and has
artists, craftsmen, shops and
restaurants. Leashed dogs can
accompany you along the
streets and window shop or
enjoy the architecture of the
historic Adobe and Victorian
buildings. For dining, try
Guadalajara Grill, where well-
behaved, leashed dogs are
allowed at the outdoor tables.
La Villita is located on the east
bank of the San Antonio River,
near The Alamo. It is located
between the following streets:
Villita, S. Presa, Alamo and
Nueva.

Market Square - El Mercado
W. Commerce Street
San Antonio, TX
210-207-8600

Leashed dogs are allowed at
this outdoor market. Inside
Market Square is El Mercado,
which is the largest Mexican
marketplace outside of Mexico.
Here you can find pinatas,
pottery, clothing and more. You
also might be able to listen to
some live music throughout the
market. The market is open
daily, except for Easter,
Thanksgiving, Christmas, and
New Year's Day. It is located in
downtown San Antonio, at W.
Commerce Street and San
Mateo Street.

Riverwalk
South Alamo
San Antonio, TX
210-207-3000
Dogs are allowed on this world
famous landmark, but they must
be leashed. The Riverwalk is the
second most visited attraction in
Texas (the Alamo is the top
tourist attraction). The 2 mile
walkway follows the San Antonio
River, and passes by many
outdoor restaurants and shops.
Some of the outdoor restaurants
are dog-friendly. Please visit our
restaurant section under San
Antonio for listings. The
Riverwalk is located in
downtown San Antonio. There
are many access points
including the following streets:
South Alamo, Losoya, Market,
and Commerce.

Veterans Memorial Plaza
100 Auditorium Circle
San Antonio, TX
800-447-3372
This plaza honors veterans of
the Vietnam, World War II, and
Korean wars, as well as all other
veterans of war. The memorials
are located throughout the
plaza. The plaza is located at
the intersection of Jefferson and
Martin streets, between Martin
and Municipal Way.

Yellow Rose Carriage Co.
Crockett Street
San Antonio, TX

210-337-6495
Take an elegant horse and carriage with your well-behaved pooch and view some historic sites in San Antonio. Most of the carriage drivers are animal lovers and will allow your pooch. Occasionally some of the drivers might not allow dogs, but the majority of them will accept dogs. Tours leave from the Alamo Plaza and include many historic sites including historic hotels, buildings and the Riverwalk. You can choose between a narrated tour or opt for a quiet romantic ride. A short tour is about 20 minutes and costs $25 per couple. A 40 minute tour runs $45 per couple and the King William tour is 1 hour and costs $65 per couple. Children under 10 ride free with a paying adult. Additional children under 10 years cost $5 each. Dogs ride for free. Carriage rides run from 7pm to 11:30pm daily, weather permitting. If it is too hot outside, the tours will not start until about 8pm. You can either pick up a carriage on Crockett Street next to the Alamo or call ahead and make a reservation at 210-337-6495.

Parks

San Antonio

Brackenridge Park
3910 N. St. Marys Street
San Antonio, TX
210-207-3000
There are walking and bicycling paths throughout this 343 acre urban park. Dogs on leash are allowed, and owners must clean up after their pets. The park is located near downtown San Antonio.

Braunig Park
17500 Donop Road
San Antonio, TX
210-207-3000
The lake located in this park is a popular fishing and boating spot. Swimming is not permitted in the lake. Picnic tables, restrooms, and concession stands are available. There is a minimal day use fee. Dogs on leash are allowed, and owners must clean up after their pets. The park is located southeast of downtown, off Highway 37 and Exit 130.

Calaveras Park
12991 Bernhardt Road
San Antonio, TX
210-207-3000
This 140 plus acre park offers picnic tables, restrooms, and concession stands. Dogs on leash are allowed, and owners must clean up after their pets. The park is located southeast of downtown, off Loop 1604.

Eisenhower Park
19399 Northwest Military Drive
San Antonio, TX
210-207-3000
This 320 acre park offers 5 miles of hiking and running trails. Picnic areas and restrooms are available. Dogs on leash are allowed, and owners must clean up after their pets. The park is located south of Camp Bullis.

McAllister Park
Jones-Maltsberger Rd
San Antonio, TX
210-207-3000
There are over 6 miles of hiking and biking trails at this 800 plus acre park. Dogs on leash are allowed, and owners must clean up after their pets. The park is adjacent to the San Antonio International Airport.

Restaurants

San Antonio

Boudro's Bistro on the Riverwalk
421 E. Commerce St
San Antonio, TX
210-224-8484
Boudro's offers a variety of dishes like smoked shrimp enchiladas, blackened prime rib and fresh gulf coast seafood. While dogs are not allowed on the outdoor patio, they are allowed at the outdoor tables by the river. Dogs should be well-behaved and leashed.

Cappy's
5011 Broadway Ave
San Antonio, TX 78209
210-828-9669
Entrees at this restaurant include pasta, chicken, prime rib, and more. Well-behaved, leashed dogs are allowed at the outdoor tables.

Crumpets Restaurant and Bakery
3920 Harry Wurzback Rd
San Antonio, TX 78209
210-821-5600
Enjoy salads, pasta, chicken, seafood or beef at this restaurant that has been voted one of Esquires' 100 best restaurants. The outdoor tables are located in a relaxing setting surrounded by oak trees, ponds and running waterfalls. They are open for lunch and dinner daily, and brunch on Sunday. Well-behaved, leashed dogs are allowed at the outdoor tables.

Dolores Del Rio
106 E. River Walk
San Antonio, TX
210-223-0609
Located on the Riverwalk, this Italian restaurant allows well-behaved, leashed dogs are allowed at their outdoor tables.

Guadalajara Grill
301 S. Alamo Street
San Antonio, TX
210-222-1992
Located in La Villita, a shopping and crafts area, this restaurant offers authentic Mexican food and Tex-Mex favorites like fajitas and burgers. They are

located steps away from the Riverwalk. Well-behaved, leashed dogs are allowed at the outdoor tables.

Kangaroo Court
512 River Walk
San Antonio, TX
210-224-6821
This restaurant, located on the Riverwalk, is open for breakfast, lunch and dinner. Menu items include waffles for breakfast, and salad, pasta, seafood, chicken and beef for lunch or dinner. Well-behaved, leashed dogs are allowed at the outdoor tables.

La Margarita Restaurant
120 Produce Row
San Antonio, TX
210-227-7140
Located in Market Square, this Mexican restaurant is popular for its fajitas. Well-behaved, leashed dogs are allowed at the outdoor tables.

Madhatters Tea House and Cafe
320 Beauregard
San Antonio, TX 78204
210-212-4832
Located in the King William Historic District, this cafe offers over 50 teas, as well as sandwiches and salads. Well-behaved, leashed dogs are allowed at the outdoor tables.

Rio Rio Cantina
421 E Commerce
San Antonio, TX
210-226-8462
Tex-Mex food is served at this restaurant which is located on the Riverwalk. Dogs are only allowed at the downstairs outdoor tables next to the river. Dogs should be well-behaved and leashed.

Zuni Grill
223 Losoya St.
San Antonio, TX
210-227-0864
Located on the Riverwalk, this restaurant offers southwest cuisine. Well-behaved, leashed dogs are allowed at the outdoor tables.

South Padre Island City Guide
Accommodations
South Padre Island

Best Western Fiesta Isles Hotel
5701 Padre Blvd
South Padre Island, TX 78597
956-761-4913
There is a $25 refundable pet deposit.

Econo Lodge
3813 Padre Blvd.
South Padre Island, TX 78597
956-761-8500
There is a $25 per day pet charge.

Island Inn
5100 Gulf Blvd.
South Padre Island, TX 78597
956-761-7677
There is a $10 per day pet fee.

Motel 6
4013 Padre Blvd
South Padre Island, TX 78597
956-761-7911
Well-behaved pets are allowed.

Accommodations - Vacation Home Rentals
South Padre Island

Naturally's Beach House Suites
5712 Padre Blvd.
South Padre Island, TX
956-761-8750
They offer pet-friendly condos and vacation home rentals.

Beaches
South Padre Island

Andy Bowie Park
Park Road 100
South Padre Island, TX
956-761-3704
Dogs on leash are allowed on the beach. People need to clean up after their pets. There is a minimal day use fee. This park is located on the northern end of South Padre Island.

Edwin K. Atwood Park
Park Road 100
South Padre Island, TX
956-761-3704
This beach offers 20 miles of beach driving. Dogs on leash are allowed on the beach. People need to clean up after their pets. There is a minimal day use fee. This park is located almost 1.5 miles north of Andy Bowie Park.

Isla Blanca Park
Park Road 100
South Padre Island, TX
956-761-5493
This popular beach offers about a mile of clean, white beach. Picnic tables, restrooms, and RV spaces are available at this park. Dogs on leash are allowed on the beach. People need to clean up after their pets. There is a minimal day use fee. The park is located on the southern tip of South Padre Island.

Restaurants
South Padre Island

Ben and Jack Island Shack
3508 Padre Blvd.
South Padre Island, TX
956-761-2254
This restaurant serves hamburgers, pizzas, salads and more. Well-behaved, leashed dogs are allowed at the outdoor tables.

Bubba's Bar B Que
1313 Padre Blvd.
South Padre Island, TX

956-772-8000
Well-behaved, leashed dogs are allowed at the outdoor tables.

Naturally's Veggie Cafe
5712 Padre Blvd.
South Padre Island, TX
956-761-5332
This cafe and juice bar allows well-behaved, leashed dogs at the outdoor tables.

Yummies Coffee Shack
708 Padre Blvd
South Padre Island, TX
956-761-2526
Enjoy breakfast, lunch or dinner at the outside patio. Well-behaved, leashed dogs are allowed at the outdoor tables.

Denver City Guide
Accommodations

Aurora

Comfort Inn Airport
16921 E 32nd Ave
Aurora, CO 80011
303-367-5000
There is no pet fee. A credit card will be required.

La Quinta Inn Denver Aurora
1011 South Abilene Street
Aurora, CO
303-337-0206
Dogs of all sizes are allowed at the hotel.

Aurura

Motel 6 - Aurura
14031 E Iliff Ave
Aurura, CO 80014
303-873-0286
There are no additional pet fees.

Denver

Denver East Drury Inn
4380 Peoria Street
Denver, CO 80239
303-373-1983
Dogs of all sizes are permitted.

Pets are not allowed in the breakfast area of the hotel. Pets are not to be left unattended, and each guest must assume liability for damage of property or other guest complaints. There is a limit of one pet per room.

Denver Marriott City Center
1701 California St.
Denver, CO 80202
303-297-1300
There is no pet charge.

Executive Tower Hotel
1405 Curtis Street
Denver, CO 80202
303-571-0300
There is a $50 refundable pet deposit.

Guest House Inn
3737 Quebec St.
Denver, CO 80207
303-388-6161
There is a $100 refundable pet deposit.

Hotel Monaco Denver
1717 Champa Street at 17th
Denver, CO 80202
303-296-1717
Well-behaved dogs of all sizes are welcome at this pet-friendly hotel. The luxury boutique hotel offers both rooms and suites. Hotel amenities include complimentary evening wine service, a 24 hour on-site fitness room, and a gift shop. There are no pet fees, just sign a pet liability form.

Hotel Teatro
1100 Fourteenth Street
Denver, CO 80202
303-228-1100
Dogs are allowed at this luxury boutique hotel. There is no extra pet charge.

La Quinta Inn & Suites Denver Airport/DIA
6801 Tower Road
Denver, CO
303-371-0888
Dogs of all sizes are allowed at

the hotel.

La Quinta Inn Denver Central
3500 Park Avenue West
Denver, CO
303-458-1222
Dogs of all sizes are allowed at the hotel.

La Quinta Inn Denver South
1975 S Colorado Boulevard
Denver, CO
303-758-8886
Dogs up to 75 pounds are allowed at the hotel.

Loews Denver Hotel
4150 East Mississippi Ave.
Denver, CO 80246
303-782-9300
All well-behaved dogs of any size are welcome. This upscale hotel offers their "Loews Loves Pets" program which includes special pet treats, local dog walking routes, and a list of nearby pet-friendly places to visit. There are no pet fees.

Marriott TownePlace Suites - Downtown
685 Speer Blvd
Denver, CO 80204
303-722-2322
Marriott TownePlace Suites is an all suite hotel designed for the extended stay traveler. All studio, one, and two-bedroom suites offer full kitchens and weekly housekeeping. Pets are welcome for a non-refundable fee of $20 a day up to $200.00. On-site amenities include guest laundry, business center, fitness room and free parking.

Motel 6 - Airport
12020 E 39th Ave
Denver, CO 80239
303-371-1980
There are no additional pet fees.

Quality Inn South - DTC
6300 E Hampden Ave
Denver, CO 80222
303-758-2211
There is a pet fee of $6 per day.

Englewood

Comfort Suites Tech Center South
7374 South Clinton St
Englewood, CO 80172
303-858-0700
There is a pet deposit of $50 and a pet fee of $5 per day. Pets are allowed on the first floor only.

Denver Tech Center Drury Inn & Suites
9445 East Dry Creek Road
Englewood, CO 80112
303-694-3400
Dogs of all sizes are permitted. Pets are not allowed in the breakfast area of the hotel. Pets are not to be left unattended, and each guest must assume liability for damage of property or other guest complaints. There is a limit of one pet per room.

Sheraton Denver Tech Center Hotel
7007 South Clinton Street
Englewood, CO 80112
303-799-6200
There is no weight limit for dogs. There are no pet fees.

Golden

La Quinta Inn Denver Wheat Ridge - Golden
3301 Youngfield Service Road
Golden, CO
303-279-5565
Dogs of all sizes are allowed at the hotel.

Greenwood Village

Mainstay Suites
9253 E Costilla Ave
Greenwood Village, CO 80112
303-858-1669
There is a one time pet fee of $25.

Sleep Inn Denver Tech
9257 E Costilla Ave
Greenwood Village, CO 80112

303-662-9950
There is a one time pet fee of $25.

Lakewood

Quality Suites
7260 W. Jefferson
Lakewood, CO 80235
303-988-8600
There is a one time fee of $10.

Sheraton Denver West Hotel
360 Union Boulevard
Lakewood, CO 80228
303-987-2000
Dogs up to 80 pounds are allowed. There are no additional pet fees.

Lone Tree

Staybridge Suites
7820 Park Meadows Drive
Lone Tree, CO 80124
303-649-1010
There is a $10 per day or $75 per month additional pet fee.

Northglenn

Holiday Inn
10 E. 120th Ave at I-25
Northglenn, CO 80233
303-452-4100
There is a $50 refundable pet deposit. Exit Hwy 128 from I-25.

Westminster

La Quinta Inn & Suites Westminster - Promanade
10179 Church Ranch Way
Westminster, CO
303-438-5800
Dogs of all sizes are allowed at the hotel.

La Quinta Inn Denver - Westminster Mall
8701 Turnpike Drive
Westminster, CO
303-425-9099
Dogs of all sizes are allowed at

the hotel.

La Quinta Inn Denver Northglenn - Westminster
345 West 120th Avenue
Westminster, CO
303-252-9800
Dogs of all sizes are allowed at the hotel.

Wheat Ridge

Holiday Inn Express - Denver West
4700 Kipling St
Wheat Ridge, CO 80033
303-423-4000
There is a $10 one time pet fee. Exit I-70 at Kipling St.

Attractions

Aurora

Cherry Creek Marina Boat Rentals
Cherry Creek State Park
Aurora, CO
303-779-6144
Located just minutes from downtown Denver, this marina allows dogs on their fishing boat rentals. You and your pup can rent a boat and explore the reservoir located in the dog-friendly Cherry Creek State Park. Boat rental rates start at about $25 for 1 hour.

Denver

Denver Pavilions
15th Street and Tremont
Denver, CO
303-260-6000
This open air shopping center allows leashed dogs at the outdoor areas. Located downtown, this is Denver's premier retail and entertainment complex. The center features 50 stores and restaurants in four three-story buildings linked by walkways. Dogs are also welcome to dine at the 16th Street Deli's outdoor tables,

located in the shopping center. To get there from Interstate 25, exit Colfax Avenue. Cross Speer Blvd. and take the first left onto Welton Street. Cross 15th Street to the Denver Pavilions. The entrance to the underground parking garage is on the right. There is a minimal fee for parking.

Larimer Square
Larimer Street
Denver, CO

Popular with both the locals and tourists, this area offers specialty stores, galleries, and restaurants. Some of the restaurants allow dogs at the outdoor tables, including the Del Mar Crab House and The Market Restaurant. If you want to do some shopping with your pooch, some stores allow your well-behaved dog inside including the Larimer Mission Gift Shop, Cry Baby Ranch and Z Gallerie. Look for details about the restaurants and stores in our Denver City Guide. The square is located on Larimer Street, between 14th and 15th Streets, and Market and Lawrence Streets.

Golden

Lookout Mountain Park
Lookout Mountain Road
Golden, CO
303-964-2589
Dogs on leash are allowed at this Denver mountain park. The park is over 65 acres and offers scenic views including an overlook of Denver and the plains. William "Buffalo Bill" Cody was buried in this park back in 1917. Dogs are not allowed inside the Buffalo Bill Museum. However, you and your pooch can visit the outdoor gravesite of this popular cowboy and frontiersman. You can also take your dog on one of the many hiking trails at the park. To

get to the park, take Interstate 70 west to exit 256 (marked as Buffalo Bill Grave). Follow the signs to the park (Buffalo Bills Grave). It will be a winding uphill road.

Morrison

Dinosaur Ridge
16831 West Alameda Parkway
Morrison, CO 80465
303-697-3466
Leashed dogs are allowed, including on the self-guided walking tour. Dinosaur Ridge is a geographically famous National Natural Landmark, located just 15 minutes west of downtown Denver. The site features historically famous Jurassic dinosaur bones. The bones were discovered in 1877 and over 300 Cretaceous dinosaur footprints have also been found. The self-guided tour is one mile long and features 16 interpretive signs that describe fossil remains and other important features. There is no charge for the self guided walk. Booklets are available for purchase in the Visitor Center. The booklets offer more details of the walking tour. To get there from Interstate 70, take exit 259 (Morrison/Golden exit) and head south (towards Red Rocks Park) on Highway 93/26. As you near Red Rocks Park, there will be a turn off to the left for Highway 26. Follow the signs for Dinosaur Ridge.

Parks

Aurora

Cherry Creek State Park
4201 South Parker Road
Aurora, CO
303-699-3860
Dogs on a 6 foot or less leash are allowed, except on wetland trails, and swim beaches. But there are plenty of dog-friendly

hiking trails in this park. There is also an off-leash area in this park, located near Parker and Orchard Roads. For details of which hiking trails allow dogs, please visit one of the Entrance Stations at the park.

Denver

Bible Park
Yale Avenue
Denver, CO
303-964-2580
This is a 70 acre park and about half of it is developed with sports fields, picnic areas and restrooms. The park has many walking trails and it is bordered by the High Line Canal Trail and the Cherry Creek Trail. The park is located at Yale Avenue and Pontiac Street. Dogs must be leashed.

City Park
17th Avenue
Denver, CO
303-964-2580
This park is Denver's largest city park. It covers over 300 acres and offers tennis courts, fountains, flower gardens, sports fields, a lake and more. The park is located just east of downtown on 17th Avenue and York Street. Pets must be on a leash.

Denver's Off Leash Dog Park
666 South Jason Street
Denver, CO
303-698-0076
This park is Denver's first off leash dog park. It is open from sunrise to sunset, seven days a week. The park is located directly behind the Denver Animal Control building.

Littleton

Chatfield State Park
11500 N Roxborough Park Rd
Littleton, CO
303-791-7275
Hiking, fishing and picnicking are popular activities in this

park. Dogs are allowed at this park, but not at the swim beaches. There are other areas that are non-swim beaches where dogs are allowed to go into the water. Dogs must be leashed, except for the off leash area near Wadsworth Blvd. For maps and more information, please call 303-791-7275 or stop by the visitor center.

Restaurants

Denver

16th Street Deli
Denver Pavilions
Denver, CO
720-956-0440
Dogs are allowed at the outdoor tables. The deli is located on 16th Street in the Denver Pavilions.

Armida's
840 Lincoln
Denver, CO
303-837-8921
This Mexican restaurant offers a variety of food like burritos, fajitas, flautas, and tacos. They also offer sandwiches and salads. Dogs are allowed at the outdoor tables.

Corner Bakery Cafe
500 16th Street
Denver, CO 80202
303-572-0170
Dogs are allowed at the outdoor tables.

Croc's Cafe
1630 Market Street
Denver, CO
303-436-1144
This Mexican restaurant allows dogs at their outdoor tables.

Del Mar Crab House
1453 Larimer Square
Denver, CO
303-825-4747
Dogs need to be tied to the fence, but on the same side of the fence as your outdoor table,

and your pooch can sit right next to you. This restaurant, located in Larimer Square, specializes in crab, seafood, and steaks.

Gelato D'Italia
250 Detroit
Denver, CO
303-316-9154
Dogs are allowed at the outdoor tables. This is a popular spot for dogs and their owners. Gelato D' Italia serves a variety of gelato.

Il Fornaio
1631 Wazee Street
Denver, CO
303-573-5050
This Italian restaurant allows dogs at the outdoor tables.

Palettes
100 West 14th Avenue Parkway
Denver, CO
303-629-0889
Dogs are allowed at the perimeter outdoor tables.

Paris Coffee Roasting
1553 Platte Street
Denver, CO
303-455-2451
Dogs are allowed at the outdoor tables.

Schlotzsky's Deli
727 Colorado Blvd.
Denver, CO 80206
303-333-1200
This chain offers a variety of hot and cold sandwiches, salads and more. Dogs are allowed at the outdoor tables.

Schlotzsky's Deli
7325 East Iliff
Denver, CO 80231
303-696-1100
Dogs are allowed at the outdoor tables.

The Market
1445 Larimer Street
Denver, CO
303-534-5140

This restaurant, located in Larimer Square, allows dogs at their outdoor tables.

Tiramisu
2191 Arapahoe Street
Denver, CO
303-308-0764
This Italian restaurant allows dogs at the perimeter outdoor tables.

Tosh's Hacienda
3090 Downing Street
Denver, CO
303-295-1861
This Mexican restaurant allows dogs at their outdoor tables.

Wall Street Deli
1801 California Street
Denver, CO
303-296-6277
This chain restaurant serves gourmet sandwiches, salads and soups. Dogs are allowed at the outdoor tables.

Wynkoop Brewery
1634 18th Street
Denver, CO
303-297-2700
Dogs are allowed at the outdoor tables at this brewery, which is one of the largest brewpubs in the world.

Greenwood Village

Yia Yia's Eurocafe
8310 East Belleview Avenue
Greenwood Village, CO 80111
303-741-1110
This Mediterranean restaurant features bistro specialties, pasta, pizza and more. Dogs are allowed at the outdoor tables.

Stores

Denver

Cry Baby Ranch
1422 Larimer Street
Denver, CO
303-623-3979

This store offers Western gear for men, women, children and babies. They also offer unique Western-themed items including kitchen supplies, bedding, bath supplies, signs, and even lunchboxes. Well-behaved, leashed dogs are allowed inside.

Larimer Mission Gift Shop
1421 Larimer Street
Denver, CO
720-904-2789
This gift shop allows well-behaved, leashed dogs inside.

Z Gallerie
1465 Larimer Street
Denver, CO
303-615-9646
This home furnishings store allows leashed, well-behaved dogs inside.

Durango City Guide
Accommodations

Durango

Best Western Lodge at Purgatory
49617 Hwy 550
Durango, CO 81301
970-247-9669
There is a $10 per day pet fee.

Days Inn
1700 County Road
Durango, CO 81301
970-259-1430
There are no additional pet fees.

Doubletree Hotel
501 Camino Del Rio
Durango, CO 81301
970-259-6580
There is a $15 per day pet charge.

Holiday Inn
800 Camino Del Rio
Durango, CO 81301
970-247-5393
There is a $10 per day additional pet fee.

Quality Inn & Suites
455 S. Camino Del Rio
Durango, CO 81301
970-259-7900
There is a pet deposit of $50. Pets are allowed on the first and second floors only.

Rochester Hotel
726 E. Second Ave.
Durango, CO 81301
970-385-1920
This beautifully renovated hotel offers fifteen spacious rooms with high ceilings, king or queen beds, and private baths, and is decorated in an Old West motif. This hotel, located in downtown Durango, was designated as "The Flagship Hotel of Colorado" by Conde' Nast Traveler. They are very pet-friendly and offer two pet rooms, with a $20 per day pet charge.

Attractions

Durango

Carriages For Hire
7th and Main Ave
Durango, CO
970-247-5699
Treat yourself to a horse and carriage ride. Carriages for Hire offers two different 30 minute carriage rides. One will take you and your well-behaved pooch on a tour of the historic district of Durango. The other ride takes you on pleasant country roads. Rates are subject to change, but when we checked the cost was $10 per adult, $8 for teens, $6 for kids and free for your pooch. The carriage rides are located at the corner of 7th and Main, across from the Strater Hotel.

Rent A Wreck of Durango
21760 Highway 160 West
Durango, CO
970-259-5858
Go for a mountain adventure in your own rental Jeep 4x4.

There are some great off-road trails which pass by several old ghost towns in Silverton, about an hour and a half drive north of Durango. Rent A Wreck of Durango allows dogs in their Jeep rentals. Don't let the name fool you, they actually do rent new 4x4 Jeep Wranglers. According to Rent A Wreck, they are the only year round off-road 4x4 rental in the area. The charge for a one day Jeep rental is approximately $110 which is pretty much the going rate for a 4x4 in Durango. There is a $20 extra pet fee if the Jeep has lots of doggie hair upon return. Reservations are not required, but it's probably a good idea to reserve a Jeep about a week in advance just in case.

Parks

Durango

Animas City Mountain Trail
West 4th Avenue
Durango, CO

This is a 5-6 mile dirt trail that rises up to the top of a mesa where you can get a great view of the area. Please note that there is a separate trail for mountain bikers and for hikers. From downtown Durango, head north on Main Street. Turn left on 32nd Street and then right on West 4th Avenue. Dogs must be leashed on the trail.

Animas River Trail
32nd Avenue (at East 2nd Ave)
Durango, CO

The Animas River Trail is a 5 mile paved trail that runs along the river and through Durango. It is a popular trail with walkers, runners, in-line skaters and of course, dogs. If your pooch wants to cool off along the way, he or she can take a dip in the refreshing river. The north end of the trail is located at 32nd

Avenue and East 2nd Avenue. Dogs must be leashed on the trail.

Restaurants

Durango

Cyprus Cafe
725 East Second Avenue
Durango, CO
970-385-6884
This restaurant, located in downtown Durango, welcomes dogs to their popular outdoor patio. This award-winning Mediterranean restaurant serves lunch and dinner. Try the grilled salmon sandwich, lamb, chicken salad, or gyro for lunch. If you come for the dinner, they serve a variety of entrees including rock shrimp linguini, roasted butternet squash risotto, and portabello mushroom. In addition to the delicious food, you and your pooch can enjoy the live jazz on the patio.

Durango Natural Foods Deli
575 East 8th Avenue
Durango, CO
970-247-8129
This deli offers organic and natural sandwiches, soups, salads and more. Dogs are allowed at the outdoor tables.

The Buzz House Cafe
1019 Main Street
Durango, CO
970-385-5831
Friendly, well-behaved dogs are allowed at their outdoor tables. Come here for breakfast or lunch. They serve coffee, fruit smoothies, pastries, and vegetarian and low-fat meals.

Stores

Durango

Half-Price Tees
758 Main Street
Durango, CO

970-259-5601
Well-behaved, leashed dogs are allowed in the store.

Mountain Treasures Gifts
108 East 5th Street
Durango, CO
970-375-9270
Well-behaved, leashed dogs are allowed in the store.

Southwest Book Trader
175 E. 5th Street
Durango, CO
970-247-8479
Well-behaved, leashed dogs are allowed in the store.

The Shirt Off My Back
680 Main Street
Durango, CO
970-247-9644
Well-behaved, leashed dogs are allowed in the store.

Toh-Atin Gallery
145 West 9th Street
Durango, CO
970-247-8277
Art gallery specializing in Native American and Southwestern arts and crafts. Well-behaved, leashed dogs are allowed in the store.

Waldenbooks-Downtown
104 E. 5th Street
Durango, CO
970-247-3838
Well-behaved, leashed dogs are allowed in the store.

Yellowstone - Grand Teton City Guide

Accommodations

Jackson

Motel 6
600 S Hwy 89
Jackson, WY 83001
307-733-1620
There are no additional pet

fees. A well-behaved pet is allowed in each room.

Quality 49er Inn and Suites
330 W Pearl St
Jackson, WY 83001
307-733-7550
There are no additional pet fees.

Jackson Hole

Painted Buffalo Inn
400 West Broadway
Jackson Hole, WY 83001
307-733-4340
There is a $10 one time pet fee.

Snow King Resort
400 E Snow King Ave
Jackson Hole, WY 83001
307-733-5200
There is a $100 pet deposit. $50 of this is refundable.

Pray

Chico Hot Springs Resort
#1 Chico Road
Pray, MT 59065
406-333-4933
"We're pet-friendly, so bring your four-legged friends along." This resort has a lodge and cabins which sit on 150 acres. There are miles of hiking trails for you and your pup. They are located 30 miles from the north Yellowstone National Park entrance. There is a $10 per day pet fee.

Wapiti

Green Creek Inn
2908 Yellowstone Hwy
Wapiti, WY 82450
307-587-5004
There is a $5 per day pet fee.

West Yellowstone

Best Western Weston Inn
103 Gibbon Street
West Yellowstone, MT 59758
406-646-7373

There are no additional pet fees.

Yellowstone National Park

Flagg Ranch Village
Hwy 89 Yellowstone South Entrance
Yellowstone National Park, WY 83013
307-543-2861
Dogs are allowed in cabins. This is a seasonal hotel and is not open year round. There is a $5 per day additional pet fee.

Attractions

Moose

Grand Teton National Park

Moose, WY
307-739-3300
Pets are only allowed in your car, on roads and road shoulders, campgrounds, picnic areas, parking lots, etc. Dogs must be leashed. Dogs are not allowed on any park trails or in the backcountry. With national parks like this, it is very nice to have an adjacent national forest, like the Bridger-Teton National Forest, that allows dogs on trails.

Yellowstone National Park

Yellowstone National Park
various
Yellowstone National Park, WY
307-344-7381
While this national park is not dog-friendly, you will still be able to see, in a limited fashion, some of the major attractions. Dogs are allowed in parking areas, campgrounds and within 100 feet of roads. Pets must be on a 6 foot or less leash or crated or caged at all times. Pets are not allowed on the trails, boardwalks, or in thermal areas where the geysers, including Old Faithful, are located. While dogs are not

allowed next to the Old Faithful Geyser, you and your pooch will be able to view its large eruptions from about 200 feet back. And if you drive the Grand Loop Road, you will be able to view some points of interest and perhaps see some wildlife including black bears, grizzly bears, bison and elk. If you are looking for some hiking trails, there are numerous dog-friendly trails in the nearby Shoshone National Forest, located between the town of Cody and Yellowstone National Park.

Parks

Cody

Shoshone National Forest
808 Meadow Lane
Cody, WY 82414
307-527-6241
There are numerous dog-friendly trails in the forest, many of which are located between the town of Cody and Yellowstone National Park. One of the trails is the Eagle Creek Trail, which is about 16 miles long, at an elevation of 6700 to 9900 feet with a hiking difficulty of moderate. This trail is located off Highways 14 and 16, between Cody and Yellowstone.

Jackson

Bridger-Teton National Forest
various
Jackson, WY
307-739-5500
This national forest offers over 1200 miles of trails for you and your pooch to enjoy. You can take a short hike or take a week-long backpacking trip. There are many trails near Jackson and Buffalo. Here are two trails located near Jackson. The first is Cache Creek Trail

which is about 6 miles long and follows the creek. It is a popular trail and offers good views of the town and surrounding area. You might spot wildlife like moose, deer, elk and more during the summertime. This hike has a gentle grade which makes it a good trail for the entire family. To get there from the town square, travel east on Broadway to Redmond Street. Follow Redmond to Cache Creek Drive then follow Cache Creek Drive to parking lot. Another trail is the Black Canyon Overlook/Pass Ridge Trail. This trail is rated moderate and is about 2 miles long. The trail follows the ridge and travels through meadows and forest, with views of Jackson Hole and the surrounding mountains. To get there from Jackson, follow Highway 22 West to the summit of Teton Pass. Park at the top of Teton Pass on the left. The trailhead is well marked on the south side of the road at the parking area.

Restaurants

Jackson

The Cadillac Grille
55 North Cache
Jackson, WY 83001
307-733-3279
Only quiet, well-behaved, leashed dogs are allowed at the outdoor tables.

West Yellowstone

Firehole Grill
611 Highway 20
West Yellowstone, MT
406-646-4948
Dogs are allowed at the outdoor tables. This restaurant is open for breakfast, lunch and dinner.

Old Town Cafe
128 Madison Avenue
West Yellowstone, MT

406-646-0126
Dogs are allowed at the outdoor tables.

Petes Rocky Mountain Pizza and Pasta
Canyon Street and Madison Ave.
West Yellowstone, MT
406-646-7820
Enjoy pizza, pasta, chicken, salads and more. Dogs are allowed at the outdoor tables.

Wilson

Pearl Street Bagels
Fish Creek Center
Wilson, WY
307-739-1261
Dogs are allowed at the outdoor tables.

Tucson City Guide
Accommodations

Tucson

Best Western Executive Inn
333 West Drachman Street
Tucson, AZ 85705
520-791-7551
There is a $15 one time pet fee per visit.

Clarion Hotel & Suites Santa Rita
88 E. Broadway Blvd.
Tucson, AZ 85701
520-622-4000
There is a $50 pet deposit of which $25 is non-refundable.

Comfort Suites
6935 S. Tucson Blvd.
Tucson, AZ 85706-
520-295-4400
There is a non-refundable pet deposit of $50.

Comfort Suites at Tucson Mall
515 W. Automall Dr.
Tucson, AZ 85705
520-888-6676
There is a one time pet fee of

$10.

Doubletree Guest Suites
6555 E Speedway Blvd
Tucson, AZ 85710
520-721-7100
There is a $25 per visit pet fee.

Hawthorn Suites LTD
7007 E Tanque Verde Rd
Tucson, AZ 85715
520-298-2300
There is a $25 pet fee per visit.

Loews Ventana Canyon Resort
7000 North Resort Drive
Tucson, AZ 85750
520-299-2020
All well-behaved dogs of any size are welcome. This upscale hotel offers their "Loews Loves Pets" program which includes special pet treats, local dog walking routes, and a list of nearby pet-friendly places to visit. There are no pet fees.

Motel 6 - 22nd Street
1222 S Frwy
Tucson, AZ 85713
520-624-2516
A clean well-behaved large dog is okay. Exit 22nd Street from I-10 and go west. There are no additional pet fees.

Motel 6 - Airport
1031 E Benson Hwy
Tucson, AZ 85713
520-628-1264
There are no additional pet fees.

Motel 6 - Benson Hwy N
755 E Benson Hwy
Tucson, AZ 85713
520-622-4614
There are no additional pet fees.

Motel 6 - Congess St
960 S. Freeway
Tucson, AZ 85745
520-628-1339
Exit I-10 at exit 258, take the frontage road south. There are no additional pet fees.

Motel 6 - North
4630 W Ina Rd
Tucson, AZ 85741
520-744-9300
Take Ina Rd exit off of I-10. There are no additional pet fees.

Red Roof Inn Tucson North
4940 W Ina Rd
Tucson, AZ 85743
520-744-8199
There are no additional pet fees. Dogs up to 80 pounds are allowed. Pets must never be left alone in the rooms.

Residence Inn by Marriott
6477 E Speedway Blvd
Tucson, AZ 85710
520-721-0991
There is a $50 one time pet fee per visit.

Sheraton Tucson Hotel and Suites
5151 East Grant Road
Tucson, AZ
520-323-6262
Dogs up to 80 pounds are allowed. There is a $25 per night additional pet fee. Dogs may not be left in the room by themselves.

Studio 6
4950 S. Outlet Center Dr
Tucson, AZ 85706
520-746-0030
There is a $10 per day or $50 per week additional pet fee.

Westward Look Resort
245 East Ina Road
Tucson, AZ 85704
520-297-1151
This resort comes highly recommended from one of our readers. They said it was the most pet-friendly resort around and they can't say enough good things about it. This former 1912 guest ranch, now a desert resort hideaway, is nestled in the foothills of Tucson's picturesque Santa Catalina Mountains. It offers guests a Southwestern experience on 80 desert acres.

They have walking trails at the resort, tennis, swimming pools and much more. Special room rates can be as low as $69 during certain times and seasons. There is a $50 one time additional pet fee.

Windmill Inn at St Philip's Plaza
4250 N Campbell Ave
Tucson, AZ 85718
520-577-0007
There are no additional pet fees.

Attractions

Tucson

Old Tucson Studios
201 S. Kinney Road
Tucson, AZ 85735
520-883-0100
Well-behaved, leashed dogs are welcome at this outdoor studio which offers "Hollywood" stunt shows, re-enacted gunfights and more. See locations in this Old West town where popular Wild West films were shot. There are also many shops in the town that offer authentic western wear, gifts, books and collectibles. Well-behaved leashed dogs are also allowed inside the stores.

Pima Air and Space Museum
6000 East Valencia Road
Tucson, AZ 85706
520-574-0462
Dogs are allowed at the outdoor exhibits at this air museum. This museum has over 250 aircraft on display on 80 acres. Please make sure your pooch does not lift a leg on the aircraft. Have him or her take care of business before entering the museum.

Parks

Tucson

Christopher Columbus Park Dog Run

600 N. Silverbell Rd.
Tucson, AZ
520-791-4873
There is almost 15,000 square feet of enclosed space for your pooch to run leash-free. About 5,500 square feet has grass. Other doggie amenities include doggie bags, water, trees, and more.

Rillito River Trail
La Cholla Blvd
Tucson, AZ
520-877-6000
This popular paved trail stretches for miles, offering plenty of opportunity for your pooch to stretch his or her legs. Just be careful to go early in the morning or early evening if it is a hot day, as the paved path and the adjacent desert sand can become too hot for paws. A popular section of the trail is located between La Cholla Blvd. and Campbell Avenue, along the Rillito River. There is parking and restrooms available near La Cholla Boulevard.

Restaurants

Tucson

El Charro Cafe
311 North Court Avenue
Tucson, AZ
520-622-1922
Well-behaved dogs are allowed at the outdoor tables. Choose from a selection of fajitas, tamales, chalupas, enchiladas, salads and more.

Famous Sam's Restaurant and Bar
8058 North Oracle Rd
Tucson, AZ
520-531-9464
Dogs are allowed at the outdoor tables, but need to enter through the patio gate. Have a server open the gate for you.

Li'l Abner's Steakhouse
8501 North Silverbell Rd
Tucson, AZ
520-744-2800
Dogs are allowed at the outdoor tables.

Mama's Famous Pizza and Heros
7965 North Oracle Rd
Tucson, AZ
520-297-3993
Enjoy pizza or sandwiches at this restaurant. Dogs are allowed at the outdoor tables.

Ric's Cafe
5605 East River Rd
Tucson, AZ 85750
520-577-7272
Dogs are allowed at the outdoor tables.

Schlotzsky's Deli
6301 East Broadway Blvd.
Tucson, AZ 85710
520-722-1100
Dogs are allowed at the outdoor tables. Choose from a variety of hot and cold sandwiches, salads and more.

Schlotzsky's Deli
5121 East Grant Rd
Tucson, AZ 85712
520-325-5185
Dogs are allowed at the outdoor tables. Choose from a variety of hot and cold sandwiches, salads and more.

Schlotzsky's Deli
3270 East Valencia
Tucson, AZ 85706
520-741-2333
Dogs are allowed at the outdoor tables. Choose from a variety of hot and cold sandwiches, salads and more.

Tombstone City Guide

Accommodations

Tombstone

Best Western Lookout Lodge
Highway 80 West
Tombstone, AZ 85638
520-457-2223
This is Tombstone's newest motel. Amenities include a pool. It is located within a short drive to historic Tombstone. There is a $5 per day pet charge.

Trail Rider's Inn
13 N. 7th Street
Tombstone, AZ 85638
520-457-3573
You and your pup can walk to the historic Tombstone district from this inn. They offer large, clean, quiet rooms and cable TV. There is a $5 per day pet fee.

Attractions

Tombstone

1880 Historic Tombstone
70 miles from Tucson
Tombstone, AZ
800-457-3423
This historic Western town is one of the most famous and glamorized mining towns in America. Prospector Ed Schieffelin was told he would only find his tombstone in the San Pedro Valley. He named his first silver claim Tombstone, and it later became the name of the town. The town is situated on a mesa at an elevation of 4,540 feet. While the area became notorious for saloons, gambling houses and the O.K. Corral shootout, in the 1880s Tombstone had become the most cultivated city in the West. Surviving the Great Depression and relocation of the County Seat to Bisbee, in the 1930s Tombstone became known as "The Town Too Tough To Die." You an your leashed dog are welcome to take a step back in time and walk along the wooden sidewalks and dirt streets. Here is a side note about the town: dogs are not allowed inside the

O.K. Corral shoot-out area. This historic town is a must visit when you go to Arizona!

Old Tombstone Stagecoach Tours
Allen Street (between 4th and 5th Streets)
Tombstone, AZ
520-457-3018
You and your pooch are welcome to hop on the stagecoach and tour the old town of Tombstone. They offer horse drawn tours daily. Prices run about $10 for a 10-15 minute tour.

WF Trading Company
418 Allen St
Tombstone, AZ 85638
520-457-3664
Located in the heart of historic Tombstone, this retail store allows your well-behaved leashed dog inside the store. They sell gift items, jewelry, clothing and more.

Restaurants

Tombstone

O.K. Cafe
220 E. Allen Street
Tombstone, AZ 85638
520-457-3980
Come here for breakfast and lunch. Dogs are allowed at the outdoor tables.

Phoenix City Guide
Accommodations

Phoenix

Comfort Inn
5050 N. Black Canyon Highway
Phoenix, AZ 85017
602-242-8011
There is a $25 pet deposit if the room is paid for in cash. If the room is paid for by credit card there is no fee.

Comfort Inn

255 North Kyrene Blvd
Phoenix, AZ 85226
480-705-8882
There is no pet fee.

Comfort Suites
8473 West Paradise Ln.
Phoenix, AZ 85382
623-334-3993
There is a $50 pet deposit.

Crowne Plaza
2532 W. Peoria Ave
Phoenix, AZ 85029
602-943-2341
Exit I-17 at Peoria Ave.

Embassy Suites Hotel - Thomas Rd
2333 E Thomas Rd
Phoenix, AZ 85016
602-957-1910
There is a $15 per day pet fee.

Hampton Inn
8101 N Black Canyon Hwy
Phoenix, AZ 85021
602-864-6233
There is a $25 one time fee for pets.

Hilton Suites
10 E Thomas Road
Phoenix, AZ 85012
602-222-1111
There are no additional pet fees.

Holiday Inn - West
1500 N 51st Ave
Phoenix, AZ 85043
602-484-9009
There is a $25 one time pet fee.

Holiday Inn Express
3401 E University Dr
Phoenix, AZ 85034
602-453-9900
There are no additional pet fees

Holiday Inn Express Hotel & Suites
15221 S. 50th St
Phoenix, AZ 85044
480-785-8500
There is a $5 per day additional pet fee.

Holiday Inn Select - Airport

4300 E. Washington St
Phoenix, AZ 85034
602-273-7778
There is a $25 refundable pet deposit.

Howard Johnson Inn
124 S 24th St.
Phoenix, AZ 35034
602-220-0044
Dogs up to 60 pounds are allowed. There is a $20 one time pet fee.

La Quinta Inn Phoenix AP North
4727 E. Thomas Rd.
Phoenix, AZ
602-956-6500
Dogs up to 50 pounds are allowed at the hotel.

La Quinta Inn Phoenix North
2510 West Greenway
Phoenix, AZ
602-993-0800
Dogs of all sizes are allowed at the hotel.

La Quinta Inn Phoenix Thomas Road
2725 N Black Canyon Highway
Phoenix, AZ
602-258-6271
Dogs up to 75 pounds are allowed at the hotel.

Lexington Hotel at City Square
100 W Clarendon Ave
Phoenix, AZ 85013
602-279-9811
There is a $100 refundable deposit required for dogs.

Motel 6
2330 W Bell Rd
Phoenix, AZ 85023
602-993-2353
Pets may never be left alone in the room.

Motel 6
4130 N Black Canyon Hwy
Phoenix, AZ 85017
602-277-5501
Pets may not be left unattended in the room and must be on a leash when outside the room.

The hotel is at the Indian School exit on I-17.

Motel 6
8152 N. Black Canyon Hwy
Phoenix, AZ 85051
602-995-7592
The hotel is at the Northern Ave exit on I-17.

Motel 6
5315 E Van Buren Street
Phoenix, AZ 85008
602-267-8555
Pets may not be left alone in the room.

Premier Inn
10402 N Black Canyon Hwy
Phoenix, AZ 85051
602-943-2371
There are no additional pet fees. Pets are not allowed in deluxe rooms.

Quality Hotel & Resort
3600 N 2nd Ave
Phoenix, AZ 85013
602-248-0222
There is a one time non-refundable fee of $25.

Quality Inn South Mountain
5121 E. La Puente Ave.
Phoenix, AZ 85044
480-893-3900
Pets may not be left alone. There is a $50 pet fee of which $25 is refundable.

Quality Suites
3101 N. 32nd St
Phoenix, AZ 85018
602-956-4900
There is a $10 per day pet fee.

Red Lion Metrocenter
12027 N 28th Dr
Phoenix, AZ 85029
602-866-7000
There are no additional pet fees.

Red Roof Inn
5215 W Willetta
Phoenix, AZ 85043
602-233-8004
Dogs under about 80 pounds

are allowed. There are no additional pet fees.

Residence Inn
8242 N Black Canyon Hwy
Phoenix, AZ 85051
602-864-1900
There is a $50 non-refundable pet fee.

Sheraton Crescent Hotel
2620 West Dunlap Avenue
Phoenix, AZ 85021
602-943-8200
Dogs up to 80 pounds are allowed. There is no additional pet fee.

Sheraton Wild Horse Pass Resort and Spa
Gila River Indian Community
Phoenix, AZ
602-225-0100
Dogs up to 55 pounds are allowed. All rooms are non-smoking. There are no pet fees.

Sleep Inn
6347 E. Southern Ave.
Phoenix, AZ 85206
480-807-7760
There is a $25 pet deposit. Pets may not be left alone.

Sleep Inn North
18235 N. 27th Ave.
Phoenix, AZ 85053
602-504-1200
There is a $25 pet deposit.

Sleep Inn Sky Harbor Airport
2621 S 47th Pl
Phoenix, AZ 85034
480-967-7100
There is a $25 one time pet fee.

Studio 6
8405 North 27th Avenue
Phoenix, AZ 85053
602-843-1151
There is a $10 per day additional pet fee. Exit Union Hills Drive west from I-17.

Townplace Suites
9425-B N Black Canyon Hwy
Phoenix, AZ 85021
602-943-9510

There is a one-time $100 pet fee.

Tempe

Holiday Inn - Tempe
915 E. Apache Blvd
Tempe, AZ 85281
480-968-3451
One well-behaved large dog is okay.

La Quinta Inn Phoenix Sky Harbor Tempe
911 South 48th Street
Tempe, AZ
480-967-4465
Dogs of all sizes are allowed at the hotel.

Motel 6
1720 S. Priest Drive
Tempe, AZ 85281
480-968-4401
There are no additional pet fees.

Motel 6
1612 N Scottsdale Rd/Rural Rd
Tempe, AZ 85281
480-945-9506
Pets may not be left alone in the room.

Quality
1375 E. University Dr.
Tempe, AZ 85251
480-774-2500
There is no pet fee. A credit card will be required.

Studio 6
4909 South Wendler Dr.
Tempe, AZ 85282
602-414-4470
There is a $10 per day or $30 per week pet fee.

Accommodations - Vacation Home Rentals

Phoenix

South Mountain Village Pet Friendly Vacation Apartment
113 E. La Mirada Drive
Phoenix, AZ 85042

602-243-3452
Located in the foothills of South Mountain Park. 1 bedroom, 1 bath apartment, completely furnished, including dishes, utensils, cookware, linens and much more for a self-catering vacation. Pets have free range of completely fenced 1/8 acre gated yard. Pool, spa, laundry, off-street parking for one automobile. Horse riding stables, golf, hiking trials nearby. Rates are seasonal, starting at $300 per week and $975 per month for 2 adults and 1 pet (fees apply for additional guests/pets). Tax and cleaning fees are extra.

Attractions

Phoenix

Biltmore Fashion Park
2502 E. Camelback Rd.
Phoenix, AZ 85016
602-955-8400
Well-behaved leashed dogs are welcome at this outdoor shopping mall and most of the stores are pet-friendly. This mall even has a list of pet-friendly stores on their website. Some of the stores that allow dogs include Macy's, Sak's Fifth Avenue, Restoration Hardware, Pottery Barn, Godiva Chocolatier, The Sharper Image, Williams-Sonoma, Three Dog Bakery, and Baily, Banks & Biddle. Many of the outdoor restaurant also allow dogs. Please check our restaurant section for listings.

Deer Valley Rock Art Center
3711 West Deer Valley Rd.
Phoenix, AZ
623-582-8007
Run by Arizona State University, this 47 acre attraction offers a self-guided walking tour to an archeological site where you can view petroglyphs with your pooch.

The Hedgpeth Hills site has over 1,500 petroglyphs on almost 600 boulders. Researchers believe the petroglyphs are 200 to 2,000 years old. Dogs are not allowed inside the building, but can accompany you on the self-guided trail. A map of the trail is included with admission. Pets must be leashed and please clean up after your pet.

Pioneer Living History Village
3901 West Pioneer Road
Phoenix, AZ 85086
623-465-1052
This living history museum offers over 90 acres of an old 1800's village with original buildings and historically accurate reproductions. You will find costumed interpreters, cowboys, lawmen, Victorian ladies plus a working blacksmith shop and more. There are also "shootouts" that start daily at 11: 30am. Well-behaved leashed dogs are welcome. The village is located 30 minutes north of Phoenix. This attraction is open year-round, but the best time is during the winter when it's not too hot for your dog to walk around. Winter hours are from mid-September through the end of May.

Parks

Phoenix

Camelback Mountain
Cholla Lane
Phoenix, AZ
602-262-6862
This park offers sheer red sandstone cliffs and strenuous hiking trails. There are some easier trails which allow for a close-up view around Camelback's base. The easy trails and one of the strenuous trails begin off of Echo Canyon Parkway near McDonald Drive. Parking is very limited at the trailheads. Pets must be leashed and please clean up after them.

North Mountain Area
7th Street
Phoenix, AZ
602-262-6862
North Mountain is over 2,100 feet and offers panoramic views of Phoenix. There are a variety of trails rated easy to difficult. The trailheads for two of the easy to moderate trails are located at the north end of Mountain View Park at 7th Avenue and Cheryl Drive. The North Mountain National Trail is rated moderate to difficult hiking and the trailhead is located at the Maricopa picnic area off 7th Street (not 7th Avenue). Parking is available. Pets must be leashed and please clean up after them.

Papago Park
Galvin Parkway
Phoenix, AZ
602-262-6862
This park offers sandstone buttes and mostly easy hikes with little elevation gain. One of the trails is called the Hole-In-The-Rock Trail which is a short trail that leads to a popular landmark with some good views. Parking is available. Pets must be leashed and please clean up after them.

Pecos Park Dog Park
48th Street
Phoenix, AZ
602-262-6862
This dog park is scheduled to open in the fall of 2003. It will be located in Pecos Park which is at 48th Street and Pecos Parkway.

PetsMart Dog Park
21st Avenue
Phoenix, AZ
602-262-6971
This fully fenced dog park has over 2.5 grassy acres. Amenities include a water fountain and two watering stations for dogs, benches, bag dispensers and garbage cans. This off-leash

park is located in Washington Park on 21st Avenue north of Maryland (between Bethany Home and Glendale roads).

Reach 11 Recreation Area
Cave Creek Road
Phoenix, AZ
602-262-6862
This 1,500 acre park is about 7 miles long and less than 1/2 mile wide. The park runs along the north side of the Central Arizona Project canal. There are about 18 miles of multi-use trails to enjoy. In general the trails are flat and easy. The trails run the length of the recreation area from Cave Creek Road east to Scottsdale Road. Access points include Cave Creek Road, Tatum Blvd., Scottsdale Road and 56th Street. Pets must be leashed and please clean up after them.

South Mountain Park
10919 S. Central Avenue
Phoenix, AZ 85040
602-534-6324
At 16,000 acres, this park is the largest municipal park in the world. It is popular for hiking, biking and horseback riding. There are over 58 miles of trails rated easy to difficult. Many of the trails start off of or near Central Avenue or San Juan Road. Pets must be leashed and please clean up after them.

Squaw Peak/Dreamy Draw Area
Squaw Peak Drive
Phoenix, AZ
602-262-6862
Squaw Peak is 2,608 feet high and is one of the best known peaks in Phoenix. The summit trail is rated moderate to difficult hiking and is one of the most popular trails. There are also several easy trails. Some of the trails begin off Squaw Peak Drive. Parking is available. Pets must be leashed and please clean up after them.

Aunt Chilada's
7330 N. Dreamy Draw Drive
Phoenix, AZ 85020
602-944-1286
This Southwestern restaurant offers a variety of food including quesadillas, soup, salads, tacos, enchiladas, fajitas, and burritos. Well-behaved leashed dogs are allowed at the outdoor tables.

Baja Fresh Mexican Grill
1615 E Camelback Rd Ste F
Phoenix, AZ
602-263-0110
This Mexican restaurant chain offers a variety of items on their menu including burritos, tacos, salads, quesadillas, fajitas, and enchiladas. Well-behaved leashed dogs are allowed at the outdoor tables.

Baja Fresh Mexican Grill
10810 N. Tatum Blvd, Ste 108
Phoenix, AZ
602-569-8600
This Mexican restaurant chain offers a variety of items on their menu including burritos, tacos, salads, quesadillas, fajitas, and enchiladas. Well-behaved leashed dogs are allowed at the outdoor tables.

Baja Fresh Mexican Grill
430 East Bell Rd.
Phoenix, AZ
602-843-6770
This Mexican restaurant chain offers a variety of items on their menu including burritos, tacos, salads, quesadillas, fajitas, and enchiladas. Well-behaved leashed dogs are allowed at the outdoor tables.

Baja Fresh Mexican Grill
3923 E. Thomas Rd. Ste B-5
Phoenix, AZ
602-914-9000
This Mexican restaurant chain offers a variety of items on their

menu including burritos, tacos, salads, quesadillas, fajitas, and enchiladas. Well-behaved leashed dogs are allowed at the outdoor tables.

Baja Fresh Mexican Grill
50 N. Central Ave
Phoenix, AZ
602-256-9200
This Mexican restaurant chain offers a variety of items on their menu including burritos, tacos, salads, quesadillas, fajitas, and enchiladas. Well-behaved leashed dogs are allowed at the outdoor tables.

Bamboo Club
2596 E. Camelback Rd.
Phoenix, AZ 85016
602-955-1288
This restaurant offers Pacific Rim food, including Thailand, Korean, Vietnam, and Chinese. Well-behaved leashed dogs are allowed at the outdoor tables. This restaurant is located in the dog-friendly Biltmore Fashion Park.

Christopher's Fermier Brasserie
2584 E. Camelback Rd.
Phoenix, AZ
602-522-2344
This restaurant offers a combination French and American cuisine. Some of their specialty items include house-smoked salmon, and lightly smoked truffle-cured sirloin. Well-behaved leashed dogs are allowed at the outdoor tables. This restaurant is located in the dog-friendly Biltmore Fashion Park.

Coffee Plantation
2468 E. Camelback Rd.
Phoenix, AZ 85016
602-553-0203
This is a tropical coffeehouse and bean store. They offer cofee, espresso, iced drinks, fresh Artisan Breads, Baguettes, specialty bread loaves and more. Well-behaved leashed

dogs are allowed at the outdoor tables. This restaurant is located in the dog-friendly Biltmore Fashion Park.

Duck and Decanter
1651 East Camelback Road
Phoenix, AZ 85016
602-274-5429
This restaurant offers a variety of sandwiches, salads, and soups. Some of their Signature Sandwiches include The Duckling with smoked duck, The Pocket with your choice of meat, and Where's the Beef which is their veggie sandwich. Well-behaved leashed dogs are allowed at the outdoor tables. The restaurant is located to the east of Albertson's, behind Copenhagen Furniture.

Haagen-Dazs
2454 E. Camelback Rd.
Phoenix, AZ 85016
602-508-8053
This popular ice cream shop offers a variety of ice creams, sorbet, frozen yogurt, sundaes, banana split, specialty shakes, espresso, and ice cream cakes. Well-behaved leashed dogs are allowed at the outdoor tables. This restaurant is located in the dog-friendly Biltmore Fashion Park.

Juice Works
10895 North Tatum Boulevard
Phoenix, AZ
480-922-5337
This juice bar serves fresh fruit smoothies and juices. Well-behaved leashed dogs are allowed at the outdoor tables.

Rubio's Fresh Mexican Grill
4340 E. Indian School Rd., Ste. 1
Phoenix, Az 85018
602-508-1732
This Mexican restaurant chain serves items like char-grilled steak and chicken burritos, tacos, quesadillas, seafood including lobster, shrimp, Mahi-Mahi, and their famous fish

taco. Well-behaved leashed dogs are allowed at the outdoor tables.

Rubio's Fresh Mexican Grill
4747 East Bell Road #17
Phoenix, AZ 85032
602-867-1454
This Mexican restaurant chain serves items like char-grilled steak and chicken burritos, tacos, quesadillas, seafood including lobster, shrimp, Mahi-Mahi, and their famous fish taco. Well-behaved leashed dogs are allowed at the outdoor tables.

Sam's Cafe
2566 E. Camelback Rd.
Phoenix, AZ 85016
602-954-7100
This restaurant specializes in Southwestern cuisine and welcomes dogs to their outdoor patio. Their entrees include the Fire Grilled Tuna, Desert Fire Pasta, Blackened Salmon Caesar, Grilled Vegetable Paella and the classic Southwest steak. Well-behaved leashed dogs are welcome at the outdoor tables. This restaurant is located in the dog-friendly Biltmore Fashion Park.

The Capital Grille
2502 E. Camelback Rd.
Phoenix, AZ 85016
602-952-8900
This steak house offers dry aged steaks, North Atlantic lobsters and fresh seafood. Well-behaved leashed dogs are allowed at the outdoor tables. This restaurant is located in the dog-friendly Biltmore Fashion Park.

The Farm at South Mountain
6106 South 32nd Street
Phoenix, AZ
602-276-6360
This restaurant specializes in organic and natural foods. All seating is outdoors, either in their patio under pecan trees or at picnic tables. An organic garden is on the premises and

they often use ingredients from it. They serve sandwiches, salads, and baked goods. Well-behaved leashed dogs are allowed at the outdoor tables. The restaurant is open daily weather permitting from 8am to 3pm, except they are closed on Mondays.

Vintage Market
2442 B East Camelback Rd.
Phoenix, AZ 85016
602-955-4444
This cafe also has a wine bar and gourmet gift shop. They are open for dinner. Well-behaved leashed dogs are allowed at the outdoor tables. This restaurant is located in the dog-friendly Biltmore Fashion Park.

Wild Oats Natural Marketplace
3933 E. Camelback Rd.
Phoenix, AZ
602-954-0584
This natural food market has a deli with outdoor seats. Well-behaved leashed dogs are allowed at the outdoor tables.

Tempe

Baja Fresh Mexican Grill
414 W. University Drive
Tempe, AZ
480-446-3116
This Mexican restaurant chain offers a variety of items on their menu including burritos, tacos, salads, quesadillas, fajitas, and enchiladas. Well-behaved leashed dogs are allowed at the outdoor tables.

Rubio's Fresh Mexican Grill
1712 East Guadalupe Rd., Ste. 109
Tempe, AZ 85283
480-897-3884
This Mexican restaurant chain serves items like char-grilled steak and chicken burritos, tacos, quesadillas, seafood including lobster, shrimp, Mahi-Mahi, and their famous fish taco. Well-behaved leashed dogs are

allowed at the outdoor tables.

Grand Canyon City Guide

Accommodations

Grand Canyon

Rodeway Inn-Red Feather Lodge
Highway 64
Grand Canyon, AZ 86023
928-638-2414
This motel is located just one mile south of the south entrance to the Grand Canyon National Park. Pets are welcome, but they must not be left unattended in the room. There is a $50 refundable pet deposit and a $10 pet fee per night per pet.

Williams

Highlander Motel
533 W. Bill Williams Avenue
Williams, AZ 86046
928-635-2541
There is a $5/day pet charge. Room prices are in the $50 range. This motel is about 1 hour from the Grand Canyon.

Holiday Inn
950 N. Grand Canyon Blvd
Williams, AZ 86046
928-635-4114
There are no additional pet fees.

Motel 6 - Grand Canyon
831 W Rt 66
Williams, AZ 86046
520-635-9000
There are no additional pet fees.

Motel 6 Park Inn
710 W. Bill Williams Avenue
Williams, AZ 86046
928-635-4464

This motel is about 1 hour from the Grand Canyon. There are no additional pet fees.

Quality Inn - Mountain Ranch Resort
6701 E. Mountain Ranch Road
Williams, AZ 86046
928-635-2693
Amenities include tennis courts, a heated pool and whirlpool (closed during the winter). There is a one time $20 charge for pets. Room prices range from $50-100. This motel is about 1 hour from the Grand Canyon.

Attractions

Grand Canyon

Grand Canyon National Park
Hwy 64
Grand Canyon, AZ 86023
928-638-7888
The Grand Canyon, located in the northwest corner of Arizona, is considered to be one of the most impressive natural splendors in the world. It is 277 miles long, 18 miles wide, and at its deepest point, is 6000 vertical feet (more than 1 mile) from rim to river. The Grand Canyon has several entrance areas, but the most popular is the South Rim. Dogs are not allowed on any trails below the rim, but leashed dogs are allowed on the paved rim trail. This dog-friendly trail is about 2.7 miles each way and offers excellent views of the Grand Canyon. Remember that the elevation at the rim is 7,000 feet, so you or your pup may need to rest more often than usual. Also, the weather can be very hot during the summer and can be snowing during the winter, so plan accordingly. And be sure you or your pup do not get too close to the edge! Feel like taking a tour? Well-behaved dogs are allowed on the Geology Walk. This is a one hour park ranger guided tour and consists of a leisurely walk

along a 3/4 mile paved rim trail. They discuss how the Grand Canyon was created and more. The tour departs at 11am daily (weather permitting) from the Yavapai Observation Station. The Grand Canyon park entrance fee is currently $20.00 per private vehicle, payable upon entry to the park. Admission is for 7 days, includes both South and North Rims, and covers the entrance fee only.

Williams

Historic Route 66 Driving Tour
Bill Williams Avenue
Williams, AZ

Route 66 was the main route between Los Angeles and Chicago during the 1920's through the 1960's. It was completely paved in 1938. This historic route symbolizes the American adventure and romance of the open road. Begin your self-guided driving tour on Bill Williams Avenue in Williams. This portion of Route 66 is considered "America's Main Street," where you will find gas stations, restaurants, shops and motels that have served travelers since the 1920's. Then head east on Old 66 to the I-40 interchange. Continue east on I-40 for 6 miles. Take the Pittman Valley exit and left left, pass over I-40, and turn right onto historic Route 66. This portion of the road was originally paved in 1939. Stop and park at the Oak Hill Snowplay Area. You and your pooch can take a 2 mile round trip hike to the Keyhole Sink petroglyphs. After your walk, continue driving and you will come to a community called Parks. Located here is a country store that has been in operation since about 1910. At this point you can turn around and head back to Williams via I-40. Directions and descriptions are from the USDA Forest

Service in Williams, Arizona.

Parks

Williams

Kaibab National Forest
800 South 6th Street
Williams, AZ 86046
928-635-8200
Dogs on leash are allowed on many trails throughout this national forest. Hiking trails range greatly in difficulty, from easy to very difficult. A couple of the more popular trails are the Keyhole Sink Trail and the Bill Williams Mountain Trail. The Keyhole Sink Trails is an easy trail that is 2 miles round trip. Walk through a ponderosa pine forest until you reach a box canyon. At the canyon, you will find petroglyphs (prehistoric sketches on the rock), that are about 1,000 years old. The message suggests that the area was an important hunting ground. To get there from Williams, take I-40 east to the Pitman Valley Exit (#171). Turn left and cross over the Interstate. Proceed east on Historic Route 66 for about 2 miles to the Oak Hill Snowplay Area. The trail begins on the north side of the road. Park in the lot provided. The Bill Williams Mountain Trail is rated moderate and is about 4 miles long. The trailhead starts at 7,000 feet. To get there, go west from downtown Williams on Bill Williams Avenue about one mile; turn left at Clover Hill and proceed along the frontage road to the turnoff to Williams Ranger District office. Follow the signs to the trailhead.

Restaurants

Grand Canyon

Grand Canyon Snack Bars
Grand Canyon National Park

Grand Canyon, AZ

Dogs are permitted at the outdoor benches at park operated snack bars located at the South Rim area. Please note that these snack bars typically have benches only and not tables. There were no other restaurants we found at the Grand Canyon that had outdoor tables. The closest outdoor dining we found was in Williams, Arizona.

Williams

Cruiser's Cafe
233 West Route 66
Williams, AZ
928-635-2445
This cafe is located on Old Route 66 in historic downtown Williams. The cafe is located in a renovated gas station and displays hundreds of Route 66 memorabilia items. Dogs are allowed at the outdoor tables.

Grand Canyon Coffee Cafe
125 West Route 66
Williams, AZ
928-635-1255
There is one outdoor table. Dogs are allowed at the outdoor table.

Smash Hit Subs and Pizza
5235 North Highway 64
Williams, AZ
928-635-1487
There are a few benches and tables outside. This restaurant also serve bakery items. Dogs are allowed at the outdoor tables.

Subway Sandwiches
1050 North Grand Canyon Blvd.
Williams, AZ
928-635-0955
Dogs are allowed at the outdoor table.

The Route 66 Place
417 East Route 66
Williams, AZ
928-635-0266

Dogs are allowed at the outdoor tables. This cafe is named after the Old Route 66, which was the main route between Los Angeles and Chicago during the 1920's through the 1960's.

Las Vegas City Guide

Accommodations

Boulder City

Super 8
704 Nevada Hwy
Boulder City, NV 89005
702-294-8888
There is a $10 per day pet fee.

Henderson

Residence Inn
2190 Olympic Road
Henderson, NV 89014
702-434-2700
There is a $50 one time pet fee and a $10 per day pet fee. One dog is allowed per room and dogs up to 65 pounds are allowed.

Las Vegas

Best Western Nellis
5330 East Craig Street
Las Vegas, NV 89115
702-643-6111
This motel is located away from the busy downtown area, but within minutes from the Las Vegas Strip. Amenities include an outdoor pool, a playground, laundry/valet services and complimentary continental breakfast on the weekends. There is a $10 per day pet charge.

Best Western Parkview
921 Las Vegas Blvd North
Las Vegas, NV 89101
702-385-1213
This motel is located within a 15 minute drive from the Las Vegas Strip. Amenities include an outdoor pool and a guest laundry. There is a $8 per day pet charge.

Comfort Inn
910 E. Cheyenne Rd.
Las Vegas, NV 89030
702-399-1500
This motel is located about three miles from the Las Vegas Strip. Amenities at this motel include a heated outdoor pool & hot tub, gift shop, free continental breakfast and wheelchair accessibility. There is a $5 per day pet charge.

Hampton Inn
7100 Cascade Valley Court
Las Vegas, NV 89128
702-360-5700
There is a $25 one time pet fee.

Hawthorn Suites-The Strip
5051 Duke Ellington Way
Las Vegas, NV 89119
702-739-7000
This suites hotel has no size restrictions for dogs as long as they are well-behaved (no barking, potty trained, etc.). There is a $125 pet deposit and $25 of it is non-refundable. Hotel amenities include a guest laundry, outdoor pool, exercise room and more.

Holiday Inn Express-The Lakes
8669 W. Sahara Avenue
Las Vegas, NV 89117
702-256-3766
Dogs are welcome at this inn. There is a $20 one time pet charge. Amenities include guest laundry facilities. They are located about 6.5 miles from downtown Las Vegas.

La Quinta Inn Las Vegas - Nellis
4288 N. Nellis Rd.
Las Vegas, NV
702-632-0229
Dogs of all sizes are allowed at the hotel.

La Quinta Inn Las Vegas - Tropicana
4975 South Valley View
Las Vegas, NV
702-798-7736
Dogs of all sizes are allowed at the hotel.

La Quinta Suites Las Vegas - West/Lakes
9570 W. Sahara
Las Vegas, NV
702-243-0356
Dogs of all sizes are allowed at the hotel.

Residence Inn - Hughes Center
370 Hughes Center Drive
Las Vegas, NV 89109
702-650-0040
There is a $50 one time pet fee and a $10 per day pet charge.

Rodeway Inn & Suites
167 E. Tropicana Ave
Las Vegas, NV 89109
702-795-3311
There is a $100 refundable pet deposit.

Mt. Charleston

Mount Charleston Lodge and Cabins
HCR 38 Box 325
Mt. Charleston, NV
702-872-5408
800-955-1314
The lodge sits at over 7,700 feet above sea level and about 35 miles from the Las Vegas Strip. There are several dog-friendly trails nearby for hikers. Dogs are welcome for an additional $10 per day pet charge.

Accommodations - Vacation Home Rentals

Boulder City

Seven Crown Resorts Houseboats
322 Lake Shore Road
Boulder City, NV 89005
800-752-9669
Rent a houseboat on Lake Mead

at the Lake Mead Resort Marina and bring your pooch with you. Lake Mead is approximately 25 miles from downtown Las Vegas. Pets are welcome on houseboats at no additional charge. Advance reservations are required. Call 800-752-9669 to make your reservation.

Green Valley

Green Valley Vacation Home Rental
Call to Arrange.
Green Valley, NV
702-433-6786
This Spanish-style 3 bedroom, 2 bathroom house, located in Green Valley, is about 10 miles from the Las Vegas Strip. This pet-friendly home offers a doggy door in the sliding glass door which leads to a large, private enclosed grassy backyard. Families welcome.

Las Vegas

Desert Shores Vacation Rental
Call to Arrange.
Las Vegas, NV
702-656-8905
This 2 bedroom, 2 bathroom condo vacation rental allows pets.

Las Vegas Vacation Home Rental
Call to Arrange.
Las Vegas, NV
702-395-7065
This 4 bedroom, 3 bathroom house is only 5 minutes from the Las Vegas Strip. Lake Mead and Hoover Dam are about 25 minutes away. Pets are allowed in this vacation home. Amenities include a backyard with a pool/spa combo and gas BBQ.

Las Vegas Vacation Villas
Call to Arrange.
Las Vegas, NV
702-798-9808
This company offers pet-friendly townhouse vacation and estate

vacation rentals. It is located in a gated community with views of green fairways.

Attractions

Blue Diamond

Bonnie Springs Old Nevada
1 Gunfighter Lane
Blue Diamond, NV 89004
702-875-4191
Visit a replica of an 1880's mining town near Las Vegas. While dogs are not allowed on the miniature train ride, in the restaurant or in the zoo, there are still other activities you can do with your best friend. Watch a gunfight in the street and check out all the historic replica buildings. Well-behaved, leashed dogs are welcome.

Las Vegas

Historic Spring Mountain Ranch
State Route 159
Las Vegas, NV 89004
15 miles W of Las Vegas
702-875-4141
Previous owners of this historic ranch include Chester Lauck of the comedy team "Lum & Abner," German actress Vera Krupp, and millionaire Howard Hughes. Guided tours through the Ranch House and other historic ranch buildings are available on weekends and holidays. The visitor center is open Monday through Friday and on holidays. Dogs on leash are allowed on the grounds, but not inside the buildings. Other amenities at this park include a tree-shaded picnic area and scenic hiking trails.

Las Vegas Strip Walking Tour
3300-3900 Las Vegas Blvd.
Las Vegas, NV

Since dogs are not allowed inside the buildings or

attractions on the Vegas strip, we have put together an outdoor self-guided walking tour that you can take with your pooch. It is kid-friendly too! While you can take the tour any time of day, probably the best time is late afternoon or early evening because of the special effects and light shows at some of the points of interest. All places mentioned can be viewed from the sidewalk. Start the walk at the Treasure Island Hotel at 3300 South Las Vegas Blvd. In the front of this hotel you can view two battle ships duke it out. Every 90 minutes, each evening at Buccaneer Bay, musket and cannon fire are exchanged in a pyrotechnic battle between the pirate ship Hispaniola and the British frigate H.M.S. Britannia. This is a popular attraction and it can become very crowded on the sidewalk. Next stop is the Volcano in front of the Mirage Hotel at 3400 South Las Vegas Blvd. From dusk to midnight, every 15 minutes, flames shoot into the sky, spewing smoke and fire 100 feet above the water, transforming a tranquil waterfall into streams of molten lava. For a little musical entertainment, walk over to the Musical Fountains at the Bellagio Hotel at 3600 South Las Vegas Blvd. Here you will find spectacular fountains that fill a 1/4 mile long lake in front of the hotel. Every evening there is a water show that is timed to music. The show takes place every 15 minutes. For some interesting architecture, walk over to the Eiffel Tower at the Paris Hotel at 3655 South Las Vegas Blvd. While your pooch cannot go into the Paris Hotel or the tower, you can view this half size Paris replica from the street. You can also visit the Statue of Liberty right in Las Vegas. Walk over to the New York, New York Hotel at 3790 South Las Vegas Blvd. Again, your pooch cannot go inside this hotel, but you can view the replica from the street. The last stop is the Luxor Hotel at 3900 South Las Vegas Blvd. From the sidewalk you will see the large pyramid with hotel rooms inside and a large sphinx in the front of the hotel. Please note that some of the attractions might be closed during certain times of the year or during bad weather, especially when it is windy.

Old Las Vegas Mormon Fort

500 E Washington Ave
Las Vegas, NV 89101
702-486-3511
This park includes a remnant of the original adobe fort which housed the first permanent non-native Mormon missionary settlers in the Las Vegas Valley. They successfully diverted water from the Las Vegas Creek in 1855 for farming. There are future plans to re-create many more historic features at this park. The park is open all year and allows leashed dogs on the outside grounds.

Parks

Boulder City

Lake Mead National Recreation Area

Lakeshore Rd/166
Boulder City, NV 89005
702-293-8907
This recreation area covers 1.5 million acres. The west side of the park is about 25 miles from downtown Las Vegas. We didn't see any designated trails, but leashed dogs are allowed on many of the trails and at the lake. To get there from Las Vegas, take Hwy 146 east to Lakeshore Rd./166. Lakeshore Rd. is the scenic drive along Lake Mead.

Las Vegas

Desert Breeze County Park

8425 W. Spring Mtn. Road
Las Vegas, NV
Durango Drive

This county park has picnic tables, sports fields, a bike/walking path and a dog park. It is located approximately 5 miles east of downtown Las Vegas and the Strip. From Flamingo Road/589 in downtown, head west and pass Hwy 15. Turn right on Durango Drive. Then turn right onto Spring Mountain Road and the park will be on the corner. Dogs must be leashed, except for in the dog park.

Desert Breeze Dog Run

8425 W. Spring Mtn. Road
Las Vegas, NV
Durango Drive

This dog park/run is fully enclosed. Thanks to one of our readers who recommended this park. She also suggested that we remind people that they shouldn't bring their puppies to the dog park until they have had all their shots. Young puppies can be very susceptible to Parvo. The park is located approximately 5 miles east of downtown Las Vegas and the Strip. From Flamingo Road/589 in downtown, head west and pass Hwy 15. Turn right on Durango Drive. Then turn right onto Spring Mountain Road. The dog park is located off Spring Mountain Rd., between the Community Center and Desert Breeze County Park.

Dog Fancier's Park

5800 E. Flamingo Rd.
Las Vegas, NV
702-455-8200
Dog Fancier's Park is a 12 acre park that allows canine enthusiasts to train their dogs off leash. Owner's must still have control over their dogs and may be cited if their dogs (while off leash) interfere with

other animals training at the park. This dog park has benches, poop bags and water taps.

Lorenzi Park

3333 W. Washington Ave.
Las Vegas, NV
702-229-6297
This park is about a mile west of downtown Las Vegas. Leashed dogs are allowed. Lorenzi Park features tennis courts, playgrounds, picnic tables and a five acre lake.

Red Rock Canyon National Area

Charleston Blvd/159
Las Vegas, NV
702-363-1921
Located just 20-25 minutes west of downtown Las Vegas is the beautiful Red Rock Canyon National Conservation Area. This preserve has over 60,000 acres and includes unique geological formations. There is a popular 13 mile one-way scenic loop road that winds around the park, providing sightseeing, vistas and overlooks. Many of the hiking trails begin off this road. Leashed dogs are allowed on most of the trails. Some of the trails they are not allowed on are more like rock climbing expeditions than hiking trails. There are a variety of hiking trails ranging from easy to difficult. The visitor center is open daily and should have trail maps. On the trails, be aware of extreme heat or cold. Also watch out for flash floods, especially near creeks and streams. According to the BLM (Bureau of Land Management), violent downpours can cause flash flooding in areas untouched by rain. Do not cross low places when water is running through a stream. The park entrance fee is $5 per vehicle and $5 per dog. To get there from downtown Las Vegas, take Charleston Blvd./159 and head west.

Shadow Rock Dog Run
2650 Los Feliz on Sunrise Mountain
Las Vegas, NV
702-455-8200
This is a 1.5 acre dog park with benches, poop bags and water taps.

Sunset Park Dog Run
2601 E. Sunset Rd
Las Vegas, NV
702-455-8200
Located in Sunset Park, this dog park offers about 1.5 acres of land for your pooch to play. The dog park has benches, poop bags and water taps.

Mt. Charleston

Spring Mountain National Recreation Area
Echo Road
Mt. Charleston, NV
702-515-5404
This 316,000 acre park, part of the Toiyabe National Forest, is located about 35 miles northwest of Las Vegas. Mt. Charleston is located in this dog-friendly park and has many hiking trails. Temperatures here can average 25 to 30 degrees cooler than in Las Vegas. The Mary Jane Falls trail, located on Mt. Charleston, is one of the more popular trails. The trail passes a seasonal waterfall and several small caves. The trail is about 2.4 miles and starts at about 7840 foot elevation. To reach the trailhead, take State Route 157, travel 2 miles west of the ranger station to Echo Road. After traveling .35 mile, take the left fork off Echo Road and continue up until the road ends. Dogs must be on leash.

Restaurants

Henderson

Jitters Gourmet Coffee
75 S. Valle Verde Drive
Henderson, NV 89012
702-990-7900
Thanks to one of our readers for recommending this restaurant. Here is what they said about it. "You order inside at this strip-mall place, but they have a really nice patio that is separated from the street and well-landscaped. The owners are dog-lovers, and they make sure dogs are comfortable on the patio by making huge water bowls available."

Manhattan Bagel
1500 N. Green Valley Parkway
Henderson, NV
702-260-9511
Dogs are allowed at the outdoor tables.

Las Vegas

Baja Fresh Mexican Grill
1380 E Flamingo Rd
Las Vegas, NV
702-699-8920
Dogs are allowed at the outdoor tables.

Baja Fresh Mexican Grill
8780 W Charleston Blvd # 100
Las Vegas, NV
702-948-4043
Dogs are allowed at the outdoor tables.

Baja Fresh Mexican Grill
7501 W Lake Mead Blvd # 100
Las Vegas, NV
702-838-4100
Dogs are allowed at the outdoor tables.

Baja Fresh Mexican Grill
9310 S Eastern Ave
Las Vegas, NV
702-563-2800
Dogs on leash are allowed at the outdoor tables.

Einstein Brothers Bagels
9031 W. Sahara Ave
Las Vegas, NV
702-254-0919
Dogs are allowed at the outdoor tables.

In-N-Out Burger
2900 W. Sahara Ave.
Las Vegas, NV
800-786-1000
This fast food restaurant serves great hamburgers and fries.

Java Joint
23 N Nellis Blvd
Las Vegas, NV
702-459-8166
Dogs are allowed at the outdoor tables.

Joey's Only Seafood Restaurants
114 Durango Drive
Las Vegas, NV 89129
702-242-2888
This restaurant serves seafood appetizers, soups, salads, main dishes and more. Dogs are allowed at the outdoor tables.

Leo's Deli
4055 S. Maryland Parkway
Las Vegas, NV
702-733-7827
Dogs are allowed at the outdoor tables. The deli, located in the Target shopping center, is named after the owner's dog, Leo.

Mountain Ham Deli
920 S Rampart Blvd
Las Vegas, NV
702-933-4262
Dogs are allowed at the outdoor tables.

Mountain Springs Saloon
Highway 160
Las Vegas, NV
702-875-4266
Dogs are welcome at the outdoor dining area. This bar has a limited food menu and serves a variety of beer. The bar has live music Friday and Saturday nights. They are located near the Mountain Springs Summit, about 15-20 minutes west of downtown Las Vegas.

Wild Sage Cafe
600 E Warm Springs Rd
Las Vegas, NV
702-944-7243
Dogs are allowed at the outdoor tables.

Stores

Las Vegas

Harley-Davidson Store
2605 S. Eastern Avenue
Las Vegas, NV 89109
702-431-8500
Well-behaved, leashed dogs are allowed inside this store, which is the world's largest Harley dealership. Whether you own a Harley or just wish you could own one, stop by the store and take a look around. This is a popular place for locals and tourists. The store is located about 15 minutes north of downtown Las Vegas.

Vets and Kennels

Las Vegas

A-V.I.P. Kennel
6808 La Cienega
Las Vegas, NV
s. of McCarran Airport
702-361-8900
This kennel offers day boarding and long-term boarding. They have indoor/outdoor kennel runs and a grass exercise yard. The indoor facilities are climate controlled. The day boarding runs about $14 per day for a large dog (possibly less for a small dog). They are open Monday through Saturday from 8am-5pm and Sunday from 10am-2pm. There are no specific drop off or pick up times. However, you might want to call ahead and make a reservation just in case. The kennel is located about 5 minutes from the Strip, and the airport and their slogan is "Where Your Pets Are Treated

Like Family".

Animal Emergency Service
1914 E Sahara Ave
Las Vegas, NV 89104
near Eastern Ave
702-457-8050
Monday - Friday 6 pm to 8 am, Saturday noon - Monday 8 am.

The Animal Inn Kennels
3460 W Oquendo Road
Las Vegas, NV 89118
702-736-0036
Full service boarding kennel. Well established in Las Vegas for over 40 years. Conveniently located right off of I-15. Daycare, overnight and long term boarders welcome. $14 - $18 standard daily rate. Discounts for 2 or more dogs boarding together. Weekly and monthly discounts available. Large individual indoor/outdoor climate controlled runs. Special diets or medications administered at no extra charge. 1/2 acre tree lined grass play yard. Office hours are Mon - Fri 8 am - 6 pm, Sat - Sun 8 am - 5 pm. Please call 702-736-0036 to make a reservation.

Reno City Guide

Accommodations

Carson City

Best Value Motel
2731 S Carson St
Carson City, NV
775-882-2007
There is a $30 refundable pet deposit.

Super 8 Motel
2829 S. Carson Street
Carson City, NV
775-883-7800
There is a $6 per day pet fee.

Reno

Days Inn

701 E 7th
Reno, NV 89512
775-786-4070
There is a $10 per day pet fee.

Holiday Inn
1000 E. 6th St.
Reno, NV 89512
775-786-5151
This hotel is located only 4 blocks from Reno's famous gaming strip and within walking distance to the Reno Livestock & Events Center. Amenities include a heated pool and gift shop. There is a $10 per day pet charge.

Motel 6 - Virginia/Plumb
1901 S. Virginia St
Reno, NV 89502
775-827-0255
There are no additional pet fees.

Residence Inn by Marriott
9845 Gateway Drive
Reno, NV 89511
775-853-8800
Every room is a suite with a bedroom area, living room area and kitchen. Amenities include room service, self service laundry facilities, complimentary continental breakfast, an outdoor pool and exercise room. Rooms include hairdryers and iron/ironing boards. There is a one time non-refundable $80 pet charge and an additional $6 per day for pets.

Rodeway Inn
2050 Market Street
Reno, NV 89502
775-786-2500
This hotel (previously Travelodge) is about a mile from the Reno gambling strip. Amenities include a complimentary continental breakfast, heated outdoor pool, kitchenettes in some rooms, and wheelchair accessible rooms. There is a $10 per day pet charge.

Truckee River Lodge
501 W. 1st Street

Reno, NV 89503
775-786-8888
There is a $10 per day pet fee.
All rooms in the hotel are non-smoking. There is a park across the street.

Vagabond Inn
3131 S. Virginia St.
Reno, NV 89502
775-825-7134
This motel is located less than a couple miles from the downtown casinos and the Convention Center. Amenities include a swimming pool, 24 hour cable television, air conditioning, and more. There is a $10 per day pet fee.

Attractions

Virginia City

Virginia & Truckee Railroad Co.
565 S. K Street
Virginia City, NV 89440
775-847-0380
You and your dog can ride back in time on this steam train. The train takes you on a leisurely 35 minute round trip to the historic station in the city of Gold Hill. Passengers can get off the train at Gold Hill, visit the historic old town and then board the next train. The conductor gives a narration of the many historic sites you will view from the train. Your dog is welcome to join you on either the open air railcar or the enclosed railcar. Trains operate everyday from May through October. The round trip fare is about $5 for adults and about $3 for children. Prices are subject to change. Tickets can be purchased at the railcar on C Street or next to the train depot near Washington and F Streets. The train ride is located in Virginia City, about 30-40 minutes south of Reno.

Virginia City
Hwy 341

Virginia City, NV 89440
775-847-0311
This small town was built in the late 1800s and was a booming mining town. The restored Old Western town now has a variety of shops with wooden walkways. Dogs are allowed to window shop with you. Dogs are also welcome to ride the Virginia & Truckee Steam Train with you. Virginia City is located about 30-40 minutes south of Reno.

Parks

Carson City

Toiyabe National Forest
Hwy 395
Carson City, NV
S. Stewart St.

There are several dog-friendly hiking trails on the national forest land in Carson City. These are desert-like trails, so only go with your dog when the weather is cooler. If it's hot, the sand may burn your pup's paws. Visit the Carson Ranger Station for maps and trail information about the Toiyable National Forest. The station is located on Hwy 395, near S. Stewart Street. Dogs should be leashed.

Washoe Lake State Park
4855 East Lake Blvd.
Carson City, NV 89704
775-687-4319
This park is frequently used for bird watching, hiking, horseback riding, picnicking, windsurfing, water skiing, jet skiing, fishing and during certain times of the year, hunting. There are many trails at this park for hikers, mountain bikers, and equestrians. Pets must be leashed at all times, except at the Wetlands during hunting season. The park is located off U.S. 395, 10 miles north of Carson City and 15

miles south of Reno.

Reno

Donnelly Park
Mayberry Drive
Reno, NV
at McCarran Blvd.

This is a small, but nice park to walk around with your dog. It is across the street from Scraps Dog Bakery and Walden's Coffee. Dogs must be leashed.

Rancho San Rafael Park
Hillside Drive
Reno, NV
N. Sierra St.

Dogs are allowed in the undeveloped areas of this park. Leashed dogs are allowed on a hiking and walking path which crosses over McCarren Blvd. It is a dirt trail which narrows to a single track trail once you cross over McCarren Blvd. Just be careful when crossing over McCarren - the speed limit is about 45-50mph. To get there from Hwy 80, exit Keystone Ave. Head north on Keystone. Turn right onto Coleman Drive. Take Coleman until it almost ends and turn right into the park. Park near the Coleman intersection and the trailhead will be nearby. Dogs must be leashed.

Sutcliffe

Pyramid Lake
Hwy 445
Sutcliffe, NV
775-574-1000
Pyramid Lake is located in an Indian reservation, but visitors to the lake are welcomed guests of the Pyramid Lake Tribe of the Paiute Indians. Your leashed dog is also welcome. The lake is a beautiful contrast to the desert sandstone mountains which surround it. It is about 15 miles long by 11 miles wide, and among interesting rock

formations. Pyramid Lake is Nevada's largest natural lake. It is popular for fishing and photography. The north end of the lake is off-limits to visitors because it is a sacred area to the Paiutes. There is a beach area near the ranger's station in Sutcliffe. Be careful when wading into the water, as there are some ledges which drop off into deeper water. Also, do not wade in the water at the south end of the lake because the dirt acts like quick sand. The lake is about 35-40 minutes north of Reno, off Hwy 445.

Restaurants

Carson City

Comma Coffee
312 S. Carson Street
Carson City, NV 775-883-2662

This cafe serves breakfast and lunch, as well as fruit smoothies, juices, cappuccinos, lattes, mochas and more. Dogs are welcome at the outdoor patio tables.

Mom and Pop's Diner
224 S. Carson St.
Carson City, NV 89701
775-884-4411
This restaurant serves breakfast, lunch and dinner. Dogs are allowed at the outdoor tables.

Quiznos
3228 N. Carson Street
Carson City, NV
775-882-7849
This restaurant serves a variety of sandwiches. Dogs are allowed at the outdoor tables.

Schlotzsky's Deli
1410 East Williams St.
Carson City, NV
775-882-5777
They have a few tables outside. Dogs are allowed at the outdoor tables.

Reno

Archie's Grill
2195 N. Virginia St.
Reno, NV 89503
775-322-9595
This restaurant serves breakfast, lunch and dinner. Your dog is allowed at the outdoor tables.

Chevy's Fresh Mex Restaurant
4955 S. Virginia Street
Reno, NV
775-829-8008
Dogs are allowed at the outdoor tables.

Java Jungle
246 W. 1st Street
Reno, NV 89509
775-329-4484
Java Jungle was voted "Best Espresso and Cappuccino of Reno" in the Reno Gazette-Journal reader surveys. The wide variety of their customers include lawyers and judges on their way to the Washoe County Courthouse as well as joggers and dog walkers. It is located in downtown Reno, near the Truckee River. Dogs are welcome at the outdoor tables.

My Favorite Muffin & Bagel Cafe
340 California Ave.
Reno, NV 89509
775-333-1025
This cafe was voted Reno's Best Bagels. As the name of the cafe implies, they serve bagels and muffins. Your dog is allowed at the outdoor tables.

Peg's Glorified Ham & Eggs
425 S. Sierra St.
Reno, NV 89501
775-329-2600
This restaurant is located in downtown and has a few outdoor tables. Your dog is allowed at the outdoor tables.

Quiznos
4965 S. Virginia Street
Reno, NV
775-828-5252
They serve a variety of sandwiches. Dogs are allowed at the outdoor tables.

Romanos Macaroni Grill
5505 S. Virginia St.
Reno, NV
775-448-9994
Well-behaved, leashed dogs are allowed at some of the perimeter tables.

Sage Creek Grill and Taproom
5851 South Virginia Street
Reno, NV
775-829-4600
Well-behaved dogs are allowed at the outdoor tables, but must be leashed. The restaurant is open for lunch and dinner.

Schlotzsky's Deli
10590 N McCarran Blvd.
Reno, NV
775-746-8284
Dogs are allowed at the outdoor tables.

Schlotzsky's Deli
8030 S. Virginia Street
Reno, NV
775-852-3354
Dogs are allowed at the outdoor tables. Please remember to keep your dog leashed.

Walden's Coffee Co.
3940 Mayberry Drive
Reno, NV 89509
775-787-3307
Your dog is welcome at the outdoor tables at coffee house. They have a variety of pastries and snacks available. The Scraps Dog Bakery is in the same shopping center (see Attractions.)

Sparks

Rapscallions' Roadhouse Grill
1250 Disc Drive
Sparks, NV
775-626-7066

Dogs are allowed at one of their perimeter tables.

Virginia City

Angel Station Deli
204 South C Street
Virginia City, NV

This deli serves a variety of sandwiches, wraps and salads. Dogs are allowed at the outdoor tables. They usually have a dog bowl of water for visiting pooches.

Firehouse BBQ
204 South C Street
Virginia City, NV 89440
775-847-4774
You and your pup will be tempted to stop here for lunch or dinner after you smell the delicious BBQ. This restaurant is located on the main street in historic Virginia City. Dogs are allowed at the outdoor tables.

Stores

Reno

Harley Davidson of Reno
2295 Market Street
Reno, NV 89502
775-329-2913
Well-behaved leashed dogs are allowed in this store. In addition to the motorcycles, they also sell collectibles, riding gear and accessories.

Scraps Dog Bakery
3890 Mayberry Drive
Reno, NV 89509
775-787-3647
Your dog is welcome inside this bakery which sells cookies and goodies for your pup. They also have a general store which sells other doggie items.

Virginia City

Bogie's Beer Collectibles
182 South C

Virginia City, NV 89440
Hwy 341
775-847-9300
Bogie's Beer Collectibles is a small retail store in historic Virginia City. They sell beer collectibles, brew bags and other fun collectible items. The owner is a dog lover and allows your dog inside the store. They even have a sign outside that says "Kids, Dogs & Cats Welcome in Bogie's. Please Tie Horses & Mules Outside."

Vets and Kennels

Carson City

Carson Tahoe Veterinary Hospital
3389 S. Carson Street
Carson City, NV
775-883-8238
Weekdays 7:30 am - 6 pm. Emergencies will be seen 24 hours with an additional $60 emergency fee.

Reno

Animal Emergency Center
6427 S Virginia St
Reno, NV 89511
Hwy 395 and Del Monte Lane
775-851-3600
Monday - Friday 6 pm to 8 am, Saturday noon - Monday 8 am.

San Diego City Guide

Accommodations

Chula Vista

Motel 6
745 E Street
Chula Vista, CA 91910
619-422-4200
A well-behaved large dog is okay. Dogs must be attended at all times.

Vagabond Inn
230 Broadway St.
Chula Vista, CA 91910
619-422-8305
This motel is located within several miles of downtown San Diego. Amenities include two swimming pools, continental breakfast, cable television and more hotel amenities. Pets are an additional $10 per day.

Coronado

Crown City Inn
520 Orange Ave
Coronado, CA 92118
619-435-3116
This inn is located in beautiful Coronado which is across the harbor from downtown San Diego. Walk to several outdoor restaurants or to the Coronado Centennial Park. Room service is available. Pet charges are $8 per day for a designated pet room and $25 per day for a non-designated pet room. They have non-smoking rooms available. Pets must never be left unattended in the room.

Loews Coronado Bay Resort
4000 Coronado Bay Road
Coronado, CA 92118
619-424-4000
All well-behaved dogs of any size are welcome. This upscale hotel offers their "Loews Loves Pets" program which includes special pet treats, local dog walking routes, and a list of nearby pet-friendly places to visit. There are no pet fees.

El Cajon

Motel 6
550 Montrose Court
El Cajon, CA 92020
619-588-6100
There are no additional pet fees.

La Jolla

Andrea Villa Inn

2402 Torrey Pines Rd
La Jolla, CA 92037
858-459-3311
Nestled in the heart of beautiful La Jolla, this inn is conveniently located near cosmopolitan shopping and dining experiences. The beaches of La Jolla Shores are within easy walking distance. There is a $25 one time pet charge.

La Jolla Village Lodge
1141 Silverado Street
La Jolla, CA 92037
858-551-2001
There is a $20 one time pet fee. Thanks to a reader for recommending this hotel.

Residence Inn by Marriott
8901 Gilman Dr.
La Jolla, CA 92037
858-587-1770
Every room is a suite that includes a bedroom area, living room, and kitchen. This inn is located about 3-4 miles north of downtown La Jolla. There is a $50 one time pet fee and a $10 per day pet fee.

National City

Super 8
425 Roosevelt Ave
National City, CA 91950
619-474-8811
There is a $15 per day additional pet fee.

San Diego

Best Western Lamplighter Inn & Suites
6474 El Cajon Blvd
San Diego, CA 92115
800-545-0778
This motel is located in the suburbs of San Diego. If you are visiting someone from San Diego State University, this motel is nearby. It's also about 7-8 miles from the dog-friendly Mission Trails Regional Park. There is a $10 per day pet charge.

Harborview Inn & Suites
550 West Grape St
San Diego, CA
619-233-7799
There is a $15 per day pet fee.

Holiday Inn on the Bay
1355 N Harbor Dr
San Diego, CA 92101
619-232-3861
This Holiday Inn has a 5 and 14 story building which overlooks the harbor. Across the street from the hotel is a harborside walkway. There is a $100 pet deposit ($75 refundable and $25 non-refundable).

Homestead Suites
7444 Mission Valley Rd
San Diego, CA
619-299-2292
There is a $75 one time pet fee per visit.

La Quinta Inn San Diego - Rancho Penasquitos
10185 Paseo Montril
San Diego, CA
858-484-8800
Dogs up to 50 pounds are allowed at the hotel.

Marriott San Diego Marina
333 West Harbor Drive
San Diego, CA 92101
619-234-1500
This hotel is right next to the the San Diego Harbor. If you want to stretch your legs, there is also a nice walkway that goes about a mile along the harborside. There are no pet charges.

Ocean Villa Inn
5142 West Point Loma Blvd.
San Diego, CA 92107
619-224-3481
There is a $100 per deposit for up to 2 pets. Of this $25 is non-refundable and $75 is refundable. There is an additional charge for more than 2 pets.

Pacific Inn Hotel & Suites

1655 Pacific Hwy
San Diego, CA
619-232-6391
There is a $10 per day additional pet fee.

Red Lion Hanalei Hotel
2270 Hotel Circle North
San Diego, CA 92108
619-297-1101
This hotel is located in the heart of Mission Valley. Dogs under 50 pounds are allowed. There is a $50 refundable pet deposit.

Residence Inn
11002 Rancho Carmel Dr
San Diego, CA 92128
858-673-1900
There is a $150 one time pet fee and a $10 per day additional pet fee.

Residence Inn
5995 Pacific Mesa Court
San Diego, CA 92121
858-552-9100
There is a $150 one time pet fee and a $10 per day additional pet fee.

Residence Inn - Downtown
1747 Pacific Highway
San Diego, CA 92101
619-338-8200
There is a $100 one time pet fee and a $10 per day additional pet fee.

Residence Inn by Marriott
5400 Kearny Mesa Rd
San Diego, CA 92111
858-278-2100
This suite style inn is located north of San Diego. Dinner delivery service is available from local restaurants. Limit two pets per room. They charge a $100 non-refundable pet fee and $7 per day pet charge. Dogs up to 65 pounds are allowed.

San Diego Marriott - Mission Valley
8757 Rio San Diego Dr
San Diego, CA 92108
619-692-3800
This hotel is about 3-4 miles

from Old Town State Historic Park and approximately 5-6 miles from the Mission Trails Regional Park. Room service is available. There is a $200 pet deposit ($150 is refundable and $50 is non-refundable.)

San Diego Marriott Suites
701 A Street
San Diego, CA 92101
619-696-9800
There is a $50 one time pet fee per visit.

Sheraton San Diego Hotel and Marina
1380 Harbor Island Drive
San Diego, CA 92101
619-291-2900
Dogs up to 80 pounds are allowed. There are no additional pet fees. Only one dog is permitted per room.

Sheraton Suites San Diego
701 A. Street
San Diego, CA 92101
619-696-9800
Dogs of all sizes are allowed. There is a $100 one time pet fee per stay. There is a $50 refundable deposit per stay for pets.

Staybridge Suites
6639 Mira Mesa Blvd
San Diego, CA 92121
800-238-8000
There is a $75 one time pet fee.

Vagabond Inn-Mission Bay
4540 Mission Bay Dr.
San Diego, CA 92109
858-274-7888
This motel is located within several miles of the Old Town Historic State Park and SeaWorld. It is also close to the popular Dog Beach in Ocean Beach. The motel features an outdoor swimming pool, cable television, guest laundry service and more hotel amenities. There is an additional pet charge of $10 per day.

Vagabond Inn-Point Loma

1325 Scott St.
San Diego, CA 92106
619-224-3371
This motel is located less than five miles from downtown San Diego and Sea World. It is close to the popular Dog Beach in Ocean Beach. The motel features an outdoor swimming pool, family unit rooms, cable television and more hotel amenities. Dogs up to about 70-75 pounds are allowed and there is an additional $10 per day pet fee.

W San Diego
421 West B. Street
San Diego, CA 92101
619-231-8220
Dogs up to 80 pounds are allowed. There is a $100 non-refundable cleaning fee for pets. There is a $25 per night pet fee.

Motel 6 - Border
160 E Calie Primera
San Ysidro, CA 92173
619-690-6663
This hotel is very close to the Mexican border in San Diego.

The Hohe House
4905 Dixie Drive
San Diego, CA 92109
858-273-0324
The Hohe (Hoy) House is a spacious, non-smoking, 2 bedroom/2 bath, Ocean View, Private residence in a unique Pacific Beach neighborhood; close to all (Beach, Boardwalk, Restaurants, Nightlife, & Shopping), yet quietly removed from the hubs of activity. The Hohe House sleeps 6 (1 King, 2 Doubles, and a queen sleeper sofa) and is fully furnished with all linens

provided. Amenities include: Beach chairs, Beach towels, Boogie boards, Umbrellas, Coolers, & Bicycles for your Beach enjoyment... This is a great dog friendly area. There is a 4 night minimum during the low season, $200 nightly, (Mid-Sept to Mid-June), and rates vary for low to high season, from $1275 to $1875 weekly. Additional 10.5% hotel room tax applies and rates are subject to change. A $350 refundable, security deposit is required to reserve a week's stay and balance is due 30 days prior to arrival. There is a $10 per night pet fee. Well-behaved dogs over 18 months and under 80 pounds are welcome. They will gladly email the entire pet policy to you.

Cinderella Carriage Rides

San Diego, CA
619-239-8080
You and your dog can enjoy a carriage ride throughout downtown San Diego. The horse and carriages are located in the Gaslamp Quarter at 5th and F Streets, or call ahead and get a carriage to pick you up from your downtown hotel. The rides are from 6pm-11pm. Rates start at $15 for about a 10 minute ride and go up to $95 for 60 minutes. Prices are subject to change. The carriages hold 3-4 people plus a dog. They accept cash or credit card.

Family Kayak Adventure Center
4217 Swift Avenue
San Diego, CA 92104
619-282-3520
This company offers guided kayaking adventure tours to people of all ages and abilities. For beginners they offer paddles

on flat water in stable tandem kayaks that hold one to four people. All equipment and instruction is provided for an enjoyable first outing. Well-behaved dogs are also welcome. There is even a "Dog Paddles" tour which is an evening tour on Mission Bay that includes quality time on the water and on Fiesta Island's leash free area.

Old Town State Historic Park
San Diego Ave & Twiggs St
San Diego, CA
619-220-5422
Old Town demonstrates life in the Mexican and early American periods of 1821 to 1872 (including 5 original adobe buildings). There are shops, several outdoor cafes and live music. Since pups are not allowed inside the buildings, you can shop at the many outdoor retail kiosks throughout the town. There are several food concessions where you can order the food and then take it to an outdoor table. After walking around, relax with your best friend by listening to a variety of live music. If your dog wants to see more trees and green grass, take a quick drive over to Presidio Park which is close to Old Town (see Parks).

SeaWorld of California-Kennels
1720 South Shore Rd.
San Diego, CA 92109
in Mission Bay
619-226-3901
This may not be your dog's idea of an attraction, but it is nice to know that SeaWorld has day kennels at the main entrance of their Adventure Park. The kennels are attended at all times and you can visit your dog throughout the day when you need a break from the attractions. The day boarding is open the same hours as the park and cost only $5 for the whole day. Kennels range in

size from small to large. Thanks to one of our San Diego readers for telling us about this.

Seaforth Boat Rentals
333 W Harbor Dr
San Diego, CA 92101
Marriott Marina-Gate 1
619-239-BOAT
Rent a sail or power boat from this shop located between Seaport Village and the Marriott San Diego Marina Hotel. You'll find much to see in the San Diego Bay, but remember you'll also be sharing the space with fishing boats and some Navy ships like aircraft carriers. Prices start at $25/hr for a 14' sail boat (up to 30' available) and $65/hr for a 17' power boat (up to 27' available). They say dogs are allowed as long as you clean up after them. Prices are subject to change.

Beaches

Coronado

North Beach Dog Run
Ocean Blvd.
Coronado, CA
Ocean Drive

This dog beach is located in the city of Coronado at the end of Ocean Blvd next to the U.S. Naval Station entrance. Park on the street and walk along the Naval Station fence until you reach the ocean and then bear right. There will be signs posted for the North Beach Dog Run.

La Jolla

La Jolla Shores Beach
Camino Del Oro
La Jolla, CA
Vallecitos Ct
619-221-8900
Leashed dogs are allowed on this beach and the adjacent Kellogg Park from 6pm to 9am.

The beach is about 1/2 mile long. To get there, take Hwy 5 to the La Jolla Village Drive exit heading west. Turn left onto Torrey Pines Rd. Then turn right onto La Jolla Shores Drive. Go 4-5 blocks and turn left onto Vallecitos. Go straight until you reach the beach and Kellogg Park.

Point La Jolla Beaches
Coast Blvd.
La Jolla, CA
near Prospect & Ivanhoe
619-221-8900
Leashed dogs are allowed on this beach and the walkway (paved and dirt trails) from 6pm to 9am. The beaches and walkway are at least a 1/2 mile long and might continue further. To get there, exit La Jolla Village Drive West from Hwy 5. Turn left onto Torrey Pines Rd. Turn right on Prospect and then park or turn right onto Coast Blvd. Parking is limited around the village area.

Ocean Beach

Dog Beach
Point Loma Blvd.
Ocean Beach, CA
619-221-8900
Dogs are allowed to run off leash at this beach anytime during the day. This is a very popular dog beach which attracts lots and lots of dogs on warm days. To get there, take Hwy 8 West until it ends and then it becomes Sunset Cliffs Blvd. Then make a right turn onto Point Loma Blvd and follow the signs to Ocean Beach's Dog Beach.

Ocean Beach
Point Loma Blvd.
Ocean Beach, CA
619-221-8900
Leashed dogs are allowed on this beach from 6pm to 9am. The beach is about 1/2 mile long. To get there, take Hwy 8

West until it ends and then it becomes Sunset Cliffs Blvd. Then make a right turn onto Point Loma Blvd and follow the signs to Ocean Beach Park. A separate beach called Dog Beach is at the north end of this beach which allows dogs to run off-leash.

San Diego

Fiesta Island
Fiesta Island Road
San Diego, CA
Mission Bay Drive
619-221-8900
On this island, dogs are allowed to run off-leash anywhere outside the fenced areas, anytime during the day. It is mostly sand which is perfect for those beach loving hounds. You might, however, want to stay on the north end of the island. The south end was used as the city's sludge area (mud and sediment, and possibly smelly) processing facility. The island is often used to launch jet-skis and motorboats. There is a one-way road that goes around the island and there are no fences, so please make sure your dog stays away from the road. About half way around the island, there is a completely fenced area on the beach. Please note that the fully enclosed area is not a dog park. The city of San Diego informed us that is supposed to be locked and is not intended to be used as a dog park even though there may occasionally be dogs running in this off-limits area.

Parks

Coronado

Bayshore Bikeway
Silver Strand Blvd.
Coronado, CA
(Glorietta Bay Park)

If you are in Coronado and really want to stretch your legs, you can go for a run or walk on the Bayshore Bikeway. The path is about 6 miles long each way. It starts by the Glorietta Bay Park and continues south along Silver Strand Blvd. There's not too much shade along this path, so your pup might not want to go on a hot day. Dogs need to be leashed.

Centennial & Tidelands Parks
Orange Ave and First St.
Coronado, CA

We have combined these two parks because there is a scenic 1/2 - 1 mile path between them. Both of these parks provide nice photo opportunities of downtown San Diego and the San Diego Bay. Dogs must be leashed.

La Mesa

Harry Griffen Park
9550 Milden Street
La Mesa, CA
619-667-1307
Thanks to one of our readers who writes: "A leash-free dog area - very nice area of the park and no restrictions on dog size."

Ocean Beach

Dusty Rhodes Dog Park
Sunset Cliffs Blvd.
Ocean Beach, CA
619-236-5555
This dog park is located in Dusty Rhodes Neighborhood Park. The park is on Sunset Cliffs Blvd. between Nimitz and West Point Loma.

San Diego

Balboa Park
El Prado St
San Diego, CA
Hwy 163

619-235-1121
Balboa Park is a 1200 acre urban cultural park located just east of downtown. Dogs must be leashed and under control of the owner at all times, including on the trails and in the canyons. The park is known for its brilliant displays of seasonal flowers, an award-winning rose garden, shady groves of trees, and meandering paths. Many of Balboa Park's museums are magnificent Spanish Colonial Revival buildings, originally constructed for the 1915-1916 Panama-California Exposition. If you are interested in the architecture, you and your pup can take an outdoor walking tour around the various buildings. Work up an appetite after walking around? There is a concession stand called In the Park. It has many outdoor seats and is located at the corner of Village Place and Old Globe Way. For a map of the park, stop by the Visitors Center on El Prado St near Hwy 163. There is also an unfenced dog run on the west side of the park by El Prado and Balboa Drive.

Balboa Park Dog Run
Balboa Dr
San Diego, CA
El Prado St
619-235-1100
The dog-friendly Balboa Park has set aside a portion of land for an off leash dog run. It's not fenced, so make sure your pup listens to voice commands. It is located between Balboa Drive and Hwy 163.

Mission Bay Park
Mission Bay Drive
San Diego, CA
Clairemont Dr & Hwy 5
619-221-8900
Leashed dogs are allowed in this park from 6pm to 9am. There are over 20 miles of beaches that make up this park (including Fiesta Island). If you come during the above

mentioned hours, there is also a nice path that meanders through the grass and trees.

Mission Beach & Promenade
Mission Blvd.
San Diego, CA
Mission Bay Drive
619-221-8900
Leashed dogs are allowed on this beach and promenade walkway from 6pm to 9am. It is about 3 miles long and located west of Mission Bay Park.

Mission Trails Regional Park
1 Father Junipero Serra Trail
San Diego, CA 92119
Mission Gorge Rd
619-668-3275
This 6,000 acre regional park has a nice variety of trails ranging from an easy 1 mile loop to a strenuous 5 mile hike with elevation gains of up to 1150 feet. Dogs are allowed, but must be leashed at all times. Don't forget to bring enough water since it can get pretty warm here year-round. The park is located off Mission Gorge Rd at the corners of Father Junipero Serra Trail and Echo Dell Rd. It is located about 8-9 northeast of downtown San Diego. Maps are available at the Visitor and Interpretive Center on Father Junipero Serra Trail.

Presidio Park
Jackson St
San Diego, CA
by Old Town
619-235-1100
This is a nice park for your pup to stretch his or her legs before or after you visit Old Town State Historic Park which is located about 2-3 blocks away. Dogs must be leashed in the park.

Tecolote Canyon Natural Park
Tecolote Road
San Diego, CA
Hwy 5
619-581-9952
This is a very nice natural park with over 6 miles (12 round trip)

of walking, running or mountain biking trails. There are nine entry points into the park, but we recommend you start at the Visitors and Nature Center where you can pick up a trail map from the ranger. If you start at the Nature Center, most of the trail (first five miles) is relatively flat. It gets steeper in the last mile and there could be some creek crossings. From the Nature Center, follow the path which will take you past a golf course. At the end of the golf course, you'll need to take Snead Ave which will join up with the rest of the path. There might be a few more street crossings, but the majority of the walk is on the dirt trail. With the all the natural surroundings it seems like it is far from the city, but it's located only 6-7 miles from downtown. To get there, take Tecolote Road until it ends. Dogs must be on leash in the park.

Restaurants

Coronado

Cafe 1134
1134 Orange Ave
Coronado, CA
619-437-1134
Cafe 1134 offers coffee and a full bistro menu. Dogs are allowed at the outdoor tables.

PrimaVera Pastry Caffe
956 Orange Ave
Coronado, CA
619-435-4191
Come to this bakery and deli for breakfast, lunch or dinner. Dogs are allowed at the outdoor tables.

Rhinoceros Cafe and Grill
1166 Orange Ave
Coronado, CA
619-435-2121
The folks we spoke with here said they are very dog-friendly. For lunch and dinner, they

serve steaks, ribs, chicken and pasta dishes seven days a week. Breakfast is served on the weekends. Dogs are welcome at the outdoor tables.

La Jolla

Elijah's
8861 Villa La Jolla Drive
La Jolla, CA
858-455-1461
Dogs are allowed at the outdoor tables.

Girard Gourmet
7837 Girard Ave
La Jolla, CA
858-454-3321
This cafe and bakery serves gourmet deli food and baked goods. They have several outdoor tables.

Putnam's Restaurant & Bar
910 Prospect St
La Jolla, CA
858-454-2181
Located in the Grand Colonial Inn, Putnam's serves breakfast, lunch, dinner and Sunday brunch. They offer contemporary world cuisine by an award-winning chef. Dogs are allowed at the outdoor tables.

San Diego

Gulf Coast Grill
4130 Park Blvd
San Diego, CA 92103
619-295-2244
Gulf Coast Grill serves lunch and dinner daily. The specialty is southern and southwestern cuisine. Dogs may dine with you on the outside patio.

Hard Rock Cafe
801 4th Ave
San Diego, CA
(downtown)
619-615-7625
This is one of the Hard Rock Cafe chain locations. They have 2-3 outdoor tables for dining. The menu offers a variety of

burgers, chicken, desserts and more.

Rubio's Baja Grill
901 4th Ave
San Diego, CA
(downtown)
619-231-7731
Rubio's prides themselves on their fish tacos, but they also have a variety of other food like tacos, burritos, and even healthy low fat items. They are a large chain located throughout Southern California. Dogs are allowed at the outdoor tables.

Sally's Restaurant & Bar
1 Market Place
San Diego, CA
(by Seaport Village)
619-687-6080
Dogs are welcome at the tables that are next to the lawn. Dogs need to sit or lay on the grass, which is next to your table. This popular seafood restaurant usually draws a crowd at the outdoor tables, so call ahead so that they can hold a table near the grass. There are nice views of the marina and San Diego Bay from the patio. Sally's is located between Seaport Village and the Marriott San Diego Marina Hotel. The restaurant is open for lunch and dinner.

Seven 17 Restaurant
717 4th Ave
San Diego, CA
(downtown)
619-232-4440
The restaurant allows well-behaved dogs at their outside tables. They are open 7 days a week for dinner.

Terra
3900 Block of Vermont
San Diego, CA 92103
619-293-7088
This restaurant comes highly recommended from one of our readers who says "It has dog food from The Original Paw Pleasers on the menu and lets you bring your dogs to eat with

you at their outdoor dining area... Sometimes they have pet parties too." They are located in the Hillcrest area of San Diego.

The Alamo
2502 San Diego Ave
San Diego, CA 92110
619-296-1112
This Mexican restaurant serves some tasty dishes and is located next to Old Town State Historic Park. Dogs are allowed at the outdoor tables.

Trattoria Fantastica
1735 India Street
San Diego, CA 92101
619-234-1735
Dogs are allowed at the tables on the front patio.

Stores

La Jolla

Restoration Hardware
4405 La Jolla Village Drive
La Jolla, CA
858-784-0575
Your well-behaved leashed dog is allowed inside this store.

San Diego

Neiman Marcus
7027 Friars Road
San Diego, CA 92108
Fashion Valley Center
619-692-9100
This famous department store, which sells everything from clothing to home furnishings, allows your well-behaved leashed dog to shop with you. It is located in Fashion Valley Center.

The Original Paw Pleasers Bakery
1220 Cleveland Ave
San Diego, CA 92103
Vermont
619-293-PAWS
Has your dog every dreamed of

going to a bakery where the fresh baked cookies and cakes are made just for canines? Your pup will be sure to drool over the specialty goodies like Tail Waggin' Treats, Bark-La-Va, Carob Brownies, Birthday Cakes and more. The cakes look perfect enough for human consumption, but they are actually for dogs. You'll be able to tell from the sign, "Pets Welcome, Owners Optional", that your pooch is more than welcome to peruse and drool over the treats. And if your pup is thirsty, these nice folks will provide a bowl of water. Also, make sure your pet tries the dog and cat yogurt bar with soft-serve frozen yogurt and a toppings bar that includes freeze-dried liver. The yogurt bar is available weekends in May & June and open daily in July & August. When in San Diego, be sure to stop by. If you don't have time, you can order via phone at 888-670-PAWS.

Vets and Kennels

San Diego

Animal ER of San Diego
5610 Kearny Mesa Rd
San Diego, CA 92111
Hwy 52
858-569-0600
Monday - Friday 6 pm to 8 am, 24 hours on weekends.

Animal Emergency Clinic
13240 Evening Creek Dr S
San Diego, CA 92128
858-748-7387
24 hours everyday.

Emergency Animal Clinic
2317 Hotel Cir S # A
San Diego, CA 92108
619-299-2400
Monday - Friday 6 pm to 8 am, 24 hours on weekends.

Los Angeles City Guide

Accommodations

Arcadia

Residence Inn - Arcadia
321 E. Huntington Dr/Gateway
Arcadia, CA 91006
626-446-6500
There is a $250 refundable deposit for pets. There is a $50 one time pet fee and a $6 per day additional pet fee.

Beverly Hills

Loews Beverly Hills Hotel
1224 S. Beverwil Drive
Beverly Hills, CA 90035
310-277-2800
All well-behaved dogs of any size are welcome. This upscale hotel offers their "Loews Loves Pets" program which includes room service for pets, special pet treats, local dog walking routes, and a list of nearby pet-friendly places to visit. There are no pet fees.

Culver City

Four Points by Sheraton
5990 Green Valley Circle
Culver City, CA 90230
310-641-7740
There is a $25 one time pet fee. Dogs are allowed only on the first floor.

Glendale

Vagabond Inn
120 W. Colorado Street
Glendale, CA 91204
818-240-1700
This motel is located near Universal Studios. Amenities include a complimentary breakfast and during the week, a free USA Today newspaper. There is a $10 per day pet fee.

Long Beach

Guesthouse International
5325 East Pacific Coast Highway
Long Beach, CA 90804
562-597-1341
There is a $10 one time pet fee.

Holiday Inn
2640 Lakewood Blvd
Long Beach, CA 90815
562-597-4401
Dogs are not allowed in the main tower. There is a $25 one time additional pet fee.

Los Angeles

Beverly Laurel Hotel
8018 Beverly Blvd
Los Angeles, CA 90048
323-651-2441
There is a $10 per day pet fee. Up to two pets per room are allowed. Thanks to one of our readers who wrote "Our large German Shepherd was welcome."

Four Points by Sheraton - LAX
9750 Airport Blvd
Los Angeles, CA 90045
310-645-4600
There is a $50 refundable deposit and a $10 per day pet fee. Dogs must be on a leash at all times on the premises.

Holiday Inn - Downtown
750 Garland Ave @ 8th St.
Los Angeles, CA 90017
213-628-9900
There is a $15 per day pet fee. A well-behaved large dog is okay.

Hotel Sofitel
8555 Beverly Blvd
Los Angeles, CA 90052
310-278-5444
This upscale hotel is located next to West Hollywood and Beverly Hills. You and your dog will feel most welcome at this hotel. Since parking is limited in this area, your car will be valet parked. They open the car doors not only for you, but for your dog too. You can feel comfortable registering at the front desk with your pup at your side and then taking the elevator to the room that awaits you. There is a restaurant at this hotel that has outdoor dining where your dog is also welcome. Room rates run about $150-250 per night, but your dog will be treated first class.

Le Meridien Hotel
465 South La Cienega Blvd.
Los Angeles, CA 90048
310-247-0400
Dogs up to 50 pounds are allowed. This luxury class hotel is located in one of the most prestigious areas in Los Angeles. They welcome both business and leisure travelers, as well as your dog of any size. Room rates at this first class hotel start at the low $300s per night. They sometimes offer special weekend rates. There is an additional $100 pet fee for the first night and an additional $25 for each additional day.

Los Angeles Airport Marriott Hotel
5885 W. Century Blvd.
Los Angeles, CA 90045
310-641-5700
Dogs are allowed on the ground floor only of this 18 story hotel, so be sure to call ahead and reserve a room. They have 24-hour room service. The hotel is located approximately a 1/2 mile from the Los Angeles Airport. Parking is $9 per day and valet parking is $11 per day. It's located on Century Blvd between Sepulveda & Aviation Blvds.

Travelodge Hotel at LAX
5547 W. Century Blvd.
Los Angeles, CA 90045
310-649-4000
This inn offers free parking, a feature not found with many of

the L.A./West Hollywood hotels. They welcome pets here at this 2 story inn which has interior/exterior corridors, a gift shop and heated pool. It is located about one mile east of the Los Angeles Airport. There is a $10 per day additional pet fee per pet.

Vagabond Inn
3101 S. Figueroa St.
Los Angeles, CA 90007
213-746-1531
This motel is located just 2 blocks from the University of Southern California (USC) and 2 miles from the LA Convention Center. It features an outdoor swimming pool, cable television, air conditioning and many more amenities. There is a $10 per day pet fee.

Manhattan Beach

Residence Inn by Marriott
1700 N Sepulveda Blvd
Manhattan Beach, CA 90266
310-546-7627
Every room at this inn is a suite with a living room, kitchen and bedroom. Amenities include an outdoor pool, complimentary continental breakfast, self service laundry facilities, and dinner delivery service from local restaurants. Room rates start at $125 and up. There is a $75 one time pet charge and an additional $8 per day for pets. If you reserve one of the penthouses, then there is a $100 one time pet charge.

Pico Rivera

Days Inn - Pico Rivera
6540 S. Rosemead Blvd
Pico Rivera, CA 90660
562-942-1003
There is a $15 per day pet fee.

Santa Monica

Le Merigot Beach Hotel and

Spa
1740 Ocean Avenue
Santa Monica, CA
310-395-9700
The hotel provides pet dishes and toys upon arrival. There is a $35 one time pet fee. There is also a $150 refundable pet deposit.

Loews Santa Monica Beach Hotel
1700 Ocean Avenue
Santa Monica, CA 90401
310-458-6700
All well-behaved dogs of any size are welcome. This upscale hotel offers their "Loews Loves Pets" program which includes special pet treats, local dog walking routes, and a list of nearby pet-friendly places to visit. There are no pet fees.

Torrance

Residence Inn - Torrance
3701 Torrance Blvd
Torrance, CA 90503
310-543-4566
There is a $40 one time pet fee and a $8 per day additional pet fee. There is also a $4 per day fee for each additional pet.

Universal City

Sheraton Universal Hotel
333 Universal Hollywood Drive
Universal City, CA 91608
818-980-1212
Dogs up to 80 pounds are allowed. There are no additional pet fees.

West Covina

Hampton Inn
3145 E. Garvey Ave
West Covina, CA 91791
626-967-5800
There are no additional pet fees.

Attractions

Beverly Hills

Hollywood Star's Homes
Self-Guided Walking Tour
Beverly Hills, CA

Want to check out the Star's homes in Beverly Hills with your dog? How about a self-guided walking tour of the Star's homes? All you need is a map and a good starting point. Maps can be purchased at many of the tourist shops on Hollywood Blvd. A good place to begin is at the Will Rogers Memorial Park in Beverly Hills (between Sunset Blvd, Beverly Dr and Canon Drive). It's a small park but still a good place for both of you to stretch your legs before beginning the walk. You can certainly plot out your own tour, but we have a few samples tours that will help you get started. TOUR 1 (approx 1 mile): From the park and Canon Street, turn left (heading west) onto Sunset Blvd. Turn right on Roxbury. Cross Benedict Canyon Rd and the road becomes Hartford Way. Take Hartford Way back to the park. TOUR 2 (approx 3 miles): From the park, head north on Beverly Drive and cross Sunset Blvd. Turn right on Rexford Drive. Turn right on Lomitas Ave and then left onto Crescent Drive. Make a right at Elevado Ave, walk for about 5 blocks and turn right onto Bedford Dr. Then turn left on Lomitas Ave, right on Whittier Dr and left on Greeway. Then turn right on Sunset Blvd and head back to the park.

Burbank

Los Angeles Equestrian Center
480 Riverside Drive
Burbank, CA 91506
818-840-9066
This is a nice diversion for those pups that enjoy being around horses. Southern California's

largest Equestrian Center has a covered arena where many top-rated horse shows are held throughout the year. Your dog is welcome to watch the horse shows if he or she doesn't bark and distract the horses. To see their upcoming events list, check out the official website at http://www.la-equestriancenter.com or call 818-840-9066. When there are no shows, you can still walk around on the grounds. There is a horse trail to the right of the main entrance where you can walk your dog. Or if you want to do some shopping, your dog is welcome in 1 of the 2 equestrian stores (which also has some dog treats and toys). The dog-friendly store is called Dominion Saddlery and is located behind the store that is next to the parking lot. They even have water bowls in the store for your pup.

Los Angeles

Century City Shopping Center
10250 Santa Monica Blvd
Los Angeles, CA 93309
310-277-3898
This dog-friendly outdoor shopping center, located just one mile from Rodeo Drive in Beverly Hills, is popular with many Hollywood actors and actresses. Your well-behaved dog is allowed inside many of the stores. For a list of dog-friendly stores, please look at our stores category.Your dog is also welcome to join you at the outdoor cafe tables in the food court area.

Griffith Observatory
2800 East Observatory Road
Los Angeles, CA 90027
(In Griffith Park)
323-664-1181
Please note: The Observatory will close in January 2002 and re-open to the public in late 2004. This observatory has been a major Los Angeles landmark since 1935. Star-gazing dogs are not allowed inside the Observatory, but you are allowed to walk to the roof (on the outside stairs) and get some great views of the Los Angeles basin and the Hollywood sign. Located across the parking lot from the Observatory is the Griffith Park snack shop and the Mt. Hollywood Trail (about 6 miles of dog-friendly trails). To get to there, take Hwy 5 to the Los Feliz Blvd exit and head west. Turn right on Hillhurst or Vermont Ave (they merge later). Go past the Bird Sanctuary and Greek Theater. Stay on Vermont Ave and you'll come to the Griffith Observatory.

Griffith Park Southern Railroad
4400 Crystal Springs Drive
Los Angeles, CA
Los Feliz Blvd.
323-664-6788
Does your pup want to try a train ride? This small train ride (serving the public since 1948) is popular with kids, but your dog will love it too. The seating area is kind of small and larger dogs will need to sit or stand on the floor by your feet. But don't worry, it's a pretty short ride whichs goes about 1 mile in distance. It'll give your pup a chance to decide if he/she is made for the rails. It's located in Griffith Park which also has several nice hikes that of course allow dogs. Hungry? There is a small snack stand located nearby with many picnic tables. While you eat lunch, you can watch the kids ride the rental ponies. Griffith Park is pretty large, so to find the train ride, take Los Feliz Bvld (near Hwy 5) to Crystal Springs Drive/Griffith Park Drive. Head north on Crystal Springs and the train ride will be on your right.

Hollywood Walk of Fame
6100-6900 Hollywood Blvd.
Los Angeles, CA
323-469-8311
Want to see the star that was dedicated to your favorite actor or actress? Then come to the famous Hollywood Walk of Fame on Hollywood Blvd. You'll find about 10-15 blocks of Hollywood stars placed in the sidewalks of Hollywood Blvd. Don't forget to look at the famous Footprints located at the Mann's Chinese Theatre on Hollywood Blvd between Orange Drive and Orchid Ave. Want to see an actor or actress receive their honorary Star? This takes place throughout the year in front of the Hollywood Galaxy General Cinemas on Hollywood Blvd. It may be too crowded for your pup to stand directly in front of the Cinemas, but you can see plenty from across the street. Just make sure your dog is comfortable with crowds yelling and cheering as this will happen when the actor/actress arrives. Our pup was able to see Nicolas Cage receive his Hollywood Star. To find out the schedule of when the next actor/actress will receive their star, look at the Hollywood Chamber of Commerce website at http://www.hollywoodcoc.org or call 323-469-8311. To get to the Hollywood Walk of Fame, take Hwy 101 North past Sunset Blvd. Take the next exit which is Hollywood Blvd and turn left (west). The Hollywood Stars are located on 6100-6900 Hollywood Blvd. between Gower Street and Sycamore Avenue.

Travel Town Museum
5200 Zoo Drive
Los Angeles, CA
In Griffith Park
323-662-5874
Dogs are allowed on leash throughout the Travel Town Museum in Griffith Park in LA. Here you can see many trains, cars and lots more. Your well-

behaved dog is also allowed on the miniature train ride.

Pacific Palisades

Will Rogers State Hist. Park
1501 Will Rogers State Park Rd.
Pacific Palisades, CA
Sunset Blvd.
310-454-8212
This park was Will Roger's personal home and ranch. Mr. Rogers was famous for his horse and rope tricks. He performed on Broadway and then moved on to Hollywood to star in many movies. The ranch was made into a state historic park in 1944 after the death of Mrs. Rogers and it reflects Will Rogers avid horsemanship. On the ranch there is a large polo field, which is the only outdoor polo field in Los Angeles county and the only field that is regulation size. The polo field has been featured in many movies and TV shows. The ranch buildings and grounds have been maintained to show how the Rogers' family lived back in the late 1920s and 1930s. Today, the grounds are also a working ranch with a variety of western equestrian activities. Leashed dogs are allowed on the property, in the horse barn, and on the Inspiration Point Trail. They are not allowed inside the ranch house. Dogs, along with people and children, should not touch the horses. The ranch staff enforces the leash law and will fine violators $82. The entrance fee to the park is $6 per car and $1 per dog.

Pasadena

Frisbee Golf Course
Oak Grove Drive
Pasadena, CA
in Hahamongna Watershed Park

This disc golf course in Pasadena is the world's first disc

golf course. It is an extremely popular course, with over 100 golfers playing daily during the week and twice that on the weekends. If you are a beginner, this might not be the right course for you, but you can watch some of the pros at work. Disc golf is similar to golf with clubs and balls, but the main difference is the equipment. Discs are shot into elevated baskets/holes. Your dog is allowed to go with you on this course, just watch out for flying discs. Dogs must be leashed and poop bags/scoopers are necessary. During the summer months, there can be rattlesnakes, so make sure your dog stays leashed. You'll also want to keep your pup away from the ground squirrels (they can potentially be rabid). This course is located in Hahamongna Watershed Park (formerly Oak Grove Park). If you don't have any discs, you can purchase them online at http: //www.gottagogottathrow.com. The prices range from $8-12. Directions to the course are on their website. The park is off Hwy 210 near Altadena.

Old Town Pasadena
100W-100E Colorado Blvd.
Pasadena, CA 91106

Old Town Pasadena is Pasadena's premier shopping and dining district. This area is a nice place to walk around with your pup. While dogs are not allowed inside the stores (with the exception of the Three Dog Bakery), they can sit at one of the many dog-friendly outdoor cafes and dine with you (see Restaurants). A major portion of the popular annual Rose Parade takes place on this part of Colorado Boulevard. The shopping area is the 100 West to 100 East blocks of Colorado Blvd., and between

Marengo & Pasadena Avenues.

Universal City

Universal Studios Kennel
Hollywood Frwy (Hwy 101)
Universal City, CA
Lankershim Blvd.
818-508-9600
This isn't really an attraction for your pup, but will allow humans to spend several hours in the world's largest film and TV studio. Universal Studios has a day kennel located at the main entrance. There is no full time attendant, but the kennels are locked. Simply stop at one of the information booths and ask for assistance. There is no fee for this service. At Universal Studios, you can learn how movies are made, visit set and sound stages, and enjoy a variety of special effect rides.

Beaches

Long Beach

Haute Dogs on the Beach
on the beach
Long Beach, CA
562-570-3100
Once a month, during the spring and summer months, a certain section of the beach is open to dogs. Between 300 to 450 dogs come to play leash free in the shore each time. The special once a month event is organized by a private citizen and his website is http: //www.hautedogs.org/. Take a look at his website for dates and times.

Long Beach Dog Beach Zone
between Roycroft and Argonne Avenues
Long Beach, CA 20803

This is a new three acre off-leash dog beach zone during specified hours daily. This is the only off leash beach that we are aware of in Los Angeles County and one of the few in Southern California. The hours vary by season and are 6 - 9 am & 6 - 8 pm during the summer from Memorial Day to Labor Day. During the rest of the year the hours are 6 - 9 am & 4 - 6 pm. Dogs are not permitted on the beach at any other time other than the scheduled hours. Dogs must be under visual and voice control of the owners. You can check with the website http://www.hautedogs.org for updates and additional rules about the Long Beach Dog Beach Zone.

Malibu

Leo Carrillo State Beach
Hwy 1
Malibu, CA
30 miles n. of Santa Monica
818-880-0350
This beach is one of the very few dog-friendly beaches in the Los Angeles area. In a press release dated November 27, 2002, the California State Parks clarified the rules for dogs at Leo Carrillo State Beach. We thank the State Parks for this clear announcement of the regulations. Dogs are allowed on a maximum 6 foot leash when accompanied by a person capable of controlling the dog on all beach WEST (up coast) of lifeguard tower 3 at Leo Carrillo State Park, Staircase Beach, County Line Beach, and all Beaches within Point Mugu State Park. Dogs are NOT allowed EAST of lifeguard tower 3 at Leo Carrillo State Beach at any time. And please note that dogs are not allowed in the tide pools at Leo Carrillo. There should be signs posted. A small general store is located on the mountain side of the freeway. Here you can grab some snacks and other items. The park is located on Hwy 1, approximately 30 miles northwest of Santa

Monica. We ask that all dog people closely obey these regulations so that the beach continues to be dog-friendly.

Parks

El Segundo

El Segundo Recreation Park
Grande Ave at Eucalyptus Dr
El Segundo, CA

This park allows dogs during all hours that the park is open, but they must be on leash at all times. Please clean up after your dogs, so the city continues to allow their presence. This park is bounded by the following streets: North by E. Pine St, South by Grande Ave, West by Eucalyptus Dr. and East by Penn St. Thanks to one of our readers for recommending this park.

Long Beach

Recreation Park Dog Park
7th St & Federation Dr
Long Beach, CA
562-570-3100
Licensed dogs over four months are allowed to run leash-free in this area by the casting pond. As usual with all dog parks, owners are responsible for their dogs and must supervise them at all times. The Recreation Park Dog Park is located off 7th Street and Federation Drive behind the Casting Pond. It is open daily until 10 p.m. Thanks to one of our readers for recommending this park.

Los Angeles

Griffith Park
Los Feliz Blvd.
Los Angeles, CA
Hwy 5

This is the park that allows

dogs on their small trains (see Attractions), has the Griffith Observatory, the famous Hollywood sign and plenty of hiking trails. The Mt. Hollywood Trail is about a 6 mile round trip and can get very hot in the summer season, so head out early or later in the evening during those hot days. There is also a more shaded trail that begins by the Bird Sanctuary. Be careful not to go into the Sanctuary because dogs are not allowed there. Instead go to the trail to the left of the Sanctuary entrance. That trail should go around the perimeter of the Bird Sanctuary. For more trail info, pick up a map at one of the Ranger stations (main Ranger's station is at Crystal Springs/Griffith Park Drive near Los Feliz Blvd). To get to there, take Hwy 5 to the Los Feliz Blvd exit and head west. Turn right on Hillhurst or Vermont Ave (they merge later). The trail by the Bird Sanctuary will be on the right, past the Greek Theater. To get to the Mt. Hollywood Trail, continue until you come to the Griffith Observatory. Park here and the trail is across the parking lot from the Observatory (near the outdoor cafe). Please note that no one is allowed to actually hike to the famous Hollywood sign - it is very well guarded. But from some of the trails in this park, you can get a long distance view of the sign. Dogs must be leashed in the park.

Griffith Park Dog Park
North 200 Drive
Los Angeles, CA
323-913-7390
This dog park is located 1/2 mile west of the 134 Fwy.

Laurel Canyon Park
8260 Mulholland Dr.
Los Angeles, CA 90046

This nice dog park is located in the hills of Studio City. It is completely fenced with water and even a hot dog stand. The on-leash hours are 10am-3pm and off-leash hours are 6am to10am and 3pm to dusk. To get there, take Laurel Canyon Blvd and go west on Mulholland Blvd. Go about a 1/4 mile and turn left. There is a parking lot below.

Runyon Canyon Park
Mulholland Hwy
Los Angeles, CA
Desmond Street

This park has off-leash hiking trails. There is not a fenced dog park area, but your pup can hike with you without his or her leash under voice control. It is located off Mulholland Hwy at Desmond Street in the Hollywood Hills. You can also get there by taking the Hollywood Fwy (Hwy 101) to Highland Avenue south. Then head west on Franklin Ave. Go north on Fuller Street until it ends. Parking is available on the street.

Silverlake Dog Park
2000 West Silverlake Blvd.
Los Angeles, CA
South part of the reservoir

This is one of the best dog parks in the Los Angeles area and it usually averages 30-40 dogs. It is located at approximately 2000 West Silverlake Blvd. It's on the south side of the reservoir in Silverlake, which is between Hollywood and downtown L.A. between Sunset Blvd. and the 5 Freeway. The easiest way to get there is to take the 101 Freeway to Silverlake Blvd. and go east. Be careful about street parking because they ticket in some areas. Thanks to one of our readers for recommending this dog park.

Pasadena

Hahamongna Watershed
Oak Grove Drive

Pasadena, CA
near Hwy 210

The Hahamongna Watershed Park (formerly Oak Grove Park) allows leashed dogs on the trails and on the world's first disc golf course. During the summer months, there can be rattlesnakes here, so make sure your dog stays leashed. You'll also want to keep your pup away from the ground squirrels. Some squirrels in this mountain range have been known to carry rabies. Aside from being a very popular disc golf course, this park is also very popular with bird watchers. To get there from Hwy 210, take the Berkshire Ave. exit and head east. Turn left onto Oak Grove Drive and the park will be on the right. To get to one of the trails, follow the signs to the disc golf course. After going downhill, turn right and the trail begins.

Redondo Beach

Redondo Beach Dog Park
Flagler Lane
Redondo Beach, CA
at 190th St.
310-378-8555
This dog park is located next to Dominguez Park. Local dogs and vacationing dogs are welcome at the dog park. There is a separate section for small dogs and big dogs. It is completely fenced and has pooper scooper bags available.

San Fernando

Angeles National Forest
Little Tujunga Canyon Rd.
San Fernando, CA
near Hwy 210
626-574-1613
This forest is over 690,000 acres and covers one-fourth of the land in Los Angeles County. We have selected a couple of trails near San

Fernando Valley ranging from 2.5 to 3 miles. Dogs are allowed on leash or leash free but under voice control. Both of the trails are single-track, foot trails. The first trail is called Gold Creek Trail. It is about 2.5 miles long. The second trail is called Oaks Springs Trail and it is about 3 miles long. To get there from Hwy 215, take the Foothill Blvd. exit and head north towards the mountains. Turn left onto Little Tujunga Canyon Rd. You will see the Little Tujunga Forest Station on the left. After you pass the station, continue on Little Tujunga Canyon Rd. Go about 1-1.5 miles and then turn right onto Gold Creek Rd. Go about 1 mile and on the right you will see the trailhead for Oak Springs Trail. If you continue to the end of Gold Creek Rd, you will see the trailhead for Gold Creek Trail. There should be parking along the road.

Santa Monica

Memorial Park
1401 Olympic Blvd
Santa Monica, CA
310-450-1121
There is an off-leash dog run located in this park.

Venice

Westminster Dog Park
1234 Pacific Ave
Venice, CA 90291
310-392-5566
Thanks to one of our readers who writes: "Spacious (half a block in size), clean (mulched) dog run in dog-friendly Venice. Only five minutes walk from Hydrant Cafe."

Restaurants

Burbank

The Riverside Cafe
1221 Riverside Dr

Burbank, CA
818-563-3567
This British style bistro allows dogs at its outdoor seats. It is closed Mondays. The restaurant is open for lunch and dinner on Tuesday through Friday, and for brunch, lunch and dinner on weekends. According to a reader dogs get their own bowl of water and maybe a dog bone.

Irwindale

Picasso's Cafe
6070 N. Irwindale Ave.
Irwindale, CA 91706
626-969-6100
The owners of this restaurant are very dog-friendly. This restaurant was one of the sponsors in the spcaLA's 1999 Petelethon. Your pup is welcome to dine with you at the outdoor tables. They serve a full breakfast and lunch. Also enjoy some great dessert from their bakery. The hours are Monday through Friday from 7am-2:30pm. To get there from the 210 Freeway, exit Irwindale and head south. Turn right at Gateway Business and Picasso's is on the corner.

Los Angeles

Fred's 62
1854 N Vermont Ave
Los Angeles, CA 90027
323-667-0062
Dogs are allowed at the outdoor tables.

Griffith Park snack stand
Vermont Ave
Los Angeles, CA
(Griffith Observatory)

This is a basic snack stand but what makes it nice is the fact that it's in Griffith Park between the Griffith Observatory and the Mt. Hollywood Trail. Your pup can't go in the Observatory, but can walk up the outside stairs to the roof and check out the view

of Los Angeles. At the Mt. Hollywood Trail, there is a 6 mile round trip dog-friendly trail. Load up on snacks and water at this stand. To get to there, take Hwy 5 to the Los Feliz Blvd exit and head west. Turn right on Hillhurst or Vermont Ave (they merge later). Go past the Bird Sanctuary and Greek Theater. Stay on Vermont Ave and you'll come to the Griffith Observatory and snack shop parking.

Hollywood Blvd restaurants
Hollywood Blvd.
Los Angeles, CA
various

While you are looking at the Stars on the Hollywood Walk of Fame at Hollywood Blvd., you can take a lunch or snack break at one of the many outdoor cafes that line this popular street. Many of them only have a few tables, but you should be able to find one.

In-N-Out Burgers
7009 Sunset Blvd.
Los Angeles, CA 90028
Orange Drive
800-786-1000
We decided to mention this specific In-N-Out Burgers because it's very close to the Hollywood Blvd. Walk of Fame. It's a few blocks south of Hollywood Blvd (Walk of Fame). Head south on Orange Drive which is near the Mann's Chinese Theatre. The In-N-Out is near the corner of Sunset Blvd. and Orange. Dogs are allowed at the outdoor tables.

Johnny Rockets
1000 N. La Cienga Blvd.
Los Angeles, CA
(between 3rd & Beverly Blvd.)
310-657-6073
Johnny Rockets is a popular chain that serves hamburgers, fries and malts with a traditional 1950's style. Dogs are allowed at the outdoor tables.

Mel's Drive-In
8585 Sunset Blvd.
Los Angeles, CA
La Cienga Blvd.
310-854-7200
This 24 hour West Hollywood restaurant serves you and your pup breakfast, lunch or dinner outside.

Tail O The Pup
329 N. San Vicente Blvd.
Los Angeles, CA
Beverly Blvd.
310-652-4517
This food stand serves a fast-food type of breakfast and then for lunch they serve hamburgers and hot dogs. Order with your pup at the "Hot Dog" window and then sit at one of their several outdoor tables.

The Back Door Bakery
1710 Silver Lake Blvd
Los Angeles, CA 90026
323-662-7927
This restaurant is two blocks from the Silver Lake Dog Park, so it gets a regular group of 4 legged customers at the outdoor tables. They have dog biscuits for the dogs. The hours are 7:30 am to 7 pm Tuesday through Sunday.

The Pig, Memphis-Style BBQ
612 N. La Brea Ave
Los Angeles, CA 90036
323-935-1116
This restaurant is very dog friendly. There are a lot of doggy regulars at the "Pig". Closed Mondays. Open from 11 am to at least 10 pm other days. Dogs are welcome to dine with you at the outdoor tables.

Manhattan Beach

Johnny Rockets
1550 Rosecrans Ave.
Manhattan Beach, CA 90266
310-536-9464
Dogs are allowed at the outdoor tables at this Johnny Rockets.

North Hollywood

Chez Nous
10550 Riverside Drive
North Hollywood, CA
Cahueriga Blvd.
818-760-0288
Enjoy lunch dining and table service at this restaurant located in North Hollywood. Dogs are allowed at the outdoor tables.

Pasadena

All India Cafe
39 S Fair Oaks Ave
Pasadena, CA 91105
626-440-0309
Dogs are allowed at the outdoor tables.

Barney's Ltd
93 W. Colorado Blvd.
Pasadena, CA 91105
in Old Town Pasadena
626-577-2739
This restaurant has good chili, salads, sandwiches and a large selection of beers. Your pup is welcome to join you at the outdoor tables.

Crocodile Cafe
88 W. Colorado Blvd.
Pasadena, CA 91105
in Old Town Pasadena
626-568-9310
You are welcome to dine with your dog at the outdoor tables.

Gaucho Grill
121 W. Colorado Blvd.
Pasadena, CA 91105
in Old Town Pasadena
626-683-3580
This restaurant allows dogs to dine with you at their outdoor tables.

Jake's Diner & Billiards
38 W. Colorado Blvd.
Pasadena, CA 91105
in Old Town Pasadena
626-568-1602
Come here for some English-style meat pies, burgers or just a beer. Dogs are welcome to join

their people and the restaurant staff will even bring out some water for your pup.

Trattoria Farfalla
43 E. Colorado Blvd.
Pasadena, CA 91105
in Old Town Pasadena
626-564-8696
The outdoor tables are pretty close together, but your dog is welcome to join you for lunch or dinner.

Wok n Roll
55 E. Colorado Blvd.
Pasadena, CA 91105
in Old Town Pasadena
626-304-1000
Not only does this restaurant allow your dog, they will also bring him or her water. Dogs are allowed at the outdoor tables.

Studio City

Gaucho Grill
12050 Ventura Blvd.
Studio City, CA 91604
Laurel Canyon Blvd.
818-508-1030
This Argentinian restaurant is located on the second floor of a strip mall in Studio City. The outdoor seats are pretty popular during the lunch and dinner rush hours, so try to come a little early to ensure a seat.

Louise's Trattoria
12050 Ventura Blvd.
Studio City, CA 91604
Laurel Canyon Blvd.
818-762-2662
This Italian restaurant is located on the second floor of a strip mall in Studio City. The outdoor seats are pretty popular during the lunch and dinner rush hours, so try to come a little early to ensure a seat.

West Hollywood

Basix Cafe
8333 Santa Monica Blvd.
West Hollywood, CA 90069
323-848-2460
This cafe offers flavor-infused, health-conscious cuisine using the freshest ingredients. Here you can enjoy specialties like fresh-baked breads, pastas, sandwiches, wood-fired pizzas. They also serve breakfast including items like eggs and omelettes, pancakes and more. Well-behaved leashed dogs are allowed at the outdoor tables. Thanks to one of our readers for recommending this dog-friendly cafe.

Westwood

Native Foods
1110 1/2 Gayley Avenue
Westwood, CA 90025
310-209-1055
This restaurants serves organic vegetarian food. Dogs are allowed at the outdoor tables.

Stores

Beverly Hills

Anthropologie
320 North Beverly Dr.
Beverly Hills, CA
310-385-7390
Thanks to one of our readers who writes "They have always been especially lovely when Hector and I go in!"

Los Angeles

Brentano's Books
Century City Shopping Center
Los Angeles, CA 93309
310-785-0204
Your well-behaved leashed dog is allowed inside this store.

Foot Locker
Century City Shopping Center
Los Angeles, CA 93309
310-556-1498
Your well-behaved leashed dog

is allowed inside this store.

Gap
Century City Shopping Center
Los Angeles, CA 93309
310-556-1080
Your well-behaved leashed dog
is allowed inside this store.

Illiterature
452 S La Brea Ave
Los Angeles, CA 90036
323-937-3505
Dogs are allowed but they must
be leashed.

Laura Ashley
Century City Shopping Center
Los Angeles, CA 93309
310-553-0807
Your well-behaved leashed dog
is allowed inside this store.

Origins
Century City Shopping Center
Los Angeles, CA 93309
310-772-0272
Your well-behaved leashed dog
is allowed inside this store.

Pottery Barn
Century City Shopping Center
Los Angeles, CA 93309
310-552-0170
Your well-behaved leashed dog
is allowed inside this store.

Restoration Hardware
Century City Shopping Center
Los Angeles, CA 93309
310-551-4995
Your well-behaved leashed dog
is allowed inside this store.

Rocket Video
726 N La Brea Ave
Los Angeles, CA 90038
323-965-1100
Well-behaved leashed dogs are
welcome in this store which is
Los Angeles' premier
independent video store.

Pasadena

Saks Fifth Avenue
35 N De Lacey Ave

Pasadena, CA 91103
626-396-7100
Leashed, well - behaved dogs
are allowed in the store.

Three Dog Bakery
24 Smith Alley A
Pasadena, CA 91106
in One Colorado
626-440-0443
Your pup is invited inside this
dog bakery store which is
located in Old Town Pasadena.
Here he or she can choose
from a variety of special dog
cookies and pastries. The
goodies look yummy enough
for people to eat, but remember
they are for dogs, not for
humans. After your pup has
indulged in the treats, both of
you can dine at one of the
many dog-friendly outdoor
restaurants located within
walking distance (see
Restaurants).

Santa Monica

Barnes and Noble Bookstore
1201 3rd Street
Santa Monica, CA 90401
310-260-9110
Your well-behaved leashed dog
is allowed inside this store. One
of our readers writes "They
(dogs) are totally welcome
there!"

West Hollywood

Video West
805 Larrabee Street
West Hollywood, CA
310-659-5762
Very dog friendly video store.
Dogs always welcome and
usually they have dog biscuits.
The owner is a dog lover and is
active in dog rescue. The store
is open 10am-midnight, 7 days
a week.

Vets and Kennels

Culver City

Affordable Emergency Clinic
5558 Sepulveda Blvd
Culver City, CA 90230
Jefferson Blvd
310-397-4883
9:30 am - 12 midnight 7 days a
week

El Monte

Emergency Pet Clinic
3254 Santa Anita Ave
El Monte, CA 91733
Hwy 10
626-579-4550
Monday - Friday 6 pm to 8 am,
Noon Saturday to 8 am Monday.

Glendale

Animal Emergency Clinic
831 Milford St
Glendale, CA 91203
near I-5 and 134
818-247-3973
Mon - Tues 8 am - 7 pm. Wed -
Fri 8 am - 6 pm, Sat 8 am - 12
noon, Closed Sunday.

Long Beach

Evening Pet Clinic
6803 Cherry Ave
Long Beach, CA 90805
Hwy 91
562-422-1223
Mon - Fri 8 am - 9 pm with
certain lunch and dinner breaks,
Sat - Sun 12 - 6 pm.

Los Angeles

Animal Emergency Clinic
1736 S Sepulveda Blvd #A
Los Angeles, CA 90025
Santa Monica Blvd
310-473-1561
Monday - Friday 6 pm - 8 am. 24
hours weekends and holidays.

**Eagle Rock Emergency Pet
Clinic**
4252 Eagle Rock Blvd
Los Angeles, CA 90065

near Occidental College
323-254-7382
Monday - Friday 6 pm - 8 am.
Saturday 12 noon - Monday 8
am.

Norwalk

Crossroads Animal Emergency Hospital
11057 Rosecrans Ave
Norwalk, CA 90650
Hwy 605
562-863-2522
Monday - Thursday 6 pm to 8
am, Friday 6 pm to 8 am
Monday.

Pasadena

Animal Emergency Clinic
2121 E Foothill Blvd
Pasadena, CA 91107
Lola Ave
626-564-0704
Monday - Friday 6 pm - 8 am.
Saturday 12 noon - Monday 8
am.

Studio City

Animal Emergency Center
11740 Ventura Blvd
Studio City, CA 91604
818-760-3882
Monday - Friday 6 pm to 8 am,
Saturday 2 pm - Monday 8 am.

Monterey – Carmel City Guide

Accommodations

Carmel

Carmel Country Inn
P.O. Box 3756
Carmel, CA 93921
831-625-3263
This dog-friendly bed and
breakfast has 12 rooms and
allows dogs in several of these
rooms. It's close to many
downtown outdoor dog-friendly
restaurants (see Restaurants). A

20-25 minute walk will take you
to the dog-friendly Carmel City
Beach. There is a $20 per night
per pet charge.

Carmel Tradewinds Inn
Mission St & 3rd Ave.
Carmel, CA 93921
831-624-2776
This motel allows dogs in
several of their rooms. They are
a non-smoking inn. It's located
about 3-4 blocks north of
Ocean Ave and close to many
outdoor dog-friendly
restaurants in downtown
Carmel. A 20-25 minute walk
will take you to the dog-friendly
Carmel City beach. There is a
$25 per day pet charge. Dogs
are not allowed on the bed.

Casa De Carmel
Monte Verde & Ocean Ave
Carmel, CA
831-624-2429
There is an additional fee of
$20 per day for 1 pet, and $30
a day for 2 pets.

Coachman's Inn
San Carlos St. & 7th
Carmel, CA 93921
831-624-6421
Located in downtown, this
motel allows dogs. It's close to
many downtown outdoor dog-
friendly restaurants (see
Restaurants). A 20-25 minute
walk will take you to the Carmel
City beach which allows dogs.
There is a $15 per day
additional pet fee.

Cypress Inn
Lincoln & 7th
Carmel, CA 93921
831-624-3871
This hotel is located within
walking distance to many dog-
friendly outdoor restaurants in
the quaint town of Carmel and
walking distance to the Carmel
City Beach. This is definitely a
pet-friendly hotel. Here is an
excerpt from the Cypress Inn's
web page "Co-owned by
actress and animal rights

activist Doris Day, the Cypress
Inn welcomes pets with open
arms -- a policy which draws a
high percentage of repeat
guests. It's not unusual to see
people strolling in and out of the
lobby with dogs of all sizes.
Upon arrival, animals are
greeted with dog biscuits, and
other pet pamperings." Room
rates are about $125 - $375 per
night. If you have more than 2
people per room (including a
child or baby), you will be
required to stay in their deluxe
room which runs approximately
$375 per night. There is a $25
per day pet charge.

Hofsas House Hotel
San Carlos Street
Carmel, CA 93921
831-624-2745
There is a $15 per day additional
pet fee. The hotel is located
between 3rd Ave and 4th Ave in
Carmel. Thanks to one of our
readers for recommending this
hotel.

Lincoln Green Inn
PO Box 2747
Carmel, CA
831-624-7738
These cottages are owned and
booked through the dog-friendly
Vagabond's House Inn in
Carmel. One big difference
between the two
accommodations is that the
Vagabond's House does not
allow children, whereas the
Lincoln Green does allow
children. The Lincoln Green is
located very close to a beach.
All cottages are non-smoking
and there is a $20 per day pet
fee.

Sunset House
Camino Real and Ocean Ave
Carmel, CA 93923
831-624-4884
There is a $20 one time pet fee.
Thanks to one of our readers
who writes "Great B&B,
breakfast brought to your room
every morning."

The Forest Lodge Cottages
Ocean Ave. and Torres St. (P.O. Box 1316)
Carmel, CA 93921
831-624-7055
These cottages are surrounded by oak and pine trees among a large garden area. They are conveniently located within walking distance to many dog-friendly restaurants and the dog-friendly Carmel City Beach. There is a $10 one time additional pet fee.

Vagabond's House Inn B&B
P.O. Box 2747
Carmel, CA 93921
831-624-7738
This dog-friendly bed and breakfast is located in downtown and has 11 rooms. It's close to many downtown outdoor dog-friendly restaurants. A 20-25 minute walk will take you to the dog-friendly Carmel City beach. Children 12 years and older are allowed at this B&B inn.

Wayside Inn
Mission St & 7th Ave.
Carmel, CA 93921
831-624-5336
This motel allows dogs in several of their rooms and is close to many downtown outdoor dog-friendly restaurants. A 20-25 minute walk will take you to the dog-friendly Carmel City beach. Pets are welcome at no extra charge. Dogs up to about 75 pounds are allowed.

Carmel Valley

Best Western Carmel Mission Inn
3665 Rio Rd.
Carmel Valley, CA 93921
831-624-1841
Located in Carmel Valley off Hwy 1, this inn is a few blocks from The Crossroads Shopping Center which has several outdoor dog-friendly restaurants and a pet store. The Garland Ranch Park is located within a 10-15 minute drive. There is also a $35 one time pet fee.

Carmel Valley Lodge
Carmel Valley Rd
Carmel Valley, CA 93924
831-659-2261
Your dog will feel welcome at this country retreat. Pet amenities include heart-shaped, organic homemade dog biscuits and a pawtographed picture of Lucky the Lodge Dog. Dogs must be on leash, but for your convenience, there are doggy-hitches at the front door of every unit that has a patio or deck and at the pool. There are 31 units which range from standard rooms to two bedroom cottages. A great community park is located across the street and several restaurants with outdoor seating are within a 5 minute walk. Drive about 15 minutes from the lodge and you'll be in downtown Carmel or at one of the dog-friendly beaches. Rates with seasonal changes are from $139 to $319 per night. Dogs are an extra $10 per day and up to two dogs per room. There is no charge for childen under 16. The lodge is located in Carmel Valley. From Carmel, head south on Hwy 1. Turn left on Carmel Valley Rd., drive about 11-12 miles and the lodge will be located at Ford Rd.

Los Laureles Lodge
313 West Carmel Valley Road
Carmel Valley, CA 93924
831-659-2233
There is a $20 per day pet fee. Dogs may not be left in the room unattended. This large ranch lodge sits on 10 acres in rural Carmel Valley, about 10 minutes from the Carmel seaside and near world class golf, hiking, wineries and everything else Carmel has to offer. Nearby Garland Ranch is available for hiking.

Monterey

Bay Park Hotel
1425 Munras Ave
Monterey, CA
831-649-1020
There is a $10 per day pet fee. Pets may not be left alone in the room.

Best Western Monterey Beach Hotel
2600 Sand Dunes Drive
Monterey, CA 93940
831-394-3321
This beach front hotel allows dogs. Dogs stay in the first floor rooms on the garden side (not facing the beach). They originally just allowed small dogs, but now they allow all dogs that are well-behaved and well-trained. While there are no restaurants within an easy walking distance, the sandy beach is right at the hotel. Dogs are allowed on the beaches that stretch from this hotel down to Fisherman's Wharf - about 2 miles. If you want a longer walk, once at Fisherman's Wharf, continue on the paved Monterey Recreation Trail. The hotel is located off Hwy 1 at the Del Rey Oaks exit. There is a $25 one time fee for pets.

Best Western Victorian Inn
487 Foam Street
Monterey, CA 93940
831-373-8000
This inn is a few blocks from the beautiful dog-friendly Monterey Recreation Trail that parallels the ocean. The inn has nice spacious rooms with fireplaces and of course it has a great location for ocean lovers and their water dogs. There is a $100 refundable pet deposit and a one time $35 pet cleaning charge for the room. Thanks to one of our readers who writes: "...He received upon arriving to our room the "pooch package" of treats overflowing in a bowl, and his own bottle of water for walks along the surf. "

El Adobe Inn
936 Munras Ave.
Monterey, CA 93940
831-372-5409
This inn is located on Munras Ave. about 1/2 mile east of Hwy 1. There is a $10 per day additional pet fee.

Hyatt Resort
1 Od Golf Course Rd
Monterey, CA
831-372-1234
There is a $50 one time pet fee for each dog. Dogs must be on leash and certain areas of the hotel are off limits to pets. The front desk will explain the restrictions upon check in.

Monterey Fireside Lodge
1131 10th Street
Monterey, CA 93940
831-373-4172
All 24 rooms have gas fireplaces. There is an additional $20/day pet charge.

Pacific Grove

Andril Fireplace Cottages
569 Asilomar Blvd
Pacific Grove, CA
831-375-0994
There is an additional fee of $14 per day for a pet. Well-behaved dogs are allowed.

Lighthouse Lodge and Suites
1249 Lighthouse Ave
Pacific Grove, CA
831-655-2111
There are no additional pet fees.e high $400s per night and up.

Attractions

Carmel

Carmel Village Shopping Area
Ocean Ave
Carmel, CA
between Mission & Casanova St.

This shopping expedition is more of a window shopping adventure, however there are some dog-friendly stores throughout this popular and quaint village. Just ask a store clerk before entering into a store with your pooch. We do know that the Galerie Blue Dog (Blue Dog Gallery) located at 6th Ave. and Lincoln St. is dog-friendly. There are also many dog-friendly restaurants throughout the village (see Restaurants).

Carmel Walks-Walking Tours
Lincoln and Ocean Streets
Carmel, CA
courtyard of The Pine Inn
831-642-2700
Discover the special charms and secrets of Carmel on this two hour guided walking tour. Walk through award-winning gardens, by enchanting fairytale cottages and learn the homes, haunts, and history of famous artists, writers, and movie stars. Your leashed dog is welcome to join you. Tours are offered every Saturday at 10am and 2pm. Tuesday thru Friday, the tours are at 10am. The cost is $20 per person and dogs get the tour for free. Prices are subject to change. Reservations are required.

Seventeen Mile Drive
Seventeen Mile Drive
Carmel, CA

This toll road costs $8 and allows you to access a very scenic section of coastline, walking trails and beaches. Dogs are allowed all along 17 mile drive on leash.

Carmel Valley

Crossroads Shopping Center
Cabrillo Hwy (Hwy 1)
Carmel Valley, CA
near Carmel Valley Rd.

This is an outdoor shopping mall with many dog-friendly outdoor restaurants and a pet store. While your dog cannot go into the shops, he or she is more than welcome inside the pet store.

Quail Lodge Golf Club
8205 Valley Greens Drive
Carmel Valley, CA 93922
831-624-2888
Well-behaved, leashed dogs are welcome at this 18-hole championship golf course. Dogs must be leashed and either in your golf cart or tied to your pull cart. The course is open to members, resort guests (dogs are allowed at the hotel) and non-resort guests.

Monterey

Monterey Bay Whale Watch Boat Tours
Fisherman's Wharf
Monterey, CA
at Sam's Fishing Fleet
831-375-4658
Monterey Bay Whale Watch offers year-round whale watching trips to observe whales and dolphins in Monterey Bay. Tours are 3 - 6 hours. Well-behaved dogs on leash are allowed. The tours are located at Sam's Fishing Fleet on Fisherman's Wharf in Monterey.

Old Fisherman's Wharf
Del Monte & Washington
Monterey, CA
831-373-0600
Old Fisherman's Wharf in Monterey contains many outdoor ordering fish markets and cafes, boat tours (some of which allow dogs) and an observation deck where you can view sea lions and other animals.

Sea Life Tours
90 Fishermans Wharf
Monterey, CA 93940
831-372-7150

This boat allows leashed dogs on its 45 minute tours of the Monterey bay where you can view sea lions and sometimes whales and other sea life.

Beaches

Carmel

Carmel City Beach
Ocean Avenue
Carmel, CA
At end of Ocean Ave.
831-624-9423
This beach is within walking distance (about 7 blocks) from the quaint village of Carmel. There are a couple of hotels and several restaurants that are within walking distance of the beach. Your pooch is allowed to run off-leash as long as he or she is under voice control. To get there, take the Ocean Avenue exit from Hwy 1 and follow Ocean Ave to the end.

Carmel River State Beach
Carmelo Street
Carmel, CA
831-624-9423
This beach is just south of Carmel. It has approximately a mile of beach and leashes are required. It's located on Carmelo Street.

Monterey

Monterey Recreation Trail
various (see comments)
Monterey, CA
Hwy 1

Take a walk on the Monterey Recreation Trail and experience the beautiful scenery that makes Monterey so famous. This paved trail extends for miles, starting at Fisherman's Wharf and ending in the city of Pacific Grove. Dogs must be leashed. Along the path there are a few small beaches that allow dogs such as the one south of Fisherman's Wharf and

another beach behind Ghiradelli Ice Cream on Cannery Row. Along the path you'll find a few more outdoor places to eat near Cannery Row and by the Monterey Bay Aquarium. Look at the Restaurants section for more info.

Monterey State Beach
various (see comments)
Monterey, CA
Hwy 1
831-649-2836
Take your water loving and beach loving dog to this awesome beach in Monterey. There are various starting points, but it basically stretches from Hwy 1 and the Del Rey Oaks Exit down to Fisherman's Wharf. Various beaches make up this 2 mile (each way) stretch of beach, but leashed dogs are allowed on all of them . If you want to extend your walk, you can continue on the paved Monterey Recreation Trail which goes all the way to Pacific Grove. There are a few smaller dog-friendly beaches along the paved trail.

Pacific Grove

Asilomar State Beach
Along Sunset Drive
Pacific Grove, CA
Pico
831-372-4076
Dogs are permitted on leash on the beach and the scenic walking trails. If you walk south along the beach and go across the stream that leads into the ocean, you can take your dog off-leash, but he or she must be under strict voice control and within your sight at all times.

Parks

Big Sur

Los Padres National Forest

Big Sur Station #1
Big Sur, CA 93920
831-385-5434
While dogs are not allowed in the state park in Big Sur, they are welcome in the adjacent Los Padres National Forest. Dogs should be on leash. One of the most popular trails is the Pine Ridge Trail. This trail is miles long and goes through the Los Padres National Forest to the dog-friendly Ventana Wilderness. To get there, take Highway 1 south, about 25-30 miles south of Carmel. Park at the Big Sur Station for a minimal fee. From the Big Sur Station in Big Sur, you can head out onto the Pine Ridge Trail. The Los Padres National Forest actually stretches over 200 miles from the Carmel Valley all the way down to Los Angeles County. For maps and more information about the trails, contact the Monterey Ranger District at 831-385-5434 or at the Forest Headquarters in Goleta at 805-968-6640.

Carmel Valley

Garland Ranch Regional Park
Carmel Valley Rd.
Carmel Valley, CA
831-659-4488
This dog-friendly 4,500 acre regional park offers approx. 5-6 miles of dirt single-track and fire road trails. The trail offers a variety of landscapes, with elevations ranging from 200 to 2000 feet. If you are looking for some exercise in addition to the beaches, this is the spot. Dogs must be on leash. The park is located 8.6 miles east of Highway 1 on Carmel Valley Road.

Monterey

El Estero Park
Camino El Estero & Fremont St
Monterey, CA 93940
831-646-3860

This is a city park with a lake, trails around the lake, a children's play area and many places to walk your dog. It's located on the east side of town.

Jack's Peak Regional Park
Jack's Peak Drive
Monterey, CA 93940
831-647-7799
This park has about 11 miles of trails, mostly hilly. It is about 5 minutes out of town to the east.

Restaurants

Carmel

Casanova Restaurant
Mission & 5th
Carmel, CA
831-625-0501
This dog-friendly restaurant has several outdoor tables in the front with heaters. It's located in downtown near several hotels and within a 20-25 minute walk to the dog-friendly beach.

Forge in the Forest
5th and Junipero, SW Corner
Carmel, CA 93921
831-624-2233
Dogs are allowed to dine in this elegantly designed outdoor patio. Dogs are only allowed at certain tables on the upper patio.

Le Coq D'Or
Mission between 4th & 5th
Carmel, CA
831-626-9319
Your well-behaved dog is welcome on their heated outdoor patio. This is a European country restaurant that serves an innovative menu of German and French specialties. Your pooch will feel welcome here.

Nico Restaurant
San Carlos & Ocean Ave
Carmel, CA
831-624-6545
Dogs are allowed at the outdoor tables.

PortaBella
Ocean Ave
Carmel, CA
between Lincoln & Monte Verde
831-624-4395
Dogs... come here to be treated first class. Your waiter will bring your pup water in a champagne bucket. They have several outdoor tables with heaters. It's located in downtown near several hotels and within a 20-25 minute walk to the beach.

Carmel Valley

Cafe Stravaganza
241 The Crossroads
Carmel Valley, CA
Crossroads Shopping Center
831-625-3733
Located in the Crossroads Shopping Center in Carmel Valley, this restaurant offers dog-friendly outdoor dining. A pet store is nearby.

Carmen's Place
211 The Crossroads
Carmel Valley, CA
Crossroads Shopping Center
831-625-3030
This restaurant offers a delicious breakfast. Lunch is also served here. It's located in the Crossroads Shopping Center in Carmel Valley. A pet store is nearby.

Oak Deli
24 W Carmel Valley Rd
Carmel Valley, CA 93924
Carmel Valley Village
831-659-3416
Dogs are allowed at the outdoor tables.

Plaza Linda
9 Del Fino Pl
Carmel Valley, CA 93924
831-659-4229
This "dog-friendly" restaurant has a sign out front that says so. Sit on the front patio.

Sole Mio Caffe Trattoria
3 Del Fino Pl
Carmel Valley, CA 93924
Carmel Valley Village
831-659-9119
Dogs are allowed at the outdoor tables.

The Corkscrew Cafe
55 W Carmel Valley Rd
Carmel Valley, CA 93924
831-659-8888
Their daily menu reflects the use of fresh herbs and seasonal produce from their large gardens, paired with local fish and meats. Dogs are allowed at the outdoor tables.

Monterey

Archie's Hamburgers & Breakfast
125 Ocean View Blvd.
Monterey, CA
(by Monterey Bay Aquarium)
831-375-6939
Enjoy a hamburger or chicken sandwich for lunch and dinner or come early and have some breakfast at this restaurant that overlooks the ocean. The Monterey Recreation Trail is directly across the street.

Captain's Gig Restaurant
6 Fishermans Wharf #1
Monterey, CA 93940
831-373-5559
This restaurant has outdoor seating on Fisherman's Wharf in Monterey.

El Palomar Mexican Restaurant
724 Abrego St
Monterey, CA 93940
831-372-1032
Dogs are allowed at the outdoor tables.

Ghiradelli Ice Cream
616 Cannery Row
Monterey, CA
on Cannery Row
831-373-0997
Come here for some of the best

tasting ice cream. While there, you have a choice of outdoor seating. They have nice patio seating shaded by a large tree or ocean view seating that is covered. Afterwards you and your pup can enjoy the small beach below (dogs on leash only).

Lighthouse Bistro
401 Lighthouse Ave
Monterey, CA 93940
831-649-0320
This restaurant has a large number of outdoor seats and heaters.

London Bridge Pub & Restaurant
Municipal Wharf
Monterey, CA
(north of Fisherman's Wharf)
831-655-2879
Enjoy tasty English food at this British Pub located on the Municipal Wharf between Fisherman's Wharf and the Monterey Beaches. They serve lunch outside and possibly dinner depending how cold it gets at night.

Mi Casita Taqueria
638 Wave St
Monterey, CA 93940
831-655-4419
This restaurant has a few outdoor tables and heaters. Dogs are welcome at these tables.

Monterey Bay Pie Company
481 Alvarado St
Monterey, CA 93940
831-656-9743
Monterey Bay Pie Company is in Old Monterey. Dogs are allowed at the outdoor tables.

Morgan's Coffee Shop
498 Washington St
Monterey, CA 93940
831-373-5601
Morgan's Coffee Shop has a large number of outdoor seats in the Old Monterey area.

Peter B's Brewery & Restaurant
2 Portola Plaza
Monterey, CA 93940
Doubletree Hotel
831-649-4511
This restaurant is located in the Doubletree Hotel just east of Fisherman's Wharf and near the Monterey State Historic Park. They do not always offer the outdoor dining so call ahead. If they are serving outside you can order a good lunch and great beer.

Pino's Italian Cafe & Ice Cream
211 Alvarado St
Monterey, CA
(east of Fisherman's Wharf)
831-649-1930
This Italian cafe & ice cream/gelato shop has a few outdoor seats and is located between Fisherman's Wharf and the Doubletree Hotel near the Monterey State Historic Park.

Shnarley's Pizza
685 Cannery Row #100
Monterey, CA 93940
831-373-8463
This pizza place has outdoor seats and heaters for you and your dog.

Tarpy's Road House
2999 Monterey Salinas Hwy #1
Monterey, CA 93940
831-647-1444
This 1800's looking complex is an interesting atmosphere for dining with your dog. There is a courtyard with a large number of outdoor tables. The restaurant is about 5 miles out of town on the Salinas highway.

Trailside Cafe
550 Wave Street
Monterey, CA
near Cannery Row
831-649-8600
Thanks to one of our readers for recommending this dog-friendly restaurant: "A terrific restaurant we found for breakfast during our morning walks is the Trailside Cafe. I know you request an address, but i don't have a specific one, except to say it is on the Monterey Rail Trail (Monterey Recreation Trail). ...my pooch loved the ocean view of the trail, but most importantly the special biscuit treats he received from the waitstaff when we ordered our wonderful breakfasts. the food is marvelous and staff very good... the patio has a breathtaking view of the pacific. Remember,,,, TRAILSIDE CAFE...on the rail trail in Monterey, only 2 blocks from the Victorian Inn."

Turtle Bay Taqueria
431 Tyler St
Monterey, CA 93940
831-333-1500
Turtle Bay Taqueria is in Old Monterey. It has a few outdoor tables for dining with your pup.

Pacific Grove

Bagel Bakery
1132 Forest Ave
Pacific Grove, CA 93950
831-649-6272
Dogs are allowed at the outdoor tables.

First Awakenings
125 Ocean View Blvd #105
Pacific Grove, CA 93950
831-372-1125
Dogs are allowed at the outdoor tables.

Seventeenth Street Grill
617 Lighthouse Ave
Pacific Grove, CA 93950
831-373-5474
Dogs are allowed at the outdoor tables.

Tinnery at the Beach
631 Ocean View Blvd
Pacific Grove, CA 93950
831-646-1040
This restaurant is at Lovers

Point Park, at the western end of the Monterey/Pacific Grove Recreation Trail.

Toasties Cafe
702 Lighthouse Ave
Pacific Grove, CA 93950
831-373-7543
Toasties Cafe has a large number of outdoor tables for you and your dog.

Seaside

Bagel Bakery
2160 California Ave
Seaside, CA
831-392-1581
Dogs are allowed at the outdoor tables.

Jamba Juice
2160 California Ave
Seaside, CA
831-583-9696
Dogs are allowed at the outdoor tables.

Stores

Carmel

Blue Dog Gallery
6th Ave. and Lincoln St.
Carmel, CA
831-626-4444
First created in 1984, Blue Dog is based on the mythical "loup garou," a French-Cajun ghost dog, and Tiffany, Rodrique's own pooch who had passed away a few years prior to the notoriety. Blue Dog represents a dog who is between heaven and earth. Ask about the story behind Blue Dog when you visit this gallery. The painter, Rodrique, is an internationally acclaimed painter. Blue Dog will probably look familiar to you because Absolut Vodka and other companies have used it for their marketing campaigns. This gallery usually has some cookies and treats for visiting pooches. Thanks to one of our

readers who writes: "A most wonderful place, I called asking for information after Rodrigue did a picture for Neiman Marcus . . . the lady with whom I spoke sent us information plus dog biscuits for our corgi.."

Yellow Dog Gallery
Dolores & 5th Ave
Carmel, CA 93923
831-624-3238
This contemporary art gallery has a large number of dog works and allows your dog to visit with you.

Pacific Grove

Best Friends Pet Wash
167 Central Ave # A
Pacific Grove, CA 93950
831-375-2477
After a day at the beach with your pup you may want to wash the sand away here at a self serve pet wash.

Vets and Kennels

Monterey

Monterey Peninsula - Salinas Emergency Vet
2 Harris Court Suite A1
Monterey, CA
Ryan Ranch and Hwy 68
831-373-7374
Monday - Thursday 5:30 pm to 8 am. Friday 5:30 pm to Monday 8 am.

Monterey Peninsula - Salinas Emergency Vet
2 Harris Court Suite A1
Monterey, CA
Ryan Ranch and Hwy 68
831-373-7374
Monday - Thursday 5:30 pm to 8 am. Friday 5:30 pm to Monday 8 am.

San Francisco City Guide
Accommodations

San Francisco

Best Western Tuscan Inn
425 Northpoint Street
San Francisco, CA
415-561-1100
Well-behaved dogs of all sizes are allowed on the first floor only, which consists of half smoking and half non-smoking rooms. There is a $50 one time per stay pet fee.

Campton Place Hotel
340 Stockton Street
San Francisco, CA 94108
415-781-5555
This dog-friendly hotel holds many awards including "Top 100 Hotels in the World" by Conde Nast Traveler. Room rates are approximately $230 to $345 a night. There is a $35 per day additional pet fee.

Days Inn - Lombard St
2358 Lombard Street
San Francisco, CA 94123
415-922-2010
There is a $10 per day pet fee. A well-behaved large dog is okay. Dogs may not be left alone in the rooms and you are responsible for any damage to the room by your pet.

Harbor Court Hotel
165 Steuart Street
San Francisco, CA 94105
415-882-1300
Well-behaved dogs of all sizes are welcome at this pet-friendly hotel. Amenities include a complimentary evening wine reception, and an adjacent fitness room. There are no pet fees, just sign a pet liability form.

Hotel Cosmo
761 Post Street
San Francisco, CA 94109
415-673-6040

Well-behaved dogs of all sizes are welcome at this pet-friendly hotel. The boutique hotel offers both rooms and suites. Hotel amenities include a complimentary evening wine service. There are no pet fees, just sign a pet liability form.

Hotel Juliana
590 Bush Street
San Francisco, CA 94108
415-392-2540
Well-behaved dogs of all sizes are welcome at this pet-friendly hotel. The luxury boutique hotel offers both rooms and suites. Hotel amenities include a complimentary evening wine reception, and a 24 hour on-site fitness room. There are no pet fees, just sign a pet liability form.

Hotel Palomar
12 Fourth Street
San Francisco, CA 94103
415-348-1111
Well-behaved dogs of all sizes are welcome at this pet-friendly hotel. The boutique hotel offers both rooms and suites. Hotel amenities include room service, an on-site 24 hour fitness room and complimentary high speed Internet access. There are no pet fees, just sign a pet liability form. Pets cannot be left alone in the room.

Hotel Triton
342 Grant Avenue
San Francisco, CA 94108
415-394-0500
Well-behaved dogs of all sizes are welcome at this pet-friendly hotel. The boutique hotel offers both rooms and suites. Hotel amenities include a complimentary evening wine reception, room service, and a 24 hour on-site fitness room. There are no pet fees, just sign a pet liability form.

Marina Motel - on Lombard Street
2576 Lombard St.
San Francisco, CA 94123

415-921-9406
All friendly dogs welcome regardless of size. Walk to the Golden Gate Bridge along Crissy Field beach five blocks away. Miles of pastoral hiking trails in the historical Presidio Park one block away. Numerous outdoor dog-friendly cafes around the corner. All rooms have refrigerators, coffee makers, irons and hair dryers. There is a $10 per night per dog pet fee. Dogs may not be left unattended in the room at any time.

Monticello Inn
127 Ellis Street
San Francisco, CA 94102
415-392-8800
Well-behaved dogs of all sizes are welcome at this pet-friendly hotel. The boutique hotel offers both rooms and suites. Hotel amenities include complimentary evening wine service, evening room service, hotel library with magazines, newspapers and books, and a Borders Books and Music room service. There are no pet fees, just sign a pet liability form.

Palace Hotel
2 New Montgomery Street
San Francisco, CA 94105
415-512-1111
There is a $75 one time pet fee. This is a Sheraton Hotel.

Prescott Hotel
545 Post Street
San Francisco, CA 94102
415-563-0303
Well-behaved dogs of all sizes are allowed at this pet-friendly hotel. The luxury boutique hotel is located in Union Square and offers both rooms and suites. Hotel amenities include room service and an on-site 24 hour fitness room. There are no pet fees, just sign a pet liability form.

Residence Inn
Oyster Point Blvd & 101

San Francisco, CA 94080
650-837-9000
There is a $75 one time pet fee and a $10 per day additional pet fee.

Serrano Hotel
405 Taylor Street
San Francisco, CA 94102
415-885-2500
Well-behaved dogs of all sizes are welcome at this pet-friendly hotel. The luxury boutique hotel offers both rooms and suites. Hotel amenities include an evening hospitality hour, and a 24 hour on-site fitness room. There are no pet fees, just sign a pet liability form.

The Laurel Inn
444 Presidio Ave.
San Francisco, CA 94115
415-567-8467
This pet-friendly hotel is a boutique hotel in San Francisco's atmospheric Pacific Heights neighborhood. This newly renovated hotel includes a classic 1960's modern architectural design. Amenities include a complimentary continental breakfast served daily in the lobby, free indoor parking, laundry and valet service, room service from Dine-One-One and more.

W San Francisco
181 Third Street
San Francisco, CA 94103
415-777-5300
Dogs up to 80 pounds are allowed. There is a $25 per day additional pet fee.

Attractions

San Francisco

Barbary Coast Trail

San Francisco, CA
415-775-1111
The Barbary Coast Trail is a 3.8-mile walk through historic San Francisco. Bronze medallions

and arrows in the sidewalk mark the trail and guide you to 20 of the City's most important historic sites. It was created by the San Francisco Historical Society. Begin the self-guided walking tour at the Old U.S. Mint building on the corner of Mission and 5th Street. Along the trail you will find historic Union Square, the oldest Chinatown in North America, Plymouth Square, the Pony Express site and more.

Blue & Gold Fleet Ferry Rides
Pier 43 1/2
San Francisco, CA
415-773-1188
Take a ferry ride with your dog on the San Francisco Bay. There are several beautiful destinations. You can take the ferry from San Francisco Pier 43 1/2 (close to Fisherman's Wharf) to Tiburon or Sausalito (other city destinations are available, but mostly for commuting). Pets are not allowed on Alcatraz Island or Angel Island since these are both State Parks. Parking is next to Pier 43 1/2 or on Beach Street. Operations may depend upon weather, so please call ahead to confirm dates/hours.

Fisherman's Wharf Shopping
Jefferson Street
San Francisco, CA

Fisherman's Wharf is a classic tourist attraction. The walkways follow the bayshore and are complete with all types of street vendors and performers. It's a great dog-friendly place to walk your dog as long as your pup doesn't mind crowds. You can start at Ghirardelli Square and walk along the bayshore to Jefferson Street. Some of the piers don't allow dogs, but there are plenty of things to see and do on Jefferson Street.

Ghirardelli Square Shopping Center
900 North Point Street

San Francisco, CA 94109
(between Polk and Larkin)
415-775-5500
Back in 1893, the famous Ghirardelli chocolate factory occupied these buildings. Today, it is a popular shopping center with numerous shops including the dog-friendly Beastro By the Bay (your dog is welcome inside this unique animal motif gift store). At Ghirardelli Square, you and your pup can take the self-guided outside walking tour and learn about the area's history. Just pick up a free map at the information booth at the west end of Fountain Plaza.

Golden Gate Bridge Walk
Hwy 1/Hwy 101
San Francisco, CA

You and your dog can walk across this famous California and San Francisco landmark. The Golden Gate Bridge has been heralded as one of the top ten construction achievements of the 20th Century. The bridge was constructed in 1937 and is 1.7 miles long. Make sure your dog (and kids) stay away from the small gaps between the walking path and the road which go the water below. And don't forget to take a jacket, because it can get windy. There is a parking lot off Marine Street by Fort Point which is at the south end of the bridge (San Francisco side). You'll walk along a dirt and/or paved bike path to get to the Bridge Walk.

Pac Bell Park
24 Willie Mays Plaza
San Francisco, CA 94107
415-972-2000
There is a viewing deck along the water where you can view a few minutes of the game from way out in right field without entering the ballpark. You may take a leashed and well-behaved dog here. Also, one

game a year the bleachers are open to you and your well-behaved pup. It is usually in August and is known as Dog Days of Summer. Get tickets early.

Waterfront Carriage Rides
Jefferson Street
San Francisco, CA
Pier 41
415-771-8687
Want to tour San Francisco in style? Take an elegant horse and carriage ride with your well-behaved dog. They'll take you and your pup on a tour of Fisherman's Wharf. The carriages are located by Pier 41.

Beaches

San Francisco

Baker Beach
Golden Gate Natl Rec Area
San Francisco, CA
Lincoln Blvd/Bowley St

This dog-friendly beach in the Golden Gate National Recreation Area has a great view of the Golden Gate Bridge. The beach is located approx. 1.5 to 2 miles south of the Golden Gate Bridge. From Lincoln Avenue, turn onto Bowley Street and head towards the ocean. There is a parking lot next to the beach.

Fort Funston/Burton Beach
Skyline Blvd./Hwy 35
San Francisco, CA
John Muir Drive

This is a very popular dog-friendly park and beach. In the past, dogs have been allowed off-leash. However, currently all dogs must be on leash. Fort Funston is part of the Golden Gate National Recreation Area. There are trails that run through the dunes & ice plant from the parking lot above with good access to the beach below. It overlooks the southern end of Ocean Beach, with a large parking area accessible from Skyline Boulevard. There is also a water faucet and trough at the parking lot for thirsty pups. It's located off Skyline Blvd. (also known Hwy 35) by John Muir Drive. It is south of Ocean Beach. Thanks to one of our readers for this info. Expect to see lots and lots of dogs having a great time. But not to worry, there is plenty of room for everyone.

Ocean Beach
Great Hwy
San Francisco, CA
Sloat Blvd.
415-556-8642
You'll get a chance to stretch your legs at this beach which has about 4 miles of sand. The beach runs parallel to the Great Highway (north of Fort Funston). There are several access points including Sloat Blvd., Fulton Street or Lincoln Way. This beach has a mix of off-leash and leash required areas. Thanks to the San Francisco Dog Owners Group (SFDOG) for providing the following information: Dogs must be on leash on Ocean Beach between Sloat Blvd and Stairwell #21 (roughly at Fulton). North of Fulton to the Cliff House and South of Sloat for several miles are still okay for off-leash dogs, however parts of these areas may be impassible at high tide. The Golden Gate National Rec Area (GGNRA) strictly enforces the on-leash area between Sloat and Fulton. They usually give no warning tickets ($50 fine). As with all other leash required areas, we encourage dog owners to comply with the rules.

Parks

San Francisco

Alta Plaza Park

Clay Street
San Francisco, CA

This park is bordered by Jackson, Clay, Steiner and Scott streets. It is across from the tennis courts. The first Sunday of every month is Pug Day at this dog park. It's a casual meeting of pug owners which takes place at the north end of park, usually between 3: 30 - 5:00, weather permitting. At the gathering, there can be 20-50 pugs.

Golden Gate National Recreation Area

San Francisco, CA
415-556-0560
This dog-friendly Recreation Area spans 76,500 acres of land and water. It starts at the coastline south of San Francisco, goes into San Francisco and then north of the Golden Gate Bridge. Many of the San Francisco beaches and parks are part of this Rec Area including Baker Beach, Fort Funston and Ocean Beach. One of the trails is located south of Baker Beach. From Lincoln Avenue, turn onto Bowley Street and head towards the ocean. There is a parking lot next to the beach.

Golden Gate Park Dog Run
Fulton Street
San Francisco, CA
38th Avenue

This dog run is completely fenced in with water bowls. Located at 38th Ave & Fulton Street.

Lafayette Park
Sacramento St
San Francisco, CA
Gough St/Laguna St
415-831-2700
Lafayette Park allows leashed dogs. It's located on Sacramento Street and about two blocks west of Van Ness

Ave.

Presidio of San Francisco
Hwy 1/Park Presidio Blvd.
San Francisco, CA
Lake Street
415-561-4323
This land was an Army base and is now a dog-friendly national park (borders up to the Golden Gate Recreation Area.) The park has over 500 historic buildings and miles of nice hiking trails. Leashes are required. It's located south of the Golden Gate Bridge. From the Bridge and Hwy101, take Hwy 1 south. It will turn into Park Presidio Blvd. You can also enter the park from Arguello Blvd.

Restaurants

San Francisco

24th Street Cafe and Grill
3853 24th Street
San Francisco, CA 94114
415-282-1213
Dogs are allowed at the outdoor tables.

Bechelli's
2346 Chestnut St
San Francisco, CA 94123
415-346-1801
Dogs are allowed at the outdoor tables.

Blue Danube Coffee House
306 Clement St
San Francisco, CA 94118
Richmond District
415-221-9041
There is an outside counter where you can sit with your dog.

Cafe De La Presse
352 Grant Ave
San Francisco, CA 94108
Bush St(by Chinatown)
415-398-2680
It is located next to the Hotel Triton and Chinatown. This cafe also serves beer. Dogs are allowed at the outdoor tables.

Cafe Niebaum-Coppola
916 Kearny Street
San Francisco, CA 94133
415-291-1700
Dogs are allowed at the outdoor
tables.

Cafe Triste
1465 25th Street
San Francisco, CA 94107
415-550-1107
Dogs are allowed at the outdoor
tables.

Calzone's
430 Columbus Ave
San Francisco, CA 94133
North Beach
415-397-3600
Located in North Beach, this
Euro bistro features pasta, pizza
and much more. Well-behaved,
leashed dogs are allowed at the
outdoor tables. The restaurant is
open everyday from 9am-1am.

Cioppino's
Jefferson St
San Francisco, CA
(Fisherman's Wharf)

Cioppino's is located in the
Fisherman's Wharf area. It's on
the 400 block of Jefferson Street
by Leavenworth Street. Dogs
are allowed at the outdoor
tables.

Coffee Bean and Tea Leaf
2201 Fillmore St
San Francisco, CA 94115
Fillmore District
415-447-9733
This coffee shop is very popular
with the dogs. Dogs are allowed
at the outdoor tables.

Coffee Roastery
2191 Union Street
San Francisco, CA 94123
415-922-9559
Dogs are allowed at the outdoor
tables.

Crepes a Go Go
2165 Union St
San Francisco, CA 94123
415-928-1919

Dogs are allowed at the
outdoor tables.

Dolores Park Cafe
18th and Dolores
San Francisco, CA
at Dolores Park
415-621-2936
Dogs are allowed at the
outdoor tables.

Expo Family Restaurant
160 Jefferson St
San Francisco, CA 94133
(Fisherman's Wharf)
415-673-9400
Expo is located in the
Fisherman's Wharf area on
Jefferson by Taylor Street.
Dogs are allowed at the
outdoor tables.

Flippers
482 Hayes Street
San Francisco, CA 94102
415-552-8880
Dogs are allowed at the
outdoor tables.

**Ghirardelli Ice Cream
Fountain**
Ghirardelli Square
San Francisco, CA
Beach Street
415-771-4903
Come here to taste some of the
best ice cream around. It's in
Ghirardelli Square by the Clock
Tower on the first floor (by
Larkin Street). This place is
almost always crowded, but
there are several outdoor
tables. You'll need to order
inside and then grab one of the
outdoor tables.

I Love Chocolate
397 Arguello Blvd
San Francisco, CA 94118
415-750-9460
Dogs are allowed at the
outdoor tables.

Judy's Cafe
2269 Chestnut St #248
San Francisco, CA 94123
415-922-4588
Dogs are allowed at the

outdoor tables.

Lou's Pier 47 Restaurant
300 Jefferson St
San Francisco, CA 94133
(Fisherman's Wharf)
415-771-5687
Lou's is located in the
Fisherman's Wharf area on
Jefferson by Jones Street. They
have live bands seven days a
week and you might be able to
hear the music from outside.

**Martha & Brothers Coffee
Company**
1551 Church Street
San Francisco, CA 94131
415-648-1166
Dogs are allowed at the outdoor
tables.

Meze's
2373 Chestnut Street
San Francisco, CA 94123
415-409-7111
Dogs are allowed at the outdoor
tables.

Mona Lisa
353 Columbus Ave
San Francisco, CA 94133
415-989-4917
Dogs are allowed at the outdoor
tables.

Noe's Bar
1199 Church Street
San Francisco, CA 94114
415-282-4007
Dogs are allowed at the outside
tables and may be allowed
inside as well.

Park Chow
9th and Irving
San Francisco, CA
Sunset District
415-665-9912
Dogs are allowed at the outdoor
tables.

Peet's Coffee
2156 Chestnut St
San Francisco, CA 94123
415-931-8302
Dogs are allowed at the outdoor
tables.

Peet's Coffee and Tea
2197 Fillmore St
San Francisco, CA 94115
Fillmore District
415-563-9930
This coffee shop is very popular
with pups and their people.

Pluto's Fresh Food
3258 Scott St
San Francisco, CA 94123
Chestnut
415-775-8867
Dogs are allowed at the outdoor
tables.

Pompei's Grotto
340 Jefferson St
San Francisco, CA
(Fisherman's Wharf)
415-776-9265
Pompei's Grotto is located in the
Fisherman's Wharf area on the
300-400 block of Jefferson
Street by Jones Street. Dogs are
allowed at the outdoor tables.

Royal Ground Coffee
2060 Fillmore St
San Francisco, CA 94115
Fillmore District
415-567-8822
Dogs are allowed at the outdoor
tables.

Ti Couz
3108 16th St
San Francisco, CA
Mission/Castro
415-252-7373
Dogs are allowed at the outdoor
tables.

Stores

San Francisco

Le Video
1231 and 1239 9th Avenue
San Francisco, CA 94122
415-566-3606
Your well-behaved leashed dog
is allowed inside this store.

Neiman Marcus
150 Stockton Street

San Francisco, CA 94108
877-634-6264
This famous department store,
which sells everything from
clothing to home furnishings,
allows your well-behaved
leashed dog to shop with you.

Vets and Kennels

San Francisco

All Animals Emergency
Hospital
1333 9th Ave
San Francisco, CA 94122
415-566-0531
Monday - Friday 6 pm to 8 am,
Saturday noon - Monday 8 am.

Sacramento
City Guide
Accommodations

Davis

Best Western University
Lodge
123 B Street
Davis, CA 95616
530-756-7890
There is no additional pet
charge.

Econo Lodge
221 D Street
Davis, CA 95616
530-756-1040
There are no additional pet
fees.

Howard Johnson Hotel
4100 Chiles Road
Davis, CA 95616
530-792-0800
Dogs of all sizes are welcome.
There is a $10 per day pet fee.
They have one non-smoking
pet room, but cannot guarantee
it will be available.

University Inn Bed and
Breakfast
340 A Street
Davis, CA 95616

530-756-8648
All rooms are non-smoking.
There are no pet fees. Children
are also allowed.

University Park Inn & Suites
1111 Richards Blvd.
Davis, CA 95616
530-756-0910
Located within walking distance
of downtown Davis. They have
one pet room available and
there is a $10 per night pet
charge.

Folsom

Lake Natoma Inn
702 Gold Lake Drive
Folsom, CA 95630
916-351-1500
This inn offers 120 guest rooms
and 12 Lakeview Suites nestled
in a wooded natural environment
overlooking Lake Natoma. Enjoy
over 20 miles of beautiful bike
and dog-friendly walking trails
along the American river. This
inn is also located next to
Historic Folsom. There is a $45
one time per stay pet fee and a
$15 per day pet charge per pet.

Residence Inn
2555 Iron Point Road
Folsom, CA 95630
916-983-7289
This extended-stay inn offers a
complimentary continental
breakfast and an indoor pool.
There is a $100 one time per
stay pet charge and a $10 per
day pet fee.

North Highlands

Motel 6
4600 Watt Ave
North Highlands, CA 95660
916-973-8637
A large, well-behaved dog is
okay. Dogs may not be left
unattended in a room.

Rancho Cordova

Inns of America
12249 Folsom Blvd
Rancho Cordova, CA 95670
916-351-1213
This motel offers a complimentary continental breakfast. To get there from Sacramento, take Hwy 5 and exit Hazel Ave. Turn right onto Hazel. Then turn right onto Folsom Blvd. The hotel will be on the right. There is a $5 per day additional pet fee.

Residence Inn by Marriott
2779 Prospect Park Drive
Rancho Cordova, CA 95670
916-851-1550
This hotel offers 90 spacious suites. Amenities include an indoor pool and an exercise room, a complimentary breakfast and more. There is a $50 pet fee and a $10 per day pet charge.

Roseville

Best Western Roseville Inn
220 Harding Blvd.
Roseville, CA 95678
916-782-4434
They have a pet building at this inn. There is a $10 pet charge.

Oxford Suites
130 N Sunrise Ave
Roseville, CA 95661
916-784-2222
This inn features a health club, self-service laundry, heated pool and spa, and video rentals. Each room has a separate living area, 2 phones, 2 TVs, a microwave, refrigerator and more. To get there from Hwy 80, exit Douglas Blvd. and head east. Then turn left on N Sunrise Ave. There is a $15 one time pet fee.

Sacramento

Candlewood Suites
555 Howe Ave.
Sacramento, CA 95825
916-646-1212
This hotel offers studio and one

bedroom suites fully equipped with kitchens, oversized work areas and more. Amenities include a fitness center and spa. There is a $75 pet charge.

Canterbury Inn Hotel
1900 Canterbury Rd
Sacramento, CA 95815
916-927-0927
This inn is located about a 5-10 minute drive from Old Sacramento. Guest laundry services are available. To get there from Hwy 160, take the Leisure Lane ramp towards Canterbury Rd. Turn right onto Canterbury Rd. There is a $5 per day additional pet fee.

Motel 6
1254 Halyard Dr
Sacramento, CA 95691
916-372-3624
There are no additional pet fees.

Ramada Inn
2600 Auburn Blvd
Sacramento, CA 95821
916-487-7600
This inn offers complimentary continental breakfast, an exercise room and an outdoor pool. There is a $100 refundable pet deposit. To get there from Business Route 80, exit Fulton Ave and head south. Then turn left onto Auburn Blvd.

Residence Inn by Marriott
1530 Howe Ave
Sacramento, CA 95825
916-920-9111
This inn offers a complimentary continental breakfast, self service laundry facilities and a complimentary newspaper. Each guest room is a two room suite which includes hair dryers, ironing boards and data ports on phones. Fireplaces are available in some rooms. This Residence Inn charges a one-time $100 pet cleaning fee for the room. The inn is located about 1/2 mile from Howe Dog Park (see Parks). To get there

from Hwy 80, exit Arden Way and head east. Turn right on Howe Ave. It is located on Howe Ave, between Arden Way and Hallmark Drive.

Residence Inn by Marriott - South Natomas
2410 West El Camino Avenue
Sacramento, CA 95833
916-649-1300
This hotel offers 126 spacious suites. Amenities include an outdoor pool and an exercise room, a complimentary breakfast and more. Dinner delivery service is available from local restaurants. There is a $50 pet fee and a $6 per day pet charge.

Sheraton Grand Sacramento Hotel
1230 J Street
Sacramento, CA 95814
916-447-1700
Dogs up to 85 pounds are allowed. Dogs may not be taken into the bar or restaurant areas. There are no additional pet fees.

Attractions

Folsom

Old Towne Folsom
Sutter St & Riley St
Folsom, CA

This few block area of Folsom represents the historic mid 1800's gold rush days. There are shops, restaurants, and places to explore. Some of the restaurants will allow your well-behaved, leashed dog at their outdoor tables.

Rancho Cordova

Nimbus Fish Hatchery
2001 Nimbus Rd
Rancho Cordova, CA 95670
near Highway 50 and Hazel
916-358-2884
There is a free self-guided tour of the fish hatchery, where

salmon eggs are hatched every year. Your well-behaved dog may accompany you leashed. The hours are daily 9 am - 3 pm.

Sacramento

Capitol Park-Self-Guided Walk
10th and L Streets
Sacramento, CA
916-324-0333
At this park, you can enjoy the historic nostalgia of California's State Capitol. The Capitol Building has been the home of the California Legislature since 1869. While dogs are not allowed inside the Capitol Building, you can walk up to it and around it on the 40 acres known as Capitol Park. This park is home to a variety of different trees from around the world. There is a self-guided tour that explains the origin of the trees and plants. Squirrels are also in abundance here, so be sure to hold on to the leash if your pup likes those little creatures. Capitol Park is located in downtown Sacramento at 10th and L Streets.

Old Sacramento Historic Area
between I and L Streets
Sacramento, CA 95814
near Hwy 5 & Sacramento River
916-442-7644
Old Sacramento is a state historic park located in downtown Sacramento, next to the Sacramento River. This National Registered Landmark covers 28 acres and includes a variety of shops and restaurants (see Restaurants). Take the self-guided audio tour of Old Sacramento and learn about life in the 1860's. There are nine audio stations ($.50 per station) placed throughout Old Sacramento. The California State Railroad Museum is also located here. Dogs aren't allowed inside the museum, but there are several locomotives

outside. You and your pup can investigate these large trains outside of the museum. Dogs are allowed on the horse and carriage rides located throughout town. Top Hand Ranch Carriage Rides will be more than happy to take you and your well-behaved pup on their carriages. (see Attractions). Old Sacramento is located in downtown Sacramento, between I and L Streets, and Hwy 5 and the Sacramento River. Parking garages are located at 3rd and J Streets or at Capitol Mall and Front Streets. There is a minimal fee for parking.

Top Hand Ranch Carriage Rides
Old Sacramento
Sacramento, CA 95814
J Street & 2nd Street
916-655-3444
Top Hand Ranch offers horse and carriage rides in Old Sacramento and around the State Capitol. Your pooch is welcome in the carriage. Prices are subject to change, but when we checked it cost $10 for a 15 minute ride or $30 for a 35 minute ride around Old Sacramento. If you want to tour Sacramento in style, take the horse and carriage from Old Sacramento to the State Capitol Building and back. This ride lasts about 50 minutes and costs $50. The carriage rides are available daily in Old Sacramento. The carriages are located in several spots, but the main location is at the Old Supreme Court building near J and 2nd Streets. Old Sacramento is located in downtown Sacramento, between I and L Streets, and Hwy 5 and the Sacramento River. Parking garages are located at 3rd and J Streets or at Capitol Mall and Front Streets. There is a minimal fee for parking.

Parks

Carmichael

Carmichael Park and Dog Park
Fair Oaks Blvd & Grant Ave
Carmichael, CA
Grant Ave
916-485-5322
This is a one acre off leash dog park. It is located in Carmichael Park which can be accessed from Fair Oaks Blvd in Carmichael. The rest of the park is nice for picnics and other activities. Dogs must be leashed when not inside the dog park.

Citrus Heights

Rusch Community Park and Gardens
Antelope Road & Auburn Blvd
Citrus Heights, CA
Auburn Blvd

This is a nice city park with walkways, bridges and views plus a botanical garden to explore. The botanical garden is accessed from Antelope Rd and Rosswood. Dogs must be on leash at all times.

Davis

Cemetery Dog Run Park
Poleline Rd at East 8th
Davis, CA

Dogs are allowed on the east side of the cemetery over the small hill. Here three sides are fenced but the other side is open but not to heavy traffic. All other off-leash parks in Davis are entirely open and not fenced. Your dog should be well-behaved and reliably able to come when called to use this off leash park.

Community Park
1405 F Street
Davis, CA
14th Street

Dogs on leash are permitted in this and most parks in Davis. The park is 28 acres in size.

Folsom

Folsom Lake State Recreation Area
various (see comments)
Folsom, CA
916-988-0205
This popular lake and recreation area is located in the Sierra Foothills. The Folsom Lake State Rec Area is approximately 18,000 acres, of which, 45% is land. Leashed dogs are allowed almost everywhere in this park except on the main beaches (there will be signs posted). But there are many other non-main beaches all around Folsom Lake where your dog is welcome. There are about 80 miles of dog-friendly trails in this park. This park is also adjacent to the American River Parkway, a 32 mile paved and dirt path, which stretches from Folsom Lake to downtown Sacramento. Folsom Lake has various entry points and can be reached via Hwy 80 or Hwy 50. It is located about 25 miles east of Sacramento. From Hwy 80, exit Douglas Blvd in Roseville and head east. From Hwy 50, exit Folsom Blvd. and head north. There is a minimal day use fee.

North Highlands

Gibson Ranch Park
Elverta Rd West of Watt Ave
North Highlands, CA
Watt Ave
916-875-6961
This park allows dogs on leash. There are a lot of dirt walking or jogging trails which must be shared with horses as this is predominantly an equestrian park. There is a lake in the center with picnic areas and fishing available.

Orangevale

Orangevale Community Park
Oak Ave & Filbert Ave
Orangevale, CA
916-988-4373
Dogs must be on leash at this city park.

Roseville

Maidu Park
Rocky Ridge Rd & Maidu Dr
Roseville, CA
916-774-5969
Dogs must be on leash in this new 152 acre park in Roseville.

Marco Dog Park
1800 Sierra Gardens Drive
Roseville, CA
Douglas Blvd.
916-774-5950
RDOG (Roseville Dog Owners Group) helped to establish this 2 acre dog park which is Roseville's first off-leash dog park. This park was named Marco Dog Park in memory of a Roseville Police Department canine named Marco who was killed in the line of duty. The park has a large grassy area with a few trees and doggie fire hydrants. It is closed on Wednesdays from dawn until 3:30pm for weekly maintenance. Like other dog parks, it may also be closed some days during the winter due to mud. To get there from Hwy 80, exit Douglas Blvd. heading east. Go about 1/2 mile and turn left on Sierra Gardens Drive. Marco Dog Park will be on the right.

Sacramento

American River Parkway
various (see comments)
Sacramento, CA
916-875-6672
The American River Parkway is a very popular recreation trail for locals and visitors. There are over 32 miles of paved and dirt paths that stretch from

Folsom Lake in the Sierra Foothills to Old Sacramento in downtown Sacramento. It is enjoyed by hikers, wildlife viewers, boaters, equestrians and bicyclists. And of course, by dogs. Dogs must be on leash. There are various starting points, like the Folsom Lake State Recreation Area in Folsom or just north of downtown Sacramento. To start just north of downtown, take Hwy 5 north of downtown and exit Richards Blvd. Turn left onto Richards Blvd. Then turn right on Jibboom Street. Take Jibboom St to the parking lot.

Bannon Creek Dog Park
Bannon Creek Drive near West El Camino
Sacramento, CA
West El Camino
916-264-5200
This off leash dog park is in Bannon Creek Park. Its hours are 5am to 10 pm daily. The park is 0.6 acres in size.

Granite Park Dog Park
Ramona Avenue near Power Inn Rd
Sacramento, CA
916-264-5200
This dog park is in Granite Regional Park. Its hours are 5 am to 10 pm daily. It is 2 acres in size.

Howe Dog Park
2201 Cottage Way
Sacramento, CA 95825
Howe Ave
916-927-3802
Howe Dog Park is completely fenced and located in Howe Park. It has grass and several trees. To get there, take Business Route 80 and exit El Camino Ave. Head east on El Camino Ave. Turn right on Howe Ave. Howe Park will be on the left. Turn left onto Cottage Way and park in the lot. From the parking lot, the dog park is located to the right of the tennis courts.

Partner Park Dog Park
5699 South Land Park Drive
Sacramento, CA
916-264-5200
This dog park is located behind
the Bell Cooledge Community
Center. The park is 2.5 acres
and its hours are 5 am to 10 pm
daily. There are lights at the
park.

Restaurants

Carmichael

Bella Bru Coffee Co
5038 Fair Oaks Blvd
Carmichael, CA 95608
near Arden Way
916-485-2883
They allow dogs at their outdoor
tables and may even have dog
cookies for your pup.

Citrus Heights

Krispy Kreme Doughnuts
7901 Greenback Lane
Citrus Heights, CA
Sunrise
916-721-3667
Dogs are allowed at the outdoor
tables.

Davis

Ben & Jerry's
500 1st St #9
Davis, CA
530-756-5964
This Ben & Jerry's Ice Cream is
at the Davis Common in
Downtown. Dogs are allowed at
the outdoor tables.

Bruegger's Bagels
206 F Street
Davis, CA
530-753-6770
This bagel shop is in downtown
Davis. Dogs are allowed at the
outdoor tables.

Chico's Tecate Grill
425 2nd Street

Davis, CA
530-750-2252
This Mexican restaurant is
located in downtown Davis.
Dogs are allowed at the
outdoor tables.

Jamba Juice
500 1st Street #3
Davis, CA
530-757-8499
This Juice Bar is located at the
Davis Common in downtown.
Dogs are allowed at the
outdoor tables.

Mishka's
514 2nd Street
Davis, CA
530-759-0811
Dogs are allowed at the
outdoor tables.

Redrum
978 Olive Drive
Davis, CA 95616
Richards Blvd.
530-756-2142
This burger place is a local
favorite in this college town (the
original name was Murder
Burger and the new name is
Redrum Burger). They serve
regular hamburgers and ostrich
burgers, chicken sandwiches,
shakes and more. You can
order with your pup from the
outside window. Then enjoy the
food at the covered seating
next to the building or under a
large shade tree in the back. To
get there from Sacramento,
take Hwy 80 south and exit
Richards Blvd. Turn right onto
Richards Blvd. Then turn left
onto Olive Drive.

**Steve's Place Pizza, Pasta &
Grill**
314 F Street
Davis, CA
530-758-2800
Steve's Place has a nice
outdoor seating area for you
and your leashed dog.

Subway
4748 Chiles Rd

Davis, CA 95616
530-753-2141
Dogs are allowed at the outdoor
tables.

Fair Oaks

Steve's Place Pizza
11711 Fair Oaks Blvd
Fair Oaks, CA 95628
Madison Ave
916-961-1800
Dogs are allowed at the outdoor
tables.

Folsom

Bella Bru Coffee
1115 E Bidwell St #126
Folsom, CA
916-983-4003
Dogs are allowed at the outdoor
tables.

Chevy's Fresh Mex
705 Gold Lake Dr #200
Folsom, CA 95630
Old Towne Folsom
916-985-4696
Dogs are allowed at the outdoor
tables.

Coffee Republic
6610 Folsom Auburn Rd
Folsom, CA 95630
Old Towne Folsom
916-987-8001
Dogs are allowed at the outdoor
tables.

Lanza's Restaurant
718 Sutter St #200
Folsom, CA 95630
Old Towne Folsom
916-353-0273
Dogs are allowed in the outdoor
seats in the back only, not on
the front deck.

Pizzeria Classico
702 Sutter St
Folsom, CA 95630
Old Towne Folsom
916-351-1430
Outdoor seating is available
during the summer months only.

Snook's Candies and Ice Cream
702 Sutter St #G
Folsom, CA 95630
Old Towne Folsom
916-985-0620
Dogs are allowed at the outdoor tables.

Yager's Tap House and Grille
727 Traders Lane
Folsom, CA 95630
Old Towne Folsom
916-985-4677
Dogs are allowed at the outdoor tables.

Granite Bay

La Bou
4110 Douglas Blvd
Granite Bay, CA 95746
Sierra College Blvd
916-791-2142
Dogs are allowed at the outdoor tables.

Rancho Cordova

The Cellar Cafe
12401 Folsom Blvd
Rancho Cordova, CA 95742
Hazel Ave
916-985-0202
Enjoy lunch or dinner at this cafe. It is located in the Nimbus Winery Center. To get there from Sacramento, take Hwy 5 east and exit Hazel Ave. Turn right on Hazel and then left on Folsom Blvd. The cafe is on the left.

Rocklin

Jasper's Giant Hamburgers
4820 Granite Dr
Rocklin, CA 95677
Rocklin Rd - Sierra Meadows Plaza
916-624-9055
Dogs are allowed at the outdoor tables.

Redrum Burger
5070 Rocklin Rd

Rocklin, CA 95677
at Sierra College
916-624-4040
Dogs are allowed at the outdoor tables.

Roseville

Baja Mexican Grille
1850 Douglas Blvd #512
Roseville, CA 95661
916-773-2252
Dogs are allowed at the outdoor tables.

Dos Coyotes Border Cafe
2030 Douglas Blvd #4
Roseville, CA 95661
Eureka
916-772-0775
Dogs are allowed at the outdoor tables.

Quizno's Classic Subs
1228 Galleria Blvd #130
Roseville, CA 95678
916-787-1940
Dogs are allowed at the outdoor tables.

Togo's Eatery
1825 Douglas Blvd
Roseville, CA 95661
Sierra Gardens Drive
916-782-4546
This is a fast food sandwich place. It is within walking distance of Marco Dog Park (see Sacramento Parks). To get there, take Hwy 80 and exit Douglas Blvd. east (towards Folsom). Turn left at the third street which is Sierra Gardens Drive. Then make a left turn into the parking lot. Dogs are allowed at the outdoor tables.

Sacramento

Annabelle's Pizza-Pasta
200 J Street
Sacramento, CA 94086
2rd Street
916-448-6239
Located in Old Sacramento, this restaurant allows dogs at the outdoor seating area in the

back of the restaurant. There you will find several picnic tables.

Danielle's Creperie
3535 B Fair Oaks Blvd
Sacramento, CA 95864
Watt Ave
916-972-1911
The outdoor tables here are seasonal. Well-behaved dogs on leash are permitted at the outdoor tables.

Krispy Kreme Doughnuts
3409 Arden Way
Sacramento, CA
916-485-3006
Dogs are allowed at the outdoor tables.

La Bou
5420 Madison Ave
Sacramento, CA 95841
Garfield
916-349-1002
They gave our pup a dog cookie at the drive-thru. Dogs are allowed at the outdoor tables.

La Bou
10395 Rockingham Dr
Sacramento, CA 95827
at Mather Field Rd and Highway 50
916-369-7824
Dogs are allowed at the outdoor tables.

Metro Expresso
1030 K St
Sacramento, CA 95814
Downtown
916-444-8129
Dogs are allowed at the outdoor tables.

The Bread Store
1716 J Street
Sacramento, CA
916-557-1600
This sandwich shoppe allows dogs at the outdoor patio. The patio is covered.

Tony Roma's
1441 Howe Ave
Sacramento, CA 95825

Hallmark Drive
916-922-8787
This restaurant is one of the Tony Roma's U.S. chain of restaurants. It is famous for its BBQ ribs. They also serve chicken, steak, seafood and delicious desserts. You and your pup are welcome at the outdoor seats located in the front of the restaurant. To get there from Hwy 160, exit Arden Way heading east. Then turn right onto Howe Ave.

Stores

Davis

The Cultured Canine
231 G Street #3
Davis, CA 95616
530-753-3470
Well-behaved dogs are allowed inside this gift store.

Sacramento

Home Depot
3611 Truxel Rd
Sacramento, CA 95834
916-928-0722
Your well-behaved leashed dog is allowed inside this store.

My Best Friend's Barkery
1050 Front Street #120
Sacramento, CA 95814
In Old Sacramento
916-448-3436
Your dog will be drooling over the freshly baked treats here. They are welcome to sniff around the store and pick out their favorite goodies. This store is located in Old Sacramento in the Public Market area which is next to the train tracks and along the waterfront (next to Bike Sacramento). After a trip to the bakery, wander around dog-friendly Old Sacramento or take a horse and carriage ride with your pooch.

Vets and Kennels

Carmichael

Kenar Pet Resort
3633 Garfield Ave
Carmichael, CA 95608
near Whitney Ave
916-487-5221
Monday - Saturday 7 am - 6 pm, Sunday 3 pm - 6 pm pickup with extra day fee.

Fair Oaks

Greenback Pet Resort
8311 Greenback Lane
Fair Oaks, CA 95628
Overhill Rd
916-726-3400
This kennel is attached to a veterinary clinic. The kennel hours are Monday - Friday 8am to 6 pm, Saturday 8am - 5pm, Sunday 10am - 5pm.

Greenback Veterinary Hospital
8311 Greenback Lane
Fair Oaks, CA 95628
Overhill Rd
916-725-1541
There is also an on site kennel - Greenback Pet Resort. This is a 24 hour emergency veterinarian.

Roseville

Pet Emergency Center
1100 Atlantic St
Roseville, CA 95678
Hwy 80
916-632-9111
The vet is open 24 hours for emergencies.

Sacramento

Emergency Animal Clinic
9700 Business Park Dr #404
Sacramento, CA 95827
Hwy 50 and Bradshaw
916-362-3146
Monday - Saturday 9 am - 6 pm, Emergencies handled 24 hours.

Sacramento Emergency Vet Clinic
2201 El Camino Ave
Sacramento, CA 95821
Howe Ave
916-922-3425
Monday - Friday 6 pm to 8 am, 24 hours on the weekend.

Lake Tahoe City Guide
Accommodations

Hope Valley

Sorensen's Resort
14255 Highway 88
Hope Valley, CA 96120
530-694-2203
This secluded mountain resort is located in beautiful Hope Valley which is about 30 minutes south of South Lake Tahoe. Dogs are allowed in several of the cabins. The dog-friendly cabins sleep from two up to four people. Each cabin has a wood-burning stove (for heat) and kitchen. The Hope Valley Cross Country Ski Rentals are located on the premises (see Attractions). Hiking is available during the summer on the trails of the Toiyable National Forest. There are also several nearby lakes. Cabin rates start at $85 per night and go up to about $450 for a large bedroom cabin. There are no additional pet fees.

South Lake Tahoe

Alder Inn
1072 Ski Run Blvd.
South Lake Tahoe, CA 96150
530-544-4485
This dog-friendly motel can schedule their local pet-sitter to watch your dog if you want to try your luck at the casinos. The sitter will take care of your pup in the motel room. There is a $12 per day pet fee.

Colony Inn at South Lake Tahoe

3794 Montreal Road
South Lake Tahoe, CA 96150
530-544-6481
The Colony Inn at South Lake Tahoe is located just 1.5 blocks from Harrah's and the other casinos and just down the street from Heavenly Ski Resort. Want to experience the beautiful outdoors? The Colony Inn's backyard is National Forest Land, featuring dog-friendly hiking, mountain biking, and peace and quiet. There is a $25 refundable pet deposit, and pets cannot be left unattended in the rooms.

Fireside Lodge

515 Emerald Bay Rd.
South Lake Tahoe, CA 96150
530-544-5515
This inn offers log cabin style suites. The rooms have a unique "Country Mountain" theme decor with crafted fireplaces, and custom woodwork. Each room offers a microwave, refrigerator and coffee-maker, private bath w/shower, cable TV and VCR with numerous free videos available in their Gathering Room. Full kitchen units are available as well as private 1 to 4 bedroom cabins, off the property. There is a $20 per day pet charge.

Inn at Heavenly B&B

1261 Ski Run Boulevard
South Lake Tahoe, CA 96150
530-544-4244
You and your dog are welcome at this log-cabin style bed and breakfast lodge. The property is all dog-friendly and dogs are allowed everywhere but their Gathering Room. They offer 14 individual rooms each with a private bath and shower. Room conveniences include refrigerators, microwaves and VCRs. Some rooms have a fireplace. Three to four bedroom cabins are also available. The lodge is located on a 2-acre

wooded park complete with picnic areas, BBQs and log swings. Continental breakfast is served and snacks are available throughout the day. One large dog is allowed per room and pet charges apply. Room rates range from the low to mid $100s per night. Call for cabin prices. The owners have friendly dogs on the premises. The lodge is located in South Lake Tahoe. There is a $20 per day pet fee per pet.

Sandor's Chateau Motel

1137 Emerald Bay Road
South Lake Tahoe, CA 96150
530-541-6312
This pet-friendly motel is located on the quiet end of South Lake Tahoe just as you come into town on Highway 50, away from the congestion and noise of the casinos. They are situated in a park-like setting just minutes from beautiful Lake Tahoe. There are no extra pet charges.

Spruce Grove Cabins

P.O. Box 16390
South Lake Tahoe, CA 96150
530-544-0549
Spruce Grove puts you amidst a private, quiet secluded mountain resort off Ski Run Blvd., at the foot of Heavenly Ski Area and walking distance from Lake Tahoe. Spruce Grove offers private cabins and suites, with shady grounds for relaxing or BBQs. Close to shopping, restaurants, skiing, biking, hiking, entertainment and casinos. Children and well-behaved dogs are welcome. This dog friendly retreat is a fully fenced acre of land that is next to an open field of pine trees. There is a dog beach at the lake and lots of places to hike with your dogs. There is a $10 per night pet fee and a $100 refundable pet deposit ($25 for cleaning and $75 for damage). Please review the pet policy on the website or ask

when making a reservation.

Super 8 Motel

3600 Lake Tahoe Blvd.
South Lake Tahoe, CA 96150
530-544-3476
This motel offers good size rooms and a nice front lawn where you can walk your dog or sit at the various tables. There is a restaurant on the premises with a few outdoor picnic tables. They sometimes serve food outside - I guess it depends on how many waiters/waitresses they have. At night, you can walk up to the bar window, place your order, and then sit outside at the picnic tables with your dog while you enjoy a beer or wine. The motel also has an outdoor pool and spa. Pets are allowed only on the first floor of this two story accommodation, so if you are looking for a non-smoking room, call ahead as they tend to fill up fast. It's located on Hwy 50, west of Ski Run Blvd. There is a $10 per day pet fee per pet.

Tahoe Vista

Rustic Cottages

7449 North Lake Blvd
Tahoe Vista, CA 96148
530-546-3523
There is a $10 per day pet fee.

Tahoma

Norfolk Woods Inn

6941 West Lake Blvd.
Tahoma, CA 96142
530-525-5000
This inn only allows dogs in the cabins...but your pup won't mind. They have wonderful cozy cottages with kitchens. They only have 4 cabins, so call ahead. Also note that the entire premises is smoke free. Located directly in front of this inn is the Tahoe bike trail where you and your pup can walk or run for several miles. The trail is mostly paved except for a small dirt path section. The inn is located

approx. 8-9 miles south of Tahoe City on Hwy 89. There is a $10 per day additional pet fee per pet.

Tahoma Meadows Bed and Breakfast
6821 W. Lake Blvd.
Tahoma, CA 96141
530-525-1553
A well-behaved dog is allowed only if you let them know in advance that you are bringing your dog. Pets are allowed in one of their cabins, the Mountain Hideaway (previously known as Dogwood). This cabin includes a Queen bed, a fireplace, claw foot soaking tub, private deck and an efficiency kitchen. There is an extra $25 one time pet charge per stay, plus a security deposit. Cabin rates start at $145 per night.

Truckee

The Inn at Truckee
11506 Deerfield Drive
Truckee, CA 96161
530-587-8888
The Inn at Truckee specializes in relaxed accommodations and fun filled days for Truckee Tahoe Visitors. North Lake Tahoe resorts are located within a few minutes of this inn's doorstep. There is a $11 per day pet charge.

Zephyr Cove

Zephyr Cove Resort
460 Highway 50
Zephyr Cove, NV 89448
775-588-6644
Thanks to one of our readers for recommending this resort. Dogs are allowed in the cabins but not in the lodge or cabin number one. That still leaves a nice selection of cabins to choose from. There is a $10 per day pet fee. This resort is located near South Lake Tahoe on the Nevada side. Dogs are not allowed on the beach or at the outdoor seats at the restaurant.

Accommodations - Vacation Home Rentals

Kings Beach

Tahoe Rental House
Call to Arrange.
Kings Beach, CA
510-665-8100
This four bedroom, three bathroom house in north Tahoe is available for weekend, weekday, and holiday rentals. Dogs are welcome. This house can sleep up to 12 people. There is a $15 per day pet charge and a one time cleaning fee of $125.00.

South Lake Tahoe

Accommodation Station
2516 Lake Tahoe Blvd.
South Lake Tahoe, CA 96150
S. of Hwy 50
530-542-5850
The Accommodation Station is a property management company that rents out vacation homes, cabins, and condos in the South Lake Tahoe area. Each unit is completely furnished and features a fully equipped kitchen and fireplace. There are also many parks and hikes in the area that allow dogs (see Lake Tahoe Parks). They have a few properties that currently allow pets, but are working on getting more owners to accommodate the dog-friendly demand. They do not charge guests for pets in a particular property, but do charge a fully refundable security deposit provided no damage occurs. To find out which properties allow dogs, call 800-344-9364 or send an email to stay@tahoelodging.com. They will find out which rentals allow your pup.

Lake Tahoe

Accommodations
Call to Arrange.
South Lake Tahoe, CA
800-544-3234
This vacation home company offers luxury vacation rentals. Many are located near Lake Tahoe's world class golf courses and ski resorts. They have three pet-friendly vacation units. There are no extra pet fees.

Salsa's Chalet
South Lake Tahoe, CA
707-565-3740
This 2 bedroom, 1 bathroom vacation cabin rental is dog-friendly. Heavenly Ski Resort and major casinos are within one and a half miles of this cabin. It is a non-smoking cabin. Families, couples and children are welcome. Dogs are welcome with a $100 refundable pet deposit.

South Lake Tahoe Vacation Rental
Call to arrange.
South Lake Tahoe, CA
415-388-8170
This two story chalet vacation home rental is located in a residential neighborhood close to Lake Tahoe, Camp Richardson beach, and Emerald Bay. It has three bedrooms and two bathrooms, a yard and a deck. A well-behaved dog is allowed. There is a $10 per day pet charge and a $100 refundable pet deposit.

Stonehenge Vacation Properties
Call to Arrange.
South Lake Tahoe, CA 96158
800-822-1460
This vacation rental company offers several elegant and unique dog-friendly vacation homes located around South Lake Tahoe.

Tahoe Keys Resort
599 Tahoe Keys Blvd
South Lake Tahoe, CA 96150

530-544-5397
They feature approximately 50 pet friendly cabins, condos and homes in South Lake Tahoe. All dogs receive treats upon check-in. A $25.00 pet fee is taken per reservation. There is also a $100.00 refundable security deposit upon check in.

The Nash Cabin
Shirley Avenue
South Lake Tahoe, CA 96150
415-759-6583
This two bedroom, two bath cabin has everything you need; hot tub, wood stove, fire wood, full kitchen. They provide linens and towels and clean up after your stay. The cabin is located on a quiet street with a large fenced yard that backs onto a sunlit meadow. Dogs are welcome with a $100 pet deposit. There are miles of dog-friendly forest hikes within a five minute drive.

Squaw Valley

Squaw Valley Chalet
1730 Navajo Ct
Squaw Valley, CA 96146
530-550-8600
With views of Squaw Valley's Mountains, this is a comfortable one bedroom home. Granite counters, a jetted tub, new big screen TV, large deck with B.B.Q. and a plush leather couch are just a few of the upgrades to make you feel at home. Dogs are welcomed with a squeaky toy, dog cookies, clean dog towel, furniture sheet and more. Dogs stay Free!!!

Tahoe City

Tahoe Moon Properties
P.O. Box 7521
Tahoe City, CA 96145
530-581-2771
They have over 15 beautiful homes that allow well-behaved dogs. All of the houses are close to Tahoe City or ski areas. Bath

and bed linens are provided. There are a few dog rules; no dogs on the furniture, dogs are not to be left alone in the house, you must clean up after your dog and pet owners are responsible for any damages. Rates start at $150 per night with a 2 night minimum. There is a $30 per dog charge.

West Lake Properties
55 West Lake Blvd., P.O. Box 1768
Tahoe City, CA 96145
530-583-0268
Dogs are allowed in two of their vacation home rentals. The Log Cabin is within walking distance of Tahoe City and the Banovich Home, with a fenced yard for your dog, is located near Tahoe City.

Truckee

Andrea's Grinnin Bear Cabin
Call to Arrange.
Truckee, CA
530-582-8703
Located on a quiet cul-de-sac on a pine tree lot, this spacious 3 bedroom home is available for rent to people with pets. Nearby there are dog walks, hikes and places to explore. The Truckee river, Mardis Creek, Donner Lake and beach, Boca, Stampede and Prosser Reservoirs are all less than 15 minutes away.

Fore Paw Cottage
14906 Davos Drive
Truckee, CA 96161
530-587-4082
A cottage in a peaceful setting with fantastic views of Tahoe Donner golf course. Sleeps 6 comfortably with two queen beds, one king bed plus a bunk bed and a pull out queen bed. There is a maximum of two dogs, which always stay free. There is skiing at any of six major downhill ski areas located within 15 minutes.

Zephyr Cove

Lake Tahoe Lodging
P.O. Box 11489
Zephyr Cove, NV 89448
775-588-5253
Lake Tahoe Lodging has over 22 pet friendly vacation rentals in South Lake Tahoe. The properties range from 2 bedroom ski condos to 5 bedroom luxury lakefront estates. There is a $75.00 non-refundable pet security deposit. Also available is a homeopathic hourly pet sitting service through a local veterinarian.

Lake Village Resort
301 Highway 50
Zephyr Cove, NV 89448
775-589-6065
This vacation home rental company offers several pet-friendly condo rentals in Lake Tahoe. There is a $20 per day pet charge.

Attractions

Homewood

Mountain High Weddings
PO Box 294
Homewood, CA 96141
530-525-9320
Want to get married AND have your pooch with you to enjoy that special moment? Mountain High Weddings performs ceremonies on the North and West Shores of Lake Tahoe and they invite you to bring your dog. They have performed many ceremonies where rings were taken off the collars of special canine ring bearers. Couples have been married on skis on top of a mountain, under the full moon on the lake, or at a small intimate dinner party in the middle of a meadow. The weddings can be as traditional or unique as you desire. So if you are getting ready to tie the knot, now you can include your pooch in the wedding party.

Hope Valley

Hope Valley Cross Country Skis
14255 Hwy 88
Hope Valley, CA
east of Hwy 89
530-694-2203
Thirty minutes south of South Lake Tahoe is beautiful Hope Valley. The Hope Valley Cross Country Ski Center is located at the dog-friendly Sorensen's Resort (see Accommodations). Rent cross-country skis here (about $15-prices subject to change) and then take your pooch with you on the ungroomed trails in the Toiyabe National Forest. There are some advanced (uphill) trails next to the rental center. Beginners can take the skis and drive about a mile down the road to some easier trails. The Burnside Lake Trail is a flat, 14 mile cross-country loop trail around the lake. A smaller loop (about 4-5 miles) can be found at the Sawmill Trail. The rental center will be able to provide directions and/or maps.

Kirkwood

Kirkwood Cross Country Ski Center
Highway 88
Kirkwood, CA
209-258-7248
This ski resort allow dogs on two cross-country ski trails. They are the High Trail, located behind the Kirkwood Inn Restaurant, and the Inner Loop on the meadow. Adult passes are about $20 per day, children $6 per day and doggie passes are only $3 per day. Kirkwood is located about 45 minutes from South Lake Tahoe, on Hwy 88. The closest pet-friendly lodging to Kirkwood, that we know of, is in South Lake Tahoe. Thanks to one of our readers for recommending this attraction.

Olympic Valley

Ann Poole Weddings, Nature's Chapel
P.O. Box 3768
Olympic Valley, CA 96146
530-412-5436
This business offers Lake Tahoe and Bay Area Weddings. Make it a special day by bringing your dog along with you. Here is an excerpt from the Wedding Minister: "You are planning to marry the Love of Your Life... so naturally, you will bring your 'best friend' to your wedding, won't you? Dogs do great at weddings... they are excellent ring bearers or proudly stand up with you, with flowers around their collars. They seem to simply KNOW that this is a Special Day for you and that they have an important part in it." They have many Wedding locations to choose from. You can choose your own unique location or have your wedding in a wedding chapel, nestled in the woods, or at one of their favorite locations like on a cliff overlooking beautiful Lake Tahoe, surrounded by tall pine trees.

Squaw Valley Chapel
440 Squaw Peak Road
Olympic Valley, CA
530-525-4714
This chapel, supported by a local congregation of the United Church of Christ, welcomes persons of all faiths, and is very open to having your dog be part of the wedding ceremony. The chapel can seat up to 120 peple and offers a piano and a CD and tape player sound system. They can also refer you to local florists, photographers and musicians if needed.

Squaw Valley USA-Gondola
1910 Squaw Valley Rd
Olympic Valley, CA 96146
off Hwy 89
530-583-5585
This is a summer only attraction. Dogs are allowed in the Gondola/Cable Car, but make sure your best friend is not claustrophobic. You can take the cable car from the parking lot (6,200 ft elevation) to High Camp (8,200 ft elevation). Once at the top, your well-behaved leashed pooch is welcome inside the lobby and the gift shop. Want some exercise? From High Camp, hike down the mountain along the ski path. Want a more strenuous hike? Try hiking up to High Camp. Squaw Valley is located off Hwy 89 on the northwest shore of Lake Tahoe. Dogs are not allowed on the cable car on the 4th of July weekend because of the crowds and fireworks. Squaw Valley does have special events during the summer, like Full Moon Hikes and Stargazing at High Camp. Dogs are welcome at both events.

South Lake Tahoe

Tahoe Keys Boat Rentals
2435 Venice Drive E.
South Lake Tahoe, CA
Tahoe Keys Blvd.
530-544-8888
Rent a boat and cruise around on beautiful Lake Tahoe with your pup. Dogs are allowed as long as you clean up any 'accidents' your pup may do on the boat. Boat rentals can be seasonal, so please call ahead. It's located in Tahoe Keys. To get there from Hwy 89 north, take Hwy 50 east. Turn left onto Tahoe Keys Blvd and then right at Venice Drive East. Park at the end of Venice Drive and follow the signs to the rental office.

Tahoe Sport Fishing
900 Ski Run Boulevard
South Lake Tahoe, CA 96150
530-541-5448
This company offers sport fishing charters in the morning or

afternoon and your pooch can go with you. Travel from the south shore up to the north shore of Lake Tahoe and back. They have six fishing boats ranging from 30 to 45 foot boats. They will clean and bag the fish (trout) you catch. They can even suggest local restaurants that will cook your fresh catch for you. Call ahead to make a reservation. Rates for the morning charter are $80 per person and for the afternoon charter are $70 per person.

Tallac Historic Site
Highway 89
South Lake Tahoe, CA 96150

Three of Lake Tahoe's most luxurious playgrounds of the rich and famous were here on its south shore, including the Pope Estate. The Pope Estate is used as the interpretive center for the Tallac Historic Site; it features historic tours, exhibits, and living history programs. Dogs are allowed at the trails and outside of the historic buildings. The grounds are open year-round, though most of the buildings are open only during summer. From the intersection of highways 50 and 89 in South Lake Tahoe, travel 3.5 miles west on Highway 89. The entrance and parking areas are on the lake side of the highway.

Taylor Creek/Fallen Leaf-XCountry Ski
off Highway 89
South Lake Tahoe, CA

The Taylor Creek/Fallen Leaf area provides the newcomer to cross-country skiing an opportunity to enjoy winter adventure. Developed for the beginner, this well marked series of trails allows skiers to explore an area of forest with the knowledge that other people are near and there is no avalanche danger. The terrain is mostly flat and provides an excellent day

tour for the whole family. The developed trails cover a large area and although heavily used, are not congested. The loop trail traverses through open meadows and aspen groves. To get there, take Highway 89 north from South Lake Tahoe approximately 3-1/2 miles to the Taylor Creek Sno-Park. Snowmobiles are not allowed. You'll need to bring your own cross-country skis.

Stateline

Borges Sleigh and Carriage Rides
P.O. Box 5905
Stateline, NV 89449
775-588-2953
Take your pooch on a carriage or sleigh ride in Lake Tahoe. The carriage rides start in the casino area between Harveys and Horizon, and in front of Embassy Suites. The sleigh rides begin in the field next to Caesars Tahoe (on the corner of hwy 50 and Lake Parkway). The carriages and sleighs are pulled by their 2000 pound Blond Belgium horses or one of their rare American- Russian Baskhir Curlies which have been featured in Pasadena's Tournament of Rose Parade over the past few years. Carriage rides open noon until sunset daily, weather permitting. Prices are $15 per adult $7.50 per child under 11. Sleigh rides are given during the winter. Sleigh rides are open 10:00am to sunset (about 4:45pm). Sleigh rides are $15 per Adult $7.50 per child under 11.

Tahoe City

Blackwood Canyon Rd-XCountry Ski
off Highway 89
Tahoe City, CA

Picturesque scenery can be

seen along this unmarked road winding through Blackwood Canyon. Follow the road to an obvious junction and stay to the right. This path will lead you to a beautiful meadow where snowmobiles are not allowed. For a longer, more strenuous outing, continue upward to Barker Pass. Snowmobiles are allowed on this part of the trail. Take Highway 89 three miles south of Tahoe City to Blackwood Canyon Road, across from Kaspian Picnic Area. Continue to the Blackwood Canyon Sno-Park. You'll need to bring your own cross-country skis.

Page Meadow-XCountry Ski & Snowshoeing
off Highway 89
Tahoe City, CA

Try this pleasant ski or snowshoeing trip through a meadow surrounded by a scenic forest. Here are directions from the Lake Tahoe Basin Management Unit: From Highway 89, two miles south of Tahoe City, turn on Fountain Ave. just north of William Kent Campground. Turn right on Pine Ave., left on Tahoe Park Heights Dr., right on Big Pine Dr. and left on Silvertip. Park along the street where the snowplowing ends. Parking is extremely limited. Ski down the road to the meadow. There are no designated trails. Snowmobiles are not allowed. You'll need to bring your own skis or snowshoes.

Reel Deal Sport Fishing & Lake Tours
P.O. Box 7724
Tahoe City, CA 96145
530-581-0924
This dog-friendly fishing charter runs year-round. After your fishing trip, they will clean the fish for you. They also offer lake tours during the summer months. Rates are $75 per

person during the winter and $80 per person during the summer. Dogs are allowed on both the fishing tour and the lake tours.

Tahoe Cross Country Ski Area
Country Club Drive
Tahoe City, CA
near Hwy 28
530-583-5475
This is a winter only attraction. Tahoe Cross Country offers some of the best dog skiing in Lake Tahoe. It is a great place for dog lovers who want to enjoy cross country skiing with their pooch. They welcome dogs on 7.5 kilometers of trails (beginner and intermediate terrain). They also allow skijoring on their trails and offer skijoring equipment for sale (ask the store clerk to see the skijoring equipment). The dog trails are open on limited days (5.5 days a week, non-holiday). Bring your dog Monday through Friday 8:30am-5:00pm, and Sundays 2:00pm-5:00pm, non-holiday. Dog passes are $3.00 per dog per day, and season passes are $45.00 for the entire season. Prices are subject to change. Dogs are allowed on Special Green and Blue Trails and complimentary poop bags are provided.

Truckee River Raft Rentals
185 River Road
Tahoe City, CA 96145
530-581-0123
Your pooch is welcome to join you on a self-guided river rafting adventure. They just ask that your dog doesn't keep going in and out of the raft constantly because their nails can damage the raft. Enjoy a 2-3 hour leisurely, self guided, 5-mile float on the Truckee River from Tahoe City to the River Ranch Bar, Restaurant & Hotel. From there you can catch a free shuttle bus back to your car any time until 6 p.m. daily.

Parks

Glenbrook

Lake Tahoe State Park/Spooner Lake
Hwy 28
Glenbrook, NV
close to Hwy 50
775-831-0494
This hiking trail is known as the world famous "Flume Trail". This is one of the most beautiful places in the world to mountain bike. But as a hiker, you'll hardly notice the bicyclists because this trail is so long and a good portion of the path consists of nice wide fire trails. It starts at Spooner Lake and the entire loop of the Flume Trail is about 25 miles which can satisfy even the most avid hiker. For a shorter hike, try the trail that loops around Spooner Lake. For a longer 10-12 mile out and back hike, start at Spooner Lake and hike up to Marlette Lake. Although there is a rise in elevation, it's not a rock climbing path as most of this is a fire road trail. Even if you are used to hiking 10 miles, don't forget about the altitude which will make you tired quicker. Also, do not forget to bring enough water and food. To get to the start of the trail, from South Lake Tahoe, take Hwy 50 towards Nevada (north). Then turn left onto Hwy 28. Follow the signs to the Lake Tahoe State Park and Spooner Lake. Parking for Spooner Lake is on the right. There is a parking fee of approx. $5-7. This includes an extra fee for the pup - but well worth it. From South Lake Tahoe, it's about a 25-30 minute drive to Spooner Lake. Dogs must be leashed in the park.

Kings Beach

Coon Street Beach

Coon Street
Kings Beach, CA

Located at the end of Coon Street, on the east side of Kings Beach is a small but popular dog beach. There are also picnic tables, BBQs and restrooms at this beach.

North Tahoe Regional Park
National Avenue
Kings Beach, CA
Donner Road

In the summer this park is used for hiking and during the winter, it's used by cross-country skiers. There are about 3-4 miles of wooded trails at this park. Want to go for a longer hike? There is a National Forest that borders up to this regional park and dogs are allowed on those trails as well. To get there, take Hwy 28 by Kings Beach to Gun Club Road (north). Turn left on Donner Road and then right on National Avenue. There is a large parking lot at the end. Dogs must be on a leash in the park.

Olympic Valley

Squaw Valley USA
1960 Squaw Valley Rd
Olympic Valley, CA 96146
off Hwy 89
530-583-6985
In the summer (non-snow season) you and your pup can hike on the trails at this ski resort. Both of you will feel very welcome at Squaw. You can take your dog into the lobby to purchase the tickets for the dog-friendly Cable Car ride and/or snacks. As for the trails, there are many miles of hiking trails. One of the main hikes is from High Camp to the main parking lot or visa versa. It's the trail designed for night skiing (follow the light posts). During the summer, Squaw Valley has several dog-friendly events like

the Star Gazing and Full Moon Hikes where dogs are welcome. Dogs must be leashed at all times.

South Lake Tahoe

Cove East
Venice Drive East
South Lake Tahoe, CA
Tahoe Keys Blvd.

This short but nice path is located near the boat rentals and Tahoe Keys Resort. It's approximately 1-2 miles and will give your pup a chance to take care of business before hopping on board your rental boat. To get there from Hwy 89 north, take Hwy 50 east. Turn left onto Tahoe Keys Blvd and then right at Venice Drive East. Dogs must be leashed.

Eagle Falls
Hwy 89
South Lake Tahoe, CA

This beautiful moderate to strenuous hiking trail in the Desolation Wilderness starts at Hwy 89 and goes up to Eagle Lake. This trail is pretty popular because it's about a 1 mile hike from the road to the lake. If you want a longer hike, you can go another 4-5 miles where there are 3 other lakes. Dogs must be leashed. To get there from the intersection of Hwys 50 and 89, take Hwy 89 north and go approximately 8 miles. The Eagle Falls Picnic Area and parking are on the left. Day and Camping Wilderness Permits are required. Go here early because it is extremely popular and parking spots fill up fast. There is a minimal fee for parking. Dogs must be on leash on the trail.

Echo Lakes Trail
off Johnson Pass Road
South Lake Tahoe, CA

See a variety of alpine lakes on this moderate rated trail. Take Highway 50 to Echo Summit and turn onto Johnson Pass Road. Stay left and the road will lead you to the parking area by Lower Echo Lake. For a short hike, go to the far end of Upper Echo Lake. A longer hike leads you to one of the many lakes further down the trail. Day hikers, pick up your permit at the self serve area just to the left of the Echo Lake Chalet. Dogs should always be on leash.

Fallen Leaf Lake
Fallen Leaf Lake Rd off Hwy 89
South Lake Tahoe, CA

There are some nice walking trails on the north shore of Fallen Leaf Lake and the surrounding areas. To get there from the intersection of Hwys 89 and 50, take Hwy 89 north approximately 2.5 to 3 miles to Fallen Leaf Lake Rd. Turn left and in about 1/2 mile there will be parking on the right. The Fallen Leaf Lake Trail begins here. For a longer hike, there are two other options. For the first option, instead of taking the trailhead on the right, take the trail on the left side of Fallen Leaf Lake Rd. This trail is also known as the Tahoe Mountain Bike Trail. Option number two is to take Fallen Leaf Lake Rd further to the south side of Fallen Leaf Lake. Park at the Glen Alpine trailhead which offers about 3-4 miles of trails (parking is across from Lily Lake). There is also a trail here that heads off to the Desolation Wilderness which has miles and miles of trails. Dogs should be leashed.

Kiva Beach
Hwy 89
South Lake Tahoe, CA
530-573-2600
This small but lovely beach is a perfect place for your pup to

take a dip in Lake Tahoe. Dogs must be on leash. To get there from the intersection of Hwys 89 and 50, take Hwy 89 north approx 2-3 miles to the entrance on your right. Follow the road and towards the end, bear left to the parking lot. Then follow the path to the beach.

Tahoe City

Pebble Beach/Dog Beach
Hwy 89
Tahoe City, CA

This beach is not officially called "pebble beach" but it is an accurate description. No sand at this beach, but your water-loving dog won't mind. The water is crisp and clear and perfect for a little swimming. It's not a large area, but it is very popular with many dogs. There is also a paved bike trail that is parallel to the beach. There was no official name posted for this beach, but it's located about 1-2 miles south of Tahoe City on Hwy 89. From Tahoe City, the beach and parking will be on your left. Dogs should be on leash on the beach.

Truckee River Bike Path
Hwy 89
Tahoe City, CA

This paved path starts at Tahoe City and heads towards Squaw Valley, paralleling Highway 89. It's about 5 miles each way with spots for your water dog to take a dip in the Truckee River (just be careful of any quick moving currents.) To get there, the path starts near the intersection of Hwys 89 and 28 in Tahoe City. You can also join the path 1/2 - 1 mile out of town by heading north on Hwy 89 and then there are 1 or 2 parking areas on the left side which are adjacent to the path. Dogs must be on leash.

Pet Sitters

Tahoe City

Doggie Love Daycare
Call to Arrange.
Tahoe City, CA
530-525-6189
They offer either full day packages as well as sleepover packages. Doggie Love provides exercise & lots of playtime, socialization with other dogs, and love and nurturing. NO kennels, just plenty of doggie sofas, toys, warm fireplace and a comfy Tahoe home. They are open 7 days a week, 24 hours a day and provide your dog with around the clock care. Doggie daycare check-in begins at 7am daily and check-out is at 6 pm. Pick up/drop off service is available, please call for availability.

Truckee

Truckee Tails Pet Sitting and Doggy Day Care
P.O. Box 2945
Truckee, CA 96160
530-582-6964
At Truckee Tails Ranch your dog can run free on their beautiful 13-acre forest property chasing balls, splashing in kiddie pools, rolling in snow and romping with other friendly dogs. At lunch the dogs listen to classical music in a cozy bunkhouse while napping and snacking on treats. There's also trips to the lake, hiking in the mountains, doggy arts and crafts, agility games and photo sessions. Lots of one on one time with petting, love and attention for the older or independent dogs who can hang out, nap under trees and explore the forest. Open every day. Overnight camping also available.

Zephyr Cove

Zephyr Feed & Boarding
396 Dorla Court - PO Box 10548
Zephyr Cove, NV 89448
775-588-3907
Zephyr Feed & Boarding is Tahoe's dog & cat boarding place for stress free boarding for you and your pet, so you can relax on your vacation. Located just 2 miles east of the South Shore's casinos, they offer daycare & overnight boarding. Doggie daycare is available by the hour or day, so you can tour around the sites and know your pet is having a day of fun. The kennel is climate controlled inside, full walls for stress free boarding, veterinarian on call, an outside area for potty time, inside exercise runs, and a large playroom. Your pet will receive daily individual exercise, playtime with the other boarders during social time, belly rubs, and lots of love and cookies.

Restaurants

Carnelian Bay

Old Post Office Coffee Shop
5245 North Lake Blvd
Carnelian Bay, CA
530-546-3205
This restaurant is open for breakfast and lunch. They welcome well-behaved dogs at their outdoor seats. Dogs need to be leashed while sitting at the table with you.

Homewood

Pisanos Pizza
5335 West Lake Blvd
Homewood, CA
530-525-6464
Enjoy pizza at one of the several outdoor tables. The restaurant (formerly West Side Pizza) is located off Hwy 89 in Homewood (between Tahoe

City and Tahoma on the west shore of Lake Tahoe.)

West Shore Cafe
5180 West Lake Blvd.
Homewood, CA 96145
530-525-5200
This restaurant comes highly recommended from one of our readers. They said the food was delicious and the place is very dog-friendly. They went there with several people and about 7 dogs. The outdoor dining area is located on a pier right next to beautiful Lake Tahoe. Take a look at their website for the lunch and dinner menu. The restaurant is open seven days a week during the summer, weather permitting, from about Memorial Day to Labor Day. Lunch is served from 11:30am to 3:00pm, Happy Hour is from 3:00pm-5:30pm, and Dinner is from 5:30pm-10:00pm.

Incline Village

Grog & Grist Market & Deli
800 Tahoe Blvd
Incline Village, NV 89451
775-831-1123
They have a few tables and some benches outside where your dog is welcome.

T's Rotisserie
901 Tahoe Blvd
Incline Village, NV 89451
775-831-2832
This restaurant serves rotisserie sandwiches and more. Your dog can sit with you at the outdoor tables.

Kings Beach

Brockway Bakery
8710 North Lake Blvd
Kings Beach, CA
530-546-2431
Grab one of the several outdoor tables at this bakery and enjoy. It's located on Hwy 28 in Kings Beach.

Olympic Valley

Thunder Ridge Cafe
150 Alpine Meadows Rd # 2
Olympic Valley, CA 96146
530-583-6896
Dogs are allowed at the outdoor tables.

South Lake Tahoe

Bountiful Cafe
717 Emerald Bay Rd
South Lake Tahoe, CA 96150
near 10th Street
530-542-4060
Leashed dogs are welcome to sit at the outdoor tables.

Carina's Cafe
3469 Lake Tahoe Blvd
South Lake Tahoe, CA 96150
530-541-3354
They are open for breakfast and lunch. Dogs are allowed at the outdoor tables. This cafe is located near the shoreline of Lake Tahoe.

Chris' Cafe
3140 Highway 50
South Lake Tahoe, CA 96150
530-577-5132
This cafe is located in Meyers which is off Highway 50, before you enter into South Lake Tahoe. Your dog is welcome at their outdoor picnic tables.

Colombo's Burgers A-Go-Go
841 US Hwy 89 Emerald Bay Rd
South Lake Tahoe, CA 96150
530-541-4646
Dogs are welcome at the outdoor tables.

Dixon's Restaurant & Brewery
675 Emerald Bay Rd
South Lake Tahoe, CA 96150
530-542-3389
Dogs are welcome at the outdoor tables.

Izzy's Burger Spa
2591 Highway 50
South Lake Tahoe, CA 96150
530-544-5030

Dogs are welcome at the outdoor tables.

J&J Pizza
2660 Lake Tahoe Blvd
South Lake Tahoe, CA 96150
near Sierra Blvd.
530-542-2780
They have a few outdoor tables on the sidewalk. The outdoor tables are seasonal.

Marie Callender's Restaurant
3599 Lake Tahoe Boulevard
South Lake Tahoe, CA 96150
near Ski Run Blvd.
530-544-5535
Dine with your pooch at the outdoor tables. The outside dining is seasonal.

Meyer's Downtown Cafe
3200 Highway 50
South Lake Tahoe, CA 96150
530-573-0228
This dog-friendly cafe is off Highway 50 in Meyers, before entering South Lake Tahoe.

Rude Brothers Bakery and Coffee House
3117 Harrison Ave #B
South Lake Tahoe, CA 96150
530-541-8195
Dogs are allowed at the outdoor tables.

Shoreline Cafe
3310 Lake Tahoe Blvd
South Lake Tahoe, CA 96150
530-541-7858
Dogs are allowed at the outdoor tables. They are open for breakfast and lunch. This cafe is located near the shoreline of Lake Tahoe.

Sno-Flake Drive In
966 Modesto Avenue
South Lake Tahoe, CA

This is a great place for a burger or chicken sandwich. You can walk up to the outside order window and then sit on the small patio and enjoy your lunch or dinner. To get there from the intersection of Hwys 50 and 89, take Hwy 50 south. It will be on your right at Modesto Ave.

Tahoe City

Black Bear Tavern
2255 West Lake Blvd.
Tahoe City, CA 96145
530-583-8626
Dogs are allowed at the outdoor tables at this upscale restaurant. The restaurant is located on Hwy 89, south of downtown Tahoe City.

Coyotes Mexican Grill
521 N Lake Blvd
Tahoe City, CA 96145
530-583-6653
Dogs are allowed at the outdoor tables.

Fast Eddies Texas Bar-B-Que
690 N Lake Blvd
Tahoe City, CA 96145
530-583-0950
Dogs are allowed at the outdoor tables.

Fiamma
521 North Lake Blvd
Tahoe City, CA
530-581-1416
This Italian restaurant has a few seats outside where dogs are welcome. Arrive early to get one of the tables.

Naughty Dawg Saloon & Grill
255 North Lake Blvd
Tahoe City, CA
530-581-3294
This is definitely a dog-friendly restaurant. They welcome your pup which is obvious from the dog dishes full of water on the patio. This is a very popular place for both local and vacationing dogs. Choose from a variety of foods on their menu (many of which have doggie names.). This is absolutely a place worth visiting either for lunch, dinner, or just a beer. It's located in Tahoe City on Hwy 28 which is on the northwest shore

of Lake Tahoe.

Rosie's Cafe
571 North Lake Blvd
Tahoe City, CA
530-583-8504
Enjoy a delicious breakfast, lunch or dinner on the porch at this cafe. It's located in Tahoe City off Hwy 28 which is located on the northwest shore of Lake Tahoe.

Sierra Vista Lakefront Dining
700 N Lake Blvd
Tahoe City, CA 96145
530-583-0233
Dogs are allowed at the outdoor tables at this lakefront restaurant in the heart of Tahoe City. They have outside heaters if it gets a little too chilly. This restaurant offers a variety of dishes including Chinese Stir Fry, Jambalaya, San Francisco Style Ciopinno and Chicken Cordon Bleu.

Syd's Bagelery & Expresso
550 N Lake Blvd
Tahoe City, CA 96145
530-583-2666
Your dog is welcome at the outdoor picnic tables.

Tahoe House Bakery and Gourmet Store
625 W Lake Blvd
Tahoe City, CA 96145
530-583-1377
They offer fresh baked breads, pastries, coffee drinks, cookies, European style tortes, deli lunches fully prepared meals to go with gourmet chesses, meats and more. Dogs are allowed at the outdoor tables.

Truckee

Earthly Delights
10087 W River St
Truckee, CA 95603
530-587-7793
This deli cafe allows dogs at their outdoor tables. They also offer freshly baked breads and

pastries.

Stores

Tahoe City

Bone Jour-Gift Store
521 North Lake Blvd.
Tahoe City, CA
530-581-2304
Dogs are welcome inside this specialty gift store for dogs, cats and people. They also have a selection of dog treats and toys. It is on the second story near Fiamma Restaurant. Bone Jour is located in Tahoe City on Hwy 28 which is on the northwest shore of Lake Tahoe.

Vets and Kennels

Carson City

Carson Tahoe Veterinary Hospital
3389 S. Carson Street
Carson City, NV
775-883-8238
Weekdays 7:30 am - 6 pm. Emergencies will be seen 24 hours with an additional $60 emergency fee.

Portland City Guide

Accommodations

Gresham

Hawthorn Inn & Suites
2323 NE 181st Ave
Gresham, OR 97230
503-492-4000
There is a $10 per stay pet fee.

Lake Oswego

Crowne Plaza
14811 Kruse Oaks Dr
Lake Oswego, OR 97035
503-624-8400
There is a $10 per day pet fee.

Portland

5th Avenue Suites
506 S.W. Washington
Portland, OR 97204
503-222-0001
Well-behaved dogs of all sizes are welcome at this pet-friendly hotel. The luxury boutique hotel offers both rooms and suites. Hotel amenities include complimentary evening wine service, and a 24 hour on-site fitness room. There are no pet fees, just sign a pet liability form.

Best Western Inn at the Meadows
1215 N Hayden Meadows Dr
Portland, OR 97217
503-286-9600
There is a $21.80 one time pet fee.

Comfort Inn
8855 SW Citizen Dr.
Portland, OR 97070`
503-682-9000
There is a pet fee of $10 per day.

Days Inn
9930 N Whitaker Rd
Portland, OR 97217
503-289-1800
There is a $15 one time pet fee.

Hotel Lucia
400 SW Broadway
Portland, OR 97205
503-228-7221
There is a $100 refundable pet deposit.

Hotel Vintage Plaza
422 SW Broadway
Portland, OR 97205
503-228-1212
Well-behaved dogs of all sizes are welcome at this pet-friendly hotel. The luxury boutique hotel offers both rooms and suites. Hotel amenities include complimentary evening wine service, complimentary high-speed Internet access in all guest rooms, 24 hour room service and an on-site fitness

room. There are no pet fees, just sign a pet liability form.

Howard Johnson Hotel
7101 NE 82nd Ave.
Portland, OR 97220
503-255-6722
Dogs of all sizes are welcome. There is a $15 per day pet fee.

La Quinta Inn & Suites Portland Northwest
4319 NW Yeon
Portland, OR
503-497-9044
Dogs of all sizes are allowed at the hotel.

La Quinta Inn Portland - Lloyd
431 NE Multnomah
Portland, OR
503-233-7933
Dogs up to 75 pounds are allowed at the hotel.

Mallory Hotel
729 SW 15th
Portland, OR 97205
503-223-6311
There is a $10 one time fee for pets.

Motel 6
3104 SE Powell Blvd
Portland, OR 97202
503-238-0600
There are no pet fees. Pets must never be left alone in rooms.

Quality Inn Portland Airport
8247 NE Sandy Blvd.
Portland, OR 97220
503-256-4111
There is a pet fee of $15 per day.

Sheraton Portland Airport Hotel
8235 NE Airport Way
Portland, OR 97220
503-281-2500
Dogs of all sizes are allowed. There is a $25 one time per stay pet fee.

Sleep Inn
2261 NE 181st Ave.
Portland, OR 97230

503-618-8400
There is a pet fee of $10 per day, to a maximum of $50.

Staybridge Suites
11936 NE Glenn Widing Drive
Portland, OR 97220
503-262-8888
There is a $25 one time pet fee plus a pet fee of $10 per day.

Tigard

Motel 6
17950 SW McEwan Rd
Tigard, OR 97224
503-620-2066
There are no additional pet fees. Pets must not be left alone in rooms.

Tualatin

Sweetbrier Inn
7125 SW Nyberg
Tualatin, OR 97062
503-692-5800
There is a $25 refundable pet deposit for standard rooms, $50 for suites.

Wilsonville

Holiday Inn Select
25425 SW 95th Ave
Wilsonville, OR 97070
503-570-8500
There is a $10 per day pet fee.

Attractions

Portland

Portland Saturday Market
108 West Burnside
Portland, OR
503-222-6072
This is the largest outdoor arts and crafts market in continuous operation in the United States. It is also one of Portland's top tourist attractions. You will find over 350 artisans, live music and lots of food vendors. There are also many pet-related

booths that sell anything from dog cookies, bandanas, and dog beds to waterproof fleece-lined dog coats. Well-behaved leashed dogs are allowed. This market is open Saturdays from 10am to 5pm and on Sundays from 11am to 4:30pm. The market is located between Front Avenue and SW 1st Avenue under the Burnside Bridge.

Portland Walking Tours
SW Broadway and Yamhill
Portland, OR 97205
503-774-4522
Take an award-winning guided outdoor walking tour of Portland. Their most popular tour is called The Best of Portland. This 2 to 2.5 hour morning tour features an overview of Portland including history, architecture, artwork, and more. The tour goes through downtown Portland, the Cultural District, Historic Yamhill and along the riverfront. Tours are held rain or shine on Friday, Saturday and Sunday at 10:30am and 3pm, from April through November. The cost is $15 per person and free for dogs and young children. At the beginning of the tour, the guide will ask if everyone is okay with dogs. If there is anyone in your tour that is uncomfortable around dogs, you might have to keep your pooch away from that person by staying on the other side of the group. The overwhelming majority of people on these tours are okay with dogs. All tours leave from the Pioneer Courthouse Square. Please note that they strongly recommend reservations, even a week or two in advance.

The Grotto
NE 85th and Sandy Blvd.
Portland, OR 97294
503-254-7371
This is a 62 acre Catholic Shrine and botanical garden. While dogs are not allowed on the upper level, they are allowed

outdoors on the first level, both in the plaza and in the botanical garden. The Grotto holds special events throughout the year, including a Blessing of the Animals each July. Well-behaved leashed dogs are allowed. The main public entrance to the Grotto is located on Sandy Blvd (Hwy 30) at Northeast 85th Avenue. It is near the junction of the I-205 and I-84 freeways just minutes from downtown Portland.

Parks

Portland

Chimney Dog Park
9360 N. Columbia Blvd
Portland, OR
503-823-7529
This entire 16-acre park is designated as an off-leash area. The park has meadows and trails but is not fenced and no water is available. The park is open year-round and is located next to the City Archives Building.

East Delta Park Off-Leash Area
N. Union Court
Portland, OR
503-823-7529
This 5 acre off-leash fenced field has trees and benches, but no water. It is open during the dry season only, from May through October. Dogs are allowed off-leash, but not on the sports fields. The park is located off exit 307 on I-5 across from the East Delta Sports Complex.

Gabriel Park and Off-Leash Area
SW 45 Ave and Vermont
Portland, OR
503-823-7529
This popular regional park offers trails, a natural area and picnic tables. Dogs are not allowed on the playgrounds, sports fields, tennis courts, or in the wetlands

and creeks. They are allowed in the rest of the park but must be leashed, except for the designated off-leash area. There is a 1.5 acre fenced dog park that has trees, picnic tables and water. The dog park is only open during the dry season, from May through October.

Portland Rose Gardens
various locations
Portland, OR
503-823-7529
There are three main rose gardens in Portland. The Internation Rose Test Garden in Washington Park is one of the world's most famous rose gardens. It is a popular tourist site with great views and more than 8,000 roses. Ladd's Addition Rose Garden, located at SE 16th and Harrison, displays over 3,000 roses. The Peninsula Park Rose Garden, located at N. Ainsworth between Kerby and Albina, offers more than 8,800 fragrant roses. Dogs may accompany you to all of the rose gardens, but pets must be leashed and you are required to clean up after your dog.

Powell Butte Nature Park
SE 162nd Avenue and Powell Blvd
Portland, OR 97230
503-823-7529
This 592 acre park is an extinct volcano and is Portland's second largest park. There are over 9 miles of hiking trails which are popular with mountain bicyclists, horseback riders, and hikers. Dogs must be leashed and people must clean up after their dogs.

Tom McCall Waterfront Park
Naito Parkway
Portland, OR
503-823-7529
This waterfront park follows the Willamette River, between SW Clay and NW Glisan. The park

offers walking and bicycling trails. Dogs are allowed but must be leashed and people need to clean up after their pets.

Washington Park
SW Park Place
Portland, OR 97210
503-823-7529
This 129 acre park offers hiking trails and a popular rose garden. Dogs must be leashed and people must clean up after their dogs.

West Delta Park Off-Leash Area
N. Expo Road & Broadacre
Portland, OR
503-823-7529
This 3 acre field is not fenced and there is no water available. It is open year-round but the ground gets soggy after heavy rains. Dogs are allowed off-leash. The park is located off exit 306B on I-5 next to the entrance to Portland International Raceway (PIR).

Restaurants

Portland

Baja Fresh Mexican Grill
1121 W. Burnside St.
Portland, OR
503-595-2252
This Mexican restaurant chain offers a variety of items on their menu including burritos, tacos, salads, quesadillas, fajitas, and enchiladas. Well-behaved leashed dogs are allowed at the outdoor tables.

Baja Fresh Mexican Grill
1505 NE 40th Ave
Portland, OR
503-331-1000
This Mexican restaurant chain offers a variety of items on their menu including burritos, tacos, salads, quesadillas, fajitas, and enchiladas. Well-behaved leashed dogs are allowed at the outdoor tables.

Bibo Juice
1445 NE Weidler St.
Portland, OR
503-288-5932
This juice bar offers a variety of smoothies and fruit juices. They also have nutritional supplements that can be added to the drinks. Well-behaved leashed dogs are allowed at the outdoor tables.

Dogs Dig Vegetarian Deli
212 NW Davis, Old Town Area
Portland, OR
503-223-3362
This small deli has a few outdoor tables. Well-behaved leashed dogs are allowed at the outdoor tables.

Garbonzo's
6341 S.W. Capitol Highway
Portland, OR 97201
503-293-7335
This Middle Eastern fast food restaurant has patio dining. Well-behaved leashed dogs are allowed at the outdoor tables.

Jake's Famous Crawfish
401 SW 12th Ave.
Portland, OR
at Stark St
503-226-1419
This seafood restaurant is part of the McCormick & Schmick's chain. Well-behaved leashed dogs are allowed at the outdoor tables.

Lucky Labrador Brewing Co.
915 SE Hawthorne Blvd.
Portland, OR
503-236-3555
This dog-friendly brew pub has a labrador retriever as their mascot and on their beer labels. At the outside seating area, your pooch can relax at your feet while you unwind with some beer or food. The pub offers a nice variety of food including veggie and meat sandwiches, bentos (chicken or veggies over rice), soup and more. Of course, if you love beer, you will also have to try their ales like the Black Lab Stout, the Dog Day India Pale Ale or the Top Dog Extra Special Pale Ale. And if you visit during the month of October, don't miss their Dogtoberfest usually held on a Saturday. They celebrate the pub's anniversary on this day. The highlight of the day is the dog wash, which helps to raise money for dog-related causes or dog organizations. For treats, humans can try a special Dogtoberfest ale and doggies can get dog cookies and biscuits. The pub might even have a band for musical entertainment as well. Please keep pets leashed.

Lucky Labrador Public House
7675 SW Capitol Highway
Portland, OR
503-244-2537
This restaurant is a spin-off from the original Lucky Labrador Brewing Co. Dogs are welcome at the outdoor tables. The restaurant serves pizza, salads, and draught ale direct from their brewery in southeast Portland. They are located on Capitol Highway, near 31st Street. Please keep pets leashed.

McCormick and Schmick's Harborside Restaurant
309 SW Montgomery
Portland, OR
503-220-1865
This seafood restaurant is located in the RiverPlace Marina. Well-behaved leashed dogs are allowed at the outdoor tables.

Rubio's Fresh Mexican Grill
1307 NE 102nd Avenue
Portland, OR 97220
503-258-8340
This Mexican restaurant chain serves items like chargrilled steak and chicken burritos, tacos, quesadillas, seafood including lobster, shrimp, Mahi-Mahi, and their famous fish taco. Well-behaved leashed dogs are allowed at the outdoor tables.

The Divine Cafe
9th and SW Alder Street
Portland, OR
503-314-9606
This outdoor food vendor offers vegan and organic foods. There are a few outdoor seats. Well-behaved leashed dogs are allowed at the outdoor tables.

Vita Cafe
3024 NE Alberta
Portland, OR
503-335-8233
This natural food restaurant specializes in vegan dishes, but they also offer meat too. Organic foods and ingredients are used whenever possible. Well-behaved leashed dogs are allowed at the outdoor tables.

Wild Oats Natural Marketplace
3535 15th Ave.
Portland, OR
503-288-3414
This natural food market has a deli with outdoor seats. Well-behaved leashed dogs are allowed at the outdoor tables. They are located on 15th Avenue at Fremont.

Wild Oats Natural Marketplace
6344 SW Capitol Highway
Portland, OR
503-244-3110
This natural food market has a deli with a couple of outdoor seats. Well-behaved leashed dogs are allowed at the outdoor tables. The deli is located in the Hillsdale Shopping Center.

Wild Oats Natural Marketplace
2825 East Burnside Street
Portland, OR
503-232-6601
This natural food market has a deli with outdoor seats. Well-behaved leashed dogs are allowed at the outdoor tables.

Seattle City Guide

Accommodations

Issaquah

Motel 6
1885 15th Pl NW
Issaquah, WA 98027
425-392-8405
There are no additional pet fees.

Kirkland

Best Western Kirkland Inn
12223 NE 116th St
Kirkland, WA 98034
425-822-2300
There is a $50 refundable pet deposit. There are only a few non-smoking pet rooms so make a reservation early.

La Quinta Inn Bellevue - Kirkland
10530 NE Northup Way
Kirkland, WA
425-828-6585
Dogs up to 75 pounds are allowed at the hotel.

Motel 6
12010 120th Pl NE
Kirkland, WA 98034
425-821-5618
One well-behaved dog is allowed per room. Pets must be attended at all times.

Seattle

Alexis Hotel
1007 First Avenue
Seattle, WA 98104
206-624-4844
Well-behaved dogs up to 200 pounds are welcome at this pet-friendly hotel. The luxury boutique hotel offers both rooms and suites. Hotel amenities include complimentary evening wine service, 24 hour room service and an on-site fitness room. This hotel is located near the historic Pioneer Square and Pike's Place Market. There are no pet fees, just sign a pet

liability form.

Crowne Plaza - Downtown
1113 6th Ave
Seattle, WA 98101
206-464-1980
There is a $75 refundable pet deposit. Dogs up to 75 pounds are allowed.

Hotel Monaco Seattle
1101 4th Avenue
Seattle, WA 98101
206-621-1770
Well-behaved dogs of all sizes are welcome at this pet-friendly hotel. The luxury boutique hotel offers both rooms and suites. Hotel amenities include complimentary evening wine service, complimentary high speed Internet access in all guest rooms, 24 hour room service and a 24 hour on-site fitness room. There are no pet fees, just sign a pet liability form.

Hotel Vintage Park
1100 Fifth Avenue
Seattle, WA 98101
206-624-8000
Well-behaved dogs of all sizes are welcome at this pet-friendly hotel. The luxury boutique hotel offers both rooms and suites. Hotel amenities include complimentary evening wine service, complimentary high speed Internet access, and 24 hour room service. There are no pet fees, just sign a pet liability form.

La Quinta Inn & Suites Seattle
2224 Eighth Ave.
Seattle, WA
206-624-6820
Dogs of all sizes are allowed at the hotel.

La Quinta Inn Sea-Tac - Seattle
2824 S 188th St
Seattle, WA
206-241-5211
Dogs of all sizes are allowed at

the hotel.

Motel 6
20651 Military Rd
Seattle, WA 98198
206-824-9902
There are no additional pet fees. One well-behaved pet per room is permitted.

Motel 6 - Airport
18900 47th Ave S
Seattle, WA 98188
206-241-1648
There are no additional pet fees.

Pensione Nichols Bed and Breakfast
1923 1st Avenue
Seattle, WA 98101
206-441-7125
Thanks to one of our readers who writes: "A charming and very dog-friendly place to stay in downtown Seattle." Large dogs are allowed to stay here if they are well-behaved. This B&B also requires that you do not leave your dog in the room alone. The Pensione Nichols is the only bed-and-breakfast located in the retail and entertainment core of downtown Seattle. Housed in a remodeled, turn-of-the-century building in the historic Smith Block, Pensione Nichols overlooks the Pike Place Market. This B&B has 10 guest rooms and suites (the suites have private bathrooms). Rates are approximately $75 (guest rooms) to $175 (suites). During the summer, there is a 2 night minimum.

Residence Inn Seattle Downtown
800 Fairview Ave N
Seattle, WA 98109
206-624-6000
There is a $10 per day pet charge.

The Sheraton Seattle Hotel and Towers
1400 Sixth Avenue
Seattle, WA 98101
206-621-9000

Dogs up to 80 pounds are allowed. There are no additional pet fees. You must sign a pet waiver.

Vagabond Inn by the Space Needle
325 Aurora Ave N
Seattle, WA 98109
206-441-0400
This motel is located just several blocks from the Space Needle, the waterfront and Washington St. Convention Center. The motel has a heated swimming pool and jacuzzi, 24 hour cable television and more. There is a $10 per day pet charge

W Seattle
1112 Fourth Avenue
Seattle, WA 98101
206-264-6000
Dogs of any size are allowed. There is a $25 per day additional pet fee.

Attractions

Kenmore

Kenmore Air Seaplanes
6321 Northeast 175th
Kenmore, WA 98028
800-543-9595
Well-behaved, leashed dogs are allowed on these seaplanes. Small dogs can sit on your lap. For larger dogs, you will need to purchase an extra seat. To board the seaplanes, you will need to walk up a step ladder. Since seaplanes are usually noisier inside than large commercial airplanes, the staff or pilot usually hands out earplugs to help keep the noise down. Seaplanes fly lower than commercial airliners and therefore you are able to see a lot more sights than if you where flying at over at 30,000 feet. They offer many scheduled flight routes to or from Seattle including the San Juan Islands, Oak Harbor, Victoria and Vancouver. Or you and your

pooch can try the 20 minute sightseeing tour of Seattle. Charter packages are also available. For trips to or from Canada, customs regulations apply. You can hop aboard their seaplanes at the Kenmore Air Harbor at 6321 N 175th Street in Kenmore, or at the Lake Union Terminal at 950 Westlake Avenue in Seattle.

Seattle

Emerald Country Carriages
Piers 55-56
Seattle, WA
425-868-0621
Emerald Country Carriages allows well-behaved dogs on their elegant horse and carriage rides. They offer both open and closed carriages which seat up to six. The standard tour includes the waterfront and Pioneer Square. You can catch one of their white and burgundy carriages on the waterfront, between Piers 55 and 56. The cost is about $35 for a standard 30 minute tour and an extra $10 if you make a reservation in advance.

Pike Place Market
First and Pike
Seattle, WA
206-682-7453
The popular Pike Place Market is a historic area that covers nine acres, has about 15 residential and retail buildings, and gets about nine million visitors per year. This marketplace offers fresh seafood (watch out for flying fish!), vegetables, fruit, flowers, cafes, shops, artists, street performers and more. The place might look familiar if you have seen the movie, "Sleepless in Seattle," which was filmed at this marketplace. Canines are welcome at the marketplace, but are not allowed inside the food stores or cafes.

Pioneer Square
First Street and Yesler Way
Seattle, WA

Pioneer Square is Seattle's oldest neighborhood. It is preserved as a National Historic District. Please note that dogs are not allowed on the Underground Tour at Pioneer Square. In this district, you can stroll through the area and see the historic buildings, or better yet, take an elegant horse and carriage ride from Emerald Country Carriages.

Seattle Center
Mercer Street and Broad St.
Seattle, WA
206-684-7200
The Seattle Center is a 74 acre urban park which was home to the 1962 World Fair. While your pooch cannot go into the buildings, he or she is allowed to walk around the center with you and spot out several points of interest. The famed Seattle Space Needle resides at the center and is always a good photo opportunity. You and your pooch can also visit the Sculpture Garden and watch jugglers, musicians, face painters, and more. Pets must be on leash. If you have a doggie that happens to be under 20 pounds, you can even carry him or her on the Seattle Monorail.

Washington State Ferries
Pier 52
Seattle, WA
206-464-6400
The Washington State Ferries is the nation's largest ferry system and the state's number one tourist attraction. This ferry service offers many ferry routes, including Seattle to Bainbridge Island, Seattle to Bremerton, Edmonds to Kingston, Anacortes to Friday Harbor (San Juan Islands), and Anacortes to Sidney in British Columbia,

Canada. Please see our Washington State Ferry listing in our Victoria, British Columbia, Canada City Guide for customs requirements for both people and dogs. While leashed dogs are allowed on the ferry routes mentioned above, the following pet regulations apply. On the newer ferries that have outside stairwells, dogs are allowed on the car deck and on the outdoor decks above the car deck. If the ferry has indoor stairwells, dogs are only allowed on the deck where they boarded the ferry. For example, if your dog comes onto the ferry in your car, he or she has to remain on the car deck. If you walk onto the ferry with your dog, your pooch is allowed on the outside deck where you boarded but cannot go onto other decks. In cases where your pet has to remain on the car deck, you can venture to the above decks without your pet to get food at the snack bars. However, the ferry system recommends in general that you stay with your pooch in the car. For any of the ferries, dogs are not allowed inside the ferry terminals. Ferry prices for people and autos are determined by the route and peak times, but in general tickets for people can start under $10 round trip, and more for autos. Dogs ride free!

Beaches

Seattle

Sand Point Magnuson Park Dog Off-Leash Beach and Area
7400 Sand Point Way NE
Seattle, WA
206-684-4075
This leash free dog park covers about 9 acres and is the biggest fully fenced off-leash park in Seattle. It also offers an access point to the lake where your pooch is welcome to take a dip

in the fresh lake water. To find the dog park, take Sand Point Way Northeast and enter the park at Northeast 74th Street. Go straight and park near the playground and sports fields. The main gate to the off-leash area is located at the southeast corner of the main parking lot. Dogs must be leashed until you enter the off-leash area.

Parks

Redmond

Marymoor Park and Off-Leash Area
6046 West Lake Sammamish Pkwy NE
Redmond, WA
206-296-8687
This park offers 640 acres of land for recreational activities. Some special areas in the park include a velodrome (for bicyclist training and racing), a climbing rock, a model airplane flying field, and the historic Willowmoor Farm. Dogs on leash are allowed at the park. There is also a 40 acre off-leash dog exercise area where dogs can run free while under voice control. To get there from I-5 or I-405, take State Route 520 east to the West Lake Sammamish Pkwy exit. At the bottom of the ramp, go right (south) on W. Lake Sammamish Parkway NE. The park entrance is the next left at the traffic light.

Seattle

Discovery Park
3801 W. Government Way
Seattle, WA
206-386-4236
Discovery Park is located northwest of downtown Seattle. It has over 500 acres and is the city's largest park. It offers views of both the Olympic and Cascade mountain ranges.

Dogs on leash are allowed on about 7 miles of trails except for beaches, ponds, wetlands and the Wolf Tree Nature Trail.

Sand Point Magnuson Park
7400 Sand Point Way NE
Seattle, WA
206-684-4075
The park is northeast of Seattle and is located across the lake from the city of Kirkland. This park has about 350 acres and is Seattle's second largest park. You will find over four miles of walking trails along Lake Washington, through grassy fields, trees and brush. Dogs are not allowed in the water at Lake Washington, except at the off-leash area.

Sand Point Magnuson Park Dog Off-Leash Area
7400 Sand Point Way NE
Seattle, WA
206-684-4946
This leash free dog park covers about 9 acres and is the biggest fully fenced off-leash park in Seattle. It also offers an access point to the lake where your pooch is welcome to take a dip in the fresh lake water. To find the dog park, take Sand Point Way Northeast and enter the park at Northeast 74th Street. Go straight and park near the playground and sports fields. The main gate to the off-leash area is located at the southeast corner of the main parking lot. Dogs must be leashed until you enter the off-leash area.

Restaurants

Seattle

Il Bistro
93A Pike Street
Seattle, WA
206-682-3040
This Italian restaurant, located in Pike Place Market, has three outdoor tables where your well-behaved dog can lay next to

you. The dinner menu includes seafood specials, pasta and more.

Ivar's Salmon House
401 NE Northlake Way
Seattle, WA
206-632-0767
There are several different outdoor areas where they serve food, and dogs are only allowed at the Fish Bar area.

Lombardi's Cucina
2200 N.W. Market Street
Seattle, WA 98107
206-783-0055
This restaurant offers traditional Italian cuisine. Well-behaved dogs are allowed at the outdoor tables. If they are busy, they will try to find a spot away from the crowd for your pooch.

Madison Park Cafe
1807 42nd Ave East
Seattle, WA
206-324-2626
Well-behaved, leashed dogs can accompany you to the outdoor tables at this French bistro. The restaurant is open on the weekends for brunch and Tuesday through Saturday for dinner. The dinner menu includes entrees like Lemon Parsley Raviolis, Lavender Honey Marinated Rack of Lamb, duck, and steak. Prices start at about $15 per entree.

Maggie Bluff's Marina Grill
2601 W. Marina Place
Seattle, WA
206-283-8322
This restaurant, open for breakfast and lunch, serves hamburgers, salads, pastas, and more. Dogs are allowed at the outdoor tables. Heaters are usually available.

McCormick and Schmick's
1200 Westlake Avenue North
Seattle, WA
206-270-9052
This restaurant is located on Lake Union and offers a variety

of seafood. Enjoy views of downtown Seattle and Lake Union. Dogs are allowed at the outdoor tables on the lakeside deck.

Portage Bay Cafe
4140 Roosevelt Way NE
Seattle, WA 98105
206-547-8230
Open for breakfast and lunch, this cafe allows dogs are their outdoor tables. A children's menu is available.

Sister's Cafe
Pike Place Market
Seattle, WA
206-623-6723
Located in Pike Place Market, this cafe serves sandwiches and more. Dogs are allowed at the outdoor tables.

Stores

Seattle

Three Dog Bakery
1408 1st Avenue
Seattle, WA
206-364-9999
You can purchase all kinds of fresh home-made treats for your pooch at this dog cookie bakery.

Vancouver City Guide

Accommodations

Coquitlam

Best Western Chelsea Inn
725 Brunette Avenue
Coquitlam, BC V3K 1C3
604-525-7777
There is an $20 per day pet fee.

Holiday Inn
631 Lougheed Highway
Coquitlam, BC V3K 3S5
604-931-4433
There is a $30 one time pet fee.

Pitt Meadows

Ramada Inn
19267 Lougheed Hwy
Pitt Meadows, BC V3Y 2J5
604-460-9859
Pets must be well-behaved. There are no additional pet fees.

Vancouver

Best Western Sands Hotel
1755 Davie Street
Vancouver, BC V6G 1W5
604-682-1831
Situated in Downtown Vancouver down the block from Stanley Park and across from English Bay Beach. 2 Lounges, Restaurant, Room Service, Fitness Room and Sauna. The pet fee is $10.00 per day. Pets receive a welcome doggy bag upon arrival, includes Pet Lovers Digest, treats and scoop bags.

Coast Plaza Suite Hotel at Stanley Park
1763 Comox Street
Vancouver, BC V6G 1P6
604-688-7711
All Coast Hotels have on hand extra pet amenities if you forget something. For dogs, they have extra doggy dishes, sleeping cushions, nylon chew toys and dog food. If your dog needs one of these items, just ask the front desk. There is a $20 per day additional pet fee.

Granville Island Hotel
1253 Johnston St
Vancouver, BC
604-683-7373
This hotel has a restaurant on the premises called the Dockside Restaurant. You can dine there with your pet at the outdoor tables that are closest to the grass. The hotel charges a $25 per night pet fee per room.

Metropolitan Hotel
645 Howe Street
Vancouver, BC
604-687-1122

There are no additional pet fees.

Pacific Palisades Hotel
1277 Robson Street
Vancouver, BC
604-688-0461
Well-behaved dogs of all sizes are welcome at this hotel which offers both rooms and suites. Amenities include workout rooms, an indoor swimming pool, and 24 hour room service. There is a $25 one time per stay pet fee and $5 of this is sent to the SPCA.

Quality Hotel Downtown
1335 Howe St
Vancouver, BC V6Z1R7
604-682-0229
There is a pet fee of $15 per day.

Ramada Inn
1221 Granville St
Vancouver, BC V6Z 1M6
604-685-1111
There is a $20 per day additional pet fee.

Residence Inn by Marriott
1234 Hornby St
Vancouver, BC
604-688-1234
There is a $75 pet fee per visit plus $5 per night for your pet

Sylvia Hotel
1154 Gilford St
Vancouver, BC
604-681-9321
There are no additional pet fees.

Attractions

Albion

Albion Ferry
off River Road
Albion, BC
604-467-7298
This ferry transports passengers and vehicles across the River, between Fort Langley and Albion. Crossing time is 10 minutes. Pets are allowed. If you walk onto the ferry with no car,

your pet must be leashed. If your dog comes onto the ferry in your vehicle, he or she needs to stay in the car. This ferry is run by the Fraser River Marine Transportation company and is a subsidiary of TransLink. The ferry is located east of Vancouver.

Boston Bar

Hell's Gate Airtram
43111 Trans Canada Highway
Boston Bar, BC
604-867-9277
Come and visit the steepest non-supported air tram in North America. You will experience breath-taking views, above the river's fishways, in one of their comfortable 25 passenger air tram cabins. After the tram ride, walk over to the Salmon House Restaurant where you can enjoy mouth-watering salmon at the outdoor tables. For some dessert visit the Fudge Factory where they have over 30 flavors of homemade fudge. Also on the premises is the Patio Cafe, which is home to British Columbia's smallest outdoor pub. Your dog can even enjoy a nice cold drink of water from the "Pup Pub" bucket at the cafe. Dogs on leash are welcome in the air tram, at the outdoor restaurant and at the outdoor pub. This attraction is located about 2 and 1/2 hours from Vancouver off the Trans Canada Highway.

North Vancouver

Capilano Suspension Bridge and Park
3735 Capilano Road
North Vancouver, BC V7R 4J1
604-985-7474
This is Vancouver's oldest and most famous attraction which draws over 800,000 visitors each year. The park is home to the world's greatest suspension footbridge, which was original

built in 1889. Today's bridge is the fourth bridge at this location. It spans 450 feet across and is 230 feet above the Capilano River. Located on the other side of the bridge is a West Coast rain forest. The forest is a popular attraction for visitors and offers trails that pass by trout ponds and old growth evergreens. The park's trails are located in the rain forest and some of the trails offer interactive displays that explain the local flora and fauna. Near the main entrance you can visit the Totem Park with over 25 authentic totem poles from the 1930s. Then stop by the Big House which features First Nations carvers who explain and demonstrate their skills, and techniques. Walk through the Story Centre, where you can pose with the "tramps", view artifacts, antiques and hear "voices from the past". While there at the park, dine at the outdoor tables at either the Bridge House Restaurant or the Canyon Cafe and Logger's Grill. Dogs on leash are allowed everywhere except in the Trading Post Gift Shop and inside the restaurants. Tour greeters and guides are available at the park for complimentary history and nature tours from May to October. The bridge and park are open daily except for Christmas Day. Summer hours are 8:30am until dusk and winter hours are 9am to 5pm. This park is located just 10 minutes from downtown Vancouver. To get there, go through Stanley Park, over the Lions Gate Bridge and go north 1 mile on Capilano Road. From the Trans-Canada Highway, take the Capilano road exit and go north for a half a mile.

Rosedale

Minter Gardens

52892 Bunker Road
Rosedale, BC
604-794-7191
Enjoy a world class show garden with your pooch. This attraction has 11 beautifully themed gardens spread out over 32 acres. Leashed pets are welcome outside and owners need to clean up after their pets. The gardens are open daily from April to mid-October. They are located 90 minutes east of Vancouver. From Highway 1, take Exit 135.

Vancouver

AquaBus Ferries
230-1333 Johnston Street/Granville Island
Vancouver, BC
604-689-5858
Sightseeing cruises are available on these small ferries. The cruises last about 25 minutes and pass by a floating village, kayakers, tugboats towing barges, fishermen, sail boaters and more. No reservations are required. Cruises depart from the Granville Island dock every twenty minutes daily from 9am to 7pm. Well-behaved leashed dogs are welcome.

Granville Island

Vancouver, BC V6H 3S3
604-666-6655
Once home to industrial factories, this area is popular for it's public market, art studios, and restaurants. Pets are not allowed inside the public marketplace because of the food, but your pooch can walk along the sidewalks and the Sea Wall with you. Along the sidewalks there are usually entertaining street performers. Dog-friendly establishments on Granville Island include the Granville Island Hotel, AquaBus ferries and a dog bakery called Woofles. Granville Island is

located just south of downtown Vancouver.

Historic Gastown
Water Street
Vancouver, BC
604-683-5650
This historic area is where Vancouver was founded. Gastown is named after the man John "Gassy Jack" Deighton who opened his saloon in 1867 on a shoestring budget. He got his name "Gassy Jack" because he talked a lot. The locals called the place Gassy's Town which was later shortened to Gastown. You can find Gassy Jack's statue at the corner of Water and Carrall Streets. In Gastown, you and your pooch can walk on the cobble-stoned streets and view the Victorian architecture. Be sure to stop by the Gastown Steam Clock, which is the world's first steam-powered clock. It blows every 15 minutes. Also in Gastown you can watch street performers or visit a dog-friendly outdoor restaurant on Powell Street like Gassy Jack's Deli or Cafe Dolcino.

Historic Gastown Guided Walking Tours
Water and Carrall Streets
Vancouver, BC
604-683-5650
Take a free guided historic walking tour of Gastown with your well-behaved dog. The GBIS (Gastown Business Improvement Society) offers tours that highlight the history and architecture of Vancouver's birthplace. The tours are held each summer from mid-June through August at 2pm daily. Tours last about 90 minutes. Meet at Gassy Jack's statue, on the corner of Water and Carrall Streets.

Sam Kee Building
Pender Street
Vancouver, BC

Visit the second largest Chinatown in North American and take a look at the Sam Kee Building. This building is the world's thinnest office building according to the Guiness Book of World Records. The two-story building was built in 1913 and is only 6 feet wide. The back of the building is right next to another building and it visually looks like it is part of the other building. But look closely and you will see that is it actually only 6 feet wide. The second floor has an overhang that the owner added in order to increase office space. At one time this building housed thirteen little businesses. Today the building is still used for office space. It is located in Chinatown at the corner of Pender and Carrall Streets.

Victoria

BC Ferries
1112 Fort Street
Victoria, BC V8V 4V2
250-386-3431
Pets are allowed on most of the BC ferries, including the route from Vancouver to Victoria. This route departs from Tsawwassen which is south of Vancouver and arrives at Swartz Bay, which is north of Victoria. You will need to bring your car on the ferry in order to visit most of the dog-friendly places in Victoria. Dogs are only allowed on the open air car deck and must stay in the car or tied in a designated pet area. Owners must stay with their pets. The travel time for this route is approximately 1 hour and 35 minutes. Guide dogs and certified assistance dogs are not required to stay on the car decks.

Vancouver to Alaska Ferries
1112 Fort Street
Victoria, BC V8V 4V2
250-386-3431
While we do not recommend this

route for pet owners because you cannot always be with your pet, here is some information about taking a ferry with your dog from Vancouver to Alaska. First take a BC Ferry from Port Hardy to Prince Ruppert via the Inside Passage. The ferry ride is about 15 hours. Dogs are allowed on the car decks and pet owners are not allowed to stay with their pets. You can still visit your pet about 4 to 5 times during the day only when crew members designate certain visiting times. From Prince Rupert in Canada to Seward in Alaska, you will need to take an Alaska State Ferry. This route takes about 4 days. Pets are required to have current health certificates within 30 days of travel. Pets must remain in your car or in your carrier, on the car decks only. People are not allowed to stay with their pets. The captain will announce "pet calls" so pet owners can take their pets out for a short walk onboard in the designated pet area. While there are usually three pet visitation times per day, it is entirely up to the captain. The captain's decision is based on the weather and other factors. On both ferries, there is a designated pet area where your pets can relieve themselves. Owners must clean up after their pets. Guide dogs and certified assistance dogs are not required to stay on the car decks.

Beaches

Vancouver

Spanish Banks West
NW Marine Drive
Vancouver, BC
604-257-8400
This beach allows dogs off-leash. Dogs are allowed from 6am to 10pm. People are required to clean up after their dogs. The beach is located in

the Queen Elizabeth District. It is off NW Marine Drive, at the entrance to Pacific Spirit Park.

Sunset Beach
off Beach Avenue
Vancouver, BC
604-257-8400
This bay beach allows dogs off-leash. Dogs are allowed from 6am to 10pm. People are required to clean up after their dogs. The beach is located in the Stanley District, near Beach Avenue, under the Burrard Bridge. It is behind the Aquatic Centre east of the ferry dock.

Vanier Park
Chestnut
Vancouver, BC
604-257-8400
This beach allows dogs off-leash. Dogs are allowed from 6am to 10am and then from 5pm to 10pm. People are required to clean up after their dogs. The beach is located in the Queen Elizabeth District. It is on Chestnut at English Bay.

Parks

Burnaby

Burnaby Lake Regional Park
Sprott Street
Burnaby, BC
604-294-7450
Dogs on leash are allowed at this park and on the trails. This park is popular for bird-watching. Be on the lookout for bald eagles, great blue herons, or even green-backed herons. Along the shoreline you might see beavers, ducks and turtles. For some good exercise, try one of the trails that circles the lake.

Burnaby Mountain Park
Centennial Way
Burnaby, BC
604-294-7450
Dogs on leash are allowed at this park and on the trails. The

park offers mountain, water and city views from the top of Burnaby Mountain. You might even see some deer or bald eagles. To get there, take Lougheed Highway and turn north on Gaglardi Way to Centennial Way.

Central Park
Boundary Road
Burnaby, BC
604-294-7450
Dogs on leash are allowed at this park and on the trails. This park is an urban forest with douglas fir, western hemlock, poplar and maple trees. To get there, take the Trans Canada Highway to Boundary Road. Go south to get to the park.

Confederation Park
Willingdon Avenue
Burnaby, BC
604-294-7450
Dogs on leash are allowed at this park and on the trails. There is an off-leash area located north of Penzance Drive, roughly between Willingdon and Gamma Avenues. To get to the park, take Hastings Road and then go North on Willingdon Avenue.

Confederation Park Off-Leash Area
Willingdon Avenue
Burnaby, BC
604-294-7450
Dogs are allowed off-leash year-round in a designated area. The area is located north of Penzance Drive, roughly between Willingdon and Gamma Avenues. There will be signs posted indicating the off-leash area. The following off-leash codes apply: clean up after your pet, you must be present and in verbal control of your dog at all times, dogs must wear a valid rabies tag, no aggressive dogs allowed, and dogs must be leashed before and after using the off-leash area. Dogs on leash are allowed throughout Confederation Park.

Coquitlam

Colony Farm Regional Park
Colony Farm Road
Coquitlam, BC
604-224-5739
This park offers large open fields with wildflowers. It is a good birdwatching spot to find hawks and herons. Dogs on leash are allowed on the trails, except for beaches or where posted. To get there, take the Trans Canada Highway (Highway 1) east. Take the Cape Horn Interchange to Highway 7 (Lougheed), then turn right onto Colony Farm Road.

North Vancouver

Capilano River Regional Park
Capilano Park Road
North Vancouver, BC
604-224-5739
This park offers lush forest trails and is also home to the Capilano Fish Hatchery. Dogs on leash are allowed on the trails, except for beaches or where posted. The park is located in North Vancouver, next to the Cleveland Dam.

South Burnaby

Burnaby Fraser Foreshore Park Off-Leash Area
Byrne Road
South Burnaby, BC
604-294-7450
From October through March, dogs are allowed off-leash in a designated area near the Fraser River. The area is located near the end of Byrne Road. The following off-leash codes apply: clean up after your pet, you must be present and in verbal control of your dog at all times, dogs must wear a valid rabies tag, no aggressive dogs allowed, and dogs must be leashed before and after using the off-leash area. Dogs on leash are allowed in the rest of the park, but not on the banks of the Fraser River.

Vancouver

Charleson Park Off-Leash Area
6th Avenue
Vancouver, BC
604-257-8400
Dogs are allowed off-leash year-round in the Grass Bowl from 6am to 10pm. At the Waterfall Pond, dogs are allowed off-leash before 10am and after 7pm from June through September. During the rest of the year, there are no restricted off-leash hours at the Waterfall Pond.

Pacific Spirit Regional Park
Southwest Marine Drive
Vancouver, BC
604-224-5739
This is a popular park for jogging and running. The park offers over 30 miles or 54 kilometers of trails. Dogs on leash are allowed on the trails, except for beaches or where posted. There is also an off-leash area in this park which will be posted with signs.

Queen Elizabeth Park
Cambie Boulevard
Vancouver, BC
604-257-8400
This 130 acre (52 hectare) park has about 6 million visitors per year. The popular Quarry Gardens is located at the top of the hill in the park. This land used to be an actual quarry before it became a city park. Dogs are allowed in the park and on the walkways and trails, except where posted. Dogs must be on leash. The park is located off Cambie Boulevard and is surrounded by the following streets: Cambie Blvd., Kersland Dr., 37th Ave., Midlothian Ave., and 27th Ave.

Queen Elizabeth Park Off-Leash Area
37th Avenue and Columbia St.
Vancouver, BC
604-257-8400

Dogs are allowed off-leash from 6am to 10pm only in the designated area. The off-leash area is located at approximately 37th Avenue and Columbia Street.

Stanley Park
Georgia Street
Vancouver, BC
604-257-8400
This park is the largest city park in Canada and the third largest urban park in North America. It attracts about 8 million people per year. The park has 1,000 forested acres and offers miles of trails, including a 6.2 mile paved trail around the perimeter. On the north side of the park, you will get a view of Lion's Gate Bridge. This bridge connects Vancouver and North Vancouver and is similar in size to the San Francisco Golden Gate Bridge. Dogs are allowed in the park, except on beaches or where posted. Your dog is welcome to walk or jog with you on the trails. Stanley Park is located is just north of downtown Vancouver. To get there, take Georgia Street towards North Vancouver. Dogs must be leashed.

Restaurants

Coquitlam

Bread Garden Bakery Cafe
2991 Lougheed Highway
Coquitlam, BC
604-945-9494
This cafe is open for breakfast, lunch and dinner. For breakfast they serve breakfast sandwiches, pastries, fruit salads and smoothies. For lunch and dinner they offer pasta and rice bowls, salads, sandwiches, wrapps, smoothies and desserts. Well-behaved, leashed dogs are allowed at the outdoor tables.

Bread Garden Bakery Cafe
100 Schoolhouse Street

Coquuitlam, BC V3K 6V9
604-515-0295
This cafe is open for breakfast, lunch and dinner. For breakfast they serve breakfast sandwiches, pastries, fruit salads and smoothies. For lunch and dinner they offer pasta and rice bowls, salads, sandwiches, wrapps, smoothies and desserts. Well-behaved, leashed dogs are allowed at the outdoor tables.

Vancouver

Andale's Mexican Restaurant
3211 Broadway West
Vancouver, BC V6K 2H5
604-738-9782
Well-behaved, leashed dogs are allowed at the outdoor tables.

Apple Deli
849 Davie Street
Vancouver, BC
604-669-1309
Well-behaved, leashed dogs are allowed at the outdoor tables.

Bread Garden Bakery Cafe
889 West Pender Street
Vancouver, BC V6C 3B2
604-638-3982
This cafe is open for breakfast, lunch and dinner. For breakfast they serve breakfast sandwiches, pastries, fruit salads and smoothies. For lunch and dinner they offer pasta and rice bowls, salads, sandwiches, wrapps, smoothies and desserts. Well-behaved, leashed dogs are allowed at the outdoor tables.

Cafe Dolcino
12 Powell Street
Vancouver, BC V6A 1E7
604-801-5118
This cafe serves breakfast all day as well as Italian food. The cafe has two outdoor tables. Well-behaved, leashed dogs are allowed at the outdoor tables.

Cafe Il Nido

780 Thurlow Street
Vancouver, BC V6E 1V8
604-685-6436
This restaurant is open for lunch and dinner. Well-behaved, leashed dogs are allowed at the outdoor tables.

Dockside Patio Restaurant
1253 Johnston Street
Vancouver, BC V6H 3R9
604-683-7373
This restaurant is located in the pet-friendly Granville Island Hotel. They are open for breakfast, lunch and dinner. Well-behaved, leashed dogs are allowed at the outdoor tables that are closest to the grass. The patio offers great views of False Creek and Vancouver City's skyline.

Don Francesco Ristorante
860 Burrard Street
Vancouver, BC
604-685-7770
This restaurant offers Italian cuisine with a Mediterranean flair. Well-behaved, leashed dogs are allowed at the outdoor tables.

Gassy Jack Deli
26 Powell Street
Vancouver, BC V6A 1E7
604-683-1222
This deli serves Mediterranean and Indian fast food. Well-behaved, leashed dogs are allowed at the outdoor tables.

Hermitage Restaurant
115 - 1025 Robson Street
Vancouver, BC V6E 4A9
604-689-3237
This French Restaurant is located in downtown Vancouver on popular Robson Street. Well-behaved, leashed dogs are allowed at the outdoor tables. They recommend that you make a reservation in advance because the outdoor seating can fill up quickly.

Le Gavroche Restaurant
1616 Alberni Street

Vancouver, BC
604-685-3924
This French restaurant is located within walking distance of Historic Gastown and Stanley Park. Well-behaved, leashed dogs are allowed at the outdoor tables.

Quattro on Fourth
2611 West 4th Avenue
Vancouver, BC
604-734-4444
This upscale Italian restaurant offers soups, salads, pastas, seafood, beef and more. Well-behaved, leashed dogs are allowed at the corner outdoor tables. They recommend calling in advance to reserve a table.

West Vancouver

Beach House at Dundarave Pier
150 - 25th Street
West Vancouver, BC
604-922-1414
This restaurant specializes in fresh fish and shellfish dishes. Well-behaved, leashed dogs are allowed at the outdoor tables. They recommend that you make a reservation in advance because the outdoor seating can book up several days in advance.

Bread Garden Bakery Cafe
550 Park Royal North
West Vancouver, BC V7T 1H9
604-925-0181
This cafe is open for breakfast, lunch and dinner. For breakfast they serve breakfast sandwiches, pastries, fruit salads and smoothies. For lunch and dinner they offer pasta and rice bowls, salads, sandwiches, wrapps, smoothies and desserts. Well-behaved, leashed dogs are allowed at the outdoor tables.

Hot Dog Jonny's
#120 - 1425 Marine Drive
West Vancouver, BC

604-913-3647
This restaurant has been voted "Best Hot Dogs in Vancouver" by the Vancouver Sun and Georgia Straight Readers Choice Award. They serve a dozen different hot dogs and sausages including all-beef Kosher, pork, poultry, veggie and smokies. A complete list of all ingredients and nutritional data is included on their web site. They have a few tables outside where well-behaved, leashed dogs are welcome.

Stores

Vancouver

O.K. Boot Corral
205 Carrall Street
Vancouver, BC V6B 2J2
604-684-2668
Only well-behaved leashed dogs are allowed inside this store. They offer boots, hats, replica antique firearms, and accessories like belt buckles. The store is located in Historic Gastown.

Woofles Doggilicious Deli
1496 Cartright Street
Vancouver, BC
604-689-3647
This specialty pet store offers 100% natural homemade dog and cat treats, pet jewelry, and toys. They even host doggie weddings and doggie parties. The store is located on Granville Island in the Kids Market. They are open seven days a week. Dogs are welcome!

Victoria City Guide
Accommodations

Saanichton

Quality Inn Wadding Dog
2476 Mt Newton Crossroad
Saanichton, BC
250-652-1146
There is a $5.00 per night dog

fee.

Super 8 Victoria/Saanichton
2477 Mount Newton Crossroad
Saanichton, BC
250-652-6888
There is a $10 one time pet fee.

Sidney

Best Western Emerald Isle
2306 Beacon Ave
Sidney, BC V8L 1X2
250-656-4441
There is a $20 one time pet fee per visit.

Cedarwood Motel
9522 Lochside Dr
Sidney, BC
250-656-5551
There is a $15 per day additional pet fee.

Victoria Airport Travelodge
2280 Beacon Ave
Sidney, BC
250-656-1176
There is a $10 per day additional pet fee.

Sooke

Gordon's Beach Farm Stay B&B
4530 Otter Point Road
Sooke, BC V0S 1N0
250-642-5291
A well-behaved dog is allowed in one of their suite rooms that has marble flooring. There is a $10 one time per stay pet fee.

Ocean Wilderness Country Inn
109 W Coast Rd
Sooke, BC
250-646-2116
There is a $15 pet fee per visit.

Sooke Harbour House
1528 Whiffen Spit Rd
Sooke, BC
250-642-3421
There is a $30 per night pet fee.

Victoria

Accent Inn
3233 Maple Street
Victoria, BC
250-475-7500
There is a $10 one time pet fee.

Annabelles Cottage B&B
152 Joseph Street
Victoria, BC V8S 3H5
250-384-4351
Both pets and children are welcome. There is a $10 one time per stay pet fee. The inn is located near Beacon Hill Park.

Coast Harbourside Hotel and Marina
146 Kingston Street
Victoria, BC V8V 1V4
250-360-1211
All Coast Hotels have on hand extra pet amenities if you forget something. For dogs, they have extra doggy dishes, sleeping cushions, nylon chew toys and dog food. If your dog needs one of these items, just ask the front desk. There is a $20 per day additional pet fee.

Dashwood Seaside Manor
1 Cook Street
Victoria, BC
250-385-5517
There is a $25 per stay pet fee.

Executive House Hotel
777 Douglas Street
Victoria, BC V8W 2B5
250-388-5111
Enjoy European ambience in a downtown Victoria hotel. The hotel is directly across from the Victoria Conference Centre, one block from the magnificent Inner Harbour, Royal BC Museum, National Geographic Theatre, shopping and attractions. Pets are welcome for $15 per night extra.

Harbour Towers Hotel
345 Quebec St
Victoria, BC
250-385-2405
There is a $15 per day additional

pet fee.

Howard Johnson Hotel
310 George Rd. East
Victoria, BC
250-382-2151
Dogs up to 60 pounds are
allowed. There is a refundable
pet deposit required.

Howard Johnson Hotel
4670 Elk Lake Drive
Victoria, BC
250-704-4656
Dogs of all sizes are welcome.
There is a $15 per day pet fee.

Ryan's Bed and Breakfast
224 Superior St
Victoria, BC
250-389-0012
There is a $10 per night pet fee.

Tally Ho Motor Inn
3020 Douglas St
Victoria, BC
250-386-6141
There are no additional pet fees.

Attractions

Anacortes

Washington State Ferries
2100 Ferry Terminal Rd
Anacortes, WA
206-464-6400
This ferry service offers many
routes in Washington State, as
well as a route from Sidney,
near Victoria, to Anacortes in
Washington. The ferry ride is
about 3 hours long and the ferry
carries both passengers and
vehicles. You can also catch a
ferry to Sidney from Friday
Harbor, Washington, in the San
Juan Islands. This ferry ride is
about 1 hour and 15 minutes.
While leashed dogs are allowed
on the ferry routes mentioned
above, the following pet
regulations apply. On the newer
ferries that have outside
stairwells, dogs are allowed on
the car deck and on the outdoor
decks above the car deck. If the

ferry has indoor stairwells, dogs
are only allowed on the deck
where they boarded the ferry.
For example, if your dog comes
onto the ferry in your car, he or
she has to remain on the car
deck. If you walk onto the ferry
with your dog, your pooch is
allowed on the outside deck
where you boarded but cannot
go onto other decks. In cases
where your pet has to remain
on the car deck, you can
venture to the above decks
without your pet to get food at
the snack bars. However, the
ferry system recommends in
general that you stay with your
pooch in the car. For any of the
ferries, dogs are not allowed
inside the ferry terminals. The
ferries in Anacortes leave from
2100 Ferry Terminal Road. The
ferries in Friday Harbor leave
from 91 Front Street and the
ferries in Sidney leave from
2499 Ocean Avenue.
Reservations are
recommended 48 hours or
more in advance if you are
bringing a vehicle. Because
you will be crossing over an
international border,
identification for Customs and
Immigration is required. U.S.
and Canadian citizens traveling
across the border will need
proof of citizenship such as
your passport or a certified
copy of your birth certificate
issued by the city, county or
state/province where you were
born. You will also need photo
identification such as a current
valid driver's license. People
with children need to bring their
child's birth certificate. Single
parents, grandparents or
guardians traveling with
children often need proof or
notarized letters from the other
parent authorizing travel. Dogs
traveling to Canada or returning
to Canada need a certificate
from their vet showing a rabies
vaccination within the past 3
years. Dogs traveling to the
U.S. or returning to the U.S.

need to have a valid rabies
vaccination certificate (including
an expiration date and vet
signature). The certificate must
show that the dog had the rabies
vaccine at least 30 days prior to
entry and within the past 12
months unless a later expiration
date is shown on the certificate.

Vancouver Island

The Butchart Gardens

Vancouver Island, BC

Leashed dogs are allowed at
this 50-acre show-place of floral
finery offering spectacular views
of gardens. You and your pup
can stroll along meandering
paths and expansive lawns. But
Butchart Gardens does more
than just allow dogs. These dog-
friendly folks have placed
running dog drinking fountains
throughout the entire garden.
Thanks to one of our readers for
recommending this place. The
Butchart Gardens is a must visit
if you are on Vancouver Island!

Victoria

BC Ferries
1112 Fort Street
Victoria, BC V8V 4V2
250-386-3431
Pets are allowed on most of the
BC ferries, including the route
from Vancouver to Victoria.
These ferries depart from
Tsawwassen which is south of
Vancouver and arrives at Swartz
Bay, which is north of Victoria.
Dogs are only allowed on the
open air car deck and must stay
in your car or tied in a
designated pet area on the car
deck. Owners must stay with
their pets. The travel time for this
route is approximately 1 hour
and 35 minutes. Guide dogs and
certified assistance dogs are not
required to stay on the car
decks.

Grandpas Antique Photo Studio

1252 Wharf Street
Victoria, BC V8W 1T8
250-920-3800
Create an old time photo in one of the following themes of your choice; The Old West, Victorian Era, Roaring 20's, Southern Belle, US Military and more. Most costumes fit over street clothing and fit all ages and sizes. Bring your well-behaved dog and include him or her in your photo. The studio is open from 10am to 10pm year-round. Prints are usually ready in 10 minutes.

Victoria Carriage Tours

Menzies and Belleville Street
Victoria, BC
250-383-2207
Take a guided horse and carriage tour of the waterfront, Beacon Hill Park, historical buildings and more. Choose from 30 minute to 90 minute tours. Prices start at $70 Canadian Dollars for the entire carriage which holds about 4 to 6 people. Well-behaved, leashed dogs are welcome. Carriages usually run from 9am until midnight, 7 days per week, weather permitting.

Victoria Express

Belleville Street
Victoria, BC
250-361-9144
This passenger ferry service runs between Port Angeles in Washington and Victoria. Crossing time is about one hour. Dogs are allowed and must be leashed. The ferries in Port Angeles leave from the Landing Mall on Railroad Avenue. The ferries in Victoria leave from the port on Belleville Street. Currency exchange is available at the Port Angeles Reservation Office. Their toll free number in the U.S. is 1-800-633-1589. Reservations are recommended. Because you will be crossing over an international border,

identification for Customs and Immigration is required. U.S. and Canadian citizens traveling across the border will need proof of citizenship such as your passport or a certified copy of your birth certificate issued by the city, county or state/province where you were born. You will also need photo identification such as a current valid driver's license. People with children need to bring their child's birth certificate. Single parents, grandparents or guardians traveling with children often need proof of or notarized letters from the other parent authorizing travel. Dogs traveling to Canada or returning to Canada need a certificate from their vet showing a rabies vaccination within the past 3 years. Dogs traveling to the U.S. or returning to the U.S. need to have a valid rabies vaccination certificate (including an expiration date and vet signature). The certificate must show that the dog had the rabies vaccine at least 30 days prior to entry and within the past 12 months unless a later expiration date is shown on the certificate.

Beaches

Victoria

Beacon Hill Park Off-Leash Beach

Dallas Road
Victoria, BC
250-385-5711
Dogs are allowed off-leash at the gravel beach in Beacon Hill Park. People are required to clean up after their dogs. The beach is located in downtown Victoria, along Dallas Road, between Douglas Street and Cook Street.

Parks

Saanich

Francis/King Regional Park

Munn Road
Saanich, BC
250-478-3344
There are many hiking trails in this park. One of the trails is the Elsi King Trail. This interpretive trail is accessible and also good for families with young children. Dogs must be leashed in all high use areas including the Elsi King Trail. Dogs may be allowed off-leash in other areas as long as they are under voice control. The park is located about 30 minutes from Victoria. Take the Trans-Canada Highway from Victoria and then take the Helmcken Road exit. Turn left onto Burnside Road West and then turn right on Prospect Lake Road. Keep left on Munns Road and it will lead to the park entrance on the right.

Sooke

East Sooke Regional Park

East Sooke Road
Sooke, BC
250-478-3344
This park offers miles of trails through forests and along the rugged coastline. Enjoy views of the Olympic Mountains and the Strait of Juan de Fuca. The trails are rated easy to challenging. Dogs are welcome at the park and on the trails, but not on the beaches during the summer. The park district recommends that you keep your pets on leash in all high use areas and that pets need to be under your control at all times. The park is located about one hour from Victoria. To get there, take the Trans Canada Highway from Victoria and take the Colwood exit. Follow Old Island Highway which turns into Sooke Road. Turn left onto Gillespie Road and then turn right onto East Sooke Road.

Victoria

Beacon Hill Park
Douglas Street
Victoria, BC
250-385-5711
Views from oceanside bluffs and wildflowers on slopes can both be enjoyed at this park. The interior of the park features manicured flowerbeds and bridges over streams. Dogs on leash are allowed. Dogs can be off-leash at the gravel beach located along Dallas Road, between Douglas and Cook Street.

Restaurants

Victoria

17 Mile House Pub and Restaurant
5126 Sooke Road
Victoria, BC V9C 4C4
250-642-5942
Well-behaved, leashed dogs are allowed at the outdoor tables that are closest to the lawn.

Baja Grill
1600 Bay Street
Victoria, BC V8R 2B6
250-592-0027
This Mexican restaurant allows well-behaved, leashed dogs at their outdoor tables.

Cafe Brio
944 Fort Street
Victoria, BC
250-383-0009
This restaurant serves West Coast contemporary food with a Tuscan hint. They focus on using local, certified organic produce whenever possible. Menu items include salads, pasta, seafood, meat, poultry and dessert. Reservations are recommended. Well-behaved, leashed dogs are allowed at the outdoor tables.

Gino Cappuccino
777 Royal Oak Drive

Victoria, BC V8X 4V1
250-727-7722
This coffee house welcomes dogs to their outdoor tables. They will even give your dog a bowl of water. Items on the menu include coffee, cappuccino, tea, Italian Sodas, steamed milk, bagels, muffins and scones.

Golden Saigon Vietnamese Restaurant
1002 Johnson Street
Victoria, BC V8V 3N7
250-361-0015
Well-behaved, leashed dogs are allowed at the outdoor tables.

Pagliacci's
1011 Broad Street
Victoria, BC V8W 2A1
250-386-1662
This Italian restaurant offers homemade pasta, focaccia bread, cheesecake and more. Well-behaved, leashed dogs are allowed at the outdoor sidewalk tables.

Chapter 2

Dog-Friendly Accommodations

UNITED STATES ACCOMMODATIONS

Alabama Listings

Abbeville

Best Western Abbeville Inn
Hwy 431 South, Route 2
Abbeville, AL
334-585-5060
There are no additional pet fees.

Andalusia

Comfort Inn
1311 East Bypass
Andalusia, AL
334-222-8891
There is a $10 per day pet fee.

Athens

Best Western Athens Inn
1329 Hwy 72 East
Athens, AL
256-233-4030
There is a $7 per day pet fee.

Attalla

Holiday Inn Express
801 Cleveland Avenue
Attalla, AL
256-538-7861
Dogs are given complimentary welcome bags upon registration. Unlimited free doggie biscuits are available at the front desk 24 hours a day. There is a $10 pet fee that is non-refundable.

Auburn

Comfort Inn
2283 South College Street
Auburn, AL
334-821-6699
There is a $5 per day pet fee.

Birmingham

Comfort Inn Oxmoor
195 Oxmoor Rd
Birmingham, AL
205-941-0990
There is no pet fee.

Holiday Inn - Airport
5000 10th Ave N
Birmingham, AL
205-591-6900
There is a $25 one time pet fee.

La Quinta Inn Birmingham Northwest
905 11th Court West
Birmingham, AL
205-324-4510
Dogs of all sizes are allowed at the hotel.

Microtel
251 Summit Pkwy
Birmingham, AL
205-945-5550
There is a pet waiver to sign.

Motel Birmingham Garden Courtyards
7905 Crestwood Blvd
Birmingham, AL
205-956-4440
There is a $10 per day additional pet fee.

Residence Inn by Marriott
3 Green Hill Pkwy
Birmingham, AL
205-991-8686
There is a $75.00 one time pet fee.

Calera

Holiday Inn Express
357 Hwy 304
Calera, AL
205-668-3641
There is a $20 one time pet fee per visit.

Dothan

Holiday Inn - Dothan South
2195 Ross Clark Circle SE
Dothan, AL
334-794-8711

There is a $15 one time pet fee per visit.

Holiday Inn - Dothan West
3053 Ross Clark Circle
Dothan, AL
334-794-6601
Pets must be out of the room when housekeeping cleans the room.

Motel 6
2907 Ross Clark Circle SW
Dothan, AL
334-793-6013
There are no additional pet fees.

Enterprise

Comfort Inn
615 Bol Weevil Circle
Enterprise, AL
334-393-2304
There is a pet fee of $25 per day.

Eufaula

Comfort Suites
12 Paul Lee Pkwy
Eufaula, AL
334-616-0114
There is a one time pet fee of $25.

Evergreen

Comfort Inn
83 Bates Rd
Evergreen, AL
251-578-4701
There is a pet fee of $5 per day.

Foley

Holiday Inn Express
2682 S. McKenzie St
Foley, AL
251-943-9100
There is a $21.60 one time pet fee per visit.

Greenville

Comfort Inn

1029 Fort Dale Rd
Greenville, AL
334-383-9595
There is a pet fee of $5 per day.

Heflin

Howard Johnson Express Inn
1957 Almon Street
Heflin, AL
256-463-2900
Dogs of all sizes are welcome.
There is a $5 one time pet fee.

Huntsville

Guest House Suites
4020 Independence Dr
Huntsville, AL
256-837-8907
There is a $50 one time pet fee.

**La Quinta Inn Huntsville
Research Park**
4870 University Drive
Huntsville, AL
256-830-2070
Dogs up to 50 pounds are
allowed at the hotel.

**La Quinta Inn Huntsville
Space Center**
3141 University Drive
Huntsville, AL
256-533-0756
Dogs of all sizes are allowed at
the hotel.

Mobile

Days Inn
5480 Inn Rd
Mobile, AL
251-661-8181
There is an $8 per day pet fee.

Drury Inn
824 West I-65 Service Road
South
Mobile, AL
251-344-7700
Dogs of all sizes are permitted.
Pets are not allowed in the
breakfast area of the hotel. Pets
are not to be left unattended,
and each guest must assume

liability for damage of property
or other guest complaints. There
is a limit of one pet per room.

Holiday Inn
5465 Hwy 90 W (Gov't Blvd)
Mobile, AL
251-666-5600
There is a $25 one time pet fee
per visit.

Ramada Inn
850 S. Beltline Hwy
Mobile, AL
251-342-3220
Pets must never be left alone in
the room.

Red Roof Inn South
5450 Coca Cola Rd
Mobile, AL
334-666-1044
There are no additional pet fees.

Montgomery

Best Western Monticello Inn
5837 Monticello Drive
Montgomery, AL
334-277-4442
There is a $10 per day pet fee.

Days Inn
2625 Zelda Rd
Montgomery, AL
334-269-9611
There is a $5 per day pet fee.

Holiday Inn - East I-85
1185 Eastern Blvd
Montgomery, AL
334-272-0370
There is a $24 one time pet fee
for dogs less than 25 pounds. If
the dog weighs more than 25
pounds the one time fee is $50.

Holiday Inn - South/Airport
1100 W South Blvd
Montgomery, AL
334-281-1660
There is a $10 one time pet fee.

Residence Inn
1200 Hillmar Court
Montgomery, AL
334-270-3300

There is a $90.00 one time pet
fee.

Oxford

Howard Johnson Express Inn
PO Box 3308
Oxford, AL
256-835-3988
Dogs of all sizes are welcome.
There are no additional pet fees.

Motel 6
202 Grace Street
Oxford, AL
256-831-5463
There are no additional pet fees.

Ozark

Best Western Ozark Inn
US 231 South and Deese Rd
Ozark, AL
334-774-5166
There are no additional pet fees.

Holiday Inn
151 Hwy 231 North
Ozark, AL
334-774-7300
There is a $25 one time pet fee.

Priceville

Comfort Inn
3239 Point Mallard Pkwy
Priceville, AL
256-355-1037
There is a $10 per day pet fee.

Troy

Holiday Inn Express
Hwy 231 at Hwy 29
Troy, AL
334-670-0012
There are no additional pet fees.

Tuscaloosa

La Quinta Inn Tuscaloosa
4122 McFarland Blvd East
Tuscaloosa, AL
205-349-3270
Dogs of all sizes are allowed at

the hotel.

Motel 6
4700 McFarland Blvd E (Hwy 82E)
Tuscaloosa, AL
205-759-4942
There are no additional pet fees.

Alaska Listings

Anchorage

Aurora Winds Resort Bed and Breakfast
7501 Upper O'Malley Rd
Anchorage, AK
907-346-2533
This B&B offers five rooms with private baths. They offer two acres of privacy. Pets must be leashed when outside of the room.

Best Western Barratt Inn
4616 Spenard Rd
Anchorage, AK
907-243-3131
There is a $10 per day pet fee.

Merrill Field Inn
420 Sitka St
Anchorage, AK
907-276-4547
There is a $7 per day pet fee.

Millennium Alaskan Hotel
4800 Spenard Rd
Anchorage, AK
907-243-2300
This 248-room hotel is located on the eastern shore of Lake Spenard. There is a $50 refundable pet deposit.

Parkwood Inn
4455 Juneau St
Anchorage, AK
907-563-3590
There is a $5 one time pet fee and a $50 refundable pet deposit if paying with cash.

Sourdough Visitors Lodge

801 E Erikson St
Anchorage, AK
907-279-4148
There is a $100 refundable deposit and a $50 one time pet fee.

Cantwell

Backwoods Lodge
At George Parks Hwy, Milepost 210
Cantwell, AK
907-768-2232
This motel's log building offers nine large comfortable rooms with satellite TVs, microwaves, refrigerators and BBQs. The property has a view of Mt. McKinley. They have hiking trails and a canoe which guests can use on a nearby small pond. Call ahead for reservations because they do tend to book up early, especially during the summer. The nice folks here give out pet blankets to put over the furniture if your dog is going to be on the bed or chairs. They are located about 30 miles from Denali National Park. Pets must be on leash when outside of the rooms and may not be left unattended in the room or in your car. Dogs under 70 pounds are allowed.

Fairbanks

Chena Hot Springs Resort
P.O. Box 73440
Fairbanks, AK
907-452-7867
This resort is a great place to view the Aurora Borealis due to it's location in the northern region and it's distance from the city lights. They offer hotel rooms, cabins, RV parking and camping. There are lots of outdoor activities to do on this 440 acre resort. They are located approximately 60 miles east of Fairbanks. There is a $100 refundable deposit for pets.

Comfort Inn
1908 Chena Landings Loop
Fairbanks, AK
907-479-8080
There is a pet fee of $10 per day. Pets are allowed on the first floor only. There are only 2 non-smoking pet rooms, reserve early.

Super 8 Motel
1909 Airport Rd
Fairbanks, AK
907-451-8888
There is a $10 one time pet fee per pet.

Glennallen

The New Caribou Hotel
Box 329
Glennallen, AK
907-822-3302
Rooms are in a log cabin style building. There is a $10 per day pet fee.

Gustavus

Bear Track Inn
255 Rink Creek Rd
Gustavus, AK
907-697-3017
This log cabin style inn is located on 17 acres. They offer 14 rooms each with a private bath. They are open from January 1 to October 1. There is a $100 refundable pet deposit. The owners have a large dog. There are no roads leading to this inn, so you will need to take the ferry or plane from Juneau. Dogs must be crated on the boat or plane.

Puffin's Bed and Breakfast
1/4 Mile Logging Rd
Gustavus, AK
907-697-2260
This B&B is open May - September. They offer 5 cabins situated on 7 acres of land. There are no roads leading to this inn, so you will need to take the ferry or plane from Juneau.

Dogs must be crated on the boat or plane.

Haines

Captain's Choice Motel
108 2nd Ave N
Haines, AK
907-766-3111
There is a $10 one time pet fee.

Homer

Best Western Bidarka Inn
575 Sterling Hwy
Homer, AK
907-235-8148
There is a $10 per day pet fee.

Heritage Hotel
147 E Pioneer Ave
Homer, AK
907-235-7787
There is a $10 per day pet fee. They usually place pets in smoking rooms but will give you a non-smoking room if requested.

Lakewood Inn Bed and Breakfast
984 Ocean Dr #1
Homer, AK
907-235-6144
There is a $10 per day pet fee.

Juneau

Best Western Country Lane Inn
9300 Glacier Hwy
Juneau, AK
907-789-5005
Pets are allowed in the motel section not the bed and breakfast. There is a $10 pet fee each day.

Super 8 Motel
2295 Trout St
Juneau, AK
907-789-4858
There is a $25 refundable deposit.

The Driftwood Lodge

435 Willoughby Ave
Juneau, AK
907-586-2280
There is a $5 per day pet fee.

Ketchikan

Best Western Landing
3434 Tongass Ave
Ketchikan, AK
907-225-5166
There is a $50 refundable pet deposit. Dogs are allowed in the outer court rooms.

Tok

Cleft on the Rock Bed and Breakfast
Mile 0.5 Sundog Trail
Tok, AK
907-883-4219
Pets are not allowed on the furniture. The owner has a cat and your dog needs to be ok around cats. There is a $25 one time pet fee.

Valdez

Tiekel River Lodge
Richardson Hwy, Mile 56
Valdez, AK
907-822-3259
There is a $10 per day pet fee. The lodge is open from March through September. There are no designated smoking or non-smoking rooms.

Arizona Listings

Benson

Motel 6
637 S. Whetstone Commerce Dr
Benson, AZ
520-586-0066
There are no additional pet fees.

Bisbee

Sleepy Dog Guest House
212A Opera Drive
Bisbee, AZ
520-432-3057
There is a one bedroom and two bedroom guest house overlooking Bisbee. No credit cards, smoking outside only. There are no additional pet fees.

Camp Verde

Comfort Inn
340 N Industrial Dr
Camp Verde, AZ
928-567-9000
There is a $15 pet fee.

Carefree

Boulders Resort
34631 N Tom Darlington Rd
Carefree, AZ
480-488-9009
There is a one-time $100 dog fee.

Casa Grande

Holiday Inn
777 N Pinal Ave
Casa Grande, AZ
520-426-3500
There are no additional pet fees.

Chambers

Best Western Chieftain Inn
Hwy 40 and Chambers
Chambers, AZ
928-688-2754
There is a $10 per day pet fee.

Chandler

Red Roof Inn
7400 W Boston St
Chandler, AZ
480-857-4969
There are no additional pet fees.

Sheraton San Marcos Golf Resort and Conference Center

One San Marcos Place
Chandler, AZ
480-812-0900
Dogs up to 80 pounds are allowed. Larger dogs are put in rooms that are closer to the walking areas. There is a $100 refundable deposit for dogs.

Windmill Inn of Chandler
3535 W Chandler Blvd
Chandler, AZ
480-812-9600
There is no additional pet fee. There is a special pet section of the hotel.

Eagar

Best Western Sunrise Inn
128 N Main Street
Eagar, AZ
928-333-2540
There is a $25 refundable pet deposit if you are paying with cash.

Ehrenberg

Flying J Motel
I-10, Exit 1
Ehrenberg, AZ
928-923-9711
This hotel has a couple of pet rooms. There is a $10 refundable pet deposit.

Flagstaff

Comfort Inn I-17 & I40
2355 S Beulah Blvd.
Flagstaff, AZ
928-774-2225
There is a $5 per day pet fee.

Days Inn - Highway 66
1000 West Business 40
Flagstaff, AZ
928-774-5221
There is a $10 per day pet fee.

Holiday Inn
2320 E Lucky Lane
Flagstaff, AZ
928-714-1000
There is a $25 one time pet fee

per visit.

Howard Johnson Inn
3300 E. Rt. 66
Flagstaff, AZ
800-437-7137
Dogs of all sizes are welcome. There is a $7 one time pet fee.

La Quinta Inn & Suites Flagstaff
2015 South Beulah Blvd.
Flagstaff, AZ
928-556-8666
Dogs of all sizes are allowed at the hotel.

Motel 6
2010 E Butler Ave
Flagstaff, AZ
928-774-1801
One large well-behaved dog is okay.

Ramada Suites Limited
2755 Woodland Village Blvd
Flagstaff, AZ
928-773-1111
There is a $10 per day pet fee.

Red Roof Inn
2520 E Lucky Ln
Flagstaff, AZ
928-779-5121
There is a $20 refundable deposit for pets. Large dogs ok, if well-behaved.

Sleep Inn
2765 S. Woodlands Village Blvd.
Flagstaff, AZ
928-556-3000
There is a $50 non-refundable deposit.

Gila Bend

Best Western Space Age Lodge
401 E Pima
Gila Bend, AZ
928-683-2273
There are no pet fees. You just need to sign a pet agreement.

Globe

Comfort Inn at Round Mountain Park
1515 South St.
Globe, AZ
928-425-7575
There is a $20 per night pet fee.

Goodyear

Best Western Goodyear Inn
55 N Litchfield Rd
Goodyear, AZ
623-932-3210
There is a $10 per day pet fee.

Hampton Inn and Suites
2000 N Litchfield Rd
Goodyear, AZ
623-536-1313
There are no additional pet fees.

Holiday Inn Express
1313 Litchfield Rd
Goodyear, AZ
623-535-1313
Exit I-10 at Litchfield Rd.

Grand Canyon

Rodeway Inn-Red Feather Lodge
Highway 64
Grand Canyon, AZ
928-638-2414
This motel is located just one mile south of the south entrance to the Grand Canyon National Park. Pets are welcome, but they must not be left unattended in the room. There is a $50 refundable pet deposit and a $10 pet fee per night per pet.

Heber

Best Western Sawmill Inn
1877 Hwy 260
Heber, AZ
928-535-5053
There is a $5 per day pet fee.

Holbrook

Best Western Adobe Inn
615 W Hopi Dr
Holbrook, AZ
928-524-3948
There is a $25 refundable pet deposit.

Best Western Arizonian Inn
2508 Navajo Blvd
Holbrook, AZ
928-524-2611
There is a $30 refundable pet deposit.

Comfort Inn
2602 E. Navajo Blvd.
Holbrook, AZ
928-524-6131
There is no pet fee. A credit card will be required.

Holiday Inn Express
1308 E Navajo Blvd
Holbrook, AZ
928-524-1466
There is a $10 per day additional pet fee.

Motel 6
2514 Navajo Blvd
Holbrook, AZ
928-524-6101
There are no additional pet fees.

Kingman

Best Western A Wayfarer's Inn
2815 East Andy Devine
Kingman, AZ
928-753-6271
There is a $25 refundable pet deposit. Nice clean rooms.

Best Western King's Inn
2930 East Andy Devine
Kingman, AZ
928-753-6101
There are no additional pet fees.

Days Inn East
3381 E Andy Devine
Kingman, AZ
928-757-7337
There is a $10 per day additional pet fee.

Motel 6

3351 E Andy Devine Ave
Kingman, AZ
928-757-7151
There are no additional pet fees.

Quality Inn
1400 E. Andy Devine Ave.
Kingman, AZ
928-753-4747
There is a one time pet fee of $10.

Super 8 Motel
3401 E. Andy Devine
Kingman, AZ
928-757-4808
There is a $10 per day pet charge.

Lake Havasu City

Best Western Lake Place Inn
31 Wings Loop
Lake Havasu City, AZ
928-855-2146
There is a $10 per day pet fee.

Holiday Inn
245 London Bridge Rd
Lake Havasu City, AZ
928-855-2379
There is a $10 per day additional pet fee.

Island Inn Hotel
1300 W McCulloch Blvd
Lake Havasu City, AZ
928-680-0606
There is a $10 per day pet charge.

Motel 6
111 London Bridge Rd
Lake Havasu City, AZ
928-855-3200
Dogs may not be left alone in the room.

Mesa

Arizona Golf Resort
425 S Power Road
Mesa, AZ
480-832-3202
There are no additional pet charges.

Best Western Mesa Inn
1625 E Main St
Mesa, AZ
480-964-8000
There is a $5 per day additional pet fee.

Holiday Inn Hotel and Suites
1600 S Country Club
Mesa, AZ
480-964-7000
There is a $20 one time pet fee.

Homestead Village
1920 W Isabella
Mesa, AZ
480-752-2266
There is a $75 one time pet fee.

Motel 6
336 W Hampton Ave
Mesa, AZ
480-844-8899
One large well-behaved dog is okay.

Motel 6
630 W Main Street
Mesa, AZ
480-969-8111
There are no additional pet fees.

Motel 6
1511 S. Country Club Dr
Mesa, AZ
480-834-0066
One well-behaved pet is allowed per room.

Residence Inn
941 W Grove Ave
Mesa, AZ
480-610-0100
There is a $50 one time pet fee and $10 each day.

Sleep Inn
6347 E Southern Ave
Mesa, AZ
480-807-7760
There is a one-time $25 fee for pets.

Page

Best Western Arizonainn

716 Rimview Drive
Page, AZ
928-645-2466
There is a $10 per day pet fee.
This hotel is near Lake Powell
on the Arizona and Utah border.

**Best Western Weston Inn &
Suites**
207 N Lake Powell Blvd
Page, AZ
928-645-2451
There is a $10 per day pet fee.
This hotel is near Lake Powell.

Motel 6
637 S. Lake Powell Blvd
Page, AZ
928-645-5888
There are no additional pet fees.

Quality Inn
287 N. Lake Powell Blvd.
Page, AZ
928-645-8851
There is no fee for pets. Pets are
allowed on the first floor only.

Wahweap Lodge and Marina
2.5 miles SE of US 89 at Lake
Powell
Page, AZ
928-645-2433
This lodge is next to beautiful
Lake Powell. There are boat
rentals here for you and your
pup. There are no additional pet
fees.

Paradise Valley

Hermosa Inn
5532 N Palo Cristi Rd
Paradise Valley, AZ
602-955-8614
There is a $50 refundable pet
deposit.

Parker

Motel 6
604 California
Parker, AZ
928-669-2133
There are no additional pet fees.

Phoenix

Comfort Inn
5050 N. Black Canyon Highway
Phoenix, AZ
602-242-8011
There is a $25 pet deposit if the
room is paid for in cash. If the
room is paid for by credit card
there is no fee.

Comfort Inn
255 North Kyrene Blvd
Phoenix, AZ
480-705-8882
There is no pet fee.

Comfort Suites
8473 West Paradise Ln.
Phoenix, AZ
623-334-3993
There is a $50 pet deposit.

Crowne Plaza
2532 W. Peoria Ave
Phoenix, AZ
602-943-2341
Exit I-17 at Peoria Ave.

**Embassy Suites Hotel -
Thomas Rd**
2333 E Thomas Rd
Phoenix, AZ
602-957-1910
There is a $15 per day pet fee.

Hampton Inn
8101 N Black Canyon Hwy
Phoenix, AZ
602-864-6233
There is a $25 one time fee for
pets.

Hilton Suites
10 E Thomas Road
Phoenix, AZ
602-222-1111
There are no additional pet
fees.

Holiday Inn - West
1500 N 51st Ave
Phoenix, AZ
602-484-9009
There is a $25 one time pet fee.

Holiday Inn Express
3401 E University Dr

Phoenix, AZ
602-453-9900
There are no additional pet fees

**Holiday Inn Express Hotel &
Suites**
15221 S. 50th St
Phoenix, AZ
480-785-8500
There is a $5 per day additional
pet fee.

Holiday Inn Select - Airport
4300 E. Washington St
Phoenix, AZ
602-273-7778
There is a $25 refundable pet
deposit.

Howard Johnson Inn
124 S 24th St.
Phoenix, AZ
602-220-0044
Dogs up to 60 pounds are
allowed. There is a $20 one time
pet fee.

**La Quinta Inn Phoenix AP
North**
4727 E. Thomas Rd.
Phoenix, AZ
602-956-6500
Dogs up to 50 pounds are
allowed at the hotel.

La Quinta Inn Phoenix North
2510 West Greenway
Phoenix, AZ
602-993-0800
Dogs of all sizes are allowed at
the hotel.

**La Quinta Inn Phoenix
Thomas Road**
2725 N Black Canyon Highway
Phoenix, AZ
602-258-6271
Dogs up to 75 pounds are
allowed at the hotel.

Lexington Hotel at City Square
100 W Clarendon Ave
Phoenix, AZ
602-279-9811
There is a $100 refundable
deposit required for dogs.

Motel 6

2330 W Bell Rd
Phoenix, AZ
602-993-2353
Pets may never be left alone in the room.

Motel 6
4130 N Black Canyon Hwy
Phoenix, AZ
602-277-5501
Pets may not be left unattended in the room and must be on a leash when outside the room. The hotel is at the Indian School exit on I-17.

Motel 6
8152 N. Black Canyon Hwy
Phoenix, AZ
602-995-7592
The hotel is at the Northern Ave exit on I-17.

Motel 6
5315 E Van Buren Street
Phoenix, AZ
602-267-8555
Pets may not be left alone in the room.

Premier Inn
10402 N Black Canyon Hwy
Phoenix, AZ
602-943-2371
There are no additional pet fees. Pets are not allowed in deluxe rooms.

Quality Hotel & Resort
3600 N 2nd Ave
Phoenix, AZ
602-248-0222
There is a one time non-refundable fee of $25.

Quality Inn South Mountain
5121 E. La Puente Ave.
Phoenix, AZ
480-893-3900
Pets may not be left alone. There is a $50 pet fee of which $25 is refundable.

Quality Suites
3101 N. 32nd St
Phoenix, AZ
602-956-4900
There is a $10 per day pet fee.

Red Lion Metrocenter
12027 N 28th Dr
Phoenix, AZ
602-866-7000
There are no additional pet fees.

Red Roof Inn
5215 W Willetta
Phoenix, AZ
602-233-8004
Dogs under about 80 pounds are allowed. There are no additional pet fees.

Residence Inn
8242 N Black Canyon Hwy
Phoenix, AZ
602-864-1900
There is a $50 non-refundable pet fee.

Sheraton Crescent Hotel
2620 West Dunlap Avenue
Phoenix, AZ
602-943-8200
Dogs up to 80 pounds are allowed. There is no additional pet fee.

Sheraton Wild Horse Pass Resort and Spa
Gila River Indian Community
Phoenix, AZ
602-225-0100
Dogs up to 55 pounds are allowed. All rooms are non-smoking. There are no pet fees.

Sleep Inn
6347 E. Southern Ave.
Phoenix, AZ
480-807-7760
There is a $25 pet deposit. Pets may not be left alone.

Sleep Inn North
18235 N. 27th Ave.
Phoenix, AZ
602-504-1200
There is a $25 pet deposit.

Sleep Inn Sky Harbor Airport
2621 S 47th Pl
Phoenix, AZ
480-967-7100
There is a $25 one time pet fee.

South Mountain Village Pet Friendly Vacation Apartment
113 E. La Mirada Drive
Phoenix, AZ
602-243-3452
Located in the foothills of South Mountain Park. 1 bedroom, 1 bath apartment, completely furnished, including dishes, utensils, cookware, linens and much more for a self-catering vacation. Pets have free range of completely fenced 1/8 acre gated yard. Pool, spa, laundry, off-street parking for one automobile. Horse riding stables, golf, hiking trials nearby. Rates are seasonal, starting at $300 per week and $975 per month for 2 adults and 1 pet (fees apply for additional guests/pets). Tax and cleaning fees are extra.

Studio 6
8405 North 27th Avenue
Phoenix, AZ
602-843-1151
There is a $10 per day additional pet fee. Exit Union Hills Drive west from I-17.

Townplace Suites
9425-B N Black Canyon Hwy
Phoenix, AZ
602-943-9510
There is a one-time $100 pet fee.

Pinetop

Best Western Inn of Pinetop
404 S. White Mountain Blvd
Pinetop, AZ
928-367-6667
There is a $10 per day pet fee.

Prescott

Comfort Inn
1290 White Spar Rd.
Prescott, AZ
928-778-5770
There is no pet fee in a smoking room. There is a $10 pet fee in a non-smoking room. There are

walking trails nearby.

Lynx Creek Farm Bed and Breakfast
SR69 and Onyx Rd
Prescott, AZ
928-778-9573
There is an additional $10 per day pet fee. Pets may not be left in the room unattended.

Super 8 Motel - Prescott
1105 E. Sheldon Street
Prescott, AZ
928-776-1282
$10/stay for up to 3 dogs in one room. FREE 8-minute long distance call each night. FREE continental breakfast. Coffee maker, night light, clock/radio, safe in each room. Seasonal outdoor pool. On-site guest laundry. Kids 12 & under stay free. On Sheldon St (BR 89), West of intersection of US 89 & AZ 69.

Prescott Valley

Days Inn
7875 E AZ 69
Prescott Valley, AZ
928-772-8600
There is a $50 refundable pet deposit.

Safford

Best Western Desert Inn
1391 Thatcher Blvd
Safford, AZ
928-428-0521
There is a $6 per day pet fee.

Scottsdale

Hampton Inn Oldtown
4415 N Civic Center Plaza
Scottsdale, AZ
480-941-9400
There is a one-time $50 pet fee.

Homestead Village
3560 N Marshall Way
Scottsdale, AZ
480-994-0297

There is a $75 one time pet fee.

Inn at the Citadel
8700 E Pinnacle Peak Rd
Scottsdale, AZ
480-585-6133
This B&B is located in an adobe-like complex of stores and next to the foothills of Pinnacle Peak. There are no additional pet fees.

La Quinta Inn & Suites Scottsdale
8888 East Shea Blvd.
Scottsdale, AZ
480-614-5300
Dogs of all sizes are allowed at the hotel.

Motel 6
6848 E Camelback Rd
Scottsdale, AZ
480-946-2280
Pets must be attended at all times.

Pima Inn and Suites
7330 N Pima Rd
Scottsdale, AZ
480-948-3800
There is a $10 one time pet fee. Dogs are not allowed in the lobby.

Residence Inn
6040 N Scottsdale Rd
Scottsdale, AZ
480-948-8666
There is a $50 one time pet fee plus $6 per day pet fee.

Sleep Inn
16630 N. Scottsdale Rd
Scottsdale, AZ
480-998-9211
This hotel has 107 rooms which have either 2 double beds or one King bed. They offer a deluxe continental breakfast, outdoor heated pool, spa, and fitness room. They accept all types of pets and charge a $10 per day fee for the first 5 days of your stay. No deposits are required.

Sedona

Best Western Inn of Sedona
1200 Hwy 89A
Sedona, AZ
928-282-3072
There is a $10 per day pet fee.

Matterhorn Motor Lodge
230 Apple Ave
Sedona, AZ
928-282-7176
This inn is located in the center of uptown Sedona.

Oak Creek Terrace Resort
4548 N. Hwy. 89A
Sedona, AZ
928-282-3562
Relax by the creek or in one of the jacuzzi rooms. Dogs welcome with a $35 non-refundable pet fee. Amenities include in-room fireplaces, barbeque and picnic areas, air conditioning and cable TV.

Quail Ridge Resort
120 Canyon Circle Dr
Sedona, AZ
928-284-9327
There is a $10 per day pet fee.

Sky Ranch Lodge
Airport Rd
Sedona, AZ
928-282-6400
There is a $10.00 per day pet fee, dogs up to 75 pounds ok.

Show Low

Best Western Paint Pony Lodge
581 W Deuce of Clubs
Show Low, AZ
928-537-5773
There is a $15 refundable pet deposit.

Motel 6
1941 E Deuce of Clubs
Show Low, AZ
928-537-7694
There are no additional pet fees.

Sleep Inn

1751 W. Deuce of Clubs
Show Low, AZ
928-532-7323
There is a $25 per day pet fee.

Sierra Vista

Best Western Mission Inn
3460 E Fry Blvd
Sierra Vista, AZ
520-458-8500
There is a $5 per day additional pet fee.

Motel 6
1551 E Fry Blvd
Sierra Vista, AZ
520-459-5035
There are no additional pet fees.

Super 8 Motel - Sierra Vista
100 Fab Avenue
Sierra Vista, AZ
520-459-5380
$10/stay for up to 3 dogs in one room. FREE 8-minute long distance call each night. FREE continental breakfast. Coffee maker, refrigerator, night light, clock/radio, safe in each room. Seasonal outdoor pool. On-site guest laundry. Kids 12 & under stay free. I-10, Exit 302, straight on Buffalo Soldier Trail, 30 miles, through light to Fry Blvd.; Left 1 blk.

Tempe

Holiday Inn - Tempe
915 E. Apache Blvd
Tempe, AZ
480-968-3451
One well-behaved large dog is okay.

La Quinta Inn Phoenix Sky Harbor Tempe
911 South 48th Street
Tempe, AZ
480-967-4465
Dogs of all sizes are allowed at the hotel.

Motel 6
1720 S. Priest Drive
Tempe, AZ

480-968-4401
There are no additional pet fees.

Motel 6
1612 N Scottsdale Rd/Rural Rd
Tempe, AZ
480-945-9506
Pets may not be left alone in the room.

Quality
1375 E. University Dr.
Tempe, AZ
480-774-2500
There is no pet fee. A credit card will be required.

Studio 6
4909 South Wendler Dr.
Tempe, AZ
602-414-4470
There is a $10 per day or $30 per week pet fee.

Tombstone

Best Western Lookout Lodge
Highway 80 West
Tombstone, AZ
520-457-2223
This is Tombstone's newest motel. Amenities include a pool. It is located within a short drive to historic Tombstone. There is a $5 per day pet charge.

Trail Rider's Inn
13 N. 7th Street
Tombstone, AZ
520-457-3573
You and your pup can walk to the historic Tombstone district from this inn. They offer large, clean, quiet rooms and cable TV. There is a $5 per day pet fee.

Tucson

Best Western Executive Inn
333 West Drachman Street
Tucson, AZ
520-791-7551
There is a $15 one time pet fee per visit.

Clarion Hotel & Suites Santa Rita
88 E. Broadway Blvd.
Tucson, AZ
520-622-4000
There is a $50 pet deposit of which $25 is non-refundable.

Comfort Suites
6935 S. Tucson Blvd.
Tucson, AZ
520-295-4400
There is a non-refundable pet deposit of $50.

Comfort Suites at Tucson Mall
515 W. Automall Dr.
Tucson, AZ
520-888-6676
There is a one time pet fee of $10.

Doubletree Guest Suites
6555 E Speedway Blvd
Tucson, AZ
520-721-7100
There is a $25 per visit pet fee.

Hawthorn Suites Ltd
7007 E Tanque Verde Rd
Tucson, AZ
520-298-2300
There is a $25 pet fee per visit.

Loews Ventana Canyon Resort
7000 North Resort Drive
Tucson, AZ
520-299-2020
All well-behaved dogs of any size are welcome. This upscale hotel offers their "Loews Loves Pets" program which includes special pet treats, local dog walking routes, and a list of nearby pet-friendly places to visit. There are no pet fees.

Motel 6 - 22nd Street
1222 S Frwy
Tucson, AZ
520-624-2516
A clean well-behaved large dog is okay. Exit 22nd Street from I-10 and go west. There are no additional pet fees.

Motel 6 - Airport
1031 E Benson Hwy
Tucson, AZ
520-628-1264
There are no additional pet fees.

Motel 6 - Benson Hwy N
755 E Benson Hwy
Tucson, AZ
520-622-4614
There are no additional pet fees.

Motel 6 - Congess St
960 S. Freeway
Tucson, AZ
520-628-1339
Exit I-10 at exit 258, take the frontage road south. There are no additional pet fees.

Motel 6 - North
4630 W Ina Rd
Tucson, AZ
520-744-9300
Take Ina Rd exit off of I-10.
There are no additional pet fees.

Red Roof Inn Tucson North
4940 W Ina Rd
Tucson, AZ
520-744-8199
There are no additional pet fees.
Dogs up to 80 pounds are allowed. Pets must never be left alone in the rooms.

Residence Inn by Marriott
6477 E Speedway Blvd
Tucson, AZ
520-721-0991
There is a $50 one time pet fee per visit.

Sheraton Tucson Hotel and Suites
5151 East Grant Road
Tucson, AZ
520-323-6262
Dogs up to 80 pounds are allowed. There is a $25 per night additional pet fee. Dogs may not be left in the room by themselves.

Studio 6
4950 S. Outlet Center Dr
Tucson, AZ
520-746-0030

There is a $10 per day or $50 per week additional pet fee.

Westward Look Resort
245 East Ina Road
Tucson, AZ
520-297-1151
This resort comes highly recommended from one of our readers. They said it was the most pet-friendly resort around and they can't say enough good things about it. This former 1912 guest ranch, now a desert resort hideaway, is nestled in the foothills of Tucson's picturesque Santa Catalina Mountains. It offers guests a Southwestern experience on 80 desert acres. They have walking trails at the resort, tennis, swimming pools and much more. Special room rates can be as low as $69 during certain times and seasons. There is a $50 one time additional pet fee.

Windmill Inn at St Philip's Plaza
4250 N Campbell Ave
Tucson, AZ
520-577-0007
There are no additional pet fees.

Wickenburg

Best Western Rancho Grande
293 E Wickenburg Way
Wickenburg, AZ
928-684-5445
There are no additional pet fees.

Wilcox

Best Western Plaza Inn
1100 W Rex Allen Dr
Wilcox, AZ
520-384-3556
There is an $8 per day additional pet fee.

Motel 6
921 N Bisbee Ave
Wilcox, AZ

520-384-2201
From I-10, take Rex Allen Dr East, then north on Bisbee.

Williams

Highlander Motel
533 W. Bill Williams Avenue
Williams, AZ
928-635-2541
There is a $5/day pet charge. Room prices are in the $50 range. This motel is about 1 hour from the Grand Canyon.

Holiday Inn
950 N. Grand Canyon Blvd
Williams, AZ
928-635-4114
There are no additional pet fees.

Motel 6 - Grand Canyon
831 W Rt 66
Williams, AZ
520-635-9000
There are no additional pet fees.

Motel 6 Park Inn
710 W. Bill Williams Avenue
Williams, AZ
928-635-4464
This motel is about 1 hour from the Grand Canyon. There are no additional pet fees.

Quality Inn - Mountain Ranch Resort
6701 E. Mountain Ranch Road
Williams, AZ
928-635-2693
Amenities include tennis courts, a heated pool and whirlpool (closed during the winter). There is a one time $20 charge for pets. Room prices range from $50-100. This motel is about 1 hour from the Grand Canyon.

Winslow

Days Inn
2035 W. Hwy 66
Winslow, AZ
928-289-1010
There is a $20 refundable pet deposit.

Econo Lodge
I40 & Exit 253 North Park Dr
Winslow, AZ
928-289-4687
There is a $5 per day additional
pet fee.

Holiday Inn Express
816 Transcon Lane
Winslow, AZ
928-289-2960
There is a $10 per day additional
pet fee.

Woodlands Village

Motel 6
2745 S. Woodlands Village
Woodlands Village, AZ
928-779-3757
There are no pet fees. Just let
them know that you have a pet
when you check in.

Yuma

Comfort Inn
1691 S. Riley Ave.
Yuma, AZ
928-782-1200
There is a pet fee of $5 per day.

Holiday Inn Express
3181 S. 4th Ave
Yuma, AZ
928-344-1420
There are no additional pet fees.

Motel 6 - Downtown
1640 S Arizona Ave
Yuma, AZ
928-782-6561
There are no additional pet fees.

Motel 6 - East
1445 E 16th St
Yuma, AZ
928-782-9521
There are no additional pet fees.

Arkansas Listings

Arkadelphia

Best Western Continental Inn
136 Valley Road
Arkadelphia, AR
870-246-5592
There are no additional pet
fees.

Quality Inn
I-30 & Senic Byway 7
Arkadelphia, AR
870-246-5855
There is no pet fee.

Blytheville

Comfort Inn
1520 E Main St
Blytheville, AR
870-763-7081
There is no pet fee.

Pear Tree Inn
239 North Service Road
Blytheville, AR
870-763-2300
Dogs of all sizes are permitted.
Pets are not allowed in the
breakfast area of the hotel.
Pets are not to be left
unattended, and each guest
must assume liability for
damage of property or other
guest complaints. There is a
limit of one pet per room.

Carlisle

Best Western Carlisle
I-40 & State Hwy 13
Carlisle, AR
870-552-7566
There are no additional pet
fees.

Clarksville

**Best Western Sherwood
Motor Inn**
I-40 & Exit 58
Clarksville, AR
501-754-7900
There are no additional pet
fees.

Comfort Inn

1167 S. Rogers Ave
Clarksville, AR
501-754-3000
There is a pet fee of $5 per day.

Clinton

Best Western Hillside Inn
Hwy 65 & 65B
Clinton, AR
501-745-4700
There is a $7 per day pet fee.

Conway

Comfort Inn
150 US 65 N.
Conway, AR
501-329-0300
There is a refundable pet
deposit of $20.

Howard Johnson Inn
I-40 & Hwy 65N
Conway, AR
501-329-2961
House dogs up to 60 pounds are
ok. There is a $10 one time pet
fee.

Motel 6
1105 Hwy 65 N
Conway, AR
501-327-6623
There are no additional pet fees.

El Dorado

**Best Western Kings Inn
Conference Center**
1920 Junction City Rd
El Dorado, AR
870-862-5191
There are no additional pet fees.

Comfort Inn
2303 Junction City Rd
El Dorado, AR
870-863-6677
There is no pet fee.

Eureka Springs

Alpen-Dorf
6554 US 62

Eureka Springs, AR
501-253-9475
There is a $5 per day pet fee.

Best Western Inn of the Ozarks
Hwy 62 West
Eureka Springs, AR
501-253-9768
There are no additional pet fees.

Colonial Mansion Inn
154 Huntsville Rd
Eureka Springs, AR
501-253-7300
There is a $2 per day pet fee.

Lake Lucerne Resort

Eureka Springs, AR
479-253-8085
This resort is off the beaten path and offers considerable privacy, yet is close to all downtown shops, activities and restaurants. It is located on 40 acres in the Ozark Mountains, in a secluded valley. This place has been a summer and winter retreat for families, including the family dog, for many generations. They offer dog-friendly cabins, cottages, suites and 1-3 bedroom chalets. There is a $10 one time pet fee. While at the resort, swim or rent a row boat at Lake Lucerne with your best friend.

Lazee Daze Log Cabin Resort
5432 Hwy 23S
Eureka Springs, AR
501-253-7026
There is a $50 cash deposit required for pets. $30 of this will be refunded by mail. Well-behaved dogs only.

Motel 6
3169 East Van Buren
Eureka Springs, AR
501-253-5600
Pets may not be left alone in the room.

Fayetteville

Quality Inn
523 South Shiloh Drive
Fayetteville, AR
501-444-9800
There is a one time pet fee of $15.

Ramada Inn
3901 N College Ave
Fayetteville, AR
479-443-3431
There is a $50 refundable pet deposit and a $10 one time pet fee.

Red Roof Inn
1000 US 71
Fayetteville, AR
479-442-3041
There are no additional pet fees.

Sleep Inn
728 Millsap Rd
Fayetteville, AR
501-587-8700
There is no pet fee.

Fort Smith

Comfort Inn
2120 Burnham Rd
Fort Smith, AR
501-484-0227
There is no pet fee.

Days Inn
1021 Garrison Ave
Fort Smith, AR
479-783-0548
There is a $10 per day pet fee.

Motel 6
6001 Rogers Ave
Fort Smith, AR
501-484-0576
Pets must be kept on a leash when outside the room.

Ramada Inn
5711 Rogers Ave
Fort Smith, AR
479-452-4110
There is a $20 one time pet fee.

Ramada Inn
5103 Towson Ave

Fort Smith, AR
479-646-2931
There are no additional pet fees.

Harrison

Super 8
1330 US 62/65N
Harrison, AR
870-741-1741
There is a $10 per day pet fee.

Hope

Holiday Inn Express
2600 N Hervey
Hope, AR
870-722-6262
Exit I-30 at Hwy 278.

Hot Springs

Historic Park Hotel
211 Fountain St
Hot Springs, AR
501-624-5323
Dogs of all sizes are allowed. There is a $10 per night pet fee for large dogs, $5 for small dogs.

Quality Inn
1125 E. Grand Ave
Hot Springs, AR
501-624-3321
There is a pet fee of $10 per day.

Jonesboro

Best Western
2901 Phillips Dr
Jonesboro, AR
870-932-6600
There is a $5 per day pet fee.

Days Inn
2406 Phillips Dr
Jonesboro, AR
870-932-9339
There is a $6 per day additional pet fee.

Holiday Inn
3006 S. Caraway Rd
Jonesboro, AR

870-935-2030
There are no additional pet fees.

Motel 6
2300 S Caraway Rd
Jonesboro, AR
870-932-1050
There are no additional pet fees.

Quality Suites
2909 Kazi St
Jonesboro, AR
870-802-3212
There is no pet fee.

Ramada Limited
3000 Apache Dr
Jonesboro, AR
870-932-5757
There is a $10 per day additional pet fee.

Lakeview

Gaston's White River Resort
1777 River Rd
Lakeview, AR
870-431-5202
There are no pet fees. There are no designated smoking or non-smoking cottages.

Little Rock

Motel 6
7501 Interstate 30
Little Rock, AR
501-568-8888
There are no additional pet fees.

Red Roof Inn
7900 Scott Hamilton Dr
Little Rock, AR
501-562-2694
There are no pet fees. One pet per room is allowed.

Mountain Home

Best Western Carriage Inn
963 Highway 62 East
Mountain Home, AR
870-425-6001
There are no additional pet fees.

Sunrise Point Resort

88 Sunrise Point Lane
Mountain Home, AR
870-491-5188
The owners are big animal lovers and welcome your pets at their resort. These dog-friendly and animal-friendly folks have 2 dogs, a miniature horse and a pot bellied pig named 'Hamlet'. So bring your pup and stay in one of their 11 cottages. There is an $8 per day pet fee. There are no designated smoking or non-smoking cottages.

Teal Point Resort
715 Teal Point Rd
Mountain Home, AR
870-492-5145
There is a $35 per week pet fee. Dogs are allowed in some of the cabins. There are no designated smoking or non-smoking cabins.

N Little Rock

Motel 6 - North
400 W 29th St
N Little Rock, AR
501-758-5100
Pets must be attended at all times.

North Little Rock

Comfort Suites
14322 Frontier Dr
North Little Rock, AR
501-851-8444
There is a pet fee of $20 per day.

Howard Johnson Hotel
111 W. Pershing Blvd.
North Little Rock, AR
501-758-1440
Dogs of all sizes are welcome. There is a $10 one time pet fee.

La Quinta Inn Little Rock North
4100 McCain Boulevard
North Little Rock, AR
501-945-0808
Dogs of all sizes are allowed at

the hotel.

Pine Bluff

Best Western Pines
2700 E Harding
Pine Bluff, AR
870-535-8640
There is a $25 refundable pet deposit.

Russellville

Holiday Inn
2407 N. Arkansas
Russellville, AR
501-968-4300
There are no additional pet fees.

Searcy

Comfort Inn
107 N. Rand Dr
Searcy, AR
501-279-9100
There is no pet fee.

Springdale

Executive Inn
2005 S US 71B
Springdale, AR
479-756-6101
There is a $10 one time pet fee.

Holiday Inn
1500 S. 48th St
Springdale, AR
501-751-8300
There are no additional pet fees.

Stuffgart

Holiday Inn Express
708 W. Michigan
Stuffgart, AR
870-673-3616
There is a $5 per day additional pet fee.

Stuttgart

Best Western Duck Inn
704 W. Michigan

Stuttgart, AR
870-673-2575
There are no additional pet fees.

Texarkana

Holiday Inn
5100 N. Stateline Rd
Texarkana, AR
870-774-3521
There is a $25 one time pet fee.

Van Buren

Comfort Inn
3131 Cloverleaf St
Van Buren, AR
501-474-2223
There is a refundable pet deposit of $50.

Holiday Inn Express
1903 N. 6th Street
Van Buren, AR
501-474-8100
There is a $10 per day additional pet fee. Exit Hwy 59 from I-40.

Motel 6
1716 Fayetteville Rd
Van Buren, AR
501-474-8001
A well-behaved large dog is okay.

California Listings

Albion

The Doors
North Hwy 1
Albion, CA
707-937-9200
This vacation home rental is dog-friendly. There are no additional pet fees. Please call to make reservations.

Alturas

Best Western Trailside Inn
343 North Main Street
Alturas, CA

530-233-4111
There is a $5 per day pet charge.

Hacienda Motel
201 E 12th St
Alturas, CA
530-233-3459
There are no additional pet fees.

Anaheim

Anaheim Marriott
700 W. Convention Way
Anaheim, CA
714-750-8000
This hotel is located within walking distance of Disneyland. Pets are allowed only on the first floor and they allow pets of all sizes. No deposit or fee, just be a responsible owner and pay for any damages. Room service is available. If you go to Disneyland, there are day kennels at the entrance of the Disneyland amusement park. Thanks to one of our readers for recommending this hotel.

Econolodge at the Park
1126 West Katella Ave
Anaheim, CA
714-533-4505
There is a $10 daily pet fee.

Embassy Suites Hotel
3100 E. Frontera Ave
Anaheim, CA
714-632-1221
There is a $50 one time pet fee per visit.

Hawthorn Suites
1752 S. Clementine
Anaheim, CA
714-635-5000
There is a $150 one time pet fee.

Quality Hotel Maingate
616 W Convention Way
Anaheim, CA
714-750-3131
This hotel is located about two blocks from Disneyland. The

hotel offers room service, self service laundry facilities and more. Rooms start at the low $100s and up. Parking is $8 per night. There is a $10 per night per pet and a non-refundable pet cleaning fee of $25.00. If you go to Disneyland for the day, please don't leave your dog in the room. Instead, take him or her to the Disneyland Kennel which offers friendly day boarding for your dog. (see Attractions).

Red Roof Inn
1251 N Harbor Blvd
Anaheim, CA
714-635-6461
There is a $10 per day additional pet fee.

Residence Inn by Marriott
1700 S. Clementine Street
Anaheim, CA
714-533-3555
There is a $40 one time pet fee and a $10 per day pet charge.

Staybridge Suites
1845 S. Manchester Ave
Anaheim, CA
714-748-7700
There is a $75 one time pet fee. This hotel is near Disneyland in Anaheim.

WestCoast Anaheim Hotel
1855 S. Harbor Blvd.
Anaheim, CA
714-750-1811
Call hotel direct for additional information or to check for availability.

Anderson

AmeriHost Inn
2040 Factory Outlets Dr
Anderson, CA
530-365-6100
There are no additional pet fees.

Best Western Knight's Inn
2688 Gateway Drive
Anderson, CA
530-365-2753

Well-trained, leashed dogs are allowed. There is no extra pet charge.

Angels Camp

Best Western Cedar Inn & Suites
444 South Main Street
Angels Camp, CA
209-736-4000
There is a $10 per day pet charge and dogs must be over one year old. Pets are not to be left alone in the room.

Aptos

Apple Lane Inn B&B
6265 Soquel Drive
Aptos, CA
831-475-6868
You and your well-behaved dog are allowed at this Victorian farmhouse built in the 1870s. It is situated on over 2 acres with fields, gardens, and apple orchards. There are also many farm animals such as horses, chickens, goats, ducks and geese. They have three double rooms and two suites with antique furniture. Each of the five rooms have private baths. Room stay includes a full breakfast, and afternoon and evening refreshments. Rates are $120 per night and up. There is a $25 charge for a dog, extra person or crib. No smoking is allowed indoors. This bed and breakfast is located on Soquel Drive, near Cabrillo Jr. College. From Hwy 17 south, exit Hwy 1 south towards Watsonville. Take the Park Avenue/New Brighton Beach exit. Turn left onto Park Ave. Turn right onto Soquel. It will be near Atherton Drive and before Cabrillo College.

Arcadia

Residence Inn - Arcadia
321 E. Huntington Dr/Gateway
Arcadia, CA

626-446-6500
There is a $250 refundable deposit for pets. There is a $50 one time pet fee and a $6 per day additional pet fee.

Arcata

Best Western Arcata Inn
4827 Valley West Boulevard
Arcata, CA
707-826-0313
There is a $10 per dog per day pet charge. Amenities include free continental breakfast, an indoor/outdoor pool and spa, large deluxe rooms including Jacuzzi® rooms and complimentary cable television with HBO.

Hotel Arcata
708 Ninth Street
Arcata, CA
707-826-0217
This hotel comes highly recommended from one of our readers who says "In Arcata, just north of Eureka, we stayed in an old refurbished hotel, the Hotel Arcata. It's in the center of town, right on the town square. Ask for a room that doesn't face the square, as it can get noisy at night. Bringing a dog into the elevator is fun." There is a $5 per day additional pet fee.

Quality Inn
3535 Janes Rd
Arcata, CA
707-822-0409
There is a $10 per day pet fee.

Super 8
4887 Valley W. Blvd
Arcata, CA
707-822-8888
There are no additional pet fees.

Arnold

Ebbetts Pass Lodge
1173 Highway 4, Box 2591
Arnold, CA

209-795-1563
There is a $5 per day pet charge.

Sierra Vacation Rentals
908 Moran Road
Arnold, CA
209-795-2422
Pets are allowed in some of the vacation homes and cabins. You must tell them you are bringing a dog when you make your reservation. There is a $50 refundable pet deposit. Children are also welcome in most of the rentals.

Arroyo Grande

Best Western Casa Grande Inn
850 Oak Park Road
Arroyo Grande, CA
805-481-7398
Dogs up to 75 pounds are okay. There is a $25 refundable pet deposit required.

Atascadero

Motel 6
9400 El Camino Real
Atascadero, CA
805-466-6701
There are no additional pet fees.

Auburn

Best Western Golden Key
13450 Lincoln Way
Auburn, CA
530-885-8611
There is a $15 one time pet charge. Dogs are allowed in certain pet rooms.

Holiday Inn
120 Grass Valley Highway
Auburn, CA
530-887-8787
Amenities include room service, a heated pool, spa and fitness room. There is a $20 one time pet charge.

Travelodge

13490 Lincoln Way
Auburn, CA
530-885-7025
There is a $10 per day pet fee.

Bakersfield

Best Western Crystal Palace Inn & Suites
2620 Buck Owens Blvd.
Bakersfield, CA
661-327-9651
There is a $10 per day pet charge. Dogs are allowed in certain pet rooms.

Best Western Hill House
700 Truxton Avenue
Bakersfield, CA
661-327-4064
They offer spacious guest rooms with a well-lit workspace, refrigerator in all rooms, free cable television with Showtime, free locals and more. There is a $10 per day pet charge.

Days Hotel and Golf
4500 Buck Owens Blvd
Bakersfield, CA
661-324-5555
There is a $20 one time pet fee.

Doubletree Hotel
3100 Camino Del Rio Ct
Bakersfield, CA
661-323-7111
There is a $15 per day additional pet fee.

La Quinta Inn Bakersfield
3232 Riverside Drive
Bakersfield, CA
661-325-7400
Dogs of all sizes are allowed at the hotel.

Ramada Inn
830 Wible Rd
Bakersfield, CA
661-831-1922
There is a $5 per day pet fee.

Residence Inn
4241 Chester Lane
Bakersfield, CA
661-321-9800

$40 one time fee for a studio room, more for a larger room. There is also a $6 per day pet fee.

Rio Bravo Resort
11200 Lake Ming Rd
Bakersfield, CA
661-872-5000
There is a $50 refundable pet deposit.

Super 8
901 Real Rd
Bakersfield, CA
661-322-1012
There is a $10 refundable deposit for pets.

Banning

Super 8
1690 W. Ramsey St
Banning, CA
909-849-6887
There is a $5 per day additional pet fee.

Travelodge
1700 W. Ramsey Street
Banning, CA
909-849-1000
A well-behaved large dog is allowed. There is a $5 per day pet charge.

Barstow

Days Inn
1590 Coolwater Lane
Barstow, CA
760-256-1737
There is a $10 per day pet fee.

Econo Lodge
1230 E. Main Street
Barstow, CA
760-256-2133
One large well-behaved dog is permitted per room. There is a $5 per day pet fee.

Holiday Inn Express
1861 W. Main St.
Barstow, CA
760-256-1300
This 3 story motel, located

along Historic Route 66, offers rooms with microwaves, refrigerators, iron/ironing boards, hair dryers and data ports. There is $20 refundable pet deposit.

Motel 6
150 N Tucca Ave
Barstow, CA
760-256-1752
There are no additional pet fees.

Ramada Inn
1511 E Main Street
Barstow, CA
760-256-5673
There is a $20 one time pet fee per visit.

Super 8 Motel
170 Coolwater Lane
Barstow, CA
760-256-8443
There is a $5 per day pet charge.

Beaumont

Best Western El Rancho Motor Inn
480 East 5th Street
Beaumont, CA
909-845-2176
There is a $16 per day pet charge. Dogs are allowed in certain pet rooms.

Belmont

Motel 6
1101 Shoreway Rd.
Belmont, CA
650-591-1471
There is no extra pet charge in the regular rooms. There is a $25 one time pet charge in the studio rooms.

Benicia

Best Western Heritage Inn
1955 East Second Street
Benicia, CA
707-746-0401
There is a $25 one time pet fee.

Berkeley

Beau Sky Hotel
2520 Durant Ave
Berkeley, CA
510-540-7688
This small hotel offers personalized service. Some rooms have balconies. If your room doesn't, you can sit at the chairs and tables in the patio at the front of the hotel. Your small, medium or large dog will feel welcome here because they don't discriminate against dog size. It is located close to the UC Berkeley campus and less than a block from the popular Telegraph Ave (see Attractions). There aren't too many hotels in Berkeley, especially around the campus. So if you are going, be sure to book a room in advance. To get there from Hwy 880 heading north, take the Hwy 980 exit towards Hwy 24/Walnut Creek. Then take the Hwy 24 exit on the left towards Berkeley/Walnut Creek. Exit at Claremont Ave and turn left onto Claremont Ave. Make a slight left onto College Ave. Turn left onto Haste St. Turn right onto Telegraph Ave and then right onto Durant. The hotel will be on the right. There are no additional pet fees. All rooms are non-smoking.

Golden Bear Motel
1620 San Pablo Ave
Berkeley, CA
510-525-6770
This motel has over 40 rooms. Eight of the rooms have two-bedroom units and there are four two-bedroom cottages with kitchens. Parking is free. To get there from Hwy 80 heading north, exit University Ave. Turn right onto University Ave, and then left on San Pablo Ave. The motel is on the left. There is a $10 per day additional pet fee.

Berry Creek

Lake Oroville Bed and Breakfast
240 Sunday Drive
Berry Creek, CA
530-589-0700
Dogs are welcome, but should be okay around other dogs. The owner has dogs and cats on the premises. There is a $10 per day pet fee. Children are also welcome.

Beverly Hills

Loews Beverly Hills Hotel
1224 S. Beverwil Drive
Beverly Hills, CA
310-277-2800
All well-behaved dogs of any size are welcome. This upscale hotel offers their "Loews Loves Pets" program which includes room service for pets, special pet treats, local dog walking routes, and a list of nearby pet-friendly places to visit. There are no pet fees.

Big Bear City

Cienaga Creek Ranch
P.O. Box 2773
Big Bear City, CA
909-584-1147
There is a $10 per day pet fee. Pets may not be left unattended in the cottages. According to a reader "4 cozy, clean and comfortable cottages on 40 acres adjoining BLM land. Very relaxed, run by nice people. Plenty of leash-free hiking right from your door."

Big Bear Lake

Big Bear Front Desk - Vacation Rental
Call to Arrange.
Big Bear Lake, CA
800-801-5253
2 bedroom cabin. Fully equipped kitchen and fireplace. 2 bedroom with king size bed and two single beds. Ask for unit number 54.

Big Bear Frontier
40472 Big Bear Blvd
Big Bear Lake, CA
909-866-5888
The Big Bear Frontier is a group of cabins and motel rooms nestled in a beautiful mountain setting. The Big Bear Frontier is located on Big Bear Lake. It is located in easy walking distance to Big Bear Village. Amenities include pool, jacuzzi, gym and more. There is a $15 per night pet fee. Pets may not be left unattended and must be kept on a leash when out of the room.

Big Bear Vacations
40729 Village Drive #2, Box 110410
Big Bear Lake, CA
909-866-1580
Most of their vacation home rentals allow pets. Many of the cabins and houses are near the lake and near hiking trails. All cabins are non-smoking. Pet charges may vary.

Eagle's Nest Lodge
41675 Big Bear Blvd.
Big Bear Lake, CA
909-866-6465
There are 5 cabins and only 1 allows dogs, but it is a pretty nice cabin. It's called the Sierra Madre and includes a kitchen, fireplace and separate bedroom. You can order breakfast delivered to the room for an additional $10 per person.

Grey Squirrel Resort
39372 Big Bear Blvd
Big Bear Lake, CA
909-866-4335
This dog-friendly resort has cabins that accommodate from 1-2 people up to 20 people. They have a heated pool, indoor spa, basketball and horseshoes. Some of the cabins have fireplaces and kitchens. All units have VCRs and microwaves. There is a $10 per day additional pet fee.

Holiday Inn
42200 Moonridge Rd
Big Bear Lake, CA
909-866-6666
There is a $15 per day pet fee.
Dogs may not be left alone in
the room.

Mountain Lodging Unlimited
41135 Big Bear Blvd
Big Bear Lake, CA
909-866-5500
Dogs are allowed in some of the
vacation rentals, cabins, and
motels. They will tell you which
rentals allow dogs.

Mtn. Resort Adventure Hostel
PO Box 1951
Big Bear Lake, CA
909-866-8900
According to the people at the
Hostel "Rent beds or private
rooms in our cozy hostel
overlooking Big Bear Lake.
Fenced grass yard for dogs to
play in. All dogs welcome as
long as they are friendly with our
dogs."

Shore Acres Lodge
40090 Lakeview Drive
Big Bear Lake, CA
909-866-8200
This resort has 11 cabins and is
next to Big Bear Lake and has
its own private boat dock. Other
amenities include BBQs,
volleyball, a children's
playground, pool and spa.

Timber Haven Lodge
877 Tulip Lane
Big Bear Lake, CA
909-866-7207
Dogs are not allowed to remain
unattended in the cabins. There
is a $10 per day additional pet
fee.

Timberline Lodge
39921 Big Bear Blvd.
Big Bear Lake, CA
909-866-4141
The "Pets Welcome" sign at the
main entrance will let you know
your pup is more than welcome
here. Some of the 13 cabins

have fireplaces and full
kitchens. There is also a
playground for kids. There is a
$10 per day additional pet fee
per pet.

Wildwood Resort
40210 Big Bear Blvd.
Big Bear Lake, CA
909-878-2178
This cabin resort has about 15
cabins of various sizes. Most
rooms have fireplaces and all
cabins have private picnic
benches and BBQs. There is
also a pool & spa and if your
pup is well-behaved, he or she
can be tied to the rails on the
inside of the pool area. It's a
close drive to town and to some
of the parks and attractions.
Not too many restaurants within
walking distance, but there is a
local service that delivers food -
check with the front desk. This
is a nice place to relax and
unwind. There is a $10 per day
additional pet fee. There are no
designed smoking or non-
smoking cabins.

Big Pine

Big Pine Motel
370 S Main St
Big Pine, CA
760-938-2282
There is a $4 per day additional
pet fee.

Bristlecone Motel
101 N. Main St.
Big Pine, CA
760-938-2067
According to one of our website
readers "Neat,inexpensive
rooms with kitchens or fridge
and microwave. Barbecue and
fish cleaning area. Easy day
trip to the ancient Bristlecone
Pine Forest, which is extremely
dog friendly."

Bishop

Best Western Bishop Holiday
Spa Lodge

1025 North Main Street
Bishop, CA
760-873-3543
There are no extra pet charges.
Dogs are allowed in certain
rooms.

Comfort Inn
805 N. Main Street
Bishop, CA
760-873-4284
The hotel has three non-
smoking pet rooms.

Motel 6
1005 N Man Street
Bishop, CA
760-873-8426
There are no additional pet fees.

Rodeway Inn
150 E Elm Street
Bishop, CA
760-873-3564
There is a $5 per day pet fee.
Dogs are allowed in certain
rooms only.

Vagabond Inn
1030 N Main Street
Bishop, CA
760-873-6351
There is a $5 per day pet fee.

Blythe

Best Western Sahara Motel
825 W. Hobson Way
Blythe, CA
760-922-7105
Pets are allowed with no
restrictions and there are no pet
fees. Amenities include a free
continental breakfast, pool, spa,
and microwave and VCRs in
some rooms.

Holiday Inn Express
600 W. Donion St
Blythe, CA
760-921-2300
There is a $10 per day pet fee.

Bonny Doon

Redwood Croft B&B
275 Northwest Drive

Bonny Doon, CA
831-458-1939
This bed and breakfast, located in the Santa Cruz Mountains, is set on a sunny hill amidst the redwood forest. It is the perfect country getaway, especially since they allow dogs. They are very dog-friendly. This B&B has two rooms each with a private bath and full amenities. The Garden Room has its own entrance, private deck with a secluded 7 foot Jacuzzi spa, full-size bed, wood-burning stone fireplace and a sky lit loft with a queen futon. The West Room is sunny and spacious, has a California king bed and large bathroom with a double shower and roman tub. Room stay includes a lavish country breakfast. Room rates are $145 per night. The dog-friendly Davenport Beach (see Parks) is only about 10-15 minutes away. Call the inn for directions or for a brochure.

Boonville

Boonville Hotel
Highway 128
Boonville, CA
707-895-2210
This historic hotel was built in 1862. Dogs and children are allowed in the Bungalow and the Studio rooms which are separate from the main building. Both of these rooms are in the Creekside building with private entrances and yards. Room rates start at $225 per night and there is a $15 per day pet charge. Please note that their restaurant is closed on Tuesdays and Wednesdays. This hotel is in Anderson Valley, which is located 2 1/2 hours north of San Francisco.

Borrego Springs

Borrego Valley Inn
405 Palm Canyon Drive
Borrego Springs, CA

760-767-0311
Built in 1998, the Borrego Valley Inn is a 15 room Inn situated on 10 acres of property that borders the Anza-Borrego Desert State Park. Surrounded by mountain peaks that range from 4,000 to 7,000 feet, the inn's natural desert landscaping blends perfectly with the surrounding environment. All of the rooms are decorated in Southwestern/Mexican decor and have private patios and walk-in showers. Breakfast is included with your room. There is lots of room for your pet to roam here. You can even take your dog for some exercise at the back of the property where there's a walking trail that leads up to the mountain's ledge. There is a one time $25 pet fee per dog per stay.

Bridgeport

Best Western Ruby Inn
333 Main Street
Bridgeport, CA
760-931-7241
Dogs are allowed in certain pet rooms. There are no extra pet fees. Amenities include refrigerators and hairdryers in some rooms, an outdoor spa and BBQ area. This inn is located 20 miles from Bodie Ghost Town.

Buellton

Motel 6
333 McMurray Rd
Buellton, CA
805-688-7797
Dogs are not to be left alone in the room.

Rodeway Inn
630 Ave of Flags
Buellton, CA
805-688-0022
This motel (formerly Econo Lodge) is located about 4 miles from the village of Solvang. Amenities include cable TV and

movies. Handicap accessible rooms are available. There is a $25 one time pet charge.

Burbank

Hilton Burbank
2500 Hollywood Way
Burbank, CA
800-840-6450
This hotel is located across from the Burbank Airport. It offers 24 hour room service, two on-site fitness centers, pools, spas and saunas. There is a $25 non-refundable pet fee.

Burlingame

Embassy Suites
150 Anza Blvd.
Burlingame, CA
650-342-4600
This majestic hotel which overlooks the San Francisco Bay has no size restrictions for your well-behaved dog. Inside, you will find a nine-story atrium filled with lush tropical palms, flowers and waterfalls. Amenities include a heated indoor pool and more. The hotel is located about two miles south of the San Francisco Airport and 16 miles from downtown San Francisco. There is a $50 one time pet fee.

Vagabond Inn
1640 Bayshore Highway
Burlingame, CA
650-692-4040
This motel overlooks the San Francisco Bay. It is located just south of the airport and about 16 miles from downtown San Francisco. All rooms include coffee makers, cable television and air conditioning. Pets are an additional $10 per day.

Burney

Shasta Pines Motel
37386 Main Street
Burney, CA

(530) 335-2201
Dogs of all sizes are allowed. There are no additional pet fees.

Buttonwillow

Super 8
20681 Tracy Ave
Buttonwillow, CA
661-764-5117
There are no additional pet fees.

Calistoga

Hillcrest Bed and Breakfast
3225 Lake County Hwy.
Calistoga, CA
707-942-6334
This inn is located near the base of Mt. St. Helena and within a five minute drive to downtown Calistoga. This bed and breakfast also offers swimming, hiking and fishing on 40 acres. Dogs are welcome. The owner also has two dogs. There is a $10 per day pet charge.

Pink Mansion Bed and Breakfast
1415 Foothill Blvd.
Calistoga, CA
707-942-0558
This restored 1875 home offers modern amenities for wine country travellers. The Pink Mansion has been featured in The Wine Spectator, Best Places To Kiss and the New York Post. Dogs are allowed in one of their six rooms. Each room has a private bathroom. There is a $30 per day pet charge.

Cambria

Cambria Pines Lodge
2905 Burton Drive
Cambria, CA
805-927-4200
This lodge is a 125 room retreat with accommodations ranging from rustic cabins to fireplace suites. It is nestled among 25 acres of Monterey Pines with

forested paths and flower gardens. There is a $25 one time pet charge.

Cambria Shores Inn
6276 Moonstone Beach Dr.
Cambria, CA
805-927-8644
This motel offers a beautiful ocean view from just about every room. You and your pup can enjoy ocean views, coastal walks (along the bluff, not on the beach) and pacific sunsets. Amenities include an in-room continental breakfast delivered to your door, in-room refrigerators and more. Dogs over 18 months old are allowed and there is a $10 per day pet charge.

Fogcatcher Inn
6400 Moonstone Beach Drive
Cambria, CA
805-927-1400
There is a $25 per day additional pet fee. Two pet rooms are available. Thanks to one of our readers for recommending this place.

Cameron Park

Best Western Cameron Park Inn
3361 Coach Lane
Cameron Park, CA
530-677-2203
Amenities include a complimentary continental breakfast, pool, and hairdryers in rooms. There is a $25 one time pet charge.

Campbell

Residence Inn by Marriott
2761 S Bascom Ave
Campbell, CA
408-559-1551
Every one of their 80 suites offers separate living and sleeping areas, complete with a full kitchen. There is a $75 one time pet charge and a $10 per day additional pet fee per pet.

Capistrano Beach

Seaside Inn
34862 Pacific Coast Hwy.
Capistrano Beach, CA
949-496-1399
There is a $25 one time pet fee.

Capitola

Best Western Capitola By-the-Sea
1435 41st Ave
Capitola, CA
831-477-0607
There is a $10 per day pet fee.

Capitola Inn
822 Bay Ave
Capitola, CA
831-462-3004
This inn is located a few blocks from Capitola Village. They offer 56 rooms with either a private patio or balcony. There is a $20 per day pet charge.

Carlsbad

Chamberlain Property Management
2653 Roosevelt Street, Suite D
Carlsbad, CA
760-434-7373
Dogs are allowed in one of their vacation home rentals. There is a refundable pet deposit.

Inns of America
751 Raintree
Carlsbad, CA
760-931-1185
There is a $10 one time pet fee.

Residence Inn - Carlsbad
2000 Faraday Ave
Carlsbad, CA
760-431-9999
There is a $150 one time pet fee and a $10 per day additional pet fee.

Carmel

Carmel Country Inn
P.O. Box 3756

Carmel, CA
831-625-3263
This dog-friendly bed and breakfast has 12 rooms and allows dogs in several of these rooms. It's close to many downtown outdoor dog-friendly restaurants (see Restaurants). A 20-25 minute walk will take you to the dog-friendly Carmel City Beach. There is a $20 per night per pet charge.

Carmel Tradewinds Inn
Mission St & 3rd Ave.
Carmel, CA
831-624-2776
This motel allows dogs in several of their rooms. They are a non-smoking inn. It's located about 3-4 blocks north of Ocean Ave and close to many outdoor dog-friendly restaurants in downtown Carmel. A 20-25 minute walk will take you to the dog-friendly Carmel City beach. There is a $25 per day pet charge. Dogs are not allowed on the bed.

Casa De Carmel
Monte Verde & Ocean Ave
Carmel, CA
831-624-2429
There is an additional fee of $20 per day for 1 pet, and $30 a day for 2 pets.

Coachman's Inn
San Carlos St. & 7th
Carmel, CA
831-624-6421
Located in downtown, this motel allows dogs. It's close to many downtown outdoor dog-friendly restaurants (see Restaurants). A 20-25 minute walk will take you to the Carmel City beach which allows dogs. There is a $15 per day additional pet fee.

Cypress Inn
Lincoln & 7th
Carmel, CA
831-624-3871
This hotel is located within walking distance to many dog-friendly outdoor restaurants in the quaint town of Carmel and walking distance to the Carmel City Beach. This is definitely a pet-friendly hotel. Here is an excerpt from the Cypress Inn's web page "Co-owned by actress and animal rights activist Doris Day, the Cypress Inn welcomes pets with open arms -- a policy which draws a high percentage of repeat guests. It's not unusual to see people strolling in and out of the lobby with dogs of all sizes. Upon arrival, animals are greeted with dog biscuits, and other pet pamperings." Room rates are about $125 - $375 per night. If you have more than 2 people per room (including a child or baby), you will be required to stay in their deluxe room which runs approximately $375 per night. There is a $25 per day pet charge.

Hofsas House Hotel
San Carlos Street
Carmel, CA
831-624-2745
There is a $15 per day additional pet fee. The hotel is located between 3rd Ave and 4th Ave in Carmel. Thanks to one of our readers for recommending this hotel.

Lincoln Green Inn
PO Box 2747
Carmel, CA
831-624-7738
These cottages are owned and booked through the dog-friendly Vagabond's House Inn in Carmel. One big difference between the two accommodations is that the Vagabond's House does not allow children, whereas the Lincoln Green does allow children. The Lincoln Green is located very close to a beach. All cottages are non-smoking and there is a $20 per day pet fee.

Sunset House
Camino Real and Ocean Ave
Carmel, CA
831-624-4884
There is a $20 one time pet fee. Thanks to one of our readers who writes "Great B&B, breakfast brought to your room every morning."

The Forest Lodge Cottages
Ocean Ave. and Torres St. (P.O. Box 1316)
Carmel, CA
831-624-7055
These cottages are surrounded by oak and pine trees among a large garden area. They are conveniently located within walking distance to many dog-friendly restaurants and the dog-friendly Carmel City Beach. There is a $10 one time additional pet fee.

Vagabond's House Inn B&B
P.O. Box 2747
Carmel, CA
831-624-7738
This dog-friendly bed and breakfast is located in downtown and has 11 rooms. It's close to many downtown outdoor dog-friendly restaurants. A 20-25 minute walk will take you to the dog-friendly Carmel City beach. Children 12 years and older are allowed at this B&B inn.

Wayside Inn
Mission St & 7th Ave.
Carmel, CA
831-624-5336
This motel allows dogs in several of their rooms and is close to many downtown outdoor dog-friendly restaurants. A 20-25 minute walk will take you to the dog-friendly Carmel City beach. Pets are welcome at no extra charge. Dogs up to about 75 pounds are allowed.

Carmel Valley

Best Western Carmel Mission Inn
3665 Rio Rd.
Carmel Valley, CA

831-624-1841
Located in Carmel Valley off Hwy 1, this inn is a few blocks from The Crossroads Shopping Center which has several outdoor dog-friendly restaurants and a pet store. The Garland Ranch Park is located within a 10-15 minute drive. There is also a $35 one time pet fee.

Carmel Valley Lodge
Carmel Valley Rd
Carmel Valley, CA
831-659-2261
Your dog will feel welcome at this country retreat. Pet amenities include heart-shaped, organic homemade dog biscuits and a pawtographed picture of Lucky the Lodge Dog. Dogs must be on leash, but for your convenience, there are doggy-hitches at the front door of every unit that has a patio or deck and at the pool. There are 31 units which range from standard rooms to two bedroom cottages. A great community park is located across the street and several restaurants with outdoor seating are within a 5 minute walk. Drive about 15 minutes from the lodge and you'll be in downtown Carmel or at one of the dog-friendly beaches. Rates with seasonal changes are from $139 to $319 per night. Dogs are an extra $10 per day and up to two dogs per room. There is no charge for childen under 16. The lodge is located in Carmel Valley. From Carmel, head south on Hwy 1. Turn left on Carmel Valley Rd., drive about 11-12 miles and the lodge will be located at Ford Rd.

Los Laureles Lodge
313 West Carmel Valley Road
Carmel Valley, CA
831-659-2233
There is a $20 per day pet fee. Dogs may not be left in the room unattended. This large ranch lodge sits on 10 acres in rural Carmel Valley, about 10 minutes from the Carmel seaside and

near world class golf, hiking, wineries and everything else Carmel has to offer. Nearby Garland Ranch is available for hiking.

Carpinteria

Motel 6
4200 Via Real
Carpinteria, CA
805-684-6921
There are no additional pet fees.

Motel 6 - South
5550 Carpinteria Ave
Carpinteria, CA
805-684-8602
Dogs must never be left unattended in rooms.

Cayucos

Cayucos Beach Inn
333 South Ocean Avenue
Cayucos, CA
805-995-2828
There is a $10 one time pet fee. All rooms in the inn are non-smoking. Family pets are welcome. The inn even has a dog walk and dog wash area. Thanks to one of our readers for this recommendation.

Cypress Tree Motel
125 S. Ocean Avenue
Cayucos, CA
805-995-3917
This pet-friendly 12-unit motel is located within walking distance to everything in town. Amenities include a garden area with lawn furniture and a barbecue. There is a $10 one time pet charge.

Dolphin Inn
399 S Ocean Ave
Cayucos, CA
805-995-3810
There is a $10 per day pet charge.

Shoreline Inn
1 North Ocean Avenue

Cayucos, CA
805-995-3681
This dog-friendly motel is located on the beach (dogs are not allowed on this State Beach). Dogs are allowed in the first floor rooms which have direct access to a patio area. There is a $10 per day charge for dogs.

Cedarville

Sunrise Motel & RV Park
54889 Highway 200 West
Cedarville, CA
530-279-2161
Located at the base of the dog-friendly Modoc National Forest, this motel offers all non-smoking rooms. There are no pet fees. If you are out during the day and cannot bring your pooch with you, they do have an outdoor kennel available for an extra $5.

Chico

Esplanade Bed & Breakfast
620 The Esplanade
Chico, CA
530-345-8084
Built in 1915, this Craftsman Bungalow has been completely restored. This B&B is located just steps from downtown Chico and Chico State University. Each room has a private bathroom and cable television. Enjoy their hearty breakfast served in the dining room or on the patio. Well-behaved dogs are allowed with a $20 refundable deposit. Children are also allowed.

Holiday Inn
685 Manzanita Ct
Chico, CA
530-345-2491
There is a $25 one time pet fee per visit.

Motel 6
665 Manzanita Ct
Chico, CA
530-345-5500

One pet per room is permitted.

Music Express Inn Bed and Breakfast
1091El Monte Avenue
Chico, CA
530-891-9833
This B&B is located near the dog-friendly Bidwell Park, the third largest municipal park in the United States. The B&B offers nine rooms all with private baths, refrigerators and microwaves. All rooms are non-smoking. A well-behaved dog is allowed, but must be leashed when outside your room. Pets must be attended at all times. There are no pet fees. Children are also allowed.

Super 8
655 Manzanita Ct
Chico, CA
530-345-2533
There is a $4 per day additional pet fee.

Chowchilla

Days Inn
Hwy 99 & Robertson Blvd
Chowchilla, CA
559-665-4821
There is a $5 per day additional pet fee.

Chula Vista

La Quinta Inn San Diego - Chula Vista
150 Bonita Road
Chula Vista, CA
619-691-1211
Dogs of all sizes are allowed at the hotel.

Motel 6
745 E Street
Chula Vista, CA
619-422-4200
A well-behaved large dog is okay. Dogs must be attended at all times.

Vagabond Inn
230 Broadway St.
Chula Vista, CA
619-422-8305
This motel is located within several miles of downtown San Diego. Amenities include two swimming pools, continental breakfast, cable television and more hotel amenities. Pets are an additional $10 per day.

Claremont

Ramada Inn
840 South Indian Hill Blvd
Claremont, CA
909-621-4831
There are no additional pet fees.

Coalinga

Motel 6
25008 W Dorris Ave
Coalinga, CA
559-935-1536
There are no additional pet fees.

Pleasant Valley Inn
25278 W Doris St
Coalinga, CA
559-935-2063
There is a $5 per day additional pet fee.

Coffee Creek

Becker's Bounty Lodge and Cottage
HCR #2 Box 4659
Coffee Creek, CA
530-266-3277
The lodge is a secluded mountain hideaway at the edge of the one-half million acre Trinity Alps Wilderness. Dogs are not allowed on the furniture. There is a $50 one time pet charge.

Blackberry Creek Garden Cottage
On SR-3
Coffee Creek, CA
530-266-3502
There is a $15 per day additional pet fee. According to a reader "We just spent a week at this wonderful cottage, and it is a little piece of heaven for you and your dog. Nestled under the pines, cedars and redwoods the cottage has everything you need for the perfect vacation in the woods. Down the road is the greatest swimming hole in the Trinity River, and great hikes await you in every direction. Our dogs did not want to leave and neither did we. "

Coleville

Andruss Motel
106964 Highway 395
Coleville, CA
530-495-2216
There are no additional pet fees.

Coloma

Golden Lotus Bed and Breakfast Inn
1006 Lotus Road
Coloma, CA
530-621-4562
This pre-Victorian B&B, located in the historic town of Coloma, is surrounded by herb gardens. Dogs are allowed in one of their rooms. Dogs must be well-behaved and owners must agree to pay for any damages. There is a $20 per day additional pet fee.

Colton

Days Inn
2830 Iowa Ave
Colton, CA
909-788-9900
A well-behaved large dog is okay. There is a $5 per day additional pet fee.

Columbia

Columbia Gem Motel
22131 Parrotts Ferry Rd

Columbia, CA
209-532-4508
This dog-friendly motel offers gracious, country hospitality, comfort and privacy. The motel is set on a sunny park-like acre beneath towering, majestic pines, cedars and sequoias, which provide a shady umbrella over their 6 cozy log cabins and 4 motel rooms. For a little extra, they can provide the perfect getaway with champagne on ice, flowers, wine, cheese, crackers, chocolates, or bubblebath waiting for you in your room. They can also arrange breakfast in bed or can help with any other ideas. The motel is located within walking distance (about 1 mile) from the popular dog-friendly Columbia State Historic Park. The Gold Mine Winery/Micro-Brewery is located about 1 block away from the motel. The winery has a nice outdoor covered patio and lawn area. They have free wine and beer tasting and they also make pizza from scratch, any way you like it. The management are of the belief that people who travel with their "best friends" are responsible pet owners and a pleasure to have as guests at The Gem. Dog owners are not penalized with an extra fee here. Instead, management has a simple, common sense pet regulation form they have each owner read and sign. Dogs are not to be left unattended in the rooms.

Concord

Holiday Inn
1050 Burnett Ave
Concord, CA
925-687-5500
There is a $100 refundable pet deposit and a $5 per day pet fee.

Convict Lake

Convict Lake Resort

Convict Lake, CA
760-934-3800
There is a $15 per day pet fee. Cabins are not designated as smoking or non-smoking.

Corning

Best Western Inn-Corning
2165 Solano Street
Corning, CA
530-824-2468
Amenities include a free continental breakfast and an outdoor swimming pool. There is a $5 per day pet charge.

Shilo Inn Suites
3350 Sunrise Way
Corning, CA
530-824-2940
Your pet is welcome. The hotel has complimentary continental breakfast, Mini-suites with microwave, refrigerator & wet bar, in-room iron, ironing board, coffee maker & hair dryer, guest laundromat, seasonal outdoor pool & spa, sauna, steam room and a fitness center. Conveniently located off I-5 and Highway 99 at the South Avenue Exit, 18 miles from Red Bluff, 47 miles from Redding, and 30 miles from Chico.

Corona

Motel 6
200 N Lincoln Ave
Corona, CA
909-735-6408
There are no additional pet fees.

Coronado

Crown City Inn
520 Orange Ave
Coronado, CA
619-435-3116
This inn is located in beautiful Coronado which is across the harbor from downtown San

Diego. Walk to several outdoor restaurants or to the Coronado Centennial Park. Room service is available. Pet charges are $8 per day for a designated pet room and $25 per day for a non-designated pet room. They have non-smoking rooms available. Pets must never be left unattended in the room.

Loews Coronado Bay Resort
4000 Coronado Bay Road
Coronado, CA
619-424-4000
All well-behaved dogs of any size are welcome. This upscale hotel offers their "Loews Loves Pets" program which includes special pet treats, local dog walking routes, and a list of nearby pet-friendly places to visit. There are no pet fees.

Costa Mesa

La Quinta Inn Costa Mesa
1515 South Coast Drive
Costa Mesa, CA
714-957-5841
Dogs up to 75 pounds are allowed at the hotel.

Residence Inn by Marriott
881 Baker St
Costa Mesa, CA
714-241-8800
There is a $60 one time pet fee and a $10 per day additional pet charge. Every room at this inn is a suite with a bedroom area, living room and kitchen. Rooms start at the low $100s and up. A few cafes are located next door and have no outdoor seating, but you can take food back to the room. The Bark Park dog park is located nearby. (see Parks.)

Vagabond Inn
3205 Harbor Blvd
Costa Mesa, CA
714-557-8360
This motel offers a complimentary continental breakfast. The Bark Park dog

park is located nearby. There is a $5 per day pet fee.

Coulterville

Yosemite Gold Country Motel
10407 Highway 49
Coulterville, CA
209-878-3400
All rooms are completely furnished with a heater and air conditioner, color TV, telephones, bathroom with tub-shower and free coffee. Your dog is more than welcome here, but he or she must stay on a leash when outside and should use their Doggie Park when going to the bathroom. Also, they require that you do not leave your dog outside unattended. This motel is located about hour from Yosemite Valley (40 min. to the main gate and 20 min. to the valley). There are no additional pet fees.

Crescent City

Gardenia Motel
119 L Street
Crescent City, CA
707-464-2181
There is a $5 per day additional pet fee.

Super 8
685 Hwy 101 S.
Crescent City, CA
707-464-4111
There is a $10 per day pet fee.

Town House Motel
444 US Highway 101 South
Crescent City, CA
707-464-4176
They offer one non-smoking pet room for well-behaved dogs. There is no pet charge.

Culver City

Four Points by Sheraton
5990 Green Valley Circle
Culver City, CA

310-641-7740
There is a $25 one time pet fee. Dogs are allowed only on the first floor.

Cupertino

Cypress Hotel
10050 S. DeAnza Blvd.
Cupertino, CA
408-253-8900
Well-behaved dogs of all sizes are welcome at this pet-friendly hotel. The boutique hotel offers both rooms and suites. Hotel amenities include complimentary evening wine service, an a 24 hour on-site fitness room. There are no pet fees, just sign a pet liability form.

Cypress

Woodfin Suite Hotel
5905 Corporate Ave
Cypress, CA
714-828-4000
All rooms are non-smoking. All well-behaved dogs are welcome. Every room is a suite with wetbars or full kitchens. Hotel amenities include a pool, exercise facility, complimentary video movies, and a complimentary hot breakfast buffet. There is a $5 per day pet fee and you will need to sign a pet waiver.

Dana Point

Marriott's Laguna Cliffs Resort
25135 Park Lantern
Dana Point, CA
949-661-5000
Thanks to one of our readers for recommending this hotel. This Marriott allows dogs of all sizes. Directly in front of the hotel, there is a big open park which overlooks the ocean. Hotel amenities include a pool and tennis courts. Room amenities include hairdryers,

iron and ironing boards and more. Room service is also available. Rooms rates start at about $120 and up. There is a $50 non-refundable fee for pets. The hotel is located on Park Lantern, just west of Hwy 1.

Davis

Best Western University Lodge
123 B Street
Davis, CA
530-756-7890
There is no additional pet charge.

Econo Lodge
221 D Street
Davis, CA
530-756-1040
There are no additional pet fees.

Howard Johnson Hotel
4100 Chiles Road
Davis, CA
530-792-0800
Dogs of all sizes are welcome. There is a $10 per day pet fee. They have one non-smoking pet room, but cannot guarantee it will be available.

University Inn Bed and Breakfast
340 A Street
Davis, CA
530-756-8648
All rooms are non-smoking. There are no pet fees. Children are also allowed.

University Park Inn & Suites
1111 Richards Blvd.
Davis, CA
530-756-0910
Located within walking distance of downtown Davis. They have one pet room available and there is a $10 per night pet charge.

Del Mar

Best Western Stratford Inn

710 Camino del Mar
Del Mar, CA
858-755-1501
There is a $50 one time pet fee.
Dogs up to 50 pounds are
allowed.

Les Artistes Hotel
944 Camino Del Mar
Del Mar, CA
858-755-4646
There is a $50 refundable
deposit and a one time $20 pet
fee. Well-behaved dogs are ok
at the hotel.

Delano

Shilo Inn
2231 Girard Street
Delano, CA
661-725-7551
Your pet is welcome. Amenities
include complimentary
continental breakfast, in-room
iron, ironing board & hair dryer,
guest laundromat, seasonal
outdoor pool & spa.
Conveniently located between
Fresno & Bakersfield off
Highway 99.

Dixon

Super 8
2500 Plaza Court
Dixon, CA
707-678-3399
There is a $10 per day additional
pet fee.

Downieville

**Downieville Carriage House
Inn**
110 Commercial Street
Downieville, CA
530-289-3573
This 9 room inn is located in
historic downtown Downieville
and is open year round. Well-
behaved dogs are allowed. Dogs
should be able to get along well
with other guests, as this is a
house. There is a $15 per day
pet fee.

**Downieville River Inn &
Resort**
PO Box 412 Downieville, CA
Downieville, CA
530-289-3308
A historic resort set on the
North Yuba River in Downieville
at the north end California?s
Gold Country. There are no
size restrictions on dogs. The
entire inn is non-smoking.

**Downieville River Inn and
Resort**
121 River Street
Downieville, CA
530-289-3308
This pet-friendly inn,
surrounded by Tahoe National
Forest, is nestled in the historic
town of Downieville. The inn is
located on the North Yuba
River, along Highway 49 and
the Yuba-Donner Scenic
Byway. They offer guest rooms
and cottages, each with a
private bath and porch or
balcony. Fully equipped
kitchens and suites are also
available. Enjoy their English
gardens, picnic areas with
barbecue grills, wet/dry sauna,
and heated swimming pool in
season. The Downieville area
offers year round outdoor
activities including trout fishing,
hiking, gold panning, cross
country skiing, and
snowshoeing. There are no pet
fees.

Drytown

Old Well Motel
15947 State Highway 49
Drytown, CA
209-245-6467
This motel is located near the
Shenandoah Valley. There is a
$5 per day additional pet fee.

Dunnigan

Best Western Country
3930 County Rd. 89
Dunnigan, CA

530-724-3471
Amenities include a free
continental breakfast and a
refrigerator in each room. There
are no extra pet fees.

Dunsmuir

Oak Tree Inn
6604 Dunsmuir Avenue
Dunsmuir, CA
530-235-2884
There is a $6 per day pet
charge.

Railroad Park Resort
100 Railroad Park Road
Dunsmuir, CA
530-235-4440
Spend a night or more inside a
restored antique railroad car at
this unique resort. Dogs are
allowed for an additional $10 per
day. This resort also offers RV
hookup spaces.

Travelodge
5400 Dunsmuir Ave
Dunsmuir, CA
530-235-4395
There are no additional pet fees.

El Cajon

Motel 6
550 Montrose Court
El Cajon, CA
619-588-6100
There are no additional pet fees.

Emeryville

Woodfin Suite Hotel
5800 Shellmound
Emeryville, CA
510-601-5880
All rooms are suites and all are
non-smoking. Hotel amenities
include a pool, exercise facility,
complimentary video movies or
books and a complimentary
breakfast buffet. There is a $5
per day pet fee and a $150
refundable pet deposit. All well-
behaved dogs are welcome.

Escondido

Castle Creek Inn Resort
29850 Circle R Way
Escondido, CA
760-751-8800
There are no additional pet fees.

Palm Tree Lodge
425 W Mission Ave
Escondido, CA
760-745-7613
There is a $10 per day pet fee.

Eureka

Best Western Bayshore Inn
3500 Broadway
Eureka, CA
707-268-8005
There are no pet fees if paying by credit card. If you pay with cash, a $100 refundable deposit is required.

Discovery Inn
2832 Broadway
Eureka, CA
707-441-8442
There is a $7 per day additional pet fee.

Motel 6
1934 Broadway
Eureka, CA
707-445-9631
One large dog is allowed per room.

Quality Inn
1209 Fourth Street
Eureka, CA
707-443-1601
You must pay for the room with a major credit card when traveling with a pet.

Ramada Inn
270 5th Street
Eureka, CA
707-443-2206
There is an $8 per day pet fee. Dogs up to 50 pounds are allowed.

Red Lion Hotel
1929 Fourth Street

Eureka, CA
707-445-0844
This hotel offers spacious guest rooms, with amenities like data ports, room service, hairdryers, fitness center and outdoor pool. There is a $30 one time fee for dogs.

The Eureka Inn
518 Seventh Street
Eureka, CA
707-442-6441
This inn has been named a National Historical Place, and is a member of Historic Hotels of America. Dogs are allowed on the first floor and there is no pet fee. They have allowed well-behaved St. Bernards here before.

Fairfield

Motel 6
1473 Holiday Ln
Fairfield, CA
707-425-4565
There are no additional pet fees.

Fall River Mills

Lava Creek Lodge
1 Island Rd
Fall River Mills, CA
530-336-6288
The lodge is located on 60 wooded acres interspersed with recent lava flows along the banks of Eastman Lake (Little Tule River). They offer eight rooms attached to the main lodge and seven cabins, all with private, full bathrooms. This lodge offers a full service restaurant including the option of ordering a box lunch to enjoy on a trail or riverside. There is a $10 per day pet charge and dogs must be leashed.

Fawnskin

Quail Cove
P.O. Box 117

Fawnskin, CA
800-595-2683
This lodge offers rustic and cozy cabins in a quiet wooded surrounding on Big Bear Lake. They are located within walking distance to several restaurants, markets, marinas and some of the hiking trails and fishing spots. Pets are always welcome. There is a $10 per day pet charge. Never leave your pet unattended in the cabin.

Fish Camp

Apple Tree Inn at Yosemite
1110 Highway 41
Fish Camp, CA
559-683-5111
This 54 unit inn is nestled among acres of trees. It is located two miles from the southern entrance to Yosemite National Park (about 45 minutes to Yosemite Valley). There is a $50 one time pet charge.

Narrow Gauge Inn
48571 Highway 41
Fish Camp, CA
559-683-7720
This inn is located amidst pine trees in the Sierra Mountains. They are located about four miles from the southern entrance to Yosemite National Park (about 45 minutes to Yosemite Valley). There are some trails nearby in the dog-friendly Sierra National Forest near Bass Lake. All rooms are non-smoking. Dogs are allowed in the main level rooms and there is a $25 one time per stay pet fee. Children are also welcome.

Folsom

Lake Natoma Inn
702 Gold Lake Drive
Folsom, CA
916-351-1500
This inn offers 120 guest rooms and 12 Lakeview Suites nestled in a wooded natural environment

overlooking Lake Natoma. Enjoy over 20 miles of beautiful bike and dog-friendly walking trails along the American river. This inn is also located next to Historic Folsom. There is a $45 one time per stay pet fee and a $15 per day pet charge per pet.

Residence Inn
2555 Iron Point Road
Folsom, CA
916-983-7289
This extended-stay inn offers a complimentary continental breakfast and an indoor pool. There is a $100 one time per stay pet charge and a $10 per day pet fee.

Fort Bragg

Beachcomber Motel
1111 N. Main Street
Fort Bragg, CA
707-964-2402
This ocean front motel is next to a walking, jogging, and cycling trail that stretches for miles along the coast. Many rooms have ocean views. They allow well-behaved dogs up to about 75-80 pounds. There is an additional $10 per day pet charge.

Cleone Gardens Inn
24600 N. Hwy 1
Fort Bragg, CA
707-964-2788
This park-like inn is on 5 acres. There are three pet rooms and an additional pet charge of $6 per day.

Delamere Cottages
16821 Ocean Drive
Fort Bragg, CA
707-964-9188
This establishment comes highly recommended from one of our readers who says: "They are located in Fort Bragg just minutes away from Mendocino. Last weekend my boyfriend and I stayed there with our two dogs. The stay was wonderful. The

hostess was nice and the overall feeling was downright friendly and warm. The cottage we stayed in had dog treats for the dogs and a gazebo out the back for a peaceful breakfast. You had your own private walk down to a secluded beach. Your dog could romp freely at the beach. Mendocino is just a short drive away." There are no additional pet fees.

Harbor View Seasonal Rental
Call to arrange.
Fort Bragg, CA
760-438-2563
Watch the boats go in and out of the harbor and listen to the sea lions and fog horns from this dog-friendly vacation rental. This 3,000 square foot house is entirely furnished. The main floor has a living room, dining room, kitchen, 2 bedrooms, 1 bathroom and a deck with a view of the harbor. The upstairs has a large master suite with a deck and a view of the bridge and ocean. The downstairs level has an apartment with a sofa bed and full bathroom. The yard has redwood trees and even deer wandering through. This area is popular for year-round fishing. The rental is available throughout the year. Please call to inquire about rates and available dates at 760-438-2563 or 760-809-8889 (cell phone).

Lodging & Llamas
18301 Old Coast Highway
Fort Bragg, CA
707-964-7191
Cottages are fully furnished. Cottages have a living room with upholstered reading chairs and a fireplace. An attached sunroom provides a cozy spot for morning breakfast or moonlit dinners. As you drive up the road to the cottages llamas and pygmy goats may greet you. There is a $10 pet fee per night.

Shoreline Vacation Rentals
18200 Old Coast Hwy
Fort Bragg, CA
707-964-1444
This vacation home rental company offers many dog-friendly homes on the Mendocino Coast including the Sea Dream, Cypress Cottage, Alder Creek Cottage, Whale Watch, Brentwood and more. Children are also welcome in most of the homes. There is a $20 per day pet charge.

Fortuna

Best Western Country Inn
2025 Riverwalk Drive
Fortuna, CA
707-725-6822
There are no extra pet fees. Dogs are allowed in certain pet rooms. Large dogs are okay if they do not bark.

Super 8
1805 Alamar Way
Fortuna, CA
707-725-2888
There is a $10 per day pet fee.

Fountain Valley

Residence Inn
9930 Slater Ave
Fountain Valley, CA
714-965-8000
There is a $100 one time fee for pets and a $10 per day additional pet fee.

Fremont

Howard Johnson Express Inn
43643 Mission Blvd.
Fremont, CA
510-656-2366
* Howard Johnson Express Inn remodeled in 2001
* 24 Hour Front Desk Service
* Perfect for Business and Leisure Travel
* 15 minutes from regional parks and BART station

Accommodations - Please always call ahead to make sure an establishment is still dog-friendly.

* Complimentary Continental Breakfast
* Exterior corridors
* Some rooms w/microwave and refrigerator
* Free Parking for RV and Trucks
* Fax/Copy Services
* Laundry Room
* Extended rates Available
* Free local calls
* Free Incoming fax/Outgoing fax $1:00 per page

La Quinta Inn & Suites Fremont
46200 Landing Parkway
Fremont, CA
510-445-0808
Dogs of all sizes are allowed at the hotel.

Residence Inn by Marriott
5400 Farwell Place
Fremont, CA
510-794-5900
There is a $75 one time pet fee and an additional $10 per day pet fee. All rooms have full kitchens, irons/ironing boards, hairdryers, and data ports on phones. The inn has self-service laundry facilities, and dinner delivery service from local restaurants. To get there from Hwy 880 heading north, exit Mowry Ave towards central Fremont. Turn right onto Mowry Ave. Turn left on Farwell Drive, then left onto Farwell Place. There is a $75 one time pet fee and a $10 per day additional pet fee.

Fresno

Best Western Garden Court
2141 N Parkway Dr
Fresno, CA
559-237-1881
Pets are welcome at this Best Western. Most rooms face a one acre courtyard. There is a $10 per day pet charge. To get there from Hwy 99 south, take the Motel Drive exit towards Clinton Ave. Turn right onto Clinton Ave

and then left onto North Parkway Drive. The motel will be on the right.

Best Western Parkside Inn
1415 West Olive Avenue
Fresno, CA
559-237-2086
There is a $10 per day pet charge. Large dogs are okay if they are well-behaved and leashed.

Days Inn-Parkway
1101 N Parkway Dr
Fresno, CA
559-268-6211
This motel has a playground for the kids. They also have 2 two bedroom suites available. Room rates include a free breakfast. To get there from Hwy 99 south, take the Olive Ave exit. Turn right onto Olive Ave and then left onto North Parkway Drive. The motel will be on the right. There is a $5 per day additional pet fee.

Econo Lodge
445 N Parkway Dr
Fresno, CA
559-485-5019
A large well-behaved dog is okay. There is a $10 refundable pet deposit.

Holiday Inn Express and Suites
5046 N. Barcus Rd
Fresno, CA
559-277-5700
There is a $20 one time pet fee per visit.

Knights Inn
3093 N Parkway Dr
Fresno, CA
559-275-7766
This motel shares a lobby with the Travelodge. To get there from Hwy 99 south, take the Shields Ave exit. Then turn right onto N Parkway Drive. There is a $7 per day additional pet fee.

Ramada Limited

1804 W Olive Ave
Fresno, CA
559-442-1082
There is a McDonald's restaurant next door to this motel (previously a National 9 Inn). To get there from Hwy 99 south, take the Olive Ave exit. The motel will be on the right. There is a $10 per day additional pet fee.

Red Roof Inn - Hwy 99
5021 N Barcus Avenue
Fresno, CA
559-276-1910
There is a $20 one time pet fee per visit.

Red Roof Inn - North
6730 Blackstone
Fresno, CA
559-431-3557
If paying by cash there is a $25 refundable pet deposit.

Residence Inn by Marriott
5322 N. Diana Avenue
Fresno, CA
559-222-8900
Every room at this inn is a suite. Amenities include an outdoor pool, exercise room, room service, complimentary breakfast, self-service laundry facilities and more. Room amenities include full kitchens, refrigerators, data ports, work desk with lamp and more. There is a one time non-refundable $50 pet charge and a $5 per day additional pet fee.

Travelodge
3093 N Parkway Dr
Fresno, CA
559-276-7745
This motel shares a lobby with the Knights Inn. There is a $10 per day pet charge. To get there from Hwy 99 south, take the Shields Ave exit. Then turn right onto N Parkway Drive.

Fullerton

Marriott - Fullerton

2701 East Nutwood Ave
Fullerton, CA
714-738-7800
There is a $100 pet deposit, of
this $75 is refundable. The hotel
is near Cal State Fullerton
University.

Georgetown

American River Bed and Breakfast Inn
Main and Orleans Streets
Georgetown, CA
530-333-4499
They have certain pet rooms
and you need to call in advance
to make a reservation. All rooms
are non-smoking. There is a
refundable pet deposit.

Glendale

Vagabond Inn
120 W. Colorado Street
Glendale, CA
818-240-1700
This motel is located near
Universal Studios. Amenities
include a complimentary
breakfast and during the week, a
free USA Today newspaper.
There is a $10 per day pet fee.

Gorman

Econo Lodge
49713 Gorman Post Rd
Gorman, CA
661-248-6411
There is a $10 per day pet fee.

Graeagle

Gray Eagle Lodge
5000 Gold Lake Rd.
Graeagle, CA
800-635-8778
Stay in a rustic cabin at this
mountain getaway located in the
Sierra Mountains, about 1.5
hours north of Truckee. There
are many hiking trails within a
short walk from the cabins.
There are over 40 alpine lakes

nearby. There is a $20 per pet,
per day, fee with a maximum of
2 pets per cabin. Guests are
expected to follow guidelines
provided by the lodge and will
sign a pet policy form upon
arrival. Dogs up to 50 pounds
are allowed.

Grass Valley

Bear River Retreat and Lodge
20010 Hwy 174
Grass Valley, CA
530-346-0078
According to one of our readers
"Nestled on 13+ acres of pine
and oak trees and various
hiking trails, the lodge is a
perfect doggie getaway."

Best Western Gold Country Inn
11972 Sutton Way
Grass Valley, CA
530-273-1393
There is a $10 one time pet
charge. Dogs cannot be left
alone in the room and they
need to be leashed when
outside of the room.

Swan Levine House Bed and Breakfast
328 South Church Street
Grass Valley, CA
916-272-1873
This renovated historic house
was built in 1880. It was
originally owned by a local
merchant who made his fortune
by selling mining equipment.
He sold it to a doctor who
converted the house into a
hospital and it served as a
community medical center until
1968. There are four rooms,
each with a private bath. They
have one room available for
guests who bring a large dog.
Dogs are not to be left alone in
the room. There is a $15 per
day pet charge. They are also
kid-friendly. They do have a cat
that resides in the house.

Groveland

Historic Groveland Hotel
18767 Main Street
Groveland, CA
209-962-4000
Your dog or cat is welcome at
this 1849 historic inn. Country
Inns Magazine rated the
Groveland Hotel as one of the
Top 10 Inns in the United States.
The inn is located 23 miles from
Yosemite's main gate. Their
restaurant can pack a gourmet
picnic basket for your day trip to
Yosemite. Make your
reservations early as they book
up quickly. This inn is located
about an hour from Yosemite
Valley. There are no additional
pet fees. All rooms are non-
smoking.

Sunset Inn
33569 Hardin Flat Rd.
Groveland, CA
209-962-4360
This inn offers three cabins near
Yosemite National Park. The
cabins are located on two acres
and are surrounded by a dog-
friendly National Forest at a
4500 foot elevation. All cabins
are non-smoking and include
kitchens and private bathrooms.
Children are also welcome. The
Sunset Inn is located just 2
miles from the west entrance to
Yosemite, one mile from
Highway 120.There is a $10 per
day pet charge and a $150
refundable pet deposit.

Yosemite Westgate Motel
7633 Hwy 120
Groveland, CA
209-962-5281
This motel has one pet room
available and it is a non-smoking
room. There is a $10 per night
pet fee. The motel is located
about 40 minutes from Yosemite
Valley.

Gualala

Mar Vista Cottages
35101 South Highway One

Gualala, CA
707-884-3522
They are very pet-friendly. Well-behaved pets are welcome and there are lots of paths (and a beach) where you can walk with them. The owners have remodeled their twelve cottages specifically with pets in mind, creating a pet and child friendly environment. They have hardwood floors, country furniture, slipcovers, and things that dogs need as well as humans, like beds, or a dog sheet if they sleep with you, a dog bath and towels. There is no additional pet charge and they have no designated smoking or non-smoking cottages, but they discourage guests from smoking inside the cottages.

Ocean View Properties
P.O. Box 1285
Gualala, CA
707-884-3538
Ocean View Properties offers vacation home rentals on The Sea Ranch and Mendocino Coast. Some of their vacation homes are pet-friendly. They offer a wide variety of special vacation home rentals, located on the oceanfront, oceanside and hillside at The Sea Ranch. Each of the rental homes has a fully equipped kitchen, a fireplace or wood stove, blankets, pillows, and telephones. Most have hot tubs, televisions, VCR's, radios, CD/cassette players, and washer/dryers. Guests provide kindling, bed linens, and towels. With advance notice, linens can be rented and maid service can be hired. Please call and ask them which rentals are dog-friendly.

Serenisea Vacation Homes
36100 Highway 1 S.
Gualala, CA
707-884-3836
Serenisea maintains and manages a number of vacation homes and cottages in this community on the Mendocino coast. Some of them allow dogs of all sizes.

Surf Motel
39170 S. Highway 1
Gualala, CA
707-884-3571
There is a $10 per day pet charge.

Guerneville

Creekside Inn & Resort
16180 Neeley Rd
Guerneville, CA
707-869-3623
Dogs are allowed in one of their cottages. During the summer it books up fast, so please make an early reservation. The inn will be able to help you find some pet-friendly hiking trails and beaches nearby.

River Village Resort and Spa
14880 River Road
Guerneville, CA
800-529-3376
This inn is located just minutes from the Russian River. At this inn, dogs are allowed in certain cottages and there is a $10 per day pet fee. Please do not walk pets on the lawn. Children are also welcome.

Russian River Getaways
14075 Mill Street, P.O. Box 1673
Guerneville, CA
707-869-4560
About 40 dog-friendly vacation homes in Russian River wine country with leash free beaches nearby. There are no pet fees and no size limits for dogs. There is a $75 refundable pet deposit.

Half Moon Bay

Holiday Inn Express
230 S Cabrillo Hwy
Half Moon Bay, CA
650-726-3400
Amenities at this motel include a deluxe complimentary continental breakfast. There is an additional $10 per day pet charge.

Ramada Limited
3020 N Cabrillo Hwy
Half Moon Bay, CA
650-726-9700
There is a $15 per day pet fee.

Hayfork

Trinity County Vacation Rental
Call to Arrange.
Hayfork, CA
415-252-9590
Get away from it all at this lovely 800 square foot cabin on a year round creek. Enjoy seven acres of privacy with your best friend. There is a fenced yard around the house. The home has a fully equipped kitchen, washer dryer, garbage disposal and satellite television with VCR. Located in Trinity County about 5 hours from the Bay Area and 4 hours from Sacramento. The cabin is available for weekly rentals year round.

Hayward

Super 8 Motel - Hayward I-880
2460 Whipple Road
Hayward, CA
510-489-3888
$10/stay for up to 3 dogs in one room. FREE 8-minute long distance call each night. FREE continental breakfast. Coffee maker, night light, clock/radio, safe in each room. On-site guest laundry. Kids 12 & under stay free. I-880, Exit Whipple Road East.

Vagabond Inn
20455 Hesperian Blvd.
Hayward, CA
510-785-5480
This two story motel offers a heated pool and spa. To get there from Hwy 880 heading north, exit A Street/San Lorenzo. Turn left onto A Street. Then

turn right onto Hesperian Blvd. There is a $10 per day additional pet fee per pet.

Healdsburg

Best Western Dry Creek Inn
198 Dry Creek Road
Healdsburg, CA
707-433-0300
Amenities include a Complimentary Continental Breakfast and a Gift bottle of Sonoma County Wine. There is a $20 one time pet charge.

Duchamp Hotel
421 Foss Street
Healdsburg, CA
707-431-1300
This hotel, located in Healdsburg, allows dogs in two of their cottages. Every cottage features a king bed, oversized spa shower, private terrace, fireplace, mini bar, and more. Children over 16 years old are allowed. The entire premises is non-smoking. Dogs are not allowed in the pool area and they request that you take your dog away from the cottages and hotel when they go to the bathroom.

Redwood Tree House Vacation Rental
Call to Arrange.
Healdsburg, CA
707-433-8899
This dog-friendly vacation rental is located in the heart of the wine country. It is called The Redwood Tree House because you actually enter through a 200-year-old Redwood Tree. There are two bedrooms and separate guest cottage. The home also offers a wraparound deck overlooking a private beach, and views of the Russian River. There is a $150 one time pet charge and pet owners need to fill out and sign a pet form. You can also call to arrange at 707-433-4443.

Hemet

Super 8
3510 W. Florida
Hemet, CA
909-658-2281
There is a $5 per day additional pet fee.

Hesperia

Days Suites
14865 Bear Valley Rd
Hesperia, CA
760-948-0600
There is a $7 per day pet fee.

Hope Valley

Sorensen's Resort
14255 Highway 88
Hope Valley, CA
530-694-2203
This secluded mountain resort is located in beautiful Hope Valley which is about 30 minutes south of South Lake Tahoe. Dogs are allowed in several of the cabins. The dog-friendly cabins sleep from two up to four people. Each cabin has a wood-burning stove (for heat) and kitchen. The Hope Valley Cross Country Ski Rentals are located on the premises (see Attractions). Hiking is available during the summer on the trails of the Toiyable National Forest. There are also several nearby lakes. Cabin rates start at $85 per night and go up to about $450 for a large bedroom cabin. There are no additional pet fees.

Hyampom

Ziegler's Trails End
1 Main St, P.O. Box 150
Hyampom, CA
530-628-4929
These cabins are on the South Fork of the Trinity River. This is in the middle of the dog-friendly Six Rivers National Forest.

Idyllwild

Silver Pines Lodge
25955 Cedar St
Idyllwild, CA
909-659-4335
This lodge sits on 1 1/2 acres of wooded pine forest overlooking Strawberry Creek. The lodge is approximately 2 blocks from the main village of Idyllwild where there are many eateries and shops. Each cabin is individually decorated and has its own unique features. Most rooms have fireplaces and about half have kitchens. Every room has its own refrigerator, bathroom, color cable TV and complimentary coffee. Dogs are welcome in all of the cabins, except the Foley Cabin. There is a $10 one time pet charge. They also ask that you please abide by the following pet rules. Never leave pets alone in the room. Pets should not go on the beds or furniture. Keep your dog leashed when on the property. Clean up after your pooch. Please wipe off your pets paws if it's snowy, rainy or muddy outside (they provide dog towels).

Tahquitz Inn
25840 Highway 243
Idyllwild, CA
909-659-4554
This inn is located in the heart of scenic Idyllwild and allows all well-behaved dogs. They offer one and two bedroom suites with a separate bedroom, kitchen and porches. The inn has also been a location for several Hollywood film shoots. All of their rooms accommodate dogs. There is a $10 per day pet charge, but mention DogFriendly.com when making your reservation, and your pet stays for only $5 per night!

Independence

Independence Courthouse

Motel
157 N Edwards Street
Independence, CA
760-878-2732
There is a $6 per day additional pet fee. All rooms are non-smoking.

Ray's Den Motel
405 N Edwards St
Independence, CA
760-878-2122
There is a $6 per day additional pet fee.

Wilder House Bed & Breakfast
325 Dusty Lane
Independence, CA
760-878-2119
There are no additional pet fees.

Indio

Holiday Inn Express
84-096 Indio Springs Pkwy
Indio, CA
760-342-6344
There is a $50 refundable deposit if you pay with cash.

Palm Shadow Inn
80-761 Highway 111
Indio, CA
760-347-3476
A well-behaved large dog is okay. Nestled among date palm groves, there are eighteen guest rooms which overlook nearly three acres of lawns, flowers and citrus trees. There is a $5 per day pet charge.

Quality Inn
43505 Monroe Street
Indio, CA
760-347-4044
There are no additional pet fees.

Royal Plaza Inn
82347 Hwy 111
Indio, CA
760-347-0911
This motel offers a laundry room, whirlpool and room refrigerators. There is a $10 per day additional pet fee.

Inverness

Rosemary Cottage
75 Balboa Ave
Inverness, CA
415-663-9338
Dogs are welcome at the Rosemary Cottage and The Ark Cottage. Families are also welcome. The Rosemary Cottage is a two room cottage with a deck and garden. It is adjacent to the Point Reyes National Seashore. The Ark Cottage is a two room cottage tucked in the forest a mile up the ridge from the village of Inverness. There is a $25 one time pet charge for one dog or a $35 one time pet charge for two dogs.

Inverness Park

Apple Cottage Vacation Rental
Call to arrange.
Inverness Park, CA
415-663-2000
This vacation cottage rental is set among apple trees and bordered by gardens. Dogs are allowed for an additional $25 one time fee. The cottage is non-smoking.

Irvine

La Quinta Inn East Irvine
14972 Sand Canyon Avenue
Irvine, CA
949-551-0909
Dogs up to 50 pounds are allowed at the hotel.

Residence Inn - Irvine
10 Morgan
Irvine, CA
949-380-3000
There is a $40 one time pet fee and a $6 per day pet fee.

Jackson

Amador Motel
12408 Kennedy Flat Rd
Jackson, CA
209-223-0970
This motel has a large backyard, not completely enclosed, where you can walk your dog. They allow all well-behaved dogs. There are no additional pet fees.

Jackson Gold Lodge
850 N. State Hwy 49
Jackson, CA
209-223-0486
This lodge has been dog-friendly for years. They allow dogs in the motel rooms and in the cottages. They have eight duplex cottages, each with a separate living room, kitchen, dining room, bedroom and patio. Amenities include a free continental breakfast. Dogs are an additional $10 per day. There are no designated smoking or non-smoking cottages.

Jamestown

Quality Inn
18730 SR 108
Jamestown, CA
209-984-0315
There is a $10 per day pet fee.

Royal Hotel Bed and Breakfast
18239 Main Street
Jamestown, CA
209-984-5271
Dogs are not allowed in the hotel, but are allowed in one of the private cottages. This hotel is located in historic Jamestown, near Yosemite National Park. There is a $10 per day pet charge.

The National Hotel
18183 Main Street
Jamestown, CA
209-984-3446
Established in 1859, this is one of the oldest continuously operating hotels in California. Taking a day trip or going for a hike? Just ask for a picnic basket the day before and their chef will provide you with a meal to take with you and enjoy next

to a cool Sierra Nevada stream or at one of the many picnic areas throughout the dog-friendly Stanislaus National Forest. There is a $10 per day pet charge. All rooms are non-smoking.

Julian

Apple Tree Inn
4360 Highway 78
Julian, CA
800-410-8683
This is a small country motel located near the historic gold mining town of Julian. Families are always welcome. There is a $10 per day pet charge and a $50 refundable pet deposit.

Flat Top Mountain Retreat
Call to Arrange.
Julian, CA
800-810-1170
Secluded mountain vacation home on eight acres. Located 1 1/2 miles north of the old gold mining town of Julian. This home has panoramic views of the mountain countryside to the ocean. It is fully furnished, with a wood burning stove, TV, VCR, and fully equipped kitchen. There are three bedrooms, sleeping 8 people, and 3 decks for viewing the peaceful surroundings and wildlife including deer, and wild turkey birds. Rates range from $170 to $220 per night and there is a 9% lodging tax added. Minimum stay is two nights.

McGilvray House
2506 C Street
Julian, CA
800-758-5426
They offer a fully equipped vacation cottage which is located within walking distance of downtown Julian. A well-behaved dog is welcome and children are also welcome. Dogs must be leashed on the premises when outside. There is no pet charge.

Pine Haven Cabin Rental
Call to Arrange.
Julian, CA
619-231-9988
Enjoy this charming dog-friendly mountain getaway on 1.25 acres! The entire lot is securely fenced, offering your pet the freedom to run off-leash. The Pine Haven cabin rental offers a comfortable main room with a picturesque view of a local meadow. The cabin has one bedroom plus a small loft upstairs, a bathroom with a tiled walk-in shower (no tub), and a fully equipped kitchen. The cabin sleeps 2 people. Other amenities include air conditioning, stereo system, VCR with hit movie library, karaoke machine, back patio with a picnic table, Weber grill and more! The cabin is off a small private lane, so you will have lots of privacy. Located in the Pine Hills area of Julian (about one hour east of San Diego), the cabin is only 4 miles from historic downtown Julian. No smoking allowed. Cabin rental rates range from $160 to $180 per night. There is a $30 pet fee. For reservations call Teresa at 619-231-9988 or email to pinehavenca@cox.net.

Sea Star Guest Cottage
Call to Arrange.
Julian, CA
760-765-0502
This separate cottage is styled like an old-fashioned barn. It has a separate bedroom, sleeping loft, kitchen, and woodstove. Amenities include a large outside deck and hot tub. Because there are many antiques in the cottage, small children are not allowed. A well-behaved and clean dog is allowed. There is no pet charge. A two night minimum is required. The cottage is located three miles from downtown Julian.

Falling Waters River Resort
15729 Sierra Way
Kernville, CA
(760) 376-2242
Dogs up to around 75 pounds are allowed. There is a $10 one time additional pet fee. All rooms are non-smoking.

Kettleman City

Super 8
33415 Powers Drive
Kettleman City, CA
559-386-9530
There is a $40 refundable pet deposit and a $10 per day additional pet fee.

Kings Beach

Tahoe Rental House
Call to Arrange.
Kings Beach, CA
510-665-8100
This four bedroom, three bathroom house in north Tahoe is available for weekend, weekday, and holiday rentals. Dogs are welcome. This house can sleep up to 12 people. There is a $15 per day pet charge and a one time cleaning fee of $125.00.

Kyburz

Kyburz Resort Motel
13666 Highway 50
Kyburz, CA
530-293-3382
Nestled among the pines along 300 feet of the South Fork of the American River, this motel is located in the heart of the El Dorado National Forest. It is located about 30 minutes east of Placerville and about 15-20 minutes from Apple Hill. Well-behaved dogs are allowed and they must be leashed when outside your room. There is a $10 per day pet fee.

La Jolla

Andrea Villa Inn
2402 Torrey Pines Rd
La Jolla, CA
858-459-3311
Nestled in the heart of beautiful La Jolla, this inn is conveniently located near cosmopolitan shopping and dining experiences. The beaches of La Jolla Shores are within easy walking distance. There is a $25 one time pet charge.

La Jolla Village Lodge
1141 Silverado Street
La Jolla, CA
858-551-2001
There is a $20 one time pet fee. Thanks to a reader for recommending this hotel.

Residence Inn by Marriott
8901 Gilman Dr.
La Jolla, CA
858-587-1770
Every room is a suite that includes a bedroom area, living room, and kitchen. This inn is located about 3-4 miles north of downtown La Jolla. There is a $50 one time pet fee and a $10 per day pet fee.

La Mirada

Residence Inn - La Mirada
14419 Firestone Blvd
La Mirada, CA
714-523-2800
There is a $75 one time pet fee and a $6 per day additional pet fee.

La Palma

La Quinta Inn La Palma/Theme Park Area
3 Centerpointe Drive
La Palma, CA
714-670-1400
Dogs of all sizes are allowed at the hotel.

Laguna Beach

Carriage House Bed and Breakfast
1322 Catalina Street
Laguna Beach, CA
949-494-8945
The Carriage House, a country style bed & breakfast, was built in the early 1920's and is a designated landmark. They are located one mile south of downtown Laguna Beach in a quiet neighborhood. Well-mannered, flea protected, friendly dogs over 18 months old are allowed at an extra charge of $10 per pet per night. Please cover the beds with your own blanket, or ask for a sheet, if your dog sleeps on the bed. Towels are provided upon request for your pet. Never leave your pet unattended, unless they are "crated" and you'll need to leave a cell phone or number where you can be reached. Owners are responsible for any damages caused by pets. There is also a resident dog & cat on the property. Dogs must always be leashed in Laguna, even on the beach. There is a dog park for off-leash exercise in Laguna Canyon (closed on Wednesday's year round). During the summer, dogs are allowed on the beach from June 1-September 16 before 8 a.m. and after 6 p.m. only.

Casa Laguna Inn
2510 S. Coast Hwy
Laguna Beach, CA
949-494-2996
This lovely Spanish-style bed and breakfast is on a nicely landscape hillside with panoramic views of the ocean. It was voted Orange County's Best B&B four years in a row. The rooms are decorated with a blend of antique and contemporary furnishings. There are 15 guest rooms plus several guest suites and cottages. While in Laguna Beach, browse the variety of speciality shops or dine at one of the dog-friendly restaurants. Interested in a stroll on the beach? Main Beach (certain dog hours) is a short drive from the inn. There is a $10 per day additional pet fee.

Lake Arrowhead

Arrowhead Saddleback Inn
PO Box 1890
Lake Arrowhead, CA
800-858-3334
This historic inn was originally constructed in 1917 as the Raven Hotel. It is now totally restored and a historical landmark. The inn is located at the entrance of the Lake Arrowhead Village. Dogs are allowed in some of the cottages. The cottages feature stone fireplaces, double whirlpool baths, heated towel racks and refrigerators. There is an $8 per day pet fee. Dog owners also need to sign a pet agreement.

Arrowhead Tree Top Lodge
27992 Rainbow Drive
Lake Arrowhead, CA
909-337-2311
This inn is nestled among the tall pines on four acres of heavily forested grounds. You and your pup can enjoy a stroll on their private nature trail or find a spot at Deep Creek to sit, relax and watch the squirrels and birds. Amenities include microwaves in each of the rustic alpine rooms. It is located within walking distance of the Lake Arrowhead Village. There is an $8 per day pet fee.

Gray Squirrel Inn
326 State Hwy 173
Lake Arrowhead, CA
909-336-3602
This inn is near Lake Arrowhead and has ten guest rooms. Room amenities include mini-refrigerators and coffee makers. Dogs are welcome in some of the rooms. There are no

additional pet fees.

Prophet's Paradise B&B
26845 Modoc Lane
Lake Arrowhead, CA
909-336-1969
This bed and breakfast has five stories which cascade down its alpine hillside. This provides guests with privacy and intimate decks. All rooms have private baths. Amenities include a gym, a pool room, ping-pong, and darts, a horseshoe pit and a nearby hiking trail. Room rates start at $100 per night and include a gourmet breakfast. Your well-behaved dog is welcome. The owners also have pets. There are no additional pet fees.

Lake San Marcos

Quails Inn Hotel
1025 La Bonita Drive
Lake San Marcos, CA
760-744-0120
There is a $10 per day pet fee. This resort has a number of golf packages available.

Lancaster

Best Western Antelope Valley Inn
44055 North Sierra Highway
Lancaster, CA
661-948-4651
There is a $35 one time pet charge.

Lathrop

Days Inn
14750 South Harlan Rd
Lathrop, CA
209-982-1959
There is a $10 per day pet fee.

Lee Vining

Inn at Lee Vining
45 2nd St
Lee Vining, CA

760-647-6300
There are no additional pet fees.

Murphey's Hotel
51493 Hwy 395
Lee Vining, CA
760-647-6316
There is a $5 per day additional pet fee. Dogs are not to be left alone in rooms.

Lindsay

Super 8
390 Hwy 65
Lindsay, CA
559-562-5188
There is a $10 per visit one time pet charge.

Little River

Inn at Schoolhouse Creek
7051 N. Highway One
Little River, CA
707-937-5525
This bed and breakfast inn is located 2 miles south of Mendocino. The proprietors like dogs and welcome your pooch. They provide pet sheets and paw pads for cleaning after your dog comes back from a run in the woods or on the beach. The dog-friendly Van Damme State Beach is located nearby. Dogs are welcome in four of the inn's rooms/cottages. There is a $25 fee per pet in Sun & Sea Lodge and a $40 fee per pet in Thyme & Tansy Cottages. Maximum of two pets per room. Room rates start at the low $100s and up. Thanks to one of our readers for highly recommending this inn. Children are also welcome at this inn.

Livermore

Residence Inn by Marriott
1000 Airway Blvd.
Livermore, CA
925-373-1800

There is a $75 one time pet fee and an additional fee of $6 per day. Each room at this motel is a suite with a kitchen. Some of the rooms have loft bedrooms or two bedroom suites. To get there from Hwy 580 heading east, take the Airway/Collier Canyon Rd exit. Turn left onto Airway. There is a $75 one time pet fee and a $10 per day additional pet fee per pet.

Lompoc

Days Inn - Vandenberg Village
3955 Apollo Way
Lompoc, CA
805-733-5000
There is a $250 refundable deposit and a $20 one time pet fee. Dogs may not be left alone in the rooms.

Motel 6
1521 North H Street
Lompoc, CA
805-735-7631
There are no additional pet fees.

Quality Inn & Suites
1621 N. H Street
Lompoc, CA
805-735-8555
There is a $25 one time pet fee.

Lone Pine

Alabama Hills Inn
1920 South Main
Lone Pine, CA
760-876-8700
There is a $5 per day pet fee. There is a large grass area near the hotel to walk your dog. The area around the hotel is where many Western films have been made.

Best Western Frontier Motel
1008 South Main Street
Lone Pine, CA
760-876-5571
There are no extra pet charges. Mt. Whitney is about 13 miles from this motel.

Long Beach

Guesthouse International
5325 East Pacific Coast
Highway
Long Beach, CA
562-597-1341
There is a $10 one time pet fee.

Holiday Inn
2640 Lakewood Blvd
Long Beach, CA
562-597-4401
Dogs are not allowed in the main
tower. There is a $25 one time
additional pet fee.

Los Angeles

Beverly Laurel Hotel
8018 Beverly Blvd
Los Angeles, CA
323-651-2441
There is a $10 per day pet fee.
Up to two pets per room are
allowed. Thanks to one of our
readers who wrote "Our large
German Shepherd was
welcome."

Four Points by Sheraton - LAX
9750 Airport Blvd
Los Angeles, CA
310-645-4600
There is a $50 refundable
deposit and a $10 per day pet
fee. Dogs must be on a leash at
all times on the premises.

Holiday Inn - Downtown
750 Garland Ave @ 8th St.
Los Angeles, CA
213-628-9900
There is a $15 per day pet fee. A
well-behaved large dog is okay.

Hotel Sofitel
8555 Beverly Blvd
Los Angeles, CA
310-278-5444
This upscale hotel is located
next to West Hollywood and
Beverly Hills. You and your dog
will feel most welcome at this
hotel. Since parking is limited in
this area, your car will be valet
parked. They open the car doors

not only for you, but for your
dog too. You can feel
comfortable registering at the
front desk with your pup at your
side and then taking the
elevator to the room that awaits
you. There is a restaurant at
this hotel that has outdoor
dining where your dog is also
welcome. Room rates run
about $150-250 per night, but
your dog will be treated first
class.

Le Meridien Hotel
465 South La Cienega Blvd.
Los Angeles, CA
310-247-0400
Dogs up to 50 pounds are
allowed. This luxury class hotel
is located in one of the most
prestigious areas in Los
Angeles. They welcome both
business and leisure travelers,
as well as your dog of any size.
Room rates at this first class
hotel start at the low $300s per
night. They sometimes offer
special weekend rates. There is
an additional $100 pet fee for
the first night and an additional
$25 for each additional day.

**Los Angeles Airport Marriott
Hotel**
5885 W. Century Blvd.
Los Angeles, CA
310-641-5700
Dogs are allowed on the
ground floor only of this 18
story hotel, so be sure to call
ahead and reserve a room.
They have 24-hour room
service. The hotel is located
approximately a 1/2 mile from
the Los Angeles Airport.
Parking is $9 per day and valet
parking is $11 per day. It's
located on Century Blvd
between Sepulveda & Aviation
Blvds.

Travelodge Hotel at LAX
5547 W. Century Blvd.
Los Angeles, CA
310-649-4000
This inn offers free parking, a
feature not found with many of

the L.A./West Hollywood hotels.
They welcome pets here at this
2 story inn which has
interior/exterior corridors, a gift
shop and heated pool. It is
located about one mile east of
the Los Angeles Airport. There is
a $10 per day additional pet fee
per pet.

Vagabond Inn
3101 S. Figueroa St.
Los Angeles, CA
213-746-1531
This motel is located just 2
blocks from the University of
Southern California (USC) and 2
miles from the LA Convention
Center. It features an outdoor
swimming pool, cable television,
air conditioning and many more
amenities. There is a $10 per
day pet fee.

Los Banos

Days Inn
2169 East Pacheco Blvd
Los Banos, CA
209-826-9690
There is a $5 per day pet fee.

Sunstar Inn
839 W. Pacheco Blvd
Los Banos, CA
209-826-3805
There is a $10 per day additional
pet fee.

Lost Hills

Days Inn
14684 Aloma St
Lost Hills, CA
661-797-2371
There are no additional pet fees.

Motel 6
14685 Warren St
Lost Hills, CA
661-797-2346
A well-behaved large dog is ok.

Madera

Best Western Madera Valley

Inn
317 North G Street
Madera, CA
559-673-5164
There is a $30 one time pet charge. If you are paying with cash, there is a $100 refundable deposit. Pets must not be left alone in rooms.

Days Inn
25327 Ave 16
Madera, CA
559-674-8817
There is a $5 per day pet fee.

Super 8
1855 W. Cleveland Ave
Madera, CA
559-661-1131
There is a $5 per day additional pet fee.

Mammoth Lakes

Crystal Crag Lodge
P.O. Box 88
Mammoth Lakes, CA
760-934-2436
This lodge offers cabins at 9,000 feet elevation on beautiful Lake Mary in the dog-friendly Inyo National Forest. Lake Mary is known as one of the best fishing spots in the Eastern Sierra, regularly producing trophy size trout. You will find a number of other lakes, most of the best hiking trailheads, Lake Mary Store, and some of the best scenery that the Eastern Sierra has to offer within walking distance of your cabin. The cabins, all non-smoking, have full kitchens and baths. Most cabins have living rooms with fireplaces. The lodge also offers 14-foot aluminum boats with or without a motor. Dogs are allowed on the boats as well. Please note that the lodge is only open during the summer season, from about late May to early October. Dogs are allowed for an additional $8 per day charge. Pets must never be left unattended in the cabins.

Discovery 4 Condominiums
Call to Arrange.
Mammoth Lakes, CA
760-934-6410
Dogs are allowed in certain pet designated condos. They offer one and two bedroom condos. There is a $20 per day pet charge.

Edelweiss Lodge
1872 Old Mammoth Road
Mammoth Lakes, CA
760-934-2445
Cabins on a 1 acre wooded site near hiking trails, lakes and streams. Dogs of all sizes are allowed. There is a $10 per day pet fee. All rooms are non-smoking.

Mammoth Ski and Racquet Club
Call to Arrange.
Mammoth Lakes, CA
760-934-7368
They offer fully equipped condominium rentals nestled in the forest with scenic mountain views. They have a couple of condos that allow pets. All condos are non-smoking. There is a $10 per day pet charge.

Motel 6
3372 Main St
Mammoth Lakes, CA
760-934-6660
There are no additional pet fees.

Shilo Inn
2963 Main Street
Mammoth Lakes, CA
760-934-4500
Your dog is welcome here. Each room in this motel is a mini-suite complete with microwaves, refrigerators and more. This motel is located across the street from the Visitors Center which has trails that border up to the Shady Rest Park where there are many hiking trails. If you are there in the winter, try some cross-country skiing with your pup. The cross country ski rental store is very close to this motel (see Attractions.) There is a $10 per day additional pet fee per pet.

Travelodge
54 Sierra Blvd.
Mammoth Lakes, CA
760-934-8240
There are no additional pet fees.

Villa De Los Pinos #3
3252 Chateau Rd
Mammoth Lakes, CA
760-722-5369
A year-round vacation rental townhouse-style condominium in Mammoth Lakes. This condo has two downstairs bedrooms, two bathrooms, a large living room, dining room, and kitchen. The condo is fronted by a large deck overlooking the development courtyard (where dogs are allowed off-leash), swimming pool, and Jacuzzi building. This is not a hotel-style lodging; rather it is a comfortable, nicely decorated, cozy mountain home in a small development, with a wood-burning stove. All dogs are welcome. The $25 per visit pet fee helps with the cleaning.

Manhattan Beach

Residence Inn by Marriott
1700 N Sepulveda Blvd
Manhattan Beach, CA
310-546-7627
Every room at this inn is a suite with a living room, kitchen and bedroom. Amenities include an outdoor pool, complimentary continental breakfast, self service laundry facilities, and dinner delivery service from local restaurants. Room rates start at $125 and up. There is a $75 one time pet charge and an additional $8 per day for pets. If you reserve one of the penthouses, then there is a $100 one time pet charge.

Mariposa

Best Western Yosemite Way Station
4999 S. Highway 140
Mariposa, CA
209-966-7545
There is a $5 per day pet charge. The oldest courthouse in California is located just 7 blocks from this inn. If you take Highway 140, this motel is located about 50 minutes from Yosemite Valley.

The Mariposa Lodge
5052 Hwy 140
Mariposa, CA
209-966-3607
Thanks to one of our readers for recommending this hotel. Here is what they said about it: "We stayed here after a clogged 4 hour drive from San Jose, CA. Mia at the front desk was courteous and friendly -- not what you always get when you are traveling with a 90 pound dog (black lab). The room was large, new and very nice. Lovely pool and jacuzzi. A little sitting area under a patch of trees with benches. It was very warm and Mia recommended a restaurant where we could sit outside and take our dog. Castillos on 5th Street. Our extra nice waitress brought him water and us an excellent Mexican dinner. Couldn't have been nicer. All in all Mariposa and the hotel was an A+ experience." If you take Highway 140, this motel is located about 50 minutes from Yosemite Valley (45 min. to the main gate and about 10 min. to the valley). Pets are an additional $10 per pet per night.

McCloud

Stony Brook Inn
309 Colombero
McCloud, CA
800-369-6118
There is a $15 per day pet fee. There are only 2 pet rooms so

you need to call ahead.

Mendocino

Coastal Getaways
10501 Ford Street POB1355
Mendocino, CA
707-937-9200
Coastal Getaways has over 5 vacation homes that allow dogs. Most of the homes have ocean front views and one is located in the quaint village of Mendocino. The rates range from $140 to $250 and up per night. They also have weekly rates. For more information, please call 800-525-0049.

Inn at Schoolhouse Creek
7051 N. Highway 1
Mendocino, CA
707-937-5525
With 8+ acres of ocean view gardens, meadows, forest, hiking trails and a secluded beach cove you and your pets will truly feel like you've gotten away from it all. To help your pets get in the vacation mood they will be welcomed with their own pet basket that includes a bed, towel, blanket and a treat. At the end of your day, relax in the ocean view hot tub.

MacCallum House
45020 Albion Street
Mendocino, CA
707-937-0289
Pets of all varieties are welcomed at the MacCallum House Inn and Restaurant, located in the heart of the Mendocino Village. Pets are allowed in the cottages and Barn and are provided with blankets and sheets. The original Victorian mansion, built in 1882 by William H. Kelley, was a wedding gift to his daughter, Daisy MacCallum, and is a historic landmark. Rooms include a full breakfast and a complimentary wine hour is served in the Grey Whale Bar featuring wines from

throughout the California wine country. Children are also welcomed.

McElroys Cottage Inn
Main and Evergreen Streets
Mendocino, CA
707-937-1734
All of the four rooms at this bed and breakfast inn have private baths and all rooms are non-smoking. There is a $15 per day pet charge. Dogs must be on leash and never left unattended in the room. Dogs are not allowed on the furniture or beds, so you might want to bring your own pet bedding.

Mendocino Seaside Cottages
10940 Lansing St
Mendocino, CA
707-485-0239
Accommodations have jacuzzi spas, wet bars,& fireplaces. It is located within easy walking distance of Mendocino.

Stanford Inn by the Sea
44850 Comptche-Ukiah Rd
Mendocino, CA
707-937-5615
This is a very dog friendly inn. It is known both as the Stanford Inn by the Sea and Big River Lodge. In the room there are doggie dishes, pet sheets and upon arrival, a ribbon wrapped biscuit. For the humans, all rooms are non-smoking, have fireplaces, VCRs, refrigerators and CD players/stereos. The only places dogs aren't allowed on this 10 acres are the lobby (they have resident cats), the restaurant and the pool area. Other than that, you and your pooch are more than welcome to stroll the 10 acre grounds which have several gardens as well as several llamas. Room rates are $245 and up. There is a $25 charge per stay, for the first pet. Additional pets are $12.50. If you are into adventure, walk over to the canoe rentals, take one of the canoes and spend an hour or all day going up the river

with your pup (see Attractions).

Sweetwater Spa & Inn
44840 Main Street
Mendocino, CA
707-937-4076
Sweetwater Spa & Inn offers a unique variety of accommodations, including cabin and vacation home rentals. They give dog treats at check-in as well as sheets for the guests to cover furniture and towels for wet paws in the rainy season. Some of the rentals are located in the village of Mendocino. The other rentals are located around the Mendocino area. There is a two night minimum on weekends and three night minimum on most holidays. All units are non-smoking. Your well-behaved dog is welcome. Room rates start at the low $100s and up. There is a $15 per day additional pet fee.

Whitegate Inn Village Retreat
P.O. Box 150, 499 Howard St.
Mendocino, CA
707-937-4892
Pets are welcome in this Victorian house in the heart of Mendocino on the rugged Pacific coast. The Whitegate Inn Village Retreat includes the main house and cottage with 4 bedrooms and 3 baths. The house has ocean views, TV, VCR, fine linens, deck, BBQ, gas fireplace, hot tub, sauna, phone, washer and dryer. Stroll with your dog in beautiful Mendocino and nearby state parks.

Merced

Best Western Sequoia Inn
1213 V Street
Merced, CA
209-723-3711
There is an additional $15 pet charge per stay.

Motel 6
1410 V St

Merced, CA
209-384-2131
There are no additional pet fees.

Super 8
1983 E. Childs Ave
Merced, CA
209-384-1303
There is a $5 per day additional pet fee.

Travelodge
1260 Yosemite Park Way
Merced, CA
209-722-6225
There is a $10 per day additional pet fee.

Vagabond Inn
1215 R Street
Merced, CA
209-722-2737
There are no additional pet fees.

Mill Creek

Child's Meadow Resort
41500 Highway 36E
Mill Creek, CA
530-595-3383
Dogs are allowed in this all season resort. Located between the towns of Susanville and Red Bluff, this quiet resort is on 18 acres of picturesque meadows and streams at the end of the Shasta/Cascade Mountain Range. The resort is just 9 miles from the southwest entrance to Lassen Volcanic National Park. RV hookups are available at the resort. There is no pet charge.

Millbrae

Clarion Hotel
250 El Camino Real
Millbrae, CA
650-692-6363
There is a $30 per day additional pet fee.

Milpitas

Best Western Brookside Inn
400 Valley Way
Milpitas, CA
408-263-5566
This motel has over 70 renovated rooms. Some rooms have a private balcony, refrigerator and microwave. The motel also offers a heated pool. There is a $15 per day pet charge. To get there from Hwy 880 heading north, exit Hwy 237/Calaveras Blvd towards Milpitas-Alviso Rd. Merge onto Calaveras Blvd and then turn left at the first street which is Abbott Ave. Then turn left onto Valley Way.

Residence Inn by Marriott
1501 California Circle
Milpitas, CA
408-941-9222
There is a one time pet fee of $75 and an additional daily pet charge of $10. All rooms have full kitchens, irons/ironing boards, hairdryers, and data ports on phones. They have self-service laundry facilities, and dinner delivery service from local restaurants. To get there from Hwy 880 heading north, exit Dixon Landing Rd. Turn right onto California Circle and the motel will be on the right. There is a $75 one time pet fee and a $10 per day additional pet fee.

Miranda

Miranda Gardens Resort
6766 Avenue of the Giants
Miranda, CA
707-943-3011
The cottages are surrounded by flowering gardens and surrounded by ancient redwoods. From this resort, you can take day trips to the Avenue of the Giants or the Lost Coast. All cottages are non-smoking. Children are welcome and the resort has a children's play area.

Pets are allowed in certain cabins and there is a $50 one time pet charge.

Modesto

Best Western Town House Lodge
909 16th Street
Modesto, CA
209-524-7261
There is a $25 refundable pet deposit required.

Red Lion Hotel
1612 Sisk Rd
Modesto, CA
209-521-1612
There are no additional pet fees.

Vagabond Inn
2025 W Orangeburg Ave
Modesto, CA
209-577-8008
A well-behaved large dog is okay.

Mojave

Econo Lodge
2145 SR 58
Mojave, CA
661-824-2463
There is a $5 per day pet fee.

Motel 6
16958 Hwy 58
Mojave, CA
661-824-4571
There are no additional pet fees.

Monte Rio

Grandma's House Bed and Breakfast
20280 River Blvd
Monte Rio, CA
707-865-1865
This dog-friendly bed and breakfast inn is located on the Russian River. The inn offers three rooms, all with private bathrooms. Each room also includes a private phone line, TV and VCR, refrigerator, microwave, and more. One of

the rooms is handicapped accessible. Clean, well-behaved dogs may accompany their owners, with advance notice, for $10 per dog per day. There is a $75 damage and cleaning deposit, refundable (if not needed) at departure. Owners are expected to clean up behind their dog on the grounds. Pooper-scooper bags are available for this purpose. Dogs must not be left unattended in the room for long periods. Owners are responsible for not letting their dog disturb other guests and making sure their dog is not destructive to the property.

Monterey

Bay Park Hotel
1425 Munras Ave
Monterey, CA
831-649-1020
There is a $10 per day pet fee. Pets may not be left alone in the room.

Best Western Monterey Beach Hotel
2600 Sand Dunes Drive
Monterey, CA
831-394-3321
This beach front hotel allows dogs. Dogs stay in the first floor rooms on the garden side (not facing the beach). They originally just allowed small dogs, but now they allow all dogs that are well-behaved and well-trained. While there are no restaurants within an easy walking distance, the sandy beach is right at the hotel. Dogs are allowed on the beaches that stretch from this hotel down to Fisherman's Wharf - about 2 miles. If you want a longer walk, once at Fisherman's Wharf, continue on the paved Monterey Recreation Trail. The hotel is located off Hwy 1 at the Del Rey Oaks exit. There is a $25 one time fee for pets.

Best Western Victorian Inn
487 Foam Street
Monterey, CA
831-373-8000
This inn is a few blocks from the beautiful dog-friendly Monterey Recreation Trail that parallels the ocean. The inn has nice spacious rooms with fireplaces and of course it has a great location for ocean lovers and their water dogs. There is a $100 refundable pet deposit and a one time $35 pet cleaning charge for the room. Thanks to one of our readers who writes: "...He received upon arriving to our room the "pooch package" of treats overflowing in a bowl, and his own bottle of water for walks along the surf. "

El Adobe Inn
936 Munras Ave.
Monterey, CA
831-372-5409
This inn is located on Munras Ave. about 1/2 mile east of Hwy 1. There is a $10 per day additional pet fee.

Hyatt Resort
1 Od Golf Course Rd
Monterey, CA
831-372-1234
There is a $50 one time pet fee for each dog. Dogs must be on leash and certain areas of the hotel are off limits to pets. The front desk will explain the restrictions upon check in.

Monterey Fireside Lodge
1131 10th Street
Monterey, CA
831-373-4172
All 24 rooms have gas fireplaces. There is an additional $20/day pet charge.

Moreno Valley

Econo Lodge
24412 Sunnymead Blvd
Moreno Valley, CA
909-247-6699

There is a $50 refundable pet deposit and a $5 per day pet fee.

Morro Bay

Adventure Inn On The Sea
1150 Embarcadero
Morro Bay, CA
805-772-5607
Amenities include a continental breakfast served pool-side each morning and an onsite gourmet restaurant serving lunch and dinner. There is a $10 per day pet charge.

Days Inn
1095 Main Street
Morro Bay, CA
805-772-2711
There is an $11 per day pet fee.

Pleasant Inn Motel
235 Harbor Street
Morro Bay, CA
805-772-8521
This motel, family owned and operated, is just one block east of the beautiful Morro Bay waterfront and one block west of old downtown. All rooms are non-smoking. Dogs and cats are welcome for an extra $5 per day.

Mount Shasta

Best Western Tree House Motor Inn
111 Morgan Way
Mount Shasta, CA
530-926-3101
Hotel amenities include a complimentary full breakfast, heated indoor pool, room refrigerators, hair dryers, iron/ironing boards and more. There is an additional $10 per day pet charge.

Dream Inn Bed and Breakfast
326 Chestnut Street
Mount Shasta, CA
530-926-1536
Dogs (and children) are welcome at this bed and breakfast inn. The Victorian

home, built in 1904 and completely restored, is located at 3,500 ft. in downtown Mount Shasta. Lying at the base of 14,162 ft. Mount Shasta, they are surrounded by National Forest. The inn offers 4 bedrooms with shared bathrooms. The owners also have a dog on the premises. There are no pet fees.

Econo Lodge
908 S. Mt. Shasta Blvd.
Mount Shasta, CA
530-926-3145
There is an additional $5 per day pet charge. There is a limit of one dog per room.

Mount Shasta Ranch Bed and Breakfast
1008 W. A. Barr Rd.
Mount Shasta, CA
530-926-3870
Dogs are allowed at this ranch style house bed and breakfast built in 1923. This B&B offers 12 bedrooms including a cottage. Five of the rooms have private bathrooms. There is a $10 one time per stay, per pet fee. Children are also welcome.

Mountain Air Lodge
1121 S Mount Shasta Blvd
Mount Shasta, CA
530-926-3411
There is an additional $7 per day pet charge.

Swiss Holiday Lodge
2400 S. Mt. Shasta Blvd.
Mount Shasta, CA
530-926-3446
There is an additional $5 per day pet charge.

Mountain View

Residence Inn by Marriott
1854 W El Camino Real
Mountain View, CA
650-940-1300
This is an apartment style inn that has suite style rooms. There is a $50 non-refundable

room cleaning fee for pets and a $10 per day additional pet fee per pet.

Tropicana Lodge
1720 El Camino Real
Mountain View, CA
650-961-0220
Pets may not be left alone in the rooms.

Napa

The Chablis Inn
3360 Solono Ave
Napa, CA
707-257-1944
There is a 150 pound limit for dogs. There is a $10 per day additional pet fee. All rooms are non-smoking.

The Napa Inn Bed and Breakfast
1137 Warren Street
Napa, CA
707-257-1444
Located on a quiet street in historic, downtown Napa, this inn is within an easy walking distance of shops and restaurants. Dogs are allowed in one room, the garden cottage. This private cottage is decorated in French Provincial prints. It has a queen size bed, sofa, fireplace, French doors overlooking a private flower garden, skylight, wet bar with refrigerator and microwave, and an outdoor spa. It sleeps up to four people. There is a $20 per day pet charge.

National City

Super 8
425 Roosevelt Ave
National City, CA
619-474-8811
There is a $15 per day additional pet fee.

Needles

Days Inn and Suites

1215 Hospitality Lane
Needles, CA
760-326-5836
There are no additional pet fees.

Econo Lodge
1910 N. Needles Hwy
Needles, CA
760-326-3881
There is a $5 per day pet fee.

Motel 6
1420 J St
Needles, CA
760-326-3399
A well-behaved large dog is allowed. The motel is located 26 miles from the Laughlin Casinos.

Super 8
1102 E Broadway
Needles, CA
760-326-4501
There is a $5 per day additional pet fee.

Travelers Inn
1195 3rd Street Hill
Needles, CA
760-326-4900
There are no additional pet fees.

Nevada City

Nevada Street Cottages
690 Nevada Street
Nevada City, CA
530-265-2808
Nevada Street Cottages in the Wild Wood are five cottages originally built as a hunting and fishing camp just on the outskirts of Nevada City. Children and well-behaved leashed dogs are welcome. The cottages are scattered under mature trees amid gardens, flowers, lawn furniture and toys for the kids. The cottages are located within a ten minute walk to the downtown Nevada City area through a historic neighborhood. All of the cottages are non-smoking. There is a $10 one time pet charge.

The Outside Inn

575 E. Broad Street
Nevada City, CA
530-265-2233
This inn is located in a quiet residential neighborhood two blocks from downtown Nevada City. This completely renovated 1940's era motor court features never smoked in rooms under tall pines. Children and pets are welcome. There is a $10 per night pet charge.

Newark

W Silicon Valley - Newark
8200 Gateway Boulevard
Newark, CA
510-494-8800   .
Dogs of all sizes are allowed. There is a $50 one time additional pet fee.

Woodfin Suite Hotel
39150 Cedar Blvd.
Newark, CA
510-795-1200
All well-behaved dogs are welcome. Every room is a suite with a full kitchen. Hotel amenities include free video movies and a complimentary hot breakfast buffet. There is a $50 one time per stay pet fee.

Newport Beach

Newport Beach Marriott Hotel
900 Newport Center Dr
Newport Beach, CA
949-640-4000
This hotel is across the street from the dog-friendly Fashion Island Shopping Mall (see Attractions). The hotel offers room service and self-service laundry facilities. It is also close to the Three Dog Bakery (see Attractions). There are no pet fees. Dogs up to about 75 pounds are allowed, but must never be left alone in the room.

North Highlands

Motel 6

4600 Watt Ave
North Highlands, CA
916-973-8637
A large, well-behaved dog is okay. Dogs may not be left unattended in a room.

Novato

Inn Marin
250 Entrada Drive
Novato, CA
415-883-5952
Inn Marin invites both business and leisure travelers. Nestled in a beautiful resort setting and richly restored, this inn welcomes your best friend. Amenities include a large outdoor heated pool and spa, garden patio area with barbecue, exercise facility, guest laundry facility and a continental breakfast. Rooms include data ports, voice mail and two line speaker phone, iron and ironing board, and handicapped rooms/facilities are available. They are located just off Highway 101, perfect for the business or tourist traveler. There is a $20 one time pet fee. You are required to bring a crate if you plan to leave your dog alone in the room.

Travelodge
7600 Redwood Blvd
Novato, CA
415-892-7500
There is a $10 per day pet fee. Dogs are allowed on the first floor only.

Oakhurst

Best Western Yosemite Gateway Inn
40530 Highway 41
Oakhurst, CA
559-683-2378
This inn is located in the mountain town of Oakhurst. Amenities include laundry services, an indoor and outdoor pool and more. There are no additional pet fees, but pets

must not be left alone in the room. Yosemite Valley is about a one hour drive from this inn.

Pine Rose Inn Bed and Breakfast
41703 Road 222
Oakhurst, CA
559-642-2800
The inn is located 13 miles from the south gate of Yosemite National Park, 2 miles from Bass Lake and surrounded by the Sierra National Forest. The entire inn is non-smoking, except for outside. There is a $10 per day pet charge. Dogs and other pets are welcome.

Oakland

Motel 6
1801 Embarcadero
Oakland, CA
510-436-0103
Dogs may never be left alone in the rooms.

Occidental

Occidental Hotel
3610 Bohemian Hwy
Occidental, CA
707-874-3623
There is an $8.70 per day pet fee for each pet. Dogs must be on leash and may not be left alone in the rooms.

Sonoma Cottage Vacation Rental
3657 Church Street
Occidental, CA
707-874-1047
Dogs are welcome at the Inn at Occidental's vacation rental, the Sonoma Cottage. There is a $25 one time pet fee. Children are also welcome.

Oceanside

Motel 6
3708 Plaza Dr
Oceanside, CA
760-941-1011

There are no additional pet fees.

Ramada Limited
1140 Mission Ave
Oceanside, CA
760-967-4100
There is a $50 refundable deposit for pets.

Olancha

Ranch Motel
2051 S Highway 395
Olancha, CA
760-764-2387
There are no additional pet fees.

Olema

Ridgetop Inn and Cottage
9876 Sir Francis Drake Blvd.
Olema, CA
415-663-1500
Dogs are allowed in the cottage. It is a non-smoking, one bedroom cottage with a private bathroom and a full kitchen. They stock the kitchen with breakfast items so you can serve yourself breakfast in the morning. The cottage is located above the Village of Olema, less than a mile from the Point Reyes National Seashore headquarters. There is a $25 one time pet fee. Children are also welcome.

Ontario

Country Suites by Carlson
231 N. Vineyard Ave.
Ontario, CA
909-937-6000
This motel offers studio rooms, and one to two bedroom suites. Amenities include a heated pool, whirlpool, complimentary breakfast & evening beverages, and coin operated laundry facilities. Management suggests that large dogs stay in the one bedroom units and up. The studio rooms are okay for

small and medium size dogs. There is a $10 per day pet charge.

Holiday Inn
3400 Shelby Street
Ontario, CA
909-466-9600
Amenities include a heated pool, spa, exercise room, sauna, billiards, ping pong tables, video games and basketball courts. Rooms include refrigerators with free juices and bottled water, microwave ovens with free popcorn, hair dryers, and iron/ironing boards. There is a $50 pet deposit and $25 is refundable.

Marriott - Ontario Airport
2200 E. Holt Blvd
Ontario, CA
909-975-5000
There is a $250 refundable pet deposit. There is also a $50 one time pet fee per visit.

Red Roof Inn
1818 E Holt Blvd.
Ontario, CA
909-988-8466
Amenities include a heated pool, sauna and whirlpool. There are no additional pet fees.

Orange

Residence Inn - Orange
3101 W. Chapman Avenue
Orange, CA
714-976-7700
There is a $100 one time pet fee and a $10 per day additional pet fee.

Oroville

Days Inn
1745 Feather River Blvd
Oroville, CA
530-533-3297
One large dog per room is okay. There is a $7 per day pet fee.

Motel 6
505 Montgomery St

Oroville, CA
530-534-7653
One large dog is permitted per room. Dogs may never be left unattended.

Travelodge
580 Oroville Dam Blvd
Oroville, CA
530-533-7070
There is a $40 refundable pet deposit.

Oxnard

Casa Sirena Hotel and Resort
3605 Peninsula Rd
Oxnard, CA
805-985-6311
There is a $50 one time pet fee. There is an on-site tennis court and an exercise room. Some rooms have views of the Channel Islands Harbor.

Radisson Hotel Oxnard
600 E. Esplanade Drive
Oxnard, CA
805-485-9666
There is a $50 one time pet fee. Dogs up to 50 pounds are allowed.

Residence Inn by Marriott
2101 West Vineyard Avenue
Oxnard, CA
805-278-2200
Every room in this motel is a suite with a separate living area, kitchen and bedroom. Amenities include an outdoor pool, tennis court, exercise room, self service laundry and dinner delivery service from local restaurants. Room rates start at around $100. There is a non-refundable $100 pet deposit and $6 per day pet charge. They allow pets up to about 75 pounds.

Vagabond Inn
1245 N. Oxnard Blvd.
Oxnard, CA
805-983-0251
Amenities at this motel include a free continental breakfast and

weekday newspaper. They also have an on-site coffee shop, which might be helpful in getting food to go for the room. Pets are an additional $5 per day.

Pacific Grove

Andril Fireplace Cottages
569 Asilomar Blvd
Pacific Grove, CA
831-375-0994
There is an additional fee of $14 per day for a pet. Well-behaved dogs are allowed.

Lighthouse Lodge and Suites
1249 Lighthouse Ave
Pacific Grove, CA
831-655-2111
There are no additional pet fees.

Palm Desert

Comfort Suites
39-585 Washington St
Palm Desert, CA
760-360-3337
There is a $25 refundable pet deposit.

The Inn at Deep Canyon
74470 Abronia Trail
Palm Desert, CA
760-346-8061
This hotel features a palm garden, pool and fully-equipped kitchenettes. They have pet-friendly rooms available. There is a $10 per day additional pet fee.

Palm Springs

7 Springs Inn and Suites
950 N. Indian Canyon Dr.
Palm Springs, CA
760-320-9110
7 Springs Inn and Suites offers a variety of accommodations in the heart of Palm Springs. Enjoy fully furnished suites with Kitchens, free daily Continental Breakfast, Heated Pool,

Jacuzzi, BBQ area, Remote control T.V., direct dial telephones, free parking. Close to area shopping, restaurants, casinos, golf, tennis, and Indian canyons. Pets are welcome for a $15 per night fee. Pets cannot be left unattended and must be kept on a leash when out of the room.

Casa Cody Country Inn
175 S. Cahuilla Rd.
Palm Springs, CA
760-320-9346
This is a quaint romantic historic inn that was founded in the 1920s. The founder, Harriet Cody, was a cousin of Buffalo Bill. The inn is nestled against the mountains and has adobe buildings. The rooms have fireplaces, kitchens and private patios. There is a $10 per day pet charge.

Casa Opuntia Vacation Rental
Call to Arrange.
Palm Springs, CA
877-898-1043
This 4 bedroom vacation rental is nestled in a quiet neighborhood, adjacent to the famed "Movie Colony". The house has a pool and hot tub. Walk to downtown Palm Springs and Palm Canyon Drive. There is no pet charge. You may also call 760-327-2866 to arrange.

Hacienda de Orchid Tree Vacation Rental
Call to Arrange.
Palm Springs, CA
877-898-1043
This 3 bedroom 2 bath vacation rental home with private grounds is dog-friendly. The home is located about a mile from downtown Palm Springs. There is no pet charge. You may also call 760-327-2866.

Hilton Palm Springs Resort
400 E. Tahquitz Canyon Way
Palm Springs, CA
760-320-6868
This 13-acre resort is about a

block from the Palm Canyon Drive Shopping Area. It is an ideal location if you want to be within walking distance of the many key local attractions like sidewalk cafes, shops and more. All rooms have balconies or patios and refrigerators. There is a required pet deposit.

La Serena Villas
339 South Belardo Road
Palm Springs, CA
760-325-3216
These dog-friendly villas cater to those who prefer a relaxing, secluded hideaway in Palm Springs. Built in the 1930's, the villas are nestled in the foothills of the San Jacinto Mountains. Palm Springs Village is within walking distance. Your pet is welcome. There is a $10 per day pet charge. Pets must be on leash and please pick up after your dog.

Orchid Tree Inn
261 South Belardo Road
Palm Springs, CA
760-325-2791
This inn has two pet rooms. Dogs must be attended at all times and leashed when outside the room. There is a $250 refundable pet deposit.

Porto Romantico
596 W. Via Escuela
Palm Springs, CA
760-323-4944
Situated in the Little Tuscany section of Old Palm Springs, this dog-friendly guest cottage is charming and spacious. Enjoy beautiful accommodations with king bed, down comforter, custom furniture, original artwork, kitchenette, two person whirlpool tub, climate control and a view of the San Jacinto Mountains. There is a continental breakfast each morning and plenty of room for your dog to play. Porto Romantico is a mile and a half from downtown Palm Springs in a quiet, casual setting. Read by

the pool, lounge in the covered loggia or just hang out in your cottage. Porto Romantico is entirely non-smoking. There is no additional pet fee but there is a $50 refundable pet deposit. The owners of this B&B also have a dog on the premises.

San Marino Hotel
225 West Baristo Road
Palm Springs, CA
800-676-1214
The hotel, a favorite of writers and artists, is the closest lodging to the Palm Springs historic shopping area. Dogs are allowed, but not in the poolside rooms. There is a $10 per day pet charge.

Super 8 Lodge - Palm Springs
1900 N. Palm Canyon Drive
Palm Springs, CA
760-322-3757
$10/stay for up to 3 dogs in one room. FREE 8-minute long distance call each night. FREE continental breakfast. Coffee maker, refrigerator, night light, clock/radio, safe in each room. Outdoor pool. On-site guest laundry. Kids 12 & under stay free. Off I-10, from West take Hwy 111 (N. Palm Canyon Drive); from East take Indian Avenue. Next to Billy Reed's restaurant.

Villa Angelica Vacation Rental
Call to Arrange.
Palm Springs, CA
714-434-4786
Set on a half of an acre, this three bedroom, 2 bathroom home features a large heated pool, two gazebos, mountain views and more. A large well-behaved dog is permitted. There is a $750 refundable pet deposit.

Palmdale

Residence Inn

514 West Avenue P
Palmdale, CA
661-947-4105
There is a $100 one time pet fee and a $10 per day additional pet fee.

Palo Alto

Sheraton Palo Alto Hotel
625 El Camino Real
Palo Alto, CA
650-328-2800
Dogs up to 80 pounds are allowed. There are no additional pet fees.

Panamint Springs

Panamint Springs Resort
Highway 190
Panamint Springs, CA
775-482-7680
There is a $5 per day additional pet fee. The resort is located on Highway 190, 48 miles east of Lone Pine and 31 miles west of Stovepipe Wells.

Paradise

Lime Saddle Marina Houseboat Rentals
Call to Arrange.
Paradise, CA
530-877-2414
Take a vacation with your dog on a houseboat. There is a $35 one time pet fee.

Pescadero

Estancia del Mar Cottages
San Mateo County Coastside
Pescadero, CA
650-879-1500
Enjoy a romantic getaway or a family vacation at one of the six cottages that overlook the ocean. Dogs are allowed as well as children. Estancia del Mar is also a working horse ranch where the owners breed, raise and train purebred Peruvian Paso horses.

Petaluma

Sheraton Sonoma County - Petaluma
745 Baywood Drive
Petaluma, CA
707-283-2888
Dogs up to 80 pounds are allowed. There are no additional pet fees. The entire hotel is non-smoking.

Pico Rivera

Days Inn - Pico Rivera
6540 S. Rosemead Blvd
Pico Rivera, CA
562-942-1003
There is a $15 per day pet fee.

Pismo Beach

Motel 6
860 4th St
Pismo Beach, CA
805-773-2665
There are no additional pet fees.

Oxford Suites
651 Five Cities Drive
Pismo Beach, CA
805-773-3773
This motel is located within a short drive of the dog-friendly Pismo State Beach. Amenities include a year-round pool & spa, complimentary full breakfast buffet, an evening reception with beverages & light hor d'oeuvres. Room amenities for the guest suites include a work table, sofa, microwave oven, refrigerator, TV/VCR, and wheelchair accessibility. There is a $10 per day pet charge. Dogs must never be left unattended in the room, even if they are in a crate.

Sandcastle Inn
100 Stimson Avenue
Pismo Beach, CA
805-773-2422
This inn has one non-smoking pet room. There is a $10 per day pet charge.

Sea Gypsy Motel
1020 Cypress Street
Pismo Beach, CA
805-773-1801
This motel is located on the beach and they allow dogs of any size. There is a $15 per day pet charge.

Placerville

Best Western Placerville Inn
6850 Green Leaf Dr.
Placerville, CA
530-622-9100
This motel overlooks the Sierra Foothills and allows dogs in the first floor rooms. Amenities include a heated pool and Jacuzzi. There is a coffee shop next door if you want to order food to go for the motel room. The motel is located within a short drive to historic downtown Placerville.

Pleasant Hill

Residence Inn
700 Ellinwood Way
Pleasant Hill, CA
925-689-1010
There is a $75 one time pet fee and a $6 per day additional pet fee.

Pleasanton

Candlewood Suites
5535 Johnson Ct
Pleasanton, CA
925-463-1212
There is a $75 one time pet fee. This suite motel has a kitchen in every room. To get there from Hwy 580 heading east, take the Hopyard Rd Exit. Turn right on Hopyard and then right on Owens Drive. Then turn right onto Johnson Ct. There is a $75 one time pet fee.

Motel 6
5102 Hopyard Rd
Pleasanton, CA
925-463-2626

A well-behaved large dog is allowed.

Ramada Inn
5375 Owens Court
Pleasanton, CA
925-463-1300
There is a $50 refundable pet deposit.

Residence Inn - Pleasanton
11920 Dublin Canyon Rd
Pleasanton, CA
925-227-0500
There is a $100 one time pet fee and a $10 per day additional pet fee.

Point Reyes Station

Berry Patch Cottage
P.O. Box 712
Point Reyes Station, CA
415-663-1942
This old-fashioned cottage welcomes children and well-behaved pets. Just be sure to let them know you will be bringing a dog.

Point Reyes Station Inn Bed and Breakfast
11591 Highway One, Box 824
Point Reyes Station, CA
415-663-9372
They offer private, romantic rooms with thirteen foot vaulted ceilings, whirlpool baths, fireplaces and views of rolling hills. This inn is located at the gateway of the Point Reyes National Seashore. Well-behaved dogs are welcome and there is no extra pet charge. Children are also welcome.

Tree House Bed and Breakfast Inn
73 Drake Summit, P.O. Box 1075
Point Reyes Station, CA
415-663-8720
This inn offers a secluded and peaceful getaway in West Marin. It is located on the tip of Inverness Ridge with a view of Point Reyes Station. The Point

Reyes National Seashore is nearby. All three rooms have a private bathroom. Pets and children are always welcome. Smoking is allowed outdoors. There are no pet fees.

Pomona

Sheraton Suites Fairplex
601 West McKinley Avenue
Pomona, CA
909-622-2220
Dogs of all sizes are allowed. There is a $50 one time pet fee.

Shilo Inn
3200 Temple Ave
Pomona, CA
909-598-0073
Amenities include a complimentary breakfast buffet, outdoor pool & spa, guest laundromat, fitness center and fresh fruit, popcorn & coffee. Rooms include microwaves, refrigerators, hair dryers, iron/ironing boards and more. There is a $10 per day additional pet fee.

Porterville

Motel 6
935 W Morton Ave
Porterville, CA
559-781-7600
There are no additional pet fees.

Quincy

Bucks Lake Lodge
23685 Bucks Lake
Quincy, CA
530-283-2262
There is a $10 per day additional pet fee. Dogs are allowed in the cabins, but not the motel section. The cabins are not designated as smoking or non-smoking. Thanks to one of our readers for this recommendation.

Rancho Cordova

Inns of America
12249 Folsom Blvd
Rancho Cordova, CA
916-351-1213
This motel offers a complimentary continental breakfast. To get there from Sacramento, take Hwy 5 and exit Hazel Ave. Turn right onto Hazel. Then turn right onto Folsom Blvd. The hotel will be on the right. There is a $5 per day additional pet fee.

Residence Inn by Marriott
2779 Prospect Park Drive
Rancho Cordova, CA
916-851-1550
This hotel offers 90 spacious suites. Amenities include an indoor pool and an exercise room, a complimentary breakfast and more. There is a $50 pet fee and a $10 per day pet charge.

Rancho Mirage

Motel 6
69-570 Hwy 111
Rancho Mirage, CA
760-324-8475
One large dog is allowed per room

Rancho Santa Fe

Rancho Valencia Resort
5921 Valencia Circle
Rancho Santa Fe, CA
858-756-1123
This upscale golf and tennis resort allows well-behaved dogs of all sizes. There is a $25 per day pet fee.

Red Bluff

Motel 6
20 Williams Ave
Red Bluff, CA
530-527-9200
There are no additional pet fees.

Super 8
203 Antelope Blvd
Red Bluff, CA
530-527-8882
A $100 refundable pet deposit is required only if paying with cash.

Travelodge
38 Antelope Blvd
Red Bluff, CA
530-527-6020
There is a $6 per day pet fee.

Redding

Best Western Ponderosa Inn
2220 Pine Street
Redding, CA
530-241-6300
There is a $100 refundable pet deposit.

Comfort Inn
2059 Hilltop Drive
Redding, CA
530-221-6530
There is a $15 one time pet fee.

Fawndale Lodge and RV Resort
15215 Fawndale Road
Redding, CA
800-338-0941
Nestled in the pines, this lodge offers acres of lawn, a pool and easy access to many recreational activities. All rooms are non-smoking. There is a $50 refundable pet deposit and a $6 per day pet charge.

Holiday Inn Express
1080 Twin View Blvd
Redding, CA
530-241-5500
There is a $30 one time pet fee or a $20 pet fee if you are an AAA or AARP member.

La Quinta Inn Redding
2180 Hilltop Drive
Redding, CA
530-221-8200
Dogs of all sizes are allowed at the hotel.

Motel 6

1640 Hilltop Dr
Redding, CA
530-221-1800
There are no additional pet fees.

Motel 6 - North
1250 Twin View Blvd
Redding, CA
530-246-4470
A well-behaved large dog is okay.

Motel 6 - South
2385 Bechelli Ln
Redding, CA
530-221-0562
One pet is allowed per room.

Ramada Limited
1286 Twin View Blvd
Redding, CA
530-246-2222
There is a $15 one time pet fee.

Red Lion Hotel
1830 Hilltop Drive
Redding, CA
530-221-8700
Dogs up to 50 pounds are allowed. This full service hotel features room service, several pools and an exercise room.

River Inn
1835 Park Marina Drive
Redding, CA
530-241-9500
This inn is adjacent to the Sacramento River and has a private grass area next to their lake. There is a $6 per day pet charge. Thanks to one of our readers for recommending this inn.

Seven Crown Resorts Houseboats
10300 Bridge Bay Road
Redding, CA
800-752-9669
Rent a houseboat on beautiful Shasta Lake at the Bridge Bay Resort and bring your pooch along. When not on your boat, take your leashed dog for a walk or a swim at dog-friendly Lake Shasta. Pets are welcome on houseboats at no additional charge. Advance reservations are required. Call 800-752-9669 to make your reservation.

Shasta Lodge
1245 Pine Street
Redding, CA
530-243-6133
There is a $20 refundable pet deposit. There is also a $5 per day pet fee.

Redwood City

Hotel Sofitel
223 Twin Dolphin Dr
Redwood City, CA
650-598-9000
This nice 8 story dog-friendly hotel is located off Hwy 101 and Marine World Parkway. There is a $25 one time pet fee.

Rialto

Best Western Empire Inn
475 W Valley Blvd
Rialto, CA
909-877-0690
There is an additional $5 per day pet fee.

Ridgecrest

Motel 6
535 S China Lake Blvd
Ridgecrest, CA
760-375-6866
There are no additional pet fees.

Riverside

Best Western of Riverside
10518 Magnolia Avenue
Riverside, CA
909-359-0770
There is a $10 per day pet charge and a $100 refundable pet deposit. Large dogs are okay if they are well-behaved and leashed.

Motel 6 - East
1260 University Ave
Riverside, CA
909-784-2131
Pets are not to be left unattended in rooms.

Rohnert Park

Motel 6
6145 Commerce Blvd
Rohnert Park, CA
707-585-8888
A large well-behaved dog is okay. Dogs must be leashed when outside and never left alone in the room.

Roseville

Best Western Roseville Inn
220 Harding Blvd.
Roseville, CA
916-782-4434
They have a pet building at this inn. There is a $10 pet charge.

Oxford Suites
130 N Sunrise Ave
Roseville, CA
916-784-2222
This inn features a health club, self-service laundry, heated pool and spa, and video rentals. Each room has a separate living area, 2 phones, 2 TVs, a microwave, refrigerator and more. To get there from Hwy 80, exit Douglas Blvd. and head east. Then turn left on N Sunrise Ave. There is a $15 one time pet fee.

Sacramento

Candlewood Suites
555 Howe Ave.
Sacramento, CA
916-646-1212
This hotel offers studio and one bedroom suites fully equipped with kitchens, oversized work areas and more. Amenities include a fitness center and spa. There is a $75 pet charge.

Canterbury Inn Hotel

1900 Canterbury Rd
Sacramento, CA
916-927-0927
This inn is located about a 5-10 minute drive from Old Sacramento. Guest laundry services are available. To get there from Hwy 160, take the Leisure Lane ramp towards Canterbury Rd. Turn right onto Canterbury Rd. There is a $5 per day additional pet fee.

Motel 6
1254 Halyard Dr
Sacramento, CA
916-372-3624
There are no additional pet fees.

Ramada Inn
2600 Auburn Blvd
Sacramento, CA
916-487-7600
This inn offers complimentary continental breakfast, an exercise room and an outdoor pool. There is a $100 refundable pet deposit. To get there from Business Route 80, exit Fulton Ave and head south. Then turn left onto Auburn Blvd.

Residence Inn by Marriott
1530 Howe Ave
Sacramento, CA
916-920-9111
This inn offers a complimentary continental breakfast, self service laundry facilities and a complimentary newspaper. Each guest room is a two room suite which includes hair dryers, ironing boards and data ports on phones. Fireplaces are available in some rooms. This Residence Inn charges a one-time $100 pet cleaning fee for the room. The inn is located about 1/2 mile from Howe Dog Park (see Parks). To get there from Hwy 80, exit Arden Way and head east. Turn right on Howe Ave. It is located on Howe Ave, between Arden Way and Hallmark Drive.

Residence Inn by Marriott - South Natomas

2410 West El Camino Avenue
Sacramento, CA
916-649-1300
This hotel offers 126 spacious suites. Amenities include an outdoor pool and an exercise room, a complimentary breakfast and more. Dinner delivery service is available from local restaurants. There is a $50 pet fee and a $6 per day pet charge.

Sheraton Grand Sacramento Hotel
1230 J Street
Sacramento, CA
916-447-1700
Dogs up to 85 pounds are allowed. Dogs may not be taken into the bar or restaurant areas. There are no additional pet fees.

San Bernardino

Motel 6
111 Redlands Blvd
San Bernardino, CA
909-825-6666
Well-behaved large dogs are okay.

San Carlos

Inns of America
555 Skyway Road
San Carlos, CA
650-631-0777
Amenities include a free continental breakfast, swimming pool, coin-op laundry, exercise room and more. They are located off Hwy 101 at the Holly Street Exit.

San Clemente

Holiday Inn
111 S. Ave. De Estrella
San Clemente, CA
949-361-3000
There is a $10 per day pet fee.

San Diego

Best Western Lamplighter Inn & Suites
6474 El Cajon Blvd
San Diego, CA
800-545-0778
This motel is located in the suburbs of San Diego. If you are visiting someone from San Diego State University, this motel is nearby. It's also about 7-8 miles from the dog-friendly Mission Trails Regional Park. There is a $10 per day pet charge.

Harborview Inn & Suites
550 West Grape St
San Diego, CA
619-233-7799
There is a $15 per day pet fee.

Holiday Inn on the Bay
1355 N Harbor Dr
San Diego, CA
619-232-3861
This Holiday Inn has a 5 and 14 story building which overlooks the harbor. Across the street from the hotel is a harborside walkway. There is a $100 pet deposit ($75 refundable and $25 non-refundable).

Homestead Suites
7444 Mission Valley Rd
San Diego, CA
619-299-2292
There is a $75 one time pet fee per visit.

La Quinta Inn San Diego - Rancho Penasquitos
10185 Paseo Montril
San Diego, CA
858-484-8800
Dogs up to 50 pounds are allowed at the hotel.

Marriott San Diego Marina
333 West Harbor Drive
San Diego, CA
619-234-1500
This hotel is right next to the the San Diego Harbor. If you want to stretch your legs, there is also a nice walkway that goes about a mile along the harborside. There

are no pet charges.

Ocean Villa Inn
5142 West Point Loma Blvd.
San Diego, CA
619-224-3481
There is a $100 per deposit for up to 2 pets. Of this $25 is non-refundable and $75 is refundable. There is an additional charge for more than 2 pets.

Pacific Inn Hotel & Suites
1655 Pacific Hwy
San Diego, CA
619-232-6391
There is a $10 per day additional pet fee.

Red Lion Hanalei Hotel
2270 Hotel Circle North
San Diego, CA
619-297-1101
This hotel is located in the heart of Mission Valley. Dogs under 50 pounds are allowed. There is a $50 refundable pet deposit.

Residence Inn
11002 Rancho Carmel Dr
San Diego, CA
858-673-1900
There is a $150 one time pet fee and a $10 per day additional pet fee.

Residence Inn
5995 Pacific Mesa Court
San Diego, CA
858-552-9100
There is a $150 one time pet fee and a $10 per day additional pet fee.

Residence Inn - Downtown
1747 Pacific Highway
San Diego, CA
619-338-8200
There is a $100 one time pet fee and a $10 per day additional pet fee.

Residence Inn by Marriott
5400 Kearny Mesa Rd
San Diego, CA
858-278-2100
This suite style inn is located

north of San Diego. Dinner delivery service is available from local restaurants. Limit two pets per room. They charge a $100 non-refundable pet fee and $7 per day pet charge. Dogs up to 65 pounds are allowed.

San Diego Marriott - Mission Valley
8757 Rio San Diego Dr
San Diego, CA
619-692-3800
This hotel is about 3-4 miles from Old Town State Historic Park and approximately 5-6 miles from the Mission Trails Regional Park. Room service is available. There is a $200 pet deposit ($150 is refundable and $50 is non-refundable.)

San Diego Marriott Suites
701 A Street
San Diego, CA
619-696-9800
There is a $50 one time pet fee per visit.

Sheraton San Diego Hotel and Marina
1380 Harbor Island Drive
San Diego, CA
619-291-2900
Dogs up to 80 pounds are allowed. There are no additional pet fees. Only one dog is permitted per room.

Sheraton Suites San Diego
701 A. Street
San Diego, CA
619-696-9800
Dogs of all sizes are allowed. There is a $100 one time pet fee per stay. There is a $50 refundable deposit per stay for pets.

Staybridge Suites
6639 Mira Mesa Blvd
San Diego, CA
800-238-8000
There is a $75 one time pet fee.

The Hohe House
4905 Dixie Drive

San Diego, CA
858-273-0324
The Hohe (Hoy) House is a spacious, non-smoking, 2 bedroom/2 bath, Ocean View, Private residence in a unique Pacific Beach neighborhood; close to all (Beach, Boardwalk, Restaurants, Nightlife, & Shopping), yet quietly removed from the hubs of activity. The Hohe House sleeps 6 (1 King, 2 Doubles, and a queen sleeper sofa) and is fully furnished with all linens provided. Amenities include: Beach chairs, Beach towels, Boogie boards, Umbrellas, Coolers, & Bicycles for your Beach enjoyment... This is a great dog friendly area. There is a 4 night minimum during the low season, $200 nightly, (Mid-Sept to Mid-June), and rates vary for low to high season, from $1275 to $1875 weekly. Additional 10.5% hotel room tax applies and rates are subject to change. A $350 refundable, security deposit is required to reserve a week's stay and balance is due 30 days prior to arrival. There is a $10 per night pet fee. Well-behaved dogs over 18 months and under 80 pounds are welcome. They will gladly email the entire pet policy to you.

Vagabond Inn-Mission Bay
4540 Mission Bay Dr.
San Diego, CA
858-274-7888
This motel is located within several miles of the Old Town Historic State Park and SeaWorld. It is also close to the popular Dog Beach in Ocean Beach. The motel features an outdoor swimming pool, cable television, guest laundry service and more hotel amenities. There is an additional pet charge of $10 per day.

Vagabond Inn-Point Loma
1325 Scott St.
San Diego, CA
619-224-3371

This motel is located less than five miles from downtown San Diego and Sea World. It is close to the popular Dog Beach in Ocean Beach. The motel features an outdoor swimming pool, family unit rooms, cable television and more hotel amenities. Dogs up to about 70-75 pounds are allowed and there is an additional $10 per day pet fee.

W San Diego
421 West B. Street
San Diego, CA
619-231-8220
Dogs up to 80 pounds are allowed. There is a $100 non-refundable cleaning fee for pets. There is a $25 per night pet fee.

San Francisco

Best Western Tuscan Inn
425 Northpoint Street
San Francisco, CA
415-561-1100
Well-behaved dogs of all sizes are allowed on the first floor only, which consists of half smoking and half non-smoking rooms. There is a $50 one time per stay pet fee.

Campton Place Hotel
340 Stockton Street
San Francisco, CA
415-781-5555
This dog-friendly hotel holds many awards including "Top 100 Hotels in the World" by Conde Nast Traveler. Room rates are approximately $230 to $345 a night. There is a $35 per day additional pet fee.

Days Inn - Lombard St
2358 Lombard Street
San Francisco, CA
415-922-2010
There is a $10 per day pet fee. A well-behaved large dog is okay. Dogs may not be left alone in the rooms and you are responsible for any damage to the room by your pet.

Harbor Court Hotel
165 Steuart Street
San Francisco, CA
415-882-1300
Well-behaved dogs of all sizes are welcome at this pet-friendly hotel. Amenities include a complimentary evening wine reception, and an adjacent fitness room. There are no pet fees, just sign a pet liability form.

Hotel Cosmo
761 Post Street
San Francisco, CA
415-673-6040
Well-behaved dogs of all sizes are welcome at this pet-friendly hotel. The boutique hotel offers both rooms and suites. Hotel amenities include a complimentary evening wine service. There are no pet fees, just sign a pet liability form.

Hotel Juliana
590 Bush Street
San Francisco, CA
415-392-2540
Well-behaved dogs of all sizes are welcome at this pet-friendly hotel. The luxury boutique hotel offers both rooms and suites. Hotel amenities include a complimentary evening wine reception, and a 24 hour on-site fitness room. There are no pet fees, just sign a pet liability form.

Hotel Palomar
12 Fourth Street
San Francisco, CA
415-348-1111
Well-behaved dogs of all sizes are welcome at this pet-friendly hotel. The boutique hotel offers both rooms and suites. Hotel amenities include room service, an on-site 24 hour fitness room and complimentary high speed Internet access. There are no pet fees, just sign a pet liability form. Pets cannot be left alone in the room.

Hotel Triton
342 Grant Avenue
San Francisco, CA
415-394-0500
Well-behaved dogs of all sizes are welcome at this pet-friendly hotel. The boutique hotel offers both rooms and suites. Hotel amenities include a complimentary evening wine reception, room service, and a 24 hour on-site fitness room. There are no pet fees, just sign a pet liability form.

Marina Motel - on Lombard Street
2576 Lombard St.
San Francisco, CA
415-921-9406
All friendly dogs welcome regardless of size. Walk to the Golden Gate Bridge along Crissy Field beach five blocks away. Miles of pastoral hiking trails in the historical Presidio Park one block away. Numerous outdoor dog-friendly cafes around the corner. All rooms have refrigerators, coffee makers, irons and hair dryers. There is a $10 per night per dog pet fee. Dogs may not be left unattended in the room at any time.

Monticello Inn
127 Ellis Street
San Francisco, CA
415-392-8800
Well-behaved dogs of all sizes are welcome at this pet-friendly hotel. The boutique hotel offers both rooms and suites. Hotel amenities include complimentary evening wine service, evening room service, hotel library with magazines, newspapers and books, and a Borders Books and Music room service. There are no pet fees, just sign a pet liability form.

Palace Hotel
2 New Montgomery Street
San Francisco, CA
415-512-1111
There is a $75 one time pet fee.

This is a Sheraton Hotel.

Prescott Hotel
545 Post Street
San Francisco, CA
415-563-0303
Well-behaved dogs of all sizes are allowed at this pet-friendly hotel. The luxury boutique hotel is located in Union Square and offers both rooms and suites. Hotel amenities include room service and an on-site 24 hour fitness room. There are no pet fees, just sign a pet liability form.

Residence Inn
Oyster Point Blvd & 101
San Francisco, CA
650-837-9000
There is a $75 one time pet fee and a $10 per day additional pet fee.

Serrano Hotel
405 Taylor Street
San Francisco, CA
415-885-2500
Well-behaved dogs of all sizes are welcome at this pet-friendly hotel. The luxury boutique hotel offers both rooms and suites. Hotel amenities include an evening hospitality hour, and a 24 hour on-site fitness room. There are no pet fees, just sign a pet liability form.

The Laurel Inn
444 Presidio Ave.
San Francisco, CA
415-567-8467
This pet-friendly hotel is a boutique hotel in San Francisco's atmospheric Pacific Heights neighborhood. This newly renovated hotel includes a classic 1960's modern architectural design. Amenities include a complimentary continental breakfast served daily in the lobby, free indoor parking, laundry and valet service, room service from Dine-One-One and more.

W San Francisco
181 Third Street

San Francisco, CA
415-777-5300
Dogs up to 80 pounds are allowed. There is a $25 per day additional pet fee.

San Jose

Doubletree Hotel
2050 Gateway Pl
San Jose, CA
408-453-4000
Dogs are allowed on the first floor only.

Hilton San Jose
300 Almaden Blvd
San Jose, CA
408-287-2100
Dogs up to 50 pounds are ok. There is a $100 refundable pet deposit required.

Homewood Suites
10 W Trimble Rd
San Jose, CA
408-428-9900
This inn is located in north San Jose, near Milpitas. The inn offers kitchens in each room. There are about half a dozen restaurants next door in a strip mall, many of which have outdoor seating. They require a $275 deposit, and $200 is refundable. The $75 fee is a one time pet charge.

Motel 6 - South
2560 Fontaine Rd
San Jose, CA
408-270-3131
There are no additional pet fees.

Residence Inn - South
6111 San Ignacio Ave
San Jose, CA
408-559-1551
There is a $75 one time pet fee and a $10 per day additional pet fee.

San Luis Obispo

Best Western Royal Oak
214 Madonna Rd.

San Luis Obispo, CA
805-544-4410
This motel is located near Cal Poly. Amenities include a heated pool and jacuzzi, complimentary continental breakfast, guest laundry, wheelchair accessible rooms and more. There is a $10 per day pet charge.

Motel 6 - South
1625 Calle Joaquin
San Luis Obispo, CA
805-541-6992
One pet is permitted per room.

Sands Suites & Motel
1930 Monterey Street
San Luis Obispo, CA
805-544-0500
This motel is close to Cal Poly. Amenities include a heated pool and spa, free continental breakfast, self serve laundry facilities and wheelchair accessibility. There is a $10 one time pet fee.

Vagabond Inn
210 Madonna Rd.
San Luis Obispo, CA
805-544-4710
This motel is located near Cal Poly. Amenities include a heated pool and whirlpool, complimentary continental breakfast, dry cleaning/laundry service and more. There is a $5 per day pet charge.

San Mateo

Residence Inn by Marriott
2000 Winward Way
San Mateo, CA
650-574-4700
This is an apartment style inn that has suite style rooms. There is a $75 non-refundable room cleaning fee for pets and a $6 per day additional pet fee.

San Ramon

Residence Inn - San Ramon
1071 Market Place
San Ramon, CA

925-277-9292
There is a $75 one time pet fee and a $5 per day additional pet fee.

San Ramon Marriott
2600 Bishop Drive
San Ramon, CA
925-867-9200
This Marriott allows dogs of all sizes. They have had Great Danes stay here before. Amenities include room service, self service laundry facilities, gift shop, an outdoor pool, fitness room and more. Room amenities include hairdryers and iron/ironing boards. Thanks to one of our readers for recommending this dog-friendly hotel. There is a $75 one time pet fee for dogs.

San Simeon

Best Western Cavalier Oceanfront Resort
9415 Hearst Drive
San Simeon, CA
805-927-4688
This dog-friendly motel is located next to the beach. Thanks to one of our readers, who has a 95 pound German Shepherd, for recommending this place. The motel sits on a bluff overlooking the ocean. Walk down one of the paths and you'll be on the beach. Amenities include beach access, two pools & a spa, room service, guest laundry facilities and a fitness center. All rooms feature a refrigerator, hair dryer, honor bar, remote cable TV with video cassette player, phone voice mail, and computer port. Some of the rooms offer ocean views with a wet bar, wood-burning fireplace and private patio. If you want to sit outside, there are firepits, surrounded by chairs which overlook the ocean. The firepits are lit at sunset and left burning through the night for those folks that want to enjoy the fire, the sound of the ocean

and the distant light from the Piedras Blancas Lighthouse. There are no additional pet fees. All rooms are non-smoking.

Motel 6
9070 Castillo Dr
San Simeon, CA
805-927-8691
A large well-behaved dog is okay. Dogs may not be left alone in the room.

Silver Surf Motel
9390 Castillo Drive
San Simeon, CA
805-927-4661
This coastal motel is situated around a courtyard in a park like setting. There are beautiful flower gardens, majestic pine trees, and scenic ocean views. Some rooms offer private balconies, fireplaces or ocean views. Amenities include an indoor pool & spa, and guest laundry facility. There is a $10 per day pet charge.

San Ysidro

Motel 6 - Border
160 E Calie Primera
San Ysidro, CA
619-690-6663
This hotel is very close to the Mexican border in San Diego.

Santa Ana

Red Roof Inn
2600 N Main Street
Santa Ana, CA
714-542-0311
There is a $10 one time pet fee.

Santa Barbara

Casa Del Mar Hotel
18 Bath Street
Santa Barbara, CA
805-963-4418
This popular Mediterranean-style inn is within walking distance of several restaurants,

shops and parks. Amenities include a relaxing courtyard Jacuzzi and sun deck surrounded by lush gardens year round. All rooms are non-smoking and equipped with a writing desk and chair or table, telephone, color TV with remote control, and private bathroom. There is a 2 or 3 night minimum stay on the weekends. Pets are welcome. They allow up to two pets per room and there is a $10 per pet charge. Pets must never be left alone or unattended, especially in the rooms. Children under 12 are free and there is no charge for a crib. State Street, a popular shopping area, is within walking distance.

Fess Parker's Doubletree Resort
633 E. Cabrillo Boulevard
Santa Barbara, CA
805-564-4333
This beautiful 24 acre ocean front Spanish-style tropical resort allows your best friend in the elegant rooms. This especially pet-friendly resort includes special amenities for your best friend like a gourmet pet welcome gift at check-in and an in-room pet service menu available- this includes ground sirloin (for dogs) and seared ahi tuna (for cats). Their spa even offers pet treatments such as massages. Other hotel amenities for people include a fitness room, 24 hour room service, coin laundry, a walking path around the resort, a heated outdoor pool (dogs are not allowed in the pool area) and more. Room amenities include private patios or balconies, hairdryers, newspapers, private stocked refrigerator, modem lines and more. Room rates range from approximately $179 to $270 and up per night. There is no additional pet charge. This resort is within walking distance of several restaurants, shops and parks.

Montecito Del Mar
316 W Montecito St
Santa Barbara, CA
805-962-2006
There is a $10 per day pet fee.
Dogs up to 50 pounds are
permitted.

San Ysidro Ranch
900 San Ysidro Lane
Santa Barbara, CA
805-969-5046
This is an especially dog-friendly
upscale resort located in Santa
Barbara. They offer many dog
amenities including a Privileged
Pet Program doggie turn down
and several miles of trails and
exercise areas. Pet Massage
Service is available. Choose
from the Slow & Gentle
Massage or the Authentic Reiki
massage for your dog. Dogs are
allowed in the freestanding
cottages and prices start around
$600 and up per night. There is
a $100 per pet non-refundable
cleaning fee.

Secret Garden Inn & Cottages
1908 Bath Street
Santa Barbara, CA
805-687-2300
Dogs are allowed in the cabins
only. There is a $50 refundable
pet deposit.

Santa Clara

Guesthouse Inn & Suites
2930 El Camino Real
Santa Clara, CA
408-241-3010
All rooms have microwaves and
refrigerators. There is a $10 per
day additional pet fee.

Marriott Hotel
2700 Mission College Blvd
Santa Clara, CA
408-988-1500
Dogs are allowed on the first
floor only. There is a $100
refundable pet deposit.

Santa Cruz

1600 West Cliff
1600 West Cliff Drive
Santa Cruz, CA
408-266-4453
Want to stay across the street
from the ocean in beautiful
Santa Cruz? 1600 West Cliff is
a private 3 bedroom, 2 bath
vacation rental home with
lodging for 1 to 8 people. Relax
on the enclosed back patio, or
grab a chair and sit on the front
yard patio and enjoy the
beautiful ocean view. The living
room faces the ocean and the
kitchen is fully stocked. The
West Cliff Drive Walkway is
located directly across the
street on the ocean side. This
is a nice 2 mile walking and
running path. West Lighthouse
Beach, a leash free dog beach,
is also located nearby. The
owners of this vacation home
are true dog lovers and believe
the family dog should be
welcome. Rates start at $350
per night and up. There is a 2
day minimum. A $500 security
deposit is required, but can be
charged on a credit card. To
get there, head south on Hwy
17. Take the Hwy 1 North exit,
heading towards Half Moon
Bay and Hwy 9. Merge onto
Mission Street (Hwy 1). Turn
left onto Swift Street, and then
turn right on West Cliff Drive.

Beach Bungalow Vacation Rentals
Call to Arrange.
Santa Cruz, CA
831-469-6161
This rental company offers
year-round vacation rental
accommodations in Santa Cruz
and Capitola. Many of their
vacation rental homes are dog-
friendly. They offer a nice
selection of beach-front and
ocean view homes. You may
also call 877-557-2567 to
arrange.

Edgewater Beach Motel
525 Second Street
Santa Cruz, CA

831-423-0440
This motel has ocean views,
beach views, and 17 uniquely
designed suites (for one to eight
people). Some of the rooms
have ocean views, microwaves,
refrigerators. A couple of the
rooms have fireplaces, private
lawns and full kitchens. Non-
smoking rooms are available.
While dogs are not allowed on
the Boardwalk or on the nearby
beach, they are allowed on the
West Cliff Drive Walkway. Walk
to the waterfront, then go north
(away from the Boardwalk)
along the sidewalk on the street
closest to the ocean. It will
become a walkway that is used
by walkers, joggers and
bicyclists. If you walk about 1
1/2 - 2 miles, you'll reach several
dog beaches (see Parks). To get
to the motel, take Hwy 17 south.
Take the Hwy 1 North exit. Then
take the Ocean St exit on the left
towards the beaches. Head
towards the beach on Ocean St
and then turn right on San
Lorenzo Blvd. Turn left on
Riverside Ave and then right on
2nd St. The motel will be on the
left. Ample parking is available
in their parking lot. There is a
$20 one time additional pet fee.

Guesthouse International
330 Ocean Street
Santa Cruz, CA
831-425-3722
There is a $10 per day pet fee.

Redtail Ranch by the Sea
Call to Arrange.
Santa Cruz, CA
831-429-1322
This 3 bedroom, 1 1/2 bath
ranch house is located on a 72
acre horse ranch, the Redtail
Ranch. The house features a
180 degree ocean view of the
Monterey Bay and views of the
coastal hills. The house sleeps 1
to 8 people and comes with a
complete full kitchen. The home
is located about a 5 minute drive
to local beaches, a 1 hour drive
to Monterey, Carmel and Big

Sur, and a 1 1/2 hour scenic coastal drive to San Francisco. The rental is available year-round for nightly, weekly, and extended vacation rentals.

Santa Maria

Best Western Big America
1725 North Broadway
Santa Maria, CA
805-922-5200
Thanks to one of our readers for recommending this hotel. Here is what they had to say about it: "We stayed here with our Lab last month and were very pleased. There was no extra charge for our dog and it was one of the nicest rooms we have ever stayed in. The room rates are very reasonable. It's just outside the wine tasting trail for those who want a day of picnics and wine tasting." Dogs are not to be left alone in the rooms.

Motel 6
2040 N Preisker Lane
Santa Maria, CA
805-928-8111
There are no additional pet fees.

Santa Monica

Le Merigot Beach Hotel and Spa
1740 Ocean Avenue
Santa Monica, CA
310-395-9700
The hotel provides pet dishes and toys upon arrival. There is a $35 one time pet fee. There is also a $150 refundable pet deposit.

Loews Santa Monica Beach Hotel
1700 Ocean Avenue
Santa Monica, CA
310-458-6700
All well-behaved dogs of any size are welcome. This upscale hotel offers their "Loews Loves Pets" program which includes special pet treats, local dog walking routes, and a list of

nearby pet-friendly places to visit. There are no pet fees.

Santa Nella

Holiday Inn Express
28976 W. Plaza Drive
Santa Nella, CA
209-826-8282
There are no additional pet fees.

Motel 6
12733 S Hwy 33
Santa Nella, CA
209-826-6644
There are no additional pet fees.

Ramada Inn
13070 S Hwy 33
Santa Nella, CA
209-826-4444
There is a $10 per night additional pet fee.

Santa Rosa

Comfort Inn
2632 Cleveland Ave
Santa Rosa, CA
707-542-5544
There is a $10 per day pet fee.

Days Inn
3345 Santa Rosa Ave
Santa Rosa, CA
707-568-1011
There is a $10 per day additional pet fee.

Hilton Sonoma County
3555 Round Barn Blvd
Santa Rosa, CA
707-523-7555
Located in the heart of Sonoma's wine country, this hotel is nestled on a hillside with 13 acres of landscaped grounds. There is a $15 per day pet charge.

Los Robles Lodge
1985 Cleveland Ave
Santa Rosa, CA
707-545-6330
Dogs are allowed, but not in the

pool-side rooms or executive suites. There is a $10 per day pet charge.

Motel 6 - North
3145 Cleveland Ave
Santa Rosa, CA
707-525-9010
A large well maintained and well-behaved dog is okay.

Motel 6 - South
2760 Cleveland Ave
Santa Rosa, CA
707-546-1500
One pet per room is permitted.

Santa Rosa Motor Inn
1800 Santa Rosa Ave
Santa Rosa, CA
707-523-3480
There is a $10 per day pet fee and a refundable pet deposit.

Scotts Valley

Hilton Scotts Valley
6001 La Madrona Dr
Scotts Valley, CA
831-440-1000
There is a $25 per day pet fee.

Selma

Best Western Selma Inn
2799 Floral Avenue
Selma, CA
559-891-0300
There is a $20 one time pet charge. Dogs are allowed in certain pet rooms.

Solvang

Royal Copenhagen Inn
1579 Mission Drive
Solvang, CA
800-624-6604
This inn is located in the heart of the Solvang village. Walk to dog-friendly restaurants, stores and parks. Well-behaved dogs are allowed. There is no pet fee.

Sonoma

Best Western Sonoma Valley
550 Second St. West
Sonoma, CA
707-938-9200
This motel is within walking distance of the small downtown shopping area in Sonoma. Amenities include a gift bottle of wine, complimentary continental breakfast delivered to your room, heated pool and more. Room amenities include refrigerators and a fireplace or jacuzzi. Room rates start at $130 per night and up. There is a $20 per day pet charge. The entire hotel is non-smoking.

Villa Castillo
1100 Castle Rd
Sonoma, CA
707-996-4616
Vacation rental cottage on a three acre landscaped estate available by the month, week, or day. Includes a full kitchen and use of the lap pool/hot tub. Queen bed, full kitchen, cable, phone, fireplace, BBQ and fenced patio. The Olive Grove Cottage is pet-friendly. Please follow the pet rules: any damages will be the responsibility of the dog owner, clean up after pets, pets must be leashed whenever outside the cottage and fenced patio (there is a resident cat, so dogs must not run free), pets not allowed on the bed, and no barking dogs.

Sonora

Best Western Sonora Oaks
19551 Hess Avenue
Sonora, CA
209-533-4400
There is a $10 per day pet charge. They are located within a short drive of the dog-friendly Columbia State Historic Park.

Sonora Aladdin Motor Inn
14260 Mono Way (Hwy 108)
Sonora, CA

209-533-4971
This motel's rooms offer Southwest decor with king or queen sized beds, table & chairs, refrigerators, coffee makers, climate control, cable TV & HBO, and direct dial phones with free local & credit card calls. They also feature a guest laundry. Dogs are welcome with a $5 one time charge. The motel is about an hour and a half from Yosemite.

Soquel

Blue Spruce Inn Bed and Breakfast
2815 Main Street
Soquel, CA
831-464-1137
A well-behaved dog is allowed in the Secret Garden Room. This room offers a private enclosed garden that includes an outdoor hot tub for two, a small sitting area with gas fireplace and comfortable reading chairs, private bathroom and more. There is a $25 one time pet charge. Please abide by the following pet rules. If your dog will be allowed on the furniture, please cover it first with a sheet. If you take your pooch to the dog beach, please rinse him or her off in the outside hot and cold shower before entering the room. This bed and breakfast does offer a VIP (Very Important Pets) program for your pooch. This includes a dog bone, water bowl and poop bags upon arrival.

South Lake Tahoe

Accommodation Station
2516 Lake Tahoe Blvd.
South Lake Tahoe, CA
530-542-5850
The Accommodation Station is a property management company that rents out vacation homes, cabins, and condos in the South Lake

Tahoe area. Each unit is completely furnished and features a fully equipped kitchen and fireplace. There are also many parks and hikes in the area that allow dogs (see Lake Tahoe Parks). They have a few properties that currently allow pets, but are working on getting more owners to accommodate the dog-friendly demand. They do not charge guests for pets in a particular property, but do charge a fully refundable security deposit provided no damage occurs. To find out which properties allow dogs, call 800-344-9364 or send an email to stay@tahoelodging.com. They will find out which rentals allow your pup.

Alder Inn
1072 Ski Run Blvd.
South Lake Tahoe, CA
530-544-4485
This dog-friendly motel can schedule their local pet-sitter to watch your dog if you want to try your luck at the casinos. The sitter will take care of your pup in the motel room. There is a $12 per day pet fee.

Colony Inn at South Lake Tahoe
3794 Montreal Road
South Lake Tahoe, CA
530-544-6481
The Colony Inn at South Lake Tahoe is located just 1.5 blocks from Harrah's and the other casinos and just down the street from Heavenly Ski Resort. Want to experience the beautiful outdoors? The Colony Inn's backyard is National Forest Land, featuring dog-friendly hiking, mountain biking, and peace and quiet. There is a $25 refundable pet deposit, and pets cannot be left unattended in the rooms.

Fireside Lodge
515 Emerald Bay Rd.
South Lake Tahoe, CA
530-544-5515

This inn offers log cabin style suites. The rooms have a unique "Country Mountain" theme decor with crafted fireplaces, and custom woodwork. Each room offers a microwave, refrigerator and coffee-maker, private bath w/shower, cable TV and VCR with numerous free videos available in their Gathering Room. Full kitchen units are available as well as private 1 to 4 bedroom cabins, off the property. There is a $20 per day pet charge.

Inn at Heavenly B&B

1261 Ski Run Boulevard
South Lake Tahoe, CA
530-544-4244
You and your dog are welcome at this log-cabin style bed and breakfast lodge. The property is all dog-friendly and dogs are allowed everywhere but their Gathering Room. They offer 14 individual rooms each with a private bath and shower. Room conveniences include refrigerators, microwaves and VCRs. Some rooms have a fireplace. Three to four bedroom cabins are also available. The lodge is located on a 2-acre wooded park complete with picnic areas, BBQs and log swings. Continental breakfast is served and snacks are available throughout the day. One large dog is allowed per room and pet charges apply. Room rates range from the low to mid $100s per night. Call for cabin prices. The owners have friendly dogs on the premises. The lodge is located in South Lake Tahoe. There is a $20 per day pet fee per pet.

Lake Tahoe Accommodations

Call to Arrange.
South Lake Tahoe, CA
800-544-3234
This vacation home company offers luxury vacation rentals. Many are located near Lake Tahoe's world class golf courses and ski resorts. They have three

pet-friendly vacation units. There are no extra pet fees.

Salsa's Chalet

South Lake Tahoe, CA
707-565-3740
This 2 bedroom, 1 bathroom vacation cabin rental is dog-friendly. Heavenly Ski Resort and major casinos are within one and a half miles of this cabin. It is a non-smoking cabin. Families, couples and children are welcome. Dogs are welcome with a $100 refundable pet deposit.

Sandor's Chateau Motel

1137 Emerald Bay Road
South Lake Tahoe, CA
530-541-6312
This pet-friendly motel is located on the quiet end of South Lake Tahoe just as you come into town on Highway 50, away from the congestion and noise of the casinos. They are situated in a park-like setting just minutes from beautiful Lake Tahoe. There are no extra pet charges.

South Lake Tahoe Vacation Rental

Call to arrange.
South Lake Tahoe, CA
415-388-8170
This two story chalet vacation home rental is located in a residential neighborhood close to Lake Tahoe, Camp Richardson beach, and Emerald Bay. It has three bedrooms and two bathrooms, a yard and a deck. A well-behaved dog is allowed. There is a $10 per day pet charge and a $100 refundable pet deposit.

Spruce Grove Cabins

P.O. Box 16390
South Lake Tahoe, CA
530-544-0549
Spruce Grove puts you amidst a private, quiet secluded mountain resort off Ski Run Blvd., at the foot of Heavenly

Ski Area and walking distance from Lake Tahoe. Spruce Grove offers private cabins and suites, with shady grounds for relaxing or BBQs. Close to shopping, restaurants, skiing, biking, hiking, entertainment and casinos. Children and well-behaved dogs are welcome. This dog friendly retreat is a fully fenced acre of land that is next to an open field of pine trees. There is a dog beach at the lake and lots of places to hike with your dogs. There is a $10 per night pet fee and a $100 refundable pet deposit ($25 for cleaning and $75 for damage). Please review the pet policy on the website or ask when making a reservation.

Stonehenge Vacation Properties

Call to Arrange.
South Lake Tahoe, CA
800-822-1460
This vacation rental company offers several elegant and unique dog-friendly vacation homes located around South Lake Tahoe.

Super 8 Motel

3600 Lake Tahoe Blvd.
South Lake Tahoe, CA
530-544-3476
This motel offers good size rooms and a nice front lawn where you can walk your dog or sit at the various tables. There is a restaurant on the premises with a few outdoor picnic tables. They sometimes serve food outside - I guess it depends on how many waiters/waitresses they have. At night, you can walk up to the bar window, place your order, and then sit outside at the picnic tables with your dog while you enjoy a beer or wine. The motel also has an outdoor pool and spa. Pets are allowed only on the first floor of this two story accommodation, so if you are looking for a non-smoking room, call ahead as they tend to fill up fast. It's located on Hwy

50, west of Ski Run Blvd. There is a $10 per day pet fee per pet.

Tahoe Keys Resort
599 Tahoe Keys Blvd
South Lake Tahoe, CA
530-544-5397
They feature approximately 50 pet friendly cabins, condos and homes in South Lake Tahoe. All dogs receive treats upon check-in. A $25.00 pet fee is taken per reservation. There is also a $100.00 refundable security deposit upon check in.

The Nash Cabin
Shirley Avenue
South Lake Tahoe, CA
415-759-6583
This two bedroom, two bath cabin has everything you need; hot tub, wood stove, fire wood, full kitchen. They provide linens and towels and clean up after your stay. The cabin is located on a quiet street with a large fenced yard that backs onto a sunlit meadow. Dogs are welcome with a $100 pet deposit. There are miles of dog-friendly forest hikes within a five minute drive.

South San Francisco

Howard Johnson Express Inn
222 South Airport Blvd.
South San Francisco, CA
650-589-9055
Dogs of all sizes are welcome. There is a $10 per day pet fee.

La Quinta Inn South San Francisco
20 Airport Blvd
South San Francisco, CA
650-583-2223
Dogs up to 75 pounds are allowed at the hotel.

Motel 6
111 Mitchell Ave.
South San Francisco, CA
650-871-0770
Pets are allowed, but they are not to be left in the room alone.

There is no extra pet charge.

Vagabond Inn
222 S. Airport Blvd
South San Francisco, CA
650-589-9055
Amenities include microwaves and refrigerators in some rooms. There is a $10 per day pet charge. This inn was formerly a Howard Johnson Inn.

Squaw Valley

Squaw Valley Chalet
1730 Navajo Ct
Squaw Valley, CA
530-550-8600
With views of Squaw Valley's Mountains, this is a comfortable one bedroom home. Granite counters, a jetted tub, new big screen TV, large deck with B.B.Q. and a plush leather couch are just a few of the upgrades to make you feel at home. Dogs are welcomed with a squeaky toy, dog cookies, clean dog towel, furniture sheet and more. Dogs stay Free!!!

St Helena

El Bonita Motel
195 Main Street
St Helena, CA
707-963-3216
Amenities at this motel include a continental breakfast, pool, whirlpool, sauna, and over two acres of peaceful gardens. Room amenities include microwaves, refrigerators, and more. Room rates start at about $130 per night and up. There is a $5 per day pet charge.

Harvest Inn
One Main Street
St Helena, CA
707-963-9463
This inn is nestled among 8-acres of award winning landscape. Most guest rooms feature wet bars, unique brick fireplaces and private terraces.

Amenities include two outdoor heated pools and whirlpool spas and jogging and bike trails bordering the grounds. Dogs are allowed in the standard rooms. There is a $75 one time pet charge.

Stinson Beach

Beach Front Retreat
90 Calle Del Ribera
Stinson Beach, CA
415-383-7870
This vacation home rental offers 3 bedrooms, 2 baths, a fireplace and a beach deck with BBQ. You can view the ocean from the balcony located next to the master bedroom. There is an additional $50 one time per stay pet charge

Stockton

La Quinta Inn Stockton
2710 West March Lane
Stockton, CA
209-952-7800
Dogs of all sizes are allowed at the hotel.

Motel 6 - Southeast
1625 French Camp Turnpike Rd
Stockton, CA
209-467-3600
There are no additional pet fees.

Motel 6 - West
817 Navy Drive
Stockton, CA
209-946-0923
Dogs must be attended at all times.

Residence Inn - Stockton
March Lane & Brookside
Stockton, CA
209-472-9800
There is a $60 one time pet fee and a $10 per day additional pet fee. Dogs are not allowed in the lobby.

Seven Crown Resorts Houseboats
8095 Rio Blanco Road

Stockton, CA
800-752-9669
Rent a houseboat on the California Delta and bring your dog too. The California Delta offers rivers, tributaries and channels for your houseboating experience. The waterways were used by the miners and settlers who came to California for the 1884 Gold Rush. Pets are welcome on houseboats at no additional charge. Advance reservations are required. Call 800-752-9669 to make your reservation.

Travelodge
1707 Fremont St
Stockton, CA
209-466-7777
There is a $25 refundable pet deposit.

Sunnyvale

Maple Tree Inn
711 E. El Camino Real
Sunnyvale, CA
408-720-9700
Dogs of all sizes are allowed. There are no additional pet fees.

Residence Inn - SV I
750 Lakeway
Sunnyvale, CA
408-720-1000
There is a $75 one time pet fee and a $10 per day additional pet fee. This hotel is called Residence Inn, Sunnyvale - Silicon Valley I.

Residence Inn - SV II
1080 Stewart Dr
Sunnyvale, CA
408-720-8893
There is a $75 one time pet fee and a $10 per day additional pet fee. This hotel is called Residence Inn - Sunnyvale, Silicon Valley II.

Summerfield Suites
900 Hamlin Court
Sunnyvale, CA
408-745-1515

There is a $150 one time pet fee. 1 and 2 bedroom suites are available.

Woodfin Suite Hotel
635 E. El Camino Real
Sunnyvale, CA
408-738-1700
All well-behaved dogs are welcome. All rooms are suites with full kitchens. Hotel amenities include a heated pool. There is a $5 per day pet fee.

Sunset Beach

Pelican's Nest Ocean Front House

Sunset Beach, CA
831-685-3500
This spacious ocean front flat, located at Sunset Beach, between Santa Cruz and Monterey welcomes dogs. It is right at the beach in the middle of a state park with lots of dog-friendly trails. The owners two dogs, Amy and Daisy, enjoy weekly visitors and are disappointed when visitors don't bring their dogs with them. A pet departure fee of $100 is required. Rates start at $250 per night and up for the vacation rental.

Susanville

Budget Host Frontier Inn
2685 Main St
Susanville, CA
530-257-4141
There are no additional pet fees.

River Inn
1710 Main St
Susanville, CA
530-257-6051
There is an $11 per day additional pet fee. One large dog per room is allowed.

Tahoe City

Tahoe Moon Properties
P.O. Box 7521
Tahoe City, CA
530-581-2771
They have over 15 beautiful homes that allow well-behaved dogs. All of the houses are close to Tahoe City or ski areas. Bath and bed linens are provided. There are a few dog rules; no dogs on the furniture, dogs are not to be left alone in the house, you must clean up after your dog and pet owners are responsible for any damages. Rates start at $150 per night with a 2 night minimum. There is a $30 per dog charge.

West Lake Properties
55 West Lake Blvd., P.O. Box 1768
Tahoe City, CA
530-583-0268
Dogs are allowed in two of their vacation home rentals. The Log Cabin is within walking distance of Tahoe City and the Banovich Home, with a fenced yard for your dog, is located near Tahoe City.

Tahoe Vista

Rustic Cottages
7449 North Lake Blvd
Tahoe Vista, CA
530-546-3523
There is a $10 per day pet fee.

Tahoma

Norfolk Woods Inn
6941 West Lake Blvd.
Tahoma, CA
530-525-5000
This inn only allows dogs in the cabins...but your pup won't mind. They have wonderful cozy cottages with kitchens. They only have 4 cabins, so call ahead. Also note that the entire premises is smoke free. Located directly in front of this inn is the Tahoe bike trail where you and your pup can walk or run for

several miles. The trail is mostly paved except for a small dirt path section. The inn is located approx. 8-9 miles south of Tahoe City on Hwy 89. There is a $10 per day additional pet fee per pet.

Tahoma Meadows Bed and Breakfast
6821 W. Lake Blvd.
Tahoma, CA
530-525-1553
A well-behaved dog is allowed only if you let them know in advance that you are bringing your dog. Pets are allowed in one of their cabins, the Mountain Hideaway (previously known as Dogwood). This cabin includes a Queen bed, a fireplace, claw foot soaking tub, private deck and an efficiency kitchen. There is an extra $25 one time pet charge per stay, plus a security deposit. Cabin rates start at $145 per night.

Tehachapi

Best Western Mountain Inn
416 West Tehachapi Boulevard
Tehachapi, CA
661-822-5591
There are no extra pet charges.

Travelodge
500 Steuber Rd
Tehachapi, CA
661-823-8000
There is a $7 per day pet fee.

Temecula

Comfort Inn
27338 Jefferson Ave.
Temecula, CA
909-296-3788
There is a $20 per night pet charge.

Motel 6
41900 Moreno Rd
Temecula, CA
909-676-6383
One well-behaved dog per room is allowed.

Temecula Vacation Rental
Call to Arrange.
Temecula, CA
310-390-7778
Pets are allowed at this two bedroom, two bathroom condo vacation rental located in Southern California's wine country. The condo offers central air conditioning and heating. There are no pet fees.

Thousand Oaks

Motel 6
1516 Newbury Rd
Thousand Oaks, CA
805-499-0711
One pet per room is permitted.

Thousand Oaks Inn
75 W. Thousand Oaks Blvd.
Thousand Oaks, CA
805-497-3701
This motel allows both dogs and cats. They have a $75 non-refundable pet deposit.

Three Rivers

Best Western Holiday Lodge
40105 Sierra Dr
Three Rivers, CA
559-561-4119
There are no additional pet fees.

Torrance

Residence Inn - Torrance
3701 Torrance Blvd
Torrance, CA
310-543-4566
There is a $40 one time pet fee and a $8 per day additional pet fee. There is also a $4 per day fee for each additional pet.

Tracy

Motel 6
3810 Tracy Blvd
Tracy, CA
209-836-4900

There are no additional pet fees.

Truckee

Andrea's Grinnin Bear Cabin
Call to Arrange.
Truckee, CA
530-582-8703
Located on a quiet cul-de-sac on a pine tree lot, this spacious 3 bedroom home is available for rent to people with pets. Nearby there are dog walks, hikes and places to explore. The Truckee river, Mardis Creek, Donner Lake and beach, Boca, Stampede and Prosser Reservoirs are all less than 15 minutes away.

Fore Paw Cottage
14906 Davos Drive
Truckee, CA
530-587-4082
A cottage in a peaceful setting with fantastic views of Tahoe Donner golf course. Sleeps 6 comfortably with two queen beds, one king bed plus a bunk bed and a pull out queen bed. There is a maximum of two dogs, which always stay free. There is skiing at any of six major downhill ski areas located within 15 minutes.

The Inn at Truckee
11506 Deerfield Drive
Truckee, CA
530-587-8888
The Inn at Truckee specializes in relaxed accommodations and fun filled days for Truckee Tahoe Visitors. North Lake Tahoe resorts are located within a few minutes of this inn's doorstep. There is a $11 per day pet charge.

Tulare

Best Western Town and Country
1051 N Blackstone Ave
Tulare, CA
559-688-7537
Dogs may not be left alone in

the rooms.

Days Inn
1183 N Blackstone St
Tulare, CA
559-686-0985
There is a $5 per day pet fee.

Howard Johnson Express Inn
1050 E Rankin Ave
Tulare, CA
559-688-6671
There is a $6 per day pet fee.

Motel 6
1111 N Blackstone Dr
Tulare, CA
559-686-6374
There are no additional pet fees.

Turlock

Best Western Orchard Inn
5025 N Golden State Blvd
Turlock, CA
209-667-2827
There is a $25 one time pet fee
per visit.

Motel 6
250 S Walnut Ave
Turlock, CA
209-667-4100
A large well-behaved dog is
okay.

Twentynine Palms

**Best Western Garden Inn &
Suites**
71487 Twentynine Palms
Highway
Twentynine Palms, CA
760-367-9141
There is a $10 per day pet
charge and a $100 refundable
pet deposit.

Ukiah

Days Inn
950 North State St
Ukiah, CA
707-462-7584
There is a $5 per day pet fee.

Motel 6
1208 S State Street
Ukiah, CA
707-468-5404
There are no additional pet
fees.

Universal City

Sheraton Universal Hotel
333 Universal Hollywood Drive
Universal City, CA
818-980-1212
Dogs up to 80 pounds are
allowed. There are no
additional pet fees.

Vacaville

Residence Inn
360 Orange Dr
Vacaville, CA
707-469-0300
There is a $100 one time pet
fee and a $10 per day
additional pet fee.

Super 8 Motel - Vacaville
101 Allison Court
Vacaville, CA
707-449-8884
$10/stay for up to 3 dogs in one
room. FREE 8-minute long
distance call each night. FREE
continental breakfast. Coffee
maker, night light, clock/radio,
safe in each room. Seasonal
outdoor pool. On-site guest
laundry. Kids 12 & under stay
free. I-80, Monte Vista Exit to
Allison Drive, then Allison
Court. Motel is behind Wendy's.

Vallejo

Holiday Inn
1000 Fairgrounds Dr
Vallejo, CA
707-644-1200
There is a $25 one time pet fee.
Dogs are allowed only on the
first floor.

Ventura

Best Western Inn of Ventura
708 E. Thompson Blvd.
Ventura, CA
805-648-3101
Amenities at this motel include
an outdoor pool & hot tub, and a
free continental breakfast. There
is a $25 per day pet charge up
to a maximum of $50 per visit.

La Quinta Inn Ventura
5818 Valentine Road
Ventura, CA
805-658-6200
Dogs of all sizes are allowed at
the hotel.

Motel 6
2145 E Harbor Blvd
Ventura, CA
805-643-5100
There are no additional pet fees.

Vagabond Inn
756 E. Thompson Blvd.
Ventura, CA
805-648-5371
Amenities at this motel include a
free continental breakfast,
weekday newspaper, and
heated jacuzzi. They also have
an on-site coffee shop, which
might be helpful in getting food
to go for the room. There is a
$10 per day pet fee. Dogs are
allowed in a few of the non-
smoking rooms.

Victorville

Howard Johnson Express Inn
16868 Stoddard Wells Rd.
Victorville, CA
760-243-7700
Dogs of all sizes are welcome.
There is a $10 per day pet fee
per pet.

Ramada Inn
15494 Palmdale Road
Victorville, CA
760-245-6565
There is a $25 one time pet fee.

Red Roof Inn
13409 Mariposa Rd
Victorville, CA

760-241-1577
There is a $10 one time pet fee.

Visalia

Holiday Inn
9000 W. Airport Drive
Visalia, CA
559-651-5000
There is a $25 one time pet fee.

Super 8
4801 W Noble Ave
Visalia, CA
559-627-2885
A large well-behaved dog is
okay. Sequoia National Park is
50 miles away.

Vista

La Quinta Inn Vista
630 Sycamore Avenue
Vista, CA
760-727-8180
Dogs up to 75 pounds are
allowed at the hotel.

Volcano

The St. George Hotel
16104 Main Street
Volcano, CA
209-296-4458
A well-behaved large dog is
allowed in one of the bungalow
rooms. The non-smoking pet-
friendly room has hardwood
floors, a queen bed, a private
bath and garden views. Upon
arrival, your pooch will receive
treats and an extra blanket.
There is a $20 per day pet
charge.

Walnut Creek

Holiday Inn
2730 N Main Street
Walnut Creek, CA
925-932-3332
There is a $25 one time pet fee.

Watsonville

Best Western Inn
740 Freedom Boulevard
Watsonville, CA
831-724-3367
There is a $5 per day pet
charge.

Red Roof Inn
1620 West Beach Street
Watsonville, CA
831-740-4520
There are no additional pet
fees.

Weed

Holiday Inn Express
1830 Black Butte Drive
Weed, CA
530-938-1308
There is a $10 one time pet fee.
A well-behaved large dog is
okay.

Lake Shastina Golf Resort
5925 Country Club Drive
Weed, CA
530-938-3201
Dogs are allowed in some of
the condos at this 18 hole golf
course resort. There is a $25
one time pet charge.

West Covina

Hampton Inn
3145 E. Garvey Ave
West Covina, CA
626-967-5800
There are no additional pet
fees.

Westley

Days Inn
7144 McCracken Rd
Westley, CA
209-894-5500
There is a $10 per day
additional pet fee.

Econo Lodge
7100 McCracken Rd
Westley, CA
209-894-3900
There is a $10 per day pet fee.

Super 8
7115 McCracken Rd
Westley, CA
209-894-3888
There is a $5 per day additional
pet fee.

Westport

Howard Creek Ranch Inn B&B
40501 N. Highway 1
Westport, CA
707-964-6725
Howard Creek Ranch is a
historic, 40 acre ocean front
farm located about 5-6 hours
north of San Francisco.
Accommodations include
cabins, suites and rooms. It is
bordered by miles of beach and
mountains. They offer award
winning gardens, fireplaces or
wood stoves, farm animals, a
hot tub, and a sauna. Dog-
friendly beaches nearby include
Westport Union Landing State
Beach in Westport,
MacKerricher State Park 3-4
miles north of Fort Bragg and
the 60 mile Sinkyone Wilderness
Area (Lost Coast). Outdoor
restaurants nearby are Jenny's
Giant Burgers and Sea Pal (in
Fort Bragg). Room rates are $80
and up (includes a full hearty
ranch breakfast). There is a $10
plus tax per day pet charge.
Certain dog rules apply: don't
leave your dog alone in the
room, dogs must be supervised
and attended at all times, bring
towels to clean up your pooch if
he/she gets dirty from outside,
clean up after your dog, and if
your dog will be on the bed,
please use a sheet to cover the
quilt (sheets can be provided).
The inn is located 3 miles north
of Westport.

Williams

Comfort Inn
400 C St
Williams, CA
530-473-2381

There is a $5 per day pet fee.

Motel 6
455 4th Street
Williams, CA
530-473-5337
A large well-behaved dog is okay.

Willows

Best Western Gold Pheasant Inn
249 North Humboldt Avenue
Willows, CA
530-934-4603
There is a $10 per day pet charge. Guests are responsible for any damage caused by pets.

Days Inn
475 N Humboldt Ave
Willows, CA
530-934-4444
There is a $5 per day additional pet fee.

Super 8
457 Humboldt Ave
Willows, CA
530-934-2871
There is a $20 refundable pet deposit.

Woodlake

Wickyup Bed and Breakfast Cottage
22702 Avenue 344
Woodlake, CA
559-564-8898
Dogs are allowed in the Calico Room Cottage. It offers bunk beds, a half-bath, and a discrete, enclosed outdoor shower. The cottage is located in the garden and has a private entrance.

Woodland

Motel 6
1564 Main Street
Woodland, CA
530-666-6777
There are no additional pet fees.

Sacramento - Days Inn
1524 East Main Street
Woodland, CA
530-666-3800
There is a $10 per day pet fee.

Woodland Hills

Vagabond Inn
20157 Ventura Blvd.
Woodland Hills, CA
818-347-8080
Amenities at this motel include a heated pool and a free breakfast. An adjacent coffee shop is open 24 hours a day, which might be helpful for getting food to go. There is a $5 per day pet fee.

Yorkville

Sheep Dung Estates
P.O. Box 49
Yorkville, CA
707-894-5322
This unique country hideaway has five private cottages on 320 acres in beautiful Anderson Valley. It is located about 1 1/2 hours from Mendocino and 2 hours north of San Francisco. The property has hiking trails and a swimming pond. The cottages are solar powered and eco-friendly. Each cottage is at the end of its own private driveway on l0 to 40 acres. This is such a popular spot for dogs and dog owners that the cottages usually book out well in advance. Dogs and children are welcome. There are no size restrictions for dogs, and the only requirement is that you place a sheet to cover the down comforter if your canine gets on the bed. Dogs are welcome off leash as long as they are under voice control.

Yosemite National Park

The Redwoods in Yosemite
Wawona Station/P.O. Box 2085
Yosemite National Park, CA
209-375-6666
This dog-friendly rental establishment is located within Yosemite National Park. They offer year-round vacation home and cabin rentals that welcome four legged friends and their humans. Please specify your need for a pet unit when you make your reservation. They cannot allow pets in non-pet homes, so please don't bring your pet unless you hold a confirmed reservation in a pet unit. There is a $10 per day additional pet fee. Guests are expected to abide by Yosemite's pet regulations, which require that pets be leashed at all times and are not permitted on any park trails, with the exception of paved trails on the floor of Yosemite Valley. If you want some other hiking options, The Redwoods in Yosemite management will be able to direct you to hiking trails in the adjacent Sierra National Forest where you can hike with your leashed pet. The home and cabins rentals are located in Yosemite and about an hour from Yosemite Valley.

Yountville

Vintage Inn
6541 Washington St.
Yountville, CA
707-944-1112
This inn is located in the small town of Yountville and is located within walking distance of several dog-friendly restaurants. Amenities at this pet-friendly inn include a continental champagne breakfast, afternoon tea, coffee & cookies, a heated pool, two tennis courts, and award winning gardens. Room amenities include a wood burning fireplace in every room, refrigerator with a chilled welcome bottle of wine, terry robes, nightly turn down service, hair dryer, in room iron & ironing board and more. If you need to

leave your room, but can't take your pooch with you, the concierge can arrange for a dog sitter. They also have a list of nearby dog-friendly outdoor restaurants. Room rates start at about $200 per night and up. There is a $30 one time pet charge.

Yreka

Ben-Ber Motel
1210 S Main St
Yreka, CA
530-842-2791
There is a $6 per day pet charge.

Best Western Miner's Inn
122 East Miner Street
Yreka, CA
530-842-4355
There is a $10 one time pet charge. There is a self-guided walking tour of historic Yreka about one block from this motel. Ask the motel for more information.

Days Inn
1804 B Fort Jones Rd
Yreka, CA
530-842-1612
There is a $20 refundable pet deposit.

Motel 6
1785 S Main Street
Yreka, CA
530-842-4111
There are no additional pet fees.

Yuba City

Comfort Inn
730 Palora Ave
Yuba City, CA
530-674-1592
There is a $10 per day pet fee.

Days Inn
700 N Palora Ave
Yuba City, CA
530-674-1711
There is a $7 per day pet fee.

Yucca Valley

Super 8
57096 29 Palms Hwy
Yucca Valley, CA
760-228-1773
There is a $20 refundable pet deposit and a $5 per day pet fee. The hotel is 10 miles from Joshua Tree National Park.

Zephyr Cove

Lake Tahoe Lodging
P.O. Box 11489
Zephyr Cove, NV
775-588-5253
Lake Tahoe Lodging has over 22 pet friendly vacation rentals in South Lake Tahoe. The properties range from 2 bedroom ski condos to 5 bedroom luxury lakefront estates. There is a $75.00 non-refundable pet security deposit. Also available is a homeopathic hourly pet sitting service through a local veterinarian.

Lake Village Resort
301 Highway 50
Zephyr Cove, NV
775-589-6065
This vacation home rental company offers several pet-friendly condo rentals in Lake Tahoe. There is a $20 per day pet charge.

Zephyr Cove Resort
460 Highway 50
Zephyr Cove, NV
775-588-6644
Thanks to one of our readers for recommending this resort. Dogs are allowed in the cabins but not in the lodge or cabin number one. That still leaves a nice selection of cabins to choose from. There is a $10 per day pet fee. This resort is located near South Lake Tahoe on the Nevada side. Dogs are not allowed on the beach or at the outdoor seats at the restaurant.

Colorado Listings

Alamosa

Best Western Alamosa Inn
1919 Main Street
Alamosa, CO
719-589-2567
There is a $6 per day pet fee.

Comfort Inn
6301 US 160
Alamosa, CO
719-587-9000
There is a one time pet fee of $15.

Holiday Inn
333 Santa Fe Ave
Alamosa, CO
719-589-5833
There is a $25 refundable pet deposit.

Almont

Harmel's Ranch Resort
P.O. Box 399
Almont, CO
970-641-1740
Harmel's offers an exciting dude ranch experience for the entire family, including pets. They are located in the middle of Gunnison National Forest. They offer horseback riding, flyfishing, whitewater rafting, great dining, BBQ's, hayrides, square-dances, and numerous activities. The resort is located near Crested Butte and Gunnison.

Aspen

Hotel Aspen
110 W. Main Street
Aspen, CO
970-925-3441
This dog-friendly hotel is located right on Main Street in Aspen. Rooms are large and beautifully appointed and they come

equipped with a wet bar, small refrigerator, coffee maker, microwave, iron, ironing board, hairdryer, humidifier, VCR, and air conditioning. Most rooms open onto terraces or balconies and some have private jacuzzis. They have a $20 per night charge for pets.

Hotel Jerome
330 E. Main Street
Aspen, CO
970-920-1000
There is a one time $25 pet charge.

Little Nell
675 E. Durant Ave.
Aspen, CO
970-920-4600
No pet fees, but need to sign a pet waiver.

The Sky Hotel
709 East Durant Avenue
Aspen, CO
970-925-6760
Well-behaved dogs of all kinds and sizes are welcome at this pet-friendly hotel. The luxury boutique hotel offers both rooms and suites. Hotel amenities include a heated outdoor pool, and a fitness room. There are no pet fees, just sign a pet waiver.

The St. Regis Hotel
315 East Dean Street
Aspen, CO
970-920-3300
There is a one time $50 pet charge. The hotel can also arrange a dog sitter or dog walker if you need to leave the room and cannot take your dog.

Aurora

Comfort Inn Airport
16921 E 32nd Ave
Aurora, CO
303-367-5000
There is no pet fee. A credit card will be required.

La Quinta Inn Denver Aurora

1011 South Abilene Street
Aurora, CO
303-337-0206
Dogs of all sizes are allowed at the hotel.

Aurura

Motel 6 - Aurura
14031 E Iliff Ave
Aurura, CO
303-873-0286
There are no additional pet fees.

Bailey

Glen Isle Resort
Highway 285 (near milepost marker 221)
Bailey, CO
303-838-5461
Dogs are welcome in the cabins (no designated smoking or non-smoking cabins). All cabins contain fully equipped kitchens, private baths, easy chairs, bedding and linens, fireplaces (wood provided) and gas heat. Resort amenities include a children's playground, games and game room and a library. The resort is within walking distance of the Pike National Forest and the Platte River. There you will find hours of dog-friendly hiking trails. There is a $5 per day pet charge. The resort is located 45 miles southwest of Denver.

Boulder

Foot of the Mountain Motel
200 Arapahoe Ave.
Boulder, CO
303-442-5688
Pets are welcome at this log cabin motel. There is an additional $5 per day pet charge. There are no designated smoking or non-smoking cabins.

Homewood Suites
4950 Baseline Rd.

Boulder, CO
303-499-9922
There is a one time $50 pet charge.

Residence Inn by Marriott
3030 Center Green Drive
Boulder, CO
303-449-5545
There is a one time $50 pet charge.

Breckenridge

Breckenridge Wayside Inn
165 Tiger Rd.
Breckenridge, CO
970-453-5540
Clean, comfortable motel rooms which are centrally located in Summit County, just 5 minutes to Breckenridge. Thanks to one of our readers who writes "Low-key, no-frills motel. A few miles from the heart of town but right on the main highway." Amenities include a free continental breakfast and free Hot Spiced Cider with cheese & crackers. Dogs are allowed at the motel, but not allowed in lodge area because they have three dogs of their own. There is a $20 refundable pet deposit.

Discover Resorts International
203 North Main Street
Breckenridge, CO
970-453-4422
Call to inquire about our Pet Policy Addendum for pet lovers who want to travel with their dog. Discover Resorts offers distinctive private properties from two to six bedrooms in size that are limited in number, please call so we can help you meet your occupancy needs. Units are offered upon availability. All Pet Policy Addendum requirements must be met prior to reservation.

Brush

Best Western Brush
1208 N. Colorado Ave

Brush, CO
970-842-5146
There is a $10 per day pet fee.

Burlington

Comfort Inn
282 S. Lincoln
Burlington, CO
719-346-7676
There is a refundable pet deposit of $50. There is a pet fee of $10 per day. Pets 100lbs and under welcome.

Canon City

Comfort Inn
311 Royal Gorge Blvd
Canon City, CO
719-276-6900
There is a pet fee of $10 per day.

Carbondale

Comfort Inn & Suites
920 Cowen Dr
Carbondale, CO
970-963-8880
There is a pet fee of $10 per day.

Castle Rock

Comfort Suites
4755 Castleton Way
Castle Rock, CO
303-814-9999
There is a pet fee of $10 per day.

Holiday Inn Express
884 Park Street
Castle Rock, CO
303-660-9733
There are no additional pet fees.

Cedaredge

Howard Johnson Express Inn
530 So. Grand Mesa Drive
Cedaredge, CO
970-856-7824
Dogs of all sizes are welcome.

There is a $10 per day pet fee per pet.

Colorado Springs

Best Western Palmer House
3010 North Chestnut Street
Colorado Springs, CO
719-636-5201
There is a $10 per day pet charge.

Comfort Inn North
6450 Corporate Center Dr
Colorado Springs, CO
719-262-9000
There is a pet fee of $10 per day.

Doubletree Hotel
1775 E. Cheyenne Mountain Blvd.
Colorado Springs, CO
719-576-8900
There is a $10 per day pet charge.

La Quinta Inn Colorado Springs
4385 Sinton Road
Colorado Springs, CO
719-528-5060
Dogs of all sizes are allowed at the hotel.

Motel 6
3228 N Chestnut St
Colorado Springs, CO
719-520-5400
Pets can never be left alone in the room. One well-behaved large dog is okay.

Quality Inn Garden of the Gods
555 W. Garden of the Gods Rd
Colorado Springs, CO
719-593-9119
There is a pet deposit of $50.

Residence Inn by Marriott
3880 North Academy Boulevard
Colorado Springs, CO
719-574-0370
There is a $50 one time pet fee.

Sheraton Colorado Springs Hotel
2886 S. Circle Drive
Colorado Springs, CO
719-576-5900
There is not a weight limit for dogs. There are no pet fees. Pets may not be left unattended in the room.

Cortez

Anasazi Motor Inn
640 S. Broadway
Cortez, CO
970-565-3773
There is a $50 refundable pet deposit.

Best Western Turquoise Inn & Suites
535 E. Main Street
Cortez, CO
970-565-3778
There is a $15 one time pet fee per visit.

Comfort Inn
2321 E Main
Cortez, CO
970-565-3400
There is no pet fee.

Days Inn
US Highway 160 and State Route 145
Cortez, CO
970-565-8577
There are no additional pet fees.

Craig

Holiday Inn Hotel & Suites
300 S. Colorado Hwy 13
Craig, CO
970-824-4000
There are no additional pet fees.

Delta

Comfort Inn
180 Gunnison River Dr
Delta, CO
970-874-1000
There is a pet fee of $5 per day.

Denver

Denver East Drury Inn
4380 Peoria Street
Denver, CO
303-373-1983
Dogs of all sizes are permitted. Pets are not allowed in the breakfast area of the hotel. Pets are not to be left unattended, and each guest must assume liability for damage of property or other guest complaints. There is a limit of one pet per room.

Denver Marriott City Center
1701 California St.
Denver, CO
303-297-1300
There is no pet charge.

Executive Tower Hotel
1405 Curtis Street
Denver, CO
303-571-0300
There is a $50 refundable pet deposit.

Guest House Inn
3737 Quebec St.
Denver, CO
303-388-6161
There is a $100 refundable pet deposit.

Hotel Monaco Denver
1717 Champa Street at 17th
Denver, CO
303-296-1717
Well-behaved dogs of all sizes are welcome at this pet-friendly hotel. The luxury boutique hotel offers both rooms and suites. Hotel amenities include complimentary evening wine service, a 24 hour on-site fitness room, and a gift shop. There are no pet fees, just sign a pet liability form.

Hotel Teatro
1100 Fourteenth Street
Denver, CO
303-228-1100
Dogs are allowed at this luxury boutique hotel. There is no extra pet charge.

La Quinta Inn & Suites Denver Airport/DIA
6801 Tower Road
Denver, CO
303-371-0888
Dogs of all sizes are allowed at the hotel.

La Quinta Inn Denver Central
3500 Park Avenue West
Denver, CO
303-458-1222
Dogs of all sizes are allowed at the hotel.

La Quinta Inn Denver South
1975 S Colorado Boulevard
Denver, CO
303-758-8886
Dogs up to 75 pounds are allowed at the hotel.

Loews Denver Hotel
4150 East Mississippi Ave.
Denver, CO
303-782-9300
All well-behaved dogs of any size are welcome. This upscale hotel offers their "Loews Loves Pets" program which includes special pet treats, local dog walking routes, and a list of nearby pet-friendly places to visit. There are no pet fees.

Marriott TownePlace Suites - Downtown
685 Speer Blvd
Denver, CO
303-722-2322
Marriott TownePlace Suites is an all suite hotel designed for the extended stay traveler. All studio, one, and two-bedroom suites offer full kitchens and weekly housekeeping. Pets are welcome for a non-refundable fee of $20 a day up to $200.00. On-site amenities include guest laundry, business center, fitness room and free parking.

Motel 6 - Airport
12020 E 39th Ave
Denver, CO
303-371-1980
There are no additional pet fees.

Quality Inn South - DTC
6300 E Hampden Ave
Denver, CO
303-758-2211
There is a pet fee of $6 per day.

Durango

Best Western Lodge at Purgatory
49617 Hwy 550
Durango, CO
970-247-9669
There is a $10 per day pet fee.

Days Inn
1700 County Road
Durango, CO
970-259-1430
There are no additional pet fees.

Doubletree Hotel
501 Camino Del Rio
Durango, CO
970-259-6580
There is a $15 per day pet charge.

Holiday Inn
800 Camino Del Rio
Durango, CO
970-247-5393
There is a $10 per day additional pet fee.

Quality Inn & Suites
455 S. Camino Del Rio
Durango, CO
970-259-7900
There is a pet deposit of $50. Pets are allowed on the first and second floors only.

Rochester Hotel
726 E. Second Ave.
Durango, CO
970-385-1920
This beautifully renovated hotel offers fifteen spacious rooms with high ceilings, king or queen beds, and private baths, and is decorated in an Old West motif. This hotel, located in downtown Durango, was designated as "The Flagship Hotel of Colorado" by Conde' Nast Traveler. They

are very pet-friendly and offer two pet rooms, with a $20 per day pet charge.

Eagle

Holiday Inn Express
I-70 Exit 147 & Pond Rd
Eagle, CO
970-328-8088
There is a $20 one time pet fee per visit.

Englewood

Comfort Suites Tech Center South
7374 South Clinton St
Englewood, CO
303-858-0700
There is a pet deposit of $50 and a pet fee of $5 per day. Pets are allowed on the first floor only.

Denver Tech Center Drury Inn & Suites
9445 East Dry Creek Road
Englewood, CO
303-694-3400
Dogs of all sizes are permitted. Pets are not allowed in the breakfast area of the hotel. Pets are not to be left unattended, and each guest must assume liability for damage of property or other guest complaints. There is a limit of one pet per room.

Sheraton Denver Tech Center Hotel
7007 South Clinton Street
Englewood, CO
303-799-6200
There is no weight limit for dogs. There are no pet fees.

Evans

Motel 6
3015 8th Ave
Evans, CO
970-351-6481
One pet per room is permitted. Pets may not be left unattended in the rooms.

Sleep Inn
3025 8th Ave
Evans, CO
970-356-2180
There is a one time pet fee of $10.

Evergreen

Quality Suites
19300 U.S. 40
Evergreen, CO
303-526-2000
There is a one time pet fee of $10. Pets may not be left alone.

Fort Collins

Best Western University Inn
914 S. College Ave
Fort Collins, CO
970-484-1984
There is a $5 per day additional pet fee.

Comfort Suites
1415 Oakridge Drive
Fort Collins, CO
970-206-4597
There is a one time pet fee of $15.

Holiday Inn
425 W. Prospect Rd
Fort Collins, CO
970-482-2626
Exit I-25 at Prospect Rd.

Holiday Inn
3836 E. Mulberry
Fort Collins, CO
970-484-4660
Pets must stay in rooms with exterior entrances. There is a $30 one time pet fee.

Holiday Inn-University Park
425 W. Prospect Rd.
Fort Collins, CO
970-482-2626
Dogs up to about 80 pounds are allowed.

Motel 6
3900 E Mulberry / State Hwy 14

Fort Collins, CO
970-482-6466
One well-behaved dog is allowed. The dog must be attended at all times.

Sleep Inn
3808 E. Mulberry St
Fort Collins, CO
970-484-5515
There is a pet fee of $5 per day.

Sundance Trail Guest Ranch
17931 Red Feather Lakes Rd
Fort Collins, CO
970-224-1222
This is a summer family Dude Ranch. During Fall, Winter and Spring this is a Country Lodge with horse back riding. There are no additional pet fees and the entire ranch is non-smoking.

Super 8 Motel
409 Centro Way
Fort Collins, CO
970-493-7701
There is a $5 per day additional pet fee.

Fort Lupton

Motel 6
65 South Grand
Fort Lupton, CO
303-857-1800
Pets must be attended at all times.

Fort Morgan

Best Western Terrace
725 Main Street
Fort Morgan, CO
970-867-8256
There is a $5 per day additional pet fee.

Frisco

Discover Resorts International
912 North Summit Boulevard
Frisco, CO
970-668-5151
Call to inquire about our Pet Policy Addendum for pet lovers

who want to travel with their dog. Discover Resorts offers distinctive private properties from two to six bedrooms in size that are limited in number, please call so we can help you meet your occupancy needs. Units are offered upon availability. All Pet Policy Addendum requirements must be met prior to reservation.

Holiday Inn
1129 N. Summit Blvd
Frisco, CO
970-668-5000
There is a $20 one time pet fee.

Hotel Frisco
308 Main Street
Frisco, CO
970-668-5009
Dogs are welcome at this classic Rocky Mountain lodge which is located on Frisco's historic Main Street. The hotel offers two dog-friendly rooms with access to the back porch and to the doggie run. Enjoy hiking and swimming with your dog right from the hotel's front door! Dog amenities include dog beds and treats. Dog sitting and walking service is also available. There is a $10 per day pet fee. This hotel is located 9 miles from Breckenridge.

Woods Inn Bed and Breakfast
Second Ave and Granite St
Frisco, CO
970-668-2255
This bed and breakfast inn and suites is located in the heart of Colorado ski country. They offer a range of accommodations, from full condo-style suites to single bunks. Breckenridge is just minutes away and Vail is not far. There is a $15 one time per stay pet charge.

Glenwood Springs

Quality Inn & Suites
2650 Gilstrap Court
Glenwood Springs, CO

970-945-5995
There is a pet fee of $10 per day. For a non-smoking room there is an additional $20 one time fee.

Golden

La Quinta Inn Denver Wheat Ridge - Golden
3301 Youngfield Service Road
Golden, CO
303-279-5565
Dogs of all sizes are allowed at the hotel.

Grand Junction

Best Western Horizon Inn
754 Horizon Drive
Grand Junction, CO
970-245-1410
Pets may not be left alone in the room.

Days Inn
733 Horizon Drive
Grand Junction, CO
800-329-7466
There are no additional pet fees.

Holiday Inn
755 Horizon Drive
Grand Junction, CO
970-243-6790
Dogs must stay in first floor rooms. They may not be left unattended at any time. Pets must also be on leash on the premises.

La Quinta Inn & Suites Grand Junction
2761 Crossroads Blvd.
Grand Junction, CO
970-241-2929
Dogs of all sizes are allowed at the hotel.

Motel 6
776 Horizon Dr
Grand Junction, CO
970-243-2628
One well-behaved dog is allowed per room. Pets may not

be left unattended at any time.

Greeley

Best Western Ramkota Inn
701 Eighth Street
Greeley, CO
970-353-8444
There is a $20 one time pet fee. In addition, pet owners must sign a pet contract.

Holiday Inn Express
2563 W 29th Street
Greeley, CO
970-330-7495
There is a $20 one time pet fee.

Greenwood Village

Mainstay Suites
9253 E Costilla Ave
Greenwood Village, CO
303-858-1669
There is a one time pet fee of $25.

Sleep Inn Denver Tech
9257 E Costilla Ave
Greenwood Village, CO
303-662-9950
There is a one time pet fee of $25.

Gunnison

Inn at Rockhouse Ranch
13931 County Rd 730
Gunnison, CO
970-641-0601
Upon arrival pets receive a bed and chew toy. Upscale kennels are available and there is a bottomless treat jar in the kitchen. Pet fee and policy apply.

La Junta

Quality Inn
1325 E. 3rd St
La Junta, CO
719-384-2571
There is no pet fee.

Lakewood

Quality Suites
7260 W. Jefferson
Lakewood, CO
303-988-8600
There is a one time fee of $10.

Sheraton Denver West Hotel
360 Union Boulevard
Lakewood, CO
303-987-2000
Dogs up to 80 pounds are allowed. There are no additional pet fees.

Lamar

Best Western Cow Palace Inn
1301 N. Main
Lamar, CO
719-336-7753
There are no additional pet fees.

Las Animas

Best Western Bent's Fort Inn
East Hwy 50
Las Animas, CO
719-456-0011
There are no additional pet fees.

Limon

Best Western Limon Inn
925 T Avenue, I-70 & Hwy 24
Limon, CO
719-775-0277
There is a $10 per day additional pet fee.

Lone Tree

Staybridge Suites
7820 Park Meadows Drive
Lone Tree, CO
303-649-1010
There is a $10 per day or $75 per month additional pet fee.

Loveland

Best Western Coach House
5542 E US Hwy 34
Loveland, CO

970-667-7810
There is a $15 one time pet fee.

Mancos

Far View Lodge
Mesa Verde National Park
Mancos, CO
970-529-4421
Far View Lodge sits on a high shoulder of the Mesa Verde, offering panoramic vistas into three states. There is a $50 refundable pet deposit. Pets are allowed in some of the standard rooms.

Monte Vista

Comfort Inn
1519 Grande Ave
Monte Vista, CO
719-852-0612
There is no pet fee. Pets may not be left alone.

Montrose

Black Canyon Motel
1605 E. Main Street
Montrose, CO
970-249-3495
There is a $5 per day additional pet fee.

Comfort Inn
2100 E. Main St
Montrose, CO
970-240-8000
There is a pet fee of $10 per day.

Holiday Inn Express Hotel & Suites
1391 South Townsend Ave
Montrose, CO
970-240-1800
Pets must stay in the first floor rooms.

San Juan Inn
1480 Highway 550 South
Montrose, CO
970-249-6644
There is a $12 per day pet charge.

Northglenn

Holiday Inn
10 E. 120th Ave at I-25
Northglenn, CO
303-452-4100
There is a $50 refundable pet deposit. Exit Hwy 128 from I-25.

Ouray

Ouray Victorian Inn
50 Third Avenue
Ouray, CO
800-846-8729
They have several pet rooms.

Rivers Edge Motel
110 7th Avenue
Ouray, CO
970-325-4621
There is a $5 per day pet charge.

Pagosa Springs

Fireside Inn
1600 E Hwy 160
Pagosa Springs, CO
970-264-9204
They offer modern one and two bedroom cabins (built in 1996) with fireplaces, hot tubs, kitchens and more. The cabins are located on seven acres on the San Juan River. Dogs and horses are welcome. There are no additional pet fees.

High Country Lodge
3821 E Hwy 160
Pagosa Springs, CO
970-264-4181
Dogs are allowed in the cabins. There is a $15 one time pet charge. All cabins are non-smoking.

Pueblo

Best Western Town House
730 N. Santa Fe
Pueblo, CO
719-543-6530
There is a $10 one time pet fee.

Motel 6
960 Hwy 50 W
Pueblo, CO
719-543-8900
There are no additional pet fees.

Motel 6
4103 Elizabeth St
Pueblo, CO
719-543-6221
There is a $25 one time pet fee
only if you stay in studio rooms.
Regular rooms have no pet fees.

Rifle

Buckskin Inn
101 Ray Avenue
Rifle, CO
970-625-1741
Amenities include Satellite TV,
multiple HBO, microwaves,
refrigerators, and free local calls.
There is no charge for a pet, but
please let staff know when
reserving a room. Pets cannot
be left unattended in the rooms.

Silverthorne

Quality Inn & Suites
530 Silverthorne Lane
Silverthorne, CO
970-513-1222
There is pet fee of $10 per day.
There is no pet deposit if paying
by credit card. There is a $50
pet deposit if paying by cash.
There are only 2 smoking and 2
non-smoking pet rooms.
Reserve early.

Silverton

The Wyman Hotel and Inn
1371 Greene (Main) Street
Silverton, CO
970-387-5372
Dogs are welcome on the
ground level floor and there is a
$15 per day pet charge. Dog
biscuits are handed out to the
doggie guests. This historic bed
and breakfast inn is closed
during November.

South Fork

Comfort Inn
182 E. Frontage Rd
South Fork, CO
719-873-5600
There is a pet fee of $10 per
day.

Steamboat Springs

Alpiner Lodge
424 Lincoln Ave.
Steamboat Springs, CO
970-879-1430
There is an $15 one time pet
fee.

Holiday Inn
3190 S. Lincoln Ave
Steamboat Springs, CO
970-879-2250
There is a $25 refundable pet
deposit. Pets must never be left
alone in the room.

Sheraton Steamboat Springs Resort and Conference Center
2200 Village Inn Court, P.O.
Box 774808
Steamboat Springs, CO
970-879-2220
Dogs up to 80 pounds are
allowed. There is a $25 one
time pet fee per stay. Dogs are
allowed on a certain floor. The
entire hotel is non-smoking.

Stratton

Best Western Golden Prairie Inn
700 Colorado Ave
Stratton, CO
719-348-5311
They have one non-smoking
pet room.

Telluride

Hotel Columbia Telluride
300 W. San Juan Ave.
Telluride, CO
970-728-0660
This full service resort hotel
welcomes your best friend. They
are located just two blocks from
the downtown shops and
restaurants. There is a $15 per
day pet charge. All rooms are
non-smoking.

Wyndham Peaks Resort
136 Country Club Drive
Telluride, CO
970-728-6800
There is a $50 per day pet
charge.

Thornton

Sleep Inn
12101 N. Grant St
Thornton, CO
303-280-9818
There is a pet fee of $5 per day.
Pets must be kept on a leash.

Trinidad

Holiday Inn
3125 Toupal Drive
Trinidad, CO
719-846-4491
There are no additional pet fees.

Vail

Antlers at Vail
680 W. Lionshead Place
Vail, CO
970-476-2471
This hotel and condo complex is
definitely dog-friendly. They
have had large doggie guests
like a 250 pound mastiff. They
have several pet rooms and
there is a $15 per day pet
charge. There are no designated
smoking or non-smoking units.

Westminster

La Quinta Inn & Suites Westminster - Promanade
10179 Church Ranch Way
Westminster, CO
303-438-5800
Dogs of all sizes are allowed at
the hotel.

La Quinta Inn Denver - Westminster Mall
8701 Turnpike Drive
Westminster, CO
303-425-9099
Dogs of all sizes are allowed at the hotel.

La Quinta Inn Denver Northglenn - Westminster
345 West 120th Avenue
Westminster, CO
303-252-9800
Dogs of all sizes are allowed at the hotel.

Wheat Ridge

Holiday Inn Express - Denver West
4700 Kipling St
Wheat Ridge, CO
303-423-4000
There is a $10 one time pet fee. Exit I-70 at Kipling St.

Winter Park

Best Western Winter Park Mountain Lodge
81699 US Highway 40
Winter Park, CO
970-726-4211
The pet rooms are on the eighth floor of the hotel.

Connecticut Listings

Brookfield

Twin Tree Inn
1030 Federal Rd
Brookfield, CT
203-775-0220
There is a $10.00 one time pet fee.

Cromwell

Comfort Inn

111 Berlin Rd
Cromwell, CT
860-635-4100
There is a pet fee of $15 per day.

Danbury

Holiday Inn
80 Newtown Rd
Danbury, CT
203-792-4000
Pets may not be left alone in rooms after 8 pm.

Ramada Inn
Highway 84 Exit 8
Danbury, CT
203-792-3800
There are no additional pet fees.

Dayville

Holiday Inn Express & Suites
16 Tracy Road Killingly
Dayville, CT
860-779-3200
There is a $10 per day additional pet fee. Pets are not allowed in the lobby.

East Hartford

Holiday Inn
363 Roberts St
East Hartford, CT
860-528-9611
There are no pet fees.

Sheraton Hartford Hotel
100 East River Drive
East Hartford, CT
860-528-9703
There is no weight limit for dogs. There are no pet fees.

Enfield

Motel 6
11 Hazard Ave
Enfield, CT
860-741-3685
There are no additional pet fees. One pet per room is

allowed.

Red Roof Inn
5 Hazard Ave
Enfield, CT
860-741-2571
You need to sign a pet waiver. Pets up to 80 pounds are okay.

Farmington

Centennial Inn
5 Spring Lane
Farmington, CT
860-677-4647
There is a $15 per day additional pet fee.

Greenwich

The Delamar
500 Steamboat Road
Greenwich, CT
203-661-9800
There is a $20 per day additional pet fee. There are a number of non-smoking pet rooms.

Groton

Clarion Inn
156 Kings Highway
Groton, CT
860-446-0660
There is a pet fee of $10 per day. Pets may not be left alone.

Hartford

Motel 6 - Bradley Airport
3 National Dr
Hartford, CT
860-292-6200
Pets must be under control and well-behaved.

Motel 6 - Enfield
11 Hazard Ave
Hartford, CT
860-741-3685
There are no additional pet fees.

Motel 6 - Southington
625 Queen St
Hartford, CT

860-621-7351
Pets may not be left alone in rooms.

Red Roof Inn
100 Weston St
Hartford, CT
860-724-0222
There are no additional pet fees.

Lakeville

Interlaken Inn
74 Interlaken Road
Lakeville, CT
860-435-9878
30 open acres, a great property with lake frontage to frolic on and off-leash play areas too! Miles of pet-friendly walking and hiking trails nearby. Be sure to ask about the PUPS Package. There is a $10 per day pet fee.

Manchester

Clarion Suites Inn
191 Spencer St
Manchester, CT
860-643-5811
There is a pet fee of $10 per day.

Milford

Red Roof Inn
10 Rowe Avenue
Milford, CT
203-877-6060
There are no additional pet fees.

Mystic

Harbour Inne & Cottage
15 Edgemont Street
Mystic, CT
860-572-9253
Harbour Inne & Cottage B&B is an easy walk to all the shops, restaurants and sights of downtown Mystic including boat rides and tall ships. The inn at the Harbour Inne & Cottage has a social area with fireplace and piano. The four bedrooms each

have a private bath, kitchen privileges, cable television and are air conditioned. The Inne is the perfect setting for family get-togethers or small gatherings of any kind. In the hustle and bustle of Mystic, the Harbour Inne & Cottage offers relaxing accommodations in a quiet and quaint section of town. Pets are welcome for $10 per night.

New Haven

Days Inn
270 Foxon Blvd
New Haven, CT
203-469-0343
There is a $7 per day pet fee.

Residence Inn by Marriott
3 Long Wharf Dr
New Haven, CT
203-777-5337
For a one to four night stay, the pet fee is a flat rate of $150. For a five day or longer stay, the pet fee is $15 per day.

New London

Red Roof Inn
707 Coleman St
New London, CT
860-444-0001
There are no additional pet fees.

Niantic

Motel 6
269 Flanders Rd
Niantic, CT
860-739-6991
One large dog per room is permitted.

North Haven

Holiday Inn
201 Washington Ave
North Haven, CT
203-239-4225
There are no additional pet

fees.

Old Lyme

Old Lyme
85 Lyme St
Old Lyme, CT
860-434-2600
There are no additional pet fees.

Putnam

King's Inn
5 Heritage Rd
Putnam, CT
860-928-7961
There are no additional pet fees.

Shelton

Residence Inn by Marriott
1001 Bridgeport Ave
Shelton, CT
203-926-9000
There is a $20 per day pet charge up to 14 nights. The pet charge is a total of $350.00 if you stay more than 14 nights.

Simsbury

Iron Horse Inn
969 Hopmeadow St
Simsbury, CT
860-658-2216
There are no additional pet fees.

Southbury

Hilton
1284 Strongtown Rd
Southbury, CT
203-598-7600
Pets allowed on 1st floor only. There is a $50 refundable deposit and a pet waiver needs to be signed. Dogs up to 50 pounds are allowed.

Southington

Howard Johnson Express Inn
462 Queen Street
Southington, CT

860-621-0181
Dogs of all sizes are welcome.
There is a $10 per day pet fee.

Stamford

Sheraton Stamford Hotel
2701 Summer Street
Stamford, CT
203-359-1300
There is no weight limit for dogs.
There are no pet fees.

Vernon

Howard Johnson Express Inn
451 Hartford Turnpike
Vernon, CT
860-875-0781
Dogs of all sizes are welcome.
There is a $10 per day pet fee
per pet.

Westbrook

Beach Plum Inn
1935 Boston Post Rd
Westbrook, CT
860-399-9345
There are no additional pet fees.
Dogs are allowed in the cabins.

Wethersfield

Ramada Inn
1330 Silas Deane Hwy
Wethersfield, CT
860-563-2311
You need to sign a pet policy
statement.

Willington

Sleep Inn
327 Ruby Rd
Willington, CT
860-684-1400
There is a $20 refundable pet
deposit.

Windsor

Residence Inn by Marriott
100 Dunfey Lane

Windsor, CT
860-688-7474
There is a $100 one time pet
charge.

Windsor Locks

Baymont Inn and Suites
64 Ella T Grasso Tpk
Windsor Locks, CT
860-623-3336
Dogs up to 75 pounds ok.

Homewood Suites
65 Ella Grasso Turnpike
Windsor Locks, CT
860-627-8463
There is a $150 one time pet
charge and guests need to sign
a pet policy.

**Sheraton Bradley Airport
Hotel**
Bradley International Airport
Windsor Locks, CT
860-627-5311
There is no weight limit for
dogs. There are no pet fees.

District of Columbia Listings

Arlington

Potomac Suites Rosslyn
1730 Arlington Blvd
Arlington, VA
703-528-2900
Located just across the
Potomac River from historic
Washington, DC in a quiet
neighborhood in Rosslyn,
Virginia, Potomac Suites
Rosslyn offers quick access to
the shopping and dining of
Georgetown and the
excitement of the museums
and monuments on the
National Mall. You and your pet
will enjoy fully spacious suites
with fully equipped kitchens,
cable TV with HBO, high speed
Internet access, and more.

Washington

Hotel Helix
1430 Rhode Island Ave
Washington, DC
202-462-9001
Well-behaved dogs of all sizes
are welcome at this hotel. The
boutique hotel offers both rooms
and suites. Amenities include
room service, and a 24 hour on-
site exercise room. There are no
pet fees.

Hotel Madera
1310 New Hampshire Ave
Washington, DC
202-296-7600
Well-behaved dogs of all sizes
are welcome at this boutique
hotel. Amenities include an
evening wine hour, and room
service. There are no pet fees.

Hotel Rouge
1315 16th Street NW
Washington, DC
202-232-8000
Well-behaved dogs of all sizes
are welcome at this luxury
boutique hotel. Amenities
include complimentary high
speed Internet access in the
rooms, 24 hour room service,
and a 24 hour on-site fitness
room. There are no pet fees.

Hotel Sofitel
1914 Connecticut Ave
Washington, DC
202-737-8800
There are no additional pet fees.

Hotel Washington
515 15th St NW
Washington, DC
202-638-5900
There are no additional pet fees.

Loews L'Enfant Plaza Hotel
480 L'Enfant Plaza
Washington, DC
202-484-1000
All well-behaved dogs of any
size are welcome. This upscale
hotel offers their "Loews Loves
Pets" program which includes
special pet treats, local dog

walking routes, and a list of nearby pet-friendly places to visit. There are no pet fees.

Park Hyatt Washington
1201 24th St NW
Washington, DC
202-789-1234
There are no additional pet fees.

The Jefferson Hotel, a Loews Hotel
1200 16th St. NW
Washington, DC
202-347-2200
All well-behaved dogs of any size are welcome. This upscale hotel offers their "Loews Loves Pets" program which includes special pet treats, local dog walking routes, and a list of nearby pet-friendly places to visit. There are no pet fees.

Willard Inter-Continental
1401 Pennsylvania Ave
Washington, DC
202-628-9100
Pet owners must sign a pet waiver. There are no pet fees.

Delaware Listings

Claymont

Holiday Inn Select
630 Naamans Rd
Claymont, DE
302-792-2700
There is a $50 one time pet fee.

Dewey Beach

Sea-Esta Motel I
2306 Hwy 1
Dewey Beach, DE
302-227-7666
There is a $6.00 charge per pet per night. There are no designated smoking or non-smoking rooms.

Dover

Red Roof Inn
415 Stanton Christiana Rd
Dover, DE
302-292-2870
There are no additional pet fees.

Georgetown

Comfort Inn
507 N. Dupont Highway
Georgetown, DE
302-854-9400
There is a pet fee of $5 per day.

Lewes

Lazy L at Willow Creek - A B&B Resort
11 Willow Creek Road
Lewes, DE
302-644-7220
Located on 8 secluded acres overlooking a marsh and creek, the Lazy L offers creature comforts for pets and pet owners. They offer 5 large rooms with Queen sized beds, a swimming pool, hot tub, pool table, guest kitchen and a barbeque. The dogs have a fenced in 1 acre run area, are allowed to sleep in the guest rooms and stay by themselves while you shop or go to dinner.

New Castle

Motel 6
1200 W Ave / S Hwy 9
New Castle, DE
302-571-1200
There are no additional pet fees.

Quality Inn Skyways
147 N DuPont Hwy
New Castle, DE
302-328-6666
There is a $10.00 one time fee for pets.

Rodeway Inn
111 S Dupont Hwy
New Castle, DE
302-328-6246
There is a $10 per day pet fee.

Newark

Best Western Delaware Inn
260 Chapman Rd
Newark, DE
302-738-3400
There is a $10 per day pet fee.

Comfort Inn
1120 S. College Ave.
Newark, DE
302-368-8715
There is a one time pet fee of $10. Pets are allowed on the second floor only. Pets must use the stairs.

Howard Johnson Inn
1119 South College Avenue
Newark, DE
302-368-8521
Dogs of all sizes are welcome. There is a $10 per day pet fee.

Residence Inn by Marriott
240 Chapman Rd
Newark, DE
302-453-9200
There is an additional $50.00 charge per night for the first 4 nights.

Sleep Inn
630 S. College Ave
Newark, DE
302-453-1700
There is a one time pet fee of $15.

Rehoboth Beach

Sea Esta Motel III
1409 DE 1
Rehoboth Beach, DE
302-227-4343
There is a $6 per day additional pet fee.

Wilmington

Best Western Brandywine Valley Inn

1807 Concord Pike
Wilmington, DE
302-656-9436
There are no additional pet fees.

Sheraton Suites Wilmington
422 Delaware Avenue
Wilmington, DE
302-654-8300
Dogs up to 70 pounds are allowed. There are no additional pet fees.

Florida Listings

Altamonte Springs

Embassy Suites Orlando North
225 East Altamonte Drive
Altamonte Springs, FL
407-834-2400
There is a $15 per day pet charge.

Amelia Island

Florida House Inn
22 South 3rd Street
Amelia Island, FL
800-258-3301
Built in 1857, this registered historic inn/bed and breakfast is located in the heart of the Fernandina Beach Historic District. This dog-friendly inn offers nine comfortable bedrooms and two suites, all with private baths. Six rooms have working fireplaces, two have old fashioned claw-footed tubs and two have large jacuzzi tubs. All accommodations are air-conditioned and offer access to their spacious porches, perfect for rocking and relaxing. They are located near the Victorian seaport village. Walk through the 30 block historic district. Browse a variety of quaint stores, antique shops and restaurants along Centre Street, the main thoroughfare. There is a $15 per day pet fee. Dogs

must be on a flea program.

Apalachicola

Rancho Inn
240 Hwy 98
Apalachicola, FL
850-653-9435
There is a $6 per day pet charge.

The Gibson Inn
Market St and Avenue C
Apalachicola, FL
850-653-2191
Restored in 1983, this historic country inn overlooks the water and St. George Island. Rooms are furnished in period, with four-poster beds, ceiling fans, antique armoires, brass and porcelain bathroom fixtures, and claw-foot tubs. There is a $5.30 per day pet charge.

Apopka

Howard Johnson Express Inn
1317 S. Orange Blossom Trail
Apopka, FL
407-886-1010
Dogs of all sizes are welcome. There is a $10 per day pet fee. The hotel has two pet rooms, one smoking and one non-smoking.

Bal Harbour

Sheraton Bal Harbour Beach Resort
9701 Collins Avenue
Bal Harbour, FL
305-865-7511
Dogs up to 80 pounds are allowed. There are no additional pet fees.

Boca Raton

Radisson Suite
7920 Glades Road
Boca Raton, FL
561-483-3600
There is a $100 one time pet

charge.

Residence Inn by Marriott
525 NW 77th Street
Boca Raton, FL
561-994-3222
The non-refundable pet charge is as follows; $75 for studios, $85 for 1-bedroom suites and $95 for penthouses.

Bradenton

Howard Johnson Express Inn
6511 14th St. W (US 41)
Bradenton, FL
941-756-8399
Dogs of all sizes are welcome. There is a $5 per day pet fee for pets under 20 pounds, $10 per day pet fee for pets over 20 pounds.

Motel 6
660 67 Street Cir E
Bradenton, FL
941-747-6005
There are no additional pet fees.

Brooksville

Holiday Inn
30307 Cortez Blvd
Brooksville, FL
352-796-9481
There is a $25 one time pet fee.

Bushnell

Best Western Guest House
I-75 & SR-48
Bushnell, FL
352-793-5010
There is a $10 per day additional pet fee.

Cape Coral

Bayview B&B
PO Box 35, 12251 Shoreview Dr
Cape Coral, FL
941-283-7510
The bed and breakfast has one room that allows pets. There is a $100 refundable pet deposit.

Quality Inn
1538 Cape Coral Pkwy
Cape Coral, FL
941-542-2121
Dogs are allowed in the first floor rooms. There is a $8 per day pet charge.

Clearwater

Residence Inn by Marriott-St. Petersburg
5050 Ulmerton Road
Clearwater, FL
727-573-4444
There is a $150 one time pet charge.

Clearwater Beach

Mar - Jac Apartment / Motel
144 Brightwater Drive
Clearwater Beach, FL
727-442-6009
Located on beautiful Clearwater Bay, this pet-friendly motel is within walking distance to the Gulf of Mexico and its white sandy beaches. Also close by is big pier fishing, deep sea fishing boats, shopping and fine restaurants. Mar - Jac offers lovely large rooms with carpeting and spacious walk-in closets. All accommodations are immaculately clean, fully equipped and completely furnished. Room amenities include air-conditioning, electric heat, color cable television, fresh towels provided daily and phones in all apartments. Weekly maid service is available. You will enjoy the friendly, home-like atmosphere along with our private fishing dock, lawn, bayside patio with BBQ grill, bayside Whirlpool Bath, washer/dryer and shuffleboard. Everything is done to make your stay with us a most pleasant and relaxing one. Come as our guests, leave as our friends.

Sea Spray Inn
331 Coronado Drive
Clearwater Beach, FL
727-442-0432
Sea Spray Inn is just a one minute walk to the Gulf of Mexico. There are 6 rooms, 4 with full kitchens, 2 rooms have refrigerators. Microwaves in rooms, phones, cable TV and a swimming pool. A quiet setting yet close to attractions, restaurants, marina and the pier.

Clermont

Howard Johnson Express Inn
20329 US Hwy 27
Clermont, FL
352-429-9033
Dogs of all sizes are welcome. There is a $10 per day pet fee.

Secluded Sunsets
10616 South Phillips Road
Clermont, FL
352-429-0512
This is a pet friendly duplex on Pine Island Lake. It has a two bedroom unit sleeping up to 6 adults and 3 pets and a one bedroom unit sleeping up to 4 adults and 2 pets overlooking a central Florida spring fed lake. Pet fees are $5 per pet per night. Amenities include a Hot tub, 4 person paddle boat, 2 person canoe, gas and charcoal grills, fire pit area for evening campfires, swimming, fishing, satellite tv and fully furnished kitchens.

Cocoa

Best Western Cocoa Inn
4225 West King Street
Cocoa, FL
321-632-1065
There is a $6 per day additional pet fee.

Cocoa Beach

A Beach House
3393-5 South Atlantic Avenue
Cocoa Beach, FL
321-258-1355
This vacation rental is a direct Oceanfront Duplex with 2 bedroom, 2 bathroom or a 3 bedroom, 3 bathroom available. There is a $50 one time per stay pet fee.

Holiday Inn
1300 N. Atlantic Ave
Cocoa Beach, FL
321-783-2271
Dogs up to about 50 pounds are ok. There is a $50 one time pet fee and a $10 per day additional pet charge.

Howard Johnson Express Inn
2082 North America Avenue
Cocoa Beach, FL
321-783-8855
Dogs of all sizes are welcome. There is a $20 one time pet fee per visit.

South Beach Inn
1701 South Atlantic Ave
Cocoa Beach, FL
321-784-3333
There is a $15 per day pet fee. There are no designated smoking or non-smoking rooms.

Surf Studio Beach Resort
1801 S. Atlantic Ave.
Cocoa Beach, FL
321-783-7100
There is a $25 per day pet charge. There are no designated smoking or non-smoking rooms, but they keep the rooms very clean.

Cutler Ridge

Howard Johnson Hotel
10779 Caribbean Blvd.
Cutler Ridge, FL
305-253-9960
Dogs up to 20 pounds are allowed. There is a $20 per day pet fee.

Dania

Sheraton Fort Lauderdale

Airport Hotel
1825 Griffin Road
Dania, FL
954-920-3500
Dogs up to 80 pounds are allowed. There are no additional pet fees.

Daytona Beach

Days Inn Speedway
2900 W International Speedway Blvd
Daytona Beach, FL
386-255-0541
There is a $10 per day additional pet fee.

Super 8
2992 W International Speedway Blvd
Daytona Beach, FL
386-253-0643
There is a $10 per day additional pet fee.

Daytona Beach Shores

Quality Inn Ocean Palms
2323 S. Atlantic Ave.
Daytona Beach Shores, FL
386-255-0476
There is a pet fee of $10 per day.

De Funiak Springs

Best Western Crossroads Inn
2343 Freeport Rd, I-10 & US 331S
De Funiak Springs, FL
850-892-5111
There are no additional pet fees.

De Land

Comfort Inn
400 E. Speedway Blvd
De Land, FL
386-736-3100
There are no additional pet fees.

Deland

Holiday Inn

350 E. Int'l Speedway Blvd
Deland, FL
386-738-5200
There is a $10 per day pet fee.

Howard Johnson Express Inn
2801 E. New York Ave.
Deland, FL
386-736-3440
Dogs of all sizes are welcome. There is a $10 per day pet fee.

Destin

Howard Johnson Express Inn
713 Hwy 98E
Destin, FL
850-650-2236
Dogs of all sizes are welcome. There is a $10 per day pet fee.

Elkton

Comfort Inn
2625 SR 207
Elkton, FL
904-829-3435
There is a one time pet fee of $10.

Ellenton

Ramada Limited
5218 17th Street E
Ellenton, FL
941-729-8505
There is a $10 one time pet fee.

Shoney's Inn-Bradenton
4915 17th Street East
Ellenton, FL
941-729-0600
There is a $10 one time pet charge.

Flagler Beach

Whale Watch Motel
2448 S Oceanshore Blvd
Flagler Beach, FL
386-439-2545
This is a quaint, Old Florida, beach cottage motel, recently renovated. There is a patio area with umbrella tables and

BBQ grill, and an observation deck on the dune. The rooms are clean, comfortable and pleasant. Flagler Beach is a quaint, unspoiled, northeast Florida beach town. The town offers several great restaurants and most allow dogs on their outside decks. There are seven miles of pristine, dog-friendly beaches (dogs allowed by law on leash). There are also twenty miles of oceanside bike and walking paths. Flagler Beach is conveniently located between St. Augustine and Daytona Beach. There is a $10 per day additional pet fee. The motel has one non-smoking pet room.

Florida City

Hampton Inn-Miami
124 E. Palm Drive
Florida City, FL
305-247-8833
There are no additional pet fees.

Fort Lauderdale

Birch Patio Motel
617 N Birch Rd
Fort Lauderdale, FL
954-563-9540
There is a $10 per day pet charge.

Motel 6
1801 SR 84
Fort Lauderdale, FL
954-760-7999
There are no additional pet fees.

Red Roof Inn
4800 Powerline Rd
Fort Lauderdale, FL
954-776-6333
There are no additional pet fees. Pets under 85 pounds are allowed.

Sheraton Suites Cypress Creek Ft. Lauderdale
555 N.W. 62nd Street
Fort Lauderdale, FL
954-772-5400
Dogs up to 80 pounds are

allowed. There is a $100 one time per stay pet fee.

Fort Myers

Best Western Springs Resort
18051 S. Tamiami Trail Hwy 41
Fort Myers, FL
941-267-7900
There is a $10 per day additional pet fee.

Comfort Inn
4171 Boatways Road
Fort Myers, FL
941-694-9200
There is a one time pet fee of $10.

Comfort Suites Airport
13651-A Indian Paint Ln
Fort Myers, FL
941-768-0005
There is a $10 per day pet fee. Pets may not be left alone.

Howard Johnson Express Inn
13000 North Cleveland Ave.
Fort Myers, FL
239-656-4000
Dogs of all sizes are welcome. There is a $10 per day pet fee per pet.

Howard Johnson Inn
4811 Cleveland Ave.
Fort Myers, FL
239-936-3229
Dogs of all sizes are welcome. There is a $25 pet fee every 3 days.

Motel 6
3350 Marinatown Lane
Fort Myers, FL
941-656-5544
There are no additional pet fees.

Radisson Inn Sanibel Gateway
20091 Summerlin Road
Fort Myers, FL
941-466-1200
There is a $25 one time pet charge.

Fort Pierce

Days Inn
6651 Darter Court
Fort Pierce, FL
561-466-4066
There is a $10 one time pet charge.

Holiday Inn Express
7151 Okeechobee Rd.
Fort Pierce, FL
561-464-5000
There is a $25 one time pet charge.

Royal Inn
222 Hernando Street
Fort Pierce, FL
561-464-0405
There is a $25 one time pet charge.

Fort Walton Beach

Howard Johnson Inn
203 Miracle Strip Pkwy.
Fort Walton Beach, FL
850-244-8663
Dogs of all sizes are welcome. There is a $25 one time pet fee.

Gainesville

La Quinta Inn Gainesville
920 NW 69th Terrace
Gainesville, FL
352-332-6466
Dogs of all sizes are allowed at the hotel.

Motel 6
4000 SW 40th Blvd
Gainesville, FL
352-373-1604
Pets must be attended at all times.

Red Roof Inn
3500 SW 42nd St
Gainesville, FL
352-336-3311
Dogs up to 80 pounds are allowed. There are no additional pet fees.

Grayton Beach

Hibiscus Coffee Guest House
85 Defuniak St
Grayton Beach, FL
850-231-2733
There are no additional pet fees. There is one room available for pets.

Haines City

Howard Johnson Inn
33224 US Hwy. 27 South
Haines City, FL
863-422-8621
Dogs of all sizes are welcome. There is a $10 pet fee for the first night and $5 for the second night.

Hollywood

Days Inn
2601 N. 29th Avenue
Hollywood, FL
954-923-7300
There is a $10 per day pet charge.

Indian Shores

Barrett Beach Bungalows
19646 Gulf Blvd
Indian Shores, FL
727-455-2832
Beachfront bungalows plus a cottage in the heart of picturesque Indian Shores. One, two and three bedroom bungalows and a pool. Any number and size of pets welcome. Private dog runs with each bungalow. Enjoy sunsets, volleyball and BBQs in your own backyard.

Jacksonville

Amerisuites-Baymeadows
8277 Western Way Circle
Jacksonville, FL
904-737-4477
There is a $10 one time pet fee.

Hampton Inn
1170 Airport Entrance Road

Jacksonville, FL
904-741-4980
There are no additional pet fees.

Holiday Inn
9150 Baymeadows Rd
Jacksonville, FL
904-737-1700
There is a $35 one time pet fee.

Holiday Inn - Airport North
I-95 & Airport Rd
Jacksonville, FL
904-741-4404
Pets are allowed in the 2 floor
section of the hotel. There are
no pet fees.

Homewood Suites
8737 Baymeadows Rd
Jacksonville, FL
904-733-9299
There is a $75 one time pet fee.

**La Quinta Inn & Suites
Jacksonville Butler Blvd**
4686 Lenoir Avenue South
Jacksonville, FL
904-296-0703
Dogs of all sizes are allowed at
the hotel.

**La Quinta Inn Jacksonville
Airport North**
812 Dunn Avenue
Jacksonville, FL
904-751-6960
Dogs of all sizes are allowed at
the hotel.

**La Quinta Inn Jacksonville
Baymeadows**
8255 Dix Ellis Trail
Jacksonville, FL
904-731-9940
Dogs of all sizes are allowed at
the hotel.

Motel 6
6107 Youngerman Circle
Jacksonville, FL
904-777-6100
There are no additional pet fees.

**Ramada Inn - Mandarin
Conference Center**
3130 Hartley Rd

Jacksonville, FL
904-268-8080
There is a daily pet charge of
$15 for the first day, $5 for each
additional day, and a $100
refundable pet deposit.

Red Roof Inn
6099 Youngerman Circle
Jacksonville, FL
904-777-1000
Dogs under 80 pounds are
allowed. There are no
additional pet fees.

Red Roof Inn
14701 Airport Entrance Rd
Jacksonville, FL
904-741-4488
There are no additional pet
fees.

Red Roof Inn - Southpoint
6969 Lenoir Avenue E
Jacksonville, FL
904-296-1006
There are no additional pet
fees.

Red Roof Inn South
6099 Youngerman Circle
Jacksonville, FL
904-777-1000
There are no additional pet
fees.

Residence Inn
8365 Dix Ellis Tr
Jacksonville, FL
904-733-8088
There is a $75 one time pet fee.

Residence Inn
1310 Airport Rd
Jacksonville, FL
904-741-6550
There is a $100 one time pet
fee per visit.

Studio 6
8765 Baymeadows Rd
Jacksonville, FL
904-731-7317
There is a $10 per day pet fee.
One large well-behaved dog is
permitted per room.

Juno Beach

**Holiday Inn Express-North
Palm Beach**
13950 US Hwy 1
Juno Beach, FL
561-622-4366
There is a $25 one time pet
charge.

Key Largo

Howard Johnson Hotel
Bayside MM 102 Overseas Hwy.
Key Largo, FL
305-451-1400
Dogs of all sizes are welcome.
There is a $10 per day pet fee.

Key West

**Ambrosia House Tropical
Lodging**
622 Fleming Street
Key West, FL
305-296-9838
This inn, located on almost two
private acres, offers a variety of
well-appointed rooms, suites,
town houses and a cottage, all
with private baths. The inn is
located in the heart of historic
Old Town. There is a one time
non-refundable pet fee of $25.
All pets are welcome. There is
no weight limit or limit to the
number of pets.

**Center Court Historic Inn &
Cottages**
916 Center Street
Key West, FL
305-296-9292
Dogs are allowed in the suites
and cottages. There is a $10 per
day pet charge.

Chelsea House
707 Truman Avenue
Key West, FL
305-296-2211
There is a $15 per day pet
charge.

Courtney's Place
720 Whitmarsh Lane

Key West, FL
305-294-3480
This inn has historic guest cottages. There are no designated smoking or non-smoking cottages.

Douglas House and Cuban Club Suites
419 Amelia St
Key West, FL
305-294-5269
Small dogs are welcome at the Douglas House. Large dogs are welcome at the Cuban Club Suites. There is a $10 per day pet fee. There are no designated smoking or non-smoking rooms.

Francis Street Bottle Inn
535 Francis Street
Key West, FL
305-294-8530
Dogs are allowed, including well-behaved large dogs. There is a $25 one time pet fee.

Key West Hideaways
915 Eisenhower Drive
Key West, FL
305-296-9090
Cottages, condominiums, suites and rooms in Key West. Escape the real world while enjoying the perfect alternative to a luxury hotel with the added value of total privacy and many locations in Key West. Call to request pet policy and to inquire about which rentals allow pets.

Key West's Center Court - Bed and Breakfast and Cottages
915 Center Street
Key West, FL
800-797-8787
Special doggy treats upon check-in. Pets welcome in suites, cottages, condos and homes. Amenities include 4 pools and most suites offer private jacuzzis. Specializing in weddings, honeymoons, and romantic escapes. There is a $10 per pet per night charge. Dogs of all sizes and breeds are welcome.

Key West's Travelers Palm - Inn and Cottages
915 Center Street
Key West, FL
800-294-9560
Special dog treats upon check-in. Dogs are welcome in the suites and cottages. Amenities include premier Old Town locations and 3 heated pools. Dogs of all sizes and breeds are welcome.

Seascape Tropical Inn
420 Olivia St
Key West, FL
305-296-7776
Pets are allowed in all of the cottages and two rooms in the main guesthouse. There is a $25 one time pet fee. All rooms are non-smoking. Children are allowed in the cottages. The owner has two dogs on the premises.

Sheraton Suites Key West
2001 South Roosevelt Blvd
Key West, FL
305-292-9800
Dogs up to 80 pounds are allowed. There are no additional pet fees. Pet treats are available as well.

Whispers
409 William St
Key West, FL
305-294-5969
Dogs are allowed, but no puppies please. There is a $25 one time pet fee. Children over 10 years old are allowed.

Kissimmee

Holiday Inn
7601 Black Lake Rd
Kissimmee, FL
407-396-1100
There is a $75 one time pet deposit of which $50 is refundable and $25 is not refundable.

Holiday Inn
7300 Irlo Bronson Memorial Hwy
Kissimmee, FL
407-396-7300
There is a $125 refundable pet deposit.

Homewood Suites Orlando-Disney Resort
3100 Parkway Blvd.
Kissimmee, FL
407-396-2229
There is a $250 pet deposit and $200 of the deposit is refundable. ($50 pet charge)

Howard Johnson Express Inn
4311 W. Vine Street/W Hwy 192
Kissimmee, FL
407-396-7100
Dogs of all sizes are welcome. There is a $10 per day pet fee per pet and a $25 one time pet fee.

Howard Johnson Hotel
2323 Hwy 192 East
Kissimmee, FL
407-846-4900
Dogs of all sizes are welcome. There is a $10 per day pet fee.

Howard Johnson Hotel
8660 W. Irlo Bronson Memorial Hwy
Kissimmee, FL
407-396-4500
Dogs up to 50 pounds are allowed. There is a $25 per week pet fee.

Larson's Family Inn
6075 West U.S. Hwy. 192
Kissimmee, FL
407-396-6100
There is a $150 refundable pet deposit and a $10 per day pet charge. Dogs up to 50 pounds are allowed.

Motel 6 - Main Gate East
5731 W Irlo Bronson Memorial Hwy
Kissimmee, FL
407-396-6333
Pets must not be left unattended.

Red Roof Inn

4970 Kyng's Heath Rd
Kissimmee, FL
407-396-0065
There are no additional pet fees.

Sun N Fun Vacation Homes
Bear Path
Kissimmee, FL
407-932-4079
Vacation Homes are located just 5 minutes to Disney and very close to other area attractions. All homes have private screened pools and fenced yards. Most homes welcome well-behaved pets and their families. Their is a pet fee of $30 per pet, per week plus a $300 security deposit, which is refundable assuming no damage, etc.

Lake City

Best Western Inn
4720 US 90 West
Lake City, FL
386-752-3801
There is a $5 per day additional pet fee.

Lakeland

Howard Johnson Inn
4645 Socrum Loop Rd.
Lakeland, FL
863-858-1411
Dogs of all sizes are welcome. There is a $10 per day pet fee.

Madeira Beach

Snug Harbor Inn Waterfront Bed and Breakfast
13655 Gulf Blvd
Madeira Beach, FL
727-395-9256
This bed and breakfast offers a location on the waterfront, continental breakfast, and a boat slip. Wake up with the sunrise from the spacious Key West-style deck overlooking beautiful Boca Ciega Bay. Check for availability. Snug Harbor Inn is on the Suncoast Trolley line.

Marianna

Comfort Inn
2175 Highway 71 South
Marianna, FL
850-526-5600
There is a pet fee of $12 per day.

Melbourne

Baymont Inn
7200 George T. Edwards Drive
Melbourne, FL
321-242-9400
There are no additional pet fees.

Best Western Harborview
964 S. Harbor City Blvd
Melbourne, FL
321-724-4422
There is a $10 per day pet fee.

Crane Creek Inn
909 E Melbourne Ave
Melbourne, FL
321-768-6416
The Inn is at 909 and 907 E. Melbourne Ave. There are no additional pet fees. Children are not allowed at the inn.

Hilton Oceanfront
3003 North Highway
Melbourne, FL
321-777-5000
They have had all kinds of well-behaved large dogs stay here, including Rottweilers. There is a $25 refundable pet deposit and a $10 per day pet charge.

Quality Suites Oceanside
1665 SR A1A N.
Melbourne, FL
321-723-4222
There is a non-refundable pet charge of $25. There is a per day pet fee of $10.60.

Miami

Amerisuites
3655 NW 82nd Ave.
Miami, FL

305-718-8292
There is a $10 per day pet charge.

Hampton Inn-Downtown
2500 Brickell Ave.
Miami, FL
305-854-2070
There are no additional pet fees.

Homestead Village-Miami Airport
8720 NW 33rd Street
Miami, FL
305-436-1811
There is a $75 one time pet charge.

La Quinta Inn Miami Airport North
7401 NW 36th St
Miami, FL
305-599-9902
Dogs up to 70 pounds are allowed at the hotel.

Quality Inn South-Kendall
14501 S. Dixie Highway
Miami, FL
305-251-2000
There is no pet fee.

Staybridge Suites
3265 NW 87th Avenue
Miami, FL
305-500-9100
There is a $125 one time pet fee per visit.

Miami Beach

Brigham Gardens Guesthouse
1411 Collins Avenue
Miami Beach, FL
305-531-1331
Hotel Rooms, Studios and one Bedroom Apartments - Each uniquely and comfort appointed in bright tropical linens and decor. Pets are welcome for a nightly fee of $6.00.

Hotel Leon
841 Collins Avenue
Miami Beach, FL
305-673-3767
Stone's throw from the beach, in

the heart of the Art Deco District of Miami Beach.

Hotel Ocean
1230 Ocean Drive
Miami Beach, FL
800-783-1725
Hotel Ocean's accommodations, mostly suites, are appointed in a warm Mediterranean style, where decor varies from room to room in colors, shapes, and accents. Furnished with 1930's collectible pieces, original art-deco fireplaces and exquisite bathrooms all units feature sound proofed windows, central A/C, in room safes, complimentary breakfast and cable tv. Pets are welcome. They have created a special package that includes a bed, treats, and walking service for only $19.95 per pet per day. The regular pet fee is $15.00 per pet per day.

Loews Miami Beach Hotel
1601 Collins Avenue
Miami Beach, FL
305-604-1601
All well-behaved dogs of any size are welcome. This upscale hotel offers their "Loews Loves Pets" program which includes special pet treats, local dog walking routes, and a list of nearby pet-friendly places to visit. While pets are not allowed in the pool, they are welcome to join you at the side of the pool or at the pool bar. There are no pet fees.

Miami Springs

Mainstay Suites
101 Fairway Dr
Miami Springs, FL
305-870-0448
There is a non-refundable pet charge of $25.

Milton

Comfort Inn
4962 SR 87 South

Milton, FL
850-623-1511
There is a pet fee of $10.85 per day.

Red Roof Inn & Suites
2972 Avalon Blvd
Milton, FL
850-995-6100
Dogs up to 90 pounds are allowed. There are no additional pet fees.

Naples

Charming Naples Home
746 98th Ave N.
Naples, FL
230-250-6888
Newly renovated, charming 2 bedroom, 2 bathroom home located five minutes from the beach. Fenced in back yard and one car garage. Master bedroom with queen, second bedroom with 2 twins. All amenities provided.

Red Roof Inn & Suites
1925 Davis Blvd
Naples, FL
941-774-3117
There are no additional pet fees.

Staybridge Suites
4805 Tamiami Trail North
Naples, FL
941-643-8002
There is a $75 one time pet fee.

Navarre

Comfort Inn & Conference Center
8700 Navarre Pkwy
Navarre, FL
850-939-1761
There is a pet fee of $10 per day.

Ocala

Comfort Inn
4040 W. Silver Springs Blvd
Ocala, FL

352-629-8850
There is a pet fee of $5 per day.

Holiday Inn
3621 W. Silver Springs Blvd
Ocala, FL
352-629-0381
There is a $20 one time pet fee.

Howard Johnson Inn
3951 NW Blitchton Rd.
Ocala, FL
352-629-7021
Dogs of all sizes are welcome. There is a $10 per day pet fee.

La Quinta Inn & Suites Ocala
3530 SW 36th Street
Ocala, FL
352-861-1137
Dogs of all sizes are allowed at the hotel.

Quality Inn I-75
3767 N. W. Blitchton Rd.
Ocala, FL
352-732-2300
There is a one time pet fee of $25.

Orange Park

Comfort Inn
341 Park Ave.
Orange Park, FL
904-264-3297
There is a non-refundable pet charge of $25.

Orlando

Howard Johnson Inn
7101 S. Orange Blossom Trail
Orlando, FL
407-851-4300
Dogs up to 25 pounds are allowed. There are no additional pet fees.

La Quinta Inn Orlando International Drive
8300 Jamaican Court
Orlando, FL
407-351-1660
Dogs of all sizes are allowed at the hotel.

Motel 6 - Winter Park
5300 Adanson Rd
Orlando, FL
407-647-1444
There are no additional pet fees.

Quality Inn At International Drive
7600 International Drive
Orlando, FL
407-996-1600
There is a pet fee of $6.66 per day.

Red Roof Inn
9922 Hawaiian Ct
Orlando, FL
407-352-1507
Dogs up to 80 pounds are allowed. Only one pet per room is allowed. There are no additional pet fees.

Residence Inn SeaWorld
11000 Westwood Blvd.
Orlando, FL
407-313-3600
There is a $150 one time pet fee.

Sheraton Suites Orlando Airport
7550 Augusta National Drive
Orlando, FL
407-240-5555
Dogs of any weight are allowed. There is a $25 per day additional pet fee.

Travelodge Orlando Centroplex
409 N. Magnolia Ave.
Orlando, FL
407-423-1671
There is a $10 per day pet charge. Dogs up to 50 pounds are allowed.

Ormond Beach

Super 8
1634 N. US Hwy 1 & I-95
Ormond Beach, FL
386-672-6222
There are no additional pet fees.

Palm Bay

Motel 6
1170 Malabar Rd, SE
Palm Bay, FL
321-951-8222
There are no additional pet fees.

Palm Beach

Heart of Palm Beach
160 Royal Palm Way
Palm Beach, FL
561-655-5600
There are no pet fees. Pet owners must sign a pet waiver.

Plaza Inn
215 Brazilian Avenue
Palm Beach, FL
561-832-8666
This pet friendly hotel has accommodated dogs up to 100 pounds. This inn, located on the Island of Palm Beach, is a historic 50 room hotel which has been fully renovated with warm textures of lace, polished wood, antiques and quality reproductions. Take a look at their website for pictures of this elegant inn. There are no pet fees.

Palm Harbor

Red Roof Inn
32000 US 19 North
Palm Harbor, FL
727-786-2529
There are no additional pet fees.

Pass-a-Grille

Pass-a-Grille Beach House
111 Eleventh Avenue
Pass-a-Grille, FL
casita.111@prodigy.net
Enjoy Florida, the way it used to be, with no high rise condos blocking the beach views. This pet-friendly house has all the modern amenities, yet it is in the heart of the historic district

at Pass-a-Grille Beach. Just a half block from the Gulf of Mexico in one direction, a half block from Boca Ceiga Bay in the other direction, yet, you'll be staying three blocks from restaurants and shops, and minutes from downtown St. Petersburg. Pets are welcomed, no size limits. There is a $100 pet fee.

Pensacola

Comfort Inn N.A.S.-Corry
3 New Warrington Rd
Pensacola, FL
850-455-3233
There is a non-refundable pet fee of $25.

Motel 6
7226 Plantation Rd
Pensacola, FL
850-474-1060
There are no additional pet fees.

Motel 6 - North
7827 N Davis Hwy
Pensacola, FL
850-476-5386
There are no additional pet fees.

Ramada Inn North
6550 Pensacola Blvd
Pensacola, FL
850-477-0711
This hotel regularly hosts dog shows and events. There is a $25 one time pet fee per stay.

Red Roof Inn
7340 Plantation Rd.
Pensacola, FL
850-476-7960
They usually allow small dogs, but will allow one well-behaved large dog. There are no additional pet fees.

Red Roof Inn - North
6919 Pensacola Blvd
Pensacola, FL
850-478-4499
Dogs under 50 pounds are allowed. Pets must be attended at all times.

Red Roof Inn - Univ. Mall
7340 Plantation Rd
Pensacola, FL
850-476-7960
There are no additional pet fees.

Shoney's Inn
8080 North Davis Highway
Pensacola, FL
850-484-8070
There is a $25 one time pet fee.
Dogs are not allowed in the
lobby and there is a place in the
back to walk your dog.

Super 8 Motel
7220 Plantation Rd.
Pensacola, FL
850-476-8038
There is a $5 per day pet fee.

Plantation

Holiday Inn
1711 N. University Dr
Plantation, FL
954-472-5600
There is a $10 per day additional
pet fee.

Residence Inn by Marriott-Ft. Lauderdale
130 N. University Drive
Plantation, FL
954-723-0300
There is a $20 per day pet
charge.

Staybridge Suites
410 North Pine Island Rd
Plantation, FL
954-577-9696
Dogs up to 70 pounds are
allowed and there is a $100 one
time per stay pet charge.

Pompano Beach

Motel 6
1201 NW 31st Ave
Pompano Beach, FL
954-977-8011
One large dog is okay.

Port Richey

Comfort Inn
11810 US 19
Port Richey, FL
727-863-3336
There is a pet fee of $6 per
day.

Punta Gorda

Holiday Inn
33 Tamiami Trail
Punta Gorda, FL
941-639-2167
There is a $25 one time pet fee.

Sanford

Rose Cottage Inn & Tea Room
1301 S Park Ave
Sanford, FL
407-323-9448
There is a $10 per day
additional dog fee. Dogs are
not allowed on the furniture.

Sanibel

Signal Inn
1811 Olde Middle Gulf Drive
Sanibel, FL
800-992-4690
Signal Inn, situated in a quiet,
peaceful and casual
atmosphere on the Gulf,
consists of 19 furnished
elevated beach houses. The
pet fee (per pet) is $80 per
week or $55 for 3 nights. Only
particular units allow pets,
please inquire at
1-800-992-4690.

Sarasota

Calais Motel Apartments
1735 Stickney Point Road
Sarasota, FL
941-921-5797
There is a $15 per day pet
charge and there are no
designated smoking or non-
smoking rooms.

Comfort Inn Airport
4800 N. Tamiami Trail
Sarasota, FL
941-355-7091
There is a pet fee of $10 per
day.

Coquina On the Beach Resort
1008 Ben Franklin Drive
Sarasota, FL
941-388-2141
There is a $30 one time pet
charge. There are no designated
smoking or non-smoking rooms.

Howard Johnson Express Inn
811 S Taimiami Trail
Sarasota, FL
941-365-0350
Dogs of all sizes are welcome.
There is a $10 per day pet fee.

Sebring

Quality Suites & Conference Center
6525 US 27 North
Sebring, FL
863-385-4500
There is a non-refundable pet
charge of $25. There is a per
day pet fee of $10.

Siesta Key

Turtle Beach Resort
9049 Midnight Pass Road
Siesta Key, FL
941-349-4554
This resort was featured in the
Florida Living Magazine as one
of the best romantic escapes in
Florida. There is a pet charge
added, which is about 10% of
the daily room rate.

Singer Island

Days Inn-Oceanfront Resort, W. Palm Beach
2700 N. Ocean Drive
Singer Island, FL
561-848-8661
There is a $10 per day pet
charge. This motel is located on
the beach.

St Augustine

Days Inn Historic
2800 N Ponce de Leon Blvd
St Augustine, FL
904-829-6581
There is a $10 per day pet fee.

Howard Johnson Express Inn
137 San Marco Ave.
St Augustine, FL
904-824-6181
Dogs of all sizes are welcome.
There is a $10 per day pet fee.

La Quinta Inn St Augustine
1300 N Ponce De Leon Blvd
St Augustine, FL
904-824-3383
Dogs of all sizes are allowed at
the hotel.

Ramada Inn Historic
116 San Marco
St Augustine, FL
904-824-4352
There is a $10 per day pet fee.

Ramada Ltd
2535 SR 16
St Augustine, FL
904-829-5643
There is a $15 per day pet fee.

St Augustine Beach

Holiday Inn
860 A1A Beach Blvd
St Augustine Beach, FL
904-471-2555
There is a $20 per day pet fee.

St Petersburg

Valley Forge Motel
6825 Central Avenue
St Petersburg, FL
727-345-0135
There is a $5 per day pet charge
or a fee of $25 per week for a
pet.

Stuart

**Pirates Cove Resort and
Marina**

4307 S.E. Bayview Street
Stuart, FL
561-287-2500
There is a $20 per day pet fee.
The pet rooms are usually the
smoking rooms, but if you
speak with the hotel manager,
they should be able to give you
a non-smoking room.

Tallahassee

Econo Lodge
2681 N. Monroe St.
Tallahassee, FL
850-385-6155
There is a $10 per day pet fee.

Howard Johnson Express Inn
2726 North Monroe Street
Tallahassee, FL
850-386-5000
Dogs of all sizes are welcome.
There is a $10 per day pet fee.

**La Quinta Inn Tallahassee
North**
2905 North Monroe
Tallahassee, FL
850-385-7172
Dogs up to 50 pounds are
allowed at the hotel.

**La Quinta Inn Tallahassee
South**
2850 Apalachee Parkway
Tallahassee, FL
850-878-5099
Dogs of all sizes are allowed at
the hotel.

Red Roof Inn
2930 Hospitality St.
Tallahassee, FL
850-385-7884
Housekeeping will not come
into the room while a dog is in
the room. So if you want the
room cleaned, take your pup
out for a walk. Dogs under 80
pounds are allowed. There are
no additional pet fees.

Tampa

Best Western All Suites Hotel

3001 University Center Dr
Tampa, FL
813-971-8930
There is a $10 one time pet fee.

**Days Inn-Busch Gardens
North**
701 E. Fletcher Ave.
Tampa, FL
813-977-1550
There is a $6 per day pet
charge.

**Holiday Inn Express Hotel &
Suites**
4732 N. Dale Mabry
Tampa, FL
813-877-6061
There is a $25 one time pet fee.

Howard Johnson Express Inn
2520 N. 50th St.
Tampa, FL
813-247-3300
Dogs of all sizes are welcome.
There is a $20 per day pet fee.

Howard Johnson Hotel
4139 E. Busch Blvd.
Tampa, FL
813-988-9191
Dogs of all sizes are welcome.
There is a $25 one time pet fee.

**La Quinta Inn & Suites Tampa
Bay - Brandon**
310 Grand Regency Blvd.
Tampa, FL
813-643-0574
Dogs of all sizes are allowed at
the hotel.

**La Quinta Inn & Suites Tampa
Bay USF**
3701 East Fowler
Tampa, FL
813-910-7500
Dogs up to 50 pounds are
allowed at the hotel.

Quality Hotel Westshore
1200 N. Westshore Blvd
Tampa, FL
813-282-3636
There is a non-refundable pet
charge of $25.

Red Roof Inn - Brandon
10121 Horace Ave
Tampa, FL
813-681-8484
There are no additional pet fees.

Red Roof Inn - Fairgrounds
5001 North US301
Tampa, FL
813-623-5245
There are no additional pet fees.

Sheraton Suites Tampa Airport
4400 West Cypress Street
Tampa, FL
813-873-8675
Dogs up to 80 pounds are allowed. There are no additional pet fees. There are certain rooms designated as pet rooms.

Tarpon Springs

Best Western Tahitian Resort
2337 US Hwy 19
Tarpon Springs, FL
727-937-4121
There is a $5 per day additional pet fee. Dogs are not allowed in the pool area.

Titusville

Days Inn-Kennedy Space Center
3755 Cheney Highway
Titusville, FL
321-269-4480
There is a $10 per day pet charge.

Riverside Inn
1829 Riverside Drive
Titusville, FL
321-267-7900
This inn was formerly the Howard Johnson Lodge. There is a $5 per day additional pet fee.

Venice

Days Inn
1710 S. Tamiami Trail
Venice, FL

941-493-4558
There is a $30 one time pet charge.

West Melbourne

Howard Johnson Inn
4431 West New Haven Ave.
West Melbourne, FL
321-768-8439
Dogs up to 50 pounds are allowed. There is a $20 one time per day pet fee.

West Palm Beach

Hibiscus House Bed & Breakfast
501 30th Street
West Palm Beach, FL
561-863-5633
This bed and breakfast was ranked by the Miami Herald as one of the ten best in Florida. The owner has a dog, and there are no pet charges. Large dogs usually stay in the cottage.

La Quinta Inn West Palm Beach
5981 Okeechobee Blvd.
West Palm Beach, FL
866-725-1661
Most La Quinta Hotels allow a 50 pound dog or a cat.

Studio 6
1535 Centrepark Dr, North
West Palm Beach, FL
561-640-3335
There is a $10 per day additional pet fee. Large dogs are allowed if well-behaved.

Yulee

Comfort Inn
126 Sidney Place
Yulee, FL
904-225-2600
There is a pet fee of $10 per day.

Georgia Listings

Adairsville

Comfort Inn
107 Princeton Blvd
Adairsville, GA
770-773-2886
There is a pet fee of $5 per day.

Albany

Holiday Inn Express
911 E. Oglethorpe Blvd
Albany, GA
229-883-1650
There is a $50 one time pet fee.

Knights Inn
1201 Schley Avenue
Albany, GA
229-888-9600
There is a $10 one time pet charge.

Motel 6
201 S Thornton Dr
Albany, GA
229-439-0078
One large dog is allowed in a room.

Ramada Inn
2505 N. Slappey Blvd.
Albany, GA
229-883-3211
There is a $20 one time pet fee.

Athens

Holiday Inn
197 E. Broad Street
Athens, GA
706-549-4433
Pets are allowed in the courtyard section of the hotel.

Holiday Inn Express
513 W. Broad St
Athens, GA
706-546-8122
There is a $25 one time pet fee.

Atlanta

Airport Drury Inn & Suites
1270 Virginia Avenue
Atlanta, GA
404-761-4900
Dogs of all sizes are permitted. Pets are not allowed in the breakfast area of the hotel. Pets are not to be left unattended, and each guest must assume liability for damage of property or other guest complaints. There is a limit of one pet per room.

AmeriSuites-Atlanta/Perimeter Center
1005 Crestline Parkway
Atlanta, GA
770-730-9300
There are no additional pet fees.

Crowne Plaza - Airport
1325 Virginia Ave
Atlanta, GA
404-768-6660
There is a $100 refundable pet deposit and a one-time $25 non-refundable pet fee.

Hawthorn Suites
1500 Parkwood Circle
Atlanta, GA
770-952-9595
There is a $100 one time pet fee and there is a 2 dog limit per room. There is also a $50 refundable pet deposit.

Holiday Inn - Airport North
1380 Virginia Ave
Atlanta, GA
404-762-8411
There is a $100 refundable pet deposit and a $25 one-time pet fee.

Holiday Inn Select-Atlanta Perimeter
4386 Chamblee-Dunwoody Rd.
Atlanta, GA
770-457-6363
There is a $25 one time pet fee and a 2 dog per room limit.

Marriott Atlanta Airport
4711 Best Road
Atlanta, GA
404-766-7900

There is a $50 refundable pet deposit, dogs allowed on first floor only, and limit 1 dog.

Motel 6 - Northeast (I-85)
2820 Chamblee - Tucker Rd
Atlanta, GA
770-458-6626
There is a $50 refundable pet deposit.

Red Roof Inn
2471 Old National Pkwy
Atlanta, GA
404-761-9701
There is no extra pet fee, limit 3-4 well-behaved dogs.

Red Roof Inn-Druid Hills
1960 N Druid Hills Rd.
Atlanta, GA
404-321-1653
There is no extra pet charge, limit 2 dogs. There is an eighty pound weight limit.

Residence Inn by Marriott
134 Peachtree Street NW
Atlanta, GA
404-522-0950
Located in downtown Atlanta. There is a 2 dog limit and a $150 non-refundable pet fee.

Residence Inn by Marriott-Midtown
1041 W Peachtree Street
Atlanta, GA
404-872-8885
There is a $100 one time pet charge, and a 2 dog per room limit.

Sheraton Midtown Atlanta at Colony Square
188 14th Street at Peachtree
Atlanta, GA
404-892-6000
There is no size limit for dogs. There is a $25 one time additional pet fee. There is one floor for pets. It is a non-smoking floor.

Staybridge Suites - Perimeter
4601 Ridgeview Rd
Atlanta, GA
678-320-0111

There is a $75 one time pet fee.

Summerfield Suites-Buckhead
505 Pharr Road
Atlanta, GA
404-262-7880
There is a $150 one time pet charge. There is a 60 pound weight limit for dogs.

W Atlanta
111 Perimeter Center West
Atlanta, GA
770-396-6800
Dogs up to 60 pounds are allowed. There is a $25 per day additional pet fee.

Augusta

Amerisuites
1062 Claussen Rd.
Augusta, GA
706-733-4656
There is a $30 one time pet charge.

Comfort Inn
629 Frontage Rd. N. W.
Augusta, GA
706-855-6060
There is a non-refundable pet charge of $50.

Holiday Inn
2155 Gordon Hwy
Augusta, GA
706-737-2300
There is a $35 one time pet fee.

Howard Johnson Inn
601 NW Frontage Rd.
Augusta, GA
706-863-2882
Dogs of all sizes are welcome. There is a $7 per day pet fee per pet.

La Quinta Inn Augusta
3020 Washington Road
Augusta, GA
706-733-2660
Dogs up to 75 pounds are allowed at the hotel.

Sheraton Augusta Hotel
2651 Perimeter Parkway

Augusta, GA
706-855-8100
Dogs of all sizes are allowed.
There is no additional pet fee.
Pets are allowed on the first floor
which has smoking and non-
smoking rooms.

Austell

La Quinta Inn Atlanta West
7377 Six Flags Drive
Austell, GA
770-944-2110
Dogs of all sizes are allowed at
the hotel.

Brunswick

Best Western Brunswick Inn
5323 New Jesup Highway
Brunswick, GA
912-264-0144
There are no additional pet fees.

Embassy Suites
500 Mall Blvd.
Brunswick, GA
912-264-6100
There is a $10 per day pet
charge.

Holiday Inn
5252 New Jesup Hwy
Brunswick, GA
912-264-4033
There is a $10 per day additional
pet fee.

Byron

Comfort Inn
115 Chapman Rd
Byron, GA
478-956-1600
There is a pet fee of $10 per
day.

**Holiday Inn Express Hotel &
Suites**
102 Holiday Court
Byron, GA
478-956-7829
There is a $25 one time pet fee.

Calhoun

Quality Inn
915 Highway 53 East
Calhoun, GA
706-629-9501
There is a pet fee of $6 per
day.

Carrollton

Crossroads Hotel
1202 S. Park Street
Carrollton, GA
770-832-2611
There is a $25 one time pet fee.

Cartersville

Comfort Inn
28 SR Spur
Cartersville, GA
770-387-1800
There is a pet fee of $5 per
day.

Howard Johnson Express Inn
25 Carson Loop NW
Cartersville, GA
770-386-0700
Dogs of all sizes are welcome.
There is a $5 per day pet fee.

College Park

Howard Johnson Express Inn
2480 Old National Pkwy.
College Park, GA
404-766-0000
Dogs of all sizes are welcome.
There is a $10 per day pet fee.

Columbus

La Quinta Inn Columbus
3201 Macon Road
Columbus, GA
706-568-1740
Dogs of all sizes are allowed at
the hotel.

Motel 6
3050 Victory Dr
Columbus, GA
706-687-7214

There are no additional pet fees.

Super 8 Motel
2935 Warm Springs Rd
Columbus, GA
706-322-6580
There is a $25 one time pet fee.

Commerce

Comfort Inn
165 Eisenhower Dr
Commerce, GA
706-335-9001
There is a pet fee of $20 per day
during busy times. There is a pet
fee of $10 per day during non-
busy times.

Holiday Inn Express
30747 Hwy 441 S.
Commerce, GA
706-335-5183
There is a $15 one time pet fee.

Howard Johnson Inn
148 Eisenhower Drive
Commerce, GA
706-335-5581
Dogs of all sizes are welcome.
There is a $10 one time pet fee.

Cordele

**Best Western Colonial Inn
Cordele**
1706 East 16th Ave
Cordele, GA
229-273-5420
There is a $10 one time pet fee.

Dahlonega

Cabins at Horseshoe Bend
1104 Horseshoe Bend Rd.
Dahlonega, GA
770-518-9942
Cabins with fenced yards. All
cabins are non-smoking. There
is a $25 per visit pet fee up to 3
nights. There is a $50 pet fee if
you stay over 3 nights.

Dalton

Comfort Inn & Suites
905 West Bridge Road
Dalton, GA
706-259-2583
There is a pet fee of $15 per day.

Holiday Inn
515 Holiday Dr
Dalton, GA
706-278-0500
There is a $10 one time pet fee.

Motel 6
2200 Chattanooga Rd
Dalton, GA
706-278-5522
There are no additional pet fees.

Darien

Comfort Inn
703 Frontage Rd
Darien, GA
912-437-4200
There is a pet fee of $10 per day.

Super 8
Hwy 251 and I-95
Darien, GA
912-437-6660
There is a $10 per day additional pet fee.

Dawsonville

Comfort Inn
127 Beartooth Pkwy
Dawsonville, GA
706-216-1900
There is a pet fee of $5 per day.

Douglas

Holiday Inn
1750 S. Peterson Ave
Douglas, GA
912-384-9100
There is a $15 one time pet fee.

Duluth

Studio 6 - Gwinnett Place
3525 Breckinridge Blvd

Duluth, GA
770-931-3113
There is a $10 per day pet fee.

Ellijay

Sliding Rock Cabins
177 Mossy Rock Lane
Ellijay, GA
706-636-5895
Located midway between Ellijay and Blue Ridge, Sliding Rock Cabins offers beautifully decorated full log and rustic style cabins with large hot tubs. Pets always stay free and Sliding Rock Cabins provides a large bed for them along with food and water bowls, all natural treats, toys, and towels for the water loving dogs.

Forsyth

Best Western Hilltop Inn
I-75 & GA 42
Forsyth, GA
478-994-9260
There is a $15 one time pet fee.

Comfort Inn
333 Harold G. Clark Pkwy
Forsyth, GA
478-994-3400
There is a pet fee of $10 per day. There is only 1 non-smoking pet room, reserve early.

Gainesville

Holiday Inn
726 Jesse Jewell Pkwy
Gainesville, GA
770-536-4451
There is a $25 refundable pet deposit.

Jekyll Island

Clarion Resort Buccaneer
85 S. Beachview Dr.
Jekyll Island, GA
912-635-2261
There is a pet fee of $10 per

day.

Comfort Inn Island Suites
711 Beachview Dr.
Jekyll Island, GA
912-635-2211
This beachfront motel's amenities include a playground and room service. There is a $10 per day pet charge.

Holiday Inn Beach Resort
200 S. Beachview Drive
Jekyll Island, GA
912-635-3311
There is a $10 per day pet charge.

Jekyll Inn Resort
975 North Benchview Drive
Jekyll Island, GA
912-635-2531
This 15 acre resort is the largest oceanfront resort hotel in Jekyll Island. The resort is also home to the largest public golf course in Georgia. Amenities include an outdoor pool, playground and more. All guest rooms are non-smoking and have either one king bed or two double beds. Rollaways, cribs, microwaves and refrigerators are also available for a minimal fee. Or you can stay in one of the Villas, which are two-level townhouses that come with a separate bedroom, kitchen, dining area, living room, bathrooms, and private patio. There is a $10 per night pet charge plus tax and resort fee.

Seafarer Inn & Suites
700 North Beachview Drive
Jekyll Island, GA
912-635-2202
There is a $10 per day pet charge.

Villas By The Sea
1175 N. Beachview Dr.
Jekyll Island, GA
912-635-2521
This resort has villas with kitchens, private living rooms and separate bedrooms, located along a wooded beachfront.

There is a $50 one time pet charge for 1 bedroom units, $75 pet charge for the 2 bedroom units and $100 for the 3 bedroom units.

Jesup

Holiday Inn Express
1100 Express Lane
Jesup, GA
912-427-3549
There is a $25 one time pet fee.

Jonesboro

Holiday Inn - Atlanta South
6288 Old Dixie Hwy
Jonesboro, GA
770-968-4300
There is a $15 one time pet fee.

Kennesaw

Best Western Kennesaw Inn
3375 Busbee Drive
Kennesaw, GA
770-424-7666
There is a $10 per day additional pet fee.

Comfort Inn
750 Cobb Place
Kennesaw, GA
770-419-1530
There is a pet fee of $15 per day.

Kingsland

Best Western Kings Bay
1353 Hwy 40 East
Kingsland, GA
912-729-7666
There is a $30 refundable pet deposit.

Super 8
120 Edenfield Dr
Kingsland, GA
912-729-6888
There is a $5 per day additional pet fee.

Lake Park

Holiday Inn Express
1198 Lakes Blvd
Lake Park, GA
229-559-5181
There is a $10 per day additional pet fee.

Lavonia

Best Western Regency Inn & Suites
13705 Jones Street
Lavonia, GA
706-356-4000
There is a $10 per day pet fee.

Lithia Springs

Motel 6
920 Bob Arnold Blvd
Lithia Springs, GA
678-945-0606
There are no additional pet fees.

Macon

Best Western Inn & Suites
4861 Chambers Road
Macon, GA
478-781-5300
There is a $10 one time pet charge. Amenities include an indoor pool and an exercise room.

Comfort Inn North
2690 Riverside Dr.
Macon, GA
478-746-8855
There is no pet fee.

Holiday Inn Express
2720 Riverside Dr
Macon, GA
478-743-1482
There is a $20 one time pet fee.

La Quinta Inn & Suites Macon
3944 River Place Dr.
Macon, GA
478-475-0206
Dogs of all sizes are allowed at the hotel.

Quality Inn
4630 Chambers Rd
Macon, GA
478-781-7000
There is a pet fee of $5 per day.

Marietta

Comfort Inn
2100 Northwest Pkwy
Marietta, GA
770-952-3000
There is a non-refundable pet charge of $75.

La Quinta Inn Atlanta Delk Road - Marietta
2170 Delk Road
Marietta, GA
770-951-0026
Dogs of all sizes are allowed at the hotel.

Motel 6 - Marietta
2360 Delk Rd
Marietta, GA
770-952-8161
There are no additional pet fees.

McDonough

Comfort Inn
80 SR 81 W.
McDonough, GA
770-954-9110
There is a pet fee of $5 per day.

Holiday Inn
930 Hwy 155 S.
McDonough, GA
770-957-5291
There are no pet fees. The hotel is at Exit 216 off I-75.

Metter

Comfort Inn
1300 Fortner Rd
Metter, GA
912-685-4100
There is a pet fee of $10 per day.

Milledgeville

Accommodations - Please always call ahead to make sure an establishment is still dog-friendly.

Ramada Limited
2627 North Columbia Street
Milledgeville, GA
478-452-3502
There is a $4 per day additional
pet fee.

Morrow

Quality Inn Southlake
6597 Joneboro Rd
Morrow, GA
770-960-1957
There is a pet fee of $10 per
day.

Sleep Inn
2185 Mt. Zion Pkwy
Morrow, GA
770-472-9800
There is a pet fee of $10 per
day.

South Drury Inn & Suites
6520 S. Lee Street
Morrow, GA
770-960-0500
Dogs of all sizes are permitted.
Pets are not allowed in the
breakfast area of the hotel. Pets
are not to be left unattended,
and each guest must assume
liability for damage of property or
other guest complaints. There is
a limit of one pet per room.

Norcross

**La Quinta Inn Atlanta
Peachtree Ind - Norcross**
5375 Peachtree Industrial Blvd
Norcross, GA
770-449-5144
Dogs of all sizes are allowed at
the hotel.

Northeast Drury Inn & Suites
5655 Jimmy Carter Blvd
Norcross, GA
770-729-0060
Dogs of all sizes are permitted.
Pets are not allowed in the
breakfast area of the hotel. Pets
are not to be left unattended,
and each guest must assume
liability for damage of property or
other guest complaints. There is

a limit of one pet per room.

North Georgia

Toccoa Riverfront Cabin
Call to Arrange.
North Georgia, GA
352-237-4335
North Georgia mountain cabin
on the Toccoa River. Located
near Blue
Ridge/Blairsville/Dahlonega.
Very private. Sleeps 6. Central
heat/AC, fireplace, satellite TV,
BBQ grill, swings, screened
porch, catfish pond and river
fishing year-round. Fenced
acreage and barn for horses.
Pets are welcome.

Peachtree City

**Best Western Peachtree City
Inn**
976 Crosstown Drive
Peachtree City, GA
770-632-9700
There is a $10 per day
additional pet fee.

Perry

Comfort Inn
1602 Sam Nunn Blvd
Perry, GA
478-987-7710
There is a one time pet fee of
$15.

Pooler

Econo Lodge
500 E. US 80
Pooler, GA
912-748-4124
There is a $10 additional pet
fee. Pets are allowed in the pet
rooms on the ground floor. The
hotel offers free cable w/HBO,
a continental breakfast, free
local calls, an outdoor pool, and
in-room coffee. The hotel is
newly renovated and has AAA,
AARP, corporate and military
rates. The hotel is located 11

miles from downtown Savannah
near Interstate 95.

Rome

Holiday Inn
#20 Hwy 411 East
Rome, GA
706-295-1100
There is a $25 refundable pet
deposit.

Howard Johnson Express Inn
1610 Martha Berry Blvd.
Rome, GA
706-291-1994
Dogs of all sizes are welcome.
There is a $5 per day pet fee.

Roswell

Studio 6 - Roswell
9955 Old Dogwood Rd
Roswell, GA
770-992-9449
There is a $10 per day pet fee or
a $50 per week pet fee.

Savannah

Holiday Inn
I-95 & GA 204
Savannah, GA
912-925-2770
There is a $15 one time pet fee.

Howard Johnson Express Inn
17003 Abercorn Street
Savannah, GA
912-925-7050
There is a $10 per day per pet
fee.

**Joan's on Jones Bed and
Breakfast**
17 West Jones Street
Savannah, GA
912-234-3863
This bed and breakfast has one
pet suite. There is a $50 one
time pet charge.

La Quinta Inn Savannah
6805 Abercorn Street
Savannah, GA
912-355-3004

Dogs of all sizes are allowed at the hotel.

La Quinta Inn Savannah I-95
6 Gateway Boulevard South
Savannah, GA
912-925-9505
Dogs of all sizes are allowed at the hotel.

Motel 6
4071 Highway 17
Savannah, GA
912-756-3543
There are no additional pet fees.

Red Roof Inn
405 Al Henderson Blvd
Savannah, GA
912-920-3535
Dogs are only allowed on the 3rd floor. Dogs under 50 pounds are allowed.

Sleep Inn
17013 Abercorn St
Savannah, GA
912-921-1010
There is a pet fee of $10 per day.

Southern Chic Guesthouse
418 East Charlton Street
Savannah, GA
(678) 859-0674
Located in historic district of Savannah, Georgia. There are no additional pet fees.

Super 8 Motel - Savannah I-95
15 Ft. Argyle Rd.
Savannah, GA
912-927-8550
Convenient I-95 location, minutes from the Historic District. $10/stay for up to 3 dogs in one room. FREE 8-minute long distance call each night. FREE continental breakfast. Coffee maker, night light, clock/radio, safe in each room. Seasonal outdoor pool. On-site guest laundry. Kids 12 & under stay free. I-95, Exit 94 West (Hwy 204/Abercorn). South of I-16.

The Manor House Bed &

Breakfast
201 West Liberty Street
Savannah, GA
912-233-9597
There are no pet fees. There are no designated smoking or non-smoking rooms.

Smyrna

Comfort Inn & Suites
2800 Highlands Parkway
Smyrna, GA
678-309-1200
This is a phone number central reservation center, so make sure you specify which property you are calling about. There is a $25 refundable deposit and a daily fee of $10.

Suwanee

Comfort Inn
2945 Highway 317
Suwanee, GA
770-945-1608
There is a non-refundable pet charge of $25.

Holiday Inn
2955 Hwy 317
Suwanee, GA
770-945-4921
There is a $25 one time pet fee.

Thomson

Best Western White Columns Inn
1890 Washington
Thomson, GA
706-595-8000
There is a $10 per day pet fee.

Tifton

Holiday Inn
I-75 & US 82W
Tifton, GA
229-382-6687
There are no additional pet fees.

Motel 6

579 Old Omega Rd
Tifton, GA
229-388-8777
There are no additional pet fees.

Tucker

Studio 6 - Northlake
1795 Crescent Blvd
Tucker, GA
770-934-4040
There is a $10 per day additional pet fee.

Valdosta

Best Western King of the Road
1403 St. Augustine Rd
Valdosta, GA
229-244-7600
There are no additional pet fees.

Holiday Inn
1309 St Augustine Rd
Valdosta, GA
229-242-3881
There is a $10 per day additional pet fee.

Howard Johnson Express Inn
1330 St. Augustine Rd.
Valdosta, GA
229-249-8900
Dogs up to 65 pounds are allowed. There is a $5 per day pet fee.

Motel 6
2003 W Hill Ave
Valdosta, GA
229-333-0047
A well-behaved large dog is okay.

Quality Inn North
1209 Augustine Rd
Valdosta, GA
229-244-8510
There is no pet fee.

Quality Inn South
1902 W. Hill Ave.
Valdosta, GA
229-244-4520
There is no pet fee. Pets may

not be left alone.

Ramada Inn
Interstate Highway 75 & State
Route 84
Valdosta, GA
229-242-1225
There is a $5 per day pet
charge.

Vidalia

Holiday Inn Express
2619 E. 1st Street
Vidalia, GA
912-537-9000
There are no additional pet fees.

Warner Robins

Best Western Peach Inn
2739 Watson Blvd
Warner Robins, GA
478-953-3800
There is a $5 per day additional
pet fee.

**Comfort Inn & Suites at
Robins Air Force Base**
95 S. SR 247
Warner Robins, GA
478-922-7555
There is a one time non-
refundable pet charge of $25.

Waycross

Holiday Inn
1725 Memorial Drive
Waycross, GA
912-283-4490
There are no additional pet fees.

Hawaii Listings
The State of Hawaii law states
that pets are required to
complete a 120-day confinement
in the State Animal Quarantine
Station. However, if specific pre-
arrival and post-arrival
requirements are met, animals
may qualify for a 30-day
quarantine or a new 5-day-or-
less quarantine that became

effective on June 30, 2003.
There is a three page checklist
for the 5-day-or-less program
on Hawaii's Agricultural web
site at http:
//www.hawaiiag.org/AQS/aqs-
checklist-5.pdf. In general, the
program requires stringent
rabies vaccine requirements, a
rabies blood test (which states
that the test was given *at least*
120 days before arrival into
Hawaii), a readable microchip,
complete documents filled out,
payment of about $225 per pet,
and a "direct release" from the
airplane to the Airport Animal
Quarantine Holding Facility
located only at the Honolulu
International Airport. All pets
arriving into Hawaii must be in
a sealed carrier or crate and
the seal can only be removed
by quarantine officials. If you
remove the seal yourself, your
dog may have to go into a 5 to
120 day quarantine. All
requirements must be met
exactly according to their
documentation, otherwise dogs
will dog into the lengthy
quarantine.

Haiku

Haiku Private Home Rental
Call to Arrange.
Haiku, HI
808-575-9610
This 3 bedroom, 3 bathroom
house rental is on 4 acres of
landscaped grounds. Well-
behaved dogs are allowed.

North Shore Vacation Rental
Call to Arrange.
Haiku, HI
307-733-3903
This 3 bedroom, 2 bathroom
vacation home allows well-
behaved dogs.

Hilo

Hale Kai Bed and Breakfast
111 Honolii Pali
Hilo, HI

808-935-6330
Well-behaved dogs are allowed.
Please note that at the time of
this publication, the ownership of
this inn was changing and the
inn may or may not allow dogs
in the future. Please call in
advance to make sure they still
allow dogs. This B&B offers four
ocean front guest rooms all with
private bathrooms.

Hilo Seaside Retreat Rentals
Call to Arrange.
Hilo, HI
808-961-6178
This private home offers two
private suites available for rent.
The rentals are located about 10
minutes from the Hilo Airport.
Well-behaved dogs are allowed.

Hilo Vacation Rental
Call to Arrange.
Hilo, HI
707-865-1200
This 3 bedroom, 2 bathroom
vacation home rental allows
well-behaved dogs.

Ka Waile'a
Call to Arrange.
Hilo, HI
808-933-1451
This studio cabin rental is
located about 15 miles north of
Hilo. Well-behaved dogs are
allowed.

Honolulu

Sheraton Waikiki Hotel
2255 Kalakaua Avenue
Honolulu, HI
808-922-4422
Dogs up to 80 pounds are
allowed. There are no additional
pet fees.

W Honolulu - Diamond Head
2885 Kalakaua Avenue
Honolulu, HI
808-922-1700
Dogs up to 80 pounds are
allowed. There is a $25 per day
pet fee and a $100 one time per
stay pet fee.

Kaihua

Paradise Cottage Vacation Rental
Call to Arrange.
Kaihua, HI
808-254-3332
This private cottage rental sleeps six people, and has air-conditioning. Well-behaved dogs are allowed for an extra charge.

Kailua

Kailua Beach Vacation Home
Call to Arrange.
Kailua, HI
808-230-2176
This 5 bedroom, 2 bathroom vacation home allows well-behaved dogs. It is located about 30 minutes from the Honolulu Airport.

Kailua Vacation Home
Call to Arrange.
Kailua, HI
808-263-0039
This 3 bedroom, 2 bathroom house is located within a short drive to the town of Kailua, and just a few miles to the ocean. Dogs are allowed.

Vacation Cottage Rental
Call to Arrange.
Kailua, HI
808-261-6220
This 2 bedroom, 1 bathroom cottage with a pool allows well-behaved dogs. The yard is completely fenced for children and pets.

Kapaa

Makaleha Mountain Retreat
Call to Arrange.
Kapaa, HI
808-822-5131
This vacation rental home has 2 bedroom and 1 bathroom, plus a studio. Well-behaved dogs are allowed.

Koloa

Sheraton Kauai Resort
2440 Hoonani Road
Koloa, HI
808-742-1661
Dogs of all sizes are allowed. There are no additional pet fees.

Makaweli

Coco's Kauai B&B Rental
Call to Arrange.
Makaweli, HI
808-338-0722
This 2 bedroom, 1 bathroom vacation rental allows well-behaved dogs. The rental is about five minutes from historic Waimea.

Maunaloa

Sheraton Molokai Lodge and Beach Village
8 Maunaloa Highway
Maunaloa, HI
808-552-2741
Dogs up to 80 pounds are allowed. There are no additional pet fees.

Poipu

Poipu Beachfront Condo Rental
Call to Arrange.
Poipu, HI
503-590-2528
This 2 bedroom, 2 bathroom condo vacation rental allows well-behaved dogs.

Princeville

Vacation Rental on Princeville Golf Course
Call to Arrange.
Princeville, HI
415-584-1134
This 3 bedroom, 3.5 bathroom home on the golf course allows well-behaved dogs.

Waipio

Hale Kukui Cottage Rentals
Call to Arrange.
Waipio, HI
808-775-7130
They offer one to three bedroom cottages, all with private baths. Well-behaved dogs are allowed.

Idaho Listings

Boise

Doubletree Hotel Boise, Riverside
2900 Chinden Blvd.
Boise, ID
208-343-1871
There is a 50 pound weight limit for dogs and a $25 one time pet fee.

Econo Lodge
4060 W. Fairview Ave.
Boise, ID
208-344-4030
Dogs up to 70 pounds allowed. There is a $10 per day pet fee.

Holiday Inn - Airport
3300 Vista Ave
Boise, ID
208-344-8365
There is a $10 per day pet fee.

Motel 6
2323 Airport Way
Boise, ID
208-344-3506
There are no additional pet fees.

Caldwell

La Quinta Inn Caldwell
901 Specht Avenue
Caldwell, ID
208-454-2222
Dogs of all sizes are allowed at the hotel.

Coeur d'Alene

Best Inn & Suites

280 W. Appleway
Coeur d'Alene, ID
208-765-5500
There are no pet fees. This was formerly the Comfort Inn

Coeur d'Alene Inn & Conference Center
414 W. Appleway
Coeur d'Alene, ID
208-765-3200
There is a $10 per day pet charge.

Shilo Inn
702 W. Appleway
Coeur d'Alene, ID
208-664-2300
There is a $10 one time pet charge.

Idaho Falls

Best Western Driftwood Inn
575 River Pkwy
Idaho Falls, ID
208-523-2242
There is a $10 one time pet fee.

Comfort Inn
195 S. Colorado Ave.
Idaho Falls, ID
208-528-2804
There is a pet fee of $5 per day.

Motel 6
1448 W Broadway
Idaho Falls, ID
208-522-0112
Pets must be attended at all times.

Shilo Conference Hotel
780 Lindsay Blvd
Idaho Falls, ID
208-523-0088
There are no additional pet fees.

Jerome

Best Western Sawtooth Inn & Suites
2653 South Lincoln
Jerome, ID
208-324-9200
There is a $50 refundable pet

deposit.

Ketchum

Best Western Tyrolean Lodge
260 Cottonwood
Ketchum, ID
208-726-5336
Dogs are allowed in rooms on the first floor only. There is a $10 per day pet fee.

Clarion Inn
600 Main St
Ketchum, ID
208-726-5900
There is a pet fee of $10 per day.

Lewiston

Comfort Inn
2128 8th Ave
Lewiston, ID
208-798-8090
There is a pet fee of $10 per day.

Howard Johnson Express Inn
1716 Main St.
Lewiston, ID
208-743-9526
Dogs of all sizes are welcome. There is a $4 per day pet fee and a $15 one time pet fee.

McCall

Best Western McCall
415 Third Street
McCall, ID
208-634-6300
There are no additional pet fees.

Montpelier

Best Western Clover Creek Inn
243 N 4th Street
Montpelier, ID
208-847-1782
There is a $6 per day pet fee.

Moscow

Best Western University Inn
1516 Pullman Road
Moscow, ID
208-882-0550
Dogs are allowed, but not in the poolside rooms or suites. There is a $25 one time pet fee.

Hillcrest Motel
706 North Main Street
Moscow, ID
208-882-7579
There is a $5 per day pet charge.

Palouse Inn
101 Baker Street
Moscow, ID
208-882-5511
Palouse Inn allows pets into a few rooms, both smoking and non-smoking. There is an $8 per day additional pet fee for 1 pet, $2 more per additional pet.

Mountain Home

Best Western Foothills Motor Inn
1080 Hwy 20
Mountain Home, ID
208-587-8477
There is a $5 per day pet fee.

Sleep Inn
1180 US 20
Mountain Home, ID
208-587-9743
There is a pet fee of $5 per day.

Nampa

Sleep Inn
1315 Industrial Rd
Nampa, ID
208-463-6300
There is a pet fee of $10 per day.

Nordman

Elkin's Resort on Priest Lake
404 Elkins Road
Nordman, ID
208-443-2432

There is a $15 per day pet charge and there are no designated smoking or non-smoking cabins.

Pocatello

Best Western CottonTree Inn
1415 Bench Rd
Pocatello, ID
208-237-7650
There are no additional pet fees.

Cavanaughs Pocatello Hotel
1555 Pocatello Creek Road
Pocatello, ID
208-233-2200
There are no additional pet fees.

Comfort Inn
1333 Bench Rd
Pocatello, ID
208-237-8155
There is a pet fee of $7 per day. Pets must not be left alone. Pets must be on a leash when not in the room.

Holiday Inn
1399 Bench Rd
Pocatello, ID
208-237-1400
Pets are allowed in the rooms with exterior entrances only. There are no additional pet fees.

Post Falls

Holiday Inn Express
3105 E. Seltice Way
Post Falls, ID
208-773-8900
Well-behaved dogs of all sizes are welcome. There is a $10 one time pet fee.

Howard Johnson Express Inn
West 3647 5th Ave.
Post Falls, ID
208-773-4541
Dogs of all sizes are welcome. There is a $5 per day pet fee.

Sleep Inn
100 N. Pleasant View Rd
Post Falls, ID
208-777-9394

There is a one time pet fee of $15. Pets must not be left alone and must be on a leash when out of the room.

Priest Lake

Hill's Resort
4777 W. Lakeshore Rd.
Priest Lake, ID
208-443-2551
There is a $150 per week pet charge. Dogs are also allowed on the beaches.

Rexburg

Comfort Inn
1565 W. Main St
Rexburg, ID
208-359-1311
There is no pet fee.

Sandpoint

Edgewater Resort
56 Bridge Street
Sandpoint, ID
208-263-3194
There is a $5 one time pet charge.

La Quinta Inn Sandpoint
415 Cedar Street
Sandpoint, ID
208-263-9581
Dogs of all sizes are allowed at the hotel.

Motel 6
477255 Hwy 95 N
Sandpoint, ID
208-263-5383
There are no additional pet fees.

Quality Inn
807 N. 5th Ave.
Sandpoint, ID
208-263-2111
There is a pet fee of $5 per day.

Sandpoint Super 8 Motel
476841 Hwy 95 North
Sandpoint, ID

208-263-2210
There are no additional pet fees.

Twin Falls

Best Western Apollo Motor Inn
296 Addison Ave West
Twin Falls, ID
208-733-2010
There is a $50 refundable pet deposit.

Comfort Inn
1893 Canyon Springs Rd
Twin Falls, ID
208-734-7494
There is a pet fee of $7 per day. Pets may not be left alone.

Motel 6
1472 Blue Lake Blvd N
Twin Falls, ID
208-734-3993
Pets must never be left unattended.

Illinois Listings

Alton

Holiday Inn
3800 Homer Adams Pkwy
Alton, IL
618-462-1220
There is a $15 one time pet fee.

Super 8 Motel
1800 Homer Adams Pkwy.
Alton, IL
618-465-8885
There are no additional pet fees.

Arcola

Comfort Inn
610 East Springfield
Arcola, IL
217-268-4000
There is a pet fee of $7 per day.

Arlington Heights

La Quinta Inn Chicago - Arlington Heights
1415 W Dundee Road
Arlington Heights, IL
847-253-8777
Dogs of all sizes are allowed at the hotel.

Motel 6 - North Central
441 W Algonquin Rd
Arlington Heights, IL
847-806-1230
There are no additional pet fees.

Sheraton Chicago Northwest
3400 West Euclid Avenue
Arlington Heights, IL
847-394-2000
Dogs up to 80 pounds are allowed. There is a $50 one time pet fee per stay. Pets may only be left alone in the room in a crate.

Belleville

Super 8 Motel
600 E. Main
Belleville, IL
618-234-9670
There is a $5 per day pet charge.

Bolingbrook

Holiday Inn Hotel & Suites
205 Remington Blvd
Bolingbrook, IL
630-679-1600
There is a $35 one time pet fee per visit.

Bourbonnais

Motel 6
1311 Illinois Rt 50 North
Bourbonnais, IL
815-933-2300
There are no additional pet fees.

Carlinville

Holiday Inn
I-55 & Rt 108
Carlinville, IL

217-324-2100
There is a $10 one time pet fee per visit.

Casey

Comfort Inn
933 SR 49
Casey, IL
217-932-2212
There is a one time [et fee of $5.

Caseyville

Motel 6
2431 Old Country Inn Rd
Caseyville, IL
618-397-8867
There are no additional pet fees.

Champaign

Comfort Inn
305 Market View Drive
Champaign, IL
217-352-4055
There is a pet fee of $5 per day.

Drury Inn & Suites
905 W. Anthony Drive
Champaign, IL
217-398-0030
Dogs of all sizes are permitted. Pets are not allowed in the breakfast area of the hotel. Pets are not to be left unattended, and each guest must assume liability for damage of property or other guest complaints. There is a limit of one pet per room.

La Quinta Inn Champaign
1900 Center Drive
Champaign, IL
217-356-4000
Dogs of all sizes are allowed at the hotel.

Red Roof Inn
212 W. Anthony Drive
Champaign, IL
217-352-0101

There are no additional pet fees.

Chicago

Claridge Hotel
1244 North Dearborn Parkway
Chicago, IL
312-787-4980
There is a $25 refundable pet deposit.

Holiday Inn - Mart Plaza
350 N. Orleans St
Chicago, IL
312-836-5000
There are no additional pet fees.

Hotel Allegro
171 West Randolph Street
Chicago, IL
312-236-0123
Well-behaved dogs of all sizes are welcome at this pet-friendly hotel. The luxury boutique hotel offers both rooms and suites. Hotel amenities include complimentary evening wine served in the living room, a gift shop, and an on-site fitness center. There are no pet fees.

Hotel Burnham
1 West Washington
Chicago, IL
312-782-1111
Dogs of all kinds and sizes are welcome at this pet-friendly hotel. The luxury boutique hotel offers both rooms and suites. Hotel amenities include a fully equipped fitness room, and complimentary evening wine in the lobby. There are no pet fees, just sign a pet liability form.

Hotel Monaco Chicago
225 North Wabash
Chicago, IL
312-960-8500
Well-behaved dogs of all sizes are welcome at this pet-friendly hotel. The luxury boutique hotel offers both rooms and suites. Hotel amenities include complimentary evening wine service, 24 hour room service, and an on-site fitness room.

There are no pet fees, just sign a pet liability form.

Palmer House Hilton
17 East Monroe Street
Chicago, IL
312-726-7500
No pet charge, just sign a pet waiver for any possible damages to the room.

Residence Inn by Marriott-Downtown
201 East Walton Place
Chicago, IL
312-943-9800
There is a $15 per day pet charge.

W Chicago - Lakeshore
644 North Lake Shore Drive
Chicago, IL
312-943-9200
Dogs up to 80 pounds are allowed. There is a $125 one time pet fee per stay and a $25 per day additional pet fee.

Collinsville

Collinsville Drury Inn
602 N. Bluff
Collinsville, IL
618-345-7700
Dogs of all sizes are permitted. Pets are not allowed in the breakfast area of the hotel. Pets are not to be left unattended, and each guest must assume liability for damage of property or other guest complaints. There is a limit of one pet per room.

Crystal Lake

Comfort Inn
595 E. Tracy Trail
Crystal Lake, IL
815-444-0040
There is a pet fee of $10 per day.

Danville

Comfort Inn
383 Lynch Dr

Danville, IL
217-443-8004
There is no pet fee.

Sleep Inn & Suites
361 Lynch Dr
Danville, IL
217-442-6600
There is a $10 non-refundable pet charge. There is a refundable pet deposit of $25.

Dixon

Best Western Brandywine Lodge
443 IL Route 2
Dixon, IL
815-284-1890
There is a $25 refundable pet deposit.

Comfort Inn
Plaza Dr
Dixon, IL
815-284-0500
There is a pet fee of $15 per day. A credit card will be required.

Downers Grove

Red Roof Inn
1113 Butterfield Road
Downers Grove, IL
630-963-4205
There are no additional pet fees.

East Peoria

Motel 6
104 W Camp Street
East Peoria, IL
309-699-7281
A large well-behaved dog is okay. Pets may not be left unattended at any time in the rooms.

Effingham

Holiday Inn Express
1103 Ave of Mid America
Effingham, IL

217-540-1111
There are no additional pet fees.

Howard Johnson Express Inn
1606 W Fayette Ave.
Effingham, IL
217-342-4667
Dogs of all sizes are welcome. There is a $5 per day pet fee per pet.

Elmhurst

Holiday Inn
624 N. York Rd
Elmhurst, IL
630-279-1100
There is a $25 refundable pet deposit.

Fairview Heights

Fairview Heights Drury Inn & Suites
12 Ludwig Drive
Fairview Heights, IL
618-398-8530
Dogs of all sizes are permitted. Pets are not allowed in the breakfast area of the hotel. Pets are not to be left unattended, and each guest must assume liability for damage of property or other guest complaints. There is a limit of one pet per room.

Forsyth

Comfort Inn
134 Barnett Ave.
Forsyth, IL
217-875-1166
There is no pet fee.

Franklin Park

Comfort Inn
3001 N. Mannheim Rd
Franklin Park, IL
847-233-9292
There is a pet fee of $7 per day. If paying with cash a refundable deposit of $50 will be required.

Galena

Best Western Quiet House & Suites
Highway 20 East
Galena, IL
815-777-2577
There is a $15 per day additional pet fee.

Galesburg

Comfort Inn
907 W. Carl Sandburg Dr
Galesburg, IL
309-344-5445
There is no pet fee for a smoking room. There is a pet fee of $15 for a non-smoking room.

Glenview

Motel 6 - North
1535 Milwaukee Ave
Glenview, IL
847-390-7200
Pets must be attended at all times.

Hammond

Holiday Inn - Southeast
3830 179th St
Hammond, IL
219-844-2140
There is a $35 one time pet fee. Pets may not be left alone in rooms.

Joliet

Comfort Inn North
3235 Norman Ave
Joliet, IL
815-436-5141
There is no pet fee. Pets are allowed on the first floor only.

Motel 6 - Joliet
3551 Mall Loop Drive
Joliet, IL
815-439-1332
From I-80 take I-55 north to US 30 exit.

Lincoln

Comfort Inn
2811 Woodlawn Rd
Lincoln, IL
217-735-3960
There is a pet fee of $10 per day.

Holiday Inn Express
130 Olson Rd
Lincoln, IL
217-735-5800
There are no additional pet fees.

Litchfield

Comfort Inn
1010 East Columbian N Blvd
Litchfield, IL
217-324-9260
There is a one time pet fee of $15.

Marion

Drury Inn
2706 W. DeYoung
Marion, IL
618-997-9600
Dogs of all sizes are permitted. Pets are not allowed in the breakfast area of the hotel. Pets are not to be left unattended, and each guest must assume liability for damage of property or other guest complaints. There is a limit of one pet per room.

Motel 6
1008 Halfway Rd
Marion, IL
618-993-2631
Pets must be attended at all times.

Red Carpet Inn & Suites
8101 Express Dr, Rte 8, Box 348-1
Marion, IL
618-993-3222
There is a $5 per day additional pet fee. Dogs may not be left alone in the rooms.

Mendota

Comfort Inn
1307 Kilash Dr
Mendota, IL
815-538-3355
There is no pet fee. Pets may not be left alone. Only well behaved dogs allowed.

Metropolis

Best Western Metropolis Inn
2119 East Fifth Street
Metropolis, IL
618-524-3723
There are no additional pet fees.

Comfort Inn
2118 E. 5th St
Metropolis, IL
618-524-7227
There is a one time pet fee of $25.

Moline

Hampton Inn
6920 27th Street
Moline, IL
309-762-1711
Well-behaved dogs allowed.

Holiday Inn Express - Airport
6910 27th Street
Moline, IL
309-762-8300
There are no additional pet fees.

Motel 6
2359 69th Ave
Moline, IL
309-764-8711
Pets must never be left alone in the room.

Morris

Days Inn & Suites
Rt 47 at Hampton Street
Morris, IL
815-942-9000
There are no additional pet fees.

Morton

Holiday Inn Express
115 E. Ashland
Morton, IL
309-266-8310
There are no additional pet fees.

Mount Vernon

Drury Inn
145 N 44th Street
Mount Vernon, IL
618-244-4550
Dogs of all sizes are permitted. Pets are not allowed in the breakfast area of the hotel. Pets are not to be left unattended, and each guest must assume liability for damage of property or other guest complaints. There is a limit of one pet per room.

Holiday Inn
222 Potomac Blvd
Mount Vernon, IL
618-244-7100
There are no additional pet fees.

Motel 6
333 S 44th St
Mount Vernon, IL
618-244-2383
Interstate 64

Thrifty Inn
100 North 44th Street
Mount Vernon, IL
618-244-7750
Dogs of all sizes are permitted. Pets are not allowed in the breakfast area of the hotel. Pets are not to be left unattended, and each guest must assume liability for damage of property or other guest complaints. There is a limit of one pet per room.

Normal

Best Western University Inn
6 Traders Circle
Normal, IL
309-454-4070
There are no additional pet fees.

Holiday Inn
8 Traders Circle

Normal, IL
309-452-8300
There is a $15 one time pet fee.

Holiday Inn Express Hotel & Suites
1715 Parkway Plaza Drive
Normal, IL
309-862-1600
There is a $15 one time pet fee.

Motel 6
1600 N Main Street
Normal, IL
309-452-0422
Pets must not be left unattended in the room at any time.

O'Fallon

Comfort Inn
1100 Eastgate Dr.
O'Fallon, IL
618-624-6060
There is a refundable deposit of $50.

Palatine

Motel 6 - Northwest
1450 E Dundee Rd
Palatine, IL
847-359-0046
There are no additional pet fees.

Peoria

Holiday Inn
4400 N. Brandywine Dr
Peoria, IL
309-686-8000
There is a $50 refundable pet deposit.

Hotel Pere Marquette
501 Main Street
Peoria, IL
309-637-6500
There is a $100 refundable pet deposit.

Jumer's Castle Lodge
117 N. Western Avenue
Peoria, IL

309-673-8040
There is a $25 refundable pet deposit.

Red Roof Inn
4031 N War Memorial Drive
Peoria, IL
309-685-3911
There are no additional pet fees.

Pontiac

Comfort Inn
1821 W. Reynolds St
Pontiac, IL
815-842-2777
There is a pet fee of $10 per day.

Quincy

Comfort Inn
4122 Broadway
Quincy, IL
217-228-2700
There is a pet fee of $10 per day.

Holiday Inn
201 S. 3rd
Quincy, IL
217-222-2666
There is a $10 per day pet fee.

Rantoul

Best Western Heritage Inn
420 South Murray Rd
Rantoul, IL
217-892-9292
There are no additional pet fees.

Robinson

Best Western Robinson Inn
1500 West Main Street
Robinson, IL
618-544-8448
There is a $5 per day additional pet fee.

Rochelle

Comfort Inn & Suites
1133 N. 7th St

Rochelle, IL
815-562-5551
There is a pet fee of $15 per day.

Rockford

Best Western Colonial Inn
4850 East State Street
Rockford, IL
815-398-5050
Dogs are allowed in the first floor rooms. There is a $25 one time per stay pet fee.

Residence Inn by Marriott
7542 Colosseum Drive
Rockford, IL
815-227-0013
There is a $100 one time pet charge.

Rosemont

Holiday Inn Select
10233 West Higgins Rd
Rosemont, IL
847-954-8600
There is a $25 one time pet fee.

Sheraton Gateway Suites Chicago O'Hare
6501 N. Mannheim Rd
Rosemont, IL
847-699-6300
Dogs up to 75 pounds are allowed. There are no additional pet fees.

Schaumburg

Chicago - Schaumburg Drury Inn
600 N. Martingale
Schaumburg, IL
847-517-7737
Dogs of all sizes are permitted. Pets are not allowed in the breakfast area of the hotel. Pets are not to be left unattended, and each guest must assume liability for damage of property or other guest complaints. There is a limit of one pet per room.

La Quinta Inn Chicago -

Schaumburg
1730 East Higgins Road
Schaumburg, IL
847-517-8484
Dogs of all sizes are allowed at the hotel.

Skokie

Howard Johnson Hotel
9333 Skokie Blvd.
Skokie, IL
847-679-4200
One large dog is permitted per room. There are no pet fees.

Springfield

Drury Inn & Suites
3180 S. Dirksen Parkway
Springfield, IL
217-529-3900
Dogs of all sizes are permitted. Pets are not allowed in the breakfast area of the hotel. Pets are not to be left unattended, and each guest must assume liability for damage of property or other guest complaints. There is a limit of one pet per room.

Motel 6
6011 S 6th St
Springfield, IL
217-529-1633
Pets must be attended at all times.

Pear Tree Inn
3190 S. Dirksen Parkway
Springfield, IL
217-529-9100
Dogs of all sizes are permitted. Pets are not allowed in the breakfast area of the hotel. Pets are not to be left unattended, and each guest must assume liability for damage of property or other guest complaints. There is a limit of one pet per room.

Sleep Inn
3470 Freedom Dr
Springfield, IL
217-787-6200

There is a pet charge of $25.

Super 8 Motel-South
3675 S 6th St
Springfield, IL
217-529-8898
There is a $25 refundable pet deposit.

Urbana

Motel 6
1906 N Cunningham Ave
Urbana, IL
217-344-1082
From I-57 take I-74 E to Hwy 45 Exit.

Indiana Listings

Anderson

Comfort Inn
2205 E. 59th St
Anderson, IN
765-644-4422
There is a one time pet fee of $15.

Bloomington

Best Western Fireside Inn
4501 E Third Street
Bloomington, IN
812-332-2141
There is a $20 refundable pet deposit.

Days Inn
200 Matlock Road
Bloomington, IN
812-336-0905
There is a $10 one time pet charge.

Cloverdale

Holiday Inn Express
1017 N. Main St
Cloverdale, IN
765-795-5050
There is a $15 one time pet fee.

Columbus

Holiday Inn
2480 Jonathon Moore Pike
Columbus, IN
812-372-1541
Pets are only allowed in the
exterior rooms.

Corydon

Capitol Inn
St Rd 135 & I-64, PO Box 773
Corydon, IN
812-738-4192
There is a $10 per day additional
pet fee.

Dale

Motel 6
20840 N US Hwy 231
Dale, IN
812-937-2294
There are no additional pet fees.

Edinburgh

Best Western Horizon Inn
11780 N US 31
Edinburgh, IN
812-526-9883
There is a $10 per day additional
pet fee.

Evansville

Comfort Inn
19622 Elpers Rd
Evansville, IN
812-867-1600
There is a pet fee of $10 per
day.

Comfort Inn
5006 E. Morgan Ave.
Evansville, IN
812-477-2211
There are no additional pet fees.

Motel 6
4321 Hwy 41 N
Evansville, IN
812-424-6431
There are no additional pet fees.

North Drury Inn
3901 US 41 North
Evansville, IN
812-423-5818
Dogs of all sizes are permitted.
Pets are not allowed in the
breakfast area of the hotel.
Pets are not to be left
unattended, and each guest
must assume liability for
damage of property or other
guest complaints. There is a
limit of one pet per room.

Fishers

Sleep Inn
9791 North By Northeast Blvd
Fishers, IN
317-558-4100
There is no pet fee. A credit
card will be required.

Studio 6 - North
8250 North By Northeast Blvd
Fishers, IN
317-913-1920
There is a $25 one time pet fee.

Fort Wayne

Marriott Hotel
305 E Washington Ctr Road
Fort Wayne, IN
219-484-0411
No pet charge, just sign a pet
waiver for any possible room
damage.

Motel 6
3003 Coliseum Blvd W
Fort Wayne, IN
219-482-3972
Pets may not be left
unattended in the rooms.

Red Roof Inn
2920 Goshen Road
Fort Wayne, IN
219-484-8641
There are no additional pet
fees.

Sleep Inn & Suites
2881 DuPont Rd.
Fort Wayne, IN

219-484-6262
There is a non-refundable pet
charge of $25.

Greenfield

Comfort Inn
178 E. Martindale Dr
Greenfield, IN
317-467-9999
There is a one time pet fee of
$5.

Hammond

Motel 6
3840 179th Street
Hammond, IN
219-845-0330
There are no additional pet fees.

Indianapolis

Comfort Inn North
3880 W. 92nd St
Indianapolis, IN
317-872-3100
There is a one time pet fee of
$25.

Drury Inn
9320 N. Michigan Road
Indianapolis, IN
317-876-9777
Dogs of all sizes are permitted.
Pets are not allowed in the
breakfast area of the hotel. Pets
are not to be left unattended,
and each guest must assume
liability for damage of property or
other guest complaints. There is
a limit of one pet per room.

Holiday Inn
6990 E. 21st St
Indianapolis, IN
317-359-5341
There are no additional pet fees.
Pets may not be left unattended
and they are not allowed in the
restaurant.

Holiday Inn
5120 Victory Drive
Indianapolis, IN
317-783-7751

Pets may not be left unattended in the rooms. There are no additional pet fees.

La Quinta Inn Indianapolis East
7304 East 21st Street
Indianapolis, IN
317-359-1021
Dogs up to 50 pounds are allowed at the hotel.

Mainstay Suites
8520 Northwest Blvd
Indianapolis, IN
317-334-7829
There is a pet fee of $10 per day.

Marriott Hotel
7202 East 21st Street
Indianapolis, IN
317-352-1231
There are no additional pet fees.

Motel 6 - Airport
5241 W Bradbury Ave (at Lynhurst Dr)
Indianapolis, IN
317-248-1231
There are no additional pet fees.

Motel 6 - East
2851 Shadeland Ave
Indianapolis, IN
317-546-5864
There are no additional pet fees.

Motel 6 - Keystone
9402 Haver Way
Indianapolis, IN
317-848-2423
There are no additional pet fees.

Motel 6 - South
5151 Elmwood Dr
Indianapolis, IN
317-783-5555
A large dog is okay if it is kept on a leash when it is outside of the room.

Sheraton Indianapolis Hotel and Suites
8787 Keystone Crossing
Indianapolis, IN
317-846-2700
Dogs of all sizes are allowed. If your dog is over 80 pounds there is a $50 one time pet fee.

Jeffersonville

Motel 6
2016 Old Hwy 31 E
Jeffersonville, IN
812-283-7703
There are no additional pet fees.

Kokomo

Comfort Inn
522 Essex Dr
Kokomo, IN
765-452-5050
There is a pet fee of $5 per day. Pets may not be left alone.

Lafayette

Comfort Suites
31 Frontage Rd
Lafayette, IN
765-447-9980
There is a one time pet fee of $10.

Holiday Inn
I-65 & SR 43
Lafayette, IN
765-567-2131
There are no additional pet fees.

Holiday Inn Express
201 Frontage Rd
Lafayette, IN
765-449-4808
There are no additional pet fees. Pets must be on leash outside the room.

Ramada Inn
4221 State Road 26 East
Lafayette, IN
765-447-9460
There are no additional pet fees.

Logansport

Holiday Inn
3550 E. Market
Logansport, IN
219-753-6351
There are no additional pet fees.

Madison

Best Western of Madison
700 Clifty Drive, Hwy 62
Madison, IN
812-273-5151
There is a $5 per day additional pet fee.

Markle

Sleep Inn
730 W. Logan St.
Markle, IN
219-758-8111
There is no pet fee.

Merrillville

Motel 6
8290 Louisiana Street
Merrillville, IN
219-738-2701
Pets must never be left unattended.

Muncie

Comfort Inn
4011 W. Bethel
Muncie, IN
765-282-6666
There is a non-refundable pet fee of $25.

Days Inn
3509 N. Everbrook Lane
Muncie, IN
765-288-2311
There is a $10 per day pet fee.

Radisson Hotel
420 S. High Street
Muncie, IN
765-741-7777
There are no additional pet fees.

New Albany

Holiday Inn Express

411 W. Springs St
New Albany, IN
812-945-2771
There are no additional pet fees.

North Vernon

Comfort Inn
150 FDR Dr
North Vernon, IN
812-352-9999
If paying with a credit card there is no fee. If paying with cash there is a refundable pet deposit of $20.

Richmond

Best Western Imperial Motor Lodge
3020 East Main Street
Richmond, IN
765-966-1505
There is a $5 per day additional pet fee.

Holiday Inn
5501 National Rd E
Richmond, IN
765-966-7511
There are no additional pet fees.

Lee's Inn
6030 National Rd. E.
Richmond, IN
765-966-6559
There are no additional pet fees.

Motel 6
419 Commerce Dr
Richmond, IN
765-966-6682
There are no additional pet fees.

Seymour

Holiday Inn
2025 E. Tipton St
Seymour, IN
812-522-6767
There are no additional pet fees.

Motel 6
365 Tanger Blvd
Seymour, IN
812-524-7443

A well-behaved large dog is okay.

South Bend

Motel 6
52624 US Hwy 31 N
South Bend, IN
219-272-7072
There are no additional pet fees.

Taylorsville

Comfort Inn
10330 N. US 31
Taylorsville, IN
812-526-9747
There is a pet fee of $5 per day.

Tell City

Holiday Inn Express Hotel & Suites
310 Orchard Hill Drive
Tell City, IN
812-547-0800
There is a $10 one time pet fee. The pet fee is spent on food for animals at the local shelter. Pets under 50 pounds are allowed.

Terre Haute

Comfort Suites
501 E. Margaret Ave.
Terre Haute, IN
812-235-1770
There is a pet fee of $15 pet day.

Drury Inn
3040 South US Hwy 41
Terre Haute, IN
812-238-1206
Dogs of all sizes are permitted. Pets are not allowed in the breakfast area of the hotel. Pets are not to be left unattended, and each guest must assume liability for damage of property or other guest complaints. There is a

limit of one pet per room.

Holiday Inn
3300 US 41 S.
Terre Haute, IN
812-232-6081
Pet owners must sign a pet damage waiver. There are no additional pet fees.

Motel 6
1 W Honey Creek Dr
Terre Haute, IN
812-238-1586
There are no additional pet fees.

Pear Tree Inn
3050 South US Hwy 41
Terre Haute, IN
812-234-4268
Dogs of all sizes are permitted. Pets are not allowed in the breakfast area of the hotel. Pets are not to be left unattended, and each guest must assume liability for damage of property or other guest complaints. There is a limit of one pet per room.

Vicennes

Quality Inn
600 Wheatland Rd
Vicennes, IN
812-886-9900
There are no additional pet fees. A large dog is okay if it is kept under control and leashed at all times when outside the room.

Iowa Listings

Altoona

Howard Johnson Express Inn
2701 Adventureland Drive
Altoona, IA
515-967-4886
Dogs of all sizes are welcome. There is a $6 per day pet fee per pet.

Amana

Holiday Inn
I-80 Exit 225
Amana, IA
319-668-1175
There are no pet fees. Dog owners must sign a pet waiver.

Ames

Howard Johnson Express Inn
1709 S Duff Ave.
Ames, IA
515-232-8363
Dogs of all sizes are welcome. There is a $10 per day pet fee.

Bettendorf

Jumer's Castle Lodge
I-74 at Spruce Hills Drive
Bettendorf, IA
319-359-7141
There is a $25 refundable pet deposit.

Burlington

Comfort Inn
3051 Kirkwood
Burlington, IA
319-753-0000
There is a pet fee of $5 per day.

Cedar Rapids

Best Western Cooper's Mill Hotel
100 F Avenue, Northeast
Cedar Rapids, IA
319-366-5323
There is a $5 per day pet charge.

Howard Johnson Express Inn
9100 Atlantic Dr. SW
Cedar Rapids, IA
319-363-3789
Dogs of all sizes are welcome. There is a $8 per day pet fee.

Clear Lake

Best Western Holiday Lodge
I-35 & Hwy 18, Box J

Clear Lake, IA
641-357-5253
There is a $10 one time pet fee.

Clive

Chase Suite Hotel by Woodfin
11 428 Forest Ave.
Clive, IA
515-223-7700
All well-behaved dogs are welcome. Every room is a suite with a full kitchen. Hotel amenities include a pool, exercise facility, and a complimentary breakfast buffet. There is a $5 per day pet fee and a $50 refundable pet deposit.

Coralville

Motel 6
810 1st Ave
Coralville, IA
319-354-0030
Pets may not be left unattended in the room.

Council Bluffs

Motel 6
3032 S Expwy
Council Bluffs, IA
712-366-2405
There are no additional pet fees.

Davenport

Best Western SteepleGate Inn
100 West 76th Street
Davenport, IA
319-386-6900
There is a $3 per day pet charge.

Clarion Hotel
227 LeClaire Street
Davenport, IA
563-324-1921
There is no pet fee.

Comfort Inn
7222 Northwest Blvd
Davenport, IA
563-391-8222
There is a pet fee of $10 per day.

Motel 6
6111 N Brady St
Davenport, IA
563-391-8997
There are no additional pet fees.

Des Moines

Best Western Colonial
5020 NE 14th Street
Des Moines, IA
515-265-7511
There are no additional pet fees.

Holiday Inn
5000 Merle Hay Rd
Des Moines, IA
515-278-0271
There is a $20 one time pet charge.

Hotel Fort Des Moines
1000 Walnut Street
Des Moines, IA
515-243-1161
This dog-friendly hotel is on the National Register of Historic Places.

Motel 6 - North
4940 NE 14th St
Des Moines, IA
515-266-5456
Please declare your pet when you check-in. Pets may not be left unattended in the room.

Dubuque

Comfort Inn
4055 McDonald Dr
Dubuque, IA
563-556-3006
There is a refundable pet fee of $15. Well behaved pets only.

Dyersville

Comfort Inn

527 16th Ave SE
Dyersville, IA
563-875-7700
There is a $50 refundable pet deposit.

Johnston

Inn At Merle Hay
5055 Merle Hay Rd
Johnston, IA
515-270-1111
There is a $30 refundable deposit and a $10 one time pet charge.

Le Claire

Comfort Inn Riverview
902 Mississippi View Court
Le Claire, IA
563-289-4747
If paying by credit card there is no fee. If paying by cash a refundable deposit of $25 will be required. Pets may not be left alone.

Marshalltown

Comfort Inn
2613 S. Center St
Marshalltown, IA
641-752-6000
There is a pet fee of $10 per day.

Mason City

Holiday Inn
2101 4th St, SW
Mason City, IA
641-423-1640
There is a $10 one time pet fee. Pets are not allowed in the lobby or the pool area.

Mount Pleasant

Ramada Limited
1200 East Baker St.
Mount Pleasant, IA
319-385-0571
The hotel offers King and Queen Rooms, 18 Suites, hot and cold

Breakfast, an Indoor Pool and Hot Tubs. There is plenty of open space to walk your pet. The pet fee is a one time $8.00 charge.

Muscatine

Comfort Inn
115 Cleveland St
Muscatine, IA
563-263-1500
There is a pet fee of $10 per day. Pets may not be left alone.

Newton

Best Western Newton Inn
I-80 and Hwy 14, Exit 164
Newton, IA
641-792-4200
There are no additional pet fees.

Holiday Inn Express
1700 W. 19th St S.
Newton, IA
641-792-7722
There is a $25 one time pet fee. Pets must not be left alone in the rooms.

Osceola

Best Western Regal Inn
1520 Jeffrey's Dr, PO Box 238
Osceola, IA
641-342-2123
There are no additional pet fees.

Sioux City

Comfort Inn
4202 S. Lakeport St.
Sioux City, IA
712-274-1300
There is a pet fee of $10 per day.

Motel 6
6166 Harbor Dr
Sioux City, IA
712-277-3131
Pets may not be left

unattended in the room.

Urbandale

Comfort Inn
5900 Sutton Dr
Urbandale, IA
515-270-1037
There is a pet fee of $5 per day.

Waterloo

Best Western Starlite Village
214 Washington Street
Waterloo, IA
319-235-0321
There is a $10 per day pet charge.

Holiday Inn-Civic Center
205 W. 4th Street
Waterloo, IA
319-233-7560
There are no additional pet fees.

Quality Inn & Suites
226 W. 5th St.
Waterloo, IA
319-235-0301
There is no pet fee.

Ramada Inn
205 W. 4th Street
Waterloo, IA
319-233-7560
There are no additional pet fees.

West Des Moines

Motel 6 - West
7655 Office Plaza Dr N
West Des Moines, IA
515-267-8885
There are no additional pet fees.

Williamsburg

Best Western Quiet House Suites
1708 N. Highland
Williamsburg, IA
319-668-9777
There is a $15 per day pet charge.

Kansas Listings

Abilene

Best Western Abilene's Pride
1709 N Buckeye Ave, PO Box 536
Abilene, KS
785-263-2800
There is a $10 per day additional pet fee.

Best Western President's Inn
2210 N Buckeye, PO Box 458
Abilene, KS
785-263-2050
Well-behaved large dogs are okay.

Holiday Inn Express Hotel & Suites
110 East Lafayette St
Abilene, KS
785-263-4049
There is a $5 per day additional pet fee.

Colby

Best Western Crown Motel
2320 S. Range Ave
Colby, KS
785-462-3943
There are no additional pet fees.

Comfort Inn
2225 S. Range Ave
Colby, KS
785-462-3833
There is a pet fee of $5 per day.

Days Inn
Highway 70 and Highway 25
Colby, KS
785-462-8691
There is a $5 per day pet fee.

Dodge City

Nendels Inn and Suites
2523 E Wyatt Earp Blvd
Dodge City, KS
316-225-3000

There are no additional pet fees.

Super 8
1708 W Wyatt Earp Blvd
Dodge City, KS
316-225-3924
There is a $50 refundable deposit.

El Dorado

Best Western Red Coach Inn
2525 W. Central
El Dorado, KS
316-321-6900
There are no additional pet fees.

Emporia

Best Western Hospitality House
3021 W. Hwy 50
Emporia, KS
620-342-7587
Pets are not allowed in poolside rooms.

Super 8 Motel - Emporia
2913 W. Highway 50
Emporia, KS
620-342-7567
$10/stay for up to 3 dogs in one room. FREE 8-minute long distance call each night. FREE continental breakfast. Coffee maker, night light, clock/radio, safe in each room. On-site guest laundry. Kids 12 & under stay free. KS Turnpike, Exit 127 or 127B. I-35, Exit 128 (Industrial Rd). South to US 50, Right 1 block.

Fort Scott

First Interstate Inn
2222 S Main St
Fort Scott, KS
316-223-5330
There is a $5 per day pet fee.

Garden City

Best Western Red Baron Hotel
US Hwy 50 E Side at Hwy 83
Garden City, KS
620-275-4164
There are no additional pet fees.

Best Western Wheat Lands
1311 E. Fulton
Garden City, KS
620-276-2387
There are no additional pet fees.

Days Inn
1818 Commanche Dr
Garden City, KS
620-275-5095
There are no additional pet fees.

Holiday Inn Express Hotel & Suites
2502 E. Kansas Ave
Garden City, KS
620-275-5900
There are no additional pet fees.

Goodland

Comfort Inn
2519 Enterprise Rd
Goodland, KS
785-899-7181
There is a pet fee of $15 per day.

Great Bend

Super 8 Motel - Great Bend
3500 Tenth Street
Great Bend, KS
620-793-8486
$10/stay for up to 3 dogs in one room. FREE 8-minute long distance call each night. FREE continental breakfast. Coffee maker, night light, clock/radio, safe in each room. Indoor pool. On-site guest laundry. Kids 12 & under stay free. US 56, West of US 281 btwn Lincoln & Harrison, near Wal-Mart.

Greensburg

Best Western J-Hawk Motel
515 West Kansas Ave
Greensburg, KS

620-723-2121
Well-behaved large dogs are okay.

Hays

Best Western Vagabond Motel
2524 Vine Street
Hays, KS
785-625-2511
There are no additional pet fees.

Hampton Inn
3801 Vine St
Hays, KS
785-625-8103
There are no additional pet fees.

Holiday Inn
3603 Vine St
Hays, KS
785-625-7371
There are no additional pet fees.

Motel 6
3404 Vine St
Hays, KS
785-625-4282
There are no pet fees.

Hutchinson

Best Western Sun Dome
11 Des Moines SH
Hutchinson, KS
620-663-4444
The entire hotel is non-smoking.

Super 8 Motel - Hutchinson
1315 E. 11th Avenue
Hutchinson, KS
620-662-6394
Home of the KS State Fair.
$10/stay for up to 3 dogs in one room. FREE 8-minute long distance call each night. FREE continental breakfast. Coffee maker, night light, clock/radio, safe in each room. On-site guest laundry. Kids 12 & under stay free. KS 61 & E 11th Avenue.

Independence

Best Western Prairie Inn
3222 West Main

Independence, KS
620-331-7300
There is a $10 one time pet fee per visit.

Junction City

Motel 6
1931 Lacy Drive
Junction City, KS
785-762-2215
There are no additional pet fees.

Kansas City

Best Western Inn & Conf Center
501 Southwest Blvd
Kansas City, KS
913-677-3060
Dogs may not be left alone in the room.

Lansing

Holiday Inn Express Hotel & Suites
120 Express Drive
Lansing, KS
913-250-1000
There is a $20 one time pet fee.

Larned

Best Western Townsman Motel
123 E 14th
Larned, KS
620-285-3114
There are no additional pet fees.

Lawrence

Holiday Inn
200 McDonald Drive
Lawrence, KS
785-841-7077
There is a $100 refundable pet deposit.

Super 8 Motel - Lawrence
515 McDonald Drive
Lawrence, KS

785-842-5721
Home of KU Jayhawks. $10/stay for up to 3 dogs in one room. FREE 8-minute long distance call each night. FREE continental breakfast. Coffee maker, night light, clock/radio, safe in each room. On-site guest laundry. Kids 12 & under stay free. I-70 (KS Turnpike), Exit 202, South 1 mile.

Lenexa

La Quinta Inn Kansas City - Lenexa
9461 Lenexa Drive
Lenexa, KS
913-492-5500
Dogs of all sizes are allowed at the hotel.

Manhattan

Holiday Inn
530 Richards Drive
Manhattan, KS
785-539-5311
There are no additional pet fees.

Motel 6
510 Tuttle Creek Blvd
Manhattan, KS
785-537-1022
There are no additional pet fees.
Pets must be on leash when outside the room.

McPherson

Super 8 Motel - McPherson
2110 E. Kansas
McPherson, KS
620-241-8881
$10/stay for up to 3 dogs in one room. FREE 8-minute long distance call each night. FREE continental breakfast. Coffee maker, night light, clock/radio, safe in each room. On-site guest laundry. Kids 12 & under stay free. I-135, Exit 60, on US 56 (Kansas Ave Frontage Road) near Wal-Mart & KFC.

Newton

Best Western Red Coach Inn
1301 East First
Newton, KS
316-283-9120
There is a $6 per day pet fee.
Dogs may not be left alone in
the room.

Super 8 Motel - Newton
1620 E. 2nd Street
Newton, KS
316-283-7611
Located just 20 miles North of
Wichita. $10/stay for up to 3
dogs in one room. FREE 8-
minute long distance call each
night. FREE continental
breakfast. Coffee maker, night
light, clock/radio, safe in each
room. On-site guest laundry.
Kids 12 & under stay free. I-135,
Exit 31, East 1-1/2 blocks to
Spencer, Left on Spencer.

Olathe

Sleep Inn
20662 W 151st St
Olathe, KS
913-390-9500
There is a one time pet fee of
$10. Pets must be kept in a
kennel when alone in the room.

Overland Park

Chase Suite Hotel by Woodfin
6300 W. 11Oth
Overland Park, KS
913-491-3333
All well-behaved dogs are
welcome. Every room is a suite
and hotel amenities includes an
exercise room and a
complimentary hot breakfast
buffet. There is a $10 per day
pet fee.

Holiday Inn
7240 Shawnee Mission Pkwy
Overland Park, KS
913-262-3010
There is a $25 one time pet fee.

Pratt

Best Western Hillcrest
1336 East First
Pratt, KS
620-672-6407
There are no additional pet
fees.

Holiday Inn Express
1401 W. Hwy 54
Pratt, KS
620-672-9433
There are no additional pet
fees.

Salina

Best Western Mid-America Inn
1846 North 9th Street
Salina, KS
785-827-0356
There are no additional pet
fees.

Comfort Inn
1820 W. Crawford St
Salina, KS
785-826-1711
The non-smoking room pet fee
is $15 per day. The smoking
room pet fee is $10 per day.

Holiday Inn
1616 W Crawford
Salina, KS
785-823-1739
There are no additional pet
fees.

Motel 6
635 W. Diamond Drive
Salina, KS
785-827-8397
There are no additional pet
fees. Pets must not be left
unattended in the room.

Topeka

Motel 6
1224 Wanamaker Rd SW
Topeka, KS
785-273-9888
There are no additional pet
fees.

Ramada Inn
420 E 6th St
Topeka, KS
785-234-5400
There are no additional pet fees.

Wichita

Best Western Red Coach Inn
915 E 53rd Street North
Wichita, KS
316-832-9387
There is a $15 one time pet fee.

Comfort Inn East
9525 E.Corporate Hills
Wichita, KS
316-686-2844
There is a one time pet fee of
$10.

Holiday Inn - Airport
5500 W. Kellogg
Wichita, KS
316-943-2181
There is a $25 one time pet fee.

La Quinta Inn Wichita
7700 East Kellogg
Wichita, KS
316-681-2881
Dogs up to 50 pounds are
allowed at the hotel.

Motel 6
5736 W. Kellogg
Wichita, KS
316-945-8440
There are no additional pet fees.
One large dog per room is okay.

Residence Inn by Marriott - East
411 S Webb Rd
Wichita, KS
316-686-7331
There are studios and 1
bedroom suites. There is a $30
one time fee and a $10 daily pet
fee for the studios. There is a
$50 one time fee and a $10 daily
pet fee for the 1 bedrooms.

Kentucky Listings

Bardstown

Holiday Inn
Hwy 31 E & Bluegrass Pwy
Bardstown, KY
502-348-9253
There is a $10 per day additional pet fee.

Benton

Holiday Inn Express Hotel & Suites
173 Carroll Rd
Benton, KY
270-527-5300
There is a $10 per day additional pet fee.

Berea

Boone Tavern Hotel
100 Main Street
Berea, KY
606-986-9358
This hotel is one of the registered Historic Hotels of America. It is owned by Berea College and is staffed by students.

Bowling Green

Best Western Continental Inn
700 Interstate Drive
Bowling Green, KY
270-781-5200
There are no additional pet fees.

Drury Inn
3250 Scottsville Road
Bowling Green, KY
270-842-7100
Dogs of all sizes are permitted. Pets are not allowed in the breakfast area of the hotel. Pets are not to be left unattended, and each guest must assume liability for damage of property or other guest complaints. There is a limit of one pet per room.

Holiday Inn
3240 Scottsville Rd
Bowling Green, KY
270-781-1500
There are no additional pet fees.

Motel 6
3139 Scottsville Rd
Bowling Green, KY
270-843-0140
There are no additional pet fees.

Quality Inn
1919 Mel Browning Street
Bowling Green, KY
270-846-4588
There is a pet fee of $10 per day.

Brooks

Comfort Inn
149 Willabrook Dr.
Brooks, KY
502-957-6900
There is no pet fee.

Cave City

Comfort Inn
801 Mammoth Cave St
Cave City, KY
270-773-2030
There is a pet fee of $5 per day. Pets may not be left alone and must be on a leash when out of the room.

Quality Inn
1006 A Doyle Rd.
Cave City, KY
502-773-2181
There is a $10 per day pet charge.

Corbin

Best Western Corbin Inn
2630 Cumberland Falls Rd
Corbin, KY
606-528-2100
There is a $10 per day pet fee.

Quality Inn

264 W. Cumberland Gap Pkwy
Corbin, KY
606-528-4802
There is no pet fee.

Danville

Holiday Inn Express
96 Daniel Dr
Danville, KY
859-236-8600
There is a $50 refundable pet deposit.

Dry Ridge

Holiday Inn Express
1050 Fashion Ridge Rd
Dry Ridge, KY
859-824-7121
There is a $7 per day additional pet fee.

Elizabethtown

Holiday Inn
1058 N. Mulberry
Elizabethtown, KY
270-769-2344
A large dog is okay if it is quiet and well-behaved. There are no additional pet fees.

Super 8 Motel
2028 N. Mulberry Street
Elizabethtown, KY
270-737-1088
There is a $7 per day pet charge.

Erlanger

Residence Inn by Marriott
2811 Circleport Drive
Erlanger, KY
606-282-7400
There is a $100 one time pet charge.

Florence

Best Western Inn Florence
7821 Commerce Drive
Florence, KY
859-525-0090

There is a $10 per day pet fee.

Motel 6
7937 Dream St
Florence, KY
859-283-0909
There are no additional pet fees.

Super 8 Motel - Frankfort
1225 U.S. Highway 127 S.
Frankfort, KY
502-875-3220
Located between Louisville &
Lexington. $10/stay for up to 3
dogs in one room. FREE 8-
minute long distance call each
night. FREE continental
breakfast. Coffee maker, night
light, clock/radio, safe in each
room. On-site guest laundry.
Kids 12 & under stay free. I-64,
Exit 53B to US 127. 1 mile
North.

Comfort Inn
3794 Nashville Road
Franklin, KY
270-586-6100
There is a pet fee of $7 per day.

Holiday Inn Express
3811 Nashville Rd
Franklin, KY
270-586-5090
There is a $10 per day additional
pet fee.

Motel 6
401 Cherryblossom Way
Georgetown, KY
502-863-1166
There are no additional pet fees.

Comfort Inn
210 Calvary Dr
Glasgow, KY
270-651-9099

There is a pet fee of $10 per
day.

Holiday Inn
2910 Ft. Campbell Blvd
Hopkinsville, KY
270-886-4413
Pets must be on leash while
outside of the room.

Best Western Regency
I-75 at US Hwy 60 Exit 110
Lexington, KY
859-293-2202
There is a $10 per day
additional pet fee.

Holiday Inn
5532 Athens-Boonesboro Rd
Lexington, KY
859-263-5241
There are no additional pet
fees.

Marriott's Griffin Gate Resort
1800 Newtown Pike
Lexington, KY
859-231-5100
There is a $40 one time pet
charge.

Motel 6
2260 Elkhorn Rd
Lexington, KY
859-293-1431
There are no additional pet
fees.

Quality Inn Northwest
750 Newtown Ct.
Lexington, KY
859-233-0561
There is a one time pet fee of
$10.

Red Roof Inn
483 Haggard Lane
Lexington, KY
859-293-2626
There is a limit of two dogs per
room. There are no pet fees.

Sheraton Suites Lexington
2601 Richmond Rd
Lexington, KY
859-268-0060
Dogs of all sizes are allowed.
There is a $50 one time pet fee
per dog.

Sleep Inn
1920 Plaudit Pl
Lexington, KY
859-543-8400
There is a pet fee of $10 per
day.

Budget Host Westgate Inn
254 W Daniel Boone Parkway
London, KY
606-878-7330
There are no additional pet fees.

Days Inn
2035 Hwy. 192 West
London, KY
606-864-7331
There is a $5.50 per day pet
charge.

Park Inn
400 GOP
London, KY
606-878-7678
There are no additional pet fees.

Best Western Village Inn
Madison & Lock Avenue
Louisa, KY
606-638-9417
There is a $5 per day additional
pet fee.

**Aleksander House Bed and
Breakfast**
1213 South First Street
Louisville, KY
502-637-4985
Stay at an 1882 Victorian home
located in "Old Louisville." They
take well-behaved dogs and
cats. Animals must have a bath

before they visit. There is no pet fee and they may be left in the room alone as long as they are quiet and not destructive.

Breckinridge Inn
2800 Breckinridge Lane
Louisville, KY
502-456-5050
There is a $50 one time pet charge.

Comfort Suites
1850 Resouce Way
Louisville, KY
502-266-6509
There is a pet fee of $10 per day. Pets may not be left alone.

Drury Inn & Suites
9501 Blairwood Road
Louisville, KY
502-326-4170
Dogs of all sizes are permitted. Pets are not allowed in the breakfast area of the hotel. Pets are not to be left unattended, and each guest must assume liability for damage of property or other guest complaints. There is a limit of one pet per room.

Holiday Inn
1325 S. Hurstbourne Pkwy
Louisville, KY
502-426-2600
There is a $25 one time pet fee.

Holiday Inn
4004 Gardiner Point Drive
Louisville, KY
502-452-6361
There are no additional pet fees.

Holiday Inn - Airport
3317 Fern Valley Rd
Louisville, KY
502-964-3311
There is a $35 one time pet fee.

Holiday Inn - Downtown
120 W Broadway
Louisville, KY
502-582-2241
Dogs under 50 pounds are allowed. There are no additional pet fees.

Mainstay Suites
1650 Alliant Ave.
Louisville, KY
502-267-4454
There is a pet fee of $10 per day. If paying cash a refundable $50 deposit is required.

Motel 6
3200 Kemmons Drive
Louisville, KY
502-473-0000
There are no additional pet fees. Pets must always be attended in the room.

Red Roof Inn-East
9330 Blairwood Road
Louisville, KY
502-426-7621
There are no additional pet fees. The hotel allows one large dog per room.

Seelbach Hilton
500 Fourth Avenue
Louisville, KY
502-585-3200
There is a $50 refundable pet deposit.

Sleep Inn
1850 Priority Way
Louisville, KY
502-266-6776
There is a pet fee of $10 per day. Pets may not be left alone.

Sleep Inn
3330 Preston Hwy, Gate 6
Louisville, KY
502-368-9597
There is a pet fee of $8 per day.

Staybridge Suites
11711 Gateworth Way
Louisville, KY
502-244-9511
There is a $75 one time pet fee.

Travelodge
9340 Blairwood Rd.
Louisville, KY
502-425-8010
There is a $15 one time pet charge.

Madisonville

Days Inn
1900 Lantaff Blvd.
Madisonville, KY
270-821-8620
There is a $10 per day pet charge.

Morgantown

Motel 6
1460 S. Main Street
Morgantown, KY
270-526-9481
There are no additional pet fees. One well-behaved pet is allowed per room.

Morton's Gap

Best Western Pennyrile Inn
Pennyrile Pkwy Exit 37
Morton's Gap, KY
270-258-5201
There is a $20 per day additional pet fee.

Murray

Days Inn
517 S. 12th Street
Murray, KY
270-753-6706
There is a $10 per day pet charge. They usually put dogs in a smoking room, but if you request a non-smoking room, they will try to accommodate your request.

Murray Plaza Court
502 S. 12th Street
Murray, KY
270-753-2682
There are no pet fees.

Owensboro

Holiday Inn
3136 W. 2nd St
Owensboro, KY
270-685-3941
There are no additional pet fees. Pets must be attended at all

times.

Motel 6
4585 Frederica St
Owensboro, KY
270-686-8606
There are no additional pet fees.

Paducah

Drury Inn
3975 Hinkleville Road
Paducah, KY
270-443-3313
Dogs of all sizes are permitted.
Pets are not allowed in the
breakfast area of the hotel. Pets
are not to be left unattended,
and each guest must assume
liability for damage of property or
other guest complaints. There is
a limit of one pet per room.

Drury Suites
2930 James-Sanders Blvd
Paducah, KY
270-441-0024
Dogs of all sizes are permitted.
Pets are not allowed in the
breakfast area of the hotel. Pets
are not to be left unattended,
and each guest must assume
liability for damage of property or
other guest complaints. There is
a limit of one pet per room.

Hampton Inn
4930 Hinkleville Rd.
Paducah, KY
270-442-4500
There are no additional pet fees.

Motel 6
5120 Hinkleville Rd
Paducah, KY
270-443-3672
There are no additional pet fees.
Pets must be on leash when
outside of the room.

Pear Tree Inn
5002 Hinkleville Road
Paducah, KY
270-444-7200
Dogs of all sizes are permitted.
Pets are not allowed in the
breakfast area of the hotel. Pets

are not to be left unattended,
and each guest must assume
liability for damage of property
or other guest complaints.
There is a limit of one pet per
room.

Travel Inn
1380 S. Irvin Cobb Dr.
Paducah, KY
270-443-8751
There are no additional pet
fees.

Versailles

Rose Hill Inn Bed & Breakfast
233 Rose Hill
Versailles, KY
859-873-5957
Dogs are welcome in the
cottage and the apartment at
this bed & breakfast. The
owners also have dogs which
reside on the premise. There is
a $15 one time pet charge.

Winchester

Best Western Country Squire
1307 West Lexington Avenue
Winchester, KY
859-744-7210
There is a $5.35 per day
additional pet fee.

Louisiana Listings

Alexandria

Best Western
2720 W MacArthur Dr
Alexandria, LA
318-445-5530
Pets are allowed in the hotel,
but not in the indoor pool area.
There are no additional pet
fees.

Holiday Inn
701 4th Street
Alexandria, LA
318-442-9000

There is a $25 one time pet fee.

**La Quinta Inn & Suites
Alexandria**
6116 West Calhoun Drive
Alexandria, LA
318-442-3700
Dogs of all sizes are allowed at
the hotel.

Ramada Limited
742 MacArthur Drive
Alexandria, LA
318-448-1611
There is a $25 one time pet fee.

Baton Rouge

Chase Suite Hotel by Woodfin
5522 Corporate Blvd
Baton Rouge, LA
225-927-5630
All well-behaved dogs are
welcome. Every room is a suite
and hotel amenities include a
video rental library. There is a $5
per day pet fee.

La Quinta Inn Baton Rouge
2333 South Acadian Thruway
Baton Rouge, LA
225-924-9600
Dogs up to 75 pounds are
allowed at the hotel.

Motel 6
9901 Gwen Adele Ave
Baton Rouge, LA
225-924-2130
There are no additional pet fees.

Bossier City

La Quinta Inn Bossier City
309 Preston Boulevard
Bossier City, LA
318-747-4400
Dogs of all sizes are allowed at
the hotel.

Motel 6
210 John Wesley Blvd
Bossier City, LA
318-742-3472
There are no additional pet fees.

Quality Inn
4300 Industrial Drive
Bossier City, LA
318-746-5050
There is a one time pet fee of
$20.

Residence Inn
1001 Gould Dr
Bossier City, LA
318-747-6220
There is a $100 one time pet fee
and a $5 per day pet fee.

Breaux Bridge

Best Western
2088-B Rees Street
Breaux Bridge, LA
337-332-1114
There is a $20 per day additional
pet fee.

Holiday Inn Express
2942H Grand Point Highway
Breaux Bridge, LA
337-667-8913
There is a $25 one time pet fee.
Pets need to use the side
entrances. Exit I-10 at Highway
347.

Delhi

Best Western Delhi Inn
35 Snider Rd, I20 & 17 S.
Delhi, LA
318-878-5126
There is a $5 per day additional
pet fee.

Gretna

**La Quinta Inn New Orleans
West Bank - Gretna**
50 Terry Parkway
Gretna, LA
504-368-5600
Dogs of all sizes are allowed at
the hotel.

Hammond

**Best Western Hammond Inn &
Suites**

107 Duo Drive
Hammond, LA
985-419-2001
There is a $10 per day
additional pet fee.

Quality Inn
14175 Highway 190
Hammond, LA
985-542-8555
There is a pet fee of $10 per
day.

Iowa

Howard Johnson Express Inn
107 E Frontage Rd.
Iowa, LA
337-582-2440
Dogs of all sizes are welcome.
There are no additional pet
fees.

Kinder

**Holiday Inn Express Hotel &
Suites**
11750 US Hwy 165
Kinder, LA
337-738-3381
There are no additional pet
fees.

La Place

Best Western La Place Inn
4289 Main Street
La Place, LA
985-651-4000
There is a $20 refundable pet
deposit.

Lafayette

Comfort Inn
1421 S.E. Evangeline Thruway
Lafayette, LA
337-232-9000
There is no pet fee. Pets may
not be left alone.

La Quinta Inn Lafayette
2100 NE Evangeline Thruway
Lafayette, LA
337-233-5610

Dogs of all sizes are allowed at
the hotel.

Quality Inn
2216 NE Evangeline Thruway
Lafayette, LA
337-234-0383
There are no pet fees.

Red Roof Inn
1718 N University Ave
Lafayette, LA
337-233-3339
Dogs up to 80 pounds are
allowed. There are no additional
pet fees.

Lafayette/Scott

Howard Johnson Express Inn
103 Nibor Lane
Lafayette/Scott, LA
337-593-0849
Dogs of all sizes are welcome.
There is a $25 refundable pet
deposit.

Lake Charles

Best Suites of America
401 Lakeshore Drive
Lake Charles, LA
337-439-2444
There are no additional pet fees.

Metairie

**La Quinta Inn New Orleans
Veterans - Metairie**
5900 Veterans Memorial Blvd
Metairie, LA
504-456-0003
Dogs of all sizes are allowed at
the hotel.

**Quality Hotel & Conference
Center**
2261 N. Causeway Blvd.
Metairie, LA
504-833-8211
There is no pet fee.

Minden

Best Western Minden Inn

1411 Sibley Rd
Minden, LA
318-377-1001
There are no additional pet fees.

Monroe

Days Inn
5650 Frontage Rd
Monroe, LA
318-345-2220
There are no additional pet fees.

Morgan City

Holiday Inn
520 Roderick St
Morgan City, LA
504-385-2200
There is a $50 one time pet fee.

New Iberia

Best Western Inn & Suites
2714 Highway 14
New Iberia, LA
337-364-3030
There is a $50 refundable pet deposit.

New Orleans

Ambassador Hotel
535 Tchoupitoulas St
New Orleans, LA
504-527-5271
There is a $25 one time pet fee.

Best Western Patio Downtown Motel
2820 Tulane Avenue
New Orleans, LA
504-822-0200
Centrally located, The Best Western Patio is located just minutes from destinations such as The French Quarter, Harrah's Casino, The Riverwalk and the historic Garden District. There is a $35.00 pet fee per stay.

Chimes Bed and Breakfast
Constantinople St & Coliseum St
New Orleans, LA
504-899-2621

Dogs that stay here need to like children and cats. Please clean up after your pet. Pets are not to be left alone in the room.

Drury Inn & Suites
820 Poydras Street
New Orleans, LA
504-529-7800
Dogs of all sizes are permitted. Pets are not allowed in the breakfast area of the hotel. Pets are not to be left unattended, and each guest must assume liability for damage of property or other guest complaints. There is a limit of one pet per room.

French Quarter Courtyard
1101 N Rampart
New Orleans, LA
504-522-7333
There is a $25 one time pet fee.

Hotel Monaco New Orleans
333 St. Charles Avenue
New Orleans, LA
504-561-0010
Well-behaved dogs of all sizes are welcome at this pet-friendly hotel. The luxury boutique hotel offers both rooms and suites. Hotel amenities include complimentary evening wine service, 24 hour room service, and a 24 hour on-site fitness room. There are no pet fees, just sign a pet liability form.

Hotel de la Monnaie
405 Esplanade Ave
New Orleans, LA
504-947-0009
There is a $50 non-refundable one time pet fee.

Royal Street Courtyard
2438 Royal Street
New Orleans, LA
504-943-6818
Stay in a beautiful Antebellum home within easy walking distance of all French Quarter Attractions. Pets welcome at a nightly fee of $5 extra. A leash free dog park is only 2 blocks away. Grooming and Boarding

services are within walking distance.

Sheraton New Orleans Hotel
500 Canal Street
New Orleans, LA
504-525-2500
Dogs up to 80 pounds are allowed. There are no additional pet fees.

Studio 6
12330 I-10 Service Rd
New Orleans, LA
504-240-9778
There is a $10 per day pet fee, to a maximum pet fee of $50.

Opelousas

Best Western of Opelousas
5791 I-49 Service Rd South
Opelousas, LA
337-942-5540
There is a $10 per day additional pet fee.

Shreveport

La Quinta Inn & Suites Shreveport
6700 Financial Circle
Shreveport, LA
318-671-1100
Dogs of all sizes are allowed at the hotel.

Red Roof Inn
7296 Greenwood Rd
Shreveport, LA
318-938-5342
Pets up to 50 pounds are allowed. There are no additional pet fees.

Slidell

La Quinta Inn New Orleans Slidell
794 E. I-10 Service Rd.
Slidell, LA
985-643-9770
Dogs of all sizes are allowed at the hotel.

Motel 6

136 Taos St
Slidell, LA
985-649-7925
There are no additional pet fees.

Sulphur

La Quinta Inn Lake Charles - Sulphur
2600 South Ruth
Sulphur, LA
337-527-8303
Dogs of all sizes are allowed at the hotel.

Maine Listings

Augusta

Augusta Hotel and Suites
390 Western Avenue
Augusta, ME
207-622-6371
There are no pet fees unless you stay more than one week. Then there is a $20 one time pet fee.

Best Western Senator Inn & Spa
284 Western Avenue
Augusta, ME
207-622-5804
There is a $9 per day pet charge.

Comfort Inn Civic Center
281 Civic Center Drive
Augusta, ME
207-623-1000
There is no pet fee.

Motel 6
18 Edison Dr
Augusta, ME
207-622-0000
One large dog is allowed per room. There are no additional pet fees.

Bangor

Best Western White House Inn

155 Littlefield Avenue
Bangor, ME
207-862-3737
There are no pet fees.

Comfort Inn
750 Hogan Rd
Bangor, ME
207-942-7899
There is a pet fee of $6 per day.

Motel 6
1100 Hammond St
Bangor, ME
207-947-6921
One well-behaved large dog is permitted per room. There are no pet fees.

The Phenix Inn
20 Broad Street
Bangor, ME
207-947-0411
Pets are welcome in the first floor rooms. They have two non-smoking pet rooms. There is a $5 per day additional pet fee.

Bar Harbor

Balance Rock Inn
21 Albert Meadow
Bar Harbor, ME
207-288-2610
The oceanfront inn is within walking distance of many restaurants and shops in downtown Bar Harbor. Choose from fourteen individually decorated rooms at the inn, many of which offer an ocean view and private balcony. They also offer a heated outdoor pool and fitness room. Room rates for this inn average $200 to $300 per night but can start at $95 and go up to almost $600 per night. There is also a $30 per day pet fee.

Hanscom's Motel and Cottages
Route 3
Bar Harbor, ME
207-288-3744

This motel is located just 3 miles from downtown Bar Harbor. Rates for the motel range from $54 to $120 per night, with an extra $8 per pet.

Rose Eden Cottages
864 State Highway 3
Bar Harbor, ME
207-288-3038
This small cottage complex offers ten non-smoking cottages and some of them have kitchenettes. They are located just 4 miles to the entrance of Acadia National Park and about 10 minutes from downtown Bar Harbor. Harbor Point Beach, which allows leashed dogs, is located within walking distance. Room rates range from about $40 to $80 per night depending on the season and size of the cottage. One dog is allowed per cottage and there is a $10 per day pet charge.

Summertime Cottages
Call to arrange.
Bar Harbor, ME
207-288-2893
These vacation rental cottages border the Acadia National Park. They are located near downtown Bar Harbor. The rentals are available year-round. Children and family pets are welcome.

The Ledgelawn Inn
66 Mount Desert Street
Bar Harbor, ME
207-288-4596
This bed and breakfast inn has a $15 one time pet charge. There are no designated smoking or non-smoking rooms.

Bath

Holiday Inn
139 Richardson Street
Bath, ME
207-443-9741
There are no additional pet fees.

Belfast

Comfort Inn
159 Searsport Ave
Belfast, ME
207-338-2090
There is a pet fee of $10 per day. Pets are allowed on the first floor only.

Bucksport

Best Western Jed Prouty Motor Inn
52 Main Street (Rt 15)
Bucksport, ME
207-469-3113
There are no additional pet fees.

Calais

Calais Motor Inn
293 Main Street
Calais, ME
207-454-7111
There is a $10 per day pet charge.

International Motel
276 Main Street
Calais, ME
207-454-7515
Dogs are allowed in the older building only and not in the motel office. There are no additional pet fees.

Camden

Blue Harbor House
67 Elm Street
Camden, ME
207-236-3196
Dogs are allowed in one of the suites in the Carriage House at this Village Inn. There are no additional pet fees.

Camden Harbour Inn
83 Bayview Street
Camden, ME
207-236-4200
The Camden Harbour Inn, built in 1874, overlooks the historic and picturesque Camden harbor. Be sure to ask for their "Pooch Package" which includes dog cookies upon arrival, pet

bowls for food and water, cushioned dog bed or bedspread cover, a basket of treats and towels for muddy paws. Thanks to one of our readers who writes "Great hotel and home to a beautiful elderly yellow labrador named Bo. Great lobster restaurant at the marina which on our visit had 7 dogs with owners... beautiful place." There is a $20 one time pet fee.

Cape Elizabeth

Inn By The Sea
40 Bowery Beach Road
Cape Elizabeth, ME
207-799-3134
Thanks to one of our readers for these comments: "This hotel is an amazing place for dog lovers. It's a four star hotel that treats your puppy like any other hotel guest. There are two suites (bedroom, kitchen, living room) that are specifically appointed for dogs. Water dishes, biscuits, towels for paws, and outside hoses are provided. There are four nearby state parks and the hotel itself borders a feral area which my dog spent hours on end exploring. There's even a fenced-in kennel area, complete with a dog house, if you want to leave your pet for an hour and go for dinner. Wonderful place, they love dogs, great recreation, beautiful rooms, great hotel restaurant - truly a superb experience." This hotel also offers dog walking service with 24-hour notification. They even have a special pet menu with items like gourmet chuck burgers, grilled range chicken, NY sirloin strip steak with potatoes and vegetables, and for dessert, vanilla ice cream or doggie bon bons. If you are there during Thanksgiving, Christmas or the Fourth of July, they offer a special pet holiday menu. The

hotel asks that all pets be kept on a leash when not in their suite and that pets are not left alone in the suite. When making a reservation, they do require that you tell them you are bringing your pet. There are no pet fees. All rooms are non-smoking.

Kennebunkport

Captain Jefferds Inn
5 Pearl Street
Kennebunkport, ME
207-967-2311
This historic inn has a $20 per day pet charge. They ask that you please never leave your dog alone in the room.

Lodge At Turbat's Creek
Turbats Creek Rd at Ocean Avenue
Kennebunkport, ME
207-967-8700
There are no additional pet fees.

The Colony Hotel
140 Ocean Ave
Kennebunkport, ME
207-967-3331
There is a $25 per day pet charge.

Lewiston

Motel 6
516 Pleasant St
Lewiston, ME
207-782-6558
There are no pet fees. A large dog is allowed but must stay on the first floor.

Millinocket

Best Western Heritage Motor Inn
935 Central St
Millinocket, ME
207-723-9777
There are no additional pet fees.

Orono

Best Western Black Bear Inn
4 Godfrey Dr
Orono, ME
207-866-7120
There is a $3 per day pet fee.

Howard Johnson Plaza Hotel
155 Riverside
Portland, ME
207-774-5861
Dogs of all sizes are welcome.
There is a $50 refundable pet
deposit.

Motel 6
1 Riverside St
Portland, ME
207-775-0111
Dogs up to 75 pounds are
allowed. There are no additional
pet fees.

The Inn at St. John
939 Congress Street
Portland, ME
207-773-6481
There are no additional pet fees.

Best Western Merry Manor Inn
700 Main Street
South Portland, ME
207-774-6151
There are no additional pet fees.

Howard Johnson Hotel
675 Main St.
South Portland, ME
207-775-5343
Dogs of all sizes are welcome.
There are no additional pet fees.

Harbor Watch Motel

Swans Island, ME
207-526-4563
To get to this motel on Swans
Island, take the ferry from Bass
Harbor in Southwest Harbor to
Swans Island. Leashed dogs

and cars are allowed on the
Maine State Ferries. Dogs are
allowed for an additional $10
per day pet fee. Rooms rates
range from about $60 to $80
per night.

Best Western Waterville Inn
356 Main Street
Waterville, ME
207-873-3335
There are no additional pet
fees.

Holiday Inn
375 Main Street
Waterville, ME
207-873-0111
There are no additional pet
fees. Pets may not be left alone
in the room.

Maryland Listings

Days Inn
783 W. Bel Air Ave
Aberdeen, MD
410-272-8500
There is a $5 per day pet
charge and a 2 dog limit per
room.

**Four Points Hotels by
Sheraton**
980 Hospitality Way
Aberdeen, MD
410-273-6300
There are no additional pet
fees.

**Holiday Inn Chesapeake
House**
1007 Beards Hill Rd
Aberdeen, MD
410-272-8100
There are no additional pet
fees.

Red Roof Inn
988 Hospitality Way

Aberdeen, MD
410-273-7800
There are no additional pet fees.

Loews Annapolis Hotel
126 West Street
Annapolis, MD
410-263-7777
There are no additional pet fees.

Residence Inn by Marriott
170 Admiral Cochrane Dr
Annapolis, MD
410-573-0300
There is a $100 pet charge per
stay.

Brookshire Suites
120 E. Lombard Street
Baltimore, MD
410-625-1300
All well-behaved dogs are
welcome at this suites hotel.
There are no pet fees.

Comfort Inn Airport
6921 Baltimore-Annap. Blvd
Baltimore, MD
410-789-9100
There are no pet fees.

Pier 5 Hotel
711 Eastern Avenue
Baltimore, MD
410-539-2000
The entire hotel offers a smoke
free environment. All well-
behaved dogs are welcome and
there are no pet fees.

**Sheraton Baltimore North
Hotel**
903 Dulaney Valley Road
Baltimore, MD
410-321-7400
Dogs up to 100 pounds are
allowed. There is a $100 one
time pet fee.

Sheraton Inner Harbor Hotel
300 South Charles Street
Baltimore, MD

410-962-8300
Dogs up to 80 pounds are allowed. There are no additional pet fees. The hotel has specific pet rooms.

Sheraton International Hotel on BWI Airport
7032 Elm Road
Baltimore, MD
410-859-3300
Dogs of any size are allowed. There is a $25 one time additional pet fee.

Sleep Inn and Suites Airport
6055 Belle Grove Road
Baltimore, MD
410-789-7223
There are no pet fees.

The Admiral Fell Inn
888 South Broadway
Baltimore, MD
410-522-7377
All well-behaved dogs are welcome and there no pet fees.

Bethesda

Residence Inn by Marriott
7335 Wisconsin Ave
Bethesda, MD
301-718-0200
There is a $100 one time pet fee and an additional $5 per day pet charge.

Brooklyn

Comfort Inn Airport
6921 Baltimore-Annap. Blvd
Brooklyn, MD
410-789-9100
There is no pet fee.

Cockeysville

Chase Suite Hotel by Woodfin
1071 0 Beaver Dam Road
Cockeysville, MD
All well-behaved dogs are welcome. All rooms are suites with a full kitchen. Hotel amenities include a complimentary breakfast buffet.

There is a $5 per day pet fee. There are no additional pet fees.

Columbia

Staybridge Suites
8844 Columbia 100 Pkwy
Columbia, MD
410-964-9494
There is a $75 one time pet fee.

Cumberland

Holiday Inn
100 S. George St
Cumberland, MD
301-724-8800
There are no additional pet fees.

Easton

Comfort Inn
8523 Ocean Gateway
Easton, MD
410-820-8333
There is no pet fee. A credit card will be required.

Days Inn
7018 Ocean Gateway
Easton, MD
410-822-4600
There is an $12 per day pet charge.

Edgewood

Best Western Invitation Inn
1709 Edgewood Road
Edgewood, MD
410-679-9700
There is a $50 refundable pet deposit.

Elkton

Knights Inn
262 Belle Hill Rd
Elkton, MD
410-392-6680
There is a $10 per day pet fee.

Motel 6

223 Belle Hill Rd
Elkton, MD
410-392-5020
There are no additional pet fees.

Frederick

Holiday Inn
999 W. Patrick St
Frederick, MD
301-662-5141
There are no additional pet fees.

Holiday Inn
5400 Holiday Drive
Frederick, MD
301-694-7500
There are no additional pet fees. Pets must be crated if left alone in rooms.

Holiday Inn - Frederick
999 W Patrick St
Frederick, MD
301-662-5141
There are no additional pet fees.

Holiday Inn - Holidome
5400 Holiday Dr
Frederick, MD
301-694-7500
There are no additional pet fees.

Holiday Inn Express
5579 Spectrum Drive
Frederick, MD
301-695-2881
There is a $25 refundable pet deposit.

Quality Inn
420 Prospect Blvd
Frederick, MD
301-695-6200
There is no pet fee.

Frostburg

Days Inn & Suites
11100 New Georges Creek Rd
Frostburg, MD
301-689-2050
There is a $10.00 per day additional pet fee.

Gaithersburg

Comfort Inn at Shady Grove
16216 Frederick Rd
Gaithersburg, MD
301-330-0023
There is no pet fee.

Holiday Inn - Gaithersburg
2 Montgomery Village Ave
Gaithersburg, MD
301-948-8900
There are no additional pet fees.

Red Roof Inn - Gaithersburg
497 Quince Orchard Rd
Gaithersburg, MD
301-977-3311
There are no additional pet fees.

Residence Inn by Marriott
9721 Washington Blvd
Gaithersburg, MD
301-590-3003
There is a $100 one time pet charge and an additional $6 a day pet fee.

Glen Burnie

Days Inn - Glen Burnie
6600 Richie Hwy
Glen Burnie, MD
410-761-8300
There is a $10 per day additional pet fee per pet.

Grantsville

Holiday Inn
2541 Chestnut Ridge Rd
Grantsville, MD
301-895-5993
Pets may not be left alone in the room.

Hagerstown

Econo Lodge
18221 Mason Dixon Rd
Hagerstown, MD
301-791-3560
There is a $3 per day pet fee.

Four Points by Sheraton
1910 Dual Hwy
Hagerstown, MD

301-790-3010
There are no additional pet fees.

Motel 6
11321 Massey Blvd
Hagerstown, MD
301-582-4445
There are no additional pet fees.

Sleep Inn & Suites
18216 Colonel H K Douglas Dr
Hagerstown, MD
301-766-9449
There is a pet fee of $10 per day.

Hanover

Red Roof Inn
7306 Parkway Dr South
Hanover, MD
410-712-4070
There are no additional pet fees.

Jessup

Red Roof Inn
8000 Washington Blvd
Jessup, MD
410-796-0380
Dogs up to 75 pounds are allowed. One pet per room is allowed. There are no additional pet fees.

La Plata

Best Western La Plata Inn
6900 Crain Hwy, Rt 301
La Plata, MD
301-934-4900
There is a $25 one time pet fee.

Laurel

Comfort Suites Laurel Lakes
14402 Laurel Pl.
Laurel, MD
301-206-2600
There is a $50 refundable pet deposit.

Red Roof Inn - Laurel
12525 Laurel Bowie Rd
Laurel, MD
301-498-8811
One pet per room is permitted. Dogs up to 85 pounds are allowed. There are no additional pet fees.

Linthicum

Hampton Inn - BWI
829 Elkridge Landing Rd
Linthicum, MD
410-850-0600
There are no pet fees.

Holiday Inn - BWI
890 Elkridge Landing Rd
Linthicum, MD
410-859-8400
There is a $20 one time per stay pet fee.

Linthicum Heights

Comfort Inn Airport
6921 Baltimore Annapolis Blvd
Linthicum Heights, MD
410-789-9100
There are no additional pet fees.

Homestead Hotel - BWI
939 International Drive
Linthicum Heights, MD
410-691-2500
All studio suite rooms offer a fully equipped kitchen. There is a $75 one time per stay pet fee.

Homewood Suites Hotel BWI
1181 Winterson Rd
Linthicum Heights, MD
410-684-6100
There is a $200.00 one time pet fee.

Motel 6
5179 Raynor Ave
Linthicum Heights, MD
410-636-9070
There are no additional pet fees. Pets must be attended at all times.

McHenry

Accommodations - Please always call ahead to make sure an establishment is still dog-friendly.

Comfort Inn at Deep Creek Lake
2704 Deep Creek Dr
McHenry, MD
301-387-4200
There is a one time pet fee of $10.

Ocean City

Clarion Resort Fontainebleau
10100 Coastal Highway
Ocean City, MD
410-524-3535
There is a pet fee of $25 per day.

Oxon Hill

Red Roof Inn - Oxon Hill
6170 Oxon Hill Rd
Oxon Hill, MD
301-567-8030
There are no additional pet fees.

Pocomoke City

Days Inn
1540 Ocean Hwy
Pocomoke City, MD
410-957-3000
There is a $5.00 per day pet fee.

Quality Inn
825 Ocean Highway
Pocomoke City, MD
410-957-1300
There is no pet fee.

Rock Hall

Huntingfield Manor Bed & Breakfast
4928 Eastern Neck Rd
Rock Hall, MD
410-639-7779
This B&B is located on a 70 acre working farm. Pets are allowed in the cottage which is not designated as smoking or non-smoking. There are no additional pet fees.

Rockville

Best Western Washington Gateway Hotel
1251 W Montgomery Ave
Rockville, MD
301-424-4940
There is a $10 per day additional pet fee.

Quality Suites and Conference Center
3 Research Ct
Rockville, MD
301-840-0200
There is a $25 pet fee.

Sleep Inn Shady Grove
2 Research Ct
Rockville, MD
301-948-8000
There is a pet fee of $25.

Woodfin Suite Hotel
1380 Piccard Drive
Rockville, MD
301-590-9880
All well-behaved dogs are welcome. Every room is a suite with either a wet bar or full kitchen. Hotel amenities includes a pool, free video movies and a complimentary hot breakfast buffet. There is a $5 per day pet fee per pet. If you are staying for one month, the pet fee is $50 for the month.

Salisbury

Best Western Salisbury Plaza
1735 N Salisbury Blvd
Salisbury, MD
410-546-1300
There is a $10 per day additional pet fee.

Comfort Inn
2701 N. Salisbury Blvd
Salisbury, MD
410-543-4666
There is no pet fee.

Ramada Inn
300 S. Salisbury Blvd
Salisbury, MD
410-546-4400
There is a $25 one time pet fee.

Snow Hill

River House Inn Bed and Breakfast
201 E Market St
Snow Hill, MD
410-632-2722
This B&B is a National Register Victorian home located on the Pocomoke River on Maryland's Eastern Shore.

Timonium

Red Roof Inn - Timonium
111 W Timonium Rd
Timonium, MD
410-666-0380
There are no additional pet fees.

Towson

Days Inn - Baltimore East
8801 Loch Raven Blvd
Towson, MD
410-882-0900
There is a $15 per day pet charge.

Waldorf

Days Inn of Waldorf
11370 Days Court
Waldorf, MD
301-932-9200
There is a $10 one time fee per pet.

Massachusetts Listings

Andover

Staybridge Suites
4 Tech Drive
Andover, MA
978-686-2000
There is a $50 one time pet fee.

Auburn

Baymont Inn & Suites

288

444 Southbridge Street
Auburn, MA
508-832-7000
Thanks to one of our readers for recommending this inn. There are no additional pet fees.

Boston

Boston Harbor Hotel
70 Rowes Wharf
Boston, MA
617-439-7000
There are no additional pet fees. Pet owners must sign a pet waiver.

Seaport Hotel
1 Seaport Ln
Boston, MA
617-385-4000
Dogs up to 50 pounds allowed.

Sheraton Boston Hotel
39 Dalton Street
Boston, MA
617-236-2000
Dogs up to 50 pounds are allowed. There are no additional pet fees. Pets may not be left alone in rooms.

Swissotel Boston
One Ave de Lafayette
Boston, MA
617-451-2600
Pet owners must sign a pet waiver. You need to specifically request a non-smoking pet room if you want one. Dogs need to stay in the first through fourth floors only. Pets may not be left alone in the rooms. The hotel can recommend pet sitters if needed.

The Eliot Suite Hotel
370 Commonwealth Ave
Boston, MA
617-267-1607
There are no additional pet fees. Pets may not be left alone in the rooms.

Boxborough

Holiday Inn

242 Adams Place
Boxborough, MA
978-263-8701
There is a $25 one time pet fee.

Braintree

Motel 6
125 Union Street
Braintree, MA
781-848-7890
Well-behaved large dogs allowed. Dogs must be leashed on premises and may not be left alone in the room. There are no additional pet fees.

Brewster

Greylin House
2311 Main St
Brewster, MA
508-896-0004
1 room, non-smoking for pets. Dog must be able to get along with the owners 2 dogs.

High Brewster Inn
964 Satucket Rd
Brewster, MA
508-898-3636
There are no additional pet fees.

Burlington

Candlewood Suites
130 Middlesex Turnpike
Burlington, MA
781-229-4300
There is a $150 one time pet fee.

Staybridge Suites
11 Old Concord Rd
Burlington, MA
781-221-2233
There is a $150 one time pet fee.

Buzzards Bay

Bay Motor Inn
223 Main St
Buzzards Bay, MA

508-759-3989
There is a $10 per day pet fee. The motel has no designated smoking or non-smoking rooms. Pets must be attended at all times.

Cambridge

Hotel Marlowe
25 Edwin H. Land Blvd.
Cambridge, MA
617-868-8000
Dogs of all kinds and sizes are welcome at this pet-friendly and family-friendly hotel. The luxury boutique hotel offers both rooms and suites. Hotel amenities include a fitness room and 24 hour room service. There are no pet fees, just sign a pet waiver.

Sheraton Commander Hotel
16 Garden Street
Cambridge, MA
617-547-4800
Dogs up to 80 pounds are allowed. There are no additional pet fees. The dog owner must fill out a pet agreement.

The Charles Hotel in Harvard Square
1 Bennett St
Cambridge, MA
617-864-1200
There is a $50 one time pet fee. Pets may not be left alone in the rooms, and pet owners must sign a pet agreement.

Centerville

Centerville Corners Motor Lodge
369 S Main St
Centerville, MA
508-775-7223
There is a $5 per day pet fee.

Concord

Best Western at Historic Concord
740 Elm St
Concord, MA

978-369-6100
There is a $10 per day charge for pets.

Danvers

Motel 6
65 Newbury St/US Rt 1 N
Danvers, MA
978-774-8045
Dogs are allowed up to around 75 pounds.

Residence Inn - North Shore
51 Newbury St, Rt
Danvers, MA
978-777-7171
There is a $100 one time pet fee and an additional $10 per day pet fee.

Dedham

Residence Inn - Dedham
259 Elm Street
Dedham, MA
781-407-0999
There is a $100 one time pet fee and a $10 per day pet fee.

Edgartown

Colonial Inn
38 North Water Street
Edgartown, MA
508-627-4711
This family friendly inn offers two pet-friendly suites for travelers with dogs. You can enjoy the daily complimentary continental breakfast outside in the Garden Courtyard with your pooch. There is a $30 per day pet fee. The entire inn is non-smoking.

Martha's Vineyard Vacation Homes
Call to Arrange.
Edgartown, MA
203-374-8624
Some of the vacation homes are pet-friendly. There is a $100 weekly pet fee, and a $150 security deposit for pet damage or additional cleaning.

Shiverick Inn
5 Pease Point Way
Edgartown, MA
508-627-3797
Pets up to about 75 pounds are allowed in the three bedroom suite which is located just off the library. Dogs are not allowed in the indoor common areas, just inside your room and outside. There is a $50 pet deposit. Pets cannot be left alone in the room. The entire inn is non-smoking.

The Point Way Inn Bed and Breakfast
104 Main Street
Edgartown, MA

All rooms are non-smoking, have private bathrooms and some have private entrances. This inn allows dogs and they have even had previous guests with large dogs like Newfoundlands and Mastiffs. Complimentary continental breakfast is included and you may dine with your pooch in your room, or in the garden. Afternoon tea or espresso can also be enjoyed outside. There may be a 3 night minimum stay on weekends. There is a $50 per day pet fee during the summer, and a $25 per day pet fee in the off-season.

Fairhaven

Holiday Inn Express
110 Middle St.
Fairhaven, MA
508-997-1281
There is a $10 per day additional pet fee.

Foxborough

Residence Inn - Foxborough
250 Foxborough Blvd
Foxborough, MA
508-698-2800
There is a $150 one time pet fee and a $10 per day pet fee.

Framingham

Motel 6
1668 Worcester Rd
Framingham, MA
508-620-0500
There are no additional pet fees. A well-behaved dog is allowed and must be attended at all times.

Sheraton Framingham Hotel
1657 Worcester Road
Framingham, MA
508-879-7200
Dogs up to 80 pounds are allowed. There are no additional pet fees.

Gloucester

Ocean View Inn
171 Atlantic Rd
Gloucester, MA
978-283-6200
Dogs are allowed, but not in the Main Building (restaurant building). There are no additional pet fees.

Hyannis

Comfort Inn
1470 SR 132
Hyannis, MA
508-771-4804
There is a refundable pet deposit of $50.

Sheraton Hyannis Resort
35 Scudder Avenue
Hyannis, MA
508-775-7775
Dogs up to 80 pounds are allowed. There are no additional pet fees.

Hyannis Port

Simmons Homestead Inn
288 Scudder Ave.
Hyannis Port, MA
800-637-1649
The B & B is at an 1800 Sea Captain's estate in Hyannis Port in the center of Cape Cod. 14

rooms in two buildings. Full breakfasts, wine hour(s), free bikes, beach stuff, billiards and a bunch more. A chance to see the collection of over 50 classic red sports cars behind the Inn at Toad Hall is probably worth the trip by itself.

Lawrence

Hampton Inn Boston/North Andover
224 Winthrop Ave
Lawrence, MA
978-683-7143
There are no additional pet fees.

Lenox

Seven Hills Country Inn
40 Plunkett Street
Lenox, MA
413-637-0060
The Seven Hills Inn offers accommodations in the Manor House, the neighboring Terrace House and Carriage House. Thanks to one of our readers who writes: "They are on 27 beautifully groomed acres with lots of room for pets to roam." There is a $20 per night pet fee.

Lexington

Holiday Inn Express
440 Bedford Street
Lexington, MA
781-861-0850
There is a $75 one time pet fee per visit.

Sheraton Lexington Inn
727 Marrett Road
Lexington, MA
781-862-8700
Dogs up to 80 pounds are allowed. There is a $15 one time pet fee. The only place dogs aren't allowed is in the food and beverage areas.

Mansfield

Red Roof Inn
60 Forbes Blvd
Mansfield, MA
508-339-2323
There are no additional pet fees.

Nantucket

Brass Lantern Inn
11 North Water Street
Nantucket, MA
508-228-4064
Dogs up to about 65 pounds are allowed. Call to inquire if you have a larger dog. There is a $30 per day pet fee. All rooms are non-smoking.

Quidnuck Vacation Rental
Call to Arrange.
Nantucket, MA
202-663-8439
One dog is allowed at this vacation rental home. They ask that you do not bring a puppy and to never leave your dog alone in the house. There is a $75 one time per stay pet fee which will be used towards spraying the house for fleas. Ask for Jack when calling.

Safe Harbor Guest House
2 Harbor View Way
Nantucket, MA
508-228-3222
Dogs are allowed at this guest house. All rooms have private bathrooms. If your dog will be on the bed, please bring a sheet with you to place over the bedspread. There is no pet fee, they just request that you give the housekeeper a tip for extra cleaning, if necessary.

The Cottages at the Boat Basin
P.O. Box 1139
Nantucket, MA
866-838-9253
Dogs and cats are welcome in "The Woof Cottages." These cottages are one and two bedroom cottages which include special pet amenities like a welcome basket of pet treats and play toys, a pet bed, food and water bowls, and a Nantucket bandana. When you make a reservation, let them know what size your pet is, so they can have the appropriate size pet bed and bowls in the room. All cottages are non-smoking. There is a $25 one time per stay pet fee.

The Grey Lady
P.O. Box 1292
Nantucket, MA
508-228-9552
Pets and children are welcome at this guest house. While there is no pet fee, they have certain pet rooms which cost more per night than a standard room. All rooms are non-smoking. There may be a two or three night minimum stay during the summer. They also offer weekly cottage rentals at the Boat House.

Newton

Sheraton Newton Hotel
320 Washington Street
Newton, MA
617-969-3010
Dogs of all sizes are allowed. There are no additional pet fees. Pets cannot be left unattended in rooms.

Provincetown

BayShore on the Water
493 Commercial Street
Provincetown, MA
508-487-9133
This five house complex has been converted to studios, one bedroom and two bedroom units. There are a few non-smoking units and the rest are not designated as smoking or non-smoking. There is a $15 per day pet fee for 1 dog, or a $20 per day pet fee for 2 dogs.

Keep Inn
698 Commercial St

Provincetown, MA
508-487-1711
There are no additional pet fees.
Pets must be attended at all
times.

The Sandpiper Beach House
165 Commercial Street
Provincetown, MA
508-487-1928
There is a $25 per visit pet fee.

White Wind Inn
174 Commercial St
Provincetown, MA
508-487-1526
There are no additional pet fees.

Holiday Inn Express
909 Hingham St
Rockland, MA
781-871-5660
There is a $6 per day additional
pet fee.

Sandy Bay Motor Inn
173 Main St
Rockport, MA
978-546-7155
There is a $10 per day pet
charge. The hotel has two non-
smoking rooms in their pet
building.

Hawthorne Hotel
18 Washington Sq W
Salem, MA
978-744-4080
There is a $7.50 per night
charge for pets.

Sandwich Lodge and Resort
54 Route 6A
Sandwich, MA
508-888-2275
There is a $15.00 one time pet
fee.

**The Earl of Sandwich Motor
Manor**
378 Rt 6A
Sandwich, MA
508-888-1415
There are no additional pet
fees.

Motel 6
36 Burnett Rd
Springfield, MA
413-592-5141
There are no additional pet
fees.

**Comfort Inn & Suites
Colonial**
215 Charlton Rd
Sturbridge, MA
508-347-3306
There is a pet fee of $15 per
day.

Days Inn
66-68 Old Rt 15, Haynes St
Sturbridge, MA
508-347-3391
There is a $7 per day pet fee.

Publick House Historic Inn
On the Common, Route 131
Sturbridge, MA
508-347-3313
There is a $5 per day additional
pet fee.

Sturbridge Host Hotel
366 Main Street
Sturbridge, MA
508-347-7393
Overlooking Cedar Lake, the
Resort offers lake view rooms,
some with Illuminating
fireplaces, just minutes from
Old Sturbridge Village. This
resort property features a
variety of recreational activities
such as an indoor pool, boating
and fitness center. Children
under 18 stay free. Pet fees do
apply.

Holiday Inn
4 Highwood Drive
Tewksbury, MA
978-640-9000
Pet owners must sign a pet
waiver.

Motel 6
95 Main St
Tewksbury, MA
978-851-8677
There are no additional pet fees.

Residence Inn by Marriott
1775 Andover St
Tewksbury, MA
978-640-1003
There is a $100 pet charge per
stay and a $10 per day pet
charge.

**Martha's Vineyard Rental
Houses**
Call to Arrange.
Vineyard Haven, MA
508-693-6222
Select from a variety of pet-
friendly rental homes. Pet fees
may vary per property.

**Sheraton Colonial Hotel and
Golf Club Boston North**
One Audubon Road
Wakefield, MA
781-245-9300
Dogs up to 80 pounds are
allowed. There are no additional
pet fees.

Homestead Village
52 Fourth Ave
Waltham, MA
781-890-1333
$75 one time fee. This is a long
term stay hotel.

Red Roof Inn
1254 Riverdale St
West Springfield, MA
413-731-1010
There is a 2 dog limit. There are no additional pet fees.

Williamstown

Cozy Corner Motel
284 Sand Springs Rd
Williamstown, MA
413-458-8006
There is a $10 per day additional pet fee.

The Villager Motel
953 Simonds Rd
Williamstown, MA
413-458-9611
There are 2 pet rooms, one non-smoking.

Winthrop

The Inn at Crystal Cove
600 Shirley Street
Winthrop, MA
617-846-9217
Great view and wonderful dog-friendly people. The inn is located on Boston Harbor. The inn is a comfortable, colonial-style hotel located in a residential neighborhood of Winthrop, just minutes from downtown Boston. Their swimming pool and jacuzzi make comfortable lodging at a reasonable rate.

Woburn

Radisson Hotel
15 Middlesex Canal Park Rd
Woburn, MA
781-935-8760
There is a $50 refundable pet deposit.

Yarmouth Port

Colonial House
Old Kings Hwy
Yarmouth Port, MA
508-362-4348
There is a $5.00 per day pet charge.

Michigan Listings

Alpena

Fletcher Motel
1001 US 23N
Alpena, MI
989-354-4191
Dogs allowed in all rooms except the luxury rooms.

Holiday Inn
1000 US 23 N.
Alpena, MI
989-356-2151
Pets are not allowed in public areas of the hotel such as the lobby. Pets must be leashed outside the room and may not be left alone in the room.

Ann Arbor

Comfort Inn & Business Center
2455 Carpenter Rd
Ann Arbor, MI
734-973-6100
There is no pet fee. Pets may not be left alone.

Residence Inn by Marriott
800 Victors Way
Ann Arbor, MI
734-996-5666
There is a $125 one time pet fee.

Auburn Hills

Staybridge Suites
2050 Featherstone Rd
Auburn Hills, MI
248-322-4600
There is a $75 one time pet fee.

Battle Creek

Days Inn
4786 Beckley Rd
Battle Creek, MI
616-979-3561
There is a $25 one time pet fee.

Motel 6
4775 Beckley Rd
Battle Creek, MI
616-979-1141
There are no additional pet fees.

Bay City

Americinn of Bay City
3915 Three Mile Rd
Bay City, MI
989-671-0071
There are no additional pet fees.

Belleville

Comfort Inn
45945 S. I-94 Service Drive
Belleville, MI
734-697-8556
There is a pet fee of $10 per day.

Red Roof Inn - Detroit Airport-Belleville
45501 North Expressway Service Drive
Belleville, MI
734-697-2244
Dogs up to 80 pounds are allowed and one dog is permitted per room. There are no pet fees.

Benton Harbor

Comfort Inn
1598 Mall Dr.
Benton Harbor, MI
616-925-1880
There is a refundable pet deposit of $20.

Cadillac

Best Western - Bill Oliver's
5676 E M55
Cadillac, MI
231-775-2458

There is a $10 per day pet fee.

Econo Lodge
2501 Sunnyside Dr
Cadillac, MI
231-775-6700
There is a $10 per day pet fee
for the first three days of a stay.

Canton

Baymont Inn and Suites
41211 Ford Rd
Canton, MI
734-981-1808
One large dog per room is
permitted.

Cedarville

Comfort Inn
106 W. SR 134
Cedarville, MI
906-484-2266
There is a pet fee of $10 per
day.

Charlevoix

Lodge of Charlevoix
120 Michigan Ave
Charlevoix, MI
231-547-6565
There is a $10 per day pet fee.

Points North Inn
101 Michigan Ave
Charlevoix, MI
231-547-0055
There is a $5 per day pet fee.

Sleep Inn
800 Petoskey Ave
Charlevoix, MI
231-547-0300
If paying by credit card there is
no deposit. If paying by cash
there is a refundable deposit of
$25. Pets may not be left alone.

Chelsea

Comfort Inn
1645 Commerce Park Dr
Chelsea, MI

734-433-8000
There is a refundable pet
deposit of $50. A credit card
will be required.

Dearborn

Red Roof Inn
24130 Michigan Ave
Dearborn, MI
313-278-9732
There are no additional pet
fees.

**Residence Inn Detroit
Dearborn**
5777 Southfield Service Drive
Dearborn, MI
313-441-1700
Amenities include a
complimentary buffet breakfast,
guest laundry, outdoor pool and
an exercise room. Room
amenities include a full kitchen
in each room. There is a $100
one time pet fee.

Ritz-Carlton
300 Town Center Drive
Dearborn, MI
313-441-2000
There is a $150 one time pet
fee.

TownePlace Suites
6141 Mercury Drive
Dearborn, MI
313-271-0200
Amenities include full kitchens
in each suite room. Hotel
amenities include a guest
laundry room, outdoor pool and
an exercise room. There is a
$100 one time per stay pet fee
and a $5 per day pet fee.

Detroit

Hotel St. Regis
3071 West Grand Blvd
Detroit, MI
313-873-3000
There are no pet fees.
Amenities include room
service.

Ramada Inn Downtown

Detroit
400 Bagley Avenue
Detroit, MI
313-962-2300
Dogs are welcome but must be
on a leash. There are no pet
fees.

Residence Inn by Marriott
5777 Southfield Service Dr
Detroit, MI
313-441-1700
There is a $100 one time pet
fee.

Dundee

Comfort Inn
621 Tecumseh
Dundee, MI
734-529-5505
There is a pet fee of $10 per
day.

Farmington Hills

Motel 6
38300 Grand River Ave
Farmington Hills, MI
248-471-0590
There are no additional pet fees.
A large well-behaved dog is
allowed.

Red Roof Inn
24300 Sinacola Ct
Farmington Hills, MI
248-478-8640
There are no additional pet fees.

Flint

Holiday Inn Express
1150 Robert T. Longway Blvd
Flint, MI
810-238-7744
From I-75 take I-475 to Exit 8A.
There is a $50 one time pet fee.
Pets are allowed in first floor
rooms.

Howard Johnson Express Inn
G-3277 Miller Road
Flint, MI
810-733-5910
Dogs of all sizes are welcome.

There is a $10 per day pet fee.

Motel 6
2324 Austin Pkwy
Flint, MI
810-767-7100
There are no additional pet fees.

Red Roof Inn
G-3219 Miller Rd
Flint, MI
810-733-1660
There are no additional pet fees.

Frankenmuth

Drury Inn & Suites
260 South Main
Frankenmuth, MI
989-652-2800
Dogs of all sizes are permitted.
Pets are not allowed in the
breakfast area of the hotel. Pets
are not to be left unattended,
and each guest must assume
liability for damage of property or
other guest complaints. There is
a limit of one pet per room.

Gaylord

Gaylord Inn
833 W. Main Street
Gaylord, MI
989-732-2431
There are no additional pet fees.

Gladstone

Norway Pines Motel
7111 US 2, 41 and M-35
Gladstone, MI
906-786-5119
There are no additional pet fees.

Grand Rapids

Comfort Inn Airport
4155 28th St S.E.
Grand Rapids, MI
616-957-2080
There is no pet fee.

Days Inn - Downtown
310 Pearl St NW

Grand Rapids, MI
616-235-7611
There is a $20 per day pet fee.

Homewood Suites
3920 Stahl Dr SE
Grand Rapids, MI
616-285-7100
There is an $80 one time pet
fee and a $5 per day pet fee.

Howard Johnson Plaza Hotel
255 28th St. SW
Grand Rapids, MI
616-241-6444
Dogs of all sizes are welcome.
There is a $10 one time pet fee.

Grayling

Holiday Inn
2650 S. I-75 Business Loop
Grayling, MI
989-348-7611
Pets must be housebroken and
should not be left alone in the
room. There are no additional
pet fees.

Hancock

**Best Western Copper Crown
Motel**
235 Hancock Avenue
Hancock, MI
906-482-6111
There are no additional pet
fees.

Hart

Comfort Inn
2248 Comfort Drive
Hart, MI
231-873-3456
There is a pet fee of $10 per
day.

Houghton

Best Western King's Inn
215 Shelden Avenue
Houghton, MI
906-482-5000
There is a $4 per day additional

pet fee.

Iron Mountain

Best Western Executive Inn
1518 S Stephenson Ave
Iron Mountain, MI
906-774-2040
There is a $9 per day pet fee.

Ironwood

Super 8 Motel
160 E Cloverland Dr
Ironwood, MI
906-932-3395
There is a $25 refundable
deposit for pets. Pets are
allowed on the first floor only.

Jackson

Motel 6
830 Royal Dr
Jackson, MI
517-789-7186
There are no additional pet fees.

Kalamazoo

Comfort Inn Airport
3820 Sprinkle Rd
Kalamazoo, MI
616-381-7000
There is a non-refundable pet
charge of $50.

Knights Inn
1211 S Westernedge Ave
Kalamazoo, MI
616-381-5000
There is a $25 refundable
deposit for pets.

Motel 6
3704 Van Rick Rd
Kalamazoo, MI
616-344-9255
There are no additional pet fees.
A large well-behaved dog is
allowed.

Quality Inn & Suites
3750 Easy St
Kalamazoo, MI

616-388-3551
There is no pet fee.

Red Roof Inn - East
5425 W Michigan Ave
Kalamazoo, MI
616-375-7400
There are no additional pet fees.

Residence Inn by Marriott
1500 E Kilgore
Kalamazoo, MI
616-349-0855
There is a $50 one time pet fee.

Lake

Crooked Lake Resort
8071 Mystic lake Dr
Lake, MI
(989)544-2383
Furnished Cabins on the Lake
Located in Clare County
Michigan.6 cabins range from 2
bedrooms,to 3 bedrooms. There
are no additional pet fees.
Cabins are not designated as
smoking or non-smoking.

Lansing

**Best Western Governor's Inn
& Conf Ctr**
6133 S. Pennsylvania
Lansing, MI
517-393-5500
There are no additional pet fees.

**Clarion Hotel and Conference
Center**
3600 Dunckel Dr
Lansing, MI
517-351-7600
There is a non-refundable pet
charge of $35. Please keep a
"Do Not Disturb" sign on the
door when your pet is in the
room. Pets must always be
attended in rooms.

Motel 6
7326 W. Saginaw Hwy
Lansing, MI
517-321-1444
There are no additional pet fees.

Red Roof Inn - East
3615 Dunckel Rd
Lansing, MI
517-332-2575
There are no additional pet
fees.

Residence Inn by Marriott
922 Delta Commerce Dr
Lansing, MI
517-886-5030
There is a $100 one time pet
fee.

Livonia

**TownePlace Suites Detroit
Livonia**
17450 Fox Drive
Livonia, MI
734-542-7400
Hotel amenities include an
outdoor pool. There is a $125
one time pet fee.

Ludington

Holiday Inn Express
5323 W. US 10
Ludington, MI
231-845-7004
There is a $10 one time pet fee.

**Nader's Lake Shore Motor
Lodge**
612 N Lakeshore Dr
Ludington, MI
231-843-8757
There are two non-smoking pet
rooms. The hotel is closed
during the winter months. Pets
must be leashed and attended
at all times.

Mackinaw City

Motel 6
206 Nicolet St
Mackinaw City, MI
231-436-8961
There are no additional pet
fees.

Madison Heights

Motel 6
32700 Barrington Rd
Madison Heights, MI
248-583-0500
There are no additional pet fees.
One well-behaved dog is
allowed per room.

Manistique

Comfort Inn
726 E. Lakeshore Drive
Manistique, MI
906-341-6981
There is a pet fee of $10 per
day.

Marquette

Holiday Inn
1951 US 41 West
Marquette, MI
906-225-1351
There are no additional pet fees.

Ramada Inn
412 W Washington St
Marquette, MI
906-228-6000
There are no additional pet fees.

Menominee

Econo Lodge
2516 10th St
Menominee, MI
906-863-4431
There is a $5 per day additional
pet fee.

Midland

Fairview Inn
2200 W Wackerly St
Midland, MI
517-631-0070
There is a $25 refundable
deposit for pets.

Sleep Inn
2100 W. Wackerly St
Midland, MI
989-837-1010
There is no pet fee. Pets may
not be left alone.

Mount Pleasant

Holiday Inn
5665 E Pickard Rd
Mount Pleasant, MI
517-772-2905
There are no additional pet fees.

Petoskey

Comfort Inn
1314 US 31 N.
Petoskey, MI
231-347-3220
There is no pet fee.

Plainwell

Comfort Inn
622 Allegan St
Plainwell, MI
616-685-9891
There is a non-refundable pet charge of $10. There is a pet fee of $5 per day.

Pontiac

Residence Inn Detroit Pontiac/Auburn Hills
333 Centerpoint Parkway
Pontiac, MI
248-858-8664
Amenities include a complimentary buffet breakfast, guest laundry, indoor pool and an exercise room. Room amenities include a full kitchen in each room. There is a $100 one time per stay pet fee and a $5 per day pet charge.

Port Huron

Knights Inn
2160 Water St
Port Huron, MI
810-982-1022
There is a $10 per day additional pet fee.

Romulus

Romulus Marriott Detroit Airport
30559 Flynn Dr
Romulus, MI
734-729-7555
There is a $75 one time pet fee.

Saginaw

Best Western Saginaw
1408 S. Outer Drive
Saginaw, MI
989-755-0461
There are no additional pet fees.

Knights Inn - Saginaw South
1415 S Outer Dr
Saginaw, MI
989-754-9200
There is a $10 one time pet fee.

Red Roof Inn
966 S Outer Dr
Saginaw, MI
989-754-8414
There are no additional pet fees.

Sault Ste Marie

Seaway Motel
1800 Ashmun St
Sault Ste Marie, MI
906-632-8201
Hotel is open May through October only. There is one non-smoking pet room. There are no additional pet fees.

Super 8
3826 I-75 Business Spur
Sault Ste Marie, MI
906-632-8882
There is a $50 refundable deposit if paying with cash.

Sault Ste. Marie

Quality Inn & Conference Center
3290 I-75 Business Spur
Sault Ste. Marie, MI
906-635-6918
There is a pet fee of $25 per day.

Silver City

Best Western Porcupine Mountain Lodge
120 Lincoln at Beaser
Silver City, MI
906-885-5311
There is a $10 per day additional pet fee.

St Ignace

Hotel Dupont
913 Boulevard Dr
St Ignace, MI
906-643-9700
There is a $10 per day pet fee.

Sterling Heights

TownePlace Suites
14800 Lakeside Circle
Sterling Heights, MI
586-566-0900
Hotel amenities include an outdoor pool. There is a $125 one time per stay pet fee and a $5 per day pet charge.

Tawas City

Tawas Motel - Resort
1124 W. Lake Street
Tawas City, MI
989-362-3822
Motel amenities include individual heating and cooling, free local calls, free continental breakfast, Jacuzzi, heated outdoor pool and a picnic area with grills. Well-behaved dogs are welcome. There are no pet fees.

Traverse City

Best Western Four Seasons Motel
305 Munson Ave
Traverse City, MI
231-946-8424
There is a $7 per day additional pet fee. Dogs should not be left alone in rooms or cars at the hotel.

Holiday Inn
615 E. Front Street
Traverse City, MI
231-947-3700
There is a $10 per day pet fee.
Pets must not be left unattended
in the room.

Motel 6
1582 US 31 North
Traverse City, MI
231-938-3002
There is a $7 per day pet fee.

Quality Inn by the Bay
1492 US 31 N.
Traverse City, MI
231-929-4423
There is a pet fee of $10 per
day.

Troy

Drury Inn
575 W. Big Beaver Road
Troy, MI
248-528-3330
Dogs of all sizes are permitted.
Pets are not allowed in the
breakfast area of the hotel. Pets
are not to be left unattended,
and each guest must assume
liability for damage of property or
other guest complaints. There is
a limit of one pet per room.

Holiday Inn
2537 Rochester Court
Troy, MI
248-689-7500
At I-75 and Rochester Road.
There is a $5 per day additional
pet fee.

Union Pier

Blue Fish Vacation Rentals
10234 Community Hall Rd.
Union Pier, MI
269-469-0468
Blue Fish Vacation Rentals has
a wide selection of vacation
homes, from one-bedroom
cottage bungalows, to 2 to 5
bedroom properties. Some of
the listings have lake views, or
are in close proximity to the
lake and beaches, while others
are country or village homes.
Inquire about pet friendly
rentals at 269-469-0468,
extension 112.

Warren

Residence Inn Detroit Warren
30120 Civic Center North
Warren, MI
586-558-8050
Amenities include a
complimentary buffet breakfast,
guest laundry, outdoor pool and
an exercise room. Room
amenities include a full kitchen
in each room. There is a $75
one time pet fee.

Minnesota Listings

Albert Lea

Comfort Inn
810 Happy Trails Lane
Albert Lea, MN
507-377-1100
There is a pet fee of $10 per
day.

Alexandria

Holiday Inn
5637 State Hwy 29 S.
Alexandria, MN
320-763-6577
There are no additional pet
fees. Exit I-94 at Hwy 29.

Babbitt

**Timber Bay Lodge and
Houseboats**

Babbitt, MN
218-827-3682
There is a $14 additional pet
fee per day for a cabin or a
houseboat. The cabins and
houseboats are not designated
as smoking or non-smoking.

Brooklyn Center

Comfort Inn
1600 James Circle N.
Brooklyn Center, MN
763-560-7464
If paying with cash there is a
refundable deposit fo $20. If
paying with a credit card there is
no deposit.

Motel 6
2741 Freeway Blvd
Brooklyn Center, MN
763-560-9789
There are no additional pet fees.
One pet per room is allowed.

Burnsville

Super 8 Motel - Burnsville
1101 Burnsville Parkway
Burnsville, MN
952-894-3400
Convenient to all Twin Cities
attractions. $10/stay for up to 3
dogs in one room. FREE 8-
minute long distance call each
night. FREE continental
breakfast. Coffee maker, night
light, clock/radio, safe in each
room. On-site guest laundry.
Kids 12 & under stay free.
I-35W, Exit 2 (Burnsville Pkwy)
West on Burnsville Pkwy 1
block.

Duluth

**Best Western Downtown
Motel**
131 W. 2nd Street
Duluth, MN
218-727-6851
There are no additional pet fees.

Days Inn
909 Cottonwood Ave
Duluth, MN
218-727-3110
There are no additional pet fees.

Motel 6
200 South 27th Ave W.
Duluth, MN
218-723-1123

There are no additional pet fees. Pets must be attended at all times.

Ely

Westgate
110 N 2nd Ave W
Ely, MN
218-365-4513
There is a $10 one time pet fee.

Grand Marais

Aspen Lodge
310 East U.S. Hwy. 61
Grand Marais, MN
218-387-2500
Pets are allowed in the motel section. There are no additional pet fees.

Best Western Superior Inn & Suites
PO Box 456, Hwy 61 East
Grand Marais, MN
218-387-2240
There are no additional pet fees.

Clearwater Lodge
774 Clearwater Rd
Grand Marais, MN
218-388-2254
There is a $60 per week pet fee. Dogs are allowed in cabins only, not in the main lodge.

Grand Rapids

Best Western Rainbow Inn
1300 E US 169
Grand Rapids, MN
218-326-9651
There is a $50 refundable pet deposit.

Country Inn
2601 US 169S
Grand Rapids, MN
218-327-4960
There are no additional pet fees.

Lakeville

Motel 6

11274 210th St
Lakeville, MN
952-469-1900
There are no additional pet fees. A large well-behaved dog is okay.

Mankato

Comfort Inn
131 Apache Place
Mankato, MN
507-388-5107
There is no pet fee.

Holiday Inn
101 E. Main Street
Mankato, MN
507-345-1234
There are no additional pet fees.

Maple Grove

Staybridge Suites
7821 Elm Creek Blvd
Maple Grove, MN
763-494-8856
There is a $75 one time pet fee. Pets up to 75 pounds are allowed.

Marshall

Best Western Marshall Inn
1500 E College Dr, Jct 19/23
Marshall, MN
507-532-3221
There is a $10 per day pet fee.

Minneapolis

Holiday Inn
1500 Washington Ave S.
Minneapolis, MN
612-333-4646
There is a $25 one time pet fee. The hotel is off I-35W at Exit 17C. (W. Bank)

The Marquette Hilton
710 Marquette Ave
Minneapolis, MN
612-333-4545
There are no additional pet fees. A large well-behaved dog is okay. Pet owners will need to sign a pet waiver.

Richfield

Motel 6
7640 Cedar Ave S
Richfield, MN
612-861-4491
There are no additional pet fees.

Rochester

Holiday Inn
1630 S. Broadway
Rochester, MN
507-288-1844
A large dog is okay if it is well-behaved and quiet. There are no additional pet fees.

Quality Inn & Suites
1620 1st Ave.
Rochester, MN
507-282-8091
There is no pet fee. A credit card will be required. Pets may not be left alone. Well behaved pets only.

St Cloud

Comfort Inn
4040 Second St.
St Cloud, MN
320-251-1500
There is a pet fee of $10 per day.

Holiday Inn Express
4322 Clearwater Rd
St Cloud, MN
320-240-8000
There are no additional pet fees. Pets must be attended at all times.

Holiday Inn Hotel & Suites
75 S. 37th Avenue
St Cloud, MN
320-253-9000
There are no additional pet fees.

Motel 6
815 1st St S

St Cloud, MN
320-253-7070
There are no additional pet fees.

Taylors Falls

The Springs Country Inn
361 Government St
Taylors Falls, MN
651-465-6565
There is a $7 per day pet fee.
Dogs are allowed on the first 2
floors.

White Bear Lake

Best Western Bear Country Inn
4940 State Hwy 61
White Bear Lake, MN
651-429-5393
Dogs up to 50 pounds okay.
There is a $10 per day additional
pet fee.

Winona

Quality Inn
956 Mankato Ave.
Winona, MN
507-454-4390
There is no pet fee. Pets may
not be left alone.

Woodbury

Red Roof Inn
1806 Wooddale Dr
Woodbury, MN
651-738-7160
There are no additional pet fees.

Mississippi Listings

Biloxi

Breakers Inn
2506 Beach Blvd
Biloxi, MS
228-388-6320
There is a $30 one time pet fee.
There are no designated

smoking or non-smoking
rooms.

Holiday Inn - Beachfront
2400 Beach Blvd
Biloxi, MS
228-388-3551
There is a $25 one time pet fee.

Holiday Inn Express
2416 Beach Blvd
Biloxi, MS
228-388-1000
There is a $25 one time pet fee.

Motel 6
2476 Beach Blvd
Biloxi, MS
228-388-5130
There are no additional pet
fees.

Canton

Best Western Canton Inn
137 Soldier Colony Road
Canton, MS
601-859-8600
There is a $7.50 per day
additional pet fee.

Corinth

Comfort Inn
2101 Highway 72, West
P.O.Box 1557
Corinth, MS
662-287-4421
There is a refundable pet
deposit of $20.

Forest

Apple Tree Inn
I-20 at Highway 35, PO Box
402
Forest, MS
601-469-2640
There are no additional pet
fees.

Greenville

Holiday Inn Express
2428 Hwy 82 E.

Greenville, MS
662-334-6900
There is a $30 one time pet fee.

Grenada

Holiday Inn
1796 Sunset Dr
Grenada, MS
601-226-2851
There are no additional pet fees.

Gulfport

Best Western Seaway Inn
9475 US Hwy 49 & I-10
Gulfport, MS
228-864-0050
There are no additional pet fees.

Holiday Inn Express
9435 US Hwy 49
Gulfport, MS
228-864-7222
There is a $35 one time pet fee.
Take I-10 exit 34-A South to the
hotel.

Hattiesburg

Comfort Inn at Convention Center
6595 US 49 N.
Hattiesburg, MS
601-268-2170
There is a non-refundable pet
fee of $25.

Howard Johnson Express Inn
6553 Hwy 49 North
Hattiesburg, MS
601-268-1410
Dogs of all sizes are welcome.
There is a $10 per day pet fee.

Motel 6
6508 US Hwy 49
Hattiesburg, MS
601-544-6096
There are no additional pet fees.
A large well-behaved dog is
okay.

Horn Lake

South Drury Inn & Suites
735 Goodman Road West
Horn Lake, MS
662-349-6622
Dogs of all sizes are permitted. Pets are not allowed in the breakfast area of the hotel. Pets are not to be left unattended, and each guest must assume liability for damage of property or other guest complaints. There is a limit of one pet per room.

South Drury Inn & Suites
735 Goodman Road West
Horn Lake, MS
662-349-6622
Dogs of all sizes are permitted. Pets are not allowed in the breakfast area of the hotel. Pets are not to be left unattended, and each guest must assume liability for damage of property or other guest complaints. There is a limit of one pet per room.

Indianola

Comfort Inn
910 US 82 E.
Indianola, MS
662-887-6611
There is no pet fee. Pets may not be left alone.

Jackson

Clarion Hotel
400 Greymont Ave.
Jackson, MS
601-969-2141
There is a non-refundable pet fee of $25.

Crowne Plaza - Downtown
200 E. Amite Street
Jackson, MS
601-969-5100
There is a $150 refundable pet deposit.

Edison Walthall Hotel
225 E Capitol St
Jackson, MS
601-948-6161
There is a $10 per day pet fee.

Holiday Inn Hotel & Suites
5075 I-55 North
Jackson, MS
601-366-9411
There is a $125 refundable pet deposit and a $25 one time pet fee.

La Quinta Inn Jackson North
616 Briarwood Drive
Jackson, MS
601-957-1741
Dogs of all sizes are allowed at the hotel.

Leland Inn
150 Angle St
Jackson, MS
601-373-6110
There are no additional pet fees.

Motel 6
6145 I-55 N
Jackson, MS
601-956-8848
There are no additional pet fees.

Quality Hotel Southwest
2649 Highway 80 West
Jackson, MS
601-355-3472
There is a pet fee of $20 per day.

Sleep Inn
2620 US 80 West
Jackson, MS
601-354-3900
There is a pet fee of $10 per day.

McComb

Days Inn
2298 Delaware Ave
McComb, MS
601-684-5566
There is an $8 daily pet fee.

Ramada Inn
1900 Delaware Ave
McComb, MS
601-684-6211
There is a $7.50 per day additional pet fee.

Meridian

Holiday Inn
111 US Hwy 11 & 80
Meridian, MS
601-485-5101
There is a $20 one time pet fee.

Motel 6
2309 S. Frontage Rd
Meridian, MS
601-482-1182
There are no additional pet fees.

Quality Inn
1401 Roebuck Dr
Meridian, MS
601-693-4521
There are no additional pet fees.

Ocean Springs

Comfort Inn
7827 Lamar Poole Rd.
Ocean Springs, MS
228-818-0300
There is a $50 pet fee.

Pearl

Motel 6
216 N Pearson Rd
Pearl, MS
601-936-9988
There are no additional pet fees.

Picayune

Comfort Inn
550 South Lofton Dr.
Picayune, MS
601-799-2833
There is a pet fee of $10 per day.

Ridgeland

Drury Inn & Suites
610 E. County Line Road
Ridgeland, MS
601-956-6100
Dogs of all sizes are permitted. Pets are not allowed in the breakfast area of the hotel. Pets are not to be left unattended,

and each guest must assume liability for damage of property or other guest complaints. There is a limit of one pet per room.

Tupelo

Executive Inn
1011 N Gloster St
Tupelo, MS
601-841-2222
There is a $15 one time pet fee.

Red Roof Inn
1500 McCullough Blvd
Tupelo, MS
662-844-1904
There are no additional pet fees.

Vicksburg

Battlefield Inn
4137 I-20 Frontage Rd
Vicksburg, MS
601-638-5811
There is a $5 per day pet fee.

Duff Green Mansion
1114 First East St
Vicksburg, MS
601-638-6662
There are no designated smoking or non-smoking rooms.

La Quinta Inn Vicksburg
4216 Washington Street
Vicksburg, MS
601-638-5750
Dogs up to 50 pounds are allowed at the hotel.

The Corners Bed and Breakfast Inn
601 Klien St
Vicksburg, MS
601-636-7421
There are no additional pet fees.

Yazoo City

Comfort Inn
1600 N. Jerry Clower Blvd.
Yazoo City, MS
662-746-6444
There is a non-refundable pet fee of $50 for the first 5 days

and on the 6th day another $50 non-refundable fee is required.

Missouri Listings

Arnold

St Louis - Arnold Drury Inn
1201 Drury Lane
Arnold, MO
636-296-9600
Dogs of all sizes are permitted. Pets are not allowed in the breakfast area of the hotel. Pets are not to be left unattended, and each guest must assume liability for damage of property or other guest complaints. There is a limit of one pet per room.

Blue Springs

Sleep Inn
451 N.W. Jefferson St.
Blue Springs, MO
816-224-1199
There is no pet fee.

Branson

Best Western Branson Rustic Oak
403 W Hwy 76
Branson, MO
417-334-6464
There are no additional pet fees.

Branson Inn
448 MO 248
Branson, MO
417-334-5121
There is a $5 per day pet fee. Pets must be out of the room for maid service.

Howard Johnson Hotel
3027-A West Hwy 76
Branson, MO
417-336-5151
Dogs of all sizes are welcome. There is a $10 per day pet fee.

Settle Inn
3050 Green Mt Dr
Branson, MO
417-335-4700
There is a $10 per day pet fee. Pets are not allowed in theme rooms.

Cameron

Best Western Acorn Inn
I-35 & US 36
Cameron, MO
816-632-2187
There are no additional pet fees.

Comfort Inn
1803 Comfort Lane
Cameron, MO
816-632-5655
There is no pet fee.

Cape Girardeau

Cape Girardeau Drury Lodge
104 S. Vantage Drive
Cape Girardeau, MO
573-334-7151
Dogs of all sizes are permitted. Pets are not allowed in the breakfast area of the hotel. Pets are not to be left unattended, and each guest must assume liability for damage of property or other guest complaints. There is a limit of one pet per room.

Cape Girardeau Drury Suites
3303 Campster Drive
Cape Girardeau, MO
573-339-9500
Dogs of all sizes are permitted. Pets are not allowed in the breakfast area of the hotel. Pets are not to be left unattended, and each guest must assume liability for damage of property or other guest complaints. There is a limit of one pet per room.

Cape Girardeau Pear Tree Inn
3248 William Street
Cape Girardeau, MO
573-334-3000
Dogs of all sizes are permitted. Pets are not allowed in the

breakfast area of the hotel. Pets are not to be left unattended, and each guest must assume liability for damage of property or other guest complaints. There is a limit of one pet per room.

Holiday Inn - West Park
I-55 & William St
Cape Girardeau, MO
573-334-4491
There is a $55 refundable pet deposit.

Pear Tree Inn
3248 William St
Cape Girardeau, MO
573-334-3000
One large dog is allowed pet room.

Chillicothe

Best Western Inn
1020 S. Washington
Chillicothe, MO
660-646-0572
There is a $5 per day additional pet fee.

Columbia

Columbia Drury Inn
1000 Knipp Street
Columbia, MO
573-445-1800
Dogs of all sizes are permitted. Pets are not allowed in the breakfast area of the hotel. Pets are not to be left unattended, and each guest must assume liability for damage of property or other guest complaints. There is a limit of one pet per room.

Holiday Inn Executive Center
2200 I-70 Dr SW
Columbia, MO
573-445-8531
There are no additional pet fees.

Holiday Inn Express
801 Keene St
Columbia, MO
573-449-4422
There are no additional pet fees.

Holiday Inn Select
2200 I-70 Dr. SW
Columbia, MO
573-445-8531
There are no additional pet fees.

Motel 6
1800 I-70 Dr SW
Columbia, MO
573-445-8433
There are no additional pet fees.

Quality Inn
1612 N. Providence Road
Columbia, MO
573-449-2491
There is a pet fee of $10 per day.

Travelodge
900 Vandover Dr
Columbia, MO
573-449-1065
There is a $5 per day pet fee.

Creve Coeur

St Louis - Creve Coeur Drury Inn & Suites
11980 Olive Blvd
Creve Coeur, MO
314-989-1100
Dogs of all sizes are permitted. Pets are not allowed in the breakfast area of the hotel. Pets are not to be left unattended, and each guest must assume liability for damage of property or other guest complaints. There is a limit of one pet per room.

Fenton

Motel 6
1860 Bowles Ave
Fenton, MO
636-349-1800
There are no additional pet fees.

St Louis - Fenton Drury Inn & Suites
1088 South Highway Drive

Fenton, MO
636-343-7822
Dogs of all sizes are permitted. Pets are not allowed in the breakfast area of the hotel. Pets are not to be left unattended, and each guest must assume liability for damage of property or other guest complaints. There is a limit of one pet per room.

St Louis - Fenton Pear Tree Inn
1100 S. Highway Drive
Fenton, MO
636-343-8820
Dogs of all sizes are permitted. Pets are not allowed in the breakfast area of the hotel. Pets are not to be left unattended, and each guest must assume liability for damage of property or other guest complaints. There is a limit of one pet per room.

Foristell

Best Western West 70 Inn
12 Hwy W, PO Box 10
Foristell, MO
636-673-2900
There is a $10 per day additional pet fee.

Hayti

Comfort Inn
I-55 Highway 84 East
Hayti, MO
573-359-0023
There is a pet fee of $10 per day.

Hayti Drury Inn & Suites
1317 Hwy 84
Hayti, MO
573-359-2702
Dogs of all sizes are permitted. Pets are not allowed in the breakfast area of the hotel. Pets are not to be left unattended, and each guest must assume liability for damage of property or other guest complaints. There is a limit of one pet per room.

Hazelwood

La Quinta Inn St. Louis - Hazelwood
5781 Campus Court
Hazelwood, MO
314-731-3881
Dogs up to 50 pounds are allowed at the hotel.

Independence

Comfort Inn East
4200 South Noland Rd.
Independence, MO
816-373-8856
There is a non-refundable pet fee of $25.

Jackson

Jackson Drury Inn & Suites
225 Drury Lane
Jackson, MO
573-243-9200
Dogs of all sizes are permitted. Pets are not allowed in the breakfast area of the hotel. Pets are not to be left unattended, and each guest must assume liability for damage of property or other guest complaints. There is a limit of one pet per room.

Joplin

Best Western Sands Inn
1611 Rangeline Rd
Joplin, MO
417-624-8300
Dogs may not be left alone in rooms.

Joplin Drury Inn & Suites
3601 Range Line Road
Joplin, MO
417-781-8000
Dogs of all sizes are permitted. Pets are not allowed in the breakfast area of the hotel. Pets are not to be left unattended, and each guest must assume liability for damage of property or other guest complaints. There is a limit of one pet per room.

Sleep Inn
I-44 SR 43 S.
Joplin, MO
417-782-1212
There is a one time pet fee of $10.

Kansas City

Best Western Seville Plaza Hotel
4309 Main Street
Kansas City, MO
816-561-9600
There is a $10 per day additional pet fee.

Chase Suite Hotel by Woodfin
9900 NW Prairie View Road
Kansas City, MO
816-891-9009
All well-behaved dogs are welcome. Every room is a suite and hotel amenities include an exercise room. There is a $5 per day pet fee.

Clarion Hotel
1601 N. Universal Ave.
Kansas City, MO
816-483-9900
There is a non-refundable pet fee of $50.

Comfort Suites
8200 N. Church Rd.
Kansas City, MO
816-781-7273
There is a pet fee of $10 per day.

Kansas City - Stadium Drury Inn & Suites
3830 Blue Ridge Cutoff
Kansas City, MO
816-923-3000
Dogs of all sizes are permitted. Pets are not allowed in the breakfast area of the hotel. Pets are not to be left unattended, and each guest must assume liability for damage of property or other guest complaints. There is a limit of one pet per room.

Mainstay Suites
9701 N. Shannon Ave.
Kansas City, MO
816-891-8500
There is a refundable deposit of $100. There is a pet fee of $5 per day.

Motel 6
6400 E 87th St
Kansas City, MO
816-333-4468
There are no additional pet fees.

Super 8 Motel
6900 NW 83rd Terrace
Kansas City, MO
816-587-0808
There is a $10 per day pet fee per pet.

The Westin Crown Center
One Pershing Road
Kansas City, MO
816-474-4400
Dogs are allowed in the 6th floor Lanai rooms. These rooms have a sliding glass door which leads to a lawn on the 6th floor, so you can walk your dog. There is a $50 one time pet charge.

Kirksville

Best Western Shamrock Inn
PO Box 1005
Kirksville, MO
660-665-8352
There is a $10 per day additional pet fee.

Budget Host Village Inn
1304 S Baltimore
Kirksville, MO
660-665-3722
There is a $5 per day pet fee.

Lake Ozark

Sunspree Resort
Business Hwy 54
Lake Ozark, MO
573-365-2334
There is a $25 refundable pet deposit and a $6 per day additional pet fee.

Lebanon

Best Western Wyota Inn
I-44 at Exit 130
Lebanon, MO
417-532-6171
There are no additional pet fees.

Macon

Best Western Inn
28933 Sunset Dr
Macon, MO
660-385-2125
There is a $20 refundable pet deposit.

Maryland Heights

Westport Drury Inn & Suites
12220 Dorsett Road
Maryland Heights, MO
314-576-9966
Dogs of all sizes are permitted. Pets are not allowed in the breakfast area of the hotel. Pets are not to be left unattended, and each guest must assume liability for damage of property or other guest complaints. There is a limit of one pet per room.

North Kansas City

Days Inn Motel - North Kansas City
2232 Taney Street
North Kansas City, MO
816-421-6000
$10/stay for up to 3 dogs in one room. FREE 8-minute long distance call each night. FREE deluxe continental breakfast. Coffee maker, night light, clock/radio, hairdryer, safe in each room. On-site guest laundry. Kids 12 & under stay free. From I-35/I-29, take Hwy 210/Armour Road exit, East to Taney Street, then Left/North to motel.

Ozark

Comfort Inn

1900 West Evangel St
Ozark, MO
417-485-6688
There is a one time pet fee of $10.

Perryville

Best Western Colonial Inn
I-55 & Hwy 51 S.
Perryville, MO
573-547-1091
Pets may never be left alone in rooms.

Poplar Bluff

Comfort Inn
2582 N. Westwood Blvd.
Poplar Bluff, MO
573-686-5200
There is a one time pet fee of $10.

Poplar Bluff Drury Inn
2220 Westwood Blvd North
Poplar Bluff, MO
573-686-2451
Dogs of all sizes are permitted. Pets are not allowed in the breakfast area of the hotel. Pets are not to be left unattended, and each guest must assume liability for damage of property or other guest complaints. There is a limit of one pet per room.

Poplar Bluff Pear Tree Inn
2218 N. Westwood Blvd
Poplar Bluff, MO
573-785-7100
Dogs of all sizes are permitted. Pets are not allowed in the breakfast area of the hotel. Pets are not to be left unattended, and each guest must assume liability for damage of property or other guest complaints. There is a limit of one pet per room.

Rolla

Best Western Coachlight
1403 Martin Spring Dr, Box 826

Rolla, MO
573-341-2511
There are no additional pet fees.

Howard Johnson Inn
127 HJ Drive at I-44
Rolla, MO
573-364-7111
Dogs of all sizes are welcome. There is a $10 per day pet fee.

Sikeston

Sikeston Drury Inn
2602 East Malone
Sikeston, MO
573-471-4100
Dogs of all sizes are permitted. Pets are not allowed in the breakfast area of the hotel. Pets are not to be left unattended, and each guest must assume liability for damage of property or other guest complaints. There is a limit of one pet per room.

Sikeston Pear Tree Inn
2602 Rear East Malone
Sikeston, MO
573-471-8660
Dogs of all sizes are permitted. Pets are not allowed in the breakfast area of the hotel. Pets are not to be left unattended, and each guest must assume liability for damage of property or other guest complaints. There is a limit of one pet per room.

Springfield

Best Western Coach House Inn
2535 N Glenstone
Springfield, MO
417-862-0701
There are no additional pet fees.

Best Western Route 66 Rail Haven
203 S. Glenstone
Springfield, MO
417-866-1963
There is a $10 per day additional pet fee.

Clarion Hotel
3333 S. Glenstone Ave
Springfield, MO
417-883-6550
There is a pet fee of $10 per
day.

Comfort Suites
1260 E. Independence St.
Springfield, MO
417-886-5090
There is a pet fee of $10 per
week.

Howard Johnson Express Inn
2535 S Campbell Ave.
Springfield, MO
417-890-6060
Dogs of all sizes are welcome.
There is a $15 per day pet fee.

Motel 6
3114 N Kentwood
Springfield, MO
417-833-0880
There are no additional pet fees.

Sheraton Hawthorn Park Hotel
2431 North Glenstone
Springfield, MO
417-831-3131
Dogs of all sizes are allowed.
There is a $50 one time per stay
pet fee.

Sleep Inn
233 E. Camino Alto
Springfield, MO
417-886-2464
There is a pet fee of $10 per
day. Pets may not be left alone.

Springfield Drury Inn & Suites
2715 N. Glenstone Avenue
Springfield, MO
417-863-8400
Dogs of all sizes are permitted.
Pets are not allowed in the
breakfast area of the hotel. Pets
are not to be left unattended,
and each guest must assume
liability for damage of property or
other guest complaints. There is
a limit of one pet per room.

St Charles

Comfort Suites
1400 S. 5th St.
St Charles, MO
636-949-0694
There is no pet fee.

Motel 6
3800 Harry S. Truman Blvd
St Charles, MO
636-925-2020
There are no pet fees. A well-
behaved large dog is okay.

St Joseph

Holiday Inn
102 S. 3rd Street
St Joseph, MO
816-279-8000
There is a $10 one time pet fee.

St. Joseph Drury Inn
4213 Frederick Blvd
St Joseph, MO
816-364-4700
Dogs of all sizes are permitted.
Pets are not allowed in the
breakfast area of the hotel.
Pets are not to be left
unattended, and each guest
must assume liability for
damage of property or other
guest complaints. There is a
limit of one pet per room.

St Josephs

Motel 6
4021 Frederick Blvd
St Josephs, MO
816-232-2311
There are no additional pet
fees.

St Louis

Comfort Inn Westport
12031 Lackland Rd.
St Louis, MO
314-878-1400
There is a one time non-
refundable pet fee of $25.
There is a per day pet fee of
$10.

Holiday Inn

4234 Butler Hill Rd
St Louis, MO
314-894-0700
There are no additional pet fees.
Pets must never be left alone in
the room.

Motel 6
1405 Dunn Rd
St Louis, MO
314-869-9400
There are no pet fees. A large
well-behaved dog is okay.

Residence Inn by Marriott
1881 Craigshire Rd
St Louis, MO
314-469-0060
There is a $100 one time pet
fee, and a fee of $6 per day.

**Sheraton St. Louis City Center
Hotel and Suites**
400 South 14th Street
St Louis, MO
314-231-5007
Dogs up to 80 pounds are
allowed. There are no additional
pet fees, but you need to fill out
a pet waiver form.

St Louis - Airport Drury Inn
10490 Natural Bridge Road
St Louis, MO
314-423-7700
Dogs of all sizes are permitted.
Pets are not allowed in the
breakfast area of the hotel. Pets
are not to be left unattended,
and each guest must assume
liability for damage of property or
other guest complaints. There is
a limit of one pet per room.

**St Louis - Convention Center
Drury Inn & Suites**
711 North Broadway
St Louis, MO
314-231-8100
Dogs of all sizes are permitted.
Pets are not allowed in the
breakfast area of the hotel. Pets
are not to be left unattended,
and each guest must assume
liability for damage of property or
other guest complaints. There is
a limit of one pet per room.

St Louis - Drury Plaza Hotel
Fourth & Market Streets
St Louis, MO
314-231-3003
Dogs of all sizes are permitted. Pets are not allowed in the breakfast area of the hotel. Pets are not to be left unattended, and each guest must assume liability for damage of property or other guest complaints. There is a limit of one pet per room.

St Louis - Union Station Drury Inn
201 South 20th Street
St Louis, MO
314-231-3900
Dogs of all sizes are permitted. Pets are not allowed in the breakfast area of the hotel. Pets are not to be left unattended, and each guest must assume liability for damage of property or other guest complaints. There is a limit of one pet per room.

St Peters

Holiday Inn Select
4221 S. Outer Rd
St Peters, MO
636-928-1500
There are no additional pet fees.

St Louis - St. Peters Drury Inn
170 Westfield Drive
St Peters, MO
636-397-9700
Dogs of all sizes are permitted. Pets are not allowed in the breakfast area of the hotel. Pets are not to be left unattended, and each guest must assume liability for damage of property or other guest complaints. There is a limit of one pet per room.

Villa Ridge

Best Western Diamond Inn
2875 Hwy 100
Villa Ridge, MO
636-742-3501
There is a $10 per day additional pet fee.

West Plains

Best Western Grand Villa
220 Jan Howard Expressway
West Plains, MO
417-257-2711
There is a $10 per day additional pet fee.

Montana Listings

Belgrade

Holiday Inn Express
6261 Jackrabbit Lane
Belgrade, MT
406-388-0800
Pets must be on leash and should never be left unattended in the room. There are no additional pet fees. The entire hotel is non-smoking.

Big Sky

Best Western Buck's T-4 Lodge
Hwy 191, PO Box 160279
Big Sky, MT
406-995-4111
There is a $5 per day additional pet fee. Pets may not be left alone in the room.

Bigfork

O'Duachain Country Inn Bed and Breakfast
675 Ferndale Dr
Bigfork, MT
406-837-6851
There is a $25 one time pet fee. The owner has a dog and a peacock, so your dog needs to be ok with them.

Timbers Motel
8540 Hwy. 35 South
Bigfork, MT
406-837-6200
There is a $5 per day pet fee.

Billings

Comfort Inn
2030 Overland Ave.
Billings, MT
406-652-5200
There is a one time pet fee of $10.

Hilltop Inn
1116 N 28th St
Billings, MT
406-245-5000
There is a $5 per day pet fee.

Holiday Inn - Grand Montana
5500 Midland Rd
Billings, MT
406-248-7701
There is a $10 one time pet fee.

Howard Johnson Express Inn
1001 S 27th St.
Billings, MT
406-248-4656
Dogs of all sizes are welcome. There are no additional pet fees.

Motel 6
5400 Midland Rd
Billings, MT
406-252-0093
There are no additional pet fees.

Quality Inn Homestead Park
2036 Overland Ave.
Billings, MT
406-652-1320
There is a refundable pet deposit of $25.

Super 8 Motel
5400 Southgate Dr
Billings, MT
406-248-8842
There is a $20 refundable pet deposit.

Bozeman

Holiday Inn
5 Baxtor Lane
Bozeman, MT
406-587-4561
There are no additional pet fees.

La Quinta Inn & Suites Bozeman - Belgrade

6445 Jackrabbit Lane
Bozeman, MT
406-388-2222
Dogs of all sizes are allowed at
the hotel.

Ramada Limited
2020 Wheat Drive
Bozeman, MT
406-585-2626
There are no additional pet fees.

Western Heritage Inn
1200 E Main St
Bozeman, MT
406-586-8534
There is a $5 per day pet
charge.

Butte

Comfort Inn
2777 Harrison Ave.
Butte, MT
406-494-8850
There is a pet fee of $5 per day.

Days Inn
2700 Harrison Avenue
Butte, MT
406-494-7000
There are no additional pet fees.

Ramada Inn
4655 Harrison Ave.
Butte, MT
406-494-6666
There is a $10 per day pet fee.

Dillon

Best Western Paradise Inn
650 N. Montana Street
Dillon, MT
406-683-4214
There are no additional pet fees.

Comfort Inn
450 N. Interchange
Dillon, MT
406-683-6831
There is a pet fee of $5 per day.

Forsyth

Best Western Sundowner Inn

1018 Front St, PO Box 1080
Forsyth, MT
406-356-2115
There is a $3 per day additional
pet fee.

Glasgow

Cottonwood Inn
45 1st Avenue
Glasgow, MT
406-228-8213
There are no additional pet
fees.

Glendive

Days Inn
2000 N Merrill Avenue
Glendive, MT
406-365-6011
There are no additional pet
fees.

Super 8 Motel
1904 N. Merrill Ave.
Glendive, MT
406-365-5671
There is a $5 per day additional
pet fee.

Great Falls

Best Western Heritage Inn
1700 Fox Farm Road
Great Falls, MT
406-761-1900
There are no additional pet
fees.

Holiday Inn
400 10th Ave S.
Great Falls, MT
406-727-7200
There is a $10 per day pet fee.
Pets must be on leash when
outside the room.

Townhouse Inn
1411 10th Avenue South
Great Falls, MT
406-761-4600
There is a $5 per day pet
charge.

Hamilton

Comfort Inn
1113 N. First St.
Hamilton, MT
406-363-6600
There is a pet fee of $10 per
day.

Havre

Townhouse Inn
601 1st Street West
Havre, MT
406-265-6711
There is a $5 per day pet
charge.

Helena

Barrister Bed and Breakfast
416 North Ewing
Helena, MT
406-443-7330
There are no additional pet fees.

Holiday Inn
22 N. Last Chance Gulch
Helena, MT
406-443-2200
There is a $10 one time pet fee.

Motel 6
800 N Oregon St
Helena, MT
406-442-9990
There are no additional pet fees.

Shilo Inn
2020 Prospect Avenue
Helena, MT
406-442-0320
There is a $10 per day pet
charge.

Kalispell

Cavanaugh's
20 N Main St
Kalispell, MT
406-752-6660
There is a $15 one time pet fee.

Hampton Inn
1140 Hwy 2 West
Kalispell, MT

406-755-7900
No extra pet fees, just sign a pet waiver.

Kalispell Grand Hotel
100 Main St
Kalispell, MT
406-755-8100
There are no additional pet fees.

La Quinta Inn & Suites Kalispell
255 Montclair Dr.
Kalispell, MT
406-257-5255
Dogs of all sizes are allowed at the hotel.

Motel 6
1540 Hwy 93 S
Kalispell, MT
406-752-6355
There are no additional pet fees. One pet per room is allowed. Pets must be leashed when outside of the room.

Libby

Super 8 Motel
448 Hwy 2 West
Libby, MT
406-293-2771
There is a $5 one time pet charge.

Livingston

Best Western Yellowstone Inn
1515 W. Park Street
Livingston, MT
406-222-6110
There is a $10 per day pet charge.

Miles City

Best Western War Bonnet Inn
1015 S. Haynes, Box 1055
Miles City, MT
406-232-4560
There are no additional pet fees.

Budget Inn
1006 S. Haynes Ave.
Miles City, MT

406-232-3550
There is a $5 per day pet charge.

Motel 6
1314 Haynes Ave Rt 2, Box 3396
Miles City, MT
406-232-7040
There are no additional pet fees.

Missoula

Best Western Executive Inn
201 East Main Street
Missoula, MT
406-543-7221
There is a $25 refundable pet deposit.

Best Western Grant Creek Inn
5280 Grant Creek Rd
Missoula, MT
406-543-0700
There are no additional pet fees.

Hampton Inn
4805 North Reserve St
Missoula, MT
406-549-1800
There is a $10 one time pet charge.

Holiday Inn
200 S. Pattee St
Missoula, MT
406-721-8550
There are no additional pet fees.

Motel 6
3035 Expo Pkwy Commerce Ctr
Missoula, MT
406-549-6665
There are no additional pet fees.

Shelby

Comfort Inn
50 Frontage Rd.
Shelby, MT

406-434-2212
There is no pet fee.

Whitefish

Quality Inn Pine Lodge
920 Spokane Ave
Whitefish, MT
406-862-7600
There are no additional pet fees.

Nebraska Listings

Beatrice

Holiday Inn Express Hotel & Suites
N. Hwy 77
Beatrice, NE
402-228-7000
There is a $25 one time pet fee.

Cozad

Motel 6
809 S Meridian
Cozad, NE
308-784-4900
There are no additional pet fees.

Fremont

Comfort Inn
1649 E. 23rd St.
Fremont, NE
402-721-1109
There is no pet fee.

Grand Island

Holiday Inn
I-80 & Hwy 281
Grand Island, NE
308-384-7770
There is a $15 one time pet fee. Pets must be on leash when outside the room.

Howard Johnson Hotel
3333 Ramada Road
Grand Island, NE
308-384-5150

Dogs of all sizes are welcome. There is a $10 one time pet fee.

Hastings

Holiday Inn
2205 Osborne Dr East
Hastings, NE
402-463-6721
There are no additional pet fees.

Super 8
2200 N Kansas
Hastings, NE
402-463-8888
There are no additional pet fees.

Kearney

Best Western Inn of Kearney
1010 3rd Ave
Kearney, NE
308-237-5185
There is a $10 one time pet fee.

Motel 6
101 Talmadge Rd
Kearney, NE
308-338-0705
There are no additional pet fees.

Super 8 Motel - Kearney
15 W. 8th Street
Kearney, NE
308-234-5513
$10/stay for up to 3 dogs in one room. FREE 8-minute long distance call each night. FREE continental breakfast. Coffee maker, night light, clock/radio, safe in each room. On-site guest laundry. Kids 12 & under stay free. I-80, Exit 272, N 1/2 mile to W. 8th St. Turn Right.

Lexington

Budget Host Minute Man Motel
801 Plum Creek Pkwy
Lexington, NE
308-324-5544
There is a $5 per day pet fee. Usually pets are in smoking rooms, but they will make exceptions.

Holiday Inn Express & Suites
2605 Plum Creek Pkwy
Lexington, NE
308-324-9900
There is a $10 one time pet fee. Pets are allowed on the third floor only. Take US 283 exit off of I-80.

Lincoln

Comfort Inn
2940 NW 12th St
Lincoln, NE
402-475-2200
There is a $5 one time pet fee.

Comfort Suites
4231 Industrial Ave.
Lincoln, NE
402-476-8080
There is a pet fee of $10 per day.

Holiday Inn Express
1133 Belmont Ave
Lincoln, NE
402-435-0200
There are no additional pet fees.

Motel 6
5600 Cornhusker Hwy
Lincoln, NE
402-464-5971
There are no pet fees.

Motel 6
3001 NW 12th St
Lincoln, NE
402-475-3211
There are no pet fees. Pets may never be left alone in the room.

Staybridge Suites
2701 Fletcher Avenue
Lincoln, NE
402-438-7829
The one time pet fee is $25 for 1-4 days, $50 for 5 - 29 days, and $75 for 30 or more days.

North Platte

Best Western Chalet Lodge
920 N Jeffers
North Platte, NE
308-532-2313
There is a $3 per day additional pet fee.

Best Western Circle C S. Motor Inn
1211 South Dewey Street
North Platte, NE
308-532-0130
There is a $6 per day additional pet fee.

Motel 6
1520 S Jeffers St
North Platte, NE
308-534-6200
There are no additional pet fees.

Quality Inn & Suites
2102 S. Jeffers
North Platte, NE
308-532-9090
There is a one time pet fee of $10.

Stanford Motel
1400 E 4th Street
North Platte, NE
308-532-9380
There is a $3 per day pet fee. Puppies are not allowed but dogs are permitted.

Ogallala

Holiday Inn Express
501 Stage Coach Drive
Ogallala, NE
308-284-2266
Pets must stay on the first floor. There is no pet fee most of the time. During busy times there may be a pet fee.

Omaha

Comfort Inn
10919 J St.
Omaha, NE
402-592-2882
There is a one time pet fee of $10.

Accommodations - Please always call ahead to make sure an establishment is still dog-friendly.

Crowne Plaza
655 N. 108th Ave
Omaha, NE
402-496-0850
There is a $25 one time pet fee.

La Quinta Inn Omaha
3330 North 104th Avenue
Omaha, NE
402-493-1900
Dogs of all sizes are allowed at the hotel.

Marriott
10220 Regency Circle
Omaha, NE
402-399-9000
There is a $30 one time pet fee.

Motel 6
10708 M St
Omaha, NE
402-331-3161
There are no pet fees. A large well-behaved dog is okay.

clarion Hotel
4888 S 118th St
Omaha, NE
402-895-1000
There is a $10 per day pet fee.

Scottsbluff

Best Western Scottsbluff Inn
1901 21st Ave
Scottsbluff, NE
308-635-3111
There is a $5 per day pet fee.

Lamplighter American Inn
606 E 27th St
Scottsbluff, NE
308-632-7108
There is a $6 per day additional pet fee.

Sidney

Holiday Inn
664 Chase Blvd
Sidney, NE
308-254-2000
There is a $10 one time pet fee. Use the Hwy 385 exit off of I-80.

York

Best Western Palmer Inn
2426 S. Lincoln Ave
York, NE
402-362-5585
There is a $5 per day additional pet fee.

Nevada Listings

Battle Mountain

Comfort Inn
521 E. Front Street
Battle Mountain, NV
775-635-5880
There is a $100 refundable pet deposit.

Boulder City

Seven Crown Resorts Houseboats
322 Lake Shore Road
Boulder City, NV
800-752-9669
Rent a houseboat on Lake Mead at the Lake Mead Resort Marina and bring your pooch with you. Lake Mead is approximately 25 miles from downtown Las Vegas. Pets are welcome on houseboats at no additional charge. Advance reservations are required. Call 800-752-9669 to make your reservation.

Super 8
704 Nevada Hwy
Boulder City, NV
702-294-8888
There is a $10 per day pet fee.

Bullhead City

Best Western Inn
1126 Highway 95
Bullhead City, AZ
928-754-3000
This hotel is in Bullhead City, Arizona. This is across the river from Laughlin, NV. There is a $10 per day pet fee.

Seven Crown Resorts Houseboats
Katherine Landing
Bullhead City, AZ
800-752-9669
Rent a houseboat on Lake Mohave at the Lake Mohave Resort-Katherine Landing and bring your pooch too. Lake Mohave is a short drive north of Laughlin, Nevada and Bullhead City, Arizona. Pets are welcome on houseboats at no additional charge. Advance reservations are required. Call 800-752-9669 to make your reservation.

Carson City

Best Value Motel
2731 S Carson St
Carson City, NV
775-882-2007
There is a $30 refundable pet deposit.

Super 8 Motel
2829 S. Carson Street
Carson City, NV
775-883-7800
There is a $6 per day pet fee.

Elko

Best Western Gold Country Inn
2050 Idaho Street
Elko, NV
775-738-8421
There is a $15 one time pet fee.

Comfort Inn
2970 Idaho St
Elko, NV
775-777-8762
There is a $10 per day pet fee.

High Desert Inn
3015 Idaho Street
Elko, NV
775-738-8425
There is a $15 one time pet charge.

Motel 6
3021 Idaho Street
Elko, NV
775-738-4337
There are no additional pet fees.

Red Lion Casino
2065 Idaho Street
Elko, NV
775-738-2111
There is a $15 one time pet fee.

Shilo Inn
2401 Mountain City Highway
Elko, NV
775-738-5522
There is a $10 per day pet charge.

Best Western Main Motel
1101 Aultman
Ely, NV
775-289-4529
There is a $20 one time pet fee.

Best Western Park Vue
930 Aultman
Ely, NV
775-289-4497
There is a $20 one time pet fee.

Ramada Inn Copper Queen Casino
805 Great Basin Blvd
Ely, NV
775-289-4884
There are no additional pet fees.

Super 8
855 W. Williams Ave
Fallon, NV
775-423-6031
There is a $5 per day additional pet fee.

Best Western Fernley Inn
1405 E Newlands Dr
Fernley, NV
775-575-6776

There is a $7 per day addition pet fee.

Soldier Meadows Guest Ranch and Lodge
Soldier Meadows Rd
Gerlach, NV
530-233-4881
Dating back to 1865 when it was known as Camp McGarry, this historic cattle ranch lies in the Black Rock Desert about three hours north of Reno. Soldier Meadows is a family owned working cattle ranch with over 500,000 acres of public and private land to enjoy. It is one of the largest and remotest guest ranches in the nation. There are no phones, faxes, or computers here. Horseback riders can work with the cowboys, take trail rides to track wild mustangs and other wildlife, or ride out to the natural hot springs for a soak. Or you may chose to go mule deer hunting, fishing, hiking, mountain biking or 4-wheeling. The lodge offers 10 guest rooms, and one suite with a private bathroom and kitchenette. The main lodge has a common living room with a large fireplace. Pets are not allowed in the kitchen area. There is a $20 one time pet charge.

Green Valley Vacation Home Rental
Call to Arrange.
Green Valley, NV
702-433-6786
This Spanish-style 3 bedroom, 2 bathroom house, located in Green Valley, is about 10 miles from the Las Vegas Strip. This pet-friendly home offers a doggy door in the sliding glass door which leads to a large, private enclosed grassy backyard. Families welcome.

Residence Inn
2190 Olympic Road
Henderson, NV
702-434-2700
There is a $50 one time pet fee and a $10 per day pet fee. One dog is allowed per room and dogs up to 65 pounds are allowed.

Best Western Nellis
5330 East Craig Street
Las Vegas, NV
702-643-6111
This motel is located away from the busy downtown area, but within minutes from the Las Vegas Strip. Amenities include an outdoor pool, a playground, laundry/valet services and complimentary continental breakfast on the weekends. There is a $10 per day pet charge.

Best Western Parkview
921 Las Vegas Blvd North
Las Vegas, NV
702-385-1213
This motel is located within a 15 minute drive from the Las Vegas Strip. Amenities include an outdoor pool and a guest laundry. There is a $8 per day pet charge.

Comfort Inn
910 E. Cheyenne Rd.
Las Vegas, NV
702-399-1500
This motel is located about three miles from the Las Vegas Strip. Amenities at this motel include a heated outdoor pool & hot tub, gift shop, free continental breakfast and wheelchair accessibility. There is a $5 per day pet charge.

Desert Shores Vacation Rental
Call to Arrange.
Las Vegas, NV
702-656-8905

This 2 bedroom, 2 bathroom condo vacation rental allows pets.

Hampton Inn
7100 Cascade Valley Court
Las Vegas, NV
702-360-5700
There is a $25 one time pet fee.

Hawthorn Suites-The Strip
5051 Duke Ellington Way
Las Vegas, NV
702-739-7000
This suites hotel has no size restrictions for dogs as long as they are well-behaved (no barking, potty trained, etc.). There is a $125 pet deposit and $25 of it is non-refundable. Hotel amenities include a guest laundry, outdoor pool, exercise room and more.

Holiday Inn Express-The Lakes
8669 W. Sahara Avenue
Las Vegas, NV
702-256-3766
Dogs are welcome at this inn. There is a $20 one time pet charge. Amenities include guest laundry facilities. They are located about 6.5 miles from downtown Las Vegas.

La Quinta Inn Las Vegas - Nellis
4288 N. Nellis Rd.
Las Vegas, NV
702-632-0229
Dogs of all sizes are allowed at the hotel.

La Quinta Inn Las Vegas - Tropicana
4975 South Valley View
Las Vegas, NV
702-798-7736
Dogs of all sizes are allowed at the hotel.

La Quinta Suites Las Vegas - West/Lakes
9570 W. Sahara
Las Vegas, NV
702-243-0356
Dogs of all sizes are allowed at

the hotel.

Las Vegas Vacation Home Rental
Call to Arrange.
Las Vegas, NV
702-395-7065
This 4 bedroom, 3 bathroom house is only 5 minutes from the Las Vegas Strip. Lake Mead and Hoover Dam are about 25 minutes away. Pets are allowed in this vacation home. Amenities include a backyard with a pool/spa combo and gas BBQ.

Las Vegas Vacation Villas
Call to Arrange.
Las Vegas, NV
702-798-9808
This company offers pet-friendly townhouse vacation and estate vacation rentals. It is located in a gated community with views of green fairways.

Residence Inn - Hughes Center
370 Hughes Center Drive
Las Vegas, NV
702-650-0040
There is a $50 one time pet fee and a $10 per day pet charge.

Rodeway Inn & Suites
167 E. Tropicana Ave
Las Vegas, NV
702-795-3311
There is a $100 refundable pet deposit.

Pioneer Hotel and Gambling Hall
2200 S. Casino Drive
Laughlin, NV
702-298-2442
This hotel casino allows dogs of all sizes. However, there are only ten pet rooms and these are all smoking rooms. We normally do not include smoking room only pet rooms but since the selection of pet friendly lodging in Laughlin is

so limited we have listed this one.

Ramada Inn Sturgeon's Casino
1420 Cornell Ave
Lovelock, NV
775-273-2971
There is a $100 refundable pet deposit.

Mount Charleston Lodge and Cabins
HCR 38 Box 325
Mount Charleston, NV
800-955-1314
The lodge sits at over 7,700 feet above sea level and about 35 miles from the Las Vegas Strip. There are several dog-friendly trails nearby for hikers. Dogs are welcome for an additional $10 per day pet charge.

Best Western North Shore Inn
520 N. Moapa Valley Blvd
Overton, NV
702-397-6000
There is a $50 refundable pet deposit. The hotel is 10 miles from Lake Mead.

Days Inn
701 E 7th
Reno, NV
775-786-4070
There is a $10 per day pet fee.

Holiday Inn
1000 E. 6th St.
Reno, NV
775-786-5151
This hotel is located only 4 blocks from Reno's famous gaming strip and within walking distance to the Reno Livestock & Events Center. Amenities

include a heated pool and gift shop. There is a $10 per day pet charge.

Motel 6 - Virginia/Plumb
1901 S. Virginia St
Reno, NV
775-827-0255
There are no additional pet fees.

Residence Inn by Marriott
9845 Gateway Drive
Reno, NV
775-853-8800
Every room is a suite with a bedroom area, living room area and kitchen. Amenities include room service, self service laundry facilities, complimentary continental breakfast, an outdoor pool and exercise room. Rooms include hairdryers and iron/ironing boards. There is a one time non-refundable $80 pet charge and an additional $6 per day for pets.

Rodeway Inn
2050 Market Street
Reno, NV
775-786-2500
This hotel (previously Travelodge) is about a mile from the Reno gambling strip. Amenities include a complimentary continental breakfast, heated outdoor pool, kitchenettes in some rooms, and wheelchair accessible rooms. There is a $10 per day pet charge.

Truckee River Lodge
501 W. 1st Street
Reno, NV
775-786-8888
There is a $10 per day pet fee. All rooms in the hotel are non-smoking. There is a park across the street.

Vagabond Inn
3131 S. Virginia St.
Reno, NV
775-825-7134
This motel is located less than a couple miles from the downtown casinos and the Convention

Center. Amenities include a swimming pool, 24 hour cable television, air conditioning, and more. There is a $10 per day pet fee.

Tonopah

Best Western Hi-Desert Inn
320 Main Street
Tonopah, NV
775-482-3511
Pets may not be left unattended in the room. There are no pet fees.

Wendover

Super 8
Wendover Blvd (I-80 Exit 410)
Wendover, NV
775-664-2888
There is a $7.50 per day pet fee. Take exit 410 off of I-80 and turn right on Wendover Blvd.

Winnemucca

Best Western Gold Country Inn
921 West Winnemucca Boulevard
Winnemucca, NV
775-623-6999
There is a $10 one time pet charge.

Best Western Holiday Motel
670 W. Winnemucca Blvd
Winnemucca, NV
775-623-3684
There are no additional pet fees.

Days Inn
511 W. Winnemucca Blvd
Winnemucca, NV
775-623-3661
There is a $10 per day pet fee.

Holiday Inn Express
1987 W. Winnemucca Blvd
Winnemucca, NV
775-625-3100
There is a $50 pet deposit and

$10 of the deposit is non-refundable.

Motel 6
1600 Winnemucca Blvd
Winnemucca, NV
775-623-1180
Pets may not be left unattended in rooms at any time.

Red Lion Inn & Casino
741 West Winnemucca Boulevard
Winnemucca, NV
775-623-2565
There is a $20 refundable pet deposit. They have a 24 hour restaurant on the premises.

Santa Fe Motel
1620 W. Winnemucca Blvd
Winnemucca, NV
775-623-1119
There are no additional pet fees.

Super 8
1157 Winnemucca Blvd
Winnemucca, NV
775-625-1818
There is a $5 per day pet fee.

New Hampshire Listings

Bedford

Wayfarer Inn
121 South River Rd
Bedford, NH
603-622-3766
There is a $25.00 one time pet fee.

Bennington

Highland Inn
634 Francestown Rd
Bennington, NH
603-588-2777
There is a $10 one time pet fee.

Claremont

Claremont Motor Lodge
Beauregard St, near SR 103
Claremont, NH
603-542-2540
There are no additional pet fees.

Northern Comfort Motel
RR 1, Box 520
Colebrook, NH
603-237-4440
There is a $5.00 per day pet charge.

Comfort Inn
71 Hall St.
Concord, NH
603-226-4100
There is a pet fee of $10 per day. Pets must be well-behaved.

Days Inn
481 Central Ave
Dover, NH
603-742-0400
There is a $50 refundable pet deposit.

Hickory Pond Inn & Golf Course
1 Stagecoach Rd
Durham, NH
603-659-2227
There are several designated pet rooms. All rooms are non-smoking. There is a $10 one time pet fee.

Franconia Notch Vacations
PO Box 605
Franconia, NH
800-247-5536
Not all homes advertised accept pets. Please call for more information.

Horse & Hound
205 Wells Rd
Franconia, NH
603-823-5501
There are no designated smoking or non-smoking rooms. There is an $8.50 per day additional pet fee.

Lovetts Inn by Lafayette Brook
SR 18
Franconia, NH
603-823-7761
There are two pet rooms, both non-smoking. There is a $10 one time additional pet fee.

Temperance Tavern
Old Providence Rd
Gilmanton, NH
603-267-7349
Owners have a dog and welcome well-trained potty trained dogs only. There is a $5 per day additional pet fee.

Top Notch Motor Inn
265 Main St
Gorham, NH
603-466-5496
$25 refundable deposit for pets.

Town & Country Motor Inn
US 2
Gorham, NH
603-466-3315
There are no additional pet fees.

Hanover Inn at Dartmouth College
Box 151, at Main & Wheelock Sts
Hanover, NH
603-643-4300
There is a $30 per day pet charge.

Yankee Trail Motel
US 3
Holderness, NH
603-968-3535
There are no additional pet fees.

Swiss Chalets Village Inn
Old Route 16A
Intervale, NH
603-356-2232
Swiss Chalets Village Inn offers comfortable lodgings, some with fireplace jacuzzi suites, plenty of indoor and outdoor activities, and a bit of Swiss charm right in the midst of New Hampshire's White Mountains. Pets are welcome.

Dana Place Inn
SR 16
Jackson, NH
603-383-6822
There are no additional pet fees.

The Village House
PO Box 359 Rt 16A
Jackson, NH
603-383-6666
This bed and breakfast's rooms are located in a 100 year old barn behind the main house that houses the Yellow Snow Dog Gear collar and lead business. Rooms have kitchenettes, balconies, jacuzzi tubs, and are decorated in the style of a B&B. There are 15 guest rooms and 13 have private baths. They welcome all well-behaved dogs and there are no size restrictions. Rates range from $65-140 depending on the season. There is a $10 per day pet fee.

Econo Lodge
75 W Hancock St

Manchester, NH
603-624-0111
There is a $100 refundable deposit and a $10 per day pet fee.

Mount Sunapee

Best Western Sunapee Lake Lodge
1403 Route 103
Mount Sunapee, NH
603-763-2010
There is an $8 per day additional pet fee.

Nashua

Holiday Inn
9 Northeastern Blvd
Nashua, NH
603-888-1551
There are no additional pet fees.

Sheraton Nashua Hotel
11 Tara Boulevard
Nashua, NH
603-888-9970
Dogs up to 80 pounds are allowed. There are no additional pet fees.

Pittsburg

The Glen
77 The Glen Rd
Pittsburg, NH
603-538-6500
Pets are allowed in the cottages only. There are no pet fees. There are no designated smoking or non-smoking cottages.

Portsmouth

Motel 6
3 Gosling Rd
Portsmouth, NH
603-334-6606
One pet per room is permitted. Well-behaved large dogs are okay.

Residence Inn

1 International Dr
Portsmouth, NH
603-436-8880
There is a $250.00 one time pet charge.

Rochester

Anchorage Inn
80 Main St
Rochester, NH
603-332-3350
There is a $10 per day additional pet fee.

Salem

Red Roof Inn
15 Red Roof Ln
Salem, NH
603-898-6422
There are no additional pet fees. Pets must be attended at all times.

Sugar Hill

The Hilltop Inn Bed and Breakfast
Main St
Sugar Hill, NH
603-823-5695
There is a $10 per day dog fee. The owner has two dogs on the premises.

Weirs Beach

Victorian Cottage
#30 Veterans Ave
Weirs Beach, NH
603-279-4583
Remodeled antique home located at Weirs Beach, NH. Spectacular view of Lake Winnipesaukee and surrounding mountains from the house and porch. 3 bedrooms/sleeps 6. Pets are welcome in this beautiful home. $1300/wk with $300 security deposit. Contact Sally Garden at 604-279-4583.

West Chesterfield

Chesterfield Inn
HCR 10 Box 59
West Chesterfield, NH
603-256-3211
There are no additional pet fees.

West Lebanon

Airport Economy Inn
45 Airport Rd
West Lebanon, NH
603-298-8888
There is a $10 per day pet fee.

Radisson Inn - North Country
25 Airport Rd
West Lebanon, NH
603-298-5906
There is a $10 per day pet fee for each pet.

Woodsville

All Seasons Motel
36 Smith St
Woodsville, NH
603-747-2157
There is a $6 per day pet fee. Dogs must not be left alone in the rooms.

New Jersey Listings

Blackwood

Howard Johnson Express Inn
832 North Black Horse Pike
Blackwood, NJ
856-228-4040
Dogs of all sizes are welcome. There is a $10 per day pet fee.

Cherry Hill

Residence Inn by Marriott
1821 Old Cuthbert Rd
Cherry Hill, NJ
856-429-6111
There is a $200 one time per stay pet fee and a 2 pet per room limit. This apartment-style hotel is designed for a long term

stay.

East Brunswick

Motel 6
244 Rt 18
East Brunswick, NJ
732-390-4545
There are no additional pet fees.

East Rutherford

Sheraton Meadowlands Hotel and Conference Center
2 Meadowlands Plaza
East Rutherford, NJ
201-896-0500
Dogs of all sizes are allowed. There is a $75 one time per stay pet fee.

Eatontown

Sheraton Eatontown Hotel
Route 35 at Industrial Way East
Eatontown, NJ
732-542-6500
Dogs up to 80 pounds are allowed. There are no additional pet fees. The hotel only has two non-smoking pet rooms.

Edison

Red Roof Inn
860 New Durham Rd
Edison, NJ
732-248-9300
There are no additional pet fees.

Sheraton Edison Hotel Raritan Center
125 Raritan Center Parkway
Edison, NJ
732-225-8300
Dogs of all sizes are allowed. There are no additional pet fees.

Englewood

Radisson
401 S Van Brunt St
Englewood, NJ
201-871-2020
There are no additional pet fees.

Lawrenceville

Howard Johnson Inn
2995 Rt. 1 South
Lawrenceville, NJ
609-896-1100
Dogs of all sizes are welcome. There is a $10 per day pet fee.

Lyndhurst

Quality Inn Meadowlands
10 Polito Ave.
Lyndhurst, NJ
201-933-9800
There is no pet fee.

Mahwah

Sheraton Crossroads Hotel
1 International Boulevard
Mahwah, NJ
201-529-1660
Dogs of all sizes are allowed. There are no additional pet fees.

Maple Shade

Motel 6
Rt 73 North
Maple Shade, NJ
856-235-3550
There are no additional pet fees. Use Exit 4 on the NJ Turnpike.

Middletown

Howard Johnson Inn
750 Hwy 35 South
Middletown, NJ
732-671-3400
Dogs of all sizes are welcome. There is a $15 per day pet fee.

Mount Holly

Best Western Burlington Inn
2020 Rt 541, RD 1
Mount Holly, NJ
609-261-3800
There is a $5 per day additional pet fee.

North Wildwood

Surf 16 Motel
1600 Surf Avenue
North Wildwood, NJ
609-522-1010
Open during the summer only. We have a dog-friendly motel. We accept all sizes, in fact we have a Doberman and a Staffordshire Terrior ourselves. We are open from May 1st through mid-October. We are 1/2 blocks from the beach and boardwalk. Dogs are allowed on the beach before May 15 and after September 15. We have a fenced in dog run and people can leave the dog in the room as long as it is quiet. We have motel rooms and apartments. There is a $10 per day pet charge. All of the motel's rooms are not designated smoking or non-smoking.

Paramus

Radisson
601 From Rd
Paramus, NJ
201-262-6900
Dogs up to 50 pounds are allowed. There is a $25 per week pet fee.

Parsippany

Sheraton Parsippany Hotel
199 Smith Road
Parsippany, NJ
973-515-2000
Dogs up to 80 pounds are allowed. There are no additional pet fees.

Phillipsburg

Clarion
1314 US 22
Phillipsburg, NJ
908-454-9771
There are no additional pet fees. Use the Hwy 22 exit off of I-78.

Princeton

Summerfield Suites Hotel
4375 US 1 S
Princeton, NJ
609-951-0009
There is a $150 pet charge per each stay.

Secaucus

Mainstay Suites Meadowlands
1 Plaza Drive
Secaucus, NJ
201-553-9700
There is a pet fee of $10 per day.

Radisson Suite
350 NJ 3 W
Secaucus, NJ
201-863-8700
There is a $25 one time pet fee.

Somers Point

Residence Inn
900 Mays Landing Rd
Somers Point, NJ
609-927-6400
There is a $75.00 one time pet charge.

Somerset

Holiday Inn
195 Davidson Ave
Somerset, NJ
732-356-1700
There are no additional pet fees. Pets may never be left alone in the room. Housekeeping will need to schedule your room for cleaning if you have a pet.

South Plainfield

Holiday Inn
4701 Stelton Rd
South Plainfield, NJ
908-753-5500
There are no additional pet fees.

Springfield

Holiday Inn
304 Rt 22 W
Springfield, NJ
973-376-9400
There are no pet fees. Pets must be on leash when they are outside of the room.

Tinton Falls

Red Roof Inn
11 Centre Plaza
Tinton Falls, NJ
732-389-4646
Dogs are allowed on first floor only. There are no additional pet fees.

Weehawken

Sheraton Suites on the Hudson
500 Harbor Boulevard
Weehawken, NJ
201-617-5600
Dogs up to 70 pounds are allowed. There is a one time pet fee of $64.00 per stay.

New Mexico Listings

Alamogordo

Best Western Desert Aire Motor Inn
1021 S White Sands Blvd
Alamogordo, NM
505-437-2110
There is a $50 refundable pet deposit.

Holiday Inn Express
1401 S. White Sands Blvd
Alamogordo, NM
505-437-7100
There is a $50 refundable pet deposit.

Motel 6
251 Panorama Blvd
Alamogordo, NM
505-434-5970

There are no additional pet fees.

Albuquerque

Best Western American Motor Inn
12999 Central Ave NE
Albuquerque, NM
505-298-7426
There is a $15 per day additional pet fee.

Brittania and WE Mauger Estate
701 Roma Ave NW
Albuquerque, NM
505-242-8755
This bed and breakfast has one pet room. This room has a doggie door which leads to an enclosed lawn area for your dog. There is a $30 one time additional pet fee.

Comfort Inn & Suites North
5811 Signal Ave. N.E.
Albuquerque, NM
505-822-1090
There is a pet fee of $10 per day.

Comfort Inn Airport
2300 Yale Blvd.
Albuquerque, NM
505-243-2244
There is a $10 per day pet fee.

Econo Lodge
13211 Central Ave NE
Albuquerque, NM
505-292-7600
There is a $10 per day pet fee.

Hampton Inn
5101 Ellison NE
Albuquerque, NM
505-344-1555
There are no additional pet fees.

Holiday Inn - Mountain View
2020 Menaul Blvd NE
Albuquerque, NM
505-884-2511
There is a $25 one time pet fee.

Holiday Inn Express
6100 Iliff Rd

Albuquerque, NM
505-836-8600
There is a $10 per day additional pet fee. A well-behaved and quiet large dog is okay.

Holiday Inn Express
10330 Hotel Ave NE
Albuquerque, NM
505-275-8900
There is a $5 per day additional pet fee.

Howard Johnson Express Inn
7630 Pan American Freeway NE
Albuquerque, NM
505-828-1600
Dogs of all sizes are welcome. There is a $5 per day pet fee.

Howard Johnson Hotel
15 Hotel Circle NE
Albuquerque, NM
505-296-4852
Dogs of all sizes are welcome. There is a $20 one time pet fee.

La Quinta Inn Albuquerque Airport
2116 Yale Boulevard
Albuquerque, NM
505-243-5500
Dogs up to 50 pounds are allowed at the hotel.

La Quinta Inn Albuquerque North
5241 San Antonio Drive NE
Albuquerque, NM
505-821-9000
Dogs of all sizes are allowed at the hotel.

Motel 6
1000 Avenida Cesar Chavez SE
Albuquerque, NM
505-243-8017
There are no additional pet fees.

Motel 6
3400 Prospect Ave NE
Albuquerque, NM
505-883-8813
There are no additional pet fees.

Motel 6
1701 University Blvd NE
Albuquerque, NM

505-843-9228
There are no additional pet fees. One pet per room is allowed.

Plaza Inn
900 Medical Arts Ave NE
Albuquerque, NM
505-243-5693
There is a $25 one time pet fee.

Sleep Inn Airport
2300 International Ave. SE
Albuquerque, NM
505-244-3325
There is a refundable deposit of $50. Pets must be well-behaved.

Travelodge
13139 Central Ave NE
Albuquerque, NM
505-292-4878
There is a $5.00 per day pet fee.

Artesia

Holiday Inn Express
2204 W. Main Street
Artesia, NM
505-748-3904
There is a $15 one time pet fee.

Belen

Best Western Belen
2111 Sosimo Padilla Blvd
Belen, NM
505-861-3181
There is a $5 per day additional pet fee. There is also a $20 refundable pet deposit.

Carlsbad

Holiday Inn
601 S. Canal
Carlsbad, NM
505-885-8500
There is a $25 one time pet fee.

Motel 6
3824 National Parks Hwy
Carlsbad, NM
505-885-0011

There are no additional pet fees. Pets may never be left unattended in the rooms.

Quality Inn
3706 National Parks Highway
Carlsbad, NM
505-887-2861
There is no pet fee.

Clayton

Best Western Kokopelli Lodge
702 S 1st Street
Clayton, NM
505-374-2589
There is a $5 per day pet fee.

Clovis

Comfort Inn
1616 Mabry Dr.
Clovis, NM
505-762-4591
There is a one time pet fee of $10.

Howard Johnson Express Inn
2920 Mabry Drive
Clovis, NM
505-769-1953
Dogs up to 50 pounds are allowed. There is a $10 per day pet fee.

Motel 6
2620 Mabry Dr
Clovis, NM
505-762-2995
There are no pet fees.

Deming

Holiday Inn
Exit 85 I-10
Deming, NM
505-546-2661
There are no additional pet fees.

Motel 6
I-10 & Motel Drive
Deming, NM
505-546-2623
There are no additional pet fees.

Accommodations - Please always call ahead to make sure an establishment is still dog-friendly.

Dulce

Best Western Jicarilla Inn
233 Jicarilla Blvd/US Hwy 64
Dulce, NM
505-759-3663
There is a $5 per day additional pet fee. There is also a $20 refundable pet deposit.

Espanola

Comfort Inn
604-B S. Riverside Dr.
Espanola, NM
505-753-2419
There is a one time pet fee of $5. Pets may not be left alone.

Farmington

Comfort Inn
555 Scott Ave.
Farmington, NM
505-325-2626
There is a pet fee of $5 per day.

Holiday Inn
600 E. Broadway
Farmington, NM
505-327-9811
There is a $20 one time pet fee.

Holiday Inn Express
2110 Bloomfield Blvd
Farmington, NM
505-325-2545
There is a $20 one time pet fee.

La Quinta Inn Farmington
675 Scott Avenue
Farmington, NM
505-327-4706
Dogs of all sizes are allowed at the hotel.

Gallup

Best Western Inn and Suites
3009 W. Highway 66
Gallup, NM
505-722-2221
There are no additional pet fees.

Best Western Royal Holiday Motel

1903 W Hwy 66
Gallup, NM
505-722-4900
There is a $5 per day additional pet fee.

Comfort Inn
3208 W. US 66
Gallup, NM
505-722-0982
There is a pet fee of $5 per day. Pets may not be left alone.

Days Inn-East
1603 W Highway 66
Gallup, NM
505-863-3891
There is a $5 per day additional pet fee.

Holiday Inn
2915 W. Hwy 66
Gallup, NM
505-722-2201
There are no additional pet fees.

Motel 6
3306 W 66
Gallup, NM
505-863-4492
There are no additional pet fees.

Sleep Inn
3820 US 66 E.
Gallup, NM
505-863-3535
There is a pet fee of $5 per day.

Grants

Holiday Inn Express
1496 E Santa Fe Ave
Grants, NM
505-285-4676
There are no additional pet fees.

Motel 6
1505 E Santa Fe Ave
Grants, NM
505-285-4607
There are no additional pet fees.

Hobbs

Howard Johnson Inn
501 N Marland Blvd.
Hobbs, NM
505-397-3251
Dogs up to 50 pounds are allowed. There is a $20 refundable pet deposit.

Las Cruces

Best Western Mesilla Valley Inn
901 Avenida de Mesilla
Las Cruces, NM
505-524-8603
There are no additional pet fees.

Holiday Inn
201 University Ave
Las Cruces, NM
505-526-4411
There are no additional pet fees.

Holiday Inn Express
2200 S. Valley Drive
Las Cruces, NM
505-527-9947
There are no additional pet fees.

La Quinta Inn Las Cruces
790 Avenida De Mesilla
Las Cruces, NM
505-524-0331
Dogs up to 50 pounds are allowed at the hotel.

Motel 6
235 La Posada Ln
Las Cruces, NM
505-525-1010
There are no additional pet fees.

Lordsburg

Best Western American Motor Inn
944 East Motel Drive
Lordsburg, NM
505-542-3591
There is a $5 per day additional pet fee.

Best Western Skies Inn
1303 South Main

320

Lordsburg, NM
505-542-8807
There is a $5 per day additional pet fee.

Los Lunas

Comfort Inn
1711 Main St. S.W.
Los Lunas, NM
505-865-5100
There is a refundable pet deposit of $50.

Moriarty

Holiday Inn Express
1507 Route 66
Moriarty, NM
505-832-5000
There is an $8 per day additional pet fee.

Motel 6
109 Rt 66 East
Moriarty, NM
505-832-6666
There are no additional pet fees.

Raton

Motel 6
1600 Cedar St
Raton, NM
505-445-2777
There are no pet fees. One pet per room is allowed.

Rio Rancho

Best Western Inn at Rio Rancho
1465 Rio Rancho Drive
Rio Rancho, NM
505-892-1700
There is a $25 refundable pet deposit.

Roswell

Best Western El Rancho Palacio
2205 N Main Street
Roswell, NM
505-622-2721

There are no additional pet fees.

Comfort Inn
3595 N. Main St.
Roswell, NM
505-623-4567
There is a pet fee of $6 per day.

Frontier Motel
3010 N Main St
Roswell, NM
505-622-1400
There are no additional pet fees.

Motel 6
3307 N Main Street
Roswell, NM
505-625-6666
There is a $5 per day pet fee. Pets are allowed in third floor rooms.

Ramada Inn
2803 W 2nd St
Roswell, NM
505-623-9440
There is a $50 refundable pet deposit.

Ruidoso

Holiday Inn Express
400 West Hwy 70
Ruidoso, NM
505-257-3736
There are no additional pet fees.

Santa Fe

Best Western Inn of Santa Fe
3650 Cerrillos Rd
Santa Fe, NM
505-438-3822
Pets may not be left alone in the room.

Eldorado Hotel
309 W San Francisco
Santa Fe, NM
505-988-4455
There is a $50 one time pet fee.

Inn of the Anasazi
113 Washington Ave
Santa Fe, NM
505-988-3030
There is a $20 one time pet fee.

La Quinta Inn Santa Fe
4298 Cerrillos Road
Santa Fe, NM
505-471-1142
Dogs of all sizes are allowed at the hotel.

Motel 6
3007 Cerrillos Rd
Santa Fe, NM
505-473-1380
There are no additional pet fees.

Quality Inn
3011 Cerrillos Rd.
Santa Fe, NM
505-471-1211
There is no pet fee.

Residence Inn
1698 Galisteo St
Santa Fe, NM
505-988-7300
There is a $10 per day pet fee and a $150 refundable pet deposit.

Sleep Inn
8376 Cerrillos Rd.
Santa Fe, NM
505-474-9500
There is a one time pet fee of $10.

Santa Rosa

Best Western Adobe Inn
1501 E. Will Rogers Drive
Santa Rosa, NM
505-472-3446
There are no additional pet fees.

Best Western Santa Rosa Inn
3022 E. Will Rogers Drive
Santa Rosa, NM
505-472-5877
There are no additional pet fees.

Comfort Inn
3343 E. Will Rogers Blvd.
Santa Rosa, NM

505-472-5570
There is a pet fee of $10 per day.

Socorro

Motel 6
807 S US Hwy 85
Socorro, NM
505-835-4300
There are no additional pet fees.

Taos

Alpine Village Suites
PO Box 917
Taos, NM
505-776-8540
Located in Taos Ski Valley, this hotel offers a completely non-smoking environment. All 24 Suites and Studios have mini-kitchens, and most have private balconies with views. Many of our suites have fireplaces, and all suites have TV/VCR's, full baths and telephones. They are located steps from the lifts, restaurants, nightlife, and shopping. The Alpine Village complex houses two full service ski shops, a restaurant and bar. They welcome kids of all ages and the family pet. There is a $10 per day pet charge.

Holiday Inn
1005 Paseo Del Pueblo Sur
Taos, NM
505-758-4444
There is a $75 refundable pet deposit.

La Dona Luz Inn
114 Kit Carson Road
Taos, NM
505-758-4874
Thanks to one of our readers for recommending this dog-friendly bed and breakfast. A large dog is welcome to stay here if they are well-behaved and if the dog owner agrees to pay for room damages caused by their dog. There is a $10 per night pet fee. This historic B&B offers 5 rooms (up a narrow spiral stairway), all

with private baths. Room rates are approximately $75 to $150 per night. This B&B has been recommended by both The New York Times and USA Today Weekend.

Quality Inn
1043 Camino del Pueblo Sur
Taos, NM
505-758-2200
There is a pet fee of $7 per day.

Truth or Consequences

Best Western Hot Springs Inn
2270 N Date Street
Truth or Consequences, NM
505-894-6665
Young puppies are not allowed, but dogs are okay.

Holiday Inn
2000 N. Date Street
Truth or Consequences, NM
505-894-1660
There are no additional pet fees.

Tucumcari

Best Western Discovery Inn
200 East Estrella Ave
Tucumcari, NM
505-461-4884
There is a $5 per day additional pet fee.

Best Western Pow Wow Inn
801 W Tucumcari Blvd
Tucumcari, NM
505-461-0500
There is a $10 per day additional pet fee.

Comfort Inn
2800 E. Tucumcari Blvd
Tucumcari, NM
505-461-4094
There is a pet fee of $6 per day.

Holiday Inn
3716 E. Tucumcari Blvd
Tucumcari, NM
505-461-3780

There is a $6 per day pet fee.

Howard Johnson Express Inn
3604 E. Rt. 66 Blvd.
Tucumcari, NM
505-461-2747
Dogs of all sizes are welcome. There is a $6 per day pet fee.

Motel 6
2900 E Tucumcari Blvd
Tucumcari, NM
505-461-4791
There are no additional pet fees.

New York Listings

Amherst

Lord Amherst
5000 Main St
Amherst, NY
716-839-2200
There are no additional pet fees.

Marriott - Niagara
1340 Millersport Hwy
Amherst, NY
716-689-6900
Dogs allowed on first floor only. There is a $50.00 one time pet charge.

Red Roof Inn - Amherst
42 Flint Road
Amherst, NY
716-689-7474
Dogs up to 80 pounds are allowed. There are no additional pet fees.

Amsterdam

Best Western Amsterdam
10 Market Street
Amsterdam, NY
518-843-5760
There are no additional pet fees.

Auburn

Days Inn
37 Williams St

Auburn, NY
315-252-7567
There is a $10 per day pet fee.

Avoca

Caboose Motel
8620 State Route 415
Avoca, NY
607-566-2216
Large dogs are allowed in the
cabooses. There are no
additional pet fees.

Bath

Days Inn
330 W Morris
Bath, NY
607-776-7644
There are no additional pet fees.

Binghamton

Comfort Inn
1156 Front St.
Binghamton, NY
607-722-5353
There is a refundable pet
deposit of $50.

Holiday Inn Arena
2-8 Hawley St
Binghamton, NY
607-722-1212
There is a $25 one time pet
charge.

Motel 6
1012 Front St
Binghamton, NY
607-771-0400
There are no pet fees. Pets may
never be left alone in the room.
A large well-behaved dog is
okay.

Super 8 Motel - Binghamton
650 Old Front Street
Binghamton, NY
607-773-8111
There may be a $35 pet deposit
for larger dogs.

Super 8 Upper Court Street
771 Upper Court Street

Binghamton, NY
607-775-3443
There are no additional pet
fees.

Brockport

Holiday Inn Express
4908 South Lake Rd
Brockport, NY
716-395-1000
There is a $15 one time pet fee.

Buffalo

Comfort Suites
901 Dick Rd
Buffalo, NY
716-633-6000
There is no pet fee. Pets may
not be left alone.

Canandaigua

Econo Lodge
170 Eastern Blvd
Canandaigua, NY
716-394-9000
There are no additional pet
fees.

Inn On The Lake
777 S. Main St
Canandaigua, NY
716-394-7800
There is a $5 per day additional
pet fee.

Catskill Mountains

Inn at Lake Joseph
400 Saint Joseph Road
Catskill Mountains, NY
845-791-9506
The inn is a romantic 135-year-
old Victorian Country Estate on
a 250-acre private lake,
surrounded by thousands of
acres of hardwood forest and
wildlife preserve. The Inn
provides a variety of summer
and winter recreational facilities
including the use of their
nearby full service health and
fitness club. Breakfast is served

on the screened-in Veranda
allowing you to enjoy the sounds
and feel of the lush green forest.
When glassed in during winter,
you can experience the beauty
of a surrounding snowscape.
Dogs are welcomed in their
Carriage House and Cottage.
The inn is located in Forestburgh
at Lake Joseph.

Cazenovia

Lincklaen House
79 Albany St
Cazenovia, NY
315-655-3461
A landmark since 1836, this
hotel was built as a luxurious
stopover for colonial travelers.
All rooms are non-smoking.
There are no additional pet fees.

Cobleskill

Best Western Inn of Cobleskill
12 Campus Drive Extension
Cobleskill, NY
518-234-4321
There is a $20 refundable pet
deposit.

Corning

Stiles Motel
9239 Victory Highway
Corning, NY
607-962-5221
There is a $3 per day pet
charge.

Dunkirk

**Best Western Dunkirk and
Fredonia**
3912 Vineyard Drive
Dunkirk, NY
716-366-7100
There is a $10 per day additional
pet fee.

Comfort Inn
3925 Vinyard Dr.
Dunkirk, NY
716-672-4450

There is a pet fee of $10 per day.

East Syracuse

Holiday Inn
6555 Old Collamer Rd South
East Syracuse, NY
315-437-2761
There is a $25 one time pet fee.

Fishkill

Mainstay Suites
25 Merritt Blvd
Fishkill, NY
845-897-2800
There is a refundable deposit of $100. There is a pet fee of $10 per day.

Geneva

Motel 6
485 Hamilton St
Geneva, NY
315-789-4050
There are no additional pet fees.

Ramada Inn Geneva LakeFront
41 Lakefront Drive
Geneva, NY
315-789-0400
There is a $10 per day additional pet fee.

Grand Island

Chateau Motor Lodge
1810 Grand Island Blvd
Grand Island, NY
716-773-2868
There is an $8 per day pet fee.

Hamburg

Comfort Inn
3615 Commerce Place
Hamburg, NY
716-648-2922
There is a pet fee of $10 per day.

Hampton Bays

Bowen's by the Bays
117 West Montauk Highway
Hampton Bays, NY
631-728-1158
Bowen's by the Bays offers a choice of one, two or three bedroom cottages. The resort is set on four lovely acres and amenities include lighted tennis, swimming pool, playground, shuffleboard courts and a putting green. Hampton Bays is located in the heart of the Hamptons - the ideal setting for a special vacation. Pets are welcome in the cottages and prior arrangements must be made. Pet owners are required to abide by the published pet rules,i.e. clean up after your pet, keep pets under their direct control, do not disturb other guests, etc. There is a $15.00 per day/per pet fee.

Henrietta

Red Roof Inn
4820 W Henrietta Rd
Henrietta, NY
716-359-1100
There are no additional pet fees.

Herkimer

Herkimer Motel
100 Marginal Rd
Herkimer, NY
315-866-0490
There are no additional pet fees. Dogs must not be left alone in the rooms.

Horseheads

Best Western Marshall Manor
3527 Watkins Glen Rd
Horseheads, NY
607-739-3891
There is a $4 per day additional pet fee.

Ithaca

Clarion University Hotel & Conference Center
1 Sheraton Dr.
Ithaca, NY
607-257-2000
There is a non-refundable pet fee of $20.

Econo Lodge
Cayuga Mall
Ithaca, NY
607-257-1400
There is a $10 per day pet charge.

Jamestown

Comfort Inn
2800 N. Main St. Extension
Jamestown, NY
716-664-5920
There is a one time pet fee of $10.

Johnstown

Holiday Inn
308 N. Comrie Ave
Johnstown, NY
518-762-4686
There are no additional pet fees.

Kings Park

Villa Rosa B&B Inn
121 Highland Street
Kings Park, NY
631-724-4872
Built in 1920, this bed and breakfast inn is surrounded by spacious landscaped grounds. Some of the inn's rooms have private baths. This dog-friendly inn offers a fenced dog park area. Guests are welcome to bring their well-behaved dog, but pets must be leashed when in shared areas. There is a $20 per day pet charge. Room rates start around $130 per night and up. Weekly and monthly rates are available. They also have parking for larger vehicles like motorhomes and trailers.

Accommodations - Please always call ahead to make sure an establishment is still dog-friendly.

Kingston

Holiday Inn
503 Washington Ave
Kingston, NY
845-338-0400
There are no additional pet fees.
Pets may not be left alone in
rooms.

Super 8
487 Washington Ave
Kingston, NY
845-338-3078
There are no additional pet fees.

Lake Luzerne

Luzerne Court
508 Lake Ave
Lake Luzerne, NY
518-696-2734
There are no additional pet fees.
Dogs must not be left alone in
the rooms.

Lake Placid

Art Devline's Olympic
350 Main St
Lake Placid, NY
518-523-3700
There are no additional pet fees.

Best Western Golden Arrow
150 Main St
Lake Placid, NY
518-523-3353
$25.00 one time pet fee. Pets
must stay on the first floor.
There is a 12 store mini-mall in
the hotel. The entire hotel is
non-smoking.

Edge of the Lake Motel
56 Saranac Ave
Lake Placid, NY
518-523-9430
There is a $10.00 per night
charge per dog. Dogs are
permitted up to 75 pounds.
There are no designated
smoking or non-smoking rooms.

**Fourpeaks - Adirondack
Camps & Guest Barns**

Stonehouse Road
Lake Placid, NY
518-946-7313
Looking for a vacation with your
dog? Fourpeaks Adirondack
Camps & Guest Barns is an
outdoor adventure resort in the
dog-friendly High Peaks. 4
mountains. 1 river. 700 acres.
Dog-friendly hiking/skiing trails.
River swimming. Rates range
from $85 to $150 per night.

Hilton - Lake Placid Resort
1 Mirror Lake Dr.
Lake Placid, NY
518-523-4411
There is a $25 one time pet fee.

Holiday Inn
1 Olympic Drive
Lake Placid, NY
518-523-2556
There are no additional pet
fees. Pets may not be left
unattended in rooms.

Howard Johnson Inn
90 Saramac Ave.
Lake Placid, NY
518-523-9555
Dogs of all sizes are welcome.
There are no additional pet
fees. Dogs cannot be left
unattended in the room.

Lake Placid Lodge
Whiteface Inn Rd.
Lake Placid, NY
518-523-2700
There is a $50 one time pet fee.
Pets are allowed in the cabins.

**Lake Placid Resort Hotel and
Golf Club**
One Olympic Dr.
Lake Placid, NY
518-523-2556
Management requests that you
do not leave your pet alone in
the rooms. There are no
additional pet fees.

Ramada Inn
8-12 Saranac Ave
Lake Placid, NY
518-523-2587
There are no additional pet

fees.

Latham

Century House Inn
997 New Loudon Road
Latham, NY
518-785-0931
There is a $15 one time pet fee.

Microtel
7 Rensselaer Ave
Latham, NY
518-782-9161
There are no additional pet fees.

Liberty

Ramada Limited
7 Route 52 E
Liberty, NY
845-292-7171
There is a $10 per day pet
charge.

Little Falls

**Best Western Little Falls
Motor Inn**
20 Albany Street
Little Falls, NY
315-823-4954
There are no additional pet fees.

Liverpool

Econo Lodge
401 7th North St
Liverpool, NY
315-451-6000
There is a $10 per day pet
charge.

Holiday Inn
441 Electronics Pkwy
Liverpool, NY
315-457-1122
There are no additional pet fees.

Knights Inn
430 Electronics Pkwy
Liverpool, NY
315-453-6330
There is a $8 per day pet
charge.

Livingston Manor

The Guest House
408 Debruce Road
Livingston Manor, NY
845-439-4000
The Guest House bed and breakfast is a beautiful 40 acre estate on the banks of the Willowemoc trout stream in the western Catskill Mountains. All of the rooms are individually decorated with private bathrooms and there are three cottages. All but two rooms are suitable for dogs. They have four Labradors and two Spaniels themselves. Dogs are $10 per night. Grooming is available.

Middletown

Howard Johnson Hotel
551 Rt. 211 East
Middletown, NY
845-342-5822
Dogs of all sizes are welcome. There are no additional pet fees.

Super 8 Lodge
563 Route 211 East
Middletown, NY
518-483-0500
There is a $25.00 non-refundable deposit for pets.

Mount Kisco

Holiday Inn
1 Holiday Inn Dr
Mount Kisco, NY
914-241-2600
There is a $25 one time pet charge.

New Hartford

Holiday Inn
1777 Burrstone Rd
New Hartford, NY
315-797-2131
There are no additional pet fees.

New York

Holiday Inn - Wall Street
15 Gold Street
New York, New York
212-232-7700
There is a $25 one time pet fee.

Novotel Hotel
226 West 52nd Street
New York, NY
212-315-0100
This hotel is located in Midtown Manhattan, in the Broadway theater district. Amenities include room service, an exercise room and gift shop. The hotel lobby is located on the 7th floor. The Novotel allows dogs up to 50 pounds. There are no pet fees, but owners must sign a pet waiver.

Regency Hotel
540 Park Avenue
New York, NY
212-759-4100
All well-behaved dogs of any size are welcome. This upscale hotel offers their "Loews Loves Pets" program which includes special pet treats, local dog walking routes, and a list of nearby pet-friendly places to visit. There are no pet fees.

Renaissance New York Hotel
714 7th Avenue
New York, NY
212-765-7676
They allow dogs up to about 70 pounds. This hotel is located in Times Square. It is located at the intersection of Broadway and Seventh Avenue. Amenities include room service, an in-room refreshment center, and an exercise/weight room. The hotel lobby is located on the third floor. There is a $65 one time charge for pets.

Sheraton New York Hotel and Towers
811 7th Avenue on 53rd Street
New York, NY
212-581-1000
Dogs up to 75 pounds are allowed. There are no additional pet fees.

Sofitel Hotel
45 West 44th Street
New York, NY
212-354-8844
This French hotel overlooks 5th Ave. Amenities include a fitness room. There are no additional pet fees.

Soho Grand Hotel
310 West Broadway
New York, NY
212-965-3000
This hotel is VERY pet-friendly and there are no size restrictions at all for dogs. They are owned by the Hartz Mountain Company which manufactures the 2 in 1 pet products. The hotel is located in the artistic heart of New York's cultural capital SoHo (South of Houston Street), and within an easy walking distance to the surrounding neighborhoods of Tribeca, Greenwich Village, Little Italy and Chinatown. The hotel is also just steps from Wall Street, and only minutes from Midtown Manhattan. Amenities include 24 room service and a fitness center. One of our readers has this to say about the hotel: "This is the most incredibly dog friendly hotel. Bellboys carry dog treats, there is a dog room service menu, doggie day care is provided. It's also one of New York's super chic hotels." There are no pet fees.

Swissotel NY -The Drake
440 Park Avenue
New York, NY
212-421-0900
Located in Midtown Manhattan, The Drake is just a couple of blocks from several dog-friendly stores and only 5 blocks from Central Park. Amenities include 24 hour room service and a fitness center/spa. No extra pet charge, just sign a pet waiver. Dogs up to about eighty pounds are allowed.

The Muse
130 West 46th Street
New York, NY
212-485-2400
There are no additional pet fees.
They offer a pampered pooch
package for an additional fee.

Tribeca Grand Hotel
2 Avenue of the Americas
New York, NY
212-519-6600
This dog-friendly hotel is located
just 2 blocks from it's sister
hotel, the dog-friendly Soho
Grand Hotel. This hotel is
located within walking distance
of Little Italy, Chinatown,
Greenwich Village, and many
department stores. Room rates
begin at $399 and up. There are
no pet fees.

W New York
541 Lexington Avenue
New York, NY
212-755-1200
Dogs up to 70 pounds are
allowed. There is a $25 one time
per stay pet fee.

W New York - The Court
130 East 39th Street
New York, NY
212-685-1100
Dogs up to 80 pounds are
allowed. There is a $100 one
time pet fee and a $25 per day
additional pet fee.

W New York - The Tuscany
120 East 39th Street
New York, NY
212-686-1600
Dogs up to 80 pounds are
allowed. There is a $25 per day
additional pet fee.

W New York - Times Square
1567 Broadway at 47th Street
New York, NY
212-930-7400
Dogs up to 80 pounds are
allowed. There is a $100 per
stay pet fee and a $25 per night
additional pet fee.

W New York - Union Square

201 Park Avenue South
New York, NY
212-253-9119
Dogs up to 80 pounds are
allowed. There is a $100 one
time per stay pet fee and a $25
per day additional pet fee.
Dogs may not be left alone in
the room.

Niagara Falls

Best Western Summit Inn
9500 Niagara Falls Blvd
Niagara Falls, NY
716-297-5050
There is an $8 per day pet fee.

Howard Johnson Hotel
454 Main St.
Niagara Falls, NY
716-285-5261
Dogs of all sizes are welcome.
There is a $10 per day pet fee.
Dogs are allowed in all rooms.

Quality Hotel & Suites
240 Rainbow Blvd.
Niagara Falls, NY
716-282-1212
There is a pet fee of $10 per
day.

Travelodge
201 Rainbow Blvd
Niagara Falls, NY
716-285-9321
There is a $10.00 per day
charge for pets.

Oneonta

Holiday Inn
Rt 23 Southside
Oneonta, NY
607-433-2250
There are no additional pet
fees.

Super 8
4973 St Hwy 23
Oneonta, NY
607-432-9505
There are no additional pet
fees.

Painted Post

**Best Western Lodge on the
Green**
3171 Canada Road
Painted Post, NY
607-962-2456
There are no additional pet fees.

Peekskill

Peekskill Inn
634 Main St
Peekskill, NY
914-739-1500
There are no additional pet fees.

Plainview

Residence Inn by Marriott
9 Gerhard Rd
Plainview, NY
516-433-6200
There is a $150 one time pet
charge and a $10.00 per day pet
charge.

Rochester

Crowne Plaza
70 State St
Rochester, NY
716-546-3450
There are no additional pet fees.

Hampton Inn
500 Center Place
Rochester, NY
585-663-6070
There are no additional pet fees.
Pet owners must sign a pet
waiver.

Motel 6
155 Buell Rd
Rochester, NY
716-436-2170
There are no pet fees. Pets must
be leashed when outside the
room.

Ramada Inn
800 Jefferson Rd
Rochester, NY
716-475-9190
There are no additional pet fees.

Dog owners must sign a pet waiver.

Residence Inn by Marriott
1300 Jefferson Rd
Rochester, NY
716-272-8850
There is a $125 one time pet charge.

Holiday Inn
173 Sunrise Hwy Rt 27
Rockville Center, NY
516-678-1300
There is a $15 per day pet fee.

Quality Inn
200 S. James St.
Rome, NY
315-336-4300
There is a pet fee of $25 per day.

Lake Flower Inn
15 Lake Flower Ave
Saranac Lake, NY
518-891-2310
Management requests that dogs are not left alone in the rooms and that guests clean up after their pets. Dogs are not allowed on the beds.

Lake Side
27 Lake Flower Ave
Saranac Lake, NY
518-891-4333
There are a limited number of pets allowed in the hotel at a time. There are no additional pet fees.

Holiday Inn
232 Broadway Rt 9
Saratoga Springs, NY
518-584-4550
There are no additional pet fees.

Holiday Inn
100 Nott Terrace
Schenectady, NY
518-393-4141
There are no additional pet fees. Pets must stay in the first floor rooms and may not be left unattended. From I-90 take I-890 to Broadway exit.

Blue Ridge Motel
Route 9
Schroon Lake, NY
518-532-7521
There are no additional pet fees.

Bird's Nest
1601 E Genesee St
Skaneateles, NY
315-685-5641
There is a $150.00 refundable pet deposit.

Comfort Inn
6491 Thompson Rd
Syracuse, NY
315-437-0222
There is no pet fee. Pets may only stay on the first floor.

Comfort Inn Fairgrounds
7010 Interstate Island Rd.
Syracuse, NY
315-453-0045
There is a one time pet fee of $10.

Holiday Inn
State Fair Blvd & Farrell Rd
Syracuse, NY
315-457-8700
There is a $25 refundable pet deposit.

Red Roof Inn
6614 N Thompson Rd
Syracuse, NY
315-437-3309
There are no additional pet fees.

Residence Inn by Marriott
6420 Yorktown Circle
Syracuse, NY
315-432-4488
There is a $50 one time pet fee and a $5 per day pet charge.

Circle Court
440 Montcalm St
Ticonderoga, NY
518-585-7660
There are no additional pet fees.

Microtel
1 Hospitality Centre Way
Tonawanda, NY
716-693-8100
There is a $10 per day additional pet fee.

Best Western Gateway Adirondack Inn
175 N Genesee Street
Utica, NY
315-732-4121
There are no additional pet fees.

Holiday Inn
4105 Vestal Pkwy E Rt 434
Vestal, NY
607-729-6371
There is a $25 one time pet fee.

Best Western Carriage House Inn
300 Washington Street
Watertown, NY
315-782-8000
There are no additional pet fees.

Best Western Weedsport Inn
2709 Erie Drive
Weedsport, NY
315-834-6623
There is a $10 per day pet fee.

West Coxsackie

Best Western New Baltimore Inn
12600 Route 9W
West Coxsackie, NY
518-731-8100
There is a $5 per day additional pet fee.

Williamsville

Residence Inn by Marriott
100 Maple Rd
Williamsville, NY
716-632-6622
There is a $50 one time pet fee and a $6 per day pet charge.

Wilmington

Hungry Trout
(on Route 86)
Wilmington, NY
518-946-2217
Additional $5 per day charge for a pet.

North Carolina Listings

Asheville

Holiday Inn - Blue Ridge Pkwy
1450 Tunnel Rd
Asheville, NC
828-298-5611
There are no additional pet fees.

Motel 6
1415 Tunnel Rd
Asheville, NC
828-299-3040
There are no additional pet fees.

Banner Elk

Holiday Inn
Hwy 184
Banner Elk, NC
828-898-4571
There are no additional pet fees.

Battleboro

Howard Johnson Inn
7568 NC 48
Battleboro, NC
252-977-9595
Dogs of all sizes are welcome. There is a $5 per day pet fee.

Burlington

Holiday Inn - Outlet Center
2444 Maple Avenue
Burlington, NC
336-229-5203
There is a $50 one time pet fee.

Cary

La Quinta Inn & Suites Raleigh - Cary
191 Crescent Commons
Cary, NC
919-851-2850
Dogs of all sizes are allowed at the hotel.

Charlotte

Clarion Hotel
321 West Woodlawn Road
Charlotte, NC
704-523-1400
Room amenities include a microwave, refrigerator, hairdryers and more. Hotel amenities include a fitness center, onsite restaurant and more. There is a $25 one time per stay pet charge.

Drury Inn & Suites
415 West W.T. Harris Blvd.
Charlotte, NC
704-593-0700
Dogs of all sizes are permitted.

Pets are not allowed in the breakfast area of the hotel. Pets are not to be left unattended, and each guest must assume liability for damage of property or other guest complaints. There is a limit of one pet per room.

La Quinta Inn & Suites Charlotte Coliseum
4900 South Tryon Street
Charlotte, NC
704-523-5599
Dogs of all sizes are allowed at the hotel.

Residence Inn - South Park
6030 J.A. Jones Drive
Charlotte, NC
704-554-7001
There is a $150 one time per stay pet fee. Every suite at this eight floor inn offers a separate living and sleeping area. Amenities include an indoor pool, complimentary buffet breakfast, free parking, dinner delivery from local restaurants and more.

Residence Inn - Uptown
404 South Mint Street
Charlotte, NC
704-340-4000
There is a $100 one time per stay pet charge and an additional $5 per day pet fee. Every room in this eleven story inn is a suite with a living area, bedroom and kitchen. The inn is located within walking distance to downtown and Uptown. Amenities include a 24 hour exercise room, complimentary hot breakfast, complimentary evening happy hour and more. There is a fee for parking.

Residence Inn by Marriott
5816 Westpark Drive
Charlotte, NC
704-527-8110
There is a $150 one time pet fee.

Sleep Inn
8525 N Tryon St.
Charlotte, NC

704-549-4544
There is a $25 one time pet charge.

Staybridge Suites
7924 Forest Pine Drive
Charlotte, NC
704-527-6767
There is a $75 one time pet fee.

Studio 6
3420 I-85 Service Rd South
Charlotte, NC
704-394-4993
There is a $10 per day pet fee. Well-behaved dogs are allowed at the hotel.

Cornelius

Holiday Inn
19901 Holiday Lane
Cornelius, NC
704-892-9120
There is a $25 one time pet fee.

Dunn

Best Western Midway Inn
603 Spring Branch Rd
Dunn, NC
910-892-2162
There is a $5 per day pet fee.

Durham

Best Western Skyland Inn
5400 U.S. 70
Durham, NC
919-383-2508
The Best Western Skyland Inn is a unique family style inn in a country setting. Moderately priced, they offer a pool, picnic area and playground with convenient parking at your room door. Your dog is welcome here for an additional $10 daily charge.

La Quinta Inn & Suites Raleigh-Research Triangle Park
1910 West Park Drive
Durham, NC
919-484-1422

Dogs up to 50 pounds are allowed at the hotel.

Emerald Isle

Bluewater GMAC Vacation Rentals
200 Mangrove Dr, PO Box 4340
Emerald Isle, NC
252-354-2323
Bluewater GMAC Real Estate offers over 500 Ocean Vacation Rental Homes on the Southern Outer Banks of North Carolina. Many homes allow dogs (2 maximum) for an additional $100 per pet. No size or breed limitations. Leash and Pooper Scooper Laws in effect.

Fayetteville

Best Western Fayetteville - Ft Bragg
2910 Sigman Street
Fayetteville, NC
910-485-0520
There is a $15 one time pet fee per visit.

Holiday Inn
1707 Owen Drive
Fayetteville, NC
910-323-0111
There is a $100 refundable pet deposit. There is a $15 one time pet fee.

Red Roof Inn
1569 Jim Johnson Rd
Fayetteville, NC
910-321-1460
There is a $10 per day pet fee.

Fort Mill

Motel 6
255 Carowinds Blvd
Fort Mill, NC
803-548-9656
There are no additional pet fees.

Franklin

Patterson Realty, Vacation Home Rentals
145 E. Palmer Street
Franklin, NC
800-742-0719
Choose from several of their vacation rental homes that allow pets. The Armstrong's River House, located on the Cullasaja River, is a 2 bedroom, 2 bathroom home and accommodates up to 7 people. Courson's Cottages, located close to Franklin, are cute new 1 bedroom cottages which accommodate up to 4 people. They have porches with nice views of the mountains.

Gastonia

Motel 6
1721 Broadcast St
Gastonia, NC
704-868-4900
There are no pet fees. Well-behaved dogs are welcome.

Glendale Springs

Mountain View Lodge & Cabins
Blue Ridge Parkway Mile Post 256
Glendale Springs, NC
336-982-2233
Vacation with your pet at this retreat on the Blue Ridge Parkway in the northern mountains of North Carolina. Trails, grassy lawn for romping, nearby pond for swimming. 1-2 bedroom cabins with kitchenettes, full bathrooms and porches. There is no size limit for dogs.

Goldsboro

Best Western Goldsboro Inn
801 Hwy 70 Bypass East
Goldsboro, NC
919-735-7911
Convenient to downtown and Seymour Johnson Air Force

Base. 116 Rooms - 25 kings, 3 suites, 89 doubles. Continental breakfast included, dogs allowed with $15 non-refundable pet fee.

Days Inn
2000 Wayne Memorial Drive
Goldsboro, NC
919-734-9471
There is a $5 per day pet charge.

Motel 6
701 Bypass 70E
Goldsboro, NC
919-734-4542
There are no additional pet fees.

Ramada Inn
808 West Grantham Street
Goldsboro, NC
919-736-4590
There is a $10 one time pet charge.

Greensboro

Drury Inn & Suites
3220 High Point Road
Greensboro, NC
336-856-9696
Dogs of all sizes are permitted. Pets are not allowed in the breakfast area of the hotel. Pets are not to be left unattended, and each guest must assume liability for damage of property or other guest complaints. There is a limit of one pet per room.

La Quinta Inn & Suites Greensboro
1201 Lanada
Greensboro, NC
336-316-0100
Dogs of all sizes are allowed at the hotel.

Motel 6
605 S Regional Rd
Greensboro, NC
336-668-2085
There are no additional pet fees. One pet per room is allowed. Pets must be attended at all times.

Motel 6
831 Greenhaven Dr
Greensboro, NC
336-854-0993
There are no additional pet fees. Dogs up to 50 pounds are allowed.

Red Roof Inn-Coliseum
2101 W. Meadowview Road
Greensboro, NC
336-852-6560
There are no additional pet fees.

Residence Inn by Marriott
2000 Veasley Street
Greensboro, NC
336-294-8600
There is a $150 one time pet charge.

Greenville

Red Roof Inn
301 SE Greenville Boulevard
Greenville, NC
252-756-2792
There are no additional pet fees.

Hickory

Red Roof Inn
1184 Lenoir-Rhyne Boulevard
Hickory, NC
828-323-1500
Dogs up to 80 pounds are allowed.

Jacksonville

Super 8 Motel - Jacksonville
2149 N. Marine Blvd.
Jacksonville, NC
910-455-6888
$10/stay for up to 3 dogs in one room. FREE 8-minute long distance call each night. FREE continental breakfast. Coffee maker, night light, clock/radio, safe in each room. Seasonal outdoor pool. On-site guest laundry. Kids 12 & under stay free. US Hwy 17, 1/2 mile North of Western Blvd.

Kill Devil Hills

Ramada Inn at Nags Head Beach
1701 S. Virginia Dare Trail
Kill Devil Hills, NC
252-441-2151
There are six rooms that allow dogs, all of which are on the ground floor and don't have a beach view. They accept all kinds of pets here and all sizes of dogs. There is a $5 per day pet charge.

Lumberton

Best Western
201 Jackson Court
Lumberton, NC
910-618-9799
There is a $10 per day pet fee.

Motel 6
2361 Lackey Rd
Lumberton, NC
910-738-2410
Dogs may not be left unattended in rooms. Well-behaved large dogs are accepted.

Quality Inn & Suites
3608 Kahn Dr.
Lumberton, NC
910-738-8261
There is a $10 one time pet charge.

Super 8
150 Jackson Court
Lumberton, NC
910-671-4444
There is a $5 per day additional pet fee.

Murphy

Best Western of Murphy
1522 Andrews Road
Murphy, NC
828-837-3060
There is a $10 per day additional pet fee.

Piney Creek

Weddens Way, Too
231 Legra Rd
Piney Creek, NC
336-372-2985
Fully furnished cabin over looking the New River. Sleeps up to 7, rate for two is $80 plus tax per night. Pets are welcome for a $50 fee for the entire stay. Fish, canoe or enjoy the view.

Raleigh

Best Western Crabtree
6619 Glenwood Ave
Raleigh, NC
919-782-8650
There is a $25 one time pet fee.

Holiday Inn
4100 Glenwood Ave
Raleigh, NC
919-782-8600
There is a $50 one time pet fee.

Motel 6
1401 Buck Jones Rd
Raleigh, NC
919-467-6171
There are no additional pet fees.

Motel 6
3921 Arrow Dr
Raleigh, NC
919-782-7071
There are no additional pet fees.

Red Roof Inn-North
3201 Wake Forest Road
Raleigh, NC
919-878-9310
There is a $25 refundable pet deposit.

Red Roof Inn-Raleigh East
3520 Maitland Drive
Raleigh, NC
919-231-0200
There are no additional pet fees.

Roanoke Rapids

Motel 6
1911 Julian R. Allsbrook Hwy
Roanoke Rapids, NC
252-537-5252

There are no additional pet fees.

Rocky Mount

Residence Inn
230 Gateway Blvd
Rocky Mount, NC
252-451-5600
There is a $100 one time pet fee.

Saluda

Spring Pond Cabin
640 E US Hwy 176
Saluda, NC
828-749-9824
This cozy cabin in the woods is available for rent to you and your pets. There is a covered porch with fenced in area as well as a half mile hiking loop on the property which is wooded and has two spring fed ponds. The cabin is fully equipped and sleeps five. They ask that you bring your own linens if your dog sleeps on the bed.

Smithfield

Super 8 Motel
735 Industrial Park Rd.
Smithfield, NC
919-989-8988
There is a $4 per day pet charge.

Southern Pines

Holiday Inn
US 1 at Morganton Rd Exit
Southern Pines, NC
910-692-8585
Pets are allowed only in the first floor rooms. There is a $25 one time pet fee.

Sparta

Wedden's Farm B & B
312 Brookfield Rd
Sparta, NC

336-372-2985
Beautifully appointed farm house on 18 acres of land. Full breakfast, private upstairs offers 2 bedrooms plus den. Pets accepted for $20 for the entire stay. Come and enjoy some Blue Ridge Mountain hospitality for $80 per double plus tax. Located 8 miles from the Blue Ridge Parkway.

Wilmington

Camellia Cottage Bed and Breakfast
118 S. 4th Street
Wilmington, NC
910-763-9171
Well-behaved dogs are welcome in the Crane Suite at this bed and breakfast inn. The pet-friendly room is located next to the front door, on the first floor. There are no pet fees.

Hampton Inn & Suites-Landfall Park
1989 Eastwood Road
Wilmington, NC
910-256-9600
There is a $45 one time pet charge.

Hilton Riverside
301 N. Water Street
Wilmington, NC
910-763-5900
There is a $75 one time per stay pet fee. Dogs under 100 pounds are allowed.

Waterway Lodge
7246 Wrightsville Avenue
Wilmington, NC
910-256-3771
The Waterway Lodge offers standard motel rooms as well as one bedroom condo units with full kitchens. It is located on the Intercoastal Waterway, and a short walk to numerous shops, restaurants, marinas and the beach.

Winston-Salem

Holiday Inn Select
5790 University Pkwy
Winston-Salem, NC
336-767-9595
There is a $25 one time pet fee.

Motel 6
3810 Patterson Ave
Winston-Salem, NC
336-661-1588
There are no additional pet fees.

Residence Inn by Marriott
7835 North Point Boulevard
Winston-Salem, NC
336-759-0777
There is a $100 one time pet charge for studios, and a $150 one time pet charge for penthouses.

North Dakota Listings

Bismarck

Best Western Doublewood Inn
1400 E. Interchange Ave
Bismarck, ND
701-258-7000
There is a $10 per day additional pet fee.

Comfort Inn
1030 Interstate Ave
Bismarck, ND
701-223-1911
There are no additional pet fees.

Holiday Inn
605 E. Broadway
Bismarck, ND
701-255-6000
Pets must be on leash when outside of the room. Pets may not be left alone in the room.

Motel 6
2433 State St
Bismarck, ND
701-255-6878
There are no pet fees. Pets must be attended at all times.

Dickinson

Best Western Badlands Inn
71 Museum Dr
Dickinson, ND
701-225-9510
There is a $50 refundable pet deposit.

Fargo

Best Western Doublewood Inn
3333 13th Ave S
Fargo, ND
701-235-3333
There is a $20 refundable pet deposit.

Holiday Inn
3803 13th Ave. S.
Fargo, ND
701-282-2700
There are no additional pet fees. Pets must be attended at all times.

Holiday Inn Express
1040 40th St S.
Fargo, ND
701-282-2000
There are no additional pet fees.

Motel 6
1202 36th St S
Fargo, ND
701-232-9251
There are no additional pet fees. One pet per room is allowed. Pets may never be left unattended in the room.

Red Roof Inn
901 38th St SW
Fargo, ND
701-282-9100
There are no additional pet fees.

Grand Forks

Econo Lodge
900 N 43rd St
Grand Forks, ND
701-746-6666

There is a $5 per day additional pet fee.

Medora

Americinn Motel and Suites
75 E River Rd
Medora, ND
701-623-4800
There is a $20 one time pet fee.

Minot

Comfort Inn
1515 22nd Ave SW
Minot, ND
701-852-2201
There are no additional pet fees.

Select Inn
225 22nd Ave NW
Minot, ND
701-852-3411
There is a $25 refundable pet deposit and a $5 per day pet fee.

New Town

Four Bears Lodge
SR 23W
New Town, ND
701-627-4018
There is a $50 one time pet fee.

Wahpeton

Holiday Inn Express
1800 Two Ten Drive
Wahpeton, ND
701-642-5000
There are no additional pet fees. Pets must be on a leash when outside the room.

Ohio Listings

Akron

Best Western Inn & Suites
160 Montrose West Ave
Akron, OH

330-670-0888
There are no additional pet fees.

Holiday Inn Express
2940 Chenoweth Rd
Akron, OH
330-644-7126
There is a $50 one time pet fee.

Amherst

Motel 6
704 N Leavitt Rd
Amherst, OH
440-988-3266
There are no pet fees. One pet per room is allowed.

Ashland

Holiday Inn Express Hotel & Suites
1392 TR 743
Ashland, OH
419-281-2900
There is a $35 refundable pet deposit.

Cambridge

Best Western Cambridge
1945 Southgate Parkway
Cambridge, OH
740-439-3581
There are no additional pet fees.

Holiday Inn
2248 Southgate Pkwy
Cambridge, OH
740-432-7313
There are no additional pet fees.

Canton

Holiday Inn
4520 Everhard Rd
Canton, OH
330-494-2770
There are no pet fees. Dogs under 50 pounds are allowed in the hotel. Pets must be attended at all times.

Residence Inn by Marriott
5280 Broadmoor Circle NW

Canton, OH
330-493-0004
There is a $50 one time pet charge plus a $5 per day additional pet fee. If you stay more than 5 days, there is a $100 one time pet fee only.

Cincinnati

Howard Johnson Inn
5410 Ridge Ave.
Cincinnati, OH
513-631-8500
Dogs of all sizes are welcome. There are no additional pet fees.

Howard Johnson Inn
400 Glensprings Drive
Cincinnati, OH
513-825-3129
Dogs of all sizes are welcome. There is a $20 refundable pet deposit.

Motel 6
3960 Nine Mile Rd
Cincinnati, OH
513-752-2262
There are no additional pet fees.

Red Roof Inn-Sharonville
11345 Chester Road
Cincinnati, OH
513-771-5141
There are no additional pet fees.

Cleveland

Marriott Hotel
4277 West 150th. Street
Cleveland, OH
216-252-5333
There is a $50 one time pet charge.

Columbus

Holiday Inn
328 W. Lane Ave
Columbus, OH
614-294-4848
There are no pet fees.

Holiday Inn
175 Hutchinson Ave
Columbus, OH
614-885-3334
There are no additional pet fees.

Holiday Inn
4560 Hilton Corporate Drive
Columbus, OH
614-868-1380
There is a $20 per day pet fee.

Holiday Inn-City Center
175 E. Town Street
Columbus, OH
614-221-3281
There is a $15 per day additional pet fee.

Holiday Inn-Worthington
175 Hutchinson Ave
Columbus, OH
614-885-3334
There are no additional pet fees.

Motel 6
5910 Scarborough Blvd
Columbus, OH
614-755-2250
There are no additional pet fees.

Motel 6
3950 Parkway Lane
Columbus, OH
614-771-1500
There are no additional pet fees.

Motel 6
1289 E Dublin-Granville Rd
Columbus, OH
614-846-9860
There are no additional pet fees.

Motel 6
5500 Renner Rd
Columbus, OH
614-870-0993
There are no additional pet fees. One pet per room is allowed.

Red Roof Inn-North
750 Morse Road
Columbus, OH
614-846-8520
There are no additional pet fees.

Sheraton Suites Columbus

201 Hutchinson Avenue
Columbus, OH
614-436-0004
Dogs up to 80 pounds are allowed. There are no additional pet fees, but you must sign a pet waiver form.

Dayton

Howard Johnson Express Inn
7575 Poe Avenue
Dayton, OH
937-454-0550
Dogs of all sizes are welcome. There is a $20 per day pet fee.

Marriott Hotel
1414 S. Patterson Boulevard
Dayton, OH
937-223-1000
There is a $50 one time pet fee for 3 nights or less. If you stay 4 nights or more then there is a $100 one time pet fee. Dogs are allowed in the first floor rooms.

Red Roof Inn-North
7370 Miller Lane
Dayton, OH
937-898-1054
There are no additional pet fees.

Dublin

Northwest Drury Inn & Suites
6170 Parkcenter Circle
Dublin, OH
614-798-8802
Dogs of all sizes are permitted. Pets are not allowed in the breakfast area of the hotel. Pets are not to be left unattended, and each guest must assume liability for damage of property or other guest complaints. There is a limit of one pet per room.

Woodfin Suite Hotel
4130 Tuller Road
Dublin, OH
614-766-7762
All well-behaved dogs are welcome. Every room is a suite with a full kitchen. Hotel amenities include a pool, exercise facility, complimentary video movies and a complimentary hot breakfast buffet. There is a $50 one time per stay pet charge.

Englewood

Motel 6
1212 S Main St
Englewood, OH
937-832-3770
There are no pet fees. Pets up to 75 pounds are allowed.

Fairborn

Homewood Suites-Fairborn
2750 Presidential Drive
Fairborn, OH
937-429-0600
There is a $100 one time pet charge.

Gallipolis

Holiday Inn
577 State Rt 7 N
Gallipolis, OH
740-446-0090
Pets need to be quiet and must be on a leash when outside the room.

Kings Island

Holiday Inn Express
5589 Kings Mills Rd
Kings Island, OH
513-398-8075
There are no additional pet fees. A large dog is okay if it is quiet and well-behaved.

Macedonia

Motel 6
311 E Highland Rd
Macedonia, OH
330-468-1670
There are no pet fees. A large well-behaved dog is okay.

Marietta

Best Western Marietta
279 Muskingum Drive
Marietta, OH
740-374-7211
Pets may not be left alone in the room.

Maumee

Days Inn-Maumee
150 Dussel Drive
Maumee, OH
419-893-9960
There is a $5 per day additional pet fee.

Mentor

Studio 6
7677 Reynolds Rd
Mentor, OH
440-946-0749
There is a $10 per day pet fee up to a maximum of $50 per visit. Pets must be attended when housekeeping cleans the room.

Miamisburg

Motel 6
8101 Springboro Pike
Miamisburg, OH
937-434-8750
There is a $10 per day pet fee, up to a maximum of $50.

Middleburg Heights

Motel 6
7219 Engle Rd
Middleburg Heights, OH
440-234-0990
There are no additional pet fees.

Red Roof Inn
17555 Bagley Road
Middleburg Heights, OH
440-243-2441
There are no additional pet fees. Pets may not be left alone in the room.

N Canton

Motel 6
6880 Sunset Strip Ave NW
N Canton, OH
330-494-7611
There are no pet fees. Pets must be attended at all times.

Holiday Inn
131 Bluebell Dr SW
New Philadelphia, OH
330-339-7731
There is a $15 one time pet fee.

Motel 6
181 Bluebell Dr
New Philadelphia, OH
330-339-6446
There are no additional pet fees.

Red Roof Inn
5353 Inn Circle Court, NW
North Canton, OH
330-499-1970
There are no additional pet fees.

Howard Johnson Inn
I-280 & Hanley Road
Perrysburg, OH
419-837-5245
Dogs of all sizes are welcome.
There is a $10 per day pet fee.

Holiday Inn
4742 Brecksville Road
Richfield, OH
330-659-6151
There is a $25 one time pet fee.

Motel 6
3850 Hauck Rd
Sharonville, OH
513-563-1123
There are no additional pet fees.
Only one pet per room is allowed.

Motel 6
2000 E Kemper Rd
Sharonville, OH
513-772-5944
There are no pet fees. One pet per room is allowed.

Residence Inn by Marriott-Sharonville
11689 Chester Road
Sharonville, OH
513-771-2525
There is a $100 one time pet charge.

Best Western Southern Hills Inn
803 Solida Road
South Point, OH
740-894-3391
There is a $6 per day additional pet fee.

Comfort Inn & Suites
70 Private Rd 302
South Point, OH
740-377-2786
There is a pet fee of $5 per day.

Best Western Country Inn
111 McCauley Drive
Uhrichsville, OH
740-922-0774
There is a $15 one time pet fee.

Best Western Wapakoneta
1510 Saturn Drive
Wapakoneta, OH
419-738-8181
There is a $10 per day additional pet fee. Pets must be on leash while outside of the room.

Best Western Downtown

Motor Inn
777 Mahoning Ave NW
Warren, OH
330-392-2515
There are no additional pet fees.

Holiday Inn Express
155 Holiday Drive
Wilmington, OH
937-382-5858
There is a $20 one time pet fee.

Best Western Regency Inn
600 Little Main Street
Xenia, OH
937-372-9954
There is a $7 per day additional pet fee.

Oklahoma Listings

Holiday Inn
400 N.E. Richardson Loop
Ada, OK
580-332-9000
There is a $25 one time pet fee.

Best Western Altus
2804 N Main Street
Altus, OK
580-482-9300
There are no additional pet fees.

Best Western Ardmore Inn
6 Holiday Drive
Ardmore, OK
580-223-7525
There is a $20 refundable pet deposit.

Comfort Inn
2700 W Broadway

Accommodations - Please always call ahead to make sure an establishment is still dog-friendly.

Ardmore, OK
580-226-1250
There are no additional pet fees.

Holiday Inn
2705 Holiday Drive
Ardmore, OK
580-223-7130
There is a $10 one time pet fee.

La Quinta Inn Ardmore
2432 Veterans Blvd
Ardmore, OK
580-223-7976
Dogs up to 50 pounds are
allowed at the hotel.

Motel 6
120 Holiday Dr
Ardmore, OK
580-226-7666
There are no additional pet fees.
Pets must be attended at all
times.

Super 8
2120 Hwy 142 W
Ardmore, OK
580-223-2201
There is a $5 per night pet fee.

Bartlesville

Super 8
211 SE Washington Blvd
Bartlesville, OK
918-335-1122
There are no additional pet fees.

Broken Arrow

Holiday Inn
2600 N. Aspen
Broken Arrow, OK
918-258-7085
There is a $15 one time pet fee.

Claremore

Best Western Will Rogers Inn
940 S. Lynn Riggs Blvd
Claremore, OK
918-341-4410
There are no additional pet fees.

Clinton

**Best Western Trade Winds
Courtyard Inn**
2128 Gary Blvd
Clinton, OK
580-323-2610
There is a $5 per day additional
pet fee.

El Reno

Best Western Hensley's
2701 S. Country Club Road
El Reno, OK
405-262-6490
There is a $25 refundable pet
deposit. There is also a $5 per
day additional pet fee.

Elk City

Holiday Inn
101 Meadow Ridge
Elk City, OK
580-225-6637
There are no additional pet
fees.

Motel 6
2500 E Hwy 66
Elk City, OK
580-225-6661
There are no additional pet
fees.

Ramada Inn
102 B J Hughes Access Rd
Elk City, OK
580-225-8140
There is a $5 per day pet fee.
There is 1 non-smoking pet
room.

Ramada Inn
2500 S Main Street
Elk City, OK
580-225-0305
There is a $5 per day pet fee.

Rodeway Inn
1100 Hwy 34
Elk City, OK
580-225-9210
There is a $5 per day pet fee.

Enid

Holiday Inn
2901 S. Van Buren
Enid, OK
580-237-6000
There are no additional pet fees.

Frontier City

Motel 6
12121 North I-35 Service Rd
Frontier City, Oklahoma
405-478-4030
There are no additional pet fees.

Grove

Best Western TimberRidge Inn
120 E. 18th Street
Grove, OK
918-786-6900
There is a $5 per day additional
pet fee.

Guymon

Ambassador Inn
1909 N Highway 64
Guymon, OK
580-338-5555
There are no additional pet fees.

Henryetta

Gateway Inn
Hwy 75 and Trudgeon St
Henryetta, OK
918-652-4448
There is a $25 refundable
deposit.

Lawton

Holiday Inn
3134 NW Cache Road
Lawton, OK
580-353-1682
There is a $25 one time pet fee.

Howard Johnson Hotel
1125 E. Gore Blvd.
Lawton, OK
580-353-0200
Dogs of all sizes are welcome.

There is a $25 one time pet fee.

Motel 6
202 SE Lee Blvd
Lawton, OK
580-355-9765
There are no additional pet fees.

Best Western Inn of McAlester
1215 George Nigh Expressway
McAlester, OK
918-426-0115
There are no additional pet fees.

Holiday Inn Express Hotel & Suites
650 George Nigh Expwy
Mcalester, OK
918-302-0001
There is a $25 one time pet fee.

Best Western Inn of Miami
2225 E Steve Owens Blvd
Miami, OK
918-542-6681
There are no additional pet fees.

Motel 6
903 S 32nd St
Muskogee, OK
918-683-8369
There are no additional pet fees.

La Quinta Inn & Suites Norman
930 Ed Noble Drive
Norman, OK
405-579-4000
Dogs of all sizes are allowed at the hotel.

Best Western Saddleback Inn

4300 SW 3rd St
Oklahoma City, OK
405-947-7000
There is a $25 refundable pet deposit.

Comfort Inn and Suites
5405 N Lincoln Blvd
Oklahoma City, OK
405-528-7563
There is a $10 one time pet fee.

Days Inn North
12013 N I-35 Service Rd
Oklahoma City, OK
405-478-2554
There are no additional pet fees.

Embassy Suites
1815 S Meridian Ave
Oklahoma City, OK
405-682-6000
There is a $35 one time pet fee.

Holiday Inn
6200 North Robinson
Oklahoma City, OK
405-843-5558
There is a $25 one time pet fee.

Holiday Inn Express
13520 Plaza Terrace
Oklahoma City, OK
405-755-8686
There is a $10 one time pet fee.

Holiday Inn Hotel & Suites
6200 N. Robinson
Oklahoma City, OK
405-843-5558
There is a $25 one time pet fee.

Howard Johnson Express Inn
400 South Meridian
Oklahoma City, OK
405-943-9841
Dogs of all sizes are welcome. There is a $6 per day pet fee.

La Quinta Inn & Suites Oklahoma City-Northwest Expressway
4829 Northwest Expressway
Oklahoma City, OK
405-773-5575
Dogs of all sizes are allowed at the hotel.

La Quinta Inn Oklahoma City South
8315 South Interstate 35
Oklahoma City, OK
405-631-8661
Dogs of all sizes are allowed at the hotel.

Motel 6
820 S Meridian Ave
Oklahoma City, OK
405-946-6662
There are no additional pet fees.

Motel 6
4200 W Interstate 40
Oklahoma City, OK
405-947-6550
There are no additional pet fees.

Residence Inn by Marriott
4361 W Reno Ave
Oklahoma City, OK
405-942-4500
There is a $25 per day pet fee for the first 3 nights and no additional pet fees after that.

Studio 6
5801 Tinker Diagonal
Oklahoma City, OK
405-737-8851
There is a $10 per day additional pet fee, up to a maximum of $50 per visit. A large well-behaved dog is okay.

Super 8 Motel
924 S Kerr Blvd
Sallisaw, OK
918-775-8900
There is a $5 per day pet fee.

Best Western Sand Springs Inn & Suites
211 S. Lake Dr.
Sand Springs, OK
918-245-4999
There is a $10 per day additional pet fee. Dogs may not be left alone in the room. They must be

on leash when outside of the room.

Shawnee

Best Western Cinderella Motor Inn
623 Kickapoo Spur
Shawnee, OK
405-273-7010
There is a $10 per day additional pet fee.

Motel 6
4981 N Harrison St
Shawnee, OK
405-275-5310
There are no additional pet fees.

Stillwater

Motel 6
5122 W 6th Ave
Stillwater, OK
405-624-0433
There are no pet fees. Pets must be attended at all times.

Stroud

Best Western Stroud Motor Lodge
1200 N Eighth Ave
Stroud, OK
918-968-9515
There is a $5 per day additional pet fee.

Tulsa

Cambridge Suites
8181 E 41st St
Tulsa, OK
918-664-7241
There is an $75 one time pet fee.

Days Inn West
5525 W Skelly Dr
Tulsa, OK
918-446-1561
There is an $8 per day additional pet fee.

Doubletree Hotel at Warren

Place
6110 S Yale Ave
Tulsa, OK
918-495-1000
There is a $25 one time pet fee.

Holiday Inn
1010 N. Garnett
Tulsa, OK
918-437-7660
There is a $25 one time pet fee.

Holiday Inn Express
9010 E. 71st St
Tulsa, OK
918-459-5321
There is a $30 one time pet fee.

La Quinta Inn Tulsa 41st Street
10829 E 41st Street
Tulsa, OK
918-665-0220
Dogs of all sizes are allowed at the hotel.

La Quinta Inn Tulsa South
12525 East 52nd Street South
Tulsa, OK
918-254-1626
Dogs up to 75 pounds are allowed at the hotel.

Motel 6
5828 W Skelly Dr
Tulsa, OK
918-445-0223
There are no additional pet fees.

Sheraton Tulsa Hotel
10918 E. 41st Street
Tulsa, OK
918-627-5000
Dogs up to 80 pounds are allowed. There are no additional pet fees.

Woodward

Northwest Inn
Hwy. 270 and First St
Woodward, OK
580-256-7600
There is a $10 one time pet fee.

Wayfarer Inn

2901 Williams Ave
Woodward, OK
580-256-5553
There are no additional pet fees.

Yukon

Best Western Inn & Suites
11440 West I-40 Service Rd
Yukon, OK
405-265-2995
There is a $25 refundable pet deposit.

Oregon Listings

Albany

La Quinta Inn & Suites Albany
251 Airport Road SE
Albany, OR
541-928-0921
Dogs of all sizes are allowed at the hotel.

Ashland

Best Western Bard's Inn
132 N Main Street
Ashland, OR
541-482-0049
There is a $15 per day additional pet fee. All rooms are non-smoking. Pets may not be left alone in the rooms.

Best Western Windsor Inn
2520 Ashland St
Ashland, OR
541-488-2330
There is a $10 per day additional pet fee.

La Quinta Inn & Suites Ashland
434 S. Valley View Road
Ashland, OR
541-482-6932
Dogs of all sizes are allowed at the hotel.

Astoria

Red Lion Inn
400 Industry St
Astoria, OR
503-325-7373
There is a $10 per day pet fee.

Baker City

Quality Inn
810 Campbell St.
Baker City, OR
541-523-2242
There is a pet fee of $5 per day.

Bandon

Best Western Inn at Face Rock
3225 Beach Loop Rd
Bandon, OR
541-347-9441
There is a $15 one time pet fee.

Driftwood Motel
460 Hwy 101
Bandon, OR
541-347-9022
There is a $10 per day pet fee.

Sunset Motel
1755 Beach Loop Rd
Bandon, OR
541-347-2453
There is a $10 per day pet charge. All rooms are non-smoking.

Bend

Best Western Inn and Suites
721 NE 3rd St
Bend, OR
541-382-1515
There is a $5 per day additional pet fee.

Entrada Lodge
19221 Century Dr
Bend, OR
541-382-4080
There is a $5 per day pet fee. Pets may not be left alone in the room.

Holiday Inn Express Hotel
20615 Grandview Drive

Bend, OR
541-317-8500
There is a $5 per day pet fee.

Motel 6
201 NE Third St
Bend, OR
541-382-8282
There are no additional pet fees.

Red Lion Inn North
1415 NE 3rd St
Bend, OR
541-382-7011
There are no additional pet fees.

Sleep Inn
600 NE Bellvue
Bend, OR
541-330-0050
There is a one time fee of $8. Pets may not be left alone in the room.

The Riverhouse Resort
3075 N Hwy 97
Bend, OR
541-389-3111
You need to sign a pet policy.

Cannon Beach

Best Western Cannon Beach
3215 S. Hemlock
Cannon Beach, OR
503-436-9085
There is a $10 per day pet fee. A maximum of two pets per room is allowed.

Surfsand Resort
148 W. Gower
Cannon Beach, OR
503-436-2274
This resort offers views of Haystack Rock and the Pacific Ocean from oceanfront and ocean-view rooms. The Surfsand is a nice vacation spot for families and couples. The hotel caters to four-legged family members and they host an annual "For Fun" Dog Show. The resort is entirely non-smoking and it is located near a

dog-friendly restaurant called The Local Scoop. There is a $12 per day pet fee.

The Haystack Resort
3361 S. Hemlock
Cannon Beach, OR
503-436-1577
Every room and suite at the Haystack Resort offers complete ocean views. Your pet is always welcome. They are located near a dog-friendly restaurant called "The Local Scoop. There is a $10 per day additional pet fee.

Cave Junction

Junction Inn
406 Redwood Hwy
Cave Junction, OR
541-592-3106
There is a $5 per day additional pet fee. They normally put dogs in smoking rooms, but will make exceptions.

Coos Bay

Motel 6
1445 Bayshore Dr
Coos Bay, OR
541-267-7171
There are no pet fees. A large dog is okay if it is well-behaved.

Cottage Grove

Best Western - The Village Green
725 Row River Rd.
Cottage Grove, OR
541-942-2491
The hotel is at exit 174 on I-5.

Comfort Inn
845 Gateway Blvd.
Cottage Grove, OR
541-942-9747
There is a $10 pet deposit.

Holiday Inn Express
1601 Gateway Blvd
Cottage Grove, OR
541-942-1000
There is a $10 per day pet fee.

Eugene

Best Western Greentree Inn
1759 Franklin Blvd
Eugene, OR
541-485-2727
There is a $25.00 refundable pet deposit.

Best Western New Oregon Motel
1655 Franklin Blvd
Eugene, OR
541-683-3669
There are no additional pet fees.

Eugene Hilton
66 East 6th Avenue
Eugene, OR
541-342-2000
There is a $25 one time pet fee.

La Quinta Inn & Suites Eugene
155 Day Island Rd.
Eugene, OR
541-344-8335
Dogs of all sizes are allowed at the hotel.

Motel 6
3690 Glenwood Dr
Eugene, OR
541-687-2395
There are no additional pet fees.

Quality Inn & Suites
2121 Franklin Blvd
Eugene, OR
541-342-1243
There is no pet fee.

Ramada Inn
225 Coburg Rd
Eugene, OR
541-342-5181
There is a $15 one time pet fee.

The Valley River Inn
1000 Valley River Way
Eugene, OR
541-687-0123
There are no additional pet fees.

Gold Beach

Econo Lodge
29171 Eltensburg Ave

Gold Beach, OR
541-247-6606
There is a $5 one time pet fee.

Jot's Resort
94360 Wedderburn Loop
Gold Beach, OR
541-247-6676
There is a $10 per day pet fee. Pets are allowed in the deluxe rooms overlooking the river.

Grants Pass

Best Western Grants Pass Inn
111 NE Agness Ave
Grants Pass, OR
541-476-1117
There is a $5 per day additional pet fee.

Comfort Inn
1889 NE 6th St
Grants Pass, OR
541-479-8301
There is a $100 pet deposit.

Holiday Inn Express
105 NE Agness Ave
Grants Pass, OR
541-471-6144
There is a $5 per day additional pet fee.

La Quinta Inn & Suites Grants Pass
243 NE Morgan Lane
Grants Pass, OR
541-472-1808
Dogs of all sizes are allowed at the hotel.

Motel 6
1800 Northeast 7th St
Grants Pass, OR
541-474-1331
There are no additional pet fees.

Gresham

Hawthorn Inn & Suites
2323 NE 181st Ave
Gresham, OR
503-492-4000

There is a $10 per stay pet fee.

Harbor

Best Western Beachfront Inn
16008 Boat Basin Rd
Harbor, OR
541-469-7779
There is a $5 per day pet fee. You need to tell the hotel that you are bringing a dog when you make a reservation. There are a limited number of pet rooms.

Hillsboro

Best Western Cavanaughs Hillsboro Hotel
3500 NE Cornell Rd
Hillsboro, OR
503-648-3500
There is a $5 per day additional pet fee. A maximum to 2 pets per room are allowed.

Hines

Comfort Inn
504 N Hwy 20
Hines, OR
541-573-3370
There is a $50 pet deposit if paid with cash. If using a credit card there is no fee.

Hood River

Best Western Hood River Inn
1108 E. Marina Way
Hood River, OR
541-386-2200
There is a $12 per day additional pet fee.

Columbia Gorge
4000 Westcliff Dr
Hood River, OR
541-386-5566
There is a $25 pet charge.

Vagabond Lodge
4070 Westcliff Dr
Hood River, OR
541-386-2992
There are no additional pet fees.

King City

Best Western Northwind Inn & Suites
16105 SW Pacific Hwy
King City, OR
503-431-2100
There is a $20 one time pet fee.

Klamath Falls

Best Western Klamath Inn
4061 South Sixth Street
Klamath Falls, OR
541-882-1200
There are no additional pet fees.

Cimarron Motor Inn
3060 S Sixth St
Klamath Falls, OR
541-882-4601
There is a $5 one time fee for pets.

CrystalWood Lodge
38625 Westside Road
Klamath Falls, OR
541-381-2322
Located in the Southern Oregon Cascades, this lodge welcomes all well-behaved dogs. There is no pet fee.

Motel 6
5136 S 6th St
Klamath Falls, OR
541-884-2110
There are no additional pet fees.

Quality Inn
100 Main St.
Klamath Falls, OR
541-882-4666
There are no pet fees, but a credit card will be required.

Red Lion Inn
3612 S 6th St
Klamath Falls, OR
541-882-8864
There are no additional pet fees. Pet owners must sign a pet waiver form.

Shilo Suites Hotel
2500 Almond St
Klamath Falls, OR

541-885-7980
There is a $10 per day pet fee.

LaGrande

Howard Johnson Inn
2612 Island Avenue
LaGrande, OR
541-963-7195
Dogs of all sizes are welcome. There is a $10 per day pet fee.

Lake Oswego

Crowne Plaza
14811 Kruse Oaks Dr
Lake Oswego, OR
503-624-8400
There is a $10 per day pet fee.

Lincoln City

Ester Lee Motel
3803 S.W. HWY. 101
Lincoln City, OR
541 996 3606
Pets are welcome in the cottages but not the motel. There is a $7 per day additional pet fee. Some of the cottages are non-smoking.

Looking Glass Inn
861 SW 51st Street
Lincoln City, OR
541-996-3996
They provide a basket of dog supplies when you check in. There is a $10 per day additional pet fee.

Madras

Best Western Rama Inn
12 SW 4th Street
Madras, OR
541-475-6141
There is a $10 one time pet fee.

Medford

Best Western
1154 E Barnett Rd
Medford, OR
541-779-5085

There is a $10 per day pet charge.

Doubletree Hotel
200 N Riverside
Medford, OR
541-779-5811
There are no additional pet fees.

Motel 6
2400 Biddle Rd
Medford, OR
541-779-0550
There are no additional pet fees.

Motel 6
950 Alba Dr
Medford, OR
541-773-4290
One pet is allowed per room.

Reston Hotel
2300 Crater Lake Hwy
Medford, OR
541-779-3141
There is a $20 one time pet fee.

Mount Hood

Cooper Spur Mountain Resort
10755 Cooper Spur Rd
Mount Hood, OR
541-352-6692
There are designated pet rooms. There is a $20 one time per stay additional pet fee.

Newport

Best Western
3019 North Coast Hwy
Newport, OR
541-265-9411
There is a $10 one time pet fee.

Hallmark Resort
744 SW Elizabeth St
Newport, OR
541-265-2600
There is a $5 per day pet fee, Dogs are allowed on the first floor only.

La Quinta Inn & Suites Newport
45 SE 32nd

Newport, OR
541-867-7727
Dogs up to 75 pounds are allowed at the hotel.

Shilo Oceanfront Resort
536 SW Elizabeth St
Newport, OR
541-265-7701
There is a $10 per day pet fee.

Ontario

Best Western Inn & Suites
251 Goodfellow Street
Ontario, OR
541-889-2600
There is a $50 refundable pet deposit.

Motel 6
275 NE 12th St
Ontario, OR
541-889-6617
There are no pet fees. A well-behaved large dog is okay.

Pendleton

Best Western Pendleton Inn
400 SE Nye Ave
Pendleton, OR
541-276-2135
There is a $10 per day pet fee.

Holiday Inn Express
600 SE Nye Ave
Pendleton, OR
541-966-6520
There is a $10 one time pet fee.

Motel 6
325 SE Nye Ave
Pendleton, OR
541-276-3160
There are no additional pet fees. Pets must be attended at all times.

Portland

5th Avenue Suites
506 S.W. Washington
Portland, OR
503-222-0001
Well-behaved dogs of all sizes

are welcome at this pet-friendly hotel. The luxury boutique hotel offers both rooms and suites. Hotel amenities include complimentary evening wine service, and a 24 hour on-site fitness room. There are no pet fees, just sign a pet liability form.

Best Western Inn at the Meadows
1215 N Hayden Meadows Dr
Portland, OR
503-286-9600
There is a $21.80 one time pet fee.

Comfort Inn
8855 SW Citizen Dr.
Portland, OR
503-682-9000
There is a pet fee of $10 per day.

Days Inn
9930 N Whitaker Rd
Portland, OR
503-289-1800
There is a $15 one time pet fee.

Hotel Lucia
400 SW Broadway
Portland, OR
503-228-7221
There is a $100 refundable pet deposit.

Hotel Vintage Plaza
422 SW Broadway
Portland, OR
503-228-1212
Well-behaved dogs of all sizes are welcome at this pet-friendly hotel. The luxury boutique hotel offers both rooms and suites. Hotel amenities include complimentary evening wine service, complimentary high-speed Internet access in all guest rooms, 24 hour room service and an on-site fitness room. There are no pet fees, just sign a pet liability form.

Howard Johnson Hotel
7101 NE 82nd Ave.
Portland, OR

503-255-6722
Dogs of all sizes are welcome. There is a $15 per day pet fee.

La Quinta Inn & Suites Portland Northwest
4319 NW Yeon
Portland, OR
503-497-9044
Dogs of all sizes are allowed at the hotel.

La Quinta Inn Portland - Lloyd
431 NE Multnomah
Portland, OR
503-233-7933
Dogs up to 75 pounds are allowed at the hotel.

Mallory Hotel
729 SW 15th
Portland, OR
503-223-6311
There is a $10 one time fee for pets.

Motel 6
3104 SE Powell Blvd
Portland, OR
503-238-0600
There are no pet fees. Pets must never be left alone in rooms.

Quality Inn Portland Airport
8247 NE Sandy Blvd.
Portland, OR
503-256-4111
There is a pet fee of $15 per day.

Sheraton Portland Airport Hotel
8235 NE Airport Way
Portland, OR
503-281-2500
Dogs of all sizes are allowed. There is a $25 one time per stay pet fee.

Sleep Inn
2261 NE 181st Ave.
Portland, OR
503-618-8400
There is a pet fee of $10 per day, to a maximum of $50.

Staybridge Suites
11936 NE Glenn Widing Drive

Portland, OR
503-262-8888
There is a $25 one time pet fee plus a pet fee of $10 per day.

Redmond

Motel 6
2247 S Hwy 97
Redmond, OR
541-923-2100
There are no additional pet fees.

Reedsport

Economy Inn
1593 Highway Ave 101
Reedsport, OR
541-271-3671
There is a $5 per day pet fee.

Rice Hill

Best Western Rice Hill Inn
621 John Long Rd
Rice Hill, OR
541-849-2500
There is a $10 one time pet fee.

Roseburg

Best Western Douglas Inn
511 SE Stephens
Roseburg, OR
541-673-6625
There is a $6 per day additional pet fee.

Comfort Inn
1539 Mullholland Dr.
Roseburg, OR
541-957-1100
There is a pet fee of $10 per day. All rooms are non-smoking.

Holiday Inn Express
375 Harvard Blvd
Roseburg, OR
541-673-7517
There is a $5 per day pet fee. Pets are allowed in the first floor rooms only.

Motel 6
3100 NW Aviation

Roseburg, OR
541-464-8000
There are no additional pet fees.

Sleep Inn & Suites
2855 NW Eden Bower Blvd.
Roseburg, OR
541-464-8338
There is a pet fee of $7 per day.

Salem

Holiday Inn Express
890 Hawthorne Ave SE
Salem, OR
503-391-7000
There is a $15 one time pet fee.

Motel 6
1401 Hawthorne Ave NE
Salem, OR
503-371-8024
There are no additional pet fees.

Phoenix Inn - Salem South
4370 Commercial St SE
Salem, OR
503-588-9220
There is a $10 per day pet charge.

Red Lion Hotel
3301 Market St
Salem, OR
503-370-7888
There is a $20 non-refundable pet fee.

Seaside

Best Western Ocean View Resort
414 N. Prom
Seaside, OR
503-738-3334
There is a $15 per day pet fee. Pets are allowed on the ground floor only.

Comfort Inn
545 Broadway Ave.
Seaside, OR
503-738-3011

There is a pet fee of $7 per day.

Motel 6
2369 S Roosevelt (Hwy 101)
Seaside, OR
503-738-6269
There are no additional pet fees.

Seaside Convention Center Inn
441 Second Ave
Seaside, OR
503-738-9581
There is a $10.00 per day pet charge.

Sisters

Comfort Inn
540 US 20 West
Sisters, OR
541-549-7829
There is no pet fee. Pets may stay on the first floor only.

Springfield

Motel 6
3752 International Ct
Springfield, OR
541-741-1105
There are no additional pet fees.

Sunriver

Sunray Vacation Rentals
P.O. Box 4518
Sunriver, OR
800-531-1130
They have over 200 homes and condos for rent in Sunriver (about 20 miles from Bend, OR) and most of the rentals allow pets.

The Dalles

Quality Inn Columbia River Gorge
2114 W. 6th
The Dalles, OR
541-298-5161
There is a pet fee of $10 per day.

Tigard

Motel 6
17950 SW McEwan Rd
Tigard, OR
503-620-2066
There are no additional pet fees.
Pets must not be left alone in
rooms.

Troutdale

Motel 6
1610 NW Frontage Rd
Troutdale, OR
503-665-2254
There are no pet fees. One pet
is allowed per room. Pets must
be leashed when outside the
room and cannot be left alone in
the room.

Tualatin

Sweetbrier Inn
7125 SW Nyberg
Tualatin, OR
503-692-5800
There is a $25 refundable pet
deposit for standard rooms, $50
for suites.

Warrenton

Shilo Inn
1609 E Harbor Drive
Warrenton, OR
503-861-2181
There is a $10 per day pet fee.

Wilsonville

Holiday Inn Select
25425 SW 95th Ave
Wilsonville, OR
503-570-8500
There is a $10 per day pet fee.

Woodburn

**La Quinta Inn & Suites
Woodburn**
120 Arney Road NE
Woodburn, OR
503-982-1727

Dogs of all sizes are allowed at
the hotel.

Yachats

Adobe Resort
1555 US 101
Yachats, OR
541-547-3141
There is a $10 per day pet
charge.

Shamrock Lodgettes
US 101
Yachats, OR
541-547-3312
Pets are allowed in cabins only.
There is an additional $5 per
day charge. All units are non-
smoking and have fireplaces.

The Fireside Inn
Hwy 101
Yachats, OR
800-336-3573
Located on the coast, the
Fireside is a pet-friendly facility
that encourages pet owners to
bring their companions with
them to enjoy time away
together. Each pet is charged
$7 per night which includes a
"Pet Pack" complete with self-
contained pooper scoopers,
towels to dry off after a romp in
the water, and sheets to protect
furniture and bedding in the
guest rooms. All rooms are
non-smoking. They also have
handicapped accessible units.

Pennsylvania
Listings

Adamstown

Black Forest Inn
500 Lancaster Ave
Adamstown, PA
717-484-4801
There is a $10 per day
additional pet fee.

Allentown

Allenwood Motel
1058 Hausman Rd
Allentown, PA
610-395-3707
There is a $15 per day pet fee.

Staybridge Suites
1787 A. Airport Road
Allentown, PA
610-443-5000
There is a $50 one time pet fee.

Super 8
15 St and US 22
Allentown, PA
610-435-7880
There is a $10 one time
additional pet fee.

Altoona

Motel 6
1500 Sterling St
Altoona, PA
814-946-7601
There are no additional pet fees.

Beaver Falls

Holiday Inn
7195 Eastwood Rd
Beaver Falls, PA
724-846-3700
There are no additional pet fees.

Berwyn

Residence Inn
600 W Swedesford Rd
Berwyn, PA
610-640-9494
There is a $150.00 one time pet
charge.

Blakeslee

**Best Western Inn at Blakeslee-
Pocono**
Route 115, PO Box 413
Blakeslee, PA
570-646-6000
There is a $50 refundable pet
deposit.

Breinigsville-Lehigh Valley

Holiday Inn
7736 Adrienne Drive
Breinigsville-Lehigh Valley, PA
610-391-1000
There is a $10 per day pet fee.
Pet owners must also sign a pet
waiver.

Brookville

Holiday Inn Express
235 Allegheny Blvd
Brookville, PA
814-849-8381
There is a $10 per day pet fee.

Carlisle

Holiday Inn
1450 Harrisburg Pike
Carlisle, PA
717-245-2400
There is a $10 per day pet fee.

Motel 6
1153 Harrisburg Pike
Carlisle, PA
717-249-7622
There are no additional pet fees.

Clarion

Holiday Inn
I-80 Rt 68
Clarion, PA
814-226-8850
There are no additional pet fees.

Clearfield

Best Western Motor Inn
1-80 at Exit 19, Box 286
Clearfield, PA
814-765-2441
There is a $5 per day additional
pet fee.

Coraopolis

Holiday Inn - Airport
1406 Beers School Rd
Coraopolis, PA
412-262-3600

There are no additional pet
fees.

**La Quinta Inn Pittsburgh -
Coraopolis**
1433 Beers School Road
Coraopolis, PA
412-269-0400
Dogs of all sizes are allowed at
the hotel.

Red Roof Inn
1454 Beers School Rd
Coraopolis, PA
412-264-5678
There are no additional pet
fees.

Wyndham Hotel
777 Aten Rd
Coraopolis, PA
412-788-8800
There are no additional pet
fees.

Cranberry Township

Holiday Inn Express
20003 Rt 19
Cranberry Township, PA
724-772-1000
There is a $10 per day pet fee.
A well-behaved large dog is
okay.

DuBois

Holiday Inn
Rt 219 & I-80
DuBois, PA
814-371-5100
A well-behaved large dog is
okay. Pets may not be left
unattended in the room. There
are no additional pet fees.

Dunmore

Days Inn
1226 O'Neil Hwy
Dunmore, PA
570-348-6101
There is a $3 per day additional
pet fee.

Holiday Inn

200 Tigue St
Dunmore, PA
570-343-4771
There is a $10 per day pet fee.
Pets are allowed in rooms with
an outside entrance. The hotel is
at I-81 and Junction of 380 E &
84 E.

Erie

Motel 6
7875 Peach St
Erie, PA
814-864-4811
There are no additional pet fees.

Quality Inn
8040 Perry Hwy
Erie, PA
814-864-4911
There are no additional pet fees.

Essington

Red Roof Inn - Airport
49 Industrial Hwy
Essington, PA
610-521-5090
There are no additional pet fees.
Dogs up to 80 pounds are
allowed.

Frackville

Motel 6
701 Altamont Blvd
Frackville, PA
570-874-1223
There are no additional pet fees.

Gettysburg

Gettysburg Travelodge
64 Steinwehr Ave
Gettysburg, PA
717-334-9281
There are no pet fees.

Holiday Inn
516 Baltimore St
Gettysburg, PA
717-334-6211
Pet owners must sign a pet
waiver. Pets may not be left

alone in the room.

Grantville

Holiday Inn
Hershey Exit 28 I-81
Grantville, PA
717-469-0661
There are no additional pet fees.

Hamlin

Comfort Inn
I-84 & SR 191 (Exit 5)
Hamlin, PA
570-689-4148
There is an additional $15 one
time pet fee.

Harrisburg

Best Western
300 N Mountain Rd
Harrisburg, PA
717-652-7180
There is a $5 per day pet fee.

Holiday Inn
4751 Lindle Rd
Harrisburg, PA
717-939-7841
There is a $75 refundable pet
deposit.

**Holiday Inn Express Hotel &
Suites**
5680 Allentown Blvd
Harrisburg, PA
717-657-2200
There is a $15 one time pet fee.

Hawley

Falls Port Inn
330 Main Ave
Hawley, PA
570-226-2600
Large dogs are allowed in the
larger rooms. There is a $20 one
time pet fee.

Hazleton

Best Western Genetti Lodge
Route 309, RR2, Box 37

Hazleton, PA
570-454-2494
There are no additional pet
fees.

Horsham

Residence Inn
3 Walnut Grove Rd
Horsham, PA
215-443-7330
There is a $150.00 one time pet
charge.

Hummelstown

Holiday Inn Express
610 Walton Ave
Hummelstown, PA
717-583-0500
If pets are over 25 pounds
there is a $100 refundable
deposit. Pets must be well-
behaved.

Indiana

Holiday Inn
1395 Wayne Ave
Indiana, PA
724-463-3561
There are no additional pet
fees.

Johnstown

Comfort Inn
455 Theatre Dr
Johnstown, PA
814-266-3678
There is a $15 per day pet
charge.

Holiday Inn
250 Market St
Johnstown, PA
814-535-7777
There are no pet fees. Pets
may never be left alone in
rooms.

Holiday Inn Express
1440 Scalp Ave
Johnstown, PA
814-266-8789

There are no additional pet fees.
Pets must be attended at all
times.

Motel 6
430 Napoleon Place
Johnstown, PA
814-536-1114
There are no pet fees. Pets must
be attended at all times.

Sleep Inn
453 Theatre Dr
Johnstown, PA
814-262-9292
There is an $15.00 per day pet
charge.

Kulpsville

Best Western
1750 Sumneytown Pike
Kulpsville, PA
215-368-3800
This hotel was previously a
Holiday Inn. There are no
additional pet fees.

Lake Harmony

Ramada Inn - Pocono
Route 940
Lake Harmony, PA
570-443-8471
There is a $50 refundable pet
deposit.

Lancaster

Super 8 Motel
2129 Lincoln Hwy E
Lancaster, PA
717-393-8888
There is a $10 one time pet fee.

Langhorne

Sheraton Bucks County Hotel
400 Oxford Valley Road
Langhorne, PA
215-547-4100
Dogs up to 80 pounds are
allowed. There are no additional
pet fees.

Lionville

Hampton Inn
4 N Pottstown Pike
Lionville, PA
610-363-5555
There are no additional pet fees.

Lititz

General Sutter Inn
14 E Main St
Lititz, PA
717-626-2115
Dogs up to 75 pounds are
permitted.

Lock Haven

Best Western Lock Haven
101 East Walnut Street
Lock Haven, PA
570-748-3297
There is a $6 per day additional
pet fee.

Malvern

Homewood Suites
12 E Swedesford Rd
Malvern, PA
610-296-3500
There is a $150.00 one time pet
charge.

Mars

Motel 6
19025 Perry Hwy
Mars, PA
724-776-4333
There are no additional pet fees.

Matamoras

**Best Western Inn at Hunts
Landing**
120 Routes 6 and 209
Matamoras, PA
570-491-2400
There are no additional pet fees.

Meadville

Motel 6
11237 Shaw Ave
Meadville, PA
814-724-6366
There are no additional pet
fees.

Mercer

Howard Johnson Inn
835 Perry Hwy.
Mercer, PA
724-748-3030
Dogs of all sizes are allowed.
There are no additional pet
fees.

Milesburg

Holiday Inn
I-80 & US 150 N
Milesburg, PA
814-355-7521
There are no additional pet
fees.

Morgantown

Holiday Inn
6170 Morgantown Road
Morgantown, PA
610-286-3000
If paying with cash there is a
$50 refundable pet deposit.

New Cumberland

Holiday Inn
PA Turnpike Exit 18 & I-83 Exit
18A
New Cumberland, PA
717-774-2721
There is a $10 per day
additional pet fee.

Motel 6
200 Commerce Dr
New Cumberland, PA
717-774-8910
There are no additional pet
fees.

New Holland

The Hollander Motel

320 E Main St
New Holland, PA
717-354-4377
There is a $5.00 per day pet
charge.

Oil City

Holiday Inn
1 Seneca St
Oil City, PA
814-677-1221
There is a $10 per day additional
pet fee.

Philadelphia

Crowne Plaza
1800 Market St
Philadelphia, PA
215-561-7500
There is a $50 one time pet fee.

Loews Philadelphia Hotel
1200 Market Street
Philadelphia, PA
215-627-1200
All well-behaved dogs of any
size are welcome. This upscale
hotel offers their "Loews Loves
Pets" program which includes
special pet treats, local dog
walking routes, and a list of
nearby pet-friendly places to
visit. There are no pet fees.

Philadelphia Marriott
1201 Market St
Philadelphia, PA
215-625-2900
There is a $100 one time pet
charge.

**Residence Inn - Philadelphia
Airport**
4630 Island Ave
Philadelphia, PA
215-492-1611
There is a $100 one time pet
charge.

Sheraton Society Hill
One Dock Street
Philadelphia, PA
215-238-6000
Dogs of all sizes are allowed.
There are no additional pet fees.

The Rittenhouse
210 W Rittenhouse Square
Philadelphia, PA
215-546-9000
There are no additional pet fees.

Pittsburgh

Best Western University Center
3401 Blvd of the Allies
Pittsburgh, PA
412-683-6100
There are no additional pet fees.

Doubletree Hotel
1000 Penn Ave
Pittsburgh, PA
412-281-3700
There is a $50 one time pet fee.

Hampton Inn Greentree
555 Trumbull Dr
Pittsburgh, PA
412-922-0100
There are no additional pet fees.

Holiday Inn
401 Holiday Dr
Pittsburgh, PA
412-922-8100
There are no pet fees. Pet owners must sign a pet waiver. Pets stay on first floor rooms and may not be left alone in the rooms.

Holiday Inn Select - University Center
100 Lytton Ave
Pittsburgh, PA
412-682-6200
There are no additional pet fees. Pet owners must sign a pet waiver.

Motel 6
211 Beecham Dr
Pittsburgh, PA
412-922-9400
There are no additional pet fees. One well-behaved pet is allowed. Pets must be attended at all times and leashed when outside the room.

Red Roof Inn
6404 Steubenville Pike
Pittsburgh, PA
412-787-7870
There are no pet fees. Dogs up to 80 pounds are allowed.

Sheraton Station Square Hotel
7 Station Square Drive
Pittsburgh, PA
412-261-2000
Dogs up to 80 pounds are allowed. There are no additional pet fees.

Pittston

Holiday Inn Express
30 Concorde Drive
Pittston, PA
570-654-3300
There are no additional pet fees.

Pottstown

Comfort Inn
99 Robinson St
Pottstown, PA
610-326-5000
There is a $25 refundable pet deposit.

Days Inn
29 High St
Pottstown, PA
610-970-1101
There is a $10 per day pet charge.

Reading

Best Western Dutch Colony Inn & Suites
4635 Perkiomen Avenue
Reading, PA
610-779-2345
There is a $10 per day additional pet fee.

Scranton

Howard Johnson Express Inn
320 Franklin Ave.

Scranton, PA
570-346-7061
Dogs of all sizes are welcome. There is a $10 per day pet fee.

Somerset

Best Western Executive Inn
165 Waterworks Rd
Somerset, PA
814-445-3996
There is a $7 per day additional pet fee.

Holiday Inn
202 Harmon St
Somerset, PA
814-445-9611
There are no additional pet fees.

Knights Inn
585 Ramada Rd
Somerset, PA
814-445-8933
There are no additional pet fees.

Ramada Inn
Pennsylvania Turnpike Routes 70 and 76 (Exit 10)
Somerset, PA
814-443-4646
There are no additional pet fees.

State College

Motel 6
1274 North Atherton St
State College, PA
814-234-1600
There are no additional pet fees. Pets must be well-behaved and attended at all times.

Ramada Inn
1450 S Atherton St
State College, PA
814-238-3001
There is a $10 per day additional pet fee.

Uniontown

Holiday Inn
700 W. Main Street
Uniontown, PA
724-437-2816

There are no additional pet fees.

Warren

Holiday Inn
210 Ludlow St
Warren, PA
814-726-3000
There are no additional pet fees.

Washington

Holiday Inn
340 Racetrack Rd
Washington, PA
724-222-6200
There are no additional pet fees.

Motel 6
1283 Motel 6 Drive
Washington, PA
724-223-8040
There are no additional pet fees.

West Chester

Holiday Inn
943 S. High St
West Chester, PA
610-692-1900
There is a $25 one time pet fee.
If you stay over one week there
is a $25 pet fee per week.

White Haven

Days Inn and Suites
Highway 940 East
White Haven, PA
570-443-0391
There is a $10 one time pet fee.

Wilkes-Barre

**Best Western Genetti Hotel &
Conv. Center**
77 East Market Street
Wilkes-Barre, PA
570-823-6152
There is a $10 per day additional
pet fee.

Holiday Inn
880 Kidder St, Rt 115 & 309
Wilkes-Barre, PA

570-824-8901
There are no additional pet
fees.

Williamsport

Holiday Inn
1840 E. Third St
Williamsport, PA
570-326-1981
There are no pet fees. Pets
may not be left unattended in
rooms.

York

Holiday Inn
2000 Loucks Rd
York, PA
717-846-9500
There are no additional pet
fees.

Motel 6
125 Arsenal Rd
York, PA
717-846-6260
There are no additional pet
fees.

Rhode Island Listings

Middletown

Howard Johnson Inn
351 West Main Rd.
Middletown, RI
401-849-2000
Dogs of all sizes are welcome.
There is a $5 per day pet fee.
Pets may not be left
unattended in the room.

Newport

**1 Murray House Bed &
Breakfast**
1 Murray Place
Newport, RI
401-846-3337
Located in the famous Newport

Mansion district. Short walk to
semi-private beach. Private
patios, Private baths & Private
outside entrances to each
charmingly decorated theme
room. Wonderful gourmet
breakfast served to your room or
private patio. Stunning flower
gardens surrounding in-ground
pool & hottub. Water view room
on the second level. A
delightfully, unique & relaxing
bed & breakfast. Arringtoh Bed
& Breakfast Journal voted
Murray House B&B one of the
top B&B/Country inns on the
eastern seaboard in the book of
lists for 2003. Well-behaved pets
allowed in the room with the
waterview: Pondview Room. Pet
rules apply.

Motel 6
Rt 114 at Coddington Hwy
Newport, RI
401-848-0600
There are no additional pet fees.

Wakefield

Larchwood
521 Main St
Wakefield, RI
401-783-5454
There is a $5 per day additional
pet fee.

Warwick

Crowne Plaza
801 Greenwich Ave
Warwick, RI
401-732-6000
There are no additional pet fees.

Holiday Inn Express & Suites
901 Jefferson Blvd
Warwick, RI
401-736-5000
There is a $50 refundable pet
deposit.

**Sheraton Providence Airport
Hotel**
1850 Post Road
Warwick, RI
401-738-4000

Dogs up to 80 pounds are
allowed. There is a $25 one time
per stay pet fee.

Woonsocket

Holiday Inn Express & Suites
194 Fortin Drive
Woonsocket, RI
401-769-5000
There is a $10 per day additional
pet fee.

South Carolina
Listings

Aiken

Holiday Inn Express
155 Colony Pkwy - Whiskey Rd
Aiken, SC
803-648-0999
There is a $30 one time pet fee.

Howard Johnson Express Inn
1936 Whiskey Road South
Aiken, SC
803-649-5000
Dogs of all sizes are welcome.
There is a $11.10 per day pet
fee.

Anderson

La Quinta Inn Anderson
3430 North Main Street
Anderson, SC
864-225-3721
Dogs of all sizes are allowed at
the hotel.

Beaufort

Holiday Inn
2001 Boundary St
Beaufort, SC
843-524-2144
There is a $25 one time pet fee.

Howard Johnson Express Inn
3651 Trask Parkway, US Hwy
21

Beaufort, SC
843-524-6020
Dogs of all sizes are welcome.
There is a $25 one time pet fee.

Charleston

Indigo Inn
Maiden Lane
Charleston, SC
843-577-5900
There is a $20 per day pet fee.

**Sheraton North Charleston
Hotel**
4770 Goer Drive
Charleston, SC
843-747-1900
Dogs of all sizes are allowed.
There is a 4100 one time pet
fee per stay.

Columbia

Baymont Inn - Columbia East
1538 Horseshoe Dr
Columbia, SC
803-736-6400
Dogs under 60 pounds are
allowed. There are no
additional pet fees.

Holiday Inn
7510 Two Notch Rd, I-20 &
US-1
Columbia, SC
803-736-3000
There is a $25 one time pet fee.
Pets must be leashed when
they are not in your room.

Motel 6
1776 Burning Tree Rd
Columbia, SC
803-798-9210
There are no additional pet
fees. Pets must be attended at
all times and must be on leash
when outside the room.

Red Roof Inn - West
10 Berryhill Rd
Columbia, SC
803-798-9220
There are no additional pet
fees.

**Sheraton Columbia Hotel and
Conference Center**
2100 Bush River Road
Columbia, SC
803-731-0300
Dogs of all sizes are allowed.
There is a $50 one time per stay
pet fee.

Dillon

Best Value Inn
904 Redford Blvd
Dillon, SC
843-774-5111
There is a $12 per day additional
pet fee.

Florence

Econo Lodge
1811 W Lucas St
Florence, SC
843-665-8558
There is a $6 per day additional
pet fee.

Holiday Inn Express
1819 W. Lucas Street
Florence, SC
843-664-2400
There are no additional pet fees.

Motel 6
1834 W Lucas Street
Florence, SC
843-667-6100
One large dog per room is
permitted.

Ramada Inn
2038 W Lucas St
Florence, SC
843-669-4241
There are no additional pet fees.

Red Roof Inn
2690 David McLeod Blvd
Florence, SC
843-678-9000
There are no additional pet fees.

Thunderbird Motor Inn
2004 W Lucas St
Florence, SC
843-669-1611

There are no additional pet fees.

Young's Plantation Inn
US 76 and I-95
Florence, SC
843-669-4171
There is a $4 per day pet fee.

Greenville

Crowne Plaza
851 Congaree Rd
Greenville, SC
864-297-6300
There is a $50 one time pet fee.

Days Inn
831 Congaree Rd
Greenville, SC
864-288-6221
There is a $15 one time pet fee.

Greenville Airport Inn
5009 Pelham Rd
Greenville, SC
864-297-5353
There is a $10 per day pet fee.

Guest House Suites
48 McPrice Ct
Greenville, SC
864-297-0099
There is a $25 per day additional pet fee up to a total of $100 per stay.

Holiday Inn
4295 Augusta Rd, I-85 Exit 46A
Greenville, SC
864-277-8921
There is a $30 one time pet fee.

La Quinta Inn & Suites Greenville - Haywood
65 West Orchard Park Drive
Greenville, SC
864-233-8018
Dogs of all sizes are allowed at the hotel.

Microtel Inn
20 Interstate Court
Greenville, SC
864-297-7866
There is a $25 refundable pet deposit.

Motel 6
224 Bruce Rd
Greenville, SC
864-277-8630
There are no additional pet fees.

Red Roof Inn
2801 Laurens Rd
Greenville, SC
864-297-4458
There are no additional pet fees.

Hilton Head

Hilton Head Rentals & Golf
578 William Hilton Parkway
Hilton Head, SC
843-785-8687
1 - 3 bedroom ocean oriented condos and homes on Hilton Head Island, SC. These beautifully decorated units are close to the beach, and Hilton Head beaches are accessible to pets. Dogs up to 50 pounds are welcome. There is a $300 refundable pet deposit.

Motel 6 with Extended Stay
830 William Hilton Pkwy
Hilton Head, SC
843-785-2700
There is a $25 one time pet fee if staying in a room with a kitchenette. There are no pet fees for regular rooms.

Hilton Head Island

Red Roof Inn - Hilton Head
5 Regency Pkwy
Hilton Head Island, SC
843-686-6808
Dogs under 80 pounds are allowed. There are no additional pet fees.

Little River

Days Inn Little River
1564 US 17 Hwy N
Little River, SC
843-249-3535
There is a $10 per day pet fee.

Manning

Super 8
Rte 6 (exit Hwy 261)
Manning, SC
803-473-4646
There is a $10 per day additional pet fee.

Mount Pleasant

MainStay Suites
400 McGrath Darby Blvd.
Mount Pleasant, SC
843-881-1722
We are a 71 suite hotel with a designated dog walk area, treats from our staff in the lobby and lots of hugs from all. A $10 fee per day is charged plus any damages will be repaired and charged at cost to the guest.

Masters Inn
300 Wingo Way
Mount Pleasant, SC
843-884-2814
There is a $5 per day pet fee.

Red Roof Inn
301 Johnnie Dodds Blvd
Mount Pleasant, SC
843-884-1411
There are no additional pet fees. Dogs under 80 pounds are allowed.

Myrtle Beach

Booe Realty
7728 N. Kings Hwy
Myrtle Beach, SC
800-845-0647
Serving the Myrtle Beach and Grand Strand Area for more than 31 years, Booe Realty offers many properties (condos and houses) that are pet friendly.

St. John's Inn-Unit 115
Call to Arrange.
Myrtle Beach, SC
800-845-0624
This studio apartment is available for dog-friendly rental in Myrtle Beach. The apartment

is non-smoking. Amenities include cable tv, a microwave oven and a small refrigerator. Call St. John's Inn at 800-845-0624 or Caravelle Rentals at 800-845-0893 and specifically ask for Unit 115.

St. John's Inn-Units 310, 314, 315
Call to Arrange.
Myrtle Beach, SC
800-845-0624
Stay at Myrtle Beach in one of three pet-friendly units all with full size refrigerators. Please only request units 310, 314, or 315. Call St. John's Inn at 800-845-0624 or Caravelle Rentals at 800-845-0893.

Staybridge Suites
3163 Outlet Blvd
Myrtle Beach, SC
843-903-4000
There is a $25 one time pet fee.

The Sea Mist Resort
1200 S Ocean Blvd
Myrtle Beach, SC
843-448-1551
There is a $50 pet fee per stay (per week).

North Charleston

Residence Inn by Marriott
7645 Northwoods Blvd
North Charleston, SC
843-572-5757
There is a $75 one time pet fee for studios and a $100 one time pet fee for penthouses.

North Myrtle Beach

Myrtle Beach Holiday
North Ocean Blvd
North Myrtle Beach, SC
843-390-1537
Pet friendly vacation rentals are available for all travelers and their pets. Properties range from ocean front units to casual beach cottages across the street from the ocean. A non-refundable pet fee is required.

Retreat Myrtle Beach
500 Main Street
North Myrtle Beach, SC
843-280-3015
Vacation rentals for all groups and travelers with pets! Properties range from ocean front luxury condos to rustic family beach bungalows. All rentals are equipped to provide the comforts of home and meet basic resort rental standards. Pet fees range from $50 to $100 for the stay.

Rock Hill

Best Western Inn
1106 Anderson Rd
Rock Hill, SC
803-329-1330
There is a $10 per day pet fee.

Holiday Inn
2640 N Cherry Rd
Rock Hill, SC
803-329-1122
There is a $15 one time pet fee.

Santee

Howard Johnson Express Inn
I-95 Ex 102, Rd 400
Santee, SC
803-478-7676
There is an additional $10 per day pet fee.

Spartanburg

Motel 6
105 Jones Rd
Spartanburg, SC
864-573-6383
There are no additional pet fees.

St George

Best Western St George
I95 & Hwy 78
St George, SC
843-563-2277
There is a $10 per day pet fee.

Quality Inn
I-95 & US 78
St George, SC
843-563-4581
There are no pet fees.

Super 8
114 Winningham Rd
St George, SC
843-563-5551
There is a $5 per day additional pet fee. Normally pets are placed in smoking rooms, but they can make exceptions.

Summerville

Holiday Inn Express
120 Holiday Inn Drive, I-26 Exit 199A
Summerville, SC
843-875-3300
There are no additional pet fees.

Walterboro

Econo Lodge
1145 Sniders Hwy
Walterboro, SC
843-538-3830
There are no additional pet fees.

Howard Johnson Express Inn
1120 Sniders Hwy.
Walterboro, SC
843-538-5473
Dogs of all sizes are welcome. There is a $8 per day pet fee.

Rice Planters Inn
I-95 and SR 63
Walterboro, SC
843-538-8964
There is a $5 per day additional pet fee.

Yemassee

Holiday Inn Express
40 Frampton Drive
Yemassee, SC
843-726-9400
There is a $10 one time pet fee.

South Dakota Listings

Aberdeen

Best Western Ramkota Hotel
1400 8th Avenue NW
Aberdeen, SD
605-229-4040
There are no additional pet fees.

Ramada Inn
2727 6th Ave. S.E.
Aberdeen, SD
605-225-3600
Dogs are allowed in the outside entrance rooms only. There are no additional pet fees.

White House Inn
500 6th Avenue SW
Aberdeen, SD
605-225-5000
There is a $5 per day pet charge during hunting season. There is no pet charge during the rest of the year.

Belle Fourche

Motel 6
1815 5th Ave
Belle Fourche, SD
605-892-6663
There are no pet fees. Pets must be leashed when outside the room and may not be left alone in the room.

Brandon

Holiday Inn Express
1105 North Splitrock Blvd
Brandon, SD
605-582-2901
There is a $10 per day additional pet fee.

Custer

Legion Lake Resort in Custer State Park
Highway 16a
Custer, SD
605-255-4521
Dogs are allowed in the cabins at the Blue Bell Lodge. There is a $5 per day pet charge.

State Game Lodge in Custer State Park
Highway 16
Custer, SD
605-255-4541
Dogs are allowed in the cabins only. There is a $5 per day pet charge. This lodge was known as the Summer White House after hosting Presidents Coolidge and Eisenhower. It is open from mid-May through mid-October. All cabins are non-smoking.

Huron

Best Western of Huron
2000 Dakota South
Huron, SD
605-352-2000
There are no additional pet fees.

Dakota Plains Inn
Highway 14E
Huron, SD
605-352-1400
There is a $20 refundable pet deposit.

Holiday Inn Express
100 21st Street SW
Huron, SD
605-352-6655
There is a $25 one time pet fee. Pets must be attended at all times.

Kadoka

Best Western H & H El Centro
PO Box 37
Kadoka, SD
605-837-2287
The hotel is closed annually from mid - December through the end of January.

Keystone

Kelly Inn
Highway 16a and Cemetary Road
Keystone, SD
605-666-4483
There are 1-2 pet rooms and no extra pet charges, just sign a pet damage waiver.

Mitchell

Holiday Inn
1525 W. Havens Ave
Mitchell, SD
605-996-6501
There is a $10 per day additional pet fee.

Motel 6
1309 S Ohiman St
Mitchell, SD
605-996-0530
There are no additional pet fees. They have a few pet rooms at the hotel.

Siesta Motel
1210 West Havens
Mitchell, SD
605-996-5544
There are no additional pet fees.

North Sioux City

Comfort Inn
1311 River Drive
North Sioux City, SD
605-232-3366
There is a one time pet fee of $10.

Pierre

Best Western Kings Inn
220 S Pierre
Pierre, SD
605-224-5951
There is a $10 per day additional pet fee.

Best Western Ramkota Hotel
920 W Sioux Avenue
Pierre, SD
605-224-6877
There are no additional pet fees.

Accommodations - Please always call ahead to make sure an establishment is still dog-friendly.

Capitol Inn & Suites
815 Wells Avenue
Pierre, SD
605-224-6387
There are no additional pet fees.

Super 8 Motel
320 West Sioux
Pierre, SD
605-224-1617
There is a $5 per day additional pet fee.

Rapid City

Motel 6
620 E Latrobe St
Rapid City, SD
605-343-3687
There are no additional pet fees.

Super 8 Motel
2124 LaCrosse St.
Rapid City, SD
605-348-8070
There is a $7 per day pet charge.

Sioux Falls

Best Western Ramkota Hotel
2400 N. Louise
Sioux Falls, SD
605-336-0650
Pets must not be left unattended in the rooms.

Kelly Inn
3101 W. Russell Street
Sioux Falls, SD
605-338-6242
There is no extra charge for pets, just sign a pet damage waiver.

Motel 6
3009 W Russell St
Sioux Falls, SD
605-336-7800
There are no additional pet fees. One pet per room is permitted.

Ramada Inn Airport at the Convention Center
1301 W. Russell Street

Sioux Falls, SD
605-336-1020
There is a $10 one time pet fee.

Sheraton Sioux Falls and Convention Center
1211 West Avenue North
Sioux Falls, SD
605-331-0100
Dogs up to 80 pounds are allowed. There are no additional pet fees.

Spearfish

Holiday Inn
I-90 & Exit 14, PO Box 399
Spearfish, SD
605-642-4683
There is a $10 one time pet fee.

Howard Johnson Express Inn
323 S. 27th St.
Spearfish, SD
605-642-8105
Dogs of all sizes are welcome. There is a $10 per day pet fee. Pets must be declared when making a reservation.

Sturgis

Best Western Sturgis Inn
2431 S. Junction Street, Box 777
Sturgis, SD
605-347-3604
There are no additional pet fees.

Sturgis Super 8 Motel
HC 55 Box 306
Sturgis, SD
605-347-4447
There is a $20 refundable pet deposit.

Wall

Best Western Plains Motel
712 Glenn Street, Box 393
Wall, SD
605-279-2145
There is a $10 per day additional pet fee. The hotel is closed from mid November

through February.

Watertown

Best Western Ramkota Hotel
1901 9th Avenue Southwest
Watertown, SD
605-886-8011
There are no additional pet fees.

Tennessee Listings

Antioch

Holiday Inn
201 Crossing Place
Antioch, TN
615-731-2361
There are no additional pet fees.

Brownsville Bells

Motel 6
9740 Hwy 70 E, I-40 Exit 66
Brownsville Bells, TN
731-772-9500
There are no additional pet fees.

Butler

Creekside Chalet
138 Moreland Drive
Butler, TN
423-768-2446
The wrap around porch is gated so your 4-footed friends can romp and play. There are hiking trails and a nearby lake to swim in. They do require a dog deposit which is refunded when the chalet is left free of dog hair or any damage. Dogs of all sizes are welcome.

Chattanooga

Motel 6
7707 Lee Hwy
Chattanooga, TN
423-892-7707
There are no additional pet fees.

Red Roof Inn
7014 Shallowford Road
Chattanooga, TN
423-899-0143
There are no additional pet fees.

Clarksville

Comfort Inn
1112 State Route 76
Clarksville, TN
931-358-2020
There is a $5 per day pet
charge.

Quality Inn-Downtown
803 N. 2nd St.
Clarksville, TN
931-645-9084
Dogs are allowed in the first floor
rooms. There is a $25 one time
pet charge and a $5 per day pet
fee. Pets stay in a room which
has exterior corridors and faces
the parking lot.

Ramada Limited
3100 Wilma Rudolph Blvd.
Clarksville, TN
931-552-0098
There is a $30 refundable pet
deposit.

Clinton

Best Western Clinton Inn
720 Park Place
Clinton, TN
865-457-2311
There is a $5 per day additional
pet fee.

Cookeville

Alpine Lodge & Suites
2021 E. Spring St.
Cookeville, TN
931-526-3333
They have had Great Danes
stay here before. As long as the
dog is well-behaved, size does
not matter. There is a $5 per day
pet charge.

**Best Western Thunderbird
Motel**

900 S. Jefferson Ave.
Cookeville, TN
931-526-7115
There are no additional pet
fees.

Hampton Inn
1025 Interstate Drive
Cookeville, TN
931-520-1117
There are no additional pet
fees.

Holiday Inn
870 S. Jefferson St
Cookeville, TN
931-526-7125
There are no additional pet
fees. They have had St.
Bernards stay here before.

Covington

Best Western Inn
873 Highway 51 North
Covington, TN
901-476-8561
There is a $10 per day
additional pet fee.

Dandridge

Holiday Inn Express
119 Sharon Drive
Dandridge, TN
865-397-1910
There is a $25 one time pet fee.

Dayton

Best Western Dayton
7835 Rhea Co Hwy
Dayton, TN
423-775-6560
There is a $3 per day additional
pet fee.

Dickson

**Best Western Dickson
Station Inn**
1025 East Christi Drive
Dickson, TN
615-441-5252
There is a $10 per day

additional pet fee.

Holiday Inn
2420 Hwy 46 S.
Dickson, TN
615-446-9081
There are no additional pet fees.

Elkton

Motel 6
I-65 & Bryson Rd
Elkton, TN
931-468-2594
There are no additional pet fees.

Erwin

Holiday Inn Express
2002 Temple Hill Rd
Erwin, TN
423-743-4100
There is a $50 refundable pet
deposit. There is also a $14.95
per day additional pet fee.

Fayetteville

Best Western Fayetteville Inn
3021 Thornton Taylor Pkwy
Fayetteville, TN
931-433-0100
There is a $10 per day additional
pet fee. Pet owners need to sign
a pet waiver form at check in.

Franklin

Holiday Inn Express & Suites
4202 Franklin Commons Ct
Franklin, TN
615-591-6660
There is a $15 one time pet fee.

Gatlinburg

A & B Rentals
702 East Parkway Suite #2
Gatlinburg, TN
865-430-9988
Stay in a beautiful private chalet
or cabin in the Smoky
Mountains. The busy season for
Gatlinburg is April through
October, but there is much to do

year round. Dogs are allowed at some of the rentals. Mention that you will be bringing a dog when making reservations.

Holiday Inn Sunspree Resort
520 Historic Nature Trail
Gatlinburg, TN
865-436-9201
There are no additional pet fees.

Riverside Rentals
P.O. Box 1296
Gatlinburg, TN
865-436-9496
Riverside Rentals offers 1 - 12 Bedrooms fully furnished, some of which are pet friendly. In those units that allow pets, there is a $10 per night additional pet fee. Up to two dogs are allowed in a rental and a pet security deposit is required on your credit card. One night's deposit plus a $25.00 reservation fee is required to make a reservation.

Goodlettsville

Motel 6
323 Cartwright St
Goodlettsville, TN
615-859-9674
There are no additional pet fees. Pets must be well-behaved and leashed when outside the room.

Harriman

Best Western Sundancer Motor Lodge
120 Childs Rd, PO Box 231
Harriman, TN
865-882-6200
There is a $5 per day pet fee. Pets may not be left unattended in the room.

Holiday Inn Express
1845 S. Roane St
Harriman, TN
865-882-5340
There are no additional pet fees. Pets must be attended at all times.

Huntsville

Holiday Inn Express
11597 Scott Hwy
Huntsville, TN
423-663-4100
There is a $5 per day additional pet fee.

Jackson

Garden Plaza Hotel
1770 Hwy 45
Jackson, TN
731-664-6900
There is a $5 per day additional pet fee.

Motel 6
1940 Hwy 45 Bypass, I-40 Exit 80A
Jackson, TN
731-661-0919
There are no additional pet fees.

Kingston Springs

Best Western Harpeth Inn
116 Luyben Hills Rd
Kingston Springs, TN
615-952-3961
There is a $10 per day additional pet fee.

Knoxville

Baymont Inn-West
11341 Campbell Lakes Drive
Knoxville, TN
865-671-1010
Dogs under 50 pounds are allowed. There are no additional pet fees.

La Quinta Inn Knoxville West
258 Peters Road North
Knoxville, TN
865-690-9777
Dogs of all sizes are allowed at the hotel.

Motel 6
402 Lovell Rd
Knoxville, TN
865-675-7200

There are no pet fees. One large dog per room is okay.

Residence Inn by Marriott
215 Langley Place
Knoxville, TN
865-539-5339
There is a $90 one time pet charge. They are located at Langley Place and N. Peters Rd.

Kodak

Holiday Inn Express & Suites
2863 Winfield Dunn Parkway
Kodak, TN
865-933-9448
There are no additional pet fees.

Lawrenceburg

Best Western Villa Inn
2126 N. Locust Ave
Lawrenceburg, TN
931-762-4448
There is a $10 per day additional pet fee.

Memphis

East Drury Inn & Suites
1556 Sycamore View
Memphis, TN
901-373-8200
Dogs of all sizes are permitted. Pets are not allowed in the breakfast area of the hotel. Pets are not to be left unattended, and each guest must assume liability for damage of property or other guest complaints. There is a limit of one pet per room.

Holiday Inn Select
5795 Poplar Ave
Memphis, TN
901-682-7881
There is a $25 one time pet fee.

La Quinta Inn Memphis East
6068 Macon Cove
Memphis, TN
901-382-2323
Dogs of all sizes are allowed at the hotel.

Motel 6
1321 Sycamore View Rd
Memphis, TN
901-382-8572
There are no additional pet fees.

Red Roof Inn
210 South Pauline Street
Memphis, TN
901-528-0650
There are no additional pet fees.

Red Roof Inn-East
6055 Shelby Oaks Drive
Memphis, TN
901-388-6111
There are no additional pet fees.

Studio 6
4300 American Way
Memphis, TN
901-366-9333
There is a $10 per day pet fee up to a maximum of $50 per stay.

Monteagle

Best Western Smoke House Lodge
850 West Main Street
Monteagle, TN
931-924-2091
There is a $5 per day additional pet fee.

Morristown

Holiday Inn
5435 South Davey Crockett Pkwy
Morristown, TN
423-587-2400
There are no additional pet fees.

Holiday Inn
3304 W Andrew Johnson Hwy 11E
Morristown, TN
423-581-8700
There are no additional pet fees.

Murfreesboro

Holiday Inn
2227 Old Fort Pkwy
Murfreesboro, TN
615-896-2420
There are no pet fees. Pets are allowed in the rooms with outside access.

Motel 6
148 Chaffin Place
Murfreesboro, TN
615-890-8524
There are no additional pet fees.

Nashville

Best Western Calumet Inn at the Airport
701 Stewarts Ferry Pike
Nashville, TN
615-889-9199
There are no additional pet fees.

Drury Inn & Suites
555 Donelson Pike
Nashville, TN
615-902-0400
Dogs of all sizes are permitted. Pets are not allowed in the breakfast area of the hotel. Pets are not to be left unattended, and each guest must assume liability for damage of property or other guest complaints. There is a limit of one pet per room.

Holiday Inn Select - Opryland
2200 Elm Hill Pike
Nashville, TN
615-883-9770
There is a $125 refundable pet deposit and there is a $25 one time pet fee. They are located near Briley Parkway.

Loews Vanderbilt Hotel
2100 West End Ave
Nashville, TN
615-320-1700
All well-behaved dogs of any size are welcome. This upscale hotel offers their "Loews Loves Pets" program which includes special pet treats, local dog walking routes, and a list of nearby pet-friendly places to

visit. There are no pet fees.

Motel 6
420 Metroplex Dr
Nashville, TN
615-833-8887
There are no additional pet fees.

Motel 6
311 W Trinity Lane
Nashville, TN
615-227-9696
There are no additional pet fees.

Motel 6
95 Wallace Rd
Nashville, TN
615-333-9933
There are no pet fees. Pets must be well-behaved and attended at all times.

Pear Tree Inn
343 Harding Place
Nashville, TN
615-834-4242
Dogs of all sizes are permitted. Pets are not allowed in the breakfast area of the hotel. Pets are not to be left unattended, and each guest must assume liability for damage of property or other guest complaints. There is a limit of one pet per room.

Red Roof Inn-South
4271 Sidco Drive
Nashville, TN
615-832-0093
Dogs under 75 pounds are allowed. There are no additional pet fees.

Residence Inn - Nashville Airport
2300 Elm Hill Pike
Nashville, TN
615-889-8600
There is a $50 one time pet charge. They are located near Briley Parkway.

Sheraton Music City
777 McGavok Pike
Nashville, TN
615-885-2200
Dogs up to 80 pounds are allowed. There are no additional

pet fees. Pets are allowed on the first floor which has both smoking and non-smoking rooms.

South Drury Inn
341 Harding Place
Nashville, TN
615-834-7170
Dogs of all sizes are permitted. Pets are not allowed in the breakfast area of the hotel. Pets are not to be left unattended, and each guest must assume liability for damage of property or other guest complaints. There is a limit of one pet per room.

Best Western Newport Inn
1015 Cosby Highway, PO Box 382
Newport, TN
423-623-8713
There are no additional pet fees.

Holiday Inn
1010 Cosby Hwy
Newport, TN
423-623-8622
There are no additional pet fees. Pets must be leashed when outside the room.

Motel 6
255 Heritage Blvd
Newport, TN
423-623-1850
There are no additional pet fees.

Best Western Travelers Inn
1297 East Wood Street
Paris, TN
731-642-8881
There are no additional pet fees.

Heartlander Country Resort
2385 Parkway (US 441)
Pigeon Forge, TN
865-453-4106
There is a $20 one time pet

charge.

Holiday Inn
3230 Parkway
Pigeon Forge, TN
865-428-2700
There are no additional pet fees.

Best Western Dumplin Valley Inn
3426 Winfield Dunn Parkway
Sevierville, TN
865-933-3467
There is a $10 per day additional pet fee.

Holiday Inn Express
104 Kedron Rd
Spring Hill, TN
931-486-1234
There are no additional pet fees. A well-behaved quiet dog is okay.

Best Western Crossroads Inn
21045 Hwy 22 N
Wildersville, TN
901-968-2532
There is a $5 per day additional pet fee.

Best Western Inn
1602 Dinah Shore Blvd
Winchester, TN
931-967-9444
There is a $10 per day additional pet fee.

Texas Listings

Clarion Hotel

5403 S First St
Abilene, TX
915-695-2150
Dogs are allowed in the courtyard rooms only. There is a $10 per day pet fee.

Comfort Inn
1758 E I-20
Abilene, TX
915-676-0203
There is a pet fee of $15 per day.

Comfort Suites
3165 S Danville Dr
Abilene, TX
915-795-8500
There is a non-refundable pet fee of $30.

Embassy Suites Hotel
4250 Ridgemont Dr
Abilene, TX
915-698-1234
There is a $25 one time pet charge.

La Quinta Inn Abilene
3501 West Lake Road
Abilene, TX
915-676-1676
Dogs of all sizes are allowed at the hotel.

Quality Inn
548 Ambler
Abilene, TX
800-588-0222
There are no additional pet fees.

Quality Inn Civic Center
505 Pine St
Abilene, TX
800-588-0222
There is a one time pet fee of $10.

Whitten Inn
1625 State Route 351
Abilene, TX
915-673-5271
There are no additional pet fees.

Crowne Plaza

14315 Midway Rd
Addison, TX
972-980-8877
There is a $125 refundable pet deposit and a $25 one time pet fee.

**La Quinta Inn & Suites
Addison Galleria Area**
14925 Landmark Blvd.
Addison, TX
972-404-0004
Dogs of all sizes are allowed at the hotel.

Quality Suites North/ Galleria
4555 Beltline Rd
Addison, TX
972-503-6500
There is a one time pet fee of $25.

Amarillo

Best Western Santa Fe
4600 E Interstate 40
Amarillo, TX
806-372-1885
There is a $10 per day additional pet fee. Take exit 73 on I-40.

Hampton Inn
1700 I-40 East
Amarillo, TX
806-372-1425
There are no additional pet fees.

Kiva Motel
2501 Interstate Highway 40 East
Amarillo, TX
806-379-6555
There is a $25 one time pet fee.

**La Quinta Inn Amarillo
East/Airport Area**
1708 I-40 East
Amarillo, TX
806-373-7486
Dogs of all sizes are allowed at the hotel.

**La Quinta Inn Amarillo
Medical Center**
2108 Coulter Street
Amarillo, TX
806-352-6311
Dogs of all sizes are allowed at

the hotel.

Motel 6
3930 I-40E
Amarillo, TX
806-374-6444
There are no additional pet fees.

Motel 6
6030 I-40W
Amarillo, TX
806-359-7651
There are no additional pet fees.

Quality Inn & Suites Airport
1803 Lakeside Dr
Amarillo, TX
806-335-1561
There is a one time pet fee of $10.

Residence Inn by Marriott
6700 Interstate 40 West
Amarillo, TX
806-354-2978
There is a $100 one time pet charge.

Arlington

Days Inn-Six Flags
1195 N. Watson Road
Arlington, TX
817-649-8881
There is a $5 per day pet charge.

Hawthorn Suites Hotel
2401 Brookhollow Plaza Drive
Arlington, TX
817-640-1188
There is a $50 one time pet charge.

Motel 6
2626 E Randol Mill Rd
Arlington, TX
817-649-0147
There are no additional pet fees. Pets must be well-behaved and attended at all times.

Sleep Inn Maingate Six Flags
750 Six Flags Dr

Arlington, TX
817-649-1010
There is a pet fee of $15 per night.

Studio 6
1980 West Pleasant Ridge Rd
Arlington, TX
817-465-8500
There is a $50 one time pet fee. Well-behaved dogs are allowed to stay at the hotel.

Austin

Best Western Atrium North
7928 Gessner Drive
Austin, TX
512-339-7311
There are no additional pet fees.

Comfort Suites
1701 E St. Elmo Rd
Austin, TX
512-444-6630
There is no pet fee.

Hawthorn Suites-Austin South
4020 IH 35 South
Austin, TX
512-440-7722
There is a $50 one time pet charge and a $5 per day additional pet fee.

Highland Mall Drury Inn
919 E. Koenig Lane
Austin, TX
512-454-1144
Dogs of all sizes are permitted. Pets are not allowed in the breakfast area of the hotel. Pets are not to be left unattended, and each guest must assume liability for damage of property or other guest complaints. There is a limit of one pet per room.

Holiday Inn
8901 Business Park Drive
Austin, TX
512-343-0888
There is a $25 one time pet fee.

Holiday Inn
3401 S. I-35
Austin, TX

512-448-2444
There is a $35 one time pet fee. Well-behaved housebroken dogs are allowed.

Holiday Inn
20 N I-25
Austin, TX
512-472-8211
There is a $100 refundable pet deposit and a $25 per day additional pet fee.

Holiday Inn
6911 N I-35
Austin, TX
512-459-4251
There is a $15 one time pet fee.

Holiday Inn-Northwest Plaza
8901 Business Park Drive
Austin, TX
512-343-0888
There is a $25 one time pet fee.

La Quinta Inn & Suites Southwest at Mopac
4424 S. Mopac Expressway
Austin, TX
512-899-3000
Dogs of all sizes are allowed at the hotel.

La Quinta Inn Austin Capitol
300 E. 11th St.
Austin, TX
512-476-1166
Dogs of all sizes are allowed at the hotel.

La Quinta Inn Austin North
7100 N IH 35
Austin, TX
512-452-9401
Dogs up to 50 pounds are allowed at the hotel.

La Quinta Inn Austin Oltorf
1603 E. Oltorf Blvd.
Austin, TX
512-447-6661
Dogs of all sizes are allowed at the hotel.

Motel 6
5330 N Interregional Hwy
Austin, TX
512-467-9111

There are no additional pet fees.

Motel 6
2707 Interregional Hwy S
Austin, TX
512-444-5882
There are no additional pet fees.

Red Lion Hotel
6121 I-35 North
Austin, TX
512-323-5466
There are no additional pet fees.

Staybridge Suites - Northwest
10201 Stonelake Blvd
Austin, TX
512-349-0888
There is a $12 per day pet fee. Up to two dogs are allowed and there is a weight limit of 50 pounds per pet.

Studio 6
937 Camino La Costa
Austin, TX
512-458-5453
There are no additional pet fees.

Studio 6
11901 Pavilion Blvd
Austin, TX
512-258-3556
There is a $50 one time pet fee.

Balch Springs

Howard Johnson Express Inn
12901 Seagoville Rd.
Balch Springs, TX
972-286-1010
Dogs of all sizes are welcome. There are no additional pet fees.

Baytown

Quality Inn
300 S Hwy 146 Business
Baytown, TX
281-427-7481

There is no pet fee.

Beaumont

Best Western Beaumont Inn
2155 N. 11th Street
Beaumont, TX
409-898-8150
Exit 11th Street off of I-10.

Hilton Beaumont
2355 I-10 South
Beaumont, TX
409-842-3600
There is a $25 one time pet fee.

Holiday Inn
2095 N 11th Street at I-10
Beaumont, TX
409-892-2222
There are no additional pet fees.

Holiday Inn
3950 I-10 S at Walden Rd
Beaumont, TX
409-842-5995
There is a $10 per day additional pet fee.

Holiday Inn-Midtown
2095 N. 11th St.
Beaumont, TX
409-892-2222
There is a $10 one time pet fee.

La Quinta Inn Beaumont
220 Interstate 10 N
Beaumont, TX
409-838-9991
Dogs of all sizes are allowed at the hotel.

Bedford

Comfort Inn
2904 Crystal Springs St
Bedford, TX
817-545-2555
There is a pet deposit of $50 required if paying by cash. There is no deposit or fee if paying with a credit card.

La Quinta Inn Bedford
1450 W Airport Freeway
Bedford, TX

817-267-5200
Dogs of all sizes are allowed at the hotel.

Bellmead

Motel 6
1509 Hogan Lane
Bellmead, TX
254-799-4957
There are no additional pet fees. One pet per room is permitted and pets must be attended at all times.

Big Spring

Best Western Motor Lodge
700 W IH-20
Big Spring, TX
915-267-1601
Exit 177 off of I-20.

Motel 6
600 W I-20 Rt 2
Big Spring, TX
915-267-1695
There is a $5 per day additional pet fee.

Brownfield

Best Western Caprock Inn
321 Lubbock Hwy
Brownfield, TX
806-637-9471
There is a $5 per day pet fee. A well-behaved large dog is okay.

Buffalo

Best Western Craig's Inn
I-45 & US 79, PO Box 667
Buffalo, TX
903-322-5831
Dogs must be leashed on the premises when outside of the room.

Canyon

Holiday Inn Express Hotel & Suites
2901 4th Ave
Canyon, TX

806-655-4445
There is a $10 one time pet fee.

Cedar Park

Comfort Inn
300 E. Whitestone Blvd
Cedar Park, TX
512-259-1810
There is a pet fee of $10 per day.

Channelview

Best Western Houston East
15919 I-10 East
Channelview, TX
281-452-1000
There is a $15 one time pet fee.

Childress

Best Western Childress
1805 Ave F NW
Childress, TX
940-937-6353
There is a $5 per day additional pet fee.

Comfort Inn
1804 Ave F NW
Childress, TX
940-937-6363
There is a pet fee of $5 per day.

College Station

La Quinta Inn College Station
607 Texas Avenue
College Station, TX
979-696-7777
Dogs of all sizes are allowed at the hotel.

Motel 6
2327 Texas Ave South
College Station, TX
979-696-3379
There are no additional pet fees.

Columbus

Holiday Inn Express Hotel &

Suites
4321 I-10
Columbus, TX
979-733-9300
There is a $50 refundable pet deposit and a $10 one time pet fee.

Conroe

Motel 6
820 I-45 S
Conroe, TX
936-760-4003
There are no additional pet fees.

Corpus Christi

Bayfront Inn
601 North Shoreline Blvd.
Corpus Christi, TX
361-883-7271
There is a $20 one time per stay pet fee for up to a 3 day stay.

Best Western Garden Inn
11217 IH-37
Corpus Christi, TX
361-241-6675
There is a $5 per day additional pet fee.

Holiday Inn
5549 Leopard St
Corpus Christi, TX
361-289-5100
There are no additional pet fees.

Holiday Inn
1102 S. Shoreline Blvd
Corpus Christi, TX
361-883-5731
There are no additional pet fees.

La Quinta Inn Corpus Christi South
6225 South Padre Island Dr
Corpus Christi, TX
361-991-5730
Dogs of all sizes are allowed at the hotel.

Red Roof Inn - Airport
6301 Interstate 37
Corpus Christi, TX
361-289-6925

There is a $10 per day pet fee.

Residence Inn by Marriott
5229 Blanche Moore Drive
Corpus Christi, TX
361-985-1113
There is a $100 one time per stay pet charge and a $10 per day pet fee.

Surfside Condo Apartments
15005 Windward Drive
Corpus Christi, TX
361-949-8128
Dogs up to 50 pounds are allowed. There is a $15 per day pet charge and a $200 refundable pet deposit.

Dalhart

Best Western Nursanickel Motel
102 Scott Street
Dalhart, TX
806-244-5637
There are no additional pet fees.

Dallas

Best Western Dallas North
13333 N Stemmons Fwy
Dallas, TX
972-241-8521
There is a $20 one time pet fee per visit.

Crowne Plaza Suites
7800 Alpha Rd
Dallas, TX
972-233-7600
There is a $150 refundable pet deposit and a $50 one time pet fee.

Dallas Marriott Suite Market Center
2493 North Stemmons Freeway
Dallas, TX
214-905-0050
Amenities at this hotel includes room service which might come in handy if you want to dine in with your pooch. There is a $50 one time per stay pet fee.

Harvey Hotel
7815 LBJ Freeway
Dallas, TX
972-960-7000
There is a $125 deposit for pets and $100 is refundable.

Hawthorn Suites
7900 Brookriver Dr
Dallas, TX
214-688-1010
There is a $50 one time pet fee. Dogs must be less than 75 pounds.

La Quinta Inn & Suites Dallas North Park
10001 North Central Expressway
Dallas, TX
214-361-8200
Dogs of all sizes are allowed at the hotel.

La Quinta Inn Dallas City Place
4440 N Central Expressway
Dallas, TX
214-821-4220
Dogs of all sizes are allowed at the hotel.

La Quinta Inn Dallas Lovefield
1625 Regal Row
Dallas, TX
214-630-5701
Dogs of all sizes are allowed at the hotel.

La Quinta Inn Farmers Branch NW
13235 Stemmons Freeway North
Dallas, TX
972-620-7333
Dogs of all sizes are allowed at the hotel.

Motel 6
2660 Forest Lane
Dallas, TX
972-484-9111
Use 35E to 635 East. There are no additional pet fees.

Motel 6

2753 Forest Lane
Dallas, TX
972-620-2828
Use 35E to 635 E. There are no additional pet fees.

Motel 6
4220 Independence Dr
Dallas, TX
972-296-3331
There are no additional pet fees.

Radisson - Mockingbird
1893 W Mockingbird Ln
Dallas, TX
214-634-8850
There is a $50 pet deposit. Of this, $25 is refundable.

Residence Inn by Marriott - Market Center
6950 N Stemmons Frwy
Dallas, TX
214-631-2472
There is a $50 one time pet fee.

Studio 6
2395 Stemmons Trail
Dallas, TX
214-904-1400
Use I-35 E to the Northwest Hwy exit. There is a $10 per day additional pet fee.

The Mansion on Turtle Creek
2821 Turtle Creek Blvd
Dallas, TX
214-559-2100
There is a $200 one time pet fee.

Decatur

Best Western Inn
1801 S Hwy 287
Decatur, TX
940-627-5982
There is a $5 per day additional pet fee.

Motel 6
1700 South US 81/287
Decatur, TX
940-627-0250
There is a $10 per day additional pet fee.

Del Rio

Best Western Inn of Del Rio
810 Ave F
Del Rio, TX
830-775-7511
There is a $5 per day additional
pet fee.

Motel 6
2115 Ave F
Del Rio, TX
830-774-2115
There is no additional pet fee.

Denton

La Quinta Inn Denton
700 Fort Worth Drive
Denton, TX
940-387-5840
Dogs of all sizes are allowed at
the hotel.

Motel 6
4125 Interstate 35N
Denton, TX
940-566-4798
There is no additional pet fee.

Diboll

Best Western Diboll Inn
910 North Temple Drive
Diboll, TX
936-829-2055
There is a $5 per day additional
pet fee.

Donna

Howard Johnson Express Inn
602 N Victoria Rd
Donna, TX
956-464-4656
Dogs of all sizes are welcome.
There is a $150 refundable pet
deposit and a $5 per day pet
fee.

Eagle Pass

La Quinta Inn Eagle Pass
2525 Main Street East
Eagle Pass, TX

830-773-7000
Dogs of all sizes are allowed at
the hotel.

El Paso

Best Western Airport Inn
7144 Gateway East
El Paso, TX
915-779-7700
From I-10, exit on Hawkins and
head south. A well-behaved
large dog is okay.

Camino Real Hotel
101 S El Paso St
El Paso, TX
915-534-3000
There are no additional pet
fees.

**Chase Suite Hotel by
Woodfin**
6791 Montana Ave
El Paso, TX
All well-behaved dogs are
welcome. Every room is a suite
with a full kitchen. Hotel
amenities include a
complimentary breakfast buffet.
There is a $5 per day pet fee.
There are no additional pet
fees.

Comfort Inn
7651 N. Mesa St
El Paso, TX
915-845-1906
There is a one time pet fee of
$20.

Comfort Inn Airport East
900 Yarbrough Dr
El Paso, TX
915-594-9111
There is no pet fee.

El Paso Airport Hilton
2027 Airway Blvd
El Paso, TX
915-778-4241
There is a $200 refundable pet
deposit.

**La Quinta Inn El Paso - Cielo
Vista**
9125 Gateway West

El Paso, TX
915-593-8400
Dogs up to 50 pounds are
allowed at the hotel.

La Quinta Inn El Paso West
7550 Remcon Circle
El Paso, TX
915-833-2522
Dogs of all sizes are allowed at
the hotel.

La Quinta Inn El Paso-Airport
6140 Gateway Blvd. E
El Paso, TX
915-778-9321
Dogs of all sizes are allowed at
the hotel.

La Quinta Inn Lomaland
11033 Gateway Blvd.
El Paso, TX
915-591-2244
Dogs of all sizes are allowed at
the hotel.

Sleep Inn
953 Sunland Park Dr
El Paso, TX
915-585-7577
There is a one time pet fee of
$10.

Studio 6
11049 Gateway Blvd W
El Paso, TX
915-594-8533
There is a $30 one time pet fee.

Euless

**La Quinta Inn DFW Airport
West-Euless**
1001 West Airport Freeway
Euless, TX
817-540-0233
Dogs of all sizes are allowed at
the hotel.

Motel 6
110 W Airport Frwy
Euless, TX
817-545-0141
There are no additional pet fees.

Fort Davis

Hotel Limpia
P.O. Box 1341
Fort Davis, TX
800-662-5517
This restored 1912 historic hotel
charges an additional $10 per
day pet charge.

Fort Stockton

Best Western Swiss Clock Inn
3201 W. Dickinson
Fort Stockton, TX
915-336-8521
There are no additional pet fees.

Comfort Inn
3200 W. Dickinson Blvd
Fort Stockton, TX
915-336-8531
There is a pet fee of $5 per day.

Holiday Inn Express
1308 N. Hwy 285
Fort Stockton, TX
915-336-5955
There are no additional pet fees.

Motel 6
3001 W Dickinson Blvd
Fort Stockton, TX
915-336-9737
There are no additional pet fees.
One well-behaved pet is
allowed.

Fort Worth

**Best Western Fort Worth Hotel
& Suites**
2000 Beach Street
Fort Worth, TX
817-534-4801
There is a $25 one time pet fee.
Exit Beach Street from I-30.

Green Oaks Park Hotel
6901 W Frwy
Fort Worth, TX
817-738-7311
There is a $50 refundable pet
deposit.

**La Quinta Inn & Suites Fort
Worth Southwest**

4900 Bryant Irvin Road
Fort Worth, TX
817-370-2700
Dogs up to 55 pounds are
allowed at the hotel.

**La Quinta Inn Fort Worth
West/Medical Center**
7888 I-30 West
Fort Worth, TX
817-246-5511
Dogs of all sizes are allowed at
the hotel.

Motel 6
1236 Oakland Blvd
Fort Worth, TX
817-834-7361
There are no additional pet
fees.

Motel 6
3271 Interstate 35 W
Fort Worth, TX
817-625-4359
There are no additional pet
fees.

Motel 6
6600 S Frwy
Fort Worth, TX
817-293-8595
There are no additional pet
fees. One pet per room is
allowed. Pets must be attended
at all times.

Motel 6
8701 Interstate 30 W
Fort Worth, TX
817-244-9740
There are no additional pet
fees.

Residence Inn by Marriott
1701 S University Dr
Fort Worth, TX
817-870-1011
There is a $5 per day pet fee.

Fredericksburg

Comfort Inn
908 S Adams St
Fredericksburg, TX
830-997-9811
There is no pet fee.

Fulton

Best Western Inn by the Bay
3902 N Hwy 35
Fulton, TX
361-729-8351
There is a $5 per day additional
pet fee.

Galveston

Motel 6
7404 Ave J Broadway
Galveston, TX
409-740-3794
There are no additional pet fees.
Well-behaved pets are allowed.

**Sand 'N Sea Pirates Beach
Vacation Rentals**
13706 FM 3005
Galveston, TX
800-880-2554
They offer several pet-friendly
vacation home rentals.

The Reef Resort
8502 Seawall Blvd.
Galveston, TX
409-740-0492
The weight limit for dogs is
usually 25 pounds, but they can
allow a larger dog if he or she is
well-behaved. There is a $20 per
day pet fee and a $150
refundable pet deposit. There
are no designated smoking or
non-smoking rooms.

Georgetown

Comfort Inn
1005 Leander Rd
Georgetown, TX
512-863-7504
There is a pet fee of $10 per
day.

**Holiday Inn Express Hotel &
Suites**
600 San Gabriel Village Blvd
Georgetown, TX
512-868-8555
There are no additional pet fees.

La Quinta Inn Georgetown

333 N IH 35
Georgetown, TX
512-869-2541
Dogs of all sizes are allowed at the hotel.

Gladewater

Best Western Gladewater
1009 E Broadway
Gladewater, TX
903-845-8003
There is a $20 refundable pet deposit.

Glen Rose

Best Western Dinosaur Valley Inn & Suites
1311 NE Big Bend Trail (Hwy 67)
Glen Rose, TX
254-897-4818
There is a $20 one time pet fee. The entire hotel is non-smoking.

Grand Praire

"La Quinta Inn Dallas - Grand Praire, Six Flags"
1410 NW 19th Street
Grand Praire, TX
972-641-3021
Dogs of all sizes are allowed at the hotel.

Harlingen

Comfort Inn
406 N Expressway 77
Harlingen, TX
956-412-7771
There is a pet fee of $10 per day.

La Quinta Inn Harlingen
1002 S Expressway 83
Harlingen, TX
956-428-6888
Dogs of all sizes are allowed at the hotel.

Hereford

Best Western Red Carpet Inn

830 W 1st Street
Hereford, TX
806-364-0540
There are no additional pet fees.

Houston

Comfort Inn
9041 Westheimer Rd
Houston, TX
713-783-1400
There is a pet fee of $25 per day.

Comfort Suites - Near the Galleria
6221 Richmond Ave
Houston, TX
713-787-0004
There is a one time pet fee of $25.

Doubletree Guest Suites
5353 Westheimer Rd
Houston, TX
713-961-9000
There is a $10 per day pet fee.

Holiday Inn - Airport
15222 John F. Kennedy Blvd
Houston, TX
281-449-2311
There is a $25 one time pet fee.

Holiday Inn Hotel & Suites
7787 Katy Fwy
Houston, TX
713-681-5000
There is a $25 one time pet fee.

Holiday Inn Select
14703 Park Row
Houston, TX
281-558-5580
There is a $150 one time pet fee and a $100 one time pet fee.

Houston - Near the Galleria Drury Inn & Suites
1615 West Loop South
Houston, TX
713-963-0700
Dogs of all sizes are permitted. Pets are not allowed in the breakfast area of the hotel.

Pets are not to be left unattended, and each guest must assume liability for damage of property or other guest complaints. There is a limit of one pet per room.

Houston - West Drury Inn & Suites
1000 North Highway 6
Houston, TX
281-558-7007
Dogs of all sizes are permitted. Pets are not allowed in the breakfast area of the hotel. Pets are not to be left unattended, and each guest must assume liability for damage of property or other guest complaints. There is a limit of one pet per room.

Howard Johnson Express Inn
9604 S Main St.
Houston, TX
713-666-1411
Dogs of all sizes are welcome. There is a $35 one time pet fee.

La Quinta Inn & Suites Houston - Bush Intercontinental
15510 John F Kennedy Blvd.
Houston, TX
281-219-2000
Dogs of all sizes are allowed at the hotel.

La Quinta Inn & Suites Houston Park 10
15225 Katy Freeway
Houston, TX
281-646-9200
Dogs of all sizes are allowed at the hotel.

La Quinta Inn Greenspoint
6 North Belt East
Houston, TX
866-725-1661
Dogs of all sizes are allowed at the hotel.

La Quinta Inn Houston Astrodome
9911 Buffalo Speedway
Houston, TX
713-668-8082
Dogs up to 50 pounds are

allowed at the hotel.

La Quinta Inn Houston Brookhollow
11002 Northwest Freeway
Houston, TX
713-688-2581
Dogs of all sizes are allowed at the hotel.

La Quinta Inn Houston Cyfair
13290 Fm 1960 Road West
Houston, TX
281-469-4018
Dogs up to 50 pounds are allowed at the hotel.

La Quinta Inn Houston East
11999 East Freeway
Houston, TX
713-453-5425
Dogs of all sizes are allowed at the hotel.

La Quinta Inn Houston Hobby Airport
9902 Gulf Freeway
Houston, TX
713-941-0900
Dogs of all sizes are allowed at the hotel.

La Quinta Inn Houston I-45 North
17111 North Freeway
Houston, TX
281-444-7500
Dogs of all sizes are allowed at the hotel.

La Quinta Inn Houston Wilcrest
11113 Katy Freeway
Houston, TX
713-932-0808
Dogs up to 50 pounds are allowed at the hotel.

La Quinta Inn Houston-Greenway Plaza
4015 Southwest Freeway
Houston, TX
713-623-4750
Dogs of all sizes are allowed at the hotel.

Mainstay Suites

12820 NW Freeway
Houston, TX
713-690-4035
There is a non-refundable pet fee of $75.

Motel 6
3223 S Loop W
Houston, TX
713-664-6425
There are no additional pet fees.

Motel 6
14833 Katy Frwy
Houston, TX
281-497-5000
One well-behaved pet per room is allowed.

Staybridge Suites
5190 Hidalgo
Houston, TX
713-355-8888
There is a $75 one time pet fee.

Studio 6
220 Bammel-Westfield Rd
Houston, TX
281-580-2221
There is a $50 one time pet fee.

Studio 6
12700 Featherwood
Houston, TX
281-929-5400
There is a $50 per week additional pet fee.

Studio 6
12827 Southwest Freeway
Houston, TX
281-240-6900
There is a $10 per day or $50 per week additional pet fee.

Studio 6
1255 North Highway 6
Houston, TX
281-579-6959
There is a $10 per day pet fee up to a maximum of $50.

Studio 6
3030 West Sam Houston Pkwy South
Houston, TX
713-785-8550

There is a $50 one time pet fee.

The Lovett Inn
501 Lovett Blvd
Houston, TX
713-522-5224
There is one pet room in this bed and breakfast.

Huntsville

Best Western Sam Houston Inn
613 I-45 South at 1374
Huntsville, TX
936-295-9151
There is a $10 per day additional pet fee.

Holiday Inn Express
201 West Hill Park Circle
Huntsville, TX
936-293-8800
There is a $10 per day pet fee.

La Quinta Inn & Suites Huntsville
124 I.H. 45 North
Huntsville, TX
936-295-6454
Dogs of all sizes are allowed at the hotel.

Motel 6
122 I-45
Huntsville, TX
936-291-6927
There are no additional pet fees. Well-behaved dogs are allowed.

Irving

Dallas - Ft. Worth Airport Drury Inn & Suites
4210 W. Airport Freeway
Irving, TX
972-986-1200
Dogs of all sizes are permitted. Pets are not allowed in the breakfast area of the hotel. Pets are not to be left unattended, and each guest must assume liability for damage of property or other guest complaints. There is a limit of one pet per room.

La Quinta Inn & Suites DFW-Airport North - Irving
4850 West John Carpenter Frwy
Irving, TX
972-915-4022
Dogs up to 50 pounds are allowed at the hotel.

Motel 6
510 S Loop 12
Irving, TX
972-438-4227
There are no additional pet fees.

Staybridge Suites
1201 Executive Circle
Irving, TX
972-465-9400
There is a $75 one time pet fee.

Jasper

Best Western Inn of Jasper
205 W Gibson
Jasper, TX
409-384-7767
There is a $10 per day additional pet fee.

Katy

Best Western Houston West
22455 I-10 West
Katy, TX
281-392-9800
There is a $10 per day additional pet fee.

Killeen

La Quinta Inn Killeen
1112 Fort Hood Street
Killeen, TX
254-526-8331
Dogs of all sizes are allowed at the hotel.

Motel 6
800 E Central TX Expwy
Killeen, TX
254-634-4151
There are no additional pet fees.

Kingsville

Holiday Inn
3430 Hwy 77 S
Kingsville, TX
361-595-5753
There are no additional pet fees.

Motel 6
101 N US 77
Kingsville, TX
361-592-5106
There are no additional pet fees.

Laredo

Best Western Fiesta Inn
5240 San Bernardo
Laredo, TX
956-723-3603
There is a $25 refundable pet deposit.

Family Gardens Inn
5830 San Bernardo
Laredo, TX
956-723-5300
They have onsite kennels available if you need to leave your room during the day and can't bring your pup with you. There is a $50 refundable pet deposit. You have to provide your own locks for the kennels.

La Quinta Inn Laredo
3610 Santa Ursula
Laredo, TX
956-722-0511
Dogs of all sizes are allowed at the hotel.

Motel 6
5920 San Bernardo Ave
Laredo, TX
956-722-8133
There are no additional pet fees. Well-behaved dogs are welcome.

Motel 6
5310 San Bernardo Ave
Laredo, TX
956-725-8187
There are no additional pet fees. One pet per room is allowed and pets must be

attended at all times.

Lewisville

Comfort Suites
755A Vista Ridge Mall Dr
Lewisville, TX
972-315-6464
There is a non-refundable pet fee of $50.

Motel 6
1705 Lakepointe Dr
Lewisville, TX
972-436-5008
There are no additional pet fees. A large well-behaved dog is okay.

Longview

Motel 6
110 S Access Rd
Longview, TX
903-758-5256
There are no additional pet fees. Well-behaved dogs are allowed.

Lubbock

Best Western Lubbock Windsor Inn
5410 Interstate 27
Lubbock, TX
806-762-8400
There is a $25 refundable pet deposit and a $6 per day additional pet fee.

La Quinta Inn Lubbock Medical Center
4115 Brownfield Highway
Lubbock, TX
806-792-0065
Dogs of all sizes are allowed at the hotel.

Residence Inn by Marriott
2551 S Loop 289
Lubbock, TX
806-745-1963
There is a $50 one time pet charge.

Lufkin

Accommodations - Please always call ahead to make sure an establishment is still dog-friendly.

Holiday Inn
4306 S. 1st Street
Lufkin, TX
936-639-3333
There is a $10 per day additional pet fee.

Motel 6
1110 S Timberland Dr
Lufkin, TX
936-637-7850
There are no additional pet fees.

Marshall

Motel 6
300 I-20E
Marshall, TX
903-935-4393
There are no additional pet fees.

McAllen

Drury Inn
612 W. Expressway 83
McAllen, TX
956-687-5100
Dogs of all sizes are permitted. Pets are not allowed in the breakfast area of the hotel. Pets are not to be left unattended, and each guest must assume liability for damage of property or other guest complaints. There is a limit of one pet per room.

La Quinta Inn McAllen
1100 South 10th Street
McAllen, TX
956-687-1101
Dogs of all sizes are allowed at the hotel.

Posada Ana Inn
620 W. Expressway 83
McAllen, TX
956-631-6700
Dogs of all sizes are permitted. Pets are not allowed in the breakfast area of the hotel. Pets are not to be left unattended, and each guest must assume liability for damage of property or other guest complaints. There is a limit of one pet per room.

Midland

Best Western
3904 W Wall
Midland, TX
915-694-7774
There are no additional pet fees.

La Quinta Inn Midland
4130 West Wall Avenue
Midland, TX
432-697-9900
Dogs of all sizes are allowed at the hotel.

Motel 6
1000 S Midkiff Rd
Midland, TX
915-697-3197
There are no additional pet fees.

Super 8 Motel
1000 West I-20
Midland, TX
915-684-8888
There is a $5 per day pet charge.

Mount Pleasant

Best Western Mt Pleasant Inn
102 E Burton Street
Mount Pleasant, TX
903-577-7377
Exit Hwy 271 from I-30. There is a $10 per day additional pet fee.

Nacogdoches

Comfort Inn
3400 South Street
Nacogdoches, TX
936-569-8100
There is a one time pet fee of $10.

New Braunfels

Holiday Inn
1051 I-35 E.
New Braunfels, TX
830-625-8017
There is a $15 one time pet fee.

Motel 6
1275 IH-35
New Braunfels, TX
830-626-0600
There are no additional pet fees. Well-behaved pets are allowed.

North Richland Hills

Motel 6
7804 Bedford Euless Rd
North Richland Hills, TX
817-485-3000
There are no additional pet fees. Pets must be attended at all times.

Studio 6
7450 Northeast Loop 820
North Richland Hills, TX
817-788-6000
There is a $10 per day additional pet fee to a maximum of $50 per visit.

Odessa

Best Western Garden Oasis
110 West Interstate 20
Odessa, TX
915-337-3006
Exit 116 off of I-20

Holiday Inn Hotel & Suites
6201 E. Bus I-20
Odessa, TX
915-362-2311
Dogs are allowed in the rooms with exterior entrances.

La Quinta Inn Odessa
5001 E. Highway 80
Odessa, TX
915-333-2820
Dogs of all sizes are allowed at the hotel.

Orange

Motel 6
4407 27th St
Orange, TX
409-883-4891
There are no additional pet fees.

Paris

Best Western Inn of Paris
3755 North East Loop 286
Paris, TX
903-785-5566
There are no additional pet fees.

Pecos

Best Western Swiss Clock Inn
900 West Palmer Street
Pecos, TX
915-447-2215
There are no additional pet fees.

Motel 6
3002 S Cedar St
Pecos, TX
915-445-9034
There are no additional pet fees.

Plainview

Best Western Conestoga
600 North I-27
Plainview, TX
806-293-9454
There is a $10 per day additional
pet fee.

Plano

Comfort Inn
621 Central Parkway E.
Plano, TX
972-424-5568
There is a one time pet fee of
$20.

La Quinta Inn Dallas - Plano
1820 North Central Expressway
Plano, TX
972-423-1300
Dogs of all sizes are allowed at
the hotel.

Port Arthur

Studio 6
3000 Jimmy Johnson
Port Arthur, TX
800-466-8356
There are no additional pet fees.
One well-behaved pet per room

is allowed. Pets must be
attended at all times.

Portland

Comfort Inn
1703 North Highway 181
Portland, TX
361-643-2222
There is a $5 per day pet fee.

Roanoke

Comfort Suites
801 W Hwy 114
Roanoke, TX
817-490-1455
There is a one time pet fee of
$10.

Sleep Inn & Suites Speedway
13471 Raceway Dr
Roanoke, TX
817-491-3120
There is a refundable pet
deposit of $100.

Rosenberg

**Holiday Inn Express Hotel &
Suites**
27927 S.W. Freeway
Rosenberg, TX
281-342-7888
There is a $20 one time pet fee.

Round Rock

La Quinta Inn Round Rock
2004 North I-35
Round Rock, TX
512-255-6666
Dogs of all sizes are allowed at
the hotel.

San Angelo

**Holiday Inn - Convention
Center**
441 Rio Concho Drive
San Angelo, TX
915-658-2828
There is a $25 one time pet fee.

La Quinta Inn San Angelo

Conference Center
2307 Loop 306
San Angelo, TX
915-949-0515
Dogs of all sizes are allowed at
the hotel.

San Antonio

Best Western Ingram Park Inn
6855 Northwest Loop 410
San Antonio, TX
210-520-8080
There is a refundable pet
deposit.

Clarion Suites Hotel
13101 E Loop 1604 N
San Antonio, TX
210-655-9491
There is a pet deposit of $25 for
a stay of 30 days or less. For a
stay of 30 days or more there is
a pet deposit of $100.

Comfort Inn
4403 I-10 e
San Antonio, TX
210-333-9430
There is a one time pet fee of
$10.

Comfort Inn Airport
2635 N. E. Loop 410
San Antonio, TX
210-653-9110
There is a refundable pet
deposit of $25.

Days Inn
1500 S. Laredo St.
San Antonio, TX
210-271-3334
There is a $10 one time per stay
pet fee.

Holiday Inn
318 W. Durango Blvd
San Antonio, TX
210-225-3211
There is a $125 refundable pet
deposit and a $25 one time pet
fee.

Holiday Inn - Riverwalk
217 North St. Mary's St.
San Antonio, TX

Accommodations - Please always call ahead to make sure an establishment is still dog-friendly.

210-224-2500
There is a $100 refundable pet deposit and a $25 one time pet fee.

Holiday Inn Express
9411 Wurzbach Rd
San Antonio, TX
210-561-9300
There are no additional pet fees.

Holiday Inn Riverwalk
217 St. Mary's St.
San Antonio, TX
210-224-2500
There is a $25 one time pet fee.

Holiday Inn Select
77 NE Loop 410
San Antonio, TX
210-349-9900
There is a $125 refundable pet deposit and a $25 one time pet fee.

Howard Johnson Express Inn
2755 IH-35N
San Antonio, TX
210-229-9220
Dogs of all sizes are welcome. There is a $20 one time pet fee.

La Quinta Inn & Suites San Antonio Airport
850 Halm Blvd.
San Antonio, TX
210-342-3738
Dogs of all sizes are allowed at the hotel.

La Quinta Inn I-35 North at Windsor Park
6410 N IH 35
San Antonio, TX
210-653-6619
Dogs of all sizes are allowed at the hotel.

La Quinta Inn San Antonio Lackland
6511 Military Drive West
San Antonio, TX
210-674-3200
Dogs up to 50 pounds are allowed at the hotel.

La Quinta Inn San Antonio

Wurzbach
9542 I-10 West
San Antonio, TX
210-593-0338
Dogs of all sizes are allowed at the hotel.

La Quinta Inn San Antonio-Convention Center
1001 East Commerce Street
San Antonio, TX
210-222-9181
Dogs of all sizes are allowed at the hotel.

La Quinta Inn Seaworld/Ingram Park
7134 NW Loop 410
San Antonio, TX
210-680-8883
Dogs of all sizes are allowed at the hotel.

Motel 6
138 N WW White Rd
San Antonio, TX
210-333-1850
There are no additional pet fees. One well-behaved pet per room is allowed. Pets must be attended at all times.

Motel 6
16500 IH-10 W
San Antonio, TX
210-697-0731
There are no additional pet fees.

Motel 6
7719 Louis Pasteur Court
San Antonio, TX
210-349-3100
There is a $10 per day pet fee up to a maximum of $50 per visit.

Motel 6
2185 SW Loop 410
San Antonio, TX
210-673-9020
There are no additional pet fees. One well-behaved pet of any size is allowed per room. Pets must be attended at all times.

Motel 6 - Ft Sam Houston

5522 N Pan Am Expwy
San Antonio, TX
210-661-8791
There are no additional pet fees. Pets must be attended at all times.

Motel 6 - Med Center
9400 Wurzbach Rd
San Antonio, TX
210-593-0013
There are no additional pet fees.

Motel 6 - North
9503 Interstate Hwy 35 N
San Antonio, TX
210-650-4419
There are no additional pet fees. Pets must be attended at all times.

Motel 6 - Northeast
4621 E Rittiman Rd
San Antonio, TX
210-653-8088
There are no additional pet fees. One pet per room is allowed. Pets must be attended at all times.

Motel 6 - Riverwalk
211 N Pecos St
San Antonio, TX
210-225-1111
There are no additional pet fees.

Quality Inn & Suites
222 South WW White Rd
San Antonio, TX
210-359-7200
There is a one time pet fee of $20.

Quality Inn NW Medical Center
6023 IH 10 west
San Antonio, TX
210-736-1900
There is a one time pet fee of $25.

Residence Inn by Marriott-Downtown
628 S Santa Rosa
San Antonio, TX
210-231-6000
This inn is 1.2 miles from the Alamo and .5 miles from the Riverwalk. There is a $5 per day

pet charge and a $50 one time pet charge.

Staybridge Suites
4320 Spectrum One Rd
San Antonio, TX
210-558-9009
There is a $75 one time pet fee.

Staybridge Suites - Airport
66 NE Loop 410
San Antonio, TX
210-341-3220
There is a $75 one time pet fee.

Studio 6
11802 IH 10 West
San Antonio, TX
210-691-0121
There is a $10 per day pet fee not to exceed a maximum of $50. One pet per room is permitted.

San Marcos

Motel 6
1321 I-35 N
San Marcos, TX
512-396-8705
There are no additional pet fees. One pet per room is allowed.

Seguin

Best Western of Seguin
1603 I-10/Hwy 46
Seguin, TX
830-379-9631
Use Hwy 46 exit on I-10. There is a $10 per day additional pet fee.

Holiday Inn
2950 N. Hwy 123 Bypass
Seguin, TX
830-372-0860
There are no additional pet fees.

Sherman

Comfort Suites
2900 Hwy 75 N
Sherman, TX
903-893-0499
There is a one time pet fee of

$10.

Holiday Inn
3605 Hwy 75 S.
Sherman, TX
903-868-0555
There is a $20 refundable pet deposit.

Sinton

Best Western Sinton
8108 Highway 77
Sinton, TX
361-364-2882
There are no additional pet fees.

Sonora

Best Western Sonora Inn
270 Highway 277 North
Sonora, TX
915-387-9111
Exit off of I-10 at Hwy 277.
There is a $10 per day additional pet fee.

South Padre Island

Best Western Fiesta Isles Hotel
5701 Padre Blvd
South Padre Island, TX
956-761-4913
There is a $25 refundable pet deposit.

Econo Lodge
3813 Padre Blvd.
South Padre Island, TX
956-761-8500
There is a $25 per day pet charge.

Island Inn
5100 Gulf Blvd.
South Padre Island, TX
956-761-7677
There is a $10 per day pet fee.

Motel 6
4013 Padre Blvd
South Padre Island, TX
956-761-7911
Well-behaved pets are allowed.

Naturally's Beach House Suites
5712 Padre Blvd.
South Padre Island, TX
956-761-8750
They offer pet-friendly condos and vacation home rentals.

Stephenville

Holiday Inn
2865 W. Washington
Stephenville, TX
254-968-5256
There are no additional pet fees.

Sulphur Springs

Holiday Inn
1495 E. Industrial Dr
Sulphur Springs, TX
903-885-0562
There is a $30 refundable pet deposit.

Temple

La Quinta Inn Temple
1604 West Barton Avenue
Temple, TX
254-771-2980
Dogs of all sizes are allowed at the hotel.

Texarkana

Best Western Northgate Motor Lodge
400 W 53rd Street
Texarkana, TX
903-793-6565
There is a $20 one time pet fee.

Comfort Inn
5105 Stateline Ave
Texarkana, TX
903-792-6688
There is a non-refundable pet fee of $25.

La Quinta Inn Texarkana
5201 State Line Avenue
Texarkana, TX
903-794-1900

Dogs up to 75 pounds are allowed at the hotel.

Motel 6
1924 Hampton Rd
Texarkana, TX
903-793-1413
There are no additional pet fees.

Houston - The Woodlands
Drury Inn & Suites
28099 I-45 North
The Woodlands, TX
281-362-7222
Dogs of all sizes are permitted. Pets are not allowed in the breakfast area of the hotel. Pets are not to be left unattended, and each guest must assume liability for damage of property or other guest complaints. There is a limit of one pet per room.

La Quinta Inn Houston
Woodlands North
28673 Interstate 45 N
The Woodlands, TX
281-367-7722
Dogs of all sizes are allowed at the hotel.

Holiday Inn
3310 Troup Hwy
Tyler, TX
903-593-3600
There is a $20 one time pet fee.

Holiday Inn
920 E. Main
Uvalde, TX
830-278-4511
There are no additional pet fees.

Best Western American Inn
1309 W. Broadway
Van Horn, TX
915-283-2030

There are no additional pet fees.

Best Western Inn of Van Horn
1705 W. Broadway, Box 309
Van Horn, TX
915-283-2410
There are no additional pet fees.

Comfort Inn
1601 W Broadway St
Van Horn, TX
915-283-2211
There is a pet fee of $10 per day.

Motel 6
1805 West Broadway
Van Horn, TX
915-283-2992
There are no additional pet fees.

Comfort Inn
1906 Houston Hwy
Victoria, TX
361-574-9393
There is a refundable pet deposit of $25.

La Quinta Inn Victoria
7603 North Navarro
Victoria, TX
361-572-3585
Dogs of all sizes are allowed at the hotel.

Days Inn
1504 Interstate Highway 35 North
Waco, TX
254-799-8585
There is a $10 per day pet charge.

Holiday Inn
1001 MLK Jr. Blvd
Waco, TX
254-753-0261
There is a $25 one time pet fee.

Best Western Santa Fe Inn
1927 Santa Fe Drive
Weatherford, TX
817-594-7401
Use Exit 409 off of I-20. There is a $10 per day additional pet fee.

La Quinta Inn & Suites
Weatherford
1915 Wall Street
Weatherford, TX
817-594-4481
Dogs of all sizes are allowed at the hotel.

Motel 6
1001 W NASA Rd 1
Webster, TX
281-332-4581
There are no additional pet fees.

Best Western Palm Aire Motor Inn
415 S. International Blvd
Weslaco, TX
956-969-2411
There are no additional pet fees.

Best Western Towne Crest Inn
1601 Eighth Street
Wichita Falls, TX
940-322-1182
There is a $10 per day additional pet fee.

Comfort Inn
1750 Maurine St
Wichita Falls, TX
940-322-2477
There is a pet fee of $10 per day.

La Quinta Inn Wichita Falls
1128 Central Freeway North
Wichita Falls, TX
940-322-6971
Dogs of all sizes are allowed at the hotel.

Motel 6
1812 Maurine St
Wichita Falls, TX
940-322-8817
There are no additional pet fees.
Pets must be well-behaved and
attended at all times.

Utah Listings

Beaver

**Best Western Butch Cassidy
Inn**
161 South Main, PO Box 897
Beaver, UT
435-438-2438
There is a $20 refundable pet
deposit.

Blanding

Best Western Gateway Inn
88 E Center
Blanding, UT
435-678-2278
There are no additional pet fees.

Four Corners Inn
131 E Center St
Blanding, UT
435-678-3257
There are no additional pet fees.
Dogs are not allowed on the
beds.

Brigham City

Howard Johnson Inn
1167 S Main St.
Brigham City, UT
435-723-8511
Dogs of all sizes are welcome.
There are no additional pet fees.

Bryce Canyon

Best Western Ruby Inn
Utah Highway 63
Bryce Canyon, UT
435-834-5341
Dogs are allowed in the

standard rooms.

Delta

Best Western Motor Inn
527 East Topaz Blvd
Delta, UT
435-864-3882
There is a $10 refundable pet
deposit.

Fillmore

**Best Western Paradise Inn
and Resort**
805 N Main
Fillmore, UT
435-743-6895
There are no additional pet
fees.

Green River

Motel 6
946 E Main, Box 358
Green River, UT
435-564-3436
There are no additional pet
fees. Pets under 60 pounds are
allowed.

Hurricane

**Best Western Lamplighter
Inn**
280 West State
Hurricane, UT
435-635-4647
There is a $10 per day
additional pet fee.

Kanab

Holiday Inn Express
815 E. Hwy 89
Kanab, UT
435-644-8888
There is a $10 per day pet fee.

Parry Lodge
89 East Center Street
Kanab, UT
435-644-2601
There are 3 non-smoking pet
rooms. There is a $5 per day

pet fee.

Shilo Inn
296 West 100 North
Kanab, UT
435-644-2562
There is a $10 one time pet fee.

Lehi

Best Western Timpanogos Inn
195 South 850 East
Lehi, UT
801-768-1400
There is a $10 per day additional
pet fee.

Motel 6
210 S 1200 E
Lehi, UT
801-768-2668
There are no additional pet fees.

Moab

Apache Hotel
166 S 400 East
Moab, UT
435-259-5727
There is a 1 dog limit per room.
There are no additional pet fees.

Bowen Motel
169 N Main St
Moab, UT
435-259-7132
There is a $5 per day pet fee.

Moab Valley Inn
711 S Main St
Moab, UT
435-259-4419
There are no additional pet fees.

Motel 6
1089 North Main St
Moab, UT
435-259-6686
There are no additional pet fees.

The Gonzo Inn
100 W 200 S Moab Utah
Moab, UT
435-259-2515
All rooms are non-smoking.
There is a $25 one time per stay

pet fee.

Nephi

Best Western Paradise Inn of Nephi
1025 S. Main
Nephi, UT
435-623-0624
There are no additional pet fees.

Ogden

Best Western High Country Inn
1335 W 12th St
Ogden, UT
801-394-9474
There are no additional pet fees.

Comfort Suites of Ogden
1150 W. 2150 S.
Ogden, UT
801-621-2545
There is a $30 refundable pet deposit.

Holiday Inn Express Hotel & Suites
2245 S. 1200 West
Ogden, UT
801-392-5000
There are no additional pet fees.

Motel 6
1455 Washington Blvd
Ogden, UT
801-627-4560
There are no additional pet fees. Pets must be attended at all times.

Orem

La Quinta Inn Orem
1100 West 780 North
Orem, UT
801-235-9555
Dogs of all sizes are allowed at the hotel.

Panguitch

Bryce Junction Inn
3090 E Highway 12 & Jct 89

Panguitch, UT
435-676-2221
This hotel is open from March 15 to Nov 15. There are no additional pet fees.

Park City

Best Western Landmark Inn
6560 N Landmark Drive
Park City, UT
435-649-7300
There is a $10 per day additional pet fee.

Holiday Inn Express Hotel & Suites
1501 W. Ute Blvd
Park City, UT
435-658-1600
There is a $50 refundable pet deposit. Pet owners must sign a pet waiver.

Radisson Park City
2121 Park Ave
Park City, UT
435-649-5000
There is a $15 per day pet fee.

The Gables Hotel
1335 Lowell Avenue, PO Box 905
Park City, UT
435-655-3315
Pets receive a Pet Gift basket upon arrival. The Gables Hotel features 20 one bedroom condominiums and one or two bedroom penthouse suites each with a queen or king bed in the master bedroom, fully equipped kitchen, living area with a queen sofa sleeper, dining area, fireplace, balcony and bathroom with an oversized jetted tub. Property amenities include an outdoor jacuzzi, sauna and laundry facilities. Rates start at $85.00 per night. There is a $20 per night additional pet fee. There is a $100 refundable pet deposit upon arrival.

Parowan

Best Western Swiss Village Inn
580 N Main
Parowan, UT
435-477-3391
There is a $5 per day additional pet fee. Pets may not be left alone in the room.

Price

National 9
641 W. Price River Drive
Price, UT
435-637-7000
There is a $5 per day pet fee.

Provo

La Quinta Inn Provo - BYU / Orem
1555 Canyon Road
Provo, UT
801-374-6020
Dogs up to 75 pounds are allowed at the hotel.

Motel 6
1600 S University Ave
Provo, UT
801-375-5064
Pets must be attended at all times.

Richfield

Best Western Apple Tree Inn
145 South Main
Richfield, UT
435-896-5481
There is a $6 per day additional pet fee.

Roosevelt

Frontier Motel
75 S 200 E
Roosevelt, UT
435-722-2201
There are no additional pet fees.

Salt Lake City

Days Inn - Salt Lake City Airport

1900 W N Temple
Salt Lake City, UT
801-539-8538
There are 2 pet rooms. There
are no additional pet fees.

Hotel Monaco Salt Lake City
15 West 200 South
Salt Lake City, UT
801-595-0000
Well-behaved dogs of all sizes
are welcome at this pet-friendly
hotel. The luxury boutique hotel
offers both rooms and suites.
Hotel amenities include
complimentary evening wine
service, 24 hour room service
and a 24 hour on-site fitness
room. There are no pet fees, just
sign a pet liability form.

Motel 6
1990 W N Temple St
Salt Lake City, UT
801-364-1053
There are no additional pet fees.

Motel 6 - Downtown
176 W 6th S St
Salt Lake City, UT
801-531-1252
There are no additional pet fees.

Ramada Inn
230 W 600 S
Salt Lake City, UT
801-364-5200
There is a $10 per day pet fee.

**Salt Lake City Centre
Travelodge**
524 S West Temple
Salt Lake City, UT
801-531-7100
There is a $10 per day pet fee.

Springdale

Driftwood Lodge
1515 Zion Park Blvd
Springdale, UT
435-772-3262
There is a $10 one time pet fee.

Springville

Best Western Cotton Tree Inn
1455 N 1750 West
Springville, UT
801-489-3641
There is a $10 per day
additional pet fee.

St George

Days Inn
150 N 1000 E
St George, UT
435-673-6123
There is a $10 per day
additional pet fee.

Holiday Inn
850 S. Bluff St
St George, UT
435-628-4235
There are no additional pet
fees.

Motel 6
205 N 1000 E St
St George, UT
435-628-7979
There are no additional pet
fees. One pet per room is
allowed.

Vernal

Motel 6
1092 W Highway 40
Vernal, UT
435-789-0666
There is a $5 per day additional
pet fee.

Sage Motel
54 W Main St
Vernal, UT
435-789-1442
There is a $5 one time pet fee.

Wendover

Motel 6
561 E Wendover Blvd
Wendover, UT
435-665-2267
There are no additional pet
fees. Pets must be well-
behaved and attended at all
times.

Vermont Listings

Bennington

South Gate Motel
US 7S
Bennington, VT
802-447-7525
There is a $6 per day pet fee.

Brattleboro

Motel 6
1254 Putney Rd, Rt 5N
Brattleboro, VT
802-254-6007
There are no additional pet fees.

Burlington

Residence Inn by Marriott
1 Hurricane Lane
Burlington, VT
802-878-2001
There is a $20 per day pet fee
for the first 14 days.

**Sheraton Burlington Hotel and
Conference Center**
870 Williston Road
Burlington, VT
802-865-6600
Dogs up to 80 pounds are
allowed. There is a $25 per day
pet fee.

Colchester

**Hampton Inn and Conference
Center**
8 Mountain View Dr
Colchester, VT
802-655-6177
There are no additional pet fees.

Motel 6
74 South Park Dr
Colchester, VT
802-654-6860
There are no additional pet fees.

Craftsbury Common

Inn on the Common
Main Street
Craftsbury Common, VT
802-586-9619
There is a $15 one time fee per pet.

Essex

The Inn at Essex
70 Essex Way
Essex, VT
802-878-1100
A luxury hotel featuring the acclaimed New England Culinary Institute. There is a $25 per night pet fee. There is a $300 fully refundable pet-damage deposit required.

Killington

The Cortina Inn and Resort
Route 4
Killington, VT
800-451-6108
This inn caters to pets. They have pet treats on arrival and make your pet feel welcome. There is a $10 per day additional pet fee.

Rutland

Holiday Inn
476 US Route 7 South
Rutland, VT
802-775-1911
There is a $10 per day additonal pet fee. Pets may not be left alone in the room.

S. Burlington

Holiday Inn
1068 Williston Rd
S. Burlington, VT
802-863-6363
There is a $10 one time pet fee. Pets must be attended at all times.

South Burlington

Best Western Windjammer Inn & Conf Ctr
1076 Williston Rd
South Burlington, VT
802-863-1125
There is a $5 per day additional pet fee.

South Woodstock

Kedron Valley Inn
Rt 106
South Woodstock, VT
802-457-1473
This very pet-friendly inn does not allow dogs in the main dining room, but they do allow your well-behaved best friend in the living room and the bar. The bar area has a cozy fireplace. There are no pet fees. There are no designated smoking or non-smoking rooms.

St Johnsbury

Aime's Motel
RR 1, Box 332
St Johnsbury, VT
802-748-3194
There are no additional pet fees.

Fairbanks Inn
401 Western Ave
St Johnsbury, VT
802-748-5666
There is a $5 per day pet fee.

Stowe

Andersen Lodge - An Austrian Inn
3430 Mountain Road
Stowe, VT
802-253-7336
The lodge is open from May 30 to October 25 each year. There are no additional pet fees.

Commodores Inn
823 South Main St
Stowe, VT
802-253-7131

There are no additional pet fees.

Ten Acres Lodge
14 Barrows Rd
Stowe, VT
802-253-7638
Dogs are welcome in the cottages. There are no additional pet fees.

The Mountain Road Resort
1007 Mountain Rd
Stowe, VT
802-253-4566
There is a $15 one time pet fee. Maximum of 1 pet per room.

White River Junction

Best Western at the Junction
Rt 5 & I-91
White River Junction, VT
802-295-3015
There is a $10 per day additional pet fee.

Virginia Listings

Alexandria

Comfort Inn - Mount Vernon
7212 Richmond Highway
Alexandria, VA
703-765-9000
There is a $20 per night pet fee (per pet per day). There is a $50 refundable pet deposit. There is a 2 pet limit per room. Please call for availability as there are a limited number of pet rooms.

Holiday Inn - Telegraph Rd
2460 Eisenhower Ave
Alexandria, VA
703-960-3400
There are no additional pet fees.

Red Roof Inn
5975 Richmond Highway
Alexandria, VA
703-960-5200
Dogs up to 80 pounds are allowed. There are no additional pet fees.

Arlington

Quality Inn - Iwo Jima
1501 Arlington Blvd
Arlington, VA
703-524-5000
There is a $10 per day pet fee.
Dogs are allowed in rooms with
exterior entrances.

Blacksburg

Clay Corner Inn B&B
401 Clay Street SW
Blacksburg, VA
540-953-2604
There is a $15 per day pet fee.

Comfort Inn
3705 S. Main St.
Blacksburg, VA
540-951-1500
There are no additional pet fees.

Bristol

Holiday Inn Hotel & Suites
3005 Linden Drive
Bristol, VA
276-466-4100
There is a $10 one time pet fee.

La Quinta Inn Bristol
1014 Old Airport Road
Bristol, VA
276-669-9353
Dogs of all sizes are allowed at
the hotel.

Charlottesville

Best Western Mount Vernon
1613 Emmet St, Box 7284
Charlottesville, VA
804-296-5501
Pets may not be left alone in the
rooms.

Holiday Inn
1200 5th Street
Charlottesville, VA
434-977-5100
There is a $7.50 per day
additional pet fee.

Chesapeake

Red Roof Inn
724 Woodlake Dr
Chesapeake, VA
757-523-0123
There are no additional pet
fees.

Town Place Suites
2000 Old Greenbrier Rd
Chesapeake, VA
757-523-5004
There is a $10 per day
additional pet fee.

Christiansburg

Howard Johnson Express Inn
100 Bristol Drive
Christiansburg, VA
540-381-0150
Dogs of all sizes are welcome.
There is a $7 per day pet fee
for small pets and a $10 per
day pet fee for a larger pet.

Clarksville

**Needmoor Inn Bed and
Breakfast**
801 Virginia Avenue
Clarksville, VA
434-374-2866
This Bed and Breakfast Inn is a
Virginia landmark that has
welcomed guests for over a
century. This wonderfully
restored farmhouse style B&B
can be your destination for
recreation and relaxation, or
your place of rest on a longer
journey. The inn has an area
for dogs to play, and many
parks nearby. The owners have
a dog that loves company.
Room rates are approximately
$75.

Covington

Best Value Inn
908 Valley Ridge Drive
Covington, VA
540-962-7600
There is a $10 one time pet

charge.

Best Western Mountain View
820 East Madison Street
Covington, VA
540-962-4951
There is a $10 one time pet
charge.

Comfort Inn
203 Interstate Dr.
Covington, VA
540-962-2141
There is a $10 one time pet
charge.

Daleville

Best Western Coachman Inn
437 Roanoke Rd
Daleville, VA
540-992-1234
There is a $15 one time pet fee
per visit.

Danville

Stratford Inn
2500 Riverside Dr
Danville, VA
434-793-2500
There is a $25 one time pet fee.

Emporia

Best Western Emporia
1100 W Atlantic St
Emporia, VA
434-634-3200
There is a $10 one time pet fee.

Comfort Inn
1411 Skippers Rd
Emporia, VA
434-348-3282
There are no additional pet fees.

Hampton Inn
1207 W Atlantic St
Emporia, VA
434-634-9481
There is an $8 per day additional
pet fee.

Holiday Inn
311 Florida Ave

Accommodations - Please always call ahead to make sure an establishment is still dog-friendly.

Emporia, VA
434-634-4191
There are no additional pet fees.

Fairfax

Comfort Inn University Center
11180 Main St
Fairfax, VA
703-591-5900
Pets are welcome and there are
no pet fees.

Holiday Inn Fair Oaks - Fairfax
11787 Lee Jackson Memorial
Hwy
Fairfax, VA
703-352-2525
There is a $25 non-refundable
pet fee per stay.

Fredericksburg

**Days Inn Fredericksburg
North**
14 Simpson Rd
Fredericksburg, VA
540-373-5340
There is a $5 per day pet fee.

Motel 6
401 Warrenton Rd
Fredericksburg, VA
540-371-5443
Large dogs that are well-
behaved are ok. There are no
additional pet fees.

Quality Inn
543 Warrenton Rd
Fredericksburg, VA
540-373-0000
There is an $8 per day pet fee.

Ramada Inn
2802 Plank Rd
Fredericksburg, VA
540-786-8361
There is a $15 one time pet fee.

Front Royal

Bluemont Inn
1525 N. Shenandoah Ave.
Front Royal, VA
540-635-9447

They have several pet rooms.
There are no additional pet
fees.

Super 8 Motel
111 South St.
Front Royal, VA
540-636-4888
There is a $10 per day pet
charge.

Hampton

Candlewood Suites
401 Butler Farm Rd
Hampton, VA
757-766-8976
There is a $75 one time pet fee.

**La Quinta Inn Norfolk -
Hampton**
2138 West Mercury Boulevard
Hampton, VA
757-827-8680
Dogs of all sizes are allowed at
the hotel.

Harrisonburg

Comfort Inn
1440 E Market St
Harrisonburg, VA
540-433-6066
There are no additional pet
fees.

Motel 6
10 Linda Ln
Harrisonburg, VA
540-433-6939
There are no additional pet
fees.

Sheraton Four Points Hotel
1400 E Market St
Harrisonburg, VA
540-433-2521
There are no additional pet
fees.

Herndon

Residence Inn by Marriott
315 Elden St
Herndon, VA
703-435-0044

There is a $100 one time pet fee
plus $6 per day.

Hillsville

Holiday Inn Express
85 Airport Road
Hillsville, VA
276-728-2120
There is a $5 per day additional
pet fee.

Lexington

**Best Western Inn at Hunt
Ridge**
Route 7, Box 99A
Lexington, VA
540-464-1500
There is a $25 one time pet fee.

Holiday Inn Express
850 North Lee Hwy, US 11
North at I-64.
Lexington, VA
540-463-7351
There is a $15 one time pet fee.
Pet owners must also sign a pet
waiver.

Howard Johnson Inn
2836 N. Lee Hwy.
Lexington, VA
540-463-9181
Dogs of all sizes are welcome.
There is a $5 per day pet fee.

Ramada Inn
U.S. Highway 11 and Interstate
Highway 81
Lexington, VA
540-463-6400
There is an $8 per day pet fee
per pet.

Luray

Best Western of Luray
410 W. Main St.
Luray, VA
540-743-6511
There is a $20 per day additional
pet fee. There is a limit of one
pet per room.

379

Lynchburg

Comfort Inn
3125 Albert Lankford Dr
Lynchburg, VA
434-847-9041
At US 29 and Odd Fellows Rd.
There is a $25 refundable pet
deposit.

Holiday Inn Select
601 Main Street
Lynchburg, VA
434-528-2500
There is a $25 one time pet fee.

Howard Johnson Inn
5016 S Amherst Hwy
Lynchburg, VA
434-845-7041
Dogs of all sizes are welcome.
There is a $10 one time pet fee.

Manassas

Red Roof Inn
10610 Automotive Dr
Manassas, VA
703-335-9333
There are no additional pet fees.

Marion

Best Western Marion
1424 North Main Street
Marion, VA
276-783-3193
There is a $25 refundable pet
deposit.

Martinsville

Super 8 Motel
1044 N. Memorial Boulevard
Martinsville, VA
276-666-8888
There are no additional pet fees.

Mount Jackson

**Best Western Shenandoah
Valley**
250 Conicville Rd, I-81 Exit 273
Mount Jackson, VA
540-477-2911

There is a $10 per day
additional pet fee.

New Church

**The Garden and the Sea Inn
Bed and Breakfast**
4188 Nelson Road
New Church, VA
757-824-0672
"Our Guests are welcome to
bring their pets." Escape to the
Garden and the Sea Inn for an
elegant, yet casual, respite.
Whether you're looking for a
romantic, candlelight getaway
or just a quiet, relaxed
atmosphere to return to at the
end of a day at the beach or
visiting some of the Eastern
Shore's charming, quaint towns
and marinas, the Garden and
the Sea Inn provides just the
right combination of personal
attention and Victorian
ambiance. The only
requirements are that your dog
needs to be leashed and
should be quiet when inside the
inn. There are no additional pet
fees.

Newport News

Comfort Inn
12330 Jefferson Ave
Newport News, VA
757-249-0200
There is a $10 per day
additional pet fee. Dogs are not
allowed in the lobby area
during breakfast hours.

Days Inn - Oyster Point
11829 Fishing Point Dr
Newport News, VA
757-873-6700
There is a $10 per day pet fee.

Motel 6
797 J Clyde-Morris Blvd
Newport News, VA
757-595-6336
There are no additional pet
fees.

Norfolk

Econo Lodge
9601 4th View St
Norfolk, VA
757-480-9611
There is a $5 per day pet fee.

Motel 6
853 N Military Hwy
Norfolk, VA
757-461-2380
A large well-behaved dog is
okay.

Quality Inn - Lake Wright
6280 Northampton Blvd
Norfolk, VA
757-461-6251
There is a $25 one time pet fee.

Norton

Holiday Inn
551 Hwy 58 E.
Norton, VA
276-679-7000
There are no additional pet fees.

Petersburg

Comfort Inn
11974 S Crater St
Petersburg, VA
804-732-2900
There is a $5 per day pet fee per
pet.

Days Inn
12208 S Crater Rd
Petersburg, VA
804-733-4400
There is a $10 per day pet fee.

Portsmouth

Holiday Inn
8 Crawford Pkwy
Portsmouth, VA
757-393-2573
There are no additional pet fees.

Richmond

Days Inn

2100 Dickens Rd
Richmond, VA
804-282-3300
There is a $5 per day pet fee.

Holiday Inn
4303 Commerce Rd
Richmond, VA
804-275-7891
There are no additional pet fees.

Residence Inn by Marriott
2121 Dickens Rd
Richmond, VA
804-285-8200
There is a $50 one time pet fee.

Clarion Hotel Roanoke Airport
2727 Ferndale Dr NW
Roanoke, VA
540-362-4500
There is a $35 per fee for the
first night and $10 for each
additional night.

Days Inn Civic Center
535 Orange Ave
Roanoke, VA
540-342-4551
There is a $10 per day additional
pet fee.

Holiday Inn
4468 Starkey Rd. SW
Roanoke, VA
540-774-4400
There is a $35 one time pet fee.

Howard Johnson Express Inn
23786 Rogers Clark Blvd.
Ruther Glen, VA
804-448-2499
Dogs of all sizes are welcome.
There is a $5 per day pet fee.
Please place a Do Not Disturb
Sign on the door so that
housekeepers do not open the
door while the pet is in the room.

Ramada Inn

1671 Skyview Rd
Salem, VA
540-389-7061
There is a $15 per day pet fee.

**High Meadows Inn Bed and
Breakfast**
55 High Meadows Lane
Scottsville, VA
804-286-2218
They offer 3 pet rooms. There
is a $20 per day pet charge.

Best Western South Hill
Hwy 58 & I-85
South Hill, VA
434-447-3123
There are no additional pet
fees.

Comfort Inn - Springfield
6560 Loisdale Ct
Springfield, VA
703-922-9000
There are no additional pet
fees.

Motel 6
6868 Springfield Blvd
Springfield, VA
703-644-5311
There are no additional pet
fees.

Comfort Inn Tysons Corner
1587 Spring Hill Rd
Vienna, VA
703-448-8020
There is a one time pet fee of
$25. There is also a pet fee of
$10 per day.

**Residence Inn - Tysons
Corner**
8616 Westwood Center Dr
Vienna, VA
703-893-0120

There is a $150 one time pet fee
plus $5 per day.

**La Quinta Inn Norfolk -
Virginia Beach**
192 Newtown Road
Virginia Beach, VA
757-497-6620
Dogs of all sizes are allowed at
the hotel.

Ramada Inn - Airport
5725 Northampton Blvd
Virginia Beach, VA
757-464-9351
There is a $25 one time pet fee.

Red Roof Inn
196 Ballard Court
Virginia Beach, VA
757-490-0225
There are no additional pet fees.

Howard Johnson Inn
6 Broadview Ave.
Warrenton, VA
540-347-4141
Dogs up to 85 pounds are
allowed. There is a $10 per day
pet fee.

Best Western Warsaw
4522 Richmond Rd
Warsaw, VA
804-333-1700
There is a $10 per day additional
pet fee.

**Best Western Colonial Capital
Inn**
111 Penniman Road
Williamsburg, VA
757-253-1222
There is a $10 one time pet fee
per visit.

Best Western Patrick Henry

Inn
249 E. York Street NW
Williamsburg, VA
757-229-9540
There is a $15 one time pet fee per visit. This hotel is within walking distance of Colonial Williamsburg.

Heritage Inn Motel
1324 Richmond Rd.
Williamsburg, VA
757-229-6220
There are no additional pet fees.

Holiday Inn - Colonial District
725 Bypass Rd
Williamsburg, VA
757-220-1776
Pets up to 50 pounds are allowed. There is a $25 one time pet fee.

Motel 6
3030 Richmond Rd
Williamsburg, VA
757-565-3433
There are no additional pet fees. One pet per room is okay. Pets must be attended at all times.

Ramada Inn 1776
725 Bypass Road
Williamsburg, VA
757-220-1776
All well-behaved dogs are welcome at this pet-friendly inn. The inn is located about 1 mile from Colonial Williamsburg. Amenities include a guest laundry and a seasonal pool. There are no pet size restrictions and no pet fees.

Winchester

Best Western Lee-Jackson Motor Inn
711 Millwood Avenue
Winchester, VA
540-662-4154
There is a $5 per day additional pet fee.

Wytheville

Holiday Inn
US 11 I-77/I-81
Wytheville, VA
276-228-5483
There are no additional pet fees.

Washington Listings

Aberdeen

Red Lion Inn
521 W Wishkah
Aberdeen, WA
360-532-5210
There are no additional pet fees.

Anacortes

Anacortes Inn
3006 Commercial Ave
Anacortes, WA
360-293-3153
There is a $10 per night pet fee.

Fidalgo Country Inn
7645 St Route 20
Anacortes, WA
360-293-3494
There is a $20 per day pet charge. There are 2 pet rooms.

Bellingham

Holiday Inn Express
4160 Guide Meridian
Bellingham, WA
360-671-4800
There is a $10 one time pet fee.

Motel 6
3701 Byron
Bellingham, WA
360-671-4494
There are no additional pet fees.

Centralia

Motel 6
1310 Belmont Ave
Centralia, WA
360-330-2057
There are no additional pet fees.

Chehalis

Howard Johnson Inn
122 Interstate Ave.
Chehalis, WA
360-748-0101
Dogs of all sizes are welcome. There is a $10 one time pet fee.

Clarkston

Motel 6
222 Bridge St
Clarkston, WA
509-758-1631
There are no additional pet fees.

Copalis Beach

Iron Springs Ocean Beach Resort
P. O. Box 207
Copalis Beach, WA
360-276-4230
Iron Springs is a 100 acre resort on the Washington Coast located halfway between Copalis and Pacific Beach. They offer individual cottages with fireplaces and great ocean views. The cottages are nestled among the rugged spruce trees on a low lying bluff overlooking the Pacific Ocean. They are located near miles of sandy beaches. There is a $12.00 per day charge for pets. There are no designated smoking or non-smoking cabins. They are located 130 miles from Seattle and 160 miles from Portland.

Everett

Holiday Inn
101 128th St SE
Everett, WA
425-337-2900
There is a $50 one time pet fee.

Motel 6
224 128th St SW
Everett, WA
425-353-8120
There are no additional pet fees.

Federal Way

La Quinta Inn & Suites Federal Way
32124 25th Avenue South
Federal Way, WA
253-529-4000
Dogs of all sizes are allowed at the hotel.

Forks

Kalaloch Ocean Lodge
157151 Hwy. 101
Forks, WA
360-962-2271
Perched on a bluff, overlooking the Pacific Ocean, sits the Kalaloch Lodge located in Olympic National Park. The Olympic National Forest is also located nearby. Dogs are not allowed in the lodge, but they are welcome in the cabins. This resort offers over 40 cabins and half of them have ocean views. There are no designated smoking or non-smoking cabins. Thanks to one of our readers who writes "This is a great place where you can rent cabins situated on a bluff overlooking the Pacific Ocean. Great for watching storms pound the beaches and walking wide sand beaches at low tide. Near rain forest with wooded hikes and lakes throughout. Not all units allow dogs, but you can still get a good view." There is a $12.50 per day pet fee.

Friday Harbor

Blair House Bed and Breakfast
345 Blair Street
Friday Harbor, WA
360-378-5907

Blair House is located in Friday Harbor, Washington on San Juan Island, just five short blocks from the ferry landing. The two acre grounds are wooded and landscaped. The Blair House Cottage is 800 square feet of private living where you, your children and your pets are welcome. You will need to take a car ferry to the island.

The Inn at Friday Harbor

Friday Harbor, WA
360-378-4000
There is a $50.00 one time pet fee. You need to take a car ferry to the island.

Gig Harbor

Best Western Wesley Inn of Gig Harbor
6575 Kimball
Gig Harbor, WA
253-858-9690
There is a $10 per day additional pet fee.

Glacier

Mt. Baker Lodging
7463 Mt. Baker Highway
Glacier, WA
360-599-2453
Private vacation rental homes located at the gateway to Mt. Baker. There are a wide variety of rental homes to choose, from honeymoon getaways and family cabins, to accommodations for group retreats and family reunions. All properties are privately owned, unique and completely self-contained.

Issaquah

Motel 6
1885 15th Pl NW
Issaquah, WA
425-392-8405
There are no additional pet

fees.

Kelso

Motel 6
106 Minor Rd
Kelso, WA
360-425-3229
There are no additional pet fees.

Kennewick

La Quinta Inn & Suites Kennewick
4220 West 27th Place
Kennewick, WA
509-736-3326
Dogs of all sizes are allowed at the hotel.

Kent

Howard Johnson Inn
1233 North Central
Kent, WA
253-852-7224
Dogs of all sizes are welcome. There is a $10 per day pet fee.

La Quinta Inn Kent
25100 74th Avenue South
Kent, WA
253-520-6670
Dogs of all sizes are allowed at the hotel.

Kirkland

Best Western Kirkland Inn
12223 NE 116th St
Kirkland, WA
425-822-2300
There is a $50 refundable pet deposit. There are only a few non-smoking pet rooms so make a reservation early.

La Quinta Inn Bellevue - Kirkland
10530 NE Northup Way
Kirkland, WA
425-828-6585
Dogs up to 75 pounds are allowed at the hotel.

Motel 6
12010 120th Pl NE
Kirkland, WA
425-821-5618
One well-behaved dog is
allowed per room. Pets must be
attended at all times.

Leavenworth

Howard Johnson Express Inn
405 Hwy 2
Leavenworth, WA
509-548-4326
Dogs up to 75 pounds are
allowed. There is a $12 per day
pet fee. Pets may not be left
unattended in the rooms.

Moclips

Ocean Crest Resort
4651 SR 109
Moclips, WA
360-276-4465
There is a $15 per day pet fee.
Pets are allowed in some of the
units. All rooms are non-
smoking.

Moses Lake

**Best Western Hallmark Inn &
Conf Center**
3000 Marina Dr
Moses Lake, WA
509-765-9211
There are no additional pet fees.

Motel 6
2822 Wapato Dr
Moses Lake, WA
509-766-0250
There are no additional pet fees.

Mount Vernon

Best Western College Way Inn
300 W College Way
Mount Vernon, WA
360-424-4287
There is a $10 per day additional
pet fee.

Best Western CottonTree Inn

2300 Market Place
Mount Vernon, WA
360-428-5678
There is a $10 per day
additional pet fee. Pets are
allowed on the first floor rooms
only.

Oak Harbor

Best Western Harbor Place
33175 SR20
Oak Harbor, WA
360-679-4567
There is a $15 per day
additional pet fee.

Ocean Park

**Coastal Cottages of Ocean
Park**
1511 264th Place
Ocean Park, WA
360-665-4658
The cottages are located in a
quiet setting and have full
kitchens and fireplaces. There
is a $5 per day pet charge.
There are no designated
smoking or non-smoking
rooms.

Ocean Shores

**The Polynesian
Condominium Resort**
615 Ocean Shores Blvd
Ocean Shores, WA
360-289-3361
There is a $15 per day fee for
pets. Pets are allowed on the
ground floor only.

Olympia

West Coast Inn
2300 Evergreen Park Drive
Olympia, WA
360-943-4000
There is a $45.00 one time pet
fee.

Pacific Beach

Sandpiper Ocean Beach

Resort
4159 State Route 109
Pacific Beach, WA
360-276-4580
Thanks to one of our readers
who writes "A great place on the
Washington Coast with miles of
sand beach to run." There is a
$10 per day pet fee. All rooms
are non-smoking.

Poulsbo

Holiday Inn Express
19801 7th Avenue NE
Poulsbo, WA
360-697-4400
There is a $10 one time pet fee.

Pullman

Holiday Inn Express
1190 SE Bishop Blvd
Pullman, WA
509-334-4437
There are no additional pet fees.
Pets are allowed in the first floor
rooms.

Richland

Motel 6
1751 Fowler St
Richland, WA
509-783-1250
There are no additional pet fees.

Red Lion Hotel
802 George Washington Way
Richland, WA
509-946-7611
There are no additional pet fees.

Royal Hotel
1515 George Washington Way
Richland, WA
509-946-4121
There is a $25 one time pet fee.

Seattle

Alexis Hotel
1007 First Avenue
Seattle, WA
206-624-4844

Well-behaved dogs up to 200 pounds are welcome at this pet-friendly hotel. The luxury boutique hotel offers both rooms and suites. Hotel amenities include complimentary evening wine service, 24 hour room service and an on-site fitness room. This hotel is located near the historic Pioneer Square and Pike's Place Market. There are no pet fees, just sign a pet liability form.

Crowne Plaza - Downtown
1113 6th Ave
Seattle, WA
206-464-1980
There is a $75 refundable pet deposit. Dogs up to 75 pounds are allowed.

Hotel Monaco Seattle
1101 4th Avenue
Seattle, WA
206-621-1770
Well-behaved dogs of all sizes are welcome at this pet-friendly hotel. The luxury boutique hotel offers both rooms and suites. Hotel amenities include complimentary evening wine service, complimentary high speed Internet access in all guest rooms, 24 hour room service and a 24 hour on-site fitness room. There are no pet fees, just sign a pet liability form.

Hotel Vintage Park
1100 Fifth Avenue
Seattle, WA
206-624-8000
Well-behaved dogs of all sizes are welcome at this pet-friendly hotel. The luxury boutique hotel offers both rooms and suites. Hotel amenities include complimentary evening wine service, complimentary high speed Internet access, and 24 hour room service. There are no pet fees, just sign a pet liability form.

La Quinta Inn & Suites Seattle
2224 Eighth Ave.
Seattle, WA

206-624-6820
Dogs of all sizes are allowed at the hotel.

La Quinta Inn Sea-Tac - Seattle
2824 S 188th St
Seattle, WA
206-241-5211
Dogs of all sizes are allowed at the hotel.

Motel 6
20651 Military Rd
Seattle, WA
206-824-9902
There are no additional pet fees. One well-behaved pet per room is permitted.

Motel 6 - Airport
18900 47th Ave S
Seattle, WA
206-241-1648
There are no additional pet fees.

Pensione Nichols Bed and Breakfast
1923 1st Avenue
Seattle, WA
206-441-7125
Thanks to one of our readers who writes: "A charming and very dog-friendly place to stay in downtown Seattle." Large dogs are allowed to stay here if they are well-behaved. This B&B also requires that you do not leave your dog in the room alone. The Pensione Nichols is the only bed-and-breakfast located in the retail and entertainment core of downtown Seattle. Housed in a remodeled, turn-of-the-century building in the historic Smith Block, Pensione Nichols overlooks the Pike Place Market. This B&B has 10 guest rooms and suites (the suites have private bathrooms). Rates are approximately $75 (guest rooms) to $175 (suites). During the summer, there is a 2 night minimum.

Residence Inn Seattle

Downtown
800 Fairview Ave N
Seattle, WA
206-624-6000
There is a $10 per day pet charge.

The Sheraton Seattle Hotel and Towers
1400 Sixth Avenue
Seattle, WA
206-621-9000
Dogs up to 80 pounds are allowed. There are no additional pet fees. You must sign a pet waiver.

Vagabond Inn by the Space Needle
325 Aurora Ave N
Seattle, WA
206-441-0400
This motel is located just several blocks from the Space Needle, the waterfront and Washington St. Convention Center. The motel has a heated swimming pool and jacuzzi, 24 hour cable television and more. There is a $10 per day pet charge

W Seattle
1112 Fourth Avenue
Seattle, WA
206-264-6000
Dogs of any size are allowed. There is a $25 per day additional pet fee.

Spokane

Budget Inn
E. 110 Fourth Avenue
Spokane, WA
509-838-6101
There are no additional pet fees.

Cavanaughs River Inn
N 700 Division St
Spokane, WA
509-326-5577
There are no additional pet fees.

Doubletree Hotel Spokane City Center
N. 322 Spokane Falls Ct
Spokane, WA

509-455-9600
There is a $25 one time pet fee.

Doubletree Hotel Spokane Valley
North 1100 Sullivan Road
Spokane, WA
509-924-9000
There is a $50 refundable pet deposit.

Howard Johnson Inn
South 211 Division St.
Spokane, WA
509-838-6630
Dogs of all sizes are welcome.
There is a $10 per day pet fee.

Motel 6
1508 S Rustle St
Spokane, WA
509-459-6120
There are no additional pet fees.
One well-behaved pet per room is allowed.

Motel 6
1919 N Hutchinson Rd
Spokane, WA
509-926-5399
Well-behaved dogs are allowed at the hotel.

Best Western Executive Inn
5700 Pacific Hwy E.
Tacoma, WA
253-922-0080
There is a $25 one time pet fee per visit.

Best Western Tacoma Inn
8726 S. Hosmer St
Tacoma, WA
253-535-2880
There is a $20 one time pet fee.

La Quinta Inn Tacoma
1425 E 27th St
Tacoma, WA
253-383-0146
Dogs of all sizes are allowed at the hotel.

Motel 6
1811 S 76th St

Tacoma, WA
253-473-7100
There are no additional pet fees. Pets must be attended at all times.

Best Western Tumwater Inn
5188 Capitol Blvd
Tumwater, WA
360-956-1235
There is a $5 per day additional pet fee.

Motel 6
400 W Lee St
Tumwater, WA
360-754-7320
There are no additional pet fees.

Comfort Inn
13207 NE 20th Ave.
Vancouver, WA
360-574-6000
There is a pet fee of $10 per day.

Staybridge Suites
7301 NE 41st St
Vancouver, WA
360-891-8282
There is a $50 refundable pet deposit and an additional pet fee of $10 per day.

La Quinta Inn Walla Walla
520 North Second Street
Walla Walla, WA
509-525-2522
Dogs up to 50 pounds are allowed at the hotel.

La Quinta Inn & Suites Wenatchee
1905 N. Wenatchee Ave
Wenatchee, WA
509-664-6565

Dogs of all sizes are allowed at the hotel.

Inn of the White Salmon
172 W Jewett
White Salmon, WA
509-493-2335
There is a $10 per day pet fee.
All rooms are non-smoking.

Holiday Inn Express
1001 East A Street
Yakima, WA
509-249-1000
There is a $6 per day pet fee.

Motel 6
1104 N 1st St
Yakima, WA
509-454-0080
There are no additional pet fees.
Pets must be attended at all times.

West Virginia Listings

Comfort Inn
1909 Harper Rd.
Beckley, WV
304-255-2161
There are no additional pet fees.

Econo Lodge
3400 Cumberland Rd.
Bluefield, WV
304-327-8171
There is a $10 per day pet charge.

Holiday Inn
US 460
Bluefield, WV
304-325-6170

There are no additional pet fees.

Ramada Inn
3175 East Cumberland Road
Bluefield, WV
304-325-5421
There is a $25 refundable pet deposit.

Bridgeport

Holiday Inn
100 Lodgeville Rd
Bridgeport, WV
304-842-5411
There are no additional pet fees.

Knights Inn
1235 West Main Street
Bridgeport, WV
304-842-7115
There are no additional pet fees.

Sleep Inn
115 Tolley Rd.
Bridgeport, WV
304-842-1919
There are no additional pet fees.

Buckhannon

Centennial Motel
22 N Locust St
Buckhannon, WV
304-472-4100
There are no additional pet fees.

Charleston

Motel 6
6311 MacCorkle Ave SE
Charleston, WV
304-925-0471
There are no additional pet fees.

Ramada Plaza Hotel
400 Second Avenue
Charleston, WV
304-744-4641
There is a $50 refundable pet deposit and a $10 per day pet charge.

Elkins

Days Inn
1200 Harrison Avenue
Elkins, WV
304-637-4667
There is a $5 one time pet charge.

Econo Lodge
U.S. 33 East
Elkins, WV
304-636-5311
There is a $5 per day pet charge.

Huntington

Econo Lodge
3325 US 60 E.
Huntington, WV
304-529-1331
There is a $10 per day pet charge.

Holiday Inn Hotel & Suites
800 Third Ave
Huntington, WV
304-523-8880
There is a $20 one time pet fee.

Red Roof Inn
5190 U.S. 60, East
Huntington, WV
304-733-3737
Dogs up to 80 pounds are allowed. There are no pet fees.

Stone Lodge
5600 U.S. Route 60 East
Huntington, WV
304-736-3451
There are no additional pet fees.

Kanawha City

Red Roof Inn-Kanawha City
6305 MacCorkle Avenue S.E.
Kanawha City, WV
304-925-6953
There are no additional pet fees.

Lewisburg

Days Inn
635 N. Jefferson Street

Lewisburg, WV
304-645-2345
They have 1 non-smoking pet room. There is a $15 per day pet charge.

Martinsburg

Days Inn
209 Viking Way
Martinsburg, WV
304-263-1800
There are no additional pet fees.

Holiday Inn
301 Foxcroft Ave
Martinsburg, WV
304-267-5500
There are no additional pet fees.

Knights Inn
1599 Edwin Miller Blvd
Martinsburg, WV
304-267-2211
There is a $5 per day additional pet fee.

Morgantown

Econo Lodge Coliseum
3506 Monongahela Blvd.
Morgantown, WV
304-599-8181
There are no additional pet fees.

Holiday Inn
1400 Saratoga Avenue
Morgantown, WV
304-599-1680
There is a $10 one time pet charge.

Ramada Inn
119 S. at I-68 and I-79
Morgantown, WV
304-296-3431
There are no additional pet fees.

Parkersburg

Blennerhassett Hotel
Fourth and Market Streets
Parkersburg, WV
304-422-3131
This 1889 hotel is listed on the National Register of Historic

Hotels. There is a $25 one time pet charge.

Expressway Motor Inn
6333 Emerson Ave
Parkersburg, WV
304-485-1851
There is a $5 per day pet charge.

Red Roof Inn
3714 East 7th Street
Parkersburg, WV
304-485-1741
There are no additional pet fees.

Sleep Inn
1015 Oakvale Rd.
Princeton, WV
304-431-2800
There are no additional pet fees.

Holiday Inn Express
One Hospitality Drive
Ripley, WV
304-372-5000
There are no additional pet fees.

Red Roof Inn
4006 MacCorkle Avenue
South Charleston, WV
304-744-1500
There are no additional pet fees.

Best Western Summersville Lake Motor Lodge
1203 S Broad St
Summersville, WV
304-872-6900
There is a $5 per day additional pet fee.

Oglebay's Wilson Lodge
Route 88 North
Wheeling, WV

304-243-4000
Dogs are not allowed in the lodge, but are welcome in the cottages. There are no designated smoking or non-smoking cottages. There are no additional pet fees.

Wisconsin Listings

Best Western Midway Hotel
3033 West College Avenue
Appleton, WI
920-731-4141
There is a $10 per day additional pet fee. There are 7 pet rooms located away from the pool.

Comfort Suites-Comfort Dome
3809 W. Wisconsin Ave.
Appleton, WI
920-730-3800
Thanks to one of our readers who writes: "Very Dog-Friendly. I saw at least 20 dogs and I did not spend a lot of time in the hotel. My dog was allowed to come to the bar with me and he had a great time meeting lots of friendly dog-loving people. The hotel asks that all dogs be kept on a leash (when outside your room)." Hotel amenities include an indoor fitness and recreation center. There are no pet charges.

Ramada Inn
200 N Perkins St
Appleton, WI
920-735-2733
There is a $10 per day pet fee.

Residence Inn by Marriott
310 Metro Dr
Appleton, WI
920-954-0570
There is a $25 one time pet fee and a fee of $10 per day.

Woodfield Suites

3730 W College Ave
Appleton, WI
920-734-7777
There is a $50 refundable pet deposit. There is a $10 per day pet fee. One large dog is permitted per room.

Americinn Motel and Suites
3009 Lakeshore Drive East
Ashland, WI
715-682-9950
There is a $6 per day pet charge.

Lake Aire Inn
101 E. Lake Shore Dr.
Ashland, WI
715-682-4551
There is a $10 one time pet fee.

Super 8 Motel
1610 West Lakeshore Dr.
Ashland, WI
715-682-9377
There is a $10 per day pet fee per pet.

Super 8 Motel
Harbor View Dr.
Bayfield, WI
715-373-5671
There is no additional pet fee.

Comfort Inn of Beloit
2786 Milwaukee Rd
Beloit, WI
608-362-2666
There is a $10 per day additional pet fee.

Super 8 Motel - Beloit
3002 Milwaukee Road
Beloit, WI
608-365-8680
$10/stay for up to 3 dogs in one room. FREE 8-minute long distance call each night. FREE continental breakfast. Coffee maker, night light, clock/radio,

safe in each room. On-site guest laundry. Kids 12 & under stay free. I-90, Exit 185A. Intersection of Hwy 81, I-43 & I-90.

Black River Falls

Best Western Arrowhead Lodge
600 Oasis Rd
Black River Falls, WI
715-284-9471
Pets may not be left alone in the rooms.

Brookfield

Sheraton Milwaukee Brookfield Hotel
375 S. Moorland Road
Brookfield, WI
262-364-1100
Dogs up to 90 pounds are allowed. There is no additional pet fee. You must sign a pet waiver.

Chippewa Falls

Americinn Motel and Suites
11 West South Avenue
Chippewa Falls, WI
715-723-5711
No extra pet charge, just sign a pet waiver. They have 2 non-smoking pet rooms.

Indianhead Motel
501 Summit Avenue
Chippewa Falls, WI
715-723-9171
There is a $5 per day pet charge.

DeForest

Holiday Inn Express
7184 Morrisonville Rd
DeForest, WI
608-846-8686
There is a $20 one time pet fee.

Dodgeville

Best Western Quiet House &

Suites
1130 N Johns St
Dodgeville, WI
608-935-7739
There is a $15 per day additional pet fee.

Eau Claire

Econo Lodge
4608 Royal Dr.
Eau Claire, WI
715-833-8818
No extra pet charge, just sign a pet waiver. They have a smoke free premises.

Quality Inn
809 W. Clairemont Ave.
Eau Claire, WI
715-834-6611
There is a $5 per day pet fee.

Germantown

Holiday Inn Express
W177 N9675 Riversbend Ln
Germantown, WI
262-255-1100
There are no additional pet fees.

Super 8 Motel
N96 W17490 County Line Rd
Germantown, WI
262-255-0880
There are no additional pet fees. Pets are allowed in first floor rooms or suites. Pets may not be left alone in the rooms.

Gills Rock

Harbor House Inn Bed and Breakfast
12666 SR 42
Gills Rock, WI
920-854-5196
This B&B has private beach access, outdoor grills and park-like grounds. You and your pup can also stroll through the quaint fishing village of Gills Rock. They are open late April through September. There is a $20 per day pet fee per pet.

Glendale

Residence Inn
7275 N Port Washington Rd
Glendale, WI
414-352-0070
There is a $175 one time pet fee plus $6 per day.

Woodfield Suites
5423 N Port Washington Rd
Glendale, WI
414-962-6767
There is a $10 per day pet fee.

Green Bay

Americinn
2032 Velp Ave
Green Bay, WI
920-434-9790
There is a $10 per day additional pet fee.

Motel 6
1614 Shawano Ave
Green Bay, WI
920-494-6730
There are no additional pet fees.

Residence Inn by Marriott
335 W St Joseph St
Green Bay, WI
920-435-2222
There is a $150 one time pet fee.

Super 8 Motel
2868 S Oneida St
Green Bay, WI
920-494-2042
There is a $25 refundable deposit.

Hayward

Ross Teal Lake Lodge
12425 N. Ross Rd
Hayward, WI
715-462-3631
Enjoy the Resort, Inn or rent a Cabin. Pet fees are $5 per pet per day. Pets are allowed in guest houses but special arrangements requested with housekeeping for time. Please

keep pets leashed around the main buildings in the center of the resort.

Janesville

Best Western Janesville
3900 Milton Ave
Janesville, WI
608-756-4511
There is a $10 per day additional pet fee.

Microtel Inn
3121 Wellington Pl
Janesville, WI
608-752-3121
There is a $10 one time pet fee.

Motel 6
3907 Milton Ave
Janesville, WI
608-756-1742
There are no additional pet fees. A large well-behaved dog is okay.

Select Inn
3520 Milton Ave
Janesville, WI
608-754-0251
There is a $25 refundable deposit and a $5.25 charge per day.

Ladysmith

Best Western El Rancho
8500 W Flambeau Ave
Ladysmith, WI
715-532-6666
There is a $9 per day additional pet fee.

Madison

Collins House Bed and Breakfast
704 E Gorham St
Madison, WI
608-255-4230
This B&B is listed on the National Register of Historic Places as a classic example of Prairie School Architecture. Pets are not allowed on the furniture

nor should they be left alone in a room. Pets must be leashed in all common areas. There are no additional pet fees.

Comfort Suites
1253 John Q Hammonds Dr
Madison, WI
608-836-3033
There are no additional pet fees.

Motel 6
1754 Thierer Rd
Madison, WI
608-241-8101
There are no pet fees. Pets under 60 pounds are allowed.

Red Roof Inn
4830 Hayes Rd
Madison, WI
608-241-1787
There are no additional pet fees.

Residence Inn by Marriott
4862 Hayes Rd
Madison, WI
608-244-5047
There is a $25 one time pet fee.

Woodfield Suites
5217 E Terrace Dr
Madison, WI
608-245-0123
There is a $10 one time pet fee.

Manitowoc

Comfort Inn
2200 S 44th St
Manitowoc, WI
920-683-0220
There are no additional pet fees.

Holiday Inn
4601 Calumet Ave
Manitowoc, WI
920-682-6000
There are no additional pet fees.

Marinette

Chalet Motel
1301 Marinette Ave
Marinette, WI
715-735-6687
There are no additional pet fees.

Super 8
1508 Marinette Ave
Marinette, WI
715-735-7887
There is a $50 refundable pet deposit.

Menomonie

Motel 6
2100 Stout St
Menomonie, WI
715-235-6901
There are no additional pet fees.

Mequon

Best Western Quiet House & Suites
10330 N Port Washington Rd
Mequon, WI
262-241-3677
There is a $15 per day additional pet fee.

Milwaukee

Best Western Inn Towne Hotel
710 N Old World Third Street
Milwaukee, WI
414-224-8400
There are no additional pet fees.

Hotel Wisconsin
720 N Old World 3rd St
Milwaukee, WI
414-271-4900
Built in 1913, this is a vintage Milwaukee hotel. There are no additional pet fees.

Motel 6
5037 S Howell Ave
Milwaukee, WI
414-482-4414
There are no additional pet fees.

Minocqua

Best Western Lakeview Motor Lodge
311 East Park Avenue
Minocqua, WI
715-356-5208
There is an $8 per day additional pet fee.

Oak Creek

Knights Inn - Milwaukee
9420 S 20th St
Oak Creek, WI
414-761-3807
There is a $10 per day additional pet fee.

Red Roof Inn
6360 S 13th St
Oak Creek, WI
414-764-3500
There are no additional pet fees.

Onalaska

Holiday Inn Express
9409 Hwy 16
Onalaska, WI
608-783-6555
There are no additional pet fees.

Oshkosh

Holiday Inn Express & Suites
2251 Westowne Ave
Oshkosh, WI
920-303-1300
There are no additional pet fees.

Howard Johnson Inn
1919 Omro Road
Oshkosh, WI
920-233-1200
Dogs of all sizes are welcome. There are no additional pet fees.

Prairie du Chien

Best Western Quiet House & Suites
Hwy 18, 35, 60 South
Prairie du Chien, WI
608-326-4777
There is a $15 per day additional pet fee.

Rhinelander

Best Western Claridge Motor Inn
70 North Stevens Street
Rhinelander, WI
715-362-7100
There is a $10 per day pet charge.

Comfort Inn
1490 Lincoln Street
Rhinelander, WI
715-369-1100
There is a $5 per day pet fee. Pets are not allowed in the pool area or breakfast area.

Holiday Inn
668 W. Kemp St.
Rhinelander, WI
715-369-3600
There is a $25 one time pet charge.

Rice Lake

Currier's Lakeview Lodge
2010 E. Sawyer Street
Rice Lake, WI
715-234-7474
Located on Rice Lake's scenic east side, Currier's Lakeview is the city's only all-season resort motel. The motel sits on a wooded 4-acre peninsula that is located between two beautiful bays. There are no additional pet fees.

Super 8 Motel
2401 South Main
Rice Lake, WI
715-234-6956
There is a $10 per day pet charge.

Sheboygan

Super 8 Motel - Sheboygan
3402 Wilgus Road
Sheboygan, WI
920-458-8080
$10/stay for up to 3 dogs in one room. FREE 8-minute long distance call each night. FREE continental breakfast. Coffee maker, night light, clock/radio, safe in each room. On-site guest laundry. Kids 12 & under stay free. I-43, Exit 126 onto WI 23 East to Taylor Dr; Left on Taylor Dr 1 block; Left on Wilgus 1 block.

Sparta

Country Inn by Carlson
737 Avon Rd
Sparta, WI
608-269-3110
There is a $5 per day pet fee.

Super 8
716 Avon Rd
Sparta, WI
608-269-8489
There is a $5 per day pet fee.

St Croix Falls

Holiday Inn Express & Suites
2190 US Hwy 8
St Croix Falls, WI
877-422-4097
There is a $15 one time pet fee.

Stevens Point

Super 8 Motel - Stevens Point
247 N. Division Street
Stevens Point, WI
715-341-8888
Home of University of WI - Stevens Point. $10/stay for up to 3 dogs in one room. FREE 8-minute long distance call each night. FREE continental breakfast. Coffee maker, night light, clock/radio, safe in each room. On-site guest laundry. Kids 12 & under stay free. From US 10, Take Bus. 51 North. From US 51/39, Exit 161, South on Bus. 51, 1 block.

Sturgeon Bay

Holiday Motel
29 N Second Ave
Sturgeon Bay, WI

920-743-5571
There is a $5 per day pet fee.

Superior

Best Western Bay Walk Inn
1405 Susquehanna
Superior, WI
715-392-7600
There are no additional pet fees.

Best Western Bridgeview Motor Inn
415 Hammond Ave
Superior, WI
715-392-8174
There are no additional pet fees.

Tomah

Americinn
750 Vandervort St
Tomah, WI
608-372-4100
There is a $50 refundable deposit for pets. There is one non-smoking pet room.

Cranberry Suites
319 Wittig Rd
Tomah, WI
608-374-2801
There is a $5 per day pet fee.

Econo Lodge
2005 N Superior Ave
Tomah, WI
608-372-9100
There is a $5 per day pet fee.

Lark Inn
229 N Superior Ave
Tomah, WI
608-372-5981
This inn has been sheltering travelers since the early 1900s. It is a comfortable retreat with country quilts and antiques. Dogs are allowed in the larger hotel rooms and the log cabins. There is a $6 per day pet fee.

Washington Island

Viking Village Motel
Main Road at Detroit Harbor,

P.O. Box 188.
Washington Island, WI
920-847-2551
There are no designated smoking or non-smoking rooms. There are no additional pet fees. There is an extra charge if you do not pick up after your pet.

Watertown

Holiday Inn Express
101 Aviation Way
Watertown, WI
920-262-1910
There is a $5 per day pet fee. One dog is allowed per room. Pets may never be left alone in the rooms.

Waukesha

Super 8
2501 Plaza Court
Waukesha, WI
262-785-1590
There is a $20 one time pet fee.

Wausau

Park Inn International Motel and Conf. Center
2101 N Mountain Rd
Wausau, WI
715-842-0711
Dogs are usually placed in smoking rooms. Request a non-smoking room if desired. There are no additional pet fees.

Stewart Inn
521 Grant Street
Wausau, WI
715-849-5858
The Stewart Inn is a small European Inn with modern amenities. Pets are welcome in three of the five guest rooms at no extra charge. Pet owners will need to sign a pet agreement.

Wisconsin Dells

Howard Johnson Hotel
655 Frontage Rd. North
Wisconsin Dells, WI
608-254-8306
Dogs of all sizes are welcome. There is a $10 per day pet fee. Pets may not be left unattended in the room.

Wisconsin Rapids

Best Western Rapids Motor Inn
911 Huntington Ave
Wisconsin Rapids, WI
715-423-3211
Pets may not be left alone in the room.

Super 8 Motel - Wisconsin Rapids
3410 8th Street S.
Wisconsin Rapids, WI
715-423-8080
$10/stay for up to 3 dogs in one room. FREE 8-minute long distance call each night. FREE continental breakfast. Coffee maker, night light, clock/radio, safe in each room. On-site guest laundry. Kids 12 & under stay free. South Hwy 13 btwn Cook & Two Mile Ave.

Wyoming Listings

Buffalo

Motel 6
100 Flat Iron Drive
Buffalo, WY
307-684-7000
There are no additional pet fees.

Casper

Econo Lodge
821 N Poplar St
Casper, WY
307-266-2400
There are no additional pet fees.

Holiday Inn
300 West F Street
Casper, WY
307-235-2531
There is a $50 refundable deposit when paying with cash or check.

Cheyenne

Best Western Hitching Post Inn
1700 W Lincolnway
Cheyenne, WY
307-638-3301
There are no additional pet fees.

Comfort Inn
2245 Etchepare Dr
Cheyenne, WY
307-638-7202
There is a $20 refundable deposit for pets.

Days Inn Cheyenne
2360 W Lincolnway
Cheyenne, WY
307-778-8877
There is a $25 refundable pet deposit.

Lincoln Court
1720 W Lincolnway
Cheyenne, WY
307-638-3302
There are no additional pet fees.

Windy Hills Guest House
393 Happy Jack Rd
Cheyenne, WY
307-632-6423
There are no additional pet fees.

Clearmont

The Ranch at UCross
2673 US Hwy 14 East
Clearmont, WY
307-737-2281
Secluded, inclusive resort.

Cody

Best Western Sunrise Motor Inn
1407 8th St

Cody, WY
307-587-5566
There are no additional pet fees.

Kelly Inn of Cody
2513 Greybull Hwy
Cody, WY
307-527-5505
There are no additional pet fees.

Dubois

Branding Iron Inn
401 W Ramshorn
Dubois, WY
307-455-2893
There is a $10 per day additional pet fee.

Chinook Winds Mountain Lodge
640 S 1st St
Dubois, WY
307-455-2987
There is a $5 per day pet fee.

Pinnacle Buttes Lodge and Campground
3577 US Hwy 26W
Dubois, WY
307-455-2506
There is a $50 refundable pet deposit. There are no designated smoking or non-smoking rooms.

Evanston

Days Inn
339 Wasatch Rd
Evanston, WY
307-789-2220
There is a $10 per day pet fee.

Evanston Super 8 Motel
70 Bear River Dr
Evanston, WY
307-789-7510
There is a $25 refundable pet deposit.

Jackson

Motel 6

600 S Hwy 89
Jackson, WY
307-733-1620
There are no additional pet fees. A well-behaved pet is allowed in each room.

Quality 49er Inn and Suites
330 W Pearl St
Jackson, WY
307-733-7550
There are no additional pet fees.

Jackson Hole

Painted Buffalo Inn
400 West Broadway
Jackson Hole, WY
307-733-4340
There is a $10 one time pet fee.

Snow King Resort
400 E Snow King Ave
Jackson Hole, WY
307-733-5200
There is a $100 pet deposit. $50 of this is refundable.

Lander

Best Western Inn at Lander
260 Grand View Dr
Lander, WY
307-332-2847
There is a $10 per day additional pet fee. The hotel has one non-smoking pet room.

Laramie

Best Western Gas Lite Motel
960 North Third
Laramie, WY
307-742-6616
There is a $5 per day additional pet fee.

Howard Johnson Inn
1555 Snowy Range Road
Laramie, WY
307-742-8371
Dogs of all sizes are welcome. There is a $10 per day pet fee.

Motel 6
621 Plaza Lane

Laramie, WY
307-742-2307
There are no additional pet fees.

Pray

Chico Hot Springs Resort
#1 Chico Road
Pray, MT
406-333-4933
"We're pet-friendly, so bring your four-legged friends along." This resort has a lodge and cabins which sit on 150 acres. There are miles of hiking trails for you and your pup. They are located 30 miles from the north Yellowstone National Park entrance. There is a $10 per day pet fee.

Rawlins

Sleep Inn
1400 Higley Blvd
Rawlins, WY
307-328-1732
There are no additional pet fees.

Riverton

Days Inn
909 W Main St
Riverton, WY
307-856-9677
There is a $5 per day pet fee.

Sundowner Station
1616 N Federal Blvd
Riverton, WY
307-856-6503
There are no additional pet fees.

Super 8 Motel
1040 N Federal Blvd
Riverton, WY
307-857-2400
There is a $5.35 pet fee per day.

Rock Springs

Comfort Inn
1670 Sunset Dr
Rock Springs, WY
307-382-9490

There is a $10 per day pet fee.

Holiday Inn
1675 Sunset Drive
Rock Springs, WY
307-382-9200
There is a $10 one time pet fee.

Motel 6
2615 Commercial Way
Rock Springs, WY
307-362-1850
There are no additional pet fees.

Sheridan

Guest House Motel
2007 N Main St
Sheridan, WY
307-674-7496
There is a $5 per day pet fee.

Holiday Inn
1809 Sugarland Dr
Sheridan, WY
307-672-8931
There is a $50 refundable pet deposit.

Sundance

Best Western Inn at Sundance
2179 E. Cleveland, Box 927
Sundance, WY
307-283-2800
There is a $25 refundable pet deposit.

Thermopolis

Holiday Inn
115 E Park St - Hot Springs St. Pk
Thermopolis, WY
307-864-3131
There are no additional pet fees.

Wapiti

Green Creek Inn
2908 Yellowstone Hwy
Wapiti, WY

307-587-5004
There is a $5 per day pet fee.

West Yellowstone

Best Western Weston Inn
103 Gibbon Street
West Yellowstone, MT
406-646-7373
There are no additional pet fees.

Wheatland

Best Western Torchlite Motor Inn
1809 N 16th St
Wheatland, WY
307-322-4070
There is a $25 refundable pet deposit.

Vimbo's Motel
203 16th St
Wheatland, WY
307-322-3842
There are no additional pet fees.

Yellowstone National Park

Flagg Ranch Village
Hwy 89 Yellowstone South Entrance
Yellowstone National Park, WY
307-543-2861
Dogs are allowed in cabins. This is a seasonal hotel and is not open year round. There is a $5 per day additional pet fee.

Accommodations - Please always call ahead to make sure an establishment is still dog-friendly.

CANADA ACCOMMODATIONS

Alberta Listings

Banff

Best Western Siding 29 Lodge
453 Marten Street
Banff, AB
403-762-5575
Dogs must not be left
unattended in the room. There
are no additional pet fees.

Driftwood Inn
337 Banff Avenue
Banff, AB
403-762-4496
Dogs of all sizes are allowed.
There is a $15 per night
additional pet fee. Dogs may not
be left unattended in the room.

Calgary

Coast Plaza Hotel at Calgary
1316 - 33rd Street N.E.
Calgary, AB
403-248-8888
All Coast Hotels have on hand
extra pet amenities if you forget
something. For dogs, they have
extra doggy dishes, sleeping
cushions, nylon chew toys and
dog food. If your dog needs one
of these items, just ask the front
desk. There is a $15 per day
additional pet fee.

Days Inn Calgary West
1818 16th Ave NW
Calgary, AB
403-289-1961
There is a $10 per day additional
pet fee.

Holiday Inn - Airport
1250 McKinnon Dr, NE
Calgary, AB
403-230-1999
There are no additional pet fees.

Holiday Inn - Macleod Trail

South
4206 Macleod Trail S.
Calgary, AB
403-287-2700
There is a $20 one time pet fee.
Pets must stay in first floor
rooms.

Howard Johnson Express Inn
5307 Macleod Trail South
Calgary, AB
403-258-1064
There is a $10 per day
additional pet fee. Dogs are
allowed at the hotel, cats are
not allowed.

Quality Inn Motel Village
2359 Banif Tr NW
Calgary, AB
403-289-1973
Pets may not be left alone in
the room. A credit card will be
required. There is no fee.

Ramada Limited
2363 Banff Trail NW
Calgary, AB
403-289-5571
There is a $10 per day
additional pet fee.

Sheraton Suites Calgary Eau Claire
255 Barclay Parade S.W.
Calgary, AB
403-266-7200
Dogs up to 80 pounds are
allowed. There are no
additional pet fees, just a
liability waiver.

Super 8
3030 Barlow Trail NE
Calgary, AB
403-291-9888
There is a $10 per day
additional pet fee.

Super 8
1904 Crowchild Trail NW
Calgary, AB
403-289-9211
There is a $10 per day
additional pet fee.

Super 8
60 Shawville SE Rd

Calgary, AB
403-254-8878
There is a $10 per day additional
pet fee.

Edmonton

Coast Edmonton Hotel
10155-105th Street
Edmonton, AB
780-423-4811
All Coast Hotels have on hand
extra pet amenities if you forget
something. For dogs, they have
extra doggy dishes, sleeping
cushions, nylon chew toys and
dog food. If your dog needs one
of these items, just ask the front
desk. There is an extra person
charge for dogs which is $10
Cdn. per day.

Comfort Inn West
17610 100th Ave
Edmonton, AB
780-484-4415
There is a $10 per day pet fee.

Holiday Inn
4235 Calgary Trail N.
Edmonton, AB
780-438-1222
There is a $10 per day pet fee.
The hotel has two pet rooms on
the first floor.

Holiday Inn Express & Suites
10017-179 A Street
Edmonton, AB
780-483-4000
There is a $15 per day additional
pet fee. The hotel has two pet
rooms.

Ramada Hotel and Conf. Ctr
11834 Kingsway Ave
Edmonton, AB
780-454-5454
There is a $10 per day additional
pet fee.

Sheraton Grande Edmonton Hotel
10235 101 Street
Edmonton, AB
780-428-7111
Dogs up to 80 pounds are

allowed. There is a $10 per day additional pet fee.

Super 8
3610 Calgary Trail Norhtbound NW
Edmonton, AB
780-433-8688
There is a $10 per day additional pet fee.

Fort McMurray

Super 8
321 Sakitawaw Trail
Fort McMurray, AB
780-799-8450
There is a $10 per day additional pet fee.

Grande Prairie

Super 8
10050 116 Avenue
Grande Prairie, AB
780-532-8288
There is a $10 per day additional pet fee.

Hinton

Super 8
284 Smith St
Hinton, AB
780-817-2228
There is a $10 per day additional pet fee.

Lethbridge

Comfort Inn
3225 Fairway Plaza Rd S
Lethbridge, AB
403-320-8874
There is a $10 per day pet fee.

Days Inn
100 3rd Ave South
Lethbridge, AB
403-327-6000
Pets may not be left unattended in rooms.

Holiday Inn Express & Suites
120 Stafford Drive

Lethbridge, AB
403-394-9292
There is a $35 one time pet fee.

Quality Inn
1030 Mayor Magrath Drive S
Lethbridge, AB
403-328-6636
There is a one time fee of $5 per pet.

Medicine Hat

Super 8
1280 Trans-Canada Way
Medicine Hat, AB
403-528-8888
There is a $5 per day additional pet fee. Pets are not allowed in the lobby.

Nisku

Days Inn - Airport
1101 4th Street
Nisku, AB
780-955-7744
There is a $10 per day additional pet fee.

Olds

Best Western of Olds
4512 46th Street
Olds, AB
403-556-5900
There is a $5 per day pet fee.

Slave Lake

Super 8
Main St & Highway 2
Slave Lake, AB
780-805-3100
There is a $10 per day additional pet fee.

Stettler

Super 8
5720 44 Ave
Stettler, AB
403-742-3391
There is a $10 per day additional pet fee.

Three Hills

Super 8
208 18th Ave N
Three Hills, AB
403-443-8888
There are no additional pet fees. Pets must be attended at all times.

Vermillion

Super 8
5108-47 Avenue
Vermillion, AB
780-853-4741
There is a $10 per day additional pet fee.

Whitecourt

Super 8
4121 Kepler St
Whitecourt, AB
780-778-8908
There is a $10 per day additional pet fee.

British Columbia Listings

100 Mile House

Ramada Limited
917 Alder Rd
100 Mile House, BC
250-395-2777
There is a $5 per day additional pet fee. Pets are allowed but not in the lobby. Pet rooms all have outside entrances.

Abbotsford

Holiday Inn Express
2073 Clearbrook Rd
Abbotsford, BC
604-859-6211
There is a $10 per day additional pet fee.

Ramada Inn

36035 N Parallel Rd
Abbotsford, BC
604-870-1050
There is a $10 per day additional pet fee.

Campbell River

Coast Discovery Inn and Marina
975 Shoppers Row
Campbell River, BC
250-287-7155
All Coast Hotels have on hand extra pet amenities if you forget something. For dogs, they have extra doggy dishes, sleeping cushions, nylon chew toys and dog food. If your dog needs one of these items, just ask the front desk. There is a $10 per day additional pet fee.

Castlegar

Days Inn
651-18th Street
Castlegar, BC
250-365-2700
There is a $10 per day pet pet additional fee.

Chilliwack

Best Western Rainbow Country Inn
43971 Industrial Way
Chilliwack, BC
604-795-3828
There is an $10 per day pet fee.

Comfort Inn
45405 Luckakuck Way
Chilliwack, BC
604-858-0636
There is a pet fee of $5 per day. Pets are allowed on the ground floor.

Coquitlam

Best Western Chelsea Inn
725 Brunette Avenue
Coquitlam, BC
604-525-7777

There is an $20 per day pet fee.

Holiday Inn
631 Lougheed Highway
Coquitlam, BC
604-931-4433
There is a $30 one time pet fee.

Courtenay

Best Western Collingwood Inn
1675 Cliffe Ave
Courtenay, BC
250-338-1464
There is an $8 per day pet fee.

Coast Westerly Hotel
1590 Cliffe Avenue
Courtenay, BC
250-338-7741
All Coast Hotels have on hand extra pet amenities if you forget something. For dogs, they have extra doggy dishes, sleeping cushions, nylon chew toys and dog food. If your dog needs one of these items, just ask the front desk. There is a $10 per day additional pet fee.

Cranbrook

Best Western Coach House
1417 Cranbrook St N
Cranbrook, BC
250-426-7236
There is a $10 per day pet fee.

Dawson Creek

Ramada Limited
1748 Alaska Avenue
Dawson Creek, BC
250-782-8595
There is a $10 per day additional pet fee.

Delta

Best Western Tsawwassen Inn
1665 56th Street
Delta, BC

604-943-8221
There is a $10 per day pet fee. A large well-behaved dog is okay.

Enderby

Howard Johnson Inn
1510 George St.
Enderby, BC
250-838-6825
Dogs of all sizes are welcome. There is a $5 per day pet fee.

Fort St John

Best Western Coachman Inn
8540 Alaska Road
Fort St John, BC
250-787-0651
There is a $15 per day additional pet fee.

Quality Inn
9830 100th Ave
Fort St John, BC
250-787-0521
There is a one time pet fee of $15.

Grand Forks

Ramada Limited
2729 Central Ave (Hwy 3)
Grand Forks, BC
250-442-2127
There is a $10 per day additional pet fee. Pets are not allowed on the furniture.

Hope

Quality Inn
350 Old Hope Princton Way
Hope, BC
604-869-9951
There is no pet fee. Pets may not be left alone.

Kamloops

Coast Canadian Inn
339 St. Paul Street
Kamloops, BC
250-372-5201
All Coast Hotels have on hand

extra pet amenities if you forget something. For dogs, they have extra doggy dishes, sleeping cushions, nylon chew toys and dog food. If your dog needs one of these items, just ask the front desk. There is a $10 per day additional pet fee.

Days Inn
1285 W Trans Canada Hwy
Kamloops, BC
250-374-5911
There is a $10 per day pet fee. The hotel has several pet rooms.

Howard Johnson Inn
610 West Columbia Street
Kamloops, BC
250-374-1515
Dogs of all sizes are welcome. There are no additional pet fees.

Ramada Inn
555 West Columbia St
Kamloops, BC
250-374-0358
There is a $10 per day additional pet fee.

Kelowna

Coast Capri Hotel
1171 Harvey Avenue
Kelowna, BC
250-860-6060
All Coast Hotels have on hand extra pet amenities if you forget something. For dogs, they have extra doggy dishes, sleeping cushions, nylon chew toys and dog food. If your dog needs one of these items, just ask the front desk. There is an extra person charge for dogs which is $20 -$25 Cdn. per day.

Ramada Lodge Hotel
2170 Harvey Ave (Highway 97N)
Kelowna, BC
250-860-9711
There is a $10 per day additional pet fee. Pets must be attended at all times.

Kimberley

Quality Inn
300 Wallinger Ave
Kimberley, BC
250-427-2266
There is no pet fee.

Mission

The Counting Sheep Inn
8715 Eagle Road, R.R. #3
Mission, BC
604-820-5148
They are 60 minutes from Vancouver and 45 minutes from Bellingham, Washington. This is an elegant Bed and Breakfast in the country and dogs are allowed in one of their rooms, the Carriage Suite. Check out their great season packages.

Nanaimo

Best Western Northgate Inn
6450 Metral Drive
Nanaimo, BC
250-390-2222
There is a $10 per day pet fee. Dogs are allowed on the first floor only.

Coast Bastion Inn
11 Bastion Street
Nanaimo, BC
250-753-6601
All Coast Hotels have on hand extra pet amenities if you forget something. For dogs, they have extra doggy dishes, sleeping cushions, nylon chew toys and dog food. If your dog needs one of these items, just ask the front desk. There is a $10 per day additional pet fee.

Ramada Limited on Long Lake
4700 N Island Hwy
Nanaimo, BC
250-758-1144
There is a $20 one time pet fee.

Parksville

Best Western Bayside Inn

240 Dogwood Street
Parksville, BC
250-248-8333
There is a $10 per day pet fee. The hotel has oceanside and mountain view rooms.

Penticton

Ramada Inn & Suites
1050 Eckhardt Ave West
Penticton, BC
250-492-8926
There is a $10 per day pet fee.

Pitt Meadows

Ramada Inn
19267 Lougheed Hwy
Pitt Meadows, BC
604-460-9859
Pets must be well-behaved. There are no additional pet fees.

Port Alberni

Coast Hospitality Inn
3835 Redford Street
Port Alberni, BC
250-723-8111
All Coast Hotels have on hand extra pet amenities if you forget something. For dogs, they have extra doggy dishes, sleeping cushions, nylon chew toys and dog food. If your dog needs one of these items, just ask the front desk. There are no additional pet fees.

Quality Inn
4850 Bever Creek Rd
Port Alberni, BC
250-724-2900
There is a refundable pet deposit $25. There is a pet fee of $10 per day. Non-smoking rooms are limited so please reserve early.

Powell River

Coast Town Centre Hotel
4660 Joyce Avenue
Powell River, BC

604-485-3000
All Coast Hotels have on hand extra pet amenities if you forget something. For dogs, they have extra doggy dishes, sleeping cushions, nylon chew toys and dog food. If your dog needs one of these items, just ask the front desk. There is a $10 per day additional pet fee.

Prince George

Coast Inn of the North
770 Brunswick Street
Prince George, BC
250-563-0121
All Coast Hotels have on hand extra pet amenities if you forget something. For dogs, they have extra doggy dishes, sleeping cushions, nylon chew toys and dog food. If your dog needs one of these items, just ask the front desk. There is a $10 per day additional pet fee.

Prince Rupert

Coast Prince Rupert Hotel
118 6th Street
Prince Rupert, BC
250-624-6711
All Coast Hotels have on hand extra pet amenities if you forget something. For dogs, they have extra doggy dishes, sleeping cushions, nylon chew toys and dog food. If your dog needs one of these items, just ask the front desk. There are no additional pet fees.

Quesnel

Ramada Limited
383 St Laurent Ave
Quesnel, BC
250-992-5575
One pet per room is permitted. There is a $7 per day additional pet fee.

Revelstoke

Best Western Wayside Inn
1901 Laforme Blvd
Revelstoke, BC
250-837-6161
There are no additional pet fees.

Richmond

Comfort Inn Airport
3031 Number 3 Road
Richmond, BC
604-278-5161
There is a pet fee of $10 per day. Pets are allowed on the first floor.

Saanichton

Quality Inn Wadding Dog
2476 Mt Newton Crossroad
Saanichton, BC
250-652-1146
There is a $5.00 per night dog fee.

Super 8 Victoria/Saanichton
2477 Mount Newton Crossroad
Saanichton, BC
250-652-6888
There is a $10 one time pet fee.

Saanighton

Quality Inn Waddling Dog
2476 Mt Newton Cross Rd
Saanighton, BC
250-652-1146
There is a pet fee of $5 per day.

Salmon Arm

Best Western Villager West
61-10th St SW
Salmon Arm, BC
250-832-9793
There are no additional pet fees. A large well-behaved dog is okay.

Sicamous

Sundog Bed and Breakfast
1409 Rauma Ave

Sicamous, BC
250-833-9005
There is a $15 per night pet fee with $5 going to the local SPCA. There are two pet friendly rooms.

Sidney

Best Western Emerald Isle
2306 Beacon Ave
Sidney, BC
250-656-4441
There is a $20 one time pet fee per visit.

Cedarwood Motel
9522 Lochside Dr
Sidney, BC
250-656-5551
There is a $15 per day additional pet fee.

Victoria Airport Travelodge
2280 Beacon Ave
Sidney, BC
250-656-1176
There is a $10 per day additional pet fee.

Sooke

Gordon's Beach Farm Stay B&B
4530 Otter Point Road
Sooke, BC
250-642-5291
A well-behaved dog is allowed in on of their suite rooms that has marble flooring. There is a $10 one time per stay pet fee.

Ocean Wilderness Country Inn
109 W Coast Rd
Sooke, BC
250-646-2116
There is a $15 pet fee per visit.

Sooke Harbour House
1528 Whiffen Spit Rd
Sooke, BC
250-642-3421
There is a $30 per night pet fee.

Surrey

Ramada Hotel & Suites
10410 158th St
Surrey, BC
604-930-4700
There is a $10 per day pet fee.

Ramada Limited
19225 Hwy 10
Surrey, BC
604-576-8388
There is a $10 per day pet fee per pet.

Valemount

Best Western Canadian Lodge
1501 5th Ave
Valemount, BC
250-566-8222
Dogs up to at least 75 pounds are allowed. There are no additional pet fees. The hotel has one non-smoking pet room.

Vancouver

Best Western Sands Hotel
1755 Davie Street
Vancouver, BC
604-682-1831
Situated in Downtown Vancouver down the block from Stanley Park and across from English Bay Beach. 2 Lounges, Restaurant, Room Service, Fitness Room and Sauna. The pet fee is $10.00 per day. Pets receive a welcome doggy bag upon arrival, includes Pet Lovers Digest, treats and scoop bags.

Coast Plaza Suite Hotel at Stanley Park
1763 Comox Street
Vancouver, BC
604-688-7711
All Coast Hotels have on hand extra pet amenities if you forget something. For dogs, they have extra doggy dishes, sleeping cushions, nylon chew toys and dog food. If your dog needs one of these items, just ask the front desk. There is a $20 per day additional pet fee.

Granville Island Hotel

1253 Johnston St
Vancouver, BC
604-683-7373
This hotel has a restaurant on the premises called the Dockside Restaurant. You can dine there with your pet at the outoor tables that are closest to the grass. The hotel charges a $25 per night pet fee per room.

Metropolitan Hotel
645 Howe Street
Vancouver, BC
604-687-1122
There are no additional pet fees.

Pacific Palisades Hotel
1277 Robson Street
Vancouver, BC
604-688-0461
Well-behaved dogs of all sizes are welcome at this hotel which offers both rooms and suites. Amenities include workout rooms, an indoor swimming pool, and 24 hour room service. There is a $25 one time per stay pet fee and $5 of this is sent to the SPCA.

Quality Hotel Downtown
1335 Howe St
Vancouver, BC
604-682-0229
There is a pet fee of $15 per day.

Ramada Inn
1221 Granville St
Vancouver, BC
604-685-1111
There is a $20 per day additional pet fee.

Residence Inn by Marriott
1234 Hornby St
Vancouver, BC
604-688-1234
There is a $75 pet fee per visit plus $5 per night for your pet

Sylvia Hotel
1154 Gilford St
Vancouver, BC
604-681-9321
There are no pet fees.

Victoria

Accent Inn
3233 Maple Street
Victoria, BC
250-475-7500
There is a $10 one time pet fee.

Annabelles Cottage B&B
152 Joseph Street
Victoria, BC
250-384-4351
Both pets and children are welcome. There is a $10 one time per stay pet fee. The inn is located near Beacon Hill Park.

Coast Harbourside Hotel and Marina
146 Kingston Street
Victoria, BC
250-360-1211
All Coast Hotels have on hand extra pet amenities if you forget something. For dogs, they have extra doggy dishes, sleeping cushions, nylon chew toys and dog food. If your dog needs one of these items, just ask the front desk. There is a $20 per day additional pet fee.

Dashwood Seaside Manor
1 Cook Street
Victoria, BC
250-385-5517
There is a $25 per stay pet fee.

Executive House Hotel
777 Douglas Street
Victoria, BC
250-388-5111
Enjoy European ambience in a downtown Victoria hotel. The hotel is directly across from the Victoria Conference Centre, one block from the magnificent Inner Harbour, Royal BC Museum, National Geographic Theatre, shopping and attractions. Pets are welcome for $15 per night extra.

Harbour Towers Hotel
345 Quebec St
Victoria, BC
250-385-2405
There is a $15 per day additional

pet fee.

Howard Johnson Hotel
310 George Rd. East
Victoria, BC
250-382-2151
Dogs up to 60 pounds are
allowed. There is a refundable
pet deposit required.

Howard Johnson Hotel
4670 Elk Lake Drive
Victoria, BC
250-704-4656
Dogs of all sizes are welcome.
There is a $15 per day pet fee.

Ryan's Bed and Breakfast
224 Superior St
Victoria, BC
250-389-0012
There is a $10 per night pet fee.

Tally Ho Motor Inn
3020 Douglas St
Victoria, BC
250-386-6141
There are no additional pet fees.

Westbank

Holiday Inn
2569 Dobbin Rd
Westbank, BC
250-768-8879
There is a $10 per day additional
pet fee.

Whistler

Chateau Whistler Resort
4599 Chateau Blvd
Whistler, BC
604-938-8000
This is a 5 star resort. There is
no weight limit for dogs. There is
a $25 per night additional pet
fee.

Coast Whistler Hotel
4005 Whistler Way
Whistler, BC
604-932-2522
All Coast Hotels have on hand
extra pet amenities if you forget
something. For dogs, they have
extra doggy dishes, sleeping

cushions, nylon chew toys and
dog food. If your dog needs one
of these items, just ask the
front desk. There is a $25 one
time pet fee.

Residence Inn by Marriott
4899 Painted Cliff Road
Whistler, BC
604-905-3400
Thanks to one of our readers
who writes "Offers a fantastic
outdoor playground for dogs,
located slopeside in the trees...
and the town of Whistler is dog
friendly. The town even has
"dog-sitters" available, who you
can hire to walk and play with
your dog if you need the
service (while you are out
skiing). They were great."
There is a $25 per day pet
charge.

Summit Lodge
4359 Main Street
Whistler, BC
604-932-2778
Well-behaved dogs of all sizes
are welcome at this hotel.
Amenities include a year-round
heated outdoor pool and hot
tub. There is a $15 per day pet
charge.

Manitoba Listings

Brandon

Victoria Inn
3550 Victoria Ave
Brandon, MB
204-725-1532
There is a $5 per day additional
pet fee. They have 2 non-
smoking pet rooms.

Flin Flon

Victoria Inn North
160 Hwy 10A N
Flin Flon, MB
204-687-7555
There are no additional pet

fees.

Hecla

Solmundson Gesta Hus B&B
Hwy 8 in Hecla
Hecla, MB
204-279-2088
Pets must be leashed when
outside the room. Please make
sure that your dog doesn't chase
the ducks.

Portage La Prairie

Days Inn
Highway #1 & Yellowquill Trail
Portage La Prairie, MB
204-857-9791
Pets must be attended at all
times.

Super 8
Hwy 1A W
Portage La Prairie, MB
204-857-8883
There are no additional pet fees.

The Pas

Super 8
1717 Gordon Ave
The Pas, MB
204-623-1888
There are no additional pet fees.

Winnipeg

**Place Louis Riel All-Suite
Hotel**
190 Smith St
Winnipeg, MB
204-947-6961
There are no additional pet fees.
Pet owners must sign a pet
release form.

New Brunswick Listings

Bathhurst

Comfort Inn
1170 St. Peter Ave
Bathurst, NB
506-547-8000
There is no pet fee. Pets may
not be left alone.

Bathurst

**Best Western Danny's Inn &
Conf Centre**
Hwy 134
Bathurst, NB
506-546-6621
The hotel is 4 km north of Hwy
180 on Hwy 134.

Campbellton

Comfort Inn
111 Val D'Amour Rd
Campbellton, NB
506-753-4121
There is no pet fee.

Howard Johnson Hotel
157 Water Street
Campbellton, NB
506-753-4133
Dogs of all sizes are welcome.
There are no additional pet fees.

Edmundston

Comfort Inn
5 Bateman Ave
Edmundston, NB
506-739-8361
There is no pet fee.

Fredericton

Comfort Inn
797 Prospect St
Fredericton, NB
506-453-0800
There is no pet fee. Pets are
allowed on the first floor. A
contact phone number will be
required if leaving the pet alone.

Holiday Inn
35 Mactaquac Rd
Fredericton, NB
506-363-5111

There are no pet fees. Pet
owners must sign a pet waiver.

Sheraton Fredericton Hotel
225 Woodstock Road
Fredericton, NB
506-457-7000
Dogs up to 80 pounds are
allowed. There are no
additional pet fees. There are a
few non-smoking pet rooms.

Miramichi

Comfort Inn
201 Edward St
Miramichi, NB
506-622-1215
There is no pet fee. Pets may
not be left alone.

Moncton

Comfort Inn East
20 Maplewood Dr
Moncton, NB
506-859-6868
There is no pet fee.

Comfort Inn Magnetic Hill
2495 Mountain Road
Moncton, NB
506-384-3175
There is no pet fee. Pets may
not be left alone. Pets are
allowed on the first floor.

**Holiday Inn Express Hotel &
Suites**
2515 Mountain Rd
Moncton, NB
506-384-1050
Pets may not be left alone in
the rooms.

Howard Johnson Plaza Hotel
1005 Main St.
Moncton, NB
506-854-6340
Dogs of all sizes are welcome.
There are no pet fees.

Saint John

Comfort Inn
1155 Fairville Blvd

Saint John, NB
506-674-1873
There is no pet fee.

Sussex

Quality Inn
P.O. Box 4437 Trans Canada
Highway 2
Sussex, NB
506-433-3470
There is a pet fee of $10 per
day. There is a nearby field for
walking.

Newfoundland Listings

Corner Brook

Best Western Mamateek Inn
Maple Valley Rd
Corner Brook, NF
709-639-8901
There are no additional pet fees.

Holiday Inn
48 West Street
Corner Brook, NF
709-634-5381
There are no pet fees. Pets must
be attended at all times.

Cornerbrook

Comfort Inn
41 Maple Valley Road
Cornerbrook, NF
709-639-1980
There is no pet fee.

Gander

Comfort Inn
112 Trans Canada Hwy
Gander, NF
709-256-3535
There is no pet fee. A credit card
will be required.

St Johns

Best Western Travellers Inn
199 Kenmount Rd
St Johns, NF
709-722-5540
There are no additional pet fees.

Holiday Inn
180 Portugal Cove Rd
St Johns, NF
709-722-0506
There are no pet fees.

Holiday Inn
44 Queen Street
Stephenville, NF
709-643-6666
There are no additional pet fees.

Northwest Territories Listings

Fraser Tower Suite Hotel
5303 52nd St
Yellowknife, NT
867-873-8700
There is a $5 per day additional pet fee. Pets must be crated if left alone in the room.

Super 8
308 Old Airport Rd
Yellowknife, NT
867-669-8888
There is a $25 per day additional pet fee.

Nova Scotia Listings

Comfort Inn
143 South Albion Street
Amherst, NS
902-667-0404
There is no pet fee. Pets are

allowed on the first floor.

Comfort Inn
49 North Street
Bridgewater, NS
902-543-1498
No pet fee.

Best Western Mic Mac Hotel
313 Prince Albert Rd
Dartmouth, NS
902-469-5850
There are no additional pet fees.

Holiday Inn Select
1980 Robie St
Halifax, NS
902-423-1161
There are no additional pet fees.

Howard Johnson Hotel
20 St. Margaret's Bay Rd.
Halifax, NS
902-477-5611
Dogs of all sizes are welcome. There are no pet fees.

Comfort Inn
740 Westville Rd
New Glasgow, NS
902-755-6450
There is no pet fee.

Caribou River Cottage Lodge
1308 Shore Road, RR# 3
Pictou, NS
902-485-6352
There are no additional pet fees.

Comfort Inn
368 Kings Road
Sydney, NS
902-562-0200
There is no pet fee. Pet may not be left alone.

Days Inn
480 Kings Road
Sydney, NS
902-539-6750
There are no additional pet fees.

Howard Johnson Hotel
437 Prince St.
Truro, NS
902-895-1651
Dogs of all sizes are welcome. There are no pet fees.

Comfort Inn
96 Starrs Road
Yarmouth, NS
902-742-1119
Pets are allowed in first floor rooms only.

Ontario Listings

Quality Inn
70 Madawask Blvd
Arnprior, ON
613-623-7991
There is a one time pet fee of $10.

Holiday Inn
20 Fairview Rd
Barrie, ON
705-728-6191
There are no additional pet fees.

Sleep Inn
510 Muskota Rd
Bracebridge, ON
705-645-4050
There is no pet fee. Pets may
not be left alone.

Comfort Inn
5 Rutherford Rd S
Brampton, ON
905-452-0600
There is no pet fee.

Motel 6
160 Steelwell Road
Brampton, ON
905-451-3313
A large well-behaved dog is
okay if it is kept on a leash and
is with you at all times.

Comfort Inn
58 Kng George Road
Brantford, ON
519-753-3100
There is no pet fee.

Days Inn
460 Fairview Dr
Brantford, ON
519-759-2700
There is a $10 per day additional
pet fee.

**Best Western White House
Motel**
1843 Highway 2 East
Brockville, ON
613-345-1622
There is a $10 per day pet fee.

Comfort Inn
7777 Kent Blvd
Brockville, ON
613-345-0042
There is a pet fee of $5 per day.

Comfort Inn
3290 South Service Rd
Burlington, ON
905-639-1700
There is no pet fee. Pets are
allowed in first floor rooms only.

Comfort Inn
220 Holiday Inn Drive
Cambridge, ON
519-658-1100
There is no pet fee. Pets may
not be left alone. A credit card
will be required.

Comfort Inn
1100 Richmond St
Chatham, ON
519-352-5500
There is no pet fee.

Comfort Inn
121 Densmore rd
Cobourg, ON
905-372-7007
There is no pet fee. Pets are
allowed on the first floor only.

**Best Western Parkway Inn &
Conf Centre**
1515 Vincent Massey Dr
Cornwall, ON
613-932-0451
There are no additional pet
fees.

Holiday Inn Express
1625 Vincent Massey Drive
Cornwall, ON
613-937-0111
There are no pet fees. Pets
may stay in first floor rooms.

Ramada Inn
805 Brookdale Ave
Cornwell, ON
613-933-8000
There are no additional pet fees.
A well-behaved dog is allowed.

**Quality Hotel & Suites Airport
East**
2180 Islington Ave
Etobicoke, ON
416-240-9090
There is a pet fee of $12 per
day.

**Ramada Hotel - Toronto
Airport**
2 Holiday Dr
Etobicoke, ON
416-621-2121
There is a $20 per day additional
pet fee.

Ramada Hotel & Conf. Ctr
716 Gordon St
Guelph, ON
519-836-1240
There are no additional pet fees.
Pet owners must sign a pet
waiver.

Comfort Inn
86 King William St
Huntsville, ON
705-789-1701
There is no pet fee. Pets may
not be left alone. A credit card
will be required.

Howard Johnson Inn
4022 Count Rd. 43 East
Kemptville, ON
613-258-5939
Dogs of all sizes are welcome.
There is a $10 per day pet fee.

Days Inn

920 Hwy 17 E
Kenora, ON
807-468-2003
There are no additional pet fees. Dogs are allowed in rooms with outside entrances.

Kingston

Comfort Inn Highway 401
55 Warne Cres
Kingston, ON
613-546-9500
There is no pet fee. Pets may not be left alone.

Comfort Inn Midtown
1454 Princess St
Kingston, ON
613-549-5550
There is no pet fee. Pets may not be left alone. A credit card will be required.

Howard Johnson Hotel
237 Ontario Street
Kingston, ON
613-549-6300
Dogs of all sizes are welcome. There is a $15 per day pet fee. Pets are allowed on the first and second floors only.

Kirkland

Howard Johnson Inn
50 Government Rd. East
Kirkland, ON
705-567-3241
Dogs of all sizes are welcome. There is a $5 one time pet fee.

Kitchener

Howard Johnson Hotel
1333 Weber St.
Kitchener, ON
519-893-1234
Dogs of all sizes are welcome. There is a $10 per day pet fee.

London

Quality Suites
1120 Dearness Drive

London, ON
519-680-1024
There is no pet fee. Pets are allowed on the first floor only.

Midland

Comfort Inn
980 King St
Midland, ON
705-526-2090
There is no pet fee. If your pet is left alone, a phone number must be given to the front desk.

Mississauga

Motel 6
2935 Argentia Rd
Mississauga, ON
905-814-1664
There are no additional pet fees.

Ramada Hotel Toronto Airport
5599 Ambler Dr
Mississauga, ON
905-624-9500
A large well-behaved dog is okay.

Studio 6
60 Britannia Rd East
Mississauga, ON
905-502-8897
There is a $25 one time pet fee.

Newmarket

Comfort Inn
1230 Journey's End Circle
Newmarket, ON
905-895-3355
There is no pet fee.

Niagara Falls

Camelot Inn
5640 Stanley Ave
Niagara Falls, ON
905-354-3754
There is a $10 per day additional pet fee.

Fallsview Motor Hotel
5551 Murray St
Niagara Falls, ON
905-356-0551
There is a 5 minute walk to the falls. There are no additional pet fees.

Niagara Parkway Court Motel
3708 Main Street
Niagara Falls, ON
905-295-3331
There is a $10 per day additional pet fee. The hotel only has one pet room so make your reservations early.

North Bay

Best Western North Bay
700 Lakeshore Drive
North Bay, ON
705-474-5800
There are no additional pet fees.

Clarion Resort Pinewood Park
201 Pinewood Park Drive
North Bay, ON
705-472-0810
There is no pet fee. Pets are allowed on the first floor only.

Comfort Inn
676 Lakeshore Dr.
North Bay, ON
705-494-9444
There is no pet fee.

Orillia

Comfort Inn
75 Progress Drive
Orillia, ON
705-327-7744
There is no pet fee.

Oshawa

Comfort Inn
605 Bloor Street West
Oshawa, ON
905-434-5000
There is no pet fee. Pets may not be left alone in the room.

Holiday Inn

1011 Bloor St E.
Oshawa, ON
905-576-5101
There are no pet fees. Pets may not be left unattended in the rooms.

Ottawa

Comfort Inn East
1252 Michael St
Ottawa, ON
613-744-2900
There is no pet fee. Pets are allowed on the first floor only.

Delta Ottawa Hotel and Suites
361 Queen Street
Ottawa, ON
613-238-6000
There is an additional $50 fee for a dog if you stay for 5 or more days.

Les Suites Hotel
130 Besserer St
Ottawa, ON
613-232-2000
There is a $25 one time pet fee.

Novotel Ottawa Hotel
33 Nicholas Street
Ottawa, ON
613-230-3033
There are no additional pet fees.

Ottawa Marriott Hotel
100 Kent Street
Ottawa, ON
613-238-1122
There are no additional pet fees.

Quality Hotel Downtown
290 Rideau St
Ottawa, ON
613-789-7511
There is no pet fee.

Radisson Hotel
402 Queen Street
Ottawa, ON
613-236-1133
There are no extra pet fees.

Ramada Hotel and Suites
111 Cooper Street
Ottawa, ON

613-238-1331
There are no additional pet fees.

Sheraton Ottawa Hotel
150 Albert Street
Ottawa, ON
613-238-1500
Dogs of all sizes are allowed. There are no additional pet fees.

Southway Inn
2431 Bank Street
Ottawa, ON
613-737-0811
There is a $15 pet fee for the first night and $5 each additional night.

Owen Sound

Comfort Inn
955 9th Ave E
Owen Sound, ON
519-371-5500
There is no pet fee. Pets may not be left alone in the room.

Pemborke

Comfort Inn
959 Pembroke St
Pemborke, ON
613-735-1057
There is no pet fee.

Peterborough

Comfort Inn
1209 Landsdowne St West
Peterborough, ON
705-740-7000
There is no pet fee.

Holiday Inn
150 George St N
Peterborough, ON
705-743-1144
There is a $25 one time pet fee.

King Bethune Guest House and Spa
270 King Street
Peterborough, ON
705-743-4101

Full breakfast included. Located in the the Kawartha Lakes Cottage country. There is a $10 charge per night for pets. Pets may not be left in the rooms.

Quality Inn
1074 Landsdowne St West
Peterborough, ON
705-748-6801
There is no pet fee. Pets may not be left alone in the room. A credit card will be required.

Pickering

Comfort Inn
533 Kingston Rd
Pickering, ON
905-831-6200
There is no pet fee.

Richmond Hill

Sheraton Parkway Toronto North Hotel & Suites
At Highway 404 and Highway 7
Richmond Hill, ON
905-881 2121
Dogs of all sizes are allowed, but there is only one pet room. It is a non-smoking room. There are no additional pet fees.

Sarnia

Best Western Guildwood Inn
1400 Venetian Blvd
Sarnia, ON
519-337-7577
There are no additional pet fees.

Sault Ste Marie

Holiday Inn
208 St Marys River Dr
Sault Ste Marie, ON
705-949-0611
There are no additional pet fees. Pets stay in the first floor rooms. Pets must be leashed when outside the room.

Simcoe

Best Western Little River
203 Queensway West
Simcoe, ON
519-426-2125
A well-behaved large dog is
okay. There are no additional
pet fees.

Comfort Inn
84 Queensway East
Simcoe, ON
519-426-2611
There is no pet fee.

St Catharines

Comfort Inn
2 Dunlop Dr
St Catharines, ON
905-687-8890
Dogs must stay in the first floor
rooms here. It is about a 15
minute drive to the falls. There
are no pet fees.

Holiday Inn St Catharines
2 N Service Rd
St Catharines, ON
905-934-8000
There is a $15 per day additional
pet fee.

**Ramada Parkway Inn and
Conference Centre**
327 Ontario St
St Catharines, ON
905-688-2324
There are no additional pet fees.

St Thomas

Comfort Inn
100 Centennial Ave
St Thomas, ON
519-633-4082
There is a one time pet fee of
$20.

Sudbury

Comfort Inn
2171 Regent St. S.
Sudbury, ON
705-522-1101
There is no pet fee. A credit card
or driver's license will be

required.

Thornhill

Staybridge Suites
355 SOuth Park Rd
Thornhill, ON
905-771-9333
There is a $75 one time pet fee.
Dogs are welcome to stay in
the hotel but are not allowed in
the public areas such as the
lobby and pool.

Thunder Bay

**Best Western Crossroads
Motor Inn**
655 W. Arthur Street
Thunder Bay, ON
807-577-4241
There are no additional pet
fees.

Timmins

Ramada Inn & Conf Ctr
1800 Riverside Dr
Timmins, ON
705-267-6241
If paying with cash a $50
refundable pet deposit is
required.

Toronto

**Beaches Bed and Breakfast
Inn**
174 Waverley Road
Toronto, ON
416-699-0818
This B&B, located in The
Beaches neighborhood, is just
1.5 blocks from the beach. Pets
and children are welcome at
this bed and breakfast. Most of
the rooms offer private
bathrooms. The owner has cats
on the premises.

Comfort Inn Downsview
66 Norfinch dr
Toronto, ON
416-736-4700
There is no pet fee. Pets are

allowed on the first floor only.
Pets may not be left alone.

Crowne Plaza
1250 Eglinton Ave East
Toronto, ON
416-449-4111
There is a $20 per day pet fee.
Pets stay in first floor rooms.

Delta Toronto Airport Hotel
801 Dixon Rd West
Toronto, ON
416-675-6100
There are no additional pet fees.

Four Seasons Hotel
21 Avenue Road
Toronto, ON
416-964-0411
There are no extra pet charges,
just notify reservations that you
will be bringing a pet. The hotel
needs to know in advance
because they have special pet
rooms.

Holiday Inn on King
370 King Street West
Toronto, ON
416-599-4000
There are no additional pet fees.

Howard Johnson Hotel
89 Avenue Road
Toronto, ON
416-964-1220
Dogs of all sizes are welcome.
There are no additional pet fees.

**International Plaza Hotel and
Conference Centre**
655 Dixon Rd
Toronto, ON
416-244-1711
You must sign a pet waiver for
your dog. There are no
additional pet fees.

Novotel Toronto Centre
45 The Esplanade
Toronto, ON
416-367-8900
There is a $20 per day pet
charge.

Quality Hotel
280 Bloor Street West

Toronto, ON
416-968-0010
There are no additional pet fees.

Quality Hotel Downtown
111 Lombard St
Toronto, ON
416-367-5555
There is no pet fee. Pets may
not be left alone.

Quality Suites Airport
262 Carlingview Drive
Toronto, ON
416-674-8442
There is no pet fee. Pets may
not be left alone. A credit card
wil be required.

**Sheraton Centre Toronto
Hotel**
123 Queen Street West
Toronto, ON
416-361-1000
Dogs up to 80 pounds are
allowed. There are no additional
pet fees.

Travelodge Hotel
925 Dixon Road
Toronto, ON
416-674-2222
There are no additional pet fees.

Trenton

Days Inn
10 Trenton St
Trenton, ON
613-392-9291
There are no additional pet fees.

Holiday Inn
99 Glen Miller Rd
Trenton, ON
613-394-4855
There are no additional pet fees.
Pets must be attended at all
times.

Welland

Comfort Inn
870 Niagara St.
Welland, ON
905-732-4811

There is a pet fee of $10 per
day. Pets are allowed on the
first floor only.

Whitby

Motel 6
165 Consumers Dr
Whitby, ON
905-665-8883
Pets are allowed in first floor
rooms only.

Quality Suites East
1700 Champlain Ave
Whitby, ON
905-432-8800
There is no pet deposit if a
credit card is given. There is a
pet deposit of $100 if no credit
card is given.

Windsor

Comfort Inn
2955 Dougall
Windsor, ON
519-966-7800
There is a pet fee of $10 per
day.

Holiday Inn Select
1855 Huron Church Rd
Windsor, ON
519-966-1200
There is a $10 per day pet fee.
A large well-behaved dog is
allowed.

Quality Suites Downtown
250 Dougall Ave
Windsor, ON
519-977-9707
There is a pet fee of $30 per
day.

Woodstock

Quality Hotel & Suites
580 Bruin Blvd
Woodstock, ON
519-537-5586
There is no pet fee.

Prince Edward Island Listings

Charlottetown

Comfort Inn
112 TransCanada Highway
Charlottetown, PE
902-566-4424
There is no pet fee. Pets may
not be left alone.

Holiday Inn Express & Suites
Trans Canada Hwy #1
Charlottetown, PE
902-892-1201
There are no pet fees.

Quality Inn on the Hill
150 Euston St
Charlottetown, PE
902-894-8572
There is no pet fee. Pets are
allowed on the second floor
only.

Summerside

Quality Inn Garden of the Gulf
618 Water Street East
Summerside, PE
902-436-2295
There is no pet fee. Pets are
allowed in the motel section
only.

Quebec Listings

Ancienne Lorette

Comfort Inn
1255 Duplessi
Ancienne Lorette, PQ
418-872-5900
There is no pet fee. Pets may
not be left alone.

Baie-Comeau

Comfort Inn
745 Boul Lafleche

Baie-Comeau, PQ
418-589-8252
There is no pet fee. Pets may
not be left alone.

Baie-St-Paul

Hotel Baie-Saint-Paul
911 boul Mgr Laval
Baie-St-Paul, PQ
418-435-3683
There are no additional pet fees.

Beauport

Comfort Inn
240Boul. Ste-Anne
Beauport, PQ
418-666-1226
There is no pet fee.

Boucherville

Comfort Inn
96 boul de Mortagne
Boucherville, PQ
450-641-2880
There are no additional pet fees.

Brossard

Comfort Inn
7863 boul Taschereau
Brossard, PQ
450-678-9350
There are no additional pet fees.

Chicoutimi

Comfort Inn
1595 boul. Talbot
Chicoutimi, PQ
418-693-8686
There are no additional pet fees.

Dorval

Comfort Inn
340 Avenue Michel-Jasmin
Dorval, PQ
514-636-3391
There is no pet fee.

Drummondville

Comfort Inn
1055 rue Hains
Drummondville, PQ
819-477-4000
There are no additional pet
fees.

Gatineau

Comfort Inn
630 Boulevard La Gappe
Gatineau, PQ
819-243-6010
There is a one time pet fee of
$25. Pets may not be left alone.

Hull

Holiday Inn
2 Montcalm St
Hull, PQ
819-778-3880
Pets may not be left
unattended in the room. There
are no pet fees.

La Pocatiere

Days Inn La Pocatiere
235 Rt 132
La Pocatiere, PQ
418-856-1688
There are no additional pet
fees.

Laval

Comfort Inn
2055 Autoroute Des
Laurentides
Laval, PQ
450-686-0600
There is no pet fee. Pets may
not be left alone.

Quality Suites
2035 Autorout Des Laurentides
Laval, PQ
450-686-6777
There is no pet fee.

Lennoxville

La Paysanne Motel

42 rue Queen
Lennoxville, PQ
819-569-5585
There are no additional pet fees.

Longueuil

**Holiday Inn Montreal-
Longueuil**
900 rue St-Charles E.
Longueuil, PQ
450-646-8100
There are no additional pet fees.

Louiseville

Gite du Carrefour
11 ave St-Laurent ouest
Louiseville, PQ
819-228-4932
There are no additional pet fees.

Montreal

Crowne Plaza
505 Sherbrooke St E.
Montreal, PQ
514-842-8581
There are no additional pet fees.

Delta Montreal
475 avenue Président-Kennedy
Montreal, PQ
514-286-1986
There is a 30.00 pet fee.

Holiday Inn
420 Sherbrooke St W.
Montreal, PQ
514-842-6111
There are no additional pet fees.
Pets may not be left unattended
in rooms.

Holiday Inn - Airport
6500 Cote de Liesse
Montreal, PQ
514-739-3391
There are no additional pet fees.
Pets may not be left alone in the
rooms.

Holiday Inn Montreal-Midtown
420 rue Sherbrooke ouest
Montreal, PQ
514-842-6111

There are no additional pet fees.

Hotel Maritime Plaza
1155 rue Guy
Montreal, PQ
514-932-1411
There is a $35 per night fee for the pet.

Hotel Travelodge Montreal Centre
50 boul Rene-Levesque ouest
Montreal, PQ
514-874-9090
There is a $20 per night pet fee.

Le Centre Sheraton Montreal Hotel
1201 Boulevard Rene-Levesque West
Montreal, PQ
514-878-2000
Dogs up to 80 pounds are allowed. There are no additional pet fees. You must sign a pet waiver form.

Loews Hotel Vogue
1425 Rue De La Montagne
Montreal, PQ
514-285-5555
All well-behaved dogs of any size are welcome. This upscale hotel offers their "Loews Loves Pets" program which includes special pet treats, local dog walking routes, and a list of nearby pet-friendly places to visit. There are no pet fees.

Marriott Residence Inn Montreal
2045 rue Peel
Montreal, PQ
514-982-6064
There is a one time $250.00 pet fee.

Novotel Montreal Centre
1180 rue de la Montagne
Montreal, PQ
514-861-6000
There is a $20 per night dog fee.

Quality Hotel Downtown
3440 Avenue Du Parc
Montreal, PQ
514-849-1413

There is no pet fee.

Sheraton Four Points
475 rue Sherbrooke ouest
Montreal, PQ
514-842-3961
There are no additional pet fees.

Perce

Hotel Motel Manoir de Perce
212 Route 132
Perce, PQ
418-782-2022
There are no additional pet fees.

Pointe-Claire

Holiday Inn
6700 Trans-Canada Hwy
Pointe-Claire, PQ
514-697-7110
There are no additional pet fees. Pets may not be left alone in the rooms.

Quebec

Chateau Grande-Allee
601 Grande-Allee
Quebec, PQ
418-647-4433
There is a $250 refundable deposit for a pet.

Hotel Quality Suites Quebec
1600 rue Bouvier
Quebec, PQ
418-622-4244
There are no additional pet fees.

L'Hotel du Vieux Quebec
1190 rue St-Jean
Quebec, PQ
418-692-1850
There are no additional pet fees.

Quality Suites
1600 Rue Bouvier
Quebec, PQ
418-622-4244
There is no pet fee. Pets may

not be left alone.

Quebec Hilton
1100 boul Rene-Levesque E.
Quebec, PQ
418-647-2411
There are no additional pet fees.

Quebec City

Loews Le Concorde Hotel
1225 Cours Du General De Montcalm
Quebec City, PQ
418-647-2222
All well-behaved dogs of any size are welcome. This upscale hotel offers their "Loews Loves Pets" program which includes room service for pets, special pet treats, local dog walking routes, and a list of nearby pet-friendly places to visit. There are no pet fees.

Rimouski

Comfort Inn
455 Boulevard St. Germain Quest
Rimouski, PQ
418-724-2500
There is no pet fee. Well behaved dogs only.

Riveire-Du-Loup

Days Inn
182 Fraser
Riviere-Du-Loup, PQ
418-862-6354
There is a $15 per day pet fee.

Rouyn-Noranda

Comfort Inn
1295 Avenue Lariviere
Rouyn-Noranda, PQ
819-797-1313
There is no pet fee.

Sainte-Foy

Holiday Inn
3125 Hochelaga Blvd

Sainte-Foy, PQ
418-653-4901
There are no additional pet fees.

Salaberry-de-Valleyfield

Hotel Valleyfield by Delta
40 ave du Centenaire
Salaberry-de-Valleyfield, PQ
450-373-1990
There are no additional pet fees.

Sept-Iles

Comfort Inn
854 Boulevard Laure
Sept-Iles, PQ
418-968-6005
There is no pet fee.

Shawinigan Sud

Motel Safari
4500 12e Ave
Shawinigan Sud, PQ
819-536-2664
There are no additional pet fees.

Sherbrooke

Motel La Reserve
4235 rue King ouest
Sherbrooke, PQ
819-566-6464
There is a $5 per day additional
pet fee.

St Laurent

Quality Hotel Dorval Aeroport
7700 Cote De Liessse
St Laurent, PQ
514-731-7821
There are no additional pet fees.

St-Felicien

Hotel du Jardin
1400 boul du Jardin
St-Felicien, PQ
418-679-8422
There are no additional pet fees.

St-Jean-Port-Joli

Auberge du Faubourg
280 ave de Gaspe ouest
St-Jean-Port-Joli, PQ
418-598-6455
There are no additional pet
fees.

St-Jean-sur-Richelieu

Comfort Inn
700 rue Gadbois
St-Jean-sur-Richelieu, PQ
450-359-4466
There are no additional pet
fees.

St-Laurent

Quality Hotel Dorval
7700 Cote de Liesse
St-Laurent, PQ
514-731-7821
You must sign a pet waiver.
There are no additional pet
fees.

Ste-Foy

Comfort Inn West
7320 Boulevard Wilfrid-Hamel
Ste-Foy, PQ
418-872-5038
There is no pet fee. Pets may
not be left alone.

Ste-Helene-de-Bagot

Days Inn
410 Couture
Ste-Helene-de-Bagot, PQ
450-791-2580
There is a $5.75 per day pet
fee.

Ste. Foy

Comfort Inn
7320 boul Wilfrid-Hamel
Ste. Foy, PQ
418-872-5038
There are no additional pet
fees.

Thetford Mines

Comfort Inn
123 Boulevard Smith Sud
Thetford Mines, PQ
418-338-0171
There is no pet fee.

Trois-Rivieres

Days Inn
3155 Blvd St Jean
Trois-Rivieres, PQ
819-377-4444
There is a $10 per day additional
pet fee.

Delta Trois-Rivieres
1620 rue Notre-Dame
Trois-Rivieres, PQ
819-376-1991
There are no additional pet fees.

Val D'Or

Comfort Inn
1665 3rd Avenue
Val D'Or, PQ
819-825-9360
There is no pet fee. Pets may
not be left alone.

Saskatchewan Listings

Caronport

The Pilgrim Inn
510 College Dr (Hwy 1 W)
Caronport, SK
306-756-5002
There is a $10 per day pet fee.
All rooms are non-smoking.

Kindersley

Super 8
508 12th Ave E
Kindersley, SK
306-463-8218
There are no additional pet fees.
A well-behaved large dog is

okay.

Prince Albert

Comfort Inn
3863 2nd Avenue W
Prince Albert, SK
306-763-4466
There is no pet fee.

Regina

Best Western Victoria Park
2020 E Victoria Ave
Regina, SK
306-565-2251
There are no additional pet fees.

Ramada Hotel & Conv. Ctr
1818 Victoria Ave
Regina, SK
306-569-1666
There are no additional pet fees.
Pets must be attended at all
times.

Saskatoon

**Country Inn & Suites by
Carlson**
617 Cynthia St
Saskatoon, SK
306-934-3900
There is a $10 one time pet fee.

Holiday Inn Express
315 Idylwyld Dr N
Saskatoon, SK
306-384-8844
There is a $10 pet fee for the
first night and a $5 fee for each
additional night. Pets must be on
leash when outside the room.

Radisson Hotel
405 20th St E
Saskatoon, SK
306-665-3322
There is a $20 one time pet fee.

Ramada Hotel and Golf Dome
806 Idylwyld Dr North
Saskatoon, SK
306-665-6500
There are no additional pet fees.

Sheraton Cavalier Hotel
612 Spadina Crescent
Saskatoon, SK
306-652-6770
Dogs up to 80 pounds are
allowed. There are no
additional pet fees.

Super 8
706 Circle Dr E
Saskatoon, SK
306-384-8989
There is a $5 per day additional
pet fee.

Yukon Listings

Whitehorse

Best Western Gold Rush Inn
411 Main Street
Whitehorse, YK
867-668-4500
There is a $25 per day pet fee.

Chapter 3

Dog-Friendly Coastal Beach Guides

Maine Listings

Bar Harbor

Hadley Point Beach
Highway 3
Bar Harbor, ME

Dogs are allowed on the beach, but must be leashed. The beach is located about 10 minutes northwest of downtown Bar Harbor, near Eden.

Kennebunk

Kennebunk Beaches
Beach Avenue
Kennebunk, ME

Dogs are allowed with certain restrictions. During the summertime, from about Memorial Day weekend through Labor Day weekend, leashed dogs are only allowed on the beach before 8am and after 6pm. During the rest of the year, dogs are allowed on the beach during park hours. There are a string of beaches, including Kennebunk, Gooch's and Mother's, that make up a nice stretch of wide sandy beaches. People need to clean up after their pets. The beaches are located on Beach Avenue, off Routes 9 and 35.

Kennebunkport

Goose Rocks Beach
Dyke Street
Kennebunkport, ME

Leashed dogs are allowed, with certain restrictions. From June 15 through September 15, dogs are only allowed on the beach before 8am and after 6pm. During the rest of the year, dogs are allowed on the beach during park hours. People need to clean up after their pets. The beach is located about 3 miles east of Cape Porpoise. From Route 9, exit onto Dyke Street.

Wells

Wells Beach
Route 1
Wells, ME
207-646-2451
Leashed dogs are allowed, with certain restrictions. During the summer, from June 16 through September 15, dogs are only allowed on the beach before 8am and after 6pm. The rest of the year, dogs are allowed on the beach during all park hours. There are seven miles of sandy beaches in Wells. People are required to clean up after their pets.

York

Long Sands Beach
Route 1A
York, ME
207-363-4422
Leashed dogs are allowed, with certain restrictions. During the summertime, from about Memorial Day weekend through Labor Day weekend, dogs are only allowed on the beach before 8am and after 6pm. During the off-season, dogs are allowed during all park hours. This beach offers a 1.5 mile sandy beach. Metered parking and private lots are available. The beach and bathhouse are also handicap accessible. People are required to clean up after their pets.

Short Sands Beach
Route 1A
York, ME
207-363-4422
Leashed dogs are allowed, with certain restrictions. During the summertime, from about Memorial Day weekend through Labor Day weekend, dogs are only allowed on the beach before 8am and after 6pm. During the off-season, dogs are allowed during all park hours. At the beach, there is a large parking area and a playground. People are required to clean up after their pets.

York Harbor Beach
Route 1A
York, ME
207-363-4422
Leashed dogs are allowed, with certain restrictions. During the summertime, from about Memorial Day weekend through Labor Day weekend, dogs are only allowed on the beach before 8am and after 6pm. During the off-season, dogs are allowed during all park hours. This park offers a sandy beach nestled against a rocky shoreline. There is limited parking. People are required to clean up after their pets.

Massachusetts Listings

Boston

Carson Beach
I-93 and William Day Blvd.
Boston, MA
617-727-5114
Dogs are only allowed on the beach during the off-season. Pets are not allowed from Memorial Day weekend through Labor Day weekend. Dogs must be leashed and people are required to clean up after their pets.

Cape Cod

Barnstable Town Beaches
off Route 6A
Barnstable, MA
508-790-6345
Dogs are allowed only during the off-season, from September 15 to May 15. Dogs must be on leash or under voice control. People need to clean up after

their pets. The town of Barnstable oversees Hyannis beaches and the following beaches: Craigville, Kalmus, and Sandy Neck. Before you go, always verify the seasonal dates and times when dogs are allowed on the beach.

Chatham Town Beaches
off Route 28
Chatham, MA
508-945-5100
Dogs are allowed only during the off-season, from mid September to end the end of May. Dogs must be leashed and people need to clean up after their pets. The town of Chatham oversees the following beaches: Hardings, Light, and Ridgevale. Before you go, always verify the seasonal dates and times when dogs are allowed on the beach.

Dennis Town Beaches
Route 6A
Dennis, MA
508-394-8300
Dogs are allowed only during the off-season, from after Labor Day up to Memorial Day. There is one exception. Dogs are allowed year-round on the four wheel drive area of Chapin Beach. Dogs must be leashed on all town beaches, and people need to clean up after their pets. The town of Dennis oversees the following beaches: Chapin, Mayflower, Howes Street and Sea Street. Before you go, always verify the seasonal dates and times when dogs are allowed on the beach.

Falmouth Town Beaches
off Route 28
Falmouth, MA
508-457-2567
Dogs are allowed during the summer, only before 9am and after 5pm. During the off-season, dogs are allowed all day. Dogs must be leashed and people need to clean up after their pets. The town of Falmouth oversees the following beaches:

Menauhant, Surf Drive, and Old Silver. Before you go, always verify the seasonal dates and times when dogs are allowed on the beach.

Harwich Town Beach
off Route 28
Harwich, MA
508-430-7514
Dogs are allowed only during the off-season, from October to mid-May. Dogs must be on leash or under voice control. People need to clean up after their pets. The town of Harwich oversees Red River Beach. Before you go, always verify the seasonal dates and times when dogs are allowed on the beach.

Orleans Town Beaches
off Route 28
Orleans, MA
508-240-3775
Dogs are allowed only during the off-season, from after Labor Day to the Friday before Memorial Day. Dogs are allowed off leash, but must be under voice control. People need to clean up after their pets. The town of Orleans oversees Nauset and Skaket beaches. Before you go, always verify the seasonal dates and times when dogs are allowed on the beach.

Provincetown Town Beaches
off Route 6
Provincetown, MA
508-487-7000
Dogs on leash are allowed year-round. During the summer, from 6am to 9am, dogs are allowed off-leash. The town of Provincetown oversees the following beaches: Herring Cove and Race Point. Before you go, always verify the seasonal dates and times when dogs are allowed on the beach.

Sandwich Town Beaches
off Route 6A
Sandwich, MA

508-888-4361
Dogs are allowed only during the off-season, from October through March. Dogs must be leashed and people need to clean up after their pets. The town of Sandwich oversees the following beaches: East Sandwich and Town Neck. Before you go, always verify the seasonal dates and times when dogs are allowed on the beach.

Truro Town Beaches
off Route 6
Truro, MA
508-487-2702
Dogs are allowed during the summer, only before 9am and after 6pm. This policy is in effect from about the third weekend in June through Labor Day. During the off-season, dogs are allowed all day. Dogs must be leashed and people need to clean up after their pets. The town of Truro oversees the following beaches: Ballston, Corn Hill, Fisher, Great Hollow, Head of the Meadow, Longnook and Ryder. Before you go, always verify the seasonal dates and times when dogs are allowed on the beach.

Cape Cod National Seashore
Route 6
Wellfleet, MA
508-349-3785
The park offers a 40 mile stretch of pristine sandy beaches. Dogs on leash are allowed year-round on all of the seashore beaches, except for seasonally posted nesting or lifeguard controlled beaches. Leashed pets are also allowed on fire roads, and the Head of the Meadow bicycle trail in Truro. Check with the visitor center or rangers for details about fire road locations. To get there from Boston, take Route 3 south to the Sagamore Bridge. Take Route 6 east towards Eastham.

Wellfleet Town Beaches
off Route 6

Wellfleet, MA
508-349-9818
Dogs are allowed during the summer, only before 9am and after 6pm. During the off-season, from after Labor Day to the end of June, dogs are allowed all day. Dogs must be leashed and people need to clean up after their pets. The town of Wellfleet oversees the following beaches: Marconi, Cahoon Hollow, and White Crest. Before you go, always verify the seasonal dates and times when dogs are allowed on the beach.

Martha's Vineyard

Joseph Sylvia State Beach
Beach Road
Edgartown, MA
508-696-3840
Dogs are allowed during the summer, only before 9am and after 5pm. You will need to keep your dog away from any bird nesting areas, which should have signs posted. During the off-season, from mid-September to mid-April, dogs are allowed all day. This beach is about 2 miles long. Dogs must be leashed and people need to clean up after their pets. Before you go, always verify the seasonal dates and times when dogs are allowed on the beach.

Norton Point Beach
end of Katama Road
Edgartown, MA
508-696-3840
Dogs are allowed during the summer, only before 9am and after 5pm. You will need to keep your dog away from any bird nesting areas, which should have signs posted. During the off-season, from mid-September to mid-April, dogs are allowed all day. This beach is about 2.5 miles long. Dogs must be leashed and people need to clean up after their pets. Before you go, always verify the

seasonal dates and times when dogs are allowed on the beach.

South Beach State Park
Katama Road
Edgartown, MA
508-693-0085
Dogs are allowed during the summer, only after 5pm. During the off-season, from mid-September to mid-April, dogs are allowed all day. This 3 mile beach is located on the South Shore. Dogs must be leashed and people need to clean up after their pets. Before you go, always verify the seasonal dates and times when dogs are allowed on the beach.

Eastville Point Beach
At bridge near Vineyard Haven
Oak Bluffs, MA
508-696-3840
Dogs are allowed during the summer, only before 9am and after 5pm. You will need to keep your dog away from any bird nesting areas, which should have signs posted. During the off-season, from mid-September to mid-April, dogs are allowed all day. Dogs must be leashed and people need to clean up after their pets. Before you go, always verify the seasonal dates and times when dogs are allowed on the beach.

Nantucket

Nantucket Island Beaches
various locations
Nantucket, MA
508-228-1700
Dogs are allowed during the summer on beaches with lifeguards only before 9am and after 5pm. On beaches that have no lifeguards, or during the winter months, dogs are allowed all day on the beach. Dogs must always be leashed. Before you go, always verify the seasonal dates and times when dogs are allowed on the beach.

Rhode Island Listings

Newport

Easton's Beach
Memorial Blvd.
Newport, RI
401-847-6875
Dogs are only allowed on the beach during the off-season. They are not allowed on the beach from Memorial Day weekend through Labor Day weekend. Pets must be on leash and people need to clean up after their pets. The beach is located off Route 138A (Memorial Blvd.). There is a parking fee.

Block Island

Block Island Beaches
Corn Neck Road
Block Island, RI
401-466-2982
Dogs are allowed year-round on the island beaches, but they must be leashed and people are required to clean up after their pets. To get to the beaches, take a right out of town and follow Corn Neck Road. To get to the island, you will need to take the Block Island Ferry which allows leashed dogs. The ferry from Port Judith, RI to Block Island operates daily. If you are taking the ferry from Newport, RI or New London, CT to the island, please note these ferries only operate during the summer. If you are bringing a vehicle on the ferry, reservations are required. Call the Block Island Ferry at 401-783-4613 for auto reservations.

Narragansett

Salty Brine State Beach

254 Great Road
Narragansett, RI
401-789-3563
Dogs are only allowed on the beach during the off-season, from October 1 through March 31. Pets must be on leash and people are required to clean up after their pets. To get there, take I-95 to Route 4 South. Then take Route 1 South to Route 108 South to Point Judith. If you are there during the summer, take the dog-friendly ferry at Pt. Judith to Block Island where leashed dogs are allowed year-round on the island beaches.

South Kingston

East Matunuck State Beach
950 Succotash Road
South Kingston, RI
401-789-8585
Dogs are only allowed on the beach during the off-season, from October 1 through March 31. Pets must be on leash and people are required to clean up after their pets. To get there, take I-95 to Route 4 South. Then take Route 1 South to East Matunuck Exit and follow the signs to the state beach.

Charlestown

East Beach State Beach
East Beach Road
Charlestown, RI
401-322-0450
Dogs are only allowed on the beach during the off-season, from October 1 through March 31. Pets must be on leash and people are required to clean up after their pets. To get there, take I-95 to Route 4 South. Then take Route 1 South to East Beach exit in Charlestown.

Westerly

Misquamicut State Beach
257 Atlantic Avenue
Westerly, RI

401-596-9097
Dogs are only allowed on the beach during the off-season, from October 1 through March 31. Pets must be on leash and people are required to clean up after their pets. To get there, take I-95 to Route 4 South. Then take Route 1 South to Westerly. Follow the signs to the state beach.

Connecticut Listings

Fairfield

Town of Fairfield Beaches
off Highway 1
Fairfield, CT
203-256-3010
Dogs are only allowed on the town beaches during the off-season. Pets are not allowed on the beaches from April 1 through October 1. Dogs must be on leash and people need to clean up after their pets.

New York Listings

Long Island

Camp Hero State Park
50 South Fairview Avenue
Montauk, NY
631-668-3781
The park boasts some of the best surf fishing spots in the world. Dogs on a 6 foot or less leash are allowed on the beach year-round, but not in the picnic areas. To get to the park, take Route 27 (Sunrise Highway) east to the end. The park is about 130 miles from New York City.

Hither Hills State Park
50 South Fairview Avenue
Montauk, NY

631-668-2554
This park offers visitors a sandy ocean beach. Dogs are allowed with certain restrictions. During the off-season, dogs are allowed on the beach. During the summer, dogs are not allowed on the beach, except for the undeveloped area on the other side of the freeway. Dogs must be on a 6 foot or less leash and people need to clean up after their pets. Dogs are not allowed in buildings or on walkways and they are not allowed in the camping, bathing and picnic areas.

Montauk Point State Park
50 South Fairview Avenue
Montauk, NY
631-668-3781
This park is located on the eastern tip of Long Island. Dogs are allowed on the beach, but not near the food area. Dogs must be on a 6 foot or less leash and people need to clean up after their pets. Dogs are not allowed in buildings or on walkways and they are not allowed in the camping, bathing and picnic areas. Please note that dogs are not allowed in the adjacent Montauk Downs State Park. The park is located 132 miles from Manhattan, off Sunrise Highway (Route 27).

New Jersey Listings

Seaside Park

Island Beach State Park
off Route 35
Seaside Park, NJ
732-793-0506
There are certain restrictions for pets on the beach. During the summer, dogs on a 6 foot or less leash are allowed on the beach, but not on the designated swimming beaches. Ask the ranger when you arrive, as to which part of the beach allows

dogs. During the off-season, dogs are allowed on all of the beaches, but must be on a 6 foot or less leash. People are required to clean up after their pets. To get to the park, take Route 37 east. Then take Route 35 south to the park entrance.

Cape May

Higbee Beach Wildlife Management Area
County Road 641
Cape May, NJ
609-628-2103
This park offers a 1 1/2 mile stretch of beach. The beach is managed specifically to provide habitat for migratory wildlife. Dogs on leash and under control are allowed at the beach. To get there, take SR 109 west to US9. Turn left onto US9 and go to the first traffic light. Turn left onto County Road 162 (Seashore Rd.). Then turn right onto Country Road 641 (New England Rd.). Take CR641 for 2 miles to the end and the beach access parking area. Parking areas near the beach may be closed during the summer. The park is open daily from dawn to dusk.

Cape May Point

Cape May Point State Park
Lighthouse Avenue
Cape May Point, NJ
609-884-2159
Dogs are only allowed on the beach during the off-season. Pets are not allowed from April 15 through September 15. Pets must be on a 6 foot or less leash and people need to clean up after their pets. The park is located off the southern end of the Garden State Parkway. Go over the Cape May Bridge to Lafayette Street. At the intersection, go right onto Route 606 (Sunset Blvd.), then turn left onto Lighthouse Ave.

Delaware Listings

Lewes

Cape Henlopen State Park
42 Cape Henlopen Drive
Lewes, DE
302-645-8983
This park draws thousands of visitors who enjoy sunbathing and ocean swimming. Dogs on a 6 foot or less leash are allowed on the beach, with some exceptions. Dogs are not allowed on the two swimming beaches during the summer, but they are allowed on surfing and fishing beaches, bike paths and some of the trails. Pets are not allowed on the fishing pier. People are required to clean up after their pets. The park is located one mile east of Lewes, 1/2 mile past the Cape May-Lewes Ferry Terminal.

Rehoboth Beach

Delaware Seashore State Park
Inlet 850
Rehoboth Beach, DE
302-227-2800
This park offers six miles of ocean and bay shoreline. Dogs on a 6 foot or less leash are allowed on the beach, with a couple of exceptions. Dogs are not allowed at the lifeguard controlled swimming areas. However, there are plenty of non-guarded beaches where people with dogs can walk or sunbathe. The park is located south of Dewey Beach, along Route 1.

Maryland Listings

Pasadena

Downs Park Dog Beach
8311 John Downs Loop
Pasadena, MD
410-222-6230
This dog beach is located on Chesapeake Bay, not on the ocean. People are not permitted to go swimming, but dogs can run off-leash at this beach. The dog beach is closed every Tuesday. Dogs on leash are also allowed in Downs Park. People need to clean up after their pets. Take Route 100 until it merges with Moutain Road (Rt. 177 East). Follow Mt. Road for about 3.5 miles and the park entrance will be on your right. The dog beach is located in the northeast corner of the park.

Annapolis

Quiet Waters Park Dog Beach
600 Quiet Waters Park Road
Annapolis, MD
410-222-1777
This park is located on Chesapeake Bay, not on the ocean. Dogs are welcome to run off-leash at this dog beach and dog park. The dog park is closed every Tuesday. Leashed dogs are also allowed at Quiet Waters Park. The park offers over 6 miles of scenic paved trails, and a large multi-level children's playground. People need to clean up after their pets. To get there, take Route 665 until it ends and merges with Forrest Drive. Take Forrest Drive for 2 miles and then turn right onto Hillsmere Drive. The park entrance is about 100 yards on the right. The dog beach is located to the left of the South River overlook. Park in Lot N.

Hermanville

Elm's Beach Park
Bay Forest Road
Hermanville, MD
301-475-4572
The park is located on Chesapeake Bay, not on the

ocean. Enjoy great views of the bay or swim at the beach. Dogs on leash are allowed at the beach. People need to clean up after their pets. Take Route 235 to Bay Forest Road and then go 3 miles. The park will be on the left.

Ocean City

Ocean City Beaches
Route 528
Ocean City, MD
1-800-OC-OCEAN
Dogs are only allowed during certain times of the year on this city beach. Pets are not allowed on the beach or boardwalk at any time from May 1 through September 30. The rest of the year, dogs are allowed on the beach and boardwalk, but must be on leash and people must clean up after them.

Assateague Island

Assateague Island National Seashore
Route 611
Assateague Island, MD
410-641-1441
Dogs on leash are allowed on beaches, except for any lifeguard controlled swimming beaches (will be marked off with flags). There are plenty of beaches to enjoy at this park that are not lifeguard controlled swimming beaches. Dogs are not allowed on trails in the park. The park is located eight miles south of Ocean City, at the end of Route 611.

Virginia Listings

Virginia Beach Area

Back Bay National Wildlife Refuge
Sandpiper Road

Virginia Beach, VA
757-721-2412
Dogs are only allowed on the beach during the off-season. Dogs are only allowed on the beach from October 1 through March 31. Pets must be leashed (on leashes up to 10 feet long) and people need to clean up after their pets. This park is located approximately 15 miles south of Virignia Beach. From I-64, exit to I-264 East (towards the oceanfront). Then take Birdneck Road Exit (Exit 22), turn right onto Birdneck Road. Go about 3-4 miles and then turn right on General Booth Blvd. Go about 5 miles. After crossing the Nimmo Parkway, pay attention to road signs. Get into the left lane so you can turn left at the next traffic light. Turn left onto Princess Anne Rd. The road turns into Sandbridge Rd. Keep driving and then turn right onto Sandpiper Road just past the fire station. Follow Sandpiper Road for about 4 miles to the end of the road.

First Landing State Park
2500 Shore Drive
Virginia Beach, VA
757-412-2300
Dogs on a 6 foot or less leash are allowed year-round on the beach. People need to clean up after their pet. All pets must have a rabies tag on their collar or proof of a rabies vaccine. To get there, take I-64. Then take the Northampton Blvd./US 13 North (Exit 282). You will pass eight lights and then turn right at the Shore Drive/US 60 exit. Turn right onto Shore Drive and go about 4.5 miles to the park entrance.

Virginia Beach Public Beaches
off Highway 60
Virginia Beach, VA
757-437-4919
Dogs are only allowed during off-season on Virginia Beach

public beaches. From the Friday before Memorial Day through Labor Day weekend, pets are not allowed on public sand beaches, the boardwalk or the grassy area west of the boardwalk, from Rudee Inlet to 42nd Street. People are required to clean up after their pets and dogs must be leashed.

North Carolina Listings

Nags Head

Nags Head Beach
Highway 158
Nags Head, NC
252-441-8144
Dogs on leash are allowed year-round on this beach in the Outer Banks. People need to clean up after their pets.

Manteo

Cape Hatteras National Seashore
Highway 12
Manteo, NC
252-473-2111
This park offers long stretches of pristine beach. Dogs on a 6 foot or less leash are allowed year-round, except on any designated swimming beaches. Most of the beaches are non-designated swim beaches. People are required to clean up after their pets.

Atlantic Beach

Fort Macon State Park
Highway 58
Atlantic Beach, NC
252-726-3775
This park offers beach access. Dogs on a 6 foot leash or less are allowed on the beach, but not inside the Civil War fort located in the park. People need

to clean up after their pets. The park is located on the eastern end of Bogue Banks, south of Morehead City.

Kure Beach

Ft. Fisher State Recreation Area
Highway 421
Kure Beach, NC
910-458-5798
Enjoy miles of beachcombing, sunbathing or hunting for shells at this beach. Dogs on leash are allowed everywhere on the beach, except for swimming areas that have lifeguards on duty. People need to clean up after their pets. The park is located on the southern tip of Pleasure Island, near Wilmington.

South Carolina Listings

Myrtle Beach

Myrtle Beach City Beaches
off Interstate 73
Myrtle Beach, SC
843-281-2662
There are certain restrictions for pets on the beach. Dogs are not allowed on the right of way of Ocean Blvd. (part of I-73), between 21st Avenue North and 13th Avenue South during March 1 through September 30. From Memorial Day weekend through Labor Day weekend, leashed dogs are allowed on Myrtle Beach city beaches before 9am and after 5pm. During off-season, leashed dogs are allowed on the city beaches anytime during park hours. People need to clean up after their pets.

Myrtle Beach State Park
4401 South Kings Highway

Myrtle Beach, SC
843-238-5325
This is one of the most popular public beaches on the South Carolina coast. It is located in the heart of the Grand Strand. During the summertime, dogs are only allowed during certain hours. From June through August, dogs are only allowed on the beach after 4pm. For all other months of the year, dogs are allowed on the beach anytime during park hours. Dogs must be on leash at all times. People are required to clean up after their pets.

Murrells Inlet

Huntington Beach State Park
16148 Ocean Highway
Murrells Inlet, SC
843-234-4440
This beach is the best preserved beach on the Grand Strand. Dogs on a 6 foot or less leash are allowed on the beach. People need to clean up after their pets.

Isle of Palms

Isle of Palms County Park
14th Avenue
Isle of Palms, SC
843-886-3863
Dogs on leash are allowed year-round at this beach. People are required to clean up after their pets. The park is located on the Isle of Palms, on 14th Ave., between Palm Blvd. and Ocean Blvd. Then coming to Isle of Palms from 517, continue straight at the Palm Blvd. intersection and then take the next left at the park gate.

Folly Beach

Folly Beach County Park
Ashley Avenue
Folly Beach, SC
843-588-2426
Dogs are only allowed during

the off-season at this beach. They are not allowed from May 1 through September 30. But the rest of the year, dogs on leash are allowed on the beach during park hours. People are required to clean up after their pets. The park is located on the west end of Folly Island. On the island, turn right at Ashley Avenue stoplight and go to the end of the road.

Kiawah

Beachwalker County Park
Beachwalker Drive
Kiawah, SC
843-768-2395
Dogs on leash are allowed year-round at this beach. People are required to clean up after their pets. The park is located on the west end of Kiawah Island. Take Bohicket Road to the island. Just before the island security gate, turn right on Beachwalker Drive. Follow the road to the park.

Edisto Island

Edisto Beach State Park
8377 State Cabin Road
Edisto Island, SC
843-869-2756
Sunbathe, beachcomb or hunt for seashells on this 1.5 mile long beach. This park also has a 4 mile nature trail that winds through a maritime forest with great vistas that overlook the salt marsh. Dogs on a 6 foot or less leash are allowed on the beach and on the trails. People need to clean up after their pets.

Hunting Island

Hunting Island State Park
2555 Sea Island Parkway
Hunting Island, SC
843-838-2011
This park offers over 4 miles of beach. Dogs on a 6 foot or less leash are allowed on the beach

and on the trails at this state park. People need to clean up after their pets.

Hilton Head Island

Alder Lane Beach Access
S. Forest Beach Drive
Hilton Head Island, SC
843-341-4600
This beach has restricted seasons and hours for dogs. During the summertime, from the Friday before Memorial Day through the Tuesday after Labor Day, dogs can only be on the beach before 10am and then after 5pm (they are not allowed from 10am to 5pm). Pets must be leashed. During the off-season and winter months, from April 1 through the Thursday before Memorial Day, dogs must be on a leash between 10am and 5pm. From the Tuesday after Labor Day through September 30, dogs again must be on a leash between 10am and 5pm. At all other times, dogs may be off-leash, but must be under direct, positive voice control. People are required to clean up after their pets. There are 22 metered spaces for beach parking. The cost is a quarter for each 15 minutes.

Coligny Beach Park
Coligny Circle
Hilton Head Island, SC
843-341-4600
This beach has restricted seasons and hours for dogs. During the summertime, from the Friday before Memorial Day through the Tuesday after Labor Day, dogs can only be on the beach before 10am and then after 5pm (they are not allowed from 10am to 5pm). Pets must be leashed. During the off-season and winter months, from April 1 through the Thursday before Memorial Day, dogs must be on a leash between 10am and 5pm. From the Tuesday after Labor Day through

September 30, dogs again must be on a leash between 10am and 5pm. At all other times, dogs may be off-leash, but must be under direct, positive voice control. People are required to clean up after their pets. There are 30 metered spaces for beach parking. The cost is a quarter for each 15 minutes. A flat fee of $4 is charged at the parking lot on Fridays through Sundays and holidays.

Folly Field Beach Park
Folly Field Road
Hilton Head Island, SC
843-341-4600
This beach has restricted seasons and hours for dogs. During the summertime, from the Friday before Memorial Day through the Tuesday after Labor Day, dogs can only be on the beach before 10am and then after 5pm (they are not allowed from 10am to 5pm). Pets must be leashed. During the off-season and winter months, from April 1 through the Thursday before Memorial Day, dogs must be on a leash between 10am and 5pm. From the Tuesday after Labor Day through September 30, dogs again must be on a leash between 10am and 5pm. At all other times, dogs may be off-leash, but must be under direct, positive voice control. People are required to clean up after their pets. There are 52 metered spaces for beach parking. The cost is a quarter for each 15 minutes.

Georgia Listings

St Simons Island

Little St. Simons Island Beaches
off U.S. 17
St Simons Island, GA

912-554-7566
Dogs are allowed, but only during certain hours in the summer. From Memorial Day through Labor Day, dogs are allowed on the beach before 9: 30am and after 4pm. During the rest of the year, dogs are allowed anytime during park hours. Dogs must be on leash and people need to clean up after their pets.

St. Simons Island Beaches
off U.S. 17
St Simons Island, GA
912-554-7566
Dogs are allowed, but only during certain hours in the summer. From Memorial Day through Labor Day, dogs are allowed on the beach before 9: 30am and after 4pm. During the rest of the year, dogs are allowed anytime during park hours. Dogs must be on leash and people need to clean up after their pets.

Jekyll Island

Jekyll Island Beaches
off SR 520
Jekyll Island, GA
877-453-5955
Dogs on leash are allowed on the beaches. There are about 9 to 10 miles of beach. Please clean up after your dog.

Florida Listings

Jacksonville

Huguenot Memorial Park
10980 Hecksher Drive
Jacksonville, FL
904-251-3335
Dogs are allowed in the park and on the beach. Dogs must be leashed and people need to clean up after their dogs. The park is located off A1A.

Flagler Beach

Flagler Beach
A1A
Flagler Beach, FL
386-517-2000
Dogs are allowed north of 10th Street and south of 10th Street. They are not allowed on or near the pier at 10th Street. Dogs must be on leash and people need to clean up after their dogs.

Daytona Beach

Smyrna Dunes Park
Highway 1
New Smyrna Beach, FL
386-424-2935
Dogs are not allowed on the ocean beach, but are allowed almost everywhere else, including on the inlet beach and river. Bottle-nosed dolphins are typically seen in the inlet as well as the ocean. Dogs must be leashed and people need to clean up after their pets. The park is located on the north end of New Smyrna Beach.

Space Coast

Lighthouse Point Park
A1A
Ponce Inlet, FL
386-239-7873
You might see some dolphins along the shoreline at this park. The park is also frequented by people watching a space shuttle launch out of Cape Canaveral. If you go during a shuttle launch, be sure to hold on tight to your pooch, as the shuttles can become very, very noisy and loud. Dogs on leash are allowed at the park and on the beach. Please clean up after your dog. This park is located at the southern point of Ponce Inlet.

South Florida

Dog Beach

A1A
Boynton Beach, FL

Dogs can be leash-free at this beach. Please clean up after your dog. It is a county beach, located between the cities of Boynton Beach and Ocean Ridge. The dog beach is next to Nomad Surfshop which is at 4655 North Ocean Blvd. There is no parking lot for the beach.

Fort Pierce Inlet State Park
905 Shorewinds Drive
Fort Pierce, FL
772-468-3985
Dogs are not allowed on the ocean beach, but they are allowed on the cove beach. Pets must be leashed and people need to clean up after their pets. The park is located four miles east of Ft. Pierce, via North Causeway.

Jupiter Beach
A1A at Xanadu Road
Jupiter, FL

The beach is about 2 miles long. Please follow the dog rules on the beach so that dogs will continue to be allowed here. Dogs must be leashed on the beach. Please clean up after your dog as well.

Hobe Sound National Wildlife Refuge
North Beach Road
Jupiter Island, FL
772-546-6141
This refuge has sea turtle nesting areas and endangered species like the scrub jay and gopher tortoise. Dogs on leash are allowed at the beach. The leash law is enforced and people need to clean up after their pets. The park headquarters is located 2 miles south of SR 708 (Bridge Road) on U.S. 1. The beach is located 1.5 miles north of Bridge Road on North Beach Road.

Miami

Rickenbacker Causeway Beach
Rickenbacker Causeway
Miami, FL

This beach extends the length of the Rickenbacker Causeway from Downtown Miami to Key Biscayne. Dogs are allowed on the entire stretch. There are two types of beach, a Tree lined Dirt beach and a standard type of sandy beach further towards Key Biscayne. Dogs should be leashed on the beach.

Keys

Veteran's Memorial Park
Highway 1
Duck Key, FL
305-872-2411
Dogs on leash are allowed at this park and on the beach. People need to clean up after their pets. The park is located near mile marker 40, off Highway 1.

Anne's Beach
Highway 1
Islamorada, FL

Dog on leash are allowed at this beach. Please clean up after your dog. The beach is located around mile markers 72 to 74. There should be a sign.

Key West

Dog Beach
Vernon Ave and Waddell Ave
Key West, FL

This tiny stretch of beach is the only beach we found in Key West that a dog can go to.

Naples

Delnor-Wiggins Pass State Park
11100 Gulfshore Drive
Naples, FL

239-597-6196
Dogs are not allowed on the beaches in this park, but they can take dip in the water at the boat and canoe launch only. Dogs must be on leash. Please clean up after your dog. This park is located six miles west of Exit 17 on I-75.

Fort Myers

Lee County Off-Leash Dog Beach Park
Route 865
Fort Myers Beach, FL

Dogs are allowed off-leash at this beach. Please clean up after your dog and stay within the dog park boundaries. Dog Beach is located south of Ft. Myers Beach and north of Bonita Beach on Route 865. Parking is available near New Pass Bridge.

Fort Myers Area

Algiers Beach
Algiers Lane
Sanibel, FL
239-472-6477
This beach is located in Gulfside City Park. Dogs on leash are allowed and people need to clean up after their pets. Picnic tables and restrooms are available. There is an hourly parking fee. This beach is located about mid-way on the island. From the Sanibel causeway, turn right onto Periwinkle Way. Turn left onto Casa Ybel Rd and then left on Algiers Lane.

Bowman's Beach
Bowman Beach Road
Sanibel, FL
239-472-6477
Walk over a bridge to get to the beach. Dogs on leash are allowed and people need to clean up after their pets. Picnic tables are available. This beach is located on the west side of the island, near Captiva. From the Sanibel causeway, turn right on Periwinkle Way. Turn right on Palm Ridge Rd and then continue on Sanibel-Captiva Road. Turn left onto Bowman's Beach Rd.

Lighthouse Park Beach
Periwinkle Way
Sanibel, FL
239-472-6477
This park offers a long thin stretch of beach. Dogs on leash are allowed and people need to clean up after their pets. Picnic tables are available. This park is located on the east end of the island. From Causeway Road, turn onto Periwinkle Way.

Tarpon Bay Road Beach
Tarpon Bay Road
Sanibel, FL
239-472-6477
Take a short walk from the parking lot to the beach. Dogs on leash are allowed and people need to clean up after their pets. Picnic tables and restrooms are available. There is an hourly parking fee. This beach is located mid-way on the island. From the Sanibel causeway, turn right onto Periwinkle Way. Then turn left onto Tarpon Bay Road.

Tampa Bay

Honeymoon Island State Park
1 Causeway Blvd.
Dunedin, FL
727-469-5942
Dogs on a 6 foot or less leash are allowed on part of the beach. Please ask the rangers for details when you arrive at the park. The park is located at the extreme west end of SR 586, north of Dunedin.

Gandy Bridge Causeway
Gandy Bridge east end
St Petersburg, FL

This stretch of beach allows dogs to run and go swimming. We even saw a horse here. Dogs should be leashed on the beach.

Pinellas Causeway Beach
Pinellas Bayway
St Petersburg, FL

This stretch of beach is open to humans and dogs. Dogs should be on leash on the beach.

Davis Island Dog Park
Severn Ave and Martinique Ave
Tampa, FL

This dog beach is fenced and offers a large parking area and even a doggie shower. To get there go towards Davis Island and head for the Peter Knight Airport. Loop around until you reach the water (the airport should be on the left). Thanks to one of our readers for the updated information.

Dog Island

Dog Island Park

Dog Island, FL
850-697-2585
This island is a small remote island that is accessible only by boat, ferry or airplane. Dogs are allowed on the beach, but must be on leash. This island is south of Carrabelle.

Carrabelle

Carrabelle Beach
Carrabelle Beach Rd
Carrabelle, FL
850-697-2585
Dogs are allowed on this beach, but the following rules apply. Dogs must be on leash when near sunbathers. In areas where there are no sunbathers, dogs can be off-leash, but must be under direct voice control. Picnic areas and restrooms are available. The beach is located 1.5 miles west of town.

St George Island

Public Access Beaches
Gulf Beach Drive
St George Island, FL

St. George Island beaches have been consistently ranked as one of the top 10 beaches in America. One third of the island is Florida state park land which does not allow dogs. But the rest of the island offers Franklin County public beaches, which do allow dogs on a 6 foot leash or off-leash and under direct voice control.

Alabama Listings

Gulf Shores

Bon Secour Wildlife Refuge Beach
12295 State Highway 180
Gulf Shores, AL
251-540-7720
Leashed dogs are allowed on the beach and people must clean up after their pets.

Mississippi Listings

Bay St Louis

Hancock County Beaches
Beach Blvd.
Bay St Louis, MS
228-463-9222
Dogs on leash are allowed on Hancock County beaches. People need to clean up after their pets. The county beaches are located along the coast, between the cities of Waveland and Bay St. Louis.

Louisiana Listings

Grand Isle

Grand Isle State Park
Admiral Craik Drive
Grand Isle, LA
985-797-2559
Dogs on leash are allowed at the beaches, except for some designated swimming areas. This park offers many recreational opportunities like fishing, crabbing, sunbathing, nature watching and camping. Leashed pets are also allowed at the campsites. The park is located on the east end of Grand Isle, off Highway 1 on Admiral Craik Drive. It is about 2 hours south of New Orleans.

Texas Listings

Galveston

Big Reef Nature Park
Boddeker Drive
Galveston, TX
409-765-5023
Take a walkway to the beach which runs parallel to Bolivar Rd. Dogs on leash are allowed on the beach. People need to clean up after their pets. There are no day use fees. This park is part of East Beach which does not allow dogs on the pavilion. The beach is located on the east end of Galveston Isle, off Boddeker Drive.

Dellanera RV Park
FM 3005 at 7 Mile Rd.
Galveston, TX
409-740-0390
This RV park offers 1,000 feet of sandy beach. Dogs on leash are allowed on the beach and at the RV spaces. People need to clean up after their pets. There are over 60 full RV hookups, over 20 partial hookups and day parking. Picnic tables and restrooms are available at this park. There is a $5 day parking fee. RV

spaces are about $25 and up.

Galveston Island State Park
14901 FM 3005
Galveston, TX
409-737-1222
Leashed dogs are allowed on the beach and at the campsites. There is a $3 per person (over 13 years old) day use fee. There is no charge for children 12 and under. The park can be reached from Interstate 45 by exiting right onto 61st Street and traveling south on 61st Street to its intersection with Seawall Boulevard and then right (west) on Seawall (FM 3005) 10 miles to the park entrance.

Stewart Beach
6th and Seawall Boulevard
Galveston, TX
409-765-5023
This is one of the best family beaches in Galveston. Many family-oriented events including a sandcastle competition are held at this beach. Restrooms, umbrella and chair rentals, and volleyball courts are available. There is a $7 per car admission fee. Dogs on leash are allowed on the beach. People need to clean up after their pets. The beach is located at 6th Street and Seawall Blvd.

Corpus Christi

Cole Park
Ocean Drive
Corpus Christi, TX
800-766-2322
Dogs on leash are allowed on the beach. People need to clean up after their pets.

Padre Island National Seashore
Highway 22
Padre Island, TX
361-949-8068
Visitors to this beach can swim, sunbathe, hunt for shells or just enjoy a walk. About 800,000 visitors per year come to this

park. Dogs on leash are allowed on the beach. People need to clean up after their pets. There is a minimal day use fee. The park is located on Padre Island, southeast of Corpus Christi.

South Padre Island

Andy Bowie Park
Park Road 100
South Padre Island, TX
956-761-3704
Dogs on leash are allowed on the beach. People need to clean up after their pets. There is a minimal day use fee. This park is located on the northern end of South Padre Island.

Edwin K. Atwood Park
Park Road 100
South Padre Island, TX
956-761-3704
This beach offers 20 miles of beach driving. Dogs on leash are allowed on the beach. People need to clean up after their pets. There is a minimal day use fee. This park is located almost 1.5 miles north of Andy Bowie Park.

Isla Blanca Park
Park Road 100
South Padre Island, TX
956-761-5493
This popular beach offers about a mile of clean, white beach. Picnic tables, restrooms, and RV spaces are available at this park. Dogs on leash are allowed on the beach. People need to clean up after their pets. There is a minimal day use fee. The park is located on the southern tip of South Padre Island.

California Listings

San Diego

North Beach Dog Run
Ocean Blvd.

Coronado, CA

This dog beach is located in the city of Coronado at the end of Ocean Blvd. next to the U.S. Naval Station entrance. Park on the street and walk along the Naval Station fence until you reach the ocean and then bear right. There will be signs posted for the North Beach Dog Run.

La Jolla Shores Beach
Camino Del Oro
La Jolla, CA
619-221-8900
Leashed dogs are allowed on this beach and the adjacent Kellogg Park from 6pm to 9am. The beach is about 1/2 mile long. To get there, take Hwy 5 to the La Jolla Village Drive exit heading west. Turn left onto Torrey Pines Rd. Then turn right onto La Jolla Shores Drive. Go 4-5 blocks and turn left onto Vallecitos. Go straight until you reach the beach and Kellogg Park.

Point La Jolla Beaches
Coast Blvd.
La Jolla, CA
619-221-8900
Leashed dogs are allowed on this beach and the walkway (paved and dirt trails) from 6pm to 9am. The beaches and walkway are at least a 1/2 mile long and might continue further. To get there, exit La Jolla Village Drive West from Hwy 5. Turn left onto Torrey Pines Rd. Turn right on Prospect and then park or turn right onto Coast Blvd. Parking is limited around the village area.

Dog Beach
Point Loma Blvd.
Ocean Beach, CA
619-221-8900
Dogs are allowed to run off leash at this beach anytime during the day. This is a very popular dog beach which attracts lots and lots of dogs on

warm days. To get there, take Hwy 8 West until it ends and then it becomes Sunset Cliffs Blvd. Then make a right turn onto Point Loma Blvd and follow the signs to Ocean Beach's Dog Beach.

Ocean Beach
Point Loma Blvd.
Ocean Beach, CA
619-221-8900
Leashed dogs are allowed on this beach from 6pm to 9am. The beach is about 1/2 mile long. To get there, take Hwy 8 West until it ends and then it becomes Sunset Cliffs Blvd. Then make a right turn onto Point Loma Blvd and follow the signs to Ocean Beach Park. A separate beach called Dog Beach is at the north end of this beach which allows dogs to run off-leash.

Fiesta Island
Fiesta Island Road
San Diego, CA
619-221-8900
On this island, dogs are allowed to run off-leash anywhere outside the fenced areas, anytime during the day. It is mostly sand which is perfect for those beach loving hounds. You might, however, want to stay on the north end of the island. The south end was used as the city's sludge area (mud and sediment, and possibly smelly) processing facility. The island is often used to launch jet-skis and motorboats. There is a one-way road that goes around the island and there are no fences, so please make sure your dog stays away from the road. About half way around the island, there is a completely fenced area on the beach. Please note that the fully enclosed area is not a dog park. The city of San Diego informed us that is supposed to be locked and is not intended to be used as a dog park even though there may occassionally be dogs running in this off-limits

area.

San Diego County North

Del Mar Beach
Seventeenth Street
Del Mar, CA
858-755-1556
Dogs are allowed on the beach as follows. South of 17th Street, dogs are allowed on a 6 foot leash year-round. Between 17th Street and 29th Street, dogs are allowed on a 6 foot leash from October through May (from June through September, dogs are not allowed at all). Between 29th Street and northern city limits, dogs are allowed without a leash, but must be under voice control from October through May (from June through September, dogs must be on a 6 foot leash). Owners must clean up after their dogs.

Rivermouth Beach
Highway 101
Del Mar, CA

This beach allows voice controlled dogs to run leash free from September 15 through June 15 (no specified hours). Leashes are required during mid-summer tourist season from mid June to mid Sept. Fans of this beach are trying to convince the Del Mar City council to extend the leash-free period to year round. The beach is located on Highway 101 just south of Border Avenue at the north end of the City of Del Mar. Thanks to one of our readers for recommending this beach.

Anaheim - Orange County

Huntington Dog Beach
Pacific Coast Hwy. (Hwy 1)
Huntington Beach, CA
714-536-5486
This beautiful beach is about a mile long and allows dogs from dawn to dusk. Dogs must be on leash and owners must pick up

after them. They are permitted off leash ONLY in the water and must be under control at all times. Dogs are only allowed on the beach between Golden West Street and Seapoint Ave. Please adhere to these rules as there are only a couple of dog-friendly beaches left in the entire Los Angeles area. The beach is located off the Pacific Coast Hwy (Hwy 1) at Golden West Street. Please remember to pick up after your dog... the city wanted to prohibit dogs in 1997 because of the dog waste left on the beach. But thanks to The Preservation Society of Huntington Dog Beach (http://www.dogbeach.org), it continues to be dog-friendly. City ordinances require owners to pick up after their dogs.

Main Beach
Pacific Hwy (Hwy 1)
Laguna Beach, CA
949-497-3311
Dogs are allowed on this beach between 6pm and 8am, June 1 to September 16. The rest of the year, they are allowed on the beach from dawn until dusk. Dogs must be on a leash at all times.

Los Angeles - Hollywood

Haute Dogs on the Beach
on the beach
Long Beach, CA
562-570-3100
Once a month, during the spring and summer months, a certain section of the beach is open to dogs. Between 300 to 450 dogs come to play leash free in the shore each time. The special once a month event is organized by a private citizen and his website is http://www.hautedogs.org/. Take a look at his website for dates and times.

Long Beach Dog Beach Zone
between Roycroft and Argonne

Avenues
Long Beach, CA

This is a new three acre off-leash dog beach zone during specified hours daily. This is the only off leash beach that we are aware of in Los Angeles County and one of the few in Southern California. The hours vary by season and are 6 - 9 am & 6 - 8 pm during the summer from Memorial Day to Labor Day. During the rest of the year the hours are 6 - 9 am & 4 - 6 pm. Dogs are not permitted on the beach at any other time other than the scheduled hours. Dogs must be under visual and voice control of the owners. You can check with the website http://www.hautedogs.org for updates and additional rules about the Long Beach Dog Beach Zone.

Leo Carrillo State Beach
Hwy. 1
Malibu, CA
818-880-0350
This beach is one of the very few dog-friendly beaches in the Los Angeles area. In a press release dated November 27, 2002, the California State Parks clarified the rules for dogs at Leo Carrillo State Beach. We thank the State Parks for this clear announcement of the regulations. Dogs are allowed on a maximum 6 foot leash when accompanied by a person capable of controlling the dog on all beach WEST (up coast) of lifeguard tower 3 at Leo Carrillo State Park, Staircase Beach, County Line Beach, and all Beaches within Point Mugu State Park. Dogs are NOT allowed EAST of lifeguard tower 3 at Leo Carrillo State Beach at any time. And please note that dogs are not allowed in the tide pools at Leo Carrillo. There should be signs posted. A small general store is located on the mountain side of the freeway. Here you can grab some snacks

and other items. The park is located on Hwy 1, approximately 30 miles northwest of Santa Monica. We ask that all dog people closely obey these regulations so that the beach continues to be dog-friendly.

Ventura - Oxnard

Hollywood Beach
various addresses
Oxnard, CA

This beach is located on the west side of the Channel Islands Harbor. The beach is 4 miles southwest of Oxnard. Dogs must be on leash and owners must clean up after their pets. Thanks to one of our readers for recommending this beach.

Oxnard Shores Beach
Harbor Blvd.
Oxnard, CA

This beach stretches for miles. If you enter at 5th Street and go north, there are no houses and very few people. Dogs must be on leash and owners must clean up after their pets. Thanks to one of our readers for recommending this beach.

Silver Strand Beach
various addresses
Oxnard, CA

This beach is located between the Channel Islands Harbor and the U.S. Naval Construction Battalion Center. The beach is 4 miles southwest of Oxnard. Dogs must be on leash and owners must clean up after their pets. Thanks to one of our readers for recommending this beach.

Emma Wood State Beach
Hwy. 101
Ventura, CA
805-968-1033
This is one of the few state beaches that allow dogs. Dogs

must be on leash. The beach offers a view of Anacapa Island and occasionally dolphins. It is located off Hwy 101, 2 miles west (north) of Ventura.

Santa Barbara

Goleta Beach County Park
5990 Sandspit Road
Goleta, CA
805-568-2460
Leashed dogs are allowed at this county beach. The beach and park are about 1/2 mile long. There are picnic tables and a children's playground at the park. It's located near the Santa Barbara Municipal Airport in Goleta, just north of Santa Barbara. To get there, take Hwy. 101 to Hwy 217 and head west. Before you reach UC Santa Barbara, there will be an exit for Goleta Beach.

Arroyo Burro Beach County Park
2981 Cliff Drive
Santa Barbara, CA
805-967-1300
Leashed dogs are allowed at this county beach and park. The beach is about 1/2 mile long and it is adjacent to a palm-lined grassy area with picnic tables. To get to the beach from Hwy 101, exit Las Positas Rd/Hwy 225. Head south (towards the ocean). When the street ends, turn right onto Cliff Drive. The beach will be on the left.

Arroyo Burro Off-Leash Beach
Cliff Drive
Santa Barbara, CA

While dogs are not allowed off-leash at the Arroyo Burro Beach County Park (both the beach and grass area), they are allowed to run leash free on the adjacent beach. The dog beach starts east of the slough at Arroyo Burro and stretches

almost to the stairs at Mesa Lane. To get to the off-leash area, walk your leashed dog from the parking lot to the beach, turn left and cross the slough. At this point you can remove your dog's leash.

Rincon Park and Beach
Bates Road
Santa Barbara, CA

This beach is at Rincon Point which has some of the best surfing waves in the world. In the winter, it is very popular with surfers. In the summer, it is a popular swimming beach. Year-round, leashed dogs are welcome. The beach is about 1/2-1 mile long. Next to the parking lot there are picnic tables, phones and restrooms. The beach is in Santa Barbara County, about 15-20 minutes south of Santa Barbara. To get there from Santa Barbara, take Hwy 101 south and go past Carpinteria. Take the Bates Rd exit towards the ocean. When the road ends, turn right into the Rincon Park and Beach parking lot.

San Luis Obispo

Pismo State Beach
Grand Ave.
Pismo Beach, CA
805-489-2684
Leashed dogs are allowed on this state beach. This beach is popular for walking, sunbathing, swimming and the annual winter migration of millions of monarch butterflies (the park has the largest over-wintering colony of monarch butterflies in the U.S.). To get there from Hwy. 101, exit 4th Street and head south. In about a mile, turn right onto Grand Ave. You can park along the road.

Coastal Access
off Hearst Drive
San Simeon, CA

There is parking just north of the Best Western Hotel, next to the "Coastal Access" sign. Dogs must be on leash.

Gorda

Sand Dollar Beach
Highway 1
Gorda, CA
805-434-1996
Walk down a path to one of the longest sandy beaches on the Big Sur Coast. This beach is popular for surfing, fishing and walking. Dogs must be on leash and people need to clean up after their pets. There is a minimal day use fee.

Carmel

Carmel City Beach
Ocean Avenue
Carmel, CA
831-624-9423
This beach is within walking distance (about 7 blocks) from the quaint village of Carmel. There are a couple of hotels and several restaurants that are within walking distance of the beach. Your pooch is allowed to run off-leash as long as he or she is under voice control. To get there, take the Ocean Avenue exit from Hwy. 1 and follow Ocean Ave to the end.

Carmel River State Beach
Carmelo Street
Carmel, CA
831-624-9423
This beach is just south of Carmel. It has approximately a mile of beach and leashes are required. It's located on Carmelo Street.

Monterey

Monterey Recreation Trail
various (see comments)
Monterey, CA

Take a walk on the Monterey Recreation Trail and experience the beautiful scenery that makes Monterey so famous. This paved trail extends for miles, starting at Fisherman's Wharf and ending in the city of Pacific Grove. Dogs must be leashed. Along the path there are a few small beaches that allow dogs such as the one south of Fisherman's Wharf and another beach behind Ghiradelli Ice Cream on Cannery Row. Along the path you'll find a few more outdoor places to eat near Cannery Row and by the Monterey Bay Aquarium. Look at the Restaurants section for more info.

Monterey State Beach
various (see comments)
Monterey, CA
831-649-2836
Take your water loving and beach loving dog to this awesome beach in Monterey. There are various starting points, but it basically stretches from Hwy. 1 and the Del Rey Oaks Exit down to Fisherman's Wharf. Various beaches make up this 2 mile (each way) stretch of beach, but leashed dogs are allowed on all of them. If you want to extend your walk, you can continue on the paved Monterey Recreation Trail which goes all the way to Pacific Grove. There are a few smaller dog-friendly beaches along the paved trail.

Asilomar State Beach
Along Sunset Drive
Pacific Grove, CA
831-372-4076
Dogs are permitted on leash on the beach and the scenic walking trails. If you walk south along the beach and go across the stream that leads into the ocean, you can take your dog off-leash, but he or she must be under strict voice control and within your sight at all times.

Rio Del Mar Beach
Rio Del Mar
Aptos, CA
831-685-6500
Dogs on leash are allowed at this beach which offers a wide strip of sand. From Highway 1, take the Rio Del Mar exit.

Davenport Beach
Hwy. 1
Davenport, CA
831-462-8333
This beautiful beach is surrounded by high bluffs and cliff trails. Leashes are required. To get to the beach from Santa Cruz, head north on Hwy 1 for about 10 miles.

East Cliff Coast Access Points
East Cliff Drive
Santa Cruz, CA
831-454-7900
There are many small dog-friendly beaches and coastal access points that stretch along East Cliff Drive between 12th Avenue to 41st Avenue. This is not one long beach because the water comes up to cliffs in certain areas and breaks it up into many smaller beaches. Dogs are allowed on leash. Parking is on city streets along East Cliff or the numbered avenues. To get there from Hwy 17 south, take the Hwy 1 exit south towards Watsonville. Take the exit towards Soquel Drive. Turn left onto Soquel Avenue. Turn right onto 17th Avenue. Continue straight until you reach East Cliff Drive. From here, you can head north or south on East Cliff Drive and park anywhere between 12th and 41st street to access the beaches.

Seabright Beach
Seabright Ave
Santa Cruz, CA
831-429-2850
This beach is located south of the Santa Cruz Beach Boardwalk and north of the Santa Cruz Harbor. Dogs are

allowed on leash. Fire rings are available for beach bonfires. It is open from sunrise to sunset. To get there from Hwy 17 south, exit Ocean Street on the left towards the beaches. Merge onto Ocean Street. Turn left onto East Cliff Drive and stay straight to go onto Murray Street. Then turn right onto Seabright Ave. Seabright Ave will take you to the beach (near the corner of East Cliff Drive and Seabright).

Twin Lakes State Beach
East Cliff Drive
Santa Cruz, CA
831-429-2850
This beach is one of the area's warmest beaches, due to its location at the entrance of Schwann Lagoon. Dogs are allowed on leash. The beach is located just south of the Santa Cruz Harbor where Aldo's Restaurant is located. Fire rings for beach bonfires, outdoor showers and restrooms are available. It is open from sunrise to sunset. To get there from Hwy 17 south, exit Ocean Street on the left towards the beaches. Merge onto Ocean Street. Turn left onto East Cliff Drive and stay straight to go onto Murray Street. Murray Street becomes Eaton Street. Turn right onto 7th Avenue.

West Lighthouse Beach
West Cliff Drive
Santa Cruz, CA
831-429-3777
Your dog can go leash free from sunrise to 10am and 4pm until sunset. It is not a large beach, but enough for your water loving dog to take a dip in the water and get lots of sand between his or her paws. According to the sign, dogs are not allowed between 10am and 4pm. It is located on West Cliff Drive, just north of the Lighthouse, and south of Columbia Street. It is also across from the Lighthouse Field off-leash area. To get there, head south on Hwy 17.

Take the Hwy 1 North exit, heading towards Half Moon Bay and Hwy 9. Merge onto Mission Street (Hwy 1). Turn left onto Swift Street. Then turn left on West Cliff Drive. The beach and limited parking will be on the right.

Palo Alto - Peninsula

Blufftop Coastal Park
Poplar Street
Half Moon Bay, CA
650-726-8297
Leashed dogs are allowed at this beach. The beach is located on the west end of Poplar Street, off Highway 1.

Montara State Beach
Highway 1
Half Moon Bay, CA
650-726-8819
Dogs on leash are allowed at this beach. Please clean up after your pets. The beach is located 8 miles north of Half Moon Bay on Highway 1. There are two beach access points. The first access point is across from Second Street, immediately south of the Outrigger Restaurant. The second access point is about a 1/2 mile north on the ocean side of Highway 1. Both access points have steep paths down to the beach.

Surfer's Beach
Highway 1
Half Moon Bay, CA
650-726-8297
Dogs on leash are allowed on the beach. It is located at Highway 1 and Coronado Street.

Esplanade Beach
Esplanade
Pacifica, CA
650-738-7381
This beach offers an off-leash area for dogs. To get to the beach, take the stairs at the end of Esplanade. Esplanade is

just north of Manor Drive, off Highway 1.

Bean Hollow State Beach
Highway 1
Pescadero, CA
650-879-2170
Dogs are allowed on this beach, but must be on a 6 foot or less leash. Please clean up after your pets. The beach is located 3 miles south of Pescadero on Highway 1.

San Francisco

Baker Beach
Golden Gate Natl Rec Area
San Francisco, CA

This dog-friendly beach in the Golden Gate National Recreation Area has a great view of the Golden Gate Bridge. The beach is located approx. 1.5 to 2 miles south of the Golden Gate Bridge. From Lincoln Avenue, turn onto Bowley Street and head towards the ocean. There is a parking lot next to the beach.

Fort Funston/Burton Beach
Skyline Blvd./Hwy. 35
San Francisco, CA

This is a very popular dog-friendly park and beach. In the past, dogs have been allowed off-leash. However, currently all dogs must be on leash. Fort Funston is part of the Golden Gate National Recreation Area. There are trails that run through the dunes & ice plant from the parking lot above with good access to the beach below. It overlooks the southern end of Ocean Beach, with a large parking area accessible from Skyline Boulevard. There is also a water faucet and trough at the parking lot for thirsty pups. It's located off Skyline Blvd. (also known Hwy 35) by John Muir Drive. It is south of Ocean Beach. Thanks to one of our readers for this info. Expect to see lots and lots of dogs having a great time. But not to worry, there is plenty of room for everyone.

Ocean Beach
Great Hwy
San Francisco, CA
415-556-8642
You'll get a chance to stretch your legs at this beach which has about 4 miles of sand. The beach runs parallel to the Great Highway (north of Fort Funston). There are several access points including Sloat Blvd., Fulton Street or Lincoln Way. This beach has a mix of off-leash and leash required areas. Thanks to the San Francisco Dog Owners Group (SFDOG) for providing the following information: Dogs must be on leash on Ocean Beach between Sloat Blvd and Stairwell #21 (roughly at Fulton). North of Fulton to the Cliff House and South of Sloat for several miles are still okay for off-leash dogs, however parts of these areas may be impassible at high tide. The Golden Gate National Rec Area (GGNRA) strictly enforces the on-leash area between Sloat and Fulton. They usually give no warning tickets ($50 fine). As with all other leash required areas, we encourage dog owners to comply with the rules.

Marin - North Bay

Muir Beach
Hwy. 1
Muir Beach, CA

Dogs on leash are allowed on Muir Beach with you. Please clean up after your dog on the beach. To get to Muir Beach from Hwy 101 take Hwy 1 North from the north side of the Golden Gate Bridge.

Point Reyes National Seashore
Olema, CA
415-464-5100
Leashed dogs (on a 6 foot or less leash) are allowed on four beaches. The dog-friendly beaches are the Limantour Beach, Kehoe Beach, North Beach and South Beach. Dogs are not allowed on the hiking trails. However, they are allowed on some hiking trails that are adjacent to Point Reyes. For a map of dog-friendly hiking trails, please stop by the Visitor Center. Point Reyes is located about an hour north of San Francisco. From Highway 101, exit at Sir Francis Drake Highway, and continue west on Sir Francis Drake to Olema. To find the Visitor Center, turn right in Olema onto Route 1 and then make a left onto Bear Valley Road. The Visitor Center will be on the left.

Salmon Creek

Sonoma Coast State Beach
Highway 1
Salmon Creek, CA
707-875-3483
Dogs on leash are allowed at some of the beaches in this state park. Dogs are allowed at Shell Beach, Portuguese Beach and Schoolhouse Beach. They are not allowed at Goat Rock or Salmon Creek Beach due to the protected seals and snowy plovers. Please clean up after your pets. While dogs are allowed on some of the beaches and campgrounds, they are not allowed on any hiking trails at this park.

Jenner

Stillwater Cove Regional Park
22455 Highway 1
Jenner, CA
707-565-2041
This 210 acre park includes a small beach, campground,

picnic tables, and restrooms. The park offers a great view of the Pacific Ocean from Stillwater Cove. Dogs are allowed on the beach, and in the campground, but they must be on a 6 foot or less leash. People also need to clean up after their pets. There is a $3 day use fee. The park is located off Highway 1, about 16 miles north of Jenner.

Gualala

Gualala Point Regional Park
42401 Coast Highway 1
Gualala, CA
707-565-2041
This county park offers sandy beaches, hiking trails, campsites, picnic tables and restrooms. Dogs are allowed on the beach, on the trails, and in the campground, but they must be on a 6 foot or less leash. People also need to clean up after their pets. There is a $3 day use fee.

Mendocino

Big River Beach
N. Big River Road
Mendocino, CA
707-937-5804
This small beach is located just south of downtown Mendocino. There are two ways to get there. One way is to head south of town on Hwy. 1 and turn left on N. Big River Rd. The beach will be on the right. The second way is to take Hwy 1 and exit Main Street/Jackson heading towards the coastline. In about 1/4-1/2 mile there will be a Chevron Gas Station and a historic church on the left. Park and then walk behind the church to the trailhead. Follow the trail, bearing left when appropriate, and there will be a wooden staircase that goes down to Big River Beach. Dogs must be on leash.

Van Damme State Beach

Highway 1
Mendocino, CA

This small beach is located in the town of Little River which is approximately 2 miles south of Mendocino. It is part of Van Damme State Park which is located across Highway 1. Most California State Parks, including this one, do not allow dogs on the hiking trails. Fortunately this one allows dogs on the beach. There is no parking fee at the beach and dogs must be on leash.

Fort Bragg

MacKerricher State Park
Highway 1
Fort Bragg, CA
707-964-9112
Dogs are allowed on the beach, but not on any park trails. Pets must be leashed and people need to clean up after their pets. Picnic areas, restrooms and campsites (including an ADA restroom and campsites), are available at this park. The park is located three miles north of Fort Bragg on Highway 1, near the town of Cleone.

Westport

Westport-Union Landing State Beach
Highway 1
Westport, CA
707-937-5804
This park offers about 2 miles of sandy beach. Dogs must be on a 6 foot or less leash at all times and people need to clean up after their pets. Picnic tables, restrooms (including an ADA restroom) and campsites are available at this park. Dogs are also allowed at the campsites, but not on any park trails. The park is located off Highway 1, about 2 miles north of Westport or 19 miles north of Fort Bragg.

Arcata

Mad River Beach County Park
Mad River Road
Arcata, CA
707-445-7651
Enjoy walking or jogging for several miles on this beach. Dogs on leash are allowed. The park is located about 4-5 miles north of Arcata. To get there, take Highway 101 and exit Giuntoli Lane. Then go north onto Heindon Rd. Turn left onto Miller Rd. Turn right on Mad River Road and follow it to the park.

McKinleyville

Clam Beach County Park
Highway 101
McKinleyville, CA
707-445-7651
This beach is popular for fishing, swimming, picnicking and beachcombing. Of course, there are also plenty of clams. Dogs on leash are allowed on the beach and at the campgrounds. There are no day use fees. The park is located off Highway 101, about eight miles north of Arcata.

Trinidad

Trinidad State Beach
Highway 101
Trinidad, CA
707-677-3570
Dogs are unofficially allowed at College Cove beach, as long as they are leashed and under control. The residents in this area are trying keep this beach dog-friendly, but the rules can change at any time. Please call ahead to verify.

Orick

Gold Bluffs Beach
Davison Road
Orick, CA

707-464-6101
Dogs are allowed on this beach, but not on any trails within this park. Picnic tables and campgrounds are available at the beach. Pets are also allowed at road accessible picnic areas and campgrounds. Dogs must be on a 6 foot or less leash and people need to pick up after their pets. The beach is located off Highway 101. Take Highway 101 heading north. Pass Orick and drive about 3-4 miles, then exit Davison Rd. Head towards the coast on an unpaved road (trailers are not allowed on the unpaved road).

Crescent City

Crescent Beach
Enderts Beach Road
Crescent City, CA
707-464-6101
While dogs are not allowed on any trails in Redwood National Park, they are allowed on a couple of beaches, including Crescent Beach. Enjoy beachcombing or bird watching at this beach. Pets are also allowed at road accessible picnic areas and campgrounds. Dogs must be on a 6 foot or less leash and people need to pick up after their pets. The beach is located off Highway 101, about 3 to 4 miles south of Crescent City. Exit Enderts Beach Road and head south.

Oregon Listings

Brookings

Harris Beach State Park
Highway 101
Brookings, OR
541-469-2021
The park offers sandy beaches for beachcombing, whale watching, and sunset viewing. Picnic tables, restrooms

(including an ADA restroom) and shaded campsites are available at this park. There is a minimal day use fee. Leashed dogs are allowed on the beach. Dogs are also allowed at the campgrounds. They must be on a six foot or less leash at all times and people are required to clean up after their pets. On beaches located outside of Oregon State Park boundaries, dogs might be allowed off-leash and under direct voice control, please look for signs or postings. This park is located off U.S. Highway 101, just north of Brookings.

McVay Rock State Recreation Site
Highway 101
Brookings, OR
800-551-6949
This beach is a popular spot for clamming, whale watching and walking. Picnic tables and restrooms are available at this park. There are no day use fees. Dogs are allowed on the beach. They must be on a six foot or less leash at all times and people are required to clean up after their pets. On beaches located outside of Oregon State Park boundries, dogs might be allowed off-leash and under direct voice control, please look for signs or postings. This park is located off U.S. Highway 101, just south of Brookings.

Samuel H. Boardman State Scenic Corridor
Highway 101
Brookings, OR
800-551-6949
Steep coastline at this 12 mile long corridor is interrupted by small sandy beaches. Picnic tables, restrooms (including an ADA restroom), and a hiking trail are available at this park. There are no day use fees. Leashed dogs are allowed on the beach. Dogs are also allowed on the hiking trail. They must be on a six foot or less leash at all times

and people are required to clean up after their pets. On beaches located outside of Oregon State Park boundries, dogs might be allowed off-leash and under direct voice control, please look for signs or postings. This park is located off U.S. Highway 101, 4 miles north of Brookings.

Gold Beach

Pistol River State Scenic Viewpoint
Highway 101
Gold Beach, OR
800-551-6949
This beach is popular for ocean windsurfing. There has even been windsurfing national championships held at this beach. Picnic tables and restrooms are available here. There are no day use fees. Dogs are allowed on the beach. They must be on a six foot or less leash at all times and people are required to clean up after their pets. On beaches located outside of Oregon State Park boundaries, dogs might be allowed off-leash and under direct voice control, please look for signs or postings. This park is located off U.S. Highway 101, 11 miles south of Gold Beach.

Port Orford

Cape Blanco State Park
Highway 101
Port Orford, OR
541-332-6774
Take a stroll on the beach or hike on over eight miles of trails which offer spectacular ocean vistas. Picnic tables, restrooms, hiking and campgrounds are available at this park. There is a minimal day use fee.
Leashed dogs are allowed on the beach. Dogs are also allowed on hiking trails and campgrounds. They must be on a six foot or less leash at all

times and people are required to clean up after their pets. On beaches located outside of Oregon State Park boundaries, dogs might be allowed off-leash and under direct voice control, please look for signs or postings. This park is located off U.S. Highway 101, 9 miles north of Port Orford.

Humbug Mountain State Park
Highway 101
Port Orford, OR
541-332-6774
This beach is frequented by windsurfers and scuba divers. A popular activity at this park is hiking to the top of Humbug Mountain (elevation 1,756 feet) . Picnic tables, restrooms, hiking and campgrounds are available at this park. There is a minimal day use fee. Leashed dogs are allowed on the beach. Dogs are also allowed on hiking trails and campgrounds. They must be on a six foot or less leash at all times and people are required to clean up after their pets. On beaches located outside of Oregon State Park boundries, dogs might be allowed off-leash and under direct voice control, please look for signs or postings. This park is located off U.S. Highway 101, 6 miles south of Port Orford.

Bandon

Bullards Beach State Park
Highway 101
Bandon, OR
541-347-2209
Enjoy a walk along the beach at this park. Picnic tables, restrooms, hiking and campgrounds are available at the park. There is a minimal day use fees. Leashed dogs are allowed on the beach. Dogs are also allowed on hiking trails and campgrounds. They must be on a six foot or less leash at all times and people are required to clean up after their pets. On

beaches located outside of Oregon State Park boundaries, dogs might be allowed off-leash and under direct voice control, please look for signs or postings. This park is located off U.S. Highway 101, 2 miles north of Bandon.

Seven Devils State Recreation Site
Highway 101
Bandon, OR
800-551-6949
Enjoy several miles of beach at this park. Picnic tables are available at this park. There are no day use fees. Dogs are allowed on the beach. They must be on a six foot or less leash at all times and people are required to clean up after their pets. On beaches located outside of Oregon State Park boundries, dogs might be allowed off-leash and under direct voice control, please look for signs or postings. This park is located off U.S. Highway 101, 10 miles north of Bandon.

Coos Bay

Sunset Bay State Park
Highway 101
Coos Bay, OR
541-888-4902
This park offers sandy beaches protected by towering sea cliffs. The campgrounds located at the park are within a short walk to the beach. You will also find a network of hiking trails here and in two adjacent parks. Picnic tables and restrooms (including an ADA restroom) are available at this park. There is a minimal day use fee. Leashed dogs are allowed on the beach. Dogs are also allowed on hiking trails and campgrounds. They must be on a six foot or less leash at all times and people are required to clean up after their pets. On beaches located outside of Oregon State Park boundaries, dogs might be allowed off-leash

and under direct voice control, please look for signs or postings. This park is located off U.S. Highway 101, 12 miles southwest of Coos Bay.

Florence

Carl G. Washburne Memorial State Park
Highway 101
Florence, OR
541-547-3416
This park offers five miles of sandy beach. Picnic tables, restrooms, hiking and campgrounds are available at this park. There is a day use fee. Leashed dogs are allowed on the beach. Dogs are also allowed on hiking trails and campgrounds. They must be on a six foot or less leash at all times and people are required to clean up after their pets. On beaches located outside of Oregon State Park boundaries, dogs might be allowed off-leash and under direct voice control, please look for signs or postings. This park is located off U.S. Highway 101, 14 miles north of Florence.

Heceta Head Lighthouse State Scenic Viewpoint
Highway 101
Florence, OR
800-551-6949
Go for a walk above the beach or explore the natural caves and tidepools along the beach. This is a great spot for whale watching. According to the Oregon State Parks Division, the lighthouse located on the west side of 1,000-foot-high Heceta Head (205 feet above ocean) is one of the most photographed on the Oregon coast. Picnic tables, restrooms and hiking are available at this park. There is a $3 day use fee. Leashed dogs are allowed on the beach. Dogs are also allowed on hiking trails. They must be on a six foot or less

leash at all times and people are required to clean up after their pets. On beaches located outside of Oregon State Park boundries, dogs might be allowed off-leash and under direct voice control, please look for signs or postings. This park is located off U.S. Highway 101, 13 miles north of Florence.

Yachats

Neptune State Scenic Viewpoint
Highway 101
Yachats, OR
800-551-6949
During low tide at this beach you can walk south and visit a natural cave and tide-pool. Or sit and relax at one of the picnic tables that overlooks the beach below. Restrooms (including an ADA restroom) are available at this park. There are no day use fees. Dogs are allowed on the beach. They must be on a six foot or less leash at all times and people are required to clean up after their pets. On beaches located outside of Oregon State Park boundries, dogs might be allowed off-leash and under direct voice control, please look for signs or postings. This park is located off U.S. Highway 101,

Yachats State Recreation Area
Highway 101
Yachats, OR
800-551-6949
This beach is a popular spot for whale watching, salmon fishing, and exploring tidepools. Picnic tables and restrooms are available at this park. There are no day use fees. Dogs are allowed on the beach. They must be on a six foot or less leash at all times and people are required to clean up after their pets. On beaches located outside of Oregon State Park boundries, dogs might be allowed off-leash and under direct voice control, please look

for signs or postings. This park is located off U.S. Highway 101 in Yachats.

Waldport

Beachside State Recreation Site
Highway 101
Waldport, OR
541-563-3220
Enjoy miles of broad sandy beach at this park or stay at one of the campground sites that are located just seconds from the beach. Picnic tables, restrooms (including an ADA restroom), and hiking are also available at this park. There is a day use fees. Leashed dogs are allowed on the beach. Dogs are also allowed on hiking trails and campgrounds. They must be on a six foot or less leash at all times and people are required to clean up after their pets. On beaches located outside of Oregon State Park boundaries, dogs might be allowed off-leash and under direct voice control, please look for signs or postings. This park is located off U.S. Highway 101, 4 miles south of Waldport.

Governor Patterson Memorial State Recreation Site
Highway 101
Waldport, OR
800-551-6949
This park offers miles of flat, sandy beach. It is also an excellent location for whale watching. Picnic tables and restrooms are available at this park. There are no day use fees. Dogs are allowed on the beach. They must be on a six foot or less leash at all times and people are required to clean up after their pets. On beaches located outside of Oregon State Park boundries, dogs might be allowed off-leash and under direct voice control, please look for signs or postings. This park is located off U.S. Highway 101,

1 mile south of Waldport.

Depoe Bay

Fogarty Creek State Recreation Area
Highway 101
Depoe Bay, OR
800-551-6949
This beach and park offer some of the best bird-watching and tidepooling. Picnic tables and hiking are available at this park. There is a $3 day use fees. Leashed dogs are allowed on the beach. Dogs are also allowed on hiking trails. They must be on a six foot or less leash at all times and people are required to clean up after their pets. On beaches located outside of Oregon State Park boundries, dogs might be allowed off-leash and under direct voice control, please look for signs or postings. This park is located off U.S. Highway 101, 2 miles north of Depoe Bay.

Lincoln City

D River State Recreation Site
Highway 101
Lincoln City, OR
800-551-6949
This beach, located right off the highway, is a popular and typically windy beach. According to the Oregon State Parks Division, this park is home to a pair of the world's largest kite festivals every spring and fall which gives Lincoln City the name Kite Capital of the World. Restrooms are available at the park. Dogs are allowed on the beach. They must be on a six foot or less leash at all times and people are required to clean up after their pets. On beaches located outside of Oregon State Park boundries, dogs might be allowed off-leash and under direct voice control, please look for signs or

postings. This park is located off U.S. Highway 101 in Lincoln City.

Roads End State Recreation Site
Highway 101
Lincoln City, OR
800-551-6949
There is a short trail here that leads down to the beach. Picnic tables are available at this park. There are no day use fees. Dogs are allowed on the beach. They must be on a six foot or less leash at all times and people are required to clean up after their pets. On beaches located outside of Oregon State Park boundries, dogs might be allowed off-leash and under direct voice control, please look for signs or postings. This park is located off U.S. Highway 101, 1 mile north of Lincoln City.

Neskowin

Neskowin Beach State Recreation Site
Highway 101
Neskowin, OR
800-551-6949
Not really any facilities (picnic tables, etc.) here, but a good place to enjoy the beach. Dogs are allowed on the beach. They must be on a six foot or less leash at all times and people are required to clean up after their pets. On beaches located outside of Oregon State Park boundaries, dogs might be allowed off-leash and under direct voice control, please look for signs or postings. This park is located off U.S. Highway 101 in Neskowin.

Pacific City

Bob Straub State Park
Highway 101
Pacific City, OR
800-551-6949
This is a nice stretch of beach to walk along. Picnic tables and

restrooms (including an ADA restroom) are available at this park. There are no day use fees. Dogs are allowed on the beach. They must be on a six foot or less leash at all times and people are required to clean up after their pets. On beaches located outside of Oregon State Park boundaries, dogs might be allowed off-leash and under direct voice control, please look for signs or postings. This park is located off U.S. Highway 101 in Pacific City.

Cape Kiwanda State Natural Area
Highway 101
Pacific City, OR
800-551-6949
This beach and park is a good spot for marine mammal watching, hang gliding and kite flying. Picnic tables are available at this park. There are no day use fees. Dogs are allowed on the beach. They must be on a six foot or less leash at all times and people are required to clean up after their pets. On beaches located outside of Oregon State Park boundries, dogs might be allowed off-leash and under direct voice control, please look for signs or postings. This park is located off U.S. Highway 101, 1 mile north of Pacific City.

Tillamook

Cape Lookout State Park
Highway 101
Tillamook, OR
503-842-4981
This is a popular beach during the summer. The beach is a short distance from the parking area. It is located about an hour and half west of Portland. Picnic tables, restrooms (including an ADA restroom), hiking trails and campgrounds are available at this park. There is a $3 day use fee. Leashed dogs are allowed on the beach. Dogs are also allowed on hiking trails and

campgrounds. They must be on a six foot or less leash at all times and people are required to clean up after their pets. On beaches located outside of Oregon State Park boundaries, dogs might be allowed off-leash and under direct voice control, please look for signs or postings. This park is located off U.S. Highway 101, 12 miles southwest of Tillamook.

Cape Meares State Scenic Viewpoint
Highway 101
Tillamook, OR
800-551-6949
The beach is located south of the scenic viewpoint. The viewpoint is situated on a headland, about 200 feet above the ocean. According to the Oregon State Parks Division, bird watchers can view the largest colony of nesting common murres (this site is one of the most populous colonies of nesting sea birds on the continent). Bald eagles and a peregrine falcon have also been known to nest near here. In winter and spring, this park is an excellent location for viewing whale migrations. Picnic tables, restrooms and hiking are available at this park. There are no day use fees. Leashed dogs are allowed on the beach. Dogs are also allowed on hiking trails. They must be on a six foot or less leash at all times and people are required to clean up after their pets. On beaches located outside of Oregon State Park boundries, dogs might be allowed off-leash and under direct voice control, please look for signs or postings. This park is located off U.S. Highway 101, 10 miles west of Tillamook.

Rockaway Beach

Manhattan Beach State

Recreation Site
Highway 101
Rockaway Beach, OR
800-551-6949
The beach is a short walk from the parking area. Picnic tables are available at this park. There are no day use fees. Dogs are allowed on the beach. They must be on a six foot or less leash at all times and people are required to clean up after their pets. On beaches located outside of Oregon State Park boundaries, dogs might be allowed off-leash and under direct voice control, please look for signs or postings. This park is located off U.S. Highway 101, 2 miles north of Rockaway Beach.

Manzanita

Nehalem Bay State Park
Highway 101
Manzanita, OR
503-368-5154
The beach can be reached by a short walk over the dunes. This park is a popular place for fishing and crabbing. Picnic tables, restrooms (including an ADA restroom), hiking and camping are available at this park. There is a $3 day use fee. Leashed dogs are allowed on the beach. Dogs are also allowed on hiking trails and campgrounds. They must be on a six foot or less leash at all times and people are required to clean up after their pets. On beaches located outside of Oregon State Park boundaries, dogs might be allowed off-leash and under direct voice control, please look for signs or postings. This park is located off U.S. Highway 101, 3 miles south of Manzanita Junction.

Oswald West State Park
Highway 101
Manzanita, OR
800-551-6949
The beach is located just a

quarter of a mile from the parking areas. It is a popular beach that is frequented by windsurfers and boogie boarders. Picnic tables, restrooms, hiking, and campgrounds are available at this park. There are no day use fees. Leashed dogs are allowed on the beach. Dogs are also allowed on hiking trails and campgrounds. They must be on a six foot or less leash at all times and people are required to clean up after their pets. On beaches located outside of Oregon State Park boundries, dogs might be allowed off-leash and under direct voice control, please look for signs or postings. This park is located off U.S. Highway 101, 10 miles south of Cannon Beach.

Cannon Beach

Arcadia Beach State Recreation Site
Highway 101
Cannon Beach, OR
800-551-6949
This sandy ocean beach is just a few feet from where you can park your car. Picnic tables and restrooms are available at this park. There are no day use fees. Dogs are allowed on the beach. They must be on a six foot or less leash at all times and people are required to clean up after their pets. On beaches located outside of Oregon State Park boundaries, dogs might be allowed off-leash and under direct voice control, please look for signs or postings. This park is located off U.S. Highway 101, 3 miles south of Cannon Beach.

Ecola State Park
Highway 101
Cannon Beach, OR
503-436-2844
According to the Oregon State Parks Division, this park is one of the most photographed locations in Oregon. To reach

the beach, you will need to walk down a trail. Restrooms, hiking and primitive campgrounds are available at this park. There is a $3 day use fee. Leashed dogs are allowed on the beach. Dogs are also allowed on hiking trails and campgrounds. They must be on a six foot or less leash at all times and people are required to clean up after their pets. On beaches located outside of Oregon State Park boundries, dogs might be allowed off-leash and under direct voice control, please look for signs or postings. This park is located off U.S. Highway 101, 2 miles north of Cannon Beach.

Hug Point State Recreation Site
Highway 101
Cannon Beach, OR
800-551-6949
According to the Oregon State Parks Division, people used to travel via stagecoach along this beach before the highway was built. Today you can walk along the originial trail which was carved into the point by stagecoaches. The trail is located north of the parking area. Visitors can also explore two caves around the point, but be aware of high tide. Some people have become stranded at high tide when exploring the point! This beach is easily accessible from the parking area. Picnic tables and restrooms are available at this park. There are no day use fees. Dogs are allowed on the beach. They must be on a six foot or less leash at all times and people are required to clean up after their pets. On beaches located outside of Oregon State Park boundries, dogs might be allowed off-leash and under direct voice control, please look for signs or postings. This park is located off U.S. Highway 101, 5 miles south of Cannon Beach.

Tolovana Beach State Recreation Site
Highway 101
Cannon Beach, OR
800-551-6949
Indian Beach is popular with surfers. There is a short walk down to the beach. Picnic tables are available at this park. There are no day fees. Dogs are allowed on the beach. They must be on a six foot or less leash at all times and people are required to clean up after their pets. On beaches located outside of Oregon State Park boundries, dogs might be allowed off-leash and under direct voice control, please look for signs or postings. This park is located off U.S. Highway 101, 1 mile south of Cannon Beach.

Seaside

Del Rey Beach State Recreation Site
Highway 101
Seaside, OR
800-551-6949
There is a short trail to the beach. There is no day use fee. Dogs are allowed on the beach. They must be on a six foot or less leash at all times and people are required to clean up after their pets. On beaches located outside of Oregon State Park boundaries, dogs might be allowed off-leash and under direct voice control, please look for signs or postings. This park is located off U.S. Highway 101, 2 miles north of Gearhart.

Warrenton

Fort Stevens State Park
Highway 101
Warrenton, OR
503-861-1671
There are miles of ocean beach. Picnic tables, restrooms (including an ADA restroom), hiking and campgrounds are available at this park. There is a

$3 day use fee. Leashed dogs are allowed on the beach. Dogs are also allowed on hiking trails and campgrounds. They must be on a six foot or less leash at all times and people are required to clean up after their pets. On beaches located outside of Oregon State Park boundaries, dogs might be allowed off-leash and under direct voice control, please look for signs or postings. This park is located off U.S. Highway 101, 10 miles west of Astoria.

Washington Listings

Ilwaco

Fort Canby State Park
Highway 101
Ilwaco, WA
360-902-8844
This park offers 27 miles of ocean beach and 7 miles of hiking trails. Enjoy excellent views of the ocean, Columbia River and two lighthouses. Picnic tables, restrooms (including an ADA restroom), hiking and campgrounds (includes ADA campsites) are available at this park. Leashed dogs are allowed on the beach. Dogs are also allowed on hiking trails and campgrounds. They must be on a eight foot or less leash at all times and people are required to clean up after their pets. This park is located two miles southwest of Ilwaco.From Seattle, Take I-5 south to Olympia, SR 8 west to Montesano. From there, take U.S. Hwy. 101 south to Long Beach Peninsula.

Ocean Park

Pacific Pines State Park
Highway 101
Ocean Park, WA

360-902-8844
Fishing, crabbing, clamming and beachcombing are popular activities at this beach. Picnic tables and a restroom are available at this park. Dogs are allowed on the beach. They must be on a eight foot or less leash at all times and people are required to clean up after their pets. This park is located approximately one mile north of Ocean Park. From north or south, take Hwy. 101 until you reach Ocean Park. Continue on Vernon St. until you reach 271st St.

Grayland

Grayland Beach State Park
Highway 105
Grayland, WA
360-902-8844
This 412 acre park offers beautiful ocean frontage and full hookup campsites (including ADA campsites). Leashed dogs are allowed on the beach. Dogs are also allowed at the campgrounds. They must be on a eight foot or less leash at all times and people are required to clean up after their pets. This park is located five miles south of Westport. From Aberdeen, drive 22 miles on Highway 105 south to Grayland. Traveling through the town, watch for park signs.

Ocean Shores

Damon Point State Park
Point Brown Avenue
Ocean Shores, WA
360-902-8844
Located on the southeastern tip of the Ocean Shores Peninsula, this one mile long beach offers views of the Olympic Mountains, Mount Rainer, and Grays Harbor. Picnic tables are available at this park. Dogs are allowed on the beach. They must be on a

eight foot or less leash at all times and people are required to clean up after their pets. To get there from From Hoquiam, take SR 109 and SR 115 to Point Brown Ave. in the town of Ocean Shores. Proceed south on Point Brown Ave. through town, approximately 4.5 miles. Just past the marina, turn left into park entrance.

Ocean City State Park
State Route 115
Ocean Shores, WA
360-902-8844
Beachcombing, clamming, surfing, bird watching, kite flying and winter storm watching are all popular activities at this beach. Picnic tables, restrooms, and campgrounds (including ADA campgrounds) are available at this park. Leashed dogs are allowed on the beach. Dogs are also allowed at the campgrounds. They must be on a eight foot or less leash at all times and people are required to clean up after their pets. This park is located on the coast one-and-a-half miles north of Ocean Shores on Hwy. 115. From Hoquiam, drive 16 miles west on SR 109, then turn south on SR 115 and drive 1.2 miles to the park.

Copalis Beach

Griffith-Priday State Park
State Route 109
Copalis Beach, WA
360-902-8844
This beach extends from the beach through low dunes to a river and then north to the river's mouth. Picnic tables and restrooms are available at this park. Dogs are allowed on the beach. They must be on a eight foot or less leash at all times and people are required to clean up after their pets. This park is located 21 miles northwest of Hoquiam. From Hoquiam, go north on SR 109 for 21 miles. At

Copalis Beach, at the sign for Benner Rd., turn left (west).

Pacific Beach

Pacific Beach State Park
State Route 109
Pacific Beach, WA
360-902-8844
The beach is the focal point at this 10 acre state park. This sandy ocean beach is great for beachcombing, wildlife watching, windy walks and kite flying. Picnic tables, restrooms (including an ADA restroom), and campgrounds (some are ADA accessible) are available at this park. Leashed dogs are allowed on the beach. Dogs are also allowed in the campgrounds. They must be on a eight foot or less leash at all times and people are required to clean up after their pets. This park is located 15 miles north of Ocean Shores, off SR 109. From Hoquiam, follow SR 109, 30 miles northwest to the town of Pacific Beach. The park is located in town.

Port Angeles

Kalaloch Beach
Olympic National Park
Port Angeles, WA
360-962-2283
Dogs are allowed on leash, during daytime hours only, on Kalaloch Beach along the Pacific Ocean and from Rialto Beach north to Ellen Creek. These beaches are in Olympic National Park, but please note that pets are not permitted on this national park's trails, meadows, beaches (except Kalaloch and Rialto beaches) or in any undeveloped area of the park. For those folks and dogs who want to hike on a trail, try the adjacent dog-friendly Olympic National Forest. Kalaloch Beach is located off Highway 101 in Olympic National Park.

Federal Way

Dash Point State Park
Dash Point Rd.
Federal Way, WA
360-902-8844
This beach offers great views of Puget Sound. Picnic tables, restrooms, 11 miles of hiking trails and campgrounds are available at this park. Leashed dogs are allowed on the beach. Pets are not permitted on designated swimming beaches. However, there is usually a non-designated swimming beach area as well. Dogs are also allowed on hiking trails and campgrounds. They must be on a eight foot or less leash at all times and people are required to clean up after their pets. This park is located on the west side of Federal Way in the vicinity of Seattle. From Highway 5, exit at the 320th St. exit (exit #143). Take 320th St. west approximately four miles. When 320th St. ends at a T-intersection, make a right onto 47th St. When 47th St. ends at a T-intersection, turn left onto Hwy. 509/ Dash Point Rd. Drive about two miles to the park. (West side of street is the campground side, and east side is the day-use area.)

Des Moines

Saltwater State Park
Marine View Drive
Des Moines, WA
360-902-8844
This state beach is located on Puget Sound, halfway between the cities of Tacoma and Seattle (near the Sea-Tac international airport). Picnic tables, restrooms and campgrounds are available at this park. Leashed dogs are allowed on the beach. Pets are not permitted on designated swimming beaches. However, there is usually a non-designated swimming beach

area as well. Dogs are also allowed at the campgrounds. They must be on a eight foot or less leash at all times and people are required to clean up after their pets. To get there from the north, take exit #149 off of I-5. Go west, then turn south on Hwy. 99 (sign missing). Follow the signs into the park. Turn right on 240th at the Midway Drive-in. Turn left on Marine View Dr. and turn right into the park.

Seattle

Sand Point Magnuson Park Dog Off-Leash Beach and Area
7400 Sand Point Way NE
Seattle, WA
206-684-4075
This leash free dog park covers about 9 acres and is the biggest fully fenced off-leash park in Seattle. It also offers an access point to the lake where your pooch is welcome to take a dip in the fresh lake water. To find the dog park, take Sand Point Way Northeast and enter the park at Northeast 74th Street. Go straight and park near the playground and sports fields. The main gate to the off-leash area is located at the southeast corner of the main parking lot. Dogs must be leashed until you enter the off-leash area.

Bainbridge Island

Fay Bainbridge State Park
Sunset Drive NE
Bainbridge Island, WA
360-902-8844
This park is located on the northeast side of Bainbridge Island on Puget Sound. On a clear day, you can see Mt. Rainer and Mt. Baker from the beach. Picnic tables, restrooms and campgrounds are available at this park. Leashed dogs are allowed on the beach. Pets are not permitted on designated

swimming beaches. However, there is usually a non-designated swimming beach area as well. Dogs are also allowed at the campgrounds. They must be on a eight foot or less leash at all times and people are required to clean up after their pets. To get there from From Poulsbo, take Hwy. 305 toward Bainbridge Island. Cross the Agate Pass Bridge. After three miles, come to stoplight and big brown sign with directions to park. Turn left at traffic light onto Day Rd. NE. Travel approximately two miles to a T-intersection. Turn left onto Sunrise Drive NE, and continue to park entrance, about two miles away.

Oak Harbor

Fort Ebey State Park
Hill Valley Drive
Oak Harbor, WA
360-902-8844
This 600+ acre park is popular for hiking and camping, but also offers a saltwater beach. Picnic tables and restrooms (including an ADA restroom) are available at this park. Leashed dogs are allowed on the saltwater beach. Dogs are also allowed on hiking trails and campgrounds. They must be on a eight foot or less leash at all times and people are required to clean up after their pets. To get to the park from Seattle, take exit #189 off of I-5, just south of Everett. Follow signs for the Mukilteo/ Clinton ferry. Take the ferry to Clinton on Whidbey Island. Dogs are allowed on the ferry. Once on Whidbey Island, follow Hwy. 525 north, which becomes Hwy. 20. Two miles north of Coupeville, turn left on Libbey Rd. and follow it 1.5 miles to Hill Valley Dr. Turn left and enter park.

Joseph Whidbey State Park
Swantown Rd
Oak Harbor, WA

360-902-8844
This 112 acre park offers one of the best beaches on Whidbey Island. Picnic tables, restrooms, and several miles of hiking trails (including a half mile ADA hiking trail) are available at this park. Leashed dogs are allowed on the beach. Pets are not permitted on designated swimming beaches. However, there is usually a non-designated swimming beach area as well. Dogs are also allowed on hiking trails. They must be on a eight foot or less leash at all times and people are required to clean up after their pets. To get there from the south, drive north on Hwy. 20. Just before Oak Harbor, turn left on Swantown Rd. and follow it about three miles.

Lopez Island

Spencer Spit State Park
Bakerview Road
Lopez Island, WA
360-902-8844
Located in the San Juan Islands, this lagoon beach offers great crabbing, clamming and beachcombing. Picnic tables, restrooms, campgrounds and 2 miles of hiking trails are available at this park. Leashed dogs are allowed on the beach. Pets are not permitted on designated swimming beaches. However, there is usually a non-designated swimming beach area as well. Dogs are also allowed on hiking trails and campgrounds. They must be on a eight foot or less leash at all times and people are required to clean up after their pets. This park is located on Lopez Island in the San Juan Islands. It is a 45-minute Washington State Ferry ride from Anacortes. Dogs are allowed on the ferry. Once on Lopez Island, follow Ferry Rd. Go left at Center Rd.,

then left at Cross Rd. Turn right at Port Stanley and left at Bakerview Rd. Follow Bakerview Rd. straight into park. For ferry rates and schedules, call 206-464-6400.

Friday Harbor

San Juan Island National Historic Park
125 Spring Street
Friday Harbor, WA
360-378-2902
Leashed dogs are welcome on the hiking trails. Some of the trails are self-guided tours of the area and buildings. Dogs on leash are also allowed on South Beach, which is located at the American Camp. Dogs are not allowed inside the Visitor's Center.

Blaine

Birch Bay State Park
Grandview
Blaine, WA
360-902-8844
This beach, located near the Canadian border, offers panoramic coastal views. Picnic tables, restrooms (including an ADA restroom), and campgrounds (including ADA campsites) are available at this park. Leashed dogs are allowed on the beach. Pets are not permitted on designated swimming beaches. However, there is usually a non-designated swimming beach area as well. Dogs are also allowed in the campgrounds. They must be on a eight foot or less leash at all times and people are required to clean up after their pets. This park is located 20 miles north of Bellingham and ten miles south of Blaine. From the south take exit #266 off of I-5. Go left on Grandview for seven miles, then right on Jackson for one mile, then turn left onto Helweg. From the north take exit #266 off of

I-5, and turn right onto
Grandview.

British Columbia Listings

Vancouver

Spanish Banks West
NW Marine Drive
Vancouver, BC
604-257-8400
This beach allows dogs off-
leash. Dogs are allowed from
6am to 10pm. People are
required to clean up after their
dogs. The beach is located in
the Queen Elizabeth District. It is
off NW Marine Drive, at the
entrance to Pacific Spirit Park.

Sunset Beach
off Beach Avenue
Vancouver, BC
604-257-8400
This bay beach allows dogs off-
leash. Dogs are allowed from
6am to 10pm. People are
required to clean up after their
dogs. The beach is located in
the Stanley District, near Beach
Avenue, under the Burrard
Bridge. It is behind the Aquatic
Centre east of the ferry dock.

Vanier Park
Chestnut
Vancouver, BC
604-257-8400
This beach allows dogs off-
leash. Dogs are allowed from
6am to 10am and then from 5pm
to 10pm. People are required to
clean up after their dogs. The
beach is located in the Queen
Elizabeth District. It is on
Chestnut at English Bay.

Victoria

**Beacon Hill Park Off-Leash
Beach**
Dallas Road

Victoria, BC
250-385-5711
Dogs are allowed off-leash at
the gravel beach in Beacon Hill
Park. People are required to
clean up after their dogs. The
beach is located in downtown
Victoria, along Dallas Road,
between Douglas Street and
Cook Street.

Chapter 4

Dog-Friendly Highway Guides

Interstate 5 Accommodation Listings

Washington (Interstate 5)

Bellingham Listings
Bellingham
Holiday Inn Express	360-671-4800	4160 Guide Meridian Bellingham WA
Motel 6	360-671-4494	3701 Byron Bellingham WA

Mount Vernon Listings
Mount Vernon
Best Western College Way Inn	360-424-4287	300 W College Way Mount Vernon WA
Best Western CottonTree Inn	360-428-5678	2300 Market Place Mount Vernon WA

Everett Listings
Everett
Holiday Inn	425-337-2900	101 128th St SE Everett WA
Motel 6	425-353-8120	224 128th St SW Everett WA

Seattle Listings
Seattle
Crowne Plaza - Downtown	206-464-1980	1113 6th Ave Seattle WA
La Quinta Inn & Suites Seattle	206-624-6820	2224 Eighth Ave. Seattle WA
La Quinta Inn Sea-Tac - Seattle	206-241-5211	2824 S 188th St Seattle WA
Motel 6	206-824-9902	20651 Military Rd Seattle WA
Motel 6 - Airport	206-241-1648	18900 47th Ave S Seattle WA
The Sheraton Seattle Hotel and Towers	206-621-9000	1400 Sixth Avenue Seattle WA
W Seattle	206-264-6000	1112 Fourth Avenue Seattle WA

Kent Listings
Kent
La Quinta Inn Kent	253-520-6670	25100 74th Avenue South Kent WA

Federal Way Listings
Federal Way
La Quinta Inn & Suites Federal Way	253-529-4000	32124 25th Avenue South Federal Way WA

Tacoma Listings
Tacoma
Best Western Executive Inn	253-922-0080	5700 Pacific Hwy E. Tacoma WA
Best Western Tacoma Inn	253-535-2880	8726 S. Hosmer St Tacoma WA
La Quinta Inn Tacoma	253-383-0146	1425 E 27th St Tacoma WA
Motel 6	253-473-7100	1811 S 76th St Tacoma WA

Olympia Listings
Olympia
West Coast Inn	360-943-4000	2300 Evergreen Park Drive Olympia WA

Tumwater
Best Western Tumwater Inn	360-956-1235	5188 Capitol Blvd Tumwater WA
Motel 6	360-754-7320	400 W Lee St Tumwater WA

Centralia Listings
Centralia
Motel 6	360-330-2057	1310 Belmont Ave Centralia WA

Chehalis Listings
Chehalis
Howard Johnson Inn	360-748-0101	122 Interstate Ave. Chehalis WA

Kelso Listings
Kelso
Motel 6	360-425-3229	106 Minor Rd Kelso WA

Highway Guides - Please always call ahead to make sure an establishment is still dog-friendly.

Vancouver Listings
Vancouver
Comfort Inn	360-574-6000	13207 NE 20th Ave. Vancouver WA
Staybridge Suites	360-891-8282	7301 NE 41st St Vancouver WA

Oregon (Interstate 5)

Portland Listings
Portland
Comfort Inn	503-682-9000	8855 SW Citizen Dr. Portland OR
La Quinta Inn Portland - Lloyd	503-233-7933	431 NE Multnomah Portland OR
Motel 6	503-238-0600	3104 SE Powell Blvd Portland OR
Sheraton Portland Airport Hotel	503-281-2500	8235 NE Airport Way Portland OR

Portland Area Listings
Lake Oswego
Crowne Plaza	503-624-8400	14811 Kruse Oaks Dr Lake Oswego OR

Tigard
Motel 6	503-620-2066	17950 SW McEwan Rd Tigard OR

Wilsonville
Holiday Inn Select	503-570-8500	25425 SW 95th Ave Wilsonville OR

Woodburn Listings
Woodburn
La Quinta Inn & Suites Woodburn	503-982-1727	120 Arney Road NE Woodburn OR

Salem Listings
Salem
Holiday Inn Express	503-391-7000	890 Hawthorne Ave SE Salem OR
Motel 6	503-371-8024	1401 Hawthorne Ave NE Salem OR
Phoenix Inn - Salem South	503-588-9220	4370 Commercial St SE Salem OR
Red Lion Hotel	503-370-7888	3301 Market St Salem OR

Albany Listings
Albany
La Quinta Inn & Suites Albany	541-928-0921	251 Airport Road SE Albany OR

Eugene Listings
Eugene
Best Western Greentree Inn	541-485-2727	1759 Franklin Blvd Eugene OR
Best Western New Oregon Motel	541-683-3669	1655 Franklin Blvd Eugene OR
Eugene Hilton	541-342-2000	66 East 6th Avenue Eugene OR
La Quinta Inn & Suites Eugene	541-344-8335	155 Day Island Rd. Eugene OR
Motel 6	541-687-2395	3690 Glenwood Dr Eugene OR
Quality Inn & Suites	541-342-1243	2121 Franklin Blvd Eugene OR
Ramada Inn	541-342-5181	225 Coburg Rd Eugene OR
The Valley River Inn	541-687-0123	1000 Valley River Way Eugene OR

Cottage Grove Listings
Cottage Grove
Best Western - The Village Green	541-942-2491	725 Row River Rd. Cottage Grove OR
Comfort Inn	541-942-9747	845 Gateway Blvd. Cottage Grove OR
Holiday Inn Express	541-942-1000	1601 Gateway Blvd Cottage Grove OR

Rice Hill Listings
Rice Hill
Best Western Rice Hill Inn	541-849-2500	621 John Long Rd Rice Hill OR

Roseburg Listings
Roseburg
Best Western Douglas Inn	541-673-6625	511 SE Stephens Roseburg OR
Comfort Inn	541-957-1100	1539 Mullholland Dr. Roseburg OR
Holiday Inn Express	541-673-7517	375 Harvard Blvd Roseburg OR
Motel 6	541-464-8000	3100 NW Aviation Roseburg OR

Highway Guides - Please always call ahead to make sure an establishment is still dog-friendly.

Sleep Inn & Suites	541-464-8338	2855 NW Eden Bower Blvd. Roseburg OR

Grants Pass Listings
Grants Pass
Best Western Grants Pass Inn	541-476-1117	111 NE Agness Ave Grants Pass OR
Comfort Inn	541-479-8301	1889 NE 6th St Grants Pass OR
Holiday Inn Express	541-471-6144	105 NE Agness Ave Grants Pass OR
La Quinta Inn & Suites Grants Pass	541-472-1808	243 NE Morgan Lane Grants Pass OR
Motel 6	541-474-1331	1800 Northeast 7th St Grants Pass OR

Medford Listings
Medford
Best Western	541-779-5085	1154 E Barnett Rd Medford OR
Doubletree Hotel	541-779-5811	200 N Riverside Medford OR
Motel 6	541-779-0550	2400 Biddle Rd Medford OR
Motel 6	541-773-4290	950 Alba Dr Medford OR
Reston Hotel	541-779-3141	2300 Crater Lake Hwy Medford OR

Ashland Listings
Ashland
Best Western Bard's Inn	541-482-0049	132 N Main Street Ashland OR
Best Western Windsor Inn	541-488-2330	2520 Ashland St Ashland OR
La Quinta Inn & Suites Ashland	541-482-6932	434 S. Valley View Road Ashland OR

California (Interstate 5)

Yreka Listings
Yreka
Ben-Ber Motel	530-842-2791	1210 S Main St Yreka CA
Best Western Miner's Inn	530-842-4355	122 East Miner Street Yreka CA
Days Inn	530-842-1612	1804 B Fort Jones Rd Yreka CA
Motel 6	530-842-4111	1785 S Main Street Yreka CA

Mount Shasta Listings
Dunsmuir
Oak Tree Inn	530-235-2884	6604 Dunsmuir Avenue Dunsmuir CA
Railroad Park Resort	530-235-4440	100 Railroad Park Road Dunsmuir CA
Travelodge	530-235-4395	5400 Dunsmuir Ave Dunsmuir CA
McCloud
Stony Brook Inn	800-369-6118	309 Colombero McCloud CA
Mount Shasta
Best Western Tree House Motor Inn	530-926-3101	111 Morgan Way Mount Shasta CA
Dream Inn Bed and Breakfast	530-926-1536	326 Chestnut Street Mount Shasta CA
Econo Lodge	530-926-3145	908 S. Mt. Shasta Blvd. Mount Shasta CA
Mount Shasta Ranch Bed and Breakfast	530-926-3870	1008 W. A. Barr Rd. Mount Shasta CA
Mountain Air Lodge	530-926-3411	1121 S Mount Shasta Blvd Mount Shasta CA
Swiss Holiday Lodge	530-926-3446	2400 S. Mt. Shasta Blvd. Mount Shasta CA
Weed
Holiday Inn Express	530-938-1308	1830 Black Butte Drive Weed CA
Lake Shastina Golf Resort	530-938-3201	5925 Country Club Drive Weed CA

Redding Listings
Redding
Best Western Ponderosa Inn	530-241-6300	2220 Pine Street Redding CA
Comfort Inn	530-221-6530	2059 Hilltop Drive Redding CA
Fawndale Lodge and RV Resort	800-338-0941	15215 Fawndale Road Redding CA
Holiday Inn Express	530-241-5500	1080 Twin View Blvd Redding CA
La Quinta Inn Redding	530-221-8200	2180 Hilltop Drive Redding CA
Motel 6	530-221-1800	1640 Hilltop Dr Redding CA
Motel 6 - North	530-246-4470	1250 Twin View Blvd Redding CA
Motel 6 - South	530-221-0562	2385 Bechelli Ln Redding CA
Ramada Limited	530-246-2222	1286 Twin View Blvd Redding CA

Highway Guides - Please always call ahead to make sure an establishment is still dog-friendly.

Red Lion Hotel	530-221-8700	1830 Hilltop Drive Redding CA
River Inn	530-241-9500	1835 Park Marina Drive Redding CA
Shasta Lodge	530-243-6133	1245 Pine Street Redding CA

Redding

Seven Crown Resorts Houseboats	800-752-9669	10300 Bridge Bay Road Redding CA

Anderson Listings
Anderson

AmeriHost Inn	530-365-6100	2040 Factory Outlets Dr Anderson CA
Best Western Knight's Inn	530-365-2753	2688 Gateway Drive Anderson CA

Red Bluff Listings
Red Bluff

Motel 6	530-527-9200	20 Williams Ave Red Bluff CA
Super 8	530-527-8882	203 Antelope Blvd Red Bluff CA
Travelodge	530-527-6020	38 Antelope Blvd Red Bluff CA

Corning Listings
Corning

Best Western Inn-Corning	530-824-2468	2165 Solano Street Corning CA
Shilo Inn Suites	530-824-2940	3350 Sunrise Way Corning CA

Willows Listings
Willows

Best Western Gold Pheasant Inn	530-934-4603	249 North Humboldt Avenue Willows CA
Days Inn	530-934-4444	475 N Humboldt Ave Willows CA
Super 8	530-934-2871	457 Humboldt Ave Willows CA

Williams Listings
Williams

Comfort Inn	530-473-2381	400 C St Williams CA
Motel 6	530-473-5337	455 4th Street Williams CA

Dunnigan Listings
Dunnigan

Best Western Country	530-724-3471	3930 County Rd. 89 Dunnigan CA

Woodland Listings
Woodland

Motel 6	530-666-6777	1564 Main Street Woodland CA
Sacramento - Days Inn	530-666-3800	1524 East Main Street Woodland CA

Sacramento Listings
Sacramento

Sheraton Grand Sacramento Hotel	916-447-1700	1230 J Street Sacramento CA

Stockton Listings
Stockton

La Quinta Inn Stockton	209-952-7800	2710 West March Lane Stockton CA
Motel 6 - Southeast	209-467-3600	1625 French Camp Turnpike Rd Stockton CA
Motel 6 - West	209-946-0923	817 Navy Drive Stockton CA
Residence Inn - Stockton	209-472-9800	March Lane & Brookside Stockton CA
Travelodge	209-466-7777	1707 Fremont St Stockton CA

Lathrop Listings
Lathrop

Days Inn	209-982-1959	14750 South Harlan Rd Lathrop CA

Westley Listings
Westley

Days Inn	209-894-5500	7144 McCracken Rd Westley CA
Econo Lodge	209-894-3900	7100 McCracken Rd Westley CA
Super 8	209-894-3888	7115 McCracken Rd Westley CA

Highway Guides - Please always call ahead to make sure an establishment is still dog-friendly.

Santa Nella Listings
Santa Nella
Holiday Inn Express	209-826-8282	28976 W. Plaza Drive Santa Nella CA
Motel 6	209-826-6644	12733 S Hwy 33 Santa Nella CA
Ramada Inn	209-826-4444	13070 S Hwy 33 Santa Nella CA

Los Banos Listings
Los Banos
Days Inn	209-826-9690	2169 East Pacheco Blvd Los Banos CA
Sunstar Inn	209-826-3805	839 W. Pacheco Blvd Los Banos CA

Coalinga Listings
Coalinga
Motel 6	559-935-1536	25008 W Dorris Ave Coalinga CA
Pleasant Valley Inn	559-935-2063	25278 W Doris St Coalinga CA

Kettleman City Listings
Kettleman City
Super 8	559-386-9530	33415 Powers Drive Kettleman City CA

Lost Hills Listings
Lost Hills
Days Inn	661-797-2371	14684 Aloma St Lost Hills CA
Motel 6	661-797-2346	14685 Warren St Lost Hills CA

Buttonwillow Listings
Buttonwillow
Super 8	661-764-5117	20681 Tracy Ave Buttonwillow CA

Gorman Listings
Gorman
Econo Lodge	661-248-6411	49713 Gorman Post Rd Gorman CA

Los Angeles - Hollywood Listings
Pico Rivera
Days Inn - Pico Rivera	562-942-1003	6540 S. Rosemead Blvd Pico Rivera CA

Universal City
Sheraton Universal Hotel	818-980-1212	333 Universal Hollywood Drive Universal City CA

Anaheim - Orange County Listings
Anaheim
Econolodge at the Park	714-533-4505	1126 West Katella Ave Anaheim CA
Embassy Suites Hotel	714-632-1221	3100 E. Frontera Ave Anaheim CA
Hawthorn Suites	714-635-5000	1752 S. Clementine Anaheim CA
Staybridge Suites	714-748-7700	1845 S. Manchester Ave Anaheim CA

Irvine
La Quinta Inn East Irvine	949-551-0909	14972 Sand Canyon Avenue Irvine CA

La Mirada
Residence Inn - La Mirada	714-523-2800	14419 Firestone Blvd La Mirada CA

Orange
Residence Inn - Orange	714-976-7700	3101 W. Chapman Avenue Orange CA

Santa Ana
Red Roof Inn	714-542-0311	2600 N Main Street Santa Ana CA

San Clemente Listings
San Clemente
Holiday Inn	949-361-3000	111 S. Ave. De Estrella San Clemente CA

San Diego County North Listings
Carlsbad
Inns of America	760-931-1185	751 Raintree Carlsbad CA
Residence Inn - Carlsbad	760-431-9999	2000 Faraday Ave Carlsbad CA

Oceanside

| Motel 6 | 760-941-1011 | 3708 Plaza Dr Oceanside CA |
| Ramada Limited | 760-967-4100 | 1140 Mission Ave Oceanside CA |

San Diego Listings

Chula Vista

| Motel 6 | 619-422-4200 | 745 E Street Chula Vista CA |

La Jolla

| Andrea Villa Inn | 858-459-3311 | 2402 Torrey Pines Rd La Jolla CA |

National City

| Super 8 | 619-474-8811 | 425 Roosevelt Ave National City CA |

San Diego

| Sheraton Suites San Diego | 619-696-9800 | 701 A. Street San Diego CA |
| Staybridge Suites | 800-238-8000 | 6639 Mira Mesa Blvd San Diego CA |

San Ysidro

| Motel 6 - Border | 619-690-6663 | 160 E Calie Primera San Ysidro CA |

Interstate 10 Accommodation Listings

California (Interstate 10)

Los Angeles - Hollywood Listings

Los Angeles

| Holiday Inn - Downtown | 213-628-9900 | 750 Garland Ave @ 8th St. Los Angeles CA |

Santa Monica

| Loews Santa Monica Beach Hotel | 310-458-6700 | 1700 Ocean Avenue Santa Monica CA |

West Covina

| Hampton Inn | 626-967-5800 | 3145 E. Garvey Ave West Covina CA |

Inland Empire Listings

Claremont

| Ramada Inn | 909-621-4831 | 840 South Indian Hill Blvd Claremont CA |

Ontario

| Marriott - Ontario Airport | 909-975-5000 | 2200 E. Holt Blvd Ontario CA |

Pomona

| Sheraton Suites Fairplex | 909-622-2220 | 601 West McKinley Avenue Pomona CA |

Rialto

| Best Western Empire Inn | 909-877-0690 | 475 W Valley Blvd Rialto CA |

San Bernardino

| Motel 6 | 909-825-6666 | 111 Redlands Blvd San Bernardino CA |

Beaumont Listings

Beaumont

| Best Western El Rancho Motor Inn | 909-845-2176 | 480 East 5th Street Beaumont CA |

Banning Listings

Banning

| Super 8 | 909-849-6887 | 1690 W. Ramsey St Banning CA |
| Travelodge | 909-849-1000 | 1700 W. Ramsey Street Banning CA |

Palm Springs Listings

Indio

Holiday Inn Express	760-342-6344	84-096 Indio Springs Pkwy Indio CA
Palm Shadow Inn	760-347-3476	80-761 Highway 111 Indio CA
Quality Inn	760-347-4044	43505 Monroe Street Indio CA

Palm Desert

| Comfort Suites | 760-360-3337 | 39-585 Washington St Palm Desert CA |

Palm Springs

| Super 8 Lodge - Palm Springs | 760-322-3757 | 1900 N. Palm Canyon Drive Palm Springs CA |

Rancho Mirage

| Motel 6 | 760-324-8475 | 69-570 Hwy 111 Rancho Mirage CA |

Blythe Listings
Blythe

| Best Western Sahara Motel | 760-922-7105 | 825 W. Hobson Way Blythe CA |
| Holiday Inn Express | 760-921-2300 | 600 W. Donion St Blythe CA |

Arizona (Interstate 10)

Phoenix Listings
Phoenix

Holiday Inn - West	602-484-9009	1500 N 51st Ave Phoenix AZ
Holiday Inn Express Hotel & Suites	480-785-8500	15221 S. 50th St Phoenix AZ
Motel 6	602-267-8555	5315 E Van Buren Street Phoenix AZ
Quality Hotel & Resort	602-248-0222	3600 N 2nd Ave Phoenix AZ
Quality Inn South Mountain	480-893-3900	5121 E. La Puente Ave. Phoenix AZ
Quality Suites	602-956-4900	3101 N. 32nd St Phoenix AZ

Phoenix Area Listings
Goodyear

| Holiday Inn Express | 623-535-1313 | 1313 Litchfield Rd Goodyear AZ |

Scottsdale

| Motel 6 | 480-946-2280 | 6848 E Camelback Rd Scottsdale AZ |

Tempe

La Quinta Inn Phoenix Sky Harbor Tempe	480-967-4465	911 South 48th Street Tempe AZ
Motel 6	480-968-4401	1720 S. Priest Drive Tempe AZ
Motel 6	480-945-9506	1612 N Scottsdale Rd/Rural Rd Tempe AZ
Studio 6	602-414-4470	4909 South Wendler Dr. Tempe AZ

Casa Grande Listings
Casa Grande

| Holiday Inn | 520-426-3500 | 777 N Pinal Ave Casa Grande AZ |

Tucson Listings
Tucson

Best Western Executive Inn	520-791-7551	333 West Drachman Street Tucson AZ
Clarion Hotel & Suites Santa Rita	520-622-4000	88 E. Broadway Blvd. Tucson AZ
Comfort Suites	520-295-4400	6935 S. Tucson Blvd. Tucson AZ
Motel 6 - 22nd Street	520-624-2516	1222 S Frwy Tucson AZ
Motel 6 - Airport	520-628-1264	1031 E Benson Hwy Tucson AZ
Motel 6 - Benson Hwy N	520-622-4614	755 E Benson Hwy Tucson AZ
Motel 6 - Congess St	520-628-1339	960 S. Freeway Tucson AZ
Motel 6 - North	520-744-9300	4630 W Ina Rd Tucson AZ
Studio 6	520-746-0030	4950 S. Outlet Center Dr Tucson AZ

Benson Listings
Benson

| Motel 6 | 520-586-0066 | 637 S. Whetstone Commerce Dr Benson AZ |

Wilcox Listings
Wilcox

| Best Western Plaza Inn | 520-384-3556 | 1100 W Rex Allen Dr Wilcox AZ |
| Motel 6 | 520-384-2201 | 921 N Bisbee Ave Wilcox AZ |

New Mexico (Interstate 10)

Lordsburg Listings
Lordsburg

| Best Western American Motor Inn | 505-542-3591 | 944 East Motel Drive Lordsburg NM |
| Best Western Skies Inn | 505-542-8807 | 1303 South Main Lordsburg NM |

Deming Listings
Deming

| Holiday Inn | 505-546-2661 | Exit 85 I-10 Deming NM |
| Motel 6 | 505-546-2623 | I-10 & Motel Drive Deming NM |

Las Cruces Listings

Las Cruces

Best Western Mesilla Valley Inn	505-524-8603	901 Avenida de Mesilla Las Cruces NM
Holiday Inn	505-526-4411	201 University Ave Las Cruces NM
Holiday Inn Express	505-527-9947	2200 S. Valley Drive Las Cruces NM
La Quinta Inn Las Cruces	505-524-0331	790 Avenida De Mesilla Las Cruces NM
Motel 6	505-525-1010	235 La Posada Ln Las Cruces NM

Texas (Interstate 10)

El Paso Listings

El Paso

Best Western Airport Inn	915-779-7700	7144 Gateway East El Paso TX
Comfort Inn	915-845-1906	7651 N. Mesa St El Paso TX
Comfort Inn Airport East	915-594-9111	900 Yarbrough Dr El Paso TX
La Quinta Inn El Paso - Cielo Vista	915-593-8400	9125 Gateway West El Paso TX
La Quinta Inn El Paso West	915-833-2522	7550 Remcon Circle El Paso TX
La Quinta Inn El Paso-Airport	915-778-9321	6140 Gateway Blvd. E El Paso TX
Sleep Inn	915-585-7577	953 Sunland Park Dr El Paso TX
Studio 6	915-594-8533	11049 Gateway Blvd W El Paso TX

Van Horn Listings

Van Horn

Best Western American Inn	915-283-2030	1309 W. Broadway Van Horn TX
Best Western Inn of Van Horn	915-283-2410	1705 W. Broadway, Box 309 Van Horn TX
Comfort Inn	915-283-2211	1601 W Broadway St Van Horn TX
Motel 6	915-283-2992	1805 West Broadway Van Horn TX

Fort Stockton Listings

Fort Stockton

Best Western Swiss Clock Inn	915-336-8521	3201 W. Dickinson Fort Stockton TX
Comfort Inn	915-336-8531	3200 W. Dickinson Blvd Fort Stockton TX
Holiday Inn Express	915-336-5955	1308 N. Hwy 285 Fort Stockton TX
Motel 6	915-336-9737	3001 W Dickinson Blvd Fort Stockton TX

Sonora Listings

Sonora

| Best Western Sonora Inn | 915-387-9111 | 270 Highway 277 North Sonora TX |

San Antonio Listings

San Antonio

Comfort Inn	210-333-9430	4403 I-10 e San Antonio TX
Holiday Inn	210-225-3211	318 W. Durango Blvd San Antonio TX
Holiday Inn - Riverwalk	210-224-2500	217 North St. Mary's St. San Antonio TX
Holiday Inn Express	210-561-9300	9411 Wurzbach Rd San Antonio TX
La Quinta Inn San Antonio Wurzbach	210-593-0338	9542 I-10 West San Antonio TX
Motel 6	210-333-1850	138 N WW White Rd San Antonio TX
Motel 6	210-697-0731	16500 IH-10 W San Antonio TX
Motel 6	210-349-3100	7719 Louis Pasteur Court San Antonio TX
Motel 6 - Med Center	210-593-0013	9400 Wurzbach Rd San Antonio TX
Motel 6 - Riverwalk	210-225-1111	211 N Pecos St San Antonio TX
Quality Inn & Suites	210-359-7200	222 South WW White Rd San Antonio TX
Quality Inn NW Medical Center	210-736-1900	6023 IH 10 west San Antonio TX
Staybridge Suites	210-558-9009	4320 Spectrum One Rd San Antonio TX
Studio 6	210-691-0121	11802 IH 10 West San Antonio TX

Seguin Listings

Seguin

| Best Western of Seguin | 830-379-9631 | 1603 I-10/Hwy 46 Seguin TX |
| Holiday Inn | 830-372-0860 | 2950 N. Hwy 123 Bypass Seguin TX |

Highway Guides - Please always call ahead to make sure an establishment is still dog-friendly.

Columbus Listings
Columbus

| Holiday Inn Express Hotel & Suites | 979-733-9300 | 4321 I-10 Columbus TX |

Houston Listings
Houston

Comfort Inn	713-783-1400	9041 Westheimer Rd Houston TX
Holiday Inn Hotel & Suites	713-681-5000	7787 Katy Fwy Houston TX
Holiday Inn Select	281-558-5580	14703 Park Row Houston TX
Houston - West Drury Inn & Suites	281-558-7007	1000 North Highway 6 Houston TX
La Quinta Inn & Suites Houston Park 10	281-646-9200	15225 Katy Freeway Houston TX
La Quinta Inn Houston East	713-453-5425	11999 East Freeway Houston TX
La Quinta Inn Houston Wilcrest	713-932-0808	11113 Katy Freeway Houston TX
Motel 6	281-497-5000	14833 Katy Frwy Houston TX
Studio 6	281-579-6959	1255 North Highway 6 Houston TX

Katy

| Best Western Houston West | 281-392-9800 | 22455 I-10 West Katy TX |

Houston Area Listings
Channelview

| Best Western Houston East | 281-452-1000 | 15919 I-10 East Channelview TX |

Port Arthur Listings
Port Arthur

| Studio 6 | 800-466-8356 | 3000 Jimmy Johnson Port Arthur TX |

Orange Listings
Orange

| Motel 6 | 409-883-4891 | 4407 27th St Orange TX |

Louisiana (Interstate 10)

Sulphur Listings
Sulphur

| La Quinta Inn Lake Charles - Sulphur | 337-527-8303 | 2600 South Ruth Sulphur LA |

Lake Charles Listings
Lake Charles

| Best Suites of America | 337-439-2444 | 401 Lakeshore Drive Lake Charles LA |

Iowa Listings
Iowa

| Howard Johnson Express Inn | 337-582-2440 | 107 E Frontage Rd. Iowa LA |

Lafayette Listings
Lafayette

Comfort Inn	337-232-9000	1421 S.E. Evangeline Thruway Lafayette LA
La Quinta Inn Lafayette	337-233-5610	2100 NE Evangeline Thruway Lafayette LA
Quality Inn	337-234-0383	2216 NE Evangeline Thruway Lafayette LA
Red Roof Inn	337-233-3339	1718 N University Ave Lafayette LA

Lafayette/Scott

| Howard Johnson Express Inn | 337-593-0849 | 103 Nibor Lane Lafayette/Scott LA |

Breaux Bridge Listings
Breaux Bridge

| Best Western | 337-332-1114 | 2088-B Rees Street Breaux Bridge LA |
| Holiday Inn Express | 337-667-8913 | 2942H Grand Point Highway Breaux Bridge LA |

Baton Rouge Listings
Baton Rouge

La Quinta Inn Baton Rouge	225-924-9600	2333 South Acadian Thruway Baton Rouge LA

La Place Listings
La Place

Best Western La Place Inn	985-651-4000	4289 Main Street La Place LA

New Orleans Listings
Gretna

La Quinta Inn New Orleans West Bank - Gretna	504-368-5600	50 Terry Parkway Gretna LA

Metairie

La Quinta Inn New Orleans Veterans - Metairie	504-456-0003	5900 Veterans Memorial Blvd Metairie LA
Quality Hotel & Conference Center	504-833-8211	2261 N. Causeway Blvd. Metairie LA

New Orleans

Drury Inn & Suites	504-529-7800	820 Poydras Street New Orleans LA
Studio 6	504-240-9778	12330 I-10 Service Rd New Orleans LA

Slidell

La Quinta Inn New Orleans Slidell	985-643-9770	794 E. I-10 Service Rd. Slidell LA
Motel 6	985-649-7925	136 Taos St Slidell LA

Mississippi (Interstate 10)

Gulfport Listings
Gulfport

Best Western Seaway Inn	228-864-0050	9475 US Hwy 49 & I-10 Gulfport MS
Holiday Inn Express	228-864-7222	9435 US Hwy 49 Gulfport MS

Biloxi Listings
Biloxi

Breakers Inn	228-388-6320	2506 Beach Blvd Biloxi MS
Holiday Inn - Beachfront	228-388-3551	2400 Beach Blvd Biloxi MS
Holiday Inn Express	228-388-1000	2416 Beach Blvd Biloxi MS
Motel 6	228-388-5130	2476 Beach Blvd Biloxi MS

Ocean Springs Listings
Ocean Springs

Comfort Inn	228-818-0300	7827 Lamar Poole Rd. Ocean Springs MS

Alabama (Interstate 10)

Mobile Listings
Mobile

Holiday Inn	251-666-5600	5465 Hwy 90 W (Gov't Blvd) Mobile AL
Ramada Inn	251-342-3220	850 S. Beltline Hwy Mobile AL

Florida (Interstate 10)

Pensacola Listings
Pensacola

Comfort Inn N.A.S.-Corry	850-455-3233	3 New Warrington Rd Pensacola FL
Motel 6	850-474-1060	7226 Plantation Rd Pensacola FL
Motel 6 - North	850-476-5386	7827 N Davis Hwy Pensacola FL
Red Roof Inn - North	850-478-4499	6919 Pensacola Blvd Pensacola FL
Red Roof Inn - Univ. Mall	850-476-7960	7340 Plantation Rd Pensacola FL

Milton Listings
Milton

Comfort Inn	850-623-1511	4962 SR 87 South Milton FL
Red Roof Inn & Suites	850-995-6100	2972 Avalon Blvd Milton FL

Navarre Listings
Navarre

| Comfort Inn & Conference Center | 850-939-1761 | 8700 Navarre Pkwy Navarre FL |

De Funiak Springs Listings
De Funiak Springs

| Best Western Crossroads Inn | 850-892-5111 | 2343 Freeport Rd, I-10 & US 331S De Funiak Springs FL |

Marianna Listings
Marianna

| Comfort Inn | 850-526-5600 | 2175 Highway 71 South Marianna FL |

Tallahassee Listings
Tallahassee

| Howard Johnson Express Inn | 850-386-5000 | 2726 North Monroe Street Tallahassee FL |
| La Quinta Inn Tallahassee North | 850-385-7172 | 2905 North Monroe Tallahassee FL |

Jacksonville Listings
Jacksonville

| Red Roof Inn - Southpoint | 904-296-1006 | 6969 Lenoir Avenue E Jacksonville FL |

Interstate 15 Accommodation Listings

Montana (Interstate 15)

Shelby Listings
Shelby

| Comfort Inn | 406-434-2212 | 50 Frontage Rd. Shelby MT |

Great Falls Listings
Great Falls

| Holiday Inn | 406-727-7200 | 400 10th Ave S. Great Falls MT |

Helena Listings
Helena

| Holiday Inn | 406-443-2200 | 22 N. Last Chance Gulch Helena MT |
| Motel 6 | 406-442-9990 | 800 N Oregon St Helena MT |

Butte Listings
Butte

| Comfort Inn | 406-494-8850 | 2777 Harrison Ave. Butte MT |

Dillon Listings
Dillon

| Best Western Paradise Inn | 406-683-4214 | 650 N. Montana Street Dillon MT |
| Comfort Inn | 406-683-6831 | 450 N. Interchange Dillon MT |

Idaho (Interstate 15)

Idaho Falls Listings
Idaho Falls

Best Western Driftwood Inn	208-523-2242	575 River Pkwy Idaho Falls ID
Comfort Inn	208-528-2804	195 S. Colorado Ave. Idaho Falls ID
Motel 6	208-522-0112	1448 W Broadway Idaho Falls ID

Pocatello Listings
Pocatello

Best Western CottonTree Inn	208-237-7650	1415 Bench Rd Pocatello ID
Comfort Inn	208-237-8155	1333 Bench Rd Pocatello ID
Holiday Inn	208-237-1400	1399 Bench Rd Pocatello ID

Utah (Interstate 15)

Highway Guides - Please always call ahead to make sure an establishment is still dog-friendly.

Brigham City Listings
Brigham City
Howard Johnson Inn | 435-723-8511 | 1167 S Main St. Brigham City UT

Ogden Listings
Ogden

Best Western High Country Inn	801-394-9474	1335 W 12th St Ogden UT
Comfort Suites of Ogden	801-621-2545	1150 W. 2150 S. Ogden UT
Holiday Inn Express Hotel & Suites	801-392-5000	2245 S. 1200 West Ogden UT
Motel 6	801-627-4560	1455 Washington Blvd Ogden UT

Salt Lake City Listings
Lehi

Best Western Timpanogos Inn	801-768-1400	195 South 850 East Lehi UT
Motel 6	801-768-2668	210 S 1200 E Lehi UT

Salt Lake City

Motel 6	801-364-1053	1990 W N Temple St Salt Lake City UT
Motel 6 - Downtown	801-531-1252	176 W 6th S St Salt Lake City UT

Orem Listings
Orem
La Quinta Inn Orem | 801-235-9555 | 1100 West 780 North Orem UT

Provo Listings
Provo

La Quinta Inn Provo - BYU / Orem	801-374-6020	1555 Canyon Road Provo UT
Motel 6	801-375-5064	1600 S University Ave Provo UT

Springville Listings
Springville
Best Western Cotton Tree Inn | 801-489-3641 | 1455 N 1750 West Springville UT

Nephi Listings
Nephi
Best Western Paradise Inn of Nephi | 435-623-0624 | 1025 S. Main Nephi UT

Fillmore Listings
Fillmore
Best Western Paradise Inn and Resort | 435-743-6895 | 805 N Main Fillmore UT

Beaver Listings
Beaver
Best Western Butch Cassidy Inn | 435-438-2438 | 161 South Main, PO Box 897 Beaver UT

St George Listings
St George

Holiday Inn	435-628-4235	850 S. Bluff St St George UT
Motel 6	435-628-7979	205 N 1000 E St St George UT

Nevada (Interstate 15)

Overton Listings
Overton
Best Western North Shore Inn | 702-397-6000 | 520 N. Moapa Valley Blvd Overton NV

Las Vegas Listings
Las Vegas

Best Western Nellis	702-643-6111	5330 East Craig Street Las Vegas NV
Comfort Inn	702-399-1500	910 E. Cheyenne Rd. Las Vegas NV
Hawthorn Suites-The Strip	702-739-7000	5051 Duke Ellington Way Las Vegas NV
La Quinta Inn Las Vegas - Nellis	702-632-0229	4288 N. Nellis Rd. Las Vegas NV

La Quinta Inn Las Vegas - Tropicana	702-798-7736	4975 South Valley View Las Vegas NV
Residence Inn - Hughes Center	702-650-0040	370 Hughes Center Drive Las Vegas NV
Rodeway Inn & Suites	702-795-3311	167 E. Tropicana Ave Las Vegas NV

California (Interstate 15)

Barstow Listings

Barstow

Days Inn	760-256-1737	1590 Coolwater Lane Barstow CA
Econo Lodge	760-256-2133	1230 E. Main Street Barstow CA
Holiday Inn Express	760-256-1300	1861 W. Main St. Barstow CA
Motel 6	760-256-1752	150 N Tucca Ave Barstow CA
Ramada Inn	760-256-5673	1511 E Main Street Barstow CA
Super 8 Motel	760-256-8443	170 Coolwater Lane Barstow CA

Victorville Listings

Hesperia

Days Suites	760-948-0600	14865 Bear Valley Rd Hesperia CA

Victorville

Howard Johnson Express Inn	760-243-7700	16868 Stoddard Wells Rd. Victorville CA
Ramada Inn	760-245-6565	15494 Palmdale Road Victorville CA
Red Roof Inn	760-241-1577	13409 Mariposa Rd Victorville CA

Inland Empire Listings

Claremont

Ramada Inn	909-621-4831	840 South Indian Hill Blvd Claremont CA

Corona

Motel 6	909-735-6408	200 N Lincoln Ave Corona CA

Rialto

Best Western Empire Inn	909-877-0690	475 W Valley Blvd Rialto CA

Temecula Listings

Temecula

Comfort Inn	909-296-3788	27338 Jefferson Ave. Temecula CA
Motel 6	909-676-6383	41900 Moreno Rd Temecula CA

Temecula

Temecula Vacation Rental	310-390-7778	Call to Arrange. Temecula CA

San Diego County North Listings

Escondido

Castle Creek Inn Resort	760-751-8800	29850 Circle R Way Escondido CA

San Diego Listings

National City

Super 8	619-474-8811	425 Roosevelt Ave National City CA

San Diego

La Quinta Inn San Diego - Rancho Penasquitos	858-484-8800	10185 Paseo Montril San Diego CA
Residence Inn	858-673-1900	11002 Rancho Carmel Dr San Diego CA

Interstate 20 Accommodation Listings

Texas (Interstate 20)

Pecos Listings

Pecos

Best Western Swiss Clock Inn	915-447-2215	900 West Palmer Street Pecos TX
Motel 6	915-445-9034	3002 S Cedar St Pecos TX

Odessa Listings
Odessa
Best Western Garden Oasis	915-337-3006	110 West Interstate 20 Odessa TX
Holiday Inn Hotel & Suites	915-362-2311	6201 E. Bus I-20 Odessa TX
La Quinta Inn Odessa	915-333-2820	5001 E. Highway 80 Odessa TX

Midland Listings
Midland
La Quinta Inn Midland	432-697-9900	4130 West Wall Avenue Midland TX

Big Spring Listings
Big Spring
Best Western Motor Lodge	915-267-1601	700 W IH-20 Big Spring TX
Motel 6	915-267-1695	600 W I-20 Rt 2 Big Spring TX

Abilene Listings
Abilene
Comfort Inn	915-676-0203	1758 E I-20 Abilene TX
Comfort Suites	915-795-8500	3165 S Danville Dr Abilene TX
La Quinta Inn Abilene	915-676-1676	3501 West Lake Road Abilene TX
Quality Inn Civic Center	800-588-0222	505 Pine St Abilene TX

Weatherford Listings
Weatherford
Best Western Santa Fe Inn	817-594-7401	1927 Santa Fe Drive Weatherford TX
La Quinta Inn & Suites Weatherford	817-594-4481	1915 Wall Street Weatherford TX

Fort Worth Listings
Fort Worth
La Quinta Inn & Suites Fort Worth Southwest	817-370-2700	4900 Bryant Irvin Road Fort Worth TX
Motel 6	817-244-9740	8701 Interstate 30 W Fort Worth TX

Dallas - Fort Worth Area Listings
Arlington
Studio 6	817-465-8500	1980 West Pleasant Ridge Rd Arlington TX

Balch Springs
Howard Johnson Express Inn	972-286-1010	12901 Seagoville Rd. Balch Springs TX

Dallas Listings
Dallas
Motel 6	972-296-3331	4220 Independence Dr Dallas TX

Longview Listings
Longview
Motel 6	903-758-5256	110 S Access Rd Longview TX

Marshall Listings
Marshall
Motel 6	903-935-4393	300 I-20E Marshall TX

Louisiana (Interstate 20)

Shreveport Listings
Bossier City
La Quinta Inn Bossier City	318-747-4400	309 Preston Boulevard Bossier City LA
Motel 6	318-742-3472	210 John Wesley Blvd Bossier City LA
Quality Inn	318-746-5050	4300 Industrial Drive Bossier City LA
Residence Inn	318-747-6220	1001 Gould Dr Bossier City LA

Shreveport
La Quinta Inn & Suites Shreveport	318-671-1100	6700 Financial Circle Shreveport LA
Red Roof Inn	318-938-5342	7296 Greenwood Rd Shreveport LA

Minden Listings
Minden

| Best Western Minden Inn | 318-377-1001 | 1411 Sibley Rd Minden LA |

Monroe Listings
Monroe

| Days Inn | 318-345-2220 | 5650 Frontage Rd Monroe LA |

Delhi Listings
Delhi

| Best Western Delhi Inn | 318-878-5126 | 35 Snider Rd, I20 & 17 S. Delhi LA |

Mississippi (Interstate 20)

Vicksburg Listings
Vicksburg

Battlefield Inn	601-638-5811	4137 I-20 Frontage Rd Vicksburg MS
Duff Green Mansion	601-638-6662	1114 First East St Vicksburg MS
La Quinta Inn Vicksburg	601-638-5750	4216 Washington Street Vicksburg MS
The Corners Bed and Breakfast Inn	601-636-7421	601 Klien St Vicksburg MS

Jackson Listings
Jackson

| Quality Hotel Southwest | 601-355-3472 | 2649 Highway 80 West Jackson MS |
| Sleep Inn | 601-354-3900 | 2620 US 80 West Jackson MS |

Forest Listings
Forest

| Apple Tree Inn | 601-469-2640 | I-20 at Highway 35, PO Box 402 Forest MS |

Meridian Listings
Meridian

Holiday Inn	601-485-5101	111 US Hwy 11 & 80 Meridian MS
Motel 6	601-482-1182	2309 S. Frontage Rd Meridian MS
Quality Inn	601-693-4521	1401 Roebuck Dr Meridian MS

Alabama (Interstate 20)

Tuscaloosa Listings
Tuscaloosa

| La Quinta Inn Tuscaloosa | 205-349-3270 | 4122 McFarland Blvd East Tuscaloosa AL |
| Motel 6 | 205-759-4942 | 4700 McFarland Blvd E (Hwy 82E) Tuscaloosa AL |

Birmingham Listings
Birmingham

| Holiday Inn - Airport | 205-591-6900 | 5000 10th Ave N Birmingham AL |
| La Quinta Inn Birmingham Northwest | 205-324-4510 | 905 11th Court West Birmingham AL |

Oxford Listings
Oxford

| Howard Johnson Express Inn | 256-835-3988 | PO Box 3308 Oxford AL |
| Motel 6 | 256-831-5463 | 202 Grace Street Oxford AL |

Heflin Listings
Heflin

| Howard Johnson Express Inn | 256-463-2900 | 1957 Almon Street Heflin AL |

Georgia (Interstate 20)

Lithia Springs Listings
Lithia Springs

| Motel 6 | 678-945-0606 | 920 Bob Arnold Blvd Lithia Springs GA |

Atlanta Listings

Atlanta

Airport Drury Inn & Suites	404-761-4900	1270 Virginia Avenue Atlanta GA
AmeriSuites-Atlanta/Perimeter Center	770-730-9300	1005 Crestline Parkway Atlanta GA
Crowne Plaza - Airport	404-768-6660	1325 Virginia Ave Atlanta GA
Hawthorn Suites	770-952-9595	1500 Parkwood Circle Atlanta GA
Holiday Inn - Airport North	404-762-8411	1380 Virginia Ave Atlanta GA
Holiday Inn Select-Atlanta Perimeter	770-457-6363	4386 Chamblee-Dunwoody Rd. Atlanta GA
Marriott Atlanta Airport	404-766-7900	4711 Best Road Atlanta GA
Motel 6 - Northeast (I-85)	770-458-6626	2820 Chamblee - Tucker Rd Atlanta GA
Red Roof Inn	404-761-9701	2471 Old National Pkwy Atlanta GA
Red Roof Inn-Druid Hills	404-321-1653	1960 N Druid Hills Rd. Atlanta GA
Residence Inn by Marriott	404-522-0950	134 Peachtree Street NW Atlanta GA
Residence Inn by Marriott-Midtown	404-872-8885	1041 W Peachtree Street Atlanta GA
Sheraton Midtown Atlanta at Colony Square	404-892-6000	188 14th Street at Peachtree Atlanta GA
Staybridge Suites - Perimeter	678-320-0111	4601 Ridgeview Rd Atlanta GA
Summerfield Suites-Buckhead	404-262-7880	505 Pharr Road Atlanta GA
W Atlanta	770-396-6800	111 Perimeter Center West Atlanta GA

Norcross

Northeast Drury Inn & Suites	770-729-0060	5655 Jimmy Carter Blvd Norcross GA

Atlanta Area Listings

Austell

La Quinta Inn Atlanta West	770-944-2110	7377 Six Flags Drive Austell GA

Thomson Listings

Thomson

Best Western White Columns Inn	706-595-8000	1890 Washington Thomson GA

Augusta Listings

Augusta

Amerisuites	706-733-4656	1062 Claussen Rd. Augusta GA
Comfort Inn	706-855-6060	629 Frontage Rd. N. W. Augusta GA
Holiday Inn	706-737-2300	2155 Gordon Hwy Augusta GA
Howard Johnson Inn	706-863-2882	601 NW Frontage Rd. Augusta GA
La Quinta Inn Augusta	706-733-2660	3020 Washington Road Augusta GA
Sheraton Augusta Hotel	706-855-8100	2651 Perimeter Parkway Augusta GA

South Carolina (Interstate 20)

Columbia Listings

Columbia

Holiday Inn	803-736-3000	7510 Two Notch Rd, I-20 & US-1 Columbia SC
Motel 6	803-798-9210	1776 Burning Tree Rd Columbia SC
Sheraton Columbia Hotel and Conference Center	803-731-0300	2100 Bush River Road Columbia SC

Interstate 25 Accommodation Listings

Wyoming (Interstate 25)

Buffalo Listings

Buffalo

Motel 6	307-684-7000	100 Flat Iron Drive Buffalo WY

Casper Listings

Highway Guides - Please always call ahead to make sure an establishment is still dog-friendly.

Casper
Econo Lodge	307-266-2400	821 N Poplar St Casper WY
Holiday Inn	307-235-2531	300 West F Street Casper WY

Wheatland Listings
Wheatland
Best Western Torchlite Motor Inn	307-322-4070	1809 N 16th St Wheatland WY
Vimbo's Motel	307-322-3842	203 16th St Wheatland WY

Colorado (Interstate 25)

Fort Collins Listings
Fort Collins
Best Western University Inn	970-484-1984	914 S. College Ave Fort Collins CO
Comfort Suites	970-206-4597	1415 Oakridge Drive Fort Collins CO
Holiday Inn	970-482-2626	425 W. Prospect Rd Fort Collins CO
Holiday Inn	970-484-4660	3836 E. Mulberry Fort Collins CO
Motel 6	970-482-6466	3900 E Mulberry / State Hwy 14 Fort Collins CO
Sleep Inn	970-484-5515	3808 E. Mulberry St Fort Collins CO

Loveland Listings
Loveland
Best Western Coach House	970-667-7810	5542 E US Hwy 34 Loveland CO

Greeley Listings
Greeley
Holiday Inn Express	970-330-7495	2563 W 29th Street Greeley CO

Thornton Listings
Thornton
Sleep Inn	303-280-9818	12101 N. Grant St Thornton CO

Denver Listings
Denver
La Quinta Inn Denver Central	303-458-1222	3500 Park Avenue West Denver CO
Quality Inn South - DTC	303-758-2211	6300 E Hampden Ave Denver CO

Greenwood Village
Mainstay Suites	303-858-1669	9253 E Costilla Ave Greenwood Village CO
Sleep Inn Denver Tech	303-662-9950	9257 E Costilla Ave Greenwood Village CO

Denver Area Listings
Englewood
Comfort Suites Tech Center South	303-858-0700	7374 South Clinton St Englewood CO
Denver Tech Center Drury Inn & Suites	303-694-3400	9445 East Dry Creek Road Englewood CO
Sheraton Denver Tech Center Hotel	303-799-6200	7007 South Clinton Street Englewood CO

Westminster
La Quinta Inn Denver Northglenn - Westminster	303-252-9800	345 West 120th Avenue Westminster CO

Castle Rock Listings
Castle Rock
Comfort Suites	303-814-9999	4755 Castleton Way Castle Rock CO
Holiday Inn Express	303-660-9733	884 Park Street Castle Rock CO

Colorado Springs Listings
Colorado Springs
Comfort Inn North	719-262-9000	6450 Corporate Center Dr Colorado Springs CO
La Quinta Inn Colorado Springs	719-528-5060	4385 Sinton Road Colorado Springs CO
Motel 6	719-520-5400	3228 N Chestnut St Colorado Springs CO
Quality Inn Garden of the Gods	719-593-9119	555 W. Garden of the Gods Rd Colorado Springs CO
Sheraton Colorado Springs Hotel	719-576-5900	2886 S. Circle Drive Colorado Springs CO

Pueblo Listings

Pueblo

Best Western Town House	719-543-6530	730 N. Santa Fe Pueblo CO
Motel 6	719-543-8900	960 Hwy 50 W Pueblo CO
Motel 6	719-543-6221	4103 Elizabeth St Pueblo CO

Trinidad Listings
Trinidad

Holiday Inn	719-846-4491	3125 Toupal Drive Trinidad CO

New Mexico (Interstate 25)

Raton Listings
Raton

Motel 6	505-445-2777	1600 Cedar St Raton NM

Santa Fe Listings
Santa Fe

Best Western Inn of Santa Fe	505-438-3822	3650 Cerrillos Rd Santa Fe NM
La Quinta Inn Santa Fe	505-471-1142	4298 Cerrillos Road Santa Fe NM
Motel 6	505-473-1380	3007 Cerrillos Rd Santa Fe NM
Quality Inn	505-471-1211	3011 Cerrillos Rd. Santa Fe NM
Sleep Inn	505-474-9500	8376 Cerrillos Rd. Santa Fe NM

Rio Rancho Listings
Rio Rancho

Best Western Inn at Rio Rancho	505-892-1700	1465 Rio Rancho Drive Rio Rancho NM

Albuquerque Listings
Albuquerque

Best Western American Motor Inn	505-298-7426	12999 Central Ave NE Albuquerque NM
Comfort Inn & Suites North	505-822-1090	5811 Signal Ave. N.E. Albuquerque NM
Comfort Inn Airport	505-243-2244	2300 Yale Blvd. Albuquerque NM
Holiday Inn - Mountain View	505-884-2511	2020 Menaul Blvd NE Albuquerque NM
Howard Johnson Express Inn	505-828-1600	7630 Pan American Freeway NE Albuquerque NM
La Quinta Inn Albuquerque Airport	505-243-5500	2116 Yale Boulevard Albuquerque NM
La Quinta Inn Albuquerque North	505-821-9000	5241 San Antonio Drive NE Albuquerque NM
Motel 6	505-243-8017	1000 Avenida Cesar Chavez SE Albuquerque NM
Motel 6	505-883-8813	3400 Prospect Ave NE Albuquerque NM
Motel 6	505-843-9228	1701 University Blvd NE Albuquerque NM
Sleep Inn Airport	505-244-3325	2300 International Ave. SE Albuquerque NM

Los Lunas Listings
Los Lunas

Comfort Inn	505-865-5100	1711 Main St. S.W. Los Lunas NM

Belen Listings
Belen

Best Western Belen	505-861-3181	2111 Sosimo Padilla Blvd Belen NM

Socorro Listings
Socorro

Motel 6	505-835-4300	807 S US Hwy 85 Socorro NM

Truth or Consequences Listings
Truth or Consequences

Best Western Hot Springs Inn	505-894-6665	2270 N Date Street Truth or Consequences NM
Holiday Inn	505-894-1660	2000 N. Date Street Truth or Consequences NM

Las Cruces Listings
Las Cruces

Best Western Mesilla Valley Inn	505-524-8603	901 Avenida de Mesilla Las Cruces NM
Holiday Inn	505-526-4411	201 University Ave Las Cruces NM
Holiday Inn Express	505-527-9947	2200 S. Valley Drive Las Cruces NM
La Quinta Inn Las Cruces	505-524-0331	790 Avenida De Mesilla Las Cruces NM

Interstate 35 Accommodation Listings

Minnesota (Interstate 35)

Duluth Listings
Duluth
Best Western Downtown Motel	218-727-6851	131 W. 2nd Street Duluth MN
Days Inn	218-727-3110	909 Cottonwood Ave Duluth MN
Motel 6	218-723-1123	200 South 27th Ave W. Duluth MN

Minneapolis - St Paul Listings
Brooklyn Center
Comfort Inn	763-560-7464	1600 James Circle N. Brooklyn Center MN
Motel 6	763-560-9789	2741 Freeway Blvd Brooklyn Center MN

Burnsville
Super 8 Motel - Burnsville	952-894-3400	1101 Burnsville Parkway Burnsville MN

Lakeville
Motel 6	952-469-1900	11274 210th St Lakeville MN

Maple Grove
Staybridge Suites	763-494-8856	7821 Elm Creek Blvd Maple Grove MN

Minneapolis
Holiday Inn	612-333-4646	1500 Washington Ave S. Minneapolis MN
The Marquette Hilton	612-333-4545	710 Marquette Ave Minneapolis MN

Woodbury
Red Roof Inn	651-738-7160	1806 Wooddale Dr Woodbury MN

Albert Lea Listings
Albert Lea
Comfort Inn	507-377-1100	810 Happy Trails Lane Albert Lea MN

Iowa (Interstate 35)

Clear Lake Listings
Clear Lake
Best Western Holiday Lodge	641-357-5253	I-35 & Hwy 18, Box J Clear Lake IA

Ames Listings
Ames
Howard Johnson Express Inn	515-232-8363	1709 S Duff Ave. Ames IA

Des Moines Listings
Des Moines
Best Western Colonial	515-265-7511	5020 NE 14th Street Des Moines IA
Holiday Inn	515-278-0271	5000 Merle Hay Rd Des Moines IA
Hotel Fort Des Moines	515-243-1161	1000 Walnut Street Des Moines IA
Motel 6 - North	515-266-5456	4940 NE 14th St Des Moines IA

Urbandale
Comfort Inn	515-270-1037	5900 Sutton Dr Urbandale IA

West Des Moines
Motel 6 - West	515-267-8885	7655 Office Plaza Dr N West Des Moines IA

Osceola Listings
Osceola
Best Western Regal Inn	641-342-2123	1520 Jeffrey's Dr, PO Box 238 Osceola IA

Missouri (Interstate 35)

Cameron Listings
Cameron
Best Western Acorn Inn	816-632-2187	I-35 & US 36 Cameron MO
Comfort Inn	816-632-5655	1803 Comfort Lane Cameron MO

Kansas City Listings

Kansas City

Best Western Seville Plaza Hotel	816-561-9600	4309 Main Street Kansas City MO
Chase Suite Hotel by Woodfin	816-891-9009	9900 NW Prairie View Road Kansas City MO
Clarion Hotel	816-483-9900	1601 N. Universal Ave. Kansas City MO
Comfort Suites	816-781-7273	8200 N. Church Rd. Kansas City MO
Kansas City - Stadium Drury Inn & Suites	816-923-3000	3830 Blue Ridge Cutoff Kansas City MO
Mainstay Suites	816-891-8500	9701 N. Shannon Ave. Kansas City MO
Motel 6	816-333-4468	6400 E 87th St Kansas City MO
Super 8 Motel	816-587-0808	6900 NW 83rd Terrace Kansas City MO
The Westin Crown Center	816-474-4400	One Pershing Road Kansas City MO

North Kansas City

Days Inn Motel - North Kansas City	816-421-6000	2232 Taney Street North Kansas City MO

Kansas (Interstate 35)

Olathe Listings

Olathe

Sleep Inn	913-390-9500	20662 W 151st St Olathe KS

Emporia Listings

Emporia

Best Western Hospitality House	620-342-7587	3021 W. Hwy 50 Emporia KS
Super 8 Motel - Emporia	620-342-7567	2913 W. Highway 50 Emporia KS

El Dorado Listings

El Dorado

Best Western Red Coach Inn	316-321-6900	2525 W. Central El Dorado KS

Wichita Listings

Wichita

Best Western Red Coach Inn	316-832-9387	915 E 53rd Street North Wichita KS
Comfort Inn East	316-686-2844	9525 E.Corporate Hills Wichita KS
Holiday Inn - Airport	316-943-2181	5500 W. Kellogg Wichita KS
La Quinta Inn Wichita	316-681-2881	7700 East Kellogg Wichita KS
Motel 6	316-945-8440	5736 W. Kellogg Wichita KS
Residence Inn by Marriott - East	316-686-7331	411 S Webb Rd Wichita KS

Oklahoma (Interstate 35)

Oklahoma City Listings

Oklahoma City

Best Western Saddleback Inn	405-947-7000	4300 SW 3rd St Oklahoma City OK
Comfort Inn and Suites	405-528-7563	5405 N Lincoln Blvd Oklahoma City OK
Days Inn North	405-478-2554	12013 N I-35 Service Rd Oklahoma City OK
Embassy Suites	405-682-6000	1815 S Meridian Ave Oklahoma City OK
Holiday Inn	405-843-5558	6200 North Robinson Oklahoma City OK
Holiday Inn Express	405-755-8686	13520 Plaza Terrace Oklahoma City OK
Holiday Inn Hotel & Suites	405-843-5558	6200 N. Robinson Oklahoma City OK
Howard Johnson Express Inn	405-943-9841	400 South Meridian Oklahoma City OK
La Quinta Inn & Suites Oklahoma City-Northwest Expressway	405-773-5575	4829 Northwest Expressway Oklahoma City OK
La Quinta Inn Oklahoma City South	405-631-8661	8315 South Interstate 35 Oklahoma City OK
Motel 6	405-946-6662	820 S Meridian Ave Oklahoma City OK
Motel 6	405-947-6550	4200 W Interstate 40 Oklahoma City OK
Residence Inn by Marriott	405-942-4500	4361 W Reno Ave Oklahoma City OK
Studio 6	405-737-8851	5801 Tinker Diagonal Oklahoma City OK

Norman Listings

Norman

La Quinta Inn & Suites Norman	405-579-4000	930 Ed Noble Drive Norman OK

Ardmore Listings

Ardmore

Best Western Ardmore Inn	580-223-7525	6 Holiday Drive Ardmore OK
Comfort Inn	580-226-1250	2700 W Broadway Ardmore OK
Holiday Inn	580-223-7130	2705 Holiday Drive Ardmore OK
La Quinta Inn Ardmore	580-223-7976	2432 Veterans Blvd Ardmore OK
Motel 6	580-226-7666	120 Holiday Dr Ardmore OK
Super 8	580-223-2201	2120 Hwy 142 W Ardmore OK

Texas (Interstate 35)

Denton Listings

Denton

La Quinta Inn Denton	940-387-5840	700 Fort Worth Drive Denton TX
Motel 6	940-566-4798	4125 Interstate 35N Denton TX

Roanoke Listings

Roanoke

Comfort Suites	817-490-1455	801 W Hwy 114 Roanoke TX
Sleep Inn & Suites Speedway	817-491-3120	13471 Raceway Dr Roanoke TX

Dallas Listings

Dallas

Best Western Dallas North	972-241-8521	13333 N Stemmons Fwy Dallas TX
La Quinta Inn Dallas Lovefield	214-630-5701	1625 Regal Row Dallas TX
Motel 6	972-484-9111	2660 Forest Lane Dallas TX
Motel 6	972-620-2828	2753 Forest Lane Dallas TX
Studio 6	214-904-1400	2395 Stemmons Trail Dallas TX

Dallas - Fort Worth Area Listings

Lewisville

Comfort Suites	972-315-6464	755A Vista Ridge Mall Dr Lewisville TX
Motel 6	972-436-5008	1705 Lakepointe Dr Lewisville TX

Fort Worth Listings

Fort Worth

Motel 6	817-625-4359	3271 Interstate 35 W Fort Worth TX
Motel 6	817-293-8595	6600 S Frwy Fort Worth TX

Temple Listings

Temple

La Quinta Inn Temple	254-771-2980	1604 West Barton Avenue Temple TX

Georgetown Listings

Georgetown

Comfort Inn	512-863-7504	1005 Leander Rd Georgetown TX
Holiday Inn Express Hotel & Suites	512-868-8555	600 San Gabriel Village Blvd Georgetown TX
La Quinta Inn Georgetown	512-869-2541	333 N IH 35 Georgetown TX

Cedar Park Listings

Cedar Park

Comfort Inn	512-259-1810	300 E. Whitestone Blvd Cedar Park TX

Round Rock Listings

Round Rock

La Quinta Inn Round Rock	512-255-6666	2004 North I-35 Round Rock TX

Austin Listings

Austin

Best Western Atrium North	512-339-7311	7928 Gessner Drive Austin TX
Comfort Suites	512-444-6630	1701 E St. Elmo Rd Austin TX
Highland Mall Drury Inn	512-454-1144	919 E. Koenig Lane Austin TX
Holiday Inn	512-448-2444	3401 S. I-35 Austin TX
Holiday Inn	512-472-8211	20 N I-25 Austin TX

Holiday Inn	512-459-4251	6911 N I-35 Austin TX
La Quinta Inn Austin Capitol	512-476-1166	300 E. 11th St. Austin TX
La Quinta Inn Austin North	512-452-9401	7100 N IH 35 Austin TX
La Quinta Inn Austin Oltorf	512-447-6661	1603 E. Oltorf Blvd. Austin TX
Motel 6	512-467-9111	5330 N Interregional Hwy Austin TX
Motel 6	512-444-5882	2707 Interregional Hwy S Austin TX
Studio 6	512-458-5453	937 Camino La Costa Austin TX
Studio 6	512-258-3556	11901 Pavilion Blvd Austin TX

San Marcos Listings
San Marcos

Motel 6	512-396-8705	1321 I-35 N San Marcos TX

New Braunfels Listings
New Braunfels

Holiday Inn	830-625-8017	1051 I-35 E. New Braunfels TX
Motel 6	830-626-0600	1275 IH-35 New Braunfels TX

San Antonio Listings
San Antonio

Clarion Suites Hotel	210-655-9491	13101 E Loop 1604 N San Antonio TX
Holiday Inn	210-225-3211	318 W. Durango Blvd San Antonio TX
Holiday Inn - Riverwalk	210-224-2500	217 North St. Mary's St. San Antonio TX
Howard Johnson Express Inn	210-229-9220	2755 IH-35N San Antonio TX
La Quinta Inn I-35 North at Windsor Park	210-653-6619	6410 N IH 35 San Antonio TX
Motel 6 - Ft Sam Houston	210-661-8791	5522 N Pan Am Expwy San Antonio TX
Motel 6 - North	210-650-4419	9503 Interstate Hwy 35 N San Antonio TX
Motel 6 - Northeast	210-653-8088	4621 E Rittiman Rd San Antonio TX
Motel 6 - Riverwalk	210-225-1111	211 N Pecos St San Antonio TX

Laredo Listings
Laredo

Best Western Fiesta Inn	956-723-3603	5240 San Bernardo Laredo TX
Family Gardens Inn	956-723-5300	5830 San Bernardo Laredo TX
La Quinta Inn Laredo	956-722-0511	3610 Santa Ursula Laredo TX
Motel 6	956-722-8133	5920 San Bernardo Ave Laredo TX
Motel 6	956-725-8187	5310 San Bernardo Ave Laredo TX

Interstate 40 Accommodation Listings

California (Interstate 40)

Barstow Listings
Barstow

Days Inn	760-256-1737	1590 Coolwater Lane Barstow CA
Econo Lodge	760-256-2133	1230 E. Main Street Barstow CA
Holiday Inn Express	760-256-1300	1861 W. Main St. Barstow CA
Motel 6	760-256-1752	150 N Tucca Ave Barstow CA
Ramada Inn	760-256-5673	1511 E Main Street Barstow CA
Super 8 Motel	760-256-8443	170 Coolwater Lane Barstow CA

Needles Listings
Needles

Days Inn and Suites	760-326-5836	1215 Hospitality Lane Needles CA
Econo Lodge	760-326-3881	1910 N. Needles Hwy Needles CA
Motel 6	760-326-3399	1420 J St Needles CA
Super 8	760-326-4501	1102 E Broadway Needles CA
Travelers Inn	760-326-4900	1195 3rd Street Hill Needles CA

Arizona (Interstate 40)

Kingman Listings
Kingman

Best Western A Wayfarer's Inn	928-753-6271	2815 East Andy Devine Kingman AZ
Best Western King's Inn	928-753-6101	2930 East Andy Devine Kingman AZ
Days Inn East	928-757-7337	3381 E Andy Devine Kingman AZ
Motel 6	928-757-7151	3351 E Andy Devine Ave Kingman AZ
Quality Inn	928-753-4747	1400 E. Andy Devine Ave. Kingman AZ
Super 8 Motel	928-757-4808	3401 E. Andy Devine Kingman AZ

Grand Canyon Listings
Williams

Holiday Inn	928-635-4114	950 N. Grand Canyon Blvd Williams AZ
Motel 6 - Grand Canyon	520-635-9000	831 W Rt 66 Williams AZ

Flagstaff Listings
Flagstaff

Comfort Inn I-17 & I40	928-774-2225	2355 S Beulah Blvd. Flagstaff AZ
Holiday Inn	928-714-1000	2320 E Lucky Lane Flagstaff AZ
Howard Johnson Inn	800-437-7137	3300 E. Rt. 66 Flagstaff AZ
La Quinta Inn & Suites Flagstaff	928-556-8666	2015 South Beulah Blvd. Flagstaff AZ
Motel 6	928-774-1801	2010 E Butler Ave Flagstaff AZ
Sleep Inn	928-556-3000	2765 S. Woodlands Village Blvd. Flagstaff AZ

Woodlands Village

Motel 6	928-779-3757	2745 S. Woodlands Village Woodlands Village AZ

Winslow Listings
Winslow

Days Inn	928-289-1010	2035 W. Hwy 66 Winslow AZ
Econo Lodge	928-289-4687	I40 & Exit 253 North Park Dr Winslow AZ
Holiday Inn Express	928-289-2960	816 Transcon Lane Winslow AZ

Holbrook Listings
Holbrook

Best Western Adobe Inn	928-524-3948	615 W Hopi Dr Holbrook AZ
Best Western Arizonian Inn	928-524-2611	2508 Navajo Blvd Holbrook AZ
Comfort Inn	928-524-6131	2602 E. Navajo Blvd. Holbrook AZ
Holiday Inn Express	928-524-1466	1308 E Navajo Blvd Holbrook AZ
Motel 6	928-524-6101	2514 Navajo Blvd Holbrook AZ

Chambers Listings
Chambers

Best Western Chieftain Inn	928-688-2754	Hwy 40 and Chambers Chambers AZ

New Mexico (Interstate 40)

Gallup Listings
Gallup

Best Western Inn and Suites	505-722-2221	3009 W. Highway 66 Gallup NM
Best Western Royal Holiday Motel	505-722-4900	1903 W Hwy 66 Gallup NM
Comfort Inn	505-722-0982	3208 W. US 66 Gallup NM
Days Inn-East	505-863-3891	1603 W Highway 66 Gallup NM
Holiday Inn	505-722-2201	2915 W. Hwy 66 Gallup NM
Motel 6	505-863-4492	3306 W 66 Gallup NM
Sleep Inn	505-863-3535	3820 US 66 E. Gallup NM

Grants Listings
Grants

Holiday Inn Express	505-285-4676	1496 E Santa Fe Ave Grants NM
Motel 6	505-285-4607	1505 E Santa Fe Ave Grants NM

Albuquerque Listings
Albuquerque

Best Western American Motor Inn	505-298-7426	12999 Central Ave NE Albuquerque NM
Holiday Inn - Mountain View	505-884-2511	2020 Menaul Blvd NE Albuquerque NM
Holiday Inn Express	505-836-8600	6100 Iliff Rd Albuquerque NM

Holiday Inn Express	505-275-8900	10330 Hotel Ave NE Albuquerque NM
Howard Johnson Hotel	505-296-4852	15 Hotel Circle NE Albuquerque NM
Motel 6	505-883-8813	3400 Prospect Ave NE Albuquerque NM
Motel 6	505-843-9228	1701 University Blvd NE Albuquerque NM

Moriarty Listings
Moriarty
Holiday Inn Express	505-832-5000	1507 Route 66 Moriarty NM
Motel 6	505-832-6666	109 Rt 66 East Moriarty NM

Santa Rosa Listings
Santa Rosa
Best Western Adobe Inn	505-472-3446	1501 E. Will Rogers Drive Santa Rosa NM
Best Western Santa Rosa Inn	505-472-5877	3022 E. Will Rogers Drive Santa Rosa NM
Comfort Inn	505-472-5570	3343 E. Will Rogers Blvd. Santa Rosa NM

Tucumcari Listings
Tucumcari
Best Western Discovery Inn	505-461-4884	200 East Estrella Ave Tucumcari NM
Best Western Pow Wow Inn	505-461-0500	801 W Tucumcari Blvd Tucumcari NM
Comfort Inn	505-461-4094	2800 E. Tucumcari Blvd Tucumcari NM
Holiday Inn	505-461-3780	3716 E. Tucumcari Blvd Tucumcari NM
Howard Johnson Express Inn	505-461-2747	3604 E. Rt. 66 Blvd. Tucumcari NM
Motel 6	505-461-4791	2900 E Tucumcari Blvd Tucumcari NM

Texas (Interstate 40)

Amarillo Listings
Amarillo
Best Western Santa Fe	806-372-1885	4600 E Interstate 40 Amarillo TX
La Quinta Inn Amarillo East/Airport Area	806-373-7486	1708 I-40 East Amarillo TX
Motel 6	806-374-6444	3930 I-40E Amarillo TX
Motel 6	806-359-7651	6030 I-40W Amarillo TX
Quality Inn & Suites Airport	806-335-1561	1803 Lakeside Dr Amarillo TX

Oklahoma (Interstate 40)

Elk City Listings
Elk City
Holiday Inn	580-225-6637	101 Meadow Ridge Elk City OK
Motel 6	580-225-6661	2500 E Hwy 66 Elk City OK

Clinton Listings
Clinton
Best Western Trade Winds Courtyard Inn	580-323-2610	2128 Gary Blvd Clinton OK

El Reno Listings
El Reno
Best Western Hensley's	405-262-6490	2701 S. Country Club Road El Reno OK

Yukon Listings
Yukon
Best Western Inn & Suites	405-265-2995	11440 West I-40 Service Rd Yukon OK

Oklahoma City Listings
Oklahoma City
Howard Johnson Express Inn	405-943-9841	400 South Meridian Oklahoma City OK
Motel 6	405-947-6550	4200 W Interstate 40 Oklahoma City OK
Studio 6	405-737-8851	5801 Tinker Diagonal Oklahoma City OK

Shawnee Listings
Shawnee
Best Western Cinderella Motor Inn	405-273-7010	623 Kickapoo Spur Shawnee OK

| Motel 6 | 405-275-5310 | 4981 N Harrison St Shawnee OK |

Sallisaw Listings
Sallisaw

| Super 8 Motel | 918-775-8900 | 924 S Kerr Blvd Sallisaw OK |

Arkansas (Interstate 40)

Van Buren Listings
Van Buren

Comfort Inn	501-474-2223	3131 Cloverleaf St Van Buren AR
Holiday Inn Express	501-474-8100	1903 N. 6th Street Van Buren AR
Motel 6	501-474-8001	1716 Fayetteville Rd Van Buren AR

Fort Smith Listings
Fort Smith

| Comfort Inn | 501-484-0227 | 2120 Burnham Rd Fort Smith AR |
| Motel 6 | 501-484-0576 | 6001 Rogers Ave Fort Smith AR |

Clarksville Listings
Clarksville

| Best Western Sherwood Motor Inn | 501-754-7900 | I-40 & Exit 58 Clarksville AR |
| Comfort Inn | 501-754-3000 | 1167 S. Rogers Ave Clarksville AR |

Russellville Listings
Russellville

| Holiday Inn | 501-968-4300 | 2407 N. Arkansas Russellville AR |

North Little Rock Listings
North Little Rock

Comfort Suites	501-851-8444	14322 Frontier Dr North Little Rock AR
Howard Johnson Hotel	501-758-1440	111 W. Pershing Blvd. North Little Rock AR
La Quinta Inn Little Rock North	501-945-0808	4100 McCain Boulevard North Little Rock AR

Little Rock Listings
N Little Rock

| Motel 6 - North | 501-758-5100 | 400 W 29th St N Little Rock AR |

Tennessee (Interstate 40)

Memphis Listings
Memphis

East Drury Inn & Suites	901-373-8200	1556 Sycamore View Memphis TN
La Quinta Inn Memphis East	901-382-2323	6068 Macon Cove Memphis TN
Motel 6	901-382-8572	1321 Sycamore View Rd Memphis TN

Brownsville Bells Listings
Brownsville Bells

| Motel 6 | 731-772-9500 | 9740 Hwy 70 E, I-40 Exit 66 Brownsville Bells TN |

Jackson Listings
Jackson

| Motel 6 | 731-661-0919 | 1940 Hwy 45 Bypass, I-40 Exit 80A Jackson TN |

Wildersville Listings
Wildersville

| Best Western Crossroads Inn | 901-968-2532 | 21045 Hwy 22 N Wildersville TN |

Dickson Listings
Dickson

| Best Western Dickson Station Inn | 615-441-5252 | 1025 East Christi Drive Dickson TN |
| Holiday Inn | 615-446-9081 | 2420 Hwy 46 S. Dickson TN |

Nashville Listings

Highway Guides - Please always call ahead to make sure an establishment is still dog-friendly.

Kingston Springs
Best Western Harpeth Inn	615-952-3961	116 Luyben Hills Rd Kingston Springs TN

Nashville
Best Western Calumet Inn at the Airport	615-889-9199	701 Stewarts Ferry Pike Nashville TN
Drury Inn & Suites	615-902-0400	555 Donelson Pike Nashville TN
Holiday Inn Select - Opryland	615-883-9770	2200 Elm Hill Pike Nashville TN
Motel 6	615-833-8887	420 Metroplex Dr Nashville TN
Motel 6	615-333-9933	95 Wallace Rd Nashville TN
Sheraton Music City	615-885-2200	777 McGavok Pike Nashville TN

Cookeville Listings

Cookeville
Best Western Thunderbird Motel	931-526-7115	900 S. Jefferson Ave. Cookeville TN
Holiday Inn	931-526-7125	870 S. Jefferson St Cookeville TN

Harriman Listings

Harriman
Best Western Sundancer Motor Lodge	865-882-6200	120 Childs Rd, PO Box 231 Harriman TN
Holiday Inn Express	865-882-5340	1845 S. Roane St Harriman TN

Knoxville Listings

Knoxville
La Quinta Inn Knoxville West	865-690-9777	258 Peters Road North Knoxville TN
Motel 6	865-675-7200	402 Lovell Rd Knoxville TN

Kodak Listings

Kodak
Holiday Inn Express & Suites	865-933-9448	2863 Winfield Dunn Parkway Kodak TN

Sevierville Listings

Sevierville
Best Western Dumplin Valley Inn	865-933-3467	3426 Winfield Dunn Parkway Sevierville TN

Dandridge Listings

Dandridge
Holiday Inn Express	865-397-1910	119 Sharon Drive Dandridge TN

Newport Listings

Newport
Best Western Newport Inn	423-623-8713	1015 Cosby Highway, PO Box 382 Newport TN
Holiday Inn	423-623-8622	1010 Cosby Hwy Newport TN
Motel 6	423-623-1850	255 Heritage Blvd Newport TN

North Carolina (Interstate 40)

Asheville Listings

Asheville
Holiday Inn - Blue Ridge Pkwy	828-298-5611	1450 Tunnel Rd Asheville NC
Motel 6	828-299-3040	1415 Tunnel Rd Asheville NC

Hickory Listings

Hickory
Red Roof Inn	828-323-1500	1184 Lenoir-Rhyne Boulevard Hickory NC

Greensboro Listings

Greensboro
Drury Inn & Suites	336-856-9696	3220 High Point Road Greensboro NC
La Quinta Inn & Suites Greensboro	336-316-0100	1201 Lanada Greensboro NC
Motel 6	336-668-2085	605 S Regional Rd Greensboro NC
Motel 6	336-854-0993	831 Greenhaven Dr Greensboro NC

Burlington Listings

Burlington
Holiday Inn - Outlet Center	336-229-5203	2444 Maple Avenue Burlington NC

Durham Listings

Durham
La Quinta Inn & Suites Raleigh-Research Triangle Park	919-484-1422	1910 West Park Drive Durham NC

Raleigh Listings

Raleigh
Best Western Crabtree	919-782-8650	6619 Glenwood Ave Raleigh NC
Motel 6	919-467-6171	1401 Buck Jones Rd Raleigh NC
Motel 6	919-782-7071	3921 Arrow Dr Raleigh NC

Wilmington Listings

Wilmington
Camellia Cottage Bed and Breakfast	910-763-9171	118 S. 4th Street Wilmington NC
Hampton Inn & Suites-Landfall Park	910-256-9600	1989 Eastwood Road Wilmington NC
Hilton Riverside	910-763-5900	301 N. Water Street Wilmington NC
Waterway Lodge	910-256-3771	7246 Wrightsville Avenue Wilmington NC

Interstate 55 Accommodation Listings

Illinois (Interstate 55)

Chicago Area Listings

Joliet
Comfort Inn North	815-436-5141	3235 Norman Ave Joliet IL
Motel 6 - Joliet	815-439-1332	3551 Mall Loop Drive Joliet IL

Bolingbrook Listings

Bolingbrook
Holiday Inn Hotel & Suites	630-679-1600	205 Remington Blvd Bolingbrook IL

Pontiac Listings

Pontiac
Comfort Inn	815-842-2777	1821 W. Reynolds St Pontiac IL

Normal Listings

Normal
Best Western University Inn	309-454-4070	6 Traders Circle Normal IL
Motel 6	309-452-0422	1600 N Main Street Normal IL

Lincoln Listings

Lincoln
Comfort Inn	217-735-3960	2811 Woodlawn Rd Lincoln IL
Holiday Inn Express	217-735-5800	130 Olson Rd Lincoln IL

Springfield Listings

Springfield
Drury Inn & Suites	217-529-3900	3180 S. Dirksen Parkway Springfield IL
Motel 6	217-529-1633	6011 S 6th St Springfield IL
Pear Tree Inn	217-529-9100	3190 S. Dirksen Parkway Springfield IL
Sleep Inn	217-787-6200	3470 Freedom Dr Springfield IL
Super 8 Motel-South	217-529-8898	3675 S 6th St Springfield IL

Carlinville Listings

Carlinville
Holiday Inn	217-324-2100	I-55 & Rt 108 Carlinville IL

468

Litchfield Listings
Litchfield
Comfort Inn   217-324-9260   1010 East Columbian N Blvd   Litchfield IL

St Louis Area Listings
Collinsville
Collinsville Drury Inn   618-345-7700   602 N. Bluff   Collinsville IL

Missouri (Interstate 55)

St Louis Listings
St Louis
Holiday Inn   314-894-0700   4234 Butler Hill Rd   St Louis MO
St Louis - Drury Plaza Hotel   314-231-3003   Fourth & Market Streets   St Louis MO
St Louis - Union Station Drury Inn   314-231-3900   201 South 20th Street   St Louis MO

Arnold Listings
Arnold
St Louis - Arnold Drury Inn   636-296-9600   1201 Drury Lane   Arnold MO

Perryville Listings
Perryville
Best Western Colonial Inn   573-547-1091   I-55 & Hwy 51 S.   Perryville MO

Jackson Listings
Jackson
Jackson Drury Inn & Suites   573-243-9200   225 Drury Lane   Jackson MO

Cape Girardeau Listings
Cape Girardeau
Cape Girardeau Drury Lodge   573-334-7151   104 S. Vantage Drive   Cape Girardeau MO
Cape Girardeau Drury Suites   573-339-9500   3303 Campster Drive   Cape Girardeau MO
Cape Girardeau Pear Tree Inn   573-334-3000   3248 William Street   Cape Girardeau MO

Sikeston Listings
Sikeston
Sikeston Drury Inn   573-471-4100   2602 East Malone   Sikeston MO
Sikeston Pear Tree Inn   573-471-8660   2602 Rear East Malone   Sikeston MO

Hayti Listings
Hayti
Comfort Inn   573-359-0023   I-55 Highway 84 East   Hayti MO
Hayti Drury Inn & Suites   573-359-2702   1317 Hwy 84   Hayti MO

Arkansas (Interstate 55)

Blytheville Listings
Blytheville
Comfort Inn   870-763-7081   1520 E Main St   Blytheville AR
Pear Tree Inn   870-763-2300   239 North Service Road   Blytheville AR

Mississippi (Interstate 55)

Horn Lake Listings
Horn Lake
South Drury Inn & Suites   662-349-6622   735 Goodman Road West   Horn Lake MS

Canton Listings
Canton
Best Western Canton Inn   601-859-8600   137 Soldier Colony Road   Canton MS

Ridgeland Listings
Ridgeland

| Drury Inn & Suites | 601-956-6100 | 610 E. County Line Road Ridgeland MS |

McComb Listings
McComb

| Days Inn | 601-684-5566 | 2298 Delaware Ave McComb MS |
| Ramada Inn | 601-684-6211 | 1900 Delaware Ave McComb MS |

Louisiana (Interstate 55)

Hammond Listings
Hammond

| Best Western Hammond Inn & Suites | 985-419-2001 | 107 Duo Drive Hammond LA |
| Quality Inn | 985-542-8555 | 14175 Highway 190 Hammond LA |

Interstate 59 Accommodation Listings

Alabama (Interstate 59)

Birmingham Listings
Birmingham

Comfort Inn Oxmoor	205-941-0990	195 Oxmoor Rd Birmingham AL
Holiday Inn - Airport	205-591-6900	5000 10th Ave N Birmingham AL
La Quinta Inn Birmingham Northwest	205-324-4510	905 11th Court West Birmingham AL
Microtel	205-945-5550	251 Summit Pkwy Birmingham AL
Motel Birmingham Garden Courtyards	205-956-4440	7905 Crestwood Blvd Birmingham AL
Residence Inn by Marriott	205-991-8686	3 Green Hill Pkwy Birmingham AL

Tuscaloosa Listings
Tuscaloosa

| Motel 6 | 205-759-4942 | 4700 McFarland Blvd E (Hwy 82E) Tuscaloosa AL |

Mississippi (Interstate 59)

Meridian Listings
Meridian

Holiday Inn	601-485-5101	111 US Hwy 11 & 80 Meridian MS
Motel 6	601-482-1182	2309 S. Frontage Rd Meridian MS
Quality Inn	601-693-4521	1401 Roebuck Dr Meridian MS

Hattiesburg Listings
Hattiesburg

Comfort Inn at Convention Center	601-268-2170	6595 US 49 N. Hattiesburg MS
Howard Johnson Express Inn	601-268-1410	6553 Hwy 49 North Hattiesburg MS
Motel 6	601-544-6096	6508 US Hwy 49 Hattiesburg MS

Picayune Listings
Picayune

| Comfort Inn | 601-799-2833 | 550 South Lofton Dr. Picayune MS |

Interstate 64 Accommodation Listings

Illinois (Interstate 64)

St Louis Area Listings

Fairview Heights

Fairview Heights Drury Inn & Suites	618-398-8530	12 Ludwig Drive Fairview Heights IL

Caseyville Listings
Caseyville

Motel 6	618-397-8867	2431 Old Country Inn Rd Caseyville IL

O'Fallon Listings
O'Fallon

Comfort Inn	618-624-6060	1100 Eastgate Dr. O'Fallon IL

Mount Vernon Listings
Mount Vernon

Drury Inn	618-244-4550	145 N 44th Street Mount Vernon IL
Holiday Inn	618-244-7100	222 Potomac Blvd Mount Vernon IL
Motel 6	618-244-2383	333 S 44th St Mount Vernon IL
Thrifty Inn	618-244-7750	100 North 44th Street Mount Vernon IL

Indiana (Interstate 64)

Evansville Listings
Evansville

Comfort Inn	812-867-1600	19622 Elpers Rd Evansville IN
Motel 6	812-424-6431	4321 Hwy 41 N Evansville IN

Dale Listings
Dale

Motel 6	812-937-2294	20840 N US Hwy 231 Dale IN

Corydon Listings
Corydon

Capitol Inn	812-738-4192	St Rd 135 & I-64, PO Box 773 Corydon IN

New Albany Listings
New Albany

Holiday Inn Express	812-945-2771	411 W. Springs St New Albany IN

Kentucky (Interstate 64)

Louisville Listings
Louisville

Aleksander House Bed and Breakfast	502-637-4985	1213 South First Street Louisville KY
Breckinridge Inn	502-456-5050	2800 Breckinridge Lane Louisville KY
Comfort Suites	502-266-6509	1850 Resouce Way Louisville KY
Drury Inn & Suites	502-326-4170	9501 Blairwood Road Louisville KY
Holiday Inn	502-426-2600	1325 S. Hurstbourne Pkwy Louisville KY
Holiday Inn	502-452-6361	4004 Gardiner Point Drive Louisville KY
Holiday Inn - Airport	502-964-3311	3317 Fern Valley Rd Louisville KY
Holiday Inn - Downtown	502-582-2241	120 W Broadway Louisville KY
Mainstay Suites	502-267-4454	1650 Alliant Ave. Louisville KY
Motel 6	502-473-0000	3200 Kemmons Drive Louisville KY
Red Roof Inn-East	502-426-7621	9330 Blairwood Road Louisville KY
Seelbach Hilton	502-585-3200	500 Fourth Avenue Louisville KY
Sleep Inn	502-266-6776	1850 Priority Way Louisville KY
Sleep Inn	502-368-9597	3330 Preston Hwy, Gate 6 Louisville KY
Staybridge Suites	502-244-9511	11711 Gateworth Way Louisville KY
Travelodge	502-425-8010	9340 Blairwood Rd. Louisville KY

Frankfort Listings
Frankfort

Super 8 Motel - Frankfort	502-875-3220	1225 U.S. Highway 127 S. Frankfort KY

Lexington Listings

Lexington

Best Western Regency	859-293-2202	I-75 at US Hwy 60 Exit 110 Lexington KY
Holiday Inn	859-263-5241	5532 Athens-Boonesboro Rd Lexington KY
Marriott's Griffin Gate Resort	859-231-5100	1800 Newtown Pike Lexington KY
Motel 6	859-293-1431	2260 Elkhorn Rd Lexington KY
Quality Inn Northwest	859-233-0561	750 Newtown Ct. Lexington KY
Red Roof Inn	859-293-2626	483 Haggard Lane Lexington KY
Sheraton Suites Lexington	859-268-0060	2601 Richmond Rd Lexington KY
Sleep Inn	859-543-8400	1920 Plaudit Pl Lexington KY

Versailles

Rose Hill Inn Bed & Breakfast	859-873-5957	233 Rose Hill Versailles KY

Winchester Listings

Winchester

Best Western Country Squire	859-744-7210	1307 West Lexington Avenue Winchester KY

West Virginia (Interstate 64)

Huntington Listings

Huntington

Econo Lodge	304-529-1331	3325 US 60 E. Huntington WV
Holiday Inn Hotel & Suites	304-523-8880	800 Third Ave Huntington WV
Red Roof Inn	304-733-3737	5190 U.S. 60, East Huntington WV
Stone Lodge	304-736-3451	5600 U.S. Route 60 East Huntington WV

Charleston Listings

Charleston

Motel 6	304-925-0471	6311 MacCorkle Ave SE Charleston WV
Ramada Plaza Hotel	304-744-4641	400 Second Avenue Charleston WV

Kanawha City

Red Roof Inn-Kanawha City	304-925-6953	6305 MacCorkle Avenue S.E. Kanawha City WV

South Charleston

Red Roof Inn	304-744-1500	4006 MacCorkle Avenue South Charleston WV

Beckley Listings

Beckley

Comfort Inn	304-255-2161	1909 Harper Rd. Beckley WV

Lewisburg Listings

Lewisburg

Days Inn	304-645-2345	635 N. Jefferson Street Lewisburg WV

Virginia (Interstate 64)

Covington Listings

Covington

Best Value Inn	540-962-7600	908 Valley Ridge Drive Covington VA
Best Western Mountain View	540-962-4951	820 East Madison Street Covington VA
Comfort Inn	540-962-2141	203 Interstate Dr. Covington VA

Charlottesville Listings

Charlottesville

Best Western Mount Vernon	804-296-5501	1613 Emmet St, Box 7284 Charlottesville VA
Holiday Inn	434-977-5100	1200 5th Street Charlottesville VA

Scottsville

High Meadows Inn Bed and Breakfast	804-286-2218	55 High Meadows Lane Scottsville VA

Richmond Listings

Richmond

Days Inn	804-282-3300	2100 Dickens Rd Richmond VA
Holiday Inn	804-275-7891	4303 Commerce Rd Richmond VA
Residence Inn by Marriott	804-285-8200	2121 Dickens Rd Richmond VA

Williamsburg Listings

Williamsburg

Best Western Colonial Capital Inn	757-253-1222	111 Penniman Road Williamsburg VA
Best Western Patrick Henry Inn	757-229-9540	249 E. York Street NW Williamsburg VA
Heritage Inn Motel	757-229-6220	1324 Richmond Rd. Williamsburg VA
Holiday Inn - Colonial District	757-220-1776	725 Bypass Rd Williamsburg VA
Motel 6	757-565-3433	3030 Richmond Rd Williamsburg VA
Ramada Inn 1776	757-220-1776	725 Bypass Road Williamsburg VA

Virginia Beach Area Listings

Hampton

La Quinta Inn Norfolk - Hampton	757-827-8680	2138 West Mercury Boulevard Hampton VA

Newport News

Motel 6	757-595-6336	797 J Clyde-Morris Blvd Newport News VA

Norfolk

Motel 6	757-461-2380	853 N Military Hwy Norfolk VA

Interstate 65 Accommodation Listings

Indiana (Interstate 65)

Merrillville Listings

Merrillville

Motel 6	219-738-2701	8290 Louisiana Street Merrillville IN

Lafayette Listings

Lafayette

Comfort Suites	765-447-9980	31 Frontage Rd Lafayette IN
Holiday Inn	765-567-2131	I-65 & SR 43 Lafayette IN
Holiday Inn Express	765-449-4808	201 Frontage Rd Lafayette IN

Indianapolis Listings

Indianapolis

Motel 6 - South	317-783-5555	5151 Elmwood Dr Indianapolis IN

Edinburgh Listings

Edinburgh

Best Western Horizon Inn	812-526-9883	11780 N US 31 Edinburgh IN

Taylorsville Listings

Taylorsville

Comfort Inn	812-526-9747	10330 N. US 31 Taylorsville IN

Columbus Listings

Columbus

Holiday Inn	812-372-1541	2480 Jonathon Moore Pike Columbus IN

Seymour Listings

Seymour

Holiday Inn	812-522-6767	2025 E. Tipton St Seymour IN
Motel 6	812-524-7443	365 Tanger Blvd Seymour IN

Jeffersonville Listings

Jeffersonville

Motel 6	812-283-7703	2016 Old Hwy 31 E Jeffersonville IN

Kentucky (Interstate 65)

Louisville Listings

Louisville

Holiday Inn - Airport	502-964-3311	3317 Fern Valley Rd Louisville KY

| Holiday Inn - Downtown | 502-582-2241 | 120 W Broadway Louisville KY |
| Sleep Inn | 502-368-9597 | 3330 Preston Hwy, Gate 6 Louisville KY |

Brooks Listings
Brooks

| Comfort Inn | 502-957-6900 | 149 Willabrook Dr. Brooks KY |

Elizabethtown Listings
Elizabethtown

| Holiday Inn | 270-769-2344 | 1058 N. Mulberry Elizabethtown KY |
| Super 8 Motel | 270-737-1088 | 2028 N. Mulberry Street Elizabethtown KY |

Cave City Listings
Cave City

| Comfort Inn | 270-773-2030 | 801 Mammoth Cave St Cave City KY |
| Quality Inn | 502-773-2181 | 1006 A Doyle Rd. Cave City KY |

Glasgow Listings
Glasgow

| Comfort Inn | 270-651-9099 | 210 Calvary Dr Glasgow KY |

Bowling Green Listings
Bowling Green

Best Western Continental Inn	270-781-5200	700 Interstate Drive Bowling Green KY
Drury Inn	270-842-7100	3250 Scottsville Road Bowling Green KY
Holiday Inn	270-781-1500	3240 Scottsville Rd Bowling Green KY
Motel 6	270-843-0140	3139 Scottsville Rd Bowling Green KY
Quality Inn	270-846-4588	1919 Mel Browning Street Bowling Green KY

Tennessee (Interstate 65)

Nashville Listings
Goodlettsville

| Motel 6 | 615-859-9674 | 323 Cartwright St Goodlettsville TN |

Nashville

| Motel 6 | 615-227-9696 | 311 W Trinity Lane Nashville TN |
| Motel 6 | 615-333-9933 | 95 Wallace Rd Nashville TN |

Spring Hill Listings
Spring Hill

| Holiday Inn Express | 931-486-1234 | 104 Kedron Rd Spring Hill TN |

Elkton Listings
Elkton

| Motel 6 | 931-468-2594 | I-65 & Bryson Rd Elkton TN |

Alabama (Interstate 65)

Athens Listings
Athens

| Best Western Athens Inn | 256-233-4030 | 1329 Hwy 72 East Athens AL |

Priceville Listings
Priceville

| Comfort Inn | 256-355-1037 | 3239 Point Mallard Pkwy Priceville AL |

Birmingham Listings
Birmingham

| Comfort Inn Oxmoor | 205-941-0990 | 195 Oxmoor Rd Birmingham AL |

Calera Listings
Calera

| Holiday Inn Express | 205-668-3641 | 357 Hwy 304 Calera AL |

Greenville Listings
Greenville
| Comfort Inn | 334-383-9595 | 1029 Fort Dale Rd Greenville AL |

Evergreen Listings
Evergreen
| Comfort Inn | 251-578-4701 | 83 Bates Rd Evergreen AL |

Mobile Listings
Mobile
Drury Inn	251-344-7700	824 West I-65 Service Road South Mobile AL
Holiday Inn	251-666-5600	5465 Hwy 90 W (Gov't Blvd) Mobile AL
Ramada Inn	251-342-3220	850 S. Beltline Hwy Mobile AL

Interstate 70 Accommodation Listings

Utah (Interstate 70)

Richfield Listings
Richfield
| Best Western Apple Tree Inn | 435-896-5481 | 145 South Main Richfield UT |

Green River Listings
Green River
| Motel 6 | 435-564-3436 | 946 E Main, Box 358 Green River UT |

Colorado (Interstate 70)

Grand Junction Listings
Grand Junction
Holiday Inn	970-243-6790	755 Horizon Drive Grand Junction CO
La Quinta Inn & Suites Grand Junction	970-241-2929	2761 Crossroads Blvd. Grand Junction CO
Motel 6	970-243-2628	776 Horizon Dr Grand Junction CO

Rifle Listings
Rifle
| Buckskin Inn | 970-625-1741 | 101 Ray Avenue Rifle CO |

Glenwood Springs Listings
Glenwood Springs
| Quality Inn & Suites | 970-945-5995 | 2650 Gilstrap Court Glenwood Springs CO |

Eagle Listings
Eagle
| Holiday Inn Express | 970-328-8088 | I-70 Exit 147 & Pond Rd Eagle CO |

Vail Listings
Vail
| Antlers at Vail | 970-476-2471 | 680 W. Lionshead Place Vail CO |

Frisco Listings
Frisco
Holiday Inn	970-668-5000	1129 N. Summit Blvd Frisco CO
Hotel Frisco	970-668-5009	308 Main Street Frisco CO
Woods Inn Bed and Breakfast	970-668-2255	Second Ave and Granite St Frisco CO

Frisco
| Discover Resorts International | 970-668-5151 | 912 North Summit Boulevard Frisco CO |

Silverthorne Listings

Silverthorne

Quality Inn & Suites	970-513-1222	530 Silverthorne Lane Silverthorne CO

Evergreen Listings

Evergreen

Quality Suites	303-526-2000	19300 U.S. 40 Evergreen CO

Denver Listings

Aurora

Comfort Inn Airport	303-367-5000	16921 E 32nd Ave Aurora CO

Denver

Denver East Drury Inn	303-373-1983	4380 Peoria Street Denver CO
Motel 6 - Airport	303-371-1980	12020 E 39th Ave Denver CO

Denver Area Listings

Lakewood

Sheraton Denver West Hotel	303-987-2000	360 Union Boulevard Lakewood CO

Wheat Ridge

Holiday Inn Express - Denver West	303-423-4000	4700 Kipling St Wheat Ridge CO

Limon Listings

Limon

Best Western Limon Inn	719-775-0277	925 T Avenue, I-70 & Hwy 24 Limon CO

Burlington Listings

Burlington

Comfort Inn	719-346-7676	282 S. Lincoln Burlington CO

Kansas (Interstate 70)

Goodland Listings

Goodland

Comfort Inn	785-899-7181	2519 Enterprise Rd Goodland KS

Colby Listings

Colby

Best Western Crown Motel	785-462-3943	2320 S. Range Ave Colby KS
Comfort Inn	785-462-3833	2225 S. Range Ave Colby KS
Days Inn	785-462-8691	Highway 70 and Highway 25 Colby KS

Hays Listings

Hays

Best Western Vagabond Motel	785-625-2511	2524 Vine Street Hays KS
Hampton Inn	785-625-8103	3801 Vine St Hays KS
Holiday Inn	785-625-7371	3603 Vine St Hays KS
Motel 6	785-625-4282	3404 Vine St Hays KS

Abilene Listings

Abilene

Best Western Abilene's Pride	785-263-2800	1709 N Buckeye Ave, PO Box 536 Abilene KS
Best Western President's Inn	785-263-2050	2210 N Buckeye, PO Box 458 Abilene KS
Holiday Inn Express Hotel & Suites	785-263-4049	110 East Lafayette St Abilene KS

Junction City Listings

Junction City

Motel 6	785-762-2215	1931 Lacy Drive Junction City KS

Topeka Listings

Topeka

Motel 6	785-273-9888	1224 Wanamaker Rd SW Topeka KS

Lawrence Listings

Lawrence		
Holiday Inn	785-841-7077	200 McDonald Drive Lawrence KS
Super 8 Motel - Lawrence	785-842-5721	515 McDonald Drive Lawrence KS

Kansas City Listings

Kansas City		
Best Western Inn & Conf Center	913-677-3060	501 Southwest Blvd Kansas City KS

Missouri (Interstate 70)

Blue Springs Listings

Blue Springs		
Sleep Inn	816-224-1199	451 N.W. Jefferson St. Blue Springs MO

Columbia Listings

Columbia		
Columbia Drury Inn	573-445-1800	1000 Knipp Street Columbia MO
Holiday Inn Executive Center	573-445-8531	2200 I-70 Dr SW Columbia MO
Holiday Inn Express	573-449-4422	801 Keene St Columbia MO
Holiday Inn Select	573-445-8531	2200 I-70 Dr. SW Columbia MO
Motel 6	573-445-8433	1800 I-70 Dr SW Columbia MO
Quality Inn	573-449-2491	1612 N. Providence Road Columbia MO
Travelodge	573-449-1065	900 Vandover Dr Columbia MO

Foristell Listings

Foristell		
Best Western West 70 Inn	636-673-2900	12 Hwy W, PO Box 10 Foristell MO

St Peters Listings

St Peters		
St Louis - St. Peters Drury Inn	636-397-9700	170 Westfield Drive St Peters MO

St Charles Listings

St Charles		
Comfort Suites	636-949-0694	1400 S. 5th St. St Charles MO
Motel 6	636-925-2020	3800 Harry S. Truman Blvd St Charles MO

St Louis Listings

St Louis		
St Louis - Airport Drury Inn	314-423-7700	10490 Natural Bridge Road St Louis MO
St Louis - Convention Center Drury Inn & Suites	314-231-8100	711 North Broadway St Louis MO
St Louis - Drury Plaza Hotel	314-231-3003	Fourth & Market Streets St Louis MO
St Louis - Union Station Drury Inn	314-231-3900	201 South 20th Street St Louis MO
St Peters		
Holiday Inn Select	636-928-1500	4221 S. Outer Rd St Peters MO

Illinois (Interstate 70)

St Louis Area Listings

Collinsville		
Collinsville Drury Inn	618-345-7700	602 N. Bluff Collinsville IL

Effingham Listings

Effingham		
Holiday Inn Express	217-540-1111	1103 Ave of Mid America Effingham IL
Howard Johnson Express Inn	217-342-4667	1606 W Fayette Ave. Effingham IL

Casey Listings

Casey		
Comfort Inn	217-932-2212	933 SR 49 Casey IL

Indiana (Interstate 70)

Highway Guides - Please always call ahead to make sure an establishment is still dog-friendly.

Terre Haute Listings

Terre Haute

Comfort Suites	812-235-1770	501 E. Margaret Ave. Terre Haute IN
Drury Inn	812-238-1206	3040 South US Hwy 41 Terre Haute IN
Holiday Inn	812-232-6081	3300 US 41 S. Terre Haute IN
Motel 6	812-238-1586	1 W Honey Creek Dr Terre Haute IN
Pear Tree Inn	812-234-4268	3050 South US Hwy 41 Terre Haute IN

Cloverdale Listings

Cloverdale

Holiday Inn Express	765-795-5050	1017 N. Main St Cloverdale IN

Indianapolis Listings

Indianapolis

Holiday Inn	317-359-5341	6990 E. 21st St Indianapolis IN
La Quinta Inn Indianapolis East	317-359-1021	7304 East 21st Street Indianapolis IN
Motel 6 - Airport	317-248-1231	5241 W Bradbury Ave (at Lynhurst Dr) Indianapolis IN
Motel 6 - East	317-546-5864	2851 Shadeland Ave Indianapolis IN

Richmond Listings

Richmond

Best Western Imperial Motor Lodge	765-966-1505	3020 East Main Street Richmond IN
Holiday Inn	765-966-7511	5501 National Rd E Richmond IN
Motel 6	765-966-6682	419 Commerce Dr Richmond IN

Ohio (Interstate 70)

Dayton Listings

Dayton

Howard Johnson Express Inn	937-454-0550	7575 Poe Avenue Dayton OH

Englewood

Motel 6	937-832-3770	1212 S Main St Englewood OH

Columbus Listings

Columbus

Holiday Inn	614-868-1380	4560 Hilton Corporate Drive Columbus OH
Motel 6	614-755-2250	5910 Scarborough Blvd Columbus OH
Motel 6	614-870-0993	5500 Renner Rd Columbus OH

Cambridge Listings

Cambridge

Best Western Cambridge	740-439-3581	1945 Southgate Parkway Cambridge OH
Holiday Inn	740-432-7313	2248 Southgate Pkwy Cambridge OH

Pennsylvania (Interstate 70)

Washington Listings

Washington

Holiday Inn	724-222-6200	340 Racetrack Rd Washington PA
Motel 6	724-223-8040	1283 Motel 6 Drive Washington PA

Somerset Listings

Somerset

Best Western Executive Inn	814-445-3996	165 Waterworks Rd Somerset PA
Holiday Inn	814-445-9611	202 Harmon St Somerset PA

Maryland (Interstate 70)

Hagerstown Listings

Hagerstown

Motel 6	301-582-4445	11321 Massey Blvd Hagerstown MD
Sleep Inn & Suites	301-766-9449	18216 Colonel H K Douglas Dr Hagerstown MD

Frederick Listings
Frederick

| Holiday Inn | 301-662-5141 | 999 W. Patrick St Frederick MD |
| Quality Inn | 301-695-6200 | 420 Prospect Blvd Frederick MD |

Interstate 75 Accommodation Listings

Michigan (Interstate 75)

Sault Ste. Marie Listings
Sault Ste. Marie

| Quality Inn & Conference Center | 906-635-6918 | 3290 I-75 Business Spur Sault Ste. Marie MI |

Mackinaw City Listings
Mackinaw City

| Motel 6 | 231-436-8961 | 206 Nicolet St Mackinaw City MI |

Gaylord Listings
Gaylord

| Gaylord Inn | 989-732-2431 | 833 W. Main Street Gaylord MI |

Grayling Listings
Grayling

| Holiday Inn | 989-348-7611 | 2650 S. I-75 Business Loop Grayling MI |

Saginaw Listings
Saginaw

| Best Western Saginaw | 989-755-0461 | 1408 S. Outer Drive Saginaw MI |

Frankenmuth Listings
Frankenmuth

| Drury Inn & Suites | 989-652-2800 | 260 South Main Frankenmuth MI |

Flint Listings
Flint

Holiday Inn Express	810-238-7744	1150 Robert T. Longway Blvd Flint MI
Howard Johnson Express Inn	810-733-5910	G-3277 Miller Road Flint MI
Motel 6	810-767-7100	2324 Austin Pkwy Flint MI

Detroit Area Listings
Auburn Hills

| Staybridge Suites | 248-322-4600 | 2050 Featherstone Rd Auburn Hills MI |

Madison Heights

| Motel 6 | 248-583-0500 | 32700 Barrington Rd Madison Heights MI |

Troy

| Drury Inn | 248-528-3330 | 575 W. Big Beaver Road Troy MI |
| Holiday Inn | 248-689-7500 | 2537 Rochester Court Troy MI |

Ohio (Interstate 75)

Toledo Listings
Maumee

| Days Inn-Maumee | 419-893-9960 | 150 Dussel Drive Maumee OH |

Perrysburg

| Howard Johnson Inn | 419-837-5245 | I-280 & Hanley Road Perrysburg OH |

Wapakoneta Listings
Wapakoneta

| Best Western Wapakoneta | 419-738-8181 | 1510 Saturn Drive Wapakoneta OH |

Dayton Listings

Dayton

Howard Johnson Express Inn	937-454-0550	7575 Poe Avenue Dayton OH
Marriott Hotel	937-223-1000	1414 S. Patterson Boulevard Dayton OH
Red Roof Inn-North	937-898-1054	7370 Miller Lane Dayton OH

Englewood

Motel 6	937-832-3770	1212 S Main St Englewood OH

Fairborn

Homewood Suites-Fairborn	937-429-0600	2750 Presidential Drive Fairborn OH

Miamisburg

Motel 6	937-434-8750	8101 Springboro Pike Miamisburg OH

Cincinnati Listings

Sharonville

Motel 6	513-563-1123	3850 Hauck Rd Sharonville OH
Motel 6	513-772-5944	2000 E Kemper Rd Sharonville OH

Kentucky (Interstate 75)

Florence Listings

Florence

Best Western Inn Florence	859-525-0090	7821 Commerce Drive Florence KY
Motel 6	859-283-0909	7937 Dream St Florence KY

Dry Ridge Listings

Dry Ridge

Holiday Inn Express	859-824-7121	1050 Fashion Ridge Rd Dry Ridge KY

Georgetown Listings

Georgetown

Motel 6	502-863-1166	401 Cherryblossom Way Georgetown KY

Lexington Listings

Lexington

Best Western Regency	859-293-2202	I-75 at US Hwy 60 Exit 110 Lexington KY
Holiday Inn	859-263-5241	5532 Athens-Boonesboro Rd Lexington KY
Motel 6	859-293-1431	2260 Elkhorn Rd Lexington KY
Quality Inn Northwest	859-233-0561	750 Newtown Ct. Lexington KY

Berea Listings

Berea

Boone Tavern Hotel	606-986-9358	100 Main Street Berea KY

London Listings

London

Budget Host Westgate Inn	606-878-7330	254 W Daniel Boone Parkway London KY
Days Inn	606-864-7331	2035 Hwy. 192 West London KY
Park Inn	606-878-7678	400 GOP London KY

Corbin Listings

Corbin

Best Western Corbin Inn	606-528-2100	2630 Cumberland Falls Rd Corbin KY
Quality Inn	606-528-4802	264 W. Cumberland Gap Pkwy Corbin KY

Tennessee (Interstate 75)

Clinton Listings

Clinton

Best Western Clinton Inn	865-457-2311	720 Park Place Clinton TN

Knoxville Listings

Knoxville

Baymont Inn-West	865-671-1010	11341 Campbell Lakes Drive Knoxville TN
La Quinta Inn Knoxville West	865-690-9777	258 Peters Road North Knoxville TN
Motel 6	865-675-7200	402 Lovell Rd Knoxville TN

Residence Inn by Marriott	865-539-5339	215 Langley Place Knoxville TN

Chattanooga Listings
Chattanooga
Motel 6	423-892-7707	7707 Lee Hwy Chattanooga TN
Red Roof Inn	423-899-0143	7014 Shallowford Road Chattanooga TN

Georgia (Interstate 75)

Dalton Listings
Dalton
Comfort Inn & Suites	706-259-2583	905 West Bridge Road Dalton GA
Holiday Inn	706-278-0500	515 Holiday Dr Dalton GA
Motel 6	706-278-5522	2200 Chattanooga Rd Dalton GA

Calhoun Listings
Calhoun
Quality Inn	706-629-9501	915 Highway 53 East Calhoun GA

Adairsville Listings
Adairsville
Comfort Inn	770-773-2886	107 Princeton Blvd Adairsville GA

Kennesaw Listings
Kennesaw
Best Western Kennesaw Inn	770-424-7666	3375 Busbee Drive Kennesaw GA
Comfort Inn	770-419-1530	750 Cobb Place Kennesaw GA

Atlanta Area Listings
Jonesboro
Holiday Inn - Atlanta South	770-968-4300	6288 Old Dixie Hwy Jonesboro GA
Marietta
Comfort Inn	770-952-3000	2100 Northwest Pkwy Marietta GA
La Quinta Inn Atlanta Delk Road - Marietta	770-951-0026	2170 Delk Road Marietta GA
Motel 6 - Marietta	770-952-8161	2360 Delk Rd Marietta GA
Morrow
South Drury Inn & Suites	770-960-0500	6520 S. Lee Street Morrow GA

Atlanta Listings
Atlanta
Airport Drury Inn & Suites	404-761-4900	1270 Virginia Avenue Atlanta GA

Morrow Listings
Morrow
Quality Inn Southlake	770-960-1957	6597 Joneboro Rd Morrow GA
Sleep Inn	770-472-9800	2185 Mt. Zion Pkwy Morrow GA

McDonough Listings
McDonough
Comfort Inn	770-954-9110	80 SR 81 W. McDonough GA
Holiday Inn	770-957-5291	930 Hwy 155 S. McDonough GA

Forsyth Listings
Forsyth
Best Western Hilltop Inn	478-994-9260	I-75 & GA 42 Forsyth GA
Comfort Inn	478-994-3400	333 Harold G. Clark Pkwy Forsyth GA

Macon Listings
Macon
Comfort Inn North	478-746-8855	2690 Riverside Dr. Macon GA
Holiday Inn Express	478-743-1482	2720 Riverside Dr Macon GA
La Quinta Inn & Suites Macon	478-475-0206	3944 River Place Dr. Macon GA

Byron Listings
Byron
| Comfort Inn | 478-956-1600 | 115 Chapman Rd Byron GA |
| Holiday Inn Express Hotel & Suites | 478-956-7829 | 102 Holiday Court Byron GA |

Warner Robins Listings
Warner Robins
| Best Western Peach Inn | 478-953-3800 | 2739 Watson Blvd Warner Robins GA |
| Comfort Inn & Suites at Robins Air Force Base | 478-922-7555 | 95 S. SR 247 Warner Robins GA |

Perry Listings
Perry
| Comfort Inn | 478-987-7710 | 1602 Sam Nunn Blvd Perry GA |

Cordele Listings
Cordele
| Best Western Colonial Inn Cordele | 229-273-5420 | 1706 East 16th Ave Cordele GA |

Tifton Listings
Tifton
| Holiday Inn | 229-382-6687 | I-75 & US 82W Tifton GA |
| Motel 6 | 229-388-8777 | 579 Old Omega Rd Tifton GA |

Valdosta Listings
Valdosta
Best Western King of the Road	229-244-7600	1403 St. Augustine Rd Valdosta GA
Holiday Inn	229-242-3881	1309 St Augustine Rd Valdosta GA
Howard Johnson Express Inn	229-249-8900	1330 St. Augustine Rd. Valdosta GA
Motel 6	229-333-0047	2003 W Hill Ave Valdosta GA
Quality Inn North	229-244-8510	1209 Augustine Rd Valdosta GA
Quality Inn South	229-244-4520	1902 W. Hill Ave. Valdosta GA
Ramada Inn	229-242-1225	Interstate Highway 75 & State Route 84 Valdosta GA

Lake Park Listings
Lake Park
| Holiday Inn Express | 229-559-5181 | 1198 Lakes Blvd Lake Park GA |

Florida (Interstate 75)

Gainesville Listings
Gainesville
La Quinta Inn Gainesville	352-332-6466	920 NW 69th Terrace Gainesville FL
Motel 6	352-373-1604	4000 SW 40th Blvd Gainesville FL
Red Roof Inn	352-336-3311	3500 SW 42nd St Gainesville FL

Ocala Listings
Ocala
Holiday Inn	352-629-0381	3621 W. Silver Springs Blvd Ocala FL
Howard Johnson Inn	352-629-7021	3951 NW Blitchton Rd. Ocala FL
Quality Inn I-75	352-732-2300	3767 N. W. Blitchton Rd. Ocala FL

Bushnell Listings
Bushnell
| Best Western Guest House | 352-793-5010 | I-75 & SR-48 Bushnell FL |

Brooksville Listings
Brooksville
| Holiday Inn | 352-796-9481 | 30307 Cortez Blvd Brooksville FL |

Port Richey Listings
Port Richey
| Comfort Inn | 727-863-3336 | 11810 US 19 Port Richey FL |

Tampa Bay Listings

Bradenton
Motel 6	941-747-6005	660 67 Street Cir E Bradenton FL

Ellenton
Ramada Limited	941-729-8505	5218 17th Street E Ellenton FL

Sarasota
Comfort Inn Airport	941-355-7091	4800 N. Tamiami Trail Sarasota FL

Tampa
Best Western All Suites Hotel	813-971-8930	3001 University Center Dr Tampa FL
Red Roof Inn - Brandon	813-681-8484	10121 Horace Ave Tampa FL
Red Roof Inn - Fairgrounds	813-623-5245	5001 North US301 Tampa FL

Punta Gorda Listings

Punta Gorda
Holiday Inn	941-639-2167	33 Tamiami Trail Punta Gorda FL

Fort Myers Listings

Fort Myers
Best Western Springs Resort	941-267-7900	18051 S. Tamiami Trail Hwy 41 Fort Myers FL
Comfort Inn	941-694-9200	4171 Boatways Road Fort Myers FL
Comfort Suites Airport	941-768-0005	13651-A Indian Paint Ln Fort Myers FL
Howard Johnson Inn	239-936-3229	4811 Cleveland Ave. Fort Myers FL
Motel 6	941-656-5544	3350 Marinatown Lane Fort Myers FL

Naples Listings

Naples
Red Roof Inn & Suites	941-774-3117	1925 Davis Blvd Naples FL
Staybridge Suites	941-643-8002	4805 Tamiami Trail North Naples FL

Interstate 77 Accommodation Listings

Ohio (Interstate 77)

Akron Listings

Akron
Best Western Inn & Suites	330-670-0888	160 Montrose West Ave Akron OH
Holiday Inn Express	330-644-7126	2940 Chenoweth Rd Akron OH

Canton Listings

Canton
Holiday Inn	330-494-2770	4520 Everhard Rd Canton OH
Residence Inn by Marriott	330-493-0004	5280 Broadmoor Circle NW Canton OH

N Canton
Motel 6	330-494-7611	6880 Sunset Strip Ave NW N Canton OH

North Canton
Red Roof Inn	330-499-1970	5353 Inn Circle Court, NW North Canton OH

New Philadelphia Listings

New Philadelphia
Holiday Inn	330-339-7731	131 Bluebell Dr SW New Philadelphia OH
Motel 6	330-339-6446	181 Bluebell Dr New Philadelphia OH

Cambridge Listings

Cambridge
Best Western Cambridge	740-439-3581	1945 Southgate Parkway Cambridge OH
Holiday Inn	740-432-7313	2248 Southgate Pkwy Cambridge OH

Marietta Listings

Marietta
Best Western Marietta	740-374-7211	279 Muskingum Drive Marietta OH

West Virginia (Interstate 77)

Parkersburg Listings
Parkersburg

Blennerhassett Hotel	304-422-3131	Fourth and Market Streets Parkersburg WV
Expressway Motor Inn	304-485-1851	6333 Emerson Ave Parkersburg WV
Red Roof Inn	304-485-1741	3714 East 7th Street Parkersburg WV

Ripley Listings
Ripley

Holiday Inn Express	304-372-5000	One Hospitality Drive Ripley WV

Charleston Listings
Charleston

Motel 6	304-925-0471	6311 MacCorkle Ave SE Charleston WV
Ramada Plaza Hotel	304-744-4641	400 Second Avenue Charleston WV

Kanawha City

Red Roof Inn-Kanawha City	304-925-6953	6305 MacCorkle Avenue S.E. Kanawha City WV

South Charleston

Red Roof Inn	304-744-1500	4006 MacCorkle Avenue South Charleston WV

Beckley Listings
Beckley

Comfort Inn	304-255-2161	1909 Harper Rd. Beckley WV

Princeton Listings
Princeton

Sleep Inn	304-431-2800	1015 Oakvale Rd. Princeton WV

Virginia (Interstate 77)

Wytheville Listings
Wytheville

Holiday Inn	276-228-5483	US 11 I-77/I-81 Wytheville VA

Hillsville Listings
Hillsville

Holiday Inn Express	276-728-2120	85 Airport Road Hillsville VA

North Carolina (Interstate 77)

Cornelius Listings
Cornelius

Holiday Inn	704-892-9120	19901 Holiday Lane Cornelius NC

Charlotte Listings
Charlotte

La Quinta Inn & Suites Charlotte Coliseum	704-523-5599	4900 South Tryon Street Charlotte NC
Staybridge Suites	704-527-6767	7924 Forest Pine Drive Charlotte NC

Fort Mill

Motel 6	803-548-9656	255 Carowinds Blvd Fort Mill NC

South Carolina (Interstate 77)

Rock Hill Listings
Rock Hill

Best Western Inn	803-329-1330	1106 Anderson Rd Rock Hill SC
Holiday Inn	803-329-1122	2640 N Cherry Rd Rock Hill SC

Interstate 80 Accommodation Listings

Highway Guides - Please always call ahead to make sure an establishment is still dog-friendly.

California (Interstate 80)

Vallejo Listings
Vallejo
Holiday Inn	707-644-1200	1000 Fairgrounds Dr Vallejo CA

Vacaville Listings
Vacaville
Residence Inn	707-469-0300	360 Orange Dr Vacaville CA
Super 8 Motel - Vacaville	707-449-8884	101 Allison Court Vacaville CA

Dixon Listings
Dixon
Super 8	707-678-3399	2500 Plaza Court Dixon CA

Davis Listings
Davis
Best Western University Lodge	530-756-7890	123 B Street Davis CA
Econo Lodge	530-756-1040	221 D Street Davis CA
Howard Johnson Hotel	530-792-0800	4100 Chiles Road Davis CA
University Inn Bed and Breakfast	530-756-8648	340 A Street Davis CA
University Park Inn & Suites	530-756-0910	1111 Richards Blvd. Davis CA

Sacramento Listings
North Highlands
Motel 6	916-973-8637	4600 Watt Ave North Highlands CA

Roseville
Best Western Roseville Inn	916-782-4434	220 Harding Blvd. Roseville CA
Oxford Suites	916-784-2222	130 N Sunrise Ave Roseville CA

Sacramento
Motel 6	916-372-3624	1254 Halyard Dr Sacramento CA
Sheraton Grand Sacramento Hotel	916-447-1700	1230 J Street Sacramento CA

Gold Country Listings
Auburn
Best Western Golden Key	530-885-8611	13450 Lincoln Way Auburn CA
Holiday Inn	530-887-8787	120 Grass Valley Highway Auburn CA
Travelodge	530-885-7025	13490 Lincoln Way Auburn CA

Nevada (Interstate 80)

Reno Listings
Reno
Days Inn	775-786-4070	701 E 7th Reno NV
Truckee River Lodge	775-786-8888	501 W. 1st Street Reno NV

Lovelock Listings
Lovelock
Ramada Inn Sturgeon's Casino	775-273-2971	1420 Cornell Ave Lovelock NV

Winnemucca Listings
Winnemucca
Best Western Gold Country Inn	775-623-6999	921 West Winnemucca Boulevard Winnemucca NV
Best Western Holiday Motel	775-623-3684	670 W. Winnemucca Blvd Winnemucca NV
Days Inn	775-623-3661	511 W. Winnemucca Blvd Winnemucca NV
Holiday Inn Express	775-625-3100	1987 W. Winnemucca Blvd Winnemucca NV
Motel 6	775-623-1180	1600 Winnemucca Blvd Winnemucca NV
Red Lion Inn & Casino	775-623-2565	741 West Winnemucca Boulevard Winnemucca NV
Santa Fe Motel	775-623-1119	1620 W. Winnemucca Blvd Winnemucca NV
Super 8	775-625-1818	1157 Winnemucca Blvd Winnemucca NV

Battle Mountain Listings

Battle Mountain

| Comfort Inn | 775-635-5880 | 521 E. Front Street Battle Mountain NV |

Elko Listings

Elko

Best Western Gold Country Inn	775-738-8421	2050 Idaho Street Elko NV
Comfort Inn	775-777-8762	2970 Idaho St Elko NV
High Desert Inn	775-738-8425	3015 Idaho Street Elko NV
Motel 6	775-738-4337	3021 Idaho Street Elko NV
Red Lion Casino	775-738-2111	2065 Idaho Street Elko NV
Shilo Inn	775-738-5522	2401 Mountain City Highway Elko NV

Utah (Interstate 80)

Wendover Listings

Wendover

| Motel 6 | 435-665-2267 | 561 E Wendover Blvd Wendover UT |

Salt Lake City Listings

Lehi

| Best Western Timpanogos Inn | 801-768-1400 | 195 South 850 East Lehi UT |
| Motel 6 | 801-768-2668 | 210 S 1200 E Lehi UT |

Salt Lake City

Days Inn - Salt Lake City Airport	801-539-8538	1900 W N Temple Salt Lake City UT
Hotel Monaco Salt Lake City	801-595-0000	15 West 200 South Salt Lake City UT
Motel 6	801-364-1053	1990 W N Temple St Salt Lake City UT
Motel 6 - Downtown	801-531-1252	176 W 6th S St Salt Lake City UT
Ramada Inn	801-364-5200	230 W 600 S Salt Lake City UT
Salt Lake City Centre Travelodge	801-531-7100	524 S West Temple Salt Lake City UT

Park City Listings

Park City

Best Western Landmark Inn	435-649-7300	6560 N Landmark Drive Park City UT
Holiday Inn Express Hotel & Suites	435-658-1600	1501 W. Ute Blvd Park City UT
Radisson Park City	435-649-5000	2121 Park Ave Park City UT
The Gables Hotel	435-655-3315	1335 Lowell Avenue, PO Box 905 Park City UT

Wyoming (Interstate 80)

Evanston Listings

Evanston

| Days Inn | 307-789-2220 | 339 Wasatch Rd Evanston WY |
| Evanston Super 8 Motel | 307-789-7510 | 70 Bear River Dr Evanston WY |

Rock Springs Listings

Rock Springs

Comfort Inn	307-382-9490	1670 Sunset Dr Rock Springs WY
Holiday Inn	307-382-9200	1675 Sunset Drive Rock Springs WY
Motel 6	307-362-1850	2615 Commercial Way Rock Springs WY

Rawlins Listings

Rawlins

| Sleep Inn | 307-328-1732 | 1400 Higley Blvd Rawlins WY |

Laramie Listings

Laramie

Best Western Gas Lite Motel	307-742-6616	960 North Third Laramie WY
Howard Johnson Inn	307-742-8371	1555 Snowy Range Road Laramie WY
Motel 6	307-742-2307	621 Plaza Lane Laramie WY

Cheyenne Listings

Cheyenne

| Best Western Hitching Post Inn | 307-638-3301 | 1700 W Lincolnway Cheyenne WY |
| Comfort Inn | 307-638-7202 | 2245 Etchepare Dr Cheyenne WY |

Days Inn Cheyenne	307-778-8877	2360 W Lincolnway Cheyenne WY
Lincoln Court	307-638-3302	1720 W Lincolnway Cheyenne WY
Windy Hills Guest House	307-632-6423	393 Happy Jack Rd Cheyenne WY

Nebraska (Interstate 80)

Sidney Listings
Sidney
Holiday Inn	308-254-2000	664 Chase Blvd Sidney NE

Ogallala Listings
Ogallala
Holiday Inn Express	308-284-2266	501 Stage Coach Drive Ogallala NE

North Platte Listings
North Platte
Best Western Chalet Lodge	308-532-2313	920 N Jeffers North Platte NE
Best Western Circle C S. Motor Inn	308-532-0130	1211 South Dewey Street North Platte NE
Motel 6	308-534-6200	1520 S Jeffers St North Platte NE
Quality Inn & Suites	308-532-9090	2102 S. Jeffers North Platte NE
Stanford Motel	308-532-9380	1400 E 4th Street North Platte NE

Cozad Listings
Cozad
Motel 6	308-784-4900	809 S Meridian Cozad NE

Lexington Listings
Lexington
Budget Host Minute Man Motel	308-324-5544	801 Plum Creek Pkwy Lexington NE
Holiday Inn Express & Suites	308-324-9900	2605 Plum Creek Pkwy Lexington NE

Kearney Listings
Kearney
Best Western Inn of Kearney	308-237-5185	1010 3rd Ave Kearney NE
Motel 6	308-338-0705	101 Talmadge Rd Kearney NE
Super 8 Motel - Kearney	308-234-5513	15 W. 8th Street Kearney NE

Grand Island Listings
Grand Island
Holiday Inn	308-384-7770	I-80 & Hwy 281 Grand Island NE
Howard Johnson Hotel	308-384-5150	3333 Ramada Road Grand Island NE

York Listings
York
Best Western Palmer Inn	402-362-5585	2426 S. Lincoln Ave York NE

Lincoln Listings
Lincoln
Comfort Inn	402-475-2200	2940 NW 12th St Lincoln NE
Comfort Suites	402-476-8080	4231 Industrial Ave. Lincoln NE
Holiday Inn Express	402-435-0200	1133 Belmont Ave Lincoln NE
Motel 6	402-464-5971	5600 Cornhusker Hwy Lincoln NE
Motel 6	402-475-3211	3001 NW 12th St Lincoln NE
Staybridge Suites	402-438-7829	2701 Fletcher Avenue Lincoln NE

Omaha Listings
Omaha
Comfort Inn	402-592-2882	10919 J St. Omaha NE
Crowne Plaza	402-496-0850	655 N. 108th Ave Omaha NE
La Quinta Inn Omaha	402-493-1900	3330 North 104th Avenue Omaha NE
Marriott	402-399-9000	10220 Regency Circle Omaha NE
Motel 6	402-331-3161	10708 M St Omaha NE
clarion Hotel	402-895-1000	4888 S 118th St Omaha NE

Highway Guides - Please always call ahead to make sure an establishment is still dog-friendly.

Iowa (Interstate 80)

Council Bluffs Listings
Council Bluffs
Motel 6   712-366-2405   3032 S Expwy Council Bluffs IA

Des Moines Listings
Des Moines
Best Western Colonial   515-265-7511   5020 NE 14th Street Des Moines IA
Holiday Inn   515-278-0271   5000 Merle Hay Rd Des Moines IA
Motel 6 - North   515-266-5456   4940 NE 14th St Des Moines IA
West Des Moines
Motel 6 - West   515-267-8885   7655 Office Plaza Dr N West Des Moines IA

Altoona Listings
Altoona
Howard Johnson Express Inn   515-967-4886   2701 Adventureland Drive Altoona IA

Newton Listings
Newton
Best Western Newton Inn   641-792-4200   I-80 and Hwy 14, Exit 164 Newton IA
Holiday Inn Express   641-792-7722   1700 W. 19th St S. Newton IA

Iowa City Listings
Coralville
Motel 6   319-354-0030   810 1st Ave Coralville IA

Quad Cities Listings
Bettendorf
Jumer's Castle Lodge   319-359-7141   I-74 at Spruce Hills Drive Bettendorf IA
Davenport
Best Western SteepleGate Inn   319-386-6900   100 West 76th Street Davenport IA
Clarion Hotel   563-324-1921   227 LeClaire Street Davenport IA
Comfort Inn   563-391-8222   7222 Northwest Blvd Davenport IA
Motel 6   563-391-8997   6111 N Brady St Davenport IA

Le Claire Listings
Le Claire
Comfort Inn Riverview   563-289-4747   902 Mississippi View Court Le Claire IA

Illinois (Interstate 80)

Moline Listings
Moline
Holiday Inn Express - Airport   309-762-8300   6910 27th Street Moline IL
Motel 6   309-764-8711   2359 69th Ave Moline IL

Morris Listings
Morris
Days Inn & Suites   815-942-9000   Rt 47 at Hampton Street Morris IL

Chicago Area Listings
Hammond
Holiday Inn - Southeast   219-844-2140   3830 179th St Hammond IL
Joliet
Motel 6 - Joliet   815-439-1332   3551 Mall Loop Drive Joliet IL

Indiana (Interstate 80)

Hammond Listings
Hammond
Motel 6   219-845-0330   3840 179th Street Hammond IN

South Bend Listings

South Bend

Motel 6	219-272-7072	52624 US Hwy 31 N South Bend IN

Ohio (Interstate 80)

Toledo Listings

Maumee

Days Inn-Maumee	419-893-9960	150 Dussel Drive Maumee OH

Perrysburg

Howard Johnson Inn	419-837-5245	I-280 & Hanley Road Perrysburg OH

Cleveland Area Listings

Macedonia

Motel 6	330-468-1670	311 E Highland Rd Macedonia OH

Middleburg Heights

Motel 6	440-234-0990	7219 Engle Rd Middleburg Heights OH

Richfield Listings

Richfield

Holiday Inn	330-659-6151	4742 Brecksville Road Richfield OH

Akron Listings

Akron

Best Western Inn & Suites	330-670-0888	160 Montrose West Ave Akron OH

Pennsylvania (Interstate 80)

Mercer Listings

Mercer

Howard Johnson Inn	724-748-3030	835 Perry Hwy. Mercer PA

Clarion Listings

Clarion

Holiday Inn	814-226-8850	I-80 Rt 68 Clarion PA

Brookville Listings

Brookville

Holiday Inn Express	814-849-8381	235 Allegheny Blvd Brookville PA

DuBois Listings

DuBois

Holiday Inn	814-371-5100	Rt 219 & I-80 DuBois PA

Clearfield Listings

Clearfield

Best Western Motor Inn	814-765-2441	1-80 at Exit 19, Box 286 Clearfield PA

Milesburg Listings

Milesburg

Holiday Inn	814-355-7521	I-80 & US 150 N Milesburg PA

Blakeslee Listings

Blakeslee

Best Western Inn at Blakeslee-Pocono	570-646-6000	Route 115, PO Box 413 Blakeslee PA

Interstate 81 Accommodation Listings

New York (Interstate 81)

Watertown Listings

Highway Guides - Please always call ahead to make sure an establishment is still dog-friendly.

Watertown
Best Western Carriage House Inn   315-782-8000   300 Washington Street Watertown NY

Binghamton Listings
Binghamton
| Comfort Inn | 607-722-5353 | 1156 Front St. Binghamton NY |
| Motel 6 | 607-771-0400 | 1012 Front St Binghamton NY |

Pennsylvania (Interstate 81)

Scranton Listings
Scranton
Howard Johnson Express Inn   570-346-7061   320 Franklin Ave. Scranton PA

Pittston Listings
Pittston
Holiday Inn Express   570-654-3300   30 Concorde Drive Pittston PA

Wilkes-Barre Listings
Wilkes-Barre
Holiday Inn   570-824-8901   880 Kidder St, Rt 115 & 309 Wilkes-Barre PA

Hazleton Listings
Hazleton
Best Western Genetti Lodge   570-454-2494   Route 309, RR2, Box 37 Hazleton PA

Frackville Listings
Frackville
Motel 6   570-874-1223   701 Altamont Blvd Frackville PA

Harrisburg Listings
Grantville
Holiday Inn   717-469-0661   Hershey Exit 28 I-81 Grantville PA
Harrisburg
Holiday Inn Express Hotel & Suites   717-657-2200   5680 Allentown Blvd Harrisburg PA

Maryland (Interstate 81)

Hagerstown Listings
Hagerstown
Econo Lodge	301-791-3560	18221 Mason Dixon Rd Hagerstown MD
Four Points by Sheraton	301-790-3010	1910 Dual Hwy Hagerstown MD
Motel 6	301-582-4445	11321 Massey Blvd Hagerstown MD
Sleep Inn & Suites	301-766-9449	18216 Colonel H K Douglas Dr Hagerstown MD

West Virginia (Interstate 81)

Martinsburg Listings
Martinsburg
Days Inn	304-263-1800	209 Viking Way Martinsburg WV
Holiday Inn	304-267-5500	301 Foxcroft Ave Martinsburg WV
Knights Inn	304-267-2211	1599 Edwin Miller Blvd Martinsburg WV

Virginia (Interstate 81)

Winchester Listings
Winchester
Best Western Lee-Jackson Motor Inn   540-662-4154   711 Millwood Avenue Winchester VA

Mount Jackson Listings
Mount Jackson
Best Western Shenandoah Valley   540-477-2911   250 Conicville Rd, I-81 Exit 273 Mount Jackson VA

Harrisonburg Listings
Harrisonburg

Comfort Inn	540-433-6066	1440 E Market St Harrisonburg VA
Motel 6	540-433-6939	10 Linda Ln Harrisonburg VA
Sheraton Four Points Hotel	540-433-2521	1400 E Market St Harrisonburg VA

Lexington Listings
Lexington

Best Western Inn at Hunt Ridge	540-464-1500	Route 7, Box 99A Lexington VA
Holiday Inn Express	540-463-7351	850 North Lee Hwy, US 11 North at I-64. Lexington VA
Howard Johnson Inn	540-463-9181	2836 N. Lee Hwy. Lexington VA
Ramada Inn	540-463-6400	U.S. Highway 11 and Interstate Highway 81 Lexington VA

Daleville Listings
Daleville

Best Western Coachman Inn	540-992-1234	437 Roanoke Rd Daleville VA

Salem Listings
Salem

Ramada Inn	540-389-7061	1671 Skyview Rd Salem VA

Christiansburg Listings
Christiansburg

Howard Johnson Express Inn	540-381-0150	100 Bristol Drive Christiansburg VA

Wytheville Listings
Wytheville

Holiday Inn	276-228-5483	US 11 I-77/I-81 Wytheville VA

Marion Listings
Marion

Best Western Marion	276-783-3193	1424 North Main Street Marion VA

Bristol Listings
Bristol

Holiday Inn Hotel & Suites	276-466-4100	3005 Linden Drive Bristol VA
La Quinta Inn Bristol	276-669-9353	1014 Old Airport Road Bristol VA

Tennessee (Interstate 81)

Morristown Listings
Morristown

Holiday Inn	423-587-2400	5435 South Davey Crockett Pkwy Morristown TN
Holiday Inn	423-581-8700	3304 W Andrew Johnson Hwy 11E Morristown TN

Interstate 84 Accommodation Listings

Oregon (Interstate 84)

Portland Listings
Portland

La Quinta Inn Portland - Lloyd	503-233-7933	431 NE Multnomah Portland OR
Sleep Inn	503-618-8400	2261 NE 181st Ave. Portland OR

Troutdale Listings
Troutdale

Motel 6	503-665-2254	1610 NW Frontage Rd Troutdale OR

Hood River Listings
Hood River

Best Western Hood River Inn	541-386-2200	1108 E. Marina Way Hood River OR
Columbia Gorge	541-386-5566	4000 Westcliff Dr Hood River OR
Vagabond Lodge	541-386-2992	4070 Westcliff Dr Hood River OR

The Dalles Listings
The Dalles

Quality Inn Columbia River Gorge	541-298-5161	2114 W. 6th The Dalles OR

Pendleton Listings
Pendleton

Best Western Pendleton Inn	541-276-2135	400 SE Nye Ave Pendleton OR
Holiday Inn Express	541-966-6520	600 SE Nye Ave Pendleton OR
Motel 6	541-276-3160	325 SE Nye Ave Pendleton OR

LaGrande Listings
LaGrande

Howard Johnson Inn	541-963-7195	2612 Island Avenue LaGrande OR

Baker City Listings
Baker City

Quality Inn	541-523-2242	810 Campbell St. Baker City OR

Ontario Listings
Ontario

Best Western Inn & Suites	541-889-2600	251 Goodfellow Street Ontario OR
Motel 6	541-889-6617	275 NE 12th St Ontario OR

Idaho (Interstate 84)

Caldwell Listings
Caldwell

La Quinta Inn Caldwell	208-454-2222	901 Specht Avenue Caldwell ID

Nampa Listings
Nampa

Sleep Inn	208-463-6300	1315 Industrial Rd Nampa ID

Boise Listings
Boise

Holiday Inn - Airport	208-344-8365	3300 Vista Ave Boise ID
Motel 6	208-344-3506	2323 Airport Way Boise ID

Mountain Home Listings
Mountain Home

Best Western Foothills Motor Inn	208-587-8477	1080 Hwy 20 Mountain Home ID
Sleep Inn	208-587-9743	1180 US 20 Mountain Home ID

Jerome Listings
Jerome

Best Western Sawtooth Inn & Suites	208-324-9200	2653 South Lincoln Jerome ID

Twin Falls Listings
Twin Falls

Comfort Inn	208-734-7494	1893 Canyon Springs Rd Twin Falls ID
Motel 6	208-734-3993	1472 Blue Lake Blvd N Twin Falls ID

Interstate 85 Accommodation Listings

Virginia (Interstate 85)

South Hill Listings
South Hill
Best Western South Hill | 434-447-3123 | Hwy 58 & I-85 South Hill VA

North Carolina (Interstate 85)

Burlington Listings
Burlington
Holiday Inn - Outlet Center | 336-229-5203 | 2444 Maple Avenue Burlington NC

Greensboro Listings
Greensboro
Motel 6 | 336-854-0993 | 831 Greenhaven Dr Greensboro NC

Charlotte Listings
Charlotte
Drury Inn & Suites | 704-593-0700 | 415 West W.T. Harris Blvd. Charlotte NC
Staybridge Suites | 704-527-6767 | 7924 Forest Pine Drive Charlotte NC
Studio 6 | 704-394-4993 | 3420 I-85 Service Rd South Charlotte NC

Gastonia Listings
Gastonia
Motel 6 | 704-868-4900 | 1721 Broadcast St Gastonia NC

South Carolina (Interstate 85)

Spartanburg Listings
Spartanburg
Motel 6 | 864-573-6383 | 105 Jones Rd Spartanburg SC

Greenville Listings
Greenville
Crowne Plaza | 864-297-6300 | 851 Congaree Rd Greenville SC
Holiday Inn | 864-277-8921 | 4295 Augusta Rd, I-85 Exit 46A Greenville SC
La Quinta Inn & Suites Greenville - Haywood | 864-233-8018 | 65 West Orchard Park Drive Greenville SC
Motel 6 | 864-277-8630 | 224 Bruce Rd Greenville SC

Anderson Listings
Anderson
La Quinta Inn Anderson | 864-225-3721 | 3430 North Main Street Anderson SC

Georgia (Interstate 85)

Lavonia Listings
Lavonia
Best Western Regency Inn & Suites | 706-356-4000 | 13705 Jones Street Lavonia GA

Commerce Listings
Commerce
Comfort Inn | 706-335-9001 | 165 Eisenhower Dr Commerce GA
Holiday Inn Express | 706-335-5183 | 30747 Hwy 441 S. Commerce GA

Suwanee Listings
Suwanee
Comfort Inn | 770-945-1608 | 2945 Highway 317 Suwanee GA
Holiday Inn | 770-945-4921 | 2955 Hwy 317 Suwanee GA

Norcross Listings
Norcross
La Quinta Inn Atlanta Peachtree Ind - Norcross | 770-449-5144 | 5375 Peachtree Industrial Blvd Norcross GA

Atlanta Listings

Atlanta

Airport Drury Inn & Suites	404-761-4900	1270 Virginia Avenue Atlanta GA
Crowne Plaza - Airport	404-768-6660	1325 Virginia Ave Atlanta GA
Holiday Inn - Airport North	404-762-8411	1380 Virginia Ave Atlanta GA
Motel 6 - Northeast (I-85)	770-458-6626	2820 Chamblee - Tucker Rd Atlanta GA
Sheraton Midtown Atlanta at Colony Square	404-892-6000	188 14th Street at Peachtree Atlanta GA

Norcross

Northeast Drury Inn & Suites	770-729-0060	5655 Jimmy Carter Blvd Norcross GA

Atlanta Area Listings

College Park

Howard Johnson Express Inn	404-766-0000	2480 Old National Pkwy. College Park GA

Duluth

Studio 6 - Gwinnett Place	770-931-3113	3525 Breckinridge Blvd Duluth GA

Alabama (Interstate 85)

Auburn Listings

Auburn

Comfort Inn	334-821-6699	2283 South College Street Auburn AL

Montgomery Listings

Montgomery

Holiday Inn - East I-85	334-272-0370	1185 Eastern Blvd Montgomery AL

Interstate 90 Accommodation Listings
(From Chicago to Cleveland see Highway 80 Listings)

Washington (Interstate 90)

Moses Lake Listings

Moses Lake

Best Western Hallmark Inn & Conf Center	509-765-9211	3000 Marina Dr Moses Lake WA
Motel 6	509-766-0250	2822 Wapato Dr Moses Lake WA

Spokane Listings

Spokane

Howard Johnson Inn	509-838-6630	South 211 Division St. Spokane WA
Motel 6	509-459-6120	1508 S Rustle St Spokane WA
Motel 6	509-926-5399	1919 N Hutchinson Rd Spokane WA

Idaho (Interstate 90)

Post Falls Listings

Post Falls

Holiday Inn Express	208-773-8900	3105 E. Seltice Way Post Falls ID
Howard Johnson Express Inn	208-773-4541	West 3647 5th Ave. Post Falls ID
Sleep Inn	208-777-9394	100 N. Pleasant View Rd Post Falls ID

Montana (Interstate 90)

Missoula Listings

Missoula

Best Western Executive Inn	406-543-7221	201 East Main Street Missoula MT
Best Western Grant Creek Inn	406-543-0700	5280 Grant Creek Rd Missoula MT
Motel 6	406-549-6665	3035 Expo Pkwy Commerce Ctr Missoula MT

Highway Guides - Please always call ahead to make sure an establishment is still dog-friendly.

Butte Listings
Butte
Comfort Inn	406-494-8850	2777 Harrison Ave. Butte MT
Days Inn	406-494-7000	2700 Harrison Avenue Butte MT
Ramada Inn	406-494-6666	4655 Harrison Ave. Butte MT

Belgrade Listings
Belgrade
Holiday Inn Express	406-388-0800	6261 Jackrabbit Lane Belgrade MT

Bozeman Listings
Bozeman
Holiday Inn	406-587-4561	5 Baxtor Lane Bozeman MT
La Quinta Inn & Suites Bozeman - Belgrade	406-388-2222	6445 Jackrabbit Lane Bozeman MT
Ramada Limited	406-585-2626	2020 Wheat Drive Bozeman MT
Western Heritage Inn	406-586-8534	1200 E Main St Bozeman MT

Livingston Listings
Livingston
Best Western Yellowstone Inn	406-222-6110	1515 W. Park Street Livingston MT

Billings Listings
Billings
Comfort Inn	406-652-5200	2030 Overland Ave. Billings MT
Holiday Inn - Grand Montana	406-248-7701	5500 Midland Rd Billings MT
Motel 6	406-252-0093	5400 Midland Rd Billings MT
Quality Inn Homestead Park	406-652-1320	2036 Overland Ave. Billings MT

Wyoming (Interstate 90)

Sheridan Listings
Clearmont
The Ranch at UCross	307-737-2281	2673 US Hwy 14 East Clearmont WY

Sheridan
Guest House Motel	307-674-7496	2007 N Main St Sheridan WY
Holiday Inn	307-672-8931	1809 Sugarland Dr Sheridan WY

Buffalo Listings
Buffalo
Motel 6	307-684-7000	100 Flat Iron Drive Buffalo WY

Sundance Listings
Sundance
Best Western Inn at Sundance	307-283-2800	2179 E. Cleveland, Box 927 Sundance WY

South Dakota (Interstate 90)

Belle Fourche Listings
Belle Fourche
Motel 6	605-892-6663	1815 5th Ave Belle Fourche SD

Spearfish Listings
Spearfish
Holiday Inn	605-642-4683	I-90 & Exit 14, PO Box 399 Spearfish SD
Howard Johnson Express Inn	605-642-8105	323 S. 27th St. Spearfish SD

Sturgis Listings
Sturgis
Best Western Sturgis Inn	605-347-3604	2431 S. Junction Street, Box 777 Sturgis SD
Sturgis Super 8 Motel	605-347-4447	HC 55 Box 306 Sturgis SD

Mount Rushmore Listings
Rapid City

Highway Guides - Please always call ahead to make sure an establishment is still dog-friendly.

| Motel 6 | 605-343-3687 | 620 E Latrobe St Rapid City SD |

Wall Listings
Wall

| Best Western Plains Motel | 605-279-2145 | 712 Glenn Street, Box 393 Wall SD |

Kadoka Listings
Kadoka

| Best Western H & H El Centro | 605-837-2287 | PO Box 37 Kadoka SD |

Mitchell Listings
Mitchell

Holiday Inn	605-996-6501	1525 W. Havens Ave Mitchell SD
Motel 6	605-996-0530	1309 S Ohiman St Mitchell SD
Siesta Motel	605-996-5544	1210 West Havens Mitchell SD

Sioux Falls Listings
Sioux Falls

| Best Western Ramkota Hotel | 605-336-0650 | 2400 N. Louise Sioux Falls SD |
| Motel 6 | 605-336-7800 | 3009 W Russell St Sioux Falls SD |

Brandon Listings
Brandon

| Holiday Inn Express | 605-582-2901 | 1105 North Splitrock Blvd Brandon SD |

Minnesota (Interstate 90)

Albert Lea Listings
Albert Lea

| Comfort Inn | 507-377-1100 | 810 Happy Trails Lane Albert Lea MN |

Rochester Listings
Rochester

| Quality Inn & Suites | 507-282-8091 | 1620 1st Ave. Rochester MN |

Winona Listings
Winona

| Quality Inn | 507-454-4390 | 956 Mankato Ave. Winona MN |

Wisconsin (Interstate 90)

Onalaska Listings
Onalaska

| Holiday Inn Express | 608-783-6555 | 9409 Hwy 16 Onalaska WI |

Sparta Listings
Sparta

| Country Inn by Carlson | 608-269-3110 | 737 Avon Rd Sparta WI |
| Super 8 | 608-269-8489 | 716 Avon Rd Sparta WI |

Wisconsin Dells Listings
Wisconsin Dells

| Howard Johnson Hotel | 608-254-8306 | 655 Frontage Rd. North Wisconsin Dells WI |

DeForest Listings
DeForest

| Holiday Inn Express | 608-846-8686 | 7184 Morrisonville Rd DeForest WI |

Madison Listings
Madison

Collins House Bed and Breakfast	608-255-4230	704 E Gorham St Madison WI
Comfort Suites	608-836-3033	1253 John Q Hammonds Dr Madison WI
Motel 6	608-241-8101	1754 Thierer Rd Madison WI
Red Roof Inn	608-241-1787	4830 Hayes Rd Madison WI

Residence Inn by Marriott	608-244-5047	4862 Hayes Rd Madison WI
Woodfield Suites	608-245-0123	5217 E Terrace Dr Madison WI

Janesville Listings
Janesville

Best Western Janesville	608-756-4511	3900 Milton Ave Janesville WI
Motel 6	608-756-1742	3907 Milton Ave Janesville WI

Beloit Listings
Beloit

Super 8 Motel - Beloit	608-365-8680	3002 Milwaukee Road Beloit WI

Illinois (Interstate 90)

Crystal Lake Listings
Crystal Lake

Comfort Inn	815-444-0040	595 E. Tracy Trail Crystal Lake IL

Schaumburg Listings
Schaumburg

La Quinta Inn Chicago - Schaumburg	847-517-8484	1730 East Higgins Road Schaumburg IL

Chicago Listings
Chicago

Holiday Inn - Mart Plaza	312-836-5000	350 N. Orleans St Chicago IL

Chicago Area Listings
Arlington Heights

Motel 6 - North Central	847-806-1230	441 W Algonquin Rd Arlington Heights IL
Sheraton Chicago Northwest	847-394-2000	3400 West Euclid Avenue Arlington Heights IL

Rosemont

Holiday Inn Select	847-954-8600	10233 West Higgins Rd Rosemont IL
Sheraton Gateway Suites Chicago O'Hare	847-699-6300	6501 N. Mannheim Rd Rosemont IL

Ohio (Interstate 90)

Cleveland Area Listings
Amherst

Motel 6	440-988-3266	704 N Leavitt Rd Amherst OH

Mentor

Studio 6	440-946-0749	7677 Reynolds Rd Mentor OH

Pennsylvania (Interstate 90)

Erie Listings
Erie

Motel 6	814-864-4811	7875 Peach St Erie PA

New York (Interstate 90)

Dunkirk Listings
Dunkirk

Best Western Dunkirk and Fredonia	716-366-7100	3912 Vineyard Drive Dunkirk NY
Comfort Inn	716-672-4450	3925 Vinyard Dr. Dunkirk NY

Hamburg Listings
Hamburg

Comfort Inn	716-648-2922	3615 Commerce Place Hamburg NY

Weedsport Listings
Weedsport

| Best Western Weedsport Inn | 315-834-6623 | 2709 Erie Drive Weedsport NY |

Syracuse Listings
East Syracuse

| Holiday Inn | 315-437-2761 | 6555 Old Collamer Rd South East Syracuse NY |

Syracuse

Comfort Inn	315-437-0222	6491 Thompson Rd Syracuse NY
Comfort Inn Fairgrounds	315-453-0045	7010 Interstate Island Rd. Syracuse NY
Holiday Inn	315-457-8700	State Fair Blvd & Farrell Rd Syracuse NY

Syracuse Area Listings
Liverpool

| Holiday Inn | 315-457-1122 | 441 Electronics Pkwy Liverpool NY |

Rome Listings
Rome

| Quality Inn | 315-336-4300 | 200 S. James St. Rome NY |

Utica Listings
New Hartford

| Holiday Inn | 315-797-2131 | 1777 Burrstone Rd New Hartford NY |

Utica

| Best Western Gateway Adirondack Inn | 315-732-4121 | 175 N Genesee Street Utica NY |

Little Falls Listings
Little Falls

| Best Western Little Falls Motor Inn | 315-823-4954 | 20 Albany Street Little Falls NY |

Amsterdam Listings
Amsterdam

| Best Western Amsterdam | 518-843-5760 | 10 Market Street Amsterdam NY |

Schenectady Listings
Schenectady

| Holiday Inn | 518-393-4141 | 100 Nott Terrace Schenectady NY |

Massachusetts (Interstate 90)

Springfield Listings
Springfield

| Motel 6 | 413-592-5141 | 36 Burnett Rd Springfield MA |

Boston Area Listings
Framingham

| Motel 6 | 508-620-0500 | 1668 Worcester Rd Framingham MA |
| Sheraton Framingham Hotel | 508-879-7200 | 1657 Worcester Road Framingham MA |

Newton

| Sheraton Newton Hotel | 617-969-3010 | 320 Washington Street Newton MA |

Interstate 94 Accommodation Listings

Montana (Interstate 94)

Billings Listings
Billings

Comfort Inn	406-652-5200	2030 Overland Ave. Billings MT
Hilltop Inn	406-245-5000	1116 N 28th St Billings MT
Holiday Inn - Grand Montana	406-248-7701	5500 Midland Rd Billings MT
Howard Johnson Express Inn	406-248-4656	1001 S 27th St. Billings MT
Motel 6	406-252-0093	5400 Midland Rd Billings MT

Quality Inn Homestead Park	406-652-1320	2036 Overland Ave. Billings MT
Super 8 Motel	406-248-8842	5400 Southgate Dr Billings MT

Forsyth Listings
Forsyth
Best Western Sundowner Inn	406-356-2115	1018 Front St, PO Box 1080 Forsyth MT

Miles City Listings
Miles City
Best Western War Bonnet Inn	406-232-4560	1015 S. Haynes, Box 1055 Miles City MT
Budget Inn	406-232-3550	1006 S. Haynes Ave. Miles City MT
Motel 6	406-232-7040	1314 Haynes Ave Rt 2, Box 3396 Miles City MT

Glendive Listings
Glendive
Days Inn	406-365-6011	2000 N Merrill Avenue Glendive MT
Super 8 Motel	406-365-5671	1904 N. Merrill Ave. Glendive MT

North Dakota (Interstate 94)

Dickinson Listings
Dickinson
Best Western Badlands Inn	701-225-9510	71 Museum Dr Dickinson ND

Bismarck Listings
Bismarck
Best Western Doublewood Inn	701-258-7000	1400 E. Interchange Ave Bismarck ND
Holiday Inn	701-255-6000	605 E. Broadway Bismarck ND
Motel 6	701-255-6878	2433 State St Bismarck ND

Fargo Listings
Fargo
Best Western Doublewood Inn	701-235-3333	3333 13th Ave S Fargo ND
Holiday Inn	701-282-2700	3803 13th Ave S. Fargo ND
Holiday Inn Express	701-282-2000	1040 40th St S. Fargo ND
Motel 6	701-232-9251	1202 36th St S Fargo ND
Red Roof Inn	701-282-9100	901 38th St SW Fargo ND

Minnesota (Interstate 94)

Alexandria Listings
Alexandria
Holiday Inn	320-763-6577	5637 State Hwy 29 S. Alexandria MN

St Cloud Listings
St Cloud
Comfort Inn	320-251-1500	4040 Second St. St Cloud MN
Holiday Inn Express	320-240-8000	4322 Clearwater Rd St Cloud MN
Motel 6	320-253-7070	815 1st St S St Cloud MN

Minneapolis - St Paul Listings
Brooklyn Center
Comfort Inn	763-560-7464	1600 James Circle N. Brooklyn Center MN
Motel 6	763-560-9789	2741 Freeway Blvd Brooklyn Center MN

Maple Grove
Staybridge Suites	763-494-8856	7821 Elm Creek Blvd Maple Grove MN

Minneapolis
Holiday Inn	612-333-4646	1500 Washington Ave S. Minneapolis MN

Wisconsin (Interstate 94)

Menomonie Listings
Menomonie
Motel 6	715-235-6901	2100 Stout St Menomonie WI

Eau Claire Listings

Eau Claire

Econo Lodge	715-833-8818	4608 Royal Dr. Eau Claire WI
Quality Inn	715-834-6611	809 W. Clairemont Ave. Eau Claire WI

Black River Falls Listings

Black River Falls

Best Western Arrowhead Lodge	715-284-9471	600 Oasis Rd Black River Falls WI

Tomah Listings

Tomah

Americinn	608-372-4100	750 Vandervort St Tomah WI
Cranberry Suites	608-374-2801	319 Wittig Rd Tomah WI
Econo Lodge	608-372-9100	2005 N Superior Ave Tomah WI
Lark Inn	608-372-5981	229 N Superior Ave Tomah WI

Madison Listings

Madison

Collins House Bed and Breakfast	608-255-4230	704 E Gorham St Madison WI
Comfort Suites	608-836-3033	1253 John Q Hammonds Dr Madison WI
Motel 6	608-241-8101	1754 Thierer Rd Madison WI
Red Roof Inn	608-241-1787	4830 Hayes Rd Madison WI
Residence Inn by Marriott	608-244-5047	4862 Hayes Rd Madison WI
Woodfield Suites	608-245-0123	5217 E Terrace Dr Madison WI

Watertown Listings

Watertown

Holiday Inn Express	920-262-1910	101 Aviation Way Watertown WI

Milwaukee Listings

Brookfield

Sheraton Milwaukee Brookfield Hotel	262-364-1100	375 S. Moorland Road Brookfield WI

Milwaukee

Motel 6	414-482-4414	5037 S Howell Ave Milwaukee WI

Illinois (Interstate 94)

Chicago Area Listings

Skokie

Howard Johnson Hotel	847-679-4200	9333 Skokie Blvd. Skokie IL

Michigan (Interstate 94)

Union Pier Listings

Union Pier

Blue Fish Vacation Rentals	269-469-0468	10234 Community Hall Rd. Union Pier MI

Benton Harbor Listings

Benton Harbor

Comfort Inn	616-925-1880	1598 Mall Dr. Benton Harbor MI

Kalamazoo Listings

Kalamazoo

Comfort Inn Airport	616-381-7000	3820 Sprinkle Rd Kalamazoo MI
Motel 6	616-344-9255	3704 Van Rick Rd Kalamazoo MI
Quality Inn & Suites	616-388-3551	3750 Easy St Kalamazoo MI

Battle Creek Listings

Battle Creek

Motel 6	616-979-1141	4775 Beckley Rd Battle Creek MI

Jackson Listings

Jackson		
Motel 6	517-789-7186	830 Royal Dr Jackson MI

Chelsea Listings

Chelsea		
Comfort Inn	734-433-8000	1645 Commerce Park Dr Chelsea MI

Detroit Area Listings

Belleville		
Comfort Inn	734-697-8556	45945 S. I-94 Service Drive Belleville MI

Port Huron Listings

Port Huron		
Knights Inn	810-982-1022	2160 Water St Port Huron MI

Interstate 95 Accommodation Listings

Maine (Interstate 95)

Bangor Listings

Bangor		
Best Western White House Inn	207-862-3737	155 Littlefield Avenue Bangor ME
Comfort Inn	207-942-7899	750 Hogan Rd Bangor ME
Motel 6	207-947-6921	1100 Hammond St Bangor ME
The Phenix Inn	207-947-0411	20 Broad Street Bangor ME
Orono		
Best Western Black Bear Inn	207-866-7120	4 Godfrey Dr Orono ME

Waterville Listings

Waterville		
Best Western Waterville Inn	207-873-3335	356 Main Street Waterville ME
Holiday Inn	207-873-0111	375 Main Street Waterville ME

Belfast Listings

Belfast		
Comfort Inn	207-338-2090	159 Searsport Ave Belfast ME

Augusta Listings

Augusta		
Augusta Hotel and Suites	207-622-6371	390 Western Avenue Augusta ME
Best Western Senator Inn & Spa	207-622-5804	284 Western Avenue Augusta ME
Comfort Inn Civic Center	207-623-1000	281 Civic Center Drive Augusta ME
Motel 6	207-622-0000	18 Edison Dr Augusta ME

Portland Listings

Portland		
Howard Johnson Plaza Hotel	207-774-5861	155 Riverside Portland ME
Motel 6	207-775-0111	1 Riverside St Portland ME
The Inn at St. John	207-773-6481	939 Congress Street Portland ME
South Portland		
Best Western Merry Manor Inn	207-774-6151	700 Main Street South Portland ME

South Portland Listings

South Portland		
Howard Johnson Hotel	207-775-5343	675 Main St. South Portland ME

New Hampshire (Interstate 95)

Portsmouth Listings

Portsmouth		
Motel 6	603-334-6606	3 Gosling Rd Portsmouth NH

Massachusetts (Interstate 95)

Boston Area Listings

Burlington

Staybridge Suites	781-221-2233	11 Old Concord Rd Burlington MA

Danvers

Motel 6	978-774-8045	65 Newbury St/US Rt 1 N Danvers MA
Residence Inn - North Shore	978-777-7171	51 Newbury St, Rt Danvers MA

Dedham

Residence Inn - Dedham	781-407-0999	259 Elm Street Dedham MA

Foxborough

Residence Inn - Foxborough	508-698-2800	250 Foxborough Blvd Foxborough MA

Lexington

Holiday Inn Express	781-861-0850	440 Bedford Street Lexington MA
Sheraton Lexington Inn	781-862-8700	727 Marrett Road Lexington MA

Mansfield

Red Roof Inn	508-339-2323	60 Forbes Blvd Mansfield MA

Wakefield

Sheraton Colonial Hotel and Golf Club Boston North	781-245-9300	One Audubon Road Wakefield MA

Waltham

Homestead Village	781-890-1333	52 Fourth Ave Waltham MA

Woburn

Radisson Hotel	781-935-8760	15 Middlesex Canal Park Rd Woburn MA

Rhode Island (Interstate 95)

Warwick Listings

Warwick

Crowne Plaza	401-732-6000	801 Greenwich Ave Warwick RI
Holiday Inn Express & Suites	401-736-5000	901 Jefferson Blvd Warwick RI
Sheraton Providence Airport Hotel	401-738-4000	1850 Post Road Warwick RI

Connecticut (Interstate 95)

New London Listings

New London

Red Roof Inn	860-444-0001	707 Coleman St New London CT

New Haven Listings

New Haven

Days Inn	203-469-0343	270 Foxon Blvd New Haven CT
Residence Inn by Marriott	203-777-5337	3 Long Wharf Dr New Haven CT

Milford Listings

Milford

Red Roof Inn	203-877-6060	10 Rowe Avenue Milford CT

Stamford Listings

Stamford

Sheraton Stamford Hotel	203-359-1300	2701 Summer Street Stamford CT

New Jersey (Interstate 95)

Northern New Jersey Listings

East Rutherford

Sheraton Meadowlands Hotel and Conference Center	201-896-0500	2 Meadowlands Plaza East Rutherford NJ

Edison

Red Roof Inn	732-248-9300	860 New Durham Rd Edison NJ
Sheraton Edison Hotel Raritan Center	732-225-8300	125 Raritan Center Parkway Edison NJ

Secaucus

Radisson Suite	201-863-8700	350 NJ 3 W Secaucus NJ

East Brunswick Listings
East Brunswick

Motel 6	732-390-4545	244 Rt 18 East Brunswick NJ

Trenton - Princeton Listings
Lawrenceville

Howard Johnson Inn	609-896-1100	2995 Rt. 1 South Lawrenceville NJ

Maple Shade Listings
Maple Shade

Motel 6	856-235-3550	Rt 73 North Maple Shade NJ

Mount Holly Listings
Mount Holly

Best Western Burlington Inn	609-261-3800	2020 Rt 541, RD 1 Mount Holly NJ

Cherry Hill Listings
Cherry Hill

Residence Inn by Marriott	856-429-6111	1821 Old Cuthbert Rd Cherry Hill NJ

Delaware (Interstate 95)

Wilmington Listings
Wilmington

Best Western Brandywine Valley Inn	302-656-9436	1807 Concord Pike Wilmington DE
Sheraton Suites Wilmington	302-654-8300	422 Delaware Avenue Wilmington DE

Wilmington Area Listings
New Castle

Motel 6	302-571-1200	1200 W Ave / S Hwy 9 New Castle DE

Newark

Best Western Delaware Inn	302-738-3400	260 Chapman Rd Newark DE
Comfort Inn	302-368-8715	1120 S. College Ave. Newark DE
Howard Johnson Inn	302-368-8521	1119 South College Avenue Newark DE
Residence Inn by Marriott	302-453-9200	240 Chapman Rd Newark DE
Sleep Inn	302-453-1700	630 S. College Ave Newark DE

Maryland (Interstate 95)

Elkton Listings
Elkton

Knights Inn	410-392-6680	262 Belle Hill Rd Elkton MD
Motel 6	410-392-5020	223 Belle Hill Rd Elkton MD

Aberdeen Listings
Aberdeen

Days Inn	410-272-8500	783 W. Bel Air Ave Aberdeen MD
Four Points Hotels by Sheraton	410-273-6300	980 Hospitality Way Aberdeen MD
Holiday Inn Chesapeake House	410-272-8100	1007 Beards Hill Rd Aberdeen MD
Red Roof Inn	410-273-7800	988 Hospitality Way Aberdeen MD

Baltimore Area Listings
Baltimore

Sheraton International Hotel on BWI Airport	410-859-3300	7032 Elm Road Baltimore MD

Hanover Listings
Hanover

Red Roof Inn	410-712-4070	7306 Parkway Dr South Hanover MD

Jessup Listings

Jessup
Red Roof Inn   410-796-0380   8000 Washington Blvd Jessup MD

Washington Suburbs Listings
Laurel
Comfort Suites Laurel Lakes   301-206-2600   14402 Laurel Pl. Laurel MD
Oxon Hill
Red Roof Inn - Oxon Hill   301-567-8030   6170 Oxon Hill Rd Oxon Hill MD

Virginia (Interstate 95)

Northern Virginia Listings
Alexandria
Holiday Inn - Telegraph Rd   703-960-3400   2460 Eisenhower Ave Alexandria VA
Springfield
Motel 6   703-644-5311   6868 Springfield Blvd Springfield VA

Fredericksburg Listings
Fredericksburg
Days Inn Fredericksburg North   540-373-5340   14 Simpson Rd Fredericksburg VA
Motel 6   540-371-5443   401 Warrenton Rd Fredericksburg VA
Quality Inn   · 540-373-0000   543 Warrenton Rd Fredericksburg VA
Ramada Inn   540-786-8361   2802 Plank Rd Fredericksburg VA

Ruther Glen Listings
Ruther Glen
Howard Johnson Express Inn   804-448-2499   23786 Rogers Clark Blvd. Ruther Glen VA

Richmond Listings
Richmond
Days Inn   804-282-3300   2100 Dickens Rd Richmond VA
Holiday Inn   804-275-7891   4303 Commerce Rd Richmond VA
Residence Inn by Marriott   804-285-8200   2121 Dickens Rd Richmond VA

Petersburg Listings
Petersburg
Comfort Inn   804-732-2900   11974 S Crater St Petersburg VA
Days Inn   804-733-4400   12208 S Crater Rd Petersburg VA

Emporia Listings
Emporia
Best Western Emporia   434-634-3200   1100 W Atlantic St Emporia VA
Comfort Inn   434-348-3282   1411 Skippers Rd Emporia VA
Hampton Inn   434-634-9481   1207 W Atlantic St Emporia VA
Holiday Inn   434-634-4191   · 311 Florida Ave Emporia VA

North Carolina (Interstate 95)

Roanoke Rapids Listings
Roanoke Rapids
Motel 6   252-537-5252   1911 Julian R. Allsbrook Hwy Roanoke Rapids NC

Rocky Mount Listings
Battleboro
Howard Johnson Inn   252-977-9595   7568 NC 48 Battleboro NC
Rocky Mount
Residence Inn   252-451-5600   230 Gateway Blvd Rocky Mount NC

Smithfield Listings
Smithfield
Super 8 Motel   919-989-8988   735 Industrial Park Rd. Smithfield NC

Dunn Listings
Dunn

| Best Western Midway Inn | 910-892-2162 | 603 Spring Branch Rd Dunn NC |

Fayetteville Listings
Fayetteville

Best Western Fayetteville - Ft Bragg	910-485-0520	2910 Sigman Street Fayetteville NC
Holiday Inn	910-323-0111	1707 Owen Drive Fayetteville NC
Red Roof Inn	910-321-1460	1569 Jim Johnson Rd Fayetteville NC

Lumberton Listings
Lumberton

Best Western	910-618-9799	201 Jackson Court Lumberton NC
Motel 6	910-738-2410	2361 Lackey Rd Lumberton NC
Quality Inn & Suites	910-738-8261	3608 Kahn Dr. Lumberton NC
Super 8	910-671-4444	150 Jackson Court Lumberton NC

South Carolina (Interstate 95)

Dillon Listings
Dillon

| Best Value Inn | 843-774-5111 | 904 Redford Blvd Dillon SC |

Florence Listings
Florence

Econo Lodge	843-665-8558	1811 W Lucas St Florence SC
Holiday Inn Express	843-664-2400	1819 W. Lucas Street Florence SC
Motel 6	843-667-6100	1834 W Lucas Street Florence SC
Ramada Inn	843-669-4241	2038 W Lucas St Florence SC
Red Roof Inn	843-678-9000	2690 David McLeod Blvd Florence SC
Thunderbird Motor Inn	843-669-1611	2004 W Lucas St Florence SC
Young's Plantation Inn	843-669-4171	US 76 and I-95 Florence SC

Manning Listings
Manning

| Super 8 | 803-473-4646 | Rte 6 (exit Hwy 261) Manning SC |

Santee Listings
Santee

| Howard Johnson Express Inn | 803-478-7676 | I-95 Ex 102, Rd 400 Santee SC |

St George Listings
St George

Best Western St George	843-563-2277	I95 & Hwy 78 St George SC
Quality Inn	843-563-4581	I-95 & US 78 St George SC
Super 8	843-563-5551	114 Winningham Rd St George SC

Walterboro Listings
Walterboro

| Econo Lodge | 843-538-3830 | 1145 Sniders Hwy Walterboro SC |
| Rice Planters Inn | 843-538-8964 | I-95 and SR 63 Walterboro SC |

Yemassee Listings
Yemassee

| Holiday Inn Express | 843-726-9400 | 40 Frampton Drive Yemassee SC |

Georgia (Interstate 95)

Savannah Listings
Pooler

| Econo Lodge | 912-748-4124 | 500 E. US 80 Pooler GA |

Savannah

Holiday Inn	912-925-2770	I-95 & GA 204 Savannah GA
La Quinta Inn Savannah I-95	912-925-9505	6 Gateway Boulevard South Savannah GA
Motel 6	912-756-3543	4071 Highway 17 Savannah GA
Red Roof Inn	912-920-3535	405 Al Henderson Blvd Savannah GA

Sleep Inn	912-921-1010	17013 Abercorn St Savannah GA
Super 8 Motel - Savannah I-95	912-927-8550	15 Ft. Argyle Rd. Savannah GA

Darien Listings
Darien
Comfort Inn	912-437-4200	703 Frontage Rd Darien GA
Super 8	912-437-6660	Hwy 251 and I-95 Darien GA

Brunswick Listings
Brunswick
Best Western Brunswick Inn	912-264-0144	5323 New Jesup Highway Brunswick GA
Embassy Suites	912-264-6100	500 Mall Blvd. Brunswick GA
Holiday Inn	912-264-4033	5252 New Jesup Hwy Brunswick GA

Jekyll Island Listings
Jekyll Island
Clarion Resort Buccaneer	912-635-2261	85 S. Beachview Dr. Jekyll Island GA

Kingsland Listings
Kingsland
Super 8	912-729-6888	120 Edenfield Dr Kingsland GA

St Marys Listings
Kingsland
Best Western Kings Bay	912-729-7666	1353 Hwy 40 East Kingsland GA

Florida (Interstate 95)

Yulee Listings
Yulee
Comfort Inn	904-225-2600	126 Sidney Place Yulee FL

Jacksonville Listings
Jacksonville
Amerisuites-Baymeadows	904-737-4477	8277 Western Way Circle Jacksonville FL
Hampton Inn	904-741-4980	1170 Airport Entrance Road Jacksonville FL
Holiday Inn	904-737-1700	9150 Baymeadows Rd Jacksonville FL
Holiday Inn - Airport North	904-741-4404	I-95 & Airport Rd Jacksonville FL
Homewood Suites	904-733-9299	8737 Baymeadows Rd Jacksonville FL
La Quinta Inn & Suites Jacksonville Butler Blvd	904-296-0703	4686 Lenoir Avenue South Jacksonville FL
La Quinta Inn Jacksonville Airport North	904-751-6960	812 Dunn Avenue Jacksonville FL
La Quinta Inn Jacksonville Baymeadows	904-731-9940	8255 Dix Ellis Trail Jacksonville FL
Red Roof Inn	904-777-1000	6099 Youngerman Circle Jacksonville FL
Red Roof Inn	904-741-4488	14701 Airport Entrance Rd Jacksonville FL
Red Roof Inn - Southpoint	904-296-1006	6969 Lenoir Avenue E Jacksonville FL
Residence Inn	904-733-8088	8365 Dix Ellis Tr Jacksonville FL
Residence Inn	904-741-6550	1310 Airport Rd Jacksonville FL
Studio 6	904-731-7317	8765 Baymeadows Rd Jacksonville FL

St Augustine Listings
St Augustine
Days Inn Historic	904-829-6581	2800 N Ponce de Leon Blvd St Augustine FL
Howard Johnson Express Inn	904-824-6181	137 San Marco Ave. St Augustine FL
La Quinta Inn St Augustine	904-824-3383	1300 N Ponce De Leon Blvd St Augustine FL
Ramada Inn Historic	904-824-4352	116 San Marco St Augustine FL
Ramada Ltd	904-829-5643	2535 SR 16 St Augustine FL

St Augustine Beach
Holiday Inn	904-471-2555	860 A1A Beach Blvd St Augustine Beach FL

Daytona Beach Listings
Daytona Beach
Days Inn Speedway	386-255-0541	2900 W International Speedway Blvd Daytona Beach FL

Super 8	386-253-0643	2992 W International Speedway Blvd Daytona Beach FL
Daytona Beach Shores		
Quality Inn Ocean Palms	386-255-0476	2323 S. Atlantic Ave. Daytona Beach Shores FL
Ormond Beach		
Super 8	386-672-6222	1634 N. US Hwy 1 & I-95 Ormond Beach FL

Space Coast Listings

Cocoa		
Best Western Cocoa Inn	321-632-1065	4225 West King Street Cocoa FL
Melbourne		
Baymont Inn	321-242-9400	7200 George T. Edwards Drive Melbourne FL
Quality Suites Oceanside	321-723-4222	1665 SR A1A N. Melbourne FL
Palm Bay		
Motel 6	321-951-8222	1170 Malabar Rd, SE Palm Bay FL
Titusville		
Days Inn-Kennedy Space Center	321-269-4480	3755 Cheney Highway Titusville FL
West Melbourne		
Howard Johnson Inn	321-768-8439	4431 West New Haven Ave. West Melbourne FL

South Florida Listings

Boca Raton		
Residence Inn by Marriott	561-994-3222	525 NW 77th Street Boca Raton FL
Dania		
Sheraton Fort Lauderdale Airport Hotel	954-920-3500	1825 Griffin Road Dania FL
Fort Lauderdale		
Motel 6	954-760-7999	1801 SR 84 Fort Lauderdale FL
Red Roof Inn	954-776-6333	4800 Powerline Rd Fort Lauderdale FL
Sheraton Suites Cypress Creek Ft. Lauderdale	954-772-5400	555 N.W. 62nd Street Fort Lauderdale FL
Fort Pierce		
Days Inn	561-466-4066	6651 Darter Court Fort Pierce FL
Holiday Inn Express	561-464-5000	7151 Okeechobee Rd. Fort Pierce FL
Hollywood		
Days Inn	954-923-7300	2601 N. 29th Avenue Hollywood FL
West Palm Beach		
Studio 6	561-640-3335	1535 Centrepark Dr, North West Palm Beach FL

Miami Listings

Miami Springs		
Mainstay Suites	305-870-0448	101 Fairway Dr Miami Springs FL

Highway 101 Accommodation Listings

Washington (Highway 101)

Olympia Listings

Olympia		
West Coast Inn	360-943-4000	2300 Evergreen Park Drive Olympia WA
Tumwater		
Best Western Tumwater Inn	360-956-1235	5188 Capitol Blvd Tumwater WA
Motel 6	360-754-7320	400 W Lee St Tumwater WA

Forks Listings

Forks		
Kalaloch Ocean Lodge	360-962-2271	157151 Hwy. 101 Forks WA

Aberdeen Listings

Aberdeen		
Red Lion Inn	360-532-5210	521 W Wishkah Aberdeen WA

Oregon (Highway 101)

Astoria Listings
Astoria
Red Lion Inn	503-325-7373	400 Industry St Astoria OR

Seaside Listings
Seaside
Best Western Ocean View Resort	503-738-3334	414 N. Prom Seaside OR
Comfort Inn	503-738-3011	545 Broadway Ave. Seaside OR
Motel 6	503-738-6269	2369 S Roosevelt (Hwy 101) Seaside OR
Seaside Convention Center Inn	503-738-9581	441 Second Ave Seaside OR

Cannon Beach Listings
Cannon Beach
Best Western Cannon Beach	503-436-9085	3215 S. Hemlock Cannon Beach OR
Surfsand Resort	503-436-2274	148 W. Gower Cannon Beach OR
The Haystack Resort	503-436-1577	3361 S. Hemlock Cannon Beach OR

Lincoln City Listings
Lincoln City
Ester Lee Motel	541 996 3606	3803 S.W. HWY. 101 Lincoln City OR
Looking Glass Inn	541-996-3996	861 SW 51st Street Lincoln City OR

Newport Listings
Newport
Best Western	541-265-9411	3019 North Coast Hwy Newport OR
Hallmark Resort	541-265-2600	744 SW Elizabeth St Newport OR
La Quinta Inn & Suites Newport	541-867-7727	45 SE 32nd Newport OR
Shilo Oceanfront Resort	541-265-7701	536 SW Elizabeth St Newport OR

Yachats Listings
Yachats
Adobe Resort	541-547-3141	1555 US 101 Yachats OR
Shamrock Lodgettes	541-547-3312	US 101 Yachats OR
The Fireside Inn	800-336-3573	Hwy 101 Yachats OR

Reedsport Listings
Reedsport
Economy Inn	541-271-3671	1593 Highway Ave 101 Reedsport OR

Coos Bay Listings
Coos Bay
Motel 6	541-267-7171	1445 Bayshore Dr Coos Bay OR

Bandon Listings
Bandon
Best Western Inn at Face Rock	541-347-9441	3225 Beach Loop Rd Bandon OR
Driftwood Motel	541-347-9022	460 Hwy 101 Bandon OR
Sunset Motel	541-347-2453	1755 Beach Loop Rd Bandon OR

Harbor Listings
Harbor
Best Western Beachfront Inn	541-469-7779	16008 Boat Basin Rd Harbor OR

California (Highway 101)

Crescent City Listings
Crescent City
Gardenia Motel	707-464-2181	119 L Street Crescent City CA
Super 8	707-464-4111	685 Hwy 101 S. Crescent City CA
Town House Motel	707-464-4176	444 US Highway 101 South Crescent City CA

Arcata Listings

Highway Guides - Please always call ahead to make sure an establishment is still dog-friendly.

Arcata

Best Western Arcata Inn	707-826-0313	4827 Valley West Boulevard Arcata CA
Hotel Arcata	707-826-0217	708 Ninth Street Arcata CA
Quality Inn	707-822-0409	3535 Janes Rd Arcata CA
Super 8	707-822-8888	4887 Valley W. Blvd Arcata CA

Eureka Listings

Eureka

Best Western Bayshore Inn	707-268-8005	3500 Broadway Eureka CA
Discovery Inn	707-441-8442	2832 Broadway Eureka CA
Motel 6	707-445-9631	1934 Broadway Eureka CA
Quality Inn	707-443-1601	1209 Fourth Street Eureka CA
Ramada Inn	707-443-2206	270 5th Street Eureka CA
Red Lion Hotel	707-445-0844	1929 Fourth Street Eureka CA
The Eureka Inn	707-442-6441	518 Seventh Street Eureka CA

Fortuna

Super 8	707-725-2888	1805 Alamar Way Fortuna CA

Fortuna Listings

Fortuna

Best Western Country Inn	707-725-6822	2025 Riverwalk Drive Fortuna CA

Miranda Listings

Miranda

Miranda Gardens Resort	707-943-3011	6766 Avenue of the Giants Miranda CA

Ukiah Listings

Ukiah

Days Inn	707-462-7584	950 North State St Ukiah CA
Motel 6	707-468-5404	1208 S State Street Ukiah CA

Marin - North Bay Listings

Healdsburg

Best Western Dry Creek Inn	707-433-0300	198 Dry Creek Road Healdsburg CA
Duchamp Hotel	707-431-1300	421 Foss Street Healdsburg CA

Novato

Inn Marin	415-883-5952	250 Entrada Drive Novato CA
Travelodge	415-892-7500	7600 Redwood Blvd Novato CA

Rohnert Park

Motel 6	707-585-8888	6145 Commerce Blvd Rohnert Park CA

Santa Rosa

Comfort Inn	707-542-5544	2632 Cleveland Ave Santa Rosa CA
Days Inn	707-568-1011	3345 Santa Rosa Ave Santa Rosa CA
Hilton Sonoma County	707-523-7555	3555 Round Barn Blvd Santa Rosa CA
Los Robles Lodge	707-545-6330	1985 Cleveland Ave Santa Rosa CA
Motel 6 - North	707-525-9010	3145 Cleveland Ave Santa Rosa CA
Motel 6 - South	707-546-1500	2760 Cleveland Ave Santa Rosa CA
Santa Rosa Motor Inn	707-523-3480	1800 Santa Rosa Ave Santa Rosa CA

Guerneville

Russian River Getaways	707-869-4560	14075 Mill Street, P.O. Box 1673 Guerneville CA

San Francisco Listings

San Francisco

Best Western Tuscan Inn	415-561-1100	425 Northpoint Street San Francisco CA
Campton Place Hotel	415-781-5555	340 Stockton Street San Francisco CA
Days Inn - Lombard St	415-922-2010	2358 Lombard Street San Francisco CA
Harbor Court Hotel	415-882-1300	165 Steuart Street San Francisco CA
Hotel Cosmo	415-673-6040	761 Post Street San Francisco CA
Hotel Juliana	415-392-2540	590 Bush Street San Francisco CA
Hotel Palomar	415-348-1111	12 Fourth Street San Francisco CA
Hotel Triton	415-394-0500	342 Grant Avenue San Francisco CA
Marina Motel - on Lombard Street	415-921-9406	2576 Lombard St. San Francisco CA
Monticello Inn	415-392-8800	127 Ellis Street San Francisco CA
Palace Hotel	415-512-1111	2 New Montgomery Street San Francisco CA

Prescott Hotel	415-563-0303	545 Post Street San Francisco CA
Residence Inn	650-837-9000	Oyster Point Blvd & 101 San Francisco CA
Serrano Hotel	415-885-2500	405 Taylor Street San Francisco CA
The Laurel Inn	415-567-8467	444 Presidio Ave. San Francisco CA
W San Francisco	415-777-5300	181 Third Street San Francisco CA

Palo Alto - Peninsula Listings

Belmont
Motel 6	650-591-1471	1101 Shoreway Rd. Belmont CA

Burlingame
Embassy Suites	650-342-4600	150 Anza Blvd. Burlingame CA
Vagabond Inn	650-692-4040	1640 Bayshore Highway Burlingame CA

Millbrae
Clarion Hotel	650-692-6363	250 El Camino Real Millbrae CA

Mountain View
Residence Inn by Marriott	650-940-1300	1854 W El Camino Real Mountain View CA
Tropicana Lodge	650-961-0220	1720 El Camino Real Mountain View CA

Palo Alto
Sheraton Palo Alto Hotel	650-328-2800	625 El Camino Real Palo Alto CA

Redwood City
Hotel Sofitel	650-598-9000	223 Twin Dolphin Dr Redwood City CA

San Carlos
Inns of America	650-631-0777	555 Skyway Road San Carlos CA

South San Francisco
Howard Johnson Express Inn	650-589-9055	222 South Airport Blvd. South San Francisco CA
La Quinta Inn South San Francisco	650-583-2223	20 Airport Blvd South San Francisco CA
Motel 6	650-871-0770	111 Mitchell Ave. South San Francisco CA
Vagabond Inn	650-589-9055	222 S. Airport Blvd South San Francisco CA

San Jose Listings

San Jose
Doubletree Hotel	408-453-4000	2050 Gateway Pl San Jose CA
Hilton San Jose	408-287-2100	300 Almaden Blvd San Jose CA
Motel 6 - South	408-270-3131	2560 Fontaine Rd San Jose CA

Santa Clara
Marriott Hotel	408-988-1500	2700 Mission College Blvd Santa Clara CA

Sunnyvale
Residence Inn - SV I	408-720-1000	750 Lakeway Sunnyvale CA
Residence Inn - SV II	408-720-8893	1080 Stewart Dr Sunnyvale CA
Summerfield Suites	408-745-1515	900 Hamlin Court Sunnyvale CA
Woodfin Suite Hotel	408-738-1700	635 E. El Camino Real Sunnyvale CA

San Luis Obispo Listings

Arroyo Grande
Best Western Casa Grande Inn	805-481-7398	850 Oak Park Road Arroyo Grande CA

Atascadero
Motel 6	805-466-6701	9400 El Camino Real Atascadero CA

Pismo Beach
Motel 6	805-773-2665	860 4th St Pismo Beach CA
Oxford Suites	805-773-3773	651 Five Cities Drive Pismo Beach CA
Sandcastle Inn	805-773-2422	100 Stimson Avenue Pismo Beach CA
Sea Gypsy Motel	805-773-1801	1020 Cypress Street Pismo Beach CA

San Luis Obispo
Best Western Royal Oak	805-544-4410	214 Madonna Rd. San Luis Obispo CA
Motel 6 - South	805-541-6992	1625 Calle Joaquin San Luis Obispo CA
Sands Suites & Motel	805-544-0500	1930 Monterey Street San Luis Obispo CA
Vagabond Inn	805-544-4710	210 Madonna Rd. San Luis Obispo CA

Santa Maria Listings

Santa Maria
Best Western Big America	805-922-5200	1725 North Broadway Santa Maria CA
Motel 6	805-928-8111	2040 N Preisker Lane Santa Maria CA

Solvang Listings

Buellton

Motel 6	805-688-7797	333 McMurray Rd Buellton CA
Rodeway Inn	805-688-0022	630 Ave of Flags Buellton CA

Solvang

Royal Copenhagen Inn	800-624-6604	1579 Mission Drive Solvang CA

Santa Barbara Listings

Carpinteria

Motel 6	805-684-6921	4200 Via Real Carpinteria CA
Motel 6 - South	805-684-8602	5550 Carpinteria Ave Carpinteria CA

Santa Barbara

Casa Del Mar Hotel	805-963-4418	18 Bath Street Santa Barbara CA
Fess Parker's Doubletree Resort	805-564-4333	633 E. Cabrillo Boulevard Santa Barbara CA
Montecito Del Mar	805-962-2006	316 W Montecito St Santa Barbara CA
San Ysidro Ranch	805-969-5046	900 San Ysidro Lane Santa Barbara CA
Secret Garden Inn & Cottages	805-687-2300	1908 Bath Street Santa Barbara CA

Ventura - Oxnard Listings

Oxnard

Casa Sirena Hotel and Resort	805-985-6311	3605 Peninsula Rd Oxnard CA
Radisson Hotel Oxnard	805-485-9666	600 E. Esplanade Drive Oxnard CA
Residence Inn by Marriott	805-278-2200	2101 West Vineyard Avenue Oxnard CA
Vagabond Inn	805-983-0251	1245 N. Oxnard Blvd. Oxnard CA

Ventura

Best Western Inn of Ventura	805-648-3101	708 E. Thompson Blvd. Ventura CA
La Quinta Inn Ventura	805-658-6200	5818 Valentine Road Ventura CA
Motel 6	805-643-5100	2145 E Harbor Blvd Ventura CA
Vagabond Inn	805-648-5371	756 E. Thompson Blvd. Ventura CA

San Fernando Valley Listings

Thousand Oaks

Motel 6	805-499-0711	1516 Newbury Rd Thousand Oaks CA
Thousand Oaks Inn	805-497-3701	75 W. Thousand Oaks Blvd. Thousand Oaks CA

Woodland Hills

Vagabond Inn	818-347-8080	20157 Ventura Blvd. Woodland Hills CA

Canadian Highway 1 and 5 (West) and Highway 17 (East) Accommodation Listings

British Columbia (Trans-Canada)

Vancouver Listings

Coquitlam

Holiday Inn	604-931-4433	631 Lougheed Highway Coquitlam BC

Pitt Meadows

Ramada Inn	604-460-9859	19267 Lougheed Hwy Pitt Meadows BC

Surrey Listings

Surrey

Ramada Hotel & Suites	604-930-4700	10410 158th St Surrey BC
Ramada Limited	604-576-8388	19225 Hwy 10 Surrey BC

Abbotsford Listings

Abbotsford

Holiday Inn Express	604-859-6211	2073 Clearbrook Rd Abbotsford BC
Ramada Inn	604-870-1050	36035 N Parallel Rd Abbotsford BC

Chilliwack Listings

Chilliwack

Highway Guides - Please always call ahead to make sure an establishment is still dog-friendly.

Best Western Rainbow Country Inn	604-795-3828	43971 Industrial Way Chilliwack BC
Comfort Inn	604-858-0636	45405 Luckakuck Way Chilliwack BC

Hope Listings
Hope
Quality Inn	604-869-9951	350 Old Hope Princton Way Hope BC

Kamloops Listings
Kamloops
Coast Canadian Inn	250-372-5201	339 St. Paul Street Kamloops BC
Days Inn	250-374-5911	1285 W Trans Canada Hwy Kamloops BC
Howard Johnson Inn	250-374-1515	610 West Columbia Street Kamloops BC
Ramada Inn	250-374-0358	555 West Columbia St Kamloops BC

Salmon Arm Listings
Salmon Arm
Best Western Villager West	250-832-9793	61-10th St SW Salmon Arm BC

Sicamous Listings
Sicamous
Sundog Bed and Breakfast	250-833-9005	1409 Rauma Ave Sicamous BC

Revelstoke Listings
Revelstoke
Best Western Wayside Inn	250-837-6161	1901 Laforme Blvd Revelstoke BC

Alberta (Trans-Canada)

Banff Listings
Banff
Best Western Siding 29 Lodge	403-762-5575	453 Marten Street Banff AB
Driftwood Inn	403-762-4496	337 Banff Avenue Banff AB

Calgary Listings
Calgary
Coast Plaza Hotel at Calgary	403-248-8888	1316 - 33rd Street N.E. Calgary AB
Days Inn Calgary West	403-289-1961	1818 16th Ave NW Calgary AB
Holiday Inn - Airport	403-230-1999	1250 McKinnon Dr, NE Calgary AB
Holiday Inn - Macleod Trail South	403-287-2700	4206 Macleod Trail S. Calgary AB
Howard Johnson Express Inn	403-258-1064	5307 Macleod Trail South Calgary AB
Quality Inn Motel Village	403-289-1973	2359 Banif Tr NW Calgary AB
Ramada Limited	403-289-5571	2363 Banff Trail NW Calgary AB
Sheraton Suites Calgary Eau Claire	403-266-7200	255 Barclay Parade S.W. Calgary AB
Super 8	403-291-9888	3030 Barlow Trail NE Calgary AB
Super 8	403-289-9211	1904 Crowchild Trail NW Calgary AB
Super 8	403-254-8878	60 Shawville SE Rd Calgary AB

Medicine Hat Listings
Medicine Hat
Super 8	403-528-8888	1280 Trans-Canada Way Medicine Hat AB

Saskatchewan (Trans-Canada)

Caronport Listings
Caronport
The Pilgrim Inn	306-756-5002	510 College Dr (Hwy 1 W) Caronport SK

Regina Listings
Regina
Best Western Victoria Park	306-565-2251	2020 E Victoria Ave Regina SK
Ramada Hotel & Conv. Ctr	306-569-1666	1818 Victoria Ave Regina SK

Manitoba (Trans-Canada)

Brandon Listings
Brandon
Victoria Inn	204-725-1532	3550 Victoria Ave Brandon MB

Portage La Prairie Listings
Portage La Prairie
Days Inn	204-857-9791	Highway 1 & Yellowquill Trail Portage La Pairie MB
Super 8	204-857-8883	Hwy 1A W Portage La Praire MB

Winnipeg Listings
Winnipeg
Place Louis Riel All-Suite Hotel	204-947-6961	190 Smith St Winnipeg MB

Ontario (Trans-Canada)

Kenora Listings
Kenora
Days Inn	807-468-2003	920 Hwy 17 E Kenora ON

Thunder Bay Listings
Thunder Bay
Best Western Crossroads Motor Inn	807-577-4241	655 W. Arthur Street Thunder Bay ON

Sault Ste Marie Listings
Sault Ste Marie
Holiday Inn	705-949-0611	208 St Marys River Dr Sault Ste Marie ON

Sudbury Listings
Sudbury
Comfort Inn	705-522-1101	2171 Regent St. S. Sudbury ON

North Bay Listings
North Bay
Best Western North Bay	705-474-5800	700 Lakeshore Drive North Bay ON
Clarion Resort Pinewood Park	705-472-0810	201 Pinewood Park Drive North Bay ON
Comfort Inn	705-494-9444	676 Lakeshore Dr. North Bay ON

Arnprior Listings
Arnprior
Quality Inn	613-623-7991	70 Madawask Blvd Arnprior ON

Ottawa Listings
Ottawa
Comfort Inn East	613-744-2900	1252 Michael St Ottawa ON
Delta Ottawa Hotel and Suites	613-238-6000	361 Queen Street Ottawa ON
Les Suites Hotel	613-232-2000	130 Besserer St Ottawa ON
Novotel Ottawa Hotel	613-230-3033	33 Nicholas Street Ottawa ON
Ottawa Marriott Hotel	613-238-1122	100 Kent Street Ottawa ON
Quality Hotel Downtown	613-789-7511	290 Rideau St Ottawa ON
Radisson Hotel	613-236-1133	402 Queen Street Ottawa ON
Ramada Hotel and Suites	613-238-1331	111 Cooper Street Ottawa ON
Sheraton Ottawa Hotel	613-238-1500	150 Albert Street Ottawa ON
Southway Inn	613-737-0811	2431 Bank Street Ottawa ON

Canadian Highway 16
Accommodation Listings

Alberta (Canada Highway 16)

Hinton Listings

Hinton

Super 8	780-817-2228	284 Smith St Hinton AB

Edmonton Listings

Edmonton

Coast Edmonton Hotel	780-423-4811	10155-105th Street Edmonton AB
Comfort Inn West	780-484-4415	17610 100th Ave Edmonton AB
Holiday Inn	780-438-1222	4235 Calgary Trail N. Edmonton AB
Holiday Inn Express & Suites	780-483-4000	10017-179 A Street Edmonton AB
Ramada Hotel and Conf. Ctr	780-454-5454	11834 Kingsway Ave Edmonton AB
Sheraton Grande Edmonton Hotel	780-428-7111	10235 101 Street Edmonton AB
Super 8	780-433-8688	3610 Calgary Trail Norhtbound NW Edmonton AB

Nisku

Days Inn - Airport	780-955-7744	1101 4th Street Nisku AB

Saskatchewan (Canada Highway 16)

Saskatoon Listings

Saskatoon

Country Inn & Suites by Carlson	306-934-3900	617 Cynthia St Saskatoon SK
Holiday Inn Express	306-384-8844	315 Idylwyld Dr N Saskatoon SK
Radisson Hotel	306-665-3322	405 20th St E Saskatoon SK
Ramada Hotel and Golf Dome	306-665-6500	806 Idylwyld Dr North Saskatoon SK
Sheraton Cavalier Hotel	306-652-6770	612 Spadina Crescent Saskatoon SK
Super 8	306-384-8989	706 Circle Dr E Saskatoon SK

Canadian Highway 401 (Ontario) and Highway 20 (Quebec) Accommodation Listings

Ontario (Highways 401 and 20)

Windsor Listings

Windsor

Comfort Inn	519-966-7800	2955 Dougall Windsor ON
Holiday Inn Select	519-966-1200	1855 Huron Church Rd Windsor ON
Quality Suites Downtown	519-977-9707	250 Dougall Ave Windsor ON

Chatham Listings

Chatham

Comfort Inn	519-352-5500	1100 Richmond St Chatham ON

London Listings

London

Quality Suites	519-680-1024	1120 Dearness Drive London ON

Cambridge Listings

Cambridge

Comfort Inn	519-658-1100	220 Holiday Inn Drive Cambridge ON

Toronto Listings

Toronto

Comfort Inn Downsview	416-736-4700	66 Norfinch dr Toronto ON
Crowne Plaza	416-449-4111	1250 Eglinton Ave East Toronto ON
Quality Hotel Downtown	416-367-5555	111 Lombard St Toronto ON

Pickering Listings

Pickering

Highway Guides - Please always call ahead to make sure an establishment is still dog-friendly.

Comfort Inn	905-831-6200	533 Kingston Rd Pickering ON

Oshawa Listings
Oshawa

Comfort Inn	905-434-5000	605 Bloor Street West Oshawa ON
Holiday Inn	905-576-5101	1011 Bloor St E. Oshawa ON

Cobourg Listings
Cobourg

Comfort Inn	905-372-7007	121 Densmore rd Cobourg ON

Trenton Listings
Trenton

Days Inn	613-392-9291	10 Trenton St Trenton ON
Holiday Inn	613-394-4855	99 Glen Miller Rd Trenton ON

Kingston Listings
Kingston

Comfort Inn Highway 401	613-546-9500	55 Warne Cres Kingston ON
Comfort Inn Midtown	613-549-5550	1454 Princess St Kingston ON
Howard Johnson Hotel	613-549-6300	237 Ontario Street Kingston ON

Cornwall Listings
Cornwall

Best Western Parkway Inn & Conf Centre	613-932-0451	1515 Vincent Massey Dr Cornwall ON
Holiday Inn Express	613-937-0111	1625 Vincent Massey Drive Cornwall ON

Quebec (Highways 401 and 20)

Drummondville Listings
Drummondville

Comfort Inn	819-477-4000	1055 rue Hains Drummondville PQ

Chapter 5

Other Dog-Friendly Attractions

For many more attractions see Chapter 1.

See many other Dog-Friendly Attractions in our City Guide Listings in Chapter 1.

Alabama Listings

Decatur

Civil War Self-Guided Walking Tour
Church Street
Decatur, AL
256-350-2028
Located just minutes from downtown Atlanta off I-65, the city of Decatur offers a self-guided walking tour in the Old Decatur Historic District. The tour is called the Civil War Walking Tour and it traces the clash in 1864 between the Southern and Union forces. This 13 block tour offers large markers and plaques that describe important events of the four day battle and the overall history of the community. To get there, head on I-65 north and take exit 340. Go west on Highway 20/Alt. Highway 72 approximately 1 mile to the junction of Highway 31. Continue south on Highway 31 about 1 mile to Church Street. Turn right (west) on Church Street and go about five blocks to the Old State Bank Building. The first markers for the tour begin at this point. Free maps of the area can be obtained at the Old State Bank Building or at Decatur's Convention and Visitor's Bureau.

Arizona Listings

Page

Lake Powell - Glen Canyon Recreation Area

Page, AZ
435-684-7400
Beautiful Lake Powell is called America's Natural Playground and is home to the world's largest natural bridge (standing 290 feet high), the Rainbow Bridge National Monument. The Wahweap Lodge, located in Page, rents powerboats for sight-seeing on the lake. Rent and drive your own boat, and your dog is welcome to join you. If you rent a boat, there is a one half mile trail to the Rainbow Bridge from the Rainbow Bridge courtesy dock. Also at Lake Powell near Bullfrog, there is a 3 mile round-trip hiking trail called Pedestal Alley. For boat rentals, the Wahweap Lodge is located 2.5 miles SE of US 89 at Lake Powell. The best time to visit the lake is during the fall season when temperatures are mild.

Petrified Forest National Park

Petrified Forest National Park
Entrances on Hwy 40 and Hwy 180
Petrified Forest National Park, AZ
928-524-6228
The Petrified Forest is located in northeastern Arizona and features one of the world's largest and most colorful concentrations of petrified wood. Also included in the park's 93,533 acres are the multi-hued badlands of the Painted Desert, archeological sites and displays of 225 million year old fossils. Your leashed dog is welcome on all of the paved trails and scenic overlooks. Take a walk on the self-guided Giant Logs trail or view ancient petroglyphs from an overlook. The entrance fee is $10 per private vehicle.

Sedona

Red Rock Country - Coconino National Forest
various
Sedona, AZ
928-527-3600
This park offers a colorful collection of buttes, pinnacles, mesas, canyons and red rock vistas. Over the years, this area has served as the setting of many western novels and movies and has been the subject of uncounted paintings, photographs and other works of art. Your leashed dog is allowed on the scenic Red Rock Country hiking trails with you

Williams

Historic Route 66 Driving Tour
Bill Williams Avenue
Williams, AZ

Route 66 was the main route between Los Angeles and Chicago during the 1920's through the 1960's. It was completely paved in 1938. This historic route symbolizes the American adventure and romance of the open road. Begin your self-guided driving tour on Bill Williams Avenue in Williams. This portion of Route 66 is considered "America's Main Street," where you will find gas stations, restaurants, shops and motels that have served travelers since the 1920's. Then head east on Old 66 to the I-40 interchange. Continue east on I-40 for 6 miles. Take the Pittman Valley exit and left left, pass over I-40, and turn right onto historic Route 66. This portion of the road was originally paved in 1939. Stop and park at the Oak Hill Snowplay Area. You and your pooch can take a 2 mile round trip hike to the Keyhole Sink petroglyphs. After your walk, continue driving and you will come to a community called Parks. Located here is a country store that has been in operation since about 1910. At this point you can turn around and head back to Williams via I-40. Directions and descriptions are from the USDA Forest Service in Williams, Arizona.

Winslow

Homolovi Ruins State Park
State Route 87
Winslow, AZ
928-289-4106
This site is Arizona's first archaeological state park. Homolovi, a Hopi word meaning 'place of the little hills,' consists of four major pueblo sites thought to have been occupied between A.D. 1200 and 1425 by ancestors of today's Hopi Indians. Homolovi sites I and II are accessible to visitors. Your leashed dog is welcome to view the sites with you. Just stay on the trail because there are rattlesnakes in the area. The park is located five miles northeast of Winslow on State Route 87. Tale I-40 to Exit 257, then go 1.3 miles north on Highway 87.

California Listings

Bishop

Bristlecone Pine Forest
White Mountain Rd
Bishop, CA
760-873-2500
This forest, located in the Inyo National Forest, is home to the world's oldest known trees. They are the ancient bristlecone pines. Some of these trees were growing when the Egyptians built the pyramids over four thousand years ago. At the Schulman Grove Visitor's Center, there are picnic areas, restrooms, outdoor exhibits and two self-guided nature trails. You

can also get information on hiking trails in the area from the visitor's center. Open daily from Memorial Day through October, weather permitting. July through September are usually the best months for hiking in the White Mountains. Dogs are allowed on leash. Driving time from Big Pine to Schulman Grove is approximately 45 minutes on paved roads. Take Highway 168 east 12 miles from Big Pine to White Mtn Road. Turn left and drive ten miles to the Schulman Grove Visitor Center. The Bristlecone Pines can be viewed from the parking area of the visitor center and along three nature trails.

Calistoga

Old Faithful Geyser
1299 Tubbs Lane
Calistoga, CA
707-942-6463
Your well-behaved dog is welcome to accompany you to this natural phenomena. Just keep him or her away from the hot water. This geyser is one of only three Old Faithful geysers in the world, erupting about every 40 minutes on a yearly average. The water is 350 degrees hot and shoots about 60 feet into the air for about three to four minutes, then recedes. To see the geyser, you and your pup will need to walk through the main entrance and gift shop. Purchase the tickets at the gift shop and then walk to the geyser area to watch Old Faithful errupt. There is also a snack bar and picnic areas onsite. The admission price is $6 per adult, $5 per senior, $2 per children 6-12 and FREE for dogs. Prices are subject to change.

Petrified Forest
4100 Petrified Forest Rd.
Calistoga, CA

707-942-6667
Geologists call this petrified forest, "one of the finest examples of a pliocene fossil forest in the world." The petrified forest was created from a long ago volcanic eruption, followed by torrential rains which brought giant mud-flows of volcanic ash from the eruption site to entomb the felled giants/trees. The 1/2 mile round trip meadow tour shows some of the petrified trees. Your leashed dog is welcome. Admission prices are $5 for adults, less for seniors and children, and FREE for dogs. Prices are subject to change.

Columbia

Columbia State Historic Park
Parrotts Ferry Rd.
Columbia, CA
209-532-0150
The popular Columbia State Historic Park represents a gold rush town of the 1850-1870 time period. In 1945 the State Legislature made this site a State Historic Park in order to preserve a typical Gold Rush town, an example of one of the most colorful eras in American history. The town's old Gold Rush-era business district has been preserved with many shops and restaurants. The proprietors of the shops are dressed in mid 1800s period clothing. Activities include viewing over a dozen historic structures, shopping, picnic facilities and a few hiking trails. One of the trails, The Karen Bakerville Smith Memorial Trail is a self-guided 1/2 mile loop trail which was dedicated to a teacher. The trail is located by the historic school building and there is a brochure describing the plants and surroundings. The park operates daily from 9am to 5 pm. They are closed on Thanksgiving and Christmas days. Admission is free. Your

leashed dog is welcome. It is located on Parrotts Ferry Road, between Hwy. 4 and Hwy. 49 (near Sonora).

Fish Camp

Yosemite Mountain Sugar Pine Railroad
56001 Highway 41
Fish Camp, CA
559-683-7273
Hop aboard a four mile railroad excursion with your pooch and enjoy a narrative ride through the Sierra National Forest. One of their steam engines is the heaviest operating narrow gauge Shay locomotive in use today. Well-behaved leashed dogs are welcome. The railroad is located near Yosemite Park's south gate on Highway 41.

Klamath

Trees of Mystery
15500 Highway 101 N.
Klamath, CA
800-638-3389
Located in the center of the Redwood National and State Parks, this attraction allows leashed dogs everywhere people are welcome. They have an 8/10ths of a mile groomed interpretive trail through the awe-inspiring Redwoods of California. Also located here is a world-class Native American Museum and a gondola which takes you and your pooch on an aerial ride through the redwood forest canopy. They are located along Highway 101 in Klamath. Klamath is 36 miles south of the Oregon border and 260 miles north of Santa Rosa.

Mammoth Lakes

Mammoth Mountain-Gondola
#1 Minaret Road
Mammoth Lakes, CA
760-934-0745
Want some awesome views of

Mammoth Mountain and the surrounding areas? During the summer, you and your dog can hop on the Gondola (Cable Car) ride. You'll climb about 2,000 feet to the top of the mountain. Once there, you can enjoy a nice 1 1/2 - 2 hour hike down or take the Gondola back down the mountain. Dogs should be leashed.

Newport Beach

Fashion Island Mall
1133 Newport Center Dr.
Newport Beach, CA
800-495-4753
Fashion Island Mall is known as Southern California's premier open-air shopping center. And they allow dogs. Some of the stores allow your well-behaved dog inside. Please always ask the store clerk before bringing your dog inside, just in case policies have changed. For a list of dog-friendly stores, please look at our stores category. You can also shop at the numerous outdoor retail kiosks located throughout the mall. Work up an appetite after walking around? Try dining at the fast food court located upstairs which has many outdoor seats complete with heaters.

Fun Zone Boat Tours
6000 Edgewater Place
Newport Beach, CA
949-673-0240
The people here are very dog-friendly and welcome your pup on several of their boat tours. The narrated trips range in length from 45 to 90 minutes and can include a harbor, sea lion and Lido Island tour. The prices range from $6.00 to $9.00 and less for children. Prices are subject to change. Boat tours depart every half hour seven days a week. They do have a summer and winter schedule, so please call ahead

for the hours. Whale watching tours are also available from January through March. (see Attractions). The Fun Zone Boat Co. is located at the end of Palm Street next to the Ferris Wheel.

Oxnard

Hopper Boat Rentals
3600 Harbor Blvd # 368
Oxnard, CA
805-382-1100
This boat rental company, located at Fisherman's Wharf in Oxnard, allows well-behaved dogs on their motor skiff boats. You and your pup can cruise the Channel Islands Harbor between the hours of 10am until dusk. The boat rentals are $45 per hour. Prices are subject to change.

Riverside

March Air Museum
I215 at Van Buren
Riverside, CA
909-697-6602
The air museum welcomes your well-behaved leashed dog to the outdoor areas of the museum. Most of the museum is outdoors. Dogs may walk through the main building on the way to the outdoor museum. There are a large number of modern and old aircraft on exhibit. There is also a war dog statue in front and a war dog exhibit honoring our 4 legged soldiers. The hours are 9 - 4, year round.

Solvang

Solvang Village
1500-2000 MIssion Drive
Solvang, CA
800-468-6765
As the Solvang Visitor's Bureau states, "Visiting Danes have described Solvang as 'more like Denmark than Denmark' - a remarkable tribute to the town's

passion for Danish architecture, cuisine and customs." Solvang is a quaint shopping village and a great place to walk with your dog. Several stores along Mission Drive are dog-friendly like The Book Loft and Lemo's Feed & Pet Supply (please always verify that stores are dog-friendly by asking the clerk before entering). There are also many dog-friendly restaurants in town including bakeries that have mouth watering goodies. Sunset Magazine recently voted Solvang as one of the '10 Most Beautiful Small Towns' in the Western United States.

Ventura

Ventura Harbor Village
1559 Spinnaker Drive
Ventura, CA
805-644-0169
This nice seaside shopping village allows your leashed dog. While dogs are not allowed inside the stores, there are several outdoor dog-friendly restaurants (see Restaurants). During the summer weekends, the village usually has outdoor art exhibits and concerts where your pup is welcome.

Yermo

Calico Ghost Town
PO Box 638
Yermo, CA
760-254-2122
Dogs are allowed at this old ghost town but not inside the restaurants. Founded in March 1881, it grew to a population of 1,200 with 22 saloons and more than 500 mines. Calico became one of the richest mining towns in California, producing $86 million in silver, $45 million in borax and gold. After 1907, when silver prices dropped and borax mining moved to Death Valley, Calico became a ghost town. Today, Calico is one of the few remaining original mining

towns of the western United States. It was preserved by Walter Knott (founder of Knott's Berry Farm and a relative of the owner of Calico's Silver King mine). Mr. Knott donated Calico Ghost Town to the County of San Bernardino in 1966, and it remains alive and well as a 480-acre County Regional Park. Live events like gunfights and living history reenactments are common at the park. Take a self-guided town tour or go for a hike on one of their trails. You and your pooch can also take a guided walking tour (Mon-Fri) with Calico's historian who will examine the history of the miners, the famous 20-mule team and a U.S. Postal Mail dog named Dorsey. The park also offer many festivals throughout the year. Camping and RV hookups are available here. The park is located 8 miles north of Barstow and 3 miles east of Interstate 15.

Florida Listings

Crystal River

Crystal River State Archeological Site
3400 N. Museum Point
Crystal River, FL
352-795-3817
This six-mound complex was built by a cultural group called the pre-Columbian mound builders. It is considered one of the longest continually occupied sites in Florida. For 1,600 years, beginning around 200 B.C., these 14 acres were an imposing prehistoric ceremonial center for Florida's Native Americans. Dogs are not allowed in the visitor center or on the mounds, but they are allowed on the paved trail. Dogs must be leashed. This archeological site is located on the west coast of Florida.

Naples

Collier-Seminole State Park Boat Tours
20200 E. Tamiami Trail
Naples, FL
941-642-8898
Dogs under 50 pounds are allowed on the pontoon boat tours. The tours last about an hour and include a narration about the early settlers and Everglade animals and plants. The cost is $8.50 per person and dogs ride free.

Olustee

Olustee Battlefield State Historic Site
U.S. 90
Olustee, FL
386-758-0400
Leashed dogs are allowed on this historic battlefield. There is a one-mile walking trail which educates visitors about Florida's biggest Civil War battle. The battlefield is located about 1 hour from Jacksonville. Dogs are not allowed during the Olustee Battle Re-enactment Event.

Palatka

Ravine State Gardens
Twigg Street
Palatka, FL
386-329-3721
This park has long been famous for its extensive plantings of azaleas and other ornamental plants. Leashed dogs are allowed on the nature trails throughout this 80+ acre park. Dogs are not allowed in the picnic areas. The park is located about a one hour drive from St. Augustine.

Titusville

Space Shuttle Launches
Kennedy Space Center
Titusville, FL

321-867-4636
You and your dog can view a shuttle launch from along Highway 1. Check the phone number or the web site at http://www.ksc.nasa.gov for launch schedule information. Kennedy Space Center is about 1 hour from Orlando.

New Mexico Listings

Albuquerque

Petroglyph National Monument
6001 Unser Boulevard NW
Albuquerque, NM
505-899-0205
More than 20,000 prehistoric and historic Native American and Hispanic petroglyphs (images carved in rock) stretch 17-miles along Albuquerque's West Mesa. Your leashed dog is welcome to accompany you on a dirt trail that is about 1.5 miles long and passes about 800 petroglyphs. There is no shade or water along this trail which can get very hot during the summer months. The trail starts at Unser Blvd and St. Joseph. Dogs are not allowed on the Boca Negra trail or other developed areas of the park.

Belen

The Harvey House Museum
104 North First Street
Belen, NM
505-861-0581
The Harvey House in Belen is one of 84 houses created by Fred Harvey. These houses/restaurants were located next to the railroad and they had a renown reputation for serving fine food in an elegant manner. Eastern U.S. women were recruited to work in these eating establishments throughout the Southwest U.S. The superb food

preparation and excellent dining service sustained The Harvey House through the Great Depression of the 1930s. Your well-behaved leashed dog is welcome inside this museum. The museum is adjacent to a miniature railroad museum where your dog is also welcome. The museum is located in the city of Belen, which is about an hour south of Albuquerque. It is a nice stop on the way to the dog-friendly Very Large Array (VLA) Radio Telescopes in Socorro. Admission is free, but donations are welcome.

Carrizozo

Valley of Fires Recreation Area
U.S. 380
Carrizozo, NM
505-648-2241
Valley of Fires is adjacent to the spectacular Malpais Lava Flow. It was created about 1500 years ago when Little Black Peak erupted. The lava flowed into the Tularosa Basin, filling the valley with molten rock. The lava flow is now rock that is 4-6 miles wide by 44 miles long and 160 feet deep. This lava flow is the youngest formation of this type in the continental U.S. Dogs on leash are allowed on the self-guided paved 3/4 mile each way Malpais Nature Trail. From the trail you can view the lava rock, and native plants and animals. Valley of Fires is located on U.S. Highway 380, four miles west of Carrizozo, NM. There is a minimal fee for parking.

Lincoln

Lincoln Historic Town
Highway 380
Lincoln, NM

The town of Lincoln was built in the 1800's and today it is a

National Historic Landmark. The Lincoln County war took place here, which was a fight between cowboys/ranchers and banker/politicians. Billy the Kid was one of the cowboys who fled during this battle. He was later found and brought back to Lincoln. While waiting for his trial, he escaped from the Lincoln County Courthouse. Today there are over 40 historic buildings throughout the town. You and your pup can go on a self-guided walking tour of Lincoln. Just pick up a map from the Visitor Center located on Hwy. 380. There is a minimal fee for the map.

Madrid

Old Coal Mine Museum
2846 Highway 14
Madrid, NM
505-473-0743
The Old Coal Mine Museum is located on 3 acres of what was once the epicenter of the Madrid mining operation. Here you will find a fully restored railroad engine, impressive collection of mining equipment, tools of trade, household goods and a blacksmith's shop, as well as industrial sized machinery. Dogs are welcome at this mostly outdoor museum. There is a minimal entrance fee. The museum is located in the city of Madrid, about an hour south of Santa Fe. If you are driving between Santa Fe and Albuquerque, take Highway 14 and visit this attraction in Madrid.

Roswell

International UFO Museum & Research Center
114 N. Main Street
Roswell, NM
505-625-9495
Ever wondered if there is extraterrestrial life out there? Curious about the famous

'Roswell Incident'? The Tourism Association of New Mexico has awarded this museum the 1996 "Top Tourist Destination of New Mexico." You and your dog are absolutely welcome inside this very popular and large UFO Museum and Research Center. They have many dog visitors every day. At the museum you can view exhibits about The Roswell Incident, Crop Circles, Ragsdale Crash Site, Ancient Cultures, Worldwide Sighting Map and a Children's Area. You can also sit and view videos (with your pup, of course) in their small theater room. After viewing the exhibits, your pup is welcome in the gift shop too. Admission is free, but donations are always welcome.

Socorro

Very Large Array (VLA) Radio Telescope
U.S. Hwy. 60
Socorro, NM
505-835-7000
The VLA is one of the world's premier astronomical radio observatories. It consists of 27 antennas arranged in a huge Y pattern up to 22 miles across. Dogs are not allowed in the visitor's center, but you can take your pup on the self-guided walking tour. This is where part of the movie Contact, starring Jodie Foster, was filmed. The VLA is located 50 miles west of Socorro on U.S. Highway 60. From U.S. 60, turn South on NM 52, then West on the VLA access road, which is well marked. Signs will point you to the Visitor Center. The tour is free, but donations are welcome.

Steins

Steins Railroad Ghost Town
Interstate 10, Exit 3
Steins, NM
505-542-9791
When traveling along I-10 in

New Mexico, near the Arizona border, be sure to stop at this ghost town. Steins Railroad Ghost Town was once a thriving railroad station town named after Captain Stein, a U.S. Army officer, who was the first Anglo witness to sign a treaty with the Apaches. At the town's peak, between 1905 to 1945, Steins supported 1300 residents. Take a step back in time and walk through the preserved Old West frontier town with your pup. You can purchase some souvenirs and cold drinks at the Steins Mercantile or purchase a guided tour for $2.50 per person. The self-guided tour is free. This is a nice place to stop when traveling along I-10. Just be sure to keep your dog leashed because there are several cats on the premises.

North Carolina Listings

Salem

Old Salem
601 Old Salem Road
Salem, NC
336-721-7350
Old Salem is a living history town with restored buildings and costumed interpreters. Dogs are not allowed in the buildings but you can still get a good flavor of the place.

Pennsylvania Listings

Bird In Hand

Aaron and Jessica's Buggy Rides
Route 340
Bird In Hand, PA

717-768-8828
Well-behaved dogs are allowed on the buggy rides.

Abe's Buggy Rides
2596 Old Philadelphia Pike
Bird In Hand, PA
717-392-1794
Well-behaved dogs are allowed to accompany you on these buggy rides.

Gettysburg

Gettysburg National Military Park

Gettysburg, PA
717-334-1124
Dogs are allowed to visit the outside portions of the battlefield on leash. They are not allowed into buildings or the cemetery.

Washington Listings

Friday Harbor

San Juan Island National Historic Park
125 Spring Street
Friday Harbor, WA
360-378-2902
Leashed dogs are welcome on the hiking trails. Some of the trails are self-guided tours of the area and buildings. Dogs on leash are also allowed at South Beach, which is located at the American Camp. Dogs are not allowed inside the Visitor's Center.

See many other Dog-Friendly Attractions in our City Guide Listings in Chapter 1.

Notes

Notes

Notes

Notes

Notes

Notes